FIFTH EDITION

FUNDAMENTALS OF BUSINESS LAW

Robert N. Corley
University of Georgia

Peter J. Shedd
University of Georgia

PRENTICE HALL
Englewood Cliffs, New Jersey 07632

Library of Congress Cataloging-in-Publication Data

CORLEY, ROBERT NEIL.
Fundamentals of business law.

1. Commercial law—United States. I. Shedd, Peter J. II. Title.
KF889.C64 1990 346.73'07 89-23122
ISBN 0-13-334335-9 347.3067

Editorial/production supervision: *Nancy DeWolfe*
Interior design: *Peg Kenselaar and Lorraine Mullaney*
Cover design: *Jerry Votta*
Manufacturing buyer: *Ed O'Dougherty and Mary Ann Gloriande*

A Division of Simon & Schuster
Englewood Cliffs, New Jersey 07632

Printed in the United States of America

10 9 8 7 6 5 4 3 2 1

ISBN 0-13-334335-9 01

Prentice-Hall International (UK) Limited, *London*
Prentice-Hall of Australia Pty. Limited, *Sydney*
Prentice-Hall Canada Inc., *Toronto*
Prentice-Hall Hispanoamericana, S.A., *Mexico*
Prentice-Hall of India Private Limited, *New Delhi*
Prentice-Hall of Japan, Inc., *Tokyo*
Simon & Schuster Asia Pte. Ltd., *Singapore*
Editora Prentice-Hall do Brasil, Ltda, *Rio de Janeiro*

Overview

Contents

Preface

We are delighted to introduce the fifth edition of *Fundamentals of Business Law*. When we started to work on this edition, it was our goal to retain the strengths of previous editions and to add new materials to provide up-to-date coverage of traditional business law topics. We hope you agree our efforts have been successful.

We continue to believe that the students who use this text have needs much different from those of law students. Therefore, the text stresses legal principles that are essential to the business decision-making process. This coverage of traditional business law topics uses a transactional approach to the study of business law. This approach enables the students to be exposed to the most current trends in the law from a traditional perspective.

As in the previous editions, the fifth edition continues to present its cases in a briefed form. These decisions are incorporated into the text of each chapter in order to illustrate important legal concepts with real-life examples and to demonstrate the use of legal reasoning to resolve business problems and disputes. These cases were chosen for their ability to represent clearly current general principles as well as trends in the law. Of the 257 cases in this edition, 141 are new.

In the fourth edition we introduced the pedagogical tools of previews and summaries in each chapter. Because we received many favorable comments about the previews and summaries, they are included in this edition, too. An addition to the fifth edition is the ''Business Management Decision'' at the beginning of each chapter. We believe these questions should help the student see the everyday relevance of the material to be studied. They are intended to be illustrative, not exhaustive. As always, we welcome your comments.

The 45 chapters of this fifth edition are divided into eight parts. The design enables professors to select the subjects in any order they wish to cover the material. This organization should provide sufficient flexibility for courses on either the quarter or semester system. We continue to believe that the material in this edition needs to be covered over at least two courses.

Part I serves as an introduction to various sources of the law and to the court system. Chapters 3 and 4 discuss the litigation process in detail. Chapter 5 emphasizes alternatives to litigation as methods of resolving controversies. Of particular importance in this chapter is the material on arbitration and administrative agencies. Chapter 6, on torts, places special emphasis on the various tort theories used to impose tort liability, especially on the business community. Problems related to malpractice by professional people such as accountants are highlighted. Chapter 7 is a separate chapter on the problems business managers face as a result of the high crime rate. The first seven chapters may be omitted or quickly reviewed if students have had an introductory legal studies course that covered these topics.

Part II, on contracts, is designed to give students an understanding of the basic and traditional concepts of contracts as well as of recent developments of the closely related law of sales under the Uniform Commercial Code. This Code is included as an appendix, and appropriate sections are referred to in brackets within the text. After the introductory chapter, the next four chapters (9 through 12) discuss the essential requirements for every valid contract. Contracts that are contrary to public policy are discussed in Chapter 12. Chapter 13 involves issues of form and interpretation of contracts and Chapter 14 includes a discussion of contractual performance. Chapter 15 is a new chapter in this edition. It examines the available excuses for not performing a contractual obligation as well as the methods of discharging such promises. Finally, issues created when third parties become involved in contracts are discussed in Chapter 16.

Part III includes four chapters that give additional material on the sale of goods. Without repeating the details contained in the contracts chapters, Chapters 17 and 18 emphasize the provisions of Article 2 of the Uniform Commercial Code. Chapter 19 is an in-depth examination of the law of warranties. Recognizing the continuing impact of products liability to all businesses, Chapter 20 is dedicated to this subject.

Part IV, Agency, contains four chapters. Chapter 21 deals with the creation and general principles of the agency relationship. The next two chapters discuss this agency from the perspective of the law of contracts and the law of torts. Chapter 24 emphasizes how the agency relationship can be terminated without additional liability.

Part V discusses business organization in three stages. In addition to the factors used in selecting the form of organization, these stages are (1) the method of creation of the various forms of organizations; (2) the legal aspects of operating the various forms of organization; and (3) the law as it relates to dissolution of business organizations.

Part VI on property, has been reorganized and rewritten. After an introductory chapter, methods of acquiring title to both real and personal property are discussed in Chapter 33. Next, in Chapter 34, the lease of real estate and the bailment of personal property are discussed. Chapter 35, on the use of wills and trusts in estate planning, concludes this part.

Organized as a new part to this edition, VII is devoted to commercial paper and Articles 3 and 4 of the Uniform Commercial Code. This subject has been reduced by one chapter from the fourth edition; however, we believe that the coverage continues to be complete. Our emphasis is on students gaining an appreciation for the liable parties involved in the commercial paper transaction. A discussion of the Expedited Funds Availability Act appears in the bank-collection process material in Chapter 36.

Part VIII contains six chapters dealing with the law as it relates to creditors and debtors. The first two chapters (40 and 41) examine Article 9 of the Uniform Commercial Code on secured credit transactions. Chapter 42 covers the use of real estate as security for debts. Chapter 43, on other laws assisting creditors, emphasizes the complex area of suretyship. Chapter 44 gathers in one place much of the recent legislation aimed at protecting debtors and consumers. Finally, Chapter 45 discusses bankruptcy.

Our thanks are extended to Scott Barr, our editor, and to Nancy DeWolfe, who oversaw the production process. Their assistance and encouragement was welcomed.

Most importantly, we thank Mary Evans of Athens, Georgia. Her typing of the manuscript made the preparation phase very efficient. We are grateful.

Robert N. Corley

Peter J. Shedd

Law 1

CHAPTER PREVIEW

- LAW

  Definitions of Law
  Forces That Shape the Law
  Logic • History and Custom • Religion • Social Utility
  Classification of Legal Subjects

- SOURCES OF LAW

  Basic Constitutional Principles
  Legislation
  Interpretation of Legislation
  Uniform State Laws

- CASE LAW

  Stare Decisis
  Problems Inherent in Case Law
  Rejection of Precedent
  Conflict of Laws

BUSINESS MANAGEMENT DECISION

Your import-export business becomes subject to new legislation regulating international trade transactions. A particular provision of the new law is unclear in its application to your business. You consult your company lawyer for advice. He informs you that he is not sure what the law means.

Should you hire a new lawyer?

LAW

1. Introduction

The subject matter of this text is business law. Legal concepts, principles, and rules provide the foundation for the conduct of business. The law guarantees individual rights, including the right to own private property, which right in a broad sense is involved in all business transactions. The law determines who may conduct business, how it is to be conducted, and what sanctions are to be imposed if its requirements are not met. Thus it is apparent that knowledge of the law as it relates to business is an indispensable ingredient in any successful business venture.

This text is divided into eight parts. Part I provides a background, an understanding of our legal system. We find out where our laws come from, how they are applied, and how they are changed. The emphasis is on the various methods of resolving conflicts and controversies. Litigation and arbitration as a substitute for litigation are the major areas of study. There is also a discussion of the role of ethics as an influence on individual and business conduct. Finally, there is detailed coverage of the law of torts (private wrongs) and criminal law (public wrongs) as they pertain to business. The seven parts that follow consider the law as it relates to business.

Now, more than ever in our nation's history, law impacts on business decisions. Laws written to solve many of society's problems are directed at business, regulating its activity and its processes. This text will attempt to create an awareness of the role of the rule of law in business.

2. Definitions of Law

Our view of the law will be a broad one, and our first question will be: What is law? In everyday conversation, people use the word *law* in many different ways, but it is a word that is very difficult to define. In its broad context, it expresses a variety of concepts. Law has been defined as rules and regulations established by government and applied to people in order for civilization to exist. Law and legal theory, however, are far too complex for such a simple definition.

In attempting to define *law,* it is helpful to look at its purposes or functions. A basic purpose of law in a civilized society is to maintain order. This is the prime function of that body of law known as the *criminal law.* Another role of law is to resolve disputes that arise between individuals and to impose responsibility if one person has a valid, legal claim against another, as in a suit for breach of contract. It is important that we bear in mind that the law is not simply a statement of rules of conduct but also the means whereby remedies are afforded when one person has wronged another.

In one sense, almost every issue or dispute in our society—political, social, religious, economic—ultimately becomes a legal issue to be resolved by the courts. Thus it can be said that law is simply what the courts determine it to be as an expression of the public's will in resolving these issues and disputes.

In still another sense, *law* has been defined as the rules and principles applied by the courts to decide controversies. These rules and principles fall into three categories:

1. Laws, including the federal Constitution and state constitutions, that have been passed by legislative bodies
2. Common law, or case law, derived from cases decided by the courts
3. Procedural rules, which determine how lawsuits are handled in the courts and include such matters as the rules of evidence and related issues

The first two elements provide the rules of substantive law that the courts apply to decide controversies. The third provides the machinery whereby these rules of substantive law are given effect and applied to resolve controversies.

Many legal scholars have defined *law* in relation to the sovereign. For example, Blackstone, the great legal scholar of the eighteenth century, defined law as "that rule of action which is prescribed by some superior and which the inferior is bound to obey." This concept of law as a command from a superior to an inferior is operative in many areas. For example, the tax laws command that taxes shall be paid to the sovereign.

Another view of law is that it is a method of social control—an instrument of social, political, and economic change. Law is both an instrument of change and a result of changes that take place in our society. The law brings about changes in our society; society brings about changes in the law. The law—responding to the goals, desires, needs, and aspirations of society—is in a constant state of change. Sometimes the law changes more rapidly than the attitudes of the majority. In this event, the law and our legal system provide leadership in bringing about changes. At other times society is ahead of the law in moving in new directions, and changes in the law are brought about by the people. In the field of ecology, for example, various groups have put pressure on legislators to clean up the air and water. As a result, laws have been enacted that require devices to be installed to control pollution. Here public pressure resulted in the enactment of laws, and the law was a follower rather than a leader. It is important to note that law is not static—that it is constantly changing—and the impetus for the changes may come from many different sources.

While we are on the subject of definitions, we should point out that the pronoun *he* can mean "he or she," and we intend that inclusive meaning in almost every instance. In order to save the reader from tiresome repetition of the phrase "he or she," we use *he* throughout the text.

3. Forces That Shape the Law

Throughout history, legal scholars have written about the nature and origin of law, its purposes and the factors that influence its development. Legal philosophers have generally acknowledged that logic, history, custom, religion, and social utility are among the major influences and forces that have shaped and directed the law. But there has been disagreement as to the relative importance of these forces, and the influence of each has varied throughout history.

Logic. Judicial reasoning often involves the use of prior decisions as precedents. The use of the analogy is of prime importance to the judicial process because of the need for certainty in the law. Logic may involve deductive reasoning or inductive reasoning. Deductive reasoning takes the form of a syllogism in which a conclusion concerning a particular circumstance (minor premise) is drawn from a general principle (major premise). Inductive reasoning involves the process of using specific cases to reach a general conclusion. It is often said that application of the doctrine of *stare decisis* by basing a decision on precedents announced in prior cases is inductive in nature, while applying a statute to a given set of facts is an example of deductive reasoning, but these examples are open to some criticism. In addition, the development of the law using logic would require that the law consist of a set of known rules. Since the law does not, pure logic cannot always be used to decide cases. Reasoning by example, however, is at the heart of our judicial system.

In any case, "The life of the law has not been logic; it has been experience." In making this statement and in defining law as a prediction of what courts will decide, Justice Oliver Wendell Holmes stressed the empirical and pragmatic aspects of the law, its primary reliance on facts to dictate what the law is. Yet he recognized that law is actually unpredictable and uncertain.

History and Custom. History and custom play a significant role in the development of the law in many areas. The law tends to evolve as we learn from history. As customs and practices gain popular acceptance and approval, they become formalized into rules of conduct. Law was found in the rules, and it evolved from them. Custom results from repeated approved usage, and when such usage by common adoption and acquiescence justifies each member of society in assuming that every member of society will conform thereto, a rule of conduct has been formulated. When such a rule is adopted by a court as controlling in a particular case or is enacted into legislation, law has been made.

Religion. Throughout history, religious principles have played a major role in the development of the law. Many legal theorists have argued that there exists a natural law, based on divine principles established by the Creator, which mortal man is bound to follow.

This natural-law theory softened the rigid common law of England, became the basis of courts of equity, and found its way to America in the Declaration of Independence: "certain unalienable Rights, . . . Life, Liberty, and the Pursuit of Happiness."

Social Utility. Law was previously defined as a scheme of social control. Social utility is perhaps the most significant force influencing the development of the law today. Social utility involves the use of economic, political, and social considerations as factors in formulating the law. Under the pressure of conflicting interests, legislators and courts make law. Thus, law, when enacted by legislatures or pronounced by courts, is in the end the result of finding an equilibrium between conflicting interests.

Law is not only generalization deduced from a set of facts, a recognized tradition, a prescribed formula for determining natural justice; it is also a set of rules for social control, and it grows out of the experiences of mankind. Current social mores, political ideologies, international situations and conditions, and economic and business interests are all elements to be investigated and evaluated in making the law and in determining how it operates.

4. Classification of Legal Subjects

Legal subjects may be classified in a variety of ways. As was noted in the preceding sections, laws and legal principles are sometimes classified as substantive or procedural. The law that is used to decide disputes is **substantive law.** On the other hand, the legal procedures that determine how a lawsuit is begun, how the trial is conducted, how appeals are taken, and how a judgment is enforced are called **procedural law.** Substantive law is the part of the law that defines rights; procedural law establishes the procedures whereby rights are enforced and protected. For example, A and B have entered into an agreement, and A claims that B has breached the agreement. The rules that provide for bringing B into court and for the conduct of the trial are rather mechanical, and they constitute procedural law. Whether the agreement was enforceable and whether A is entitled to damages are matters of substance and would be determined on the basis of the substantive law of contracts.

Substantive law *Law that regulates and controls the rights and duties of all persons in society.*

Procedural law *The laws that establish the process by which a lawsuit is filed, a trial is conducted, an appeal is perfected, and a judgment is enforced. In essence, these laws can be called the rules of litigation.*

Law is also frequently classified into areas of public and private law. *Public law* includes those bodies of law that affect the public generally; *private law* includes the areas of the law concerned with relationships between individuals.

Public law may be further divided into three general categories:

1. *Constitutional law* concerns itself with the rights, powers, and duties of federal and state governments under the U.S. Constitution and the constitutions of the various states.
2. *Administrative law* is concerned with the multitude of administrative agencies, such as the Federal Trade Commission and the National Labor Relations Board.
3. *Criminal law* consists of statutes that forbid certain conduct as being detrimental to the welfare of the state or the people generally and provides punishment for their violation.

Private law is that body of law that pertains to the relationships between individuals in an organized society. Private law encompasses the subjects of contracts, torts, and property. Each of these subjects includes several bodies of law. The law of contracts, for example, may be subdivided into the subjects of sales, commercial paper, agency, and business organizations. The major portion of this text covers these subjects, which constitute the body of law usually referred to as business law.

The law of torts is the primary source of litigation in the United States and is also a part of the total body of law in areas such as agency and sales. A *tort* is a wrong committed by one person against another or against his property. The law of torts is predicated upon the premise that in a civilized society people who injure other persons or their property should compensate them for their loss. Chapter 6 discusses the law of torts.

The law of property may be thought of as a branch of the law of contracts, but in many ways our concept of private property contains much more than the contract characteristics. Property is the basic ingredient in our economic system, and the subject matter may be subdivided into several areas, such as wills, trusts, estates in land, personal property, bailments, and many more. Several chapters in Part V of this text are devoted to the law of property.

Any attempt at classification of subject matter, particularly in the private law, is difficult, because the law is indeed a "seamless web." For example, assume that an agent or a servant acting on behalf of his employer commits a tort. The law of agency, although a subdivision of the law of contracts, must of necessity contain a body of law to resolve the issues of tort liability of the employer and employee. Likewise, assume that a person is injured by a product he has purchased. The law of sales, even though a part of the law of contracts, contains several aspects that could best be labeled a branch of the law of torts. Therefore it is apparent that even the general classifications of contract and tort are not accurate in describing the subject matter of various bodies of law.

SOURCES OF LAW

5. Introduction

Our law comes from four basic sources: constitutions, legislation, judicial decisions, and the rules, regulations, and decisions of administrative agencies. Assuming that administrative agencies are part of the executive branch of government, our law comes from all three branches.

A unique characteristic of American law is that a very substantial part of it is found in cases decided by our courts. This concept of decided cases as a source of law comes to us from England. It is generally referred to as the **common law.** Our common law system, which relies on case precedent as a source of law, must be contrasted with **civil law** systems, which developed on the European continent. The civil law countries have codified their laws—reduced them to statutes—so that the main source of law in those countries is to be found in the statutes rather than in the cases. Under the common law system, of course, we have a large number of statutes and ordinances, but these are only a part of our law.

Common law *That body of law deriving from judicial decisions, as opposed to legislatively enacted statutes and administrative regulations.*

Civil law *A system of law based on legislation or codes as in the European system of codified law.*

In the United States, common law has been the predominant influence. Since most of the colonists were of English origin, they naturally were controlled by the laws and customs of their mother country. But in Louisiana and, to some extent, Texas and California, the civil law has influenced the legal systems, because these states were founded by French and Spanish peoples. It must not be overlooked, however, that much of the law in every state of the United States is statutory, and statutes are becoming increasingly important. Case law, or common law, remains an important source of law because of the extreme difficulty in reducing all law to writing in advance of an issue being raised.

As you read further, remember that the judicial system has established a general priority among the various sources of law. Constitutions prevail over statutes, and statutes prevail over common law principles established in court decisions. Courts will not turn to case decisions for law if a statute is directly in point.

6. Basic Constitutional Principles

In the U.S. constitutional system, the Constitution of the United States and the constitutions of the various states provide the basis of our legal system and our supreme law. All other laws must be consistent with them, or they are void. Most state constitutions are modeled after the federal Constitution. They divide state government into executive, legislative, and judicial branches, giving each branch checks and balances on the others. Constitutions also define the powers and functions of the various branches.

The Constitution of the United States and the constitutions of the various states are the fundamental written law in this country. A federal law must not violate the U.S. Constitution. All state laws must conform to, or be in harmony with, the federal Constitution as well as with the constitution of the appropriate state.

Two very important principles of constitutional law are basic to our judicial system. They are closely related to each other and are known as the doctrine of **separation of powers** and the doctrine of **judicial review.**

Separation of powers *The doctrine that the legislative, executive, and judicial branches of government function independently of one another and that each branch serves as a check on the others.*

The doctrine of separation of powers results from the fact that both state and federal constitutions provide for a scheme of government consisting of three branches—legislative, executive, and judicial. Separation of powers has both a horizontal and a vertical aspect. The vertical aspect is that there is separation between the federal government and the state government. Each has its own functions to perform. The horizontal aspect of separation of powers ascribes to each branch a separate function and a check and balance on the functions of the other branches. The doctrine of separation of powers implies that each separate branch will not perform the function of the other and that each branch has limited powers.

Judicial review *The power of courts to declare laws and executive actions unconstitutional.*

The doctrine of judicial review is the heart of the concept of separation of powers. This doctrine and the doctrine of supremacy of the Constitution were established at an early date in our country's history in the celebrated case of *Marbury* v. *Madison.*[1] In this case, Chief Justice Marshall literally created for the court a power the founding fathers had refused to include in the Constitution. This was the power of the judiciary to review the actions of the other branches of government and to set them aside as null and void if in violation of the Constitution. In creating this power to declare laws unconstitutional, Chief Justice Marshall stated:

> Certainly, all those who have framed written constitutions contemplated them as forming the fundamental and paramount law of the nation, and consequently, the theory of every such government must be that an act of the legislature, repugnant to the constitution, is void. This theory is essentially attached to a written constitution and is, consequently, to be considered by this court as one of the fundamental principles of our society.

Justice Marshall then decided that courts have the power to review the actions of the legislative and executive branches of government to determine if they are constitutional. This doctrine of judicial review has, to some extent, made the courts the overseers of government and of all aspects of our daily lives.

7. Legislation

Much of our law is found in legislation. Legislative bodies exist at all levels of government. Legislation is created by Congress, state assemblies, city councils, and other local government bodies. The term *legislation* in its broad sense also

[1] 1 Cranch 137 (1803).

includes treaties entered into by the executive branch of government and ratified by the Senate.

Statute *A law passed by Congress or the legislative body of a state.*

Ordinance *Generally speaking, the legislative act of a municipality. A city council is a legislative body, and it passes ordinances that are the laws of the city.*

Code *A collection or compilation of the statutes passed by a legislative body on a particular subject such as automobile traffic.*

Legislation enacted by Congress or by a state legislature is usually referred to as a **statute.** Laws passed by local governments are frequently called **ordinances.** Compilations of legislation at all levels of government are called **codes.** For example, we have local traffic codes covering all aspects of driving automobiles, and state laws such as the Uniform Commercial Code that cover all aspects of commercial transactions. The statutes of the United States that attempt to regulate general conduct are known as the U.S. Code.

Legislation at all levels contains general rules for human conduct. Legislation is the result of the political process expressing the public will on an issue. Courts also play a significant role in the field of statutory law. In addition to their power of judicial review, courts interpret legislation and apply it to specific facts. Courts interpret legislation by resolving ambiguities and filling the gaps in the statutes. By its very nature, most legislation is general, and interpretation is necessary to find the intent of the legislature when the statute was enacted. This is discussed further in the next section.

Legislative bodies have procedural rules that must be followed if a law is to be valid. Among the typical procedural rules are those relating to the way amendments are added to a proposed law, the way proposed statutes are presented for consideration (reading aloud to the members, and so on), and the manner of voting by the members of the legislative body.

8. Interpretation of Legislation

Theoretically, legislation expresses the will or intent of the legislature on a particular subject. In practice, this theory suffers from certain inherent defects. First of all, it is not possible to express the legislative intent in words that will mean the same thing to everyone. Statutes, by their very nature, are written in general language that is frequently ambiguous.

Second, the search for legislative intent is often complicated by the realization that the legislative body in fact had no intent on the issue in question, and the law is incomplete. The matter involved is simply one that was not thought about when the law was passed. Therefore, sometimes the question about legislation is not what did the legislature intend, but what would it have intended had it considered the problem. Both of these problems result in an expanded role for courts in our legal system.

One technique of statutory interpretation is to examine the legislative history of an act, to determine the purpose of the legislation or the evil it was designed to correct. Legislative history includes the committee hearings, the debates, and any statement made by the executive in requesting the legislation. Legislative history does not always give a clear understanding of the legislative intent, because the legislature may not have considered many questions of interpretation that confront courts.

Judges use several accepted rules of statutory interpretation in determining legislative intent. Many of these rules are based on the type of law being construed. For example, one rule is that criminal statutes and taxing laws should be strictly or narrowly construed. As a result, doubts as to the applicability of criminal and taxing laws will be resolved in favor of the accused or the taxpayer, as the case may be.

Another rule of statutory construction is that remedial statutes (those creating a judicial remedy on behalf of one person at the expense of another) are to be liberally construed, in order that the statute will be effective in correcting the condition to be remedied.

There are also rules of construction that aid in finding the meaning of words used in legislation. Words may be given their plain or usual meaning. Technical words are usually given their technical meaning. Others are interpreted by the context in which they are used. For example, if a general word in a statute follows specific words, the general word takes its meaning from the specific words.

Statutory construction is not always based on the type of statute or the words used. For example, if a statute contains both specific and general provisions, the specific provision controls. A frequently cited rule provides: "A thing may be within the letter of the statute and yet not within the statute because it is not within the statute's spirit nor within the intention of the makers." This rule allows a court to have a great deal of flexibility and to give an interpretation contrary to the plain meaning. The power of courts to interpret legislation means that in the final analysis, a statute means what the court says it means.

9. Uniform State Laws

Since each state has its own constitution, statutes, and body of case law, there are substantial differences in the law among the various states. It is important to recognize that ours is a federal system in which each state has a substantial degree of autonomy; thus it can be said that there are really fifty-one legal systems—a system for each state plus the federal legal structure. In many legal situations it does not matter that the legal principles are not uniform throughout the country. This is true when the parties to a dispute are *citizens* of the same state and the transaction or occurrence creating the dispute happened in that state; then the controversy is strictly *intrastate* as opposed to one having *interstate* implications. But when citizens of different states are involved in a transaction (perhaps a buyer in one state contracts with a seller in another), many difficult questions can arise from the lack of uniformity in the law. Assume that a contract is valid in one state but not in the other. Which state's law controls? Although a body of law called conflict of laws (see section 13 of this chapter) has been developed to cover such cases, more uniformity is still desirable.

Two methods of achieving uniformity in business law are possible: having federal legislation govern business law and having uniform laws concerning at least certain phases of business transactions adopted by the legislatures of all states. The latter method has been attempted by a legislative drafting group known as the National Conference of Commissioners on Uniform State Laws. This group of commissioners appointed by the governors of the states endeavors to promote uniformity in state laws on all subjects for which uniformity is desirable and practical. Their goal is accomplished by drafting model acts. When approved by the National Conference, proposed uniform acts are recommended to the state legislatures for adoption.

More than one hundred uniform laws concerning such subjects as partnerships, leases, arbitration, warehouse receipts, bills of lading, and stock transfers have been drafted and presented to the various state legislatures. The response has varied. Very few of the uniform laws have been adopted by all the states. Some states have adopted the uniform law in principle but have changed some of the provisions to meet local needs or to satisfy lobbying groups, so that the result has often been "nonuniform uniform state laws."

The most significant development for business in the field of uniform state legislation has been the Uniform Commercial Code. It was prepared for the stated purpose of collecting in one body the law that "deals with all the phases which may ordinarily arise in the handling of a commercial transaction from start to finish. . . ." The detailed aspects of the Code, as it is often called, make up a significant portion of this text, and sections of the Code are referred to in brackets throughout this text where appropriate. Its provisions are set forth in the appendix.

The field of commercial law is not the only area of new uniform statutes. Many states are adopting modern procedures and concepts in criminal codes and other uniform laws dealing with social problems. In addition, the past few years have seen dynamic changes in both state and federal statutes setting forth civil procedures and revising court systems. The future will undoubtedly bring many further developments to improve the administration of justice. The trend, despite some objection, is to cover more areas of the law with statutes and to rely less on precedent in judicial decisions, or common law, as a source of law. Many of these new statutes tend to be uniform throughout the country.

CASE LAW

10. *Stare Decisis*

Stare decisis *"Stand by the decision." The law should adhere to decided cases.*

Notwithstanding the trend toward reducing law to statutory form, a substantial portion of our law has its source in decided cases. This case law, or common law, is based on the concept of *precedent* and the doctrine of ***stare decisis,*** which means "to stand by decisions and not to disturb what is settled." *Stare decisis* tells us that once a case has established a precedent, it should be followed in subsequent cases involving the same issues. Judicial decisions create precedent by interpreting legislation and by deciding issues not covered by legislation.

When a court decides a case, particularly upon an appeal from a lower court decision, the court writes an opinion setting forth, among other things, the reasons for its decision. From these written opinions rules of law can be deduced, and these make up the body of case law or common law.

Stare decisis gives both certainty and predictability to the law. It is also expedient. Through the reliance on precedent established in prior cases, the common law has resolved many legal issues and brought stability into many areas of the law, such as the law of contracts. The doctrine of *stare decisis* provides a system so businesspeople may act in a certain way, confident that their actions will have certain legal effects. People can rely on prior decisions and, knowing the legal significance of their action, can act accordingly. There is reasonable certainty as to the results of conduct.

Courts usually hesitate to renounce precedent. They generally assume that if a principle or rule of law announced in former judicial decision is unfair or contrary to public policy, it will be changed by legislation. It is important to note that an unpopular court ruling can usually be changed or overruled by statute. Precedent has more force on trial courts than on courts of review; the latter have the power to make precedent in the first instance.

The doctrine of *stare decisis* must be contrasted with the concept of ***res judicata,*** which means "the thing has been decided." *Res judicata* applies when, between the parties themselves, the matter is closed at the conclusion of the lawsuit. The losing party cannot again ask a court to decide the dispute. *Stare decisis* means that a court of competent jurisdiction has decided a controversy and has, in a written opinion, set forth the rule or principle that formed the basis for its decision, so that rule or principle will be followed by the court in deciding subsequent cases involving the same issues. Likewise, subordinate courts in the same jurisdiction will be bound by the rule of law set forth in the decision. *Stare decisis,* then, affects persons who are not parties to the lawsuit, but *res judicata* applies only to the parties involved.

Res judicata *A controversy once having been decided or adjudged upon its merits is forever settled so far as the particular parties involved are concerned.*

11. Problems Inherent in Case Law

The common law system as used in the United States has several inherent difficulties. First of all, the unbelievably large volume of judicial decisions, each possibly creating precedent, places "the law" beyond the actual knowledge of lawyers, let alone laypersons. Large law firms employ lawyers whose major task is to search case reports for "the law" to be used in lawsuits and in advising clients. Today, computers are being used to assist in the search for precedent, because legal research involves examination of cases in hundreds of volumes. Because the total body of ruling case law is so extensive, it is obvious that laypersons who are supposed to know the law and govern their conduct accordingly do not know the law and cannot always follow it, even with the advice of legal counsel.

Another major problem involving case law arises because conflicting precedents are often cited to the court by opposing lawyers. One of the major tasks of the court in such cases is to determine which precedent is applicable to the present case. In addition, even today, many questions of law arise on which there has been no prior decision or in areas where the only authority is by implication. In such situations the judicial process is "legislative" in character and involves the creation of law, not merely its discovery.

It should also be noted that there is a distinction between precedent and mere dicta. As authority for future cases, a judicial decision is coextensive only with the facts upon which it is founded and the rules of law upon which the decision is actually based. Frequently, courts make comments on matters not necessary to the decision reached. Such expressions, called **dicta,** lack the force of an adjudication and, strictly speaking, are not precedent the court will be required to follow within the rule of *stare decisis.* Dicta or implication in prior cases may be followed if sound and just, however, and dicta that have been repeated frequently are often given the force of precedent.

Dicta *Opinions of the court that are not necessary to decide the controversy before the court.*

Finally, our system of each state having its own body of case law creates serious legal problems in matters that have legal implications in more than one state. The problem is discussed in more detail in section 13 of this chapter.

12. Rejection of Precedent

The doctrine of *stare decisis* has not been applied in a fashion that renders the law rigid and inflexible. If a court, especially a reviewing court, finds that the prior decision was "palpably wrong," it may overrule and change it. By the same token, if the court finds that a rule of law established by a prior decision is no longer sound because of changing conditions, it may reverse the precedent. The strength and genius of the common law is that no decision is *stare decisis* when it has lost its usefulness or the reasons for it no longer exist. The doctrine does not require courts to multiply their errors by using former mistakes as authority and support for new errors. Thus, just as legislatures change the law by new legislation, courts change the law from time to time by reversing former precedents. Judges, like legislators, are subject to social forces and changing circumstances. As personnel of courts change, each new generation of judges deems it a responsibility to reexamine precedents and adapt them to the present.

The argument is frequently made that changes in the law should be left to the legislative process. If a rule of law does not represent the judgment of society, the people through the political process will cause the appropriate legislative body to change it. The argument that an issue is more appropriate for legislative resolution is often unpersuasive. Such an argument ignores the responsibility of courts to face difficult legal questions and to accept judicial responsibility for a needed change in the common law. Courts often meet changing times and new social demands by expanding outmoded common law concepts. Many cases produce changes that have a profound effect on social and business relationships. Many judges believe that it is the responsibility of the courts to balance competing interests. They recognize that the common law is judge-made and judge-applied. As a result, case law will be changed when changed conditions and circumstances establish that it is unjust or has become bad public policy. The dynamic quality of the law allows it to grow and meet changing conditions.

Stare decisis may not be ignored by mere whim or caprice. It must have more impact on trial courts than on reviewing courts. It must be followed rather rigidly in daily affairs. In the whole area of private law, uniformity and continuity are necessary. It is obvious that the same rules of tort and contract law must be applied from day to day. *Stare decisis* must serve to take the capricious element out of law and to give stability to a society and to business.

In the area of public law, however, especially constitutional law, the doctrine is frequently ignored. The Supreme Court recognizes that "it is a constitution which we are expounding, not the gloss which previous courts may have put on it."[2] Constitutional principles are often considered in relation to the times and circumstances in which they are raised. Public law issues are relative to the times, and precedent is often ignored so that we are not governed by the dead. Courts reexamine precedents and adapt them to changing conditions. A doctrine known as *constitutional relativity* means that the meaning of the Constitution is relative to the time in which it is being interpreted. Under this concept, great weight is attached to social forces in formulating judicial decisions. As the goals, aspirations, and needs of society change, precedent changes.

13. Conflict of Laws

Certain basic facts about our legal system must be recognized. First of all, statutes and precedents in all legal areas vary from state to state. In some states the plaintiff

[2] Chief Justice John Marshall in McCullough v. Maryland, 4 Wheat 316, 407 (1819).

in an automobile accident case must be completely free of fault in order to recover damages; in most other states the doctrine of comparative negligence is used, so that a plaintiff found to be 20 percent at fault could recover 80 percent of his damages. Second, the doctrine of *stare decisis* does not require that one state recognize the precedent or rules of law of other states. Each state is free to decide for itself questions concerning its common law and interpretation of its own constitution and statutes. (However, courts will often follow decisions of other states if they are found to be sound. They are considered persuasive authority. This is particularly true in cases involving uniform acts, when each state has adopted the same statute.) Third, many legal issues arise out of acts or transactions that have contact with more than one state. A contract may be executed in one state, performed in another, and the parties may live in still others; or an automobile accident may occur in one state involving citizens of different states.

These hypothetical situations raise the following fundamental question: Which state's *substantive* laws are applicable in a multiple-jurisdiction case in which the law differs from one state to the other? The body of law known as conflict of laws or choice of laws answers this question. It provides the court or forum with the applicable substantive law in the multistate transaction or occurrence. The law applicable to a tort is generally said to be the law of the state of place of injury. Thus, a court sitting in state X would follow its own rules or procedure, but it would use the tort law of state Y if the injury occured in Y.

Several rules are used by courts on issues involving the law of contracts:

1. The law of the state where the contract was made
2. The law of the place of performance
3. "Grouping of contracts" or "center of gravity" theory, which uses the law of the state most involved with the contract
4. The law of the state specified in the contract

Many contracts designate the applicable substantive law. A contract provision that provides "This contract shall be governed by the law of the State of New York" will be enforced if New York has at least minimal connection with the contract.

It is not the purpose of this text to teach conflict of laws, but the reader should be aware that such a body of law exists and should recognize those situations in which conflict of laws principles will be used. The trend toward uniform statutes and codes has tended to decrease these conflicts, but many of them still exist. So long as we have a federal system and fifty separate state bodies of substantive law, the area of conflict of laws will continue to be of substantial importance in the application of the doctrine of *stare decisis* and statutory law.

CHAPTER SUMMARY

Law

Definitions of Law	1. There are many definitions of law depending on the content and subject matter involved. 2. In some areas, the law is a command from the sovereign.

	3. Law is a method of controlling society and implementing change. 4. Law consists of the principles used by courts to decide controversies.
Forces That Shape the Law	1. There are many forces that shape and give direction to the law as it develops. 2. Among the more important forces are logic, history, custom, religion, and the attitudes of society.
Classification of Legal Subjects	1. Public versus private. 2. Substance versus procedure.

Sources of Law

Basic Constitutional Principles	1. Constitutional principles provide the foundation of our legal system. 2. One of the most important constitutional principles is the doctrine of judicial review.
Legislation	1. Legislation in the form of statutes, codes, and ordinances provides much of our body of law. 2. Courts have a major role to play in interpreting legislation.
Uniform State Laws	1. Uniform state laws such as the Uniform Commercial Code are an attempt to provide uniformity in business transactions throughout the country.

Case Law

Stare Decisis	1. Decided cases provide us with our common law system. 2. The goal is certainty and predictability.
Problems Inherent in Case Law	1. The volume of cases makes legal research difficult. 2. There are often conflicting precedents that are difficult to apply. 3. Precedent must be distinguished from mere dicta.
Rejection of Precedent	1. Case law may be changed if conditions change or its reasoning is no longer sound. 2. Precedent is given greater weight in the private law than in cases involving public law issues.
Conflict of Laws	1. Conflict of laws principles determine the appropriate statutes and case law to be used in litigation involving more than one jurisdiction. 2. A court in one forum may use the substantive law of another to decide a case.

REVIEW QUESTIONS AND PROBLEMS

1. Give three definitions of law, and give an example of the application of each.
2. Classify the following subjects as public law or private law:

a. Constitutional law	e. Property law
b. Contract law	f. Tort law
c. Administrative law	g. Sales law
d. Criminal law	h. Business organization law

3. Compare and contrast the following:
   a. Public law and private law
   b. Civil law and common law
   c. Torts and crimes
   d. Substance and procedure
   e. Case law and legislation
4. Describe three advantages of the common law (case law) system.
5. What are the disadvantages of the system based on the doctrine of *stare decisis?*
6. The product of the legislative process is often described by separate terms. List three such terms and distinguish them.
7. To what extent is the judiciary the overseer of the government? Explain.
8. Why are uniform state laws important to business?
9. List three rules used by courts to find the meaning of ambiguous statutes.
10. The basic characteristic of the common law is that a case once decided establishes a precedent that will be followed by the courts when similar issues arise later. Yet courts do not always follow precedent. Why?
11. *Stare decisis* is of less significance in public law subjects than in cases dealing with private law subjects. Why?
12. Why is it necessary for each state to have a system of conflict of laws principles?
13. Give two examples of conflict of laws principles.

2 Court Systems

CHAPTER PREVIEW

BUSINESS MANAGEMENT DECISION

As the operator of a small business, you have eight customers that owe you between $200 and $500 each. You consult your lawyer and learn that it would cost you at least $300 to file a suit against each customer.

How do you collect these debts?

FUNCTIONS AND POWERS OF COURTS

Our system of government has selected courts as the primary means to resolve controversies that cannot be settled by agreement of the parties involved. Litigation is the ultimate method for resolving conflict and disagreements in our society. Whether the issue is the busing of schoolchildren, the legality of abortions, the enforceability of a contract, or the liability of a wrongdoer, the dispute, if not otherwise resolved, goes to the court system for a final decision.

The basic function of the judge is to apply the law to the facts. The facts are often determined by a jury. If a jury is not used, the judge is also the finder of the facts. (Cases in which the parties are entitled to a jury are discussed later.) The rule of law applied to the facts produces a decision that settles the controversy.

The three great powers of the judiciary come into play as it performs its functions of deciding cases and controversies: the power of judicial review, the power to interpret and apply statutes, and the power to create law through precedent. The extent to which these powers are exercised varies from case to case, but all three are frequently involved.

Of course, not every dispute may be properly submitted to courts for a decision. For example, courts would not decide if a Catholic priest should be allowed to marry or the grade to be assigned a college student. Courts are ill-equipped to decide such controversial private matters and even some public issues, as the following case illustrates.

CASE

Woodruff had been a student in a master's degree program at a state university. She received an F in a course for plagiarism, but an appeals committee within the university changed the grade to an incomplete. After seven years, she received her master's degree in a program that normally took two or three years to complete. She applied to a doctoral program at another university, which required recommendations from former professors. Her former professors either refused or ignored her requests. Woodruff sued the university, her former professors, and the Board of Regents, alleging violations of her state and federal constitutional rights, breach of contract, and tort claims, such as libel, slander, and intentional infliction of mental distress. She further alleged that her professors had been hostile and sarcastic to her, had refused to help her with coursework and thesis preparation, and had given her undeservedly low grades in an attempt to block her graduation. In their depositions, her former professors gave academic reasons for withholding their recommendations, and they testified that Woodruff was troublesome, erratic in her studies, and not qualified to proceed in a doctoral program. The trial court dismissed her complaint as not justiciable.

ISSUE: Is a dispute concerning academic decisions of a public educational institution a justiciable controversy?

DECISION: No.

REASONS:

1. Courts traditionally have been reluctant to pursue courses of judicial action that would require continuing supervision of the official conduct of public officers.
2. Courts are ill-equipped to make fundamental legislative and administrative policy decisions like those involved in the everyday administration of a public school system. For example, courts are not well suited to decide how much local supplement to teachers' salaries should be paid in order to attract qualified teachers, how many levels of English or math should be taught, whether buildings should be constructed, or whether a system of pupil ability grouping should be used.
3. Other branches of government are best suited to resolve discretionary policy matters, and the courts should not interfere by imposing inferior decisions on the other governmental branches.
4. The court should refuse to adjudicate this matter for other reasons. The court's refusal to hear the case shields the judicial system from an incalculable number of lawsuits challenging grades. The court's decision protects teachers from the agony of litigation initiated by those who would rely on legal rather than learning processes.

Woodruff v. Georgia State University, 304 S.E.2d 697 (Ga. 1983).

STATE COURT SYSTEMS

The judicial system of the United States is a dual system consisting of state courts and federal courts. Most states have threee levels of courts: *trial* courts, where litigation is begun; *intermediate reviewing* courts; and a *final reviewing* court. States use different names to describe these three levels of courts. For example, some states call their trial courts the circuit court because in early times a judge rode the circuit from town to town holding court. Other states call the trial court the superior court or the district court. New York has labeled it the supreme court.

Jurisdiction *The power or authority to try causes and decide cases.*

Before examining these courts, it is necessary to define jurisdiction as it is used in the study of courts. **Jurisdiction** means the power to hear a case. There are courts in every state of general jurisdiction. This means that they have the power to hear almost any type of case. In contrast, many courts have limited powers. They can hear only certain types of cases and thus are said to have limited jurisdiction. They may be limited as to the area in which the parties live, the subject matter involved, or the amount in the controversy. For example, courts with jurisdiction limited to a city's residents often are called *municipal* courts.

Probate court *Handles the settlement of estates.*

Juvenile court *A court with jurisdiction to hear matters pertaining to those persons under a certain age.*

Courts may also be named according to the subject matter with which they deal. **Probate courts** deal with wills and the estates of deceased persons; **juvenile courts** with juvenile crime and dependent children; *municipal* and *police courts* with violators of local ordinances; and *traffic courts* with traffic violations. For an accurate classification of the courts of any state, the statutes of that state should be examined. Figure 2–1 illustrates the jurisdiction and organization of reviewing and trial courts in a typical state.

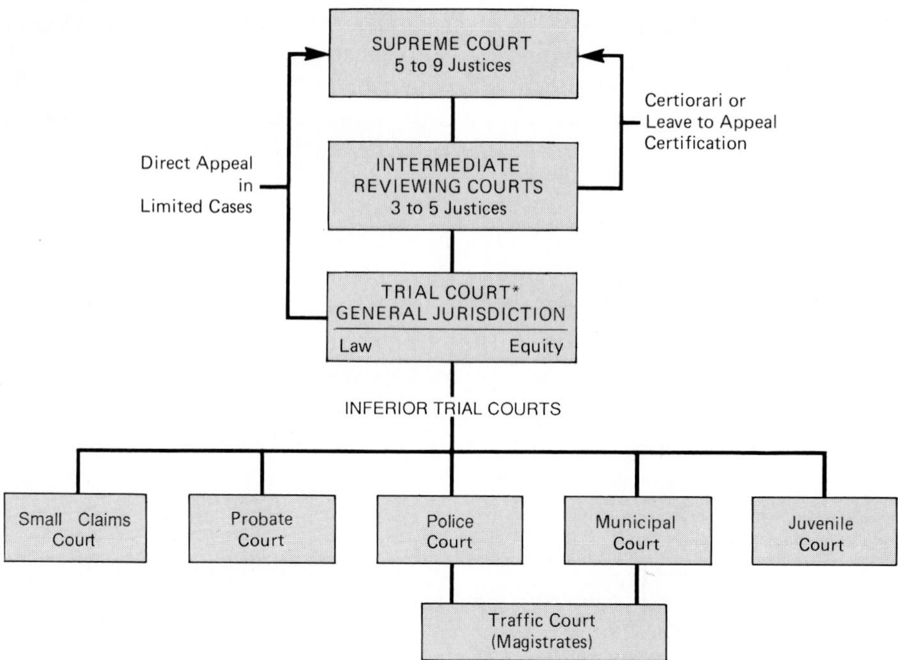

*Commonly called circuit court, district court, or superior court in many states.

FIGURE 2–1 Typical state court system

The **small claims court** is a court whose jurisdiction is limited by the amount in controversy. In recent years, these courts have assumed growing importance. In fact, a popular television program has been created out of this concept. The small claims court represents an attempt to provide a prompt and inexpensive means of settling thousands of minor disputes that often include suits by consumers against merchants for lost or damaged goods or for services poorly performed. Landlord-tenant disputes and collection suits are also quite common in small claims courts. In these courts, the usual court costs are greatly reduced. The procedures are simplified, so that the services of a lawyer are usually not required. Most of the states have authorized small claims courts and have imposed a limit on their jurisdiction. Some states keep the amount as low as $500; others exceed $2,500, but $1,500 is a typical limit.

Small claims court *A court with jurisdiction to hear cases involving a limited amount of money. The jurisdictional amount varies among the states and local communities.*

THE FEDERAL COURT SYSTEM

1. Structure

The United States Constitution created the Supreme Court and authorizes Congress to establish inferior courts from time to time. Congress has created twelve intermediate United States courts of appeal, plus a special Court of Appeals for the Federal Circuit. This special reviewing court, located in Washington, D.C., hears appeals from special courts such as the United States Claims Court and Contract Appeals, as well as from administrative decisions such as those by the Patent and Trademark

Office. Intermediate reviewing courts are not trial courts, and their jurisdiction is limited to reviewing cases. Congress has also created the United States district courts (at least one in each state), and others to handle special subject matter, such as the Court of Military Appeals. Figure 2–2 illustrates the federal court system and shows the relationship of the state courts for review purposes.

2. District Court Jurisdiction

The district courts are the trial courts of the federal judicial system. They have original jurisdiction, exclusive of the courts of the states, over all federal crimes—that is, all offenses against the laws of the United States. The accused is entitled to a trial by jury in the state and district where the crime was committed.

In civil actions, the district courts have jurisdiction only when the matter in controversy is based on either diversity of citizenship or a federal question.

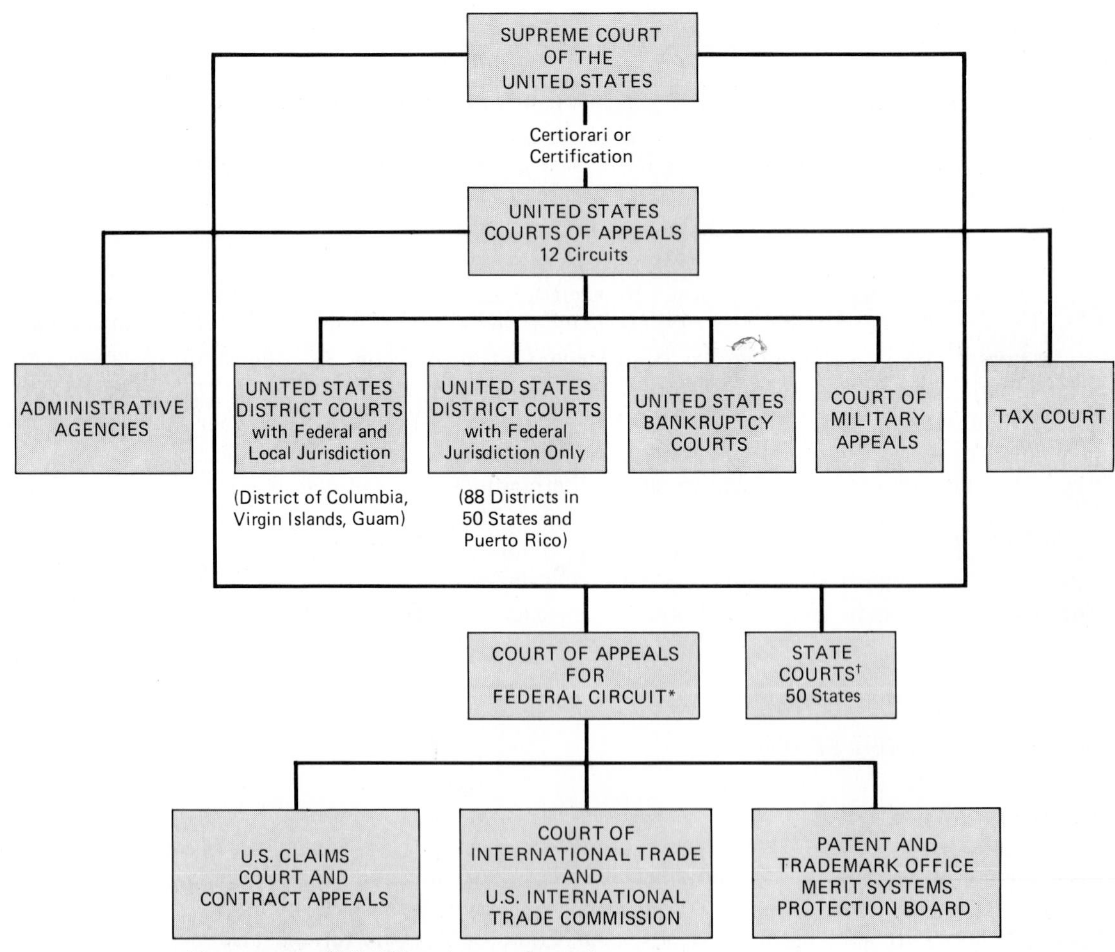

*Same as other United States courts of appeal.
†Certiorari.

FIGURE 2–2 The federal court system

Diversity of Citizenship. Diversity of citizenship exists in suits between (1) citizens of different states, (2) a citizen of a state and a citizen of a foreign country, and (3) a state and citizens of another state. For diversity of citizenship to exist, all plaintiffs must be citizens of a state different from the state in which any one of the defendants is a citizen. Diversity of citizenship does not prevent the plaintiff from bringing suit in a state court, but if diversity of citizenship exists, the defendant has the right to have the case removed to a federal court. A defendant, by having the case removed to the federal court, has an opportunity of having a jury selected from an area larger than the county where the cause arose, thus perhaps reducing the possibility of jurors tending to favor the plaintiff.

For the purpose of suit in a federal court based on diversity of citizenship, a corporation is considered a "citizen" both of the state where it is incorporated and of the state in which it has its principal place of business. As a result, there is no federal jurisdiction in many cases in which one of the parties is a corporation. If any one of the parties on the other side of the case is a citizen either of the state in which the corporation is chartered or is doing its principal business, there is no diversity of citizenship and thus no federal jurisdiction.

Jurisdictional Amount. If diversity of citizenship is the basis of federal jurisdiction, the parties must satisfy a jurisdictional amount, which is $50,000. If a case involves multiple plaintiffs with separate and distinct claims, each claim must satisfy the jurisdictional amount. Thus, in a class-action suit, the claim of each plaintiff must exceed the $50,000 minimum unless changed by statute.

Federal Question. Federal jurisdiction based on a federal question exists if the lawsuit arises out of rights granted by the Constitution, laws, or treaties of the United States. These civil actions may involve matters such as bankruptcy or suits such as those based on patents, copyrights, trademarks, taxes, elections, the rights guaranteed by the Bill of Rights, and those rights secured to individual citizens by the Fourteenth Amendment. In addition, by statute the district courts have original jurisdiction to try tort cases involving citizens who suffer damages caused by other officers or agents of the federal government, and they have the power to issue **writs of *habeas corpus*** and to grant injunctions in a variety of cases. If injunctions are sought, three judges must hear the case.

***Writ of* habeas corpus** *A court order to one holding custody of another, to produce that individual before the court for the purpose of determining whether such custody is proper.*

3. The Law in Federal Courts

The U.S. dual system of federal and state courts creates a unique problem in "conflict of laws." In all cases, federal courts use their own body of procedural law. In cases involving the U.S. Constitution, treaties, and federal statutes, federal substantive law is used. However, there is no body of federal common law in suits based on diversity of citizenship. Therefore federal courts use the substantive law, including conflict of laws principles, of the state in which they are sitting to decide diversity cases. Thus, just as the state courts are bound by federal precedent in cases involving federal law and federally protected rights, federal courts are bound by state precedent in diversity of citizenship cases. The following case established this very important principle.

CASE

While walking along the railroad's right-of-way in Pennsylvania, Tompkins was injured by a passing train of the Erie Railroad. He sued the railroad in a New York Federal District Court, basing jurisdiction on diversity of citizenship. Tompkins was a citizen of Pennsylvania, and the railroad was a New York corporation. The railroad argued that Pennsylvania law should apply since the accident occurred there. Under Pennsylvania law, Tompkins was a trespasser, which meant the railroad would not be liable for the injuries caused. Tompkins argued that the federal court could apply its own principles of law in diversity cases. The trial court applied federal common law, and the jury returned a verdict of $30,000 for Tompkins. The railroad appealed.

ISSUE: When jurisdiction is based on diversity of citizenship, can the federal district court apply its own notions of federal common law?

DECISION: No. In diversity cases, state laws are applicable.

REASONS:
1. The doctrine of federal common law prevents uniformity in the administration of the laws of the states. An out-of-state plaintiff, when suing an in-state defendant, can bring an action in state court or in federal court on the basis of diversity of citizenship. The plaintiff's choice of where to sue should not vary the outcome of the lawsuit.
2. No clause in the Constitution gives Congress or the federal courts the power to declare substantive rules of general common law. By doing so, federal courts invade rights reserved by the Constitution to the states.
3. In diversity of citizenship cases, where matters being litigated are not governed by the federal Constitution or acts of Congress, the federal court will apply state law, as if it were another court of the state. There is no federal general common law.

Erie Railroad v. Tompkins, 304 U.S. 64 (1938).

FEDERAL REVIEWING COURTS

__Writ of certiorari__ A discretionary proceeding by which an appellate court may review the ruling of an inferior tribunal.

As previously noted, there are two levels of federal reviewing courts. Cases decided in the federal district courts are reviewed by the appropriate courts of appeals. In most cases the decisions of the courts of appeals are final. Cases in the courts of appeals may be reviewed by the Supreme Court, if a **writ of certiorari** is granted upon a petition of any party before or after a decision in the courts of appeals. The granting of a writ of certiorari to review a judgment of the courts of appeals is within the discretion of the Supreme Court. The writ will be issued when necessary to secure uniformity of decision or to bring cases of grave public concern to the court of last resort for decision.

Prior to 1988, the Supreme Court was required to review certain cases. This mandatory or obligatory jurisdiction extended to certain cases heard by three judges at the district court level and to certain state Supreme Court decisions involving constitutional issues. This mandatory jurisdiction was eliminated almost entirely in 1988 in order to grant the Supreme Court the total power to control its docket. Today, the Justices of the Supreme Court themselves determine which cases they will decide on their merits.

It was noted that a petition for a writ of certiorari may be filed prior to a decision by the courts of appeals. If a federal statute is challenged on constitutional grounds, the Supreme Court may grant the writ and decide the case as quickly as it could have under the mandatory appeal process.

Decisions of state courts that could formerly be appealed as a matter of right are now subject to the discretion of the certiorari process. This relieves the Supreme Court of any obligation to review the merits of inconsequential federal challenges to state laws. If there is a significant federal issue of paramount importance, the court may, of course, hear the case.

The 1988 amendments also transferred certain appeals to the courts of appeals from the Supreme Court. For example, decisions under the Federal Election Campaign Act are now appealed to the appropriate court of appeals. Federal statutes still do authorize a few direct appeals to the Supreme Court. These involve a few civil injunctions heard by three-judge district courts. For example, direct appeals have been retained in reapportionment cases, in certain cases under the Voting Rights Act of 1965, and under the Presidential Election Campaign Fund Act of 1971. In addition, the Antitrust Procedures and Penalties Act of 1974 authorizes a direct appeal to the Supreme Court in civil antitrust cases brought by the government seeking equitable relief where immediate Supreme Court review is found by the trial judge to be "of general public importance in the administration of justice," and the Supreme Court does not determine "in its discretion" to "deny the direct appeal and remand the case to the court of appeals." These few statutory kinds of Supreme Court obligatory jurisdiction contribute very little to the Court's workload.

As a virtually all-certiorari court, the Supreme Court will review annually over 5,000 petitions for a writ of certiorari. It can be expected to grant about 150 for each term of court. Some of them will be heard because the 1988 law eliminated a number of mandatory appeals that the court would not have heard if given a choice. Today, the law recognizes that the Supreme Court is the best judge of what cases out of the thousands are from the national standpoint the most deserving of a hearing on their merits.

LAW AND EQUITY

4. Introduction

Historically, trial courts in the United States have been divided into two parts—a court of law and a court of equity or chancery. The term **equity** arose in England because the failure of the law courts to provide adequate remedies often made it impossible to obtain justice in the king's courts of law. The only remedy at law was a suit for money damages.

In order that justice might be done, the person seeking a remedy other than money damages sought redress from the king in person. Because the appeal was to the king's conscience, he referred such matters to his spiritual adviser, the chancellor, who was usually a church official and, in giving a remedy, usually favored the ecclesiastical law.

By such method, there developed a separate system of procedure and different rules for deciding matters presented to the chancellor. Suits involving these rules were said to be brought "in **chancery**" or "in equity," in contrast to suits "at law" in the king's courts. Courts of equity were courts of conscience and recognized many rights that were not recognized by common law courts. Examples of the remedies created through *equitable actions* include trusts in lands, rescission of contracts created through fraud, injunctions, and specific performance. Each of these examples is discussed in detail in the chapters that follow.

In a few states, courts of equity are still separate and distinct from courts of law. In most states, the equity and law courts are organized under a single court

Equity *Because the law courts in early English law did not always give an adequate remedy, an aggrieved party sought redress from the king. Since this appeal was to the king's conscience, he referred the case to his spiritual adviser, the chancellor. The chancellor decided the case according to rules of fairness, honesty, right, and natural justice. From this there developed the rules in equity.*

Chancery *Court of equity.*

with two dockets—one at law, the other in equity. Whether the case is in equity or at law is determined by the remedy desired. Modern civil procedure laws usually have abolished the distinction between actions at law and in equity. However, pleadings usually must denote whether the action is legal or equitable because, as a general rule, there is no right to a jury trial of an equitable action. The constitutional guarantee to a trial by jury applies only to actions at law.

5. Equitable Procedures

By statute in some states, a jury may hear the evidence in equity cases, but the determination of the jury in these cases is usually advisory only and is not binding on the court. The judge passes upon questions of both law and fact, and he may decide the case upon the pleadings without the introduction of oral testimony. If the facts are voluminous and complicated, the judge may refer the case to an attorney-at-law, usually called a **master in chancery,** to take the testimony. This is the usual procedure when a complicated accounting is required. The master in chancery hears the evidence, makes findings of fact and conclusions of law, and reports back to the judge.

Master in chancery *An officer appointed by the court to assist the court of equity in taking testimony, computing interest, auditing accounts, estimating damages, ascertaining liens, and doing other tasks incidental to a suit, as the court requires. The power of a master is merely advisory, and his tasks are largely fact finding.*

Decree *The decision of the chancellor (judge) in a suit in equity. Like a judgment at law, it is the determination of the rights between the parties and is in the form of an order that requires the decree to be carried out.*

In personam *A legal proceeding, the judgment of which binds the defeated party to a personal liability.*

Interlocutory decree *A decree of a court of equity that does not settle the complete issue but settles only some intervening part, awaiting a final decree.*

The decision of the court in equity is called a **decree.** A judgment in a court of law is measured in damages, whereas a decree of a court of equity is said to be **in personam;** that is, it is directed to the defendant, who is to do or not to do some specific thing.

Decrees are either final or interlocutory. A decree is *final* when it disposes of the issues in the case, reserving no question to be decided in the future. A decree quieting title to real estate, granting a divorce, or ordering specific performance is usually final. A decree is **interlocutory** when it reserves some question to be determined in the future. A decree granting a temporary injunction, appointing a receiver, and ordering property to be delivered to such a receiver would be interlocutory.

Failure upon the part of the defendant to obey a decree of a court of equity is contempt of court because the decree is directed not against his property but against his person. Any person in contempt of court may be placed in jail or fined by order of the court.

6. Maxims

Courts of equity use *maxims* instead of strict rules of law to decide cases. There are no *legal* rights in equity, for the decision is based on moral rights and natural justice. Some of the typical maxims of equity are

- Equity will not suffer a right to exist without a remedy.
- Equity regards as done that which ought to be done.
- Where there is equal equity, the law must prevail.
- He who comes into equity must do so with clean hands.
- He who seeks equity must do equity.
- Equity aids the vigilant.
- Equality is equity.

These maxims guide the chancellor in exercising his discretion. For example, the clean-hands doctrine prohibits a party who is guilty of misconduct in the matter in litigation from receiving the aid of a court. Likewise, a court of equity may protect one party from his own mistakes if the other party does not have clean hands or is guilty of wrongful conduct. The following case illustrates the breadth of equitable powers.

CASE

Mouw owed $291.97 to Tudor for professional land surveying services. Tudor sued Mouw and obtained a judgment of $304.22. When Mouw failed to pay the judgment, Tudor instituted proceedings to have Mouw's home sold at a judicial sale. Mouw was not served with notice of the sale. Tudor, the only bidder at the sale, purchased the property for $385.65. By statute, Mouw had an interval of time, called the period of redemption, in which he could pay off the debt and regain his home. This period expired, and Tudor received a sheriff's deed to the home. Tudor then advertised the property for sale for $49,000. Mouw filed a motion asking the court to set aside the sale or to permit him to redeem, or buy back, the property. The trial court vacated the sale and gave Mouw a right to redeem his interest in his home.

ISSUE: Should the court grant Mouw an equitable right of redemption, thus allowing him to buy back his home even though the period of redemption had expired?

DECISION: Yes.

REASONS:
1. In granting an equitable right of redemption, the court balances the equities on both sides of the dispute. For example, courts may consider whether the purchaser misled the debtor into believing the period of redemption would be extended, whether the debtor was competent during the original action, and whether the sale price at foreclosure was adequate. While one of these factors alone may not be determinative, a court may weigh them in the balance.
2. In appropriate circumstances, a court can grant an equitable right of redemption to a debtor whose property has been sold because of his failure to pay off a judgment within the period of redemption. The debtor must show fraud, mistake, or other circumstances that would justify the court's giving him the right. By granting an equitable right of redemption, the court prevents a creditor with unclean hands from benefiting from improper conduct, and strips the creditor of the title that the debtor intended to and would have otherwise redeemed. The debtor is still required to pay at a later date what he would have paid within the period of redemption.
3. In this case, the purchase price was grossly inadequate. Tudor paid $385.65 for the home and advertised it for sale for $49,000. Tudor also failed to give any of the interested parties notice of the sale. These factors constitute substantial, competent evidence in support of the trial court's decision.

Tudor Engineering Co. v. Mouw, 709 P.2d 146 (Idaho 1985).

Equity jurisprudence plays an ever-increasing role in our legal system. The movement toward social justice requires more reliance on the equitable maxims and less reliance on rigid rules of law.

OPERATING THE COURT SYSTEM

7. Judges and Justices

Highly technical, the court system must be operated by numerous persons with special training and skills; trial judges, reviewing court judges and justices, and responsible citizens to serve as jurors are required if justice is to be achieved.

Trial Judges. The trial judge owes very high duties to litigants, witnesses, and the jury. Since the court is the protector of constitutional limitations and guarantees, a judge should be temperate, attentive, patient, impartial, studious, diligent, and prompt in ascertaining the facts and applying the law. Judges should be courteous and considerate of jurors, witnesses, and others in attendance upon the court, but they should criticize and correct unprofessional conduct of attorneys.

Judges must avoid any appearance of impropriety and should not act in a controversy in which they or near relatives have an interest. They should not be swayed by public clamor or consideration of personal popularity or be apprehensive of unjust criticism.

The trial judge conducts the lawsuit. It is in the trial courts that the law is made alive and its words are given meaning. Since a trial judge is the only contact that most people have with the law, the ability of such judges is largely responsible for the effective function of the law.

Reviewing Court Judges and Justices. Members of reviewing courts are also called judges. Persons serving on final reviewing courts, such as the Supreme Court of the United States, are called justices. The reviewing judges and justices must be distinguished from trial court judges because their roles are substantially different. For example, a reviewing court judge or justice rarely has any contact with litigants. These judges or justices must do much more than simply decide a case; they usually give written reasons for their decision, so that anyone may examine them and comment on their merits. Each decision becomes precedent to some degree, a part of our body of law. Thus the legal opinion of a reviewing judge or justice—unlike that of the trial judge, whose decision has direct effect only upon the litigants—affects society as a whole. A reviewing judge or justice, in deciding a case, must consider not only the result between the parties involved but the total effect of the decision on the law. In this sense, they may assume a role similar to that of a legislator.

Because of this difference in roles, the personal qualities required for a reviewing judge or justice are somewhat different from those for a trial judge. The duties of a reviewing judge or justice are in the area of legal scholarship. These individuals are required to be articulate in presenting ideas in writing and to use the written word as the primary source of their decisions. Whereas trial judges, being a part of the trial arena, observe the witnesses and essentially use knowledge gained from their participation for their decisions, reviewing judges or justices spend hours studying briefs, the record of proceedings, and the law before preparing and handing down their decisions.

8. The Jury

In Anglo-American law, the right of trial by **jury,** particularly in criminal cases, is traced to the famous Magna Carta issued by King John of England in 1215, wherein it states:

> . . . that no freeman shall be taken or imprisoned or disseised or outlawed or exiled . . . without the judgment of his peers or by the law of the land. . . .

Jury *A group of persons, usually twelve, sworn to declare the facts of a case as they are proved from the evidence presented to them and, upon instructions from the court, to find a verdict in the cause before them.*

In early English legal history, the juror was a witness; this is, he was called to tell what he knew, not to listen to others testify. The word *jury* comes from the French word *juré,* which means "sworn." The jury gradually developed into an institution to determine facts. The function of the jury today is to ascertain facts, just as the function of the court is to ascertain the law.

The Sixth and Seventh Amendments of the United States Constitution guarantee the right of trial by jury both in criminal and civil cases. The Fifth Amendment provides for indictment by a grand jury for capital offenses and infamous crimes. (**Indictment** is a word used to describe the decision of the grand jury.) A *grand jury* differs from a *petit jury* in that the grand jury determines whether the evidence of guilt is sufficient to warrant a trial; the petit jury determines guilt or innocence in criminal cases and decides the winner in civil cases. In civil cases, the right to trial by a jury is preserved in suits at common law when the amount in controversy exceeds $20. State constitutions have like provisions guaranteeing the right of trial by jury in state courts.

Indictment *A finding by a grand jury that it has reason to believe there is sufficient evidence for the accused to be tried. It informs the accused of the offense with which he is charged, so that he may prepare its defense. It is a pleading in a criminal action.*

Historically, the jury consisted of twelve persons, but many states and some federal courts now have rules of procedure that provide for smaller juries in both criminal and civil cases. As the following case established, juries consisting of as few as six persons are constitutional.

CASE

Colgrove was a party in a diversity suit in a Montana federal district court. Judge Battin, the presiding judge, set the case for trial before a six-member jury in accordance with the local rules of this federal court. Colgrove petitioned the Court of Appeals for the Ninth Circuit to direct Judge Battin to impanel a twelve-member jury. Colgrove contended that the district court's local rule violated the Seventh Amendment to the United States Constitution, which provides that "[I]n suits at common law, the right of trial by jury shall be preserved." The court of appeals found no merit in Colgrove's contention, and sustained the validity of the local rule. Colgrove then petitioned the United States Supreme Court for a writ of certiorari, which was granted.

ISSUE: Does a jury of six persons violate the Seventh Amendment?

DECISION: No.

REASONS: 1. At the time the framers of the Constitution drafted the Seventh Amendment, juries consisted of twelve persons. However, constitutional history reveals that the framers did not intend the amendment to require that a jury be the same size as it was at common law. The framers included the Seventh Amendment because of fear that the use of juries in civil cases would be abolished unless protected in express words. The framers were not concerned with the preservation of jury characteristics such as size.

2. The function of a jury is to prevent government oppression in criminal trials and to ensure fair resolution of factual issues in criminal and civil trials. The size of a jury does not affect its ability to perform each function. Therefore, twelve-member juries are not part of the substance of the common law right to trial by jury in civil cases and are not guaranteed by the Seventh Amendment.
3. A six-member jury satisfies the Seventh Amendment's guarantee of trial by jury in civil cases because there is no discernible difference between the results reached by six-member and twelve-member juries.

Colgrove v. Battin, 93 S.Ct. 2448 (1973).

Historically, too, a jury's verdict was required to be unanimous. Today, some states authorize less than unanimous verdicts. If fewer than twelve persons serve on the jury, however, the verdict in criminal cases must be unanimous.

The jury system is much criticized by those who contend that many jurors are prejudiced, unqualified to distinguish fact from fiction, and easily swayed by skillful trial lawyers. However the "right to be tried by a jury of his peers" in criminal cases is felt by most members of the bench and bar to be as fair and effective a method as has been devised for ascertaining the truth and giving an accused his "day in court."

The persons who are selected to serve on trial juries are drawn at random from lists of qualified voters in the county or city where the trial court sits. Most states, by statute, exempt from jury duty those who are in certain occupations and professions, but such exemptions have been reduced or eliminated in recent years in an effort to make jury duty a responsibility of all citizens. Many persons called for jury duty attempt to avoid serving because it involves a loss of money or time away from a job; but because of the importance of jury duty, most judges are reluctant to excuse citizens who are able to serve.

Jury duty in long, complex cases creates a difficult situation. Because few people can afford to serve for many months, juries in complex antitrust and products liability cases frequently consist of the unemployed and retired. It has therefore been proposed to take long and complex matters out of the jury system.

CHAPTER SUMMARY

Functions and Powers of Courts

1. Judges supply the law applicable to the facts.
2. Judges find the facts if there is no jury.
3. The judiciary has the power of judicial review, to interpret legislation, and to create law through precedent.

State Court Systems

1. Each state has a trial court of general jurisdiction and inferior courts of limited jurisdiction.
2. The small claims court is of growing importance because it provides a means of handling small cases without the need for a lawyer.

The Federal Court System

Structure

1. The Constitution created the Supreme Court.
2. Congress has created thirteen courts of appeals and at least one district court in each state.

District Court Jurisdiction

1. Federal courts have limited jurisdiction. They hear cases based on federal laws (federal question cases) and cases involving diversity of citizenship.
2. Diversity of citizenship cases have a jurisdictional minimum of more than $50,000.
3. For diversity of citizenship purposes, a corporation is a citizen of two states: the state of incorporation and the state of its principal places of business.

The Law in Federal Courts

1. Federal courts use the rules of federal procedure.
2. Federal question cases are decided using federal substantive law.
3. A federal court in a diversity of citizenship case uses the substantive law of the state in which it sits to decide such a case.

Federal Reviewing Courts

1. Courts of appeals decisions are usually final.
2. Most cases in the Supreme Court are there as the result of granting a petition for a writ of certiorari.

Law and Equity

Introduction

1. Historically, courts of law handled cases involving claims for money damages.
2. Courts of equity or chancery were created where the remedy at law (money damages) was inadequate—for example, suits seeking an injunction or dissolution of a business.

Equitable Procedures

1. There is usually no right to a trial by jury.
2. Sometimes a special appointee known as a master in chancery assists with the fact finding.
3. The decision is called a decree.
4. A person may be jailed for violating a decree.

Maxims

1. Courts of equity use maxims instead of rules of law to decide cases.
2. Use of maxims allows courts to achieve justice.

Operating the Court System

Judges and Justices

1. Judges at the trial court level conduct the trial. They decide questions of procedure and instruct the jury on the law applicable to the issues to be decided by the jury. If a case is tried without a jury, the judge also finds the facts.

2. Judges of intermediate reviewing courts and justices of final reviewing courts decide cases on appeal. The questions to be decided are questions of law.
3. Reviewing courts require more legal scholarship of the reviewing judges and justices than that typically required of the trial judges.

The Jury

1. The jury function is to decide disputed questions of fact.
2. A jury may consist of as few as six persons.
3. Less than unanimous verdicts are possible with twelve-person juries.
4. Excuses from jury duty are more difficult to obtain today.

REVIEW QUESTIONS AND PROBLEMS

1. The trial courts in different states are given different names. List four names used to describe state trial courts, and indicate which is used in your state.
2. Why were small claims courts created? Give three examples of typical cases decided in such courts.
3. Henry, a resident of Nevada, sued Adam, a resident of Utah, in the federal court in California. He sought $60,000 damages for personal injuries arising out of an automobile accident that occurred in Los Angeles, California, while both parties were attending the 1987 Super Bowl.
   a. Does the federal court have jurisdiction? Why or why not?
   b. What rules of procedure will the court use? Why?
   c. What rules of substantive law will the court use? Why?
4. Paul, a citizen of Georgia, was crossing a street in New Orleans when he was struck by a car driven by David, a citizen of Texas. The car was owned by David's employer, a Delaware corporation, which has its principal place of business in Atlanta, Georgia. Paul sues both David and the corporation in the federal district court in New Orleans. Paul's complaint alleges damages in the amount of $100,000. Does this court have jurisdiction? Why?
5. What is the function of a petition for a writ of certiorari or a petition for leave to appeal? Explain.
6. John sues Ivan in a state court, seeking damages for breach of contract to sell a tennis racquet. The trial court finds for Ivan. John announces that he will appeal "all the way to the Supreme Court of the United States, if necessary, to change the decision." Assuming that John has the money to do so, will he be able to obtain review by the Supreme Court of the United States? Explain.
7. Describe three controversies that would be decided in a court of equity or chancery in states that still distinguish between courts of law and courts of equity.
8. Mario agreed to sell his house to George, but he later changed his mind. George sued Mario for specific performance. Is either party entitled to a jury trial? Why or why not?
9. For diversity of citizenship purposes, a corporation is a citizen of two states. Identify them.
10. Jane deposited $400 with her landlord to secure a lease and to pay for any damages to an apartment that she had rented. At the end of the lease, she vacated the apartment and requested the return of the deposit. Although the landlord admitted that the apartment was in good shape, the landlord refused to return the deposit. What should Jane do? Explain.
11. Why are some controversies excluded from the court system? Give examples of such issues.

Litigation: Pretrial

3

CHAPTER PREVIEW

BUSINESS MANAGEMENT DECISION

Your company, which operates in Georgia, makes and sells peanut brittle to a distributor in Atlanta that, in turn, sells the peanut brittle in Vermont. A customer in Vermont breaks a tooth on your peanut brittle. This customer files suit in Vermont against you, and a summons is served on you in Georgia.

Should you ignore the complaint and summons?

We have noted that law may be classified as substantive law or procedural law. *Substantive law* defines the rights and duties of persons. *Procedural law* specifies the method and means by which the substantive law is made, enforced, and administered. Procedural rules prescribe the methods by which courts apply substantive law to resolve conflicts. Substantive rights have no value unless there are procedures that provide a means for establishing and enforcing them.

Judicial procedure is concerned with rules by which a lawsuit is conducted. One common method of classifying judicial procedure is to divide it into two parts—criminal and civil. *Criminal procedure* prescribes the rules of law for apprehension, prosecution, and punishment of persons who have allegedly committed crimes. *Civil procedure* prescribes rules by which parties to **civil actions** use the courts to settle their disputes.

Civil action *A proceeding in a law court or a suit in equity by one person against another. Civil action is in contradistinction to criminal action, in which the state prosecutes a person for breach of a duty.*

In most cases there are three basic questions to be answered: What are the facts? What evidence is relevant and proper to prove the facts? What rules of law apply to the facts? The jury answers the first question; the court answers the second. The court also provides the answer to the third by instructing the jury as to the law applicable to the facts found by the jury.

THE PARTIES TO LITIGATION

1. Names

In a criminal case, *the people* bring the action against the named defendant. Most civil cases use the term **plaintiff** to describe the party bringing the lawsuit, and **defendant** describes the party against whom the lawsuit is brought; but in some cases, especially in courts of equity, the parties are described as the **petitioner** and the **respondent.**

Plaintiff *In an action at law, the complaining party or the one who commences the action. The person who seeks a remedy in court.*

Defendant *A person who has been sued in a court of law; the person who answers the plaintiff's complaint. In criminal actions, the defending party is referred to as the accused.*

Petitioner *The party who files a claim in a court of equity. Also the party who petitions the Supreme Court for a writ of certiorari.*

Respondent *One who answers another's bill or pleading, particularly in an equity case.*

When the result at the trial court level is appealed, the party appealing is usually referred to as **appellant,** and the successful party in the trial court is called the **appellee.** Many jurisdictions, in publishing the decisions of reviewing courts, list the appellant first and the appellee second, even though the appellant may have been the defendant in the trial court.

Appellant *The party who takes an appeal from one court or jurisdiction to another.*

Appellee *The party in a cause against whom an appeal is taken.*

In most states and in the federal courts, all persons may join in one lawsuit as plaintiffs if the causes of action arise out of the same transaction or series of transactions and involve common questions of law or fact. In addition, the plaintiffs may join as defendants all persons who are necessary to a complete determination or settlement of the questions. In addition, if a defendant alleges that a complete determination of a controversy cannot be made without other parties, that defendant may bring in new third parties as third-party defendants. This procedure is usually followed when someone is liable to a defendant who, in turn, is liable to the plaintiff.

Two problem areas or issues relating to the parties to a lawsuit frequently arise in litigation. The first of these areas is generally described as ''standing to sue.'' The second is class-action suits. These special problems are discussed more fully in the next two sections.

2. Standing to Sue

Standing to sue *The doctrine that requires the plaintiff in a lawsuit to have a sufficient legal interest in the subject matter of the case.*

The question of **standing to sue** is whether the litigant is entitled to have the court decide the dispute. The issue arises because of the limited role of courts in our society. The Constitution requires that a plaintiff must allege a case or controversy between himself and the defendant if the court is to hear the case. A plaintiff must have a personal stake in the outcome of the controversy, and this stake must be based on some threatened or actual injury resulting from the defendant's action. Without the requirement of ''standing,'' courts would be called upon to decide abstract questions of public interest. Such questions are best resolved by the political process.

When the asserted harm is a generalized grievance shared in substantially equal measure by all or a large class of citizens, that harm alone normally does not grant standing to sue. For example, a taxpayer filed suit challenging the budget of the CIA. The court held that the taxpayer lacked standing to sue. Likewise, a plaintiff must assert his own legal rights and not those of some third party. A citizen objected to the army's surveillance of civilians, but the case was dismissed without a showing that the plaintiff was one of the civilians under surveillance.

Standing to sue is in no way dependent on the merits of the plaintiff's contention that particular conduct is illegal. The presence of standing is determined by the nature and source of the plaintiff's claim. As a general rule, standing requires that a complaining party have a personal stake in the outcome of the controversy. The stake must result from adversity and must be such as to guarantee that all aspects of the issues will be presented for decision. A complainant must present facts sufficient to show that his individual needs require the remedy being sought in suits directed at government. A plaintiff must show that he has sustained or is immediately in danger of sustaining a direct injury as a result of some governmental action involved in the lawsuit. In civil rights cases and in cases involving threats to the environment, the courts have been rather liberal in finding a personal stake in a plaintiff bringing an action relating to those subjects. However, even in these areas of the law, a plaintiff must have an actual stake in the controversy. In the following case, one plaintiff had such a stake and one did not.

CASE

The Fair Housing Act of 1968 outlaws discrimination in housing and authorizes civil suits to enforce the law. Havens Realty Corporation, the operator of two apartment complexes, told Coleman, a black, that no apartments were available. Willis, a Caucasian, was told that there were vacancies. Both Coleman and Willis were "testers," or individuals who had no intent to rent or purchase a home or apartment but posed as such for the purpose of collecting evidence of unlawful practices. They filed suit against Havens Realty, alleging "racial steering" in violation of the Fair Housing Act.

The district court held that the plaintiffs lacked standing to sue and dismissed the suit. The court of appeals reversed, holding that both Willis and Coleman had standing to sue as "testers." The U.S. Supreme Court granted certiorari.

ISSUE: Do "testers," who have no desire to obtain housing, have standing to sue under the Fair Housing Act of 1968 when they receive false information concerning the availability of housing?

DECISION: Yes.

REASONS:

1. The U.S. Supreme Court has previously held that, in order to have standing to sue under the Fair Housing Act of 1968, a plaintiff has to meet only the most minimal requirements. Plaintiffs have standing in these cases as long as they allege that they have suffered "a distinct and palpable injury" as a result of a defendant's actions.
2. The Fair Housing Act of 1968 provides that it is unlawful for an individual or firm covered by the Act "[t]o represent to any person because of race, color, religion, sex, or national origin that any dwelling is not available for inspection, sale, or rental when such a dwelling is in fact so available." The Act also expressly provides for a private case of action to enforce its prohibition. Therefore the Act creates an enforceable right to truthful information concerning the availability of housing.
3. It is not the denial of available housing but the receipt of false information concerning the availability of housing that establishes the injury. Therefore, even if an individual does not intend to rent or purchase housing, once he receives false information, he has suffered the injury that the statute seeks to prevent and he has standing to sue under the Act.
4. Coleman, the black "tester," has standing to sue under the Fair Housing Act because he received false information concerning the availability of housing. However, Willis, the white "tester," did not receive any false information. Therefore he has not alleged an injury to his statutory right to truthful information concerning the availability of housing, and he does not have standing to sue under the Act. The portion of the court of appeals' decision that allowed Willis standing to sue is therefore reversed.

Havens Realty Corp. v. Coleman, 102 S.Ct. 1114 (1982).

3. Class-Action Suits

Class-action suit *A legal proceeding whereby one or more persons represent in litigation a larger group of people who might have a claim similar to the representative(s).*

A **class-action suit** is one in which a person files suit on his own behalf and on behalf of all other persons who may have a similar claim. For example, a class-action suit may be brought on behalf of all purchasers of a defective product. The number of people who comprise the class is frequently quite large. Class-action suits are popular because they often involve matters in which no one member of the class would have a sufficient financial interest to warrant filing suit. The combined interest of all members of the class not only makes litigation feasible, but often makes it very profitable for the lawyer who handles the suit.

Because many defendants consider class-action suits a form of harassment, courts have tended to discourage the suits. For example, cases have held that all members of the class be given actual notice of the lawsuit. In addition, plaintiffs who bring the class-action suit must pay all court costs of the action, including the cost of compiling names and addresses of members of the class.

CASE

A class-action suit was filed on behalf of certain stock traders against brokerage firms and a stock exchange for alleged violations of the antitrust and securities laws. Plaintiffs asked the court to order the defendants to furnish the names and addresses of all members of the class because defendants could easily gather the information and because plaintiffs had limited funds.

ISSUE: Must the defendants assist the plaintiffs in meeting the notice requirement?

DECISION: No.

REASON: The notice requirement cannot be tailored to fit the pocketbooks of the particular plaintiffs. The total cost of notice to members of the class must be borne by the plaintiffs filing the class-action suit, and a portion of the cost cannot be imposed on the defendants on the grounds that the plaintiff was more likely to win the case.

Eisen v. Carlisle & Jacquelin, 94 S.Ct. 2140 (1974).

If a class-action suit is in federal court because of diversity of citizenship, the claim of each member of the class must meet the jurisdictional amount of $50,000. This requirement, together with the requirement of notice to each member of the class, has greatly reduced the number of class-action suits in the federal courts. However, the practice of plaintiffs' lawyers combining a single grievance into a lawsuit on behalf of every possible litigant is quite common in state courts. There are numerous state class-action statutes that allow consumers and others to file suit in state courts on behalf of all citizens of that state.

THE PLACE OF LITIGATION

4. Jurisdiction

The first requirement in any lawsuit is that it must be brought before a court that has the power to hear the case. This power to hear the case is known as *jurisdiction,* and it has two aspects: jurisdiction over the subject matter and jurisdiction over the parties.

Subject Matter. Jurisdiction over the *subject matter* means that the lawsuit is of the type that the court was created to decide. A probate court would have no jurisdiction to determine questions of law involving a civil suit for damages. A criminal court would have no jurisdiction in a divorce matter. As previously noted, courts may also be limited by the amounts of money involved in the case.

Sometimes the subject-matter jurisdiction of a court is exclusive. This means that no other court has the *power* to hear such cases. The Supreme Court of the

United States has exclusive jurisdiction in all proceedings affecting ambassadors, public ministers, and consuls and in all actions in which a state is a party.

Parties. A court must also have jurisdiction over the parties—the plaintiff and the defendant. A plaintiff voluntarily submits to the jurisdiction of the court when the suit is filed.

Summons *A writ issued by a court to the sheriff, directing him to notify the defendant that the plaintiff claims to have a cause of action against the defendant and that he is required to answer. If the defendant does not answer, judgment will be taken by default.*

Jurisdiction over the defendant is accomplished by the service of a **summons** issued by the court. It is delivered to a sheriff or other person, to be served upon the defendant. Jurisdiction over a defendant in a limited number of cases may be obtained by publishing a notice in a newspaper. This method is possible in a suit for divorce or one concerning real estate—something important enough to be written up in a public notice that would be deemed adequate to notify the defendant.

Publication may also be accompanied by proper attachment proceedings. In such cases, service by publication brings under the court's jurisdiction all attached property of a nonresident defendant if it lies within the territorial limits of the court. When this technique is employed, the attached property may be used to satisfy any judgment.

Most cases, however, require the actual service of a summons to the defendant in order to give him notice of the suit. Many states allow a summons to be served upon any member of the family above a specified age, such as ten years, at the defendant's home. In such cases, a copy is also mailed to the defendant.

5. Long-Arm Statutes

Historically, the jurisdiction of courts to enter judgment against a person required actual personal service of the summons on the defendant in the state in which the suit was brought. This was necessary in order to give the defendant notice of the suit and an opportunity to defend. Because the jurisdiction of courts was limited to geographic areas such as a state, the power to issue and serve a summons beyond the borders of the state did not exist.

Limiting the jurisdiction of courts to persons physically present in the state is no longer accepted. Personal jurisdiction over nonresidents has been expanded because modern transportation and communication facilities have minimized the inconveniences to a nonresident defendant who must defend himself in courts beyond his home state. There is no longer any logical reason to deny a local citizen a remedy in local courts for an injury caused by a nonresident temporarily present in the state.

Long-arm statute *A law which allows courts in the state court systems to extend their personal jurisdiction beyond the state boundaries to nonresident defendants if such defendants have had sufficient minimal contacts with the state to justify the exercise of personal jurisdiction.*

The first extension of jurisdiction over nonresidents occurred in auto accident cases. This extension was made by creating a legal ''fiction'' that resulted in the summons being served within the state whose court issued the summons. This legal fiction was created by the enactment of statutes providing that a nonresident, by using the state highways, automatically appointed a designated state official, usually the secretary of state, as his agent to accept service of process. The summons would be served on the secretary of state, who would notify the defendant of the suit, and the defendant was then subject to the power of the court.

These nonresident motorist statutes opened the door for adoption of other statutes called **long-arm statutes,** which further extend the jurisdiction of courts over nonresidents, whether individuals or corporations. Long-arm statutes typically extend the jurisdiction of courts to cases in which a tort injury has been caused by a nonresident temporarily present in the state. They also usually extend jurisdiction to cases arising out of the ownership of property located within the state. Of course, the conduct of business such as entering into contracts confers jurisdiction. Thus, a nonresident individual or a corporation may be subject to a suit for injuries if either has certain "minimal contacts" within the state, so long as the maintenance of the suit does not offend traditional notions of fair play and substantial justice.

What "minimal contacts" and activities are necessary to bring the defendant into a state is a fact question depending on each particular case. Whatever the basis for the action may be, either in contract or in tort, the court can acquire jurisdiction over the defendant if these minimal contacts are present. If there are no minimal contacts, there is no jurisdiction because requiring a defense would be a denial of due process of law. The following landmark case illustrates that long-arm statutes do have limitations.

CASE

The Robinsons lived in New York. They purchased an Audi automobile from Seaway Motors, a dealership in New York. Seaway had purchased the car from World-Wide Volkswagen Corporation, a New York Audi distributor for the New York-Connecticut-New Jersey region. While the Robinsons were driving the Audi to their new home in Arizona, they were involved in an accident on an Oklahoma freeway when another car rear-ended their Audi, rupturing the gas tank and causing a fire. The Robinsons brought a products liability action for their injuries against Seaway, World-Wide Volkswagen, and others in an Oklahoma court claiming the wreck was due to a manufacturing defect in the Audi. The defendants were served under an Oklahoma long-arm statute. Neither Seaway nor World-Wide Volkswagen did any business in Oklahoma, and they filed a motion to dismiss for lack of personal jurisdiction. The trial judge denied the motion. The Oklahoma Supreme Court held that the defendants were subject to the Oklahoma trial court's jurisdiction. The U.S. Supreme Court granted the defendants' petition for a writ of certiorari.

ISSUE: Can an Oklahoma court exercise *in personam* jurisdiction over a nonresident automobile retailer and its wholesaler in a products liability action when the defendants' only connection with Oklahoma is the fact that an automobile sold in New York to New York residents became involved in an accident in Oklahoma?

DECISION: No.

REASONS:

1. The due process clause of the Fourteenth Amendment to the Constitution requires that our legal system be characterized by some degree of predictability, so that citizens can at least estimate the legal consequences of their behavior, such as where they must answer a lawsuit. Citizens can then either accept the risks of potentially adverse legal consequences or adjust their behavior to lessen those risks.
2. Due process not only ensures fairness and predictability, but also prohibits the states from reaching out though their courts beyond the limits imposed on them by their status as co-equal sovereigns in our federal system. States would transgress those limits if they exercised jurisdiction over nonresidents who had not purposefully established some sort of contact with the state that would justify their exercise of jurisdiction.

3. Therefore, this court has held that due process prevents state courts from exercising personal jurisdiction over a nonresident defendant unless "minimum contacts" exist between the defendant and the forum state. This "minimum contacts" requirement ensures that states will not force a nonresident to litigate in their courts, a possibly distant and inconvenient forum, unless doing so is fair to the defendant and does not violate the sovereignty of their fellow states.
4. Standing alone, the fortuitous circumstance that one automobile, sold in New York by the defendants to New York residents, happened to suffer an accident in Oklahoma and cause injury to Oklahoma citizens, does not satisfy the "minimum contacts" test of due process.
5. The Oklahoma court's exercise of jurisdiction over the defendants would be reasonable if the accident were not an isolated occurrence, but arose from the defendants' efforts to serve, either directly or indirectly, the market for their cars in Oklahoma. However, the defendants have made no efforts, through salespeople or advertising reasonably calculated to reach Oklahoma, to sell any products or services in the state. They do not serve or seek to serve, directly or indirectly, the Oklahoma market.
6. Therefore the defendants' conduct and connection with the state are not such that they should have reasonably anticipated being hailed into an Oklahoma court. In other words, "minimum contacts" between the defendants and Oklahoma do not exist. The Oklahoma court may not exercise jurisdiction over Seaway or World-Wide Volkswagen.

World-Wide Volkswagen Corp. v. Woodson, 100 S.Ct. 559 (1980).

6. Venue

Venue *The geographical area over which a court presides. Venue designates the county in which the action is tried. Change of venue means to move to another county.*

As previously discussed, the term *jurisdiction* describes the power of the court to hear and adjudicate the case. Jurisdiction includes the court's power to inquire into the facts, apply the law to the facts, make a decision, and declare and enforce a judgment. **Venue** relates to, and defines, the particular territorial area within the state, county, or district in which the civil case should be brought and tried. Matters of venue are usually determined by statute. In a few states, the subject of venue is covered in the state constitution.

Venue statutes usually provide that actions concerning interests in land must be commenced and tried in the county or district in which the land is located. Actions for the recovery of penalties imposed by statute against public officers must be commenced and tried in the county or district in which the cause of action arose. Suits for divorce must be commenced and tried in the county in which one of the parties resides. All other suits or actions must be commenced and tried in the county in which one or all of the defendants reside or in the county in which the transaction took place or where the wrong was committed. A tort action may be commenced and tried either in the county or district where the tort was committed or where the defendant resides or may be found. If the defendants are nonresidents, and assuming that proper service can be made upon them under a long-arm statute, the suit may be commenced and tried in any county the plaintiff designates in his complaint.

The judge may change the place of trial at the request of either party when it appears from an affidavit of either party that the action was not commenced in the proper venue. A change of venue may also be requested on the ground that the judge has an interest in the suit or is related to any parties to the action or has manifested a prejudice so that he cannot be expected to conduct a fair and impartial trial. A change of venue is often requested in criminal trials when the inhabitants of the county allegedly are so prejudiced against the defendant that a fair trial is not possible. The convenience of witnesses and the parties may also justify a change of venue.

PLEADINGS

7. Introduction

Pleading *Process by which the parties in a lawsuit arrive at an issue.*

A **pleading** is a legal document filed with the court that sets forth the position and contentions of a party. The purpose of pleadings in civil actions is to define the issues of the lawsuit. This is accomplished by each party making allegations of fact and the other party either admitting the allegations or denying them. The procedure begins when the plaintiff files with the clerk of the court a pleading usually called a **complaint.** In some types of cases this initial pleading is called a *declaration* or a *petition*. The clerk then issues a summons that, together with a copy of the complaint, is served on the defendant. The summons notifies the defendant of the date by which he is required to file a pleading in answer to the allegations of the complaint or to file some other pleading attacking the complaint.

Complaint *The first pleading a plaintiff files in a court in a lawsuit. It is a statement of the facts upon which the plaintiff rests his cause of action.*

If the defendant has no legal basis to attack the sufficiency of the complaint, he may simply file an entry of appearance, or he may file an *answer* either admitting or denying each material allegation of the complaint. This answer will put in issue all allegations of the complaint that are denied. A simple entry of appearance is an admission of the truth of all allegations of the complaint.

In addition to admissions and denials, an answer may contain affirmative defenses, which if proved will defeat the plaintiff's claim. The answer may also contain **counterclaims,** causes of action the defendant has against the plaintiff. Upon receipt of the defendant's answer, the plaintiff will, unless the applicable rules of procedure do not so require, file a reply that specifically admits or denies each new allegation in the defendant's answer. These new allegations are those found in the affirmative defenses and counterclaims. Thus the allegations of each party are admitted or denied in the pleadings. Allegations of fact claimed by either party and denied by the other become the issues to be decided at the trial.

Counterclaims *By cross-action, the defendant cl… that he is entitled to r… from the plaintiff. … must arise out … transaction … plaintiff's … connec… subj… th…*

A defendant that fails to answer the allegations of the plaintiff is in default, and a court of law may enter a default judgment against him. In effect, the defendant has admitted the allegations of the plaintiff. A court of equity would enter a similar order known as a decree *pro confesso*. A plaintiff who fails to reply to new matte… such as a counterclaim is also subject to a judgment or decree by default.

8. Motions Attacking Pleadings

The first pleading (complaint) in order to be legally sufficient, must allege facts sufficient to set forth a right of action or the plaintiff's right to legal relief. The defendant's attorney, after studying the complaint, may (instead of answering) choose one of several different ways to challenge its legal sufficiency. For example, by motion to the court, the defendant may object to the complaint, pointing out specifically its defects. The defendant, through such motion, admits for purposes of argument all the facts alleged in the complaint. His position is that those facts are not legally sufficient to give the plaintiff the right to what is sought in the complaint. Such motion, called a **demurrer** at common law, raises questions of law, not questions of fact. If the court finds that the complaint does set forth facts sufficient to give the plaintiff what is sought, it will deny the motion. Some states require that the complaint state a cause of action. Others require only that the facts alleged establish a right to the relief sought. In either case, it is reversible error to dismiss a complaint that is legally sufficient.

Demurrer *A common law procedural method by which the defendant admits all the facts alleged in the plaintiff's complaint but denies that such facts state a cause of action. It raises a question of law on the facts, which must be decided by the court.*

If the motion is denied, the defendant will then be granted time to answer the complaint. Should he fail to do so within the time limit set by the court, a judgment by default may be entered for the plaintiff. If the court finds, however, that the complaint fails to state facts sufficient to give the plaintiff the relief sought, the court will allow the motion and dismiss the suit, but will give to the plaintiff permission to file an amended complaint. The plaintiff will thus be given an opportunity to restate the allegations so that he may be able to set forth a right to recover from the defendant.

In addition to a motion to dismiss for failure to allege a valid cause of action, a defendant may also move to dismiss the suit for reasons that as a matter of law would prevent the plaintiff from winning his suit. Such matters as a discharge in bankruptcy, a lack of jurisdiction of the court to hear the suit, or an expiration of the time limit during which the defendant is subject to suit may be raised by such a motion. These are technical matters that raise questions of law for the court's decision.

In order to expedite litigation, many states require that all motions attacking a complaint be included with an answer to the allegations set forth in the complaint. This requirement reduces the time required for the pleading stage of the litigation.

9. Decisions Prior to a Trial

Judgment on the Pleadings. Most states and the federal courts also have procedures known as motions for *judgment on the pleadings,* by which either party may seek a final decision without a trial. In hearings on these motions, the court examines the pleadings on file in the case to see if a genuine material issue of fact remains. If there is no such question of fact, the court will then decide the legal question raised by the facts and find for one party or the other. In such cases, the pleadings alone establish that there is no reason for a trial, and the issues between the parties are pure questions of law.

mmary judgment *A ial determination that nuine factual dispute nd that one party to uit is entitled to as a matter of law.*

Summary Judgment. If a litigant asks the trial judge to decide a case based on the pleadings plus supporting materials, a motion for **summary judgment** is involved—a procedure created to avoid trials when the facts are not disputed. If the only issue before the court is the legal effect of those facts, this issue can be decided by the court on motion by one of the parties.

Either party may ask the court for a summary judgment. The usual procedure is to attach to the motion the supporting **affidavits** that set forth the facts and to supplement these affidavits with depositions taken during the discovery process (discussed in detail in the following section). The opposing party is also permitted to file affidavits and depositions with the court. These affidavits and depositions in effect supply the court with sworn testimony. The court then examines this sworn testimony to see whether there is a genuine issue as to any material fact. If there is no such factual issue, the litigation will be decided on the facts presented to the court.

Affidavit *A voluntary statement of facts formally reduced to writing, sworn to, or affirmed before, some officer authorized to administer oaths. The officer is usually a notary public.*

CASE

Plaintiff, Benjamin, age fifteen, went swimming at a pool located in an apartment complex owned by defendant, Deffet Rentals, Inc. Eventually, plaintiff and a friend began jumping and diving off a 7-foot plastic sliding board located at the deepest end of the pool, where the water level was from 5 to 5½ feet deep.

Plaintiff initially jumped off the platform at the top of the sliding board. Next, he successfully executed a dive into the pool. However, in attempting a third dive, plaintiff's feet slipped as he pushed off the slide platform. Because of this, he inadvertently propelled himself into the pool at an acute vertical angle. His head struck the bottom of the pool, breaking his neck.

Plaintiff sued, alleging negligence on the part of Deffet Rentals for failing to reasonably provide for safe operation of the pool, for installing an unreasonably dangerous and defective slide, and for failing to warn plaintiff of latent hazards in the slide.

Defendant filed a motion for summary judgment that basically asserted the defense of assumption of the risk. It cited a prior case that had held that assumption of the risk was a complete defense. In support of that motion, defendant filed a deposition of the plaintiff in which he admitted that he knew that if he went into the water at the wrong angle, he would get hurt.

ISSUE: Is a summary judgment appropriate?

DECISION: Yes.

REASONS:

1. Defendant's motion for summary judgment was supported by the deposition. This deposition demonstrated appellee's knowledge of the risk inherent in diving into shallow water from a structure not designed for such activity.
2. The motion for summary judgment, and the evidence marshaled in support thereof, show that there is no genuine issue of material fact and demonstrates, as a matter of law, that appellee assumed the risk of his injury.

Benjamin v. Deffet Rentals, Inc., 419 N.E.2d 883 (Ohio 1981).

In most states, a court may render a summary judgment on the issue of liability alone and leave the amount of damages to be decided at the trial. Many of the cases set forth in later chapters of this text were decided by the summary judgment procedure. Remember that a summary judgment will not be granted when there is a disputed question of any material fact.

DISCOVERY

Discovery *The procedure whereby parties involved in litigation exchange information about their cases.*

During the pleading stage and in the interval before the trial, the law provides for procedures called **discovery.** Discovery is designed to take surprise out of litigation and to ensure that the results of lawsuits are based on the merits of the controversy rather than on the ability, skill, or cunning of counsel. Discovery procedures prevent a party or a witness from remaining silent about material facts. They ensure that all potential testimony and other evidence is equally available to both parties. With each side fully aware of the strengths and weaknesses of both sides, the second of the avowed purposes of discovery—to encourage settlement of suits and to avoid actual trial—is facilitated. Modern discovery procedures result in the compromise and settlement of most civil suits.

Discovery practices include deposing (oral questioning under oath) of other parties and witnesses; written questions, called interrogations, answered in writing under oath by the opposite party; compulsory physical examinations by doctors chosen by the other party in personal injury cases; orders requiring the production of statements, exhibits, documents, maps, photographs, and so on; and serving of demands by one party on the other to admit facts under oath. These procedures allow a party to learn not only about matters that may be used as evidence but also about matters that may lead to the discovery of evidence. The fact that evidence is relevant does not always mean that it is subject to discovery. The law will deny discovery when other interests such as trade secrets may outweigh the needs of a party to litigation. However, discovery is to be permitted in cases where the exchange of information will not cause irreparable damage and will lead to better informed litigants.

CASE

Bruce Mincey was killed by the explosion of a steel drum that he was cutting with a circular saw. In a wrongful death action brought by the plaintiff, Pearl Mincey, administratrix of his estate, against the defendant, Dorsey Trailers, Inc., the defendant served interrogatories upon the plaintiff seeking information concerning the facts and circumstances that supported plaintiff's claim that defendant was responsible for the death. The interrogatories requested information about the decedent's medical history, work history, and educational background. In addition, the defendant requested the identities of expert witnesses to be called by the plaintiff and the substance of their testimony. When the plaintiff refused to answer the questions, the defendant asked the trial judge to compel answers to the interrogatories. When the trial judge refused to grant the defendant's request, the defendant appealed.

ISSUE: Did the trial judge abuse his discretion in not compelling answers to the interrogatories?

DECISION: Yes.

REASONS:

1. To be discoverable, material need only be relevant to the subject matter of the action and not competent as evidence at trial.
2. The scope of discovery is broad and defendant is entitled to information on decedent's background, as it may be relative to his ability to understand any warnings on the drum.

3. It is not the prerogative of a party answering interrogatives to refuse to answer because of his opinion regarding the usefulness of the information sought. The answering party is also required to disclose the facts discovered and opinions held by his own expert witnesses.

Ex parte Dorsey Trailers, 397 S.2d 98 (Ala. 1981).

Just prior to the trial, a pretrial conference between the lawyers and the judge will be held in states with modern rules of procedure. At this conference the pleadings, results of the discovery process, and probable evidence are reviewed in an attempt to settle the suit. The issues may be further narrowed, and the judge may even predict the outcome in order to encourage settlement.

CHAPTER SUMMARY

The Parties to Litigation

1. The names used to describe the parties in litigation vary, depending on the type of lawsuit and the stage of the litigation. Cases on appeal are usually titled in the name of the appellant versus the appellee.
2. A plaintiff must have standing to sue. Standing requires that the plaintiff have an actual stake in the controversy such that all issues will be adequately raised.
3. Suits are often brought by one person on behalf of a class. Class-action suits require notice to all members of the class, and each member must meet the jurisdictional amount in the federal courts.

The Place of Litigation

Jurisdiction

1. To render a binding decision, a court must have jurisdiction of the subject matter of the litigation and over the parties.
2. Jurisdiction over the defendant is usually obtained by the service of a summons. In some cases jurisdiction may be obtained by publishing a notice in the newspaper.

Long-Arm Statutes

1. A summons may be served beyond the borders of the state if the state has a long-arm statute. Such service is not a denial of due process if the party served has sufficient contact with the state issuing the summons that requiring the out-of-state defendant to appear and defend the lawsuit does not offend our traditional notions of fair play and substantial justice.
2. A plaintiff may file a lawsuit in a state without "minimum contacts," since the plaintiff is voluntarily submitting to the jurisdiction of the court.

Venue

1. The term *venue* is used to describe the appropriate court among all of those with jurisdiction to hear the case.

Pleadings

Introduction

1. The term *pleading* is used to describe papers filed with the court by the parties in order to create the issues for trial. The plaintiff makes allegations in a complaint, and the defendant answers the complaint by admitting or denying each allegation of the complaint.

2. The pleadings may contain counterclaims of the defendant, and in some states the plaintiff must file a reply to all new matters raised in the answer.

Motions Attacking Pleadings

1. Many cases are decided on motions attacking pleadings. The law requires certain minimal allegations, and if each of these allegations is not present, a court may dismiss the complaint.
2. Motions may also be filed during the pleading stage that raise technical matters such as bankruptcy, illegality, or other matters that would indicate a trial was unnecessary

Decisions Prior to a Trial

1. If during the pleading stage it appears that there is no material fact in dispute, then there is no need for a trial. The court will decide the questions of law raised by the pleadings and other documents on file. This decision may be a judgment on the pleadings or it may be a summary judgment.

Discovery

1. During the pleading stage and thereafter, the law has several techniques that the parties use to discover facts known by the other.
2. These techniques include the taking of depositions, the furnishing of copies of documents and photographs, serving interrogatories, and compulsory physical examinations.
3. The purpose of discovery is to encourage settlement and to take the surprise element out of litigation.
4. At the close of discovery the parties and the judge meet at a pretrial conference to finish narrowing the issues for trial and to settle the case if possible.

REVIEW QUESTIONS AND PROBLEMS

1. Match each term in column A with the appropriate statement in column B.

A	B
(1) Petitioner	(a) The proper court in which to conduct a trial.
(2) Venue	(b) The party bringing a civil lawsuit.
(3) Respondent	(c) When served with a summons, this person is subject to the jurisdiction of the court.
(4) Plaintiff	(d) A person bringing a lawsuit in equity.
(5) Counterdefendant	(e) A person against whom equitable relief is sought.
(6) Long-arm statute	(f) A defendant who seeks damages from a plaintiff.
(7) Counterplaintiff	(g) A plaintiff whose damages may be reduced because of an obligation owed the defendant.
(8) Defendant	(h) A law that authorizes the service of a summons beyond the border of the state.
(9) Summary judgment	(i) The common law term for a motion to dismiss a complaint.
(10) Demurrer	(j) A final decision without a trial because no facts are in dispute.

2. The Sierra Club, an organization devoted to the conservation and maintenance of national forests, sued the Secretary of the Interior to prevent federal approval of an extensive skiing development. The secretary asked the court to dismiss the suit on the ground that the plaintiffs lacked standing to sue. What result? Why?
3. The parents of black children attending public schools in districts undergoing desegregation brought a nationwide class-action suit alleging that the Internal Revenue Service had not adopted sufficient standards and procedures to fulfill its obligation to deny tax-exempt

status to racially discriminatory private schools. Did the plaintiffs have standing to bring this class-action suit? Explain.

4. A paving contractor incorporated in Delaware with the principal place of business in Indiana was hired to oil and chip streets in a mobile home park located in Urbana, Illinois. Heavy winds developed during the spraying of oil on the street and a light film of oil was sprayed on 106 mobile homes, doing approximately $500 damage to each. A class-action suit was filed in federal court seeking $103,000 damages. Does the court have jurisdiction? Explain.

5. An accounting firm incorporated in Oregon performed accounting services in California in connection with a merger. A dispute arose later and the corporation was sued in California. The summons was served in Oregon as authorized by the California long-arm statute. The accounting firm objected to the jurisdiction of the court. Did the California court have jurisdiction over the defendant? Why?

6. Geraldine's car had been illegally repossessed in Texas by the Baker Bank, a federally chartered national bank located in the state of Tennessee. The National Bank Act requires that suits against national banks be brought in the county in which the bank is located. Geraldine sued the bank in Texas, and it moved to dismiss contending that the suit could not be brought in Texas. What result? Why?

7. Pauline filed a complaint for divorce against Daniel. The complaint and summons was left with Daniel's secretary at his office while he was out of town. Was Daniel properly served with these process papers? Why?

8. Munns suffered injuries in an automobile accident while driving his VW Beetle in Alaska. He sued Volkswagen and recovered a sizable judgment because of a defective seat belt mechanism. Volkswagen then sued Klippan, a German corporation, which had sold the seat belt mechanism to Volkswagen in Germany. This suit was filed in Alaska. Klippan contended that the court lacked personal jurisdiction over it. Could Alaska's long-arm statute properly be used in this case? Why?

9. What is the basic distinction between jurisdiction and venue? Give three reasons for granting a motion for a change of venue.

10. What is the function of a pleading stage of a lawsuit? Explain how this function is accomplished.

11. When is a motion for summary judgment proper?

12. List four types of discovery procedures. What is the principal purpose of discovery procedures in general? What sanctions are available to a court for noncompliance?

4 Trials and Appeals

CHAPTER PREVIEW

BUSINESS MANAGEMENT DECISION

As the result of a jury verdict of $3,000 against your company, you consult your lawyer. The lawyer advises you that an appeal, which would cost $2,500, would likely be successful in having the jury verdict reversed.

Should your company appeal?

THE TRIAL

1. Jury Selection

Not every case can be settled in the pretrial stage, even under modern procedures. Some must go to trial on the issues of fact raised by pleadings that remain after the pretrial conference. If the only issues are questions of law, the court will decide the case without a trial by ruling on one of the motions previously mentioned. If the case is at law and either party has demanded a jury trial, the case will be set for trial and a jury empaneled. If the case is in equity or if no jury demand has been made, it will be set down for trial before the court. For purposes of the following discussion, we shall assume a trial before a jury.

The first step of the trial is to select the jury. Prior to calling the case, the clerk of the court will have summoned potential jurors known as the **venire.** They will be selected at random from lists of eligible citizens, and the appropriate number (six or twelve) will be called into the jury box for the conduct of ***voir dire*** examination.

Venire *Potential jurors.*

Voir dire *Preliminary examination of a prospective juror.*

In *voir dire,* the court and attorneys for each party question prospective jurors to determine their fairness and impartiality. Jurors are sworn to answer truthfully and may be challenged or excused for cause, such as bias or relation to one of the parties. A certain number of **peremptory challenges,** for which no cause need be given, may also be exercised to reject potential jurors.

Peremptory challenge *An objection raised by a party to a lawsuit who rejects a person serving as a juror. No reason need be given.*

2. Introduction of Proof

After selecting the jurors, the attorneys make opening statements. An opening statement is not evidence. Its purpose is to familiarize the jury with essential facts that each side expects to prove, in order that the jury may understand the overall picture of the case and the relevancy of each piece of evidence. After the opening statements, the plaintiff presents his evidence.

Evidence *In law,* evidence *has two meanings. (1) Testimony of witnesses and facts presented to the court and jury by way of writings and exhibits, which impress the minds of the court and jury, to the extent that an allegation has been proven. (2) The rules of law, called the law of evidence, that determine what evidence shall be introduced at a trial and what shall not.*

Evidence. **Evidence** is presented in open court by means of examination of witnesses and the production of documents and other exhibits. The party calling a witness questions him to establish the facts about the case. As a general rule, a party calling a witness is not permitted to ask *leading questions,* questions in which the desired answer is indicated by the form of the question. After the party calling the witness has completed his direct examination, the other party is given the opportunity to cross-examine the witness. Matters inquired into on cross-examination are limited tc those matters that were raised on direct examination. After cross-examination, the party calling the witness again has the opportunity of examining the witness, and this examination is called redirect examination. It is limited to the scope of those matters covered on cross-examination and is used to clarify matters raised on cross-examination. After redirect examination, the opposing party is allowed recross-examination, with the corresponding limitation on scope of the questions. Witnesses may be asked to identify exhibits. Expert witnesses may be asked to give their opinion, within certain limitations, about the case, and sometimes experts are allowed to answer hypothetical questions.

Rules of Evidence. In the conduct of a trial, *rules of evidence* govern admissibility of testimony and exhibits and establish which facts may be presented to the jury. Each rule of evidence is based on some policy consideration and the desire to give each party an opportunity to present his evidence and contentions without unduly taking advantage of the other party. Rules of evidence were not created to serve as a stumbling block to meritorious litigants or to create unwarranted roadblocks to justice. On the contrary, rules of evidence were created and should be applied to ensure fair play and to aid in the goal of having controversies determined on their merits. Modern rules of evidence are liberal in the sense that they allow the introduction of most evidence that may contribute to the search for truth.

For example, with respect to written documents, courts generally have required that the original writing be presented as evidence of that document's contents. This rule, known as the *best evidence rule,* is important for businesspeople to understand and remember. The original of all contracts, promissory notes, and other written documents must be signed by the parties and preserved in case they are needed as evidence to resolve a dispute. However, when the original cannot be located, an authenticated copy generally will be accepted as evidence as an exception to the best evidence requirement.

CASE

Robert Rodenberg borrowed $900,000 on behalf of his company, RRR&G, Inc. Rodenberg signed a promissory note payable to Farmers Bank of Delaware on behalf of the corporation and as a personal guarantor. Farmers Bank had financial difficulty, and as a result, it sold many of its notes to the FDIC. Among these notes purchased by the FDIC was the RRR&G note, which was guaranteed by Rodenberg. RRR&G filed for bankruptcy, and the FDIC sued Rodenberg personally for payment of the $900,000 owed. The FDIC presented photocopies of the promissory note and personal guaranty. Rodenberg objected to these copies being admitted as evidence since they were not the original notes.

ISSUE: Should the photocopies be admitted into evidence in lieu of the original note and guaranty agreement?

DECISION: Yes.

REASONS:

1. A supplemental affidavit and extracts from Rodenberg's deposition were submitted to show that these copies were taken from the files the FDIC obtained from Farmers Bank.
2. Since Rodenberg does not deny signing the documents and the relevant terms of the note and guaranty are clear, these copies are admissible as duplicates.

Federal Deposit Insurance Corporation v. Rodenberg, 571 F. Supp. 455 (D.C. Md. 1983).

To illustrate the policy considerations that form the basis of the rules of evidence, an examination of the rules relating to privileged communications is helpful.

The policy behind the Fifth Amendment's privilege against self-incrimination is obvious. Other communications—such as between husband and wife, doctor and patient, clergy and penitent, and attorney and client—are also considered privileged by the law, in order that they can be made without fear of their subsequent use against the parties involved. Fair play requires that attorneys not be required to testify on matters told to them in confidence by their clients. The preservation of the home requires that a spouse not be required to testify against the other spouse regarding confidential communications. The existence of insurance coverage for a party is privileged because of the impact that knowledge of the existence of insurance would have on a jury. Jurors might award damages or increase the amount simply because of the ability of an insurance company to pay. By these rules of fair play, privileged matters should not be admitted into evidence. Similar policy considerations support all rules of evidence. Each rule is designed to assist in the search for truth.

3. Motions during Trial

A basic rule of evidence is that a party cannot introduce evidence unless it is competent and relevant to the issues raised by the pleadings. A connection between the pleadings and the trial stage of the lawsuit is also present in certain motions made during the trial. After the plaintiff has presented his evidence, for example, the defendant will usually make a motion for a **directed verdict.** This motion asks the court to rule as a matter of law that the plaintiff has failed to establish the case against the defendant and that a verdict should be entered for the defendant as a matter of law. The court can direct a verdict for the defendant only if the evidence taken in the light most favorable to the plaintiff establishes as a matter of law that the defendant is entitled to a verdict. The defendant argues that the plaintiff has failed to prove each allegation of his complaint. Just as a plaintiff must allege certain facts or have his complaint dismissed by motion to dismiss, he must also have some proof of each essential allegation or lose his case on a motion for a directed verdict. If he has some proof of each allegation, the motion will be denied. If a reviewing court finds that there was no evidence to support a claim, it may reverse for failure to allow for a directed verdict. The following case is typical of those in which a trial judge erred in submitting a case to a jury.

Directed verdict *If it is apparent to reasonable men and the court that the plaintiff, by his evidence, has not made out his case, the court may instruct the jury to bring in a verdict for the defendant. If, however, different inferences may be drawn from the evidence by reasonable men, then the court cannot direct a verdict.*

CASE

Willmon, a customer in a Safeway store in Malvern, Arkansas, slipped on a liquid substance and fell while pushing a cart down an aisle. He sued Safeway for his injuries. Safeway moved for a directed verdict twice during trial, once at the close of the plaintiff's presentation of his case and once at the close of all evidence. The trial court denied these motions, and thus submitted the issue of negligence to the jury.

ISSUE: Should the court have granted Safeway's motion for a directed verdict?

DECISION: Yes.

REASONS: 1. The mere fact that a patron slips and falls in a store does not raise an inference of the store's negligence. When a business invitee slips and falls on a foreign substance on the premises of a business, he may establish liability on the part of the business in two ways. He must prove either that the presence of the substance on the floor was the result of the storekeeper's negligence or, regardless of how the substance came to be on the floor, that the substance had been on the floor for such a length of time that the storekeeper knew, or reasonably should have known, of its presence and failed to use ordinary care to remove it.

2. At trial, there was no proof that the liquid was on the floor as a result of the storekeeper's negligence. There was not even any substantial evidence on how the substance came to be on the floor. Although Willmon testified that an unknown employee of Safeway told him the substance looked like soapy water, two employees who inspected the fluid identified it as clear water. The store manager testified that the water could have been brought from a water fountain at the rear of the store, or that someone could have spilled a cup of ice. One store employee testified that he inspected nearby jugs of distilled water and found none that leaked. These various speculations and conjectures do not suffice to show any evidence of negligence.

3. Similarly, there was no proof that the water had been on the floor for such a length of time that the storekeeper knew or should have known of its presence and failed to use ordinary care to remove it. Safeway's records show that the aisle had been swept one hour and fifteen minutes before the fall. Employees had walked down the aisle between the time of sweeping and the time of the fall. There was no evidence that any employee knew of the spill or reasonably should have known of it. The plaintiff only showed that if an employee had been working at the check-out counter at the end of the aisle, that employee would have been within 15 feet of the spill.

4. Probable causes of a fall would constitute substantial evidence of negligence. However, possible causes, such as those the plaintiff offered at trial, do not constitute evidence. Because there was no substantial evidence of negligence, the trial judge should have granted the motion for a directed verdict.

Safeway Stores, Inc. v. Willmon, 708 S.W.2d 623 (Ark. 1986).

In cases tried without a jury, either party may move for a finding in his favor. Such a motion will be allowed during the course of the trial if the result is not in doubt. The judge in ruling on such motions weighs the evidence, but he may end the trial before all the evidence is presented only if there is no room for a fair difference of opinion as to the result.

If the defendant's motion for directed verdict is overruled, the defendant then presents his evidence. After the defendant has presented all his evidence, the plaintiff may bring in rebuttal evidence. When neither party has any additional evidence, the attorneys and the judge retire for a conference to consider the instructions of law to be given the jury.

4. Jury Instructions

The purpose of jury instructions is to acquaint the jury with the law applicable to the case. Since the function of the jury is to find the facts, and the function of the court is to determine the applicable law, court and jury must be brought together in an orderly manner that will result in a decision. This uniting is accomplished by the court's instructing the jury, acquainting it with the law applicable to the case.

CASE

Laurie, a diabetic, rented an apartment from Donald and Patricia. Shortly after moving into her apartment, Laurie stumbled and fell in the front yard. Although it was not immediately diagnosed as serious, Laurie later discovered that her ankle had been broken. She sued her landlords. The trial jury found for the landlords, apparently believing that Laurie's diabetic condition was the cause of her falling. Laurie appeals and argues that the trial judge erred in refusing to instruct the jury that the plaintiff had to prove only that the landlords' negligence was a contributing cause to the injury suffered. In fact, the jury was instructed as follows: "When I use the expression 'proximate cause,' I mean a cause which, in natural or probable sequence, produced the injury complained of."

ISSUE: Were the judge's instructions to the jury improper?

DECISION: No.

REASONS:

1. The purpose of instructions is to convey to the jurors the correct principles of law applicable to the evidence before them.
2. The proper approach in considering the propriety of a jury instruction is whether the instructions when considered as a whole were sufficiently clear so that the jury was not misled.
3. The instruction as given does not suggest to the jury that they are limited to a determination of a single cause for plaintiff's injury.

Wilson v. Pepich, 450 N.E.2d 882 (Ill. App. 1983).

In order to prepare instructions, the court confers with attorneys for both sides. At the conference, the attorneys submit to the court the instructions they feel should be given to the jury. The court examines these instructions and allows each side to object to the other's instructions. A party who fails to submit an instruction on a point of law cannot later object to the failure to instruct on that point. Similarly, the failure to object to an instruction is a waiver of the objection. The court then decides which instructions will be given to the jury. A jury instruction tells the jury that if it finds certain facts, then its verdict should be for the plaintiff. If it fails to find these facts, then the verdict should be for the defendant.

In the federal courts and in some state courts, judges may comment on the evidence while giving instructions. They may indicate the importance of certain portions of evidence, the inferences that might be drawn therefrom, the conflicts, what statements are more likely to be true than others, and why. The judge, however, is duty bound to make clear to the jury that it is not obligated to follow the court's evaluation of the evidence and that it is the jury's duty to determine the facts of the case.

5. Burdens of Proof

Burden of proof *This term has two distinctive meanings. One meaning is used to identify the party that has the burden of coming forward with evidence of a particular fact. The second meaning is used to identify the party with the burden of persuasion.*

The term **burden of proof** has two meanings. It may describe the person with the burden of coming forward with evidence on a particular issue. The party alleging the existence of a certain fact usually has the burden of coming forward with evidence to establish that fact. The more common usage of the term, however, is to identify the party with the burden of persuasion. The party with this burden must convince the trial (judge or jury) on the factual issues. If a party with the burden of persuasion fails to do so, that party loses the issue.

The extent of proof required to satisfy the burden of persuasion varies, depending upon the issue and the type of case. There are three distinct levels of proof recognized by the law: beyond a reasonable doubt, manifest weight, and clear and convincing proof. For criminal cases, the burden of proof is described as "beyond a reasonable doubt." This means that the prosecution in a criminal case has the burden of convincing the trier, usually a jury, of fact that the defendant is guilty of the crime charged and that the jury has no reasonable doubt about guilt. This burden of proof does not require evidence beyond any doubt, but only beyond a reasonable doubt. A reasonable doubt is one that a reasonable person viewing the evidence might reasonably entertain.

In civil cases the party with the burden of proof will be subject to one of two standards: the manifest weight of the evidence standard or the clear and convincing proof standard. *Manifest weight,* the standard used most frequently, requires that a party convince the jury by a preponderance of evidence that the facts are as contended. By *preponderance of evidence* we mean that there is greater weight of evidence in support of the proposition than there is against it.

The *clear and convincing proof* requirement is used in certain situations in which the law requires more than a simple preponderance of evidence but less than proof beyond a reasonable doubt. In a securities law case, proof of fraud usually requires clear and convincing evidence if a plaintiff is to succeed. A slight preponderance of evidence in favor of the party asserting the truth of a proposition is not enough. Unless the evidence clearly establishes the proposition, the party with the burden of proof fails to sustain it and loses the lawsuit.

CASE

The plaintiffs, the Dunlops, operated a mobile home sale lot. On the rear of the property was a cottage which the Dunlops renovated for the purpose of renting to a tenant. The defendant operated a dog kennel within four feet of the cottage. The noise and odor from the kennel made the cottage uninhabitable. Plaintiffs sued defendant to enjoin the kennel operation as a private nuisance.

The trial court, using the clear and convincing proof standard, held that the plaintiffs had failed to prove that the kennel was a private nuisance.

ISSUE: In a suit to enjoin a nuisance, what is the correct standard of proof?

HELD: Preponderance of the evidence.

REASONS:

1. In a civil action the burden of proof is generally on the plaintiff to establish its case by a preponderance of the evidence.
2. Most jurisdictions specify that the existence of a nuisance must be proved by a preponderance of the evidence. We see no reason to deviate from the preponderance standard.

Dunlop v. Daigle, 444 A.2d 519 (N.H. 1982).

6. Verdicts and Judgments

After the conference on jury instructions, the attorneys argue the case before the jury. The party with the burden of proof, usually the plaintiff, is given an opportunity to open the argument and to close it. The defendant's attorney is allowed to argue only after the plaintiff's argument and is allowed to argue only once. After the arguments are completed, the court gives instructions to the jury. The jury then retires to deliberate. In some states the jurors take written instructions with them to the jury room. In others, they must remember the instructions. Whether they are able to do so is very questionable.

Upon reaching a **verdict,** the jury returns from the jury room and announces its verdict. There are two kinds of verdicts—general and special. A *general verdict* is one in which the jury makes a complete finding and single conclusion on all issues presented to it. First it finds the facts, as proven by the evidence, then applies the law as instructed by the court, and returns a verdict in one conclusion that settles the case. Such verdict is reported as follows: "We the jury find the issues for the plaintiff [or defendant, as the case may be] and assess his damages at One Thousand Dollars." The jury usually does not make separate findings of fact or report what law is applied.

Verdict *The decision of a jury, reported to the court, on matters properly submitted to the jury for consideration.*

In a **special verdict,** the jury makes findings of fact only. It is the duty of the court to apply the law to the facts as found by the jury. A special verdict is not a decision of the case; it resolves only the questions of fact. Since the jury finds only the facts, the court does not instruct it about the law. The duty of applying the law to the fact is left to the court. The circumstances under which a general or a special verdict may be used are controlled by statute.

Special verdict *The jury finds the facts only, leaving it to the court to apply the law and draw the conclusion as to the proper disposition of the case.*

After the verdict is announced, a **judgment** is entered. A judgment entered by a court of law is similar, in its impact, to a final decree entered by a court in equity. Equitable decrees are discussed in section 6 of Chapter 2. Judgments are either *in rem* or *in personam.* A **judgement *in rem*** is an adjudication entered against a thing—property, real or personal. The judgment is a determination of the status of the subject matter. Thus a judgment of forfeiture of goods for the violation of a revenue law is a judgment *in rem.* Although a judgment *in rem* is limited to the subject matter, it nevertheless affects the rights and duties of persons. A decree dissolving a marriage seriously affects persons; nevertheless, it is a decision *in rem* because it affects a "status," the marriage relation. A judgment *in rem* is binding not only on the persons previously concerned with the status or thing but on all other persons.

Judgment (in law) *The decision, pronouncement, or sentence rendered by a court upon an issue in which it has jurisdiction.*

***Judgment* in rem** *A judgment against a thing, as distinguished from a judgment against a person.*

A judgment against a particular person is a **judgment *in personam.*** It is limited in its application to such person only, whereas a judgment *in rem* is conclusive on all persons.

***Judgment* in personam** *A judgment against a person, directing the defendant to do or not to do something.*

PROCEEDINGS AFTER THE TRIAL

7. Post-trial Motions

After judgment is entered, the losing party starts the procedure of post-trial motions, which raise questions of law concerning the conduct of the lawsuit. These motions seek relief such as a new trial or a judgment notwithstanding the verdict of the jury. A motion seeking a new trial may be granted if the judge feels that the verdict of the jury is contrary to the manifest weight of the evidence. The court may enter a judgment opposite to that of the verdict of the jury if the judge finds that the verdict is, as a matter of law, erroneous. To reach such a conclusion, the court must find that reasonable men viewing the evidence could not reach the verdict returned. For example, a verdict for the plaintiff based on sympathy instead of evidence could be set aside.

After the judge rules on the post-trial motion, the losing party may appeal. It should be noted that lawsuits usually end by a ruling on a motion, either before trial, during the trial, or after the trial. Motions raise questions of law that are decided by the court. The right to appeal is absolute if perfected within the prescribed time. All litigants are entitled to a trial and a review, provided that the proper procedures are followed.

8. Appeals

A dissatisfied party—plaintiff or defendant—has a right to appeal the decision of the trial court to a higher court, provided that he proceeds promptly and properly.

Appellate Procedure. Appellate procedures are not uniform among the states, and the appellant must comply with the appropriate statute and rules of the particular court. Appeals are usually perfected by the appellant's giving *notice of appeal* to the trial court and opposing parties. This notice of appeal must be filed within a statutory time period (usually thirty days) after the trial court has entered a final judgment or order. Failure to file the notice of appeal on time denies the appellate court jurisdiction.

Most states require that within at least ten days after giving notice of appeal, the appellant must file an appeal bond, in effect guaranteeing to pay costs that may be charged against him on the appeal. This bond permits the appellee to collect costs if the appellant loses an appeal.

The statutes usually require that within a specified time after an appeal is perfected, the appellant shall file with the clerk of the appellate court a *transcript,* consisting of a record of the testimony, a copy of the judgment, decree, or order appealed from, and other papers required by rules of the court.

The transcript alone, however, is not enough to present the case to the appellate court. The appellant must prepare and file a "brief" that contains a statement of the case, a list of the assignment of errors upon which the appellant has based his appeal, his legal authorities, and argument. The brief contains the arguments on both fact and law by which the attorney attempts to show how the lower court committed the errors alleged.

The appellee (respondent) files a brief of like character, setting out his side of the case with points, authorities, and arguments. By such procedure, the case on the issues raised goes to the appellate court for decision.

Role of Appellate Court. The appellate court, upon receipt of the appeal, will place it on the calendar for hearing. Attorneys will be notified of the time and will be given an opportunity for oral argument. After the oral argument, the court prepares a written opinion stating the applicable law involved and giving the reasons for its decision. The court, by its decision, may affirm or reverse the court below, or the court may *remand* (send back) the case for a new trial. At the end of each published opinion found in the reports, a word or a few words will express the court's decision: affirmed, reversed, reversed and remanded, or whatever the case requires.

The appellate courts basically review the legal rulings made by the trial judge. Very seldom will the jury's or judge's factual findings be reversed during the appeals process. Since those at the trial had an opportunity to see and hear the witnesses in person, their determination of the factual situation is presumed to be accurate. In other words, the reviewing court will not disturb the trial court's findings of fact unless such findings are clearly erroneous. The following case is typical of those applying this important concept.

CASE

Bessemer City established a committee of four men and one woman to interview eight persons for the position of recreation director. The four men on the committee voted for a male applicant who had a degree in physical education, while the only woman voted for Ms. Anderson, who had college degrees in social studies and education. Ms. Anderson filed suit under Title VII of the Civil Rights Act of 1964. At trial, the district court found that Ms. Anderson had been denied the position on account of her gender. The court based this finding on the fact that Ms. Anderson was the most qualified candidate, that she had been asked questions during her interview regarding her spouse's feelings about her application for the position that other applicants were not asked, and that the male committee members were biased against hiring a woman. The court found that the reasons the committee gave for its decision to hire the male were a pretext for illegal discrimination. The Court of Appeals for the Fourth Circuit reversed. The court of appeals held that, due to the nature of the position of recreation director, the man was as equally well qualified as Ms. Anderson, despite his education.

The court of appeals held that the district court's findings were clearly erroneous and that the district court had therefore erred in finding that the petitioner had been discriminated against on account of gender.

ISSUE: Did the court of appeals err in holding that the district court's finding of discrimination was clearly erroneous?

DECISION: Yes.

REASONS:

1. A finding of intentional discrimination is a finding of fact.
2. Trial courts, not appellate courts, are finders of fact. A circuit court cannot set aside a district court's findings of fact unless those findings are clearly erroneous. If, upon viewing the record of the trial in its entirety, a district court's account of the evidence is plausible, the circuit court may not reverse, even if it feels it would have weighed the evidence differently.
3. An appellate court must give even greater deference to the trial court's findings when they are based on determinations regarding the credibility of witnesses. While such findings are not always beyond question, if a trial judge's finding is internally consistent, and based on his decision to credit the testimony of one of two or more witnesses, each of whom has told a coherent and factually plausible story that is not contradicted by extrinsic evidence, that finding can virtually never be clearly erroneous.
4. At least three considerations support this deference to the original trier of fact. First, the trial judge is in the better position to make determinations of credibility of witnesses. Only he can be aware of the variations in demeanor and tone of voice that bear so heavily on the listener's belief in what is said. Second, the trial judge's experience in fulfilling the role of trier of fact gives him

expertise in doing so. Finally, after having expended energies and resources on factual issues in the trial court, litigants should then be able to concentrate on legal issues in the appellate court.

5. Although the fourth circuit's interpretation was neither illogical nor implausible, its role was not to engage in its own fact finding but to affirm the district court if the factual findings of that court were not clearly erroneous. Therefore the Fourth Circuit Court of Appeals should not have reversed the district court, and the decision of the fourth circuit is reversed.

Anderson v. City of Bessemer City, N.C., 105 S.Ct. 1504 (1985).

9. Enforcement of Judgments and Decrees

A decision of a court becomes final when the time provided for a review of the decision has expired. In the trial court, a decision is final at the expiration of time for appeal. In a reviewing court, it is expiration of the time to request a rehearing or to request a further review of the case. After the decision has become final, judicial action may be required to enforce the decision. In most cases the losing party will voluntarily comply with the decision and satisfy the judgment or otherwise do what the decree requires, but the assistance of the court is sometimes required to enforce its final decision.

Execution *Execution of a judgment is the process by which the court, through the sheriff, enforces the payment of the judgment received by the successful party. The sheriff, by a "writ," levies upon the unsuccessful party's property and sells it to pay the judgment creditor.*

Writ of Execution. If a judgment for dollar damages is not paid, the judgment creditor may apply for a writ of **execution.** This writ directs the sheriff to seize personal property of the judgment debtor and to sell enough thereof to satisfy the judgment and to cover the costs and expenses of the sale. The writ authorizes the sheriff to seize both tangible and intangible personal property, such as bank accounts. If the judgment debtor's personal property seized and sold by the sheriff does not produce sufficient funds to pay the judgment, the writ of execution is returned to the court with a statement of the extent to which the judgment is unsatisfied. If an execution is returned unsatisfied in whole or in part, the judgment becomes a lien on any real estate owned by the debtor if it is within the jurisdiction of the court that issued the writ of execution. An unpaid judgment creditor is entitled to have the real estate sold at a judicial sale and to have the net proceeds of the sale applied on the judgment. A judgment creditor with an unsatisfied writ of execution has not only a lien on real property owned by the judgment debtor at the time the judgment becomes final, but also a judicial lien on any real property acquired by the judgment debtor during the life of judgment.

Garnishment *A proceeding by which a plaintiff seeks to reach the credits of the defendant that are in the hands of a third party, the garnishee.*

Garnishment. **Garnishment** is another important method used by judgment creditors to collect a judgment. A judgment creditor can "garnish" the wages of the judgment debtor or his bank account or any other obligation owing to him from a third party. In the process of garnishment, the person owing the money to a judgment debtor—the employer, bank of deposit, third party—will be directed to pay the money into court rather than to the judgment debtor, and such money will be applied against the judgment debt.

In connection with writs of execution and garnishment proceedings, it is extremely significant that the laws of the various states have statutory provisions that exempt certain property from writs of execution and garnishment. The state laws limit the amount of wages that can be garnished and usually provide for both real property and personal property exemptions. This will be discussed with the materials on bankruptcy.

Citation Proceeding. In recent years many states have adopted a *citation proceeding,* which greatly assists the creditor in collecting a judgment. The citation procedure begins with the service of a "citation" on the judgment debtor to appear in court at a stated time for examination under oath about his financial affairs. It also prohibits the judgment debtor from making any transfer of property until after the examination in court. At the hearing, the judgment creditor or his attorney questions the judgment debtor about his income, property, and affairs. Any nonexempt property that is discovered during the questioning may be ordered sold by the judge, with the proceeds applied to the judgment. The court may also order that weekly or monthly payments be made by the judgment debtor. In states that have adopted the citation proceeding, the difficulties in collecting a judgment have been substantially reduced.

Attachment. One important method of collecting a judgment is also relevant to the procedures that may be used to commence a lawsuit. The procedure with these dual purposes is known as **attachment.** Attachment is a method of acquiring *in rem* jurisdiction of a nonresident defendant who is not subject to the service of process. The court may "attach" property of the nonresident defendant, and in so doing the court acquires jurisdiction over the defendant to the extent of the value of the property attached. Attachment as a means of obtaining *in rem* jurisdiction is used in cases involving the status of a person, such as divorce, or the status of property, such as in eminent domain (acquisition of private property for public use) proceedings.

Attachment *A legal proceeding accompanying an action in court by which a plaintiff may acquire a lien on a defendant's property as a security for the payment of any judgment that the plaintiff may recover.*

Attachment as a method of ensuring collection of a judgment is used by a plaintiff who fears that the defendant will dispose of his property before the court is able to enter a final decision. The plaintiff has the property of the defendant seized, pending the outcome of the lawsuit. It is of vital importance to the success of the attachment that the creditor prove the property being attached is either owed to the debtor or is some of the debtor's property.

Attachment and the procedures controlling its use are governed by statutes that vary among the states. The attaching plaintiff-creditor must put up a bond with the court for the protection of the defendant, and the statutes provide methods whereby the attachment may be set aside by the defendant. If the plaintiff receives a judgment against the defendant, the attached property will be sold to satisfy the judgment.

Is It Worth It? In spite of the remedies the creditor may use, it frequently develops that the judgment is of little value because of the lack of assets that can be reached or because of other judgments. It must be remembered that a judgment standing alone has little value. In many cases, the debtor may file a voluntary petition in bankruptcy, which will extinguish the judgment debt.

In other cases, the creditor recognizes the futility of attempting to use additional legal process to collect, and the matter simply lies dormant until it dies a natural death by the expiration of the time allowed to collect the claim or judgment. Everyone should be aware that some people are judgment-proof and that in such cases the law has no means of collecting a judgment. Debtors are not sent to prison simply because of their inability to pay debts or judgments.

10. Full Faith and Credit

One further aspect of litigation as it relates to the enforcement of judgments and decrees must be noted. Article IV, Section 1, of the U.S. Constitution provides: "Full faith and credit shall be given in each State to the public acts, records, and judicial proceedings of every other State. . . ." This does not mean the decision in one state is binding in other states, only that the final decisions or judgments rendered in any given state by a court with jurisdiction shall be enforced as between the original parties in other states. "Full faith and credit" is applicable to the result of a specific decision as it affects the rights of the parties, not to the reasons or principles on which it was based.

Full faith and credit requires that a suit be brought to enforce the judgment on decree in the other state. However, the plaintiff need not prove any facts other than the entry of the judgment or decree in the sister state. The doctrine dispenses with the necessity of reproving one's claim.

CHAPTER SUMMARY

The Trial

Jury Selection

1. In selecting the jury, each party is entitled to challenge any potential juror for cause.
2. In addition, each party is given a specified number of peremptory challenges to reject potential jurors without giving a reason.

Introduction of Proof

1. The parties attempt to prove their factual contentions by introducing evidence in open court. Evidence is presented through questioning of witnesses, with the opposing party being given the right of cross-examination.
2. Numerous rules restrict the admissibility of evidence that may be presented. These rules are based on policy considerations. For example, the best evidence rule requires that the original document be presented if its content is at issue.

Motions during Trial

1. At the close of the plaintiff's case, a defendant will ordinarily make a motion for a directed verdict.
2. The court will grant this motion and order the jury to return a verdict for the defendant if the evidence considered in the light most favorable to the plaintiff will not support a verdict for the plaintiff.
3. The motion will be denied if there is any evidence to support each allegation of the complaint.
4. In cases tried without a jury, either party may move for a finding in his favor if the result is not in doubt.

Jury Instructions

1. After the parties have introduced all their evidence, the court instructs the jury on the law applicable to the case.
2. Jury instructions tell the jury that if it finds certain facts, then it should reach a certain result.

Burdens of Proof

1. The term *burden of proof* is used to describe the party that is required to come forward with evidence on a certain point. It is also used to describe the party with the burden of persuasion.
2. The law imposes three levels in satisfying the burden of persuasion. In criminal cases, the burden is beyond a reasonable doubt. In most civil cases, the burden is by a preponderance of greater weight of the evidence. In some special situations, there is a burden between these other two that is known as the clear and convincing proof standard.

Verdicts and Judgments

1. The decision of a jury is known as a verdict.
2. The final decision of the court, based on the verdict is known as a judgment. Judgments may be *in rem* or *in personam*.
3. In cases tried in equity, the decision of the court is known as a decree.

Proceedings after the Trial

Post-trial Motions

1. The losing party before the trial judge ordinarily files a post-trial motion. In this post-trial motion, the losing party seeks either a new trial or a judgment in its favor notwithstanding the verdict.
2. It is from the ruling on this post-trial motion that the losing party appeals.

Appeals

1. Appeals are costly and time-consuming. The party must obtain a transcript of the proceedings before the trial court and excerpt therefrom the matters to be raised on appeal. A brief must be prepared containing the points to be considered by the reviewing court and a party's legal authorities in support of the appeal.
2. The issues before the reviewing court are essentially questions of law, and great deference is given the findings of fact at the trial level.

Enforcement of Judgments and Decrees

1. It is not enough for a party to obtain a judgment against another. If the losing party does not voluntarily satisfy the judgment, then further legal proceedings may be required.
2. These may include judicial sales of property, garnishment of wages, and court orders requiring parties to take certain actions.

Full Faith and Credit

1. A final decision in a legal proceeding in one state is entitled to full faith and credit in all other states.

REVIEW QUESTIONS AND PROBLEMS

1. Match each term in column A with the most appropriate statement in column B.

A	B
(1) Beyond a reasonable doubt	(a) The removal of a prospective juror for which no cause need be given.
(2) Brief	(b) Questioning a witness under oath by the attorney on the opposing side.
(3) Venire	(c) A method of informing the jury as to the law applicable to the case.
(4) Preponderance of the evidence	(d) The questioning of prospective jurors as to their qualifications to be fair and impartial.
(5) Garnishment	(e) The burden of proof standard in criminal cases.
(6) *Voir dire* examination	(f) The usual burden of proof standard in civil cases.
(7) Peremptory challenge	(g) A method of collecting a judgment.

(8) Clear and convincing proof standard	(h) A document used in the appeal process to set forth the grounds on which the appeal is based.
(9) Cross-examination	(i) Potential jurors.
(10) Jury instruction	(j) A burden of proof standard used in limited situations where the law requires more proof than usual.

2. Ron sues Walter for personal injuries arising out of an automobile accident. Walter was allegedly driving under the influence of alcohol at the time of the accident. An investigation reveals that the list of prospective jurors includes a relative of Ron and the owner of a package liquor store. Walter does not want his case to be tried by a jury that includes these persons. What can he do? Explain.

3. List two communications that are privileged and inadmissible as evidence in criminal litigation. Also list other evidence that is privileged.

4. George enters into a written contract to sell his house to Wally. When Wally fails to pay for the house as agreed, George sells it to Henry for $10,000 less. George sued Wally for the $10,000. At the trial George took the stand and attempted to testify about the two contracts of sale. Wally's attorney objected and the judge stopped George's testimony. What was the basis of the objection? Explain.

5. At the close of the plaintiff's case in a civil jury trial, the defendant routinely makes a motion for a directed verdict. When will this motion be granted? Explain.

6. Pat sued Vince for breach of contract. Pat testified that Vince had agreed to work as a salesman for a 10 percent commission. Vince testified that the commission was to be 15 percent. There were no witnesses to the conversation that created the oral contract. Assume that the case is tried before a jury.

   a. Which party has the burden of producing evidence as to the terms of the contract? Why?
   b. Which party has the burden of persuasion?
   c. What standard of proof is required? Explain.
   d. Is it possible for the jury to find for Pat without any other evidence? Explain.

7. What is the difference between a verdict, a judgment, and a decree?

8. Motions are used to raise legal issues at various stages of a trial. Name two motions that are usually made after a trial is complete and indicate some of the grounds or basis of such motions.

9. What are jury instructions, and what purpose do they serve? Explain.

10. Appeals are costly in time and money. Give three examples of procedures used in the review process that increase both costs.

11. Moore sued Bronson on a promissory note. Bronson failed to comply with discovery and a default judgment was entered on May 1. On October 5, Bronson filed a notice of appeal. The law requires that appeals be filed within forty days of the decision. Does the appellate court have jurisdiction? Why or why not?

12. Define and explain how a *writ of execution* and a *writ of attachment* are applicable to enforcing a judgment.

13. Nancy sued John in Maryland and recovered a judgment for $10,000. John moved to Florida. Nancy has not collected the judgment. If she sues John in Florida, will the court relitigate the issues of the first case? Why?

Resolving Controversies and Influencing Conduct

5

CHAPTER PREVIEW

- COMPROMISES

  Reasons to Settle
  Personal • Economic • Obligations of Lawyers
  Mediation

- ARBITRATION

  Advantages
  Submission
  Procedure
  The Award
  Judicial Procedures in Arbitration

- ADMINISTRATIVE LAW

  The Quasi-Legislative Function
  The Quasi-Judicial Function
  Judicial Review of Agency Decisions
  Standing to Sue • Exhaustion of Remedies • Limitations

- INFLUENCING CONDUCT

  Law and Ethics
  A Typical Ethics Problem—Acceptance of Business Courtesies

BUSINESS MANAGEMENT DECISION

As president of a construction company, you have successfully bid to build a large office building. You realize, from past experience, that issues will arise with the architect and the owner during this construction project.

How do you provide for a resolution of these potential issues?

Compromise *An agreement between two or more persons to settle the matters of the controversy.*

Arbitration *The submission for determination of disputed matter to private, unofficial persons selected in a manner provided by law or agreement.*

In our society, a variety of methods other than litigation can be used to resolve conflicts and disputes. The most common is a **compromise** or settlement agreement between the parties to the dispute. A second important method for resolving unsettled conflicts and disputes is known as **arbitration,** submission of a controversy to a nonjudicial body for a binding decision. While litigation has been the traditional method of resolving disputes, today more and more disputes are being submitted to arbitration because litigation consumes much time and money.

In a third method, many issues are referred to a governmental agency for decision. Some disputes submitted to these agencies are between whole segments of society, and thus the decision is of general application in a manner similar to a statute. Other disputes resolved by agencies involve individuals and a business in a manner similar to a judicial decision. For example, the administrative process determines a worker's entitlement to workers' compensation for industrial injuries. Still other disputes decided by the administrative process involve government and business. These controversies may involve matters such as pollution of the environment or compliance with federal laws such as those relating to discrimination in employment or antitrust. In this chapter we shall learn something about the basic legal principles applicable to arbitration and of the role of administrative agencies in solving problems and resolving controversies.

Finally, individual and business conduct is influenced by ethics and ethical standards. The question is often asked: Even if conduct is legal, is it ethical? This chapter discusses ethics as an additional influence on behavior, and it will note the relationship between law and ethics.

COMPROMISES

1. Reasons to Settle

Most disputes are resolved by the parties involved, without resort to litigation or to arbitration. Only a small fraction of the disputes in our society end up in court or even in a lawyer's office. Among the multitude of reasons why compromise is so prevalent a technique for settling disputes, some may be described as personal, others as economic.

Personal. The desire to compromise is almost instinctive. Most of us dislike trouble, and many fear going to court. Our moral and ethical values encourage compromise and settlement. Opinions of persons other than the parties to the dispute are often an influential, motivating force in many compromises, adding external forces to the internal ones that encourage people to settle their differences amicably.

Economic. Compromise and settlement of disputes is also encouraged by the economics of many situations. Lawsuits are expensive to both parties. As a general rule, both parties must pay their own attorney's fees, and the losing party must pay court costs. As a matter of practical economics, the winning party in a lawsuit is a loser to the extent of the attorney's fees, which are often quite substantial.

At least two additional facts of economic life encourage business to settle disputes out of court. First, business must be concerned with its public image and the goodwill of its customers. Although the motto "The customer is always right" is not universally applicable today, the influence of the philosophy it represents cannot be underestimated. It often is simply not good business to sue a customer. Second, juries are frequently sympathetic to individuals who have suits against large corporations or defendants who are covered by insurance. Close questions of liability, as well as the size of verdicts, are more often than not resolved against business concerns because of their presumed ability to pay. As a result, business seeks to settle many disputes rather than submit them to a jury for decision.

Obligation of Lawyers. The duty of lawyers to seek and achieve compromise whenever possible may not be understood by laypersons. In providing services, lawyers devote a substantial amount of their time, energy, and talent to seeking a compromise solution of the disputes involving their clients. Attempts to compromise will be made before resort to the courts in most cases. Of all the disputes that are the subject of legal advice, the great majority are settled without resort to litigation. Of those that do result in litigation, the great majority are settled before the case goes to trial or even during the trial. Literally, the attempt of the lawyers to resolve the dispute never ends. It occurs before suit, before and during the trial, after verdict, during appeal, and even after appeal. As long as there is a controversy, it is the function of lawyers to attempt to resolve it.

Lawyers on both sides of a controversy seek compromise for a variety of reasons. A lawyer may view the client's case as weak, either on the law or on the facts. The amount of money involved, the necessity for a speedy decision, the nature of the contest, the uncertainty of legal remedy, the unfavorable publicity, and the expense entailed are some other reasons for avoiding a court trial. Each attorney must evaluate the client's cause and seek a satisfactory—though not necessarily the most desirable—settlement of the controversy. The settlement of disputes is perhaps the most significant contribution of lawyers to our society.

2. Mediation

The term **mediation** describes the process by which a third person assists the parties to a controversy when they seek a compromise. Although a mediator cannot impose a binding solution on the parties, a disinterested and objective mediator is often able to bring about a compromise that is satisfactory to them.

Mediation The process by which a third party attempts to help the parties in dispute find a resolution. The mediator has no authority to bind the parties to any particular resolution.

The mediation of labor disputes is the function of the National Mediation and Conciliation Service. This government agency, staffed with skilled negotiators, has assisted in the settlement of countless labor disputes. Mediation is playing an expanding role in the relationship between the business community and the consuming public. Better Business Bureaus and others are serving as mediators of consumer complaints and, on occasion, as arbitrators under arbitration agreements. Their efforts have resolved thousands of consumer complaints, in part because they provide some third parties to whom a consumer can turn.

An amendment to the Federal Trade Commission Act has given added impetus to mediation as a means of resolving consumer complaints. This law provides that if a business adopts an informal dispute-resolution system to handle complaints about its product warranties, then a customer cannot sue the manufacturer or seller for breach of warranty without first going through the informal procedures. This law does not deny consumers the right to sue, nor does it compel a compromise solution. It simply favors mediation by requiring an attempt at settlement before litigation.

ARBITRATION

3. Advantages

In arbitration, a person or persons other than the court make a final, binding decision of a controversy. Though rare, the law may require arbitration for certain cases. For example, several states now require arbitration of breach of contract cases involving relatively small amounts of money. The right to arbitrate usually arises from a contract; and since the right is based on a contract, the parties are obligated to arbitrate only those issues that they have agreed to arbitrate.

There are several advantages to using arbitration as a substitute for litigation. For one thing, it is much quicker and far less expensive. An issue can be submitted to arbitration and decided in less time than it takes to complete the pleading phase of a lawsuit. Then, too, arbitration creates less hostility than does litigation, and it allows the parties to continue their business relationship somewhat more peacefully while the dispute is being decided. Arbitration also provides for a decision without resort to a tribunal and allows for a hearing to be conducted without the rigid formality of strict rules of law. Arbitration is favored today because it eases the congestion of court calendars. Finally, under the arbitration process, complex issues can be submitted to an expert for decision. For example, if an issue arises concerning construction of a building, in arbitration it can be submitted to an architect for decision. Lawyers and other specialists frequently serve as arbitrators, physicians decide issues relating to physical disabilities, certified public accountants deal with those regarding the book value of stock, and engineers decide issues relating to industrial production. A substantial amount of arbitration is also conducted by the academic community, especially in the area of labor relations.

For the foregoing reasons, arbitration as a substitute for litigation is becoming increasingly useful to business. Commercial arbitration clauses are being added to many business contracts. The American Arbitration Association will furnish experienced arbitrators for parties in a dispute, and many standard contract clauses provide for submission to this group. Since arbitration costs are deductible business expenses, this speedy, inexpensive solution to conflicts should be carefully considered by business and legal counsel in all possible areas of dispute.

The Commissioners on Uniform State Laws have prepared a Uniform Arbitration Act. There is also a Federal Arbitration Act, which covers businesses engaged in maritime and interstate commerce. Both statutes authorize voluntary arbitration.

4. Submission

Submission is the act of referring an issue or issues to the arbitration process. The submitted issues may be factual, legal, or both; they may include questions concerning the interpretation of the arbitration agreement. The scope of the arbitrator's powers is controlled by the language of the submission. Doubts concerning the arbitrability of the subject matter of a dispute are usually resolved in favor of arbitration. When a contract leaves it up to the court to determine arbitrability, an order to arbitrate a particular grievance will not be denied unless it may be said with positive assurance that the arbitration clause is not susceptible to interpretation that covers the asserted dispute.

Submission may occur under two circumstances. First, the parties may enter into an agreement to arbitrate an existing dispute. The arbitration agreement serves as the "submission" in this case. Second, the parties may contractually agree to submit to arbitration all issues that *may* arise, or they may agree that either party *may* demand arbitration of any issue that arises. Submission to arbitration under the second circumstance occurs when a demand to arbitrate is served on the other party. This demand may take the form of a notice that a matter is being referred to the arbitrator agreed upon by the parties, or it may be a demand that the matter be referred to arbitration. Merely informing the other party that a controversy exists is not an act of submission or a demand for arbitration.

Most statutes authorizing voluntary arbitration require a written agreement to arbitrate. Written agreements are required as a corollary of the provision that makes the agreement to arbitrate irrevocable. Consistent with the goal of arbitration to obtain a quick resolution of disputes, most statutes require submission within a stated time after the dispute arises—usually six months.

5. Procedure

In the usual arbitration procedure the parties to the dispute are given notice of the time and place of the hearing. Testimony is given at the hearing; the arbitrator or arbitrators deliberate and render a decision. There are no formal pleadings or motions, and the strict rules of evidence used in trials are frequently not followed. Most often the decision is given without the reasons for it.

CASE

The parties had various disputes arising from the terms of a building contract. The contract provided that all disputes concerning the terms of the contract and its alleged performance were to be resolved by arbitration. The disputes were submitted to arbitrators, who rendered the following award: "We . . . award as follows: (1) Virginia Schroeder Burnham shall pay Edward C. Malecki the sum of Five Thousand Five Hundred Dollars ($5,500). (2) The administrative fees and expenses . . . of the Arbitrators shall be borne equally by the parties. . . ." Burnham on appeal objected to the award because the arbitrators did not make any specific findings with respect to any of the disputes.

ISSUE: Was the award proper?
HELD: Yes.

REASONS: 1. The submission defines the powers of the arbitrators.
2. Arbitrators are only required to render an award in conformity to the submission and an award need contain no more than the actual decision of the arbitrators. An explanation of the means by which they reached the award, unless required by the submission, is needless and superfluous.
3. The submission in this case did not require the arbitrators to make any specific reference in their award to any of the claims made by the parties.

Malecki v. Burnham, 435 A.2d 13 (Conn. 1980).

The function of the arbitrators is to find a solution to the controversy; and to that end, they have the power to fashion the remedy appropriate to the wrong. Arbitrators are not bound by principles of substantive law or the rules of evidence, unless the submission so provides. As a result, errors of law or fact do not justify a court in setting aside the decision of the arbitration process. The arbitrator is the sole and final judge of the evidence and the weight to be given it.

Once an issue is submitted for arbitration, questions of law are for the arbitrator. They are no longer open to judicial intervention or to judicial review. Arbitrators are obligated to act fairly and impartially and to decide on the basis of the evidence before them. Therefore it is misconduct for arbitrators to use outside evidence obtained by independent investigation without the consent of the parties.

6. The Award

The decision of the arbitrator, the *award*, is binding on all issues submitted and may be judicially enforced. Every presumption is in favor of the validity of an arbitration award, and doubts are resolved in its favor. The scope of judicial review of an award is limited in most states by statute as well as by the agreement to arbitrate. Any challenge to an award on the ground that the arbitrator exceeded his powers is properly limited to a comparison of the award with the submission. Once it is decreed that a matter is arbitrable, courts do not decide the issues on the merits.

When the submission does not restrict arbitrators to decide according to principles of law, they may make an award according to their own notion of justice without regard to the law. The scope of judicial review is whether or not the issues contained in the submission have been decided. An allegation that there is insufficient evidence to support an award or that it is contrary to the evidence does not constitute a ground for vacating an award. Only clear, precise, evidence of fraud, misconduct, or other grave irregularity will suffice to vacate an arbitration award. Courts do not reweigh the evidence and make independent findings of fact.

CASE

Pursuant to the terms of a lease, the parties submitted a dispute to arbitration. The arbitrators awarded the lessor $37,324.67, which was enforced by the circuit court. The court of appeals found no substantial evidence in the arbitration record to support an award of less than $75,000 and directed entry of judgment in that amount.

ISSUE: Has the court of appeals exceeded its authority by examining the evidence presented at the arbitration hearing?

DECISION: Yes.

REASONS:
1. Generally, an arbitrator's award is not reviewable by a court.
2. Inherent in the concept of arbitration is the parties' voluntary agreement that the decision of the arbitrator will be final and binding.
3. An arbitrator's award may be set aside only if there has been a gross mistake of law or fact constituting evidence of misconduct amounting to fraud or undue partiality.
4. Here there is no suggestion of fraud or undue partiality. Therefore the award and the evidence supporting that award are not reviewable by the court of appeals.

Taylor v. Fitz Coal Company, Inc., 618 S.W.2d 432 (Ky. 1981).

Submissions to arbitration are for determinations based on the ad hoc application of broad principles of justice and fairness in the particular instance. Reliance is not placed on the continuity of the tribunal personnel or operation, and predictability is not an objective. Awards do not have, nor is it intended that they should have, the precedential value that attaches to judicial determinations.

7. Judicial Procedures in Arbitration

One purpose of arbitration is to avoid the time and expense of litigation. Judicial action may be necessary if either party refuses to submit the dispute to arbitration or refuses to carry out the terms of the award. Statutes usually contemplate the following as the procedures to be followed when a party to an arbitration contract refuses to submit the dispute to arbitration as agreed:

1. The aggrieved party may petition the court for an order directing that the arbitration be carried out according to the terms of the agreement. Upon hearing, if the court finds that making the contract to arbitrate or submission to arbitrate is not an issue, the court directs the parties to proceed to arbitrate according to the terms of the agreement.
2. If there is disagreement over the making of the contract or submission, the court will try that issue, either with or without a jury. If it is found that no contract was made, the petition is dismissed. If it is found that a contract to arbitrate or to submit was made, and there was a default, the court will issue an order directing the parties to proceed with arbitration according to the contract.

The following case illustrates the application of the Federal Arbitration Act on agreements to arbitrate and the policy favoring arbitration.

CASE

Byrd invested $160,000 through Dean Witter Reynolds, a securities firm. When $100,000 was lost, Byrd filed suit in federal court alleging violations of the federal securities laws and of various state laws. The brokerage agreement provided that any dispute would be settled by arbitration. The broker sought a court order to compel arbitration of the claims based on state law (it admitted that the federal securities law issues were not subject to arbitration).

ISSUE: Must a federal court compel arbitration of the state claims when they are joined with a nonarbitrable federal claim?

DECISION: Yes.

REASONS:
1. The Federal Arbitration Act requires district courts to compel arbitration of arbitrable claims when one party files motion to compel, even where result would be possibly inefficient maintenance of separate proceedings in different forums.
2. The act leaves no room for the exercise of discretion by a district court but instead mandates that district courts *shall* direct the parties to proceed to arbitration on issues for which an arbitration agreement has been signed.
3. The act's legislative history establishes that its principal purpose is to ensure judicial enforcement of privately made arbitration agreements and not to promote the expeditious resolution of claims.

Dean Witter Reynolds Inc. v. Byrd, 105 S.Ct. 1238 (1985).

If the parties do submit the issues to arbitration as agreed, or if arbitration is conducted pursuant to a court order, certain judicial proceedings may be necessary in order to enforce the award. Most statutes prescribe the following procedures:

1. After the award is made, it is filed with the clerk of the court. After twenty days, if no exceptions are filed, it becomes a judgment upon which a writ of execution may issue in the same manner as if a judgment had been entered in a civil action.
2. A dissatisfied party may file exceptions to the award because, for example, (a) the award covered matters beyond the issues submitted, (b) the arbitrators failed to follow the statutory requirements, and (c) fraud or corruption permeated the decision. The court does *not* review the *merits* of the decision.
3. Appeals from the judgment may be taken as in any legal action, and such appeals cannot be denied by contractual provisions.
4. If it appears that the award should be vacated, the court may refer it to the arbitrators, with instructions for correction and rehearing.

ADMINISTRATIVE LAW

8. Introduction

At the beginning of this chapter it was noted that administrative agencies resolve many disputes and controversies in our system. The administrative process is in effect a fourth branch of government. It includes the independent regulatory agencies, bureaus, and commissions. Some of the controversies submitted to these agencies are policy issues affecting whole industries or even every industry. For example, what is the best means of ensuring to workers healthy and safe working conditions? This policy question was turned over to the Occupational Safety and Health Administration, not only to make laws (rules and regulations) to achieve the goal but to enforce the laws as well. Agencies that make rules and regulations in order to resolve conflict and problems are performing a function similar to that of legislatures. Agencies engaged in enforcing laws and holding hearings are performing a function similar to that of courts. Thus administrative agencies possess the functions of the other branches of government and they are involved in all aspects of our daily lives. The principles governing these agencies and the result of their functions are what is called **administrative law.**

Administrative law *The branch of public law dealing with the operation of and results from the various agencies, boards, and commissions of government.*

The fourth branch of government exists in part because laws cannot be particularized enough to cover all aspects of a problem. Therefore Congress delegates the power to make rules and regulations to fill in the gaps and to provide the specifics that make the laws workable. Agencies develop detailed rules and regulations to carry out legislative policies.

It is also difficult if not impossible for the courts to handle all the disputes and controversies that arise. For example, each year, tens of thousands of industrial accidents cause injury or death. If each accident were to result in traditional litigation, the courts simply would not have the time or personnel to handle the multitude of cases. Therefore we use the administrative process to handle them.

Many agencies exist because of the desire for experts to handle difficult problems. The Federal Reserve Board, Nuclear Regulatory Commission, and Pure Food and Drug Administration are examples of agencies with expertise above that of the Congress or the executive branch. Administrative agencies also provide continuity and consistency in the formulation, application, and enforcement of rules and regulations governing business.

Many governmental agencies exist to protect the public and the public interest. The public interest in clean water and clear air led to the creation of the Environmental Protection Agency. The protection of the investing public was a major force behind the creation of the Securities and Exchange Commission. The manufacture and sale of dangerous products led to the creation of the Consumer Product Safety Commission. It is our practice to turn to a governmental agency for assistance whenever a business or business practice may injure significant numbers of the general public. There is a belief that a legitimate function of many government agencies is to protect the public from harm.

Today, the legislative and executive branches of government are content to identify problems and to develop policies to solve them. These policies are enacted into law; the responsibility for carrying out the policies and enforcing the laws is delegated to the administrative process. The goals of society are determined by the traditional branches of government, and their achievement is the responsibility of the fourth branch.

9. The Quasi-Legislative Function

In performing the **quasi-legislative** function, rules and regulations are made to accomplish the goals of the agency. The rule-making function is based on the authority delegated to the agency by the legislature. This delegation of authority is usually stated in broad, general language. A delegation "to make such rules, regulations, and decisions as the public interest, convenience, and necessity may require" is a typical statement of the authority of an agency. These delegations usually authorize an administrative agency to "fill in the details" of legislation by making rules and regulations to carry out goals and purposes.

Quasi-legislative *The function of administrative agencies whereby rules and regulations are promulgated. This authority permits agencies to make enforceable "laws."*

Agency regulations are often challenged on the ground that the agency has exceeded its authority. The delegation of quasi-legislative power usually involves grants of substantial discretion to the board of agency involved. It must be kept in mind that the delegation of discretion is to the agency, not to the courts. Courts cannot interfere with the discretion given to the agency and cannot substitute their judgment for that of the agency simply because they disagree with a rule or regulation. Courts will hold that any agency has exceeded its authority if an analysis of legislative intent confirms the view that the agency has gone beyond that intent. However, such decisions are relatively unusual and agencies are allowed wide latitude in performing their rule-making functions.

It is the usual practice for administrative agencies in performing their quasi-legislative functions to hold hearings on proposed rules and regulations. The agency receives testimony on the need for, or desirability of, proposed rules and regulations. Notice of such hearings is usually given to the public, and all interested parties are allowed to present evidence for consideration by the agency.

10. The Quasi-Judicial Function

The adjudicating function means that administrative agencies also decide cases or disputes between private parties after they have conducted hearings. The purpose of the hearing may be to find if a rule of the agency or an applicable statute has been violated. The National Labor Relations Board (NLRB) conducts hearings to determine if an unfair labor practice has been committed. Other **quasi-judicial** hearings may be held for the purpose of fixing liability, as in a case of discrimination in employment. The quasi-judicial hearings receive detailed evidence and determine the rights and duties of the parties subject to the jurisdiction of the agency. The rules of procedure used in these quasi-judicial hearings are usually more informal in character than court trials, but on the whole they follow the general pattern set by courts. There is no right to a trial by jury in matter before administrative agencies.

Quasi-judicial
Administrative actions involving factual determinations and the discretionary application of rules and regulations.

An agency usually appoints a person to conduct the hearing—an administrative law judge, sometimes called a hearing examiner or trial examiner. This person receives the evidence, submits findings of facts, and makes recommendations to the board or commission regarding the disposition to be made in the case. The agency studies the report and issues whatever orders the law in the case appears to demand. The agency may hear objections to the hearing officer's finding, and sometimes it will hear arguments on the issues.

11. Judicial Review of Agency Decisions

Standing to sue and exhaustion of remedies are two important procedural aspects of the broad area of judicial review of administrative action.

Standing to Sue. Standing to sue, as discussed in Chapter 3, means that a person seeking to challenge the decision of an agency must be an "an aggrieved party" with a personal interest in the outcome before he or she may obtain judicial review. Persons who may suffer economic loss due to agency action have standing to sue. Also, persons who have noneconomic interests, such as First Amendment rights, now have standing to sue.

Exhaustion of Remedies. The doctrine of exhaustion of remedies is based on the proposition that courts should not decide in advance of a hearing that an agency will not conduct it fairly. In general (although there are exceptions), courts refuse to review administrative actions until a complaining party has exhausted all the administrative review procedures available. Otherwise, the administrative system would be denied important opportunities to make a factual record, to exercise its discretion, or to apply its expertise in decision making. Exhaustion gives an agency the opportunity to discover and correct its own errors and thus help to dispense with judicial review.

Exhaustion is most clearly required in cases involving the agency's expertise or specialization, so that exhaustion would not result in unusual expense, or when the administrative remedy is just as likely as the judicial one to provide appropriate relief. If nothing is to be gained from the exhaustion of administrative remedies, and the harm from the continued existence of administrative ruling is great, the courts have not been reluctant to discard this doctrine. This is especially true when very fundamental constitutional guarantees such as freedom of speech or press are involved or the administrative remedy is likely to be inadequate. When the agency is clearly acting beyond its jurisdiction (because its action is not authorized by statute, or the statute authorizing it is unconstitutional), or when the agency's action would result in irreparable injury (such as great expense) to the petitioner, a court most probably would not insist upon exhaustion.

Limitations. Judicial review of agency decisions, by its very nature, is quite limited. Since legislatures have delegated authority to agencies because of their expertise and other capabilities, courts usually exercise restraint and give great deference to agency decisions. Courts reviewing administrative interpretations of law do not always decide questions of law for themselves. It is not unusual for a court to accept an administrative interpretation of law as final if it has support in the agency's record and a rational basis. Administrative agencies are frequently called upon to interpret the statute governing the agency, and the agency's construction is persuasive to courts. Legislatures intended for agencies to interpret their own authority and the meaning of the laws which they are to enforce.

In reviewing the rules and regulations issued by agencies, courts give great deference to the agency because of its presumed expertise. Rules and regulations must not be arbitrary or capricious and agencies must give reasons for their decisions. However, agencies' actions are seldom reversed, as the following case illustrates.

CASE

The National Environmental Policy Act (NEPA) requires federal agencies to consider the environmental impact of any major federal action. This impact must be included in an environmental impact statement. The dispute in this case concerns the adoption by the Nuclear Regulatory Commission (NRC) of a series of rules to evaluate the environmental effects of a nuclear power plant's fuel cycle. The rules were challenged as arbitrary and capricious and inconsistent with the NEPA. The challenge was made because the NRC had not factored into its rules and considered the uncertainties surrounding its assumptions made in the licensing process of power plants.

ISSUE: Will a court change the rules of the NRC?
DECISION: No.

REASONS: 1. The NRC complied with the NEPA, and its decision was not arbitrary or capricious.

2. It is not the task of the court to determine what decision it would have reached if it had been the NRC. The court's only task is to determine whether the NRC had considerd the relevant factors and articulated a rational connection between the facts found and the choice made.

3. When examining an agency's prediction with its area of special expertise, a reviewing court must generally be at its most deferential.

Baltimore Gas & Electric v. Natural Resources Defense Council, 103 S.Ct. 2246 (1983).

When a court reviews the findings of fact made by an administrative body, it considers them to be prima facie correct. A court of review examines the evidence by analyzing the record of the agency's proceedings and upholds the agency's findings and conclusions on questions of fact if they are supported by substantial evidence in the record as a whole. In other words, the record must contain material evidence from which a reasonable person might reach the same conclusion as did the agency. If substantial evidence in support of the decision is present, the court will not disturb the agency's findings, even though the court itself might have reached a different conclusion on the basis of the evidence in the record. The determination of credibility of the witnesses who testify in quasi-judicial proceedings is for the agency to determine, not the courts.

INFLUENCING CONDUCT

12. Introduction

The law is not the only means of influencing conduct and regulating the behavior of individuals and businesses. Fear of or concern for the consequences of actions is probably as important an influence on behavior as is the law. Between nations, the threat of reprisal by force of arms is more effective in preventing undesirable conduct than is international law. For example, our nuclear deterrent has contributed to world peace for more than four decades. The fact that individuals and businesses fear the economic consequences of conduct is obviously an important influence on behavior. Economists believe that our economy is best understood and regulated when everyone recognizes that people usually act in their own best self-interest. Our competitive economic system is predicated upon a belief that decisions made by millions of individuals provide the most effective and efficient allocation of the nation's resources.

Furthermore, individual and institutional ethical standards and a sense of responsibility to society are having an ever-increasing impact on decisions. Almost every publicly held business has adopted a Code of Ethical Conduct for its employees. Professional associations such as the American Bar Association or the American Institute of Certified Public Accountants have adopted ethics codes for their members. There is a federal code of ethics for government employees. While these codes are not "laws," they usually provide for sanctions for noncompliance.

Conduct is also influenced by standards for which there is no sanction for noncompliance. This is sometimes described as obedience to the unenforceable. The late Albert J. Harno, for thirty-five years dean of the College of Law at the University of Illinois, discussed this influence in a graduation address in 1961. The following excerpt from that address indicates its relationship to law and to free choice:

> Life for most people is a day-to-day affair; it is ''numbered by years, daies and hours.''[1] Men live, seek diversion and comfort, have fleeting glimpses of happiness, are touched by sorrow, and pass from the scene. A few stop to contemplate and to wonder. But now and then there rises from the multitude a prophet, a Plato, an Aristotle, a Jesus of Nazareth, a Beethoven, an Abraham Lincoln, to fashion for us in words, in poetry, in music, and in song, some lasting conception of the eternal verities of life—of the good, the true, and the beautiful—and to formulate for us directives and precepts to guide us on our way.
>
> We live in an age in which materialism and, in many parts of the world, crass materialism prevails. It is a technical age in which men put their faith in mechanized force, in atomic power, missiles, earth satellites, and space ships. We look for guidance and hear only a babel of voices as men give expression to guile, deception, hate, greed, and prejudice. . . .
>
> There is a clash as to the meaning and place of law as a governing force in society. We Americans subscribe, at least outwardly, to the idea and to the ideal that ours is a government of law—that no individuals, no not even our highest governing officials, are above the law. . . .
>
> But law is not the only force that regulates human conduct. I wish to speak about three areas or domains, of human action. I am indebted to an Englishman, Lord Moulton,[2] for this classification. The development is my own. The *first* is the area of free choice; the *second*, the domain of obedience to the unenforceable; and *third*, the domain of law.
>
> The first, the domain of free choice, is a limited area. I sometimes wonder if we really appreciate how little freedom of choice we have in making decisions; we are constantly under one pressure or another. if we have an evening to ourselves, we may have a choice of reading . . . or of going to a movie. We may be able to choose whether we will or will not take sugar in our coffee. But even that choice may be denied to us by doctor's orders.
>
> The second domain, that of obedience to the unenforceable, is difficult to define. In it there is no law which determines our course of action, and yet we feel that we are not free to choose as we would. It is a very broad area. It covers those actions which we are not compelled to perform but which some inner voice directs us to discharge. It is the realm of kindliness and conscience—the domain of manners, ethics, and morals. It is the realm which recognizes the sway of duty, of fairness, of honest dealings between men, of sympathy, of taste, and of the spirit. It covers all those things that make life beautiful and a good society possible. What other than a call of conscience is it that makes us willing to take part in community enterprises and in matters relating to the public welfare?

---

[1] Guillaume De Salluste du Bartas, *Divine Weekes and Workes*, second week, third day, part two.

[2] ''Law and Manners,'' *Atlantic Monthly*, 1 (July 1924), 134.

It is the realm of courtesy. There is no compelling reason other than the inner voice that prompts us to speak kindly to our fellowmen. It is the domain of good manners and honest dealings with others. Manners signify good breeding—and more. Manners are the outward expression of an intellectual and moral conviction. Manners are based in that true and deepest self-respect, and they originate in a respect for others. Manners do not make the man, but they reveal the man.

What is it that causes men to maintain self-restraint and consideration for others in the face of danger? Instances come to mind in which many people were faced with impending disaster and death—a shipwreck, fire, or explosion. The way to escape was open to but few. While this has not always been true, often the physically strong have resisted the temptation to fight their way to safety and have permitted the weaker members, the women and children, of the group to escape. Why was this? Law did not require it. Force at that time was not a factor.

It is the realm of tolerance. When men have lost their tolerance for the views and practices of others, they have lost something that is precious to a good society. Tolerance is the premise for some important provisions that have been written into our Constitution—freedom of speech, freedom of worship, freedom of the press.

It is the realm of truth, of ethics, morals, aesthetics, the spiritual, and of those great precepts: Love thy neighbor as thyself; do unto others as you would have them do unto you.

Truly, the full measure of a man can be gauged by the extent to which he gives obedience to these guides to human conduct that are unenforceable. The extent to which its members give credence to these standards is also the measure of the greatness of a people, of the greatness of a nation. It is through obedience of the people to these precepts that a democratic society is made possible. . . .

Observe how closely the last two domains, that of obedience to the unenforceable and that of obedience to law, are interrelated. They intertwine and complement each other. Obedience to law in a free society is of the essence, but law observance would come to naught unless the members of that society were also deeply devoted to the precept of obedience to that which they cannot be forced to obey. . . .

The issue before us is one of values. There are those among us who assert, and with reason, that we have lost our sense of purposeful direction; that we are a drifting people in ideas and ideals; that we are "paralyzed in self-indulgences"; that the impact of technology upon self-government is subjecting "the processes of democracy to a complete change of scale" . . . it is imperative that we do not permit ourselves to be deflected from the supreme and enduring values. We must fortify our lives and all of our actions with these values and make them a fighting faith.

We must never waiver in our support of the democratic process, in our adherence to the rule of law, and in our fidelity to the enduring values of life. Thus accoutered, the individual can rise above the confusion of the day. To live by these values marks the supreme measure of a man, of a people, of a nation.

13. Law and Ethics

Ethics *Conduct based on a commitment of what is right. This conduct often is at a level above that required by legal standards.*

Ethics is a term used to describe good behavior. Ethical conduct is based on a commitment to what is right and a rejection of what is wrong. Ethics provides values beyond what the law requires or prohibits. Such values are important if people are to live together peacefully in a free society, because a free society depends on people's trust and confidence in each other. Ethical standards supply the foundation on which trust and confidence are built.

Ethics and the law are closely connected and interrelated. Ethical standards are frequently enacted into law because the law usually reflects society's view of right and wrong. However, it is usually recognized that ethical standards go beyond the law. The law provides a floor above which ethical conduct rises. Ethical business conduct normally exists at a level well above legal minimums. Ethical conduct often means doing more than the law requires or less than it allows.

Codes of ethics adopted by government, the professions, trade associations, and businesses should be thought of as internal laws for all persons subject to them. These codes of conscience are based on fairness, honesty, courtesy, self-restraint, and consideration for others. Most provisions only require disclosure of facts to superiors in certain situations. However, some may dictate certain decisions and conduct. They state a collective sense of right and wrong. Codes of conduct usually are general statements, because the more specific the code, the more difficult it is to obtain acceptance of the principles.

For purposes of illustrating a typical code of business conduct, we have selected the one developed by the Boeing Company of Seattle, Washington. Its code was selected because Boeing is a company conducting business worldwide in a basic industry employing thousands of people. It is a member of the aerospace industry and of the military industrial complex, both of which are subject to significant public scrutiny and substantial criticism. In 1987, *Fortune* magazine selected Boeing as its third most admired company in America. This ranking was based on the quality of Boeing's products and services, its ability to attract people, and the quality of its management. Its "Business Conduct Guidelines" and "Policy Implementation Instructions" have contributed to its outstanding reputation while being a major factor in an industry that is generally given low marks for appropriate business conduct. Boeing has apparently been very successful in obtaining acceptance of and compliance with its operating principles and ethical standards. Excerpts from its "Business Conduct Guidelines" and "Policy Implementation Instructions" will be found throughout this text to demonstrate the close connection between law, ethics, and corporate responsibility.

The Boeing guidelines are based on a corporate policy adopted by its board of directors. This policy statement provides in part as follows:[3]

> It is the policy of this Company to conduct its business affairs fairly, impartially, and in an ethical and proper manner. Conduct that may raise questions as to the Company's honesty, integrity, impartiality, or reputation, or activities that could cause embarrassment to the Company or damage its reputation are prohibited. Any activity, conduct, or transaction that could create an appearance of unethical, illegal, or improper business conduct must be avoided.
>
> The highest possible standards of ethical and business conduct are required of Company employees in the performance of their Company responsibilities. It is the responsibility of every employee and the policy of the Company to encourage its employees to ask questions, seek guidance, report suspected violations, or express their concerns regarding compliance with this standard of conduct.
>
> To this end, the Company shall maintain a program to assist its employees in understanding the standards of ethical business conduct that are required of them, and establish procedures to assist its employees in resolving questions, providing guidance, and for

[3] The excerpts throughout this chapter appear by permission of the Boeing Company.

> reporting suspected violations of, or expressing concerns regarding compliance with, these standards of conduct. The Company shall also maintain a means, separate from line management, for employees to express concerns regarding compliance with the Ethics and Business Conduct Policy of the Company.

As a result of the foregoing policy all Boeing employees are expected to conduct their business with the highest ethical standards and treat with fairness and integrity all employees, customers, suppliers, and associates to earn and maintain their trust. In a letter transmitting the guidelines to all employees, the chief executive officer of Boeing emphasized the company's long-standing commitment to maintain these principles of ethics and business conduct.

The guidelines and the materials included throughout this text include a question-and-answer format describing actual situations that have been encountered by Boeing people.

14. A Typical Ethics Problem—Acceptance of Business Courtesies

To illustrate a typical ethics problem confronting businesses today, assume that you are a Boeing manager and consider the following questions as set forth in Boeing guidelines:

1. A supplier representative knows that I am a big basketball fan. He invited me to accompany him to the All-Star game. His company was able to get tickets even though the game had been sold out for weeks. When I told him that Boeing policy would not allow me to accept his invitation, he offered to sell me the two tickets. Would purchasing the tickets violate Boeing policy?
2. My neighbor works for a Boeing supplier. We socialize frequently and have become good friends. Could our friendship create an ethics problem?
3. I attended a seminar at Boeing expense where I won a door prize worth $100. Three hundred people attended and only four door prizes were available. May I keep it?

To answer these questions, you consult the guidelines and find the following summary of company policy on the acceptance of business courtesies:

> It is the policy of the Company to conduct its business affairs fairly and to neither seek nor grant special consideration in its dealing with suppliers. The avoidance of any appearance of favoritism in the allocation of Company business is essential to this policy. Business courtesies from suppliers which could be perceived to affect any employees' impartiality must be rejected. Business decisions made by Boeing employees should be made on the basis of quality, service, price and similar competitive factors.
>
> A business courtesy is a gift or favor for which fair market value is not paid by the recipient. It might be a tangible or intangible benefit and includes all forms of hospitality, recreation, transportation, discounts, tickets, passes, promotional material, and the recipient's use of the donor's time, material or equipment.
>
> Company employees may not accept or retain business courtesies offered to them or to their immediate families if doing so would cause or create the appearance of favoritism in the allocation of Company business, or adversely affect the reputation of the Company or its employees for impartiality or fair dealing.

In the policy implementation instructions you find in part:

> Where a business courtesy of appreciable value is received by an employee, it may not be retained for the personal use of the employee unless a payment equal to its fair value is made by the employee to The Boeing Company. Approval must be obtained from The Boeing Company Vice President who has supervisory responsibility for the recipient.

Based on this policy the company answered the questions as follows:

1. Yes. The game is sold out and the tickets aren't generally available for purchase. The vendor's offer must be declined.
2. Yes, it could if you also deal with your neighbor in her business capacity as a respresentative of the supplier. If there is no business relationship, then there is no ethics problem.
3. The random selection of the prize winners helps avoid any appearance that you were singled out for a special gift intended to induce preferential treatment. However, your management may decide that you should pay the fair market value of the item to The Boeing Company before you may keep it for your personal use.

Boeing also has policies on the *offering* of business courtesies. These policies are very important because a significant portion of Boeing's business is with agencies of the federal government. These agencies also have ethical guidelines that must be met. The following is a summary of the guidelines on offering of business courtesies:

> The Boeing Company's objective is to compete in the marketplace on the basis of superior products and services and competitive prices. Our marketing practices should focus on providing accurate information to our customers so that they can make informed decisions. The Company does not seek to gain any improper advantage through the use of entertainment or other business courtesies.
>
> Employees must exercise good judgment and moderation in providing business courtesies, and should only offer them to the extent appropriate and in accordance with reasonable customs in the marketplace. No business courtesy should be intended to induce the employees of our customers to place their personal interests above those of their employers.
>
> A business courtesy or favor is a gift for which fair market value is not paid. A business courtesy may be a tangible or intangible benefit, and includes all forms of hospitality, recreation, transportation, discount tickets, passes and promotional material, and the recipient's use of the donor's time, material or equipment. Some governmental agencies and commercial companies strictly prohibit their employees from accepting business courtesies. Learn the customers' rules before offering gifts.

It is apparent that in today's environment the giving or receiving of business courtesies such as gifts, meals, entertainment or travel usually is considered unethical conduct and unacceptable business behavior. Courtesies that are extended to obtain special treatment are usually perceived to be improper conduct. The argument that "everybody else does it" is not an acceptable excuse for such conduct if a company is serious about its ethics code.

CHAPTER SUMMARY

Compromises

Reasons to Settle	1. Most disputes in our society are settled without resort to litigation. 2. A major function of lawyers is to negotiate a settlement of controversies.
Mediation	1. Mediation is a process by which a third party assists in working out a compromise of a dispute. 2. The National Mediation and Conciliation Service is available to mediate labor disputes.

Arbitration

Advantages	1. Arbitration is the submission to a person or persons other than a court for a final binding decision of a controversy. 2. Arbitration is less expensive than litigation. It generally takes far less time and allows the parties to remain more amicable than does litigation.
Submission	1. The term *submission* is used to describe the action of referring an issue to arbitration. 2. The submission governs the duties and powers of the arbitrators. 3. Submission may result from an agreement to arbitrate all disputes that may arise in the future or from an agreement to arbitrate a particular dispute.
Procedure	1. The parties are given notice of the time and place of the hearing. 2. The proceedings are less formal than a trial, and the arbitrators need not follow strict rules of evidence.
The Award	1. The decision in arbitration is known as an *award*. Awards may be judicially enforced. 2. If an award is within the power of the submission, a court will not change it because of errors of fact or errors of law.
Judicial Procedures in Arbitration	1. Litigation is often necessary to enforce an award, which is treated as if it were a judgment of a court. 2. An agreement to arbitrate may be ordered enforced by courts also. 3. There are a few grounds for challenging an award in court.

Administrative Law

Introduction	1. Administrative agencies as a fourth branch of government have the responsibility of deciding a high percentage of the controversies in our society. 2. Many agencies serve in lieu of courts to decide disputed questions of fact.
The Quasi-Legislative Function	1. Agencies adopt rules and regulations to decide issues of a general nature. This function is similar to the legislative process.
The Quasi-Judicial Function	1. In conducting quasi-judicial hearings, the rules of procedure used by administrative agencies are far less formal than the rules used by courts. 2. Issues submitted to administrative agencies are outside the scope of the right to a trial by jury.

Judicial Review of Agency Decisions

1. Courts will determine whether the party filing the complaint has "standing" to challenge an agency's action.
2. Prior to hearing a case involving an agency's action, courts examine whether the parties have exhausted their administrative remedies.
3. Courts give great deference to decisions of administrative agencies.
4. A court will not substitute its judgment for that of the agency if there is a substantial basis for the agency's decision.
5. Judicial review of agency decisions is limited to a decision as to whether or not the agency has acted within the delegation of its authority and whether or not there is a factual basis for the agency decision.

Influencing Conduct

Introduction

1. The law is not the only means of influencing conduct. Economic considerations and ethical standards often play an important role.
2. An individual's own sense of right and wrong is a major influence on conduct. This is often called "obedience to the unenforceable."

Law and Ethics

1. Law provides a floor above which conduct is judged by ethical standards.
2. Codes of conduct developed by businesses and associations are internal laws for persons subject to them for which sanctions may be imposed for violations.
3. Codes of ethics are very important for publicly held businesses today. The Boeing Company code is used as an example throughout the text.

Typical Ethics Problem

1. The giving or receiving of business courtesies such as gifts of property or entertainment frequently raises serious ethical issues.
2. Business courtesies raise special problems when the person giving or receiving is connected with government.
3. If there is any doubt, the conduct is probably a violation of ethical standards.

REVIEW QUESTIONS AND PROBLEMS

1. Match the terms in column A with the appropriate statement in column B.

A	B
(1) Mediation	(a) The decision resulting from arbitration.
(2) Arbitration	(b) A requirement of the parties challenging an administrative agency's action in court.
(3) Submission	(c) A process whereby a third party assists others in reaching a compromise of a dispute.
(4) Award	(d) The giving or receiving of gifts in a commercial sense.
(5) Administrative agencies	(e) That which may be violated even when no law has been.
(6) Rules and regulations	(f) The function of administrative agencies in resolving disputes.
(7) Quasi-judicial	(g) The action of referring a dispute to arbitration.
(8) Exhaustion of remedies	(h) The result of an administrative agency's quasi-legislative function.
(9) Ethical standards	(i) The fourth branch of government.
(10) Business courtesies	(j) The submission of a dispute to one or more persons for a final binding resolution.

2. Alexander is involved in a dispute related to his business. He is confident that he is right, and he is considering legal action. List the reasons why it may be financially advantageous to Alexander's business to avoid court and to compromise and settle for less money than he claims is owed to him.
3. Distinguish between mediation and arbitration.
4. Discuss the scope of judicial review of an arbitrator's decision. Use the terms *award* and *submission* in your answer.
5. There was a dispute between an automobile insurance company and its insured concerning value in the loss of a truck. The insurance policy required arbitration of disputes. Each party selected an arbitrator and these two, when unable to agree, selected a third party as "umpire." The umpire, without consulting anyone or receiving any testimony, fixed the value of the loss. If challenged, will a court set aside this award? Why?
6. A dispute arose between partners on a construction project. The agreement of the parties provided that if the parties were unable to agree on any matter with respect to which a decision was to be made by both parties, the dispute would be submitted to arbitration. One party asked a court to appoint a receiver for the business. The other insisted on arbitration. How will the dispute be resolved? Why?
7. While conducting a hearing, an arbitrator allowed hearsay evidence. In reaching a decision, the arbitrator ignored a federal law that would have been applicable in court. May the losing party have the award set aside on these grounds? Why or why not?
8. The law creating the EPA states that its purpose is to establish rules and regulations to "promote a healthful environment." Pursuant to this delegation of authority, the agency adopted a regulation that made it unlawful to manufacture or to utilize power plant equipment that allowed emissions "detrimental to the atmosphere." Consumers Power Company was charged with violating the agency rule. It challenged the constitutionality of the rule. What result? Why?
9. Leonard's, Inc., was charged with violating a rule of an administrative agency and a hearing was conducted by an administrative law judge. The judge found the company guilty. The rules of the agency provided for a review by the full commission, but rather than seek such a review, Leonard's filed a case in the courts to enjoin further agency action. What result? Why?
10. Pam owned a tract of real estate across the street from a major shopping center. The lot was at an intersection of the main roads leading to the shopping center, and Pam wanted to build a service station on the property. The property was zoned for single-family residences. She filed a request with the zoning body to have the classification changed to commercial. The zoning board denied Pam's request. She filed suit contending that the present and best use of the property was for commercial purposes. The zoning board contended that a buffer was needed between the shopping center and the residential area and that the only appropriate buffer was the street. What decision? Why?
11. Codes of ethics are adopted by businesses, trade associations, and professional organizations. Why are such codes so important today?
12. Discuss the relationship between law and ethics.

The Law of Torts and Business

6

CHAPTER PREVIEW

BUSINESS MANAGEMENT DECISION

You are the general sales manager for a computer-manufacturing firm. To increase your firm's competitive advantage, you offer a competitor's district sales manager a similar position with a higher salary. This sales manager indicates that he can bring at least five of his salespeople with him.

Should you hire the sales manager and his salespeople?

Tort *A wrongful act committed by one person against another person or his property. It is the breach of a legal duty imposed by law other than by contract.*

A **tort** is an omission (failure to act) or a wrongful act (other than a breach of contract) against a person or his property. The term is somewhat difficult to define, but the word *wrongful* in the definition means a violation of one person's legal duty to another. The victim of a tort may recover damages for the injuries received, usually because the other party was "at fault" in causing the injury.

Acts or omissions, to be tortious, need not involve moral turpitude or bad motive or maliciousness. Moreover, an act or an omission that does not invade another's rights is not tortious, even though the actor's motive is bad or malicious.

Torts as private wrongs must be contrasted with crimes, which are public wrongs. The purpose of the criminal law is to punish the wrongdoer, while the purpose of the law of torts is to compensate the victim of wrongful conduct. To deter intentional torts, however, the law may impose punitive in addition to actual damages.

The same act may be both a crime and a tort: An assault and battery is both a wrong against society and a wrong against the victim. Society may punish the guilty party, and the victim may sue in tort to recover damages. It must be recognized that the criminal action does not benefit the victim of the crime or compensate him for his injury. Such compensation is left to the civil law of torts.

THEORIES OF TORT LIABILITY

1. Overview

Negligence *Failure to do that which an ordinary, reasonable, prudent person would do, or the doing of some act that an ordinary, prudent person would not do.*

Strict liability *The doctrine under which a party may be required to respond in tort damages, without regard to that party's fault.*

Tort liability is predicated on two premises: In a civilized society one person should not intentionally injure another or his property, and all persons should exercise reasonable care and caution in the conduct of their affairs. The first premise has resulted in a group of torts labeled *intentional torts*. The second premise is the basis for the general field of tort liability known as **negligence.** Liability based on negligence is liability based on fault, just as it is in an intentional tort. However, because the wrong in negligence is of a lesser degree than it is in torts, the theory of damages in negligence cases does not include punishment. For simple negligence, a person is entitled to collect only actual damages from the wrongdoer, that is, enough money to make the injured party whole. He is not entitled to collect punitive damages to discourage the wrongdoer from repeating his negligence.

A third theory of tort liability, called **strict liability,** is not based on wrongful conduct in the usual sense, although the party committing the tort usually does something intentionally or negligently. Strict liability is based on peculiar factual situations and the relationship of the parties. To the extent that an activity by one party causes injury, there is liability because of the injury, not because the defendant was at fault in the traditional sense of wrongdoing. Although there is no fault in the sense of wrongdoing, there is fault in that actions caused the injuries. Strict liability is imposed when harm is caused by dangerous or trespassing animals, blasting operations, or fire.

2. Damages

The purpose of tort litigation is to require a wrongdoer or the party at fault to compensate a victim for the injury incurred.

Compensatory Damages. The theory of **damages,** or *compensatory damages*, is that the victim of a tort should receive a sum of money that will make him "whole." In other words, dollar damages are supposed to place the victim of the tort in as good a position as he would have been in had the tort not been committed. This, of course, is impossible, because no amount of money can replace an arm, a leg, or an eye, let alone a life. Therefore, in very serious cases, especially those that involve substantial pain and suffering, any money damages are probably inadequate.

Damages *A sum of money the court imposes upon a defendant as compensation for the plaintiff because the defendant has injured the plaintiff by breach of a legal duty.*

Compensatory damages in the typical tort case usually include medical expenses, lost income from earnings, property damage, and pain and suffering and loss of life or limb. These losses are those actually sustained in the past and those estimated in the future. As a result of the latter aspect, the calculation of damage awards creates significant problems. Expert witnesses use life expectancy tables and present-value discount tables to help them testify so that a jury may determine the amount of damages to award. But uncertainty about the life expectancy of injured plaintiffs and the impact of inflation make the use of these tables questionable. Also, awarding damages for pain and suffering may result from jury sympathy as much as for compensation for financial loss.

Punitive Damages. There are also **punitive damages,** which are awarded to punish defendants for committing intentional torts and, in some states, for negligent behavior considered "gross" or "willful and wanton." For an award of punitive damages the defendant's motive must be "malicious," "fraudulent," or "evil." Increasingly, punitive damages are also awarded for dangerously negligent conduct (gross negligence) that shows a conscious disregard for the interests of others. These damages are used to deter future wrongdoing. Because they make an example of the defendant, punitive damages are sometimes called *exemplary damages*. Punitive damages are a windfall to the injuried plaintiff, who has already received compensatory damages.

Punitive damages *Damages by way of punishment. Allowed for an injury caused by a wrong that is willful and malicious.*

To collect damages, most victims must hire an attorney, whose fee is usually contingent on the total amount collected. The contingent fee system means that the attorney is paid a percentage of the recovery, but nothing if the case is lost. Usual contingent fees are 33⅓ percent if a trial is held, and 40 to 50 percent if the case is appealed. Contingent fees make the legal system and the best lawyers available to all, irrespective of ability to pay. However, if the injuries are very substantial and liability is easily established, the fees of the attorney may be viewed as unfair and unreasonable. Assume that a $15 million verdict is given for the loss of two legs. It is difficult to see how the attorney's $5 million could have been earned if the liability is clear. The chance of earning similarly large fees has encouraged ''ambulance chasing'' of potentially big cases, especially in large cities.

3. Persons Liable

Every person legally responsible is *liable* for his or her own torts. It is no defense that the wrongdoer is working under the direction of another. That fact may create liability on the part of the other person, but it is no defense to the wrongdoer. The theory of liability by which one person is liable for the torts of another is known as *respondeat superior*. This theory imposes liability on principals or masters for the torts of their agents or servants if the agent or servant is acting within the scope of employment when the tort was committed. This subject is discussed more fully in Chapter 23.

Joint and several *Two or more persons have an obligation that binds them individually as well as jointly. The obligation can be enforced either by joint action against all of them or by separate actions against one or more.*

If two or more persons jointly commit a tort, all may be held liable for the total injury. The liability is said to be **joint and several.** All are liable, and each is liable for the entire damage. This principle is often criticized, and there have been numerous efforts to change it by legislation. To illustrate the argument for abolishing the concept of joint and several liability, assume that defendant A is 99 percent at fault and defendant B is 1 percent at fault. If defendant A has no assets, defendant B must pay 100 percent of the judgment even though only 1 percent at fault.

In general, an infant has tort liability, depending on the age of the infant, the nature of the tort involved, and whether the tort is intentional or based on a theory of negligence. In most states, a child under the age of seven is conclusively presumed to be incapable of negligence; from ages seven to ten, a child is still presumed to be incapable, but the presumption may be rebutted. A child older than ten is treated as any other person insofar as tort liability is concerned. Some states use the age fourteen instead of ten for these rules. A minor above the minimum age is held to the same standard as an adult. A minor driving an automobile owes the same duty of due care that an adult owes.

Another area of substantial misunderstanding of the law is concerned with parents' liability for the torts of their children. As a general rule, a parent is not responsible for such torts. Parents are liable if the child is acting as an agent of the parent, or if the parents are themselves at fault. In addition, some states have adopted the ''family-purpose'' doctrine, which provides that when an automobile is maintained by a parent for the pleasure and convenience of the family, any member of the family, including an infant, who uses it is presumed the owner's agent, and the owner is responsible for the negligence of the family member. The presumption may be rebutted, however. Other states have gone further and provided that anyone driving a car with the permission of the owner is the owner's agent, and the owner has vicarious liability to persons injured by the driver.

In recent years courts have been faced with cases in which a person is injured by a product but the person is unable to determine which company manufactured the product. Such cases are common when drugs cause injuries not only to the person taking the drug but also to their children. While there are only a few cases to date, the trend is to hold all manufacturers liable and to allocate the loss by market share. A manufacturer can avoid its share of liability only by proving that its products could not have been the cause of the injury. Otherwise, all manufacturers share responsibility for injuries.

INTENTIONAL TORTS

4. Introduction

Several intentional torts often involve the business community as either plaintiffs or defendants. The imposition of liability for these torts provides protection to basic, individual interests of people and their property. The torts may involve interference with the personal freedom of an individual, interference with property rights, interference with economic relations, and wrongful communications. Table 6–1 briefly describes each.

5. Interference with Personal Freedom

Assault, Battery, False Imprisonment. *Assault and battery* and *false imprisonment* involve business more commonly than they should. If an employee of a business

TABLE 6–1 INTENTIONAL TORTS COMMON TO BUSINESS

Theory of Liability	Description
Interference with personal freedom	
Assault	Causing the apprehension of a harmful or offensive contact with a person's body.
Battery	Intentional and unpermitted physical contact with a person's body.
Assault and battery	A combination of assault and battery (some hits and some misses).
False imprisonment	A wrongful restraint of a person's freedom of movement.
Mental distress	Wrongful interference with a person's peace of mind by insults, indignities, or outrageous conduct.
Interference with property	
Trespass to land	An unauthorized entry upon the land of another.
Trespass to chattels	A direct intentional interference with a chattel in possession of another person, such as taking it or damaging it.
Conversion	Interference with a person's chattels to the extent that the wrongdoer ought to pay for the chattel.
Nuisance	An intentional invasion or disturbance of a person's rights in land or the conduct of an abnormally dangerous activity.
Interference with economic relations	
Disparagement	Injurious falsehoods about a person's business or property, damaging prospective advantage.
Contracts	Inducing a party to a contract to breach it or interfering with its performance.
Prospective advantage	Interfering with an expectancy such as employment or an opportunity to contract.
Wrongful appropriation	Infringing goodwill, patents, trademarks, copyrights, and other business interests.
Wrongful communications	
Slander	Oral defamation. Holding a person's name or reputation up to hatred, contempt, or ridicule, or causing others to shun him.
Libel	Written defamation.
Invasion of privacy	Interfering with one's right to be let alone by (1) appropriating the name or picture of a person, (2) intruding upon a person's physical solitude, (3) the public disclosure of private facts, and (4) publicity that places a person in a false light in the public eye.
Fraud	An intentional misstatement of a material existing fact relied upon by another, to his injury.

engages in a fight with a customer, a lawsuit on the theory of assault and battery is likely to follow. Similarly, if an employee wrongfully physically restrains a customer, there may be a tort action for false imprisonment. Assume that the plaintiff is suspected of shoplifting and the defendant physically restrains him. If the defendant is wrong, and the plaintiff is not a shoplifter, a tort has been committed.

Mental Distress. Inflicting *mental distress* is a tort very important to the business community. It is an invasion of a person's peace of mind by insults or other indignities or by outrageous conduct. If someone without a privilege to do so, by extreme and outrageous conduct, intentionally or recklessly causes another person severe emotional distress with bodily harm resulting from that distress, the offender is subject to liability for the other's emotional distress and bodily harm. Liability does not exist for every case of hurt feelings or bad manners—only where conduct is so outrageous in character and so extreme in degree that it goes beyond all possible bounds of decency. For liability, the conduct must be regarded as atrocious, utterly intolerable in a civilized community. Liability exists in cases in which the facts, if told to an average person, would lead him to exclaim "Outrageous!" High-pressure tactics of collection agencies, including violent cursing and accusations of dishonesty, have often been held to be outrageous. However, a person is not liable where he has done no more than to insist on his legal rights in a permissible way, even though he is aware that such insistence is certain to cause emotional distress. Also, there is no liability for offensive conduct that is not extreme.

CASE

Munley was divorced from her husband after they jointly incurred several debts. The divorce decree required the husband to pay the debts, but he failed to do so and they fell into default. The defendant loan company's agents then began contacting the plaintiff regarding the debts and her husband's whereabouts. The agents visited her apartment on four or six different occasions, as well as asked her neighbors where she could be found and what type of furniture she owned. The agents indicated to the neighbor that Munley was in some sort of trouble.

ISSUE: Did the actions of the defendant's agents constitute an intentional infliction of emotional distress or an invasion of privacy?

DECISION: No.

REASONS:
1. The conduct here was not so "extreme and outrageous" as to reach the level of an intentional infliction of emotional distress.
2. A creditor who by extreme and outrageous conduct intentionally or recklessly causes severe emotional distress to a debtor is subject to liability for such emotional distress, and if bodily harm to the debtor results from it, for such bodily harm.
3. In a debtor-creditor relationship, the actions of the tortfeasor are compensable when they would be highly offensive to a reasonable person. Since the conduct in this case does not amount to conduct highly offensive to a reasonable person, no invasion of privacy can be found.

Munley v. ISC Financial House, Inc., 584 P.2d 1336 (Okla. 1978).

6. Interference with Property

Trespass. The tort of **trespass** is a common one and is applied both to real and personal property. Trespass to land occurs when there is an unauthorized entry upon the land of another. The person in exclusive possession of land is entitled to enjoy the use of that land free from interference of others. Entry upon the land of another is a trespass even if the one who enters is under the mistaken belief that he is the owner or has a right, license, or pivilege to enter.

Trespass *An injury to the person, property, or rights of another person committed by actual force and violence or under such circumstances that the law will infer that the injury was caused by force or violence.*

Trespass to land may be *innocent* or *willful*. An innocent trespass would occur when one goes on another's land by mistake or under the impression that he has a right to be there. It is still an intentional wrong because persons intend the natural and probable consequences of their acts. A trespass is willful if the trespasser knowingly goes on another's land, aware that he has no right to do so. In a trespass case, if the trespass if willful, the plaintiff is entitled to exemplary or punitive damages, which may include attorney's fees. It should be kept in mind that except for tort cases involving punitive damages, every litigant pays his own attorney's fees in tort cases.

A trespass to personal property—goods and the like—is unlawful interference with the control and possession of the goods of another. One is entitled to have exclusive possession and control of his personal property and may recover for any physical harm to his goods by reason of the wrongful conduct of another. The intent need not be wrongful. If a person mistakenly interferes with the goods of another, a trespass has occurred. A trespass to goods may occur by theft of the goods or by damage to the goods. In such cases, the owner recovers the property and is entitled to be paid for the damage to the property and for its loss of use during the period that the owner lost possession of the property.

Conversion. The action of conversion is quite similar to trespass. It differs in that a suit for conversion of goods is used when the interference is so significant that the wrongdoer is compelled to pay the full value of the goods as damages. Conversion, in theory, is a judicial sale of the **chattel** to the wrongdoer. Using someone else's lumber for building purposes would be a conversion. Among the factors used to determine if the interference is relatively minor (trespass) or serious (conversion) are the extent and duration of the interference, the defendant's motives, the amount of actual damages to the goods, and the inconvenience and other harm suffered by the plaintiff. Conversion results from conduct intended to affect the chattel. The intent required is not conscious wrongdoing but an intent to exercise control over the goods. For example, a purchaser of stolen goods is guilty of conversion even though he does not know the goods are stolen. An act of interference with the rights of the true owner establishes the conversion.

Chattel *A very broad term derived from the word* cattle. *It includes every kind of property that is not real property.*

Conversion frequently occurs even though the defendant's original possession of the goods is lawful. It may result from several actions, such as a transfer of the goods to another person or to another location. A laundry that delivers shirts to the wrong person is guilty of a conversion. If the laundry refuses to deliver the shirts to the owner, a conversion has occurred. Destruction, alteration, or misuse of a chattel may also constitute a conversion.

Nuisance. Tort liability may also be predicated upon the unreasonable use by a person of his own property. Any improper or indecent activity that causes harm to

Nuisance *Generally, any continuous or continued conduct that causes annoyance, inconvenience, or damage to person or property.* Nuisance *usually applies to unreasonable, wrongful use of property, causing material discomfort, hurt, and damage to the person or property of another.*

another person, to his property, or to the public generally is tortious. Such conduct is usually described as a **nuisance,** either private or public. A private nuisance disturbs only the interest of some private individual, whereas the public nuisance disturbs or interferes with the public in general. The legal theory supporting tort liability in these areas is that an owner of property, although conducting a lawful business thereon, is subject to reasonable limitations and must use his property in a way that will not unreasonably interfere with the health and comfort of his neighbors or with their right to the enjoyment of their property. The ownership of land includes the right to reasonable comfort and convenience in its occupation. In addition to tort liability, the remedy of an injunction is used to abate a nuisance. The following case considers a typical lawful activity that is, nevertheless, a private nuisance.

CASE

Ninety-eight homeowners brought action seeking to enjoin as a nuisance the construction and operation of a ready-mix concrete plant on property adjacent to a residential area. Plaintiffs live southwest, west, and east across the highway from the plant. The plant is bounded immediately on the north and south by other business concerns. The trial court found for the plaintiffs.

ISSUE: Did the defendant's operation of a concrete plant in an area zoned for light to general industrial use constitute a nuisance?

DECISION: Yes.

REASONS:
1. The essence of private nuisance is an interference with the use and enjoyment of land. So long as the interference is substantial and unreasonable, and such as would be offensive or inconvenient to the normal person, virtually any disturbance to the enjoyment of property may amount to a nuisance.
2. Location is one factor to consider in determining whether a given activity constitutes a nuisance. However, when noise levels exceed those limits expected from business for which an area was zoned, when drainage problems cause daily sediment accumulations, and when dust levels are excessive due to operating conditions, then the trial court ruling that the activity constituted a nuisance was supported by sufficient evidence.

Morgan County Concrete Co. v. Tanner, 374 So.2d 1344 (Ala. 1979).

A nuisance may result from intentional conduct or from negligence. Although malice may not be involved, most nuisances are intentional in the sense that the party creating the nuisance did so with the knowledge that harm to the interests of others would follow. A nuisance requires a substantial and unreasonable interference with the rights of others and not a mere annoyance or inconvenience.

A nuisance may exist because of the type of business activity being conducted. Operation of a drag strip or a massage parlor has been held to constitute a private nuisance to the neighbors. Many nuisances result from the manner in which business is conducted. Pollution of the air or water by a business frequently results in tort liability based on the nuisance theory. Most tort litigation dealing with private nuisances is resolved by weighing the conflicting interests of adjoining landowners. If one party is seriously injuring the other, the activity may be enjoined and dollar damages awarded. Even if the courts are unwilling to enjoin an activity, dollar damages may still be awarded because of a nuisance.

7. Interference with Economic Relations

Interference with commercial or economic relations includes three business torts: disparagement, interference with contractual relations, and interference with prospective advantage.

Disparagement. *Disparagement* is a communication of an injurious falsehood about a person's property, quality of product, or character and conduct of business in general. Such false statements are regarded as ''unfair'' competition and are not privileged. The basis of the tort is the false communications that result in interference with the prospect of sale or some other advantageous business relation. The falsehood must be communicated to a third party and must result in specific pecuniary loss. The loss of specific customers, sales, or business transactions must be demonstrated. Although closely related, slander or personal defamation of one's reputation is another tort and is discussed in section 8, on wrongful communications.

Contracts. *Interference with contractual relations* usually takes the form of inducing a breach of contract. In order to hold someone liable for interference with a contract, a direct causal relation and improper motive must be shown. Mere loss suffered from a broken contract is insufficient. Crucial to the question of liability is the balancing of the conflicting interests of the parties involved. For example, assume that a depositor tells the bank's president that she believes one of the cashiers is dishonest. She suggests that the cashier be discharged. Has the depositor committed a tort? The policy of protecting employees from wrongful interference with the employment contracts must be weighed against the desirability of ensuring that bank employees are honest. The trend of cases is to allow recovery for wrongful interferences with the rights of others. Any intentional invasion or interference with the property or contractual rights of others without just cause is a tort. The economic harm due to the breach of an existing contract is weighed against the motive and the reasonableness of the action. The courts tend to favor the sanctity of existing contracts over other interests such as unrestricted competition.

Prospective Advantage. *Interference with prospective or potential advantage* is considered a tort, in order to protect the expectancies of future contractual relations, including the prospect of obtaining employment, employees, or customers. It is no tort to use fair business practices to beat a business rival to prospective customers; however, the competitor's motive and means of accomplishment determine liability. Fraud, violence, intimidation, and threats that drive away potential customers from one's market result in liability. As in suits for lost profits, obtaining sufficient proof that losses were actually suffered is sometimes difficult.

Other Infringements. Another interference with economic relations tort is the wrongful appropriation of another's goodwill or business value. It is a tort to infringe on another's patent, trademark, or copyright. In addition, a trade name such as Holiday Inn or Coca-Cola is entitled to protection from theft or appropriation by another. Many cases involving the appropriation of another's business values involve words or actions that are deceptively similar to those of another. It is a tort to use a name or take an action that is deceptively similar to the protected interests of another. But what degree of similarity may exist before a wrong is committed? In general, it can be said that whenever the causal observer, as distinct from the careful buyer, tends to be misled into purchasing the wrong article, an injunction as well as a tort action is available to the injured party.

The remedy of injunction is perhaps more important than the tort action where there is infringement of a patent, copyright, or trademark. The injunction that prohibits the continued appropriation protects not only the owner of the right but the consuming public as well.

Trade secrets are also protected by the law of torts and courts of equity. Information about one's trade, customers, processes, or manufacture is confidential; but if it is not patented or copyrighted, another firm may make the same discoveries fairly—through research, study, or observation—and may use them freely. ''Reverse engineering'' by which one party studies another's product to come up with a similar product is permissible. If the second firm bribes or hires an employee of the first company, however, in order to obtain secrets, the second firm may be enjoined from using them. Novelty and breach of confidential relationships are not necessary before there can be a trade secret. What constitutes a trade secret is a question of fact.

8. Wrongful Communications

Libel *Malicious publication of a defamation of a person by printing, writing, signs, or pictures, for the purposes of injuring the reputation and good name of such person.*

Slander *An oral utterance that tends to injure the reputation of another.*

Defamation consists of the twin torts of libel and slander. **Libel** is generally written; **slander** is oral. A defamatory communication is one that holds a person up to hatred, contempt, or ridicule or causes a person to be shunned by others. Tort liability for defamation exists in order to protect a person's name and reputation.

Slander. As a general rule, a charge of slander requires proof of actual damage; however, four categories of statements justify the awarding of damages without actual proof of damage: imputing the commission of a crime of moral turpitude; imputing the presence of a loathsome disease; imputing unfitness relating to the conduct of a business, trade, profession, or office; and accusing a female of unchastity. All other slanders require proof of special damage. The following case is typical of potential defamation cases facing business.

CASE

Ronald Hennis sued Transcon Lines, Inc., and Michael O'Connor, Transcon's sales manager, for slanderous statements allegedly made by O'Connor after the termination of Hennis's employment as a salesman with Transcon. Hennis claimed that O'Connor had told Hennis's friends, business associates, and customers that Hennis had stolen company property. There was testimony that O'Connor had said that Hennis, while employed, had taken things, including petty cash, from the office and submitted personal receipts as business expenses. Hennis claimed these statements were false and that O'Connor had known they were false when he uttered them. Hennis and his wife testified that O'Connor's alleged statements had caused Hennis depression, anxiety, humiliation, and sleepless nights. Hennis neither alleged nor proved special damages. During the trial, the defendants sought a directed verdict in their favor since Hennis did not prove special damages. The court did not grant the defendants a directed verdict, and the jury returned a $10,000 verdict for the plaintiff.

ISSUE: Were O'Connor's alleged statements slanderous *per se*, thus preventing the defendants from obtaining a directed verdict when the plaintiff neither alleged nor proved special damages?

DECISION: Yes.

REASONS:

1. If language is slanderous *per se*, a plaintiff does not have to allege and prove special damages. To be slanderous *per se*, the alleged defamatory statements must falsely convey not only the expression of an actionable wrong committed by the person allegedly slandered but also the nature of the particular wrong. The allegedly slanderous language, by its nature and obvious meaning, must impute the commission of a crime involving moral turpitude, an infectious disease, unfitness to perform duties of an office or employment, prejudice the victim of the statements in his profession or trade, or subject him to public ridicule or disgrace.
2. To determine if words are slanderous *per se*, the court construes language in its ordinary and popular sense. The court also determines whether a crime imputed by spoken words is of such a character as to make the language slanderous *per se*. The imputation of a crime is generally slanderous *per se* if the crime is punishable by imprisonment or is regarded by public opinion as involving moral turpitude.
3. O'Connor's statements conveyed both the expression of an actionable wrong (theft) and the nature of the wrong done (theft of petty cash and fraudulent submission of expense receipts). The imputation of these crimes was slanderous *per se*.
4. Therefore the defendants were not entitled to a directed verdict, and the trial court's judgment is affirmed.

Hennis v. O'Connor, 388 N.W.2d 470 (Neb. 1986).

Libel. The law of libel is complicated by the written aspect of defamation. Freedom of the press, for example, is guaranteed by the First Amendment, to which the law must adhere. Furthermore, application of the law of libel depends on whether or not the person defamed is a public figure, subject to a set of standards different from those governing the rest of society. Celebrities must prove malice in order to collect damages. Businesses are not public figures, and they are not required to prove malice.

If a statement is libelous on its face, it is actionable without proof of special damages. If additional facts are necessary to establish that a writing is defamatory, the law for libel is the same as for slander, and—unless the statement falls into one of the four categories previously noted—proof of actual damage is required.

Exceptions. Some defamatory statements are absolutely privileged. Statements made as a part of a judicial proceeding cannot constitute a tort because of the need for all witnesses to be able to testify freely, without fear of a subsequent lawsuit. Legislative proceedings and many executive communications are also absolutely privileged.

Some defamatory statements are subject to a qualified or limited privilege. For example, many communications to public officials are privileged in order to encourage citizens to report matters to officials. In addition, fair comment on matters of public concern cannot result in tort liability.

Invasion of Privacy. In recent years, the law has developed a tort known as *invasion of the right of privacy*. The right of privacy is the right to be let alone, but it may be invaded in numerous ways, as set forth in Table 6–1. Many cases involve newspaper or magazine stories about one's private life. A detective magazine that publishes a picture of a family at the funeral of a loved one may be guilty of an invasion of privacy. But this tort must be distinguished from libel and slander. Invasion of privacy does not involve defamation. It involves wrongful intrusion into one's private life in such a manner as to outrage or to cause mental suffering, shame, or humiliation to a person of ordinary sensibilities. The protection is for a mental condition, not a financial one. Invasion of privacy is the equivalent of a battery to one's integrity; actual damage need not be proved. Unjustified invasion of privacy entitles the victim to damages. Punitive damages may be collected if malice is shown. The tort is quite similar to inflicting mental distress by outrageous conduct. Many factual situations are given both labels.

Fraud. The intentional tort of fraudulent misrepresentation is the subject of more litigation than any other of the intentional torts. It is used not only as the basis of suits for dollar damages but to avoid contract liability and as a basis to rescind or cancel otherwise valid contracts. It is discussed more fully in Part II, on contracts.

NEGLIGENCE

Duty (in law) *A legal obligation imposed by general law or voluntarily imposed by the creation of a binding promise. For every legal duty there is a corresponding legal right.*

By most definitions, negligence has four basic elements: a **duty** imposed on a person in favor of others, an act or omission that constitutes a breach of this duty (due care), proximate cause, and an injury to another. Each element must be established if the plaintiff is to be successful.

Under a doctrine known as comparative negligence, liability is assessed in proportion to the fault of each party. In states using comparative negligence, a plaintiff can collect even if partially at fault. In states that do not follow this doctrine, a plaintiff is required to be free from contributory negligence. The law in these states requires that the defendant be 100 percent at fault and the plaintiff 0 percent at fault before there is liability.

9. Duty

The concept of a legal duty means that a person must meet certain standards of conduct in order to protect others against unreasonable risks. These standards of conduct may vary, depending on the relationship of the parties. An owner of property would owe a higher duty to a business visitor than to a trespasser or a licensee. The duty owed to a trespasser is only to warn of known dangers, while the duty to business visitors is to protect them against known dangers and dangers that, with reasonable care, the landowner might discover. The duty is to make the premises reasonably safe for business visitors. However, a business is not an insurer of the safety of its customers. The duty owed to a licensee is greater than that owed to a trespasser and less than that owed to a business visitor.

Right *The phrase "legal right" is a correlative of the phrase "legal duty." One has a legal right if, upon the breach of the correlative legal duty, he can secure a remedy in a court of law.*

Whenever the law imposes a duty upon a person, another person has a **right,** and there exists a right-duty relationship. This relationship exists because the law recognizes it. Moral obligation does not impose a duty or create a right. The duty must be owed to the person claiming injury. An airline owes a duty to its passengers, and the passengers have the right to safe transportation. Assume that this duty is breached and the plane crashes, killing all on board. Assume also that one of the passengers was a key employee of a large company. The company has no claim or tort action against the airline, because the right-duty relationship did not exist between the airline and the company. In recent years courts have expanded the duty owed in cases involving physical injury to one person and emotional injury to another. Many of these cases involve bystanders.

CASE

Santa Ramirez was hit by a car and killed. Two of the children of Ramirez were present at the time of the accident and a third was told of it. The children sued the driver on a theory of negligent infliction of emotional distress. The trial court dismissed the action on the basis of a failure to state a cause of action. The children appealed, arguing that the dismissal was improper.

ISSUE: Does a cause of action exist under the law of New Mexico for negligent infliction of emotional distress to bystanders?

DECISION: Yes.

REASONS:
1. Because of the tremendous interest in protecting "the profound and abiding sentiment of parental love," it is justifiable to impose a duty to avoid negligent infliction of emotional distress.
2. The duty to avoid negligent infliction of emotional harm will only arise when there is a marital or intimate familial relationship as in this case.
3. A series of other guidelines will also be utilized by the court in determining whether an action for negligent infliction of emotional distress to bystanders can be entertained. For example, the emotional injury must result in physical injury or death to the victim.

Ramirez v. Armstrong, 673 P.2d 822 (N.M. 1983).

10. Due Care

Negligence is sometimes defined as a failure to exercise *due care*. People are required to exercise due care and caution for the safety of others when the risk of injury to another is present. Failure to do so is negligence. In determining if a person has exercised due care and caution, the law recognizes that some injuries are caused by unavoidable accidents. There is no tort liability for injuries received in unavoidable accidents. It is only when a person is guilty of unreasonable conduct that tort liability is imposed. Some conduct is declared to be unreasonable by statute, while most conduct is judged by case law standards. The basic issue is whether or not the conduct alleged to be negligent was reasonable or unreasonable.

Liability for negligence is sometimes imposed on a defendant based on a presumption of negligence. This presumption is based on a doctrine known as **res ipsa loquitur**—the thing speaks for itself. It is used in cases where injury would not have occurred unless someone was negligent and the defendant is the only

Res ipsa loquitur *The thing speaks for itself. A rebuttable presumption that a defendant was negligent.*

logical one that could have responsibility. The latter conclusion is based on exclusive control of the property causing the injury, as the following case illustrates.

CASE

Plaintiff, Haragan, filed suit for personal injuries that he incurred when the landing gear of a truck-trailer collapsed, which in turn caused the trailer to collapse. The trailer had been leased by the defendant from its owner. Plaintiff at the time of the injury was helping to unload the trailer.

The trailer had a load-carrying capacity of 70,000 pounds. It was approximately three years old and was loaded with 38,457 pounds of steel. There was evidence that the landing gear was in a corroded condition. Plaintiff proceeded under the doctrine of *res ipsa loquitur.* The defendant contends that the elements required are not present.

ISSUE: Is this a proper case to apply the doctrine of *res ipsa loquitur?*

DECISION: Yes.

REASONS:

1. There are three prerequisites to the application of *res ipsa loquitur.* (a) the event must be of a kind that normally does not occur in the absence of someone's negligence; (b) it must be caused by an agency or instrumentality within the exclusive control of the defendant; and (c) it must not have been due to any voluntary action or contribution on the part of the plaintiff.
2. For the doctrine to apply it is not necessary to show that the accident would not have occurred in the absence of defendant's negligence. Rather, a plaintiff need only show that the accident is of a type that normally does not occur unless someone has been negligent. A trailer ordinarily does not collapse unless someone has been negligent.
3. Plaintiff's proof eliminated the probability of negligence by anyone else. Thus, where several causes of an accident are equally probable, a plaintiff may still avail himself of *res ipsa loquitur* by presenting evidence which tends to eliminate all but those causes resulting from defendant's negligence. Therefore, the exclusive control element was satisfied.

Lynden Transport, Inc. v. Haragan, 623 P.2d 789 (Alaska 1981).

Negligence cases may arise out of a breach of contract. A party to a contract owes a duty to perform the contract with due care. Failure to do so is negligence and a tort. Thus the same act may result in a suit for breach of contract or in a tort suit for damages. It often may make a difference in which theory is used.

11. Proximate Cause

Proximate cause *The responsible cause of an injury.*

Proximate cause is the element of negligence perhaps most difficult to understand. Proximate cause means that the act or the omission complained of is the cause of injury. There must be a causal connection between the breach of the duty and the injury or damage. Problems in applying the rule of proximate cause arise because events sometimes break the direct sequence between an act and injury. In other words, the chain of events sometimes establishes that the injury is remote from the wrongful act. Assume that a customer slips on the floor of a store and breaks a leg. While en route to the hospital in an ambulance, there is a collision in which the customer is killed. The store would not be liable for the wrongful death because its negligence was not the proximate cause of the death, although it was one event in the chain of causation of death.

Difficult questions often arise over the issue of intervening cause. If liquor is sold to one who is intoxicated and that person later causes an accident, is the chain of causation broken? Most modern courts would say no. Moreover, many courts also find that selling alcoholic beverages to a minor is an act of negligence that is one cause of subsequent auto accidents. Proximate cause is closely linked to foreseeability in these cases.

CASE

Billy W. McClellan, individually and as administrator of the estate of Chad W. McClellan, sued Mary Jane Tottenhoff, individually and doing business as Tody's Liquors, and Michael Buffington, an employee bartender. The complaint alleged that the defendants had negligently sold liquor to a minor at a drive-in area, that the minor became intoxicated and killed Chad W. McClellan, the child of the plaintiff, in an automobile accident, and that the sale of the liquor was a proximate cause of the accident. There was a state law prohibiting the sale of alcoholic beverages to minors.

ISSUE: Does a complaint against a vendor unlawfully selling liquor to a minor who becomes intoxicated and injures a third party state a claim for relief in Wyoming?

DECISION: Yes.

REASONS:

1. A liquor vendor owes the same duty to the whole world as does any other person. Negligence consists of a duty on the part of the defendant and a violation of the duty that proximately causes injury to the plaintiff. A defendant must exercise that degree of care required of a reasonable person in light of all circumstances.
2. The statute prohibiting sales to minors was not narrowly intended to benefit only minors, but was wisely intended for the protection of members of the general public as well. Its violation is evidence of negligence.
3. Proximate cause means that the accident or injury must be the natural and probable consequence of the act of negligence. The ultimate test concerning proximate cause is whether the vendor could foresee injury to a third person. This question is one of fact based on the circumstances of each particular case. It is, however, not necessary that a specific injury be foreseen. It is sufficient if a reasonably prudent person would foresee that injury of the same general type would be likely to happen in the absence of such safeguards.
4. A tortfeasor is generally held answerable for the injuries that result in the ordinary course of events from his negligence and it is generally sufficient if his negligent conduct was a substantial factor in bringing about the injuries. The fact that there were also intervening causes that were foreseeable or were normal incidents of the risk created does not relieve the tortfeasor of liability.

McClellan v. Tottenhoff, 666 P.2d 408 (Wyo. 1983).

The issue of proximate cause must be decided on a case-by-case basis. Proximate cause requires that the injury be the natural and probable consequence of the wrong. Proximate cause means that the injury was foreseeable from the wrong; and without the wrong, the injury would not have occurred. Issues of foreseeability are often difficult.

Assume that a plaintiff suffered a heart attack when informed that her daughter and granddaughter were killed in an auto accident. The plaintiff could not collect from the party at fault in the auto accident, because her injury was not foreseeable and predictable. There was no proximate cause.

Proximate cause need not be the sole cause nor the one nearest in time. Where several causes contribute together to an injury, they each may constitute proximate cause. If two autos, each with a negligent driver, collide and injure some third party, both drivers are liable. The negligence of each is a proximate cause of the injury. Their liability is joint and several. Both have liability for the total injury, and they may be sued separately or together. The plaintiff may collect the total damages only once, however.

12. Reasonable-Person Test

Negligence presumes a uniform standard of behavior. This standard is that of a reasonable, prudent person using ordinary care and skill. The reasonable man or woman is a community ideal of reasonable behavior that varies from situation to situation. Therefore the standard is applied by asking the question: What would the reasonable person do under these circumstances?

The reasonable person's physical characteristics are those of the actor in the case being tried. If a person is disabled, so is the reasonable person. On the other hand, the actual mental capacity of the actor may be very different from that of a reasonable person. The law cannot allow a person who has bad judgment or a violent temper to injure others without liability simply because of these mental defects. While the mental capacity required ignores temperament, intellect, and education, it does take age into account, as noted in section 3.

The *reasonable-person test* implies that everyone has a minimum level of knowledge. A reasonable person is presumed to know that gasoline will burn; that ice is slippery; and that the greater the speed of an automobile, the greater the danger of injury. In addition, if the person in question has knowledge superior to most people, the law requires that he conduct himself according to his actual skill and knowledge. A skilled orthopedic surgeon is held to a higher degree of care than a general practitioner of medicine.

Among the factors that affect the application of the reasonable-person standard are community customs, emergencies, and the conduct of others. If a person conducts himself in the manner customary to the community, then such conduct probably is not negligent. If everyone does it, then it probably is not unreasonable behavior. Custom, however, does not as a matter of law establish due care, because everybody may in fact be negligent. For example, it has been held that following generally accepted accounting principles may still constitute negligence.

The effect of emergencies is obvious. A person in an emergency situation is usually not held to as high a standard as a person who is not confronted with an emergency. The actual effect of the emergency is not to lower the standard, but to qualify it by asking: Is this conduct reasonable under the circumstances?

Negligence actions often involve the conduct of others. An operator of a business may be negligent in the selection of employees or in the failure to anticipate wrongful acts of others. The law requires that we take reasonable precautions to avoid injuries that are foreseeable. If a tavern employs a bartender with violent tendencies and he injures customers, liability based on a theory of negligence may be imposed. Likewise, entrusting an automobile to one incapable of driving would be a negligent act.

13. Degrees of Negligence

Courts sometimes talk about degrees of negligence. These have been created for specific reasons, such as defining the extent of the risk involved. As a general rule, the greater the risk, the higher the duty owed to others. In addition, the fact that a person is being paid to be careful usually increases the duty owed. A common carrier is an insurer of the goods carried and is liable except for acts of God and the public enemy if the goods are damaged. A common carrier is not an insurer of passengers, however. It owes the highest degree of care to them and will be liable to passengers for injuries resulting from even slight negligence. The carrier does not owe this high duty to persons who are on the premises of the carrier but not on board it. If a farmer is traveling on a train with hogs being delivered to market, the railroad is liable as an insurer for any injury to the hogs. It is liable to the farmer only if it is negligent.

The degrees of negligence are sometimes described as *slight negligence*, which is the failure to exercise great care; *ordinary negligence*, which is the failure to use ordinary care; and *gross negligence*, which is the failure to exercise even slight care. Such distinctions are of special importance when personal property is entrusted by one person to another. The duty owed depends on the legal relationship. If the duty is to exercise great care, there is liability for slight negligence; and if the duty is to exercise only slight care, there is liability only for gross negligence. Gross negligence is sometimes known as willful and wanton misconduct or a conscious disregard for the safety of others.

14. Negligence by Professional Persons

Among the more significant trends in the law of negligence is the substantial increase in malpractice suits by patients and clients against professional persons such as doctors or accountants. A malpractice suit may be predicated on a theory of breach of contract; but the usual theory is negligence, failure to exercise the degree of care and caution that the professional calling requires. Negligence by professional persons is not subject to the reasonable person standard. Their standard is stated in terms of the knowledge, skill, and judgment usually possessed by members of the profession, because a professional person holds himself out to the public as having the degree of skill common to others in the same profession. However, professional persons do not guarantee infallibility. Although malpractice suits involve standards of professional conduct, the issue of negligence is submitted to a jury as a question of fact for a decision. Such cases usually require the testimony of experts to assist the jury in its findings of negligence. In many cases, juries find that liability exists, even though members of the profession contend and tesify that the services performed were all that could reasonably be expected under the circumstances.

Malpractice suits against doctors and hospitals have multiplied so rapidly that they have significantly affected the practice of medicine and the cost of malpractice insurance. They have also been a significant cause of spiraling medical costs. Not only has the number of malpractice suits more than doubled in recent years, but the size of the verdicts has frequently reached astronomical proportions.

Many doctors and some hospitals have been unable to obtain adequate malpractice insurance coverage. More significantly, many doctors have been reluctant to attempt medical procedures that could result in a malpractice suit. Because of the trends in malpractice litigation, most doctors are practicing defensive medicine: prescribing tests that are probably not indicated, requiring longer hospital stays, and consulting with other doctors as a matter of routine. Defensive medicine obviously is more costly.

Malpractice cases against lawyers have also increased significantly; and although their impact on the cost of legal services is not as significant as it is in medical services, their importance is growing.

15. Malpractice by Accountants

An accountant is liable to a client for breach of contract if the services are not performed as agreed upon. There is liability to the client also if the services are negligently performed. Negligence is present if the accountant fails to exercise the degree of care and caution that the professional calling requires.

Third-person liability. Accountants may have liability also to third parties, because the services are frequently performed for the benefits of others as well as the client. When third parties sue an accountant on a theory of negligence, it is necessary to distinguish between third parties that the accountant knew would rely on his work and third parties that may be described as unforeseen.

A 1931 landmark case, which is still the law in New York and some other states, held that accountants were not liable to third parties for negligence in the absence of privity of contract. Justice Candozo stated in part:

> If liability for negligence exists, a thoughtless slip or blunder, the failure to detect a theft or forgery beneath the cover of deceptive entries, may expose accountants to a liability in an indeterminate amount for an indeterminate time to an indeterminate class. The hazards of a business conducted on these terms are so extreme as to enkindle doubt whether a flaw may not exist in the implication of a duty that exposes to those consequences.[1]

This landmark case stood for the proposition that there was no liability for negligence to third parties. Since that time, courts in Wisconsin, New Hampshire, California, New Jersey, Ohio, and other states have modified and, in some cases, failed to follow the *Ultramares* decision. The trend of the cases is away from the reasoning of Justice Cardozo in *Ultramares*.

Foreseeability. Today, the majority rule is that an accountant is liable for negligence in the performance of his services to those persons whose reliance on the financial representations was actually foreseen by the accountant. In some states

[1] Ultramares Corp. v. Touche, 255 N.Y. 170 (1931).

the liability is extended to those that were reasonably foreseeable. The *Restatement of Torts* (second edition), a legal treatise, extends the liability of the accountant to persons who he knows will receive the product of his services, transmitted by his client. For example, if an accountant knows that his financial statements are to be furnished to banks as a part of the process of obtaining a loan, the negligent accountant has liability to a lending bank for negligence in the preparation of the financial statements relied upon by the bank.

The liability of the accountant for negligence is limited to the class of third persons who come within the description "actually foreseen." It is the law in most jurisdictions that an accountant is not liable on a theory of general negligence to "unforeseen" third persons, because there is no contractual connection with the third party. Third persons without a contractual connection can sue for fraudulent acts of accountants but not for mere negligence. There is no liability to unforeseen third parties for mere negligence, even though the accountant recognizes that some third party may rely on his work.

Statutory liability. It should be noted that an accountant may also be liable to third persons under the federal securities laws. This statutory liability may involve issues of negligence. Under the Securities Act of 1933, an accountant is liable to any purchaser of a security upon proof that the portion of a registration statement attributable to the accountant contains an untrue statement of a material fact or omits to state a material fact necessary to prevent the statements made from being misleading.

The accountant's defense, however, may be that he had, after reasonable investigation, reasonable grounds to believe—and did believe—that the statements contained in the registration statement were true and that there was no omission to state a material fact required or necessary to make the statements not misleading. In other words, "due diligence" or "lack of negligence" is a defense to an allegation of a 1933 Securities Act violation. In determining whether or not an accountant has made a reasonable investigation, the law provides that the standard of reasonableness is that required of a prudent man in the management of his own property.

CHAPTER SUMMARY

Theories of Tort Liability

Damages	1. The theory of damages in tort liability is that the victim will be paid a sum of money that will put a person in as good a position as the person would have been in had the tort not occurred. 2. Compensatory damages include out-of-pocket losses plus pain and suffering, decreased life expectancy, and loss of life or limb. 3. Punitive damages are awarded in some cases to punish the wrongdoer and to deter wrongful conduct.
Persons Liable	1. Employers have liability for the torts of their employees if the employee is acting within the scope of his employment. 2. If two or more persons commit a tort, they are jointly and severally liable. 3. A child may have tort liability after reaching a certain age.

4. Parents are generally not liable for the torts of their children unless the child is an agent or servant or there is a special statute imposing liability.

Intentional Torts

Interference with Personal Freedom

1. There are intentional torts for which both compensatory and punitive damages may be awarded in most cases.
2. The tort of inflicting mental distress is of growing importance. It is based on "outrageous" conduct.

Interference with Property

1. Trespass may occur as to both real and personal property. A trespass may be innocent or willful.
2. When a conversion of personal property occurs, the wrongdoer has liability for the value of the goods.
3. A nuisance is the unreasonable use of one's property that causes injury to another. A nuisance may be enjoined or may result in dollar damages to the victim.

Interference with Economic Relations

1. Interference with commercial or economic relations includes four business torts: disparagement, interference with contractual relations, interference with prospective advantage, and wrongful appropriation of business interests.
2. Disparagement is a false communication about a product or business.
3. Interference with contractual relations usually takes the form of inducing a breach of contract.
4. Interference with prospective or potential advantage is considered a tort, in order to protect the expectancies of future contractual relations, including the prospect of obtaining employment, employees, or customers.
5. It is a tort to interfere with another's copyright, patent, trademark, or goodwill.

Wrongful Communications

1. Defamation consists of the twin torts of libel and slander. Libel is generally written; slander is oral. Tort liability for defamation exists in order to protect a person's name and reputation.
2. The right of privacy is the right to be let alone. It involves wrongful intrusion into one's private life in such a manner as to outrage or to cause mental suffering, shame, or humiliation to a person of ordinary sensibilities.

Negligence

Elements

1. The four basic elements of negligence are (1) a duty owed by one person to another, and (2) a breach of that duty (3) that was the proximate cause of (4) an injury.
2. The duty owed by one person to another varies depending on the relationship of the parties.
3. Negligence is the failure to exercise due care. Due care is reasonable conduct under the circumstances.
4. The doctrine of *res ipsa loquitur* creates a presumption of negligence.
5. Proximate cause means that there is a connection between the breach of duty and the injury. Proximate cause is often based on foreseeability.
6. The standard for judging whether or not a duty has been breached is to judge the conduct against the standards of the reasonable person.

Degrees of Negligence

1. The greater the risk, the higher the duty owed to others.
2. A common carrier is an insurer of goods and owes passengers the highest degree of care.
3. Slight negligence is the failure to use great care.
4. Ordinary negligence is the failure to use ordinary care.
5. Gross negligence is the failure to use slight care.

Negligence by Professional Persons

1. Malpractice by professional persons is the failure to exercise that degree of care and caution which the profession calls for. It is the failure to meet the standards of the profession.

Malpractice by Accountants

1. Accountants are liable to clients for breach of contract the same as any other party if they fail to perform as agreed.
2. The tort theories of fraud and negligence are often used by clients in malpractice cases against accountants.
3. Negligent performance of a contract is a mixed tort and contract theory used by clients to sue accountants.
4. Many malpractice cases are based on violations of federal and state statutes relating to the sale of securities.
5. Under the *Ultramares* doctrine; accountants are not liable to third parties for negligence in the absence of privity of contract or close relationship sufficiently equivalent to privity.
6. Section 522 of the *Restatement of Torts* extends liability to third parties whom the accountant intends to supply the information or knows the recipient intends to supply it.
7. Some courts have expanded the liability to actually foreseen third parties. Others have gone further and expanded liability in favor of anyone that is reasonably foreseeable.
8. Accountants also have malpractice liability under the securities laws.

REVIEW QUESTIONS AND PROBLEMS

1. Match the terms in column A with the appropriate statement in column B.

A	B
(1) Contingent fee	(a) Unreasonable use of property.
(2) Slander	(b) The right to be left alone.
(3) Libel	(c) A doctrine that may reduce a recovery.
(4) Invasion of privacy	(d) A presumption of negligence.
(5) Nuisance	(e) Written defamation.
(6) Conversion	(f) Closely akin to foreseeability.
(7) Comparative negligence	(g) Oral defamation.
(8) *Res ipsa loquitur*	(h) Liability without wrongful conduct.
(9) Proximate use	(i) Major interference with goods.
(10) Strict liability	(j) Assures equal access to the judicial system.

2. A child whose mother had taken the drug DES developed cancer. She sued all the manufacturers of DES and proved that through no fault of her own she was unable to determine which manufacturer caused the injury. Is she entitled to recover from all the manufacturers? Why?

3. The CAT collection agency, trying to collect fees owed to a physician, called an ex-patient ten to twenty times daily for several days, using obscene and threatening language. CAT also wrote several threatening letters. The former patient sued CAT for damages, alleging severe emotional distress. Was CAT's conduct tortious? Explain.

4. Flansburgh, who lived in a rural area, sued his neighbor Harden to enjoin a hog raising and feeding operation. As the result of the operation, the air was filled with strong odors that caused plaintiff's eyes to water and rendered it difficult for him to breathe. Plaintiff was also beset with an excess of flies and rats. Assuming that hog farming is a lawful business, will a court of equity enjoin the activity? Why or why not?

5. A law firm sued several of its former associates for damages and to enjoin them from soliciting the firm's clients. These former associates actively encouraged the older firm's clients to terminate that relationship and become clients of the new firm. Was this new firm's conduct tortious? Why or why not?

6. Craig was identified in a newspaper as the father of an illegitimate child. The article dealt with teenage pregnancies and most of it concerned the unmarried teenage mother. The reporter had talked to Craig but had not sought permission to identify him. Does Craig have a tort case against the newspaper? If so, on what theory? Explain.

7. Plaintiff was traveling in a northerly direction on Belmont Avenue through an intersection, in compliance with the traffic signals, when her car collided with an automobile driven into her path by a customer exiting from the Burger King located on the east side of Belmont Avenue. The traffic signal for the northbound lane could not be seen from the parking lot. When the customer saw the southbound traffic stop, he assumed that the northbound traffic was also stopped. Instead, the lights for northbound traffic remained green as long as a green arrow was showing on the signal for left-turning northbound traffic. Plaintiff sued Burger King for her injuries. Is the defendant liable? Why or why not?

8. Helen toured a town house built by Thames. While inspecting the kitchen, she opened a cabinet and the cabinet door fell and struck her on the head. An examination revealed that no screws were affixed to the door to secure it to the cabinet. She filed suit against the cabinetmaker and offered proof of her injury relying on the doctrine of *res ipsa loquitur*. What result? Why or why not?

9. A motorist and passengers brought action for damages arising from the collision of their vehicle with a horse. The suit was brought against an individual who owned a $1/2500$ undivided interest in a ranch and recreational community, the common areas of which were managed by an association. The suit alleged negligence of the ranch in allowing the horse to escape to a public highway. Does the defendant have liability for all of the damages? Explain.

10. Marie was searching for a parking lot in downtown Baltimore that charged a reasonable fee. She found a lot surrounded by a high chain-link fence. The fence had a large open gate; inside was a "plain building" with an open door. There were some trucks on the lot but no cars. Unfortunately, she had not found a public parking lot but a truck garage facility. After she walked onto the lot, a guard dog, "Smokey," appeared, apparently unchained, "growling and snarling." Smokey knocked her to the ground, causing damage to her right knee and other injuries. Is she entitled to collect for her injuries? Why or why not?

11. Mary witnessed an automobile strike a pedestrian. She wrongfully believed that her daughter was the pedestrian. Mary collapsed and continues to suffer severe mental distress. She sued the driver of the automobile for her injuries. Should she collect? Why or why not?

12. Plaintiff was injured in an automobile accident caused entirely by the defendant. Plaintiff was not wearing his seat belt. He was thrown from his Jeep and sustained a compression-type injury to the lower back when he landed on the pavement. The defendant offered evidence that had the plaintiff been wearing his seat belt, he would not have been thrown from the Jeep. If the doctrine of comparative negligence is followed, will this fact reduce the damages to which the plaintiff is entitled? Explain.

13. A paint manufacturing company sought financing from a local bank. In order to evaluate the company's financial condition, the bank required it to submit certain financial state-

ments. To comply with this request, the company hired an accountant. The prepared statements represented the company to be solvent, when in fact it was insolvent. Relying on these statements, the bank loaned the money. Later, the bank lost a substantial portion of the money loaned. May the bank recover its losses from the accountant? Why or why not?

14. Don, a certified public accountant, conducted an audit for ABC Company. Due to a time limitation, Don did not verify the accuracy of the closing inventory but rather accepted the president of ABC's statement that the inventory was correct. Unknown to both Don and the president, the inventory was overstated by 33⅓ percent due to theft by employees. A bank that loaned money to ABC upon the strength of the financial statements sued Don on a theory of fraud. He defended, denying any intention to mislead. What result? Explain.

7 Criminal Law and Business

C H A P T E R   P R E V I E W

BUSINESS MANAGEMENT DECISION

You are the chief operating officer of a small chemicals manufacturing firm. One of your production supervisors advises you that toxic fumes, in small quantities, are leaking into the plant. To correct this leak would cost your undercapitalized firm $1.5 million. To allow the leak to continue subjects your employees to unknown dangers.

What should you do?

GENERAL PRINCIPLES

1. Introduction

Much of the law is concerned with wrongful conduct; if it is wrongful against society, it is a crime. Criminal conduct usually affects individual persons, and as noted in Chapter 6, this effect is, by definition, tortious. In this chapter, we will briefly discuss some of the general principles of the criminal law and business.

Since a crime is a public wrong against society, criminal actions are prosecuted by the government on behalf of the people. Historically, upon a person's conviction of a crime, one of the following punishments has been imposed by society: (1) death, (2) imprisonment, (3) fine, (4) removal from office, or (5) disqualification to hold and enjoy any office or to vote. Among the purposes of punishment and of the criminal law are the protection of the public and the deterrence of crime. Punishment is also imposed simply for the sake of punishment, as well as the isolation and suppression of the criminal element of society. Table 7–1 indicates the various crimes and the interest that each was created to protect.

Conduct is criminal because a legislative body has declared it to be wrongful and has authorized punishment if it occurs. Some crimes, such as murder, have always been considered wrongful by a civilized society. They are said to be *malum in se* or per se wrongful. Other crimes have been created by legislative bodies because of a desire to prevent certain conduct. Such crimes are said to be *malum prohibitum*. For example, gambling is a crime only because a legislature has declared it to be.

Some crimes are said to be administrative crimes. Administrative agencies such as the Environmental Protection Agency or the Pure Food and Drug Administration may adopt rules, the violation of which is punishable as a crime. The legislative body by statute declares the violation to be criminal and delegates the power to the agency to adopt the rules and regulations.

In most administrative crimes the statute fixes the penalty for the violation. In a few cases the statutes not only authorize the agency to create the regulations but also to fix the penalty. For example, a statute may authorize an agency to issue regulations and to set penalties not to exceed a $500 fine or 6 months in jail or both. Such statutes may be valid if the punishment is reasonable.

Agencies may not be given the power to conduct the trial as a general rule. If conduct is criminal, the accused has a right to a trial by jury. Exceptions exist for minor penalties such as revocation or suspension of licenses or levying small

TABLE 7–1 CLASSIFICATION OF CRIMES BY PURPOSE

1. **Protection of the person from physical harm**
   Assault and battery
   Kidnapping
   Manslaughter
   Mayhem
   Murder
   Sexual crimes (see number 3 below)
2. **Protection of property**
   Arson
   Blackmail
   Burglary
   Embezzlement
   Extortion
   Forgery
   Fraud
   Larceny
   Robbery
3. **Protection from sexual abuse**
   Adultery
   Bigamy
   Incest
   Rape
   Sodomy
4. **Protection of government**
   Bribery of officials
   Sabotage
   Treason
5. **Protection of the courts**
   Bribery of witnesses, judges, jurors
   Perjury
6. **Protecting the public interest**
   Antitrust
   Disorderly conduct
   Food and drug laws
   Gambling
   Liquor and drunkenness
   Narcotics
   Obscenity
   Pollution

fines. Such proceedings may be considered quasi-criminal in the nature of a civil penalty similar to traffic violations and parking meter fines.

2. Classifications of Crimes

Treason *The offense of attempting by overt acts to overthrow the government of the state to which the offender owes allegiance; or of betraying the state into the hands of a foreign power.*

Felony *All criminal offenses that are punishable by death or imprisonment in a penitentiary.*

Misdemeanor *A criminal offense, less than a felony, that is punishable by fine or jail sentence.*

Crimes are traditionally classified as treason, felonies, and misdemeanors. **Treason** against the United States consists of levying war against it or in adhering to its enemies, giving them aid and comfort. **Felonies** are offenses usually defined by statute to include all crimes punishable by incarceration in a penitentiary. Examples are murder, grand larceny, arson, and rape. Crimes of lesser importance than felonies—such as petty larceny, trespass, and disorderly conduct—are called **misdemeanors.** They are usually defined as any crimes not punishable by long imprisonment, but punishable by fine or confinement in the local jail.

Violation of traffic ordinances, building codes, and similar municipal ordinances, prosecuted before a city magistrate, are sometimes termed *petty offenses* or *public torts* instead of crimes. The distinction is insignificant; because whether they are called crimes or public torts, the result is the same—the party charged may be fined or put in jail or both. Table 7–2 lists typical felonies and misdemeanors.

3. White-Collar Crime

Historically, the criminal law was concerned with acts of violence and the wrongful application of physical force. Murder, arson, rape, burglary, robbery, and other violent crimes affected the business community, but businesses seldom committed

TABLE 7–2. CLASSIFICATION OF CRIMES BY PUNISHMENT

Typical Felonies (Imprisonment for More Than One Year and/or Fine)	Typical Misdemeanors (Jail for Less Than One Year and/or Fine)
Aggravated assault	Battery
Arson	Disorderly conduct
Bribery	Gambling
Burglary	Larceny (petty)
Embezzlement	Prostitution
Forgery	Public disturbance
Kidnapping	Simple assault
Larceny (grand)	Traffic offenses
Manslaughter	Trespass
Mayhem	
Murder	
Price-fixing	
Rape	
Robbery	

them. Today, businesspeople are guilty of hundreds of new crimes, the so-called white-collar or business crimes. In addition, in one case the operators of a business were convicted of murdering an employee who was poisoned by cyanide used on the job.

White-collar or *business* crimes are illegal acts committed by guile, deceit, and concealment, rather than by force and violence. Such crimes usually involve attempts to obtain money, property, or services without paying for them or to secure some other business advantage. Such crimes are not limited to executives; they are committed by employees at all levels. Any employee with access to cash may be guilty of **embezzlement** or theft of company property. Salespersons may engage in price-fixing in violation of the antitrust laws. Stockbrokers may engage in illegal insider trading, as may officials of companies involved in mergers and acquisitions.

Embezzlement *The fraudulent appropriation by one person, acting in a fiduciary capacity, of the money or property of another.*

Business crime is a significant cost of doing business. Losses from embezzlement and employee theft, including theft through manipulation of computers, probably exceed losses from burglary and larceny. There is evidence that shoplifting by employees exceeds shoplifting by customers. The cost of crime results in higher prices for consumers. Costs include higher insurance premiums as well as the cost of the property stolen. It has been estimated that 30 percent of all business failures are the result of internal theft, and that many retail outlets lose as much as 50 percent of their profits to unaccountable ''inventory shrinkage.'' Many stores mark up goods an extra 15 percent to cover such losses, which means that the consuming public actually pays the bill for theft.

Fraud in various forms is rampant. The fraudulent use of another's credit card, forgery, obtaining money by false pretenses, and false auto repair bills are everyday occurrences. By statute, all these are crimes. Bribery, kickbacks, and payoffs have become so common that the Securities and Exchange Commission demands that the amounts paid be included in the reports filed by major corporations.

Although business crime does not depend on force or violence, physical injury and even death can be caused by it. Defective products sold in violation of applicable statutes frequently cause injuries. Building code violations may result in fire and injury to persons and property. Some businesses, in order to compete, buy stolen merchandise or employ illegal aliens. The maintenance of a dangerous workplace may be a crime.

One reason for the massive amount of white-collar crime is that, in the past, the risk of being caught and sent to prison was slight. White-collar crime has often been considered a legitimate cost of doing business, especially overseas. A business is usually hesitant to prosecute its employees, because disclosure would have an adverse effect on the image of the business. Even when there have been successful prosecutions, sentences have been minimal in the light of the economic consequences of the crimes. In many states there are inadequate prison facilities, and as a result judges often do not send white-collar criminals to prison.

Now that the relation of crime to business has reached crisis proportions, many people are advocating new approaches in an attempt to alter criminal conduct. Perhaps the most common suggestion is to impose stiff penalties for white-collar crime. Another is to improve the internal controls of businesses, so that internal theft and wrongdoing are more likely to be discovered. Finally, there is a trend toward punishing corporate officials who commit crimes on behalf of their corporations. A corporate official who fixes prices with competitors in violation of the Sherman Antitrust Act is more likely to go to prison now than in the past, and the fine for such conduct has been greatly increased. Knowledge about the criminal law, its enforcement, and crime prevention are key elements in business decision making.

4. Damage Suits

Criminal conduct that injures a person or his property constitutes a tort. The victim is entitled to recover dollar damages in a civil suit. This is often a hollow remedy because many criminals do not have any money with which to pay the damages and there is usually no liability insurance covering criminal conduct.

Today, legislative bodies sometimes go farther and enact legislation providing for triple damages for the victims of certain crimes. These are usually white-collar crimes such as a violation of the antitrust laws. If a party is convicted of a Sherman Act violation such as price-fixing, the conviction creates a prima facie case for triple damages on behalf of all of the victims of the price-fixing conspiracy. Such parties are also entitled to attorney's fees and court costs.

One very important federal law in this regard is known as RICO, the 1970 Racketeer Influenced and Corrupt Organizations Act. Its goal is to combat organized crime by authorizing private parties to file suits for triple damages and attorney's fees when federal laws dealing with various forms of fraud have been violated. Such suits are possible when an individual or a business has twice within a ten-year period violated one of these enumerated federal statutes, which include wire and mail fraud.

The law has had an unintended impact. It has not encouraged many suits against organized crime. Rather, it has encouraged suits against accounting firms, brokerage houses, banks, and other businesses. More than 75 percent of all RICO suits involve securities frauds and other types of business fraud. Less than 10 percent involve criminal activity generally associated with organized crime. RICO cases do not require convictions to prove a case. Two violations of any applicable law in a ten-year period establish racketeering. The use of the mail or telephone makes access to RICO very easy for any plaintiff alleging fraud in a business transaction. A plaintiff need not prove a racketeering injury—only an injury resulting from the illegal act.

RICO cases often involve routine commercial transactions that generally are not considered criminal. For example, RICO has been used by the Federal Deposit Insurance Corporation (FDIC) to recover funds lost in a bank failure. RICO cases have arisen in landlord-tenant disputes, labor relations cases, the sale of land, and, of course, the sale of securities.

5. Terminology

The criminal law has developed some terminology separate and distinct from that of civil law cases. The word *prosecution* is used to describe criminal proceedings, and *prosecutor* is the name usually given to the attorney who represents the people. Although the proceedings are brought on behalf of the people of a given state or the United States, the people are generally not called the plaintiff, as in a civil case. Rather, the case is entitled *U.S.* v. *John Doe* or *State of Ohio* v. *John Doe*.

In felony cases, the usual procedure is for a court to conduct a preliminary hearing to determine if there is sufficient evidence that the accused committed the crime charged to justify submission of the case to the grand jury. If the court finds this probable cause, the accused is *bound over* to the grand jury. The grand jury examines evidence against the accused and determines if it is sufficient to cause a reasonable person to believe that the accused probably committed the offense. If this *probable cause* exists, the grand jury *indicts* the accused by returning to the court what is called a *true bill*. If it is the opinion of the grand jury that the evidence is insufficient to indict, then a *no true bill* is returned to the court. Indictment by the grand jury is discussed with the Fifth Amendment, later in this chapter.

If the crime involved is a misdemeanor or if the accused waives the presentment of the case to the grand jury, the prosecution may proceed by filing the charges in a document known as an *information*. Both an indictment and an information serve to notify and to inform the accused of the nature of the charges, so that a defense may be prepared.

The technical aspects of the various crimes are beyond the scope of this text; however, it should be recognized that every crime has elements that distinguish it from other crimes. Larceny, robbery, and burglary are crimes with many common characteristics, yet they are legally distinct. Robbery is theft with force; larceny implies no force. Burglary is breaking and entering with intent to commit a felony (usually larceny). One act may be more than one crime, and it is possible to be convicted of more than one crime for any particular act. Many crimes are actually a part of another crime and are known as *lesser included offenses*. An assault would be a lesser included offense of forcible rape.

Criminal cases differ from civil cases in the amount of proof required to convict. In a civil case, the plaintiff is entitled to a verdict if the evidence preponderates in his favor. In other words, if, when weighing the evidence, the scales tip ever so slightly in favor of the plaintiff, the plaintiff wins. In a criminal case, however, the people or prosecution must prove the defendant's guilt beyond a reasonable doubt. Note that the law does not require proof ''beyond the shadow of a doubt'' or proof that is susceptible of only one conclusion. It does require such a quantity of proof that a reasonable person viewing the evidence would have no reasonable doubt about the guilt of the defendant.

6. Act and Intent

As a general rule, a crime involves a combination of *act* and *criminal intent*. Criminal intent without an overt act to carry it out is not criminal. If Joe says to himself, ''I am going to rob the First National Bank,'' no crime has been committed. Some act toward carrying out this intent is necessary. But if Joe communicates his desire to Frank, who agrees to assist him, then a crime has been committed. This crime is known as **conspiracy.** The criminal act was the communication between Joe and Frank.

Conspiracy *An agreement by two or more persons to commit a crime.*

Just as a crime requires an act, most crimes also require criminal intent. A wrongful act committed without the requisite criminal intent is not a crime. Criminal intent may be supplied by negligence to the degree that it equals intent. If a person drives a car so recklessly that another is killed, his criminal intent may be supplied by the negligent act.

Criminal intent is not synonymous with motive. Motive is not an element of a crime. Proof of motive may help in establishing guilt, but it is not an essential element of a prosecution.

Specific Intent. Some crimes are known as *specific intent* crimes. When a crime has a specific intent as part of its definition, that specific intent must be proved beyond a reasonable doubt. In a burglary prosecution, there must be proof of intent to commit some felony, such as larceny, rape, or murder. Also, if a crime is defined in part ''with intent to defraud,'' this specific intent must be proved, as any other element of the crime must be.

Implied Intent. There is a presumption of intent in crimes that do not require a specific intent. The intent in such crimes may be implied by the facts. In other words, the doing of the criminal act implies the criminal intent. The accused may rebut this presumption, however. The accused is presumed to intend the natural and probable consequences of his acts. Thus, if one performs an act that causes a result the criminal law is designed to prevent, he is legally responsible, even though the actual result was not intended. If a robber dynamites a safe and a passerby is killed in the explosion, the robber is guilty of homicide even though he did not actually intend to kill the passerby; the robber intended the natural and probable consequences of his act.

Strict Liability. Criminal liability may be imposed without fault or without criminal intent. Such crimes are often referred to as *strict liability crimes*. The crime consists of conduct, and the law does not require that the actor have any particular intent or mental state. In effect, the crime consists of conduct that brings about a stated result. It is immaterial whether the conduct is intentional, reckless, or negligent. Usually only a misdemeanor, the conduct is declared to be criminal in order to discourage it. For example, most liquor and narcotics laws, pure food and drug laws, and traffic laws impose liability without fault. Under these statutes, proof of the state of mind of the accused is not required. Proof of the sale of alcoholic beverages to a minor is a crime, even though the seller did not intend to commit an unlawful act.

7. Capacity

At common law children under the age of seven were conclusively presumed to lack sufficient mental capacity to form criminal intent. Those over fourteen were treated as fully capable of committing a crime. Children aged seven to fourteen were subject to a rebuttable presumption that they could have criminal capacity, but this presumption could be overcome by proof of lack of mental capacity. Many states have changed these ages by statute, and all states have juvenile courts which provide for special procedures for crimes involving minors. Juvenile courts usually handle cases involving persons under eighteen. They attempt to avoid harsh punishment and seek to rehabilitate the juvenile and prevent further criminal conduct. However, most states allow the prosecution to elect to try an offender as an adult for certain serious crimes such as murder or rape. Even if a juvenile is tried as an adult for a capital offense, the death penalty may not be imposed if the defendant is under sixteen years of age. In 1988 the Supreme Court concluded that the imposition of the death penalty on a fifteen-year-old was abhorrent to the conscience of the community.

The criminal law as it pertains to juveniles differs greatly from that applied to adults. While in most cases juveniles are given preferential treatment, the following case illustrates that juveniles may be subjected to sanctions to which adults may not.

CASE

The New York Family Court Act authorizes pretrial detention of an accused juvenile delinquent. The detention must be based on a finding that there is a "serious risk" that the child "may . . . commit an act which if committed by an adult would constitute a crime." Juveniles who had been detained under that statute brought suit, contending that the statute violates the constitutional guarantee of due process of law.

ISSUE: Does preventive detention of a juvenile violate the Constitution?

DECISION: No.

REASONS:

1. Preventive detention is a legitimate state objective. Every state has a similar statute. These laws act to protect both the juvenile and society from the hazards of pretrial crime. The practice serves a legitimate regulatory purpose comparable with the "fundamental fairness" demanded by the due process clause in juvenile proceedings.
2. The procedural safeguards afforded to juveniles detained under the statute prior to trial provide sufficient protection against erroneous and unnecessary deprivations of liberty. Post-detention procedures provide a sufficient safeguard for correcting any erroneous detentions.
3. Although the due process clause applies to juveniles, one must consider that juveniles, unlike adults, are always in some form of custody. If their parents cannot control them, the state must play its part as *parens patriae.*

Schall v. Martin, 104 S.Ct. 2403 (1984).

8. Corporate Liability

In the early common law a corporation could not be held criminally liable since it was incapable of forming criminal intent. Corporations were not liable for the conduct of others, including agents and employees acting within the scope of their employment on behalf of the corporation. Today a corporation is considered a person as the word is used in most criminal statutes, and a corporation may have criminal liability.

Corporate criminal liability may be imposed under the strict liability theory or under the vicarious liability concept. A vicarious liability crime is where one person without personal fault is liable for the conduct of another. Some criminal statutes impose criminal liability on a principal for the criminal conduct of its agents and servants. For example, most states have statutes that impose liability on the employer if an agent sells articles short weight or sells liquor to a minor. This vicarious liability is imposed even though the employer may have instructed the employee not to engage in the illegal conduct. Vicarious liability is often imposed on corporations, especially if the activity is performed in part by the board of directors, an officer, or high managerial agent. Lack of criminal intent on the part of the corporate principal is no defense. Moreover, high corporate officials may have liability because of the high standards of conduct imposed on them by some statutes. Such crimes exist in order to impose strict standards of performance on certain business activities. The punishment imposed in such cases is a fine and in some cases other sanctions, such as the loss of a license to do business.

The officers and directors of a corporation are ordinarily not personally liable for the crimes of the enterprise or their subordinates. However, a few cases have imposed liability under a theory that the person was accountable for the conduct of others. The case which follows is typical of those imposing personal liability on persons with official responsibility.

CASE

Acme Markets and its chief executive officer, Park, were charged with violating the Federal Food, Drug and Cosmetic Act in allowing interstate food shipments to become contaminated. Park's defense was based on noninvolvement in the wrongful conduct. He contended that the failure to stop the contamination was the fault of others in the hierarchy of responsibility in the corporation. He admitted that, overall, he was responsible for those under him and the shipment of sanitary food. The trial court instructed the jury that no personal participation was necessary as long as Park had some responsible relationship to the wrongful conduct.

ISSUE: May criminal liability be imputed to executives under the FFDC Act?

DECISION: Yes.

REASONS:
1. Corporate officials in authority with respect to conditions that constitute a violation of the FFDC Act have the highest standard of care to correct or prevent violations of the act.
2. People are often beyond self-protection, so the government steps in. Corporations act through individuals. Therefore, the best way to ensure that the policies of the act are carried out is to impose liability, including criminal liability, on the individual officers.

United States v. Park, 95 S.Ct. 1903 (1975).

9. Defenses to Criminal Prosecutions

A defendant in a criminal case may avail himself of a variety of defenses. He may contend that he did not commit the act of which he is accused. He may present an alibi—proof that he was at another place when the crime was committed. He may also contend that if he did the act, it was not done with the requisite intent. There are also many technical defenses used on behalf of persons accused of crimes. Some of them are described in the following paragraphs.

Entrapment. This is a defense commonly raised in certain crimes, such as the illegal sale of drugs. Entrapment means that the criminal intent originated with the police. When a criminal act is committed at the instigation of the police, fundamental fairness seems to dictate that the people should not be able to contend that the accused is guilty of a crime. Assume that a police officer asked Bill to obtain some marijuana. Bill could not be found guilty of illegal possession, because the criminal intent originated with the police officer. Entrapment is sometimes described as a positive defense, because the accused must, as a basis for the defense, admit that the act was committed.

Immunity from Prosecution. This is another technical defense. The prosecution may grant **immunity** in order to obtain a "state's witness." When immunity is granted, the person receiving it can no longer be prosecuted, and thus he no longer has the privilege against compulsory self-incrimination. When several persons have committed a crime together, it is common practice for one to be given immunity so that evidence is available against the others. The one granted immunity has a complete defense.

Immunity *Freedom from the legal duties and penalties imposed upon others.*

Insanity. A person cannot be guilty of a crime if he or she lacks the mental capacity to have the required criminal intent. Likewise, a person who is insane cannot properly defend the suit, so insanity at the time of trial is also a defense.

The defense of insanity poses many difficult problems for courts and for juries. Many criminal acts are committed in fits of anger or passion. Others, by their very nature, are committed by persons whose mental state is other than normal. Therefore, a major difficulty exists in defining insanity. In the early criminal law, the usually accepted test of insanity was the "*right-from-wrong*" test. If the accused understood the nature and consequences of the act and had the ability to distinguish right from wrong at the time of the act involved, the accused was sane. If he or she did not know right from wrong or did not understand the consequences of the act, insanity was a defense.

Subsequently, the courts of some states, feeling that the right-from-wrong test did not go far enough, adopted a test known as "*irresistible impulse.*" Under this test, it was not enough that the accused knew right from wrong. If the accused was possessed of an irresistible impulse to do what was wrong, and this impulse was so strong that it compelled him or her to do what was wrong, insanity was a defense.

As psychiatry and psychology began to play a greater role in the criminal law and the rehabilitation of criminals, many courts became dissatisfied with both the "right-from-wrong" and "irresistible-impulse" tests of insanity. A new test known as the "Durham rule" was developed. Under the Durham rule, an accused is not criminally responsible if his act was the product of a mental disease or defect. This new test has not received universal acceptance. Perpetrators of some crimes almost always have some mental abnormality, and the Durham rule makes their conduct unpunishable. Sexual assault on a child is probably committed only by one with some mental depravity, but the Durham rule makes prosecution of such cases more difficult and might result in freeing many who are guilty. Today there is a wide disparity among the states as to which test of insanity will be followed. All three tests have had significant acceptance. In the years ahead, additional developments in the law of insanity are likely.

Intoxication. This defense is quite similar to insanity, but its application is much more restricted. Voluntarily becoming intoxicated is generally no defense to a crime. It is simply no excuse for wrongful conduct. However, if the crime charged is one of specific intent and the accused was so intoxicated that he could not form the specific intent required, then intoxication is a defense of sorts. It can be used to establish lack of the required specific intent. In a prosecution for an assault with intent to rape, intoxication sufficient to negate the intent would be a defense.

Other Defenses. Return of property stolen, payment for damages caused, and forgiveness by the victim of a crime are not defenses. If a person shoplifts and is caught, it is no defense that the goods were returned or that the store owner has forgiven him. Since the wrong is against society as a whole, the attitude of the actual victim is technically immaterial. As a practical matter, however, many prosecutors do not prosecute cases that the victims are willing to abandon.

Ignorance of the law is not a defense to a criminal prosecution. Everyone is presumed to know the law and to follow it. No other system would be workable. The various constitutional protections and guarantees available to a defendant may prohibit or impede prosecution of a case. They may make it impossible for the prosecution to obtain a conviction. If evidence of a crime is illegally obtained, that evidence is inadmissible; and by preventing its admission, the accused may obtain an acquittal. These constitutional and procedural aspects of the criminal law are discussed in the sections that follow.

CRIMINAL LAW AND THE CONSTITUTION

10. General Principles

The Constitution of the United States is a major source of the law as it relates to crimes. Constitutional protections and guarantees govern the procedural aspects of criminal cases. The Bill of Rights—especially the Fourth, Fifth, Sixth, and Eighth Amendments—contains these constitutional guarantees. The Fourteenth Amendment "picks up" these constitutional protections and makes them applicable to the states.

As these constitutional guarantees are studied, three aspects of constitutional law should be kept in mind. First, constitutional guarantees are not absolutes. Every one of them is limited in its application. Just as freedom of speech under the First Amendment does not allow one to cry "Fire!" in a crowded theater, the Fourth Amendment's constitutional protection against illegal search and seizure is not absolute. Both are limited protections.

Second, in determining the extent of limitations on constitutional guarantees, the courts are balancing the constitutional protections against some other legitimate legal or social policy of society or other constitutional guarantees. A state enacted a so-called hit-and-run statute requiring the driver of a motor vehicle involved in an accident to stop at the scene and give his name and address. His action obviously may be self-incriminating, in that he is admitting the identity of the driver of the vehicle involved. Thus, the law created a conflict between the state's demand for disclosures and the protection of the right against self-incrimination. The Supreme Court, in resolving this conflict, noted that the mere possibility of incrimination is insufficient to defeat the strong policies in favor of a disclosure, and it held that the law did not violate the Constitution. In criminal cases, courts are often required to balance the interest and rights of the accused with those of the victim of crime and of society as a whole.

Third, constitutional protections are variable. They change to meet the needs of modern society. The Constitution is often said to be interpreted relative to the times. The criminal law changes as the needs of society change. In recent years the rights of defendants have been narrowed in response to the perceived need of society to combat crime, especially those that are drug-related.

11. The Fourth Amendment

Several procedural issues may arise as a result of the Fourth Amendment's protection against illegal search and seizure. Among the more common Fourth Amendment issues in criminal cases are (1) the validity of searches incident to arrest without a warrant, (2) the validity of search warrants—the presence of probable cause, (3) the validity of consents to searches by persons other than the suspect, and (4) the extent of the protection afforded.

To illustrate the first issue, assume that a student is arrested for speeding. Is it a violation of the Fourth Amendment if the police officer searches the trunk of the car without a search warrant and finds cocaine? The answer is yes, and the student could not be convicted of illegal possession of drugs, because the evidence was unconstitutionally obtained.

A search may be illegal even if it is conducted pursuant to a search warrant. The Constitution provides that a search warrant may be issued only if probable cause for its issue is presented to the court.

The validity of a consent to search premises without a search warrant is frequently an issue in a criminal case. A parent may consent to a police search of a child's room in the family home. Is this a valid waiver of the constitutional protection of the Fourth Amendment? The decision depends on many factors, including the age of the child, the extent of emancipation, and the amount of control the parents have over the total premises. Similar issues are raised when a landlord consents to the search of premises leased to a tenant. As a general rule, such consents are not sufficient to eliminate the need for a search warrant.

Fourth Amendment issues frequently have an effect on civil law as well as criminal law. The protection has been extended to prohibit activities such as inspection of premises by a fire inspector without a search warrant. Criminal charges for violating building codes cannot be based on a warrantless inspection of the premises if the owner objects.

In recent years, the protection of the Fourth Amendment has been narrowed somewhat by Court decisions and legislation. Electronic surveillance is possible pursuant to a search warrant, and the "bugs" may be installed by covert entry.

Moreover, warrants may be issued based on information obtained by electronic means. The following case is one of several in which Fourth Amendment rights have been given a limited interpretation.

CASE

Burger's junkyard business consists of dismantling automobiles and selling their parts. A New York statute authorizes warrantless inspections of automobile junkyards. Police officers entered his junkyard and asked to see his license and records as to automobiles and vehicle parts in his possession. He replied that he did not have such documents, which are required by the statute. After announcing their intention to conduct an inspection of the junkyard pursuant to the statute, the officers, without objection by respondent, conducted the inspection and discovered stolen vehicles and parts. Burger, who was charged with possession of stolen property, moved to suppress the evidence obtained as a result of the inspection. He contended that the administrative inspection statute is unconstitutional when it authorizes warrantless searches.

ISSUE: Is this warrantless search a violation of the Fourth Amendment?

DECISION: No.

REASONS:

1. A business owner's expectation of privacy in commercial property is reduced with respect to commercial property employed in a "closely regulated" industry.
2. Where the owner's privacy interests are weakened and the government's interests in regulating particular businesses are heightened, a warrantless inspection of commercial premises, if it meets certain criteria, is reasonable within the meaning of the Fourth Amendment.
3. Junkyards are a closely regulated industry, and the state has a substantial interest in regulating it because of automobile theft. Warrantless searches are necessary to further the regulatory scheme. Owners are aware that regular inspections will be made.

New York v. Burger, 107 S.Ct. 2636 (1987).

One of the more controversial aspects of the Fourth Amendment is the so-called *exclusionary rule*. The exclusionary rule, which was created by the Supreme Court, is a rule of evidence. It provides that evidence illegally obtained by the police and all information flowing therefrom cannot be used to convict a person accused of crime. Thus, if evidence is obtained without a search warrant, or if the search warrant was not properly issued, then a defendant can ask the court to prevent the use of the evidence. This request is usually called a *motion to suppress evidence*.

As a result of the exclusionary rule, many persons who have in fact committed crimes are either not prosecuted or are found to be innocent because the evidence establishing their guilt is not admissible at the trial. In recent years some courts have sought to modify the exclusionary rule and have argued that justice would be better served in certain cases if evidence is admissible notwithstanding the fact that it was improperly or illegally obtained. For example, they argue that evidence illegally obtained by state and local police should nevertheless be admissible in a federal prosecution when the federal authorities were not a party to the illegal search and seizure of evidence. The case that follows illustrates an exception created in 1984 when a warrant was obtained and the police were acting in "good faith." This good-faith exception to the exclusionary rule is a further indication of the narrowing of the Fourth Amendment.

CASE

Acting on the basis of information from a confidential informant of unproven reliability, police officers initiated a drug-trafficking investigation involving surveillance of several individuals with prior records for drug possession or distribution. Based on an affidavit summarizing the police officers' observations, an application for a search warrant to search three residences and automobiles was prepared. The application was reviewed by several deputy district attorneys, and a valid search warrant was issued by a state superior court judge. The ensuing searches produced large quantities of drugs and other evidence. The defendants were indicted for federal drug offenses. The defendants filed motions to suppress the evidence seized pursuant to the warrant. The trial judge granted the motions, concluding that the affidavit was insufficient to establish probable cause even though the officers had acted in good faith.

ISSUE: Should the Fourth Amendment exclusionary rule be modified to allow the use of evidence obtained by officers acting in reasonable reliance on a search warrant issued by a neutral magistrate but ultimately found to be unsupported by probable cause?

DECISION: Yes.

REASONS:

1. The exclusionary rule is a judicially created remedy imposed to prevent unreasonable searches and seizures by excluding from the trial evidence illegally seized. Indiscriminate use of the rule—impeding the criminal justice system's truth-finding function and allowing some guilty defendants to go free—may well generate disrespect for the law. Weighing the costs and benefits of preventing the use of trustworthy evidence suggests that the rule should be modified to permit the introduction of evidence obtained by officers relying on a warrant issued by a detached and neutral magistrate.
2. This ruling does not end the exclusionary rule. Courts may still exclude evidence if the magistrate or judge issuing the warrant was misled by information in an affidavit that the affiant knew was false, or would have known was false except for his reckless disregard of the truth, or if the magistrate or judge wholly abandoned his detached and neutral judgment. Thus, where a Fourth Amendment violation has been substantial and deliberate, application of the exclusionary rule should continue.

United States v. Leon, 104 S.Ct. 3405 (1984).

12. The Fifth Amendment

Almost everyone understands that a person "pleading the Fifth Amendment" is exercising the right against compulsory self-incrimination. The Fifth Amendment also (1) contains a due process clause, which requires that all court procedures in criminal cases be fundamentally fair; (2) requires indictment by a grand jury for a capital offense or infamous crime; and (3) prohibits double jeopardy.

A grand jury decides if there is sufficient evidence of guilt to justify the accused's standing trial. It is contrasted with a petit jury, which decides guilt or innocence. Grand juries are usually made up of twenty-three persons, and it takes a majority vote to indict a defendant. It takes less proof to indict a person and to require him to stand trial than it does to convict. The grand-jury provision contains an exception for court-martial proceedings.

The grand-jury provision is limited to capital offenses and infamous crimes. *Infamous crimes* are those that involve moral turpitude. The term indicates that one convicted of such a crime will suffer infamy. Most felonies are infamous crimes.

Double jeopardy *A constitutional doctrine that prohibits an individual from being prosecuted twice for the same criminal offense.*

The prohibition against **double jeopardy** means that a person cannot be tried twice for the same offense. A defendant who is acquitted in a criminal case cannot be retried for the same offense; however, a defendant who, on appeal, obtains a reversal of a conviction may be tried again. The reversal, in effect, means that the defendant was not in jeopardy.

Notwithstanding the foregoing provisions of the Fifth Amendment, the protection against compulsory self-incrimination is still its most important constitutional protection. The prohibition against being compelled to be a witness against oneself extends to oral testimony of an accused before and during his trial, to documents, and to statements before grand juries, legislative investigation committees, and judicial bodies in civil and criminal proceedings. The following case concerns the business records of a sole proprietorship. Notice the discussion relative to business records of partnerships and corporations and the reasons for a different application of the Fifth Amendment.

CASE

Doe is the owner of several sole proprietorships. A grand jury, during the course of an investigation of corruption in the awarding of county and municipal contracts, served five subpoenas on Doe. They sought his business records, including telephone calls, bank accounts, and checks.

ISSUE: To what extent does the Fifth Amendment privilege against compelled self-incrimination apply to the business records of a sole proprietorship?

DECISION: The records are not privileged, but their production is.

REASONS:

1. An individual may not assert the Fifth Amendment privilege on behalf of a corporation, partnership, or other collective entity.
2. Where the preparation of business records is voluntary, no compulsion is present. A subpoena that demands production of documents does not compel oral testimony; nor would it ordinarily compel the individual to restate, repeat, or affirm the truth of the contents of the documents sought. The contents are not privileged.
3. Although the contents of a document may not be privileged, the act of producing the document may be. A government subpoena compels the holder of the document to perform an act that may have testimonial aspects and an incriminating effect. Compliance with the subpoena tacitly concedes the existence of the papers demanded and their possession or control by the taxpayer. It also would indicate the individual's belief that the papers are those described in the subpoena.

United States v. Doe, 104 S.Ct. 1237 (1984).

A statement or a document does not have to be a confession of crime in order to qualify under the privilege. Both are protected if they might serve as a "link in the chain of evidence" that could lead to prosecution. The protection of the Fifth Amendment is the right to remain silent and to suffer no penalty for silence.

To illustrate the extent of the protection provided by the Fifth Amendment, the Supreme Court has held that (1) a prosecutor may not comment on the failure of a defendant to explain evidence within his knowledge; (2) a court may not tell the jury that silence may be evidence of guilt; (3) an attorney may not be disbarred for claiming his privilege at a judicial inquiry into his activities, just as a policeman may not be fired for claiming the privilege before the grand jury; and (4) the privilege protects a state witness against incrimination under federal as well as state law and a federal witness against incrimination under state law as well as federal law. To illustrate this latter concept, assume that a person is granted immunity from state prosecution in order to compel him to testify. He cannot be compelled to testify if it is possible that his testimony will lead to a conviction under federal law. The granting of immunity must be complete.

Limitations on the protections afforded by the Fifth Amendment are also readily apparent. The drunk-driving laws that require a breath or blood test are one example. In a drunk-driving case the prosecution can use as evidence the analysis of a blood sample taken without consent of the accused, or a driver's license can be revoked if a person refuses to submit to a breath test. The evidence is admissible even though the accused objects to the extraction of blood or taking the breath test. The Fifth Amendment reaches an accused's communications, whatever form they might take, but compulsion that makes a suspect the source of real evidence such as voice samples does not violate the Fifth Amendment. In addition, the protection is personal and does not prevent the production of incriminating evidence by others. Thus an accountant in possession of documents of a client can be compelled to produce them. The privilege is personal and protects each person from being a witness against himself.

13. The Sixth Amendment

The Sixth Amendment contains several provisions relating to criminal cases. It guarantees to a defendant the right (1) to a speedy and public trial, (2) to a trial by jury, (3) to be informed of the charge against him, (4) to confront his accuser, (5) to subpoena witnesses in his favor, and (6) to have the assistance of an attorney.

The right to a speedy trial is of great concern today. Most states require that a defendant in jail be tried within a minimum period of time—such as four months. This limits the punishment of those not convicted of a crime.

The right to a jury trial does not extend to state juvenile court delinquency proceedings, as they are not criminal prosecutions; however, juveniles do have the right to counsel, to confront the witnesses against them, and to cross-examine them. Thus it can be seen that there are many technical aspects to the Sixth Amendment.

The Sixth Amendment gives the right to counsel and involves two fundamental questions: (1) At what stage of the proceedings does the right to counsel attach? and (2) To what types of cases is it applicable?

For many years, it was thought that the right to counsel existed only during the trial and that it did not exist during the investigation of the crime. Today, the right to counsel exists before the trial. It extends to an accused under interrogation by the police. This right to counsel must be explained to persons accused of crime. The explanation is commonly referred to as the "*Miranda* warning" because it arose in a case by that name. It warns the accused that he has the right to remain silent, that anything he says may be used against him in court, and that he has the right to the presence of an attorney and to have an attorney appointed before questioning if he cannot afford one. A defendant may waive the right to counsel, provided the waiver is made voluntarily, knowingly, and intelligently.

In recent years the Supreme Court has limited the effect of the *Miranda* decision. It has held that a confession obtained without the requisite warning being given could nevertheless be used to impeach a defendant who denied under oath committing the crime. The courts have also created a public safety exception to the *Miranda* warning. This allows the police to delay the warning if necessary to protect innocent persons.

The courts have also extended the types of cases to which the right to counsel attaches. Historically, the right existed only in felony cases. Today, it extends to any case, felony or misdemeanor, in which the accused may be incarcerated. In addition, the right to counsel extends to juveniles in juvenile proceedings. It also extends to investigations by the Internal Revenue Service. Thus, any person charged with any crime for which he may be put in jail or prison has the right to counsel at all stages of the proceedings, from the time the investigations center on him as the accused, through his last appeal.

14. The Eighth Amendment

The Eighth Amendment provides that "excessive bail shall not be required, nor excessive fines imposed, nor cruel and unusual punishment inflicted." Bail is excessive if greater than necessary to guarantee the presence of the accused in court at the appointed time. The function of bail is not to restrict the freedom of the accused prior to trial, because of the presumption of innocence. Most states today require that only a small percentage of the actual bail be posted. The law may require that 10 percent of the total bail be deposited with the court. If the defendant fails to appear, the persons signing the bail bond then owe the other 90 percent.

At one time, the Eighth Amendment was used as the basis for declaring the death penalty to be unconstitutional; however, many legislative bodies reinstated the death penalty, and some of these laws were later held to be constitutional.

CONTEMPORARY PROBLEMS

The criminal law system has generally failed to deter crime or to accomplish most of its other assumed goals. An ever-increasing crime rate, especially in larger communities, puts crimes of violence as well as the so-called white-collar crimes constantly in the news. Because our penal system has not found the means to rehabilitate the convicted, a significant portion of all crimes are committed by repeat offenders.

Many people believe that the inadequacy of criminal law results from its failure to provide swift and sure punishment for those committing wrongs against society. Delays in all steps of criminal procedure are quite common, most of them probably the result of defense tactics, as time favors the accused. But court congestion also contributes to delay, and vice versa.

15. Plea Bargaining

One of the more controversial procedures in the criminal law is commonly referred to as *plea bargaining,* by which an accused pleads guilty to a lesser offense than that which is charged, or there is an agreement for less than normal punishment in return for a plea of guilty. Plea bargaining is essential, because the caseload is too great to try all cases; however, plea bargaining has many adverse side effects. It allows persons who have committed serious crimes to go almost immediately back on the streets to commit more crimes after only paying a fine or serving a much shorter sentence than would have been imposed if they had been convicted of the crime originally charged.

16. Court Congestion

The increased criminal law caseload has had a great impact on the work of reviewing courts. Today, approximately 75 percent of those convicted of crimes appeal their convictions. This increase is largely due to the fact that the indigent defendant is now entitled to a free appeal. We do not have enough judges to handle this caseload properly, and delay is inevitable.

Many other problems arise as a result of the failures of our criminal law system. Overcrowded prisons, unworkable probation systems, unequal sentences, plea bargaining that tends to favor the wealthy, and the failure of sentencing laws to deter crime are but a few of the obvious ills.

17. Addressing the Problems

Most legal scholars agree that the criminal law system needs a drastic overhaul. In fact, the Supreme Court, in its process of reviewing convictions, is bringing about many changes. It is requiring prompt trials or the dismissal of charges. Other decisions have reduced the number of appeals that are available to a convicted defendant. Finally, the Court is reconsidering many of the highly technical aspects of the Bill of Rights as they affect criminal prosecutions. In many of these cases, the Court is balancing the competing and conflicting policies more heavily in favor of the police and the victims of crimes than in favor of the accused.

Congress is involved in changing our criminal justice system. In 1984, it passed a federal anticrime bill designed to give law enforcement tools to attack organized crime, especially drug pushers. Among the key parts of this law are the following:

1. The federal judiciary was directed to set standard penalties for federal offenses. This attempt to end sentencing inequities increases the penalties for drug violations and for persons who use guns.
2. Federal judges are authorized to deny bail to suspects they believe to be dangerous. This preventive detention is similar to that approved for juveniles.
3. Federal suspects using the insanity defense have the burden of proving insanity. Psychiatrists may testify, but may not give their opinion on sanity.
4. Assets obtained while dealing in drugs are presumed to come from the illegal activity. Such assets may be seized and sold by the government.
5. The unauthorized use of computers is outlawed if the action leads to illegal profits or access to national security information.

This law is clear evidence of the public's growing concern with the criminal justice system and its demand for improvement.

CHAPTER SUMMARY

General Principles

Classifications of Crimes

1. Crimes may be classified by their purpose, such as the protection of individuals, the protection of property, the protection of government, or the protection of the public interest.
2. Crimes are defined by the legislature. In addition, the legislature may authorize administrative agencies to adopt rules the violation of which is criminal.
3. Crimes may also be classified as felonies or misdemeanors.

White-Collar Crime

1. White-collar crimes are the result of guile, deceit, or wrongful conduct such as price-fixing or insider trading.
2. The trend is toward harsher punishment for such crimes.

Damage Suits

1. Many statutes today authorize suits for triple damages by the victims of white-collar crime.
2. RICO cases are brought against many business specialists who have used the telephone or the mails to defraud others.

Basic Concepts

1. There is special terminology used in criminal cases. Such terms as *indictment*, *information*, and *lesser included offense* have special meanings.
2. A crime is a combination of act and intent. Some crimes require a specific intent, while others require only a general intent. In a few instances conduct is criminal without intent, and doing the act is all that is required.
3. The criminal law has special rules and procedures for handling crimes committed by juveniles. These cases are handled in special courts in order to rehabilitate and deter further criminal conduct by those underage.
4. Corporations may be held criminally liable for the acts of their directors, officers, and important managerial agents. In addition to vicarious liability, corporations may be punished for strict liability crimes.
5. There are various defenses that may be used by one accused of crime to avoid liability. Some of these defenses, such as insanity, are under challenge and are in the process of change.

Criminal Law and the Constitution

Fourth Amendment

1. The Fourth Amendment protects those accused of crime from having evidence illegally obtained.
2. If evidence is illegally obtained, the exclusionary rule prevents its use at trial.
3. Evidence may be illegally obtained even though a search warrant is used if the warrant was improperly issued.
4. In recent years the courts have narrowed the meaning of the Fourth Amendment. For example, evidence obtained by electronic surveillance is not an illegal search and seizure.
5. There is a good-faith exception to the exclusionary rule.

Fifth Amendment

1. The Fifth Amendment requires indictment by a grand jury for capital offenses and infamous crimes.

2. The Fifth Amendment provision on double jeopardy protects against a person's being tried twice for the same offense.
3. The Fifth Amendment protection against compulsory self-incrimination is personal to the accused. It does not prevent others from testifying or documents in the hands of others from being used as evidence.

Sixth Amendment

1. The Sixth Amendment contains six rights of a defendant: They are the right to a speedy trial, to a trial by jury, to be informed of the charges, to confront the accuser, to subpoena witnesses, and to have the assistance of an attorney.
2. The right to an attorney exists in any proceeding in which incarceration is a possible penalty.
3. The right to an attorney exists in any stage of the proceeding in which the investigation centers on the accused.
4. Persons suspected of crime are entitled as a general rule to be given the *Miranda* warning, but there are exceptions.

Eighth Amendment

1. The Eighth Amendment prohibits excessive bail and cruel and unusual punishment.
2. The death penalty may be imposed if subject to stringent safeguards by the courts.

Contemporary Problems

1. Our criminal justice system does not provide for swift and sure punishment for those committing crimes.
2. The criminal justice system does not serve as an adequate deterrent and has not been successful in rehabilitating most persons convicted of crime.
3. Plea bargaining, a controversial criminal law procedure, is one method of resolving criminal cases, thereby relieving court congestion.
4. In 1984, Congress passed an anticrime bill designed to enhance law enforcement.

REVIEW QUESTIONS AND PROBLEMS

1. Match each term in column A with the appropriate statement in column B.

A	B
(1) *Malum in se*	(a) The process by which the prosecution and defense in effect settle a criminal case.
(2) True bill	(b) A defense in criminal cases when the criminal intent originated with the police.
(3) Strict liability crime	(c) A group that has a responsibility to determine if there is probable cause sufficient to warrant a defendant's standing trial.
(4) Entrapment	(d) An act that is historically a crime in any civilized society.
(5) Irresistible impulse	(e) The decision of a grand jury that indicts an accused.
(6) Exclusionary rule	(f) Something the police must give to inform a person of his or her rights.
(7) Grand jury	(g) Criminal conduct that is not inherently wrongful but is declared so by legislative action.
(8) *Miranda* warning	(h) An act that is criminal without proof of criminal intent.
(9) Plea bargaining	(i) A test for insanity when the defendant knows right from wrong but is compelled to do what is wrong.
(10) *Malum prohibitum*	(j) A rule of evidence that prevents the use of evidence obtained through illegal search and seizure.

2. Compare and contrast the following terms:
   a. Indictment and information
   b. Grand jury and petit jury
   c. Felony and misdemeanor
   d. General intent and specific intent
3. For a crime to be committed, the prosecutor must be able to prove a criminal intent and an overt act to carry out that intent. Jack and Mary agreed to rob a series of banks. Prior to beginning their bank robbery spree, they were arrested and charged with criminal conspiracy. What act did Jack and Mary do that justifies a finding that they committed a crime? Explain.
4. When police entered her room without a warrant, Suzy swallowed two "uppers." Portions of the capsules were recovered by the police with the use of a stomach pump. What constitutional issue will be raised by her attorneys? Explain.
5. Dan was suspected by customs and immigration officers of having information concerning the smuggling of drugs into the United States. Acting undercover, a customs and immigration official went to Dan and suggested that he bring illegal drugs into this country. Dan refused, but at the official's insistence he later agreed. After the drugs entered this country, Dan was arrested. Does Dan have a valid defense to the charge of smuggling? Explain.
6. Devin was arrested and tried for murder. After deliberating for three days, the jury informed the judge that it was hopelessly deadlocked and could not reach a verdict. The judge declared a mistrial and scheduled a new trial. Devin objected, contending that a second trial constituted double jeopardy. Is he correct? Explain.
7. Couch's financial records were kept with an accountant who prepared her tax returns. Pursuant to an IRS investigation, a summons was issued to the accountant demanding access to the records, which had been delivered to Couch's attorney by the accountant. Does the Fifth Amendment privilege against compulsory self-incrimination prevent the production of these business and tax records? Why or why not?
8. A policeman investigating a rape spotted Quarles, who matched the rapist's description. When Quarles saw the policeman, he began to run toward the back of a store. After a chase, the policeman cornered the suspect and noticed that he had an empty shoulder holster. The policeman asked where the gun was. Quarles pointed and said: "The gun is over there." The policeman retrieved the gun and then arrested Quarles. At this point, the *Miranda* warning was read to Quarles. Was the warning too late in violation of Quarles' constitutional rights? Why or why not?
9. Why are white-collar criminals often given probation instead of a prison sentence?
10. A sixteen-year-old kills his parents. The state in which the murders occurred allows juries to impose the death penalty. Can it be imposed in this case? Explain.
11. A company was suspected of emitting smoke from its factory in violation of the environmental protection law. Police officers in helicopters collected air samples above the smokestack. They did so without a search warrant. The company moved to suppress the evidence, contending the search violated the Fourth Amendment. Rule on the motion and explain your ruling.
12. To what extent do sole proprietors differ from partners and corporate officials insofar as the Fifth Amendment is concerned? Explain.

Introduction to Contracts and Remedies

8

CHAPTER PREVIEW

Elements of a Contract
Sources of Contract Law

- CONTRACT CLASSIFICATION AND TERMINOLOGY

Bilateral and Unilateral Contracts
Express and Implied-in-Fact Contracts
Implied-in-Law or Quasi-Contract
Enforcement Terminology
Performance Terminology

- LEGAL REMEDIES FOR BREACH OF CONTRACT

Nominal Damages
Compensatory Damages—Theory
Compensatory Damages—Special Aspects
Consequential Damages
Punitive Damages
Liquidated Damages Clause

- EQUITABLE REMEDIES FOR BREACH OF CONTRACT

Specific Performance
Rescission
Restitution

BUSINESS MANAGEMENT DECISION

You have been authorized to negotiate a contract wherein your employer will supply the needs of a customer for an agreed-upon time period. As a part of these negotiations, you are concerned about customer performance over the stated contractual term.

Should you insist on a clause specifying very significant damages if the customer breaches the contract?

Each of us lives and works in a legal environment. No doubt our greatest participation in this legal environment arises from our freedom to make contracts. Every day we enter into numerous contracts as we purchase goods, hire the services of others, buy a house or rent an apartment, visit the dentist, register for a college course, and so on. The legal device of contract is basic to business law, and Part II of this text covers the law of contracts in detail.

Among the various meanings of the word contract is its technical definition: a promise or several promises under which the law recognizes a duty to perform and for which, if breached, the law gives the aggrieved party a remedy. Realistically, a contract is a legal device to control the future through promises. By definition, a promise is a present commitment, however expressed, that something will or will not be done. Parties are allowed to create rights and duties between themselves, and the state will enforce them through legal systems. When people make a contract, by their mutual assent they create the terms of their contract, which set up the bounds of their liability. It is important, then, that you keep two points in mind: (1) A contract contains a present undertaking or commitment concerning future conduct of the parties and (2) the law sanctions the commitment by putting its enforcement behind it.

1. Elements of a Contract

There are four basic elements to the formation of a contract:

1. An agreement that is a manifestation of the parties' mutual assent as found in two legal concepts called offer and acceptance (Chapter 9)
2. Bargained-for consideration or other validation device, which the law uses to validate and make the mutual assent legally operative (Chapter 10)
3. Two or more parties who are legally competent; that is, they have the legal capacity to contract (be of legal age and sane) (Chapter 11)
4. A legal purpose consistent with law and sound public policy (Chapter 12)

These elements of a contract are considered in detail in the cited chapters. For the moment, the four elements are useful in giving us a way to think about contract law. As we do so, problems in contract law fall into three groupings: preformation, contract formation, and contract performance. The initial approach to any contract problem is to decide at which of the three stages it arises. In addition to the elements listed above, at the performation stage we also are concerned about sources of contract law, general contract classifications and terminology, and remedies for breaches of contract. These topics make up the material contained in this chaper. The following eight chapters deal with the contract formation and performance stages. This organization will cause you to ask the following progressive questions:

1. Has an offer been made?
2. Has there been an acceptance?
3. If there has been an offer and acceptance (mutual assent), is there a validation device like consideration to make the offer-acceptance legally operative?
4. Assuming a valid contract has been formed, are there any legal defenses such as incapacity, illegality, fraud, mistake, or the statute of frauds that may nullify the contract?
5. Assuming a valid contract with no defenses to its formation, how is the contract to be performed? (This question concerns performance problems under the general heading of the law of conditions.)
6. Do third parties have rights or duties that may be legally recognized under the contract?

At this introductory point, you are not equipped to answer any of the questions: however, when you have finished the chapters on contracts, come back and consider them. The law of contracts will then be in sharper focus.

2. Sources of Contract Law

The bulk of contract law is judge-made case law and is for the most part uncodified. The basic rules or principles are found in the written opinions of courts. Specialized areas of contract law such as labor law and insurance law have been partially codified, but even in these areas the primary source of applicable legal principles is decided cases. A few states have codified their case law.

During the 1940s, the Commissioners of Uniform State Laws drafted the Uniform Commercial Code for consideration by the legislatures of the various states. The stated purpose of the Uniform Commercial Code was to collect in one body the law that "deals with all phases which may ordinarily arise in the handling of a commercial transaction from start to finish." The Code was initially enacted in 1952 in Pennsylvania and thereafter over the next several years by every state and territory except Louisiana and Puerto Rico. The detailed aspects of the Code, as it is usually referred to, constitute a significant portion of this text, and sections of the Code are referred to in brackets where appropriate. The references pertain to sections of this law, which are presented as an appendix at the end of the text.

As a result of the enactment of the Uniform Commercial Code, some contracts are subject to its provisions and some are not. It is essential that you keep in mind the limited applicability of the Code and that you recognize which contracts are covered by the general common law and which are covered by the Code. Most contracts (employment, construction, real property, general business, and the like) follow the common law rules as developed in cases. If a contract concerns the sale of goods (personal property), then it is governed by the Code. When the Code applies to a transaction, courts follow Code rules.

Since most rules concerning contracts are the same under the common law and under the Code, these rules will be considered, whenever possible, at the same time. When the Code has special rules different from the common law, these will be set out in the text. Rules for sale-of-goods transactions that have nothing to do with the general common law of contracts are discussed in Chapters 17–20.

CONTRACT CLASSIFICATION AND TERMINOLOGY

3. Introduction

In the early common law, contracts were formal documents that included a seal. The seal was often a wax impression made by the ring of the contracting party. This impression was later replaced with the word *seal*. Today the requirement of using a seal to have a binding contract has been abolished; formality is no longer required.

In the early law, contracts that were not under seal were called *informal contracts* and were unenforceable. Today, as a general rule, contracts, either written or oral, are enforceable. However, a statute known as the *statute of frauds* does require that certain contracts be evidenced in writing to be enforceable. (This statute of frauds is discussed in depth in Chapter 13.)

In addition to being formal or informal, contracts may be classified in a variety of ways. Among the more common classifications are the following:

1. Form: bilateral or unilateral
2. Expression: express or implied-in-fact or implied-in-law (quasi-contract)
3. Enforcement: valid, void, voidable, enforceable or unenforceable
4. Performance: executed or executory

The meaning and significance of these classifications are discussed in the following sections and throughout the other chapters on contracts.

4. Bilateral and Unilateral Contracts

Contracts are either *bilateral* (a promise exchanged for another promise) or *unilateral* (a promise exchanged for an act of performance). Most contracts are bilateral, based on an exchange of mutual promises. A **bilateral contract** is formed when the promises are exchanged between the parties. It is immaterial that neither party has rendered any performance, because the law recognizes that each party has a legal duty to perform its contractual duties. In Figure 8–1, note that there are two promises, two duties, and two correlative rights. This contract is bilateral (two-sided).

Bilateral contract *One containing mutual promises, with each party being both a promisor and a promisee.*

EXAMPLE: Mary promises to sell her truck to Dan for $2,000, and Dan promises to pay $2,000 for Mary's truck.

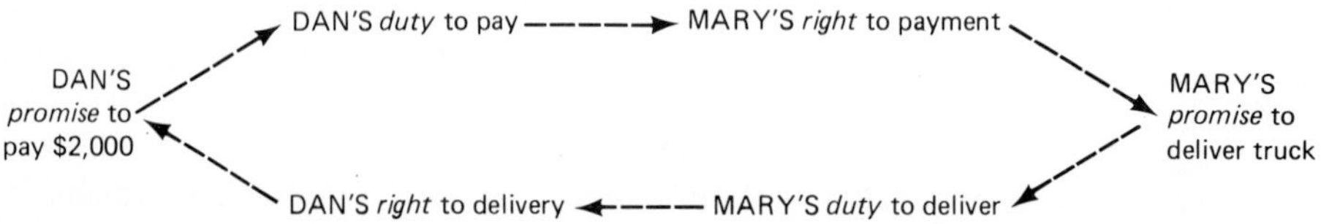

FIGURE 8–1 Bilteral contract

Whereas a bilateral contract is characterized by a promise for a promise, a **unilateral contract** is characterized by a promise for an act of performance. The *offeror* (person who makes an offer) promises the *offeree* (person to whom the offer is addressed) a benefit *if* the offeree performs some act, such as building a house, mowing the grass, fixing a car, climbing a flagpole, or programming a computer. The offerer does not bargain for a promise but for performance of an act. In Figure 8–2, note that there is only one promise, one duty, and one right. The contract is unilateral (one-sided).

Unilateral contract *A promise for an act or an act for a promise, a single enforceable promise.*

EXAMPLE April says to Bill: ''Bill, I've had enough of your promises. If you paint my house by the end of the month, I promise to pay you $4,000.'' Bill paints April's house by the end of the month.

> *Step One:* Offer for a unilateral contract (April promises to pay $4,000 if Bill paints her house by the end of the month)
>
> *Step Two:* Acceptance creates unilateral contract

When April made her promise to pay $4,000, there was no unilateral contract, only an *offer* for a unilateral contract. When Bill did the act of performance bargained for (painting the house), a unilateral contract was created. This distinction is important in later chapters, especially concerning notions of part performance of contracts.

FIGURE 8–2 Unilateral contract

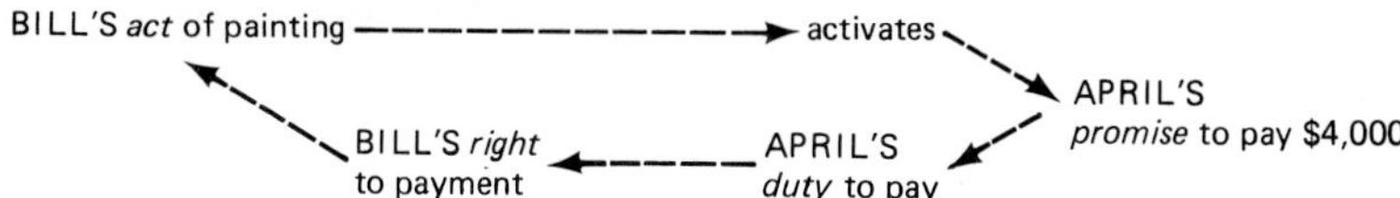

5. Express and Implied-in-Fact Contracts

An **express contract** occurs when the parties state their agreement orally or in writing. When the parties manifest their agreement by conduct rather than by words, it is said to be **implied-in fact**. You drive up to a full-service gas station and say, ''Fill it up.'' The station attendant fills it up. Although you've said nothing about paying, it is an implied-in-fact term. The contract then is partly express and partly implied. You are walking down Lexington Avenue and come upon a grocery stand filled with apples under a sign stating 35 cents per apple. You pick one up and take a bite. At that moment, an implied-in-fact contract created totally by conduct is formed.

Express contract *An agreement which is either spoken or written by the parties.*

Implied-in-fact contract *A legally enforceable agreement inferred from the circumstances and conduct of the parties.*

An additional point should be noted. At one time, sellers sometimes shipped goods to persons who had not requested them. This technique was used to sell items like religious bookmarks, neckties, tapes, and books. The seller would then make a contract (implied-in-fact) claim based on acceptance by the recipient's conduct in keeping the goods. To stop this unfair method of selling goods, the U.S. Postal Services Act, 39 U.S.C. §3009 (1970), was enacted. It allows the recipient of unsolicited goods to treat them as a gift and retain, use, discard, or dispose of the goods in any manner without obligation. There are also state statutes relieving the recipient of any duty to pay for unsolicited goods when the goods have been received through the mail or otherwise.

6. Implied-in-Law or Quasi-Contract

Quasi-contract *A situation in which there arises a legal duty that does not rest upon a promise but does involve the payment of money. In order to do justice by a legal fiction, the court enforces the duty as if a promise in fact exists.*

Implied-in-law contracts, referred to as **quasi-contracts**, are not true contracts. Rather, they are legal fictions that courts use to prevent wrongdoing and the unjust enrichment of one person at the expense of another. When one party confers a benefit upon another, the party receiving the benefit may be unjustly enriched if he were not required to pay for the benefit received. Suppose that you mistakenly thought you owned a tract of land. You paid the taxes. Certainly, the true owner should legally have to reimburse you for the taxes. To avoid any unjust enrichment, courts permit the party who conferred the benefit to recover the reasonable value of that benefit. Under common law, this legal action was brought in the form of a contract action—hence the name quasi-contract. Nonetheless, there is no real promise, and none of the other elements of a true contract is present. If a contract exists, the remedy of quasi-contract cannot be used.

This legal fiction of quasi-contract does not rest on the intention of the parties, but rather on equitable principles. The two remedies most often associated with quasi-contract because of unjust enrichment are called restitution and quantum meruit. Restitution as a remedy is discussed further in section 19 of this chapter.

Quantum meruit *"The remedy used to avoid the unjust enrichment of one party at the expenses of another. This remedy usually is in association with quasi-contract.*

The Latin term **quantum meruit** means "as much as he deserves." It is often used in cases involving the construction of real estate and the repair of personal property. As an equitable doctrine, quantum meruit is based on the concept that no one who benefits by the labor and materials of another should be unjustly enriched thereby; under those circumstances, the law implies a promise to pay a reasonable amount for the labor and materials furnished, even absent a specific contract therefor.

The elements necessary to support a claim for relief based on quantum meruit are:

1. Valuable services were rendered, or materials furnished,
2. to the party to be charged,
3. which services or materials were accepted, used and enjoyed by the party, and
4. under such circumstances which reasonably notified the party to be charged that the plaintiff, in rendering such services or furnishing such materials, expected to be paid by the party to be charged.
5. Without such payment, the party would be unjustly enriched.

Quasi-contract, as an obligation based on equity and morality, exists to achieve justice. Not every benefit received by one party at the expense of another creates liability in quasi-contract. As the following case illustrates, if receipt of a benefit is not unjust, there is no liability.

CASE

The plaintiff, a builder, arranged to purchase two lots from the defendant for $9,000 each. The plaintiff made a down payment of $500 on each lot. Both parties understood that the plaintiff would pay the defendant the balance of this purchase price when the plaintiff sold the houses he was to construct on these lots at his expense. The parties further agreed that title to these lots would not transfer until full payment was made by the plaintiff. The plaintiff partially completed the two houses but was unable to obtain financing to complete them or to find purchasers, due to general adverse economic conditions. When the plaintiff was unable to pay the defendant for the lots, the plaintiff sued, seeking to recover from the defendant the value of the partially constructed houses under the theory of unjust enrichment.

ISSUE: Is the remedy of quasi-contract available to the plaintiff due to the defendant's unjust enrichment?

DECISION: No.

REASONS:

1. A quasi-contract or a contract implied in law is an obligation created by law for reasons of justice, without any expression of assent and sometimes even against a clear expression of dissent.
2. The underlying basis for awarding quantum meruit damages in a quasi-contract case is unjust enrichment of one party and unjust detriment to the other party.
3. The evidence in this case does not support a conclusion that either party should reasonably have expected that the defendant would pay for the value of partially completed houses or expenses incurred by the plaintiff in the building of partially completed houses on his property.
4. The express contract manifests just the opposite intention; the defendant intended to convey the lots to the plaintiff in exchange for cash.
5. The plaintiff cannot, merely by erecting a house on the land of the defendant, compel him to pay for it, even if the land is benefited by the partially completed structures.

Salamon v. Terra, 477 N.E.2d 1029 (Mass. 1985).

7. Enforcement Terminology

Contract terminology regarding enforcement involves the following terms: valid, void, voidable, enforceable, and unenforceable.

A *valid* contract is one that is in all respects in accordance with the legal requirements for a contract (that is, offer, acceptance, consideration, legal capacity, and legal purpose). A **void** contract is not a contract in the eyes of the law. For example, an illegal contract is void in the sense that there is no legal machinery to protect the bargain of the parties. A **voidable** contract is one in which one or more parties have the power to end the contract. A voidable contract will be enforced unless one of those parties elects to disaffirm it. A contract executed by one who is under legal age is voidable and can be disaffirmed (set aside) by the underage party.

Void *Has no legal effect. A contract that is void is a nullity and confers no rights or duties.*

Voidable *That which is valid until one party, who has the power of avoidance, exercises such power. For example, a defrauded party has the power to avoid his contract.*

When one party is entitled to a money judgment or to specific performance because the other party failed to keep a promise, the contract is *enforceable*. Although legally there may be a contract, a defense to that contract may deny any party any remedy under the contract. Later chapters discuss these defenses to contract formation. Such a contract is said to be *unenforceable*. For example, the law requires that a contract for the sale of land be in writing; if it is oral, then it is unenforceable.

8. Performance Terminology

Executed *The term used to mean that the performances of a contract have been completed. The contract is then at an end. All is done that is to be done.*

Executory contract *Until the performance required in a contract is completed, it is said to be executory as to that part not performed.*

With respect to performance, contracts often are referred to as executed or executory. An **executed** contract is one that has been fully performed by the contracting parties. An **executory contract** is one that is yet to be performed. The traditional definition of contract, in terms of promises that are commitments regarding the future, stresses the executory nature of most contracts. For example, when Martha offers to sell Walter a beer for $1, and Walter promises to buy, the contract is executory. If Martha (rather than promising) hands Walter a beer, and he simultaneously gives her $1, then the contract is executed. Although there is nothing to perform under an executed contract, modern definitions of contract include executed in addition to executory contracts. Note also that an agreement may be mixed; that is, executed by one party and executory on the part of the other.

LEGAL REMEDIES FOR BREACH OF CONTRACT

9. Introduction

Remedy *The judicial means or court procedures by which legal and equitable rights are enforced.*

When one of the parties to a contract fails to perform as promised, a breach of contract may have occurred. If such a breach exists, the nonbreaching party may seek a **remedy.** This remedy may be classifed as legal or equitable. *Legal remedies* or *remedies at law* involve the recovery of money damages. *Equitable remedies* involve a request for something other than money. Some of the equitable remedies available for a breach of contract are discussed in sections 16 through 19.

With respect to legal remedies, four types of money damages can be awarded by the courts: *nominal* damages, *compensatory* (or general) damages, *consequential* (or special) damages, and *punitive* (or exemplary) damages. Additionally, the parties may insert in their contract a provision that attempts to state the amount of money damages to be awarded for contract breach. This *liquidated damages clause*, if fair and not a penalty, will be adopted by the court. See Section 15 of this chapter.

10. Nominal Damages

Nominal damages *A small sum assessed when no actual damages have been proven.*

For every legal wrong, there is a legal remedy. So if there is a contract breach but the nonbreaching party suffers no compensable loss, he can still recover **nominal damages.** The award (usually $1) symbolizes vindication of the wrong done by the mere breach of contract. Nominal damages thus recognize a technical injury and can be awarded even when the nonbreaching party is in a better position. Suppose that Bobby contracts to buy from Sammy 10,000 pounds of boiled peanuts at 50 cents a pound. Later, Sammy breaches and delivers nothing. If Bobby can buy boiled peanuts for 30 cents per pound on the open market, he can still recover nominal damages, even though he is not harmed by Sammy's breach.

11. Compensatory Damages—Theory

When the loss caused by the contract breach is more than nominal, the aggrieved party will sue for *compensatory (general) damages* designed to compensate for that party's loss of his bargain. Compensatory damages are the primary damages sought in most contract actions. These damages must be a *direct, foreseeable* result of the breach of contract.

The purpose and the theory of damages is to make the injured party whole. As a result of the payment of money, the injured party is in the same position he would have occupied had the breach of contract not occurred. Damages give just compensation for the losses that flowed from the breach. In other words, a person is entitled to the benefits of his bargain. If a purchaser receives less than he bargained for, the difference between the actual value and the contract price constitutes the damages. Unusual and unexpected damages resulting from peculiar facts unknown to the breaching party at the time the agreement was entered into are generally not recoverable. Nor is the injured party entitled to a profit from the breach of the contract; his recovery is limited to an amount that will place him in the same position in which he would have been had the contract been carried out.

The amount of damages is usually one of fact and therefore presented to the jury. A jury may not speculate on the amount of damage. Damages that are uncertain, contingent, remote, or speculative cannot be awarded. Loss of profits may be included as an element of recoverable damages if they can be computed with reasonable certainty from tangible and competent evidence.

A party suing for breach of contract is not entitled to recover the amount expended for attorney's fees, unless the contract so provides or special legislation permits it. Litigation is expensive, and the party who wins the lawsuit is still ''out of pocket,'' since attorney's fees will usually substantially reduce the net recovery. Court costs, which include witness fees and filing costs, are usually assessed against the losing party.

12. Compensatory Damages—Special Aspects

Mitigation of damages *A plaintiff's duty to keep the damages as low as possible.*

The injured party is duty bound to **mitigate** the damages. It is his duty to take reasonable steps to reduce the actual loss to a minimum. He cannot add to his loss or permit the damages to be enhanced when it is reasonably within his power to prevent such occurrence. An employee who has been wrongfully discharged cannot sit idly by and expect to draw his pay. A duty is imposed upon him to seek other work of a substantially similar character in the same community. He is not required to accept employment of a different or an inferior kind.

When a contract is *willfully* and *substantially* breached after partial performance has occurred, there may be some benefit conferred on the nonbreaching party. Furthermore, the benefit may be of such character that the nonbreaching party cannot surrender it to the other. In construction contracts, the benefit received from partial performance cannot be returned. Under these circumstances, the law does not require the person entitled to performance to pay for the benefit conferred upon him if the party conferring it is guilty of a substantial and willful breach. As a result, the party who has refused to complete the job is penalized because of his failure to perform. The remedy of quasi-contract is usually not available in such cases because of the existence of an express contract.

A different result occurs when the breach is unintentional—resulting from a mistake or a misunderstanding. In this situation, the party may be required to pay for the net benefit he has received. The court may award damages in the amount necessary to complete the performance, in which event the defaulting party is automatically credited for his partial performance.

In those contracts where partial performance confers benefits of such a nature that they can be returned, the recipient must return the benefits or pay for their reasonable value. This rule is applied to willful breaches as well as unintentional breaches.

13. Consequential Damages

Consequential damages *Those damages, beyond the compensatory damages, which arise from special circumstances causing special damages that are not clearly foreseeable. However, before becoming liable for these damages, the breaching party must be aware of the special circumstances that may cause consequential damages.*

Compensatory damages are general damages that arise directly and naturally from the contract breach. Everyone would expect (or foresee) these damages. Yet, special circumstances surrounding a contract might give rise to special damages that are not normally foreseeable. These damages are called **consequential damages.** Whereas compensatory damages are presumed and require no special proof, consequential damages are not presumed, since they are caused by special circumstances beyond the contract itself. To recover these special damages, evidence must be submitted that the breaching party knew (or had reason to know) that special circumstances existed and would cause the other party to suffer additional losses if the contract were breached.

This requirement of actual knowledge (or reason to know) is only fair to prevent a windfall to the nonbreaching party. This rule of a special knowledge of the ''consequential'' circumstances comes from the famous 1854 English case of *Hadley* v. *Baxendale*. Plaintiffs, owners of a mill, delivered a broken crankshaft (used in the mill operation) to the defendant, a common carrier, to be delivered to the factory for repair. Defendant delayed an unreasonable time in making the delivery. Since plaintiffs had no other crankshaft, they had to close the mill, and they lost considerable profits. At that time, it was customary (the usual situation) for large mills like theirs to have more than one crankshaft. Plaintiffs' damage recovery was limited by the court to compensatory damages, since the consequential damages (lost profits) were not reasonably foreseeable. The defendant did not have knowledge of the special circumstances—that plaintiffs had only one shaft, which if broken would cause the entire mill to shut down.

Thus, in the usual case, a plaintiff is given compensation only for injuries that one would normally and naturally expect (that is, foresee) as a probable result of the breached contract. If the injury is beyond that naturally expected, then the plaintiff must prove that the defendant knew (or had reason to know) of these special facts, so that he could foresee the injury. Plaintiffs often fail to prove that the consequential damages they seek were in the contemplation of the parties. The following case is typical of those involving such a failure.

CASE

Bart resigned as a commissioned salesman for Clarklift. Clarklift refused to pay Bart's back commissions ($55,000), which were recovered in this action. Bart also sued because without the commissions he was unable to buy real property in Florida. He sought damages measured by the "profits" he would have earned had he been able to invest the commissions in the Florida property.

ISSUE: Can Bart recover damages for lost profits from his inability to invest the unpaid commissions in the Florida property?

DECISION: No.

REASONS: 1. Since the landmark case of *Hadley* v. *Baxendale* (1854), damages for breach of contract are limited to those that may reasonably be supposed to have been within the contemplation of the parties at the time the contract was made. Lost profits are presumed to be within the contemplation of the parties when they arise out of the breached contract.

2. When lost profits arise out of another transaction, it must be shown that they were reasonably within the contemplation of the defaulting party at the time the contract was made. Here, Clarklift did not know of the Florida real estate investment opportunity. Thus, it could not know lost profits would occur if Bart's back commissions were not paid.

Bartinikas v. Clarklift of Chicago North, 508 F.Supp. 959 (Ill. 1981).

14. Punitive Damages

The term **punitive damages** or **exemplary damages** refers to money damages awarded one party to punish the other's conduct, as well as to deter others from such conduct in the future. Since punitive damages seek to punish the wrongdoer, they bear no relationship to the actual (compensatory, consequential) damages. Although it is not the purpose of a civil action to punish a party, punitive damages are frequently awarded in tort actions. Ordinarily, under common law theory, punitive damages were not allowed in contracts cases since it was not ''wrong'' to breach a contract. However, today punitive damages can be awarded in a contract case if the contract breach itself constitutes a separate tort. Moreover, the modern trend is to allow punitive damages when the contract breach is fraudulent, oppressive, malicious, or otherwise indicative of the breaching party's intent to harm the other's reasonable expectations under the contract. *Fraud* is the most often used tort theory to justify punitive damages. These damages are in addition to actual damages that may be based on either the out-of-pocket theory or the benefit of the bargain theory. Each of the these theories, as well as punitive damages, is discussed in the following case.

Exemplary damages *A sum assessed by the jury in a tort action (over and above the compensatory damages) as punishment, in order to make an example of the wrongdoer and to deter like conduct by others. Injuries caused by willful, malicious, wanton, and reckless conduct will subject the wrongdoers to exemplary damages.*

CASE

Reflections of Tulsa, Inc., a restaurant and nightclub, advertised "an all-expenses-paid Windjammer Cruise to the Caribbean for two" for the winner of the "Miss Legs of Tulsa" contest. Eileen LeFlore won the contest, and she received two tickets for the cruise. However, Ms. LeFlore was not provided with transportation to and from the point of embarking on the cruise. She sued Reflections, claiming she had been fraudently induced to enter the contest by an ad, known by Reflections to be false and misleading. Ms. LeFlore sought to recover actual damages of $900 for the cruise, $1,200 for transportation, and $15,000 in punitive damages.

ISSUE: Is Ms. LeFlore entitled to the actual and punitive damages sought?

DECISION: Yes.

REASONS: 1. Two measures of actual damages have evolved out of fraud cases—(a) out-of-pocket damages and (b) benefit of the bargain damages.

2. Under the out-of-pocket theory, Ms. LeFlore could not recover any damages since she received an amount from Reflections greater than what she gave to enter the contest.
3. Under the benefit of the bargain theory, Ms. LeFlore is entitled to the amount of actual damages sought since this is the value Reflections represented would be received by the contest winner.
4. Oklahoma had adopted a form of the benefit of the bargain measure in fraud actions. Thus Ms. LeFlore is allowed to recover the difference between the actual value received and the value represented as the contest prize.
5. Punitive damages are allowed as punishment for the benefit of society as a restraint upon a transgressor and as a warning and deterrent to those similarly situated.
6. Punitive damages may be recovered where a breach of a contract amounts to an independent tort with elements of malice, whether actual or presumed. Having found such elements in Reflections' advertisement, Ms. LeFlore is entitled to punitive damages as well as actual damages.

LeFlore v. Reflections of Tulsa, Inc., 708 P.2d 1068 (Okla. 1985).

15. Liquidated Damages Clause

Liquidated damages *A fixed sum agreed upon between the parties to a contract, to be paid as ascertained damages by the party who breaches the contract. If the sum is excessive, the courts will declare it to be a penalty and unenforceable.*

The parties to a contract may state the money damages applicable when the contract is breached. The term **liquidated damages** describes this situation, and the provision in the contract is called a *liquidated damages clause*. These provisions will be enforced unless the court considers the stipulation to be a penalty for failure to perform rather than compensation for damages. Should the court find that the term was inserted primarily to force actual performance and not to compensate for probable injury, it will be considered to be a penalty and will not be enforced. In order to be valid, the amount of recovery agreed upon must bear a reasonable relation to the probable damage to be sustained by the breach. Recovery is allowed for the amount agreed upon by the parties, although the damages actually suffered may vary somewhat from those agreed upon in the contract. In cases of doubt, the courts tend to hold that the stipulated sum is a penalty. The following case illustrates this tendency.

CASE

Pacheco had sent his son to a summer camp owned and operated by the Scoblionkos. In 1985, Pacheco paid a full camp fee of $3,100 prior to February 1, 1985. This early payment allowed Pacheco to receive a discount on the regular camp fee. The contract specified that if notice of a camper's withdrawal was received after May 1, 1985, the amount paid to the camp up to the time of the receipt of the notice would be retained by the camp.

On June 14, Pacheco was informed that because his son had failed his final exam in Spanish, he would be required to attend summer school. That same day, Pacheco telephoned Scoblionko of this fact and asked for the return of the fees paid to the camp. Scoblionko refused to refund any portion of the $3,100.

Pacheco sued for a return of the deposit.

ISSUE: Is the liquidated clause enforceable?

DECISION: No.

REASONS:
1. In order to be valid, a liquidated damages provision must meet two requirements: The damages caused by the breach are very difficult to estimate accurately and the amount so fixed is a reasonable forecast of the amount necessary to justly compensate one party for the loss occasioned by the other's breach.
2. The amount of the liquidated damages, which was 100 percent of the contract price, suggests the conclusion that it was an unenforceable penalty. An excessive sum suggests that the parties did not make a good-faith effort to preestimate the actual loss.
3. The apparent intent of the clause is to deter parents from withdrawing their children from camp at a late date, without regard to any reasonable, good-faith estimate of consequent damages.

Pacheco v. Scoblionko, 532 A.2d 1036 (Me. 1987).

EQUITABLE REMEDIES FOR BREACH OF CONTRACT

16. Introduction

As discussed previously, equitable remedies involve a request for some remedy other than money damages. These remedies generally will be allowed only if money does not provide adequate relief for the nonbreaching party. Examples of equitable remedies for breach of contracts include specific performance, rescission, and restitution. **Specific performance** is a remedy that requires the party in breach to do exactly what he agreed to do under the contract. **Rescission** disaffirms (annuls) the contract and returns the parties to the position each occupied before making the contract. *Restitution* (sometimes called quasi-contract) rectifies unjust enrichment by forcing the party who has been unjustly enriched to return the item unfairly gained or its value if the item cannot be returned. These remedies are discussed in more detail in the following sections.

Specific performance *A remedy in equity that compels performance of a contract to be substantial enough to do justice among the parties. A person who fails to obey a writ for specific performance may be put in jail for contempt of court.*

Rescission *The disaffirmance of a contract and the return of the parties to the status quo.*

17. Specific Performance

The legal remedy of dollar damages or the equitable remedy of rescission may not be adequate to provide a proper remedy to a party injured by a breach of contract. The only adequate remedy may be to require the breaching party to perform the contract. This remedy is called specific performance. It is used in contracts involving real estate and personal property; it is not available for contracts involving relationships and services.

Specific performance is granted in cases when the court in the exercise of its discretion determines that dollar damages would not be an adequate remedy. Specific performance is not a matter of right but rests in the discretion of the court. To warrant specific performance, the contract must be clear, definite, complete, and free from any suspicion of fraud or unfairness. Dollar damages are considered inadequate and specific performance is the proper remedy when the subject matter of the contract is unique. Since each parcel of real estate differs from every other parcel of real estate, all land is unique, and courts of equity will therefore specifically enforce contracts to sell real estate. Examples of unique personal property are antiques, racehorses, heirlooms, and the stock of a closely held corporation. Such stock is unique because each share has significance in the power to control the corporation. Items readily available in the marketplace are not unique.

While most suits for specific performance involve buyers suing sellers, the converse is also possible. Sellers are entitled to seek specific performance when it is equitable to grant it, as the following case illustrates.

CASE

Plaintiffs contracted to sell a house under construction to defendants for $56,000. This agreement provided that "buyers will cash out house." The defendants made partial payments, intended to assume the construction loan, and paid to partially remodel the downstairs of the house. After months of further negotiation, the defendants notified the plaintiffs that they were no longer interested in purchasing the house and lot. The plaintiffs filed suit and sought specific performance by the defendants.

ISSUE: Are sellers entitled to a court decree ordering specific performance by buyers?

DECISION: Yes.

REASONS:
1. The overwhelming weight of authority states that specific performance is as freely available to sellers as it is to buyers.
2. This house is of unique construction. It is located in a seasonal recreational area with a limited marketing season.
3. The defendant-buyers had altered the lower level of the house, and they had done substantial damage to the walls while attempting to discover building defects.
4. The buyers had sufficient cash to purchase the house, and there was no evidence that specific performance would be unjust or oppressive.

Penon v. Hale, 701 P.2d 198 (Idaho 1985).

The Uniform Commercial Code provides that specific performance may be decreed when the goods sold are *unique or in other proper circumstances* [2-716]. The Code retains the traditional requirement that the goods be unique and that there be no adequate remedy at law. However, the Code also allows this specific performance remedy "in other proper circumstances," which generally means that the goods cannot be bought elsewhere at a reasonable price. For example, peaches and oranges are not unique. But if an early severe frost destroys most of the peaches and oranges, drastically raising the price of the surviving crop, a court might award specific performance to a buyer in a contract for the purchase of peaches or oranges.

18. Rescission

The equitable remedy of rescission is available in a variety of circumstances. It may be granted by a court of equity when a transaction has been induced by fraud or mistake. Rescission will also be granted to a minor in order that he may exercise his privilege of withdrawing from a contract. It is also used as a remedy if one party's breach of a contract is so substantial that the other party should not be required to perform either. This is covered in detail in Chapter 13.

A party who discovers facts that warrant rescission of a contract has a duty to act promptly. If he elects to rescind, he must notify the other party within reasonable time, so that recission may be accomplished when parties may still be restored, as nearly as possible, to their original positions. A party entitled to rescission may either avoid the contract or affirm it. Once he makes his choice, he may not change it. Failure to rescind within a reasonable time is tantamount to affirming the contract. The party who seeks rescission must return what he has received in substantially as good condition as it was when he received it. Since this remedy is an equitable one, it is subject to the usual maxims of courts of equity.

19. Restitution

In many cases, **restitution** follows rescission. As stated above, to rescind a contract both parties must make restitution to each other; that is, they must return any benefit received under the contract. Restitution thus prevents any party from being *unjustly enriched* when a contract has been legally annulled. The purpose of restitution is to place the parties in the position they were in prior to making the contract. Goods and property received must be returned if they exist and have not been consumed. Otherwise, each party must pay for the reasonable value of the goods consumed or of the services received so that they will not be enriched unjustly.

Although restitution follows rescission, restitution alone can be a remedy. This occurs when a court imposes a contract (a quasi-contract) to prevent unjust enrichment. [Quasi-contracts are discussed earlier in this chapter.] Remember that a quasi-contract is not a true contract but is an implied-in-law contract to prevent unjust enrichment. Restitution is a flexible equitable remedy that is used whenever a court finds that natural justice and equity require compensation for benefits received. Restitution may be ordered even though the parties did not intend compensation.

CHAPTER SUMMARY

Elements of a Contract	1. Offer and acceptance 2. Consideration 3. Legal capacity to contract 4. Legal purpose of contract
Sources of Contract Law	1. Common law cases 2. Article 2 of the Uniform Commercial Code

Contract Classifications and Terminology

Bilateral and Unilateral Contracts	1. A bilateral contract is an exchange of a promise for a promise. 2. A promise exchanged for an act of performance creates a unilateral contract when the act is performed.
Express and Implied-in-Fact Contracts	1. A contract formed by words (oral, written, or a combination thereof) is an express contract. 2. A contract formed by parties' conduct, not by their words, is an implied-in-fact contract.

Implied-in-Law or Quasi-Contract

1. A court-imposed remedy (a quasi-contract) to prevent unjust enrichment.
2. It cannot be used if there is a contract.

Enforcement Terminology

1. A contract is valid if it contains the requisite legal requirements of offer, acceptance, consideration, legal capacity, and legal purpose.
2. When the term *void contract* is used, no contract legally exists (for example, illegal contract). The promises exchanged do not create legal obligations.
3. A contract one party has the option to avoid (set aside) or to enforce is a voidable contract.
4. An existing contract that cannot be legally enforced due to a legal defense is unenforceable.

Performance Terminology

1. A contract is executed when all duties are fully performed by all parties.
2. A contract is executory when duties remain to be performed by the parties.
3. A contract may be partially executed and partially executory.

Legal Remedies for Breach of Contract

Nominal Damages

1. Nominal damages ($1) are a symbolic money award to acknowledge technical injury when no actual damage from the contract breach can be proved.

Compensatory Damages

1. Compensatory damages are a money award for injuries presumed in law to arise normally and naturally from the contract breach.
2. These damages are designed to place the nonbreaching party in the same position as if the contract had been performed.

Consequential Damages

1. Consequential damages are a special money award in addition to the award of general compensatory damages.
2. The purpose of consequential damages is to compensate for indirect damage arising from special circumstances the breaching party could reasonably foresee would result from the contract breach.

Punitive Damages

1. Punitive damages are awarded to punish the breaching party and to deter others from such conduct in the future.
2. Punitive damages are generally not available in a contract action unless the contract breach itself constitutes an independent tort.

Liquidated Damages Clause

1. Liquidated damages are awarded in an amount agreed by the parties in their contract (liquidated damages clause) to be reasonable compensation for future contract breach.
2. The agreed amount of liquidated damages cannot be a penalty; it must bear a reasonable relation to the actual damages that will probably occur if the contract is breached.

Equitable Remedies for Breach of Contract

Specific Performance

1. Specific performance is a remedy that requires the party in breach to perform the contract.
2. Specific performance is granted only when money damages are an inadequate remedy. Dollar damages are usually considered inadequate when the subject matter of the contract is unique.

Rescission

1. Rescission is a remedy that cancels the contract and restores the parties to the position they occupied before the contract was formed.
2. In many cases, to rescind a contract, the parties must make restitution.

Restitution

1. Restitution is a remedy to recapture a benefit conferred to prevent that party from being unjustly enriched.
2. In restitution, actual goods or property must be returned. But if the goods or property have been consumed, an equivalent amount of money must be given.

REVIEW QUESTIONS AND PROBLEMS

1. Match each type of contract in column A with the appropriate statement in column B.

A	B
(1) Express contract	(a) Contract duties completely performed.
(2) Implied-in-fact contract	(b) Formed by parties' conduct.
(3) Implied-in-law contract	(c) Contract exists but cannot be enforced in court.
(4) Executed contract	(d) Formed either by oral or written words or both.
(5) Executory contract	(e) Imposed by law to prevent unjust enrichment.
(6) Void contract	(f) One party has option of avoiding or enforcing contract.
(7) Voidable contract	(g) Contract duties have not been performed.
(8) Unenforceable contract	(h) Illegal contract.

2. Comfort Company assumed the operation of a hotel. The previous owner had a contract with Linen Supply. Linen Supply continued to furnish services after Comfort Company assumed ownership. Comfort Company argues that it does not have to pay for the linen services because it had no express contract with Linen Supply. Can Linen Supply recover based on breach of an express contract? Why or why not?

3. A contractor was repairing a house damaged by a flood. During the course of the work, the owner asked for some repairs not called for in the contract. Upon completion, the owner refused to pay for the extras. Is the contractor entitled to be paid for them? Why or why not?

4. Architect was retained by Builder to design a motel and draft final working plans. His fee was 4 percent of the construction costs. After Architect drafted the preliminary plans, Builder decided not to build, since the land was not large enough to accommodate the motel. Builder knew the size of the lot; Architect did not. Builder claims that Architect's services were of no value to him. In Architect's lawsuit the court found for him. Did Architect recover on a contract? What kind? How much should Architect recover?

5. Dewey, an employee of American Stair Glide, had a novel idea for a safety device for elevator chairs manufactured by American. Dewey on his own time made a drawing and model of his idea and showed it to officials of American. Later, American used the safety device, thereby saving money. American refused to pay Dewey anything, claiming it had no contract with Dewey. American also proved that Dewey was not employed by American to do any engineering or design concept work. Dewey claimed that American was unjustly enriched by his idea. Can Dewey recover using the theory of quasi-contract? Explain.

6. Plaintiff was engaged by defendant to act in a musical motion picture entitled *Bloomer Girl*, her compensation to be $750,000. Prior to production, defendant notified plaintiff that *Bloomer Girl* had been canceled. She was offered a role in a Western, to be titled *Big Country*, at the same compensation. Must plaintiff accept the new role? Why or why not?

7. J. R. Drilling Company of Houston, Texas, ordered a replacement drilling shaft to substitute for a broken one. The shaft was to be shipped from Chicago to Texas via Whitlock Truck Company. J. R. told Whitlock that he (J.R.) owned only one oil well drilling rig and that he needed the replacement shaft immediately. Whitlock delayed

ten days in transporting the shaft from Chicago to Houston. Is J. R. entitled to recover the profits he lost from the lack of a prompt delivery? Explain.

8. After driving your new car for a few weeks, you discover that it was actually used. Its odometer had been set back. Are you entitled to punitive damages from the dealership? Why or why not?

9. McKibben, owner of a mining claim near Fairbanks, Alaska, signed a mining lease agreement with Mohawk Oil that provided that McKibben would receive 45 percent of the value of all ores and minerals mined. But when the ore mined had a specified low value, McKibben would receive only 10 percent of the value of the ore mined. McKibben discovered that Mohawk Oil was diluting the ore and removing precious metals without reporting this to McKibben as required by the lease. McKibben sued, seeking both compensatory and punitive damages. Can punitive damages be recovered in this breach of contract action? Why or why not?

10. Suppose that you have made reservations through American Express with the Plaza Hotel. Your reservations were confirmed by the hotel and guaranteed by American Express. Upon your arrival, the Plaza refused you a room, stating that there was none available. In addition to your out-of-pocket expenses for contract breach, are you entitled to recover punitive damages? Why or why not?

11. In December 1975, NSI contracted to provide laundry service for Secrist's nursing home for a three-year period. Secrist used the service until March 1977, when she unilaterally terminated the contract without NSI's consent. The written contract provided for liquidated damages in the event of an unlawful termination. The damages were 40 percent of the anticipated gross receipts under the contract for the unexpired term—30 percent for overhead and 10 percent for profits. NSI sued to collect the liquidated damages. The trial court found the liquidated damages provisions of the contract excessive because they included 30 percent recovery for overhead after fifteen months of contract period had been completed. Was the trial court correct in rejecting the overhead portion of the liquidated damages clause as excessive? Explain.

12. The Agosta brothers, John and Salvatore, each owned 50 percent of the capital stock of Fontana Foods, Inc. As a consequence of disagreements between them. John agreed to purchase the stock owned by Salvatore for $505,000. Before the price was paid, the warehouse of the business was destroyed by fire and John refused to pay for the stock. Is Salvatore entitled to specific performance? Why or why not?

13. Beckman signed a contract with Dillworth Lincoln-Mercury for the purchase of a Lincoln Continental. Four weeks later, Beckman inquired about the car. The dealership said the purchase order agreement was lost, so no car was ordered. The dealership offered to order another Lincoln Continental but at a price higher than the price originally agreed upon. Beckman sued the dealership for specific performance. What result? Why?

14. After buying a home and lot from Pyburn, Hutchison later discovered that the home site had not been approved by the health board because it lacked enough topsoil to sustain a septic tank and overflow field for sewage disposal. Hutchison charged that Pyburn knew of this condition and that there was no practical means of correcting it. If Hutchison's charge is true, is he entitled to rescission? Could punitive damages also be awarded?

The Agreement: Offer and Acceptance

9

CHAPTER PREVIEW

BUSINESS MANAGEMENT DECISION

As the manager of a garden/feed retail store, you order several items, specifying that they are to be packaged in ten-pound plastic bags. Your supplier responds that the requested items will be shipped in twenty-pound cardboard boxes and that the items are sold free of any express or implied warranties.

What should you do upon receiving your supplier's notice?

OBJECTIVE THEORY OF CONTRACTS

The first requirement of a valid contract is an agreement between the parties. An agreement is typically reached when one party (the *offeror*) makes an offer to another party (the *offeree*) who accepts the offer. Offer and acceptance are the acts by which the parties come to a "meeting of the minds." They reach an accord on the terms of their agreement. This accord is referred to as a *manifestation of mutual assent.*

Mutual assent *In every contract, each party must agree to the same thing. Each must know what the other intends; they must mutually assent or be in agreement.*

Mutual assent, then, is the first ingredient of a contract. Classic common law rules required that the assent of both parties exactly match at the same point in time—that is, that there be a subjective meeting of the minds. Since nobody can actually know the inner thoughts of another, this requirement proved unworkable. Rather than dealing with subjective thoughts, modern contract law follows an objective theory based on the manifestation of mutual assent. Assent to the formation of a contract is legally operative only if it is objectively manifested.

Unless there is an *objective* "meeting of the minds" of the parties on the subject matter and terms of the agreement, no contract is formed. To determine whether the minds have met, both offer and acceptance must be analyzed. The offeror may have had something in mind quite different from that of the offeree. Notwithstanding, the intention of the parties is determined not by what they think, but by their outward conduct—that is, by what each leads the other reasonably to believe.

The minds of the parties are also said to have met when they sign a written agreement. Each person possessing legal capacity to contract who signs a written document with the idea of entering into a contract is presumed to know the contents thereof. Where one who can read signs a contract without reading it, he is bound by the terms thereof unless he can show (1) that an emergency existed at the time of signing that would excuse his failure to read it; (2) that the opposite party misled him by artifice or device, which prevented him from reading it; or (3) that a fiduciary or confidential relationship existed between parties on which he relied in not reading the contract. Because the act of signing indicates a person's intention to be bound by the terms contained in the writing, he is in no position at a later date to contend effectively that he did not mean to enter into the particular agreement. All contracts should, therefore, be read carefully before they are signed.

Offers clearly made in jest or under the strain or stress of great excitement are usually not enforced because one is not reasonably justified in relying on them. Whether an offer is made in jest can be determined by applying the objective standard. If the jest is not apparent and a reasonable person would believe that an offer was being made, a contract is formed. The following case is typical of those that involve an analysis of the offeror's intent.

CASE

Treece, a vice president of Vend-a-Win, Inc., delivered a speech to the state gambling commission. During this address, Treece stated, "I'll pay $100,000 to anyone that finds a crooked punchboard; if they find it, I'll pay it." Although the audience laughed at Treece's statement, his comments were reported on a television news report and in the newspaper. Barnes had discovered two fraudulent punchboards years earlier. Barnes called Treece and inquired whether his statement to pay $100,000 was made seriously. Treece informed Barnes it was and asked Barnes to bring the punchboards to Treece's office. After Barnes delivered the fraudulent punchboards, Treece and his company refused to pay. Treece contended that his statement was made in jest. Barnes sued, claiming a contract had been formed.

ISSUE: Was Treece's statement a manifestation of an offer that could be accepted?

DECISION: Yes.

REASONS:
1. When expressions are intended as a joke and are understood or would be understood by a reasonable person as being so intended, they cannot be construed as an offer and accepted to form a contract. However, if the jest is not apparent and a reasonable hearer would believe that an offer was being made, then the speaker risks the formation of a contract that was not intended.
2. Although the original statement of Treece drew laughter from the audience, the subsequent statements, conduct, and circumstances show an intent to lead any hearer to believe the statements were made seriously.
3. The statements made by Treece and the surrounding circumstances reflect an objective manifestation of a contractual intent by Treece.
4. Treece's promise to pay $100,000 was a valid offer for a unilateral contract. Barnes performed the requested act of acceptance when he delivered rigged and fraudulent punchboards. Thus a binding unilateral contract was formed between Treece and Barnes.

Barnes v. Treece, 549 P.2d 1152 (Wash. App. 1976).

OFFERS

1. Definition of Offer

An **offer** is a conditional promise made by the offeror to the offeree. It is *conditional* because the offeror will not be bound by his promise unless the offeree responds to it in the manner sought by the offeror. This may be that the offeree (1) does something (performs an act), (2) refrains from doing something (forbearance), or (3) promises to do something or to refrain from doing something. If the offeree complies with the terms of the offer within the proper time, there is an agreement. The offeror's manifestation must create a reasonable expectation in the offeree that the offeror is willing to contract. This expectation arises when the offeror's promise demonstrates a *present commitment* in exchange for one of the three responses by the offeree listed above. The first task is to determine if an offer has been made.

Offer *A statement by one party (called the offeror) that he is prepared to be bound to a contractual position. The offer is first essential element to the meeting of the minds of the contracting parties.*

2. Test of Offer's Existence

The test for determining if an offer has been made is as follows: What would a reasonable person in the position of the offeree think the manifestation from the offeror meant? In our legal system, the reasonable person is the jury; the test asks the jury to make that factual determination. The jury looks at all the surrounding circumstances to determine what the offeree ought to have understood. It makes no difference what the offeror actually intended, because the test looks to the presumed intent of the offeror. In making the analysis of the offeror's presumed intent, juries weigh the answers to these three questions:

1. Did the offeror's manifestation demonstrate a present commitment or only an intent to bargain? (Language of present commitment is necessary for an offer.)
2. How definite were the terms as communicated? (The more definite, the more likely it was an offer.)
3. To whom was the manifestation addressed? (If addressed to a specific person rather than the public generally, then probably it was an offer.)

3. Language Used

To decide if an offer was made, the first step is to evaluate the language used. If there are no words of present commitment or undertaking, then probably the manifestation was only a preliminary negotiation or an invitation to the other party to make an offer. The following are examples of preliminary negotiation language: "I am asking," "I would consider," "I am going to sell." Such language is generally construed as inviting offers, because there is no present commitment. Consider the following examples:

1. In reply to Ronald McDonald's inquiry if Griese would sell his business (Bob Griese Fried Chicken), Griese said: "It would not be possible for me to sell unless I got $45,000 in cash." There was no offer by Griese. Griese was only saying that he would consider offers that were at least $45,000. He made no commitment to sell.

2. "I quote you $20 per hockey puck for immediate acceptance." This communication was an offer. In general, price quotations are not considered offers, because there is no present commitment. Here there is promissory language "for immediate acceptance," which would lead a reasonable person in the offeree's position to think an offer was made.

4. Definiteness of Offer

Many transactions involve lengthy negotiations between the parties, often with an exchange of numerous letters, proposals, and conversations. It is frequently difficult to establish the point at which the parties have concluded the negotiation stage and have entered into a binding contract. The key question in such situations is whether a definite offer was made and accepted *or* whether the letters, communications, and proposals were simply part of continuing negotiations. The courts must examine the facts of each case, and to those facts they must apply the basic contract rules concerning the requirements of an offer. An offer must be definite and must be made under such circumstances that the person receiving it has reason to believe that the other party (offeror) is willing to deal on the terms indicated.

One of the reasons for the requirement of definiteness is that courts may have to determine at a later date whether or not the performance is in compliance with the terms. Consequently, if the terms are vague or impossible to measure with some precision, or if major terms are absent, no contract results. Therefore, before a proposal can ripen into a contract, the offer must be sufficiently definite (when coupled with the acceptance) so a court can be reasonably certain regarding both the *nature* and *extent* of the assumed duties. Otherwise, a court has no basis for adjudicating liability. The more certain and definite the communications, the more reasonable it is to conclude that an offer is intended. But the issue remains: How definite must an offer be?

If the parties have intended to make a contract, uncertainty concerning incidental or collateral matters is not fatal to the contract's existence. For example, assume that the parties agree that certain performances shall be mutually rendered by them "immediately" or "promptly" or "as soon as possible" or "in about a month." Although these promises are indefinite, modern contract law would view them as sufficiently definite to form a contract. It should be noted, however, that the more terms the parties leave open, the less likely it is that they have intended to create a binding agreement.

In essence, the existence of a contract is determined by three rules: (1) The parties must intend (under the objective theory) to make a contract. (2) One or more material terms can be omitted from the agreement without the contract failing for indefiniteness. (3) A contract must have enough terms so a court can determine when the contract has been breached and then can fashion an appropriate remedy.

5. Gap-Filling

Courts should be willing to fill gaps or missing terms under an agreement, especially if the parties intend to contract but are silent regarding some terms. The trend of the Code and modern case law is to supply reasonable terms—even material terms. Time for performance and the price to be paid, for example, are important terms and usually are included in the contract. If no time clause is included, a court in most contracts will supply a reasonable time for performances [2–309(1)]. If no price is specified, a court will rule that a reasonable price was intended [2–305], as the following case illustrates.

CASE

Arrowhead Construction Company had a contract for the construction of a low-income housing project. Arrowhead wanted to subcontract the rough-framing carpentry work to Crotts, a subcontractor. They discussed the project and considered a "ballpark" figure of $1.25 per square foot for the carpentry work. However, no agreement was made regarding the price to be paid. Crotts began work and later received a written contract from Arrowhead specifying payment at $1.25 per square foot. Crotts refused to sign the contract but informed Arrowhead that he would require $1.35. When Crotts finished the carpentry work, he was not paid, so he sued. The trial court awarded Crotts $1.35 per square foot and Arrowhead appealed.

ISSUE: When the parties fail to agree on price for services rendered, is there a contract between the parties?

DECISION: Yes.

REASONS: 1. The actions of the parties to a contract may show conclusively that they intended to make a binding agreement, even though one or more terms are missing or are left to be agreed upon. In such cases, courts endeavor to attach a sufficiently definite meaning to the bargain. Courts will supply a term which is reasonable in the circumstances.

2. The evidence clearly shows that the parties intended to be bound by a contract. They discussed the particulars of the project beforehand, Crotts began work, Arrowhead visited the job site and was informed of Crotts' requested price, and Crotts continued working with no objection from Arrowhead. Further, the reasonableness of the price term supplied by the court is clear. Arrowhead's principal, Wayne Hunter, testified "for the amount of work they had to do, $1.35 would have been extremely reasonable."

Arrowhead Construction Co. v. Essex Corp., 662 P.2d 1195 (Kan. 1983).

Gap-filling the price term also applies when the parties have agreed that the price is to be fixed by a market or other standard and that standard fails. In a non-Code case, however, if the contract is totally executory (neither party has performed), the contract with an unspecified price term may not be enforced.

Note: A court can gap-fill a missing term but cannot rewrite the contract. Courts follow the presumption that the parties intend reasonable terms; that presumption applies only to omitted terms. If a term is vague, gap-filling is not allowed. Thus, when parties express their intention on a matter, the court cannot supply an external, reasonable term. To do so would be inconsistent with the express intention of the parties.

Although the Code allows material terms to be supplied by the court, the contract must contain sufficient terms so that the court can fashion an appropriate remedy [2–204(3)]. Quite naturally, the question arises: What term or terms are absolutely necessary before a court can state a proper remedy? The one term that must be in every contract is the *quantity* term. Without it, a court has no basis to figure damages.

6. To Whom Addressed

In addition to the language used and the definiteness of the communication, another factor to consider is the person addressed. Since an offer creates in someone the power to accept, the communication must sufficiently identify the offeree or the class from whom the offeree may emerge. The usual rule is that if the addressee is an indefinite group, as in the case of advertisements, then there is no offer. Reward offers illustrate an exception to this rule. Although the offeree is unidentified and unknown at the time a reward offer is made, the performance of the act requested in the reward is an acceptance that also identifies the offeree.

In general, advertisements, estimates, quotes, catalogs, circulars, proposals, and the like are not offers, for several reasons. There is no quantity term or language of present commitment; the goods are seldom adequately described. Practically speaking, advertisers do not intend the communication to be an offer that can ripen into a contract on the basis of the terms expressed. While it is possible for an ad or quote to constitute an offer, most do not, as the following case illustrates.

CASE

In the fall of 1977, Rhen received in the mail an advertising brochure from Purolator. The brochure stated that with an order of 100,000 Purolator products, the customer would receive a 1978 Buick Electra car as a free gift. Rhen ordered over 100,000 Purolator oil filters and requested the car. Purolator refused to fill the order and Rhen sued.

ISSUE: Was Purolator's circular advertisement an offer that Rhen accepted by placing an order?

DECISION: No.

REASONS:
1. Frequently negotiations for a contract are begun between parties by general expressions of willingness to enter into a bargain upon stated terms and yet the natural construction of the words is that one party is inviting offers or suggesting the terms of a positive future bargain. This is especially true where the words are in the form of advertisement.
2. If a proposal is not addressed to definite persons but only to the public generally, it is not an offer but only an invitation to trade. The brochure was not an offer by Purolator capable of acceptance.

Rhen Marshall, Inc. v. Purolator Filter Div., 318 N.W.2d 284 (Neb. 1982).

7. An Offer Must Be Communicated

An offer is not effective until it has been communicated to the offeree by the offeror. It can be effectively communicated only by the offeror or his duly authorized agent. If the offeree learns of the offeror's intention to make an offer from some outside source, no offer results. Also, to be effective, the offer must be communicated through the medium or channel selected by the offeror. Thus, if Terry was in Margaret's office and noticed on the desk a letter directed to Terry and containing an offer, the offer would not have been communicated to Terry. Terry would not be in a position to accept the offer.

An offer to the public may be made through newspapers or posted notices. As far as a particular individual is concerned, it is not effective until he learns that the offer has been made. As a result, a person without actual knowledge cannot accept the offer. If a reward is offered for the arrest of a fugitive and a person makes the arrest without actual knowledge of the offer of the reward, there is no contract.

An offer is effective when received even though it is delayed in reaching the offeree. Because the delay normally results from the negligence of the offeror or his chosen means of communication (for example, an overnight private mail service), he should bear the loss resulting from the delay. If the delay is apparent to the offeree, the acceptance will be effective only if it is communicated to the offeror within a reasonable time after the offer would normally have been received. If the offeree knows that there has been a delay in communicating the offer, he cannot take advantage of the delay.

It should be noted that printed material often found on the back of contract forms and occasionally on letterheads, unless embodied in the contract by reference to it, is not generally considered part of any contract set forth on the form or letterhead. It is not a part of the contract because it has not been communicated by the offeror to the offeree.

8. Auctions

Bid *An offering of money in exchange for property placed for sale. At an ordinary auction sale, a bid is an offer to purchase. It may be withdrawn before acceptance is indicated by the fall of the hammer.*

Auctions are either with reserve or without reserve. An auction is considered to be *with reserve* unless it is specifically announced to be without reserve. In a with reserve auction, the bidders are the offerors, and the acceptance occurs with the fall of the hammer. Thus the auctioneer may withdraw the property at any time, and the owner or his agents may **bid.** In a *without reserve* auction, the auctioneer makes the offer, and each bid is an acceptance subject to there being no higher bid. In either auction, the bidder can withdraw the bid freely before the fall of the hammer.

The Code has a separate section that covers sales of goods by auction [2-328]. In an auction sale, the sale is completed when the auctioneer strikes his hammer. At the point when the hammer falls, the person making the highest bid is entitled to the article and must pay for it. It sometimes happens that while the auctioneer's hammer is falling, but before it has struck the table, another bid is made. In this case, the Code provides that the auctioneer can reopen the bidding or declare the goods sold under the bid on which the hammer was falling [2-328(2)].

One who is selling goods at auction cannot bid at his own sale unless notice has been given that he retains this privilege. The Code provides that if the auctioneer knowingly receives a bid that has been made by the seller or on his behalf, and no notice has been given that the seller has the privilege of bidding at his own sale, the buyer has a choice of remedies. If the seller's wrongful bidding has bid up the price, the bidder can refuse to be bound by the sale. If he wishes to do so, he could demand that the goods be sold to him at the price of the last good-faith bid prior to the completion of the sale [2-328(4)]. The Code provisions are designed to protect people who bid at auction sales and to prevent them from being defrauded.

DURATION OF OFFERS

9. Introduction

Assuming that an offer has been made, you must consider the next legal issue, the duration of that offer; that is, how long does the offeree have the power to accept? The offeree has the power to accept until the offer is terminated. An offer that has been properly communicated continues in existence until it (1) lapses or expires, (2) is terminated by operation of law (illegality and incapacity), (3) is rejected by the offeree, or (4) is revoked (directly or indirectly) by the offeror.

10. Lapse of Time

An offer does not remain open indefinitely, even though the offeror fails to revoke it. If an offer does not stipulate the period during which it is to continue, it remains open for a reasonable time, a period that a reasonable person might conclude was intended. Whether an offer has lapsed because of the passage of time is usually a question of fact for the jury after it has given proper weight to all related circumstances, one of which is the nature of the property. An offer involving property that is constantly fluctuating in price remains open a relatively short time in comparison with property that has a more stable price. Other facts that should be considered are the circumstances under which the offer is made, the relation of the parties, and the means used in transmitting the offer. An offer made orally usually lapses when the conversation ends unless the offeror clearly indicates that the proposal may be considered further by the offeree.

If the offer stipulates the period during which it may be accepted, it automatically lapses at the end of that period. How do you measure the time period? Assume the offer is in a letter that states it will remain open for five days. The letter is dated May 1 and received by the offeree on May 3. One might argue that the offer lapsed on May 5, since the letter is dated May 1. Since an offer is not an offer until communicated, however, and if there is no contrary intent, the time will be measured from the time the offeree *receives* the offer. The rationale is to protect the offeree unless he has some reason to know that time should be measured from some earlier date. The last day for acceptance would be May 7.

11. Termination of Offer by Operation of Law

Several events will terminate an offer as a matter of law. Notice of their occurrence need not be given or communicated to the offeree or the offeror, as the offer ends instantaneously upon the occurrence of the event. Such events include the death or adjudicated insanity of either party or the destruction of the subject matter of the offer or illegality that occurs after the offer is made. The occurrence of any one of these events eliminates one of the requisites for a contract, thereby destroying the effectiveness of the acceptance of the offer to create a contract. Thus, if the offeror dies before the acceptance is effective, the offer is terminated and there is no contract. The offer terminates at the moment of death or on the date a personal representative is appointed for an insane person. Another event is the enactment of a statute making illegal the performance of any contract that would result from acceptance of the offer. Supervening illegality of the proposed contract legally terminates the offer.

There is a distinct difference between the termination of an offer and the termination of a contract. It should be emphasized that death, for example, terminates an offer but not a contract. As a general rule, death of either party does not excuse performance of contracts, although it would excuse performance in contracts for personal service. To illustrate the effect of the death of one of the parties to an offer, assume that Jeffrey offers to sell to Clint a certain electronic computer for \$15,000. After Jeffrey's death, Clint, without knowledge of the death, mails his acceptance to Jeffrey and immediately enters into a contract to resell the computer to West for \$17,000. Jeffrey's estate has no duty to deliver the machine, even though West may have a claim against Clint for breach of contract if the latter failed to deliver the computer. Had Clint's acceptance become effective before Jeffrey's death, the executor of the estate would have been obligated to deliver the computer.

12. Rejection by Offeree

An offeree's power of acceptance terminates if the offeree rejects the offer. An offeree who rejects cannot later bind the offeror by tendering an acceptance. A rejection terminates an offer even though the offeror had promised to keep the offer open for a specified time. Rejection of an offer is not effective in terminating the offer until the rejection has been received by the offeror or his authorized agent. Thus a rejection that has been sent may be withdrawn at any time prior to its delivery to the offeror. Such action does not bar a later acceptance.

It is often difficult to determine whether a communication by an offeree is a rejection or merely an expression of a desire to negotiate further on the terms of the agreement. Thus it is possible to suggest a counterproposal in a way that clearly indicates the offer is still being considered and is not being rejected. The offeree wishes a reaction from the offeror to the suggested changes. Also, the offeree may, in his acceptance, set forth terms not included in the offer, but only those that would be implied as normally included in such an agreement. The inclusion of such terms will not prevent formation of a contract.

A request for further information by an offeree who indicates that he still has the offer under consideration will not constitute a rejection of the offer. As discussed later in section 19 on the law of acceptances, a counteroffer usually is a rejection that terminates an offer.

13. Actual Revocation by Offeror

If the offer is not irrevocable, an offeror may revoke at any time before it is accepted by the offeree. As stated, the offeror may revoke even though he has promised to hold the offer open for a definite period. So long as it remains a revocable offer, it can be legally withdrawn, although morally or ethically such action may be unjustified. However, the next section discusses the three ways the law may recognize that an offer is irrevocable.

The offeror, possessing the power to revoke, can terminate the offer by communicating the revocation to the offeree. This communication can be direct or indirect. A directly communicated revocation to the offeree is effective only when received. Merely sending a notice of revocation is insufficient. It must be received, regardless of how or by whom it is conveyed. Just as the offer is not an offer until received, a revocation is not effective until receipt. As illustrated by the following case, no contract results if the revocation is effective prior to an attempted acceptance.

CASE

Farley was attempting to purchase four franchised Kentucky Fried Chicken restaurants from Champs, Ltd. Farley submitted an offer in writing that required the seller to finance the sale. Grubert, president of Champs, rejected this proposal and made a counteroffer, also by mail. This counteroffer was to expire on October 1, 1983.

On September 28, 1983, Farley telephoned Grubert. During that conversation Grubert told Farley that he was not going to enter into any agreement with him. A letter from Farley to Grubert was also dated and mailed September 28, 1983, in which Farley stated that "I am prepared to accept your offer to sell for $550,000 plus monies expended on the Drive-Thru, in cash at the time of closing." The trial court found that this letter was mailed after their telephone conversation.

ISSUE: Is there a binding contract?

DECISION: No.

REASONS: 1. A proposal may be revoked at any time before its acceptance is communicated to the proposer, but not afterward.

2. Even though a definite time in which acceptance may be made

is named in a proposal, the proposer may revoke his proposal within that period unless it was given for consideration.

3. Because Grubert withdrew his proposal before Farley's purported acceptance, no enforceable contract was formed.

Farley v. Champs Fine Foods, Inc., 404 N.W.2d 493 (N.D. 1987).

Although most revocations are made directly, the law recognizes that the revocation can occur indirectly through some third party not associated with the offeror. Indirect revocation occurs when the offeree secures reliable information from a third party that the offeror has engaged in conduct that indicates to a reasonable person that the offeror no longer wishes to make the offer. An effective indirect revocation requires that (1) the third party give correct information, (2) the offeror's conduct would indicate to a reasonable person that the offeror no longer recognizes the offer, and (3) the third party is a reliable souce.

IRREVOCABLE OFFERS

The offeror, as master of the offer, retains the power to revoke his offer. Although most offers are thus revocable, the law acknowledges that an offer may be irrevocable. The power to revoke may be lost by (1) contract, (2) legislation, and (3) conduct of the offeree. All three ways are based on option contract principles.

14. Options

The offeror can sell away his power to revoke. Recall that an offeror can revoke the offer even if he says he will not or that the offer will remain open for a specified time. For a consideration, however, the offeror can sell away his power to revoke, thereby creating an **option** contract.

Option *A right secured by a contract to accept or reject an offer to purchase property at a fixed price within a fixed time. It is an irrevocable offer sometimes called a "paid-for offer."*

An option is a contract based on some consideration, whereby the offeror binds himself to hold an offer open for an agreed period of time. It gives the holder of the option the right to accept the continuing offer within the specified time. Quite often the offeree pays or promises to pay money in order to have the option (the continuing offer) remain open. The consideration need not be money. It may be anything that the law recognizes as legal value. The significant fact is that the offer has been transformed into a contract of option because of consideration supplied by the offeree. The offer becomes irrevocable for the period of the option. Of course, the offeree in an option contract is under no obligation to accept the offer; he simply has the right to do so.

Frequently, an option is part of another contract. A lease may contain a clause that gives to the tenant the right to purchase the property within a given period at a stated price; a sale of merchandise may include a provision that obligates the seller to supply an additional amount at the same price if ordered by the purchaser within a specified time. Such options are enforceable because the initial promise to pay rent serves as consideration for both the lease and the right to buy. The original purchase price of goods serves as consideration for the goods purchased and the option to buy additional goods.

15. Firm Offers

States have statutes that make certain types of offers irrevocable. The most significant statute is found in the Code [2-205], which operates to make a merchant's offer irrevocable *without consideration.* A *merchant* is a businessperson dealing in goods [2-104(1)]. The requisites of this so-called *firm offer* under the Code are (1) assurance given in a signed writing that the offer will be held open, (2) offeror is a merchant, and (3) the transaction involves the sale of goods. The offer is then irrevocable for the time stated in the offer (but no longer than three months) or for a reasonable time not to exceed three months if the offer has no stated time period. If the writing assuring the offer will remain open is on a form supplied by the offeree, it must be separately signed by the offeror. The offeree in a firm offer can rely on the continuing legal obligation of the offeror and make other commitments on the strength of it. In effect, the firm offer by a merchant is the equivalent of an option without consideration.

16. Conduct of the Offeree

The third irrevocable offer springs from a situation analogous to an option contract. When the offeree starts to perform or relies on the offer, the law protects the offeree by holding that the offeror has lost the power to revoke. Analytically, the offeree has done something that the law sees as legal value. This legal value buys away the power to revoke, just as actual consideration does in a true option contract. The legal value consists of either part performance in the unilateral contract situation or reliance (substantial change of position) by the offeree.

Suppose Lucy says to Shirley: "I will pay you $50 to sew the letter L on four of my sweaters." When Shirley finishes sewing the L's (the act requested), that is acceptance. At that moment, a contract springs into existence. It is a unilateral contract with only one duty—to pay $50; however, problems can arise prior to complete performance. After Shirley starts to perform, can Lucy revoke her offer for a unilateral contract? In the early common law, the offer could be revoked anytime prior to *complete* performance. The offeree who had partly performed was relegated to a quasi-contract action for the reasonable value of the services bestowed upon the offeror. Since this action could cause unfair results, modern law favors the proposition that the offeree should be given a reasonable time to perform fully, once she starts to perform. The majority of courts hold that the offer is irrevocable for that reasonable time.

Sometimes it is difficult to decide if an offeree is partly performing or merely preparing to perform. Let's take the classic example. I offer to pay you $100 if you walk across the Brooklyn Bridge. You start to walk and get about halfway across the bridge, and I run up beside you and shout: "I revoke." You respond: "You cannot revoke, because my part performance has made your offer irrevocable, like an option contract." You are legally correct. But decide if any of the following are part performances or merely preparing to perform: (1) You buy a pair of running shoes to use in crossing the bridge. (2) You start on a daily exercise routine to get in shape for the walk. (3) You catch a cab that delivers you to the Brooklyn Bridge. These are only preparatory acts and do not make the offer irrevocable.

Reliance by an offeree on either a bilateral or unilateral offer can create an "option" contract. For example, assume that an offer is made which the offeror should reasonably expect will induce substantial reliance by the offeree and that such reliance happens. In such a case, the offer is binding to the extent necessary to avoid injustice, as if an option contract existed. Note that the reliance must be substantial as well as reasonably foreseeable by the offeror. In some instances, it is foreseeable that the offeree must incur substantial expense, or undertake substantial commitments, or forgo alternatives, to put himself in a position to accept by either a promise or performance. The offeree may have to borrow money, or undertake special training, or refuse other offers before he can accept. In such cases, to avoid injustice the offer is irrevocable, like an option contract.

THE LAW OF ACCEPTANCES

17. Introduction

A contract consists of an offer by one party (offeror) and its acceptance by the person (offeree) to whom it is made. An **acceptance** is an indication by the offeree of his willingness to be bound by the terms of the offer. Figuratively speaking, an offer hangs like a suspended question. The acceptance must be a positive answer to that question. For example, the offeror says: "I will sell you this article for $200. Will you buy it?" The offeree now has the legal power to accept this offer, and if he does so in proper fashion, a contract will result. A contract therefore results when the offeree (promisee) answers the question in the affirmative.

Acceptance *A statement by one party (called the offeree) that he is prepared to be bound to the contractual position stated in an offer. The acceptance is a second essential element to the meeting of the minds of the contracting parties.*

Acceptance may, if the offer permits, take the form of an act (unilateral offer), a return promise communicated to the offeror (bilateral offer), or the signing and delivery of a written instrument. The last-named method is the most common in transactions of considerable importance and in those that are more formal.

Only the person to whom the offer is made can accept the offer. Offers to the public may be accepted by any member of the public who is aware of the offer. In general, an offeree cannot assign the offer to a third party. For example, if goods are ordered from a firm that has discontinued business, that firm cannot transfer the order to another firm. If the goods are shipped by its successor, the offeror (the purchaser) is under no duty to accept the goods. If he does accept them, knowing that they were shipped by the successor, then by implication he agrees to pay the new concern for the goods at the contract price. If he does not know of the change of ownership when he accepts the goods, he is not liable for the contract price. His only liability is in quasi-contract for the reasonable value of the goods. In the alternative, the purchaser could return them to the seller if he so elected.

Despite the general rule just discussed, option contracts may be transferred by the holder of the option to another person. Such a transfer is called an **assignment.** The reason an option is transferable is that the option is a completed contract, and its offer is not considered personal.

Assignment *The transfer by one person to another of a right that usually arises out of a contract.*

18. Accepting a Bilateral Offer

An offer for a bilateral contract is accepted by the offeree making a promise in response to the promise of the offeror. The offeree's promise is to perform in the manner required by the offer. The promise of the offeree (acceptance) must be communicated to the offeror or his agent and may consist of any conduct on the part of the offeree that clearly shows an intention to be bound by the conditions prescribed in the offer.

The acceptance may take the form of a signature to a written agreement or even a nod of the head or any other indication of a willingness to perform as required by the offer. No formal procedure is generally required. If the offer is made to two or more persons, the acceptance is not complete until each of the parties has indicated acceptance. Until all have responded and accepted, the offeror is at liberty to withdraw the offer.

When it is understood that the agreement will be set forth in a written instrument, the acceptance is effective only when the document has been signed and delivered (unless it was clearly the intention of the parties that the earlier verbal agreement be binding and that the writing act merely as a memorandum or evidence of the oral contract that was already effective and binding upon the parties).

19. Counteroffers under the Mirror-Image Rule

In forming a bilateral contract, an attempted acceptance may have terms new or different from those stated in the offer. Under common law, this variance between the offer and acceptance violates the *mirror-image* or *matching acceptance* rule. Under this rule, to be effective, an acceptance must conform exactly to the terms of the offer. *Any* deviation from the terms of the offer and the acceptance will be held to be a counteroffer, which constitutes a rejection terminating the original offer.

Note: Once a counteroffer is made (that is, the acceptance is not a mirror image of the offer), then the attempted acceptance becomes a *new* offer and the original offer terminates.

It may be difficult at times to decide if the acceptance is a counteroffer or merely a counterinquiry. The original offer does not terminate if the offeree merely suggests or requests new or different terms or makes a counterinquiry. Monty offers to sell one antique cabinet to Brian for $3,500. Brian replies, ''Will you take $3,000?'' This is only a counterinquiry. Suppose Brian wires, ''Please send lowest cash price for cabinet.'' This is not a counteroffer but only a request for different terms. But in the usual case, Brian would say: ''I'll pay only $2,500.'' This is a counteroffer under the mirror-image rule and a rejection.

20. Variance under the Code

The Code rejects the mirror-image rule. Under the Code, a definite expression of acceptance of a written confirmation operates as an acceptance. This is true even though the acceptance states terms additional to, or different from, those offered or agreed upon, unless acceptance is made conditional upon agreement to the additional or different terms [2-207(1)]. This means that the additional or different terms do not prevent the formation of a contract unless they are expressed in the form of a counterproposal.

Assuming that there is acceptance, what is the status of the additional or different terms? The different terms do not become part of the contract; they are eliminated. Regarding the additional terms, the impact of these terms depends on whether either party to the contract is a merchant. If at least one party is not a merchant, the additional terms become proposals for addition to the contract. Such proposals may be accepted or rejected by the offeror. But if the contract is *between merchants*, the additional terms become part of the contract unless (1) the offer expressly limits acceptance to the terms of the offer; (2) the added terms materially alter the offer; or (3) notification of objection to them has already been given or is given within a reasonable time after notice of them is received.

The problem of variance arises in three similar situations: (1) an acceptance states terms additional to, or different from, those offered, (2) a written confirmation of an informal or oral agreement sets forth terms additional to, or different from, those previously agreed upon, and (3) the printed forms used by the parties are in conflict, especially in the "fine print." The Code takes the position that in all three situations "a proposed deal which in commercial understanding has in fact been closed is recognized as a contract" [2-207]. The following case is typical of those involving the Code change of the mirror-image rule.

CASE

Mace Industries sent a price quotation to Paddock Pool Equipment Company for certain water treatment equipment. The quotation was in the form of a sales agreement that contained the terms on which Mace proposed to sell the equipment. This agreement provided that if Paddock did purchase the equipment, it would have to pay delinquency charges on balances thirty days overdue, as well as any costs or attorney's fees incurred in collecting any past due debts. Additionally, the agreement provided for a limited warranty and disclaimed all other implied warranties. After receiving and reviewing the quotation, Paddock returned a purchase order rather than the proposed sales agreement. The terms listed on the reverse side of this purchase order did not include provisions for delinquency charges, collection costs, attorney's fees, or warranties. The equipment did not function as Paddock had expected, and Paddock refused to make any further payments, claiming that Mace had breached implied statutory warranties. Paddock claimed that these warranties applied because the sale was governed by the terms of its purchase order, which made no reference to limiting implied warranties.

Mace sued Paddock for the balance of the purchase price and collection costs, claiming that the terms of the sales agreement, including the disclaimer of implied warranties, governed the transaction. The trial judge found Mace entitled to the balance of the purchase price, interest, and collection costs. Paddock appealed.

ISSUE: Did Paddock accept Mace's terms as specified in the proposed sales agreement?

DECISION: Yes.

REASONS:
1. Common law courts, applying the mirror-image rule, require an acceptance to be identical to the terms of an offer in order to create a contract.
2. However, this state has adopted the Uniform Commercial Code, which abolishes that rule in some contracts. Under Section 2-207 of the UCC, an expression of acceptance of an offer creates a contract on the offered terms despite additional or different terms contained in the acceptance.
3. Section 2-207 also provides that the offeree's additional terms are treated as proposals for addition to the contract. These pro-

posals will become part of the contract automatically if the two parties are merchants and (1) the original offer did not limit acceptance to its terms, (2) the additional terms do not materially alter the offer, and (3) notification of objection to the additional terms has not been given or is not given in a reasonable time.

4. Paddock's purchase order constituted an acceptance under Section 2-207. Paddock did not make its acceptance expressly conditioned on Mace's acceptance of the terms of the purchase order.
5. The additional terms of the purchase order are treated as proposals for addition to the contract. These proposals, which did not materially alter the contract and were not objected to by Mace, became part of the contract, because both Mace and Paddock were merchants. However, none of these terms affected the limited warranty, so it still controls, and the trial court's judgment is affirmed.

Mace Industries, v. Paddock Pool Equipment, Co., 339 S.E.2d 527 (S.C. App. 1986).

21. Silence as Assent

As a general rule, the offeror cannot force the offeree to reply to the offer. In most cases, therefore, mere silence by the offeree does not amount to acceptance, even though the offeror in his offer may have stated that a failure to reply would constitute an acceptance. However, a previous course of dealing between the parties or the receipt of goods by the offeree under certain circumstances could impose a duty on the offeree to speak in order to avoid a contractual relationship. This duty to speak arises when the offeree has led the offeror to believe that silence or inaction is intended as a manifestation of intent to accept and the offeree believes that it is. In other words, silence where a duty exists to communicate either an acceptance or rejection is an acceptance.

Under the Code, a buyer has accepted goods when he fails to make an effective rejection or does any act inconsistent with the seller's ownership. However, failure to reject will not be construed as an acceptance unless the buyer has had a reasonable opportunity to examine the goods.

22. Communication of Acceptances

The offeror is the master of the offer. As such, the offeror has the power to control both the *manner* (promise or performance) and *mode* or *medium* of acceptance (phone, telegram, mail). If the offeror specifically seeks only a promise, then the offeree can accept only by promising (bilateral contract). Likewise, the offeror may authorize only one medium of acceptance, and that is the only medium the offeree can use in communicating the acceptance. For example, Tom mails a letter to Ralph stating the terms of a proposed contract. At the end Tom writes: "You can accept this offer only by signing on the dotted line below my signature and returning the contract by express mail." Ralph immediately sends a telegram saying: "I accept your offer." There is not contract because a telegram was not an authorized medium of acceptance.

Courts distinguish offers that merely suggest a method of acceptance from those that prescribe an exclusive method. As the following case illustrates, doubts are usually resolved in favor of suggestions rather than mandatory requirements.

CASE

Rhonda Overman agreed to sell certain property to the Browns. As evidence of the agreement, she and Patsy Brown signed a Uniform Purchase Agreement. Patsy Brown signed the agreement. Below her signature, Mrs. Overman's real estate agent signed a receipt of the offer and down payment, which stated that the Browns' offer and down payment were taken by the agent "Subject to the written approval and acceptance by the owner." Printed below this clause were the words "ACCEPTANCE ON REVERSE SIDE." At the top of the reverse side of the agreement was the heading "ACCEPTANCE." Ms. Overman signed below that heading. On a later date, the parties entered into a second Uniform Purchase Agreement under different terms. Patsy and B. G. Brown signed this agreement. However, Ms. Overman did not sign the back of the agreement. Instead, Ms. Overman sent a letter that authorized her agent to exchange the original contract for the second one. The Browns did not purchase the property, claiming Ms. Overman never accepted their offer in the proper way. Ms. Overman sued them for breach of contract, and a judgment was entered against the Browns.

ISSUE: Was the letter written by Ms. Overman a valid means of acceptance that created a contract?

DECISION: Yes.

REASONS:

1. An offer can require the offeree to accept in a specific time, place, or manner in order to create a contract. However, if the offer, as fairly interpreted, merely suggests without requiring a specific method of acceptance, the offer can be accepted in any reasonable manner.
2. Although the phrase "ACCEPTANCE ON REVERSE SIDE" was printed on the Uniform Purchase Agreement, the language was not a mandatory requirement for the acceptance of the offer.
3. While Ms. Overman's separate letter was perhaps an ill-advised or clumsy means of acceptance, it was neither ambiguous nor ineffective. An acceptance does not need to be formal, but may be shown in several different ways, including words, conduct, or acquiescence indicating agreement. The offeree's act or communication will be a valid acceptance, and therefore will create an enforceable obligation if it would lead a reasonable person to conclude that the offer had been accepted. Ms. Overman's letter was sufficient because it could be construed to express her unequivocal intent to be bound by the terms of the second agreement.
4. Therefore the acceptance was valid, and a contract came into existence. The judgment of the trial court is affirmed.

Overman v. Brown, 372 N.W.2d 102 (Neb. 1985).

In the early common law, unless the offeror stated otherwise, the only authorized medium of communication was the medium used by the offeror in communicating the offer. Assuming the offeree uses the authorized medium to accept, this question arises: When does the acceptance take effect? (1) Upon receipt by the offeror? Or (2) upon dispatch (such as mailing a letter) by the offeree?

The law generally adopted a rule that protects the offeree by making the acceptance effective at the time it is dispatched. This is known as the *deposited acceptance* or *mailbox rule*. If mail is the authorized medium, the acceptance letter is effective the moment it is mailed, even if the offeror never receives the letter of acceptance. Note that the offeror can change the mailbox rule by simply stating in the offer that the acceptance is not effective until actually received by the offeror, but few offerors so provide.

The deposited acceptance rule could be applied harshly, especially when the offeree accepted by a reasonable medium other than the one used by the offeror. In response, modern law recognizes that some offerors may be indifferent to how the offeree accepts. Some cases have held that an offer invites acceptance in any manner and by any medium reasonable under the circumstances. The Code has a provision that adopts this approach [2-206(1)(a)]. In cases under the Code, the offeror can insist on the manner and medium of acceptance. But if the offeror does not exercise his power to limit the manner or mode of acceptance, the offeree may accept in any *reasonable manner* and by any *reasonable medium*. Such acceptances are effective when deposited. What is reasonable depends on all the circumstances surrounding each situation. For example, an offer to sell certain stock is telephoned to you and nothing is said about the medium of acceptance. In a highly speculative market, a quicker medium than mail (telegram, telex, or telephone) may be the *reasonable* mediums for acceptance.

23. Accepting a Unilateral Offer

As indicated previously, an offer may be either unilateral or bilateral. Most offers are bilateral; when there is doubt as to whether they are unilateral or bilateral, the courts tend to construe them as bilateral. When an offer is unilateral, the offeror does not desire a *promise* of performance; he insists on substantial completion of the act or forbearance requested. As a general rule, substantial performance of the act requested constitutes an acceptance of a unilateral offer. If the offeree ceases performance short of substantial performance, there is no acceptance and no contract.

A difficult question arises when an offeror seeks to withdraw a unilateral offer during the course of the offeree's attempted performance of the act requested. Today, the generally accepted view is that an offeror of a unilateral offer cannot withdraw during the performance by the offeree. The offeror becomes bound when performance is commenced or tendered, and the offeree has a duty to complete performance. It is part performance by the offeree that legally "buys away" the offeror's power to revoke.

The Code makes some changes in the law of acceptance of unilateral offers. Basically, the Code provides that an order for goods may be accepted either by a shipment of the goods or by a prompt promise to ship the goods [2-206(1)(b)]. To illustrate: A merchant who desperately needs several items of merchandise mails a letter to a manufacturer asking for immediate shipment of the articles listed. This unilateral offer could be accepted by the act of shipment, even though the offeror (the buyer) had no actual knowledge of the acceptance. The buyer, however, could withdraw her offer at any time before the seller's delivery to the carrier. This revocation could harm a seller who has incurred expense by procuring, assembling, or packing the goods for shipment. Under the Code, such an offer may either be treated as a unilateral offer and accepted by shipment or be treated as a bilateral offer and accepted by a promise to ship. The seller, under the Code, is thus afforded an opportunity to bind the bargain prior to the time of shipment if he wants to do so.

CHAPTER SUMMARY

Objective Theory of Contracts

1. The formation of a contract requires a bargain in which there is a manifestation of mutual assent.
2. Manifestation of mutual assent to an exchange requires that each party either make a promise or begin to render a performance.

Offers

Definition of Offer

1. An offer is a promise to do or refrain from doing some specified thing in the future.

Tests for Offer

1. The language used must indicate a promise (present commitment), rather than bargaining language.
2. The language of an offer must be reasonably certain so that a court can determine if a breach has occurred and fashion an appropriate remedy.
3. Assuming that an offer has been made, a court can gap-fill reasonable terms like time and place of performance, price, and the like.
4. An offer *must* contain a subject matter, a quantity term, and indicate the parties' intent to be contractually bound.
5. An offer must sufficiently identify the offeree or the class from whom the offeree may emerge.

Auctions

1. Auctions may be with or without reserve.
2. In auctions with reserve, the fall of the gavel is the acceptance, and all bids may be rejected.
3. Sellers cannot bid at auctions under the Code unless notice of that fact is given.

Duration of Offers

Lapse of Time

1. If a time period for acceptance is stated in the offer, the offer lapses at the end of that time.
2. If no time period for acceptance is stated, the offer lapses at the end of a reasonable period of time.

Termination of Offer by Operation of Law

1. Death or insanity of either the offeror or offeree terminates an offer from that moment. Communication to the other part is not required.
2. Supervening illegality terminates an offer.
3. Destruction of the subject matter of the offer terminates the offer.

Rejection by Offeree

1. Rejection by the offeree terminates an offer.
2. Rejection requires words or conduct by the offeree that demonstrate a clear intent not to accept the offer. Inquiries or suggestions about the offer are not rejections.
3. A rejection is not effective until actually communicated to the offeror or his agent.
4. A counteroffer is both a rejection of the offer and a new offer.

Actual Revocation by Offeror	1. Unless the offer is irrevocable, the offer can be revoked at *any time* without liability. 2. The revocation of an offer must be communicated, directly or indirectly, to be effective. 3. Indirect revocation occurs when a *reliable* source gives *reliable* information that would cause a *reasonable* person to think the offer had been revoked.

Irrevocable Offers

Options	1. Offerors can always sell their power to revoke, which creates an option contract. 2. An option contract is based on consideration that binds the offeror to keep the offer open for a stated time period. 3. Option contracts must be strictly performed by the offeree.
Firm Offers	1. The UCC makes a merchant's written offer irrevocable without consideration. This is called a firm offer. 2. The *merchant's* offer to sell *goods* must be in *writing* and state that it will be firm. The firm offer is irrevocable for the time stated or a reasonable time, but in no event beyond three months.
Conduct of the Offeree	1. Part performance of the contract by the offeree makes the offer for a unilateral contract irrevocable. 2. Substantial reliance on the offer by the offeree that is foreseeable by the offeror makes the offer irrevocable, like an option contract.

The Law of Acceptances

Introduction	1. Acceptance of an offer is a manifestation of assent to the proffered terms made by the offeree in a manner required or invited by the offeror. 2. Offers cannot be transferred unless they are part of an option contract.
Accepting a Bilateral Offer	1. The offeree accepts a bilateral offer by making a promise. 2. The offeree's promise must be communicated to the offeror. 3. There are no formal procedures required for this communication. Written or verbal statements or conduct indicating a willingness to be bound may act as acceptance.
Counteroffers under the Mirror-Image Rule	1. Under the mirror-image rule at common law, the acceptance must be absolute, unconditional, and conform exactly to the terms of the offer. Otherwise it would be a counteroffer.
Variance under the Code	1. Under the Code, a variant acceptance *operates* as an acceptance even if it has terms *additional to* or *different from* the offer. 2. When one party is a nonmerchant, the additional terms are proposals for addition to the contract that may be accepted. 3. Between merchants, the additional terms become part of the contract unless (a) the offer limits acceptance to the terms of the offer, or (b) the new terms materially alter the contract, or (c) the new terms are rejected by reasonable notice.
Silence as Assent	1. Silence in the absence of a duty to speak does not amount to an acceptance. 2. Under the Code, a buyer accepts goods if he fails to make an effective rejection.

Communication of Acceptances	1. In cases not under the Code, acceptance of an offer for a bilateral contract is effective at the time it is deposited in the offeror's medium of communication. 2. Under the Code, an acceptance is effective when deposited in the authorized medium, or any other medium reasonable under the circumstances. 3. Modern cases adopt the Code approach for all contracts.
Accepting a Unilateral Offer	1. A unilateral offer is accepted by substantial performance of the act requested. 2. Under the Code, an order for goods may be treated as either bilateral or unilateral.

REVIEW QUESTIONS AND PROBLEMS

1. Identify the terms in column A by matching each with the appropriate statement in column B.

A	B
(1) Irrevocable offer by offeree's conduct	(a) UCC written merchant's offer.
(2) Offer terminated by operation of law	(b) Manifestation of mutual assent.
(3) Counteroffer	(c) Reliable person gives reliable information that offer is revoked.
(4) Offer terminated after reasonable time	(d) Applies only to acceptances.
(5) Irrevocable firm offer	(e) Words or conduct by offeree that reasonably shows offer is not accepted.
(6) Rejection	(f) Both a rejection and a new offer.
(7) Option contract	(g) Death or insanity of offeror or supervening illegality.
(8) Indirect revocation	(h) For consideration offeror sells power to revoke.
(9) Meeting of the minds	(i) Offer without a time limit for acceptance.
(10) Mailbox rule	(j) Part performance or reliance.

2. Suppose that I invite you over next Saturday to a catfish and hush puppy dinner, and you agree to come. You arrive next Saturday, only to find I've left town.
   a. Do you have a contract action against me?
   b. Would it make any difference if we signed a contract stating, "We intend to make this a binding obligation"?
   c. Would it make any difference if you had to drive 325 miles to my house?

3. DATASERV proposed to sell certain computer features to TFL for $100,000. The proposal contained three clauses that TFL objected to. Two of the objections were resolved, but the third was not resolved. Later DATASERV agreed to eliminate the third clause. Was there a contract? Why or why not?

4. Seller wrote a general circular to ten buyers asking, "Do you want to buy 240 good 1,000-pound cattle at $8.25? Must be sold by Friday. Phone me at Wichita, Kans." One buyer telegraphs an immediate acceptance for all 240 cattle. Is there a contract? Why or why not?

5. The following ad appeared in our local newspaper: "1 black lapin stole, beautiful, worth $139.50. $1. FIRST COME, FIRST SERVED." You are the first to appear at the store and tender $1. Is a contract formed? Why or why not?

6. Seller and Buyer execute a contract for 500 jogging shoes. The contract has all the basic terms, except the parties "agree to agree" on the price per shoe at a later date.
   a. Is there a contract?

b. If so, what happens if they later fail to agree?
c. Would your answer change if Seller says, ''I need *at least* $10 per set of shoes,'' and Buyer accepts? Explain.

7. Jimmy offers to sell Margaret a parcel of land for $5,000, stating that the offer will remain open for thirty days. Margaret replies, ''Won't you take $4,700?'' Jimmy answers ''no.'' Would an acceptance thereafter by Margaret within the thirty-day period be effective? Explain.

8. Seller offers to sell Buyer a boat for $500. Buyer replies, ''I think I want the boat, but let me have a week to consider.'' Seller replies, ''O.K. I won't sell the boat to anyone until after one week from today.'' The next day, Seller sells the boat to Popeye for $600. The day after that, Seller says he has already sold the boat. Nevertheless, Buyer tenders $500.
   a. Is Seller contractually liable to Buyer?
   b. Would your answer change if Seller were a merchant and his promise not to sell for a week were in writing?

9. The Cowgers leased certain real property to Northwestern Bell for ten years. The contract granted an option to buy the property provided that the lessee give sixty days' prior notice of its intention to purchase. Northwestern Bell gave the required sixty days' notice, but the Cowgers refused to sell because the buyer did not tender the purchase price at the time it gave notice. Northwestern Bell sued for specific performance. The Cowgers claimed that the option had not been properly exercised. Can Northwestern Bell accept the option without tendering the purchase price? Explain.

10. Dairy mails Grocery Store an offer to sell 200 quarts of milk at a stated price. Grocery Store immediately replies, ''Please send immediately 200 quarts of milk in 1-quart plastic containers.'' Dairy ignores Grocery Store's reply. If the milk is not sent, has Dairy breached a contract? Explain.

11. Valley Trout Farms used a purchase order to buy fish food from Rangen. Rangen would ship the feed, together with an invoice that provided for a 1 percent per month late charge. Valley Trout's purchase form did not mention late charges. Was the ''late charge'' language in Rangen's acceptance invoice a part of the contract terms? Why or why not?

12. Morrison made an offer to buy real property owned by Thoelke and signed a contract for sale and purchase that was mailed to Thoelke for his acceptance and signature. Thoelke signed the contract and mailed it to Morrison. Before Morrison received the contract in the mail, Thoelke called Morrison on the telephone and repudiated the contract. Nevertheless, when Morrison received the contract, he recorded it and thereby made his interest in the property a matter of public record. Thoelke then filed a suit in equity to remove Morrison's claim of interest in the property from the record. Could Thoelke repudiate the contract after he had deposited his acceptance of Morrison's offer in the mail? Explain.

13. Contractor agreed to build a building for Brooke within a certain time. Owing to extremely bad weather, Contractor asked for a time extension. Brooke sent the request to his architect but the request was eventually ignored. Although the building was not finished within the original time, should the lack of disapproval of the request for an extension be held to be an acceptance of the extension? Why or why not?

Bargained-for Consideration

10

CHAPTER PREVIEW

BUSINESS MANAGEMENT DECISION

You are the manager of your firm's accounts receivables. You receive a check in the amount of $700 from a client. This check is marked "account paid in full." Upon reviewing your records, you discover the firm believes this client owes $1,300.

What should you do with the check?

To have a valid contract, the offer and acceptance (mutual assent) must be validated by bargained-for consideration. Not every agreement (offer and acceptance) will be legally enforced. In the validation process, promises that will be enforced are separated from those that will not. If an agreement is based on a *bargain*, then the promises are legally enforceable. Something is *bargained-for* if it is sought by the promisor in exchange for his promise and is given by the promisee in exchange for that promise.

Consideration *An essential element in the creation of contract obligation. A detriment to the promisee or a benefit to the promisor. One promise is consideration for another promise. An act is consideration for a promise.*

Consideration then is defined as a *bargained-for exchange*. The exchange can be a promise exchanged for a promise, a promise exchanged for an act of performance, or a promise exchanged for a forebearance to act. The doctrine of consideration requires that the promises or performance of *both* parties be legally valid. If mutuality of consideration is not present, there is no contract.

BARGAIN THEORY OF CONSIDERATION

1. Benefits and Detriments

To have consideration, both contracting parties typically will receive a *legal benefit* and incur a *legal detriment*. Legal benefit occurs when a party receives something that he had no prior legal right to receive. *Legal detriment* is a little more difficult to define. It is either (1) a promise to perform (or act of performance) that one had no prior legal obligation to perform, *or* (2) a promise not to do something (or actually refraining from doing something) that one could legally do and had no prior legal obligation not to do.

EXAMPLE: Al promises to sell Mary his car for $2,000. Mary promises to pay Al $2,000 for his car. Al has incurred *legal detriment* (sold his car, which he had no prior obligation to do) and has received *legal benefit* (payment of $2,000, which he had no prior legal right to obtain). Mary likewise has incurred a *legal detriment* (must pay $2,000, which she had no prior legal obligation to do) and has received a *legal benefit* (legal right, which she did not previously have, to receive Al's car). Since both promises induced one another, a true bargain occurred. Therefore this bilateral contract is validated by bargained-for consideration.

Consideration is the price paid for a promise. If nothing is paid for a promise, the courts, as the following case illustrates, will not enforce it because the element of consideration is missing.

CASE

Two employees of Gerald Morel obtained a $9,000 loan from the Moorcroft State Bank. These employees executed and delivered to the bank a promissory note for $9,000, secured in part by a mortgage on their livestock. Eight days after the completion of the loan, the president of the bank asked Morel to sign a guaranty of the loan. Morel refused, but did agree to furnish grass for the livestock. The president of the bank still insisted that Morel guarantee the loan, and after much discussion and urging, Morel signed the guaranty. A year later, Morel's employees were in default, and the bank sued them and obtained a default judgment. The bank then sued Morel upon his guaranty, claiming that when he signed the guaranty he received consideration because he knew that by doing so he would receive "the continued benefit of having a good employee." Morel testified at trial that he had agreed to furnish grass for the livestock, which were collateral on the loan, because it was to his advantage to keep a good employee on his ranch. However, he denied that he had agreed to do more when the loan was made. The trial court found that there was no consideration for Morel's guaranty, and entered a judgment for Morel.

ISSUE: Did Morel receive any consideration for signing the guaranty, thus making it enforceable against him?

DECISION: No.

REASONS:

1. A guaranty of a preexisting debt, such as a guaranty of a loan that has already been completed, must meet the same requirements as any other agreement to be enforceable as a contract. Therefore the bank cannot compel Morel to pay off his employees' loan unless the guaranty agreement is supported by consideration.
2. Consideration is some benefit that the promisor receives from the promisee when he makes his promise, or some detriment that the promisee suffers in return for the promisor's promise.
3. The bank has not shown that Morel received anything from the bank in return for his promise to pay his employees' debt. If the bank had originally conditioned making the loan upon Morel's guaranty, then Morel might have received the "continued benefit of having a good employee" by guaranteeing the loan. However, the bank had already made the loan when Morel signed the guaranty. The bank simply neither suffered any detriment nor gave Morel any benefit for his signing of the guaranty.
4. Therefore there was no consideration flowing from the bank to Morel for his signing the guaranty agreement, so it cannot be enforced as a contract. The trial court's judgment is affirmed.

Moorcroft State Bank v. Morel, 701 P.2d 1159 (Wyo. 1985).

2. The Three Elements of a Bargain

A bargain results when there is causation between the legal detriment and the legal benefit. For a promise to be supported by bargained-for consideration, the following three elements must be present:

1. The promisee must suffer *legal detriment*.
2. The promise in question must *induce* the legal detriment.
3. The legal detriment must *induce* the making of the promise.

Legal detriment is not necessarily synonymous with real detriment or loss. For example, Uncle tells Niece that if she stops smoking for one month, Uncle will give her $500. If Niece refrains from smoking for a month, she incurs legal detriment. Since quitting smoking may actually be a benefit, no real detriment may be present. But because she has a legal right to smoke, she incurs legal detriment by giving up that right.

The promisor must have made the promise at least in part to exchange it for the detriment incurred by the promisee. The detriment must be the price paid for the promise. Sometimes factual patterns require one to decide if the detriment was merely a condition for a gift or was bargained for, in that it induced the promise. If the detriment is not a legal benefit to the promisor, it probably did not induce the promise. For example, suppose that you say to a tramp, "If you go around the corner to the clothing store, you may purchase an overcoat on my credit." It is a detriment to the tramp to make the walk, but the walk is not consideration because (on a reasonable construction) the walk was not requested as the price to be paid for the promise. It was merely a condition for a gratuitous promise. On the other hand, assume that Dotty writes to her sister-in-law: "If you will come down and take care of me, I promise you a place to raise your family." If the sister-in-law moves down to live with Dotty, then the sister-in-law has incurred legal detriment, which is a legal benefit to Dotty. The sister-in-law's move was thus bargained for as a trade for Dotty's promise.

3. Adequacy of Consideration

Historically, it has not been a function of law to make value judgments or economic judgments concerning contracts voluntarily entered into by the parties. As a general rule, courts have not attempted to weigh the consideration received by each party to determine if it is fair in the light of that which the other party gave. It has been sufficient in law if a party received something of legal value for which he bargained. The law is concerned only with the existence of consideration, not with its value. It does not inquire into the question of whether the bargain was a good one or bad one for either party. In the absence of fraud, oppression, undue influence, illegality, or statutory limitation, parties have been free to make any contract they please. The fact that it is onerous or burdensome for one or the other has been immaterial. The following case is typical of those finding consideration of questionable value.

CASE

Shirley Ellis retained the services of attorney Kandel after she and her children sustained personal injuries in an automobile accident. Ellis, apparently dissatisfied with Kandel's representation, subsequently retained attorney Vogelhut under a 40 percent contingent fee agreement. Vogelhut wrote a letter to Kandel advising Kandel of his retention by Ellis and requesting all the information Kandel had concerning this matter.

When Kandel delivered the files to Vogelhut, he obtained a receipt for them and an agreement that Vogelhut would pay Kandel 25 percent of any fee received in the Ellis case. When the case was settled, Kandel sued to collect his share of the fee.

ISSUE: Is the surrender of files by a discharged attorney adequate consideration to support a promise by the successor attorney to share a percentage of any fee received?

DECISION: Yes.

REASONS: 1. It is the basic contract law that courts generally will not inquire as to the adequacy of consideration.

2. Anything that fulfills the requirements of consideration, that is, one recognized as legal, will support a promise, whatever may be the comparative value of the consideration and of the thing promised.
3. A benefit to the promisor or a detriment to the promisee is sufficient valuable consideration to support a contract. Legal detriment means giving up something that immediately prior thereto the promise was privileged to retain, or doing or refraining from doing something that he was then privileged not to do, or not to refrain from doing.

Vogelhut v. Kandel, 517 A.2d 1092 (Md. 1986).

Today, this philosophy has changed somewhat. The Uniform Commercial Code provides that contracts that are so one-sided as to be unconscionable may be unenforceable [2-302]. Courts as well as legislative bodies have attempted to protect consumers by changing the historical view of one-sided contracts. These matters are discussed further in subsequent chapters dealing with consumer protection and illegal contracts.

4. Recitals of Consideration

Many written contracts have a provision reciting that there is consideration. The contract may state "For, and in consideration of, the mutual promises exchanged, the parties agree as follows." If the recital takes this form, "For, and in consideration of, $1 in hand paid," and so on, an issue may be raised related to the presence of consideration. Nominal consideration will generally validate a promise especially if it is paid. However, *sham* consideration will not. The recital of $1, even if it is paid, may be a sham (pretense). A sham is a recital of fact contrary to fact. The recital of consideration may be a sham—not because $1 is economically inadequate—but because it is not a material inducing factor. Although consideration does not have to be the sole inducement, it must be one inducement to making a promise. If out of friendship I sell you my valuable horse for $30, my promise is supported by consideration. Your detriment (paying $30) need not be the sole inducement, but it must at least be some inducement to my promise to sell. This requirement establishes the bargain, as the following case illustrates.

CASE

In an agreement dated January 10, 1972, Thomas Weinsaft gave his son, Nicholas, the option to purchase all his stock in the Crane Company upon his death. After Thomas died, Nicholas gave notice to the administrator of Thomas's estate that he was exercising the option to buy the stock. An heir of Thomas objected in this action and asserted the agreement was not supported by consideration. The agreement had this recital: "In consideration of $10 and other good and valuable consideration, including the inducement of (Nicholas) to remain the chief executive officer of the Crane Company."

ISSUE: Was the recital of consideration sufficient to validate the contract?
DECISION: Yes.

REASONS: 1. The recitation of consideration in an agreement is prima facie evidence that consideration to support the agreement was present. It creates a presumption that the recitals are true, which presumption continues unless overcome by evidence to the contrary.
2. The objecting heir produced no contrary evidence.

In re Estate of Weinsaft, 647 S.W.2d 179 (Mo. App. 1983).

There is an exception for option contracts, because the business community customarily expects them to be valid. Consequently, the law does accept a recital of $1 if there is a signed writing in a business context involving either an option contract or a guarantee of credit. An exception also exists in many states regarding recitals of consideration in *deeds* conveying real estate.

MUTUALITY OF OBLIGATION

5. Introduction

Mutuality *The binding of both parties in every contract. Each party to the contract must be bound to the other party to do something by virtue of the legal duty created.*

The doctrine of *mutuality of obligation* applies only to bilateral contracts. In a bilateral contract, each party must be bound, or neither party is bound. The problem of **mutuality** arises when one party tries to show that a promise is defective in that it does not promise anything. Since the promise is defective, it cannot provide consideration to support the other promise. When a promise is not supported by consideration, one party is not legally bound. Thus, since one party is not bound, neither is the other. One party *tries* to show that a promise is defective because it fails under one of the following:

- The promise is *illusory* (sections 6 and 7).
- A promisor is already bound (*preexisting duty*) to do what he promises to do (sections 8–12).
- The promise is to forbear from suing, but the promisor has an *invalid claim* (no right to sue) (section 13).

The following sections discuss these special problems of mutuality of obligation.

6. Illusory Promises

Illusory *That which has a false appearance. If that which appears to be a promise is not a promise, it is said to be illusory.*

An **illusory** promise is not a promise at all. What purports to be a promise is not one because the promisor need not perform it. There must be some restriction on the promisor's ability to avoid the promise; otherwise the promise cannot be construed as providing consideration. Courts require that there be a *possibility* that the promisor will incur legal detriment, otherwise the promisor's promise is illusory. In a typical illusory promise, the promisor's promise is conditional. The first step is to analyze the nature of the condition and determine if the condition is based on something beyond the promisor's control or within his control. An examination of many promises often reveals that there is in fact no promise at all. The following case illustrates a typical situation in which one party has not actually promised to do anything.

CASE

De Los Santos entered into a contract with Great Western Sugar to haul Great Western Sugar's beets. The contract specified that De Los Santos would haul "such tonnage of beets as may be loaded by the Company from piles at the beet receiving stations of the Company, and unload said beets at such factory or factories as may be designated by the Company. The term of this contract shall be from October 1, 1980 until February 15, 1981." Great Western Sugar terminated De Los Santos approximately two months after De Los Santos began transporting the beets. De Los Santos knew Great Western Sugar had entered into contracts with other contractors to carry the beets as well. De Los Santos sued, claiming that the termination constituted a breach of contract because "he was entitled to continue to haul until all of the beets had been transported to the factory." The trial court entered summary judgment for the defendant.

ISSUE: Did the trial court correctly enter summary judgment for Great Western Sugar in this action?

DECISION: Yes.

REASONS:
1. Where a promisor agrees to purchase services from the promisee on a per unit basis, but the agreement specifies no quantity and the parties did not intend that the promisor should take all of his needs from the promisee, there is no enforceable agreement, and the promisor is not obligated to accept any services from the promisee and may terminate the relationship without liability other than to pay for the services accepted.
2. Defendant's right to control the amount of beets put on plaintiff's truck was a right of termination at any point in time. The contract was void in its unexecuted portions because of the absence of mutuality.
3. Great Western was not obligated to use any of the services of De Los Santos, and thus no action arises for termination of De Los Santos.

De Los Santos v. Great Western Sugar Co., 348 N.W.2d 842 (Neb. 1984).

When the promise is conditioned on a fortuitous event (something beyond either party's control), the promise is not illusory.

EXAMPLE: I promise to buy your car for $2,500 if it rains tomorrow or if I am hired by the TNT Corporation or if the Atlanta Braves win the next World Series. Since it is possible that it will rain or that I will get the job or Atlanta may win, there is a possibility that I will have to buy your car (legal detriment).

If the condition is within the total control of the promisor, then the promise may be illusory.

EXAMPLE: "If I decide to buy a car, I'll buy yours" or "I'll buy your car if I am fully satisfied with its performance" or "I'll buy your car, but I can cancel at anytime." Since the condition in each example is within the promisor's control, the promise is illusory.

Many promises are partially within the control of one party or the other. Such promises are not illusory if there are duties implied on the promisor or the condition is met. If the condition is one of personal satisfaction for instance, courts will usually restrict the promisor's free will by imposing a promise that any dissatisfaction must be in good faith. Thus a promise to buy goods if satisfied is not illusory, since the promisor cannot refuse the goods unless actually dissatisfied. Another example is the implied promise to use best efforts regarding the condition. If I promise to buy your car only if I get a bank loan, courts will imply that I promised to use reasonable diligence to get a loan. I must take affirmative action (detriment) to attempt to satisfy the condition.

7. Requirement and Output Contracts

Requirement contracts ("I'll buy all the widgits I need from you this year") and *output contracts* ("I'll sell you all the widgits I manufacture") are not illusory. Courts find them enforceable because the seller of output or buyer of requirements has incurred legal detriment in that he has given up the right to sell to or buy from others. The Code explicitly enforces these contracts with a rule against unreasonably disproportionate quantities [2-306]. Both parties must act in good faith in their outputs or requirements. Moreover, the fact that a party to either contract might go out of business does not make the contract illusory. The Code provides protection by requiring "that no quantity unreasonably disproportionate to any stated estimate or in the absence of a stated estimate to any normal or otherwise comparable prior output or requirements may be tendered or demanded" [2-306](1)]. Therefore the promisor must conduct his business in good faith and pursuant to commercially reasonable standards, so that his output or requirements will approximate a reasonably foreseeable figure.

8. Preexisting Duty

The *preexisting duty rule* is a second way in which a party may claim no mutuality of obligation. When one promises to do what he is already legally obligated to do or promises to refrain from what he legally cannot do, then the promisor incurs no legal detriment. Therefore it is traditionally stated that a promise to perform or the performance of an existing duty is not consideration. The preexisting duty may be a duty imposed by law or a contractual duty. Notice that in the following case the plaintiff was not a law enforcement official but was performing a contractual duty.

CASE

Wells Fargo offered a $25,000 reward for information leading to the arrest and conviction of the person who shot a Wells Fargo guard. Slattery, a licensed polygraph operator, is employed by the government to interrogate persons suspected by law enforcement agencies. During a polygraph exam on an unrelated matter, a suspect admitted to Slattery that he had shot and killed the Wells Fargo guard. Slattery furnished this information to Wells Fargo, and the suspect was convicted. Slattery sued to recover the $25,000 reward.

ISSUE: Did Slattery provide consideration to validate the reward offer?

DECISION: No.

REASONS: 1. Slattery was under a preexisting contractual duty to furnish law enforcement agencies with all useful information revealed to him through interrogations. When Slattery gave the information about the killer to the authorities, he was only doing what he was bound to do as part of his employment.

2. The performance of a preexisting duty does not constitute consideration necessary to support a contract.

Slattery v. Wells Fargo Armored Service Corp., 366 So.2d 157 (Fla. 1979).

The problem of preexisting obligations has arisen in various situations. It is possible to categorize these situations under three headings: modification of non-Code contracts, modification of Code contracts, and discharge of debts.

9. Modification of Non-Code Contracts

Since the agreement to do that which one is already obligated to do does not constitute consideration, a subsequent agreement modifying an existing contract must be supported by new consideration independent of the consideration contained in the original agreement. Assume that one party to the contract refuses to continue performance unless and until the terms of the contract are modified. To ensure performance, the other party may assent to the demands and agree to terms that are more burdensome than those provided in the agreement. He may agree to pay more or accept less, but as a general rule the new promise in many cases is not supported by consideration. An employee may seek more money for the work he is already contractually bound to do, or a contractor may want more pay for the same work and materials specified in the original contract. In either case, the employee and contractor do not incur legal detriment to support the promise to modify.

Although some modifications are in bad faith or even extortionate, many are in good faith and should be validated. Assuming good-faith dealings, courts will find exceptions to the preexisting duty rule by using any of these rationales: (1) new or different duties, (2) unforeseen difficulties, and (3) rescission.

Changes in duties. If the promisor agrees to assume a new duty, give something in addition, or vary the preexisting duty (e.g., accelerating performance) the promise supplies consideration to support the promised modification. Usually an owner who promises a contractor an additional sum to complete a job under contract is not legally bound to pay the additional sum. If, however, the promisee (contractor) agrees to do anything other than, or different from, that which the original contract required, consideration is provided. The contractor who agrees to complete his work at an earlier date or in a different manner may recover on a promise by the owner to pay an additional amount.

Unforeseen difficulties. The parties to a contract often make provisions for contingencies that may arise during the course of the performance of the contract. Wisely, they recognize that problems may arise and make performance more difficult. Frequently, however, contracting parties do not provide for any contingencies, or they make some that do not encompass all the difficulties that may render performance by either party more burdensome than anticipated. In the absence of an appropriate contract clause, two questions are raised when unanticipated difficulties arise during the course of performance: (1) Will the party whose performance is rendered more difficult be required to complete performance without any adjustment in compensation? and (2) Will a promise to pay an additional sum because of the difficulty be enforceable?

Excuses for breach of contract are discussed in Chapter 15. For purposes of this discussion, it must be recognized that additional hardship is not an excuse for breach of contract as a general rule. Thus the answer to the first question is usually yes. Difficulties do not excuse performance.

The second question assumes that a promisor, although not required to do so, has promised to pay an additional sum because of the difficulty. Courts hold that where a truly unforeseen difficulty arises, and because of it a promise to pay an additional sum is made, the promise is legally valid and will be enforced. There is a definite trend toward finding consideration when the parties have agreed to a modification, as the following case illustrates.

CASE

Defendant entered into a contract with a city to collect all the trash in the city for five years for an agreed-upon compensation. The number of required collections increased substantially, and the city agreed to pay an additional $10,000 per year because of the increased amount of trash. Plaintiff, a group of citizens of the city, objected to the increased payments and sought to recover the $20,000 paid over a two-year period.

ISSUE: Was the promise to pay an additional sum enforceable?

DECISION: Yes.

REASONS:
1. The general rule is that a promise to pay more for work already required to be performed is not enforceable. There is an exception to this general rule for unforeseen difficulties.
2. The modern trend of cases recognizes that courts should enforce agreements modifying contracts when unexpected or unanticipated difficulties arise during the course of the performance of a contract, as long as the parties agree voluntarily to the modification.
3. The city was not required to promise to pay an additional sum, but when it did so, the promise was enforceable.

Angel v. Murray, 322 A.2d 630 (R.I. 1974).

Unforeseen difficulties are those that seldom occur and are extraordinary in nature. Price changes, strikes, inclement weather, and shortage of material occur frequently and are not considered unforeseen. Thus it may be that a person who has contracted to build a building finds that the cost of materials has risen since he entered the contract, or he may be faced with a carpenters' strike. Nevertheless, he must perform at the original price unless he has made provisions in the contract that some relief shall be given when such things occur.

Rescission. If the contract is rescinded, there is no longer a preexisting duty problem. The parties are now free to make a new contract on whatever terms they desire.

Note that there are three contracts involved: (1) the original contract, (2) the rescission contract, and (3) the new contract. Further, note that rescission is generally not presumed, so the facts must show an actual rescission, such as tearing up the original contract.

10. Modification of Code Contracts

The Code has made substantial inroads into the validation element of a contract, especially regarding alteration or modification of contracts by not requiring consideration to support the changes.

No consideration. Under the Code, parties to a binding contract for the sale of goods may change the terms; and if the change is mutually agreeable, no consideration is required to make it binding [2-209(1)]. This means that if a buyer agrees with the seller to pay more than the contract price for goods purchased, he will be held to the higher price. To illustrate: A car manufacturer entered into a contract with a tire dealer to purchase a certain number of tires at a stated price. Thereafter, the dealer told the manufacturer that because of higher production and labor costs, he would need to be paid $5 more per tire in order to carry on with the contract. If the automaker agrees to pay the additional sum, its promise to do so will be binding even though there is no consideration present for the new promise.

Good faith. The Code section that sustains modifications of a contract without any additional consideration could, if not limited in some way, permit a party with a superior bargaining position to take advantage of the other party to a contract. Accordingly, the Code provides that the parties must act in good faith, and the exercise of bad faith in order to escape the duty to perform under the original terms is not permitted. The "extortion" of a modification without a legitimate reason therefore is ineffective, because it violates the good-faith requirement.

To safeguard against false allegations that oral modifications have been made, it is permissible to include in the contract a provision that modifications are not effective unless they are set forth in a signed writing [2-209(2)]. If a consumer enters into such a contract, in addition to signing the contract he must sign the restrictive provision, to assure that he is aware of the limitation. Otherwise, it is not effective. If the restrictive provision is not signed, a consumer is entitled to rely upon oral modifications. The provision is apparently designed to protect the unwary consumer against reliance upon statements made to him that certain provisions of the contract do not apply to him or that others are subject to oral change. He is entitled to be forewarned not to rely upon anything but the printed word, and it is expected that the double signing will bring this message to his attention.

The Code allows necessary and desirable modifications of sales contracts without regard to technicalities that hamper such adjustments under traditional contract law. The safeguards against improper and unfair use of this freedom are found in the requirements of good faith and the "observance of reasonable commercial standards of fair dealing in the trade." There is recognition of the fact that changes and adjustments in sales contracts are daily occurrences and that the parties do not cancel their old contract and execute an entirely new one each time a change or modification is required.

11. Discharge of Liquidated Debts and Claims

As previously noted, if the consideration on each side of an agreement involves money, the consideration must be equal. Because of this rule, a debtor and creditor cannot make an enforceable agreement to have a liquidated debt of a fixed amount discharged upon payment of less than the amount agreed to be owing. In other words, there is no consideration for the agreement to accept less than the full amount owed. In most states the unpaid portion is collectible even though the lesser sum has been paid. If there is no dispute as to the amount owed, a debtor who sends in a check for less than the amount of the indebtedness and marks on the check "paid in full" will still be liable for the balance due.

Payment of a lesser sum is only performance of an existing duty; it cannot serve as consideration for a release of the balance. However, if there is sufficient evidence that the creditor intended a gift of the balance to the debtor, then the creditor may not recover the balance. A paid-in-full receipt given to the debtor by the creditor is usually regarded as evidence (though not conclusive) that a gift was intended. Likewise, where the debt is evidenced by a note, the cancellation and return of the note upon receipt of part payment is evidence that a gift of the balance was intended.

Just as a promise to pay an additional sum for the completion of an existing contract is enforceable if the promisee does something other than, or in addition to, the required performance, a debtor may obtain a discharge of the debt by paying a lesser sum than the amount owing if he gives the creditor something in addition to the money. The settlement at the lower figure will then be binding on the creditor. Since the value of consideration is ordinarily unimportant, the added consideration may take any form. Payment in advance of the due date, payment at a place other than that agreed upon, surrender of the privilege of bankruptcy, and substitution of a secured note for less than the face of the debt have all been found sufficient to discharge a larger amount than that paid. The mere giving of an unsecured note for a lesser sum than the entire debt will not release the debtor of his duty to pay the balance. The note is only a promise to pay; consequently, the promise to pay less than is due will not discharge the debt.

12. Discharge of Unliquidated Debts and Claims

Whereas a liquidated debt involves no question that the debt is due and payable, an unliquidated debt is a disputed debt. The dispute may involve the amount owed, the time or manner of payment, or related matters. An unliquidated debt may be subject to a compromise settlement. For example, when one party has a claim against another party and the amount due is disputed, a compromise settlement at a figure between the amount claimed or demanded and the amount admitted to be owing is binding on the parties. Payment of money that one party claims is not owed is consideration for the other party's loss of the right to litigate the dispute.

Accord and satisfaction
An agreement between two persons—one of whom has a right of action against the other—that the latter should do or give, and the former accept, something in satisfaction of the right of action—something different from, and usually less than, what might legally be enforced.

It does not matter whether the claim is one arising from a dispute that is contractual in nature, such as one involving damaged merchandise, or is tortious in character, such as one rising from an automobile accident. The compromise figure agreed to by both parties operates as a contract to discharge the claim. This kind of settlement contract is known legally as an **accord and satisfaction**.

An accord and satisfaction is a fully executed contract between a debtor and a creditor to settle a disputed claim. The accord consists of an agreement whereby one of the parties is to do something different by way of performance than that called for by the contract. This accord is satisfied when the substituted performance is completed and accepted by the other party. Both must be established. The cashing of a check marked "paid in full" when it is tendered to settle a *disputed* claim is a typical example of an accord and satisfaction. Keep in mind that the dispute must be in good faith.

An accord may be either oral or written. For an accord and satisfaction to discharge a claim, the claim must be disputed between the parties. If the creditor is not aware of the dispute, the cashing of a check tendered in the usual course of business with a "full payment" notation will not operate as an accord and satisfaction. An accord, like any other agreement, requires a meeting of the minds. An accord will not be implied from ambiguous language. In other words, the intent to settle the dispute must be clear.

13. Forbearance

Consideration, which usually takes the form of a promise or an action, may take the opposite form: **forbearance** from acting or a promise to forbear from taking some action. The law also considers the waiver of a right or the forbearance to exercise a right to be sufficient consideration for a contract. The right that is waived or not exercised may be one that exists either at law or in equity. It may be a waiver of a right that one has against someone other than the promisor who bargains for such a waiver.

Forbearance *Giving up the right to enforce what one honestly believes to be a valid claim, in return for a promise. It is sufficient "consideration" to make a promise binding.*

There are numerous other examples of forbearances that may constitute consideration. Relinquishment of alleged rights in an estate will furnish consideration to support a return promise to pay money. An agreement by the seller of a business not to compete with the person who has bought a business from him is another example of forbearance. Mutual promises to forbear are sufficient to support each other. They are commonly used as a part of a settlement of a dispute, as illustrated by the following case.

CASE

Mary Veilleux signed a contract to purchase a house, but before the closing she discovered that the house had a leaky basement. She attended the closing but said she would not pay until the seller (Merrill Lynch) promised to repair the basement. Merrill Lynch promised to repair it and she paid the purchase price. Merrill Lynch hired someone to repair the basement but after the work was done, the basement still leaked. Mary hired another company to fix the leak. She presented the repair bill to Merrill Lynch, which refused to pay. She brought suit to collect the repair bill. The defendant contended that there was no consideration for the promise to repair.

ISSUE: Was there consideration to support Merrill Lynch's promise to repair the basement?

DECISION: Yes.

REASONS: 1. At the time of closing Mary Veilleux made it clear that she would not proceed with the closing until she was assured the basement would be repaired. At that time she could have sought a court action to rescind the contract. She did not because the seller promised to repair.

2. When she paid the closing costs, she agreed not to sue. She gave up a valuable right.
3. The law is well settled that forebearance, or the promise of forebearance, to prosecute a well-founded or doubtful claim is sufficient consideration for a contract.

Veilleux v. Merrill Lynch Relocation Mgt., 309 S.E.2d 595 (Va. 1983).

Although forbearances generally constitute consideration, a problem can arise when the forbearance is a promise not to bring a lawsuit. Clearly, a promise to forbear from suing is a legal detriment and, if bargained for is valid consideration. The problem arises when the underlying claim is invalid. Arguably, a promise not to sue on an invalid claim really promises nothing, since the promisor has no claim on which to sue. Older cases held that the promise regarding the invalid claim was not legal detriment. Modern courts hold that a promise to surrender or forbear from suing on an invalid claim is consideration, provided two matters are proved: the promisor thought the claim was valid (subjective honesty); and the claim had some reasonable basis in law and in fact (objective test). The general rule now is that surrender of or forbearance to assert an invalid claim is detriment if the claim is asserted in good faith and is not unreasonable.

CONTRACTS VALID WITHOUT CONSIDERATION

14. Promissory Estoppel

When bargained-for consideration is not present, a court may nonetheless validate a promise based on *promissory estoppel*. A good way to view promissory estoppel (sometimes called *detrimental reliance*) is to see it as unbargained-for detriment. When a promisor's promise induces a promisee's detriment, this validation device estops the promisor from denying contractual duties because of a lack of consideration. Promissory estoppel forces the promisor to live up to his promise.

The doctrine of promissory estoppel is equitable in nature in that it compensates for harm which is caused by a promise when the harm is reasonably foreseeable by the promisor. Promissory estoppel involves as a promise which the promisor should reasonably expect [foresee] to induce a detrimental change of position by the promisee. There is reliance on the promise and a change of position. The promise is binding if injustice can be avoided only by enforcement of the promise. And the remedy granted may be as limited as justice requires. A classic example demonstrates the main elements of promissory estoppel. Uncle, knowing that Nephew is going to college, promises Nephew that he will give him $5,000 to buy a car on completion of his degree. Nephew goes to college and borrows $4,000 to buy a car. When Nephew has nearly completed his degree, Uncle notifies him that he revokes his promise. Promissory estoppel makes Uncle's promise legally binding. First, Uncle should have reasonably expected Nephew to buy a car, since Nephew knows that he will soon receive $5,000. Second, Nephew did in fact rely on the promise by borrowing $4,000 to buy a car. Third, justice under these facts require the promise to be binding. Finally, Nephew should receive only $4,000 because the remedy should be limited to the change of position, as justice requires.

The doctrine of promissory estoppel is limited in its application and provides only a limited means of enforcing promises that fail to pass the test of consideration. Although the modern tendency is to apply the doctrine to a wide variety of situations, it has been used frequently in the following situations:

1. Bidding on construction projects. The cases hold that a subcontractor's bid is irrevocable if used by the general contractor in submitting his bid for the primary contract.
2. Promised pensions and other employee benefits. Notwithstanding the fact that the employee continues to work (preexisting duty and hence no consideration), courts validate employer promises of benefits by using promissory estoppel.
3. Promises of dealer franchises. The doctrine of promissory estoppel has been used to permit recovery when there has been justifiable reliance upon preliminary negotiations, wherein a franchise was promised.

15. Moral Obligation

A promisor may from time to time make a promise based on his or her individual view of ethics and morality. The promisor feels some *moral obligation* to make a promise and to perform that promise. As a general rule, such promises are not supported by consideration, and an obligation arising out of ethics and morality alone is not enforceable.

Notwithstanding the general rule that bargained-for consideration must be present, moral obligation is sometimes used to validate a promise lacking consideration. Moral obligation in such cases may be seen as arising from an unbargained-for benefit. Some benefit previously received by the promisor is said to induce the later promise. The promise then becomes enforceable because of the moral obligation resulting from the benefit previously received. This theory is used to validate a subsequent promise only when the past benefit is a material one. Examples of such benefits conferred: someone rescues and repairs another's boat; medical services are rendered to an unconscious person; a person is injured in saving another's life. Then there is a subsequent promise by the benefited party to pay the person who gave the benefit.

Obligations discharged by law may later be the subject matter of a new promise. Such promises also may be enforceable under the moral obligation theory. For example, a new promise to pay a debt may be enforceable without consideration even though it has been discharged in bankruptcy or barred by a statute of limitations (a statute that cuts off a claim if no suit is brought within a stated time period). Some courts state that the past debt, together with the moral obligation to pay, is sufficient to validate the new promise to pay the debt. A court can infer a new promise from part payment of a debt barred by the statute of limitations, but an express written promise is required for debts discharged in bankruptcy. There are some other special rules on reaffirming debts discharged in bankruptcy. These are covered by federal law and are discussed in Chapter 45.

16. Firm Offers and Renunciations

As noted in Chapter 9, firm offers are irrevocable without consideration. More specifically, under the Code a written offer by a merchant to buy or sell goods is not revocable for lack of consideration during the time for it to remain open (but not to exceed three months). If no time is stated, it is irrevocable for a reasonable time, but again not to exceed three months.

Either party may voluntarily renounce or waive any right or claim arising out of a breach of contract. Such a renunciation or waiver is valid without consideration, provided it is in writing. A renunciation or waiver is recognized by both the Code and the common law.

CHAPTER SUMMARY

Bargain Theory of Consideration

The Three Elements of a Bargain	1. Promisee must suffer legal detriment. 2. The promise must induce the detriment. 3. The detriment must induce the promise.
Adequacy of Consideration	1. Courts will not normally inquire into the adequacy of consideration. 2. Exception: Inadequacy may be evidence of fraud, duress, or undue influence.
Recitals of Consideration	1. Sham consideration: Failure to pay the recited amount renders the contract unenforceable. 2. Nominal consideration: The recited amount, even if nominal, is sufficient if bargained for.

Mutuality of Obligation

Illusory Promises	1. A promise is illusory if there is no restriction on a party's freedom of action. 2. A promise is not illusory if based on the occurrence of conditions.
Requirement and Output Contracts	1. Requirements and output contracts generally are not illusory and thus are enforceable.
Preexisting Duty	1. If a promisor is already legally bound to do the thing promised, there is no consideration present to support the promise made.
Modification of Non-Code Contracts	1. In general, non-Code modifications must be supported by consideration. 2. Non-Code modifications are valid if new duties are assumed, unforeseeable difficulties occur, or a rescission of the original contract occurs.
Modification of Code Contracts	1. In general, modifications of Code contracts are enforceable even though consideration is lacking. 2. Modifications of Code contracts are valid if the modifications are made in good faith (i.e., made for a legitimate commercial reason).
Discharge of Debts	1. The payment of a lesser sum than a liquidated debt or claim cannot serve as consideration for a release of the balance. 2. A promise to forbear from suing on an unliquidated debt or claim is sufficient consideration, and a binding compromise results. 3. An accord and satisfaction is one example of how unliquidated debts are discharged.
Forbearance	1. Refraining from doing something that a party has a right to do is called forbearance.

2. In general, forbearance is consideration to validate another's promise.
3. A promise not to sue on valid claim is consideration.
4. A promise not to sue on invalid claim is consideration if promisor in good faith thinks the claim is valid and the claim is reasonable in law and fact.

Contracts Valid Without Consideration

Promissory Estoppel

1. A promise induces promisee to rely detrimentally on promise.
2. Elements: (a) Promisor should reasonably expect promisee to rely; (b) promisee relies to his detriment; (c) injustice can be avoided only by enforcing promise; and (d) remedy may be as limited as justice requires.

Moral Obligation

1. Moral obligation will validate a subsequent promise when the moral duty was previously a legal duty.
2. Moral obligation may validate a promise to pay for material benefits previously received.

Firm Offers and Renunciation

1. Firm offers are irrevocable even though they are not supported by consideration.
2. A renunciation is a waiver of a right or claim arising under a contract.
3. A renunciation is enforceable without supporting consideration if it is in writing.

REVIEW QUESTIONS AND PROBLEMS

1. Match each term in column A with the appropriate statement in column B.

A	B
(1) Accord and satisfaction	(a) Renunciation.
(2) Adequacy of consideration	(b) Validation device (unbargained-for benefit to promisor).
(3) Sham consideration.	(c) No possibility promisor will incur legal detriment.
(4) Written waiver of contract right	(d) Fully executed contract between debtor and creditor to settle disputed claim.
(5) Illusory promise	(e) Promisor is already bound to do matter promised.
(6) Preexisting duty	(f) Courts will not inquire into this.
(7) Mutuality of obligation	(g) Failure to pay consideration recited.
(8) Promissory estoppel	(h) Both parties are bound or nobody is bound.
(9) Moral obligation	(i) Promise valid if good-faith claim is reasonable in fact and law.
(10) Promise not to sue on invalid claim	(j) Validation device (unbargained-for detriment to promisee).

2. Dickinson was employed by Auto Center under an oral contract terminable at will. His employer agreed to sell him part ownership of the business but later refused to do so. When sued for breach of contract, Auto Center contended that there was no consideration for its promise to sell. Was it correct? Explain.

3. Brenner made a contract to enroll his son in the Little Red School House for the next school year and paid tuition of $1,080. Brenner's former wife had legal custody of his son, and she refused to enroll the boy. Brenner sought a refund. The school promised a refund, but later it refused to pay it. When Brenner sued for the promised refund,

the school defended that Brenner had incurred no legal detriment to support its promise to pay the tuition refund. Was there consideration for the school's promise to refund the tuition? Explain.

4. Humphrey pays Doug $250 for a sixty-day option to buy Doug's farm. Near the end of the option period, Humphrey asks for and gets a fifteen-day extension. No money was paid for the extension. After the original sixty-day period but within the fifteen-day extension, Doug withdraws the offer. Can Doug legally revoke the offer? Why or why not?

5. Burt pays $1 in return for a thirty-day option to purchase real estate from Reynold for $100,000. The next day Reynold tries to revoke the option. Can Reynold revoke? Why or why not?

6. Jackson Hole Builders sold Piros three condominium units that were to be built by Jackson Hole. The sales contract provided that Jackson Hole could terminate the sale contract if Jackson Hole could not sell a sufficient number of units to finance the project. The sales were made and the units were built. Piros later refused to pay for his units and Jackson Hole sued. Piros defended that the unilateral right of Jackson Hole to terminate that contract made it illusory and lacking in mutuality of obligation. Did the provision allowing Jackson Hole to terminate the contract if presale of the units would not raise enough construction capital made the contract void for lack of mutuality? Why or why not?

7. Widgit, a manufacturer of widgits, agreed to supply Midgit all the widgits that Midgit needed in his gidgit business. For several years prior to this agreement, Midgit used between 2,500 and 3,000 Widgit widgits per month. In the sixth month, Midgit ordered 10,000 widgits. Widgit said it would not honor the order. Is this a valid agreement? Is Widgit liable to Midgit for breach of contract? Why or why not?

8. Jack, a golf course architect, agrees with Sneed to direct a current construction project for a fixed fee of $5,000. During the course of the project, Jack, without excuse, takes away his plans and refuses to continue, and Sneed promises him an extra fee of $2,000 if Jack will resume work. Is Jack's resumption of work consideration for Sneed's promise of the extra fee? Explain.

9. Burgamy made a contract to furnish material and labor for plumbing modifications in Davis's house. A dispute developed over the amount that Davis owed Burgamy. Davis drafted a check on which he wrote "Payment of account IN FULL." When Burgamy received the check, he crossed out what Davis had written and wrote in "Paid on Account," and deposited it. Was there an accord and satisfaction? Explain.

10. Baillie sold lumber to Kincaid who agreed to pay $5,000. Later having financial problems, Kincaid offered to pay 35 percent of the $5,000 in full satisfaction. Kincaid paid the 35 percent in two checks, which Baillie cashed. On the second and last check, Kincaid marked "Final Installment." Can Baillie now legally recover the 65 percent of the original amount due? Why or why not?

11. Bryant personally guaranteed the debt of TLC Corporation of which she was the sole shareholder. TLC was insolvent and had been dissolved at the time Bryant signed the guaranty. This guaranty recited that it was in consideration of the creditor not suing TLC. Is the guaranty enforceable? Why or why not?

12. Hoffman wanted to acquire a franchise from Red Owl Stores. Red Owl told Hoffman that if he would sell his bakery and buy a certain tract of land, he would be given a franchise. Hoffman did these things but was not given the promised franchise. Hoffman sued and Red Owl defended on the ground that there is no consideration to support the contract. Who won? Why?

13. When Mrs. Voight died, she owed her sons money. Although Mr. Voight had no obligation to pay the money owed by his wife to his stepsons, he signed two notes for $13,500 each to the stepsons. Are the notes enforceable? Why or why not?

14. Harpo employs Zeppo to repair a vacant house. By mistake, Zeppo repairs the house next door, which belongs to Groucho. Groucho later promises to pay Zeppo the value of the repairs. Is Groucho's promise binding? What results if the reasonable value of the repairs is $400 and Groucho promises to pay $600 but later refuses to pay anything? Explain.

11 Contractual Capacity and Genuine Assent

C H A P T E R   P R E V I E W

BUSINESS MANAGEMENT DECISION

You are a sales manager for an automobile dealer. One of your salespeople wants to contract with a sixteen-year-old who is going to make a $1,000 down payment and sign a promissory note in the amount of the remainder of the purchase price.

Should you approve this sale?

In Chapter 8 it was noted that a contract has four elements:

1. Offer and acceptance
2. Consideration
3. Legal capacity
4. Legal purpose

The first two elements have been explained in the preceding two chapters. This chapter explores the third element and Chapter 12 considers the fourth element. Furthermore, some contracts are legally required to be evidenced in writing. This requirement is discussed in Chapter 13. Assuming that offer, acceptance, and consideration are present, the agreement still may not be legally "operative," that is, legally enforceable. This chapter and the two that follow consider the policing process whereby courts decide which expressions of mutual assent are legally "operative" and which are "inoperative." This process can generally be classified under one of these headings:

1. *Avoidance and reformation* (this chapter): incapacity, mistake, fraud, misrepresentation, duress, and undue influence
2. *Public policy* (Chapter 12): illegality and unconscionability
3. *Form of the agreement* (Chapter 13): statute of frauds

A valid contract may be rendered inoperative through the equitable remedy of *rescission*. When a party has the right to disaffirm or rescind a contract, that contract is said to be *voidable*. All parties must have the legal capacity to give their consent. Some parties, such as infants, insane persons, and intoxicated persons, do not have the legal capacity to assent to contract terms and they can undo (rescind) their contracts. Even if a party has the legal ability to assent or consent, that consent may not be genuine. *Genuine* consent is not present when a contracting party promises because of a mistake, fraud, duress, or undue influence. In such cases, the contract is voidable by rescission because the consent given was not real or genuine.

INCAPACITY TO CONTRACT

1. Types of Incapacity

Incapacity refers to the mental state of a party to a contract. Capacity-to-contract issues generally involve minors, mental incompetents, intoxicated persons, and drug addicts. Incapacity that makes a contract voidable may be permanent or temporary. Minors and insane persons are presumed to lack capacity to contract.

A party without mental capacity to contract (if he has not been adjudicated insane) can avoid the contract or defend a suit for breach of contract on the grounds of lack of mental capacity. The contract is voidable only by the incapacitated party. No other party may raise the issue.

If a person has been judged insane, then the contract is void, not merely voidable. If a contract is disaffirmed by an insane person, he must return all the consideration or benefit received, assuming the other party has treated him in good faith. But if the contract is unconscionable or the other party has unfairly overreached, the incapacitated party can rescind by returning whatever he has left of the consideration received.

The test of insanity for avoiding a contract is different from the test of insanity for matters involving criminal intent, making a will, commitment to a mental institution, or other purposes. In contract law, the test is whether the party was capable of understanding the nature, purpose, and consequences of his acts at the time of contract formation. A party is incompetent if he is unable to act in a reasonable manner in relation to the transaction, and the other party has reason to know of this condition.

2. Minors' Contracts

The age of majority and capacity to contract has been lowered to eighteen in most states; however, the statutory law of each state must be examined to determine the age of majority for contract purposes. Just as there are several definitions of insanity, there are numerous laws that impose minimum age requirements.

A person below the age of capacity is called an *infant* or a *minor*. Minors have the right to avoid contracts. The law grants minors this right in order to promote justice and to protect them from their presumed immaturity, lack of judgment and experience, limited willpower, and imprudence. An adult deals with a minor at his own peril. A contract between an infant and an adult is voidable only by the infant. The right to disaffirm exists, irrespective of the fairness of the contract and whether or not the adult knew he was dealing with a minor. It even extends to contracts involving two minors.

Legislation in many states has, in a limited way, altered the right of minors to avoid their contracts. Purchase of life insurance or contracts with colleges or universities are binding, and some statutes take away the minor's right to avoid contracts after marriage. A few give the courts the right to approve contracts made by emancipated minors.

3. Voiding Contracts by Minors

A minor has the right to disaffirm contracts; but until steps are taken to void the contract, the minor remains liable. A minor can disaffirm a purely executory contract by directly informing the adult of the disaffirmance or by any conduct that clearly indicates an intent to disaffirm. If the contract has been fully or partially performed, the infant also can avoid it and obtain a return of his consideration. If the infant is in possession of consideration that is passed to him, he must return it to the other party. He cannot disaffirm the contract and at the same time retain the benefits.

The courts of various states are in conflict when an infant cannot return the property in the same condition in which he purchased it. The majority of the states hold that the infant may disaffirm the contract and demand the return of the consideration with which he has parted if he returns the property that he has left. A few courts, however, hold that if the contract is advantageous to the infant and if the adult has been fair in every respect, the contract cannot be disaffirmed unless the infant returns all the consideration received. These courts take into account the depreciation of the property while in the possession of the infant.

The minor may avoid both executed and executory contracts at any time during the minority and for a reasonable period of time after majority. What constitutes a reasonable time depends on the nature of the property involved and the specific circumstances. Many states establish a maximum period, such as one or two years.

4. Ratification

Ratification means "to approve and sanction, to make valid, or to confirm." It applies to the approval of a voidable transaction by one who previously had the right to disaffirm. Applied to contracts entered into by infants, it refers to conduct of a former minor after majority, conduct that indicates approval of, or satisfaction with, a contract. It eliminates the right to disaffirm.

Generally, an executed contract is ratified if the consideration is retained for an unreasonable time after majority. Ratification also results from acceptance of the benefits incidental to ownership, such as rents, dividends, or interest. A sale of the property received or any other act that clearly indicates satisfaction with the bargain made during minority will constitute a ratification. In general, a contract that is fully executory is disaffirmed by continued silence or inaction after reaching legal age. Ratification is not possible until the infant reaches legal age, because prior to that date the contract can always be avoided. The following case illustrates these principles.

CASE

Charles Smith, a minor, bought a car from Bobby Floars Toyota, and agreed to make thirty installment payments of $100 each. After making eleven payments, Smith was financially unable to continue his payments, so he voluntarily returned the car to Bobby Floars Toyota. At that time he had been an adult for ten months. When Bobby Floars Toyota sued Smith for the unpaid installments, Smith defended on the ground that he had disaffirmed the contract upon his becoming an adult. Bobby Floars Toyota asserted that Smith had not disaffirmed within a reasonable time after becoming an adult.

ISSUE: Did Smith's voluntary return of the car ten months after attaining the age of majority constitute a timely disaffirmance of his contract?

DECISION: No.

REASONS:
1. A minor upon becoming an adult has a reasonable time to disaffirm a contract. If he waits for an unreasonable time to disaffirm, he will be held to have ratified the contract.
2. Ten months is an unreasonable time within which to elect between disaffirmance and ratification of a contract for the sale of a car that is constantly depreciating in value.

3. Modern commercial transactions require that both buyers and sellers be responsible and prompt.

Bobby Floars Toyota, Inc. v. Smith, 269 S.E.2d 320 (N.C. 1980).

5. Minors' Liability for Necessaries

The law recognizes that certain transactions are clearly for the benefit of minors and hence are binding upon them. The term *necessaries* is used to describe the subject matter of such contracts. A minor is not liable in contract for necessaries; the liability is in quasi-contract. The fact that the liability is quasi-contractual has two significant features: The liability is not for the contract price of necessaries furnished, but rather for the reasonable value of the necessaries; and there is no liability on executory contracts, but only for necessaries actually furnished.

What are necessaries? In general, the term includes whatever is needed for a minor's subsistence as measured by his age, station in life, and all his surrounding circumstances. Food and lodging, medical services, education, and clothing are the general classifications of necessaries. It is often a close question as to whether a particular item or service is to be regarded as a necessary. Even housing may not be a necessary if furnished by parents, as the following case illustrates. This case represents the extreme degree of protection that some courts often give minors. It is a powerful example of why adults must be wary of contracting with minors.

CASE

The Webster Street Partnership rented an apartment to Sheridan and Wilwerding, knowing that the two renters were minors at the time of the lease. The two minors paid a security deposit and the rent for September and October. They did not pay rent for November, and on November 12 they were evicted. Webster Street sued the two minors for the November and December rent and for the cost of repairs and re-renting the apartment. Sheridan and Wilwerding counterclaimed for a return of the rent deposit and the rent paid, contending that they had no liability on the lease. At trial, Sheridan testified that he and Wilwerding had not been forced out of their homes when they rented the apartment but had moved out voluntarily and could have left the apartment and returned home at any time. The lower court found for Webster Street.

ISSUE: Was the lease enforceable against the two minors?

DECISION: No.

REASONS:

1. As a general rule, a minor does not have the capacity to bind himself by contract. This rule protects the minor by discouraging adults from contracting with him.
2. However, there are exceptions to this rule. For example, a minor is liable for the value of necessaries furnished him. In situations involving necessaries, a contract is implied by law, and the minor is liable under this quasi-contract, even though the agreement between the minor and the other party is unenforceable.
3. The facts of each individual case determine whether an item is a necessary. Something obviously and clearly requisite for the maintenance of existence is a necessary, but beyond this category one must examine the specific facts and circumstances

of each case, including the minor's social position, fortune, health, and other factors.

4. Both of these minors could return home at any time. Therefore the apartment was not a necessary, and the contract is voidable. While this application of the rule may seem unfair, it reaches a desirable result because it discourages landlords from providing shelter to minors who can freely return home, thus compelling minors to remain with their parents.
5. Therefore Sheridan and Wilwerding had the right to avoid the lease, either during their minority or within a reasonable time after reaching majority. Their disaffirmance completely put an end to the lease, putting the parties in the same position as if no lease had ever existed. Both the minors and Webster can recover whatever they gave to the other party.
6. Therefore Sheridan and Wilwerding can recover the security deposit and the rent paid and are relieved of any further obligation under the lease. The trial court's judgment is reversed, and the case is remanded.

Webster Street Partnership, Ltd. v. Sheridan, 368 N.W.2d 439 (Neb. 1985).

6. Third-Party Rights

If an infant sells goods to an adult, the latter obtains only a voidable title to the goods. The infant can disaffirm and recover possession from the adult buyer. At common law, even a good-faith purchaser of property formerly belonging to a minor could not retain the property if the minor elected to rescind. This rule has been changed under the Code. It provides that a person with voidable title has "power to transfer a good title to a good-faith purchaser for value" [2-430]. The common law rule, however, is still applicable to sales of real property by minors. If Minor sells his farm to Adult, who in turn sells the farm to Good-Faith Purchaser, Minor may avoid against Good-Faith Purchaser and regain the farm. You may think that's unfair, but remember that Minor's name appears in the record books and is in the chain of title. Minor must return all remaining consideration to Adult. Adult, in turn, is liable on the warranty deed to Good-Faith Purchaser for failing to convey clear title.

MISTAKE

7. Introduction

Mistake is some unintended act, omission, or error that arises from ignorance, surprise, imposition, or misplaced confidence. A variety of mistakes may occur in forming a contract. They may involve errors in arithmetic, errors in transmitting the offer or acceptance, errors in drafting the written contract, or errors about existing facts. A court may or may not grant relief because of a mistake. A court may grant relief if the mistake shows that there is no real or genuine assent. The mistake must be a *material* one. The relief granted may be *contract reformation* (court changes contract to correct a mistake) or *contract avoidance* (court allows any party

Mistake (of fact) *The unconscious ignorance or forgetfulness of the existence or nonexistence of a fact, past or present, which is material and important to the creation of a legal obligation.*

adversely affected by the mistake to avoid his contract). As a general rule, courts may grant relief when there has been a bilateral mistake of material fact (both parties mistaken) as contrasted with a unilateral mistake (only one party mistaken).

8. Bilateral Mistake

To have a *bilateral* or *mutual mistake,* all parties must have the same (identical) mistake. Before making a contract, a party usually evaluates the proposed bargain based on various assumptions regarding existing facts. Many of these assumptions are shared by the other party. A bilateral mistake occurs when both parties are mistaken as to the same assumption. Relief is appropriate where a mistake of both parties has a material effect on the agreed exchange of performances. Two examples may help illustrate when relief is appropriate:

1. Al contracts to sell and Bob agrees to buy a tract of land, the value of which has depended primarily on the timber on it. Both Al and Bob believe the timber is on the land, but unknown to them a fire destroyed the timber the day before they contracted. The contract is voidable by Bob, since he is adversely affected by the material bilateral mistake. Note that the court could not reform the contract to correct the mistake.
2. Al contracts to sell and Bob agrees to buy a tract of land for $500,000 which they believe contains 200 acres. In fact, the tract contains 205 acres. The contract is not voidable by either Al or Bob unless additional facts show that the effect on the agreed exchange is material.

In business transactions, it is customary in many situations to dispose of property about which the contracting parties willingly admit that all the facts are not known. In such instances, the property is sold without regard to its quality or characteristics. Such agreements may not be rescinded if later the property appears to have characteristics that neither of the parties had reason to suspect or if it otherwise differs from their expectations. Under such conditions, the property forms the subject matter of the agreement, regardless of its nature. If shortly after a farm is sold oil is discovered on it, the agreement could not be rescinded by the seller on the grounds of bilateral mistake.

To illustrate and compare cases in which mutual mistake may be a ground for rescission, consider these two examples;

EXAMPLE ONE: A woman finds a yellow stone about the size of a bird's egg and thinks it might be a gem. She takes it to a jeweler, who honestly states that he is not sure what the stone is. Nonetheless, he offers her $15 for the stone, and she sells it. The stone is later discovered to be an uncut diamond worth $30,000. *Result*: No relief will be granted. There was no mistake of fact, only of value. Both parties bargained with the knowledge that they were consciously ignorant, both thereby assuming the risk that the stone might be worth nothing or might be a valuable gem. *Rule*: When the parties are uncertain or consciously ignorant of facts about the thing sold, there is no avoidance for mistake.

EXAMPLE TWO: A buyer and seller both mistakenly believed a cow of excellent breeding stock to be sterile. In fact, the cow could breed and was already pregnant. The cow was sold for beef at a price far below what she would otherwise have brought for breeding purposes.

Result: When the mistake became apparent, the seller could rescind. The parties were not negligent in being mistaken, nor were they consciously ignorant. Both parties thought they knew what they were buying and selling. But what they bought and sold was in fact not what they contemplated buying and selling. A sterile cow is substantially different from a breeding cow. There is as much difference between them as between a bull and a cow. Since there is no good basis to place the risk of the mistake on either party, the contract is voidable for mutual mistake. *Rule*: A mutual mistake regarding the quality of the item sold, a quality that goes to its very essence, is grounds for avoiding a contract.

9. Unilateral Mistake

When only one party is laboring under a mistake, it is said to be a *unilateral* (one-sided) *mistake*. Generally, a contract entered into because of some mistake or error by only one party affords no relief to that party. The majority of such mistakes result from carelessness or lack of diligence by the mistaken party and therefore should not affect the rights of the other party. The following case illustrates a typical unilateral mistake.

CASE

Honaker was injured in a rear-end collision while a passenger in an automobile owned by Helen Cliver. The Home Insurance Company (Home) insured Cliver's automobile and was liable for Honaker's medical and living expenses up to the limits of its policy under Delaware's no-fault statute.

Under the personal injury protection (PIP) provisions of Cliver's policy, Home paid a total of $24,907 to Honaker over a period of two years, believing that the coverage limit was $25,000. In fact, the policy limit was $10,000. Subsequently, Home discovered its error and demanded repayment. The parties conceded that the overpayment to Honaker was Home's unilateral mistake. Honaker had no actual knowledge of the policy's limits, nor access to such information.

Home filed suit for restitution of the $14,907 overpayment and damages. The court granted summary judgment for Honaker, and Home appealed.

ISSUE: Is an insurer, acting under a unilateral mistake of coverage, entitled to regain overpayments that were made to a nonpolicyholder who was unaware of the mistake?

DECISION: No.

REASONS:
1. It is clear that Honaker had no access to information about the policy's limits of coverage. Honaker could not have misled Home. Thus Honaker appears before the court with clean hands.
2. Home acted under a mistake of fact, due to its own negligence, over a two-year period.
3. An insurer must be charged with knowledge of the policies it writes. The insurer alone must bear the burden of its unilateral mistake, particularly when the error was prolonged over a two-year period.

Home Insurance Co. v. Honaker, 480 A.2d 652 (Del. Supr. 1984).

The general rule that no relief is available to a party operating under a unilateral mistake of fact is subject to certain exceptions. An offeree who has reason to know of a unilateral mistake is not permitted to snap up such an offer and profit thereby. For example, if a mistake in a bid on a construction contract is clearly apparent to the offeree, it cannot be accepted by the offeree. Sometimes the mistake is discovered prior to the bid opening and the offeror seeks to withdraw the bid. Bids are often accompanied by bid bonds, which have the effect of making them irrevocable. Most courts will allow the bidder to withdraw the bid containing the error (1) if the bidder acted in good faith, (2) if he acted without gross negligence, (3) if he was reasonably prompt in giving notice of the error in the bid to the other party, (4) if the bidder will suffer substantial detriment by forfeiture, and (5) if the other party's status has not greatly changed, and relief from forfeiture will work no substantial hardship on him. Courts clearly scrutinize the facts to make sure that all these requirements are met. It should be difficult for low bidders to claim an error in computation as the basis for escaping from a bid noticeably lower than the competition's. This is the ''bad-faith'' element of the test stated above.

10. Reformation of Written Contracts

In most instances a written contract is preceded by negotiations between the parties who agree orally upon the terms to be set forth in the final written contract. This is certainly the case when the parties contemplate a written statement signed by both as necessary to a binding agreement; that is, the oral agreement was not itself to have binding effect. Of course, the parties could intend otherwise. They could regard the oral agreement as binding without any writing, or they could regard the writing as simply a subsequent memorial of their oral agreement.

Suppose the written agreement that is finally executed by the parties contains a mistake. The signed writing does not conform to what the parties agreed to orally. Frequently, the draftsman or typist may make an error that is not discovered prior to the signing of the contract, and the party benefiting from the error seeks to hold the other party to the agreement as written. For such situations, courts of equity provide a remedy known as *reformation*; the court corrects (reforms) the contract.

The only remedy in cases of unilateral mistake apparent to the other party is rescission. Reformation is not an available remedy, since it can be used only to correct the written contract to reflect the actual intentions of both parties. Reformation is available only for a case of mutual mistake.

FRAUD AND MISREPRESENTATION

11. Elements of Actionable Fraud

A contract is voidable if one party has been induced and injured by reliance on the other's misrepresentation of a material fact. The misrepresentation may be intentional, in which case the law considers the misrepresentation to be *fraudulent*. It may be unintentional, in which case there has been no fraud but only *innocent misrepresentation*. In both cases, the victim of a misrepresentation may rescind the contract. In the case of fraudulent misrepresentation, the victim is given the choice of the additional remedy of a suit for dollar damages.

While the elements of actionable fraud are stated differently from state to state, the following are those generally required:

1. ***Scienter***, or intention to mislead. *Scienter* means knowledge of the falsity, or statements made with such utter recklessness and disregard for the truth that knowledge is inferred.
2. A false representation or the concealment of a material fact.
3. Justifiable reliance on the false statement or concealment.
4. Damages as a consequence of the reliance.

Scienter *Knowledge by a defrauding party of the falsity of a representation.*

Innocent misrepresentation does not require proof of *scienter* but does require proof of all the other elements of fraud. The absence of *scienter* is the reason that a suit for dollar damages cannot be based on an innocent misrepresentation.

Rescission is permitted only in case the defrauded party acts with reasonable promptness after he learns of the falsity of the representation. Undue delay on his part waives his right to rescind, thus limiting the defrauded party to an action for recovery of damages. A victim of fraud loses his right to rescind if, after having acquired knowledge of the fraud, he indicates an intention to affirm the contract. These principles result from the fact that rescission is an equitable remedy.

12. *Scienter*

The requirement of intent to mislead is often referred to as ***scienter***, a Latin word meaning "knowingly." *Scienter* may be present in circumstances other than the typical false statement made with actual intent to deceive. *Scienter* may be found when there has been a concealment of a material fact. Moreover, a statement that is partially or even literally true may be fraudulent in law if it is made in order to create a substantially false impression. Intention to mislead may also be established by showing that a statement was made with reckless disregard for the truth. An accountant who certifies that financial statements accurately reflect the financial condition of a company may be guilty of fraud if he has no basis for the statement. Perhaps he does not intend to mislead, but his statement is so reckless that the intention is inferred from the lack of actual knowledge.

CASE

Four oral surgeons appeal an order suspending their licenses to practice because they submitted false claims to Blue Shield. The surgeons argued that the clerical staff is responsible for filing claims and that there is no evidence that any of them knowingly or with fraudulent intent made a false claim.

ISSUE: Is the *scienter* requirement met in this case?

DECISION: Yes.

REASONS:
1. There is no evidence that the submission of false claims was the responsibility of the clerical staff. Moreover, this argument is ludicrous, since the dentists assumed full responsibility for all claims submitted over their signature to Blue Shield.
2. The dentists are responsible for the submission of false claims by reason of their reckless ignorance or because of their special circumstances.
3. The practice at their clinic indicates a reckless ignorance of the falsity of the claim. Fraud may be proven by showing false representations made knowingly or recklessly.

4. Fraud may also be proven where a duty to know of the false representations is imposed by special circumstances. Dentists who sign claims for compensation for oral surgery, thereby giving their approval, are acting in special circumstances.

Miller, D.D.S. *et al.* v. Pennsylvania State Dental Council and Examining Bd., 396 A.2d 83 (Pa. 1979).

13. False Representation

Misrepresentation *The affirmative statement or affirmation of a fact that is not true.*

To establish fraud, there must be an actual or implied **misrepresentation** of a past or existing fact. The misstatement of fact must be material or significant to the extent that it has a moving influence upon a contracting party, but it need not be the sole inducing cause for entering into the contract.

False statements in matters of opinion such as the value of property are not factual and are usually not considered actionable. Sales hype or puffery and future promises do not constitute fraud, as the franchisee learned in the following case.

CASE

Janet Van Tassel met Charles Carver, president of McDonald Corporation, a subfranchisor of Baskin-Robbins Ice Cream Company. In order to induce her to become an ice-cream store operator in a Michigan mall, Carver told Van Tassel the following:

1. The proposed location was a gold mine.
2. It would not be long before she would be driving a big car and living in a big house and she would do all right if she stuck by him.
3. He would not steer her wrong because he liked her.
4. This was the right store for her, and all she would be doing is playing golf and making bank deposits.
5. She was not going to lose money, and this would be the best thing that would happen to her.

Van Tassel invested in the franchise, but it failed to meet Carver's predictions of success. Van Tassel filed suit, seeking to reclaim her investment.

ISSUE: Did the representations constitute fraud?

DECISION: No.

REASONS:

1. An action for fraud may not be predicted upon the expression of an opinion or salesmen's talk in promoting a sale, referred to as puffery.
2. It is within normal expectations of commercial dealing for salesmen to hype their products beyond objective proof.
3. An action for fraudulent misrepresentation must be predicated upon a statement relating to a past or an existing fact. Future promises are contractual and do not constitute fraud.
4. The evidence of the alleged misrepresentations of Carver shows every statement was purely opinion, puffery, or conjecture as

to future events. Carver merely represented that plaintiff could make the store very profitable; he was apparently mistaken.

Van Tassel v. McDonald Corporation, 407 N.W.2d 6 (Mich. App. 1987).

Notwithstanding the general rules as set forth in the preceding case, statements of opinion may be considered misrepresentations of fact in certain situations. An intentional misstatement even with regard to value may be fraudulent if the person making the statement has another opinion and knowingly states a false opinion. This concept is sometimes used when the person who is allegedly fraudulent is an expert, such as a physician, or when the parties stand in a fiduciary relationship (a position of trust) to each other. Assume that a doctor, after examining a patient for an insurance company physical, states that he is of the opinion that the person has no physical disability. If his actual opinion is that the patient has cancer, the doctor is guilty of fraud. He has misstated a fact (his professional opinion). The same is true if a partner sells property to the firm of which he is a member. His false statement of opinion concerning the value of the property will supply the misstatement-of-fact element. Each partner is a fiduciary toward his fellow partners and the firm, and he must give honest opinions.

The misstatement may be oral and may in fact be partly true. A half-truth (or partial truth) that has the net effect of misleading may form the basis of fraud, just as if it were entirely false. A partial truth in response to a request for information becomes an untruth whenever it creates a false impression and is designed to do so.

An intentional misrepresentation of existing local or state law by someone other than an attorney affords no basis for rescission because it is not a statement of fact in the technical sense. Statements of law are traditionally seen as assertions of opinion; moreover, everyone is presumed to know the law, and therefore deception is not possible. However, a few courts in recent years have held such statements about the law by attorneys to be factual or the equivalent of professional opinions and thus fraudulent.

A misrepresentation may be made by conduct as well as by language. Any physical act that attempts to hide vital facts relating to property involved in the contract is, in effect, a misstatement. One who turns back the odometer on a car, fills a motor with heavy grease to keep it from knocking, or paints over an apparent defect asserts an untruth as effectively as if he were speaking. Such conduct, if it misleads the other party, amounts to fraud and makes rescission or an action for damages possible.

14. Silence as Fraud

Historically, the law of contracts has followed ***caveat emptor*** (let the buyer beware), especially in real estate transactions. The parties to a contract are required to exercise ordinary business sense in their dealings. As a result, the general rule is that silence in the absence of a duty to speak does not constitute fraud.

In at least three situations there is a duty to speak the truth, and failure to do so will constitute actionable fraud. First of all, there is a duty to speak when the parties stand in a **fiduciary** relationship (the trust that should exist among partners in a partnership, between a director and a corporation, or between an agent and a

Caveat emptor *"Let the buyer beware."*

Fiduciary *In general, a person is a fiduciary when he occupies a position of trust or confidence in relation to another person or his property. Trustees, guardians, and executors occupy fiduciary positions.*

principal). Because such parties do not deal "at arm's length," there is the duty to speak and to make a full disclosure of all facts.

The second duty is based on justice, equity, and fair dealing. This duty typically arises when a material fact is known by one party but not by the other who reasonably could not discover the fact; had the other party known the fact, there would have been no contract. For example, when there is a latent defect in property (such as termites in a home) that could not be reasonably discovered by a buyer, a seller who knows of the defect has a duty to inform the buyer. Failure to do so is fraudulent.

The third duty is that of a person who has misstated an important fact on some previous occasion and is obligated to correct the statement when negotiations are renewed or as soon as he learns about his misstatement. This is not a true exception to the silence rule, because there is in fact a positive misstatement.

The gist of these exceptions is that one of the parties has the erroneous impression that certain things are true, whereas the other party is aware that they are not true and also knows of the misunderstanding. It therefore becomes his duty to disclose the truth. Unless he does so, most courts would hold that fraud exists. This does not mean that a potential seller or buyer has to disclose all the facts about the value of property he is selling or buying. The duty to speak arises only when he knows that the other party to the agreement is harboring a misunderstanding on some vital matter.

15. Justifiable Reliance

Before a false statement can be considered fraudulent, the party to whom it has been made must reasonably believe it to be true and must act on it, to his damage. If he investigates before he acts upon it, and the falsity is revealed, no action can be brought for fraud. The cases are in conflict concerning the need to investigate. Some courts have indicated that if all the information is readily available for ascertaining the truth of the statements, blind reliance upon the misrepresentation is not justified. In such a case, the party is said to be negligent in not taking advantage of the facilities available for confirming the statement.

If a party inspects property or has an opportunity to do so, and if a reasonable investigation would have revealed that the property was not as it had been represented, he cannot be considered misled. On the other hand, some courts deny that there is any need to investigate. They hold that one who has misrepresented facts cannot avoid the legal consequences by saying in effect: "You should not have believed me. You should have checked whether what I told you was true." Generally, reliance is justified when substantial effort or expense is required to determine the actual facts. The standard of justified reliance is not whether a reasonably prudent man would be justified in relying, but whether the particular individual involved had a right to rely. When the provisions of a written contract are involved, most people cannot be defrauded by its contents because the law charges the parties with actual knowledge of its contents, as the following case illustrates.

CASE

Lewis C. Burwell, Jr., guaranteed some loans made by Pinehurst Airlines, a company he had founded and was still active in, although he had sold all of his stock in the company. When he signed the guaranty agreements, he struck out some language related to renewals and added language limiting his liability to $300,000. These loans were repaid by Pinehurst and cancelled. Later, Burwell agreed to guarantee another loan from the South Carolina National Bank. He went to the bank and executed new guaranty papers in the amount of $225,000. He looked over the documents but did not read them. The documents authorized renewals without the consent of Burwell or notice to him. When this loan was not repaid, the bank sought payment from Burwell. He filed suit against the bank, claiming that the bank fraudulently induced him to sign the guaranty agreements. The trial court found for Burwell.

ISSUE: Did the bank fraudulently induce Burwell to sign the guaranty agreement when the agreement clearly stated its terms and he did not read it?

DECISION: No.

REASONS:
1. Every contracting party owes a duty to the other party to the contract and to the public to learn the contents of a document before signing it. One cannot complain of fraud or misrepresentation in the contents of a document if the truth could have been ascertained by reading it.
2. However, if a party is ignorant and unwary, his failure to read the document may be excused. This exception is very strictly interpreted. The court considers an individual's education, business experience, and intelligence to determine if that individual should be classified as ignorant and unwary.
3. Burwell clearly cannot be classified as ignorant and unwary. He graduated from college and business school. He has been involved with various airlines and has held directorship positions with domestic and foreign companies. He testified that he had guaranteed numerous loans in the past and that this type of transaction was not new to him. Although he testified that he was not feeling well the day that he executed the guaranty, he negotiated with a bank officer and obviously understood the purposes of the transaction.
4. Therefore the trial court's judgment is reversed.

Burwell v. South Carolina National Bank, 340 S.E.2d 786 (S.C. 1986).

16. Injury or Damages

In order to prevail, the party relying on the misstatement must offer proof of resulting damage. Normally, resulting damage is proved by evidence that the property in question would have been more valuable had the statements been true. Injury results when the party is not in as good a position as he would have been had the statements been true.

In an action for damages for fraud, the plaintiff may seek to recover damages on either of two theories. He may use the benefit of the bargain theory and seek the difference between the actual market value of what he received and the value if he had received what was represented. A plaintiff may also use the out-of-pocket theory and collect the difference between the actual value of what was received and its purchase price.

Perhaps the most significant aspect of a suit for dollar damages is that the victim of fraud may be entitled to punitive damages in addition to compensatory damages. If the fraudulent representations are made maliciously, willfully, wantonly, or so recklessly that they imply a disregard of social obligations, punitive damages as determined by a jury may be awarded. (Note: For a further discussion of damages, review sections 9–15 in Chapter 8.)

UNDUE INFLUENCE AND DURESS

Equity allows a party to rescind an agreement that was not entered into voluntarily. The lack of free will may take the form of duress or undue influence. A person who has obtained property under such circumstances should not in good conscience be allowed to keep it. A person may lose his free will because of duress—some threat to his person, his family, or property. The loss may come from the more subtle pressure of undue influence, whereby one person overpowers the will of another by use of moral, social, or domestic force as contrasted wtih physical or economic force. Cases of undue influence frequently arise in situations involving the elderly, in those cases where free will is lacking, some courts hold that the minds of the parties did not meet.

Under early common law, duress would not be present when a courageous man would have possessed a free will in spite of a threat, but modern courts do not require this standard of courage or firmness as a prerequisite for the equitable remedy. If the wrongful pressure applied in fact affected the individual involved to the extent that the contract was not voluntary, there is duress. If a person has a free choice, there is no duress even though some pressure may have been exerted upon him. A threat of a lawsuit made in good faith is not duress that will allow rescission. Economic pressure may constitute duress if it is wrongful and oppressive, as the following case illustrates.

CASE

The Hamlins owed the Aurora Bank several unpaid loans. The bank decided to ask the Hamlins to sign two renewal notes as well as a deed of trust on the farm. When Mrs. Hamlin refused to sign, she was told she was responsible for her husband's debts and that the bank would foreclose on the farm if she did not sign. Mrs. Hamlin signed the documents but refused to pay the debts. In a suit by the bank on the two promissory renewal notes, the trial court found that Mrs. Hamlin's signature was obtained through threats and coercion by the bank employees. As a result, she was allowed to disaffirm the notes. The bank appealed.

ISSUE: Is Mrs. Hamlin entitled to avoid the promissory notes and the deed of trust on the grounds her signature was obtained under duress?

DECISION: Yes.

REASONS:

1. Threats to take legal action with knowledge of the falsity of the claim can amount to duress.
2. The bank officers acknowledged that when they went to the Hamlin residence, the bank had no basis for bringing a suit against Mrs. Hamlin nor any basis to levy upon the farm.
3. Duress is to be tested not by the nature of the threats, but by the state of mind induced thereby in the victim. The ultimate fact in issue is whether the victim was bereft of the free exercise of her willpower.

4. Mrs. Hamlin refused to sign the notes when first asked, but testified she signed them after the threats to sue her and to sell the farm because they convinced her that she was liable and she didn't want to lose the farm.
5. There was sufficient evidence for the trial court to find that the duress was present when Mrs. Hamlin signed the notes.

Aurora Bank v. Hamlin, 609 S.W.2d 486 (Mo. 1980).

CHAPTER SUMMARY

Incapacity to Contract

Types of Incapacity	1. A party is declared to lack capacity to contract if he cannot understand his rights, the purpose of the agreement, or the legal effect of the contract. 2. Examples of parties who may be temporarily or permanently incapacitated include minors, mental incompetents, intoxicated persons, and drug addicts. 3. Contracts made before a person is adjudged incompetent are voidable. Contracts entered into after one of the parties is declared incompetent by a court generally are void. 4. If the competent party is unaware of the other party's incompetency, the incompetent party must make restitution before the contract is voidable.
Minors' Contracts	1. In most states, everyone below the age of eighteen is considered to be a minor or an infant. 2. Minors' contracts generally may be disaffirmed by the minor but not by the competent adult party.
Voiding Contracts by Minors	1. In order to disaffirm, a minor must communicate his desire to avoid contractual liability. 2. This communication must be made to the competent adult party in writing or by spoken words or by the minor's conduct. 3. In order to avoid a contract, the minor must return all the consideration received that he still has.
Ratification	1. Ratification of a contract occurs when the party who was incompetent becomes competent and affirms or approves of the contract. 2. Ratification can be by a manifestation of intent to be bound or by retaining the consideration for an unreasonable time after majority. 3. After reaching majority, a minor must disaffirm within a reasonable time or be held to have ratified the contract.
Minors' Liability for Necessaries	1. If a contract is for necessaries, the minor is bound to pay for the reasonable value of these items instead of the contract price. (Of course, in many situations, the contract price is a very good indication of the reasonable value of the items involved.) 2. What is a necessary must often be determined from the facts of each case.
Third-Party Rights	1. A minor cannot avoid a contract if the personal property involved has been transferred by the competent adult party to a good-faith purchaser for value.

2. This rule does not apply to real property. In other words, a minor can always rescind a contract involving land even when a third party is involved.

Mistake

Bilateral Mistake

1. Bilateral mistake occurs when all parties have the identical misconception of a material fact or of the contract terms.
2. Bilateral mistake negates the element of mutuality of contract and allows either party to rescind or reform the contract.

Unilateral Mistake

1. Unilateral mistake is not grounds for rescission unless the other party knew or should have known of the mistake.

Reformation of Written Contracts

1. Reformation occurs when courts correct a written contract to reflect the parties' actual intent.
2. Reformation is not an available remedy for unilateral mistake.

Fraud and Misrepresentation

Elements of Actionable Fraud

1. *Scienter*.
2. False material representation.
3. Justifiable reliance on the representation.
4. Injury caused by such reliance.

Scienter

1. *Scienter* is the intent to mislead. It is supplied by proof of knowledge of the falsity.
2. *Scienter* is also established by proof that the statement was made with a reckless disregard for the truth.

False Representation

1. There must be a misstatement of a material existing fact.
2. Statements of opinion are not factual unless made by an expert or unless the actual opinion is not as stated.
3. Misstatements of applicable laws are not statements of fact.
4. Misstatements may be by conduct as well as language.

Silence as Fraud

1. In the absence of a duty to speak, silence is not fraud.
2. Duty to speak arises (a) from a fiduciary relationship, or (b) when equity and justice so demand, or (c) to correct a prior misrepresentation.

Justifiable Reliance

1. A party must reasonably believe the statement to be true and must act on it.
2. There is no duty to take extraordinary steps to investigate the accuracy of statements.

Injury or Damages

1. A plaintiff is entitled to the benefit of the bargain theory in some cases and to use the out-of-pocket theory in others.
2. Punitive damages may be awarded in addition to compensatory damages.

Undue Influence and Duress

1. One party exerts undue influence upon another to compel a contract.
2. Undue influence normally occurs when a fiduciary or close family relationship exists.
3. Duress is compulsion or constraint that deprives another of the ability to exercise free will in making a contract.

4. Physical threats are generally required. But economic duress is recognized in a few states, especially when a party is responsible for the economic necessity of the other party.

REVIEW QUESTIONS AND PROBLEMS

1. Match each term in column A with the appropriate statement in column B.

A	B
(1) Ratification	(a) Minor must pay for their reasonable value.
(2) *Scienter*	(b) Rescission not allowed unless other party has knowledge of it.
(3) Concealment	(c) A fiduciary or someone in close family relationship exerts pressure.
(4) Mutual mistake	(d) What minor may choose to do upon reaching majority.
(5) Necessaries	(e) Upon reaching majority, minor keeps consideration and does nothing more.
(6) Undue influence	(f) Rescission granted if a duty to speak is not performed.
(7) Unilateral mistake	(g) Physical threats usually required.
(8) Duress	(h) Misconception of material fact by all parties.
(9) Disaffirmance	(i) Intent to defraud.
(10) Reformation	(j) Court rewrites contract to make contract conform to parties' intent.

2. In 1988 David Gallagher borrowed $165,000. He signed a note secured by his father (Victor) giving a mortgage to the bank. When David defaulted on the note, the bank sued to foreclose on the mortgage. Victor defended on the ground that he did not have the requisite capacity to sign the mortgage. Victor had suffered a stroke in 1984. At trial, Victor's doctors testified that Victor could not understand a mortgage transaction. A local judge testified that Victor was incompetent in 1988. However, the bank introduced evidence of Victor's participation in complex business transactions prior to and after 1988. Did Victor have the required mental capacity to execute a mortgage agreement? Explain.

3. Bill, under guardianship by reason of mental illness, buys an old car from Larry for $700, giving a promissory note for that amount. Subsequently, Bill abandons the car. Is Bill liable on the note? Would it make any difference if the car was a necessary? Explain your answers.

4. Youngblood, a minor, sold a wrecked Ford to Blakensopp, an adult, for $350. Blakensopp took possession of the car. Unknown to Blakensopp, Youngblood took the car back, and sold it to another purchaser for $400. Youngblood was charged with theft. Was Youngblood guilty of stealing the car from Blakensopp? Explain.

5. Halbman (a minor) bought a used Oldsmobile from Lemke (an adult). About five weeks after the purchase and after Halbman had paid $1,100 of the $1,250 purchase price, the connecting rod in the engine broke. Halbman, while still a minor, disaffirmed the purchase contract and demanded all the money he had paid defendant. Is he entitled to a full refund even though the car is now damaged? Why or why not?

6. Beachcomer, a coin dealer, sues to rescind a purchase by Boskett, who paid $50 for a dime both parties thought was minted in San Francisco. In fact, it was a very valuable dime minted in Denver. Beachcomer asserts a mutual mistake of fact regarding the genuineness of the coin as San Francisco-minted. Boskett contends that the mistake was as to value only. Explain who should win.

7. Brawner Contracting was the low bidder for construction of the Marine Service Building. After the award of the contract to Brawner, it discovered an arithmetical error of $10,000 in its bid based on a similar error of like amount in a quotation made to it by a subcontractor. Correction of the error would not have caused Brawner's contract price to equal or exceed that of the next lowest bidder. Is Brawner entitled to reformation of the contract? Why or why not?

8. Ventron buried mercury on its land, which it later sold to the Wolfs without telling them about the mercury. The Department of Environmental Protection sued Ventron and the Wolfs for mercury pollution of a state waterway. Are the Wolfs entitled to rescind?

9. Big Electric Power Company formulated a plan to acquire a large area of land for a hydroelectric project. Harion owned 138 acres of land in the area. Burroughs, an undisclosed agent of the power company, offered to buy Harion's land. To Harion's inquiry about why Burroughs wanted the land, Burroughs falsely replied he had just come into a large sum of money that he wanted to invest in land. They then executed a buy-sale contract with a purchase price of $4,100. Alleging that he would have asked $27,000 if he had known the power company to be the real buyer, Harion sues to rescind. Does he win? Explain.

10. After making a visual inspection, Buyer bought property from Seller and proceeded to build a home. When the possibility of soil slippage soon became apparent, construction was halted. Buyer sued Seller to rescind the sale. Soil Expert testified that the property was not suitable for the construction of a residence. Seller was unaware of the stability hazard of the soil when the sale was transacted. Could Buyer rescind? Why or why not?

11. Purchasers of a residence sue the realtor for fraud. The purchasers allege that the realtor failed to reveal his knowledge of the extensive termite damage to the beams that supported the floors in the house. The realtor did inform that there was termite certificate, that the house had been treated for termites, and a one-year guarantee against reinfestation went with the house. Is the realtor guilty of fraudulent concealment? Why or why not?

12. An employer orally promised to institute a bonus plan for employees. Ralph, who had threatened to quit, continued in his job because of the promise. The bonus plan was not implemented, and Ralph sued for damages including punitive damages. Under what circumstances would he be entitled to them? Explain.

13. A representative for a data processing company bought a computer after the computer salesperson assured her that the machine would be adequate for her purposes. The data processing representative was aware of the specifications of the computer, but she later discovered that its printout was too slow for her company's needs. She seeks to rescind the contract on the basis of misrepresentation. With what result? Explain.

14. Phoenix Company was awarded a $6 million contract by the navy for the production of radar sets. It was a severe contract that imposed substantial penalties for late deliveries and gave the navy the right to cancel for any default by Phoenix. Phoenix then made a contract with Logan, Inc., whereby Logan agreed to furnish many of the component parts. After making a few deliveries, Logan refused to deliver any more unless the price was increased. Being unable to get the components elsewhere, Phoenix acceded to the demand. Later, Phoenix sued to have the price increase set aside. Was Phoenix successful? Explain.

Illegality and Public Policy

12

CHAPTER PREVIEW

- **STATUS OF ILLEGAL CONTRACTS**

  Litigation Disallowed
  Exceptions

- **AGREEMENTS IN VIOLATION OF STATUTES**

  Violations of License Requirements
  Usury
  Agreements and Activities in Restraint of Trade
  Sherman Antitrust Act and Contracts • Price-Fixing • Other Agreements Violating Antitrust Laws

- **AGREEMENTS IN VIOLATION OF PUBLIC POLICY**

  Agreements Not to Compete
  Unconscionability
  Contracts of Adhesion
  Contracts Disclaiming Liability
  Tickets Disclaiming Liability

BUSINESS MANAGEMENT DECISION

You are one of six accountants to enter into a partnership agreement. You recognize that one or more of your new partners may leave the firm at a future date.

What should you include in the agreement to ensure that all the clients remain with the firm?

A valid contract must have a lawful purpose or object. Contracts that do not have a lawful object are illegal and therefore unenforceable. A contract or provision of a contract may be declared illegal if it is specifically prohibited by statute, contravenes the rule of the common law, or is contrary to public policy. It may be illegal in either its subject matter, its formation, or its performance.

It is axiomatic that a contract that violates a statute or an ordinance is illegal and void. A contract provision is contrary to public policy if it is injurious to the interests of the public, contravenes some established interest of society, violates the policy or purpose of some statute, or tends to interfere with the public health, safety, morals, or general welfare. Although all agreements are subject to the paramount power of the sovereign and to the judicial power to declare contracts illegal, contracts are not to be lightly set aside on the grounds of public policy, and doubts will usually be resolved in favor of legality.

An endless variety of agreements have been held to be illegal: wagering agreements, agreements to affect the administration of justice (concealing evidence or suppressing a criminal investigation), agreements to influence legislation or executive action by bribery or undue influence, and agreements to interfere with public service. Other examples of illegal agreements are discussed throughout this chapter.

The term *public policy* is vague and variable and changes as our social, economic, and policy climates change. As society becomes more complex, courts turn more and more to statutory enactments in search of current public policy. A court's own concept of right and wrong, as well as its total philosophy, will frequently come into play in answering complex questions of public policy.

Cases involving public policy are often in conflict from jurisdiction to jurisdiction. The economic interests of a state may play a major role in the development of public policy. As the law on illegal contracts is studied, care should be taken to ascertain the reason behind each rule or decision, and the major emphasis should be on indicated trends in the law. Keep in mind that matters of illegality are discussed throughout the text.

STATUS OF ILLEGAL CONTRACTS

1. Litigation Disallowed

As a general rule, the status of an illegal contract is that a court will not allow litigation involving it. This means that if the illegal contract is executory, neither party may enforce performance by the other. If it is executed, the court will not order rescission—it will not allow recovery of what was given in performance. An illegal contract cannot be ratified by either party, and the parties can do nothing to make it enforceable. Stated simply, in an illegal contract situation, the court literally "leaves the parties where it finds them." A party to an illegal contract cannot recover damages for breach of such contract. If one party has performed, he cannot generally recover either the value of his performance or any property or goods transferred to the other. As a result of the rule, one wrongdoer may be enriched at the expense of the other wrongdoer, but the courts usually will not intercede to rectify this because the purpose is to deter illegal bargains.

2. Exceptions

There are three basic exceptions to the rule that precludes the granting of any relief to a party to an illegal contract. First, if a person falls in the category of those for whose protection the contract was made illegal, he may obtain restitution of what he has paid or parted with or may even obtain enforcement. For example, both federal and state statutes require that a corporation follow certain procedures before securities (stocks and bonds) may be offered for sale to the public. It is illegal to sell such securities without having complied with the legal requirements. Nevertheless, a purchaser is allowed to obtain a refund of the purchase price if he desires to do so. The act of one party (the seller) is more illegal than that of the other party (the buyer). Many statutes are designed to protect one party in an illegal transaction, and when this is the case, the protected party is allowed a legal remedy.

A second exception applies when a person is induced by fraud or duress to enter into an illegal agreement. In such cases, the courts do not regard the defrauded or coerced party as being an actual participant in the wrong and therefore will allow restitution of what he has rendered by way of performance. It has been suggested that the same result would occur if the party were induced by strong economic pressure to enter into an illegal agreement.

Third, there is a doctrine called *locus poenitentiae* that may provide the remedy of restitution to one who has become a party to an illegal contract. Literally, the phrase means "a place for repentance," by extension, "an opportunity for changing one's mind." As applied to an illegal contract, it means that within very strict limits, a person who repents before actually having performed any illegal part of the contract may rescind it and obtain restitution of his part performance. Thus wagers are illegal transactions except under certain circumstances. Suppose that A and B wager on the outcome of an election, and each places $100 with C, the stakeholder, who agrees to turn $200 over to the winner. Prior to the election, either A or B could recover his $100 from C by legal action, since the execution of the illegal agreement would not yet have occurred. Actually, the loser could obtain a judgment against C if he gives notice of his demand prior to the time that the stake has been turned over to the winner.

AGREEMENTS IN VIOLATION OF STATUTES

3. Violations of License Requirements

Some contracts are void and unenforceable because they involve a purpose that violates a statute. Most personal service contracts do not involve an unlawful purpose. However, personal service agreements may be unenforceable if the party performing the service is not legally entitled to do so. For example, doctors, dentists, pharmacists, architects, lawyers, accountants, surveyors, real estate brokers, and others who perform professional services must be licensed by the appropriate body before they are allowed to contract with the general public.

As a general rule, if the service rendered requires a license, the party receiving the benefit of the service can successfully refuse to pay an unlicensed plaintiff on the ground that the contract is illegal. This is true even if the person is licensed in another jurisdiction but not the one in which the services were rendered. A real estate broker licensed in one state cannot perform services in another state. If he does so, he cannot collect for the services. This rule may be applied to the sale of a business that includes real estate, as happened in the following case.

CASE

Kazmer-Standish, management consultants on mergers and acquisitions, found a buyer (Kratos) for a New Jersey corporation (Schoeffel). Schoeffel sold its entire assets, including its plant and land, to Kratos for $2.7 million. Kazmer-Standish sued Kratos and Schoeffel to collect a $100,000 business broker's or finder's fee for finding a buyer of Schoeffel's business. Since Kazmer-Standish did not have a New Jersey real estate broker's license, Kratos and Schoeffel asserted that Kazmer-Standish could not recover a broker's commission on the sale, which included real estate.

ISSUE: Can Kazmer-Standish recover a broker's fee if it does not have a real estate broker's license?

DECISION: No.

REASON: New Jersey, by statute, provides that no firm or corporation can sue in the New Jersey courts for collection of a broker's or finder's fee without proving that it was a duly licensed real estate broker at the time of sale of a business that included the business's real estate.

Kazmer-Standish Consultants, Inc. v. Schoeffel Instrument, 426 A.2d 1061 (N.J. 1981).

The practice of law by unauthorized persons is a significant problem. A person who practices law without a license is not only denied the right to a fee but also subject to criminal prosecution in many states, and such activity may also be enjoined. Since the practice of law primarily entails giving advice, difficult questions are presented when advice is given by business specialists such as certified public accountants, insurance brokers, bankers, and real estate brokers. Although the line between permissible and impermissible activities of these business specialists is often difficult to draw, some activities and services performed by various business specialists clearly constitute unauthorized practice of law. An accountant's handling of a complicated tax case has been held to constitute unauthorized practice of law, and a real estate broker's preparation of a real estate deed is illegal in most states. Business specialists should be aware that giving legal advice and preparing legal documents are illegal performances by one not licensed to practice law. A major danger in doing these things is the loss of the right to compensation for services that are otherwise legal.

4. Usury

Usury *A contract is usurious if made for a loan of money at a rate of interest in excess of that permitted by statute.*

State statutes limit the amount of interest that may be charged upon borrowed money. Any contract by which the lender is to receive more than the maximum interest allowed by the statute is usurious and illegal. In most states, the civil penalty for usury is that the lender is denied the right to collect any interest. In a few states, the lender is denied the right to collect both the interest and the principal. There are also criminal penalties for charging illegal interest.

Difficult issues often arise over what actually constitutes interest. Creditors develop ingenious schemes to charge more than the maximum legal rate of interest. For example, the calculation of interest on the basis of 360 days was held to be illegal if the computation produced in a single year more interest than would be produced by applying the maximum legal rate to a calendar year of 365 days.

The law against usury is generally not violated if the seller sets a cash price different from a credit price, but he cannot disguise interest by calling it something else, like a finder's fee or broker's fee. If the buyer is charged for making a loan, it is interest, regardless of the terminology used. As long as one lends the money of others, he may then charge a commission in addition to the maximum rate. A commission may not be legally charged when one is lending his own funds, even though he has to borrow the money with which to make the loan and expects to sell the paper shortly thereafter. The following case is typical of those holding extra charges to be usurious.

CASE

Howes borrowed $35,000 from Curtis, a financier. This loan was to be repaid in installments with 10 percent annual interest. The applicable state usury statute prohibited interest on loans in excess of 10 percent per annum. Curtis also attempted to charge Howes a 5 percent finder's fee and a 5 percent loan payment guarantee in addition to the interest. When Howes failed to pay as agreed, Curtis filed suit. Howes defended on the ground that the transaction was usurious because the total charges exceeded 10 percent.

ISSUE: Did the additional charges amount to usury?

DECISION: Yes.

REASONS:
1. Curtis could not act as a broker or as a guarantor to himself as lender since he was loaning his own money.
2. Thus the broker's 5 percent finder's fee and 5 percent loan payment guarantee were additional interest for purposes of the state usury statute.

Howes v. Curtis, 661 P.2d 729 (Idaho 1983).

The laws on usury are not violated by collection of the legal maximum interest in advance or by adding a service fee that is no larger than reasonably necessary to cover the incidental costs of making the loan (inspection, legal, and recording fees). A seller can also add a finance or carrying charge on long-term credit transactions. Some statutes allow special lenders such as pawnshops, small loan companies, or credit unions to charge in excess of the otherwise legal limit. In fact, the exceptions to the maximum interest rate in most states far exceed the situations in which the general rule is applicable. The laws relating to usury were designed to protect debtors from excessive interest. This goal has been thwarted by these exceptions, so only modest protection is actually available.

The purchase of a note at a discount greater than the maximum interest is not usurious unless the maker of the note is the person who is discounting it. A note is considered the same as any other personal property and may be sold for whatever it will bring upon the market.

Today, in most states, there is no maximum legal rate of interest when the borrower is a business, whether or not it is incorporated. Some states limit this exception to loans over a fixed sum, such as $10,000, but little protection is afforded by such laws. Loans to corporations usually are exempt in most states, regardless of the amount of the loan.

5. Agreements and Activities in Restraint of Trade

Restraint of trade *Contracts that impede free competition.*

Laws commonly referred to as the antitrust laws serve to protect our economic system from monopolies, attempts to monopolize, and activities in **restraint of trade.** In 1890, under its power to regulate interstate commerce, Congress passed the Sherman Antitrust Act, directed at these concerns. The law seeks to preserve competition by using three basic sanctions. First, violation of the Sherman Act is a federal felony punishable by fine or imprisonment or both. Second, the Sherman Act authorizes injunctions to prevent and restrain violations or continued violations of its provisions. Third, those who have been injured by violation of the act may collect treble (triple) damages plus court costs and reasonable attorney's fees. The treble-damage provision serves not only as a means of punishing the defendant for his wrongful act but also as a means of compensating the plaintiff for his injury.

Sherman Antitrust Act and Contracts. Section 1 of the Sherman Act prohibits contracts (express or implied), combinations, and conspiracies in restraint of trade. Activities that may constitute a contract, combination, or conspiracy in restraint of trade are limitless. However these agreements and practices are illegal only if they are unreasonable. In deciding if an agreement or practice is unreasonable, courts divide them into two types or categories. Some are said to be illegal ***per se.*** This means that they are conclusively presumed to be unreasonable and thus illegal. Such agreements are so plainly anticompetitive and lacking in any redeeming virtue that it is unnecessary to examine the effects of the activity. If an activity is illegal *per se*, proof of the activity is proof of a violation and proof that it is in restraint of trade. Proof of an anticompetitive effect is not required.

Per se *"By itself." Thus, a contract clause may be inherently illegal—illegal* per se.

The second type or category includes activities that are illegal only if the facts establish that they are unreasonable. An act is unreasonable if it suppresses or destroys competition. An act is reasonable if it promotes competition. In cases under this second category, courts analyze the facts to determine the significance of the activity or restraint on competition.

Price-fixing. The most common type of Sherman Act violation is price-fixing, which is illegal *per se*. It is no defense that the prices fixed are fair or reasonable. It also is no defense that price-fixing is engaged in by small competitors to allow them to compete with larger competitors. It is just as illegal to fix a low price as it is to fix a high price. Today it is as illegal to fix the price of services as it is to fix the price of goods. Price-fixing in the service sector has been engaged in by professional persons as well as by service occupations such as automobile and TV repair workers, barbers, and refuse collectors. For many years it was contended that persons performing services were not engaged in trade or commerce, but the courts today reject such arguments. The following is the landmark case applying the Sherman Act to services such as the practice of law.

CASE

A Virginia county bar association developed a schedule of minimum fees to be charged by all lawyers in the county. Goldfarb got in touch with several lawyers when he was about to buy a home, and all of them quoted the same fee for the legal services to be performed. Goldfarb sued the Virginia Bar Association, alleging that the use of the minimum-fee schedule was a violation of the Sherman Act. The Virginia Bar Association contended that legal services were not "trade or commerce" and that professional activities were exempt from the Sherman Act.

ISSUE: Is it a violation of the Sherman Act for professional persons to agree on minimum fees to be charged for services?

DECISION: Yes.

REASONS:
1. The examination of a land title is a service; the exchange of such a service for money is "commerce."
2. Section 1 of the Sherman Act is a careful attempt to bring within the act every person engaged in business whose activities might restrain or monopolize commerce among the states. In the modern world the activity of lawyers plays an important part in commerce and anticompetitive activities by lawyers can exert a restraint on commerce.
3. The Sherman Act has no exemption to protect those providing professional services, such as lawyers.

Goldfarb *et ux.* v. Virginia State Bar *et al.*, 95 S.Ct. 2004 (1975).

Some professional groups have attempted to avoid the foregoing result through the use of ethical standards. Others have attempted to determine the price of services indirectly by the use of formulas and relative value scales. Some medical organizations have determined that a given medical procedure would be allocated a relative value on a scale of one to ten. Brain surgery might be labeled a nine and a face lift a four. All members of the profession would then use these values in determining professional fees. Such attempts have been uniformly held to be illegal as a form of price fixing.

Price-fixing may be horizontal—among competitors—or it may be thought of as vertical. Vertical price-fixing occurs when a manufacturer attempts to control the retail price of its product. Resale price maintenance attempts, other than simply announcing a price and refusing to deal with customers that do not follow the announced price, are also illegal *per se*.

Other Agreements Violating Antitrust Laws. There are other agreements that may violate the Sherman Act and its amendments. Although some of these are illegal *per se*, most are judged under the rule of reason. Typical of agreements subject to question under the Sherman Act are those granting exclusive rights to sell a product or to sell in exclusive territories. An agreement among competitors to divide territories is illegal *per se*. However, if a manufacturer gives an exclusive territory to a distributor, the agreement is illegal only if it has unreasonable anticompetitive effects. Since such territorial arrangements may in fact aid competition, they may be legal.

An agreement otherwise legal may be illegal under the antitrust laws because the price charged one customer is different from the price charged for the same product to another customer. Price discrimination is declared illegal under a federal law commonly referred to as the Robinson-Patman Act. It is illegal to discriminate in price among purchasers of commodities of like grade and quality if the price discrimination substantially lessens competition or tends to create a monopoly in any line of commerce or tends to injure competition. This law does not cover transactions with consumers but only sales by manufacturers and wholesalers to retailers.

The antitrust laws also prohibit agreements that seek to tie one product to another where the effect is to lessen competition. For example, it may be illegal to make an agreement to sell or lease a product only if the buyer or lessee purchases a different product or service. A tying agreement is illegal *per se* if the seller or lessor has strong economic power over the tying product and if a substantial amount of commerce is affected. The tying of a nonpatented product, for instance, to a patented product would be a *per se* violation of the antitrust laws.

In addition to tying products, exclusive arrangements and reciprocal dealing can be illegal. In an *exclusive* dealing agreement, the parties agree to deal solely with one another. In a *reciprocal* dealing arrangement, the parties deal with each other as both buyer and seller. Both of these agreements are illegal if they significantly restrain competition. However, some agreements that limit competition, such as those between a franchisor and its franchisees, are usually found to be legal. They are legal because their effect on competition is minimal compared with the interests of the franchisor in having similarity in all of its franchised operations. Thus certain exclusive dealing contracts are legal.

AGREEMENTS IN VIOLATION OF PUBLIC POLICY

6. Agreements Not to Compete

A form of agreement that may be legal even though it is in partial restraint of trade is an agreement not to compete. An agreement by one person not to compete with another is frequently contained in a contract for the sale of a going business. The seller, by such a provision, agrees not to compete with the buyer. Agreements not to compete are also commonly found in contracts creating a business or a professional practice. Each partner or shareholder in the closely held corporation agrees not to compete with the firm or practice, should he leave the business or professional activity. In addition, as a part of their employment contract, many employees agree that they will not compete with their employer upon termination of their employment.

Such agreements will be enforced if they are reasonably necessary for the protection of a purchaser, the remaining members of a business, or an employer, provided the covenant (1) is reasonable in point of time, (2) is reasonable in the area of restraint, (3) is necessary to protect goodwill, (4) does not place an undue burden on the covenantor, and (5) does not violate the public interest. Each covenant is examined by the court to see if it is reasonable to both parties and to the general public. Factors such as uniqueness of product, patents, trade secrets, type of service, employee's contact with customers, and other goodwill factors are significant on the reasonableness issue. In the employment situation, whether or not the employee will become a burden on society and whether or not the public is being deprived of his skill are factors.

The law will look with more favor on these covenants if they involve the sale of a business interest rather than employment. In fact, an agreement not to compete may even be presumed in the case of a sale of business and its goodwill, and the seller must not thereafter directly or indirectly solicit business from his old customers, although he may advertise generally. Agreements between a buyer and seller or between partners are more likely to be held valid than are employer-employee contracts, because there is more equality of bargaining power in the first two situations than in the last. A seller or a former partner could readily refuse to sign an agreement not to compete, whereas an employee seeking a job might feel obligated to sign almost anything in order to gain employment. The following case summarizes the law in most states on agreements not to compete.

CASE

Sky, Inc., purchased the Ozark Truck Plaza from Tom Easley and his partner, Brouwer, pursuant to a written agreement. The agreement provided that for five years Easley and Brouwer would not operate, own, or have any interest in a truck stop, service station, or any business that obtained over 70 percent of its annual gross revenue from the sale of gasoline or diesel fuel within 100 miles of Alma, Arkansas. About a year after the sale, Easley began operating the Shop Stop Mini-Mart, a convenience store where gasoline and diesel fuel were sold, within the restricted area. Sky sought a permanent injunction against Easley for violating the restrictive covenant. Easley denied violating the covenant and counterclaimed, contending that the provisions regarding the nature and scope, territorial extent, and duration of the restriction were unreasonably broad and unnecessary for Sky's protection. The trial judge found the anticompetition clause valid and reasonable in all respects and necessary to protect Sky's interests. He granted a permanent injunction restraining Easley from future violations of the agreement.

ISSUE: Were the provisions of the anticompetition covenant reasonable and necessary to protect Sky's interests, so as to render the granting of the injunction proper?

DECISION: Yes.

REASONS:

1. Contracts in partial restraint of trade ancillary to a sale or business transaction are valid to the extent reasonably necessary for the purchaser's protection.
2. If the restraint lasts longer than is necessary to protect the promisee's interest, covers a geographic area larger than is necessary to protect those interests, or prohibits the promisor from engaging in activities that are unnecessary to protect the promises, it is unreasonable.
3. The duration of the restrictive covenant, five years, is not unreasonably long as a matter of law. The facts of this case especially justify a five-year period. Sky purchased the business for $1,125,000

and spent $400,000 in repairs. A co-owner of Sky testified at trial that the five-year restriction would allow Sky to amortize a large part of its initial debt, recapture a substantial part of its investment, and prevent Easley from having an unfair competitive advantage. Therefore the five-year period was necessary to protect Sky's interest.

4. The 100-mile radius is not unnecessarily large, because it is necessary for the protection of Sky's interest. Most other states view a 100-mile radius as reasonable if the business sold extends through that territory. Three parties, including Brouwer, testified at trial that trucks refuel every 100 to 200 miles. There was testimony that distributors space truck-stop franchises about 150 miles apart so that trucks could refuel at the same type of station. Easley testified that before the sale, sales to truckers made up over 90 percent of the business at Ozark Truck Plaza. This evidence shows that the geographic restriction was necessary for Sky's protection.
5. Therefore the provisions governing the duration and geographic extent of the anticompetition clause were reasonable and valid. The trial court's granting of the permanent injunction is affirmed.

Easley v. Sky, Inc., 689 S.W.2d 356 (Ark. Ct. App. 1985).

Many states by statute have limited the use of agreements not to compete. Some of these prohibit such agreements for certain professions or occupations. Other statutes set maximum limits for the area or time of the restraint. In states with statutes, such agreements tend to be more limited than in states that rely on the courts to decide legality simply on public policy.

Agreements not to compete must be a part of another contract to be legal. A bare agreement by one party not to compete with another is against public policy. If Lori threatens to open a business to compete with Elaine, and Elaine offers Lori $1,000 to agree not to do so, the contract is illegal.

Comparable to the employee's agreement not to compete is a restrictive provision in a contract for the sale or lease of real property. The landowner may wish to prevent the use of his land for any purpose that would be competitive with his own business. In a lease, the landowner may provide that the lessee cannot operate an appliance store on the leased property. In that case, the landowner (who owns an appliance store) wants to avoid competition, and he does so by the restrictive provision. Although on its face the provision does restrict trade, it is binding because other property in the community can be used for competitive purposes.

7. Unconscionability

Unconscionable *In the law of contracts, provisions that are oppressive, overreaching, or shocking to the conscience.*

Freedom of contract is not a license for a party to insert into an agreement any provision that a party deems advantageous. A concept known as **unconscionability** allows a judge to strike any portion of a contract or even the entire contract, in order to avoid any unconscionable result. Unconscionability is a question of law for the judge, and not the jury. Although no precise meaning is given, its purpose is to prevent oppression and unfair suprise. There are basically two questions presented in such cases: (1) What is the relative bargaining power of the parties, their relative economic strength, the alternative sources of supply—in a word, what are their options? and (2) Is the challenged term substantively reasonable? The concept of unconscionability is an important part of the Code [2-302] and is applicable to transactions in goods.

For a contract to be conscionable, its material terms need to be conspicuous, to be understandable by an ordinary person, and to result from a true bargain. It is not a contract of bargain when one party imposes terms on another party. Thus a party must be able to *find* and to *understand* all material terms, as well as have the right to *bargain* over them. The contract cannot be oppressively imposed and must avoid unfair surprise.

Unconscionability has sometimes been found to exist when a seller seeks to disclaim warranties. For example, all sellers of seed were disclaiming warranties. Farmers had to buy seed from someone. The unequal bargaining power convinced a court that the disclaimer was unconscionable.

Another example of an unconscionable clause was found to exist in a contract for "Yellow Pages" that limited liability for mistakes to a refund of charges. It has also been applied in cases concerning real estate brokerage contracts, home improvement contracts, leases, contracts to open a checking account, construction contracts, and so on. In modern contract law, unconscionability may be applied to any contract of adhesion, to any contract oppressively imposed by a superior party, or to any contract term that causes unfair surprise to an inferior party. Additional examples are discussed in the following section on contracts of adhesion.

Since unconscionability involves questions of public policy, it is difficult to predict when a court will or will not find a particular contract or contract provision unconscionable. As noted earlier, a court's own concept of right and wrong as well as its total philosophy will often come into play in answering complex questions of public policy. As the following case demonstrates, courts are required to conduct a hearing and to receive evidence on the issue of whether or not a contract is unconscionable.

CASE

On June 30, 1981, Ms. Jo Hudgens leased a Space Invader game, pool table, and juke box from Capital Associates. Under the terms of the lease, she was to make monthly payments of $459.85 for thirty-six months. The lease expressly provided that it was uncancellable for the three-year term, and that Hudgens would not acquire any right to obtain title to the equipment unless otherwise agreed in writing. In fine print on the reverse side, the lease provided that if Hudgens failed to pay any rental when due for a period of five days, Capital could declare the entire amount of unpaid rent for the balance of the term immediately due and payable. Hudgens made payments under the lease through April 1982. On April 23, she called Capital and requested that the equipment be removed, and All American Vending Corporation was sent to pick up the equipment on that same day. Capital notified Hudgens that it intended to sell the equipment because of her breach. Capital solicited bids for the equipment and accepted the highest bid of $1,000 from All American Vending Corporation. Capital then sued Hudgens to recover $12,093.52, which represented the balance of rental payments, taxes, late charges, and attorney's fees. At trial, Hudgens testified that when she signed the lease, she was drunk, and that at that time, agents of Capital had told her that she was signing a month-to-month lease that she cculd cancel at her option. The trial court found for Hudgens because it found that the lease agreement was unconscionable.

ISSUE: Did the trial court properly find that the lease agreement was unconscionable?

DECISION: No.

REASON:
1. A court may, of its own initiative, find that a contract or any of its clauses were unconscionable at the time it was made. If the court does so find, it may refuse to enforce the contract, enforce the remainder of the contract without the unconscionable clause, or limit the application of any unconscionable clause so as to avoid any unconscionable result.
2. When it is claimed or appears to the court that a contract or any of its clauses may be unconscionable, the court shall afford the parties a reasonable opportunity to present evidence as to the contract's commercial setting, purpose, and effect to aid the court in making a determination.
3. The record from the trial court contains prima facie evidence of unconscionability. Enforcement of the acceleration clause would allow Capital to recover unaccrued and unearned rent in an amount exceeding $12,000 for equipment that it resold for $1,000. The clause was embedded in a page of fine print, and Hudgens was an uncounseled layman. Therefore the trial court could have easily concluded that the clause was so one-sided as to be unconscionable under the circumstances existing when the contract was made.
4. However, the court did not hold a hearing to allow Capital to defend the contract's commercial reasonableness by presenting evidence as to the contract's commercial setting, purpose, and effect. Therefore the appellate court must reverse the trial court's judgment and remand the case to the trial court with instructions to hold this hearing.

Capital Associates, Inc. v. Hudgens, 455 So.2d 651 (Fla. App. 1984).

8. Contracts of Adhesion

Contract of adhesion was developed in French civil law. It has been widely used in international law, and in recent years has become important in our law of contracts. An adhesion contract is a standardized contract entirely prepared by one party. As a result of the disparity or inequality of bargaining power between the drafter and the second party, the terms are submitted on a take-it-or-leave-it basis. The standardized provisions are such that they are merely ''adhered to,'' with little choice as a practical matter on the part of the ''adherer.'' If the terms are viewed as unsatisfactory, the party cannot obtain the desired service or product.

The term *contract of adhesion* was first used in the United States in 1919 in a case involving an insurance contract. For several decades it was almost exclusively applied to insurance contracts. However, many contracts today are standardized form contracts entered into by parties who are unequal in knowledge and unequal in bargaining power. The common law ignored this inequality and applied a doctrine of *caveat emptor*. In the 1960s, courts began to police contractual abuses by superior parties using contracts of adhesion. To do that, they used the equitable principle of unconscionability.

Contracts of adhesion are not illegal but are examined for fairness, and doubts about fairness are strictly construed against the drafting party. Courts review these contracts carefully to ensure that they are conscionable, and the courts will excise clauses that are oppressive or cause unfair surprise. Employment contracts, insurance policies, and leases are frequently held to be contracts of adhesion.

Not every printed or form contract is a contract of adhesion. The case that follows sets forth the three elements required for such a finding.

CASE

The executor of the estate of Kathleen MacKay seeks a refund of the $36,950 entrance fee paid to LVL life-care retirement center. On June 16, 1983, the deceased, at age seventy-nine with a life expectancy of seven to nine years, moved into the center. On December 29, 1983, she was taken to a nursing center, where she died two days later.

The residence agreement entitled Mrs. MacKay to occupy a one-bedroom unit with a fully equipped kitchen for the rest of her life and guaranteed her admittance to the LVL nursing care center whenever required. She was also required to pay a monthly service fee (MSF) of $537 and to have medicare coverage and additional health insurance.

Mrs. MacKay had the right to terminate the agreement on ninety days' notice, if she were able to live alone and if the MSF was current and fully paid. LVL would then refund the entrance fee less "10% plus 1% for each month of residency."

To cover a resident's potential inability to pay, and the possibility that some residents would require more care and expense than anticipated by the fees, paragraph I(J) of the contract provided for no refund of the entry fee upon a resident's death.

ISSUE: Is this an unenforceable adhesion contract?

DECISION: No.

REASONS:

1. A court will refuse to enforce an adhesion contract or a provision thereof only when the contract or provision is unfair.
2. Three elements must be satisfied before an adhesion contract may be found. First, the agreement must occur in the form of a standardized contract prepared or adopted by one party for the acceptance of the other. Second, the party proffering the standardized contract must enjoy a superior bargaining position because the weaker party virtually cannot avoid doing business under the particular contract terms. Finally, the contract must be offered to the weaker party on a take-it-or-leave-it basis, without opportunity for bargaining.
3. LVL's contract with MacKay does not satisfy either the second or third elements. There was no monopoly, and no obligation was voiced to any of the terms.
4. The court also found that the contract was not unconscionable.

Guthmann v. La Vida Llena, 709 P.2d 675 (N.M. 1985).

9. Contracts Disclaiming Liability

Exculpatory clause *A provision in a contract whereby one of the parties attempts to relieve itself of tort liability.*

A party to a contract frequently includes a clause that provides that the party has no tort liability even if at fault. Such a clause is commonly called an **exculpatory clause.** These disclaimers of liability are not favored by the law and are strictly construed against the party relying on them. While some are valid, many disclaimers are frequently declared to be illegal by courts as contrary to public policy. Some states have by statute declared these clauses, in certain types of contracts such as leases, to be illegal and void.

The reasoning behind these statutes and judicial decisions is clear. Absolute freedom of contract exists in a barter situation because of the equal bargaining position of the parties. At the other extreme are the contracts with public utilities, in which there is no equality of bargaining power between the parties because of the existence of a virtual monopoly. The law therefore denies freedom of contract in the monopoly situation.

The difficulty is that many contracts involve parties and circumstances that fall between these extremes. Many contracts are entered into between parties with substantially unequal bargaining power. When the subject matter of the contracts involves items of everyday necessity, courts frequently hold that one of the parties is a quasi-public instititution and that such institutions are not entitled to complete freedom of contract because freedom of contract is not in the public interest. Thus contracts or parts of the contracts of such institutions may be held illegal whenever the quasi-public institution has taken advantage of its superior bargaining power and drawn a contract, or included a provision in a contract, that in the eyes of the court excessively favors the quasi-public institution to the detriment of the other party and the public. This is especially true when the contract provision is an exculpatory clause or passes risks to a customer that a business should bear.

Not every exculpatory clause is unconscionable, just as not every printed contract is one of adhesion. Many businesses are allowed to contract away liability when the bargaining power is essentially equal and the contract is basically a fair one. This is especially true when the service is not essential. The following case emphasizes the importance of such clauses in hazardous recreational activities.

CASE

Barbara employed Dwain and Robert to teach her to sky dive. Before her first jump, she signed an agreement releasing the instructors from all claims for personal injury resulting from parachuting and related activities. On July 1, 1979, she made her first parachute jump, flying with instructor Dwain and pilot Robert. During a difficult landing some distance from the target Barbara suffered back, arm, and leg injuries. When she sued on a negligence theory, the defendants were granted a summary judgment because of the release.

ISSUE: Does this release protect the defendants from liability caused by their negligence?

DECISION: Yes.

REASONS:
1. Wyoming courts enforce exculpatory clauses releasing parties from liability for injury or damages resulting from negligence if the clause is not contrary to public policy.
2. Generally, specific agreements absolving participants and proprietors from negligence liability during hazardous recreational activities are enforceable, subject to willful misconduct limitations. Adult private parties should not enter into a contract for hazardous recreational services lightly.
3. Private recreational businesses generally do not qualify as ser-

vices demanding a special duty to the public, nor are their services of a special, highly necessary nature.

4. The service provided by the defendants was not a matter of practical necessity for any member of the public. It was not an essential service, so no decisive bargaining advantage existed.

Schutkowski v. Carey, 725 P.2d 1057 (Wyo. 1986).

10. Tickets Disclaiming Liability

Tickets purchased for entrance into places of amusement, for evidence of a contract for transportation, or for a service often contain provisions that attempt to limit or to define the rights of the holder of the ticket. It is generally held that the printed matter on the ticket is a part of an offer that is accepted by the holder of the ticket if he is aware of the printed matter, even though he does not read it. Some cases hold that the purchaser is presumed to know about the printed matter, even though his attention is not called to it at the time the ticket is delivered.

If a ticket is received merely as evidence of ownership and is to be presented later as a means of identification, the provisions on the ticket are not a part of the contract unless the recipient is aware of them or his attention is specifically directed to them. Tickets given at checkrooms or repair shops are usually received as a means of identifying the article to be returned, rather than as setting forth the terms of a contract. Thus the fine print on such tickets is usually not a part of the offer and acceptance unless communicated.

Many terms on tickets may be unconscionable and will not be enforced in any event. The terms are unconscionable when public policy, as previously noted, would declare such a provision in a formal contract to be unconscionable. The quality of the bargaining power of the parties and the nature of the product or service are major factors to be considered in determining unconscionability.

CHAPTER SUMMARY

Status of Illegal Contracts

Litigation Disallowed Exceptions	1. An illegal agreement is legally void and courts will not provide a remedy for any party.

Exceptions

1. If a party is protected by statute, he can rescind and recover any consideration given.
2. If a party has been defrauded or unduly influenced, he can rescind and seek restitution.
3. Under the doctrine of *locus poenitentiae*, a person who repents before performing may rescind and seek restitution.

Agreements in Violation of Statutes

Violation of License Requirements	1. Unlicensed persons providing service that requires a license are not entitled to compensation.

2. Unlicensed persons practicing law cannot recover fees and may be subject to criminal prosecution.

Usury

1. Any contract by which a lender receives more interest than allowed by statute is usurious and illegal.
2. There are many exceptions to usury laws.

Agreements and Activities in Restraint of Trade

1. Antitrust laws protect our economy from monopolies, attempts to monopolize, and activities in restraint of trade.
2. Restraints of trade are either illegal *per se* or illegal only if they are unreasonable. A contract or activity is unreasonable if it suppresses or destroys competition.
3. Price-fixing, agreement among competitors to divide territories, and certain tying agreements (tying a non-patented to a patented product) are illegal *per se*.
4. Vertical price fixing (resale price maintenance) is also illegal *per se*.
5. Price discrimination is illegal if purchasers of goods of like grade and quality are given a lower price than competitors which substantially lessens competition or tends to create a monopoly or injures competition.
6. Exclusive dealing and reciprocal agreements, tying agreements, group boycotts, agreements among competitors to buy from one supplier, and an agreement of manufacturer to give dealer an exclusive territory are illegal if unreasonable.

Agreements in Violation of Public Policy

Agreements Not to Compete

1. Agreements not to compete that are unreasonable restraints of trade are illegal.
2. Reasonableness of covenants not to compete is determined by (1) length of time, (b) geographic area restrained, and (c) the need to protect goodwill.
3. To be legal, covenants not to compete must be part of another contract such as the sale of a business or an employment contract.
4. In the sale of a business, an agreement not to operate a competing business is enforceable if reasonable.
5. In employment contracts, covenants not to compete are enforceable if reasonable in time and territorial effect, considering the business interest protected and the effect on the employee.

Unconscionability

1. Unconscionability is an equitable doctrine used by courts to prevent oppression and unfair surprise in contracts.
2. To be conscionable, material terms of a contract must be conspicuous, understandable, and the result of a true bargain.
3. The doctrine of unconscionability allows a judge to strike contract terms or eliminate the entire contract or limit the unconscionable effect of a term.

Contracts of Adhesion

1. A contract of adhesion is a form contract offered on a take-it-or-leave-it basis to one with little or no bargaining power.
2. These contracts may be enforceable, but they may be found to be unconscionable if they are oppressive.

Contracts Disclaiming Liability

1. An exculpatory clause is a provision that attempts to relieve a party of all tort liability.
2. An exculpatory clause may or may not be unconscionable depending on the bargaining power of the parties.

Tickets Disclaiming Liability

1. Provisions printed on tickets that disclaim liability are binding if the ticket is purchased as admission to a business establishment or for a service.
2. Similar disclaimer provisions are not part of the contract and thus not enforceable if the ticket is merely evidence of ownership.

REVIEW QUESTIONS AND PROBLEMS

1. Match each term in column A with the appropriate statement in column B.

A	V
(1) Usury	(a) Agreement in violation of statute or public policy.
(2) Agreement in restraint of trade	(b) Equitable doctrine to prevent unfair surprise and oppression in contacts.
(3) Covenant not to compete	(c) To be legal must be reasonable in time and geographic scope.
(4) Illegal agreement	(d) Contract terms imposed on adhering party.
(5) *Locus poenitentiae*	(e) Clause that disclaims liability.
(6) Contract of adhesion	(f) Lender receives more interest that allowed by statute.
(7) Unconscionability	(g) Person who repents before performing can rescind and seek restitution.
(8) Exculpatory clause	(h) Price-fixing or other agreement to limit competition.
(9) Effect of illegality	(i) Since agreement is legally void, no remedy is available.
(10) Unlicensed practice of law	(j) Cannot recover fee for services and may violate criminal law.

2. Sam, a real estate broker, prepared a contract for the sale of land for a seller and a buyer. A state statute makes it illegal for brokers to prepare such legal agreements. What two legal dangers does Sam face? Explain.

3. The Fourth of July Company agreed to ship a quantity of fireworks to Behan. After Behan pays in full, he learns that state law prohibits this type of sale. Before the fireworks are sent, Behan calls to cancel this contract and to demand his money back. May he recover his money in court? Why or why not?

4. Melvin, an attorney licensed in California, was hired by Jane, a resident of Alabama, to represent her in an automobile accident case. The accident occurred in Alabama. Melvin was not licensed in Alabama, so he hired a local attorney to assist. Is Melvin entitled to the fees called for in the contract? Why or why not?

5. Aztec borrowed \$50,000 from Union Bank and signed a promissory note in which Aztec promised to pay Union Bank \$50,000 plus 10 percent per annum plus an "indexed principal." The note had a complicated inflation adjustment formula that yielded an additional \$500 as the "indexed principal" when the note became due. The legal rate of interest is 10 percent per annum. Is this promissory note usurious? Explain.

6. Assume that you want to open a record store in a shopping center that is being developed. How might you reduce competition by the terms of your lease with the shopping center? Explain.

7. Strickland, an insured under a Gulf Life disability policy, injured his right leg. Doctors worked unsuccessfully for 118 days to save his leg. The insurance policy provided that Gulf Life would pay disability benefits if an insured lost a leg through "dismemberment by severance" within ninety days after an accident. Gulf Life denied liability because

severance of Strickland's leg was not within the ninety-day limitation. Strickland sued, claiming the ninety-day limitation was contrary to public policy. Should Strickland collect on the policy? Why or why not?

8. Paul agreed to serve as an expert appraisal witness in a condemnation case. The attorney who hired him promised a fee of $500 for an appraisal below $200,000 and $2,500 for an appraisal over $200,000. Is the contract enforceable? Why or why not?

9. Rash signed a covenant not to compete contained in a medical partnership agreement. It prohibited a partner leaving the partnership from engaging in the practice of medicine or surgery within a 25-mile radius of the partnership office for a period of three years. Rash, in executing the covenant, expressly agreed that the covenant was reasonable and that breach of covenant would work harm to the partnership. Is the agreement enforceable? Why or why not?

10. Weniger's employment contract contained the following provision: "Weniger hereby agrees that throughout the two-year period commencing on the termination of his employment hereunder for whatever reason he will not, directly or indirectly, be or become engaged or financially interested in, or an officer or director, employee, consultant or advisor of or to, any business, firm or corporation which is engaged anywhere in the United States or Canada in any business which competes in any way with Egnall." Is the provision enforceable? Why or why not?

11. Millie, an operator of a heating and air-conditioning business for thirteen years, sued Southwestern Bell to recover damages caused by the omission of his ad from the classified section of the telephone directory. The contract contained a provision limiting the phone company's liability to the cost of the ad. Millie claimed that the provision was unconscionable. Was it? Explain.

12. Louis was hired by Kidder Corporation as a stockbroker. The employment contract provided that all disputes between the parties would be decided by arbitration. The employment agreement was a standardized form prepared by the corporation. Does Louis have a valid challenge to the legality of the contract? Explain.

13. A company made a deposit at its bank by using the night depository box. The company's account was not credited, and the bank denied any responsibility since the company's representative had signed an agreement providing that "the use of the night depository facilities shall be at the sole risk of the customer." Is this clause valid? Explain.

14. Baker rented a golf cart at the Jackson Municipal Golf Course. While he was returning the cart, the brakes failed and it overturned, resulting in personal injuries to Baker. When Baker sued, the golf course defended by pointing to a disclaimer of liability clause located on the back of a Golf Cart Rental Agreement signed by Baker. Is the defense valid? Explain.

13 Form and Interpretation of Contracts

CHAPTER PREVIEW

BUSINESS MANAGEMENT DECISION

As the general manager of a stereo store, you help a seventeen-year-old customer who wants to buy stereo equipment worth $2,750 on credit. When you object to this agreement, the customer calls her father, who tells you over the phone, "If my daughter does not pay you, I will."

Are you satisfied with this commitment?

In Chapters 8–12, the elements of a valid, enforceable contract are explained (offer, acceptance, consideration, legal capacity, and legal purpose). Even if an *oral* contract has the required five elements, it may nonetheless be unenforceable because it is not evidenced by a writing.

As a general rule, an oral contract is just as valid and enforceable as a written contract. But some oral contracts are unenforceable under a law known as the *statute of frauds*. The statute of frauds recognizes that some contracts are subject to fraudulent proofs and perjured testimony; therefore, it requires written proof of the contract for the contract to be enforceable. Numerous exceptions to the statute of frauds have been recognized by courts. This chapter considers those contracts within the statute of frauds, both common law and Code exceptions to the statute, and the nature of the writing that will satisfy the statute.

The term *within the statute* is used throughout this chapter. If a contract requires written proof, it is "within the statute." If a writing is not required, the contract is "outside" the statute.

When parties dispute the meaning of their contract, a court will be asked to decide what the contract terms mean. The process of discovering the meaning of a contract is called *interpretation*. For example, a court frequently must determine if a written contract is the sole evidence of the parties' agreement, or if other evidence may be considered. Certain statements or promises that occur prior to the written contract may not be considered because of a rule of procedure called the *parol evidence rule*. This rule and standards of contract interpretation are also covered in this chapter.

STATUTE OF FRAUDS

1. The Approach

Of English origin, the statute of frauds was first enacted in 1677. It is designed to prevent fraud by excluding legal actions on certain important contracts unless there is written evidence of the contract signed by the defendant. Those contracts are said to be unenforceable unless evidenced by a writing signed by the party sought to be bound. There are numerous exceptions to the statute, and it is often narrowly construed.

Generally, the statute is a defense, even though there is no factual dispute over the existence of the contract or its terms. A contract may come into existence at the time of the oral agreement, but it is not enforceable until written evidence of the agreement is available. The agreement is valid in every respect except for the lack of proper evidence of its existence. The statute creates a defense in suits for the breach of executory oral contracts covered by its provisions.

Study of the statute of frauds involves three questions: Is the contract at issue within the statute? If the contract is within the statute, is there written evidence of the contract that satisfies the statute? If there is not sufficient written evidence, does an exception to the statute make the oral agreement legally enforceable?

2. Contracts within the Statute

Under state law, the following contracts are within the statute of frauds and must have written evidence to be enforceable. They are discussed in the next five sections.

1. Special promise of a surety to pay the debt of another, commonly known as a guaranty contract
2. Agreements for the sale of land or an interest in land
3. Agreements that cannot be performed within one year from the date of making
4. Under the Code, contracts for the sale of goods with a price of $500 or more
5. Contracts for the sale of certain personal property other than goods

3. Guaranty Contracts

A person may seek to help another by guaranteeing the latter's debt. In such a case, the debtor is primarily liable and the **guarantor,** or surety, is secondarily liable. A guarantor is not liable to pay until it is shown that the debtor has not paid or cannot pay the debt. The statute of frauds requires a guarantor's promise to be in writing. An oral promise to be primarily liable is not within the statute. The statute protects only persons who assume a secondary liability—that is, a promise to pay another's debt only if the other person does not pay.

Guarantor *One who by contract undertakes ''to answer for the debt, default, and miscarriage of another.'' In general, a guarantor undertakes to pay if the principal debtor does not.*

In some cases, it is difficult to determine whether a party has made a promise to be secondarily liable or has incurred a direct, primary obligation to pay. A person can make a direct obligation to pay for someone else. For example, Father says to Auto Dealer: ''Deliver the car to my son, and I'll pay for it.'' This primary direct promise is not within the statute of frauds. But if someone assumes a secondary obligation to pay, that promise is a guarantee and is within the statute. For example, Father says to Auto Dealer: ''Deliver the car to my son. If he does not pay for it, then I promise to pay.'' Father is secondarily liable and his promise must be in writing to be enforceable.

At times a guarantor may intend primarily to benefit himself and not the debtor. For example, a person with a substantial financial interest in a corporation may promise orally to pay a debt of the corporation if it cannot pay. The law does not extend the protection of the statute of frauds to this type of guarantor. It analyzes the *main purpose* or *leading object* of the promisor in making the promise. When the leading object is to become a guarantor of another's debt primarily to benefit that other person, the promise is secondary and within the statute. When the leading object of the promisor is to serve some interest or purpose of his own, even though he guarantees another's debt, the promise is direct and primary; it is not within the statute. Under the leading object rule, a court must determine whether the promisor intended primarily to benefit himself or the debtor. The following case is typical of those involving the leading object rule.

CASE

Camarda, a medical doctor, and Schinella, a general contractor, entered into a partnership to develop an office building called Stevanton Plaza. In the course of that development, plumbing work was required, for which Otto was the successful bidder. Because Otto had doubts about the financial responsibility of Schinella, he refused to execute a subcontract for the plumbing work unless Camarda would personally guarantee payment. Although a separate contract of guaranty was not executed by Camarda, he did personally sign the subcontract. When Otto was not paid for his work, he sued, and the issue at trial narrowed to the personal liability of the defendant Camarda. The trial court concluded that Camarda was liable because his assurance of payment was an original undertaking not within the statute of frauds. Camarda appealed.

ISSUE: Was Camarda's promise to pay required to be evidenced by a signed writing?

DECISION: No.

REASONS:
1. The main purpose or leading object rule, which defines when an undertaking is original rather than collateral, is an exception of long standing to the statute of frauds' guaranty provision.
2. On the basis of the evidence and the record before it, the trial court could readily have inferred that the defendant, as owner, stood to benefit from the work done to complete the office building.
3. There was ample evidence that the plaintiff Otto gave credit, not to the nominal contractor, S. Schinella & Son, Inc., but rather to the owners Schinella and Camarda personally.
4. Under these circumstances, the trial court correctly concluded that the defendant Camarda made a commitment as an original undertaking not within the statute of frauds.

Otto Contracting Co. v. S. Schinella & Son, 427 A.2d 856 (Conn. 1980).

4. Contracts Involving Interests in Land

Since the law has always placed importance on contracts involving land, it is logical that the statute of frauds should require a writing for a contract creating or transferring any interest in land. In addition to contracts involving a sale of an entire interest, the statute is applicable to contracts involving interests for a person's lifetime (called life estates), to mortgages, to easements, and to leases for a period in excess of one year.

One problem under the statute is to determine what is real property. Generally, it is land and all things affixed to the land. What is the status of things such as standing timber or minerals? Is an oral contract to sell oil and gas a contract involving real estate? The general rule is that these items are real property if the title to them is to pass to the buyer before they are severed from the land; they are personal property if title to them passes subsequently. The Code provides that a contract to sell minerals, oil, and the like, or a contract for a structure or its materials to be removed from realty, is a contract for the sale of goods if they are to be severed by the seller. If the buyer is to sever them, the contract affects and involves land and is subject to the real estate provisions of the statute of frauds. The Code also provides that a contract for the sale of growing crops is a contract for the sale of goods, whether they are to be severed by the buyer or by the seller.

Note that one of the exceptions to the statute (discussed in more detail later) is the doctrine of part performance. This exception frequently applies to oral contracts granting an interest in land. For example, courts will enforce an oral contract for the sale of land if, with the seller's consent, the buyer takes possession of the land and makes a partial payment and valuable improvements on it.

5. Contracts That Cannot Be Performed within One Year

A contract is within the statute if, by its terms, it cannot be performed within one year from the time it is made. The period is measured from the time an oral contract is made to the time when the promised performance is to be completed. Thus an oral agreement to hire a person for two years or to form and carry on a partnership for ten years would not be enforceable.

The decisive factor in determining whether a long-term contract comes within the statute is whether performance is possible within a year from the date of making. If a contract, according to the intentions of the parties as shown by its terms, may be fully performed within a year from the time it is made, it is not within the statute of frauds, even though the time of its performance is uncertain and may extend—and, in fact, does extend—beyond the year. If one party has fully performed, the contract is then not within the statute of frauds.

Even though it is most unlikely that performance could be rendered within one year, the statute does not apply if there is even a remote possibility that it could. This rule is one of possibility and not probability. Thus, assuming all elements of a valid contract, a promise to pay \$10,000 "when cars are no longer polluting the air" would be enforceable even though given orally. Moreover, if a contract, otherwise to continue for more than a year, is by its own terms subject to termination within a year, it is not within the prohibition of the statute of frauds.

Thus the question is not how long performance will *probably* run, but can the contract *possibly be performed* within one year from the making of the contract. To put the matter in sharper focus, the rule should be stated: An oral contract that by its terms has no possibility of being performed within one year from the date of formation must be evidenced by a writing. If it is possible to perform it within one year from the date of making, it is not within the statute. This rule was applied in the case that follows.

CASE

Clairmont made an oral exclusive real estate listing agreement with Walker. Walker, for a commission, agrees to sell all Clairmont's real property now owned by Clairmont as well as all property later acquired by Clairmont. They agreed that this exclusive listing would last as long as they lived. When Walker sued, the trial court dismissed the case, holding that the oral contract was unenforceable under the statute of frauds.

ISSUE: Is the oral agreement within the statute of frauds?

DECISION: No.

REASONS: 1. If there is any possibility an oral contract can be performed in one year, it is not within the statute of frauds. To be within the statute, an oral contract must be impossible of performance in one year.

2. This oral contract is not within the statute even though its duration is for a lifetime because of the possibility that Walker or Clairmont may die within one year.

Berquist-Walker Real Estate v. Wm. Clairmont, 333 N.W.2d 414 (N.D. 1983).

6. Contracts for the Sale of Goods

The Uniform Commercial Code contains several provisions regarding the statute of frauds. The provision applicable to the sale of goods stipulates that a contract for the sale of goods for the price of $500 or more is not enforceable unless there is some writing sufficient to indicate that a contract for sale has been made. The writing must be signed by the defendant or his authorized agent or broker. The Code further states that a writing is not insufficient if it omits or incorrectly states a term agreed on, but the agreement will not be enforced beyond the quantity of goods mentioned in the writing.

The Code favors contract formation and performance. Given that philosophy, the Code has four exceptions to the statute of frauds provision. These exceptions are explained in sections 13–16 in this chapter.

7. Contracts for the Sale of Personal Property Other Than Goods

The Code has several additional sections that require a writing. A contract for the sale of securities such as stocks and bonds is not enforceable unless (1) there is a signed writing setting forth a stated quantity of described securities at a defined or stated price, or (2) delivery of the security has been accepted or payment has been made, or (3) within a reasonable time a confirmation in writing of the sale or purchase has been sent and received and the party receiving it has failed to object to it within ten days after receipt, or (4) the party against whom enforcement is sought admits in court that such a contract was made. Note that this relates only to contracts for the sale of securities [8-319].

Another section concerns contracts for the sale of personal property other than goods or securities. For these contracts, which involve matters such as royalty rights, patent rights, and rights under a bilateral contract, a writing is required if the amount involved exceeds $5,000 [1-206].

In the discussion of secured transactions, in Chapters 39 and 40, the Code usually requires a signed security agreement. Therefore, when a person borrows money and gives the lender an interest in his property as security, the debtor (borrower) must sign a security agreement [9-203].

8. Writing Required by the Statute of Frauds

If a contract is within the statute of frauds, there must be a signed writing sufficient to satisfy the statute of frauds. Generally, the common law requires more terms to be in the writing than does the Code. The general common law is explained in this section and the Code requirements are covered in section 9.

The statute of frauds does not require a formal written contract signed by both parties. All that is required is a note or memorandum that provides written evidence of the transaction. It must be signed by the party sought to be bound by the agreement (the defendant). The memorandum need contain only the names of the parties, a description of the subject matter, the price, and the general terms of the agreement. A memorandum of sale of real property must describe the real estate with such certainty that a court may order its conveyance, as the following case illustrates.

CASE

Truebenbach owned two adjacent tracts of land, one containing 165 acres and the other, 25 acres. He sold the 165-acre tract to Pick. The deed stated: "Grantors also guarantee Pick a right-of-way across the 25-acre tract sold to Walter Bartel." Five days later, Truebenbach sold the 25-acre tract to Bartel, who refused to recognize the easement to Pick. When Pick sued to enforce his easement, the court held Pick's deed was not a sufficient writing to satisfy the statute of frauds because the land subject to the easement was not adequately described.

ISSUE: Was the reference in Pick's deed to the "25-acre tract sold to Walter Bartel" a sufficient description?

DECISION: No.

REASONS:
1. An easement is an interest in land that is subject to the statute of frauds.
2. The description of the land subject to an easement must reasonably identify the land. The words "25-acre tract sold to Walter Bartel" does not reasonably identify the land.
3. Since the Pick and Bartel deeds were dated five days apart, the 25-acre tract had not been sold to Bartel when the Pick deed was signed. No city, county, or state is mentioned. No lot or block number is given. In fact, every essential element of the description is left to inference.

Pick v. Bartel, 659 S.W.2d 636 (Tex. 1983).

Under the statute, one party may be bound by an agreement even though the other party is not. Only the party who resists performance need have signed. Such a result is predicated on the theory that the agreement is legal in all respects, but proper evidence of such an agreement is lacking. This is furnished when the person sought to be charged with the contract has signed a writing.

The note or memorandum may consist of several writings, even though the writing containing the requisite terms is unsigned. However, it must appear from an examination of all the writings that the writing signed by the party to be charged was signed with the intention that it refer to the unsigned writing. In effect, the writings must be connected by internal reference in the signed memorandum to the unsigned one, so that they may be said to constitute one paper relating to the contract.

The unsigned document is part of the memorandum if the documents by internal reference refer to the same subject matter or transaction. But if the documents do not refer to the same subject matter, they may not be read together. Oral evidence is not admissible to connect them.

As to the signature of the party sought to be charged, it may be quite informal and need not necessarily be placed at the close of the document. It may be in the body of the writing or elsewhere, as long as it identifies the writing with the signature of the person sought to be held.

9. Writing Required for Code Contracts

The Code has three minimal requirements for the writing to satisfy the Code statute of frauds provision. First, there must be some writing sufficient to indicate that a contract for the sale of certain goods has been made between the parties. Second, the writing must contain a quantity term, which need not be accurately stated, or a means for determining quantity such as by outputs or requirements. If a contract states a quantity, it will not be enforced beyond the quantity term stated in the writing. Third, the writing must be signed by the party against whom the contract is being enforced. Thus a plaintiff who is seeking to enforce the contract is not required to have signed the writing. Beyond these three requirements, the writing need not contain the material terms of the contract.

COMMON LAW EXCEPTIONS TO THE STATUTE OF FRAUDS

10. Introduction

The statute of frauds is not applicable to executed contracts. A party who has, for example, purchased or sold land under an oral contract cannot obtain a refund of his money or cannot obtain a return deed to his land. The statute of frauds does not allow rescission; it serves only as a defense to a suit for breach of an executory contract. Likewise, a contract that cannot be performed within one year that is fully executed cannot be rescinded.

If an agreement is within the statute of frauds and no written evidence of the contract exists, the contract will still be enforced and the defense ineffectual if one of the exceptions to the statute applies. Two exceptions are applicable to all types of contracts: part performance and promissory estoppel.

11. Part Performance

When a party has partly or fully performed his oral promise or has detrimentally relied on another's oral promise, it would be inequitable in most cases to deny that party relief because of the statute of frauds. Consequently, courts have made equitable exceptions to the statute. One exception is commonly called the doctrine of part performance. When one party to an oral contract partly or fully performs, then the other party is equitably estopped from using the statute as a defense. Another name for this doctrine is **equitable estoppel.** It is used primarily in oral contracts for the sale of real property, because many oral contracts involving real estate become partially executed as a result of part payment by the buyer or surrender of possession to the buyer by the seller or both. Since the statute of frauds is a complete defense to an executory oral contract involving real estate and it is no defense to a fully executed contract, what is the status if the contract is partially performed?

Equitable estoppel *A legal theory used to prevent a party to an oral contract that has been partially performed from asserting the defense of the statute of frauds.*

Performance to satisfy the statute of frauds has two aspects. First, the performance must establish and point unmistakably and exclusively to the existence of an oral contract. Performance eliminates the statute as a defense in such cases because it eliminates any doubt that a contract was made. Thus the reason for the defense of the statute does not exist.

Second, the performance must be substantial enough to warrant judicial relief, such as specific performance of the oral contract. In other words, it must be such that returning the parties to the status quo is unreasonable. To illustrate, assume that a buyer of real property under an oral contract has paid part of the purchase price. The money can be returned, and the statute of frauds would be a defense because there would be no equitable reason to enforce the oral agreement. However, when the seller under an oral contract also delivers possession to the buyer, the defense of the statute of frauds becomes more tenuous, because returning the parties to the status quo becomes somewhat difficult. When improvements are made by one in possession, a return to the status quo becomes quite difficult, if not impossible.

It is clear that the transaction is taken out of the statute if the buyer has taken possession, paid all or part of the price, and made valuable improvements. Less part performance may also take the contract out of the statute if the buyer takes possession and pays part of the price, giving good evidence of a contract. If he also pays taxes and mortgage payments while in possession, specific performance may be warranted. Payment of the price, standing alone, is not a basis for specific performance and will not satisfy the statute since the payment of money could be interpreted as rent for a lease rather than a sale.

Part performance issues are often difficult to apply in contracts that cannot be performed within one year of the date of making. There is almost always some part performance. The following case is typical of those in which a party seeks to avoid the statute of frauds defense.

CASE

Heller Brothers Realty, the owner of a shopping center, leased space to Clarence Williams for the purpose of operating a retail clothing business. The term of the lease was five years. Later, Heller Brothers leased other space in the shopping center to Boots and Boutique, a retail store specializing in the sale of shoes. Williams sued Heller Brothers, claiming that before entering the lease agreement, they had orally agreed that no other space would be leased within the shopping center to a business that would be in direct competition with Williams's business. Williams claimed that Boots and Boutique was in direct competition with his business, and that Heller Brothers was therefore guilty of a breach of the agreement. Williams asked the court to enjoin Heller Brothers from continuing to allow this competition. Heller Brothers denied Williams's allegation of an oral agreement, and alleged that Williams's suit was barred by the statute of frauds. Williams claimed that the statute of frauds did not apply because he had partly performed his obligations under the alleged oral agreement by refraining from competing with the other tenants in the shopping center. The trial judge, finding that the statute of frauds barred the suit, dismissed the case.

ISSUE: Did the statute of frauds bar Williams's suit, despite his alleged part performance of the oral agreement?

DECISION: Yes.

REASONS: 1. The alleged oral agreement extends for five years because it would remain in effect as long as Williams was a tenant under the five-year lease. Therefore the statute of frauds applies to the oral agreement because it could not be performed within a year from the day it was made.

2. Williams's forbearance to compete with the other tenants does not constitute proof of part performance of his alleged oral agreement with Heller Brothers because there are several possible explanations for his forbearance besides the agreement. Williams might have believed that the lease's *written* provision that he was renting the space "for the purpose of operating a retail clothing business" prohibited him from engaging in another business. He may have had no skill in the conduct of other enterprises, been financially unable to expand, or simply been uninterested in undertaking a different commercial venture.
3. Therefore Williams has not shown part performance and the statute of frauds bars his suit. The trial court's judgment is affirmed.

Williams v. Heller Bros. Realty, 326 S.E.2d 661 (Va. 1985).

12. Promissory Estoppel

Chapter 10 explains promissory estoppel as a doctrine for validating contracts as an alternative to consideration. That same concept is sometimes used by courts to prevent a party to an oral contract from using the statute of frauds as a defense. When a party relies to his detriment on an oral promise, the oral promise may be enforceable, notwithstanding the statute of frauds. The reliance must be foreseeable by the promisor, and enforcement of the promise must be necessary to avoid injustice. The remedy may be limited as justice requires.

Like the part performance exception, courts may use promissory estoppel to achieve fairness and prevent an unfair result. Promissory estoppel is used whenever the plaintiff's equities are so great that any contrary decision would be inequitable. In many cases, parties will rely on oral promises. In such cases, to allow the statute of frauds to be used as a defense would itself constitute a type of fraud on the relying party. The trend of decisions is to use promissory estoppel to prevent an unfair use of the statute.

CODE EXCEPTIONS TO THE STATUTE OF FRAUDS

The Code has four exceptions to the requirement that contracts involving $500 or more must be in writing: confirmation between merchants, specially manufactured goods, judicial admissions, and part performance.

13. Written Confirmation between Merchants

This exception arises from the business practice of negotiating contracts orally, often by telephone. A merchant who contracts orally with another merchant can satisfy the statute of frauds requirement by sending a confirming writing to the other merchant [2-201(2)]. This confirmation will satisfy the statute, even though it is not signed by the party to be charged, unless written notice of objection to its contents is given within ten days after it is received. This means that a merchant who has dealt orally with another merchant will have an enforceable contract unless the merchant receiving the writing objects within the ten-day period.

For purposes of this rule, most farmers are merchants when they orally sell their grain. This is of special importance in agriculture, as oral agreements are the customary way of doing business. The following case is typical of those that arise as a result of oral grain sales.

CASE

Jim Schrant orally contracted to sell 6,500 bushels of soybeans to Agrex, Inc., for $39,130. He received a written confirmation of the sale by mail but neglected to disavow the contract. When he did not deliver the soybeans, Agrex had to purchase the beans on the open market at a higher price. Agrex sued Schrant for breach of contract. Schrant claimed, among other things, that the statute of frauds barred Agrex from suing on the contract.

ISSUE: Does the statute of frauds bar Agrex from recovering on this contract?

DECISION: No.

REASONS:

1. Nebraska has adopted the Uniform Commercial Code's statute of frauds, which provides that any contract for the sale of goods for a price of $500 or more is not enforceable unless there is some writing, signed by the party against whom enforcement is sought, which is sufficient to indicate that a contract of sale has been made.
2. However, if the parties to a contract are merchants, a written confirmation of an oral agreement satisfies the statute of frauds unless the party receiving such confirmation objects to it within ten days.
3. Experienced grain producers who regularly grow and market grain on the open market as the principal means of providing for their livelihood, and who by reason of such occupation have acquired knowledge or skill peculiar to the practices and operations of grain marketing, are merchants within the meaning of the Code's statute of frauds.
4. Since no objection to the written confirmation sent by Agrex was made by Schrant, these parties were bound to the oral contract to buy and sell soybeans.

Agrex, Inc. v. Schrant, 379 N.W.2d 751 (Neb. 1986).

14. Specially Manufactured Goods

This second exception to the writing requirement under the Code relates to conduct that clearly shows a contract has been made. The Code explicitly excludes from the statute transactions that involve goods to be specially manufactured. To fit within this exception, three requirements must be met [2-201(3)(a)]:

1. The goods are to be specially manufactured for the particular buyer and are not suitable for sale to others.

2. The seller has made a substantial beginning to manufacture or commitments to obtain the goods.
3. The circumstances reasonably indicate that the goods are for the buyer.

15. Judicial Admissions

Another substitute for writing is based on recognition that the required writing is simply a formality and that a contract may very well exist. The oral contract is unenforceable without proof of its existence; but when proper proof is available, the contract becomes enforceable. If the party who is resisting the contract admits its existence in the proper circumstances and surroundings, such admission will substitute for a writing. Thus the Code provides that an oral contract for the sale of goods is enforceable if (when legal action is brought to enforce it) the defendant admits in the court proceedings that a contract for sale was made. It is quite possible that the admission will be made in the pleadings, during discovery, or as testimony during a trial. That judicial admission satisfies the Code statutory requirement of a writing [2-201(3)(b)].

As a result of modern discovery techniques and liberal rules of evidence, this exception usually is available if a contract has in fact been entered into. There is usually no way to avoid the exception short of perjury. The following case shows how testimony can be obtained to eliminate the defense.

CASE

Anderson, a farmer, orally agreed to sell to Farmers Elevator Company 18,000 bushels of wheat at a price of $1.80 per bushel. Due to an increase in the value of his wheat, Anderson refused to deliver the required number of bushels. Instead, Anderson sold his wheat to another elevator operator at $5.35 per bushel. When sued by Farmers Elevator Company, Anderson argued that he was not bound to the contract since it was not in writing. Despite making this argument, Anderson readily admitted in a deposition and during the trial that he had orally contracted with Farmers Elevator Company.

ISSUE: Is this oral contract enforceable?

DECISION: Yes.

REASONS:

1. If the party asserting the statute of frauds defense admits the existence of an oral contract for the sale of goods, such contract will be enforced.
2. The Code attempts to make the law conform with business practices.
3. The purpose of the writing requirement of the statute of frauds is to protect against deception. That purpose is just as well served when the party against whom enforcement is sought admits the existence of the oral contract.

Farmers Elevator Co. of Reserve v. Anderson, 552 P.2d 63 (Mont. 1976).

16. Part Performance

The final exception is part performance. The Code excepts oral contracts for the sale of goods that have been paid for or received and accepted [2-201(3)(c)]. In the sale of goods, the Code takes the contract out of the statute only to the extent of the part performance. In other words, these contracts are enforceable to the extent the buyer has made payment for goods or to the extent the seller has shipped goods that the buyer has accepted. Any unperformed part of the contract is still within the statute, and some writing is required unless one of the other exceptions is applicable.

PAROL EVIDENCE RULE

17. The Theory

Courts are often asked to interpret the meaning of a contract. If the contract is written, courts may face the question of whether or not they can consider oral or other evidence that is not in the written document. The law seeks to protect the sanctity of written contracts. Therefore it is generally held that statements, promises, guarantees, and representations made by the parties prior to signing a written contract may not be considered if the written contract represents the entire agreement of the parties. This law is called the **parol evidence** rule.

Parol evidence *Legal proof based on oral statements.*

The parol evidence rule prevents the introduction of prior or contemporaneous oral or written agreements that might vary or contradict the final written contract. When parties to a contract embody the terms of their agreement in a writing intended to be the final and exclusive expression of their agreement, the written contract cannot be contradicted, explained, varied, or supplemented. Everything that happens prior to or contemporaneously with the execution of the written contract is assumed to be integrated into it. The written contract is deemed the only permissible evidence of the agreement. All earlier negotiations, understandings, representations, and agreements are said to have merged in the written contract. Therefore *parol* (extrinsic) evidence is not admissible to supplement, subtract from, alter, vary, or contradict the agreement as written.

18. Exceptions to the Parol Evidence Rule

Most legal rules have exceptions based on notions of equity, good conscience, and common sense. The parol evidence rule has several such exceptions. First, since the rule presumes all prior negotiations are merged into the written contract, it obviously cannot apply to agreements made after the written contract. Thus the rule does not prevent the use of oral evidence to establish modifications agreed upon subsequent to the execution of the written contract. Likewise, the rule is inapplicable to evidence of a cancellation of the agreement. Other exceptions include evidence of fraudulent misrepresentations, lack of delivery of an instrument when delivery is required to give it effect, and errors in drafting or reducing the contract to writing. Moreover, oral evidence is always allowed to clarify the terms of an ambiguous contract.

Perhaps the most important exception is the *partial integration rule*. This exception requires the judge to determine if the written contract is totally or merely partially integrated. A total integration occurs when the parties intend the written contract to be the *final* and *complete* statement of their agreement. If they do, evidence of prior agreements is not permitted for any reason. A partial integration occurs when the parties intend the writing to be final on the terms as written but not necessarily complete on all terms of their agreement. Although the contract cannot be *contradicted* under the partial integration rule, it can be *supplemented* or *explained* by prior agreements between the parties.

19. Parol Evidence Rule and the Code

The Code recognizes that the parol evidence rule prevents the use of oral evidence to contradict or vary the terms of a written memorandum or of a contract that is intended to be the final expression of the parties. The impact of the rule is greatly reduced, however, by the Code's provision that a written contract may be explained or supplemented by a prior course of dealing between buyer and seller, by usage of trade, or by the course of performance. The Code also allows evidence of consistent additional terms to be introduced, based on the partial integration rule [2-202]. The provisions allowing such evidence are designed to ascertain the true understanding of the parties concerning the agreement and to place the agreement in its proper perspective. The assumption is that prior dealings between the parties and the usages of the trade were taken for granted when the contract was worded. Often a contract for sale involves repetitive performance by both parties over a period of time. The course of performance is indicative of the meaning that the parties, by practical construction, have given to their agreement. It is relevant to interpretation of the agreement and thus is admissible evidence.

When oral evidence of a course of dealing, trade usage, or course of performance is introduced under the Code's exceptions to the parol evidence rule, the law recognizes an order of preference in the event of inconsistencies. Express terms will prevail over an interpretation based on the course of performance, and the course of performance will prevail over an interpretation predicated upon either the course of dealing or the usage of trade [2-208].

CONSTRUCTION AND INTERPRETATION RULES

Courts are often called upon to construe or interpret contracts. Although there is a technical distinction between *construction* (courts construe a contract's legal effect) and *interpretation* (juries interpret the parties' intentions), these words are generally interchangeable. The basic purpose of construing a contract is to determine the intention of the parties. If the language is clear and unambiguous, construction is not required, and the intent expressed in the agreement will be followed. When the language of a contract is ambiguous or obscure, courts apply certain established rules of construction in order to ascertain the supposed intent of the parties. These rules will not be used to make a new contract for the parties or to rewrite the old one. They are applied by the court merely to resolve doubts and ambiguities within the framework of the agreement.

The general standard of interpretation is to use the meaning the contract language would convey to a reasonably intelligent person who is familiar with the circumstances in which the language was used. Thus language is judged objectively rather than subjectively and is given a reasonable meaning. What one party says he or she meant or thought he or she was saying or writing is immaterial, since words are given effect in accordance with their meaning to a reasonable person in the circumstances of the parties. In determining the intention of the parties, it is the expressed intention that controls, and this will be given effect unless it conflicts with some rule of law, good morals, or public policy.

The language is judged with reference to the subject matter of the contract, its nature, objects, and purposes. Language is usually given its ordinary meaning, but technical words are given their technical meaning. Words with an established legal meaning are given that legal meaning. The law of the place where the contract was made is considered a part of the contract. Isolated words or clauses are not considered; instead, the contract is considered as a whole to ascertain the intent of the parties. If one party has prepared the agreement, an ambiguity in the contract language will be construed against him, since he had the chance to eliminate the ambiguity.

As an aid to the court in determining the intention of the parties, special provisions prevail over general provisions, handwritten provisions prevail over typewritten ones, and typewritten provisions prevail over printed ones. Furthermore, courts may consider business custom, usage, and prior dealings between the parties. The UCC encourages courts to supply contractual terms omitted by the parties. This gap-filling process is discussed in Chapter 17.

In the interpretation of contracts, the construction the parties have themselves placed on the agreement is often the most significant source of the intention of the parties. The parties themselves know best what they meant by their words of agreement, and their action under that agreement is the best indication of what that meaning was.

CHAPTER SUMMARY

Statute of Frauds

The Approach	1. Contracts within the statute of frauds are unenforceable unless evidenced by a writing. 2. The statute of frauds results in an affirmative defense that must be pleaded.
Guaranty Contracts	1. A direct primary promise to pay another's debt is not within the statute. 2. A secondary promise to pay another's debt if the debtor does not pay is within the statute and must be evidenced by a writing. 3. If the promisor's leading object or main purpose is to serve his own interests, the promise is not within the statute.
Contracts Involving Interests in Land	1. Any contract that creates or transfers any interest in land must be evidenced by a writing and signed by the party to be charged. 2. Sale of realty, leases for one year or more, liens, mortgages, and easements are within the statute. 3. Promises to transfer timber, minerals, oil and gas, and structures are within the statute *unless* the seller is to sever them from the realty. 4. Growing crops are goods, not interests in land, and are not within the statute regardless of who severs them.
Contracts That Cannot Be Performed within One Year	1. Any contract that, by its terms, is impossible to perform within one year is within the statute. 2. If there is *any possibility* a contract can be performed in one year, it is not within the statute.

Contracts for the Sale of Goods

1. Contracts for the sale of goods having a *price* of $500 or more are within the statute.

Writing Required by the Statute of Frauds

1. A writing satisfies the statute if it states with *reasonable* certainty the identity of the parties, the subject matter, and the essential terms and conditions and is signed by the party to be charged.
2. If there is more than one writing and one writing is signed, the unsigned writing is part of the signed writing if the writings by internal reference refer to the same subject matter or transaction.

Writing Required for Code Contracts

1. A writing satisfies the statute if it (a) indicates a sale of certain goods between the parties, (b) has a quantity term, and (c) is signed by the party to be charged.
2. Omission of any term other than quantity does not make writing insufficient. The quantity term may be supplied by any means such as outputs and requirements.
3. The contract will not be enforced beyond the quantity stated in the writing.

Common Law Exceptions to the Statute of Frauds

Part Performance

1. If an oral contract was fully performed by both parties, the statute is not applicable.
2. Performance must establish and point unmistakably and exclusively to the existence of an oral contract.
3. Performance must be so substantial that it would be inequitable not to grant judicial relief.
4. If it is reasonable to return the parties to the status quo, a court will rescind the transaction. A buyer who has only paid the price will have his money returned.
5. If a buyer has paid the price and taken other actions (such as making valuable improvements to land), courts will recognize an exception to the statute.
6. In contracts of long duration, full performance by one party makes the agreement enforceable.

Promissory Estoppel

1. If a party detrimentally relies on an oral promise, some courts will enforce the promise.
2. The reliance must be foreseeable by the promisor, enforcement of the promise is necessary to avoid injustice, and the remedy may be as limited as justice requires.

Code Exceptions to the Statute of Frauds

Written Confirmation between Merchants

1. The Code has four exceptions: written confirmation between merchants, specially manufactured goods, judicial admissions, and performance.
2. *Between merchants*, a signed confirmation of an oral contract sent within a reasonable time satisifes the statute if the merchant who actually receives it does not object by written notice within ten days.
3. At a minimum, the confirmation must be written, signed by the sender, evidence an actual contract between the parties, and contain a quantity term.

Specially Manufactured Goods

1. Contracts involving goods specially manufactured for the buyer are enforceable even though the contracts are not evidenced by signed writings.

Judicial Admissions

1. If the party to be charged admits in his pleadings, testimony, or otherwise in court that a contract of sale was made, the statute is satisfied.

Part Performance

1. Part or full payment or part or complete acceptance of goods satisfies the statute. The contract is enforced only to the extent of the part performance.

Parol Evidence Rule

The Theory

1. Evidence of prior or contemporaneous agreements (whether written or oral) is inadmissible to vary, contradict, or modify an unambiguous written contract.
2. Parol evidence will be excluded only if the court finds that the writing was intended as a *final and complete* agreement (totally integrated).
3. A merger or integration clause (''This is the final and complete agreement.'') is generally given effect.

Exceptions

1. Parol evidence may be used to (a) show that writing was not the final and complete agreement, (b) show defects in formation, (c) show and explain ambiguity, and (d) show subsequent agreements.

Parol Evidence Rules and the Code

1. Under the Code, agreements may be explained by evidence of course of dealing, usage of trade, or course of performance.

Construction and Interpretation Rules

1. Words are given their plain and ordinary meanings.
2. Ambiguities are construed against the party who drafted or used the ambiguous language.
3. Writings are to be interpreted as a whole and language is not to be taken out of context.
4. Specific provisions control general provisions.
5. Handwritten provisions prevail over typed provisions, and typed provisions prevail over printed provisions.
6. Courts may rely on business customs, usages of trade, and the parties' prior dealings to give meaning to a contract's language.
7. The Code supplies (gap-fills) terms omitted by the parties. Code-implied terms are applicable unless the parties provide otherwise in their agreement.

REVIEW QUESTIONS AND PROBLEMS

1. Match each term in column A with the appropriate statement in column B.

A	B
(1) Guarantor of another's debt primarily wants to benefit himself	(a) Party detrimentally relies on oral promise.
(2) Contract that cannot be performed within one year	(b) Indicates a contract between the parties, indicates quantity, and is signed by party to be charged.
(3) Promissory estoppel exception	(c) A promise to pay another's debt, grant of an interest in land, a contract that cannot be performed in one year, and sale of goods of $500 or more.
(4) Equitable estoppel exception	(d) Writing that satisfies statute but is not signed by the party to be charged.
(5) Sufficient writing required by the Code	(e) Written contract is final but not the complete agreement.
(6) Confirmation between merchants	(f) Confirmation between merchants, specially manufactured goods, judicial admissions, performance.
(7) Parol evidence rule	(g) Leading object rule.
(8) Partial integration	(h) Eliminates prior or contemporaneous evidence which varies, contradicts, or modifies a written contract.
(9) Contracts granting interests in land	(i) Part or full performance by one party.
(10) Merger or integration clause	(j) Two-year employment contract.
(11) Code exceptions to the statute of frauds	(k) "This is the parties' entire agreement."
(12) Contracts within the statute of frauds	(l) Easement, mortgage, lease for more than a year.

2. Meyers, a fashion designer, orally sold Waverly Fabrics a design known as "Cook's Stripe." The agreement prohibited licensing others to use the design. When Waverly licensed others to use the design, Meyers sued for breach of contract. Is the statute of frauds a valid defense? Why or why not?

3. A butcher sold hamburger meat on credit to the Good Eats Restaurant. When the restaurant was late in paying its bills, the butcher contacted Jim, who orally promised to pay any bill that the restaurant failed to pay. Is this oral promise enforceable in court? Why or why not? Would your answer change if Jim said: "The restaurant is on hard times. Send the bills to me, and I'll pay." Explain.

4. The Big Jim's Corporation borrowed $30,000 from Bassett. To encourage Bassett to make the loan, Griggs, the major shareholder in Big Jim's, orally promised to pay Bassett if Big Jim's did not repay the loan. In fact, Big Jim's failed to pay, and Bassett sued Griggs on his oral guarantee. Griggs contended his promise was unenforceable under the statute of frauds. Is the statute of frauds a defense? Why or why not?

5. Livesay orally agreed to sell real estate to Drake. Before the closing, Livesay sold it to someone else and wrote Drake a letter apologizing for selling it at a higher price. The letter mentioned both prices and contained an adequate reference to the real estate. When Drake sues Livesay, will the statute of frauds be an adequate defense? Why or why not?

6. Hardin Associates, a developer of shopping centers, hired Brummet to head its development division. Brummett was hired on an oral contract of employment for an indefinite time. He was later discharged, and he sued for breach of contract. Hardin asserted the statute of frauds as a defense. What result? Why?

7. On September 15, 1988, Builders orally agreed with K. Construction Company to work together on a project. Work was to begin January 1, 1989, and it was contemplated that the work would be completed by the end of 1989. Is the contract enforceable? Explain.

8. Seaman supplied fuel for ships and needed a long-term supply contract with a major oil company. In a letter, dated October 11, Standard Oil offered Seaman a ten-year supply contract with three, ten-year options for renewal. The letter made no mention of quantity requirements, price, particulars of performance, or other material terms. Seaman signed the letter indicating his acceptance of Standard's offer. When Standard later said it could not supply fuel, Seaman sued. Standard raised the defense of the statute of frauds. Is the October 11 letter a signed writing sufficient to satisfy the statute of frauds? Explain.

9. Brown entered into an oral contract to purchase a farm from Burnside. Brown took possession of the farm, made several improvements, tore down an old farmhouse, paid taxes, and made payments on the purchase price. Burnside thereafter refused to deed the farm to Brown as orally agreed. Brown sought specific performance of the oral contract. Is the oral contract to sell real property enforceable under these circumstances? Why or why not?

10. Potter hatches turkeys in Oregon, and Hatter raises turkeys in Oklahoma. Potter and Hatter orally agreed to a buy-sell contract for young turkeys, but there was a problem in transporting the young turkeys from Oregon to Oklahoma. Hatter assured Potter that he would find a solution to the transportation problem. In reliance on this assurance, Potter turned down an offer to sell his young turkeys to a California buyer. Two months later, Hatter said he would be unable to buy the turkeys and Potter sued. Is the statute of frauds a valid defense? Why or why not?

11. Associated Lithographers made an oral contract to provide Stay Wood Products with special printed business cards, letterheads and envelopes, order forms, and an etching and rubber stamp with Stay Wood Products name. When Stay Wood Products refused to pay, Associated Lithographers sued. Stay Wood raised the defense of the statute of frauds. Is the statute of frauds a defense? Explain.

12. Alex agreed to buy a car from Ford Company for $2,500. They did not sign a contract, but Alex made a $100 down payment. Later, Ford tells Alex that there was a mistake; the price is $3,500. Alex sues, and Ford defends on the basis that there is no written contract. Is the defense valid? Why or why not?

13. Roper bought a triplewide mobile home from Flamingo Home Sales. The written installment sale contract disclaimed any warranty obligation of the seller. Roper experienced several problems with the mobile home, which Flamingo refused to repair. Roper sued on Flamingo's oral promise that if problems did arise, Flamingo would "take care of them." Is this oral promise admissible in court? Explain why or why not.

14. Arlene sued Woodmen Insurance Company to recover medical benefits arising from her pregnancy. The policy covered medical expenses for a pregnancy that originates when the "Insured and the Insured's Spouse are both insured under the Policy." Arlene was insured under the policy when she became pregnant but she was not married. Before she gave birth, she married for the first time. Woodmen refused to pay because her spouse was not insured under the policy when she got pregnant. Arlene claims the requirement that "insured's spouse" be insured must be fulfilled only if the "insured" is married at the time the pregnancy occurs. Is the policy language ambiguous and should it be construed against Woodmen Insurance Company? Explain.

14 Contract Performance

CHAPTER PREVIEW

- CONDITIONS

  Definition
  Types of Conditions
  Conditions Precedent • Conditions Concurrent • Conditions Subsequent
  Express Conditions
  Express Conditions of Personal Satisfaction
  Constructive Conditions

- PERFORMANCE OF CONDITIONS

  Tender of Performance
  Substantial Performance
  Divisibility—Installment Contracts
  Anticipatory Repudiation

BUSINESS MANAGEMENT DECISION

You are the low bidder on a construction project. The proposed contract, presented to you for signing, states that "time is of the essence." This agreement contains a completion date.

Should you agree to this contract?

We have now encountered most of the basic issues in contract law. First, there has to be an agreement consisting of offer and acceptance. Second, the agreement must be validated by bargained-for consideration. Third, the valid contract may be legally unenforceable because of defenses like incapacity, illegality, public policy, or form. Based on the assumption that a valid contract exists without any defense to its formation, the discussion here concerns performance of contracts.

This chapter focuses on the problems that may arise during the period of the performance of a contract. A major emphasis is on important provisions known as *conditions*. Questions arise as to the order of performance: Who must perform first in a bilateral contract? Usually, a default or breach of a contract will occur at or after the time when performance was due, but as will be noted, a contract can be breached prior to the date for performance.

CONDITIONS

1. Definition

__Condition__ A clause in a contract, either expressed or implied, that has the effect of investing or divesting the legal rights and duties of the parties to the contract.

A **condition** is an act or event (other than the lapse of time) that, unless excused, must occur before performance under a contract becomes due. A condition is an act or event that limits or qualifies a promise. The condition must occur before the promisor has a present duty to perform. Assume that you promise to sell me your car for $3,000 and I promise to buy your car for $3,000 if I can obtain a loan of $2,000. I have no present duty to pay you $3,000. When and if I obtain a loan of $2,000, my promise to pay you is activated. My promise to pay is a conditional promise.

There is no exclusive or conclusive test to determine whether a particular contractual provision is a promise or a condition. Although no particular words are necessary for the existence of a condition, terms such as *if*, *provided that*, *on condition that*, and others that condition a party's performance usually connote an intent for a condition rather than a promise. In the absence of a clause expressly creating a condition, whether a certain contractual provision is a condition rather than a promise must be gathered from the contract as a whole and from the intent of the parties.

Conditions determine when a party has to perform. However, many promises are unconditional and absolute. The party who makes an unconditional promise has an immediate duty to perform, regardless of the other party's duties. The failure to perform such a promise is a breach of contract unless the duty is excused. Where a promise is conditional, the duty to perform it is dormant or unactivated until the condition occurs. A duty to perform is conditional if some event must occur before the duty becomes absolute.

2. Types of Conditions

Conditions may be classified by time—*when* the conditioning event must occur in relation to the promise. Under this classification, conditions are labeled *conditions precedent*, *conditions concurrent*, and *conditions subsequent*.

Condition precedent *A clause in a contract providing that immediate rights and duties shall vest only upon the happening of some event.*

Conditions precedent. A **condition precedent** is an act or event that, unless excused, must exist or occur before a duty of immediate performance of a promise arises. It usually takes the form of performance by the other party. Contracts often expressly provide that one party must perform before there is a right to performance by the other party. The first party's performance is a condition precedent to the duty of the other party to perform. Since one party must perform before the other is under a duty to do so, the failure of the first party to perform permits the other to refuse to perform and to cancel the contract. As the following case illustrates, failure to satisfy a condition precedent prevents enforcement of the contract.

CASE

K & K Pharmacy, Inc., owned Millard Pharmacy, which was located on leased space in the Millard Shopping Center. The Millard Food Mart, a grocery store, was also located there, and it had a lease giving it the exclusive right to sell grocery items in the shopping center. K & K Pharmacy entered into a written contract to sell Millard Pharmacy to James R. Barta. The sales contract contained a provision stating that the agreement would be contingent upon Barta's ability to obtain a new lease from the landlord. The sales agreement would be null and void if Barta was unable to obtain a new lease satisfactory to him. Barta operated several pharmacies and used a marketing strategy in which certain food items were sold at a low price to attract customers. During negotiations for the sale of Millard Pharmacy, Barta stated that he would require the right to sell foodstuffs in the pharmacy. After signing the sales contract, Barta began negotiations with the owner of the shopping center for a new lease. He was informed that due to the Food Mart's lease, Barta would not be allowed to sell food items. Barta refused to carry out the sales agreement, and K & K Pharmacy sued him for breach of contract.

ISSUE: Must Barta carry out the sales contract even though he tried but was unable to obtain a lease that would allow him to use his marketing strategy of selling food items?

DECISION: No.

REASONS:

1. In negotiating a contract, parties may include in their agreement a condition precedent. A condition precedent is some event or act that the parties agree must occur or be performed by one or both of the parties before the agreement becomes a legally binding contract. If the parties include a condition precedent in an agreement, then the agreement cannot be enforced until the condition occurs.
2. The provision in the sales agreement regarding Barta's obtaining a new lease satisfactory to him was clearly a condition precedent to the existence of binding contractual obligations between the parties.
3. This provision was a particular type of condition precedent known as a satisfaction clause. A reading of the clause's plain language

shows that it made the contract contingent upon Barta's satisfaction with a new lease. Therefore the condition does not occur and the sales agreement does not become legally binding if Barta was honestly dissatisfied.

4. There is no evidence of the performance of the condition precedent, even if we assume that everything K & K Pharmacy has alleged is true. The evidence is undisputed that Barta was not able to obtain a lease satisfactory to him because he could not obtain a lease allowing him to employ his established marketing strategy. He made a good-faith effort to perform the condition, and there was no evidence that his dissatisfaction was improper.
5. Therefore the condition precedent did not occur, and the sales agreement never became contractually binding.

K & K Pharmacy, Inc. v. Barta, 382 N.W.2d 363 (Neb. 1986).

Not all the terms that impose a duty of performance on a person are of sufficient importance to constitute conditions precedent. As a general rule, if a provision is relatively insignificant, its performance is not required before recovery may be obtained from the other party. In such cases, the party who was to receive performance merely deducts the damages caused by the breach.

For example, a contractor substantially follows all the plans and specifications in building a house, but completes the work ten days late. Rescission is not justified. Such a breach is of minor importance. The purchaser would have been required to pay the contract price less any damages sustained because of the delay. It is often difficult to judge whether a breach of a particular provision is so material that it justifies rescission. If the damage caused by the breach can be readily measured in money, or if the other party receives basically what he was entitled to under the contract, the clause breached is not considered a condition precedent.

Conditions concurrent. If parties are to exchange performances at the same time, their performances are **conditioned concurrently.** "I promise to sell you my car for $700 on April 1." Tender of $700 and tender of the car are concurrent conditions of exchange. Since a contract seldom states that performances are simultaneously conditioned on one another, courts will generally find concurrent conditions if both parties can perform simultaneously. Suppose, in the example above, no date for performance was set. In that case, neither party could demand that the other perform until he or she has performed or tendered performance. Each party's performance is conditioned on concurrent performance by the other party.

Conditions concurrent *Conditions concurrent are mutually dependent and must be performed at the same time by the parties to the contract. Payment of money and delivery of goods in a cash sale are conditions concurrent.*

Conditions subsequent. A **condition subsequent** stated in the contract is an event that discharges a duty of performance that has become absolute. In an insurance contract you might find the following example: "In the event of accident or loss, written notice containing all particulars shall be given by the insured to the Insurer within 30 days." The insurance company's duty to pay under the policy does not arise (become absolute) until the insured gives notice. The requirement of notice is an express condition subsequent to the insured's right to collect. Note that conditions subsequent are rare.

Condition subsequent *A clause in a contract providing for the happening of an event that divests legal rights and duties.*

Conditions may also be classified according to the way they are created. This method of classification recognizes two types of conditions: *express conditions* specifically set out in the contract and *constructive conditions* that the parties did not consider but the court imposes to achieve fundamental fairness between the parties. These two types of conditions are discussed in the following sections.

3. Express Conditions

An *express condition* is included in a contract and designated as a condition that must be strictly performed before the other party's duty to perform arises. The penalty for failure to perform an express condition properly may be the loss of the right to receive payment or otherwise to obtain the return performance. The parties may stipulate that something is a condition precedent, even though it would not ordinarily be considered so. If that stipulation is made, failure to perform exactly as specified is ground for rescission unless the court construes the clause to be a penalty provision and therefore unenforceable.

A contract may provide that "time is of the essence of this agreement." This means that performance on or before the date specified is a condition precedent to the duty of the other party to pay or to perform. The time of performance may be a condition precedent even though the contract does not specifically provide that time is of the essence. Note the contract's provisions in the following case, which make the time of performance very important.

CASE

Banker entered into a written purchase-and-sale agreement to purchase a condominium of Donald and Aldeane Siegel for $107,000. The agreement provided that part of the payment was to be financed through a wraparound mortgage bearing an interest rate "not to exceed 13% per annum" with an assumption fee of 1 percent of the principal sum of the loan. The agreement also provided that it was "contingent upon the ability of Banker to secure a firm commitment for the wraparound mortgage within 45 days from the date of acceptance of the agreement," and that the agreement would be null and void if Banker failed to obtain a commitment for the mortgage within the forty-five-day period. Banker obtained approval for the mortgage within forty-five days after the execution of the agreement. However, the assumption fee was two and one-half points, a value in excess of the one point Banker had agreed to pay. Banker was unwilling to pay these extra points. Approximately one month after the expiration of the financing contingency term, the Siegels offered to renew the original agreement and extend the period of financing. When Banker rejected this offer, the Siegels sued for specific performance. They claimed Banker had failed to proceed to settlement in accordance with terms of the con tract. Banker argued the agreement had been rendered null and void because he had been unable to obtain the agreed-upon financing within forty-five days.

ISSUE: Was time of the essence in this sales agreement, so that Banker's failure to obtain financing in forty-five days rendered the agreement null and void?

DECISION: Yes.

REASONS: 1. Parties to an agreement may make time an essential part of their agreement. In such cases, the failure by one of the parties to perform his part of the obligation within the time prescribed discharges the other party from all liability under the agreement.

2. Time will be considered of the essence where the agreement expressly provides that time is of the essence, where definite terms of the agreement show that the parties regarded the time of performance to be of vital importance, or where the nature of the property or the exigencies of the transaction make timely performance essential. Therefore the presence of the exact phrase "time is of the essence" is not necessary. Any words that provide in unequivocal language that the agreement is to be void if its terms are not fulfilled within a specified period of time will suffice.
3. The language of the clause in question expressly conditioned the agreement upon Banker obtaining specific financing within forty-five days of the execution date, with the proviso that the agreement would be null and void if the loan was not obtained within that time period. The language clearly and unambiguously expressed the parties' intention that time was of the essence.
4. The Siegels' formal offer to extend the financing contingency also suggests that they regarded the time requirement as an absolute deadline, not as a mere approximation.

Siegel v. Banker, 486 A.2d 1163 (D.C. 1984).

Another common express condition precedent, found in many construction contracts, provides that the duty of the owner to make the final payment on completion of the building is conditioned upon the builder's securing an **architect's certificate.** This is certification by the owner's architect that the construction is satisfactory and in accordance with the plans and specifications. Thus the condition is, to a large degree, outside the control of both parties and within the exclusive control of a third party, the architect.

Architect's certificate *A formal statement signed by an architect that a contractor has performed under his contract and is entitled to be paid.*

4. Express Conditions of Personal Satisfaction

A common provision in many contracts expressly conditions a party's performance on *personal satisfaction* with the other party's performance. Suppose that Wyeth agrees to paint your portrait to your personal satisfaction for $20,000. When he is finished, you say that you are not satisfied with it and refuse to pay the $20,000. The condition precedent of your personal satisfaction, you argue, has not happened to activate your duty to pay. Would it make any difference if fifty art experts state that the portrait is a masterpiece? To answer that question and to avoid unfair forfeitures, the law has adopted rules involving two categories of satisfaction cases: situations involving personal taste, fancy, or judgment (subjective dissatisfaction) and situations involving mechanical fitness, utility, or marketability (objective dissatisfaction).

When the satisfaction condition concerns your individual taste or judgment, as in the case of Wyeth's painting, the law requires that you genuinely be dissatisfied. Your dissatisfaction must be honest and in *good faith*, which is a subjective fact question. If you are dissatisfied with the bargain (paying $20,000), however, then you are refusing to pay in bad faith. The condition in that case is excused. The testimony of the art experts can therefore be used as circumstantial evidence of bad faith. This fact issue is given to the jury to determine.

When the satisfaction condition concerns something like construction or repair that can be measured objectively, the law requires reasonable rather than personal satisfaction. If the average person would be satisfied (reasonable, objective satisfaction), then you must pay, despite the fact that you personally might be dissatisfied. Thus performance that is objectively satisfactory must be paid for, notwithstanding personal (subjective) dissatisfaction.

Many cases involving the issue of satisfaction relate to financial matters such as the extension of credit on the assignment of a lease. While most cases use a reasonableness standard, the following case illustrates that a subjective evaluation is often appropriate and that such clauses are fraught with peril.

CASE

Forman contracted to buy land from Benson for $125,000 with the purchase price to be paid over a ten-year period. The contract stated: "Subject to Benson's approving Forman's credit." The credit report showed that Forman had liabilities of $80,000 and liquid assets of $24,000. Forman's tax return showed a $2,000 loss for the tax year. Benson refused to approve Forman's credit and to proceed with the sale. Forman sued for specific performance. At the trial a bank official testified that Forman had an excellent credit rating. The trial court, using the reasonableness standard, found the refusal to approve the credit to be unreasonable.

ISSUE: Did the court use the correct test to judge performance of the condition?

DECISION: No.

REASONS:

1. The reasonableness standard is favored by law when the contract concerns matters capable of objective evaluation. But when a provision is added as a personal concession, the subjective rather than the objective standard should be applied.
2. Since the relationship of the parties was to endure for ten years, the provision allowed Benson the freedom of making a personal and subjective evaluation of Forman's creditworthiness.
3. Thus there was a failure of a condition precedent, Benson's approval of Forman's credit.

Forman v. Benson, 446 N.E.2d 535 (Ill. App. 1983).

5. Constructive Conditions

A *constructive condition* is one not expressed by the parties but is read into the contract to serve justice (that is, an implied-in-law condition). In a bilateral contract, one party can perform, regardless of what the other party does. But in most cases, it would be inequitable to require one party to perform without requiring the other to perform. In the interest of fairness, courts make performances of bilateral promises constructively conditional on one another. In an employment contract, for example, one must work before getting paid. Working is a constructive condition precedent, which must occur to activate the employer's duty to pay an employee.

When parties understand that one performance must occur before the other (or such is understood by custom), the former is a constructive condition precedent to the latter. When a contractor promises to build a house for an owner who will pay him $200,000, a court will construe the builder's performance as a condition that must happen to activate the owner's duty to pay.

If both performances can be performed simultaneously, the promises are constructively concurrent. To activate the other's duty to perform, a party must tender his performances. Most contracts for the sale of goods under the Code are examples of constructive concurrent conditions of exchange.

Note: The express contract terms or custom, usage of trade, course of dealing, and the like can change the rule. A passenger, by custom, pays for an airline ticket before the airline's duty to provide transportation is activated.

PERFORMANCE OF CONDITIONS

6. Tender of Performance

A **tender** in the law of contracts is an offer to perform. When a person makes a tender, it means that he is ready, willing, and able to perform. The tender is especially significant in contracts requiring both parties to perform at the same time. One party can place the other party in default by making a tender of performance without having actually rendered the performance.

Tender *To offer and produce money in satisfaction of a debt or obligation and express to the creditor a willingness to pay.*

The concept of tender is applied not only to concurrent condition situations but also to contract performance in general. In most contracts, one party or the other is required to tender payment. Such a tender requires that there be a bona fide, unconditional offer of payment of the amount of money due, coupled with an actual production of the money or its equivalent. A tender of payment by check is not a valid tender when an objection is made to this medium of payment. When a tender is refused for other reasons, one may not later complain about the use of a check as the medium of tender. A person to whom a tender is made must specify any objection to it or waive it, so that the debtor may know and comply with the creditor's demands.

Tenders of payment are often refused for one reason or another. A party may contend that the tender was too late. The creditor may refuse to accept the offer to pay because he believes that the amount tendered is less than the amount of the debt. If it turns out that the tender was proper, the valid tender will have three important legal effects.

1. It stops interest from accruing after the date of the tender.
2. In case the creditor later brings legal action recovering no more than the amount tendered, he must pay the court costs.
3. If the debt were secured by a security interest in property belonging to the debtor, this security interest would be extinguished.

Thus a tender of payment, although it does not discharge the debt, has important advantages to the person making it.

The Uniform Commercial Code article that deals with the sale of goods has two provisions relating to tender. Unless the buyer and the seller have otherwise agreed, *tender of payment* by the buyer is a condition to the seller's duty to deliver the goods sold [2-511(1)]. Unless the seller demands payment in legal tender, the buyer is authorized to make payment by check [2-511(2)]. The Code also provides for the manner of a seller's tender of delivery of the goods involved in the contract. The Code requires that the seller make the goods available to the buyer and that he give the buyer reasonable notification that the goods are available for him [2-503(1)]. If the seller gives notice that the goods are available for the buyer and the buyer does not tender payment, then the buyer would be placed in default. Tender of delivery is a condition to the buyer's duty to accept the goods [2-507(1)].

7. Substantial Performance

Substantial performance *The performance of all the essential elements of a contract. The only permissible omissions or derivations are those that are trivial, inadvertent, and inconsequential*

Express conditions must be strictly met, or there is a material breach of contract. Constructive conditions need be only substantially performed to avoid a material breach. Because constructive conditions are imposed in the interest of good faith and fair dealing, it naturally follows that **substantial performance** of a constructive condition satisfies the condition. Thus the other party's duty to perform is activated by substantial performance. Note that substantial performance is not complete performance, so there has been an immaterial breach and dollar damages may be awarded. Although the nonbreaching party can sue for damages for this immaterial breach, the suing party must still perform, because the constructive condition precedent has been fulfilled. Thus an immaterial breach does not excuse the nonbreaching party of the duty of performance under the contract.

The consequences of a material breach are more severe. Normally, a material breach gives the nonbreaching party an option. He can opt to treat the contract as rescinded, or he can choose to continue under the contract by treating it as only a partial breach. A partial breach, in effect, continues the contract, and all parties must continue to perform. The nonbreaching party can sue for damages that accrued from the breach, and the contract is not rescinded. If a total breach is elected, the contract is at an end, and there is an immediate right to all remedies for breach of the entire contract.

Issues of substantial performance often arise in construction contracts. Seldom is there total, complete, and perfect performance. Adjustments in the price are usually made for minor deviations. However, if a contractor fails to substantially perform as agreed, the other party may rescind the contract and the contractor is not entitled to collect anything even on the theory of quasi-contract. The following case is typical of those illustrating this very important principle.

CASE

National Chain Company hired John Campbell to wallpaper an office with wallpaper that National had previously purchased. When Campbell was finished, the wallpaper had ragged and curled edges and had glue stains, contact cement, and staples on it. National refused to pay Campbell and brought suit for breach of contract to recover the amount it had paid for the wallpaper and the costs incurred in removing the wallpaper and repairing the wall surface damaged by Campbell. National did not seek any recovery for the cost of having another worker install new wallpaper. Campbell counterclaimed for the cost of services rendered. At trial, National's expert, an experienced wallpaper hanger, testified that Campbell's job looked "terrible."

The trial judge refused to instruct the jury that Campbell could not recover for the cost of his services unless he had substantially performed the contract. Instead, the judge ruled that although Campbell could not recover on the contract, he could recover on a theory of quasi-contract. The jury awarded $1 to National and $100 to Campbell on his counterclaim.

ISSUE: Can Campbell recover for the cost of his services regardless of whether he substantially performed the contract to wallpaper one of National's offices?

DECISION: No.

REASONS:

1. The underlying rationale in breach of contract actions is to place the innocent party in the position in which he would have been if the contract had been fully performed.
2. The doctrine of substantial performance recognizes that it would be unreasonable to condition the contractor's recovery on his full and complete performance of the contract. This doctrine allows the contractor to recover some of the costs of his services when the purpose of the contract has been accomplished and minor defects or omissions could be remedied by repair.
3. However, the contractor cannot recover anything where he has not substantially performed. When the contractor's performance is worthless and the work has to be redone completely, the contractor is liable for the cost to the owner of having the job redone.
4. The doctrine of substantial performance also applies when one sues under a theory of quasi-contract, as well as when one sues for breach of contract. Therefore Campbell cannot recover on a theory of quasi-contract unless he rendered substantial performance. The record indicates that the trial judge should have given the jury an instruction as the doctrine of substantial performance. The judgment is therefore reversed and the case remanded for retrial on all the issues.

National Chain Co. v. Campbell, 487 A.2d 132 (R.I. 1985).

8. Divisibility—Installment Contracts

Whereas many contracts require a single performance by each party and are completely performed at one point of time, others require or permit performance by one or both parties in installments over a period of time. The rights and obligations of parties during the period when the contract is being performed frequently depend upon whether the contract is "entire" or "divisible." A contract is said to be divisible if performance by each party is divided into two or more parts *and* performance of each part by one party is the agreed exchange for the corresponding part by the other party. It is to be noted that a contract is not divisible simply by virtue of the fact that it is to be performed in installments.

The parties may specify whether a contract is divisible or entire. Thus a contract may contain a clause stipulating that each delivery is a separate contract, or other language may be used to show the intention of the parties that their agreement is to be treated as if it were a series of contracts. Some contracts are obviously divisible. Assume Sam promises to sell and Dave promises to buy a car for $5,000 and a boat for $3,000. This contract is legally divisible into two parts, a sale of a car and a sale of a boat. If Sam tenders the car, he is entitled to $5,000 even though he has not performed the entire contract since he has not tendered the boat. Sam is liable for not tendering the boat but he can still recover for the sale of the car.

The concept of divisibility is applicable to a variety of contracts, including insurance contracts, employment contracts, construction contracts, and sales contracts. As a general proposition, employment contracts are interpreted to be divisible, but construction contracts are usually deemed to be entire. The divisibility of contracts for the sale of goods is the subject of several Code provisions [discussed later].

If a contract is divisible, the second party is under a duty to perform in part after the first party performs an installment. For example, the employer owes a duty to pay wages at the end of the pay period. A material breach of an installment justifies a rescission of the balance of the agreement. Assume that a party is to write five songs each month for a year. Only one song is written the first month. While the failure to deliver the other four would not be a substantial breach of the entire agreement, it would be a substantial breach of the installment. If the contract were treated as divisible, such a material breach would justify rescission of the contract. Likewise, if a party substantially performs an installment of a divisible contract, he may nevertheless recover the value of that installment, less damages, caused by any breach of the contract without rendering performance of the balance of the agreement.

There have been numerous cases involving the question of whether or not a contract is divisible. No general test can be derived from these cases. Courts are called upon to determine in any given case whether the parties intended that (1) each would accept part performance of the other in return for his own without regard to subsequent events or (2) the divisions of the contract were made merely for the purpose of requiring periodic payments as the work progresses. In any event, the party who breaches is liable for damages resulting from his breach.

Under the Code, unless the parties have otherwise agreed, a sales contract is entire; all the goods called for by the contract must be tendered in a single delivery, and payment in full is due upon such tender [2-307]. If the contract permits installment deliveries, the seller can demand a proportionate share of the price for each delivery as it is made, provided the price can be apportioned, as for goods sold at a certain price per item. If there is a substantial default on an installment (the goods tendered or delivered may not conform to the contract), the buyer may reject the installment [2-612(2)]. When an installment breached indicates that the seller will not satisfactorily perform the balance of the contract or that he is unreliable, the buyer can rescind the entire contract [2-612(3)]. Should the buyer accept a nonconforming installment without giving notice of cancellation or demanding that the seller deliver goods that conform, he may not use the breach as a basis for rescission.

9. Anticipatory Repudiation

Before the time specified for performance, there can be no actual breach, but there may be a breach by *anticipatory repudiation*. The expression means that repudiation occurs before performance is due. The repudiation may be express or implied. An express repudiation is a clear, positive, unequivocal refusal to perform. An implied repudiation results from conduct in which the promisor puts it out of his power to perform, making substantial performance of his promise impossible. In either case, the repudiation must be positive and unequivocal.

When a promisor repudiates his prospective duty to perform, the nonrepudiating party has an election of remedies. He can treat the repudiation as an anticipatory breach and immediately seek damages for breach of contract, rather than waiting until the time set for the repudiating party's performance. Thus the doctrine excuses any express or constructive condition to the repudiating party's duty and thereby permits an immediate lawsuit. Rather than suing, the injured party can treat the repudiation as an empty threat, wait until the time for performance arrives, and exercise his remedies for actual breach if a breach does in fact occur. If the injured party disregards the repudiation and treats the contract as still in force, the repudiation is nullified, and the injured party is left with his remedies, if any, invocable at the time of performance.

The doctrine of anticipatory breach does not apply to promises to pay money on or before a specified date. If a promissory note matures on June 1, 1990, and in 1988 the maker states that he will not pay it when the maturity date arrives, that would not give rise to present cause of action by the holder.

The Code provides that after a breach including anticipatory repudiation, the buyer may "cover" by making in good faith and without unreasonable delay any reasonable purchase of, or contract to purchase, goods in substitution for those due from the seller [2-712]. The difference between the cost of cover and the contract price, together with any incidental or consequential damages, may be recovered by the buyer from the seller. Failure of the buyer to effect cover does not bar him from recovering damages for nondelivery, but damages will be limited to those that could not have been prevented by proper cover.

A party may retract his repudiation, provided he does so prior to any material change of position by the other party in reliance upon it. The retraction would simply be a notice that he will perform the contract, after all. The Code allows a retraction of anticipatory repudiation until the repudiating party's next performance is due, unless the aggrieved party has, since the repudiation, canceled or materially changed his position or otherwise indicated that he considers the repudiation final [2-611]. Retraction may be by any method that clearly indicates to the aggrieved party that the repudiating party intends to perform, but it must include adequate assurance that he will in fact perform if the other party demands it [2-609]. Retraction reinstates the repudiating party's rights under the contract, with due excuse and allowance to the aggrieved party for any delay occasioned by the repudiation. The following case is typical of those in which a retraction nullifies a breach.

CASE

In March 1976, the University of Vermont Medical College hired Dr. David Lowe to work for a two-year term, beginning July 1, 1976, as an assistant professor. Dr. Harry Beaty was later appointed chairman of the Department of Medicine. On January 19, 1977, Dr. Beaty told Dr. Lowe that his "academic training at the institution was limited" and that he should "plan to relocate as of July 1, 1977." Dr. Lowe had not received any prior notice of dissatisfaction with his work. Dr. Lowe sought to remain in his position until August of 1977 for family reasons. He was informed he could remain on the conditions that he do all the unit's clinical work for that period and submit a letter of resignation. He refused. In February, Dr. Beaty asked Dr. Lowe to submit a letter of resignation. After this conversation, Dr. Lowe authorized his attorney to advise the university that he intended to bring suit for the breach of his employment contract. Dr. Lowe was unable to find a similar position in the Vermont area, so he decided to enter private practice in Rhode Island. In March, his attorney received a letter from the university's counsel indicating that the university intended to honor its two-year employment contract with him.

During the next few months, Dr. Lowe spent time and money traveling to Rhode Island and making the necessary arrangements for starting his private practice. He sued the University of Vermont and Dr. Beaty for breach of contract. The jury returned a verdict only against the university. The university appealed.

ISSUE: Was there a repudiation of this employment contract for which Dr. Lowe can recover damages?

DECISION: No.

REASONS:

1. To repudiate a contract, a party must clearly indicate a positive and unequivocal refusal to perform under the contract.
2. Repudiation before the time for performance under a contract constitutes an anticipatory breach of the contract.
3. The evidence shows that the University of Vermont, through its agent, Dr. Beaty, positively and unequivocally expressed its intent not to abide by the terms of the contract. Dr. Beaty strongly urged Dr. Lowe to relocate, made statements regarding the uncertainty of Dr. Lowe's future salary, and twice urged Dr. Lowe to hand in his resignation. Therefore the university repudiated the contract.
4. However, a repudiation can be withdrawn, eliminating the repudiating party's liability, provided such withdrawal occurs before the injured party materially changes his position in reliance on the repudiation. When the nonbreaching party does not materially alter its position, the breaching party's withdrawal of its repudiation nullifies the breach, absolving the breaching party of liability.
5. There is no evidence that Dr. Lowe took any action toward relocating to Rhode Island before he received notice of the university's retraction. The only actions taken by Dr. Lowe in reliance on the repudiation and before the retraction were making a few phone calls and changing his mind. These actions are insufficient, as a matter of law, to constitute a material change of position in reliance upon the university's repudiation.
5. Therefore, although the university repudiated its employment contract with Dr. Lowe, the doctor did not materially change his position and cannot recover any damages. The trial court's decision is reversed and judgment is entered for the university.

Lowe v. Beaty, 485 A.2d 1255 (Vt. 1984).

CHAPTER SUMMARY

Conditions

Definition

1. A condition is an act or event that limits or qualifies a promise.
2. A duty to perform is conditional if something other than the passage of time must occur before performance is due.

3. Conditions set the order of performance and prevent lawsuits by establishing defenses if conditions do not occur.
4. Failure of a promise gives rise to a remedy for breach; a failure of condition only excuses performance.

Types of Conditions

1. Conditions may be classified in terms of time (conditions precedent, concurrent, and subsequent) or manner of creation (express or constructive).
2. A condition precedent is an act or event that, unless excused, must occur before a duty to perform is activated.
3. Conditions concurrent require the parties to exchange performances at the same time.
4. A condition subsequent is an act or event that discharges a duty which had previously become absolute.

Express Conditions

1. An express condition is specifically stated by the parties' agreement as activating or discharging duties.
2. Express conditions must be strictly satisfied.

Express Conditions of Personal Satisfaction

1. If a condition involves personal taste or judgment, dissatisfaction is judged by a subjective standard. If good-faith dissatisfaction exists, the condition is not met.
2. If a condition involves mechanical fitness, utility, or marketability, an objective standard of dissatisfaction is used to decide if the condition has been met.

Constructive Conditions

1. A court-created condition imposed to serve justice.
2. Substantial performance of constructive conditions will make the other party's duty to perform absolute.

Performance of Conditions

Tender of Performance

1. Tender is an offer to perform. The party making the tender indicates he is ready, willing, and able to perform.
2. Tender of payment by the buyer is a condition to the seller's duty to deliver the goods.
3. Tender by the seller occurs when the goods are available to the buyer. The seller must give reasonable notice that the goods are available.

Substantial Performance

1. Substantial performance of a constructive condition is required in order to make the other party's duty absolute.
2. Substantial performance is not full performance and is an immaterial breach.
3. Failure to perform at the proper time is not substantial performance if time was of the essence.

Divisibility—Installment Contracts

1. A party can recover for performance of divisible portions of a contract.
2. Breach of one part of a divisible contract does not allow the other party to refuse to pay for the part performed.

Anticipatory Repudiation

1. Before the time for performance, a party may expressly or implicitly repudiate his duty to perform. If he does so, it is an anticipatory repudiation.
2. The repudiation is not favored and must be shown to be clear, positive, and unequivocal.
3. A repudiation may be withdrawn unless it is relied on by the other party.

REVIEW QUESTIONS AND PROBLEMS

1. Match each term in column A with the appropriate statement in column B.

A	B
(1) Condition	(a) Condition that discharges duty.
(2) Condition precedent	(b) Condition created by the court to achieve justice.
(3) Condition subsequent	(c) Party clearly indicates that he will not perform in the future.
(4) Express condition	(d) An act or event that limits or qualifies a contract duty.
(5) Constructive condition	(e) An immateral breach.
(6) Substantial performance	(f) A condition created expressly by the parties' agreement.
(7) Divisibility	(g) An offer to perform.
(8) Anticipatory repudiation	(h) Contract can be apportioned into several contracts.
(9) Tender	(i) Condition that activates a contract duty.

2. Merv and Harold contract to merge their corporate holdings into a single new company provided that the merger was not to be operative unless they raise $800,000 additional capital. What happens if they cannot raise an additional $800,000? Explain.

3. Totten hired Lampenfeld to paint his house. Totten agreed to pay in installments as the painting progressed. While Totten was on vacation, Lampenfeld started painting the house. When Totten returned, he refused to pay for the partial painting. Since he was not paid as agreed, Lampenfeld refused to complete the painting. Lampenfeld sued Totten for the value of the painting he had done. Totten claimed that Lampenfeld had materially breached the contract by not finishing the job and thus should recover nothing. Was Totten's payment for the partial painting a condition precedent to Lampenfeld's duty to complete painting the house? Explain.

4. Bob contracts with Elizabeth to paint a portrait of Elizabeth's daughter Della, for which Elizabeth promises to pay $6,000 "if entirely satisfied." Bob paints Della's portrait, but Elizabeth states that she is not satisfied with it and refuses to pay the $6,000. Elizabeth gives no reason except that the portrait does not please her. According to experts in the art field, the portrait is an admirable work of art. Will a court require Elizabeth to pay Bob $6,000? Explain.

5. John contracts with Fay to install a heating system in Fay's factory for a price of $30,000 to be paid "on condition of satisfactory completion." John installs the heating system, but Fay states that she is not satisfied with it and refuses to pay the $30,000. Fay gives no reason except that she does not approve of the heating system. According to experts, the heating system as installed is entirely satisfactory. May John successfully recover $30,000 from Fay? Explain why or why not.

6. Coots contracted to sell a farm to Bell. The sale contract required the Bells to pay the total purchase price in monthly installments with a thirty-day grace period for payments. It also contained provisions for Coots's immediate recovery of possession in the event of the Bells' default in making the monthly payments. Is time of the essence of this agreement? Why or why not?

7. Harte contracted with Connolly to install a new roof on Connolly's house. It was agreed that the roofing shingles were to be "Russet glow," a shade of brown. The roof was installed, and many of the shingles were discolored, showing streaks of yellow. Harte replaced some of the shingles, but the new shingles did not match the others. The overall appearance of the roof is that it has been patched with nonblending colors. The roof is functional and is guaranteed to last fifteen years. Must Connolly pay? Why or why not? Would your answer change if Harte were building a house for Connolly and on the scheduled completion date had done everything required by the contract except grading and paving? Why or why not?

8. Walsh contracted with the Alaska Housing Authority to construct a gravel surface road. The road was to be constructed of 12 inches of crushed rock surfacing and a 12-inch layer of compacted wood chips to be placed below the gravel surface. Instead, the wood-chip layer after the project was completed averaged 9 inches, with a 2,000-foot section averaging only 5 inches. The insufficient layer of wood-chip insulation caused increased rutting along the road, necessitating frequent maintenance. Is Walsh entitled to be paid for the road? Why or why not? If so, how much?

9. Stacey, a pro football quarterback, signed a seven-year contract with the Professional Football League for $875,000. Stacey was to receive $50,000 upon signing and another $50,000 at the end of the first year. Although he received the $50,000 upon signing, the league could pay only $20,000 at the end of the year. At that time, the league was in financial difficulties to the tune of $1,600,000 indebtedness and an overdraft at the bank for $67,000. Should Stacey treat the contract as rescinded? Why or why not?

10. Rick agreed to buy two campers from McMahon and made a deposit of $1,000 as partial payment. Rick then wired McMahon not to ship the campers and explained his reasons for delaying shipment. Later, Rick decided not to buy the campers and demanded a return of his $1,000. Was Rick's instruction not to ship an anticipatory repudiation that will justify McMahon's retention of the $1,000? Explain.

11. A bank made a loan commitment for the construction of a racquetball recreational development. After the start of construction, the bank informed the developer that it would not make the loan and that the developer could sue if it didn't like it. The developer filed suit for damages, and the bank then agreed to go ahead with the loan. Will the suit be dismissed? Why or why not?

15 Excuses for Nonperformance and Discharge of Contracts

CHAPTER PREVIEW

BUSINESS MANAGEMENT DECISION

You operate a retail paint and wallpaper store. The Handy-Man Company has purchased a variety of items on credit. One account receivable, for $425, is eighteen months old. A second account receivable is for $1,800, and it is secured by Handy-Man's spraying equipment. A third account receivable is for $175, and it is only three weeks old. Today you receive a $350 check from Handy-Man with no instructions as to its application.

How should you apply this $350 against these three accounts receivable?

EXCUSES FOR NONPERFORMANCE

Chapter 14 began our discussion of performance of contracts with special emphasis on conditions and the order of performance by the parties to a contract. Additional legal issues may arise during the performance of a contract. For example, a party may be unable to perform because of circumstances beyond his control, or he may contend that because of changed conditions, he should be excused from performing as agreed. These circumstances, known as excuses for nonperformance, begin this chapter. Finally, a contract must eventually come to an end. Most contracts end when they are fully performed, but there are other events and legal principles that may result in the discharge or termination of a contract or contract liability. These are discussed in the latter portion of this chapter.

A party to a contract may be relieved from the duty to perform or from his liability for breach if he is legally excused from contract performance. Moreover, a duty under a conditional promise may be activated not only by performance of the condition but also if the condition is excused. Actual failure of an express or a constructive condition may be legally excused in any of the following five ways: hindrance, prevention, or noncooperation; waiver, estoppel, or election; impossibility; frustration of purpose; and commercial impracticability.

1. Hindrance, Prevention, or Noncooperation

In every contract there is an implied duty of good faith and fair dealing requiring each party not to prevent or substantially hinder the other party's performance. If a party whose promise is conditional wrongfully prevents the condition from occurring, then the condition is excused. Although the cases vary, the wrongful conduct can be characterized as either hindrance, wrongful prevention, or noncooperation.

Hindrance. The conduct must be *wrongful*, which usually means that no party reasonably contemplated or assumed the risk of the kind of conduct that occurred. Seller agrees to sell Buyer a product in short supply. Seller fails to deliver because Buyer has been purchasing all of the available product from Seller's only source of supply. A court held that although Buyer did substantially hinder Seller's performance, it was not wrongful. Seller assumed the risk of such market conditions when it unconditionally agreed to supply the product.

Prevention. The wrongful prevention of performance by one party to a contract will excuse nonperformance by the other party. It is obvious that a person may not recover for nonperformance of a contract if he is responsible for the nonperformance. If a party creates a situation that makes it impossible for the other party to perform, the other party is excused. To illustrate: Barrow had leased a building to Calhoun for the operation of an ice-cream store. The rent was to be a percentage of the gross income. Thereafter, Calhoun established *another* ice cream store a block away and did very little business in the building rented to her by Barrow. Calhoun has prevented the normal performance of the contract by carrying on another business that detracted from the profits. Barrow may cancel the lease without liability because Calhoun has prevented the anticipated performance of the contract.

Noncooperation. As a part of the good-faith requirement, the law implies that the parties will reasonably cooperate with each other. If as the result of one party's failure to cooperate and to in effect act in good faith the other party breaches the contract, then the noncooperating party is not entitled to the usual contract remedies. In fact, the other party may rescind the agreement because the implied condition of good faith has been breached. The following case illustrates this implied condition of good-faith cooperation.

CASE

Fernandez rented an apartment owned by Vazquez. The lease provided that Fernandez "shall not sublease without written consent of Vazquez." When Fernandez wanted to sublease the apartment, Vazquez refused to consent without giving any reason. When Fernandez left the apartment, Vazquez sued to enforce the lease. Fernandez claimed that Vazquez arbitrarily refused to consent to the sublease justifying his cancellation.

ISSUE: Can Vazquez withhold its consent without good reason to a sublease?

DECISION: No.

REASONS:
1. The law favors free transfer of property, and a tenant, without a specific clause to the contrary, may sublease.
2. Good-faith cooperation is an implied condition precedent to performance of a contract. When a party unreasonably refuses to cooperate, he is estopped from availing himself of his own wrongdoing. Arbitrary withholding of consent to a sublease constitutes a breach of the leases agreement.

Fernandez v. Vazquez, 397 So.2d 117 (Fla. 1981).

2. Waiver

Waiver *The intentional relinquishment or giving up of a known right. It may be done by express words or conduct that involves any acts inconsistent with an intention to claim the right.*

Waiver has been defined as the passing by of an occasion to enforce a legal right, whereby the legal right is lost. As applied to contract law, it means (1) a promise to forgo the benefit of a condition to the promissor's duty or (2) an election to continue under a contract after the other party has breached. The essence of waiver is conduct that indicates an intention not to enforce certain provisions of the agreement. The waiver may be made either before or after a breach. If it is made before, it constitutes an assurance that performance of the condition will not be insisted upon. For example, a building contract provides for completion on a certain date. If the owner grants an extension of six months, he has waived his right to insist upon completion at the earlier date. The waiver may be retracted unless it is supported by consideration or the promisee has made a substantial change of position in reliance upon it. One who has waived the time for performance may withdraw the waiver if he gives the other party a reasonable opportunity to perform the condition waived.

The Uniform Commercial Code allows a party who has waived a provision of an executory contract to retract it upon giving reasonable notice that he will require strict performance of it, "unless the retraction would be unjust in view of a material change of position in reliance on the waiver" [2-209(5)]. Under the Code, the retention or acceptance of defective goods may constitute a waiver of the defect. A buyer who fails to particularize defects in goods may in fact be waiving his objections based on these defects [2-605].

3. Impossibility of Performance

Actual impossibility of performance is a valid excuse for nonperformance and releases a party from his duty to perform. Impossibility is much more than mere "additional hardship." As a general rule, in the absence of an appropriate contract provision, circumstances that impose additional hardship on one party do not constitute an excuse for breach of contract. The fact that the promised performance of a contractual obligation may be more difficult than expected at the time the promise was made does not discharge the promisor from his duty to perform. Therefore most contracts provide that manufacturers, suppliers, or builders shall be relieved from performance in case of fire, strikes, difficulty in obtaining raw materials, or other incidents imposing hardship over which they have no control. Without such a provision there would be no excuse, as they do not constitute impossibility of performance. The following case is typical of those finding no excuse in the face of significant hardship.

CASE

A building leased by Newberry as a department store was destroyed by fire. When the landlord, Marcovich, refused to rebuild, Newberry sued for damages and lost profits. Marcovich defended using impossibility as an excuse. He contended that it was not commercially feasible to rebuild due to the small amount of insurance proceeds, the blighted condition of the area, and alleged difficulty in obtaining financing.

ISSUE: Did Marcovich prove impossibility to excuse its nonperformance in failing to rebuild?

DECISION: No.

REASONS:
1. Although absolute impossibility will excuse performance, nothing here suggests absolute impossibility.
2. The evidence simply indicates that rebuilding would be a poor business decision but not one of extreme difficulty, expense, injury, or loss.

Marcovich Land Corp. v. J. J. Newberry Co., 413 N.E.2d 935 (Ind. 1980).

To have the effect of releasing a party from his duty to perform, the impossibility must render performance "physically and objectively impossible." If objective impossibility is present, the discharge is mutual; that is, the promisor is discharged, and the promisee is also discharged from his corresponding obligation. Many cases state that in order for impossibility to exist, there must be a fortuitous or unavoidable occurrence that was not reasonably foreseeable. The fact that an act of God is involved does not necessarily create an excuse. If a house under construction is destroyed by fire caused by lightning the contractor is not excused from his obligation to complete the house. The contractor takes the risk of fire unless he protects himself by expressly contracting that he shall not be held liable for such risks.

Likewise, if the situation is caused by the promisor or by developments that he could have prevented, avoided, or remedied by corrective measures, there is no excuse. For this reason, the failure of a third party, such as a supplier, to make proper delivery does not create impossibility. Impossibility will not be allowed as a defense when the obstacle was created by promisor or was within his power to eliminate. It must not exist merely because of the inability or incapacity of the promisor to do it; that is, subjective impossibility is no excuse.

4. Specific Cases of Impossibility

There are four basic situations in which impossibility of performance is frequently offered as an excuse for nonperformance.

Performance becomes illegal. In the first of these, performance becomes illegal because of the enactment of some law or governmental action. A manufacturer or supplier may be prevented from making delivery of merchandise because of government restrictions. However, government action that merely makes an agreement more burdensome than was anticipated does not afford a basis for relief.

Death or incapacitating illness. The second situation is the death or incapacitating illness of one of the contracting parties. This is not deemed to be a form of impossibility unless the contract demands the personal services of the disabled or deceased person. Ordinary contracts of production, processing, and sale of property are unaffected by the death or illness of one or both of the parties. In the event of death, it is assumed that the contract will be carried out by the estate of the deceased. If a contract is for personal services or it clearly implies that the continued services of the contracting party are essential to performance, death or illness will excuse nonperformance. In contracts for personal services, the death of the employer also terminates the relation. The estate of the employer in prematurely terminating the contract is not liable for damages to the employee.

Continued existence of certain subject matter. Many agreements involve the continued existence of certain subject matter essential to completion of the contract. The third rule is that destruction of any subject matter essential to the completion of the contract will operate to relieve the parties of the obligations assumed by their agreement. A different situation arises where property that only one of the parties expected to use in his performance is destroyed. For example, if a factory from which the owner expected to deliver certain shoes is destroyed by fire, performance is not excused, inasmuch as performance is still possible, even though an undue hardship may result. The shoes needed to fill the order can be obtained from another source. Had the contract stipulated that the shoes were to be delivered from a particular factory, however, its destruction would have operated to excuse a failure to perform. In recent years, there has been a trend toward holding that where both parties understood that delivery was to be made from a certain source, even though it was not expressly agreed, destruction of the source of supply will relieve the obligor from performing.

Lack of essential element. The last form of impossibility arises when there is an essential element lacking. This situation is difficult to define satisfactorily, but apparently the agreement may be rescinded when some element or property is lacking, although the parties assumed it existed or would exist. Some courts would hold that no contract, in fact, existed because of mutual mistake. This is said to be a form of impossibility at the time of making the contract, and courts have tended to act as if there had been no meeting of the minds. It must be definitely proved that performance is substantially impossible because of the missing element. For example, a builder contracts to build an office building at a certain location. Because of the nature of the soil, it is utterly impossible to build the type of building provided for in the agreement; the agreement must therefore be terminated. The missing element is the proper condition of the soil. In other words, from the very beginning, the contract terms could not possibly have been complied with, and in such cases the courts are prone to excuse the parties if nobody is at fault.

5. Commercial Frustration

Since the notion of requiring *absolute* impossibility may create harsh results in certain cases, courts may excuse performance using the *doctrine of commercial frustration*. The doctrine excuses performance when the essential purpose and value of the contract have been frustrated. Typically, something happens to prevent achievement of the object or purpose of the contract. If so, the courts may find an implied condition that the unforeseen development will excuse performance.

Commercial frustration arises whenever there is an intervening event or change of circumstances so fundamental it is entirely beyond that which was contemplated by the parties. Frustration is not impossibility, but it is more than mere hardship. It is an excuse created by law to eliminate liability when a fortuitous occurrence has defeated the reasonable expectations of the parties. It will not be used when the supervening event was foreseeable or assumed as a part of the agreement. Note that in the following case the significant events were obviously foreseeable.

CASE

Merritt-King Pontiac, Inc., leased from J. T. Haun the premises where Haun Pontiac Corporation had operated an automotive dealership. Contemporaneously with the signing of the lease, Haun agreed not to compete with Merritt-King Pontiac in return for a payment of $1,468.75 per month for forty-eight months. The agreement became effective on June 16, 1980, and contained a provision that R. D. King and K. G. Merritt would be "personally liable to Haun for the faithful performance of the terms" of the agreement. The agreement expressly provided that Haun relied upon the personal liability of King and Merritt in making the agreement. Haun received payments under the agreement through October 1981. The dealership closed around January 26, 1982, due to bankruptcy. King claimed the dealership went bankrupt because General Motors Acceptance Corporation, acting upon information obtained from a local bank about the financial status of Merritt-King Pontiac, discontinued the corporation's floor plan for financing new vehicles. Haun sued King and Merritt for the balance of the payments.

ISSUE: Are King and Merritt excused from paying on the contract because of GMAC's refusal to finance the dealership's purchase of new vehicles?

DECISION: No.

REASONS:

1. After the execution of a contract if some unforeseen event occurs that was neither caused by nor under the control of either party and it destroys or nearly destroys either the value of performance or the object or purpose of the contract, the parties are excused from further performance under the contract. This principle is known as the doctrine of frustration of commercial purpose.
2. The doctrine is predicated on the premise of giving relief where the parties could not protect themselves from the occurrence of the supervening event by inserting provisions in the contract. Therefore the supervening event must be wholly outside the contemplation of the parties. If the event was foreseeable, the doctrine is not a defense to liability under the contract.
3. When a party promises without qualification to do an act, his performance is not excused because it becomes onerous or unprofitable. It is deemed his own fault if he does not expressly exempt himself from responsibility if a foreseeable event occurs.
4. As a general rule, unexpected financial difficulty does not excuse a contractual promisor from performing where the contract does not provide otherwise. While such financial hardship may be unexpected, it is viewed as always foreseeable in business.
5. The surrounding circumstances suggest that the parties actually foresaw that the type of problem that occurred might happen. Haun bargained for inclusion of the personal liability of King and Merritt for the monthly payments if Merritt-King Pontiac defaulted. Clearly, the parties foresaw the possibility that Merritt-King Pontiac might encounter financial difficulty. Therefore the doctrine of frustration of commercial purpose is not a defense to the contract.

Haun v. King, 690 S.W.2d 869 (Tenn. Ct. App. 1984).

6. Commercial Impracticability under the Code

The Code uses the term *commercial impracticability* to describe a defense similar to *commercial frustration*. The Code recognizes that without the fault of either party, unexpected developments or government action may cause the promised performance to become impracticable. In some cases, the Code authorizes substituted performance. If the loading or unloading facilities of the agreed-upon carrier are unusuable, a commercially reasonable substitute must be tendered and accepted if it is available [2-614].

The Code also provides that commercial impracticability is often an excuse for a seller who fails to deliver goods or is delayed in making the delivery. The excuse is limited to cases in which unforeseen supervening circumstances not within the contemplation of the parties arise [2-615(a)]. The law does not specify all the contingencies that may justify the application of the doctrine of commercial impracticability. Increased costs will not excuse the seller unless they are due to some unforeseen contingency that alters the basic nature of the contract. Currency fluctuations may significantly impact a contract, but since they are foreseeable the impracticability defense usually does not arise, as the following case illustrates.

CASE

A distributor of sewing machines brought an action against an importer of sewing machines for interpretation of their contract, which was to last for seven years commencing in 1971. The contract provided that the exchange rate between dollars and Swiss francs was to be borne by the importer. With the precipitous decline of the dollar in relation to the Swiss franc, the importer began to surcharge the distributor 10 percent above the increased cost of purchasing Swiss francs so it "could retain sufficient profit margin to justify sales." The trial court, however, determined that the importer could not exact a profit on the additional costs incurred from the exchange rate fluctuations. The importer now claims the contract does not have to be performed due to the commerical impracticability doctrine of the Uniform Commercial Code.

ISSUE: Has the contract become impracticable due to the fluctuation of the currencies involved?

DECISION: No.

REASONS:

1. The UCC impracticability defense is not allowed where the parties have anticipated the risk and provided for its allocation. The evidence showed that the importer recognizes the possibility of exchange rate fluctuations in a letter to the distributor. The contract allows price increases only to the extent of other cost increases to the importer.
2. Cost increases alone do not render a contract impracticable. Performance may be excused when the party could perform only at a loss that would be especially severe or unreasonable. Since such is not the case here, importer is not excused from performing as promised.

Bernina Distributors, Inc. v. Bernina Sewing Machines, 646 F.2d 434 (9th Cir. 1981).

Increased costs, a rise in the market or dramatic fluctuations in currencies do not excuse performance. But a severe shortage of raw materials or of supplies due to a contingency such as war, an unforeseen shutdown of major sources of supply, or a local crop failure, which increases costs or prevents a seller from securing necessary supplies, does constitute commercial impracticability.

In order to use the excuse, the seller is required to notify customers seasonably of any delay or nondelivery. This notification is to allow the buyers to take prompt action to find another source of supply. The notice must include an estimate of the buyer's allocation when the seller is able to perform partially [2-615(c)] and is subject to the Code's allocation requirement [2-615(b)].

Upon receipt of a notice of a substantial or indefinite delay in delivery or of an allocation, the buyer has two alternative courses of action. The buyer may terminate the contract insofar as that delivery is concerned. He may also terminate and discharge the whole contract if the deficiency substantially impairs the value of the whole contract [2-616(1)]. The buyer may also modify the contract by agreeing to take his available quota in substitution. If the buyer fails to modify the contract within a reasonable time not exceeding thirty days, the contract lapses with respect to the deliveries covered by the seller's notice [2-616(2)].

DISCHARGE OF CONTRACTS

7. Introduction

The rights and duties created by a contract continue in force until the contract is discharged. The term *discharge* is used to describe the cancellation of a contract and the acts by which the enforcement of its provisions are terminated. The usual and intended method of discharge is the complete performance by both parties of their obligations under the agreement. A valid excuse is a discharge in the sense that the excused party has no liability for failure to perform. The same may be said of grounds for rescission. A rescinded contract is in effect discharged.

Release *The voluntary relinquishing of a right, lien, or any other obligation.*

Although no particular form is required for an agreement to discharge a contract duty, the term **release** has traditionally been reserved for a formal written statement by one party that the other's duty is discharged. In Chapter 10, the word *renunciation* was introduced; it is equivalent to a release. Either party may voluntarily renounce or waive any right or claim arising under a contract. A renunciation is valid without consideration provided it is in writing.

A cancellation of a written contract and the surrender of it by one party to the other will usually discharge the agreement. Such a discharge requires consideration or proof of a gift. If both parties have obligations, there is consideration on the mutual surrender of the rights to performance. If only one party has an obligation, the necessary intent to make a gift and delivery of it may be found in the delivery of the written cancelled contract. However, such evidence is not conclusive, and a jury may find that a gift was not in fact made.

The law makes a distinction between a writing that is merely the *evidence* of the obligation and one that *is* the obligation, such as a promissory note. There is no particular sanctity in the law to the physical evidence of an ordinary contract, and the destruction of this evidence does not destroy the contract. However, if the actual obligation such as a negotiable instrument is surrendered or is intentionally destroyed by the holder of it, the obligation is discharged.

There are other methods of discharge, one of which is a novation. The term *novation* has two meanings. First of all, it is used to describe the situation in which the parties to a contract substitute a new debt or obligation for an existing one. The substitution of the new agreement operates to release or discharge the old one. Novation is also used to describe an agreement whereby an original party to a contract is replaced by a new party. The concept of novation is discussed further in Chapter 16.

The legal concept of *accord and satisfaction* allows discharge of a contract by a performance different from that agreed upon in the agreement. Laws sometimes have the effect of discharging obligations by prohibiting lawsuits to enforce them. For example, passage of time without litigation to enforce one's rights will operate to discharge an obligation. A discharge in bankruptcy has the same effect. (This is the subject of Chapter 45.)

8. Payment

The obligation of one party to a contract is usually to pay the other for goods sold or services rendered. There are three especially significant issues about payment that affect the matter of discharge: What constitutes payment? What is good evidence that payment has been made and that the obligation has been discharged? When a debtor has several obligations to a creditor, how will a payment be applied?

What constitutes payment? Certainly, the transfer of money constitutes payment, but this is not necessarily the case when the payment is by a negotiable instrument such as a check or a promissory note. Generally, payment by delivery of a negotiable instrument drawn or indorsed by the debtor to the creditor is a conditional payment and not an absolute discharge of the obligation. If the instrument is paid at maturity, the debt is discharged; if it is not so paid, the debt then exists as it did prior to the conditional payment. In the latter situation, the creditor can either bring an action to recover on the defaulted instrument or pursue his rights under the original agreement.

The parties may agree that payment by a negotiable instrument is an absolute discharge, in which event, if the instrument is not paid at maturity, the only recourse of the creditor is to bring action on the instrument—the original contract is discharged. A similar situation exists when accounts receivable are assigned by a debtor to his creditor. An assignment of accounts is a conditional payment only. If the accounts are not collected, the debtor is still obligated to pay his indebtedness. If the parties intend that the receipt of negotiable instruments or accounts receivable be treated as a discharge of the obligation, they must so specify.

What is good evidence of payment and discharge? As to what constitutes acceptable evidence of payment and discharge, a receipt given by the creditor will usually suffice. Such receipt should clearly indicate the amount paid and specify the transaction to which it relates. However, the creditor may be able to rebut the receipt by evidence that it was in error that it was given under mistake. A cancelled check is also evidence of payment, but the evidence is more conclusive when the purpose for which it is given is stated on the check. The drawer of a check may specify on the instrument that the payee by indorsing or cashing it acknowledges full satisfaction of an obligation of the drawer. Mutual debts do not extinguish each other, and in order for one to constitute payment of another, in whole or in part, there must be agreement between the creditor and debtor that the one shall be applied in satisfaction of the other.

How is payment applied to multiple debts? Where a debtor owes several obligations to one creditor, the debtor may direct how any payment is to be applied. The creditor who receives such payment is obligated to follow the debtor's instructions. In the absence of any instructions, the creditor may apply the payment against any one of several obligations that are due, or may credit a portion of the payment against a claim that has been outlawed by the statute of limitations, but this will not cause the outlawed claim to revive as to the balance.

If the source of a payment is someone other than the debtor and this fact is known to the creditor, the payment must be applied in such a manner as to protect the third party who makes the payment. Hence, if the money for the payment is supplied by a surety who has guaranteed that a particular obligation will be paid by the debtor, and the creditor knows it, he is bound to apply the payment on the obligation for which the surety was liable. Finally, if the creditor fails to make a particular application, the payment will be applied by the courts to the obligation oldest in point of time. However, where the creditor holds both secured and unsecured obligations, the courts of most states are inclined to apply it on an unsecured obligation. Similarly, if both principal and interest are due, the court considers the interest to be paid first, any balance being credited on the principal.

The application of these rules often has serious consequences. Debtors who are paying their own debts or whose debts are being paid by others should always direct that the payment be applied to the intended debt. Note that in the following case, the failure to direct the application of the payment resulted in a windfall to one party (the wife) and a greatly increased debt to a business.

CASE

Nathaniel Dupont sued White Construction Company, Limerock Industries, and Old Republic Insurance Company for certain injuries he sustained. He was awarded $3,525,000 and his wife, Janey, was awarded $1,025,000 for loss of consortium. Old Republic paid $553,602.51, which represented the limits of its coverage plus interest, to the registry of the trial court. Old Republic paid this sum in partial satisfaction of the judgment without reference to any further proceedings, including appeals, and, for the benefit of the plaintiffs, without qualification. After a hearing, the court authorized the Duponts to withdraw the money without affecting their right to collect the balance from the individual defendants. The money was disbursed by paying attorney's fees and dividing the balance between the Duponts. The husband and wife each received a check and together they received a joint certificate of deposit. Later, the award of damages to Janey Dupont was reversed and remanded for retrial. The award to Nathaniel Dupont was also reversed and eventually reduced to $1,025,000.

White Construction and Limerock contended that the payment by Old Republic should be applied against the judgment in favor of Nathaniel Dupont and that none of it should be applied to the claim of Janey Dupont. The trial judge ordered that one-half of the amount paid should be applied to the claim of Nathaniel Dupont and the other one-half applied to whatever award Janey Dupont ultimately received.

ISSUE: Did the trial judge properly apply Old Republic's payment to the claims of both Janey and Nathaniel Dupont?

DECISION: Yes.

REASONS:

1. At the time a debtor makes a payment, he may direct its application to whatever account or item of indebtedness he wishes. A creditor must respect the debtor's choice of application. However, if the debtor fails to specify a particular application of his payment, the creditor may at any time apply the payment as he desires. If neither the debtor nor the creditor makes any application, the law will appropriate it to the items of indebtedness according to the justice of the case, while considering the interests of third persons.
2. The debtor has the first opportunity to direct application of the payment, so the inquiry begins with the debtor's actions. Here, none of the debtors indicated any desire to apply Old Republic's payment only to the claim of Nathaniel Dupont. The evidence suggests that Old Republic intended its payment to go toward the judgments of both husband and wife. When Old Republic

made the payment, neither White Construction nor Limerock gave any direction. Therefore White Construction and Limerock waived their right to direct application of the payment.

3. Looking next to the actions of the creditors, there is competent evidence that the Duponts made a valid election in 1981 to apply the Old Republic payment to their individual judgments. The closing statement, prepared by the Duponts' law firm, shows separate and equal payments to Nathaniel and Janey Dupont.
4. Although the payment was made to the registry of the court, White Construction and Limerock had the opportunity to direct application of the payment and failed to take advantage of these opportunities. Both debtors had the opportunity to negotiate with Old Republic and the Duponts as to the application of the payment. The Old Republic payment was initially tendered to the Dupont's counsel and only later placed in the registry of the court.
5. Therefore the creditor's application of the payment stands. The trial court's decision is affirmed.

White Construction Co., Inc. v. Dupont, 478 So.2d. 485 (Fla. App. 1985).

9. Accord and Satisfaction

An *accord* is an agreement whereby one of the parties undertakes to give or to perform and the other to accept something different from that which he is or considers himself entitled to. An accord may arise from a disputed claim in either tort or contract. The term *satisfaction* means that the substituted performance is completed.

The doctrine of accord and satisfaction requires that there be a dispute or uncertainty as to amount due and that the parties enter into an agreement that debtor will pay, and the creditor will accept, a stated amount as a compromise of their differences and in satisfaction of the debt. It must clearly appear that the parties so understood and entered into a new and substitute contract. The surrender of the legal right to litigate the dispute or the settlement agreement often serves as consideration. As the following case illustrates, there can be no accord and satisfaction without a bona fide dispute.

CASE

Barcomb Motor Sales agreed to purchase two bus bodies from School Lines, Inc., for the price of $16,464. School Lines required payment in full before delivery. Barcomb Motor delivered a check in the amount of the purchase price to School Lines, and Barcomb Motor's agents picked up the bus bodies. Later, Barcomb Motor's president stopped payment on the check and issued a new check in the amount of $15,064.66, the difference representing various costs incurred by Barcomb Motor in connection with the transaction. The language "Payment in full for bus bodies Serial #'s B18550 and B18551" appeared on the back of Barcomb Motor's new check. School Lines cashed the check after indorsing it with words, "Accepted as Partial Payment." School Lines sued Barcomb Motor for the balance of the agreed-upon purchase price. Barcomb Motor claimed that School Lines' acceptance and cashing of the check affected an accord and satisfaction.

ISSUE: Was the amount owed School Lines but withheld by Barcomb Motor the subject of a bona fide dispute so that the doctrine of accord and satisfaction would apply?

DECISION: No.

REASONS:
1. Where a debtor tenders a lesser sum than is due as payment for a liquidated or undisputed debt, acceptance by the creditor of the lesser amount does not constitute an accord and satisfaction, and the debtor will therefore still be liable for the remainder of the debt. Instead, the partial payment discharges the debt only to the extent of the payment. The creditor can still maintain an action to recover the balance.
2. The $16,464 due School Lines was a liquidated and undisputed debt. The parties agreed upon this sum. Barcomb Motor delivered a check in that amount to School Lines, and never objected to the purchase price before stopping payment on that check.
3. Barcomb Motor's unilateral decision that it should not have to pay for costs it incurred does not establish the existence of a bona fide dispute as to the purchase price owed School Lines.
4. Therefore there was no effective accord and satisfaction, and Barcomb Motor was liable for the balance of the purchase price.

School Lines, Inc. v. Barcomb Motor Sales, 503 A.2d 131 (Vt. 1975).

The usual accord and satisfaction case involves a debtor's sending a creditor a check for less than the amount claimed by the creditor to be due. This check is usually marked "Paid in full." The courts of a few states hold that the cashing of the check constitutes an accord and satisfaction without additional proof. Most states, however, require that the party asserting the accord and satisfaction also prove (1) that the debt or claim was in fact the subject of a bona fide dispute, (2) that the creditor was aware of the dispute, and (3) that the creditor was aware that the check was tendered as full payment. If the creditor cashes the check, this act constitutes the satisfaction of the accord and completes the discharge. The creditor cannot change the language of the check, deposit it, or cash it and still contend that there was no accord and satisfaction.

10. Statute of Limitations

The *statute of limitations* prescribes a time limit within which the suit must be started after a cause of action arises. Failure to file suit within the time prescribed is a complete defense to the suit.

The purpose of a statute of limitations is to prevent actions from being brought long after evidence is lost or important witnesses have died or moved away. An action for breach of any contract for sale of personal property under the Code must be commenced within four years [2-725]. The Code further provides that the parties in their agreement may reduce the period of limitation to not less than one year but may not extend it. Contracts that are not controlled by the Code are covered by a variety of limitation periods. Some states distinguish between oral and written contracts, making the period longer for the latter.

Any voluntary part payment made on a money obligation by the debtor with intent to pay the balance tolls the statute, starting it to run anew. Similarly, any voluntary part payment, new promise, or clear acknowledgment of the indebtedness made after the claim has been outlawed reinstates the obligation, and the statute commences to run again. A payment or part payment by a third person or a joint debtor does not operate to interrupt the running of the statute as to other debtors not participating in the payment. No new consideration is required to support the reinstatement promise. If the old obligation has been outlawed, a new promise may be either partial or conditional. Since there is no *duty* to pay the debt, the debtor may attach such conditions to his new promise as he sees fit or may promise to pay only part of the debt. A few states require the new promise or acknowledgment to be in writing. The Code does not alter the law on tolling of the statute of limitations [2-725(4)].

A problem exists when a party is incapacitated by minority or insanity. Most jurisdictions hold that lack of capacity stops the running of the statute and extends the period of filing suit. A minor or an insane person usually has a specified time in which to bring an action—after the minor reaches his majority or the insane person regains capacity—although the full period set by statute has expired earlier.

CHAPTER SUMMARY

Excuses for Nonperformance

Hindrance, Prevention, or Noncooperation	1. Wrongful conduct by a party that prevents or unduly hinders the other party's performance will excuse performance. 2. Wrongful conduct is conduct that was not reasonably contemplated or the risk of which was not assumed by the nonperforming party.
Waiver	1. Waiver is a voluntary and intentional relinquishment of an express or constructive condition. 2. A waiver may be retracted unless it is supported by consideration or the other party has relied on the waiver. 3. A waiver may be made prior to or after a party has breached the agreement.
Impossibility of Performance	1. When an unforeseen event makes performance impossible, all duties to perform are excused. 2. Occurrence of reasonably foreseeable events will not excuse duties to perform. 3. Change in market price, strikes, accidents, unavailability of materials, and governmental regulations are normally foreseeable. 4. Acts of God, supervening illegalities, war, and death of a party or destruction of the contract's subject matter are normally unforeseeable.
Commercial Frustration	1. An intervening event or change of circumstances that was not foreseeable which prevents achievement of the object or purpose of the contract. 2. The purpose or object frustrated must have been the *basic* purpose or object of the contract from the time the contract was made.
Commercial Impracticability under the Code	1. If the contract can be performed but performance is *unduly* burdensome, impracticability may excuse performance. 2. No excuse for change in market price but more likelihood of an excuse for foreseeable events such as strikes, government regulations, and unavailable materials.

Discharge of Contracts

Introduction	1. The term *discharge* describes the cancellation of a contract and the acts by which enforcement of its provisions is terminated. 2. The usual method of discharge is performance. 3. A contract may also be discharged as the result of excuses for nonperformance, a mutual release of terms, rescission either by agreement of the parties or operation of law, novation, accord and satisfaction, and the expiration of the period of the statute of limitations. 4. The intentional destruction of a negotiable instrument is a form of cancellation.
Payment	1. A check constitutes only conditional payment. 2. If a debtor owes several obligations, the debtor may specify which is being paid. 3. If the debtor fails to specify, the creditor may apply it to any debt. 4. If the payment is by a third party, it must be applied to the debt on which the third party is obligated.
Accord and Satisfaction	1. An accord is an agreement to change a contract, and the satisfaction is the performance of the accord. 2. If the parties agree to settle a dispute either in contract or tort, there is an accord and satisfaction. The consideration is the agreement not to litigate the dispute.
Statute of Limitations	1. The statute of limitations prescribes a time limit beyond which a suit cannot be brought on a claim. 2. There are various time periods for contracts and torts, and these vary from state to state. 3. The Code period is four years. 4. Various events may toll the running of the statute and commence the period over again. These include payment, part payment, and a new promise to pay.

REVIEW QUESTIONS AND PROBLEMS

1. Match the terms in column A with the appropriate statement in column B.

A	B
(1) Waiver	(a) This is not a defense to breach of contract.
(2) Commercial frustration	(b) Requires reasonable cooperation.
(3) Impossibility	(c) Code's version of commercial frustration.
(4) Discharge by party's agreement	(d) An unforeseen event that makes performance impossible.
(5) Discharge by operation of law	(e) Unforeseeable intervening event that prevents fulfillment of contract's main purpose.
(6) Commercial impracticability	(f) Contract avoidance, bankruptcy, and statute of limitations.
(7) Good faith	(g) Rescission, release, novation, and accord and satisfaction.
(8) Hardship	(h) A voluntary, intentional relinquishment of a condition.

2. Elmina contracts with Mickey to build a house for $60,000, payable on condition that Elmina present a certificate from Libby, Mickey's architect, showing that the construction

work has been properly completed. Elmina properly completes the work, but Libby refuses to give the certificate because of collusion with Mickey. Is the nonoccurrence of the condition therefore excused? Explain.

3. Wells contracted with the state to erect a building according to the state's specifications and to lease it to the state. Time was made of the essence in the contract. Wells completed the building two months late. The state canceled the contract and leased space elsewhere. Wells sued and proved at trial that the delay was caused by the state's failure to indicate locations for electrical fixtures, outlets, and other details as required by the contract. Did Wells win? Why or why not?

4. Crotty contracted with A & D Construction for a new house. Crotty paid $67,000 of the purchase price but refused to pay the balance because of defects in construction. A & D offered to correct the defects, but Crotty would not allow A & D on the premises unless the company agreed to waive its lien rights. Under what legal theory would A & D be able to collect the balance due without correcting the defects? Explain.

5. A real estate broker contracted to sell a piece of land to Marilyn Curry. At her request, the contract stated: "This contract is contingent upon the buyer obtaining a rezoning for a mobile home park and campground. This contract is to be void if the rezoning is not obtained within 120 days." After sixty-five days, Curry notifies the broker that she would buy the property, irrespective of a zoning change. The zoning change was not obtained during the 120-day period. The broker now refuses to convey, and Curry sues. Who wins? Why?

6. Fred agreed to take dancing lessons from Muffy for one year at a specified price. After two lessons, Fred broke his foot. Should Fred be released from the contract? Explain why or why not.

7. Pate, a contractor, agreed with the city of Kiteville to construct a golf course for the amount of $230,329.88. After Pate had completed all the clearing and dirt work, a torrential rainfall of 12.47 inches occurred in a ten-hour period. It will cost $60,000 to restore the golf course to its condition prior to the rain. Is Pate relieved from the contract by the doctrine of commercial frustration? Explain why or why not.

8. A natural gas utility entered into a long-term supply contract to purchase naphtha. Due to increase in natural gas supplies, its needs for naphtha diminished. When the price of naphtha greatly increased, the utility sought to be released from its contract because of commercial frustration. Is this a valid defense in this case? Explain.

9. John Henry Mining Company was hired to drill a coal mine. The mine failed because tunneling became too difficult. Is John Henry excused for discontinuing? Why or why not?

10. Draper agreed to sell a lot to Mohrland for $14,875. As a part of the agreement, Draper agreed to relocate a gas line that crossed the property. After signing the agreement, Draper found out that it would cost $10,050 to move the gas line. Should this fact excuse Draper's performance of the contract? Why or why not?

11. A husband was in arrears in child support. He sent his former wife a check for less than was due which was marked "paid in full." The wife cashed the check. Was there an accord and satisfaction? Why or why not?

12. King, a tree surgeon, pruned some trees at the home of Deeb. King had estimated a cost of $480 for the work. When billed for $504, Deeb contended that he had not authorized the work. Deeb's attorney forwarded a check to King in the amount of $100, with the notation to the effect that this $100 was in full and final settlement of all claims of King against Deeb for work performed. King cashed the check and sued for the balance. What result? Why?

16 Contract Rights of Third Parties

CHAPTER PREVIEW

BUSINESS MANAGEMENT DECISION

You are a loan officer at a local bank. You read in the newspaper that one of your delinquent borrowers has won a $250,000 verdict in a products liability suit. Upon contacting this borrower about payment, you agree to take an assignment of the borrower's rights against the negligent defendant.

What should you do as the assignee of this claim?

The discussion of contracts up to this point has dealt with the law of contracts as applied to the contracting parties. Frequently, persons who are not in **privity** of contract (not parties to the contract) may have rights and even duties under the contract. The rights and duties of third parties may come in play when there is (1) a *third-party beneficiary contract*—a party contracts with another party for the purpose of conferring a benefit upon a third party (beneficiary); or (2) an *assignment* of the contract—a party to a contract (assignor) transfers to a third party (assignee) his rights under the contract; or (3) a *novation*—a new party (third party) becomes a party to an existing contract as he is substituted for one of the original parties.

Privity *Mutual and successive relationship to the same interest. Offeror and offeree, assignor and assignee, grantor and grantee are in privity. Privity of estate means that one takes title from another. In contract law, privity denotes parties in mutual legal relationship to each other by virtue of being promisees and promisors. At early common law, third-party beneficiaries and assignees were said to be not in "privity."*

THIRD-PARTY BENEFICIARY CONTRACTS

1. Nature of Such Contracts

Contracts are often made for the express purpose of benefiting some third party. Such contracts, called *third-party beneficiary contracts*, are of two types—*donee-beneficiary* and *creditor-beneficiary*. Both types of third-party beneficiaries are entitled to enforce a contract made in their behalf because the promisee has provided that the performance shall go to the beneficiary rather than to himself.

Donee-beneficiary. If the promise was purchased by the promisee in order to make a gift to the third party, such party is a **donee-beneficiary.** The most typical example of such an agreement is the contract for life insurance in which the beneficiary is someone other than the insured. The insured has made a contract with the life insurance company for the purpose of conferring a benefit upon a third party, namely, the beneficiary named in the policy.

Donee-beneficiary *If a promisee is under no duty to a third party, but for a consideration secures a promise from a promisor for the purpose of making a gift to a third party, then the third party is a donee beneficiary.*

Creditor-beneficiary *One who, for a consideration, promises to discharge another's duty to a third party.*

Creditor-beneficiary. If the promisee has contracted for a promise to pay a debt that he owes to a third party, such third party is a **creditor-beneficiary**—the debtor has arranged to pay the debt by purchasing the promise of the other contracting party to satisfy his obligation. The promisee obtains a benefit because his obligation to the creditor will presumably be satisfied. To illustrate: A operates a department store. He sells his furniture, fixtures, and inventory to B, who, as part of the bargain, agrees to pay all of A's business debts. A's purpose for making this contract was to have his debts paid, and he obtained B's promise to pay them in order to confer a benefit on his creditors. A's creditors are creditor-beneficiaries and can enforce their claims directly against B. Of course, to the extent that B does not pay them, the creditors still have recourse against A.

2. Legal Requirements

Incidental beneficiary *If the performance of a promise would only indirectly benefit a person not a party to a contract, such person is an incidental beneficiary.*

A third-party beneficiary is not entitled to enforce a contract unless he can establish that the parties actually intended to benefit him. This party must be something more than a mere **incidental beneficiary.** The intent to benefit the third party must clearly appear from the terms of the contract. Construction contracts involving subcontractors and suppliers are often found to be third-party beneficiary contracts, as occurred in the following case.

CASE

Keel contracted with Titan Construction Corporation to build a house with an auxiliary solar energy system. The plans and specifications for the house were to be provided by Titan. Titan subsequently contracted with Anderson to draw plans for an auxiliary solar energy system for the house. When the solar energy system later failed to function properly, Keel sued Anderson for breach of the contract with Titan to design a proper system. Anderson defended on the ground that Keel was not a party to the contract and was not even named in the contract and therefore could not sue to enforce it.

ISSUE: Was Keel, as an intended third-party beneficiary to the Anderson-Titan contract, entitled to sue?

DECISION: Yes.

REASONS:

1. A contract made for a third person may be enforced at any time before the parties rescind it. He may sue on the contract even if he is a stranger thereto, had no knowledge of the contract, and was not identified therein if it appears the parties intended to recognize him as a beneficiary.
2. When Titan engaged Anderson to design an auxiliary solar energy system, both parties knew and intended that the purpose of the contract was to provide a benefit for Keel.
3. Therefore Keel was an intended third-party beneficiary to the Anderson-Titan contract.

Keel v. Titan Construction Corp., 639 P.2d 1228 (Okla. 1982).

The intent to benefit a third party is more easily inferred in creditor-beneficiary situations than in donee-beneficiary ones. The third party need not be named as an individual in the contract if he can show that he is a member of a group for whose direct benefit the contract was made. A third-party beneficiary need not have knowledge of the contract at the time it was made. The fact that the actual contracting party could also sue to enforce the agreement would not bar a suit by the beneficiary if he was intended to benefit directly from the contract. A third-party beneficiary need not be the exclusive beneficiary of the promise. Of course, if the benefit to the third party is only incidental, the beneficiary cannot sue.

In most states, a contract made for the express purpose of benefiting a third party may not be rescinded without the consent of the beneficiary after its terms have been accepted by the beneficiary. The latter has a vested interest in the agreement from the moment it is made and accepted. For example, an insurance company has no right to change the named beneficiary in a life insurance policy without the consent of the beneficiary unless the contract gives the insured the right to make this change. Until the third-party beneficiary has either accepted or acted upon provisions of a contract for his benefit, the parties to the contract may change the provisions and deny him the benefits of the contract. Minors, however, are presumed to accept a favorable contract upon its execution, and such contract may not be changed so as to deprive the minor of its benefits.

ASSIGNMENTS

3. General Principles

A bilateral contract creates *rights* for each party and imposes on each corresponding *duties*. Each party is an **obligor** (has an obligation to perform the duties), and each is an **obligee** (is entitled to receive the performance of the other). Either party may desire to transfer to another his rights or his rights and duties. A party *assigns* rights and *delegates* duties. The term **assignment** may mean a transfer of one's rights under a contract, or it may mean a transfer both of rights and duties. The person making the transfer is called the **assignor,** and the one receiving the transfer is called the **assignee.**

A person who has duties under a contract cannot relieve himself of those duties by transferring the contract or delegating the duties to another person. An obligor that delegates duties as well as assigns rights is not thereby relieved of liability for proper performance if the assignee fails to perform. An assignor continues to be responsible for the ultimate performance, as the court held in the following case.

Obligor *A debtor or promisor.*

Obligee *A creditor or promisee.*

Assignment *A transfer of the rights under a contract. It may include a delegation of performance by the duties of the assignor.*

Assignor *One who makes an assignment.*

Assignee *One to whom an assignment has been made.*

CASE

In 1977, Ryder leased a truck to Transportation Equipment. In 1978, Transportation, with the approval of Ryder, assigned the truck rental contract to Williams Transfer, which agreed to pay the rent. A few months later the truck was damaged, and Ryder delivered a substitute truck to Williams Transfer. When Williams subsequently failed to pay the rent for the truck, Ryder sued Transportation Equipment for the balance due on the truck lease. Transportation Equipment asserted that it was released from the contract when Ryder approved the assignment to Williams.

ISSUE: Does an assignment release the assignor from its duty to perform?

DECISION: No.

REASONS:

1. An assignor remains liable on the contract after it is assigned. To avoid liability, the assignor must be specifically released from the contract by the other party. Such a release is called a novation.
2. Neither Ryder's approval of the assignment nor the substitution of another truck expressly released Transportation Equipment from its contract obligations.

Ryder Truck Rental v. Transportation Equipment Co., 339 N.W.2d 283 (Neb. 1983).

No particular formality is essential to an assignment. Consideration, although usually present, is not required. As a general proposition, an assignment may be either oral or written, although it is, of course, desirable to have a written assignment.

Some statutes require a writing in certain assignment situations. For example, an assignment of an interest in real property must be in writing in most states.

The main feature of an assignment is a *present transfer* of a contract right. An assignment is a *completed* transaction. After the assignment, the assignor has no interest in the contract right. The assignor's right belongs exclusively to the assignee. If the assignor retains any portion of the right, there is no valid assignment and the assignee cannot sue to enforce the right.

4. Consent Required

The rights under most contracts may be assigned if both parties to the agreement are willing to let this be done. Public policy prevents the assignment of some contract rights, however. For example, many states by statute prohibit or severely limit the assignment of wages under an employment contract. In addition, rights created by the law, such as the right to collect for personal injuries, cannot be assigned in most states.

As a general rule, contract rights may be assigned by one party without the consent of the other party. In most contracts, it is immaterial to the party performing who receives the performance. A party has no right to object to most assignments.

There are certain exceptions to these general rules. Some contracts cannot be assigned without consent of the other party. Of the several classes of contracts that may not be transferred without the consent of the other party, the most important are contracts involving personal rights or personal duties. A personal right or duty is one in which personal trust and confidences are involved, or one in which skill, knowledge, or experience of one of the parties is important. In such cases, the personal acts and qualities of one or both of the parties form a material and integral part of the contract. For example, a lease contract where the rent is a percentage of sales is based on the ability of the lessee and would be unassignable without the consent of the lessor. Likewise, an exclusive agency contract would be unassignable.

If a contract involves multiple rights and duties, those that are not personal may be assigned. It is only the personal rights and duties that may not be transferred. Note that the right in the following case was not personal, although the duty was personal.

CASE

The law firm of West & Groome agreed to represent Hurst in pending criminal proceedings. The contract gave West & Groome the right after two years to sell Hurst's house and use the proceeds to pay his attorney's fees. The criminal charges against Hurst were successfully defended. Two years later when the fees were not paid, West & Groome assigned its right to sell Hurst's house to a third party. Hurst sued to prevent the sale, claiming that the assignment was illegal.

ISSUE: Can the law firm assign its right to fees from its clients?

DECISION: Yes.

REASONS:

1. Contracts may be assigned unless the performance of some term of the contract involves an element of personal skill or credit.
2. While the duty to defend Hurst involved personal skill, the right to fees and to sell his property did not.

3. Therefore West & Groome did not breach the contract by assigning it after its obligation to defend Hurst was satisfied.

Hurst v. West, 272 S.E.2d 378 (N.C. 1980).

Some duties that might appear to be personal in nature are not considered so by the courts. For example, unless the contract provides to the contrary, a building contractor may delegate responsibility for certain portions of the structure to a subcontractor without consent. Since construction is usually to be done according to specifications, the duties are delegable. It is presumed that all contractors are able to follow specifications. Of course, the delegatee must substantially complete the building according to the plans and specifications. The obligor will not be obligated to pay for it if it is not, and the assignor will be liable in event of default by the assignee.

Another example of a contract that is unassignable without consent is one in which an assignment would place an additional burden or risk upon a party—one not contemplated at the time of the agreement. Such appears to be true of an assignment of the right to purchase real estate on credit.

Most states also hold that one who has agreed to purchase goods on credit, and has been given the right to do so, may not assign his right to purchase the goods to a third party (assignee), since the latter's credit may not be as good as that of the original contracting party—the assignor. This reasoning is questionable because the seller could hold both the assignor and the assignee responsible. However, the inconvenience to the seller in connection with collecting has influenced most courts to this result. But in contracts where the seller has security for payment such as retention of title to the goods or a security interest in the goods, the seller has such substantial protection that the courts have held that the right to purchase on credit is assignable.

5. Consent Required under the Code

The Code contains provisions that generally approve the assignment of rights and delegation of duties by buyers and sellers of goods. The duties of either party may be delegated *unless* the parties have agreed otherwise or the nondelegating party has ". . . a substantial interest in having his original promisor perform or control the acts required by the contract" [2-210(1)]. Accordingly, a seller can ordinarily delegate to someone else the duty to perform the seller's obligations under the contract. This would occur when no substantial reason exists why the delegated performance would be less satisfactory than the personal performance of the assignor.

The Code does provide that rights cannot be assigned where the assignment would materially change the duty of the other party, or increase materially the burden or risk imposed on him by his contract, or impair materially his chance of obtaining return performance [2-210(2)]. These Code provisions in effect incorporate the personal rights and duties exception previously discussed.

6. Anti-assignment Clauses

Some contracts contain a clause stating that the contract cannot be assigned without the consent of the other party. Older cases often held these clauses to be against public policy and unenforceable as an unlawful restraint on alienation (right to sell one's property). Recognizing freedom of contract, modern courts usually uphold the clause prohibiting assignment and find it legally operative. Nonetheless, looking to the language of the clause in non-Code cases, courts have reached different results.

Varying interpretations. Some courts hold that if the clause *prohibits* assignment, this creates a promise (*duty* in the assignor) not to assign, but the assignor still has the *power* to assign. Thus the assignment is effective, but the obligor has a legal claim against the assignor for breach of his *promise* (duty) not to assign. Others hold that the clause *invalidates* the contract. The assignment is still effective, but the obligor has an option to avoid the contract for breach of the condition. Still others allow the parties to prohibit an assignment. Any purported assignment is void in these states, and the assignment itself is ineffective. Rather than merely creating a *duty* (promise) not to assign, this invalidation clause deprives any party of the power to assign. The following case is typical of those discussing the policy aspects of clauses attempting to prohibit assignments.

CASE

Hanigan entered into a Dairy Queen Store Agreement with LeMoine. The agreement provided that "Secondary Party shall not assign or transfer this Agreement without the written approval of First Party." LeMoine entered into a contract to sell the Dairy Queen franchise and all its assets to Wheeler. Hanigan refused to approve the sale because he felt that the price ($90,000) was too high and that an inflated sales price was detrimental to the Dairy Queen business. Hanigan also stated that Wheeler was too inexperienced and too young to run the business properly. Plaintiff Wheeler then sued Hanigan for a declaratory judgment that the contract provision disallowing the assignment of the franchise was unenforceable as against public policy.

ISSUES: Is the anti-assignment clause an unlawful restraint on alienation? If the clause is lawful, does it make an assignment ineffective?

DECISION: The contract limitation against unapproved assignments is proper and valid. The clause, however, is a mere promise not to assign; any assignment would therefore be effective.

REASONS:

1. It is a fundamental principle that one of the primary incidents of property ownership is the right of disposition or alienation. The right is not limitless; it can be defeated by a clear provision to that effect.
2. A restriction on assignment does not leave the assignor entirely powerless. Although a contract contains a promise not to assign, as in this case, the assignment is effective. The promise creates a duty in the assignor not to assign. It does not deprive the assignor of the power to assign. If the power is exercised, the assignor is liable for breach of his duty, but the assignment would be effective.

Hanigan v. Wheeler, 504 P.2d 972 (Ariz. 1972).

Code interpretation. The Code has effected significant changes regarding anti-assignment clauses. First, in Article 2 it notes the progressive undermining of the original rule invalidating these clauses. The Code observes that the courts have already construed the heart out of anti-assignment clauses. Second, in Article 9 it acknowledges the economic need of freedom of contract rights in modern commercial society. Thus an anti-assignment clause is ineffective to prohibit the assignment of an account or contract right [9-318(4)]. In a sale of business, typically both the rights are assigned and the duties are delegated. Lacking a release, the delegating party is still liable on the duties delegated. Consequently, Article 2 of the Code provides that in a sales situation, a clause prohibiting assignment should be construed as barring only the delegation of duties [2-210(3)]. Therefore a generally phrased anti-assignment clause is to be read as allowing an assignment of rights but forbidding delegation of duties. Despite the use of the term *anti-assignment*, the drafters of the Code took notice that in a sales situation the parties were usually more concerned with delegation than with assignment. Moreover, they saw great commercial need for free assignability of rights and struck the compromise of allowing assignment but prohibiting delegation when confronted with an anti-assignment clause.

7. Claims for Money

As a general rule, claims for money due or to become due under existing contracts may be assigned. An automobile dealer may assign to a bank the right to receive money due under contracts for the sale of automobiles on installment contracts. Although the law tends toward greatly reducing or eliminating the right of employees to assign wages, an employee may assign a portion of his pay to a creditor, in order to obtain credit or to satisfy an obligation. However, the Uniform Consumer Credit Code (adopted in several states) provides that a seller cannot take an assignment of earnings for payment of a debt arising out of a consumer credit sale. Lenders also are not allowed to take an assignment of earnings for payment of a debt arising out of a consumer loan. The Consumer Credit Code is a part of the trend toward greater consumer and debtor protection.

When a claim for money is assigned, an issue that frequently arises is the liability of the assignor in case the assignee is unable to collect from the debtor-obligor. If the assignee takes the assignment merely as **security** for a debt owed to him by the assignor, it is clear that if the claim is not collected the assignor still has to pay the debt to the assignee. But if someone *purchases* a claim against a third party, generally he has no recourse against the seller (assignor) if the third party (debtor-obligor) defaults. If the claim is *invalid* or sold expressly "with recourse," the assignor would be required to reimburse the assignee if the debtor-obligor did not pay.

Security *Property that a debtor places with a creditor, who may sell it if the debt is not paid.*

In all cases, an assignor *warrants* that the claim he assigns is a valid, legal claim, that the debtor-obligor is really obligated to pay, and that there are no valid defenses to the assigned claim. If this **warranty** is breached (that is, if there are valid defenses or the claim is otherwise invalid), the assignee has recourse against the assignor.

Warranty *An undertaking that a certain fact regarding the subject matter of a contract is presently true or will be true.*

8. Rights of the Assignee

An assignment is more than a mere authorization or request to pay or to perform for the assignee rather than the assignor. The obligor-debtor *must* pay or perform for the assignee, who now, in effect, owns the rights under the contract. If there is a valid assignment, the assignee owns the rights and is entitled to receive them.

Performance for the original party will not discharge the contract. Unless the contract provides otherwise, the assignee receives the identical rights of the assignor. Since the rights of the assignee are neither better nor worse than those of the assignor, any defense the third party (obligor) has against the assignor is available against the assignee. Part payment, fraud, duress, or incapacity can be used as a defense by the third party (obligor) if an action is brought against him by the assignee, just as the same defense could have been asserted against the assignor had he been the plaintiff. A common expression defining the status of the assignee is that he "stands in the shoes" of the assignor. The following case illustrates the application of this principle.

CASE

In 1979, M. DeMatteo Construction was the general contractor on a highway construction project. Dirt Movers, Inc., agreed to supply certain materials that DeMatteo needed for this project. From June through December 1979, Dirt Movers supplied the materials as agreed and was paid a total of $209,212.61. DeMatteo withheld retainages of $10,692.52. On December 6, 1979, Dirt Movers, owing $12,000 to Graves Equipment, Inc., assigned to Graves all retainages that Dirt Movers was due under the contract with DeMatteo. Dirt Movers later failed to deliver materials. DeMatteo terminated its contract with Dirt Movers and subsequently obtained the necessary materials from other suppliers at a price that was $19,170 higher than the price under its contract with Dirt Movers. DeMatteo withheld the retainages that it owed Dirt Movers, claiming that under its contract with Dirt Movers it could keep these retainages as liquidated damages. Graves, the assignee of the retainages, sued DeMatteo for payment of the retainages.

The trial court awarded Graves $10,692.52, the amount of the retainages, holding that DeMatteo could not set off any damages against any sums due Dirt Movers at the time of Dirt Movers' assignment to Graves because DeMatteo had received notice of the assignment long before any breach.

ISSUE: Was it proper for the trial judge to consider the timing of notice relative to the timing of the breach, when the right to damages arose?

DECISION: No.

REASONS:

1. The trial judge ruled that Dirt Movers' obligation under its contract with DeMatteo was for the sale of goods. The rights to the retainages, which were the rights assigned and now form the basis of this dispute, arose from this contract. Therefore the Uniform Commercial Code governs the contract and this dispute.
2. Section 9-381(1)(a) of the UCC provides that the rights of the assignee are subject to all the terms of the contract between the account debtor and assignor and subject to any defense or claim that arises from the contract. Therefore the debtor can raise, as a defense, any claim arising from his contract with the assignor regardless of the timing of the debtor's receipt of notice of the assignment relative to the timing of the accrual of the claim or defense.

   This provision of the UCC incorporates the common law rule that an assignee of contract rights stands in the shoes of the assignor and has no greater rights against the debtor than the assignor had.

3. The claims and defenses asserted by DeMatteo arose out of the terms of the material supplier contract from which the assignment was created. Therefore Section 9-318(1)(a) governs, and the timing consideration is irrelevant. The trial court's decision is reversed and the case is remanded.

Graves Equipment, Inc. v. M. DeMatteo Construction, 489 N.E.2d 1010 (Mass. 1986).

Some contracts contain a provision to the effect that "if the seller assigns the contract to a finance company or bank, the buyer agrees that he will not assert against such assignee any defense that he has against the seller-assignor." This *waiver of defense* clause is an attempt to give the contract a quality usually described as *negotiability*, a concept discussed in Chapter 37. Negotiability is a rule that cuts off defenses by giving one party a protected status. If a negotiable instrument is properly negotiated to a party, that party may have a protected status called a **holder in due course.** Thus most defenses of the original party (the buyer) cannot be asserted against the holder in due course (the finance company or bank). The purpose of the concept of negotiability is to encourage the free flow of commercial paper. Adding a provision to a contract that gives it the same effect obviously places the assignee in a favored position and makes contracts with such clauses quite marketable.

Holder in due course *One who has acquired possession of a negotiable instrument through proper negotiation for value, in good faith, and without notice of any defenses to it. Such a holder is not subject to personal defenses that would otherwise defeat the obligation embodied in the instrument.*

As a part of the growing movement toward greater consumer protection, the Federal Trade Commission has ruled that such clauses cutting off defenses of consumers against delinquent sellers when a contract is assigned constitute an unfair method of competition. They are therefore illegal. The commission has also prohibited the use of the holder in due course concept against consumers. This 1976 action by the Federal Trade Commission is discussed further in Chapter 38.

9. Duties of the Parties

As previously noted, an assignor is not relieved of his obligations by a delegation of them to the assignee. The assignor is still liable if the assignee fails to perform as agreed, in which case the assignor would have a cause of action against the assignee. If a party upon the transfer of a contract to a third person wishes to be released of liability, a legal arrangement known as a *novation* is required. The requirements for a valid novation are discussed later in this chapter.

The liability of the assignee to third persons is a much more complicated issue. The liability of the assignee is determined by a careful examination of the transactions to see whether it is an assignment of only the rights under the agreement or whether the duty has also been delegated. This is often difficult to determine when the language used refers only to an "assignment of the contract."

As a general rule, the *mere assignment* of a contract calling for the performance of affirmative duties by the assignor, with nothing more, does not impose those duties upon the assignee. As a result, an assignee is not a guarantor of the products sold by the assignor, as the following case illustrates.

CASE

Cuchine purchased a truck from Bell under a retail installment sales contract. Bell thereafter assigned the contract to Ford Motor Credit Company. Cuchine had difficulty with the truck and returned it to Bell for repair. When it was apparent that the truck could not be satisfactorily repaired, Cuchine left the truck with Bell and filed suit against Bell and the credit company seeking rescission. Cuchine maintains Ford Motor Credit Company "assumed full contract liability when the assignment was accepted." Cuchine based this claim on a clause in the contract that provided the following: "Any holder of this contract is subject to all claims and defenses which the debtor could assert against the seller of goods or services obtained pursuant hereto or with proceeds hereof."

ISSUE: Did the assignment impose complete contractual liability on Ford Motor Credit Company under the contract?

DECISION: No.

REASONS:

1. Where it is not clearly shown that the assignee under a contract expressly or implicitly assumed the assignor's liability under a contract, the assignee is not subject to the contract liability imposed by the contract on the assignor.
2. The intent of Section 9-318 of the Uniform Commercial Code "was to allow an account debtor to assert contractual defenses as a set-off; the provisions were not intended, generally, to place the assignee of a contract in the position of being held a guarantor of a product in place of the assignor."
3. The language of the contract specifying "any holder of this consumer credit contract is subject to all claims and defenses which the debtor could assert against the seller of goods or services obtained pursuant hereto . . ." does not impose full contractual liability on the assignee.

Cuchine v. H. O. Bell, Inc., 682 P.2d 723 (Mont. 1984).

Notwithstanding the foregoing case, there is a decided trend that holds that an assignment of an entire contract carries an implied assumption of the liabilities. When the assignee undertakes and agrees to perform the duties as a condition precedent to enforcement of the rights, or has assumed the obligation to perform as part of a contract of assignment, he has liability for failure to perform. To illustrate: If a tenant assigns a lease, the assignee is not liable for future rents if he vacates the property prior to expiration of the period of the lease unless he expressly assumes the burdens of the lease at the time of the assignment. He is obligated simply to pay the rent for the period of his actual occupancy. To the extent that an assignee accepts the benefits of a contract, he becomes obligated to perform the duties that are related to such benefits.

If an "entire contract" has been assigned—that is, if duties have been delegated to the assignee as well as the assignment of the rights—a failure by the assignee to render the required performance gives rise to a cause of action in favor of the third party (obligee). The obligee can sue either the assignor or the assignee or both.

Under the Code, an assignment of "the contract" or of "all my rights under the contract" or an assignment in similar general terms is an assignment of rights, and unless the language or the circumstances (as in an assignment for security) indicate the contrary, it is also a delegation of performance of the duties of the assignor and an assumption of those duties by the assignee. Its acceptance by the assignee constitutes a promise by him to perform those duties. This promise is enforceable by either the assignor or the other party to the original contract [2-210(4)].

When the assignor delegates his duties, although the assignor remains liable, the obligee may feel insecure as to the ability of the assignee to perform the delegated duties. The obligee may demand that the assignor furnish him with adequate assurance that the assignee will in fact render proper performance [2-210(5)].

10. Notice of Assignment

Immediately after the assignment, the assignee should notify the obligor or debtor of his newly acquired right. This notification is essential for two reasons.

First, in the absence of any notice of the assignment, the debtor is at liberty to perform (pay the debt or do whatever else the contract demands) for the original contracting party, the assignor. In fact, he would not know that anyone else had the right to require performance or payment. Thus, the right of the assignee to demand performance can be defeated by his failure to give this notice. The assignor who receives performance under such circumstances becomes a trustee of funds or property received from the obligor and can be compelled to turn them over to the assignee. Upon receipt of notice of assignment, the third party *must perform* for the assignee, and his payment or performance to the assignor would not relieve him of his obligation to the assignee.

Second, the notice of assignment is also for the protection of innocent third parties. The assignor has the *power*, although not the *right*, to make a second assignment of the same subject matter. If notice of the assignment has been given to the obligor, it has much the same effect as the recording of a mortgage. It furnishes protection for a party who may later consider taking an assignment of the same right. A person considering an assignment should therefore always communicate with the debtor to confirm that the right has not previously been assigned. If the debtor has not been notified of a previous assignment, and if the prospective assignee is aware of none, in many states the latter can feel free to take the assignment. He should immediately give notice to the debtor. In other words, the first assignee to give notice to the debtor, provided such assignee has no knowledge of a prior assignment, will prevail over a prior assignee in most states.

In some states, it is held that the first party to receive an assignment has a prior claim, regardless of which assignee gave notice first. In these states, the courts act on the theory that the assignor has parted with all his interest by virtue of the original assignment and has nothing left to transfer to the second assignee. In all states, however, the party who is injured by reason of the second assignment has a cause of action against the assignor, to recover the damages he has sustained. The assignor has committed a wrongful and dishonest act by making a double assignment.

NOVATION

Novation (*novo* = new) describes an agreement whereby one of the original parties to a contract is replaced by a new party. The word *novation* originated in Roman law to refer to the *substitution* of a new contract. Thus, when a *new* person becomes a party to a *new* contract by *substitution* to the same rights and duties of an original party, a novation occurs and discharges the original contract. For example, Tommy, who is indebted to Nancy on an earlier contract, agrees with Nancy and Jesse that in consideration of Nancy's discharging Tommy, Jesse promises to do what Tommy was originally obligated to do. Jesse is thus substituted for Tommy, and a new contract exists between Nancy and Jesse.

A distinction must be made between an assignment-delegation and a novation. In a novation, one party is completely dismissed from the contract as another is substituted. The dismissed party is no longer liable on the original contract. In an assignment-delegation, the original party (assignor) remains liable.

For a novation to be effective, it must be agreed to by all the parties. The remaining contracting party must agree to accept the new party and simultaneously specifically agree to release the withdrawing party. The latter must consent to withdraw and to permit the new party to take his place. The new party must agree to assume the burdens and duties of the retiring party. The agreement to release a former party and the agreement to assume the duties supplies bargained-for consideration to support the new or substituted contract. Note that a novation is never presumed. The burden of proving all the elements is on the party who claims a novation. The importance of satisfying this burden is illustrated in the following case.

CASE

Martin Stern sued for his architectural services rendered to Jacobson in Jacobson's development of a hotel and casino, known as King's Castle, on the north shore of Lake Tahoe, Nevada. In April 1969, Jacobson contracted with Stern for the architect's services and the fee. On May 1, 1969, Jacobson acquired all the stock of A.L.W., Inc., a corporation that had previously operated a casino on the site of the new development. On May 9, 1969, A.L.W. began to operate King's Castle, but it filed bankruptcy in 1972. Stern did not file a claim in the bankruptcy proceeding but rather brought this suit directly against Jacobson. When Stern was awarded $132,590.37 by the trial court, Jacobson appealed on the ground that his obligations were adopted by A.L.W., which constituted a novation.

ISSUE: Has a valid novation occurred that would release Jacobson from his personal liability?

DECISION: No.

REASONS:

1. To create a valid novation, the creditor must assent to the substitution of a new obligor. This assent may be inferred from his acceptance of part performance by the new obligor, if the performance is made with the understanding that a complete novation is proposed.
2. No evidence indicates that Stern agreed to the substitution or that he performed with the knowledge or understanding that a novation was proposed. On the contrary, Stern maintained throughout that he contracted with Jacobson personally.

Jacobson v. Stern, 605 P.2d 198 (Nev. 1980).

CHAPTER SUMMARY

Third-Party Beneficiary Contracts

Nature of Such Contracts

1. A noncontracting party may have enforceable contract rights if a party to the contract intended to confer a benefit on the third party.
2. Creditor- and donee-beneficiaries are intended beneficiaries.
3. If performance by the promisor will satisfy a duty owed to the beneficiary by the promisee, the beneficiary is a creditor-beneficiary.
4. If the promisee purchased a promise in order to make a gift to a third party, the party is a donee-beneficiary.

Legal Requirements

1. If a third party is not an intended beneficiary, he is an incidental beneficiary with no right to enforce the agreement.
2. Original parties can modify or rescind their contract until the third party's rights vest.
3. A third party's rights vest when he either relies on the contract to his detriment or manifests assent to the rights.
4. A third-party beneficiary is subject to all defenses arising out of the contract.

Assignments

General Principles

1. An assignment is a transfer of rights arising from an earlier contract.
2. A delegation is a transfer of duties arising from an earlier contract.
3. When A assigns his rights against B to C, A is the assignor, B is the promisor-obligor, and C is the assignee.
4. When A delegates his duties owed to B to C, A is the assignor (delegator), B is the promisee-obligee, and C is the assignee (delegatee).
5. "Assignment of the contract" is usually held to be both an assignment and a delegation.
6. An effective assignment requires the assignor to transfer those rights irrevocably to the assignee.
7. Neither consideration nor, generally, a writing is required.
8. An assignor is not relieved of his duties by delegating them to an assignee.

Consent Required

1. Most rights are assignable unless the assignment would (a) materially change the other party's duty, (b) materially increase the burden or risk imposed by the contract, or (c) materially impair the other party's chance of obtaining return performance.
2. The duties under contracts for personal services generally may not be delegated.
3. The right to purchase on credit cannot be assigned without consent in most states.

Consent Required under the Code

1. The Code generally approves the assignment of rights and the delegation of duties.
2. Unless the buyer has a substantial interest in having the seller perform, the seller may delegate the duty to deliver goods.

Anti-assignment Clauses

1. Contractual limitations on assignments are strictly construed in most cases to prevent only a delegation of duties.

2. A breach of such a clause may be interpeted as (a) breaching the promise not to make an assignment, (b) invalidating the contract, or (c) voiding the assignment.

Claims for Money

1. As a general rule, claims for money may be assigned but there are statutory exceptions.
2. If the assignment is as security for a debt, the assignor still owes the debt if it remains unpaid by the obligor.
3. If the assignor sells the debt, there is no recourse against the assignor if the obligor defaults.
4. An assignor warrants the genuineness of the money claims assigned.

Rights of the Assignee

1. The assignee may enforce all the rights of his assignor.
2. The obligor may raise all defenses against the assignee which the obligor had against the assignor prior to the assignment.
3. Failure of assignor to fulfill his duties to the obligor will be a defense against the assignee.
4. Contract provisions cutting off defenses of consumers are illegal under a FTC rule.

Duties of the Parties

1. An assignor is not relieved of duties by a delegation of those duties.
2. The mere assignment of rights does not include the delegation of duties.
3. Under the Code, the assignment of the contract generally includes the assignment of rights and the delegation of duties.
4. If an assignor delegates duties to an assignee, the assignee thereby becomes primarily liable to perform for the obligee.

Notice of Assignment

1. Notice of the assignment must be given by the assignee to the obligor if the assignee is to receive performance.
2. In a case of multiple assignments, the first to give notice in good faith to the obligor has priority to receive performance in most states.

Novation

1. A novation means a new contract. It involves the substitution with the express consent of all parties of a third party for one of the original parties.
2. A novation requires a prior valid contract, agreement for substitution of a third party, an express release of one party, and a new valid contract.

REVIEW QUESTIONS AND PROBLEMS

1. Match each term in column A with the appropriate statement in column B.

A	B
(1) Intended third-party beneficiary	(a) Performance will satisfy a duty the promisee owes the beneficiary.
(2) Incidental third-party beneficiary	(b) A present transfer of rights arising from an earlier contract.
(3) Creditor-beneficiary	(c) Transfer of rights would materially change the other party's duty, increase the risk imposed by the contract, or impair return performance.

(4) Donee-beneficiary	(d) Third party who has no legally enforceable rights under a contract.
(5) When beneficiary's rights vest	(e) Usually both an assignment and a delegation.
(6) Assignment	(f) Rights vest based on reliance or consent of third party.
(7) Delegation	(g) A new contract with the substitution of a third party for an original party.
(8) Nonassignable rights	(h) Third party who has legally enforceable rights under a contract.
(9) Nondelegable duties	(i) Duties of personal service or duties that may materially vary the performance given to the obligee.
(10) Novation	(j) Transfer of duties arising from an earlier contract.
(11) "Assignment of the contract"	(k) Promisee buys a promise to make a gift to a third party.

2. Boyce contracts to build a house for Anne. Pursuant to the contract, Boyce and his surety Travelers execute a payment bond to Anne by which they promise Anne that all of Boyce's debts for labor and materials on the house will be paid. Boyce later employs Sam as a carpenter and buys lumber from Larry's Lumber Company. Are Sam and Larry's Lumber Company intended beneficiaries of Travelers' promise to Anne? Explain.

3. Wichita State University leased an airplane to fly its football team. The lease provided that the university would provide liability insurance to cover any deaths or injuries from the operation of the plane. No such insurance was bought. The plane later crashed, killing all on board. Can the estates of the deceased football players sue the university as intended third-party beneficiaries? Explain why or why not.

4. A property settlement agreement that was part of a divorce decree required the former husband to pay child support until the child reached age twenty-two, if the child attended college and maintained at least a "C" average. The mother died when the child was sixteen, and the father refused to support the child after the child reached eighteen. Is the child entitled to sue the father for breach of contract? Why or why not?

5. Hunt, an employee of the Marie Reading School, was injured when the elevator he was operating fell. The school had a contract with Shaft Elevator, Inc., whereby Shaft was to inspect and service the elevator on a regular basis. Hunt contended that Shaft had not properly inspected the elevator and that its omission caused the accident. Can Hunt maintain an action against Shaft? Why or why not?

6. Gaither entered into a contract with a nonprofit corporation whereby Gaither would receive $700 per month while in medical school, provided that he would return to his small hometown, Chester, to practice medicine for ten years after becoming a licensed physician. The residents of Chester voted approval of bonds to construct a medical clinic. Gaither practiced medicine in Chester for about five weeks but then left for Mt. Clement. Do the representatives of the medical clinic and the citizens of Chester have a right to sue Gaither? Explain.

7. In violation of an injunction, the members of the defendants' unions commenced a strike, halting all mass transit in the city of New York and paralyzing its life and commerce. In contracts with the public employers, the unions had agreed not to strike. The plaintiff, a New York lawyer, brought a class action suit against the transit unions and certain of their officers, seeking damages for the mass transit strike. The unions contended that the plaintiff was not a third-party beneficiary of the contract. Were the unions correct? Explain.

8. Green, an insured of a Prudential health policy, incurred medical expenses at Kelly Health Care. She signed an authorization that stated: "I hereby authorize payment directly

to Kelly Health Care of benefits otherwise payable by me.'' Kelly sued Prudential, claiming to be an assignee of Green's insurance contract. Prudential contended that Kelly was not an assignee. Was Prudential correct? Explain.

9. Athens Lie Detector Company, for good consideration, gave Yarbrough an exclusive license to operate certain lie detector machines as part of the agreement. The company agreed to tell him how the manufacturing process works. Athens assigned its rights and delegated its duties under the contract to Travers. Are the rights assignable? Are the duties delegable? Explain.

10. Pizza of Gaithersburg contracted with Virginia Coffee Service to install cold-drink vending machines in its six restaurants. A year later, Macke bought the assets of Virginia Coffee Service and the contract was assigned to Macke. Pizza contends that the duties under the contract could not be delegated. What do you think? Explain.

11. Corey sold his property to Greer, who assigned the contract right to Bob. The original contract of sale provided for an extension of credit by Corey to Greer and did not require a total cash payment at the time of closing. Is a contract for the sale of real estate assignable by the buyer if it provides for credit from the seller to the buyer? Explain.

12. As part of his employment contract, an employee entered into a covenant not to compete with his corporate employer. The contract also contained a provision that stated: ''This agreement is personal to each of the parties hereto, and neither party may assign or delegate any of the rights or obligations hereunder without first obtaining a written consent of the other party.'' Later the corporation was dissolved, and the assets were distributed to the shareholders who operated the business as a partnership. The employee filed suit to establish that the covenant not to compete was no longer enforceable. What result? Why?

13. Suppose that contract for the sale of goods contains this clause: ''Under no circumstances may any rights under this contract be assigned.'' After the seller delivers goods to the buyer, may the seller assign the buyer's unpaid account to a third party? Explain.

14. Hudson Supply owed an open account to Eastern Brick & Tile Company (Eastern). These accounts were sold and assigned by Eastern to a finance company, the plaintiff. When plaintiff sought to collect on the assigned accounts, Hudson refused to pay on the ground that Eastern owed more money to Hudson than Hudson owed Eastern. Can a defensive setoff be asserted against the assignee of a money claim? Explain.

15. In order to get a construction contract, a contractor was required to put up a performance bond. The purpose of the bond was to ensure that the contractor would perform properly and pay all bills. The defendant bonding company agreed to write the bond provided that the contractor would assign (as security) payments due under the construction contract. The contractor agreed and the assignment was executed. Thereafter, the contractor borrowed money from plaintiff bank and assigned the same right to the same payments to the bank. The bank was the first to notify the owner of its assignment. Which party has priority? Explain.

Introduction to Sales Contracts

17

C H A P T E R   P R E V I E W

BUSINESS MANAGEMENT DECISION

You are the general manager of a wholesale mail-order distributor. The bulk of your customers are retailers who phone in their orders.

What policy would you develop for accepting these phone orders?

ARTICLE 2 OF THE UCC

1. Common Law Contract Changes

As we learned in Part II, on contracts, the Uniform Commercial Code has changed many older, classic contract rules to conform with business realities and the reasonable expectations of the contracting parties. Many common law contract rules also have been changed or modified by Article 2 of the Code to achieve a more commercially desirable result, since some basic contract rules concerning employment, construction, and real property contracts are simply inappropriate in a sale-of-goods context. The important Code modifications or changes are listed in Table 17–1. These Code rules have already been discussed in the chapters on contracts and will not be discussed further. They are summarized here for review purposes.

This chapter explores the sales contract, the transfer of title to goods, and the risk of loss when goods are destroyed, damaged, or stolen. Chapter 18 covers the remedies available to the parties when there is a breach of a sales contract.

2. Scope

A sales transaction can relate to real property, to goods, and to other forms of personal property. This chapter, however, is limited to sales transactions in goods under Article 2 of the Uniform Commercial Code. Article 2 of the Code does not define *transaction*. Although a few sections are limited either explicitly or implicitly to the sale of goods [2-204, 2-314, 2-402, 2-703], courts have extended Article 2 to transactions such as leases and bailments of goods in some cases.

When you lease a car or rent a golf cart, does Article 2 apply if problems arise? The answer is not clear. Some courts have applied the Code to all commercial leases of goods. These courts emphasize that Article 2 governs "transactions" in goods, and a lease of goods is such a transaction. On the other hand, a few courts emphasize the word *sales* in the Code and will extend Article 2 only to transactions

TABLE 17–1. SPECIAL RULES FOR CONTRACTS FOR THE SALE OF GOODS

UCC Code Section 2	Rule
Offer and acceptance	
204	All terms need not be included in negotiations in order for a contract to result.
205	Firm written offers by merchants are irrevocable for a maximum of three months.
206(1)(a)	An acceptance may be made by any reasonable means of communication and is effective when deposited.

TABLE 17–1. Cont.

UCC Code Section 2	Rule
206(1)(b)	Unilateral offers may be accepted either by a promise to ship or by shipment.
206(1)(b)	Failure to reject may constitute an acceptance.
206(2)	Acceptance by performance requires notice within a reasonable time, or the offer may be treated as lapsed.
207	Variance in terms between offer and acceptance may not be a rejection and may be an acceptance.
305	The price need not be included in a contract.
311(1)	Particulars of performance may be left open.
Consideration	
203	Adding a seal is of no effect.
209(1)	Consideration is not required to support a modification of a contract for the sale of goods.
Voidable contracts	
403	A minor may not disaffirm against an innocent third party.
721	Rescission is not a bar to a suit for dollar damages.
Illegality	
302	Unconscionable bargains will not be enforced.
Form of the agreement	
201	Statute of frauds $500 price for goods Written confirmation between merchants. Memorandum need not include all terms of agreement. Payment, acceptance, and receipt limited to quantity specified in writing. Specially manufactured goods. Admission pleadings or court proceedings that a contract for sale was made.
Rights of third parties	
210(4)	An assignment of "the contract" or of "rights under the contract" includes a delegation of duties.
Performance of contracts	
209	Claims and rights may be waived without consideration
307, 612	Rules on divisible contracts.
511	Tender of payment is a condition precedent (rather than a condition concurrent) to a tender of delivery.
610, 611	Anticipatory breach may not be withdrawn if the other party gives notice that it is final
614	Impracticability of performance in certain cases is an excuse for nonperformance.
Discharge	
725	The statute of limitations is four years, but parties can reduce it by mutual agreement to not less than one year.

in goods that are analogous to a sale of goods. Some leases, for example, contain an option to buy; and if exercised, it will cause the lease payments (rent) to be applied toward the purchase price. Cars, TV sets, stereo sets, and many other things are frequently leased with an option to buy. Most courts have applied Article 2 to these leases, since they have attributes (option to buy) that make the transactions analogous to a sale of goods.

Article 2 will not apply if the subject matter of the contract is service. But many contracts are "mixed" contracts in that they involve both sale of services and goods. You hire a painter to paint your house or a contractor to install a heating and air-conditioning system in an apartment complex, or a hairdresser to apply a special shampoo. In addition to providing services, these persons have also sold goods (the paint, heating and air unit, and shampoo). These contracts present borderline transactions, and courts must often make a decision regarding the applicability of Article 2. Most courts tend to apply Article 2 only if the goods aspect of the deal is predominant. Their approach, as in the following case, is to ask which part of the transaction is the predominant feature—sale of goods or sale of services?

CASE

Valley Farmers' Elevator contacted Lindsay Brothers Company, a distributor of agricultural equipment and industrial supplies, about expanding Valley Farmers' grain storage facilities. Lindsay Brothers' proposal was accepted, and a three-bin system was installed. Subsequently, the roof and sides of the center bin collapsed. Valley Farmers filed a suit seeking damages against Lindsay Brothers under a tort theory of negligence as well as strict liability. Lindsay Brothers argued that Valley Farmers' only claim was for a breach of warranty under Article 2 of the UCC. Therefore Lindsay Brothers asked the court to dismiss Valley Farmers' tort and strict liability claims.

ISSUE: Is this transaction governed by Article 2 of the UCC, thereby limiting Valley Farmers' potential claims?

DECISION: Yes.

REASONS:

1. Using the predominant factor test, the court concluded that the predominant purpose of this contract was the sale of goods, not the rendering of services.
2. Services are always required to convert raw materials into a useful product. That some service is required to install the product does not transform a contract of sale into a contract of services.
3. Of the full $504,000 contract price, less than $120,000 can be identified as attributable to labor. Moreover, no part of the labor charge included in the contract is designated as compensation for the defendant's design of the storage system, a factor indicating the tangential and incidental nature of these services.

Valley Farmers' Elevator v. Lindsay Brothers Company, 398 N.W.2d 553 (Minn. 1987).

Some problem areas have definite answers. Article 2 applies to specially manufactured goods [2-105(1)] and to "the serving for value of food or drink to be consumed either on the premises or elsewhere" [2-314(1)]. By statute in many states, Article 2 is inapplicable to blood transfusions, bone transfers, or organ transplants. These are considered medical services.

3. Definitions

Goods. The precise meaning of the term *goods* is sometimes a problem for the courts. In general, the term *goods* encompasses things that are movable, that is, items of personal property (chattels) that are of a tangible, physical nature [2-105(1)]. Although broadly interpreted to include even electricity, the definition of goods excludes investment securities (covered by Article 8 of the Code) and negotiable instruments (covered by Article 3 of the Code).

Being limited to goods, Article 2 necessarily excludes contracts for personal service, construction, intangible personal property, and the sale of real estate. Goods "associated" with real estate *may* be within Article 2 in sales of "structures," "minerals," and the "like" *if severance is to be made by the seller*. If severance is to be made by the buyer, the contract involves a sale of an interest in land. Growing crops, including timber, fall within Article 2, regardless of who severs them.

Another term used in Article 2 is **future goods**—goods that are not in existence at the time of the agreement or that have not been "identified," that is, designated as the specific goods that will be utilized in the transaction [2-105(2)].

Future goods *Goods that are not both existing and identified.*

Sale. The *sales transaction* involves an exchange of title to the goods for the price. The basic obligation of the seller is to tender the goods, while that of the buyer is to accept the goods and pay the price. Both responsibilities are measured by the contract [2-301]. In general, the parties to a contract for sale can agree upon any terms and conditions that are mutually acceptable.

Merchant. Special provisions of Article 2 relate to transactions involving a **merchant,** a professional businessperson who "holds himself out as having knowledge or skill peculiar to the practices or goods involved in the transaction" [2-104(1)]. This designation is of great importance and is recognition of a professional status for a businessperson, justifying standards of conduct different from those of "nonprofessionals." The courts of some states have held that farmers are merchants when selling grain and other items raised by them. Other courts have held that farmers are not merchants, so from state to state and case to case there is variation in whether or not Code provisions relating to merchants apply also to farmers. The issue is usually one of fact, as the court in the following case recognized.

Merchant *A person who deals in goods of the kind involved in a transaction; or one who otherwise, by his occupation, holds himself out as having knowledge or skill peculiar to the practices or goods involved.*

CASE

Carl Davidson, a farmer, leased 100 head of pregnant stock cows from Matthew Bauer. Davidson did not receive title to the cattle or any authority to transfer them. The cows later calved. R. P. Curran purchased sixteen of the cow-calf pairs from Davidson and resold them. Bauer sued Curran for conversion. Bauer argued that he retained ownership of the cattle despite Davidson's purported sale to Curran. Curran claimed that Davidson was a merchant as a matter of law and that Davidson's buyers therefore would have acquired title to the cattle. The court ruled that Davidson's status as a merchant was a fact to be determined by the jury. The jury found that Davidson was not a merchant, and judgment was rendered for Bauer.

ISSUE: Was Davidson's status as a merchant a question of fact for the jury, instead of a question of law to be determined by the trial judge?

DECISION: Yes.

REASONS:

1. The UCC defines a merchant in three ways. The first definition focuses on the past transactions of the potential merchant, the seller. A seller of goods is a merchant in those goods if he deals in goods of like kind. The second definition focuses on the representations the seller makes to potential buyers and the community at large. The seller is a merchant in certain goods if, by his occupation, he holds himself out as having some skill or knowledge focusing on those goods and the specific transaction involved. The third definition focuses on the principal-agent relationship. The seller is a merchant if certain knowledge or skill in the goods involved may be attributed to the seller by his employment of an agent or broker or other intermediary who holds himself out to the community or other businessmen as having special knowledge or skill concerning the goods.
2. Whether a seller is a merchant under one of these definitions is generally a question of fact for the jury. The question becomes an issue of law for determination by the court only when the facts are undisputed and reasonable minds could draw no different inferences from them. Even when the facts are not in dispute, if reasonable minds might draw different inferences, the jury must determine whether a party was a merchant with respect to the goods involved in the sale.
3. There was evidence that prior to the sale in question, Davidson had bought, sold, and leased cattle. This evidence of prior dealing in the goods involved in this case suggests that he was a merchant.
4. However, Bauer testified that although he had often bought and sold cattle in the area, he had never seen nor met Davidson before they entered into the lease agreement in question. Davidson appears to have only occasionally bought and sold cattle. Although he had earlier sold part of the cattle leased from Bauer, Davidson had done so under Bauer's direction. This evidence supports a finding that Davidson was not a merchant.
5. Therefore the evidence provides a sufficient basis for a decision either way on Davidson's status as a merchant. Reasonable minds could have drawn different inferences from the facts. The issue was therefore properly submitted to the jury, and the trial court's decision is affirmed.

Bauer v. Curran, 360 N.W.2d 88 (Iowa 1984).

Good faith ***Good faith*** *Honesty in fact in the conduct or transaction concerned. For a merchant, good faith also means the observance of reasonable commercial standards of fair dealing in the trade.*

Good faith. The Code provisions on the sale of goods are based on two assumptions: (1) that the parties should be given the maximum latitude in fixing their own terms and (2) that the parties will act in "good faith." **Good faith** means honesty in fact in the conduct or transaction [1-201(19)]. In the case of a merchant, good faith also includes the observance of reasonable commercial standards of fair dealing in the trade [2-103(1)(b)].

Returned goods. The buyer and seller may agree that the buyer has the privilege of returning the goods that have been delivered to him. If the goods are delivered primarily for use, as in a consumer purchase, the transaction is called a *sale on* *approval*. If the goods are delivered primarily for resale, it is called a *sale or return* [2-326(1)]. The distinction is an important one, because goods delivered on approval are not subject to the claims of the buyer's creditors until the buyer has indicated his acceptance of the goods; goods delivered on sale or return, however, are subject to the claims of the buyer's creditors while they are in his possession [2-326(2)]. Delivery of goods on consignment, such as a transaction in which a manufacturer or a wholesaler delivers goods to a retailer who has the privilege of returning any unsold goods, is a sale or return.

The distinction is also important if the goods are lost, stolen, damaged, or destroyed. This issue is discussed with other aspects of risk of loss later in this chapter.

4. Abbreviations

As a matter of convenience, a number of contract terms are generally expressed as abbreviations. *F.O.B.* (free on board) is the most commonly used. *F.O.B. the place of shipment* means that the seller is obligated to place the goods in possession of a carrier, so that they may be shipped to the buyer. *F.O.B. the place of destination* means that the seller is obligated to cause the goods to be delivered to the buyer [2-319(1)(b)]. Thus, if Athens, Georgia, is the seller's place of business, "F.O.B. Athens, Georgia," is a *shipment contract*. "F.O.B. Champaign, Illinois," Champaign being the place where the buyer is to receive the goods, is a *destination contract*, and the seller must provide transportation to that place at his own risk and expense. He is responsible for seeing to it that the goods are made available to the buyer at the designated place.

If the terms of the contract also specify *F.O.B. vessel, car, or other vehicle*, the seller must at his own expense and risk load the goods on board. *F.A.S.* (free alongside) *vessel* at a named port requires the seller at his own expense and risk to deliver the goods alongside the vessel in the manner usual in the port or on a dock designated and provided by the buyer [2-319(2)].

C.I.F. means that the price includes, in a lump sum, the cost of the goods and of the insurance and freight to the named destination [2-320]. The seller's obligation is to load the goods, to make provision for payment of the freight, and to obtain an insurance policy in favor of the buyer. Generally, C.I.F. means that the parties will deal in terms of the documents that represent the goods; the seller performs his obligation by tendering to the buyer the proper documents, including a negotiable bill of lading and an invoice of the goods. The buyer is required to make payment against the tender of the required documents [2-320(4)].

THE SALES CONTRACT

The terms of a sales contract are supplied by three sources: the express agreement of the parties; course of dealing, usage of trade, and course of performance; and the Code and other applicable statutes.

5. Express Agreement

The general rule in sales law is that the parties are free to make their own contract. The parties are privileged to contract expressly regarding most basic terms—quality, quantity, price, delivery, payment, and the like. In general, their agreement is sufficient to displace any otherwise applicable Code section. But the principle of freedom of contract under the Code is not without exceptions. The parties cannot "disclaim" their Code obligations of good faith, diligence, and due care. Parties may provide a liquidated damages clause, but it cannot be a penalty [2-718(1)]. Consequential damages may be limited, but the limitations cannot be unconscionable [2-719(3)].

The buyer's duty in a sales contract is to pay for the goods. In the absence of a contrary agreement, payment is due at the time and place at which the buyer is to receive the goods [2-310(a)]. The basic obligations of the parties are concurrent conditions of exchange. Accordingly, a buyer who wants credit (to get the goods before he pays in full) must specifically negotiate for it in the contract. Between merchants, most domestic sales transactions are handled on "open account" (the seller ships the goods on the buyer's simple promise to pay for them in thirty, sixty, or ninety days). The buyer is not required to sign a note evidencing obligation to pay or to grant the seller a security interest in the goods to cover his obligation.

6. Documentary Transactions

When the parties are separated by distance and the seller is unwilling to extend credit to the buyer, they may employ a *documentary exchange*. As the procedure is sometimes called, the buyer is to pay "cash against documents." In this procedure, the seller utilizes documents of title to control the goods until he is paid. The document of title may be a bill of lading issued by a railroad or trucking company, a warehouse receipt, or any other document that is evidence that the person in possession of it is entitled to the goods it covers [1-201(15)]. Documents of title are multipurpose commercial instruments. They not only act as a receipt for the goods but also state the terms of the shipment or storage contract between the seller and the transit or warehouse company.

In a typical documentary exchange, the seller may ship the goods by rail or truck to the buyer and receive from the railroad or trucking company a *negotiable* bill of lading made to the order of the seller. The carrier thereby obligates itself to deliver the goods to the holder of the bill of lading [7-403(4)]. At this point, the seller has shipped "under reservation." His procurement of the negotiable bill reserves a security interest in the goods for their price, which the buyer owes him [2-205]. The seller will indorse the bill of lading and send it to his bank. He will attach to it a sight draft or demand for immediate payment of the purchase price by the buyer. The seller's bank will forward the documents to a bank in the city of the buyer. It is the obligation of that bank to release the bill of lading to the buyer only after he has paid the draft for the purchase price [4-503(a)]. Without the bill of lading, the buyer will not be able to get the goods from the carrier. Only when he is in possession under a regular chain of indorsements is the buyer the holder to whom the carrier is obligated to deliver.

This is only one common type of documentary transaction. There are many variations. Similar protections can be obtained if the seller ships under a nonnegotiable bill of lading, taking care to consign the goods to himself or his agent. The carrier is now obligated to deliver to the consignee or to the person specified by his written instructions [7-403(4)]. The seller will withhold any instructions to deliver to the buyer until he has been paid. Under this procedure, possession of the document of title is not required to take delivery from the carrier. But note that the seller should not name the buyer as consignee in the bill of lading; if he does, control over the shipment is lost.

7. Course of Dealing, Usage of Trade, Course of Performance

The agreement of the parties includes in their bargain any previous course of dealing between the parties, general trade custom and usage, and any past course of performance on the present agreement. These three sources not only are relevant in interpreting express contract terms but also may constitute contract terms.

A **course of dealing** is a sequence of prior conduct between the parties, which gives a common basis of understanding for interpreting their communications and conduct between themselves [1-205(1)]. A **usage of trade** is a practice or custom in the particular trade, used so frequently it justifies the expectation that it will be followed in the transaction in question [1-205(2)]. **Course of performance** concerns a contract that requires repeated performances. When an earlier performance has been accepted by the other party, that performance can be used to give meaning to the agreement regarding future performance [2-208(1)].

Course of dealing A sequence of previous conduct between the parties to a particular transaction.

Usage of trade Any practice or method of dealing so regularly observed in a place, vocation, or trade that observance may justly be expected in the transaction in question.

Course of performance A term used to give meaning to a contract based on the parties having had a history of dealings.

When any of these sources is conflicting, the Code [2-208(2)] adopts the following initial hierarchy of presumed probative values:

1. Express terms
2. Course of performance
3. Course of dealing
4. Usage of trade

However, the last three do more than interpret the first. They may supplement, cut down, even subtract whole terms from the express agreement of the parties. More important, course of performance, course of dealing, and usage of trade may directly override express terms, so that an express contract term like "seven white goods" is changed to "ten black goods." This results from the fact that courts are looking for the intent of the parties, and this intent may be best found in what the parties have done rather than in what they said.

8. Gap-Filling under the Code

Written contracts have gaps in them when the parties either intentionally or inadvertently leave out basic terms. Article 2 of the Code has a number of gap-filler provisions that, taken together, comprise a type of standardized statutory contract. As stated earlier, the parties can expressly vary the effect of these provisions by their agreement (including course of dealing, trade usage, and course of performance). The most important gap-filler provisions involve price, quantity, quality, delivery, and time of performance.

Price. The price term of the contract can be left open, with the price to be fixed by later agreement of the parties or by some agreed upon market standard [2-305]. It may even be agreed that the buyer or the seller shall fix the price, in which event there is an obligation to exercise good faith in doing so. If the contract is silent on price, or if for some reason the price is not set in accordance with the method agreed upon, it will be determined as a reasonable price at the time of delivery. Thus, if it appears that it is their intention to do so, parties can bind themselves even though the exact price is not actually agreed upon.

Quantity. The Code also allows flexibility in the quantity term of a sales contract. There may be an agreement to purchase the entire output of the seller, or the quantity may be specified as all that is required by the buyer. To ensure fair dealing between the parties in "output" and "requirements" contracts, the Code provides that if parties estimate the quantity involved, no quantity that is unreasonably disproportionate to the estimate will be enforced [2-306]. If the parties have not agreed upon an estimate, a quantity that is in keeping with normal or other comparable prior output or requirements is implied.

Delivery. The term *delivery* signifies a transfer of possession of the goods from the seller to the buyer. A seller makes delivery when he physically transfers into the possession of the buyer the actual goods that conform to the requirements of the contract. He satisfies the requirement that he "transfer and deliver" when he "tenders delivery" [2-507].

Tender of delivery *The seller must put and hold conforming goods at the buyer's disposition and give the buyer any notification reasonably necessary to enable him to take delivery.*

A proper **tender of delivery** requires the seller to make available conforming goods at the buyer's disposition and to give the buyer any notification reasonably necessary to take delivery [2-503(1)]. The seller's tender must be at a reasonable hour, and he must keep the goods available for a reasonable time to enable the buyer to take possession.

Unless the contract provides to the contrary, the place for delivery is the seller's place of business. If the seller has no place of business, it is his residence [2-308(a)]. In a contract for the sale of identified goods that are known to both parties to be at some other place, that place is the place for their delivery [2-308(a)(b)].

Goods are frequently in the possession of a bailee such as a warehouseman. In this event, in order to make delivery, the seller is obligated to (1) tender a negotiable document of title (warehouse receipt) representing the goods or (2) procure acknowledgment by the bailee (warehouseman) that the buyer is entitled to the goods [2-503(4)(a)].

Unless otherwise agreed, the seller is required to tender the goods in a single delivery rather than in installments over a period of time. The buyer's obligation to pay is not due until such a tender is made [2-307]. In some situations, the seller may not be able to deliver all the goods at once, or the buyer may not be able to receive the entire quantity at one time, in which event more than a single delivery is allowed.

Time of performance. The time of delivery is often left out of contracts. Such contracts may nevertheless be generally enforceable. However, if the parties intended the written agreement to be complete and an exclusive statement of the contract and the time of performance is omitted, the contract is unenforceable. In the usual case, the time may be supplied by parol evidence if it was agreed upon. If it was not agreed upon, a reasonable time is presumed [2-309(1)].

Determining what is a reasonable time depends on what constitutes acceptable commercial conduct under all the circumstances, including the obligation of good faith and reasonable commercial standards of fair dealing in the trade. A definite time may be implied from a usage of the trade or course of dealing or performance or from the circumstances of the contract as previously noted.

Payment is due at the time when and place where the buyer is to receive the goods [2-310]. *Receipt of goods* means taking physical possession of them. The buyer is given the opportunity to inspect the goods before paying for them [2-513(1)]. However, when the shipment is C.O.D. (cash on delivery), the buyer is not entitled to inspect the goods before payment of the price [2-513(3)(a)].

The parties may enter into an open-ended contract that calls for successive performances, such as 1,000 barrels of flour per week. If the contract does not state the duration, it will be valid for a reasonable time. Unless otherwise agreed, either party can terminate it any time.

TITLE

9. Transfer of Title to Goods

The concept of **title** to goods is somewhat nebulous, but it is generally equated with the bundle of rights that constitute ownership. Issues related to the passage of title are important in the field of taxation and in areas of the law such as wills, trusts, and estates. The Code has deemphasized the importance of title, and the location of title at any given time is usually not the controlling factor in determining the rights of the parties in a contract of sale. As a general rule, the rights, obligations, and remedies of the seller, the buyer, and the third parties are determined without regard to title [2-401]. However, the concept of title is still basic to the sales transaction, since by definition a sale involves the passing of title from the seller to the buyer.

Title *This word has limited or broad meaning. When a person has the exclusive rights, powers, privileges, and immunities to property against all other persons, he has the complete title thereto. The aggregate of legal relations concerning property is the title.*

The parties can, with few restrictions, determine by their contract the manner in which title to goods passes from the seller to the buyer. They can specify any conditions that must be fulfilled in order for title to pass. Since they seldom specify, however, the Code contains specific provisions as to when title shall pass if the location of title becomes an issue. As a general rule, it provides that title passes to the buyer at the time and place at which the seller completes his performance with reference to the physical delivery of the goods.

For purposes of title, some goods are classified as future goods. These goods are not in existence at the time of the agreement, or they are not designated as the specific goods involved in the transaction [2-105(2)]. Title to future goods does not pass at the time of the contract, as is explained in the next section.

10. Identification to the Contract

Title to goods cannot pass until the goods have been *identified* to the contract [2-401(1)]. Identification requires that the seller specify the particular goods involved in the transaction [2-501(1)]. Carson may contract with Boyd to purchase 100 mahogany desks of a certain style. Boyd may have several hundred of these desks in the warehouse. Identification takes place when Carson or Boyd specifies the particular 100 desks that will be sold to Carson. There could not, of course, be a present identification of future goods (those not yet in existence or not owned by the seller). However, there can be identification of goods that are not totally in a deliverable state. The fact that the seller must do something to the goods prior to delivery does not prevent identification and the vesting of rights in the buyer.

When goods are identified to a contract, the buyer acquires a special property interest in the goods. This special interest is an insurable one and it may be created before the passing of title or delivery of possession of the goods, as the following case illustrates.

CASE

Greenwich is in the business of selling boats. Holstein, a specialist in marine financing, agreed to floor-plan boats for Greenwich. Among the boats financed was a "1976 Newport 27, Hull No. 551, Serial No. CPY27551M77A, complete with sails and appurtenances."

Greenwich executed a promissory note and a security agreement covering this boat as collateral. A financing statement was duly recorded on September 29, 1976. However, the day before the filing, on September 28, Gladych and Greenwich had signed a purchase-and-sale agreement that specifically identified the boat as the "Newport 27 #551." Gladych signed the contract without knowledge of the financing agreement between Holstein and Greenwich. Gladych paid for the boat.

The sales agreement called for the supplying of "optional equipment," which included such items as sails, a bow pulpit, lifelines, a stern rail, winches, a head, and a bilge pump. Also listed as optional extras were "commissioning in spring" and "winter storage."

On February 3, 1977, Greenwich was in default on a series of promissory notes held by Holstein. Upon learning that Greenwich was selling boats in violation of their security agreements, Holstein instituted this civil action seeking to repossess the security. At that time Hull No. 551 was still in Greenwich's yard.

ISSUE: Did Gladych have title to the described boat so as to defeat Holstein's claim against it?

DECISION: Yes.

REASONS:

1. The Code provides "A buyer in ordinary course of business takes free of a security interest created by his seller even though the security interest is perfected and even though the buyer knows of its existence." Holstein contended that Gladych could not be such a buyer because title to goods cannot pass under a contract for sale prior to their identification to a contract. The rule is correct, but its application is not.
2. The trial court concluded there was no identification of the boat because the optional equipment had not yet been put on the boat. Therefore it was not in a state "whereby delivery could be made and title would pass." However, Section 2-501 recognizes "the buyer has a 'special property . . . interest' " from the time the boats are identified to a contract of sale. Comment 4 to this section demonstrates the goods do not have to be in a deliverable state to be identifiable.
3. The boat was identified at the time of the execution of the contract by Gladych and Greenwich. The parties referred specifically to "Hull #551" in the contract. Gladych constituted a buyer in the ordinary course of business and on September 28 gained an interest superior to that security interest thereafter acquired by Holstein.

Holstein v. Greenwich Yacht Sales, Inc., 404 A.2d 842 (R.I. 1979).

Present goods. Although identification can be made at any time and in any manner "explicitly agreed to" by the parties [2-501(1)], they usually do not make provision for identification—in which event the Code rules determine when it has occurred. If goods that are the subject of a contract are in existence and designated at the time the parties enter into the contract, identification occurs and title passes at the time and place of contracting [2-501(1)(a)]. This is true even if the seller has duties to perform in respect to the goods. If the goods are in a warehouse and the seller delivers the warehouse receipt to the buyer, identification occurs and title passes at the time and place the document of title (warehouse receipt) is delivered [2-401(3)(a)].

Future goods. Contracts to sell future goods and agricultural items raise more difficult identification problems. For future goods, the seller provides identification when he ships the goods or marks them as the goods to which the contract refers [2-501(1)(b)]. The requirement is that the seller make an appropriate designation of the specific goods.

There are special provisions for agricultural items—crops and animals—because of their nature. When there is a sale of a crop to be grown, identification occurs when the crop is planted. If the sale is of the unborn young of animals, identification takes place when they are conceived [2-501(1)(c)].

Identification occurs, and title passes insofar as the specific goods are concerned, when the seller completes his performance with respect to the physical delivery of the goods. When a shipment contract specifies that a seller is to send the goods to the buyer but is not required to deliver them at the destination, title passes at the time and place of shipment [2-401(2)]. If the contract requires that the seller deliver at the destination, title will not pass until the seller has tendered the goods to the buyer at that point.

If the buyer rejects the goods when tendered to him, title will be revested in the seller. Upon the buyer's refusal to receive or retain the goods, the title automatically returns to the seller, whether or not the buyer was justified in his action. The same result obtains if the buyer has accepted the goods but subsequently revokes his acceptance for a justifiable reason [2-401(4)].

As a means of assurance that the price will be paid before the buyer can obtain title to the goods, a seller may ship or deliver goods to the buyer and reserve title in himself. Under the Code, such an attempted reservation of title does not prevent the title from passing to the buyer. It is limited to the reservation of a security interest in the goods. [2-401(1)]. To give protection to the seller, the security interest must be perfected under the provisions of Article 9. (This process is discussed in Chapters 40 and 41.) Accordingly, a seller who simply reserves a security interest will not have availed himself of protection against the claims of third parties against the property sold unless the seller complies with the law relating to secured transactions.

11. Good-Faith Purchasers

A purchaser of goods acquires the title that his transferor had or had the power to transfer. If the seller has no title, the purchaser receives no title. A purchaser from a thief has no property interest in the goods because the thief had none. The original owner still has title and may recover the goods even if a certificate of title has been issued by a governmental body.

A purchaser of a limited interest in goods has property rights only to the extent of the limited interest. If a person buys a one-half interest in a golf cart with his neighbor, his rights are limited to the one-half interest.

A purchaser of goods may acquire more rights and better title than the seller had. Such a purchaser must qualify as a good-faith purchaser for value. In addition, the seller's title must be at least voidable and not void [2-403]. The following case demonstrates the proof required for a buyer to qualify as a good-faith purchaser for value.

CASE

Darwin Dobbs Company attempted to sell a 1984 Pontiac Fiero to Steve Saffold. Saffold took possession of the car and received a sales invoice indicating that title to the car would not pass to him until his check cleared the bank. His check was returned for insufficient funds on September 24, 1984. Four days later, Saffold executed a contract to sell the car to Ledbetter Auto Sales for $9,500. At the time, Ledbetter Auto had actual knowledge that the check from Saffold to Dobbs had bounced. On October 1, 1984, the First National Bank of Alexander City received a note and security agreement secured in part by the Fiero and executed on behalf of Ledbetter Auto. The bank attempted to perfect a security interest in the car based on its floor plan agreement with Ledbetter Auto. Under this agreement, the bank provided funds for Ledbetter Auto to purchase vehicles in exchange for a security interest in those vehicles. Kenneth Ledbetter filed suit, demanding that Dobbs convey good title to the Fiero to him or that he be paid $9,500. The bank intervened and filed an answer demanding possession of the vehicle under its security agreement.

ISSUE: Did Saffold obtain any title to the car so that he could transfer any interest in it to Ledbetter or the bank?

DECISION: Yes.

REASONS:

1. Section 2-403(1)(b) of the UCC provides that when goods are delivered under a transaction of purchase in exchange for a check that was later dishonored, the purchaser obtains voidable title to the goods and the power to transfer good title to a good-faith purchaser for value. Under this section, the good-faith purchaser is protected from surprise attempts by an original seller to regain the goods. Ledbetter therefore, may fall within the protection of Section 2-403 if he was a good-faith purchaser from someone who had voidable title.
2. Saffold had voidable title. It is undisputed that Dobbs delivered the vehicle to Saffold, intending that Saffold become the owner of the car when Saffold's check cleared the bank. Therefore there had been a transaction of purchase within the meaning of Section 2-403(1)(b), and Saffold had obtained voidable title to the Fiero.
3. Although Ledbetter was a purchaser from one who had voidable title, he did not obtain good title to the car because he purchased from Saffold knowing that the check to Dobbs had bounced.
4. The bank also claims to fall within the protection of Section 2-403, and thus to be sheltered from attacks on its title to the vehicle. In order to gain this protection, the bank must be a good-faith purchaser from someone with voidable title.
5. The bank was a purchaser under the UCC because it took a

security interest in the vehicle. Section 1-201(32) of the UCC defines "purchase" broadly, and includes taking by security interest or "any other voluntary transaction creating an interest in property."

6. The bank purchased from Ledbetter, who had voidable title. The bank took the security interest from Ledbetter when it financed his purchase of the car. Ledbetter had voidable title even if he did not have good title. Ledbetter had to satisfy the good-faith requirement to take good title, but he did not have to take in good faith to obtain voidable title. There had been a delivery of possession of the Fiero from Saffold, a transferor with voidable title, to Ledbetter, a subsequent transferee, with intent that the transferee become the owner of the goods. This process was enough to establish Ledbetter's voidable title in the car.
7. There is no dispute that the bank acted in good faith. Nothing in the record indicates that the bank knew of any defect in Ledbetter's title, and there were no circumstances to put it on constructive notice of problems with the title. Therefore the bank was a good-faith purchaser from one with voidable title, and it gained good title to the Fiero.

Ledbetter v. Darwin Dobbs Co., Inc., 473 So.2d 197 (Ala. App. 1985).

The typical case in which a party has voidable title involves fraud in obtaining the title. Voidable title issues also arise when the same goods are sold to more than one buyer. For example, Franklin sells goods to Talmadge, who leaves them at Franklin's store, with the intention of picking them up later. Before Talmadge takes possession, Franklin sells them to Bell, a good-faith purchaser. Bell has title to the goods because if possession of goods is entrusted to a merchant who deals in goods of that kind, the merchant has the power to transfer all right of the entrusting owner to a buyer in the ordinary course of business [2-403(2)(3)]. A good-faith purchaser buying from a merchant in the ordinary course of business acquires good title. This rule is applicable to any delivery of possession to a merchant with the understanding that the merchant is to have possession. Thus the rule applies to consignments and bailments as well as to cash sale, but the facts of each case must be examined to ensure that the buyer qualified as a good-faith purchaser for value.

RISK OF LOSS

12. In Breach of Contract Cases

The Code sets forth a number of rules for determining which party to a sales contract must bear the risk of loss in the event of theft, destruction, or damage to the goods during the period of the performance of the contract. The approach is contractual rather than title oriented and covers two basic situations: no breach of contract cases and cases in which one of the parties is in breach. Of course, the provisions are applicable only if the contract has not allocated the risk of loss [2-303].

If the contract has been breached, the loss will be borne by the party who has breached [2-510(1)]. Thus, if the seller has tendered or delivered goods that are "nonconforming," the seller bears the risk of loss. He remains responsible until he rectifies the nonconformity or the buyer accepts the goods despite their defects.

A buyer has the privilege of revoking his acceptance of the goods under proper circumstances (discussed in Chapter 18). If the buyer rightfully revokes his acceptance, the risk of loss is back on the seller to the extent that the buyer's insurance does not cover the loss. In this situation, the seller has the benefit of any insurance carried by the buyer (the party most likely to have applicable insurance), but any uninsured loss is on the breaching seller.

Loss may occur while goods are in the seller's control, before the risk of loss has passed to the buyer. If the buyer repudiates the sale (breaches the contract) at a time when the seller has identified proper goods to the contract, the seller can impose the risk of loss upon the buyer for a reasonable time. The basic concept of the Code is that the burden of losses should be that of the party who has failed to perform as required by contract.

13. If No Breach Exists

Three situations may arise in no breach risk of loss cases. When neither party is in breach, the contract may call for shipment of the goods, the goods may be the subject of a bailment, or the contract may be silent on shipment and no bailment exists.

Shipment. A shipment contract requires only that the seller make necessary arrangements for transport; a destination contract imposes upon the seller the obligation to deliver at a destination. If a contract between buyer and seller provides for shipment by carrier under a shipment contract (F.O.B. shipping point), the risk of loss passes to the buyer when the goods are delivered to the carrier. If shipment is made under a destination contract (F.O.B. destination), risk of loss does not pass to the buyer until goods arrive at the destination and are available to the buyer for delivery [2-509(1)]. When the parties do not use symbols such as C.I.F., F.A.S., or F.O.B. or otherwise make provision for risk of loss, it is necessary to determine whether a contract does or does not require the seller to deliver at a destination. The presumption is that a contract is one of shipment, not destination, and that the buyer should bear the risk of loss until arrival, unless the seller has either specifically agreed to do so, or the circumstances indicate such an obligation. The following case is typical of those involving shipment contracts.

CASE

Pestana, a Mexican resident, entered into a contract with Karinol Corporation on March 4, 1975. The contract was reduced to a one-page invoice written in Spanish. Pestana contracted to purchase sixty-four electronic watches for $6,006. The bottom of the contract included the following written in Spanish: "Please send the merchandise in cardboard boxes duly strapped with metal bands via air parcel post to Chetumal. Documents to Banco de Commercio De Quintano Roo S.A." The seller delivered the watches to an airline for shipment. When the cartons arrived in Mexico, the watches were missing. Plaintiff buyer sued for a refund of the purchase price.

ISSUE: Does a contract for the sale of goods, which stipulates the place where the goods sold are to be sent by carrier but contains (a) no explicit provisions allocating the risk of loss while the goods are in the possession of the carrier and (b) no delivery terms such as F.O.B. place of destination, constitute a shipment contract under the Uniform Commercial Code?

DECISION: Yes.

REASONS:

1. Under Florida's Uniform Commercial Code the shipment contract and the destination contract are the two types of contracts used when a carrier is utilized to transport goods sold. On a shipment contract, the risk of loss passes to the buyer when the goods sold are duly delivered to the carrier for shipment to the buyer. Under the destination contract the seller specifically agrees to deliver the goods sold to the buyer at a particular destination and to bear the risk of loss of the goods until tender of delivery. The risk of loss under such a contract passes to the buyer when the goods sold are duly tendered to the buyer at the place of destination while in the possession of the carrier so as to enable the buyer to take delivery.
2. This case involves a shipment contract with no provision allocating risk of loss while the goods are in transit. If this is a shipment contract, Karinol fulfilled its obligations under the UCC by putting the goods sold in the possession of a carrier and making a contract for the goods' safe transportation to the plaintiff's decedent.
3. Pestana is incorrect in his contention that this was a destination contract under which risk of loss passed to him upon tender in Mexico. The fact the contract specifies "the goods were to be sent to Chetumal, Mexico" does not convert this into a destination contract. The "send to" terminology is not relevant in determining whether this was a shipment or delivery contract. Pestana, as buyer, assumed the risk of loss when the seller delivered the goods for shipment.

Pestana v. Karinol Corp., 367 So.2d 1096 (Fla. App. 1979).

Bailee *A person into whose possession personal property is delivered.*

Bailments. Often, the goods will be in the possession of a **bailee,** such as a warehouse, and the arrangement is for the buyer to take delivery at the warehouse. If the goods are represented by a negotiable document of title—a warehouse receipt, for instance—when the seller tenders the document to the buyer, the risk of loss passes to the buyer. Likewise, risk passes to the buyer upon acknowledgment by the bailee that the buyer is entitled to the goods [2-509(2)]. In this situation, it is proper that the buyer assume the risk, as the seller has done all that could be expected to make the goods available to the buyer. It should be noted that if a nonnegotiable document of title is tendered to the buyer, risk of loss does not pass until the buyer has had a reasonable time to present the document to the bailee [2-503(4)(b)]. A refusal by the bailee to honor the document defeats the tender, and the risk of loss remains with the seller.

Other cases. In cases other than shipment and bailments, the passage of risk of loss to the buyer depends upon the status of the seller. If the seller is a merchant, risk of loss will not pass to the buyer until he receives the goods [2-509(3)]. The risk of loss remains with the merchant seller even though the buyer has paid for the goods in full and has been notified that the goods are at his disposal. Continuation of the risk in this case is justified on the basis that the merchant would be likely to carry insurance on goods within his control, whereas a buyer would not likely do so until he had actually received the goods.

A nonmerchant seller transfers the risk of loss by *tendering* the goods [2-509(3)]. A *tender of delivery* occurs when the seller makes conforming goods available to the buyer and gives him reasonable notice, so that he may take delivery. Both parties are in the same position insofar as the likelihood of insurance is concerned, so the risk of loss passes to the buyer in cases where it would not do so if the seller were a merchant.

Sales on approval and sales with the right to return the goods are often involved in risk of loss cases. A characteristic of the sale on approval is that risk of loss in the event of theft or destruction of the goods does not pass to the buyer until he accepts the goods. Failure seasonably to notify the seller of his decision to return the goods will be treated as an acceptance. After notification of election to return, the seller must pay the expenses of the return and bear the risk of loss. In contrast, the buyer in a sale or return transaction has the risk of loss in the event of theft or destruction of the goods [2-327(2)] until the goods are returned to the seller.

CHAPTER SUMMARY

Article 2 of the UCC

Common Law Contract Changes

1. See Table 17–1.

Scope

1. Article 2 covers the sale of goods. It does not cover the sale of real estate or service contracts.
2. In mixed contracts, the Code is applicable if the sale of goods is the predominant part of the transaction.

Definitions

1. The term *goods* encompasses things that are movable, that is, items of personal property (chattels) that are of a tangible, physical nature.
2. A *sale* consists of the passing of title to goods from the seller to the buyer for a price.
3. A *merchant* is a professional businessperson who "holds himself out as having knowledge or skill peculiar to the practices or goods involved in the transaction."
4. *Good faith* is honesty in fact in the transaction. In the case of a merchant, it also includes the observance of reasonable commercial standards of fair dealing in the trade.
5. A *sale on approval* gives the buyer a reasonable time to decide if the sale shall take place. It is used in consumer purchases.
6. A *sale or return* is a consignment of goods whereby the buyer may return the goods not sold.

Abbreviations

1. F.O.B.—free on board.
2. F.A.S.—free along side.
3. C.I.F.—cost, insurance, and freight.

The Sales Contract

Express Agreement

1. The general rule in sales law is that the parties are free to make their own contract.
2. Parties cannot disclaim their Code obligations of good faith, diligence, and care, and unconscionable provisions will not be enforced.
3. In the absence of a contrary agreement, payment is due at the time and place at which the buyer is to receive the goods. A buyer who wants credit must specifically negotiate it in the contract.

Documentary Transactions

1. If a seller is unwilling to extend credit to the buyer, they may use a documentary exchange or cash against documents.

Course of Dealing, Usage of Trade, Course of Performance

1. A *course of dealing* is a sequence of prior conduct between the parties that gives a firm basis for interpreting their communications and conduct between themselves.
2. A *usage of trade* is a practice or custom in the particular trade used so frequently it justifies the expectation that it will be followed in the transaction in question.
3. *Course of performance* concerns a contract that requires repeated performances. When an earlier performance has been accepted by the other party, that performance can be used to give meaning to the agreement regarding future performance.

Gap-filling under the Code

1. The price term of the contract can be left open, with the price to be fixed by later agreement of the parties or by some agreed-upon market standard.
2. If the contract is silent on price, it will be a reasonable one.
3. The Code also allows flexibility in the quantity term of a sales contract. There may be an agreement to purchase the entire output of the seller, or the quantity may be specified as all that is required by the buyer.
4. If no time of delivery is stated in the contract, it may be supplied by parol evidence of the agreement. If not agreed upon, a reasonable time is assumed.
5. Unless the contract provides to the contrary, the place for delivery is the seller's place of business. If the seller has no place of business, it is his residence.
6. If the time for performance has not been agreed upon by the parties, the time for shipment or delivery or any other action under a contract shall be a reasonable time.

Title

Transfer of Title to Goods

1. The Code has deemphasized the importance of title, and the location of title at any given time is usually not the controlling factor in determining the rights of the parties in a contract of sale.
2. The parties can specify when title passes. If there is no provision, title passes to the buyer at the time and place at which the seller completes his performance with reference to the physical delivery of the goods.

Identification to the Contract

1. Title to goods cannot pass until the goods have been identified to the contract. Identification requires that the seller specify the particular goods involved in the transaction.

2. If goods that are the subject of a contract are in existence and identified at the time the parties enter into the contract, identification occurs and title passes at the time and place of contracting.
3. In a contract to sell future goods, the seller provides identification when he ships the goods or marks them as the goods to which the contract refers.
4. Identification occurs, and title passes insofar as the specific goods are concerned, when the seller completes his performance with respect to the physical delivery of the goods.
5. In a shipment contract, title passes at the time and place of shipment.
6. If the contract requires that the seller deliver at the destination, title will not pass until the seller has tendered the goods to the buyer at that point.

Good-Faith Purchasers

1. A purchase of goods usually acquires at least as good a title as the seller possessed.
2. A good-faith purchaser for value may acquire a better title than the seller had if the seller's title was voidable.

Risk of Loss

In Breach of Contract Cases

1. If the contract has been breached, the loss will be borne by the party who has breached. Thus, if the seller has tendered or delivered goods that are "non-conforming," the seller bears the risk of loss.
2. If the buyer breaches the contract at a time when the seller has identified proper goods to the contract, the risk of loss is on the buyer for a reasonable time.

If No Breach Exists

1. If a contract between buyer and seller provides for shipment by carrier under a shipment contract (F.O.B. shipping point), the risk of loss passes to the buyer when the goods are delivered to the carrier.
2. If shipment is made under a destination contract (F.O.B. destination), risk of loss does not pass to the buyer until the goods arrive at the destination and are available to the buyer for delivery.
3. It is presumed that a contract is one of shipment, not destination, and that the buyer should bear the risk of loss until arrival unless the seller has specifically agreed to do so or the circumstances indicate such an obligation.
4. If the goods are represented by a negotiable document of title, risk of loss passes to the buyer when the document is tendered.
5. In all cases other than shipment and bailment contracts, the passage of risk of loss to the buyer depends on the status of the seller. If the seller is a merchant, risk of loss will not pass to the buyer until he receives the goods, which means "takes physical possession of them."
6. A nonmerchant seller transfers the risk of loss by tendering the goods.

REVIEW QUESTIONS AND PROBLEMS

1. Match each term in column A with the appropriate statement in column B.

A	B
(1) Merchant	(a) Sale on consignment.
(2) C.I.F.	(b) A term used in shipment by merchant vessel.
(3) Bill of lading	(c) Buyer has the risk of loss if the goods are destroyed.

(4) Sale of return	(d) A requirement for title to pass.
(5) Shipment contract	(e) A farmer in many states.
(6) F.A.S.	(f) The buyer pays the cost of insuring the goods.
(7) Sale on approval	(g) Contract of shipment by a common carrier.
(8) Identification	(h) May acquire a better title than his transferor had.
(9) Good-faith purchaser	(i) Not covered by Article 2 of the Code.
(10) Organ transplant	(j) Buyer's creditors have no claim on the goods in this transaction.

2. Tom entered into a contract to sell Jerry twenty acres of sod for $1,000 per acre. Jerry was allowed to remove it any time during the next twelve-month period. Is the contract governed by the Uniform Commercial Code? Explain.

3. A contract required a subcontractor to supply labor, materials, and equipment for constructing and finishing concrete structures. Is this contract subject to the Uniform Commercial Code? Explain.

4. The Macon Whoopies, a newly formed hockey club, contracts to buy 150 hockey pucks from a wholesaler in Youngstown, Ohio. What are the wholesaler's delivery obligations if the agreement states:
   a. F.O.B. Macon?
   b. F.O.B. Youngstown?
   c. C.I.F. Macon?
   d. Ship to Macon Whoopies, Macon, Georgia?

   Explain.

5. Landrum, a collector of automobiles, was interested in buying a limited edition Chevrolet Corvette from Devenport. Devenport agreed the price would be the sticker price, $14,000 to $18,000. The car arrived with a sticker price of $14,688.21, but as a result of the demand for the car, the market price was $22,000. Is Landrum entitled to buy it for the sticker price? Why or why not?

6. Royster agreed to buy at least 31,000 tons of phosphate for three years from Columbia. When market conditions changed, Royster ordered only a fraction of the minimum and sought to renegotiate the deal. Columbia refused and sued. At trial, Royster wanted to introduce two forms of proof: (a) a usage of trade that expresses price and quantity terms in such contracts were never considered in the trade as more than mere projections, to be adjusted according to market forces; (b) course of dealing over a six-year period, which showed repeated and substantial deviations from the stated quantities or prices in other written contracts between the parties. Is the evidence admissible? Explain.

7. Plaintiff sued an oil company to recover personal property obtained by the defendant under an alleged option contract. The purported contract gave the oil company the right to purchase the property at plaintiff's cost less depreciation to be mutually agreed upon. The parties failed to agree on the amount of depreciation and plaintiff claimed that as a result, there was no valid agreement. Is the contract binding? Why?

8. On February 11, 1988, plaintiff entered into a written contract to buy three sprinkler systems from the defendant. The seller orally agreed to deliver by the middle of May 1988. The written contract contained no designated delivery date. The seller did not deliver by May 15 and plaintiff claimed a crop loss of $75,000 because of the late delivery. Is oral evidence admissible to show the agreed-upon date of delivery? Explain. Is the contract enforceable without a delivery date? Why or why not?

9. The Big Knob Volunteer Fire Department agreed to purchase a fire truck from Custom Productions, Inc. The contract provided for a down payment and for title to pass upon full payment. Custom painted the buyer's name on the truck. The seller refused to deliver the truck, and the buyer filed suit for possession of the truck. Is the buyer entitled to the truck? Why or why not?

10. A package liquor store operator was in the practice of paying for large quantities of liquor in advance in order to take advantage of quantity discounts. He would then

order the liquor as needed. A supplier was having financial difficulties, and the operator seized a large amount of undelivered liquor. The supplier went into bankruptcy, and the trustee in bankruptcy claimed the liquor. He contended that the operator did not have title to the liquor. Was the trustee in bankruptcy correct? Explain.

11. Truck Dealer had possession of a truck as the result of a lease with the truck's owner. Even though Dealer did not have title to the truck, it sold it to Peter. When Lessor discovered the sale, it demanded that Peter return the truck. Must he do so? Explain.

12. Don, engaged in the business of installing underground telephone lines, ordered three reels of underground cable from Pat to be delivered at Don's place of business. Pat delivered reels of aerial rather than underground cable. When informed of the mistake, Pat tells Don to return the cable, but he was unable to do so because of a trucking strike. The cable was stolen from Don's regular storage space, where it had been delivered. Pat sues for the purchase price. What result? Why?

13. A contract for the sale of goods contained no explicit provision on risk of loss while the goods were in transit and it contained no delivery terms such as F.O.B. destination. The goods were destroyed in transit. Which party had the risk of loss? Why?

14. A seller of a mobile home sued the buyer for the price of the home. After the parties had executed the contract of sale, but before delivery to the buyer, the mobile home was stolen from the seller's lot. What result? Why?

15. Amy delivered stereo tapes, cartridges, and stereo equipment to Tex, a service station operator, for resale. The invoice provided that the equipment would be picked up if not sold in ninety days. The service station was burglarized about two weeks later, and the stereo equipment was stolen. Who must bear the loss resulting from the burglary? Why?

Breach and Remedies 18

CHAPTER PREVIEW

BUSINESS MANAGEMENT DECISION

As the sales manager of a retail music store, you meet with a customer who has purchased a $1,500 set of drums. This customer complains that the base drum is defective.

How would you respond to this customer?

OVERVIEW OF CODE REMEDIES

1. Introduction

The law recognizes that each party to a contract for the sale of goods has certain rights and obligations unless the contract legally eliminates them. In addition, the Uniform Commercial Code has several provisions relating to the remedies of the buyer and the seller in the event of a breach of the contract by the other party. There is one provision applicable to both parties. This is known as *adequate assurance* (discussed in the next section).

As a general rule, a seller is obligated to deliver or tender delivery of goods that measure up to the requirements of the contract and to do so at the proper time and at the proper place. The goods and other performance of the seller must conform to the contract [2-106(2)].

The seller is required to tender delivery as a condition to the buyer's duty to accept the goods and pay for them [2-507(1)]. Thus the seller has performed when he has made the goods available to the buyer. The buyer, in turn, must render his performance, which means he must accept the goods and pay for them.

The parties may, in their agreement, limit or modify the remedies available to each other. The measure of damages may be limited or altered. The agreement may limit the buyer's remedies to return of the goods for refund or replacement of the goods or parts.

The parties may limit or exclude consequential damages, and such limitations and exclusions will be enforced if they are not unconscionable [2-719(3)]. A limitation of consequential damages for injury to the person in the case of *consumer goods* is prima facie unconscionable, but such limitations in commercial transactions are not presumed to be unfair.

These rights and remedies are examined in the sections that follow. Keep in mind that these sections cover sales contracts that are silent on the matter under discussion.

2. Adequate Assurance

A concept applicable to both parties in a sales transaction is known as *adequate assurance*. Under certain circumstances, either party may be concerned about the other's future performance. If a buyer is in arrears on other payments, the seller will naturally be concerned about making further deliveries. Or a buyer may discover that the seller has been delivering faulty goods to other customers and will be fearful that the goods that he is to receive may also be defective. The law recognizes that no one wants to buy a lawsuit and that merely having the right to sue for breach of contract is a somewhat hollow remedy. There is a need to protect the party whose reasonable expectation of due performance is jeopardized.

The Code grants this protection by providing that the contract for sale imposes an obligation on each party that the other's expectation of receiving due performances will not be impaired [2-609]. A party who has reasonable grounds for insecurity about the other's performance can demand *in writing* that the other offer convincing proof that he will, in fact, perform. Having made the demand, he may then suspend his own performance until he receives assurance. If none is forthcoming within a reasonable time, not to exceed thirty days, he may treat the contract as repudiated [2-609(2)].

Two factual problems are presented: What are reasonable grounds for insecurity? What constitutes an adequate assurance of performance? The Code does not particularize but does provide that between merchants commercial standards shall be applied to answer these questions [2-609(2)]. In the event of a dispute, these are questions of fact for a jury.

3. Checklist of Code Remedies

Two sections of the Code [2-703, 2-711] *list* the remedies of the seller and the remedies of the buyer. Each section provides both parties with four remedies, which are exact counterparts. Table 18–1 shows their significant correlation.

The four remedies are listed in the Code not only as equivalent actions but also as equivalent in order of importance. The Code assumes that, upon a breach by the buyer, the seller will resell the goods and sue the buyer for any difference between the resale price and the original contract price. When the seller breaches, the Code assumes that the buyer will cover by buying substitute goods and sue the seller for any difference between the cover price and the original contract price.

Obviously, before either party has one of the four remedies, the other party must have breached the contract. There are at least four possible situations in which either party may be in breach of contract.

1. *Anticipatory repudiation* by the buyer or by the seller
2. *Failure of performance* (buyer fails to pay or seller fails to deliver)
3. A rightful or wrongful *rejection* by the buyer
4. A rightful or wrongful *revocation of acceptance* by the buyer

TABLE 18.1 COMPARISON OF CODE REMEDIES

Seller's Remedies [2-703]	Buyer's Remedies [2-711]
1. Resell the goods and recover damages [2-706].	1. Cover (buy same goods elsewhere) and recover damages [2-712].
2. Cancel the contract.	2. Reject the contract.
3. Recover damages for nonacceptance [2-708].	3. Recover damages for nondelivery. [2-713]
4. Sue for the actual price of the goods [2-709].	4. Sue to get the goods (specific performance or replevy) [2-716].

Anticipatory repudiation and failure to perform are discussed in Part II, on contracts. This chapter considers the buyer's right to reject and right to revoke acceptance. If these rights are exercised properly by the buyer, the seller has breached the sales contract. If the rejection or revocation of acceptance are wrongfully exercised, the buyer has breached the contract.

BUYER'S RIGHTS AND REMEDIES

4. Right to Inspect

The buyer has a right before payment or acceptance to inspect the goods at any reasonable time and place and in any reasonable manner [2-513(1)]. The place for the inspection is determined by the nature of the contract. If the seller is to send the goods to the buyer, the inspection may be postponed until after arrival of the goods. The right to inspect is tied to the right to reject, as is illustrated in the following case.

CASE

On May 23, 1974, Heitzman Produce (defendant) agreed to purchase from G&H (plaintiff) all potatoes to be grown by G&H on its acreage in Jerome County. Heitzman's obligation to purchase was contingent upon the potatoes' meeting the size specifications set forth in the contract. The first potatoes were delivered out of storage on November 6, and the inspection of the government inspector dated November 15, 1974, showed that the potatoes did not conform to the weight requirements. When Heitzman refused to accept and pay for the potatoes, G&H sued. The trial court found for Heitzman, and G&H appealed.

ISSUE: Did Heitzman inspect and reject the goods within a reasonable time?

DECISION: Yes.

REASONS:
1. The UCC gives the buyer the right to inspect the goods at any reasonable place and time and in any reasonable manner.
2. Generally what constitutes a reasonable time is a question of fact, but where the matter can be ascertained from the language of the contract, it may be determined as a matter of law.
3. Here the contract explicitly provides that the potatoes were to be inspected for size by government inspectors at delivery. Delivery was to be made when the potatoes came out of storage.
4. Under these circumstances, Heitzman exercised his right of inspection promptly in accordance with the applicable provisions of the contract.

G&H Land & Cattle Co. v. Heitzman & Nelson, Inc., 628 P.2d 1038 (Idaho 1981).

If the contract provides for delivery C.O.D., the buyer must pay prior to inspection. Likewise, payment must be made prior to inspection if the contract calls for payment against documents of title [2-513(3)]. When the buyer is required to make payment prior to inspection, the payment does not impair his right to pursue remedies if subsequent inspection reveals defects [2-512].

The buyer must pay the expenses of inspection, but he can recover his expenses from the seller if the inspection reveals that the goods are nonconforming and he therefore rejects them [2-513(2)].

5. Right to Reject

If the goods or the tender of delivery fails to conform to the contract, the buyer has the right to reject them. Several options are available. The buyer may reject the whole, or he may accept either the whole or any commercial unit or units and reject the rest [2-601]. A commercial unit is one that is generally regarded as a single whole for purposes of sale, one that would be impaired in value if divided [2-105(6)]. When the buyer accepts nonconforming goods, he does not impair his right of recourse against the seller. Provided that he notifies the seller of the breach within a reasonable time, he may still pursue his remedy for damages for breach of contract, even though he accepts the goods.

6. Notice of Rejection

The right to reject defective or nonconforming goods is dependent on the buyer's taking action within a reasonable time after the goods are tendered or delivered to him. If the buyer rejects, he must **seasonably** notify the seller of this fact. Failing to do so would render the rejection ineffective and constitute an acceptance [2-602(1)]. If the buyer continues in possession of defective goods for an unreasonable time, he forfeits his right to reject them. This fact does not prevent the buyer from suing for breach of contract, as the court observed in the following case.

Seasonably *An action is taken "seasonably" when it is taken at, or within, the time agreed; or if no time is agreed, at or within a reasonable time.*

CASE

In the fall of 1979, Eldon Hislop was attempting to sell a used 1972 camper-trailer. When the camper was shown to Robert Duff, he became aware that the camper leaked. Upon being notified of the leak's existence, Hislop told Duff that the leak was in the roof vent and that caulking would solve the problem. In June 1980, Hislop and Duff entered into an agreement whereby Hislop would sell the camper to Duff for $1,200. Duff gave Hislop $300 on June 20 and agreed to pay the balance on October 1. Duff caulked the vent but was unable to seal the leak. He refused to tender the $900 balance. Hislop brought suit to recover the unpaid balance. The trial court entered judgment for Hislop for $900, and Duff appealed.

ISSUE: Was the trial court's award of the full balance of the purchase price proper?

DECISION: No.

REASONS:

1. Under Section 2-602(1) of the Uniform Commercial Code, a buyer's rejection of goods must be within a reasonable time after the delivery of the goods. The rejection is ineffective unless the buyer seasonably notifies the seller.
2. Duff took and maintained possession of the camper-trailer for nine months before notifying Hislop of his rejection. Therefore Duff neither rejected the goods within a reasonable time nor gave a seasonable notification to Hislop.
3. However, Duff may have a damage remedy against Hislop. By

alleging that the camper-trailer, as delivered, did not conform to the terms of the contract, Duff raised counterclaims for damages resulting from the nonconformity of the camper-trailer.

4. The trial court should have considered these claims as counterclaims, but did not do so. While Duff does technically owe Hislop the full balance of the purchase price, $900, Duff may be able to recover from Hislop on these counterclaims so that the net amount Duff owes would be reduced. Therefore the case is remanded for resolution of these claims.

Hislop v. Duff, 502 A.2d 357 (Vt. 1985).

The requirement of seasonable notice of rejection is very important. Without such notice, the rejection is ineffective [2-602(1)]. As a general rule, a notice of rejection may simply state that the goods are not conforming, without particular specification of the defects relied on by the buyer. If, however, the defect could have been corrected by the seller had he been given particularized notice, then the failure to particularize will take away from the buyer the right to rely on that defect as a breach justifying a rejection [2-605(1)(a)]. Therefore a buyer should always give detailed information relative to the reason for the rejection.

In transactions between merchants, the merchant seller is entitled to demand a full and final written statement of all the defects. If the statement is not forthcoming after a written request for it, the buyer may not rely on these defects to justify his rejection or to establish that a breach has occurred [2-605(1)(b)].

7. Rights and Duties on Rejection

A buyer who rejects the goods after taking physical possession of them is required to hold the goods with reasonable care long enough for the seller to remove them [2-602(2)(b)]. Somewhat greater obligations are imposed upon a merchant buyer who rejects goods that have been delivered to him [2-603]. The merchant is under a duty to follow the seller's reasonable instructions as to the disposition of the goods. If the seller does not furnish instructions as to the disposition of the rejected goods, the merchant buyer must make reasonable efforts to sell them for the seller's account if they are perishable or if they threaten to decline in value speedily. If a sale is not mandatory for the reasons just stated, the buyer has three options. He may store the rejected goods for the seller's account, reship them to the seller, or resell them for the seller's account [2-604].

Code Section 2-711(3) gives a buyer a security interest in the goods in his possession and the right to resell them. Thus a buyer of defective goods can reject and resell the goods, deduct all expenses regarding care, custody, resale, and other matters (such as the down payment), and then remit any money left over to the seller [2-604, 2-711(3)].

8. Right to Revoke Acceptance

Acceptance. The buyer has *accepted* goods if (1) after a reasonable opportunity to inspect them, he indicates to the seller that the goods are conforming or that he will take or retain them in spite of their nonconformity, (2) he has failed to make an effective rejection of the goods, or (3) he does any act inconsistent with the seller's ownership [2-606].

Revocation. The buyer may revoke his acceptance under certain circumstances. In many instances, the buyer will have accepted nonconforming goods because the defect was not immediately discoverable or he reasonably assumed that the seller would correct by substituting goods that did conform. In either case, the buyer has the privilege of "revoking" his acceptance by notifying the seller if, but only if, the nonconformity "substantially impairs the value to him" [2-608(1)]. Notice the importance of the word "him" in the following case.

CASE

On April 19, 1976, Clarence Miller ordered from Colonial Dodge a 1976 Dodge Royal Monaco station wagon that included a heavy-duty trailer package with extra-wide tires. On May 28, 1976, Miller picked up the wagon. Shortly after driving the car home, his wife discovered that the new car did not have a spare tire. The next morning, Miller notified Colonial Dodge that he insisted on immediately having the tire he ordered. When told there was no tire available, Miller informed Colonial's salesman that he would stop payment on the two checks that had been tendered as the purchase price, and that the car could be picked up in front of his home. Miller parked the car in front of his house. It remained there until the ten-day registration sticker expired, and the police towed the car. Miller refused the license plates for which Colonial had applied. Colonial sued Miller for the purchase price of the car. According to a witness for Colonial, the spare had not been included in the car because of a nationwide shortage caused by a labor strike. The trial court found that Miller had wrongfully revoked acceptance of the vehicle and entered judgment for Colonial.

ISSUE: Was Miller's revocation of acceptance of the station wagon wrongful?

DECISION: No.

REASONS:

1. Section 2-608(1)(b) of the Uniform Commercial Code allows a buyer to revoke his acceptance of a nonconforming good when he has accepted the goods without discovering the nonconformity. However, he may not revoke the acceptance of the goods unless two requirements are met. First, the goods' nonconformity or defect must substantially impair the goods' value to the buyer. Second, the buyer's acceptance must have been reasonably induced, either by the difficulty of discovering the defect before acceptance or by the seller's assurances that the nonconformity would be corrected.
2. Colonial's failure to include the spare tire as ordered constituted a substantial impairment in value to Miller. Ordering the special package with the special tires indicated that he sincerely valued the safety of the automobile. Miller's occupation required that he travel extensively and often in the early morning hours. He testified that he feared a tire going flat at 3 A.M., leaving him helpless until morning business hours. The dangers upon a stranded motorist are common knowledge, and Miller's fears were not unreasonable.

3. Miller's acceptance was reasonably induced because the nonconformity was difficult to discover. There was testimony that the space for the spare tire was under a fastened panel, concealed from view. This out-of-sight location satisfies the difficulty-of-discovery requirement of UCC Section 2-608(1)(b).
4. Therefore Miller's revocation of acceptance of the station wagon was proper, and the trial court's judgment is reversed.

Colonial Dodge, Inc. v. Miller, 362 N.W.2d 704 (Mich. 1984).

Revocation must take place within a reasonable time after the buyer has discovered, or should have discovered, the reason for revocation [2-608(2)]. If a buyer revokes his acceptance, he is then placed in the same position with reference to the goods as if he had rejected them in the first instance [2-608(3)]. He has a security interest in the goods for the payments made and is entitled to damages as if no acceptance had occurred.

The following case is typical of the factual situation that leads to a valid revocation of acceptance.

CASE

Newmaster bought a John Deere power seeder from Southeast Equipment. The machine was designed to break soil and drop seed in one operation. When the seeder was delivered on May 15, 1978, Newmaster used it to sow grass seed on 3 acres. Inspecting the field, Newmaster concluded that there was an insufficient number of seeds deposited by the machine per foot to produce a proper crop. He called Southeast Equipment, told them the seeder did not function properly, and was assured that someone would come to fix it. The defective nature of the machine was difficult, if not impossible, to discover without attempting to use it. When no one came to repair the machine, Newmaster over the next several weeks made fourteen telephone calls to Southeast Equipment. None of these calls resulted in the power seeder's being fixed. On July 31, 1978, Newmaster revoked his acceptance, returned the machine, and demanded a refund of the purchase price. When his payment was not returned, Newmaster sued. Southeast Equipment defended by alleging that Newmaster could not revoke acceptance because it was not made within a reasonable time.

ISSUE: Did Newmaster timely revoke his acceptance of the seeder?

DECISION: Yes.

REASONS:

1. Revocation of acceptance is possible only when the defect substantially impairs the value of the machine to Newmaster. Notification of revocation of acceptance must be made within a reasonable time after discovery of the grounds for revocation. The machine was of little value to Newmaster and he informed Southeast within a reasonable time after discovering the defect.
2. Southeast was notified of the defect three days after Newmaster accepted the machine. Repeated requests for repair were made but to no avail. The machine was properly returned to Southeast and a demand made for a refund of the purchase price.

Newmaster v. Southeast Equipment, Inc., 646 P.2d 488 (Kan. 1982).

9. Right to Cover

The buyer who has not received the goods he bargained for may **cover**—that is, arrange to purchase the goods he needs from some other source in substitution for those due from the seller [2-712]. This is a practical remedy, as the buyer must often proceed without delay in order to obtain goods needed for his own use or for resale. The buyer must act reasonably and in good faith in arranging for the cover [2-712(1)].

Cover *A good faith, prompt, reasonable purchase of, or contract to purchase, goods in substitution for those due from the seller.*

A buyer may collect from a seller the difference between what he paid for the substitute goods and the contract price [2-712(2)]. He may also collect any incidental and consequential damages. *Incidental damages* are defined as those that are reasonably incurred in connection with handling rejected goods. These damages consist of ''commercially reasonable charges, expenses or commissions in connection with effecting cover and any other reasonable expense incident to the delay or other breach'' [2-715(1)]. *Consequential damages* include ''any loss resulting from general or particular requirements and needs of which the seller at the time of contracting had reason to know and which could not reasonably be prevented by cover or otherwise'' [2-715(2)]. The buyer is obligated to keep his damages to a minimum by making an appropriate cover insofar as his right to any consequential damages is concerned.

The cover remedy has the advantage of providing certainty as to the amount of the buyer's damages. The difference between the contract price and the price paid by the buyer for substitute goods can be readily determined. Although the buyer must act reasonably and in good faith, he need not prove that he obtained the goods at the cheapest price available. However, as the following case illustrates, not all expenses may be collected under the theory of the buyer covering his needs.

CASE

McGinnis purchased a Chevrolet automobile from Wentworth Chevrolet for $5,923. McGinnis justifiably revoked her acceptance of the automobile on the basis that it was a lemon. McGinnis sued, and the trial court ruled that she was "entitled to a refund of the purchase price, less the value of her use of the automobile." On appeal, the court ruled that she was also entitled to recover the rental payments of a substitute automobile.

ISSUE: Is McGinnis, who justifiably revoked acceptance of the automobile, entitled to recover for automobile rental fees under a theory of cover?

DECISION: No.

REASONS:
1. The UCC's "cover" alternative is intended to enable the buyer to obtain the goods he needs by allowing the disappointed buyer to reenter the marketplace and make a reasonable purchase of substitute goods. When a buyer makes a reasonable "cover," the measure of damages is the difference between the actual "cover" purchased and the contract price.
2. In view of the underlying purpose of the cover remedy in providing certainty for the calculation of the buyer's loss of bargain while also allowing the buyer to obtain the needed goods, the remedy would not extend to a rental. Rental costs are not readily translat-

able into a comparable value figure for computation of the loss of bargain. A holding that the rental constitutes a cover would frustrate the purpose of the Code provision.

McGinnis v. Wentworth Chevrolet Co., 668 P.2d 365 (Oregon 1983).

10. Rights to Damages for Nondelivery

The aggrieved buyer who did not receive any goods from the seller or who received nonconforming goods is not required to cover; instead, he may bring an action for damages [2-712(3)]. The measure of damages for nondelivery or repudiation is the difference between the contract price and the market price when the buyer learned of the breach [2-713]. The buyer is also entitled to any incidental or consequential damages sustained. Damages to which a buyer is entitled consist of ''the loss resulting in the ordinary course of events from the seller's breach as determined in any manner which is reasonable'' [2-714(1)]. In a purchase for resale, it would be appropriate to measure the buyer's damage upon nondelivery as the difference between the contract price and the price at which the goods were to be resold. In other words, the damages equal the difference between the contract price and the fair market value of the goods.

Another recourse open to the buyer is the right to deduct damages from any part of the price still due under the same contract [2-717]. The buyer determines what his damages are and withholds this amount when he pays the seller. He is required to give notice to the seller of his intention to deduct damages. When the buyer's damages are established by the cover price, the amount is clear-cut. In other instances, the seller might question the amount of the deduction, and this dispute would have to be resolved between the parties or by a court.

Damages may be deducted only from the price due under the same contract. A buyer could not deduct damages for nondelivered goods under one contract from the price due under other contracts with the same seller.

11. Right to the Goods

Under proper circumstances, a buyer has rights in, and to, the actual goods purchased. The remedy of *specific performance* is available (1) when the goods are unique and (2) when other circumstances make it equitable that the seller render the required performance [2-716(1)]. To obtain specific performance, the buyer must have been unable to cover. The Code does not define ''unique,'' but it is fair to assume that it would encompass output and requirement contracts in which the goods were not readily or practically available from other sources. Even if the goods are not unique, the Code provides that the buyer may recover them under ''proper circumstances.'' When a buyer cannot practically buy the goods elsewhere, a proper circumstance for specific performance probably exists.

Replevin *A remedy given by statute for the recovery of the possession of a chattel.*

Another remedy that enables the buyer to reach the goods in the hands of the seller is the statutory remedy of replevin. **Replevin** is an action to recover the goods that one person wrongfully withholds from another. A buyer has the right to replevin goods from the seller if the goods have been *identified* to the contract and the buyer is unable to effect cover after making a reasonable effort to do so [2-716(3)].

A related remedy that also reaches the goods in the hands of the seller is the buyer's right to recover them if the seller becomes insolvent [2-502]. The right exists only if (1) the buyer has a "special property" in the goods (that is, existing goods have been identified to the contract) and (2) the seller becomes insolvent within ten days after he received the first installment payment from the buyer. Without these circumstances, the buyer is relegated to the position of a general creditor of the seller. It is apparent that if the buyer can recover the goods, he is in a much better position than he would be as a general creditor, particularly if he had paid a substantial amount of the purchase price. To exercise this remedy, the buyer must make and maintain a tender of any unpaid portion of the price.

SELLER'S RIGHTS AND REMEDIES

12. Introduction

The Code establishes certain rights and remedies for sellers, just as it does for buyers. A seller has several alternative courses of action when a buyer breaches the contract. One of the most significant rights is to *cure* a defective performance. The seller also may cancel the contract if the buyer's breach is material. Under certain circumstances, a seller may withhold delivery or stop delivery if the goods are in transit. A seller also has the right to resell the goods and recover damages or simply to recover damages for the buyer's failure to accept the goods. Finally, the seller may, under certain circumstances, file suit to recover the price of the goods. The remedies of the seller are cumulative and not exclusive. The technical aspects of "cure" and of these remedies are discussed in the following sections.

13. Right to Cure

Upon inspecting the goods, if the buyer finds that they do not conform to the contract, he may reject them, providing he acts fairly in doing so. If the rejection is for a relatively minor deviation from the contract requirements, the seller must be given an opportunity to correct the defective performance. This is called **cure.** The seller may accomplish this by notifying the buyer of his intention to cure, then tendering proper or conforming goods if the time for performance has not expired. If the time for performance has expired, the seller—if he has reasonable grounds to believe that the goods will be acceptable in spite of the nonconformity—will be granted further time to substitute goods that are in accordance with the contract.

Cure *An opportunity for the seller of defective goods to correct the defect and thereby not be held to have breached the sales contract.*

The main purpose of this rule allowing cure is to protect the seller from being forced into a breach by a surprise rejection at the last moment by the buyer. The seller, in order to take advantage of this privilege, must notify the buyer of his intention to cure.

14. Right to Reclaim Goods from an Insolvent Buyer

If a seller discovers that a buyer who has been extended credit is insolvent, the seller will want to withhold delivery before it is completed. An insolvent buyer is one "who either has ceased to pay his debts in the ordinary course of business or cannot pay his debts as they become due or is insolvent within the meaning of the federal bankruptcy law'' [1-201(23)].

A seller, upon discovering that a buyer is insolvent, may refuse to make any further deliveries except for cash, and he may demand that payment be made for all goods previously delivered under the contract [2-702(1)]. If goods are en route to the buyer, they may be stopped in transit and recovered from the carrier [2-705]. If they are in a warehouse or other place of storage awaiting delivery to the buyer, the seller may stop delivery by the bailee. Thus the seller can protect his interests by retaining or reclaiming the goods prior to the time they come into the possession of the insolvent buyer.

This right to reclaim the goods on the buyer's insolvency includes situations in which the goods have come into the buyer's possession. If the buyer has received goods on credit while he is insolvent, the seller can reclaim the goods by making a demand for them within ten days after their receipt by the buyer [2-702(2)]. By receiving the goods, the buyer has, in effect, made a representation that he is solvent and able to pay for them. If the buyer has made a written misrepresentation of solvency within the three-month period before the goods were delivered to him, and the seller has justifiably relied on the writing, the ten-day limitation period during which the seller can reclaim the goods from the insolvent buyer does not restrict the seller's right of reclamation [2-702(2)]. That is what happened in the following case.

CASE

The plaintiff, a carpet company, sold carpeting to the defendant. To obtain credit, the defendant had furnished a year-old financial statement that was false. Six weeks after this credit sales transaction, the plaintiff discovered the defendant was insolvent. As the result of the defendant's insolvency, the plaintiff reclaimed the carpeting. The defendant then filed a petition in bankruptcy, and the trustee in bankruptcy sought to recover the carpeting on the ground that the plaintiff had not acted within the ten-day time limits for reclaiming goods from an insolvent buyer.

ISSUE: Did plaintiff act within the time limits of the Code in reclaiming the goods?

DECISION: Yes.

REASONS:

1. The ten-day limitation within which to recover goods from an insolvent buyer is not applicable if the buyer has made false statements in writing about his financial condition within three months of the delivery.
2. The three-month time begins on the date that the financial statement is presented to the seller, not on the date it is originally written. Although the written statement was prepared one year before credit was extended, the delivery occurred within three months after the statement was presented.

In re Bel Air Carpets, 452 F.2d 1210 (9th Cir. 1971) (applying Calif. law).

The importance to a seller of the privilege of reclaiming goods or stopping them in transit should be clear. If the insolvent buyer is adjudicated a bankrupt, the goods will become a part of the debtor's estate and will be sold by the trustee in bankruptcy for the benefit of *all* the creditors of the buyer. If the seller is able to reclaim the goods, his loss will be kept to a minimum.

15. Right to Reclaim Goods from a Solvent Buyer

The right to stop goods in transit or to withhold delivery is not restricted to the insolvency situation. If the buyer has (1) wrongfully rejected a tender of goods, (2) revoked his acceptance, (3) failed to make a payment due on or before delivery, or (4) repudiated with respect to either a part of the goods or the whole contract, the seller can also reclaim the goods. This right extends to any goods directly affected by the breach.

To stop delivery by a carrier, the seller must give proper and timely notice to the carrier, so that there is reasonable time to follow the instructions [2-705(3)]. Once the goods have been received by the buyer, or a bailee has acknowledged that he holds the goods for the buyer, the right of stoppage is at an end. Only in the case of insolvency [2-704(2)] can the seller reclaim the goods after they are in the buyer's possession.

The right to stop delivery to a solvent buyer is restricted to carload, truckload, planeload, or larger shipments. This restriction is designed to ease the burden on carriers that could develop if the right to stop for reasons other than insolvency applied to all small shipments. The seller who is shipping to a buyer of doubtful credit can always send the goods C.O.D., and thus preclude the necessity for stopping the goods in transit. Of course, the seller must exercise care in availing himself of this remedy, as improper stoppage is a breach by the seller and would subject him to an action for damages by the buyer.

16. Right to Resell Goods

The seller who is in possession of goods at the time of the buyer's breach has the right to resell the goods [2-706]. If part of the goods has been delivered, he can resell the undelivered portion. In this way the seller can quickly realize at least some of the amount due from the buyer. He also has a claim against the buyer for the difference between the resale price and the price that the buyer had agreed to pay. The resale remedy thus affords a practical method and course of action for the seller who has possession of goods that were intended for a breaching buyer. Any person in the position of a seller of goods has the right to resell the goods when a buyer defaults.

Frequently, a buyer will breach or repudiate the contract prior to the time that goods have been identified to the contract. This occurs when goods are in the process of manufacture. This does not defeat the seller's right to resell the goods. The seller may proceed to identify goods to the contract [2-704(1)(a)] and then use his remedy of resale. When the goods are unfinished, the seller may also use his remedy of resale if he can show that the unfinished goods were intended for the particular contract [2-704(1)(b)]. The seller may also resell the unfinished goods for scrap or salvage value or take any other reasonable action in connection with the goods [2-704(2)]. The only requirement is that the seller use reasonable commercial judgment in determining which course of action he will take in order to mitigate his damages. Presumably he would take into consideration factors such as the extent to which the manufacture had been completed and the resalability of the goods if he elected to complete the manufacture. Thus the law allows the seller to proceed in a commercially reasonable manner in order to protect his interests.

When the seller elects to use his remedy of resale, the resale may be either a private sale or a public (auction) sale [2-706(2)]. The resale must be identified as one relating to the broken contract. If the resale is private, the seller must give the buyer reasonable notification of his intention to resell [2-706(3)]. If the resale is public, the seller must give the buyer reasonable notice of the time and place, so that the buyer can bid or can obtain the attendance of other bidders. With goods that are perishable or threaten to decline speedily in value, the notice is not required. The seller is permitted to buy at a public sale. The prime requirement is that the sale be conducted in a commercially reasonable manner [2-706(2)]. If the resale brings a higher price than that provided for in the contract, the seller is not accountable to the buyer for any profit [2-706(6)].

17. Right to Collect Damages

In many situations, a resale would not be an appropriate or sufficient remedy. The seller may elect to bring an action for damages if the buyer refuses to accept the goods or repudiates the contract [2-708]. The measure of damages is the difference between the market price at the place for tender and the unpaid contract price, plus incidental damages [2-708]. Incidental damages include expenses reasonably incurred as a result of the buyer's breach [2-710].

Usually, this measure of damages will not put the seller in as good a position as he would have had if the buyer had performed and the seller had not lost the sale. Under such circumstances, the measure of damages includes the profit the seller would have made from full performance by the buyer [2-708(2)] as well as incidental damages. In computing profit, the reasonable overhead of the seller may be taken into account. The measure of damages recognizes that a seller suffers a loss, even though he may ultimately resell for the same amount that he would have received from the buyer. He has lost a sale and the profit on that sale.

18. Right to Collect the Purchase Price

When the buyer fails to pay the price as it becomes due, the seller may sue for the contract price of the goods if the buyer has accepted the goods, the goods were destroyed after risk of loss passed to the buyer, or the resale remedy is not practicable. If goods are specially manufactured for a buyer and there is no market for the special goods, the seller may collect the purchase price since his right to resell is not available.

CASE

On July 9, 1976, Machlett Laboratories ordered from Plateq Corporation two steel tanks specially designed for testing x-ray tubes. On October 11, 1976, the tanks were completed. On that date an engineer from Machlett inspected the tanks and noted some deficiencies; which Plateq promised to remedy by the next day. The engineer indicated that a truck would pick up the tanks in a day or so. Instead of sending a truck, Machlett sent notice on October 4, 1976, that it was canceling the contract.

Plateq sued to recover the purchase price, and Machlett defended, stating it had not accepted the tanks.

ISSUE: Is Plateq entitled to recover the purchase price?

DECISION: Yes.

REASONS:
1. When Machlett's engineer indicated his willingness to take the tanks despite their nonconformities, Machlett accepted the tanks.
2. The Code permits a price action for contract goods when the circumstances reasonably indicate that there is no opportunity to resell the goods.
3. Since the tanks were specially manufactured according to Machlett's special needs and instructions, a reasonable opportunity to resell them is not available.

Plateq Corp. of North Haven v. Machlett Laboratories, 456 A.2d 786 (Conn. 1983).

If the seller sues for the price, the goods are held by the seller on behalf of the buyer. In effect, the goods are to be treated as if they belong to the buyer. After the seller obtains a judgment against the buyer, the seller may still resell the goods at any time prior to collection of the judgment, but he must apply the proceeds toward satisfaction of the judgment. Payment of the balance due on the judgment entitles the buyer to any goods not resold [2-709(2)].

CHAPTER SUMMARY

Overview of Code Remedies

Adequate Assurance

1. This is the one remedy that is available to both buyers and sellers.
2. The Code provides that either party may demand in writing that the other give assurance that performance will be forthcoming.
3. If assurance of performance is not given, the party who requested such assurance may treat the contract as breached.

Checklist of Code Remedies

1. See Table 18–1.

Buyer's Rights and Remedies

Right to Inspect

1. A buyer has a right before payment or acceptance to inspect the goods at any reasonable time and place.
2. If the contract is C.O.D. or calls for payment against documents, a buyer must pay before he can inspect. Payment, however, is not acceptance, and inspection still is permitted.

Right to Reject

1. If the goods fail in any respect to conform to the contract, a buyer can reject.
2. A buyer can reject the whole or accept any commercial unit and reject the rest.

Notice of Rejection

1. Rejection must be within a reasonable time and notice of rejection must be timely. Failure to do either will result in an acceptance.

Rights and Duties on Rejection	1. After rejection, a buyer who takes possession of the goods must protect them and follow any reasonable instructions from the seller. 2. A buyer has a security interest in the goods and can resell them to recover his expenses in taking possession and caring for the goods.
Right to Revoke Acceptance	1. A buyer accepts if (1) after a reasonable opportunity to inspect, he indicates he accepts despite any nonconformity, (2) he fails to make an effective rejection, or (3) he does any act inconsistent with the seller's ownership. 2. A buyer can revoke his acceptance of nonconforming goods if the nonconformity substantially impairs the value of the goods to the buyer. 3. This right might exist even if the buyer accepted the goods while thinking the seller would cure or if the nonconformity was very difficult to discover. 4. Revocation must be within a reasonable time, and the buyer has the same rights and duties as if he had rejected.
Right to Cover	1. A buyer covers when he buys the goods elsewhere and cover is a buyer's primary remedy. 2. A buyer is not required to cover. If the buyer decides to cover, it must be in good faith.
Rights to Damages for Nondelivery	1. After covering, a buyer can sue the seller for the difference between the cover price and the contract price, plus any incidental and consequential damages. 2. If a buyer does not cover, he can sue for the difference between the contract price and the market price, plus any incidental and consequential damages.
Right to the Goods	1. When the goods are unique, or in other proper circumstances, a buyer can get specific performance. The Code remedy is more flexible than the traditional remedy of specific performance in equity. 2. "Other proper circumstances" occur when the buyer simply cannot reasonably buy the goods elsewhere.

Seller's Rights and Remedies

Right to Cure	1. The right to cure exists for rejections that are for relatively minor deviations from the contract. 2. If the time for performance has not expired, a seller has an absolute right to cure (correct) his previous nonconforming tender of goods. 3. If the time for performance has expired, the seller can cure only if the seller had reasonable grounds to think his nonconforming tender would have been accepted by the buyer.
Right to Reclaim Goods from an Insolvent Buyer	1. When a seller discovers a buyer received goods while insolvent, the seller can reclaim them upon demand within ten days after receipt. If the buyer in writing three months before delivery misrepresented his solvency, the ten-day limitation does not apply. 2. The seller can also refuse to make further deliveries except for cash and can stop any goods en route to the buyer.
Right to Reclaim Goods from a Solvent Buyer	1. If the buyer has improperly rejected, wrongfully revoked acceptance, failed to pay, or repudiated the contract, the seller can reclaim the goods in transit. 2. The seller can stop goods in transit upon timely notice to the carrier. This right is limited to carload, truckload, or other large shipments.

Right to Resell Goods	1. Resale is the seller's primary remedy. 2. A seller can resell the goods and sue for the difference between the resale price and the contract price plus any incidental and consequential damages.
Right to Collect Damages	1. If the seller does not resell, he can sue for the difference between the market price at the place of tender and the contract price, plus any incidental and consequential damages.
Right to Collect the Purchase Price	1. A seller can collect the contract price if the buyer accepted to goods. 2. A seller can collect the contract price if the goods were lost or damaged within a reasonable time after the risk of loss passed to the buyer. 3. A seller can collect the contract price if the goods were identified to the contract and the seller cannot resell them, or the facts indicate the goods cannot be resold.

REVIEW QUESTIONS AND PROBLEMS

1. Match each term in column A with the appropriate statement in column B.

A	B
(1) Adequate assurance	(a) Buyer's remedy for undoing his acceptance.
(2) Inspection	(b) Seller's primary remedy.
(3) Rejection	(c) If buyer is insolvent, seller may be able to do this.
(4) Acceptance	(d) Buyer's right before he has to pay or accept.
(5) Revocation of acceptance	(e) Seller's right to correct a nonconforming tender.
(6) Cover	(f) Seller's right to collect the purchase price.
(7) Buyer's specific performance	(g) Buyer fails to make an effective rejection.
(8) Cure	(h) Buyer's primary remedy.
(9) Resale	(i) Buyer may do this if the tender of goods fails in any way to conform to the contract.
(10) Seller's specific performance	(j) Buyer's remedy if goods are unique or other proper circumstances.
(11) Seller can reclaim goods	(k) A remedy available to both parties.

2. Amy orders three white slips from a department store. They arrive C.O.D. and Amy pays the delivery person. She opens the box and discovers that black slips were sent. If she does not want these slips, what are her rights? Explain.

3. Newman bought a mobile home from Moses. On February 9, Moses delivered the mobile home to Newman's rented lot, blocked and leveled it, and connected the sewer and water pipes. Later that day, Newman's fiancee cleaned the interior of the mobile home and moved some kitchen utensils and dishes into the mobile home. She noticed a broken window and water pipe. Newman called Moses and told him about these conditions as well as having no door keys. On February 10, a windstorm totally destroyed the mobile home. When Newman refused to pay the purchase price, Moses sued, claiming that Newman must bear the loss since Newman had accepted the mobile home. Newman contended that he had not acepted the mobile home since he had complained of specific defects. Did Newman accept the mobile home? Why or why not?

4. ODA nursery sold 985 spreading juniper plants to Garcia Tree and Lawn. The plants were delivered on March 14. They were planted in July and August, but in October many of them started to die. In November, an inspection revealed that the plants were root-bound and the buyer notified the seller of the defect. Is the buyer entitled to recover the costs of the plants? Why or why not?

5. Campbell bought a pump from Kee for $6,500 that Kee had advertised as a ''mud pump.'' When the pump was delivered, Campbell discovered that the pump was not in fact a mud pump. Campbell claimed that the pump was worth $2,000 less than the mud pump advertised. He refused to pay the $6,500 purchase price but offered $4,500, which Kee refused to accept. For six months, Campbell argued with Kee over what the price should be. When a compromise could not be reached, Campbell returned the pump and refused to pay anything. When Kee sued for the $6,500 purchase price, Campbell asserted that he had rejected the pump and was not liable for anything. Did Campbell reasonably reject the pump? Explain.

6. Slacks, Inc., sells tank tops to a fashionable boutique. Upon receipt, the store inspects them, discovers defects, and seasonably rejects them. Slacks instructs the store to sell the tank tops or return them. The boutique does neither. Is it liable for anything? Explain.

7. Plaintiff, a used-car dealer, brought a car to the defendant, another dealer, for inspection in the hope that a sales agreement could be reached. Two of the defendant's employees examined the car and test-drove it. Defendant thereafter agreed to buy the car without reserving any further right to inspect. In fact, the car had several defects that were readily discernible. Can the buyer revoke in his acceptance? Why?

8. Sandra purchased a new Nissan from Rocky Mountain Nissan. During the first six months that she owned the car, it had to be towed to the dealer's shop for repairs on at least seven occasions. Sometimes the car would not start. On other occasions it would stop running and stall in traffic. Several of the dealer's mechanics told Sandra that they did not know what was wrong with the car but that it was a ''lemon.'' She estimated that the car had been in the dealer's shop four out of the first six months that she owned it. Is she entitled to revoke her acceptance? Why or why not?

9. A country music festival promoter contracted to buy 2,000 kegs of beer at $50 per keg. When the beer that arrived was found to be flat, the promoter rejected it. He could not buy that brand from any other source in time for the festival, so he bought 2,000 kegs of another beer at $55 per keg. What are the promoter's Article 2 damages? Explain.

10. Chadwell made a contract with English wherein Chadwell was given an option to purchase all of English's shares in an Oklahoma bank. On two occasions, Chadwell attempted to exercise the options, but English refused to convey the shares. Chadwell sued to recover the shares. What result? Why?

11. Pinson purchased a new Oldsmobile automobile from the defendant for $9,720.33. A few days after the purchase, Pinson noticed approximately four small indentations on the hood of the automobile and noticed some paint overspray on the left rear quarter panel of the automobile. He notified the defendant of his discovery, and it offered to correct the defects without charge under the new car warranty. The cost to repair the warranty defects was estimated to be from $75 to $100. Pinson refused to allow Freeman Oldsmobile to correct the defects and instituted suit to obtain a refund of the purchase price. What results? Why?

12. Jimmie Hart contracted to buy a certain painting through Mrs. Sims, an art dealer, for $45,000. Hart made a down payment and promised to pay the balance of the purchase price on or before November 25, 1979. Hart sent a personal check for the balance, but his check bounced due to insufficient funds in his checking account. Hart reassured Mrs. Sims that he would wire the balance to Mrs. Sims at 10:00 A.M. on November 29, 1979. On that date he called, stating he was having trouble getting the funds wired. Mrs. Sims agreed to extend the deadline to 2:00 P.M. but warned that she would sell the painting to another interested buyer if he did not meet the 2:00 P.M. deadline. Hart did wire the money, but it did not reach Mrs. Sim's bank until 3:04 P.M. At 2:30 P.M. Mrs. Sims telegraphed Hart canceling their contract. She then sold the painting to another buyer for $60,000. Hart sued, contending that Mrs. Sims did not have the right to sell the painting because he had wired the money. Did Mrs. Sims have the right to resell the painting? Why or why not?

13. The city of Louisville executed a requirements contract with plaintiff to provide the city with all its requirements of parking meters for seven months at $54.20 per meter. Two days later, a new mayor took office and repudiated the contract and entered into a contract with Duncan to supply meters at $46.92. Plaintiff sues for the price of 1,000 meters manufactured pursuant to the city's order and for the lost profits based on the number of meters the city bought from Duncan. Is plaintiff entitled to the purchase price? Why?

19 Warranties

CHAPTER PREVIEW

- TYPES OF WARRANTIES

  Express Warranties
  Warranty of Title
  Implied Warranty of Merchantability
  Implied Warranty of Fitness for a Particular Purpose

- LIMITATIONS

  Of Express Warranties
  Written Disclaimers of Implied Warranties
  Other Exclusions of Implied Warranties
  On Remedies

- OTHER ASPECTS OF WARRANTIES

  Notice
    Policies • Form • Time
  Third Parties
    Privity of contract • Abandonment of privity

BUSINESS MANAGEMENT DECISION

You inherited a retail hardware store that you do not wish to operate. After being unsuccessful in selling the business, you decide to have a going-out-of-business sale. You want to sell all the merchandise on as-is basis, but you realize that many customers rely on the expertise of your experienced sales staff.

What do you do to ensure that no express or implied warranties attach to the merchandise sold?

In the law of sales of goods, the word *warranty* describes the obligation of the seller with respect to goods that have been sold. As a general rule, a seller is responsible for transferring to the buyer a good title and goods that are of the proper quality, free from defects. He may also be responsible for the proper functioning of the article sold and for its suitability to the needs of the buyer. Thus a warranty may extend not only to the present condition for goods but also to the performance that is to be expected of them.

A warranty made by a seller is an integral part of the contract. If the warranty is breached and the buyer notifies the seller of the breach within a reasonable time, the buyer may bring an action for damages caused by the breach of warranty. A breach of warranty may also result in injuries to the buyer or to third persons. Suits may be brought to recover damages for these injuries as well.

The law takes the position that if the goods are defective, the seller should be held responsible. Various tort and contract theories impose liability on manufacturers, packers, producers, and sellers for injuries caused by defective products. This chapter discusses the breach of warranty theories. Other theories are discussed in Chapter 20, on products liability. Keep in mind that the material in this chapter is also a part of products liability.

The Uniform Commercial Code has several provisions relating to warranties. It draws a distinction between express warranties made by a seller and those implied as a matter of law from the transaction. If the seller guarantees the product directly, it is an *express warranty*. If the warranty arises out of the transaction and its circumstances, it is called an *implied warranty*. When the seller is a merchant, special treatment is sometimes afforded to warranties.

TYPES OF WARRANTIES

1. Express Warranties

An **express warranty** is one that is made as a part of the contract for sale and becomes a part of the basis of the bargain between the buyer and the seller [2-313(1)(a)]. An express warranty, as distinguished from an implied warranty, is part of the contract because it has been included as part of the individual bargain. To create an express warranty, the seller does not have to use formal words such as "warrant" or "guarantee," nor must he have the specific intention to make a warranty [2-313(3)].

Express warranty *A positive representation concerning the nature, quality, character, use, and purpose of goods, which induces the buyer to buy, and the seller intends the buyer to rely thereon.*

A seller may make a variety of statements about the goods. It is necessary to evaluate these to determine which statements are warranties and which do not impose legal responsibility because they are merely sales talk. Any positive statement by a seller of the condition of personal property made during the negotitations for its sale that indicates an intention to be bound by the truth thereof, and that was so understood and relied on by the other party, is an express warranty. A label on a bag of insecticide stated that it was developed especially to control rootworms. This was an express warranty that the insecticide was effective to control the rootworm. The word *guarantee* is often used to give an express warranty. A contract of sale of automobile tires states that the tires were guaranteed for 36,000 miles against all road hazards, including blowouts. This constituted an express warranty that the tires would not blow out during the first 36,000 miles of use.

When a statement of fact or promise about the goods is made by the seller to the buyer, an express warranty is created [2-313(1)(a)]. The express warranty is that the goods will conform to the statement of fact or promise. Any statement of fact or even of opinion, if it becomes a part of the basis of the bargain, is an express warranty. While an express warranty must become a part of the basis of the bargain, a plaintiff does not have to prove reliance on specific promises made by the seller. No particular reliance need be shown in order to weave an affirmation of fact into the fabric of the agreement.

Most statements of opinion, such as those concerning the value of the goods, do not give rise to an express warranty. As a general rule, a buyer is not justified in relying on mere opinions, and they are not usually a part of the basis of the bargain. However, the opinion of an expert, such as a jeweler, with regard to the value of a gem may justify the reliance of the buyer, and such an opinion becomes part of the basis of the bargain and a warranty. When a seller merely states his opinion or his judgment on a matter of which the seller has no special knowledge, or on which the buyer may be expected to have an opinion and exercise his judgment, then the seller's statement does not constitute an express warranty.

An express warranty may be made in a variety of ways. The seller may specifically make a factual statement about the goods. These factual statements may be on labels or in a catalog or other sales promotion material. A direct promise may state: "This grass seed is free from weeds." Generally, words that are descriptive of the product are warranties that the goods will conform to the description [2-313(1)(b)]. Descriptions may also be in the form of diagrams, pictures, blueprints, and the like. Technical specifications of the product would constitute warranties if they were part of the basis for the bargain. An express warranty can also be based on the instructions of the seller regarding use of the product.

Just as the seller may describe the goods, he may also inform the buyer by showing him a model or a sample of what is being sold. Fabrics or clothing might be purchased on the basis of samples shown to the buyer, or a seller might display a working model of an engine. In either event, there would be an express warranty that the goods will conform to the sample or model if the parties have made this a part of their bargain [2-313(1)(c)].

2. Warranty of Title

A seller may expressly warrant the title to goods but usually does not do so. Therefore the law imposes a *warranty of title* in order to protect buyers who may overlook this aspect of the sale and those who simply assume the seller has good title to the goods. The warranty of title is treated as a separate warranty under the Code.

A seller warrants that he is conveying good title to the buyer and that he has the right to sell the goods. He further warrants that there are no encumbrances or liens against the property sold and that no other person can claim a security interest in them [2-312]. In effect, the seller implicitly guarantees to the buyer that he will be able to enjoy the use of the goods free from the claims of any third party. Of course, property may be sold to a buyer who has full knowledge of liens or encumbrances, and he may buy the property subject to these claims. In this event, there would not be a breach of warranty of title. The purchase price would, however, reflect that he was obtaining less than complete title.

In Chapter 17, it is noted that a good-faith purchaser from a seller with voidable title obtains good title. Is there a breach of the warranty of title in such a sale? While there are cases answering the question both ways, most courts would find a breach of warranty even if the buyer actually receives clear title. This results from Code language that requires that the conveyance of title be rightful and free from the difficulties of establishing clear title in such cases. The good-faith purchaser thus has a choice. He may claim the goods by use of the good-faith purchaser concept, or he may recover the purchase price or any payments made by electing to sue for breach of the implied warranty of title.

Warranty of title can be excluded or modified only by specific language or by circumstances making clear that the seller is not vouching for the title [2-312(2)]. Judicial sales and sales by executors of estates would not imply that the seller guarantees the title. Also, a seller could directly inform the buyer that he is selling only the interest that he has and that the buyer takes it subject to all encumbrances.

A seller who is a merchant, regularly dealing in goods of the kind that are the subject of the sale, makes an additional warranty. He warrants that the goods are free of the rightful claim of any third person by way of infringement of the third person's interests—that the goods sold do not, for example, infringe upon a patent. But a buyer may furnish to the seller specifications for the construction of an article, and this may result in the infringement of a patent. Not only does the seller not warrant against such infringement, but the buyer must also protect the seller from any claims arising out of such infringement [2-312(3)].

3. Implied Warranty of Merchantability

Implied warranties come into being as a matter of law, without any bargaining. As an integral part of the normal sales transaction, implied warranties are legally present unless clearly disclaimed or negated. Implied warranties exist even if a seller is unable to discover the defect involved or unable to cure it if it can be ascertained. Liability for breach of an implied warranty is not based on fault, but on the public policy of protecting the buyer of goods.

A warranty that the goods shall be merchantable quality is implied in a contract for sale if the seller is a merchant who deals in goods of the kind involved in the contract. It is not enough that the defendant sold the goods. The seller-defendant must have been a merchant dealing in the goods. A person making an isolated sale is not a merchant. For example, a bank selling a repossessed car is not a merchant, and there is no implied **warranty of merchantability** in such a sale.

Warranty of merchantability *A promise implied in a sale of goods by merchants that the goods are reasonably fit for the general purpose for which they are sold.*

The warranty extends to all sales of goods by merchants. It applies to new goods and to used goods in most states, unless the warranty is excluded. The following case is typical of those extending the warranty of merchantability to used goods.

CASE

Acor purchased a truck from Roupp. Before the purchase was made, Acor told Roupp he wanted a truck with sufficient power to use in a timber-hauling business. Furthermore, he said he wanted a rebuilt truck dependable for three years. A representation was made that the truck being purchased had a completely rebuilt engine. After the purchase, the truck broke down and Acor had to buy a new engine. The engine failure resulted from a lack of oil in the bearings. Acor filed a suit based upon breach of implied warranty of merchantability.

ISSUE: Did an implied warranty of merchantability arise with the purchase of the truck?

DECISION: Yes.

REASONS:
1. A warranty of merchantability can arise with both new and used goods. The UCC doesn't draw a distinction between used and new goods in the implied warranty section.
2. An implied warranty of merchantability was created in that the truck was sold by one engaged in the sale of trucks with a representation that a rebuilt engine was installed.

Roupp v. Acor, 384 A.2d 968 (Pa. Super. 1978).

In order for a consumer to prevail in an action for damages for breach of an implied warranty of merchantability, he must demonstrate that the commodity was not reasonably suitable for the ordinary uses for which goods of that kind and description are sold, and that such defect or breach existed at the time of sale and proximately caused the damages complained of.

For goods to be merchantable, they must at least be the kind of goods that

1. Pass without objection in the trade under the contract description
2. In the case of fungible goods, are of fair average quality within the description
3. Are fit for the ordinary purposes for which such goods are used
4. Run, within the variations permitted by the agreement, of even kind, quality, and quantity within each unit and among all units involved
5. Are adequately contained, packaged, and labeled as the agreement may require
6. Conform to the promises or affirmations of fact made on the container or label if any [2-314]

Fungible goods *Fungible goods are those of which any unit is from its nature of mercantile usage treated as the equivalent of any other unit. Grain, wine, and similar items are examples.*

These standards provide the basic acceptable standards of merchantability. **Fungible goods** (point 2) are those usually sold by weight or measure, such as grain or flour. The term *fair average quality* generally relates to agricultural bulk commodities and means that they are within the middle range of quality under the description. Fitness for ordinary purposes (point 3) is not limited to use by the immediate buyer. If a person is buying for resale, the buyer is entitle to protection, and the goods must be honestly resalable by him. They must be acceptable in the ordinary market without objection. Point 5 is applicable only if the nature of the goods and of the transaction require a certain type of container, package, or label. Where there is a container or label and a representation thereon, the buyer is entitled to protection under the rule 6, so that he will not be in the position of reselling or using goods delivered under false representations appearing on the package or container. He obtains this protection even though the contract did not require either the labeling or the representation.

The implied warranty of merchantability imposes a very broad responsibility upon the merchant-seller to furnish goods that are at least of average quality. In any line of business, the word *merchantable* may have a meaning somewhat different from the Code definition, and the parties by their course of dealing may indicate a special meaning for the term.

One purpose of this warranty is to require sellers to provide goods that are reasonably safe for their ordinary intended use. Although the law does not require accident-proof products, it does require products that are reasonably safe for the purposes for which they were intended when they were placed in the stream of commerce.

The mere fact that a product injures one person does not in and of itself establish that it is not fit for the ordinary purpose for which it was intended. The following case illustrates that important limitation on the implied warranty of merchantability.

CASE

Griggs purchased and used a certain over-the-counter drug manufactured by Combe, Inc. Griggs experienced an uncommon allergic reaction to the drug and sustained injuries as a result. Combe was not aware, nor could have been aware through the exercise of reasonable diligence, that its product might have caused this reaction. Griggs sued Combe, claiming Combe had breached an implied warranty of merchantability by selling him a drug that caused him injury.

ISSUE: Is Combe liable for a breach of implied warranty merchantability?

DECISION: No.

REASONS:

1. Among the definitions of merchantability in UCC Section 2-314 is the provision that goods are "fit for the ordinary purposes for which such goods are used." Therefore, by operation of law, when a merchant sells a good, he automatically promises the buyer that the good is fit for ordinary and common use.
2. Most jurisdictions hold that if a drug is fit for use by a normal person, the manufacturer will not be liable for an uncommon allergic reaction. A product must adversely affect at least a significant number of persons before a question of merchantability arises. If the injured person suffered an allergic reaction that would be suffered by a very small or insignificant number of people, then the implied warranty of merchantability has not been breached, and the manufacturer would not be liable. However, if there were a sufficient number of people who had experienced this reaction, then the implied warranty has been breached, and liability would be imposed upon the manufacturer.
3. Judging from the record, Griggs is the only person who has suf-

fered this kind of injury during the long history of use of the drug in question. Therefore Combe has not breached its implied warranty of merchantability, and Griggs may not recover under this theory.

Griggs v. Combe, Inc., 456 So.2d 790 (Ala. 1984).

Liability for breach of the warranty of merchantability extends to direct economic loss as well as to personal injuries and to property damage. Direct economic loss includes damages based on insufficient product value. In other words, the buyer is entitled to collect the difference in value between what was received and what the product would have had if it had been of merchantable quality. Direct economic loss also includes the cost of replacements and the cost of repairs. These damages need not be established with mathematical certainty, but reasonable degrees of certainty and accuracy are required so that the damages are not based on speculation.

4. Implied Warranty of Fitness for a Particular Purpose

Warranty of fitness for a particular purpose *An implied promise by a seller of goods that arises when a buyer explains the special needs and relies on the seller's advice.*

Under the warranty of merchantability, the goods must be fit for the *ordinary purpose* for which such goods are used. The warranty of merchantability is based on a purchaser's reasonable expectation that goods purchased from a "merchant with respect to goods of that kind" will be free of significant defects and will perform in the way goods of that kind should perform. It presupposes no special relationship of trust or reliance between the seller and buyer. On the other hand, the implied **warranty of fitness for a particular purpose** is narrower, more specific, and more precise. It is created if, at the time of contracting, the seller has reason to know any particular purpose for which the buyer requires the goods and is relying on the seller's skill or judgment to select or furnish suitable goods [2-315]. In these circumstances, the seller must select goods that will accomplish the purpose for which they are being purchased. It is based on a special reliance by the buyer on the seller to provide goods that will perform a specific use required and communicated by the buyer.

The implied warranty of fitness applies both to merchants and nonmerchants but normally pertains only to merchants, since a nonmerchant does not ordinarily possess the required skills or judgment upon which buyers will rely. The buyer need not specifically state that he has a particular purpose in mind or that he is placing reliance on the seller's judgment if the circumstances are such that the seller has reason to realize the purpose intended or that the buyer is relying on him. For the warranty to apply, however, the buyer must actually rely on the seller's skill or judgment in selecting or furnishing suitable goods. If the buyer's knowledge or skill are equal to or greater than the seller's, there can be no justifiable reliance and no warranty. Both issues are questions of fact for a jury.

The difference between the implied warranty of merchantability and the implied warranty of fitness for a particular purpose is very significant. While many cases allege a breach of both warranties, the decisions often only find a breach of one or the other, but not both. The implied warranty of fitness for a particular purpose does not exist nearly as often as the implied warranty of merchantability. Particular purpose involves a specific use by the buyer; ordinary use, as expressed in the concept of merchantability, means the customary function of the goods. Thus a household dishwasher would be of merchantable quality because it could ordinarily be used to wash dishes; but it might not be fit for a restaurant's particular purpose because it would not be suited for its dishwashing needs. Goods that are of merchantable quality may not fit for a particular purpose. Goods fit for a particular purpose will almost always be of merchantable quality. Goods that are not of merchantable quality usually will not be fit for a particular purpose.

Breach of the warranty of fitness for a particular purpose may result in disaffirmance of the contract. If the product causes an injury, including economic loss, it may also result in a suit for dollar damages. The following case is one in which both the implied warranties were breached and the buyer was able to collect damages for economic losses.

CASE

Roy E. Farrar owned a produce company. He ordered from International Paper Company (IP) a shipment of boxes that would be suitable for the packaging, shipping, and storing of tomatoes. Farrar requested the boxes be the same type as those supplied to Florida packers for the shipping of tomatoes. A salesman for IP assured him that IP's computer could calculate a box with the correct dimensions. IP shipped the boxes to Farrar, and sued him when he did not pay. Farrar counterclaimed, alleging the boxes were not fit for their intended purpose. At trial, there was testimony that the salesman for IP did not obtain the dimensions of the Florida box, but instead obtained specifications for a box sold in Texas. The trial court found that these boxes were not tomato boxes, they were not the type used in Florida, and they were not strong enough for shipping. The court also found Farrar had relied upon the special knowledge and expertise of IP as a respected manufacturer of boxes used in the packing of produce.

ISSUE: Did Farrar show that IP breached implied warranties of merchantability and of fitness for a particular purpose?

DECISION: Yes.

REASONS:

1. According to UCC Section 2-314(1), the law will not imply the warranty of merchantability unless the seller is a merchant with respect to the goods of the kind involved in the transaction.
2. Section 2-314(2) defines the concept of a merchantable good. Among other requirements, the good must at least pass without objection in the trade under the contract description, and must at least be fit for the ordinary purposes for which such goods are used.
3. It was established at trial that IP was a "merchant with respect to goods of the kind" in the selling of boxes for packing produce. These boxes were unmerchantable because, under contract description, they were not fit for the ordinary purposes for which produce boxes are used. The court made specific findings that the boxes were not suitable for the packing, shipping, or storing of tomatoes. The boxes also were not the Florida-type Farrar ordered. Therefore the record supports the trial court's determination that there was a breach of the implied warranty of merchantability.
4. Section 2-315 of the UCC governs the application of the implied

warranty of fitness for a particular purpose. To recover for a breach of this warranty, the buyer must prove he has relied on the seller's skill or judgment to select or furnish suitable goods.

5. The record contains ample evidence upon which the trial court could base its finding that Farrar relied on IP's skill or judgment to provide boxes that would ship his tomatoes without collapsing during shipping and storage. Farrar's requests to IP's salesman establish reliance.
6. Clearly, the boxes were not fit for the purposes of packing, shipping, and storing tomatoes. Therefore there was also a breach of the implied warranty of fitness for a particular purpose.

International Paper Co. v. Farrar, 700 P.2d 642 (N.M. 1985).

LIMITATIONS

5. Of Express Warranties

A seller will often seek to avoid or restrict warranty liability. These attempts to limit liability may take the form of a disclaimer of warranties or a limitation of remedies. A *disclaimer of warranties* limits a seller's liability by reducing the number of circumstances in which the seller will be in breach of contract; it precludes the existence of a cause of action or greatly reduces it. A *limitation of remedies* clause restricts the remedies available to the buyer once a breach of warranty by the seller is established. The parties may also limit or alter the damages recoverable by limiting the buyer's remedy to repair or replace the nonconforming goods or parts.

The Code has provisions on exclusion or modification of warranties that are designed to protect the buyer from unexpected and unfair disclaimers of both express and implied warranties. Sometimes there are statements or conduct that create an express warranty and also statements or conduct that tend to negate or limit such warranties. To the extent that it is reasonable, the two different kinds of statements or conduct are construed as consistent with each other [2-316(1)]. However, negation of limitation of an express warranty is inoperative when such a construction is unreasonable. In other words, if the express warranty and the attempt to negate it cannot be construed as consistent, the warranty predominates. If a seller gives the buyer an express warranty and then includes in the contract a provision that purports to exclude "all warranties express or implied," that disclaimer will not be given effect. The express warranty is still enforceable.

6. Written Disclaimers of Implied Warranties

Implied warranties can be excluded if the seller makes it clear that the buyer is not to have the benefit of them. In general, to exclude or modify the implied warranty of merchantability, the word *merchantability* must be used [2-316(2)]. The warranty of merchantability may also be excluded by oral agreement or by the parties' course of performance. However, if the disclaimer is included in a written contract, it must be set forth in a conspicuous manner. The disclaimer clause of the contract should be in larger type or a different color ink or indented, so that it will be brought to the buyer's attention. A disclaimer will not be effective if it is set forth in the same type and color as the rest of the contract.

To exclude or modify any implied warranty of fitness for a particular purpose, the exclusion must be conspicuously written. The statement "there are no warranties which extend beyond the description on the face hereof" is sufficient to exclude the implied warranty of fitness for a particular purpose [2-316(2)]. An exclusionary clause should be printed in type that will set it apart from the balance of the contract. As the following case illustrates, failure to do so means that there are implied warranties.

CASE

In a sales contract between plaintiff and defendant, defendant seller had disclaimed warranties. The disclaimer appeared on the reverse side of an order confirmation slip. Although the disclaimer was in capital letters, the front side of the paper contained the following sentence: "This order subject to conditions on reverse side hereof and subject to acceptance by the company." This language was not conspicuous in any manner and, in fact, was in smaller print than the other material on the front side of the order slip. The language in capitals, which sought to disclaim warranties, was contained only on the reverse side of the order slip.

ISSUE: Is the disclaimer conspicuous as required by the UCC?

DECISION: No.

REASONS:

1. Little on the front side of the sales confirmation slip would bring to a reasonable person's attention and notice the existence of disclaimers on the reverse side.
2. While the type used for disclaiming the warranties was conspicuous, in the sense of being larger than other type in the paragraph, the presence of that paragraph on the reverse side of the order slip was not at all conspicuous, either from the general appearance of the slip or from any conspicuous language on the front side of the slip.
3. We find that the disclaimer of warranties on the reverse side of the order slip was not conspicuous so as to be valid under the Code.

Anderson v. Farmers Hybrid Companies, Inc., 408 N.E.2d 1194 (Ill. 1980).

Disclaimers of implied warranties are greatly limited by federal law today. As a part of the law relating to consumer protection, Congress passed the Magnuson-Moss warranty law (discussed in Chapter 44). This law and the Federal Trade Commission rules adopted to carry out its purposes prohibit the disclaimer of implied warranties where an express warranty is given.

7. Other Exclusions of Implied Warranties

The Code also provides for other circumstances in which implied warranties may be wholly or partially excluded. The seller may inform the buyer that he is selling goods "as is, "with all faults." Other language also may call the buyer's attention to the exclusion and make it plain that the sale involves no implied warranty [2-

316(3)(a)]. The Code does not guarantee every buyer a good deal. As the following case demonstrates, buyers frequently purchase defective products without any rights against the seller.

CASE

Forke Brothers Auctioneers conducted an auction at which vehicles owned by Magic City Trucking Service, Inc., were sold. James Smith attended this auction and registered under the name Pell City Wood, Inc. He received an auction brochure that contained disclaimers of warranties on the first three pages and descriptions of the property to be auctioned on the remaining pages. These three disclaimers all said, in effect, that the descriptions of the equipment for sale were merely a guide, were not intended as a warranty or guarantee, and that all equipment was sold "as is." James Smith purchased a truck and drove it away from the auction. Approximately seven miles down the road, the truck broke down. Smith later discovered a crack in the engine block, which required repairs totaling $8,927.

Smith filed suit for rescission, breach of warranty, and fraud against Forke Brothers and Magic City. Smith acknowledged that he read the brochure and disclaimers before bidding on the truck. He also admitted that he spoke with no one from Forke Brothers or Magic City about the truck prior to its purchase, and that other than the words of the auctioneer, the only representation concerning the truck came from the brochure. He also had the opportunity to inspect the truck prior to its purchase, and he did inspect it. The trial court granted the defendants' motion for summary judgment.

ISSUE: Did Smith create an issue of fact as to whether the representations made by the auctioneer or the descriptions printed in the brochure amounted to express warranties, thus rendering the trial court's granting of the defendants' motion for summary judgment improper?

DECISION: No.

REASONS:

1. The statements of the auctioneer that the trucks "are in good condition" and "are ready to work tomorrow" are not express warranties. These statements are either examples of puffery in an attempt to get more money at sale or are at best "statements purporting to be merely the seller's opinion or commendation of the goods." Accordingly, under UCC Section 2-313(2), this language does not rise to the level of an express warranty.
2. Smith failed to offer even a scintilla of evidence that the statements in the brochure would constitute a representation that would be express warranties. In three different places in the brochure there is language stating that the equipment was being sold "as is, where is." This "as-is" language has been held to place with the buyer the entire risk as to the quality of goods purchased. Smith stated that he read and understood the "as-is" language and the statements that the descriptions in the brochure were merely guides and not warranties.
3. Therefore Smith knew the risks and was aware of what could happen when he purchased the truck. Accordingly, the trial court's granting of summary judgment is affirmed.

Pell City Wood v. Forke Brothers Auctioneers, 474 So.2d 694 (Ala. 1985).

The buyer's examination of the goods or a sample or a model is also significant in determining the existence of implied warranties. If, before entering into the contract, the buyer has examined the goods, sample, or model as fully as he desired, there is no implied warranty on defects that an examination ought to have revealed [2-316(3)(b)]. If the seller demands that the buyer examine the goods fully, but the buyer refuses to do so, there is no implied warranty on those defects that a careful examination would have revealed. By making the demand, the seller is giving notice to the buyer that the buyer is assuming the risk with regard to defects an examination ought to reveal. However, the seller will not be protected if a demand has not been made and the buyer fails to examine the goods [2-316(3)(a)].

A course of dealing between the parties, course of performance, or usage of trade can also be the basis for exclusion or modification of implied warranties. These factors can be important in determining the nature and extent of implied warranties in any given transaction [2-316(3)(c)].

8. On Remedies

As noted in section 5, the Code also allows the parties to limit the remedies available in the event of a breach of warranty [2-719]. The agreement may provide for remedies in addition to, or in restriction of, those provided by the Code. The parties may also limit or alter the measure of damages. These provisions usually limit a buyer's damages to the repayment of the price upon return of the goods. Contracts often allow a seller to repair defective goods or replace nonconforming parts, without further liability. These provisions in effect eliminate a seller's liability for consequential damages and allow a seller to "cure" a defect or cancel a transaction by refunding the purchase price, without further liability.

Clauses limiting the liability of a seller are subject to the Code requirement on unconscionability [2-719]. Limitations of consequential damages for personal injury related to consumer goods are prima facie unconscionable. Limitations of damages for commercial loss are presumed to be valid.

OTHER ASPECTS OF WARRANTIES

9. Notice

The Code requires a buyer to give *notice* of any alleged breach of express or implied warranties [2-607(3)(a)]. This notice must be given within a reasonable time after the facts constituting the breach are discovered or should have been discovered using reasonable care. Failure to give the required notice bars all remedies. The giving of notice within a reasonable time to a seller is a condition precedent to filing a suit for damages for breach of express or implied warranties.

Policies. There are three policies behind the notice requirement. First, notice is required in order for the seller to exercise its right to cure. The seller should be given the opportunity to make adjustments to or replacement of defective products. Notice allows sellers to minimize their losses and the buyer's damages. For example, the purchaser of a computer with a defective part should not be allowed to wait several months and then sue for loss of use of the computer.

The second policy behind the notice requirement is to provide the seller an opportunity to arm itself for negotiation and litigation. The seller needs an opportunity to examine the product promptly so that it can defend itself against possible false allegations of breach of warranty. If a delay operates to deprive the seller of a reasonable opportunity to discover facts that might provide a defense or lessen its liability, the notice probably has not been given within a reasonable time.

The third policy to require the buyer to give notice of an alleged breach of warranty is to provide some psychological protection for sellers. They need to believe that their risk will end after a reasonable amount of time. The notice requirement is somewhat similar to a statute of limitations. Sellers know that after a time they can stop worrying about potential liability.

Form. The notice may be oral or in writing. Written notice is far preferable because it serves as its own proof. The notice need not be a claim for damages or a threat to file suit. All that is required is that the buyer notify the seller of the defect in the product. As a general rule, filing a lawsuit is not notice of breach of warranty, and lawsuits without prior notice are usually dismissed for failure to give the required notice. The notice of the breach of warranty requirement does not contemplate the buyer delivering a summons and complaint to the seller as notice. The Code provides no remedy for a breach of warranty until the buyer has given notice. Therefore, starting suit cannot constitute notice.

Time. The requirement that notice be given within a reasonable time is interpreted flexibly. The comments to the Code encourage courts not to close the door too quickly on ''retail consumers'' and especially those injured by defective products. The implication is that merchant-buyers are bound by a stricter notice requirement. A ''reasonable time'' for notification from retail consumer is to be judged by different standards so that in cases involving consumers it will be extended. The rule of requiring notification is not designed to deprive a good-faith consumer of his remedy, especially a consumer who suffered personal injury. In such cases, the notice policies collide with a countervailing policy that unsophisticated consumers who suffer real and perhaps grievous injury at the hands of the defendant-seller ought to have an easy road to recovery. The rule of requiring notification is designed to defeat commercial bad faith, not to deprive a good-faith consumer of his remedy.

10. Third Parties

Privity of contract. Historically, suits for breach of warranty required *privity of contract*, a contractual connection between the parties. Lack of privity of contract was a complete defense to a suit for breach of express warranty or for breach of the implied warranties. Two aspects of privity of contract requirements are sometimes described as horizontal and vertical. The *horizontal privity* issue is: To whom does the warranty extend? Does it run only in favor of the purchaser, or does it extend to others who may use or be affected by the product? The *vertical privity* issue is: Against whom can action be brought for breach of warranty? Can the party sue only the seller, or will direct action lie against wholesalers, manufacturers, producers, and growers?

When privity of contract is required, only the buyer can collect for breach of warranty, and he can collect only from the seller. A seller who is liable may recover from the person who sold to him. Thus the requirement of privity of contract not only prevented many suits for breach of warranty where privity did not exist but also encouraged multiple lawsuits over the same product.

Abandonment of privity. It is not surprising that the law has generally abandoned strict privity of contract requirements. It has done so by statute and also case by case. The abandonment has occurred in cases involving express warranties, as well as in cases involving implied warranties. Both horizontal and vertical privity have generally been eliminated or significantly reduced.

The drafters of the Code prepared three alternative provisions that states could adopt on horizontal privity [2-318]. Alternative A has been adopted by thirty jurisdictions. It provides that a warranty extends to any person in the family or household of the buyer or a guest in the home if it is reasonable to expect that such a person may consume, or be affected by, the goods and is injured by them.

Alternative B has been adopted in eight juristictions, and alternative C is the law in four states. The remaining states have either omitted the section entirely or have drafted their own version on the extent of the warranties. Alternative B and C extend warranties to any natural person who may be reasonably expected to use, consume, or be affected by the goods and who is injured by them.

These Code provisions on horizontal privity do not attempt to deal with the vertical privity issue. The Code is neutral on it and leaves the development of the law to the courts, case by case. The courts of most states have abandoned the privity of contract requirement, and persons injured by products are allowed to sue all businesses in the chain of distribution without regard to the presence of privity of contract. Some states have retained privity in suits seeking damages for economic loss even though they have abandoned it in suits for personal injuries. The following cases discusses both vertical and horizontal privity issues and illustrates the modern view on the demise of lack of privity as a defense.

CASE

Plaintiff purchased carpet for an apartment complex through an interior decorator, Lehman. Lehman in turn contracted with defendant for the purchase specifying details such as color and quality. Sometime after the carpet was installed it became apparent that the carpet was defective. Defendant refused to make any adjustment and when plaintiff sued for breach of implied warranty, the defendant moved to dismiss because of lack of privity of contract between the defendant and the plaintiff as the ultimate purchaser.

ISSUE: Is lack of privity of contract a defense?

DECISION: No.

REASONS: 1. The plaintiff is a purchaser of the goods and not a third-party beneficiary of the warranties. The issue here is vertical privity and not horizontal privity.

2. The issue of horizontal privity raises the question of whether persons other than buyer of defective goods can recover from the buyer's immediate seller on a warranty theory. The question of vertical privity is whether parties in the distributive chain prior to the immediate seller can be held liable to ultimate purchaser for loss caused by the defective product.
3. The code is silent and strictly neutral as to the necessity of vertical privity in applying implied warranties. It is up to courts to decide to what extent vertical privity of contract will be required.
4. To require vertical privity results in perpetuating a needless chain of actions whereby each buyer must seek redress from his immediate seller until the actual manufacturer is eventually reached.
5. Manufacturer may be held liable for breach of implied warranty of merchantability or fitness for particular purpose without regard to privity of contract between the manufacturer and the ultimate buyer. Plaintiff, being in the chain of distribution, may maintain a direct action against defendant to recover the benefit of his bargain in replacement of the carpet.

Old Albany Estates v. Highland Carpet Mills, 604 P.2d 849 (Okla. 1980).

CHAPTER SUMMARY

Types of Warranties

Express Warranties

1. An express warranty is a statement of fact or promise that is made as a part of the contract for sale and becomes a part of the basis of the bargain between the buyer and the seller.
2. Most statements of opinion, such as those concerning the value of the goods, do not give rise to an express warranty.
3. Express warranties may be statements about the goods in sales material or they may arise from a sale by sample or model.

Warranty of Title

1. A seller of goods makes a warranty that he has title to the goods and the right to sell them.
2. The warranty of title includes a warranty that there are no encumbrances and the buyer's use of the goods will be free from the claims of others.

Implied Warranty of Merchantability

1. A warranty that the goods shall be merchantable is implied in a contract for sale if the seller is a merchant who deals in goods of the kind involved in the contract.
2. For goods to be merchantable, they must at least be the kind of goods that are fit for the ordinary purposes for which such goods are used.
3. Liability for breach of the warranty of merchantability extends to direct economic loss, as well as to personal injuries and property damage.

Implied Warranty of Fitness for a Particular Purpose

1. An implied warranty of fitness for a particular purpose is created if, at the time of contracting, the seller has reason to know any particular purpose for which the buyer requires the goods and is relying on the seller's skill or judgment to select or furnish suitable goods.
2. The buyer need not specifically state that he has a particular purpose

in mind or that he is placing reliance on the seller's judgment if the circumstances are such that the seller has reason to realize the purpose intended or that the buyer is relying on him.

3. Breach of the warranty of fitness for a particular purpose may result in disaffirmance of the contract. If the product causes an injury including economic loss, it may also result in a suit for dollar damages.

Limitations

Of Express Warranties

1. If there is an express warranty and an attempt to limit warranties, both will be given effect if possible.
2. If not, the express warranty will prevail, and the attempt to negate it will not be given effect.

Written Disclaimers of Implied Warranties

1. To exclude or modify the implied warranty of merchantability, the word *merchantability* must be used. If the disclaimer is included in a written contract, it must be set forth in a conspicuous manner.
2. To exclude or modify any implied warranty of fitness for a particular purpose, the exclusion must be conspicuously written.
3. Disclaimers of warranties are subject to the Magnuson-Moss warranty law.

Other Exclusions of Implied Warranties

1. The Code also provides for other circumstances in which implied warranties may be wholly or partially excluded. The seller may inform the buyer that he is selling goods "as-is," "with all faults." Other language may call the buyer's attention to the exclusion and make it plain that the sale involves no implied warranty.
2. If, before entering into the contract, the buyer has examined the goods, sample, or model, there is no implied warranty on defects that an examination ought to have revealed to him [2-316(3)(b)].

On Remedies

1. Parties may agree to limit or alter the measure of damages.
2. Clauses limiting a seller's damages are subject to the Code rule on unconscionability.
3. Limiting consequential damages for personal injury is prima facie unconscionable.

Other Aspects of Warranties

Notice

1. A buyer must give notice of any breach of warranty within a reasonable time.
2. Failure to give notice prevents a suit for breach of warranty.
3. Filing suit is not notice.

Third Parties

1. The horizontal privity issue is: To whom does the warranty extend? In most states, it extends to any person in the family or household of the buyer or a guest in the home if it is reasonable to expect that such person may consume, or be affected by, the goods and is injured by them.
2. The vertical privity issue is: Against whom can action be brought for breach of warranty? The Code leaves the development of the law to the courts, case by case. The courts of most states have abandoned the vertical privity of contract requirement, and persons injured by products are allowed to sue all businesses in the chain of distribution without regard to the presence of privity of contract.

REVIEW QUESTIONS AND PROBLEMS

1. Identify the terms in column A by matching each with the appropriate statement in column B.

A	B
(1) Express warranty	(a) Made only by a merchant.
(2) Warranty of merchantability	(b) Arises because of special skill of the seller.
(3) Fungible goods	(c) To whom does the warranty extend?
(4) Warranty of fitness for a particular purpose	(d) A guarantee.
(5) Horizontal privity	(e) A condition precedent to a suit for breach of warranty.
(6) Vertical privity	(f) Sold by weight or measure.
(7) Notice	(g) Against whom can suit be brought?

2. A seller makes the following statements about goods to the buyer. Which are puffery and which are express warranties?
   a. The jukebox is a good machine and will probably not get out of order.
   b. October is not too late to plant this grass seed.
   c. This car is supposed to last a lifetime. It's in perfect condition.
   d. This dredge pipe has expandable ends that will seal upon the spill going through.
   e. This feed additive will increase your milk production and will not harm your dairy herd.
   f. These filter tanks should be able to remove iron and manganese from the water.
   g. This used car has never been wrecked.

3. Plaintiff sued the manufacturer of a backyard driving range for personal injuries. Plaintiff was hit on the head by a golf ball following a practice swing with the golf-training device. The label on the shipping carton stated in bold type: "**COMPLETELY SAFE—BALL WILL NOT HIT PLAYER.**" What theory did plaintiff use in this case? Explain.

4. Sumner, an Anchorage aircraft dealer, sold a Piper Navajo airplaine to Fel-Air, Inc., for $105,000. The title to the airplane was actually in Century Aircraft, Inc., which had leased it to Sumner with an option to purchase. Fel-Air sued Sumner for breach of the warranty of title. Sumner denied liability on the ground that Sumner as a good-faith purchaser for value received good title. Is Sumner liable? Why or why not?

5. In which of the following circumstances was the implied warranty of merchantability breached?
   a. In defendant's restaurant, plaintiff bought a martini with an unpitted olive. Plaintiff broke a tooth when he attempted to eat the olive.
   b. Plaintiff is bitten by a spider concealed in a pair of blue jeans sold by defendant's store.
   c. Seller sold cattle feed that contained the female hormone stilbestrol. It causes cattle to grow more rapidly than normal but also causes abortion in pregnant cows and sterility in bulls. The plaintiff farmer raises cattle for breeding rather than for slaughter, so he sues. The label on the cattle feed package did not mention that it contained stilbestrol.
   d. Plaintiff bought and used a power lawn mower. While the plaintiff was mowing, an unknown object was hurled out of the grass chute and penetrated the eye of plaintiff's five-year-old son.
   e. Plaintiff's Ford Pinto's gas tank exploded on impact.
   f. Plaintiff bought a cookbook from defendant retail book dealer. Four days later, while following a recipe in the book, plaintiff ate a small slice of one of the ingredients, a plant commonly known as elephant's ear, and became violently ill. Plaintiff sued for breach of the implied warranty of merchantability.
   g. Plaintiff bought a product that caused her to have an allergic reaction.

6. During training exercises, a marine was injured by a defective grenade. He sued the grenade manufacturer for breach of the implied warranty of merchantability. What result? Explain.

7. Stewart, a practicing dentist, sold his 42-foot Trojan yacht to Smith for $52,000. Three days after delivery of the boat, Smith notified Stewart that one of the boat's fuel tanks was leaking and requested that the condition be remedied at Stewart's expense. When Stewart refused, Smith sued Stewart for breach of the warranty of merchantability. What result? Explain.

8. Plaintiff, a hauler of scrap automobile bodies, bought a used truck from defendant. Defendant leases trucks but does not drive them. He operates a well-drilling business and does not have any particular expertise concerning diesel trucks. The engine blew up after the truck had been used for a short time, and plaintiff sued for breach of the warranty of fitness for a particular purpose. What result? Why?

9. An owner of cattle had them vaccinated by a veterinarian. The veterinarian purchased the vaccine from a drug company. The cattle became sick, and suit was filed against the drug company for breach of the warranty of fitness for a particular purpose. What result? Why?

10. Pat, the buyer of a tractor and backhoe, sued the seller for breach of the implied warranty of merchantability. The sales contract contained the following:

    The equipment covered hereby is sold subject only to the applicable manufacturer's standard printed warranty and no other warranties, express or implied, including the implied warranty of merchantability, shall apply.

    The type size of the foregoing was slightly larger than the rest of the contract, but it was not boldface. Was the disclaimer effective to negate the implied warranty? Explain.

11. The purchase agreement for a mobile home stated **Standard Manufacturer Warranty—** **OTHERWISE SOLD AS IS.** The buyer subsequently discovered defects and sued for breach of the implied warranty of merchantability. He contended that the disclaimer was ineffective because it did not contain the word *merchantability* and was not conspicuous. Was the buyer correct? Why or why not?

12. Plaintiff sued the manufacturer for breach of implied warranty allegedly resulting from the use and application of a herbicide. The plaintiff did not purchase the herbicide or take possession of it. He did not see the package container of the product. He merely had defendant's distributor apply it to his farmland. The container had a disclaimer of warranty printed in bold letters on its side. The herbicide severely damaged plaintiff's corn crop. Is the disclaimer of warranty effective? Why?

13. Pam purchased a contaminated cheeseburger from a vending machine where she worked. She suffered acute food poisoning and sued the baking company that baked the bun, for breach of the warranty of merchantability. It moved to dismiss for lack of privity of contract. Is lack of privity of contract a defense? Explain.

14. Crew members of a fishing vessel sued manufacturers for losses allegedly caused by manufacturers' constructing and selling a vessel with a defective rudder and component parts, resulting in the vessel's returning to shore for repairs. They sued for breach of express warranty. The seller moved to dismiss for lack of privity of contract. With what result? Why?

20 Products Liability

CHAPTER PREVIEW

- **GENERAL CONCEPTS**

Basic Principles
History of Products Liability
Trespass • Negligence • Privity • Demise of privity • Warranty • Strict liability in tort
Theories of Liability
Negligence
Res ipsa loquitur • Negligence *per se* • Failure to warn • Negligent design
Misrepresentation

- **STRICT LIABILITY**

Theory
Product Defined
Defect
Sources of product defects • Characteristics of an "adequate" warning • Consumer expectations test • Definition of defective
Proof Required
Defenses
Comparative negligence • Assumption of the risk • Misuse and abnormal use • State of the art
Comparison of Strict Tort and Warranty

BUSINESS MANAGEMENT DECISION

You are the manager responsible for the design of a proposed toy gun. To achieve a sense of realism, your design engineers envision this gun being able to fire plastic "bullets" the approximate size of real bullets.

Do you have any concerns about this proposed design?

GENERAL CONCEPTS

Products liability is a legal term that describes the liability of sellers and manufacturers of goods. One of the consequences of manufacturing or selling a product is responsibility to a consumer or user if the product is defective and causes injury to a person or to property. Injuries to property include damage to the product itself, economic losses due to the inadequate performance of the product, and injuries to the property of others.

The subject of products liability involves several legal theories. A suit for dollar damages for injuries caused by a product may be predicated on the theory of negligence; misrepresentation; breach of warranty, either express or implied; or strict liability. The legal principles relating to breach of warranty are discussed in Chapter 19 in detail. You should keep that discussion clearly in mind as a major portion of the law on products liability. The other theories and the reasons for products liability are discussed in this chapter.

1. Basic Principles

The basic principle of products liability is that a manufacturer, distributor, or seller of a product is liable to compensate a person injured by a defective product. The mere occurrence of an injury due to a product does not automatically impose liability. A manufacturer or seller is not an insurer of the safety of persons using products. They do not guarantee the safety of the consumer of their product. Products liability is not absolute liability. It is present only if there has been a violation of a legal duty to the consumer or user, and that duty is to keep a defective product out of the stream of commerce.

Products liability cases may arise out of defective design of products, defective manufacture, or the defective marketing of products. Suit may be brought against manufacturers of component parts, raw materials suppliers, anyone who provides supportive services (such as certifying, applying, or installing a product), wholesalers, and jobbers. They may be brought by the buyer, by another user of the product, or by some third party whose only connection with the product is an injury caused by it.

In most products liability cases, the injured party sues all those in the channel of distribution, including the manufacturer, the wholesaler, the distributor, and the retailer. In cases involving multiple defendants, the burden of tracing fault is on the defendant dealers and manufacturer, so that a plaintiff may be compensated while leaving it to the defendants to settle the question of responsibility among themselves. Anyone who had a hand in putting the defective product in the stream of commerce, whether technically innocent or not, may have liability to the injured party.

The trend of the law on products liability is clearly in the direction of expanding liability. A manufacturer has an obligation to the public to market a safe product, free from defects. A producer is presumed to know of defects in its products and is therefore in bad faith in selling defective products. Moreover, there is a growing philosophy that the losses caused by products must be shared by business. This shift of responsibility is premised on the notion that manufacturers and sellers best understand their products and are better able to spread the loss as a cost of production and sale. When loss is written into the cost of the product, it is shared by all buyers and users of the product. The philosophy of *shared loss*—together with the increased complexity of many products and the increased chance of errors in design, manufacturing, and marketing—has dramatically enlarged the number of products liability cases in the last two decades.

The potential liability is usually covered by products liability insurance. In recent years, the cost of this insurance has skyrocketed, and it has become a significant cost item in many products with a high exposure to products liability suits. To understand products liability law and to predict its future, we turn first to its historical development.

2. History of Products Liability

Although it cannot be precisely stated when products liability law began, it seems to have evolved through these five stages:

1. Trespass (strict tort liability)
2. Negligence (tort liability)
3. Privity (*caveat emptor*)
4. Warranty (contract liability)
5. Strict liability in tort [402A]

As you can see, the law has come full circle from its origins in strict liability, since it is now based on strict liability for defective products that cause harm.

Trespass. Prior to 1800, there were few manufacturerd products and little commerce. Times were simple, and the law reflected the values of small, interdependent communities. Injuries to persons or property were compensated by law through the tort doctrine of trespass. The trespass doctrine imposed strict liability; that is, the fact that defendant was not at fault was irrelevant.

Negligence. In the 1800s, small village life underwent dramatic changes. Population mushroomed, social and economic life grew complex, and the Industrial Revolution was born. As society's values changed, so did the law. Apparently premised on the notion that infant industries needed protection from widespread liability, the law replaced strict liability in trespass with negligence law. Product manufacturers were liable only if they failed to use "reasonable care" in the manufacture and sale of their products. But eliminating strict liability in tort apparently was not enough protection for these industries. The potential for products liability at that time was great, owing to the numerous sweatshops, factories with unguarded machinery tended by little children, and food products unregulated by government. Privity was born in 1842 to limit further products liability actions.

Privity *The connection or relationship between contracting parties.*

Privity. In 1842, the English court in *Winterbottom* v. *Wright* imposed the **privity** barrier, lest the courts be faced with ''an infinity of actions.'' The English court held that the injured driver of a defective mail coach could not maintain an action against the supplier of the coach, because no ''privity of contract'' existed between the driver and the supplier. Nineteenth-century American courts, with a similar reluctance to inhibit the free scope of industrial enterprise, generally followed the privity doctrine of *Winterbottom.*

The privity requirement limits the negligence action, since sellers owe the ''reasonable-person'' duty only to parties with whom they had actually dealt, that is, to parties with whom they had contracted. If an injured person was not the buyer of the product or had bought the product from a retailer, then the manufacturer was not liable, since no privity of contract would exist. Moreover, the retailer who was in privity could be liable only for negligence. However, the defective product was seldom the fault of the retailer who had not designed, manufactured, labeled, or packaged the product. Thus the privity rule in most cases puts the risk of harm on the injured party. The period was characterized by the rule of *caveat emptor,* ''Let the buyer beware.''

Demise of privity. With the advent of the twentieth century, infant industries matured, the United States became more prosperous, and the number and complexity of products expanded. The policy of protecting industry more than society became inapplicable, and the barrier of privity was soon dismantled first in tort, then in contract. The death knell of the privity doctrine in tort was sounded in the famous 1916 case of *MacPherson* v. *Buick Motor Company.* MacPherson was driving a Buick automobile when a wooden wheel collapsed, injuring him. (Note the factual similarity to *Winterbottom*). The defendant was the manufacturer who had sold the car to the retailer who sold the car to MacPherson. In the nineteenth century, American courts had recognized exceptions to the privity rule when products—such as drugs, foods, guns, and explosives—were ''inherently'' or ''imminently'' dangerous to life or health. The New York court in *MacPherson* found that the category of inherently dangerous products ''is not limited to poisons, explosives, and things which in their normal operation are implements of destruction.'' Rather, it held that if ''the nature of a thing is such that it is reasonably certain to place life and limb in peril when negligently made, it is then a thing of danger.'' The privity doctrine of *Winterbottom* was effectively overruled when the court stated: ''If to the element of danger there is added knowledge that the thing will be used by persons other than the purchaser, and used without new tests, then, irrespective of contract, the manufacturer of this thing of danger is under a duty to make it carefully.'' *MacPherson* has been universally followed.

Warranty. The demise of privity in contract law was not so easily accomplished, because the claim in contract was based on a theory of breach of warranty. The problem was that since the warranty theory seemed to be more in the nature of a contract right, only parties to the contract could supposedly enforce contract rights. But over time, courts were forced to adapt legal doctrine to the realities of modern marketing. The breakthrough came in the famous 1960 case of *Henningsen* v. *Bloomfield Motors, Inc.*, which is factually similar to *Winterbottom* and *MacPherson.* Mrs. Henningsen was injured when the new family car (a 1955 Plymouth ten days old with 488 odometer miles) uncontrollably left the road owing to a defective steering wheel. The New Jersey Supreme Court said: "Where the commodities sold are such that if defectively manufactured they will be dangerous to life or limb, then society's interests can only be protected by eliminating the requirement of privity between the maker and his dealers and the reasonably expected ultimate consumer." In *Henningsen*, the injured plaintiff was not the buyer of the car and therefore was not "in the distributive chain." In addition to eliminating the necessity of establishing privity between the buyer and seller, the court also held that Mrs. Henningsen, whose husband had bought the car, could maintain an action against the remote manufacturer.

The significance of the *Henningsen* principle is recognized in the Uniform Commercial Code. As noted in Chapter 19, the UCC extends the seller's warranties to parties who are not buyers of the products. But procedural problems with warranty liability, like notice of breach, caused many plaintiffs to be denied recovery. Thus one final dismantling stage remained before the law of products liability came full circle to strict tort liability.

Strict liability in tort. The year 1963 is generally regarded as the decisive date in the evolution of products liability law. Prior to that date, actions for injuries caused by defective products were based on negligence or breach of warranty. In 1963, the California Supreme Court, in the following case, adopted a theory of strict liability in tort.

CASE

Plaintiff brought this action for damages against the retailer and the manufacturer of a Shopsmith, a combination power tool that can be used as a saw, drill, and wood lathe. He saw a Shopsmith demonstrated by the retailer and studied a brochure prepared by the manufacturer. He decided he wanted a Shopsmith for his home workshop, and his wife bought and gave him one for Christmas in 1955. In 1957, he bought the necessary attachments to use the Shopsmith as a lathe for turning a large piece of wood he wished to make into a chalice. After he had worked on the piece of wood several times without difficulty, it suddenly flew out of the machine and struck him on the forehead, inflicting serious injuries. About ten and a half months later, he gave the retailer and the manufacturer written notice of claimed breaches of warranties and filed a complaint against them alleging such breaches and negligence.

ISSUE: Was this plaintiff required to prove a breach of a warranty or negligence to recover from the manufacturer for his injuries?

DECISION: No.

REASONS:
1. Expert witnesses testified that inadequate set screws were used to hold parts of the machine together so that normal vibration caused the tailstock to the lathe to move away from the piece of wood being turned, allowing it to fly out of the lathe.
2. A manufacturer is strictly liable in tort when an article placed on the market proves to have a defect that causes injury to a human being.
3. The purpose of strict liability is to ensure that the costs of injuries resulting from defective products are borne by manufacturers rather than by the injured persons.
4. To establish the manufacturer's liability, it was sufficient that plaintiff

proved that he, while using the Shopsmith in a way it was intended to be used, was injured due to a defect in the design or manufacture.

Greenman v. Yuba Power Products, inc., (377 P.2d 897 (Calif. 1963).

As a result of this case, *Greenman*, tort law is now evolving with a theory of strict liability steadfastly independent of warranty. In 1965, Section 402A of the Restatement (Second) of Torts was promulgated. Section 402A, adopted by the majority of American courts, follows the strict tort liability theory of *Greenman*. This theory is covered in detail later in this chapter.

3. Theories of Liability

As noted, both tort and contract theories are used in products liability cases. A defendant may be held liable under the contract theories of breach of express or implied warranty. The implied warranty may be either the implied warranty of merchantability or the implied warranty of fitness for a particular purpose. Most cases involve the warranty of merchantability. As noted in Chapter 19, an action can be maintained for breach of both express and implied warranty without privity of contract in most cases. An action based on such breach, being a contract action, does not require proof of negligence on the part of manufacturer or seller. A defendant in a products liability case may be found to have breached its warranty of merchantability without having been negligent.

As Table 20–1 explains, products liability cases may be based on conduct of the defendant, quality of the product, or performance of the product against the seller's promises or express representations. These may apply to both contract and tort actions.

A plaintiff, in bringing a products liability lawsuit, does not have to choose between these tort and contract theories, since all the theories may be joined into one lawsuit. Nonetheless, most plaintiffs prefer strict tort liability because it is usually the simplest remedy, as is explained later. At trial, a plaintiff may be forced to choose which theories are to be submitted to the jury. Damages incurred are sometimes not recoverable under strict liability, owing to either their nature or the

TABLE 20–1 THEORIES OF PRODUCTS LIABILITY

	Defendant's Conduct	Quality of Product	Seller's Representations
Tort	Negligence	Strict liability for product defects (402A Restatement of Torts)	Strict liability for public misrepresentations (402B Restatement of Torts)
Contract	None	Implied warranty of merchantability (UCC 2-314) and fitness (UCC 2-315)	Express warranty (UCC 2-313)

running of the tort statute of limitations. The statute of limitations for tort actions is generally a much shorter time period than it is for contract actions. However, the rights afforded by express and implied warranties may be more difficult to assert because of the contractual rules of notice of breach and disclaimers of warranties. Thus all theories are important, and each has advantages and disadvantages in comparison with the others.

4. Negligence

Contributory negligence *In a negligence suit, failure of the plaintiff to use reasonable care.*

Comparative negligence *Under this doctrine, a plaintiff's negligence is compared to that of a defendant. The plaintiff's right to recover against the defendant is reduced by the percentage of the plaintiff's negligence.*

Negligence is a tort theory used in products liability cases. In order to recover on a negligence theory, a plaintiff has to establish the failure of the defendant to exercise reasonable care. **Contributory negligence** on the part of the plaintiff in some states is a bar to recovery. In others, which follow **comparative negligence**, it will reduce the amount of recovery by the percentage of the plaintiff's fault.

The mere fact that an injury occurs from the consumption or use of a product does not ordinarily raise a presumption that the manufacturer was negligent. Negligence actions question the reasonableness of the defendant's conduct since all human activity involves an element of risk. The defendant's conduct is deemed negligent only when it is inferior to what a "reasonable" person would have done under similar circumstances. Negligence involves conduct that falls below the standard set by law for the protection of others against the unreasonably great risk of harm.

In a negligence action, privity of contract is not required, since it is not a contract action. A negligence suit can be brought not only by the person who purchased the defective product but also by any person who suffered an injury on account of a defect in the product if the defect was the proximate cause of his injury.

The Restatement of Torts (Second), Section 395, states the rules as follows:

> A manufacturer who fails to exercise reasonable care in the manufacture of a chattel which, unless carefully made, he should recognize as involving an unreasonable risk of causing physical harm to those who use it for a purpose for which the manufacturer should expect it to be used and to those whom he should expect to be endangered by its probable use, is subject to liability for physical harm caused to them by its lawful use in a manner and for a purpose for which it is supplied.

Res ipsa loquitur. The plaintiff, of course, must by appropriate evidence prove that the manufacturer was negligent—failed to exercise reasonable care. He may be able to rely on the doctrine of *res ipsa loquitur*, "the thing speaks for itself," if (1) the instrumentality involved was within the exclusive control of the defendant at the time of the act of negligence, both as to operation and inspection; (2) the injury was not the result of any voluntary action or contribution on the part of the plaintiff; and (3) the accident ordinarily would not have occurred had the defendant used due care. If an elevator falls, killing an occupant, the manufacturer has liability, because the very happening of the accident creates a presumption of negligence.

Negligence *per se*. Another method of establishing negligence is to prove that the manufacturer violated some statutory regulation in the production and distribution of his product. Some industries are subject to regulation under state or federal laws on product quality, testing, advertising, and other aspects of production and distribution. Proof of a violation of a statute may be sufficient to establish negligence of a manufacturer in such industries. Negligence established by proof of violation of a statute is called *negligence per se*.

Failure to warn. Negligence is frequently based on failure of a manufacturer to warn of a known danger related to the product. A manufacturer who knows, or should know, his product to be dangerous has a duty to exercise reasonable care and foresight in preventing it from injuring or endangering people. Reasonable care includes the duty to warn of the danger.

Negligent design. Negligence also may be based on a design defect. In determining whether a manufacturer exercised reasonable skill and knowledge concerning the design of its product, factors include the cost of safety devices, their use by competitors, their effect or function, and the extent to which the manufacturer conducted tests and kept abreast of scientific development. A manufacturer is not an insurer, nor is he required to supply accident proof merchandise; nonetheless, the responsibilities for injuries often rest with whoever is in the best position to eliminate the danger inherent in the use of the product. For example, a manufacturer of a rotary power lawn mower may be liable for negligent design if a user is able to put his hands or feet in contact with the moving blades of the mower.

5. Misrepresentation

Another tort theory used in product liability cases is known as misrepresentation. If the seller has advertised the product through newspapers, magazines, television, or otherwise and has made misrepresentations with regard to the character or quality of the product, tort liability for personal injury may be imposed on him. The Restatement of Torts (Second), Section 402B, summarizes the liability of a seller for personal injuries resulting from misrepresentation:

> One engaged in the business of selling chattels who, by advertising, labels, or otherwise, makes to the public a misrepresentation of a material fact concerning the character or quality of a chattel sold by him is subject to liability for physical harm to a consumer of the chattel caused by justifiable reliance upon the misrepresentation, even though
> (a) it is not made fraudulently or negligently, and
> (b) the consumer has not bought the chattel from or entered into any contractual relation with the seller.

The rationale of the Restatement position is that a great deal of what the consumer knows about a product comes to him through the various media, and sellers should be held responsible for injuries caused by misrepresentations made to the public.

In our complex society where sellers offer apparently similar but in reality fundamentally different products, the rationale behind the rule is most persuasive. A manufacturing seller knows the capabilities of his products, for he is the one who has designed and tested them. The consumer, on the other hand, knows only the information he has been able to glean from the seller's marketing material. Logic dictates, then, that the seller should bear the responsibility for his misrepresentation because of his superior knowledge.

Liability under Section 402B does not depend on the factors giving rise to the misrepresentation, nor does it require contractual privity. It is a rule of strict liability, which, even in the absence of bad faith or negligence, makes sellers liable if a consumer of their product suffers physical harm as a result of justifiable reliance on the seller's misrepresentation.

CASE

Winkler was an officer in the Denver Police Department. As permitted by department policy, he obtained for his own personal use a helmet, which, because of its appearance, had been discarded by the department. The helmet, manufactured by the defendant, was originally purchased by the Denver Police Department for use in crowd or riot control. It was originally packaged in a carton that depicted a motorcyclist wearing the helmet. Winkler, prior to acquiring his helmet, had become familiar with the cartons in which they were originally delivered. Believing that the helmet was intended for motorcycle use, Winkler used the helmet for that purpose. While riding his motorcycle, he collided with a pickup truck. Upon impact, the helmet, performing as designed (i.e., for quick release), came off of his head, and as a result he suffered head injuries. Although the helmet performed as designed, Winkler claims that it did not perform as represented on the packaging carton, that is, as a motorcycle helmet. It is this asserted misrepresentation upon which Winkler bases a cause of action.

ISSUE: Is the defendant liable for misrepresentation?

DECISION: Yes.

REASONS:

1. The Restatement (Second) of Torts, Section 402B, imposes strict tort liability upon sellers of products that are *not* defective in design or manufacture but are misrepresented to the consuming public.
2. Under Section 402B the seller of chattels who misrepresents material facts concerning their character or quality is subject to liability for the physical harm caused to a consumer who relies on the misrepresentation.
3. When a product fails to perform to the level, or in the manner that the consumer has been led, by the seller to believe it will, and that failure causes physical harm, the seller is liable for that harm.

Winkler v. American Safety Equipment Corp., 604 P.2d 693 (Colo. App. 1980).

STRICT LIABILITY

6. Theory

The latest development in products liability is the tort theory known as strict liability. This development imposes liability wherever damage or injury is caused by a defective product that is unreasonably dangerous to the user or consumer. It is the logical result of the elimination of the need to prove negligence and of the demise of the privity requirement in breach of warranty actions. The strict tort liability action is often preferable to the warranty action because disclaimers of warranty and notice of breach are not problems. As a result, in states that have adopted the strict liability theory, the theories of negligence and breach of warranty are becoming less significant in personal injury cases.

The theory of strict tort liability was developed by legal scholars as a part of the Restatement of the Law of Torts. Section 402A of the Restatement (Second) provides the following:

> 402A. Special Liability of Seller of Product for Physical Harm to User or Consumer.
>
> (1) One who sells any product in a defective condition unreasonably dangerous to the user or consumer, or to his property, is subject to liability for physical harm thereby caused to the ultimate user or consumer, or to his property if
> (a) the seller is engaged in the business of selling such a product, and
> (b) it is expected to and does reach the user or consumer without substantial change in the condition in which it is sold.
>
> (2) The rule stated in Subsection (1) applies although
> (a) the seller has exercised all possible care in the preparation and sale of his product, and
> (b) the user or consumer has not bought the product from or entered into any contractual relation with the seller.

The courts have relied heavily on these rules in developing the law of strict tort liability. Today, it is the law in most states.

Strict liability is imposed on manufacturers and designers, as well as on the seller of the goods. While in many states it is not applicable to the sale of used goods, there is a definite trend toward applying it to used goods. In almost every state, the liability extends not only to users and consumers but also to bystanders such as pedestrians. Strict liability has been applied both to personal injuries and to damage to the property of the user or consumer. Some courts have refused to extend it to property damage, and most courts have refused to extend it to economic loss.

The theory of strict liability has been applied to leases of goods as well as to sales. The potential liability extends to all commercial suppliers of goods.

7. Product Defined

The question of the scope and substance of the term *product* as used in strict liability cases has received considerable discussion in recent decisions. Originally, product was confined to chattels (tangible personal property), such as food for human consumption or other products intended for intimate bodily use. Using the chattel concept, many courts have had no trouble in finding many items to be products: a can of Drano, baseball sunglasses, a carpenter's hammer, and a Corvair. But with the progress of technology and changing notions of justice and strict liability, case law has progressed so that terms like *defect* and *product* remain open-ended. Recently, blood, electricity, hot water drawn from a faucet, X-radiation, and a lot "manufactured" by considerable earthmoving have been held to be products—at least in the sense that the theory of strict liability has been applied to them. Courts now focus on the public policy reasons underlying strict products liability, and they label the transaction as the sale of a product when those policies apply.

Public policy considerations advanced to support strict products liability include (1) public interest in human life and health; (2) the special responsibility of one who markets a defective product that causes harm; (3) invitations and solicitations by the manufacturer to purchase the product and representations that it is safe and suitable for use; and (4) the justice of imposing the loss on the party who created the risk and reaped the benefit by placing the item in the stream of commerce.

Note that *product* also includes its container, whether or not sold with the product. A restaurant was held strictly liable for the injuries to a customer's hand when a wine glass shattered. Moreover, a gas company that furnished a gas tank incidental to the sale of gas had to assume responsibility for injuries caused by the defective tank.

8. Defect

Sources of product defects. Product defects arise from three sources. The first and most basic is the *production defect*, arising from an error during the manufacture of the product. Production defects generally are easy to recognize. The classic example is the soft-drink bottle that explodes because of an imperfection in the glass of the bottle or inadvertent overcarbonization. A production defect, therefore, occurs when the product does not meet the manufacturer's own standards.

The second source of product defect is *design defect*. In contrast to the production defect, the product meets the standard the manufacturer intended. In a design case, the injured plaintiff will allege that the design or the manufacturer's standards were inferior and should be judged defective. The plaintiff, in order to prove that a particular product is defective in design, must show that there was some practical way in which the product could have been made safer.

Finally, there is the product that is made as intended according to a design that could not be improved but has some characteristic not brought to the attention of the user or consumer. There has been a failure to warn. A *failure to warn* (*marketing defect*) is the third source of product defect. The duty of the manufacturer to provide adequate warnings and directions for use is a prolific source of litigation today, as the following case illustrates.

CASE

In June 1974, Edward Illosky purchased a 1966 Ford Mustang from a neighbor for his daughter Karen to drive to work. At this time, Karen was twenty-two years old. At the time of purchase, the automobile was equipped with Michelin radial tires on the rear axle and either radial or conventional tires on the front axle.

At his daughter's request, Mr. Illosky took the automobile to Ferguson's Tire Company on October 22, 1974, to purchase snow tires and to have them mounted on the rear axle. Mr. Illosky purchased two recapped conventional snow tires, and a Ferguson employee mounted them on the rear axle. At Mr. Illosky's direction, the employee moved the radial tires on the rear axle to the front axle because the rear tires carried more tread than the front tires. As a result, the automobile was then equipped with radial tires on the front axle and conventional snow tires on the rear axle. Ferguson's employee did not advise Mr. Illosky that mixing tire types in this manner was not recommended or that it could create a driving condition that could result in injury.

Later that day Karen was traveling at between 20 and 30 miles per hour when she was unable to control her automobile, and it left the highway, crashing into a utility pole. She was seriously injured and sued Michelin, using the theory of strict liability. She alleged that the failure to provide an adequate warning of the dangers of mixing of tires constituted a defect that made the radial tires unreasonably dangerous.

ISSUE: Does the failure to warn create a defective product for strict liability purposes?

DECISION: Yes.

REASONS:

1. The general test for establishing strict liability in tort is whether the involved product is defective in the sense that it is not reasonably safe for its intended use. The standard of reasonable safeness is determined not by the particular manufacturer, but by what a reasonably prudent manufacturer's standards should have been at the time the product was made.
2. Use defectiveness covers situations when a product may be safe as designed and manufactured, but which becomes defective because of the failure to warn of dangers that may be present when the product is used in a particular manner.
3. For the duty to warn to exist, the use of the product must be foreseeable to the manufacturer or seller.
4. This case fits the use defectiveness category. When radials are used in combination with conventional tires in certain instances, they become dangerous, and the manufacturer or other responsible party has a duty to warn of the danger and its potential consequences.
5. This use was foreseeable and the defendant was aware of the hazard.

Illosky v. Michelin Tire Corp., 307 S.E.2d 603 (W.Va. 1983).

Characteristics of an "adequate" warning. To be ''adequate,'' the warning must have two characteristics. First, it must be in such a *form* that it could reasonably be expected to catch the attention of a reasonable person in the context of its use. Second, the *content* of the warning must be comprehensible to the average user and must convey with a degree of *intensity* that would cause a prudent person to exercise caution commensurate with the potential danger. In sum, a warning may be inadequate in factual context, inadequate in expression of facts, or inadequate in the method by which it is conveyed. But note that a manufacturer or seller is not required to warn of dangers that are known or should be known by the user of the product.

Consumer expectations test. Since any attempt to define *defect* in generalized terms can be misleading, many courts adopt a *consumer expectations test*. Other courts use a *risk/utility test*, which provides that a product is unreasonably dangerous if the risk outweighs its utility.

Under the consumer expectations or contemplation test, a product that meets all demands and expectations of society but nonetheless injures someone can hardly be the fault of the manufacturer. A manufacturer is not absolutely liable. It is not an insurer. As consumers, we know and expect some products to be dangerous.

Cars kill pedestrians; knives cut fingers; cigarettes cause cancer. These products are considered dangerous, but that fact does not make them defective. A product is defective when it does not meet the standards of safety consumers expect.

Definition of defective. Section 402A, in part, provides: "One who sells any product in a defective condition *unreasonably dangerous* to the user or consumer or to his property is subject to liability for physical harm thereby caused to the ultimate user or consumer, or to his property." The majority of courts regard the idea of "unreasonably dangerous" as inseparable from the definition of defect.

Under the comments to Section 402A, a product is defective when "it is in a condition not contemplated by the ultimate consumer, which will be unreasonably dangerous to him." A product may be found to be unreasonably dangerous when it is "dangerous to the extent beyond that which would be contemplated by the ordinary consumer." We expect that real butter, fatty meat, and good whiskey may be dangerous, but not unreasonably so. The term *defective* as interpreted by courts is applied to an almost endless variety of product design, function, and performance contexts. The following case is one example of a potentially defective product and the importance of a proper definition of *defective*.

CASE

Plaintiff suffered severe burns on his right leg when a spark from his arc welding equipment penetrated his coveralls and ignited his quilted, insulated underwear. He sued the distributor of the underwear on a strict liability theory. From a judgment for the defendant, Spencer appealed, claiming error not to instruct the jury on the word *defective*.

ISSUE: Must the trial judge instruct the jury as to the meaning of "defective" in terms of the particular factual situation?

DECISION: Yes. Reversed and remanded for a new trial.

REASONS:

1. Without knowing the meaning of "defective," the jury could not comprehend plaintiff's theory of recovery.
2. While courts employ various definitions for "defective," the court here should have instructed the jury that a garment is defective (1) if its ignitability is extraordinary, i.e., it burns more rapidly or intensely than conventional clothing and is thereby unreasonably dangerous; or (2) if it bears no warning as to the extraordinary hazards associated with its use."

Spencer v. Nelson Sales Co., Inc., 620 P.2d 477 (Okla. 1980).

9. Proof Required

To establish that a defendant is strictly liable, the plaintiff must establish that the product was defective, as just discussed. In addition, the plaintiff must prove the following:

1. The defect existed at the time the product left the defendant's control.
2. The defect caused plaintiff's injury.

Assuming the plaintiff proves the existence of a defective product, a cause of action in strict liability also requires proof that the defective product reached the plaintiff without a change of condition and that the product caused an injury to the plaintiff. For a manufacturer to have liability, the product must be defective at the time it left the manufacturer's possession. A manufacturer may introduce evidence that the product was substantially altered after leaving its possession, which evidence may rebut or overcome plaintiff's showing that his injuries were the result of the product's defect. However, before a manufacturer is put to the trouble and expense of establishing that its product was altered, the plaintiff in most cases must first establish that the product was defective when it left the manufacturer's possession.

There are a few exceptions where such proof would be impossible. For example, a victim of a propane gas explosion was not required to prove the condition of the propane gas when it left the manufacturer. The court in that case held that a plaintiff's burden on the issue of defect is limited to proof that the defect that rendered the product unreasonably dangerous to the user or consumer occurred in the course of the distribution process and before the plaintiff purchased the product. In the case of a product sold in bulk, such as propane, this burden is satisfied by evidence showing that the product was defective and unreasonably dangerous when purchased or when put to use within a reasonable time after purchase.

Even if a plaintiff proves injury from a product, he cannot recover without proving causation between that defect and the injury. As previously noted, the defect must have existed when the product left the seller's hands. A seller is not liable if a safe product is made unsafe by subsequent changes. All of a plaintiff's proof may be made by circumstantial evidence.

The crucial difference between strict liability and negligence is that the existence of due care, on the part of the seller, is irrelevant in strict liability cases. The seller is responsible for injury caused by his defective product, even if he has exercised all possible care in the preparation and sale of the product. The duty of a seller is not fulfilled by taking all reasonable measures to make the product safe. The strict liability issue focuses on whether the product was defective and unreasonably dangerous and not on the conduct of the seller.

In strict liability cases there are no issues on disclaimer or warranties, there is no problem of inconsistency with express warranties, and knowledge of the seller of the defect need not be proved. Of course, privity of contract is not required, and neither is reliance on a warranty by the injured party.

10. Defenses

Strict liability is not synonymous with *absolute liability*. There must be proof that some dangerous defect caused the injury, despite the fact that the product was being used in the manner reasonably anticipated by the seller or the manufacturer. In addition, there are defenses that may be asserted to avoid liability. It is often said that contributory negligence is not a defense to a suit based on the theory of strict liability. This is somewhat of an oversimplification, however, because misuse of a product is a defense. Moreover, a person who voluntarily encounters a known unreasonable danger is not entitled to recover. A seller of a product is entitled to have his due warnings and instructions followed; when they are disregarded and injury results, the seller is not liable. Moreover, when a user unreasonably proceeds to use a product he knows to be defective or dangerous, he relinquishes the protection of the law. There is no duty on the part of manufacturers to create products that will insure against injury to the most indifferent, adventurous, or foolhardy people.

Comparative negligence. In recent years, a doctrine known as *comparative negligence* has replaced contributory negligence in tort cases based on negligence. Under comparative negligence, an injured person's recovery is reduced by his share of fault. For example, if a plaintiff is 20 percent at fault and the defendant is 80 percent at fault, a plaintiff is entitled to recover only 80 percent of the damages sustained. Today, some courts, as in the following case, are applying comparative negligence to suits based on strict liability.

CASE

Jasper died as a result of injuries sustained while operating a hydraulic aerial work platform manufactured by defendant, J.L.G. Industries, Inc. Plaintiff, administrator of Jasper's estate, filed suit based on a strict products liability theory. Defendant asserted that Jasper was guilty of comparative negligence or fault in his operation of the platform. It also contended that Jasper's employer was also guilty of comparative negligence in failing to instruct and train Jasper on the operation of the platform and by failing to provide a groundman. In these defenses, defendant requested that its fault, if any, be compared to the total fault of all parties and any judgment against defendant reflect only its percentage of the overall liability (i.e., that defendant not be held jointly and severally liable).

ISSUE: Is the doctrine of comparative negligence applicable in strict product liability suits?

DECISION: Yes.

REASONS:
1. The imposition of strict liability does not make the manufacturer an absolute insurer. The plaintiff must prove that the injury or damage resulted from the condition of the product, that the condition was an unreasonably dangerous one, and that the condition existed at the time the product left the manufacturer's control.
2. A manufacturer can assert a user's negligence as a complete bar to recovery when it rises to the level of misuse of the product, or assumption of the risk; but contributory negligence is not a defense.
3. Comparative negligence is adopted in negligence cases in order to produce a desirable and just distribution of losses. If followed in negligence cases and not in strict liability cases, there would be different results on the same facts.
4. Comparative fault does not lessen a manufacturer's duty to produce reasonably safe products. Its responsibility for damages is lessened only by the extent to which the trier of fact finds that the consumer's conduct contributed to the injuries.
5. The risk associated with the product defect is still spread among all consumers. Only that portion due to plaintiff's own conduct or fault is borne by the plaintiff. Where the allocation of losses properly can be apportioned, there is no reason to spread the

cost of the loss resulting from plaintiff's own fault on to the consuming public.

6. Comparative negligence retains the principle of joint and several liability. Thus the fault of some other party does not reduce plaintiff's claim.

Coney v. J.L.G. Industries, Inc., 454 N.E.2d 197 (Ill. 1983).

For purposes of comparative negligence, negligence of the plaintiff is not a defense when such negligence consists merely in a failure to discover the defect in the product or to guard against the possibility of its existence. A consumer's unobservant, inattentive, ignorant, or awkward failure to discover or guard against a defect is not a damage-reducing factor. The consumer or user is entitled to believe that the product will do the job for which it was built.

When comparative negligence is used, the defenses of misuse and assumption of the risk do not bar recovery. Instead, such misconduct is compared in the apportionment of damages. Once a defendant's liability is established, and where both the defective product and plaintiff's misconduct contribute to cause the damages, the comparative fault principle operates to reduce the plaintiff's recovery by that amount which the trier of fact finds him at fault.

Assumption of the risk. Failure to heed a warning with regard to a product will bar a recovery. This, in effect, means that **assumption of the risk** is a defense to a strict liability action.

Assumption of the risk *Negligence doctrine that bars the recovery of damages by an injured party on the ground that such party acted with actual or constructive knowledge of the hazard causing the injury.*

Misuse and abnormal use. Misuse and abnormal use of a product is a defense because the manufacturer or seller could not have reasonably foreseen the misuse. If a backwoodsman uses a sharp hunting and fishing knife to shave and he cuts his throat, it is conceivable that the manufacturer would be entitled to a defense of misuse of the instrument.

State of the art. A defense that is often asserted is called *state of the art*. This defense, simply stated, is that the product was manufactured according to the best and latest technology available. If a product is manufactured using the best technology but it nevertheless injures people, should the manufacturer still have liability? As the following case illustrates, most courts do not allow the state-of-the-art defense to defeat a claim based on strict liability.

CASE

In 1976, Johnson was using a lawn mower manufactured by Hannibal Mower Corporation between October 1970 and February 1971. Johnson slipped, and his foot went under the mower housing and into the moving blade. He lost two toes as a result of this accident. He sued Hannibal, claiming that the absence of a trailing shield or "dead-man control" rendered the product defective and unreasonably dangerous to the consumer. At trial, over Johnson's objection, Hannibal introduced into evidence safety design standards for mowers promulgated by the American National Standards Institute (ANSI) in 1968. Hannibal's expert witness explained these standards at trial.

He also testified that the mower met or exceeded ANSI standards and the standards did not require trailing devices or "dead-man controls." The trial court allowed this state-of-the-art evidence. The case was submitted to the jury on a theory of strict liability for defective design of the mower, and the jury returned a verdict for the defendant.

ISSUE: Was this state-of-the-art evidence admissible in this strict liability tort case involving a product defect?

DECISION: No.

REASONS:

1. According to Section 402A(2)(a) of the Restatement (Second) of the Law of Torts, the rule of strict liability for a product defect can apply even when "the seller has exercised all possible care in the preparation and sale of his product." Therefore, in a strict liability claim, the sole subject of inquiry is the defective condition of the product, and not the manufacturer's knowledge, negligence, or fault. In a negligence action, the inquiry focuses on the reasonableness of the maker's action in designing the product. However, in an action for strict liability, the focus is on the dangerous condition of the product as put into commerce.
2. State-of-the-art evidence, or evidence of industry or federal government standards, concerns the manufacturer's standard of care, which relates to the reasonableness of the manufacturer's design choice, not of the condition of the product. Therefore this evidence is irrelevant in a strict liability case.
3. Accordingly, the plaintiff in a strict liability case need not prove the violation of the standard of reasonble care for product design, but only that the design was so defective as to make the product unreasonably dangerous for the anticipated use.
4. Evidence of ANSI standards was irrelevant and inadmissible. Additionally, the fact that these standards were widely accepted in the industry could easily have been interpreted by the jury to mean the product was safe and could have resulted in the defendant's verdict. Therefore the introduction of this evidence was prejudicial.
5. Therefore the trial court's verdict is reversed and the case is remanded for a new trial.

Johnson v. Hannibal Mower Corp., 679 S.W.2d 884 (Mo. 1984).

11. Comparison of Strict Tort and Warranty

Table 20–2 demonstrates a basic similarity between strict tort liability and the warranty of merchantability. For instance, "defective condition unreasonably dangerous" and "fit for ordinary purposes" seem to be similar tests under the notion of "defect." But plaintiffs using strict liability may prove the simplest remedy. In a breach of warranty case, the plaintiff may have to overcome contract defenses such as disclaimers of liability, the requirement of notice of breach, limitation of remedies, and lack of privity. Where there is only economic loss (no physical harm to person or property), then most courts will not allow a recovery in strict tort. Warranty liability for economic loss, however, is available. Moreover, the UCC provides a longer statute of limitations in which to bring the action. Practical considerations such as the availability or solvency of a particular defendant may also affect the choice of theory.

TABLE 20–2 COMPARISON BETWEEN STRICT TORT AND WARRANTY

	Warranty of Merchantability UCC 2-314	Strict Tort Liability Restatement (Second) Torts 402A
Condition of goods giving rise to liability	Not merchantable; that is, not fit for ordinary purpose. 2-314(1), (2)(c).	Defective condition unreasonably dangerous 402A(1).
Character of defendant	Must be seller who is a merchant with respect to goods of that kind. 2-314(1), 2-104(1).	Must be seller who is engaged in the business of selling such a product. 402A(1)(a).
Reliance	No explicit requirement. Such warranty "taken for granted." 2-314; see, however, 2-316(3)(b).	No requirement of "any reliance on the part of the consumer upon the reputation, skill or judgment of the seller." 402A Comment m.
Disclaimer	Limitation of consequential damages for injury to the person in the case of consumer goods is prima facie unconscionable. 2-316(4), 2-719(3), 2-302.	Cause of action not affected by any disclaimer or any other agreement. 402A Comment m.
Notice	Buyer must within a reasonable time after he discovers, or should have discovered, any breach notify seller of breach or be barred from any remedy. Reason of rule: to defeat commercial bad faith, not to deprive a good-faith consumer of his remedy. 2-607(3)(a).	Consumer not required to give notice to seller of his injury within a reasonable time after it occurs. 402A Comment m.
Causation	Buyer may recover consequential damages *resulting* from seller's breach, including injury to person or property *proximately resulting* from any breach of warranty. 2-714, 2-715(2)(b), 2-314; see 2-316(3)(b).	Seller subject to liability for physical harm *caused*. 402A(1); see Comment n. *Contributory negligence* is not a defense.
Protected persons	The third persons protected depend on the alternative of 2-318 adopted.	Ultimate user or consumer. 402A(1), (2)(b) and Comment 1.
Protected injuries	Injuries to person or his property. 2-318.	Physical harm to ultimate user or consumer or to his property. 402A(1).
Statute of limitations	Four years from tender of delivery. 2-725(1), (2).	State law varies (from one to three years from injury).

CHAPTER SUMMARY

General Concepts

Basic Principles

1. A manufacturer, distributor, or seller of a product is liable to compensate a person injured by a defective product.

2. Products liability cases may arise out of defective design of products, defective manufacture, or the defective marketing of products.
3. Losses caused by products are a cost of doing business to be shared by buyers and users.
4. The potential liability is usually covered by products liability insurance, the cost of which has skyrocketed in recent years.

History of Products Liability

1. Prior to 1800, liability was based on tort theory of trespass.
2. In the 1800s, negligence law and the requirement of privity of contract became law.
3. The early 1900s saw the beginning of the demise of privity of contract.
4. In the 1960s, the doctrine of strict liability was created.

Theories of Liability

1. There are both contract and tort theories.
2. The theories are based on the defendant's conduct, the quality of the product, and the seller's representations. See Table 20–1.

Negligence

1. Negligence evaluates the reasonableness of the defendant's conduct. The defendant's conduct is deemed negligent only when it is inferior to what a "reasonable" person would have done under similar circumstances.
2. A negligence suit can be brought not only by the person who purchased the defective product but also by any person who suffered an injury due to a defective product.
3. The doctrine of *res ipsa loquitur* may be used to prove negligence.
4. Negligence may be established by proof that the manufacturer violated some statutory regulation in the production and distribution of his product.
5. Negligence is frequently based on failure of a manufacturer to warn of a known danger related to the product. A manufacturer who knows, or should know, his product to be dangerous has a duty to exercise reasonable care and foresight in preventing it from injuring or endangering people.

Misrepresentation

1. If the seller has advertised the product through newspapers, magazines, television, or otherwise and has made misrepresentations regarding the character or quality of the product, strict tort liability may be imposed on him.
2. Intent to mislead is not required and neither is privity of contract.

Strict Liability

Theory

1. In strict liability cases, the focus of attention is on the product.
2. A manufacturer selling a defective product in a defective condition that is unreasonably dangerous to the user or his property is liable for physical injuries caused by the defect.
3. The theory may apply to leases as well as sales.

Product Defined

1. Products include tangible personal property, items such as electricity, and containers for goods such as soft-drink bottles.

Defect

1. Product defects may be design defects, production defects, and marketing defects.
2. The typical marketing defect is a failure to warn.
3. The consumer expectations test is used to determine if a product is defective. A product is defective if it does not meet the standards of safety that consumers expect and is unreasonably dangerous.

Proof Required	1. To establish a case of strict liability, the plaintiff must prove (a) the product was defective, (b) the defect existed at the time the product left the defendant's control, and (c) the defect caused the plaintiff's injury. 2. A plaintiff need not prove negligence of the manufacturer or seller. Disclaimers and notice of breach are not problems, and lack of privity of contract is immaterial. 3. The defective product must be unreasonably dangerous.
Defenses	1. Contributory negligence is not a defense to a suit based on the theory of strict tort liability. 2. Comparative negligence is often used to reduce verdicts in strict products liability cases. 3. Assumption of the risk is a defense. 4. Misuse and abnormal use of a product are defenses. 5. State-of-the-art defenses normally are rejected by courts.
Comparison of Strict Tort and Warranty	1. See Table 20–2.

REVIEW QUESTIONS AND PROBLEMS

1. Match the terms in column A with the appropriate statement in column B.

A	B
(1) Misrepresentation	(a) The major requirement for strict liability.
(2) *Caveat emptor*	(b) A test for defective products.
(3) Negligence *per se*	(c) A false advertisement may constitute.
(4) *Res ipsa loquitur*	(d) Violation of a statute.
(5) Marketing defect	(e) A partial defense.
(6) Consumer expectations	(f) Failure to warn may constitute.
(7) Comparative negligence	(g) Let the buyer beware.
(8) Unreasonably dangerous product	(h) The thing speaks for itself.

2. Muriel received a blood transfusion consisting of blood supplied by a blood bank. She contracted serum hepatitis as a result of the transfusion. Is the blood bank liable by reason of strict liability and breach of implied warranties? Why or why not?

3. Alan leased a mobile home, including steps, from Ben. Alan's father fell when the steps collapsed, and he sued Ben for products liability. Is there a cause of action? Why or why not?

4. Brumley purchased a radial tire. The tire had a design defect that caused it to separate, but she was not warned of this defect even though the manufacturer had received several complaints. The tire blew out and Brumley was injured. Is she entitled to recover for her injuries from the manufacturer? Why or why not?

5. Automobile Driver and Passenger brought products liability action, alleging defective design, against Automobile Manufacturer for injuries sustained when the automobile was rear-ended, causing the gas tank to rupture and burn. What theories would support such a lawsuit? Explain each.

5. Pat sued the seller of a reconditioned clothes dryer. The dryer overheated, and a blanket being dried caught fire. The fire spread to the rest of the house, causing $24,000 in damages. What theory will support the plaintiff's cause of action? Explain.

7. Smith sued Ariens for injuries sustained while operating a snowmobile in a field. The snowmobile hit a rock that was partially covered by snow. On impact, the right side of Smith's face came down and hit a brake bracket on the left side of the snowmobile. The brake bracket had two sharp metal protrusions on the inside that were toward the

plaintiff's face. What theory of recovery best supports plaintiff's case? Explain. With what result? Why?

8. The plaintiff bought a rotary power mower from the defendant. He had used similar mowers before and was thoroughly familiar with them. The rear of the housing of plaintiff's mower is embossed with the warning: "Keep Hands & Feet From Under Mower." The instruction booklet twice advises the operator to mow slopes lengthwise, not up and down. While mowing up and down, plaintiff fell and lifted the mower onto his feet. Plaintiff sues, using strict liability as his theory. With what result? Why?

9. Claude, a ski instructor, was injured while riding a chairlift at a ski area when the chair in front of him slipped back along the cable, striking his chair and knocking him 30 feet to the ground. The cause of the mishap was the failure of a cable clamp unit to secure the chain to the cable. What must Claude prove in order to recover? Explain.

10. Plaintiff was injured when a propane gas heater leaked gas and exploded. The propane did not contain ethyl mercaptan, which provides the smell of gas. Plaintiff sues on a theory of negligence. With what result? Why?

11. Maude bought a plastic waste container, and when she got it home she found the lid did not fit properly on the top of the container. In an attempt to make it fit, she hit the corner of the lid with her hand and suffered a deep gash in her hand. Will Maude successfully recover on a theory of strict liability against the manufacturer of the plastic waste container? Explain.

12. Plaintiff is a fifteen-year-old girl employed at a fast-food restaurant. She was injured when in the midst of filling a customer's order, she made a split-second decision to remove a paper towel covering a roast without turning off the power. The meat was on a moving tray approaching a stationary blade and her hand hit the blade. Is the manufacturer strictly liable? Why?

The Principal–Agent Relationship

21

CHAPTER PREVIEW

- IN GENERAL

Types of Principals
Disclosed • Undisclosed • Partially Disclosed
Types of Agents
Brokers and factors • General and special • Independent contractors
Capacity of Parties
Formal Requirements

- DUTIES OF AGENTS

Duty of Loyalty
Duty to Protect Confidential Information
Duty to Obey Instructions
Duty to Inform
Duty Not to Be Negligent
Duty to Account

- DUTIES OF PRINCIPALS

Duty to Compensate in General
Duty to Compensate Sales Representatives
Duty to Reimburse
Duty to Indemnify
Duty Not to Discriminate
Boeing Guidelines

BUSINESS MANAGEMENT DECISION

As the newly named president of a multimillion-dollar corporation, you learn that only 1 percent of your employees are black and that there are no black and no female executives.

What action would you take based on this information?

IN GENERAL

1. Introduction

The term *agency* is used to describe the fiduciary relationship that exists when one person acts on behalf, and under the control, of another person. Agency is a contract, either express or implied, by which one party confides to the other the management of some business to be transacted in his name, or on his account, and by which that other assumes to do the business and to tender an account of it. The person who acts for another is called an **agent.** The person for whom he acts, and who controls the agent, is called a *principal.* Traditionally, issues of agency law arise when the agent has attempted to enter into a contract on behalf of his principal; however, the law of agency includes several aspects of the law of torts. Although tort litigation usually uses the terms *master* and *servant,* rather than principal and agent, both relationships are encompassed within the broad legal classification of agency law.

Agent *A person authorized to act for another (principal).*

The principles of agency law are essential for the conduct of business transactions. A corporation, as a legal entity, can function only through agents. The law of partnership is, to a large degree, agency principles specially applied to that particular form of business organization.

Case law, as contrasted with statutory law, has developed most of the principles applicable to the law of agency. Agency issues are usually discussed within a framework of three parties: the principal (P), the agent (A), and the third party (T), with whom A contracts or against whom A commits a tort while in P's service. The following examples illustrate the problems and issues involved in the law of agency.

P v. A: Principal sues agent for a loss caused by A's breach of a fiduciary duty, such as to obey instructions.

P v. T: Principal sues third party for breach of a contract that A negotiated with T while A was acting on P's behalf.

A v. P: Agent sues principal for injuries suffered in the course of employment, for wrongful discharge, or for compensation owed for services rendered.

A v. T: Agent sues third party for a loss suffered by A, such as the loss of a commission due to T's interference with contractual obligations.

T v. P: Third party sues principal for breach of a contract that A negotiated with T or for damages caused by a tort committed by A.

T v. A: Third party sues agent personally for breach of a contract signed by A or for damages caused by a tort committed by A.

2. Types of Principals

From the third party's perspective, an agent may act for one of three types of principals.

Disclosed. An agent who reveals that he is working for another and who reveals the principal's identity is an agent of a *disclosed principal.* The existence of a disclosed principal will be found in most agency relationships, particularly employment situations.

Undisclosed. At the other extreme, a principal is *undisclosed* whenever a third party reasonably believes that the agent acts only on his own behalf. In essence, when an undisclosed principal is involved, the third party does not realize that any agency relationship exists. A well-known or wealthy principal may not want a third party to know he is interested in buying that third party's land, business, or merchandise. Therefore the principal hires an agent to deal with the third party. This agent would be instructed by the principal to keep that principal's existence a secret from the third party.

Partially disclosed. A third situation falls between the disclosed and undisclosed principals' circumstances. A third party may know an agent represents a principal, but that third party may not know the identity of the principal. When a third party learns of the principal's existence but not his identity, a *partially disclosed principal* is present. For the most part, legal issues treat undisclosed and partially disclosed principals in a similar manner.

3. Types of Agents

Agents have special terms to identify them.

Brokers and factors. Some agents are known as brokers and others as factors. A **broker** is an agent with special, limited authority to procure a customer in order that the owner can effect a sale or exchange of property. A real estate broker has authority to find a buyer for another's real estate, but the real estate remains under the control of the owner. A **factor** is a person who has possession and control of another's personal property, such as goods, and is authorized to sell that property. A factor has a property interest and may sell the property in his own name, whereas a broker may not. Although the term is seldom used today, a retail merchant who has a manufacturer's goods on consignment is a factor.

General and special. Agents are also classified as general or special agents. A **general agent** is one who has authority to transact all the business of the principal, of a particular kind, or in a particular case. The powers of a general agent are coextensive with the business entrusted to his care, authorizing him to act for the principal in all matters coming within the usual and ordinary scope and character of such business. A general agent has much broader authority than a special agent. Some cases define a general agent as one authorized to conduct a series of transactions involving a continuity of service, whereas a **special agent** conducts a single transaction or a series of transactions without continuity of service. A special agent is authorized

Broker *A person employed to make contacts with third persons on behalf of his principal for a commission.*

Factor *An agent for the sale of merchandise. He may hold goods in his own name or in the name of his principal. He is authorized to sell and to receive payment for the goods.*

General agent *An agent authorized to do all the acts connected with carrying on a particular trade, business, or profession.*

Special agent *An agent with a limited amount of authority. This agent usually has instructions to accomplish one specific task.*

to act for the principal only in a particular transaction or in a particular way. Most agents usually are considered to be general agents of the employer as long as they stay within the scope of their employment. However, an athlete's agent assisting in contract negotiations likely would be a special agent and generally would not be authorized to make investments or purchase property.

Independent contractor *An independent contractor is one who exercises his independent judgment on the means used to accomplish the result.*

Independent contractors. Some persons who perform services for others are known as **independent contractors.** A person may contract for the services of another in a way that gives him full and complete control over the details and manner in which the work will be conducted, or he may simply contract for a certain end result. If the agreement provides merely that the second party is to accomplish a certain result and that party has full control over the manner and methods to be pursued in bringing about the result, such a party is deemed an independent contractor. The person contracting with an independent contractor and receiving the benefit of his service is usually called a *proprietor*. A proprietor is generally not responsible to third parties for the independent contractor's actions, either in contract or in tort. On the other hand, if the second party places his services at the disposal of the first in such a manner that the action of the second is generally controlled by the former, a principal-agent relationship is established. The liabilities of these parties are discussed in the next two chapters.

4. Capacity of Parties

It is generally stated that anyone who may act for himself may act through an agent. For example, a minor may enter into a contract, and so long as he does not disaffirm it, the agreement is binding. Likewise, the majority of states have held that a contract of an agent on behalf of a minor principal is voidable. Therefore such an agreement is subject to rescission or ratification by the minor, the same as if the minor personally had entered into the contract. To this general rule concerning an infant's capacity as a principal, some states recognize an exception. There is some authority to the effect that any appointment of an agent by an infant is void, not merely voidable. Under this view, any agreement entered into by an infant's agent would be ineffective, and an attempted disaffirmance by the principal would be unnecessary.

A minor may act as an agent for an adult, and agreements he makes for his principal while acting within his authority are binding on the principal. Although the infant agent has a right to terminate his contract of agency at his will, as long as he continues in the employment, his acts within the scope of the authority conferred upon him become those of his principal.

5. Formal Requirements

As a general rule, agency relationships are based on the consent of the parties involved. No particular formalities are required to create a principal-agent relationship. A principal may appoint an agent either in writing or orally. The agency may be either expressed or implied.

Despite the general lack of formal requirements, some states require that the appointment of an agent be evidenced by a writing when the agent is to negotiate a contract required to be written by the statute of frauds. Recall from Chapter 13 that these written contracts include those involving title to real estate, guaranty contracts, performance that cannot be completed within one year of the date of making, and sales of goods for $500 or more.

When a formal instrument is used for conferring authority upon an agent, it is known as a **power of attorney.** Generally, this written document is signed by the principal in the presence of a notary public. The agent named in a power of attorney is called an **attorney in fact.** The term distinguishes this formally appointed agent from an attorney at law, who is a licensed lawyer.

Power of attorney *An instrument authorizing another to act as one's agent or attorney in fact.*

Attorney in fact *A person acting for another under a grant of special power created by an instrument in writing.*

A power of attorney may be general, which gives the agent authority to act in all respects for the principal. Sometimes an elderly person signs a power of attorney appointing a general attorney in fact to handle all the necessary matters that may arise. On the other hand, a power of attorney, known as a special power of attorney, may be narrowly written. For example, a seller of land may need to be out of town on the date set to close the sales transaction. This seller can sign a special power of attorney to act on the seller's behalf by signing the deed and other necessary papers required to complete the closing. Furthermore, a seller or buyer of real estate typically must appoint an agent via a special power of attorney in order for that agent to have authority to sign a binding contract.

Powers of attorney are usually held to grant only those powers clearly given to the agent. For example, as held in the following case, the power to sell does not include the power to make a gift.

CASE

Blankerd signed a power of attorney that authorized King to "convey, grant, bargain and/or sell" certain described real estate "on such terms as to him (King) may seem best." King later gave the property to a third party. Blankerd sued King, claiming this gift violated the terms of the power of attorney.

ISSUE: Does a power of attorney authorizing the agent to "convey, grant, bargain and/or sell" the principal's property authorize the agent to give the property away?

DECISION: No.

REASONS:
1. A power of attorney is a written document by which one party, as principal, appoints another as agent and confers upon the latter the authority to perform certain specified acts on behalf of the principal.
2. Powers of attorney are strictly construed as a general rule and are held to grant only those powers that are clearly delineated.
3. A general power of attorney authorizing an agent to sell and convey property, although it authorizes him to sell for such price and on such terms as to him shall seem proper, implies a sale for the principal's benefit.
4. It is difficult to imagine how a gift of the principal's real property would be to the benefit of the principal when the power of attorney does not authorize such a gift.

King v. Blankerd, 492 A.2d 608 (Md. 1985).

Section 14 in this chapter discusses real estate listing agreements. Although these documents are used to authorize a real estate agent to find a ready, willing, and able buyer, most states do not require these agreements to be in writing. Technically the agent cannot create a binding sales contract between the buyer and seller. In other words, the real estate agent is not authorized to sign a contract on the seller's behalf. That agent's responsibility is to bring the buyer and seller together so that these parties may sign a contract. Despite oral listing agreements being enforceable, agents generally insist upon a written one to ease the burden of proof required to establish when a commission is owed. Furthermore, a number of states do require that listing agreements be evidenced by a writing.

DUTIES OF AGENTS

6. Introduction

The nature and extent of the duties imposed upon agents and servants are governed largely by the contract of employment. In addition to the duties expressly designated, certain others are implied by the fiduciary nature of the relationship and by the legal effects on the principal of actions or omissions by the agent. The usual implied duties are (1) to be loyal to the principal, (2) to protect confidential information, (3) to obey all reasonable instructions, (4) to inform the principal of material facts that affect the relationship, (5) to refrain from being negligent, and (6) to account for all money or property received for the benefit of the principal. The sections that follow discuss how these implied duties are essential to the principal-agent relationship.

7. Duty of Loyalty

At the foundation of any fiduciary relationship is the duty of loyalty that each party owes to the other. Since an agent is in a position of trust and confidence, the agent owes an obligation of undivided loyalty to the principal. While employed, an agent should not undertake a business venture that competes or interferes in any manner with the principal's business, nor should the agent make any contract for himself that should have been made for the principal. A breach of this fundamental duty can result in the principal's enjoining the agent's new business or recovering money damages or both, as occurred in the following case.

CASE

Gaffney and McElroy were employed as executives of Ideal Tape Company, a manufacturer of tapes used in the shoe industry. During 1976 and 1977, while still employed, these men planned to form a business to compete with Ideal. They consulted with a lawyer about creating a corporation. They hired persons to locate a suitable site for a factory and to find equipment similar to that used by Ideal. During this time, these men purchased equipment for their future business instead of buying the equipment for Ideal. They made plans to solicit customers of Ideal for their own business. They also encouraged two other employees of Ideal to participate in the competing firm. All these actions occurred while the four men were being paid by Ideal. When the other officers of Ideal discovered these plans, the four men resigned. Ideal sued

Gaffney and McElroy and asked for money damages resulting from the breach of duties owed.

ISSUE: 1. Did these men breach any fiduciary duties?
2. If yes, what is their liability?

DECISION: 1. Yes.
2. Liable at least for wages received.

REASONS: 1. Employees occupying a position of trust and confidence owe a duty of loyalty to their employer and must protect that employer's interest. Because he is bound to act solely for his employer's benefit in all matters within the scope of his employment, an executive employee is barred from actively competing with his employer during the tenure of his employment even in the absence of such express prohibition.
2. Employees who breach the duty of loyalty can be required to forfeit the right to compensation even absent a showing of actual injury to the employer. Furthermore, the defendants also are liable for the compensation paid to other employees who assisted the defendants' new firm.

Chelsea Industries, Inc. v. Gaffney, 449 N.E.2d 320 (Mass. 1983).

This duty of loyalty also prevents an agent from entering into an agreement on the principal's behalf if the agent himself is the other contracting party. In order to create a binding agreement with the principal, the agent first must obtain the principal's approval. Since a contract between the agent and the principal is not a deal "at arm's length," the circumstances demand the utmost good faith from the agent. Indeed, an agent must disclose fully all facts that might materially influence the principal's decision-making process.

Likewise, an agent usually cannot represent two principals in the same transactions if the principals have differing interests. To act as dual agent often leads the agent to an unavoidable breach of the duty of loyalty to one, if not both, of the principals. In order to prevent the breach of this basic duty in this situation, the agent should inform both principals of all the facts in the transaction, including that he (the agent) is working for both principals. If these principals agree to continue negotiations, the agent in effect becomes a "go-between" or messenger. The agent is acting on behalf of both principals while avoiding active negotiations. Due to the nature of their business, real estate agents particularly must be aware of the hazards of dual agencies.

Transactions violating the duty of loyalty may always be rescinded by the principal, despite the fact that the agent acted for the best interests of his principal and the contract was as favorable as could be obtained elsewhere. The general rule is applied without favor, in order that every possible motive or incentive for unfaithfulness may be removed.

In addition to the remedy of rescission, a principal is entitled to treat any profit realized by the agent in violation of this duty as belonging to the principal. Such profits may include rebates, bonuses, commissions, or divisions of profits received by an agent for dealing with a particular third party. Here again the contracts may have been favorable to the employer, but the result is the same because the agent should not be tempted to abuse the confidence placed in him. The principal may also collect from the agent a sum equal to any damages sustained as the result of the breach of the duty of loyalty.

8. Duty to Protect Confidential Information

The duty of loyalty demands that information of a confidential character acquired while in the service of the principal shall not be used by the agent to advance his interests in opposition to those of the principal. In other words, an agent has a duty to protect the principal's confidential information. This confidential information is usually called a *trade secret.* Trade secrets include plans, processes, tools, mechanisms, compounds, and informational data used in business operations. They are known only to the owner of the business and to a limited number of other persons in whom it may be necessary to confide. An employer seeking to prevent the disclosure or use of trade secrets or information must demonstrate that he pursued an active course of conduct designed to inform his employees that such secrets and information were to remain confidential. An issue to be determined in all cases involving trade secrets is whether the information sought to be protected is, in fact and in law, confidential. The result in each case depends on the conduct of the parties and the nature of the information, as illustrated by the following case.

CASE

Parrish and Chlarson were employed as computer programmers by J&K Computer Systems, Inc. Their employment contracts provided that all programs developed would become the property of J&K. These agreements referred to such programs as special and unique assets. Parrish developed an accounts receivable program that he installed at the Arnold Machinery Company, a customer of J&K. Shortly thereafter, Parrish and Chlarson quit their jobs and formed Dynamic Software Corporation. Through this new company, Parrish contracted with Arnold Machinery Company and other customers of J&K to provide computer programming services. One service Parrish was selling was an accounts receivable program that was modified from the program developed for J&K. J&K sued Parrish, Chlarson, and their new company for misappropriation of trade secrets. The trial court awarded J&K $7,500 in damages. The defendants appealed.

ISSUE: Were the computer programs developed for J&K trade secrets that are protected from the defendants' use?

DECISION: Yes.

REASONS:

1. It is a well-established principle that the law will protect the inventor of a special process or trade secret. A trade secret includes any formula, patent, device, plan, or compilation of information that is used in one's business and that gives him an opportunity to obtain an advantage over competitiors who do not know it.
2. Just because the plaintiff's customers had access to and use of the program does not prevent the program from being classified as a trade secret. Plaintfiff in this case marked the program with the following legend: "Program Products Proprietary To—J&K Computer Systems, Inc. Authorized Use by License Agreement Only."

3. Finally, the defendants, as former employees, are not denied the use of their general knowledge, experience, memory, or skill. However, they are liable for using or disclosing any trade secret of their former employer.

J&K Computer Systems, Inc. v. Parrish, 642 P.2d 732 (Utah 1982).

An employee who learns of secret processes or formulas or comes into possession of lists of customers may not use this information to the detriment of his employer. Former employees may not use such information in a competing business, regardless of whether the trade secrets were copied or memorized. The fact that a product is on the market does not amount to a divulgence or abandonment of the secrets connected with the product. The employer may obtain an injunction to prevent their use, as use is a form of unfair competition. The rule relating to trade secrets is applied with equal severity whether the agent acts before or after he severs his connection with the principal.

Knowledge that is important but not a trade secret may be used, although its use injures the agent's former employer. That information which by experience has become a part of a former employee's general knowledge should not and cannot be enjoined from further and different uses. For this reason, there usually is nothing to hinder a person who has made the acquaintance of his employer's customers from later contacting those whom he can remember. His acquaintances are part of his acquired skill. The employer may protect himself by a clause in the employment agreement to the effect that the employee will not compete with the employer or work for a competitor for a limited period of time after his employment is terminated. See Chapter 12 for a further discussion on the proper use of agreements not to compete.

9. Duty to Obey Instructions

It is the duty of an agent to obey all instructions issued by his principal as long as they refer to duties contemplated by the contract of employment. Burdens not required by the agreement cannot be indiscriminately imposed by the employer, and any material change in an employee's duties may constitute a breach of the employment contract.

An instruction may not be regarded lightly merely because it departs from the usual procedure and seems fanciful and impractical to the agent. It is not his business to question the procedure outlined by his superior. Any loss that results while he is pursuing any other course makes him absolutely liable to the principal for such resulting loss.

Furthermore, an instruction of the principal does not become improper merely because the motive is bad, unless it is illegal or immoral. The principal may be well aware of the agent's distaste for certain tasks; yet, if those tasks are called for under the employment agreement, it becomes the agent's duty to perform them. Failure to perform often results in proper grounds for discharge.

Closely allied to the duty to follow instructions is the duty to remain within the scope of the authority conferred. Because it often becomes possible for an agent to exceed his authority and still bind his principal, the agent has a duty not to exceed the authority granted. In case the agent does so, the employee or agent becomes responsible for any resulting loss.

Occasionally, circumstances arise that nullify instructions previously given. Because of the new conditions, the old instructions would, if followed, practically destroy the purpose of the agency. Whenever such an emergency arises, it becomes the duty of the agent, provided that the principal is not available, to exercise his best judgment in meeting the situation.

10. Duty to Inform

In Chapter 22, we will see that knowledge acquired by an agent within the scope of his authority binds the principal. More succinctly, the law states that an agent's knowledge is imputed as notice to the principal. Therefore the law requires that the agent inform his principal of all facts that affect the subject matter of the agency that are obtained within the scope of the employment. The rule requiring full disclosure of all material facts that might affect the principal is equally applicable to gratuitous and to compensated agents.

This rule extends beyond the duty to inform the principal of conflicting interests of third parties or possible violations of the duty of loyalty in a particular transaction. It imposes upon the agent a duty to give his principal all information that materially affects the interest of the principal. Knowledge of facts that may have greatly advanced the value of property placed with an agent for sale must be communicated before property is sold at a price previously established by the principal. Knowledge of financial problems of a buyer on credit must also be communicated to the principal. The following case discusses the duty of an agent to get the facts and to communicate them to the principal.

CASE

Brunner, an onion farmer, hired Horton, a produce broker, to market his 1980 crop. Horton shipped four loads of onions to Valdez Brokerage in Texas, but he never collected payment. Horton had very little information about the solvency of Valdez. Horton knew that Valdez had just gone into business and that the business was not listed in the "Blue Book," a financial reference in the produce industry. Horton also knew that the previous year, when he was acting as a broker for another onion farmer, Valdez ran from 90 to 120 days late on payments. Horton did not disclose any of this information to the plaintiff, but rather, assured plaintiff that he knew Valdez and that she always paid her bills, although she was a little slow. Brunner sued Horton for the value of the onions delivered to Valdez. Brunner argued that Horton, as an agent, had breached fiduciary duties owed to Brunner.

ISSUE: Was there sufficient evidence to establish that a fiduciary relationship existed and that a fiduciary duty had been breached?

DECISION: Yes.

REASONS: 1. The question of the existence of an agency relationship is ordinarily for the fact finder. Here, defendant was responsible for arranging the sale of plaintiff's onions. This included the responsibility of arranging for transportation, selecting buyers, setting prices, as well as collecting and paying plaintiff for the net proceeds of the sales. In addition, defendant received a commission on each sale of onions. There was sufficient evidence in the record for the jury to infer the existence of an agency relationship.

2. An agent has a fiduciary duty to act with the utmost faith and loyalty in behalf of, and to act solely for, the benefit of his principal. An agent must make full and complete disclosure of all facts that might reasonably affect the principal's decision.
3. Defendant was advised that there were problems at the brokerage, but he continued to make deliveries. The trucker who delivered the first load of plaintiff's onions to Valdez at defendant's request called defendant and advised him that problems existed at the brokerage. The trucker indicated that he had problems both contacting Valdez and arranging for the unloading of the onions. Defendant did not disclose this information to the plaintiff and did not indicate that he was having trouble getting payment from Valdez until almost a month after the last shipment of onions.
4. This evidence was sufficient to support the jury's findings of breach of fiduciary duty.

Brunner v. Horton, 702 P.2d 283 (Colo. App. 1985).

11. Duty Not to Be Negligent

As is discussed more fully in Chapter 23, the doctrine of *respondeat superior* imposes liability upon a principal or master for the torts of an agent or servant acting within the scope of his employment. The agent or servant is primarily liable, and the principal or master is vicariously or secondarily liable.

It is an implied condition of employment contracts, if not otherwise expressed, that the employee has a duty to act in good faith and to exercise reasonable care and diligence in performing his tasks. Failure to do so is a breach of the employment contract. Therefore, if the employer has liability to third persons because of the employee's acts or negligent omissions, the employer may recover his loss from the employee. This right may be transferred by the doctrine of subrogation to the liability insurance carrier of the employer. For example, assume that a bakery company is held liable for damages to an injured child who was struck by a company delivery truck as the result of the employee-driver's negligence. After the company's insurance company pays the total coverage to the injured party, any unpaid damages can be collected from the company. The company in turn can sue the employee for breach of the duty not to be negligent. In some states the insurance company could also collect from the employee. However, there are some reasons to keep liability from being passed ultimately to the careless employee. These reasons are discussed in Chapter 23, on agency and tort responsibility.

12. Duty to Account

Money or property entrusted to the agent must be accounted for to the principal. Because of this fact, the agent is required to keep proper records showing receipts and expenditures, in order that a complete accounting may be rendered. Any money collected by an agent for his principal should not be mingled with funds of the agent. If they are deposited in a bank, they should be kept in a separate account.

Otherwise, any loss resulting must be borne by the agent. Also, the duty to account can arise out of the agent's breach of any other fiduciary duty.

An agent who receives money from third parties for the benefit of the principal owes no duty to account to the third parties. The only duty to account is owed to the principal. On the other hand, money paid to an agent who has no authority to collect it, and who does not turn it over to the principal, may be recovered from the agent in an action by the third party.

A different problem is presented when money is paid in error to an agent, as in the overpayment of an account. If the agent has passed the money on to his principal before the mistake is discovered, it is clear that only the principal is liable. Nevertheless, money that is still in the possession of the agent when he is notified of the error should be returned to the third party. The agent does not relieve himself of this burden by subsequently making payment to his principal.

Any payment made in error to an agent and caused by the agent's mistake or misconduct may always be recovered from him, even if he has surrendered it to his principal. Also, any overpayment may be recovered from the agent of an undisclosed principal, because the party dealing with the agent was unaware of the existence of the principal.

DUTIES OF PRINCIPALS

13. Introduction

The principal-agent relationship is a fiduciary one. Like agents, principals also have fiduciary duties. The trust and confidence of a fiduciary relationship is a two-way obligation. Thus the law requires that the principal be loyal and honest in dealing with the agents. In addition, the agent is entitled to be compensated for his services in accordance with the terms of his contract of employment. If no definite compensation has been agreed upon, there arises a duty to pay the reasonable value of such services—the customary rate in the community. Furthermore, the principal owes duties to reimburse agents for their reasonable expenses and to hold the agents harmless for liability that may be incurred while the agent is within the scope of employment. Finally, there is a duty not to discriminate in personnel decisions.

14. Duty to Compensate—in General

Many employment contracts include provisions for paying a percentage of profits to a key employee. If the employment contract does not include a detailed enumeration of the items to be considered in determining net income, it will be computed in accordance with generally accepted accounting principles, taking into consideration past custom and practice in the operation of the employer's business. It is assumed that the methods of determining net income will be consistent and that no substantial changes will be made in the methods of accounting without the mutual agreement of the parties. The employer cannot unilaterally change the accounting methods, nor can the employee require a change in order to effect an increase in his earnings.

The right of a real estate broker or agent to a commission is frequently the subject of litigation. In the absence of an express agreement, the real estate broker earns a commission (1) if he finds a buyer who is ready, willing, and able to meet the terms outlined by the seller in the listing agreement or (2) if the owner contracts with the purchaser (whether or not the price is less than the listed price), even though it later develops that the buyer is unable to meet the terms of the contract. The contract is conclusive evidence that the broker found a ready, willing, and able buyer. If a prospective purchaser conditions his obligation to purchase on an approval of credit or approval of a loan, he is not a ready, willing, and able buyer until such approval. If it is not forthcoming, the broker is not entitled to a commission.

The duty to pay a real estate commission is dependent upon which of the three types of listing has been agreed upon. An owner who lists property with several brokers is obligated to pay the first one who finds a satisfactory purchaser, at which time the agency of other brokers is automatically terminated, assuming a simple *open listing*. In an open listing, the owner is free to sell on his own behalf without a commission. The second type of listing is called an *exclusive agency listing*. For an agreed period of time, it gives the broker the exclusive right to find a buyer. In this arrangement, the seller is not free to list the property with other brokers, and a sale through other brokers would be a violation of the contract of listing, although the seller himself is free to find a buyer of his own. With the third type of listing, called an *exclusive right to sell,* even the seller is not free to find a buyer of his own choosing. If the seller does sell on his own behalf, he is obliged to pay a commission to the broker. The following case demonstrates the significance of exclusive right to sell listings when property is listed with more than one broker.

CASE

On September 5, 1979, Plaza Limited, a partnership, signed a listing agreement granting Clodfelter, a real estate broker, an exclusive right to sell certain real estate. Included in this listing agreement was the handwritten provision, "This agreement is exclusive of any sale made by the owners of their property." There was no date of termination specified.

In May or June 1980, the partners of Plaza Limited signed a second listing agreement describing the same real estate with Muchmore, also a real estate broker. On August 11, 1980, a contract of sale was signed by a buyer found by Muchmore. On August 27, 1980, the partners of Plaza Limited requested and obtained a letter from Clodfelter in which he agreed he was not entitled to a commission if the property was "sold solely through the efforts of the owners." On September 4, 1980, a sale was closed, and Muchmore received a 6 percent commission.

When he learned of all the facts, Clodfelter sued Plaza Limited for the 6 percent commission specified in the original listing agreement.

ISSUE: Was Clodfelter entitled to the commission claimed?

DECISION: Yes.

REASONS:
1. There are two types of exclusive agreements commonly used in real estate contracts, the "exclusive agency" agreement and the "exclusive right to sell" agreement.
2. The exclusive agency agreement prohibits an owner from selling the property *through another broker* during the listing period, but *allows the owner to sell his property through his own efforts.*
3. In comparison, the exclusive right to sell provision is more restrictive in that by contract it *precludes the sale of the property by anyone, including the owner,* thus protecting the broker from *any* sale other than one he arranges.

4. In the instant case, the parties agreed to an exclusive right to sell provision in the contract, but by modifying the agreement to allow the owners to sell their property, they created an exclusive agency contract.
5. Here, the owners sold their property through the agency of another broker. That action constituted a breach of contract between the first broker, Clodfelter, and the owners.
6. Clodfelter, as a broker under an exclusive agency agreement that was breached, is entitled to his full commission of $50,100.

Clodfelter v. Plaza, Ltd., 698 P.2d 1 (N.M. 1985).

Multiple listing is a method of listing property with several brokers simultaneously. These brokers belong to an organization, the members of which share listings and divide the commissions. A typical commission would be split 60 percent to the selling broker, 30 percent to the listing broker, and 10 percent to the organization for operating expenses. These multiple-listing groups give homeowners the advantage of increased exposure to potential buyers. In return for this advantage, most multiple-listing agreements are of the exclusive right to sell type.

15. Duty to Compensate Sales Representatives

Sales representatives who sell merchandise on a commission basis are confronted by problems similar to those of the broker, unless their employment contract is specific in its details. Let us assume that Low Cal Pies, Inc., appoints Albert, on a commission basis, as its exclusive sales representative in a certain territory. A grocery chain in the area involved sends a large order for pies directly to the home office of Low Cal Pies. Is Albert entitled to a commission on the sale? It is generally held that such a salesman is entitled to a commission only on sales solicited and induced by him, unless his contract of employment gives him greater rights.

The sales representative usually earns a commission as soon as an order from a responsible buyer is obtained, unless the contract of employment makes payment contingent upon delivery of the goods or collection of the sale's price. If payment is made dependent on performance by the purchaser, the employer cannot deny the sales representative's commission by terminating the agency prior to collection of the account. When the buyer ultimately pays for the goods, the seller is obligated to pay the commission.

An agent who receives a weekly or monthly advance against future commissions is not obligated to return the advance if commissions equal thereto are not earned. The advance, in the absence of a specific agreement, is considered by the courts as a minimum salary.

16. Duty to Reimburse

An agent has a general right to reimbursement for money properly expended on behalf of his principal. It must appear that the money was reasonably spent and that its expenditure was not necessitated by the misconduct or negligence of the agent. Travel-related expenses, such as airfares, mileage, lodging, and meals, are typical examples of the items that a principal must reimburse an agent for unless those parties agree otherwise.

An agent also is entitled to be reimbursed for the costs of completing an agreement when the performance was intended to benefit the principal. This is an especially true statement when the agent has performed on behalf of an undisclosed principal. That principal must protect his agent by making funds available to perform the contract as agreed. Suppose that McDonald's Hamburgers is seeking prime locations for its franchises. Not wanting to pay an additional premium just because it is the buyer, McDonald's may hire a local real estate agent to purchase a site in his own name. McDonald's must reimburse this agent for any money that the agent may have used to complete performance of any contract signed.

17. Duty to Indemnify

Whereas to *reimburse* someone means to repay him for funds already spent, to **indemnify** means to hold a person harmless or free from liability. A servant is entitled to indemnity for certain tort losses. They are limited to factual situations in which the servant is not at fault and his liability results from following the instructions of the master. An agent or a servant is justified in presuming that a principal has a lawful right to give his instructions and that performance resulting from his instructions will not injure third parties. When this is not the case, and the agent incurs a liability to some third party because of trespass or conversion, the principal must indemnify the agent against loss.

Indemnify *Literally, "to save harmless." Thus, one person agrees to protect another against loss.*

There will ordinarily be no indemnification for losses incurred in negligence actions because the servant's own conduct is involved. Any indemnification is usually of the master by the servant in tort situations. If the agent or servant is sued for actions within the course of employment in which he is not at fault, the agent or servant is entitled to be reimbursed for attorney's fees and court costs incurred if the principal does not furnish them in the first instance.

18. Duty Not to Discriminate

There are both federal and state laws that prohibit employers from discriminating in hiring, promoting, or discharging on the basis of race, color, national origin, religion, sex, age, or handicap. The federal law covers all employers with fifteen or more employees, labor unions with fifteen or more members, labor unions that operate a hiring hall, and employment agencies. It also covers state and local governments and educational institutions. The Equal Employment Opportunity Commission has primary responsibility for enforcing the law, and it does so in close cooperation with state agencies. The EEOC has the power to file a civil suit in court and to represent a person alleging a violation of the law, after it exhausts efforts to conciliate the claim. The remedies available include reinstatement with back pay for the victim of an illegal discrimination and injunctions against future violations of the law.

The duty not to discriminate may be violated even though a company's standards or policies for selecting or promoting appear to be neutral. If they have the effect of discriminating against blacks or other minorities and have no substantial, demonstrable relationship to qualification for the job in question, they are illegal. For example, refusing to hire persons because of their poor credit rating, refusing to hire those with an arrest record, and giving priority to relatives of present employees in hiring when there is a very low percentage of minority workers among these employees have been held to be illegal.

The practice of using personnel tests has also been challenged. It is not unlawful for an employer to hire or promote employees on the basis of the results of professionally developed ability tests, provided they are not designed or used to discriminate illegally. The use of a standardized general intelligence test in selecting and placing personnel is prohibited, being discriminatory on the basis of race. Tests, neutral on their face and even neutral in terms of intent, cannot be maintained if they operate to "freeze" the status quo of prior discriminatory employment practices. If an employment practice cannot be shown to be related to job performance, the practice is prohibited.

Discrimination based on sex is a major area of equal employment opportunity litigation. A federal law requires that women and men be paid equivalent wages for equivalent work, although executive personnel are exempt from the Equal Pay Act. The courts are in the process of deciding if equal pay must be paid for comparable work. The comparable worth issue is one of the most difficult issues facing business and the law today.

The Age Discrimination in Employment Act makes it illegal to discriminate against persons over forty years of age and below legal mandatory retirement age. The Rehabilitation Act applies to the executive branch of the federal government and to every employer that has a contract over $2,500 with the federal government. This law prohibits discrimination against persons who are handicapped. A *handicapped person* is anyone who has or has had a physical or mental impairment that substantially limits a major life activity. To be hired, however, that person must be "qualified," or capable of performing a particular job, with reasonable accommodation to his handicap.

The desire to eliminate the adverse effects of past discrimination prompted most governmental bodies and many private employers to adopt policies and practices described as *affirmative action programs*. These programs usually establish goals for hiring and promoting members of minority groups, to be accomplished by active recruitment programs and by giving priority to minorities. Members of minorities are to be given priority when fewer of them are working in a given job category than one would reasonably expect there should be, considering their availability.

Affirmative action programs and similar efforts have led to charges of reverse discrimination. However, the Supreme Court has held that voluntary affirmative action programs are constitutional and companies that adopt them are not in violation of the law. In a 1987 case, the Supreme Court went further and held that a governmental agency did not discriminate against male employees by taking a female employee's sex into account and promoting her over a male employee with a higher test score. The decision was made pursuant to an affirmative action plan directing that sex or race be considered for the purpose of remedying underrepresentation of women and minorities in traditionally segregated job categories. It did not unnecessarily trammel the rights of male employees or create an absolute bar to their advancement. In other cases, the Supreme Court has held that federal trial judges may approve voluntary pacts between union and public employees to give minorities hiring preferences and that a judge may order agencies to use quotas where there is a history of "egregious" racial bias. Thus affirmative action plans may be required and enforced without breaching the duty not to discriminate.

19. Boeing Guidelines

Of course, all of the Boeing Guidelines affect the employer-employee relationship. They outline the necessity for employees to keep their personal and company interests separate and provide guidance as to what is appropriate conduct in a variety of areas of importance to Boeing. One of the more important areas relate to "conflicts of interest," which is a term that directly relates to the duty of loyalty previously discussed.

The policy on conflict of interests states in part:

> It is the policy of The Boeing Company that its transactions with other business entities shall not be influenced or affected by the personal interests or activities of its employees. Employee activities or personal interests, including those of their immediate families, which could appear to influence the objective decisions required of employees in the performance of their Boeing Company responsibilities are considered to be a conflict of interest and are prohibited by this Policy unless approved in writing by The Boeing Company. Such conflicts may create a presumption of favoritism or damage the reputation of The Boeing Company or its employees in the eyes of other employees and persons with whom The Boeing Company may transact business.
>
> It must be emphasized that an actual conflict of interest need not be present to constitute a violation of this Policy. Activities or personal interests of employees or their immediate families which create the mere appearance of a conflict of interest must be avoided so as not to reflect negátively on the reputation of The Boeing Company or its employees.

In order to assist its employees in understanding the Guidelines, several examples of possible questions and answers were made available. One example follows:

> *I have been offered a job by another company which involves selling the products of that company to Boeing. Does Boeing policy allow former employees to do this?*
>
> No. Former employees are prohibited from selling to Boeing for a period of two years. Exceptions may be granted in unusual cases only by the Directors of Materiel in the individual operating companies.

CHAPTER SUMMARY

In General

Types of Principals

1. A *disclosed principal* is one whose existence and identity are known by third parties.
2. A *partially disclosed principal* is one whose existence is known but whose identity is unknown by third parties.
3. An *undisclosed principal* is one whose identity and existence are unknown by third parties.

Types of Agents

1. A *general agent* has broad authority to conduct a series of transactions with continuity of service.
2. A *special agent* has narrower authority and conducts a single transaction or lacks continuity of service.
3. A *broker* has limited authority to find a customer in order that a sale of property may be completed.

4. A *factor* has possession and control of another person's property and is authorized to sell that property.
5. An *independent contractor* retains control over the details of how work is to be accomplished. The person hiring an independent contractor contracts for a certain end result.

Capacity of Parties

1. In general, a minor may act as a principal. Actions by an adult agent on behalf of a minor principal generally are voidable by the minor.
2. In general, a minor may act as an agent. Actions by a minor agent on behalf of an adult principal generally are binding on the principal.

Formal Requirements

1. Usually, no particular requirements need to followed to create an agency.
2. Agency may be expressed or implied. Expressed relationships may be created orally or in writing.
3. The appointment of an agent must be in writing when the agent is to negotiate a contract required to be in writing under the statute of frauds.
4. A *power of attorney* is the written document used to formally appoint an agent.
5. A power of attorney may be general or special in nature.

Duties of Agents

Duty of Loyalty

1. This duty is the foundation of every agency relationship.
2. Duty is breached if agent takes for himself an opportunity intended to benefit the principal.
3. Duty is breached if agent secretly contracts with the principal.
4. Duty is breached if agent attempts to represent two principals in the same transaction. This is known as the dual agency situation.

Duty to Protect Confidential Information

1. Agent must protect principal's trade secrets and not use them for personal profit.
2. Trade secrets might include plans, processes, tools, compounds, customer lists, and other information used in business operations.
3. Principals often have agents sign agreements not to compete in order to reinforce this duty.

Duty to Obey Instructions

1. An agent must follow all reasonable instructions given by the principal.
2. An agent also must not exceed the authority granted by the principal.
3. If an emergency prevents the agent from obeying the instructions given, that agent must seek additional directions. If the principal is not available, the agent must use his best judgment.

Duty to Inform

1. Agents have the duty to give their principals all the information that materially affects the principals' interest.

Duty Not to Be Negligent

1. A principal (master) may be liable for the personal injuries caused by agents (servants) within the scope of their employment.
2. Because agents (servants) can create this liability by negligence, these parties have the legal duty to refrain from negligent acts.

Duty to Account

1. An agent always must account to the principal for any money the agent has received from or for the principal.
2. In general, an agent's duty to account is owed only to the principal, not to third parties.
3. However, an agent must account to third parties (a) if too much money is collected innocently and the agent still has the money, (b) if too much money is collected on purpose regardless of whether the agent

has the money, and (c) if too much money is collected on behalf of an undisclosed principal.

Duties of Principals

Duty to Compensate—in General

1. Compensation of agents must be reasonable if an amount is not stated in an agreement.
2. A percentage of profits is calculated using generally accepted accounting principles.
3. Real estate agents are compensated in accordance with the type of listing agreement signed.

Duty ot Compensate Sales Representatives

1. Unless their agreement states otherwise, a sales representative receives a commission only on sales solicited and induced directly.
2. The commission generally is earned as soon as an order is placed.
3. In general, an advance against commission is considered a minimum salary, and the sales representative does not have to return the excess advance.

Duty to Reimburse

1. A principal must reimburse agents who have expended reasonable amounts on behalf of the principal.
2. Expenses such as transportation costs, lodging, and meals are common reimbursable expenses.

Duty to Indemnify

1. To indemnify means to hold a person harmless or free from liability.
2. An agent is entitled to be indemnified when the agent becomes liable to third parties while that agent was following the principal's instructions.

Duty Not to Discriminate

1. Federal and state laws prohibit discrimination in the recruiting, hiring, promoting, and firing of employees based on race, color, national origin, relation, sex, age, or handicap.
2. The Age Discrimination in Employment Act protects workers in the age range of forty to mandatory retirement.
3. The Rehabilitation Act of 1973 prohibits discrimination on the basis of mental or physical handicaps of otherwise qualified persons.
4. Affirmative action programs are constitutional and legal even though the net effect may be to favor members of minority groups.

REVIEW QUESTIONS AND PROBLEMS

1. Match each term in column A with the appropriate statement in column B.

A	B
(1) Disclosed principal	(a) Principal whose identity and existence are unknown by third parties.
(2) Undisclosed principal	(b) Agent must protect these and not use them for personal profit.
(3) Broker	(c) Person who retains control over the details of how work is to be accomplished.
(4) Independent contractor	(d) Type of agent who has limited authority to find a customer in order to complete a sale of property.
(5) Power of attorney	(e) A principal whose existence and identity are known by third parties.
(6) Duty of loyalty	(f) A duty generally owed only to principals but in certain situations also to third parties.

(7) Trade secrets	(g) Means to hold a person harmless or free from liability—a duty owed by principals to agents.
(8) Duty to account	(h) The written document used to formally appoint an agent.
(9) Indemnification	(i) The foundation of every agency relationship.

2. The Pedestrian Shoe Company hired Angela, age sixteen, to work during the summer. Angela was to solicit orders from shoe stores in her hometown. She was to be paid $1 for each pair of shoes ordered. Angela was so successful that she hired Beth, age twenty-five, to help, and she promised to pay Beth 50 cents for each pair of shoes ordered. Can Angela properly be an agent for Pedestrian? Can Beth properly treat as void her appointment as an agent of Angela and submit her orders to Pedestrian for the larger compensation? Explain.

3. Jon Cady hired Telfair Realty to find a buyer for his house. On July 8, an offer to purchase was presented to Jon Cady. This offer was signed "Reta May Johnson by Jared Johnson, son" as purchaser. After studying the offer, Jon Cady accepted it, and closing was scheduled for August 25. On that date, the purchaser did not appear. Reta May Johnson notified the seller and the real estate agent that she did not intend to complete the transaction. She requested that her earnest money be refunded since she was not bound to the sales contract. She argued that her son was not authorized in writing to bind her to a real estate sales agreement. Jon Cady and Telfair Realty sued to recover their respective damages resulting from this breach of contract. Was Mrs. Johnson liable for a breach of contract? Explain.

4. New World Fashions provides guidance to persons interested in entering the retail clothing business. Anderson was hired as a sales representative of New World. After several months of working for New World, Anderson decided to start a competing business. However, prior to resigning, Anderson encouraged one of New World's prospective clients to contract with Anderson personally. He then provided to this client services typically furnished by New World. Upon discovery of these facts, New World fired Anderson and sued him to recover lost profits. Must Anderson account to New World for the financial gain he obtained in this transaction? Explain.

5. A manager of TV station was instructed by the board of directors to fire a salesperson who had a serious drinking problem. When the manager failed to do so because of the salesperson's outstanding record, the manager was fired. He filed suit for wrongful discharge. What result? Why?

6. Amos was sales manager of Plenty, a turkey-packing company. As a member of the management group, Amos was consulted on all phases of the business. He persuaded the company to enter into a contract to purchase 20,000 turkeys but concealed for some time the fact that he was the seller of the turkeys. Plenty Company did not carry out the contract, and Amos brought suit. Was the contract enforceable? Why?

7. Peterson's Florist Company hired Alex to deliver floral arrangements. One day while on a delivery, Alex fell asleep and hit a telephone pole. The delivery van was damaged to the extent of $1,600. Can Peterson's Florist Company recover this amount from Alex? Explain.

8. Perry hired the Creditor's Collection Agency to collect overdue accounts. Perry informed the agency that Terry owed $500 for merchandise received. In fact, Terry owed only $400. However, the agency did collect $500, because Terry also was mistaken about the amount owed. Later, Terry discovered the overpayment. Under what circumstances does the agency owe an accounting to Terry? Explain.

9. Patricia listed her house for sale with Rex, a real estate broker, under a listing contract that gave Rex the exclusive right to sell this house for three months. During this time, Patricia sold her house to a friend who did not know Rex. Patricia refused to pay Rex any commission because Rex was not the procuring cause of the ready, willing, and able buyer. Is Rex entitled to a commission? Why?

10. Dulcy was hired to sell merchandise in a stated territory for Paper Products, Inc. She was to receive a commission of 2 percent on all orders she submitted to the company. She received an advance of $700 a week for ten weeks, but her commissions averaged only $450 a week. If Dulcy is fired, does she owe the company the $2,500 difference? Why?

11. Douglas, a newspaper reporter, sued his former employer, a newspaper publisher. Douglas sought to recover the attorney's fees and court costs incurred in his defense of a libel action. Douglas had been sued as the result of an article written for his employer's newspaper. Douglas had won the libel case. Is the employer obligated to indemnify Douglas for his legal expenses? Explain.

12. Bowers, a refrigeration mechanic, furnished the tools necessary to do his assigned work. The tools were very heavy and were kept in two toolboxes. Three men were needed to move one toolbox; the other could be moved only by forklift. The tools were kept inside the inner building of the employer's shop. Before the Thanksgiving weekend, Bowers locked his tools in the inner office, but they were stolen in a burglary over that weekend. A statute required indemnification of losses in direct discharge of an employee's duties. Must the employer reimburse the employee for the value of the tools? Why or why not?

13. A county set a long-range goal of establishing a work force whose composition would reflect the proportion of women and minorities in the area work force. As a short-range step, it authorized officials to consider sex and ethnicity when qualified candidates were being appraised for jobs. Seven candidates qualified for a road dispatcher job. When a female candidate was selected, a male candidate who had received a higher score on the interview portion of the promotion criteria filed suit challenging the plan and the decision. What result? Why?

22 Agency and the Law of Contracts

C H A P T E R   P R E V I E W

- PURPOSE OF AGENCY RELATIONSHIP
- BASIC PRINCIPLES

  Actual Authority
  Apparent or Ostensible Authority
  Ratification
    Capacity required • Acting as agent • Full knowledge • Conduct constituting ratification

- LIABILITY OF PRINCIPALS—GENERAL

  Disclosed Principal's Liability to Agents
  Disclosed Principal's Liability to Third Parties
  Undisclosed Principal's Liability to Agents
  Undisclosed Principal's Liability to Third Parties
  Effect of Election
  Effect of Settlement

- LIABILITY OF PRINCIPALS—SPECIAL SITUATIONS

  Notice to Agents
  Agent's Power to Appoint Subagents
  Agent's Financial Powers

- LIABILITY OF AGENTS AND THIRD PARTIES

  Agent's Liability to Principals
  Agent's Liability to Third Parties
    Based on the contract • Based on breach of warranty
  Third Party's Liability to Principals
  Third Party's Liability to Agents

BUSINESS MANAGEMENT DECISION

You are a famous celebrity. A friend opens a restaurant using your name. You have made no investment of money, but you regularly eat at the restaurant for free. Otherwise you receive no benefits. Your attorney advises you about this relationship.

What should you do under these circumstances?

PURPOSE OF AGENCY RELATIONSHIP

The law of agency is essentially concerned with issues of contractual liability. Because corporations act only through agents, and because partners in a partnership are agents of the partnership, a substantial portion of all contracts entered into by businesses are entered into by agents on behalf of principals.

One ultimate goal of these transactions is to establish a relationship that binds the principal and third party contractually. In other words, although the agent negotiates with the third party, the principal is substituted for the agent in the contract with the third party. Despite this objective, whenever a contract is entered into by an agent, issues as to the liability of the various parties may arise. Is the agent personally liable on the contract? Is the principal bound? Can the principal enforce the agreement against the third party? This chapter discusses these issues and others that frequently arise out of contracts entered into by agents on behalf of principals.

However, prior to addressing these questions, the next three sections examine the fundamental legal concept of authority. Before an agent can create a binding contract between the principal and third party, that agent must have authority from the principal or his unauthorized actions must have been ratified by the principal. As we will see, authority may be actually granted to the agent by the principal, or it may be apparent to the third party from the principal's actions or inactions.

BASIC PRINCIPLES

1. Actual Authority

A principal may confer actual authority upon the agent or may unintentionally, by want of ordinary care, allow the agent to believe himself to possess it. Actual authority includes express authority and implied authority. The term *express authority* describes authority explicitly given to the agent through the principal's written or oral instructions. *Implied authority* is used to describe authority that is necessarily incidental to the express authority or that arises because of business custom and usage or prior practices of the parties. Implied authority is sometimes referred to as *incidental authority*; it is required or reasonably necessary to order to carry out the purpose for which the agency was created. Implied authority may be established by deductions or inferences from other facts and circumstances in the case, including prior habits or dealings of a similar nature between the parties.

Implied authority based on custom and usage varies from one locality to another and among different kinds of businesses. To illustrate: Perfection Fashions, Inc., appoints Andrea as its agent to sell its casual wear to retail stores. As a part of this relationship, Andrea has express authority to enter into written contracts with the purchasers and to sign Perfection Fashions' name to such agreements. Whether Andrea has implied or incidental authority to consign the merchandise, thereby allowing the purchaser to return items not sold, may depend on local custom and past dealings. Likewise, whether Andrea may sell on credit instead of cash may be determined by similar standards. If it is customary for other agents of fashion companies in this locality to sell on consignment or on credit, Andrea and the purchasers with whom she deals may assume she possesses such authority. Custom, in effect, creates a presumption of authority. Of course, if the agent or third party has actual knowledge that contradicts customs or past dealings, such knowledge limits the existence of implied or incidental authority.

Implied authority cannot be derived from the words or conduct of the agent. A third person dealing with a known agent may not act negligently in regard to the extent of the agent's authority or blindly trust his statements. The third party must use reasonable diligence and prudence in ascertaining whether the agent is acting within the scope of his authority. Similarly, if persons who deal with a purported agent desire to hold the principal liable on the contract, they must ascertain not only the fact of the agency but the nature and extent of the agent's authority. Should either the existence of the agency or the nature and extent of the authority be disputed, the burden of proof regarding these matters is upon the third party.

All agents, even presidents of corporations, have limitations on their authority. Authority is not readily implied. Possession of goods by one not engaged in the business of selling such goods does not create the implication of authority to sell. Authority to sell does not necessarily include the authority to extend credit, although custom may create such authority. The officers of a corporation must have actual authority to enter into transactions that are not in the ordinary course of the business of the corporation. For this reason, persons purchasing real estate from a corporation usually require a resolution of the board of directors specifically authorizing the sale.

2. Apparent or Ostensible Authority

To be distinguished from implied authority is *apparent* or *ostensible authority*, terms that are synonymous. These terms describe the authority a principal, intentionally or by want of ordinary care, causes or allows a third person to believe the agent possesses. Liability of the principal for the ostensible agent's acts rests on the doctrine of **estoppel.** The estoppel is created by some conduct of the principal that leads the third party to believe that a person is his agent or that an actual agent possesses the requisite authority. The third party must know about this conduct and must be injured or damaged by his reliance on it. The injury or damage may be a change of position, and the facts relied on must be such that a reasonably prudent person would believe that the authority of the agency existed. Thus three usual essential elements of an estoppel—conduct, reliance, and injury—are required to create apparent authority.

Estoppel *When one's acts, representations, or silence intentionally or through negligence induce another to believe certain facts exist, and the other person acts to his detriment on the belief that such facts are true, the first person is not allowed to deny the truth of the facts.*

The theory of apparent or ostensible authority is that if a principal's words or conduct leads others to believe that he has conferred authority upon an agent, he cannot deny his words or actions to third persons who have relied on them in good faith. The acts may include words, oral or written, or may be limited to conduct that reasonably interpreted by a third person causes that person to believe that the principal consents to have the act done on his behalf by the purported agent. Apparent authority requires more than the mere appearance of authority. The facts must be such that a person exercising ordinary prudence, acting in good faith, and conversant with business practices would be misled.

Apparent authority may be the basis for liability when the purported agent is, in fact, not an agent. It also may be the legal basis for finding that an actual agent possesses authority beyond that actually conferred. In other words, apparent authority may exist in one not an agent or it may expand the authority of an actual agent. However, an agent's apparent authority to do an act for a principal must be based on the principal's words or conduct and cannot be based on anything the agent himself has said or done. An agent cannot unilaterally create his own apparent authority.

An agency by estoppel or additional authority by estoppel may arise from the agent's dealings being constantly ratified by the principal, or it may result from a person's acting the part of an agent without any dissent from the purported principal, even though it was the principal's duty to speak, as occurred in the following case.

CASE

In December 1977, the Goldsteins leased a condominium owned by Hanna. This lease granted to the Goldsteins an option to purchase Hanna's condominium any time prior to December 9, 1978. At all times during the negotiations leading to the lease/option agreement, the Goldsteins dealt only with Callahan Realty, which was Hanna's agent concerning the condominium. During August 1978, the Goldsteins decided to exercise their option to purchase Hanna's condominium. The closing date was set for August 29, 1978. Despite some difficulties that arose, the Goldsteins informed Mr. Callahan they planned to close the sale transaction by August 29. Mr. Callahan advised the Goldsteins that they did not have to perform then since their option to buy did not expire until December 9. To make sure that Callahan's statement was accurate, the Goldsteins asked him to contact Hanna. When Callahan explained the situation to him, Hanna neither agreed nor objected to the closing date being extended. In fact, Hanna's silence led the Goldsteins to rely on Callahan's advice. In the fall, Hanna refused to sell the condominium, stating that the Goldsteins' option lapsed when the closing did not occur as scheduled. The Goldsteins sued Hanna for specific performance of the sales agreement.

ISSUE: Did Hanna's failure to speak bind Hanna to Callahan's representations?

DECISION: Yes.

REASONS:

1. A principal is obligated to exercise due care and to conduct himself as a reasonably prudent businessperson with normal regard for the interests of others.
2. A principal's silence or failure to repudiate an agent's representations can give rise to the existence of apparent authority.
3. Apparent authority is based on the theory of equitable estoppel. It is in effect an estoppel against the principal to deny agency when by his conduct (or lack of speaking) he has clothed the agent with apparent authority.

Goldstein v. Hanna, 635 P.2d 290 (Nev. 1981).

Perhaps the most common situation in which apparent authority is found to exist occurs when the actual authority is terminated, but notice of this fact is not given to those entitled to receive it. Cancellation of actual authority does not automatically terminate the apparent authority created by prior transactions. The ramification of apparent authority's surviving the termination of an agency relationship requires the principal to give notice of termination to third parties. The legal aspects of this notification are discussed in Chapter 24.

3. Ratification

Ratification *The confirmation of an act or act of another: e.g., a principal may ratify the previous unauthorized act of his agent.*

As previously noted, a purported principal may become bound by ratifying an unauthorized contract. Having knowledge of all material matters, he may express or imply adoption or confirmation of a contract entered into on his behalf by someone who had no authority to do so. **Ratification** is implied by conduct of the principal, which is inconsistent with the intent to repudiate the agent's action. It is similar to ratification by an adult of a contract entered while a minor. Ratification relates back to, and is the equivalent of, authority at the commencement of the act or time of the contract. It is the affirmance of a contract already made. It cures the defect of lack of authority and creates the relation of principal and agent.

Capacity required. Various conditions must exist before a ratification will be effective in bringing about a contractual relation between the principal and the third party. First, because ratification relates back to the time of the contract, ratification can be effective only when both the principal and the agent were capable of contracting at the time the contract was executed and are still capable at the time of ratification. For this reason, a corporation may not ratify contracts made by its promoters on the corporation's behalf before the corporation was formed. For the corporation to be bound by such agreements, a novation or an assumption of liability by the corporation must occur.

Acting as agent. Second, an agent's act may be ratified only when he holds himself out as acting for the one who is alleged to have approved the unauthorized agreement. In other words, the agent must have professed to act as an agent. A person who professes to act for himself and who makes a contract in his own name does nothing that can be ratified, even though he intends at the time to let another have the benefit of his agreement.

Full knowledge. Third, as a general rule, ratification does not bind the principal unless he acts with full knowledge of all the material facts attending negotiation and execution of the contract. Of course, when there is express ratification and the principal acts without any apparent desire to know or to learn the facts, he may not later defend himself on the ground that he was unaware of all the material facts. When, however, ratification is to be implied from the conduct of the principal, he must act with knowledge of all important details, as held in the following case.

CASE

Philbrick and Perkins were involved in an automobile accident during 1976. As a result of this mishap, Philbrick sued Perkins. In an attempt to settle this claim, Perkin's insurer offered to pay $26,000. Drafts in that amount were sent to Philbrick. Being unwilling to settle for $26,000, Philbrick gave the drafts to his lawyer and instructed that lawyer to proceed with the litigation. Without further consultation, the lawyer presented the drafts with Philbrick's forged indorsements for payment. Release forms also were forged and returned to the insurer. In early 1977, Philbrick received approximately $7,500 and was told this was part of a $10,000 advance from the insurer.

In 1979, Philbrick hired another lawyer. A second suit was filed against Perkins, seeking damages as a result of the 1976 accident. Perkins then filed this present action seeking a declaration that she was not liable since the previous suit was settled and she, Perkins, had been released from further liability. All parties agreed that Philbrick's original lawyer was not authorized to release Perkins from liability. However, Perkins claimed that Philbrick ratified the release.

ISSUE: Did Philbrick ratify the release that had been forged by accepting $7,500 of the settlement proceeds?

DECISION: No.

REASONS:

1. A lawyer with no authority other than that arising from his employment contract has no authority to settle or release a client's claim.
2. For ratification of an agent's unauthorized actions to occur, it is necessary that the principal know of all material facts.
3. It is clear from the record that Philbrick did not have knowledge of the forgery when he accepted the advance money. Therefore no ratification has occurred.

Perkins v. Philbrick, 443 A.2d 73 (Me. 1982).

Conduct constituting ratification. Ratification may be either express or implied. Any conduct that definitely indicates an intention on the part of the principal to adopt the transaction will constitute ratification. It may take the form of words of approval to the agent, a promise to perform, or actual performance, such as delivery of the product called for in the agreement. Accepting the benefits of the contract or basing a suit on the validity of an agreement clearly amounts to ratification. Knowing what the agent has done, if the principal makes no objection for an unreasonable time, ratification results by operation of law. Generally, the question of what is an unreasonable time is for the jury to decide.

The issue of whether or not ratification has occurred is also a question to be decided by the jury. Among the facts to be considered by the jury are the relationship of the parties, prior conduct, circumstances pertaining to the transaction, and the action or inaction of the alleged principal upon learning of the contract. Inaction or silence by the principal creates difficulty in determining if ratification has occurred. Failure to speak may mislead the third party, and courts frequently find that a duty to speak exists where silence will mislead. Silence and inaction by the party to be charged as a principal, or failure to dissent and speak up when ordinary human conduct and fair play would normally call for some negative assertion within a reasonable time, tends to justify the inference that the principal acquiesced in the course of events and accepted the contract as his own. Acceptance and retention of the fruits of the contract with full knowledge of the material facts of the transaction is probably the most certain evidence of implied ratification. As soon as a principal learns of an unauthorized act by his agent, he should promptly repudiate it if he is to avoid liability on the theory of ratification.

An unauthorized act may not be ratified in part and rejected in part. The principal cannot accept the benefits of the contract and refuse to assume its obligations. Because of this rule, a principal, by accepting the benefits of an authorized agreement, ratifies the means used in procuring the agreement, unless within a reasonable time after learning the actual facts he takes steps to return, as far as possible, the benefits he has received. Therefore, if an unauthorized agent commits fraud in procuring a contract, acceptance of the benefits ratifies not only the contract but the fraudulent acts as well, and the principal is liable for the fraud.

LIABILITY OF PRINCIPALS—GENERAL

4. Introduction

With respect to contractual matters, a principal may become liable to its agents and third parties. The answers to when and why such liability is created depend in part on the type of principal involved. As mentioned in the previous chapter, there are three possible choices concerning the types of principals. From the third party's perspective, a principal may be *disclosed*, *partially disclosed*, or *undisclosed*. When studying the rest of this chapter, keep in mind the distinctions between these categories. For the most part, the law treats the disclosed principals differently from the other types of principals. In general, the law views the liability of partially disclosed and undisclosed principals as being the same. Therefore, in the following sections, any mention of an undisclosed principal's liability includes the liability of a partially disclosed principal, unless the text states otherwise.

5. Disclosed Principal's Liability to Agents

Generally, a disclosed principal's liability to its agents is based on the fiduciary duties discussed in Chapter 21. From a contractual perspective, a disclosed principal implicitly agrees to protect its agents from any liability as long as these agents act within the scope of authority granted. In other words, when a disclosed principal is involved, agency principles are applied in such a way that the third party must look to the principal for contractual performance if the agent acted within the authority given. If the third party seeks to hold the agent personally liable, that agent may insist that the disclosed principal hold him harmless for liability purposes. A similar result of the principal holding the agent harmless for contractual performance occurs if a disclosed principal ratifies an unauthorized agent's actions.

However, if an agent for a disclosed principal exceeds the authority granted, the principal is not liable to the agent and is not required to protect the agent from liability. In general, the agent who exceeds authority becomes personally liable to the third party and cannot rely on the principal as a substitute for liability or indemnification. The one exception to this general rule is when the disclosed principal ratifies the unauthorized actions of an agent. When ratification does occur, the liability of the parties is the same as if the agent's acts were authorized prior to their happening.

6. Disclosed Principal's Liability to Third Parties

Because of the concept of the principal holding the agent harmless, generally a disclosed principal becomes liable to third parties who negotiate and enter into contracts with authorized agents. With respect to transactions involving disclosed principals, the agent's authority may be either actual or apparent.

Furthermore, disclosed principals become liable to third parties if the unauthorized actions of an agent are ratified. With respect to such ratification, the laws of agency state that the act of ratification must occur before the third party withdraws from the contract. The reason for protecting the third party in this way is the constant legal concern with mutuality of obligations. One party should not be bound to a contract if the other party is not also bound. Therefore the law recognizes that the third party may withdraw from an unauthorized contract entered into by an agent at any time before it is ratified by the principal. If the third party were not allowed to withdraw, the unique situation in which one party is bound and the other is not would exist. Remember, though, that ratification does not require notice to the third party. As soon as conduct constituting ratification has been indulged in by the principal, the third party loses his right to withdraw.

7. Undisclosed Principal's Liability to Agents

The fact that a principal's identity or even existence is hidden from third parties does not change the principal-agent relationship. Therefore undisclosed principals may become liable for breach of a fiduciary duty owed to agents. Furthermore, undisclosed principals are liable to agents who negotiate and enter into contracts within their actual authority. Since a third party may hold an agent of an undisclosed principal personally liable, the authorized agent may recover the amount of its liability from the undisclosed principal.

The rule of law set forth in the previous sentence limits the undisclosed principal's liability only to contracts entered pursuant to the agent's *actual* authority. When a principal is undisclosed, neither apparent authority nor ratification can occur since these happenings arise as a result of the principal-third party relationship. Of course, when the principal's identity or existence is unknown to the third party, there cannot be a principal-third party relationship. In other words, an undisclosed principal has no liability to an agent who exceeds the actual authority granted by the principal.

8. Undisclosed Principal's Liability to Third Parties

The liability of undisclosed principals to third parties is limited by two important principles. First, undisclosed principals are liable to third parties only when the agent acted within the scope of actual authority. Remember, apparent authority and ratification cannot occur when the principal is undisclosed. However, an undisclosed principal who retains the benefits of a contract is liable to the third party in quasi-contract for the value of such benefits. To allow a principal to keep the benefits would be an unacceptable form of unjust enrichment at the third party's expense.

Second, the contract entered into by an actually authorized agent must be the type that can be assigned to the undisclosed principal. For example, an employment contract requiring the personal services of the agent would not bind the undisclosed principal and the third party. Suppose a group of young engineers form an architectural design firm. Wishing to be hired to design a new fifty-story building that will serve as Exxon's headquarters, these engineers decide to submit a bid. However, being fearful that their lack of reputation will harm their chances of being employed, they hire Phillip Johnson, a renowned designer-architect, to present the bid. Mr. Johnson is instructed not to reveal the new firm's identity. In other words, the bid is to be submitted in Phillip Johnson's name alone. If Exxon awarded the design job to Mr. Johnson, it is very unlikely that the new firm and Exxon become contractually bound. This result would occur because of Exxon's belief that it was hiring the unique personal talents of Mr. Johnson. That is, the contract between the agent (Phillip Johnson) and the third party (Exxon) is not assignable to the undisclosed principal (young engineering firm) without the third party's consent. The vast majority of contracts negotiated by agents for undisclosed principals will not involve those agents' personal services. Thus most of these contracts will be freely assignable.

In addition to the requirements that the agent be actually authorized and that the contract be assignable, there are two further items to consider concerning the undisclosed principal's liability to third parties. These additional legal concepts are called *election* and *settlement*, and they are applicable to undisclosed principals only. The following discussions of elections and settlements do not apply to partially disclosed principals.

9. Effect of Election

When the existence and identity of the principal become known to the third party, the third party may look to either the agent or the principal for performance. If the third party elects to hold the principal liable, the agent is released. Similarly, if the third party elects to hold the agent liable, the previously undisclosed but now disclosed principal is released. An **election** to hold one party releases the other from liability.

Election *The third party may elect to hold either the agent or the previously undisclosed principal liable. By electing to hold one party liable, the third party has chosen not to seek a recovery against the other party.*

It is sometimes difficult to know when an election has occurred. Clearly, conduct by the third party preceding the disclosure of the principal cannot constitute an election. Because of this rule, it has been held that an unsatisfied judgment obtained against the agent before disclosure of the principal will not be a later action against the principal.

After disclosure, the third party may evidence an election by making an express declaration of his intention to hold one party and not the other liable. Most states also hold that the mere receipt, without collection, of a negotiable instrument from either the principal or agent does not constitute an election. Furthermore, it is clear that merely starting a lawsuit is not an election. However, there has been some controversy among the states about whether obtaining a judgment against the principal or agent is an election if that judgment remains uncollected. Whereas all states agree that a third party is entitled to only one satisfaction, the predominant theory is that obtaining a judgment, even if it remains uncollected, amounts to an election. This theory has been called the *judgment theory* of elections, and it was applied in the following case.

CASE

An agreement was entered between Crane-Maier and the Sherrill Trust whereby the Trust's real property located in Galveston County would be subdivided, developed, and sold by Crane-Maier. Bruce Advertising dealt with Crane-Maier by supplying services on a contractual basis for development of the realty. Bruce Advertising was not aware that the Sherrill Trust owned the property that Crane-Maier was developing. Suit was brought against Crane-Maier for the services rendered by Bruce Advertising when payment was not forthcoming. After suit was instituted, Crane-Maier, by way of its pleadings, informed Bruce Advertising that the Sherrill Trust was owner of the property that Crane-Maier was developing. The trial court sitting without a jury entered judgment against both Crane-Maier and the Sherrill Trust, holding them jointly and severally liable for the services rendered by Bruce Advertising. The Sherrill Trust appealed the judgment against it, but the judgment against Crane-Maier became final.

ISSUE: Can Bruce Advertising recover from a previously undisclosed principal if a judgment against the agent is final?

DECISION: No.

REASONS:

1. Because Bruce Advertising originally did not know that Crane-Maier was acting for anyone other than itself, the Sherrill Trust was an undisclosed principal.
2. An undisclosed principal is discharged from liability upon a contract if, with knowledge of the identity of the principal, the other party recovers judgment against the agent who made the contract, for the breach of the contract. While this rule has received some discredit, the Texas courts have consistently followed it.
3. The judgment against the agent Crane-Maier has become final. On the theory of principal and agent, the principal, the Sherrill Trust, cannot now be held liable since there is a final judgment had against its agent for breach of the contract.

Sherrill v. Bruce Advertising, Inc., 538 S.W.2d 865 (Tex. 1976).

10. Effect of Settlement

Suppose that the undisclosed principal supplied the agent with money to purchase merchandise, but the agent purchased on credit and appropriated the money. In such cases the principal has been relieved of all responsibilities. The same result may occur when the undisclosed principal *settles* with the agent after the contract is made and the merchandise is received, but before disclosure is made to the third party. A majority of states have held that a bona fide **settlement** between the principal and agent before disclosure occurs releases the principal. A settlement cannot have this effect, however, when it is made after the third party has learned of the existence of the principal. This settlement rule, adopted by most states, is based on equitable principles. It is fair to the third party in that it gives him all the protection he originally bargained for, and it is fair to the principal in that it protects him against a second demand for payment.

Settlement *By paying (or settling with) the agent, the principal is relieved of liability to the third party. This third party will look to the agent for performance of their agreement.*

LIABILITY OF PRINCIPALS—SPECIAL SITUATIONS

11. Introduction

Many special problems arise in the law of agency as it relates to contractual liability and authority of agents. Some of these problems are founded on the relationship of the parties. A spouse is generally liable for the contracts of the other spouse when the contracts involve family necessities. In most states this liability is statutory. Others involve special factual situations. An existing emergency that necessitates immediate action adds sufficiently to the agent's powers to enable him to meet the situation. If time permits and the principal is available, any proposed remedy for the difficulty must be submitted to the principal for approval. It is only when the principal is not available that the powers of the agent are extended. Furthermore, the agent receives no power greater than that sufficient to solve the difficulty.

Frequently, the liability of the principal is dependent on whether the agent is, as a matter of fact, a general agent or a special agent. If the agency is general, limitations imposed upon the usual and ordinary powers of the general agent do not prevent the principal from being liable to third parties when the agent acts in violation of such limitations, unless the attention of the third parties has been drawn to them. In other words, the third party, having established that a general agency exists and having determined in a general way the limits of the authority, is not bound to explore for unexpected and unusual restrictions. He is justified in assuming, in the absence of contrary information, that the agent possesses the powers such agents customarily have. On the other hand, if the proof is only of a special or limited agency, any action in excess of the actual authority would not bind the principal. The authority for a special agent is strictly construed; if the agent exceeds his authority, the principal is not bound.

To illustrate, assume an instruction to a sales agent not to sell to a certain individual or not to sell to him on credit, although credit sales are customary. Such a limitation cannot affect the validity of a contract made with this individual, unless the latter was aware of the limitation at the time the contract was made. The principal, by appointing an agent normally possessed of certain authority, is estopped to set up the limitation as a defense unless the limitation is made known to the third party prior to the making of the contract.

12. Notice to Agents

There are other issues directly related to the authority possessed by an agent. A common problem involves whether or not notice to an agent or knowledge possessed by him is imputed to the principal. Some of these questions are covered by statutes. Civil practice statutes contain provisions on service of a summons on an agent. They specify who may be an agent for the service of process and, in effect, provide that notice to such agents constitutes notice to the principal.

Notice to, or knowledge acquired by, an agent while acting within the scope of his authority binds the principal. This rule is based on the theory that the agent is the principal's other self; therefore what the agent knows, the principal knows. While *knowledge* possessed by an agent is *notice* to the principal, the principal may not have actual knowledge of the particular fact at all. Knowledge acquired by an agent acting outside the scope of his authority is not effective notice unless the party relying thereon has reasonable ground to believe that the agent is acting within the scope of his authority (similar to apparent authority). An agent who is acquiring property for his principal may have knowledge of certain unrecorded liens against the property. The principal purchases the property subject to those liens. Equal knowledge possessed by another agent who did not represent the principal in the particular transaction, and who did not obtain the knowledge on behalf of his principal, is not imputed to the principal.

A question exists as to whether or not knowledge acquired by an agent before he became an agent can bind the principal. The majority view is that knowledge acquired by an agent before commencement of the relationship of principal and agent is imputable to the principal if the knowledge is present and in the mind of the agent while acting for the principal in the transaction to which the information is material. There are some court decisions to the contrary that have stated the agent must acquire the knowledge during the agency relationship before the principal is presumed to have notice of that information.

Notice or knowledge received by an agent under circumstances in which the agent would not be presumed to communicate the information to the principal does not bind the principal. This is an exception to the general rule that will be observed when the agent is acting in his own behalf and adversely to the principal or when the agent is under a duty to some third party not to disclose the information. Furthermore, notice to the agent, combined with collusion or fraud between him and the third party that would defeat the purpose of the notice, would not bind the principal.

As a general rule, an agent or person ostensibly in charge of a place of business has apparent authority to accept notices in relation to the business. An employee in charge of the receipt of mail may accept written notifications.

13. Agent's Power to Appoint Subagents

Agents are usually selected because of their personal qualifications. Owing to these elements of trust and confidence, a general rule has developed that an agent may not delegate his duty to someone else and clothe the latter with authority to bind the principal. An exception has arisen to this rule in cases in which the acts of the agent are purely ministerial or mechanical. An act that requires no discretion and is purely mechanical may be delegated by the agent to the third party. Such a delegation does not make the third party the agent of the principal or give him any action against the principal for compensation unless the agent was implicitly authorized to obtain this assistance. The acts of such a third party become in reality the acts of the agent. They bind the principal if they are within the authority given to the agent. Acts that involve the exercise of skill, discretion, or judgment may not be delegated without permission from the principal.

An agent may, under certain circumstances, have the actual or implied authority to appoint other agents for the principal; in which case they become true employees of the principal and are entitled to be compensated by him. This power on the part of the agent is not often implied; but if the major power conferred cannot be exercised without the aid of other agents, the agent is authorized to hire whatever help is required. Thus a manager placed in charge of a branch store may be presumed to possess authority to hire the necessary personnel.

14. Agent's Financial Powers

An agent who delivers goods sold for cash has the implied authority to collect all payments due at the time of delivery. A salesperson taking orders calling for a down payment has implied authority to accept the down payment. By the very nature of their jobs, salespeople have no implied authority to receive payments on account, and any authority to do so must be expressly given or be implied from custom. Thus a salesperson in a store has authority to collect payments made at the time of sale, but no authority to receive payments on account. If payment to a sales agent who has no authority to collect is not delivered to the principal, it may be collected by the principal from the agent or from the party who paid the agent.

Possession of a statement of account on the billhead of the principal or in the principal's handwriting does not create implied or apparent authority to collect a debt. Payment to an agent without authority to collect does not discharge the debt.

Authority to collect gives the agent no authority to accept anything other than money in payment. Unless expressly authorized, the agent is not empowered to accept negotiable notes or property in settlement of an indebtedness. It is customary for an agent to accept checks as conditional payment. Under those circumstances, the debt is not paid unless the check is honored. If the check is not paid, the creditor principal is free to bring suit on the contract that gave rise to the indebtedness or to sue on the check, at his option.

A general agent placed in charge of a business has implied or incidental authority to purchase for cash or on credit. The implied authority is based on the nature of his position and on the fact that the public rightly concludes that a corporation or an individual acting through another person has given him the power and authority that naturally and properly belong to the character in which the agent is held out.

Authority to borrow money is not easily implied. It must be expressly granted or must qualify as incidental authority to the express authority, or the principal will not be bound. The authority to borrow should always be confirmed with the principal.

LIABILITY OF AGENTS AND THIRD PARTIES

15. Introduction

Sections 4 through 10 of this chapter discuss the general rules of the principal's liability. The following sections address the corresponding issues of when agents and third parties are liable. In essence, the legal principles attempt to make sure that if one party is bound to a contract, so is another party. For example, if a disclosed principal is liable to a third party, that third party must be liable to the disclosed principal. The law always attempts to find that parties are mutually obligated for contractual performances.

16. Agent's Liability to Principals

As long as the agent acts within the scope of authority actually granted, the agent has no liability to the principal. The one exception occurs when an undisclosed principal has settled with the agent prior to the principal's being disclosed to the third party. In that situation, the agent is liable to the principal to perform the contract as instructed.

If the agent of a disclosed principal exceeds the actual authority granted but binds the principal to the third party due to the existence of apparent authority, that agent is liable to the principal for the damages caused. The basis of holding the agent liable in this situation is that the agent has breached the duty to obey instructions. Of course, if the disclosed principal ratifies an agent's unauthorized actions, the agent does not become liable to the principal.

17. Agent's Liability to Third Parties

Agents generally do not become contractually bound to third parties, because the principal usually takes the agent's place for liability purposes. However, an agent of an undisclosed principal may become liable to the third party in one of two situations. First, if the principal settles with that agent before becoming disclosed, the agent and third party are contractually bound. Second, the third party may elect to hold the agent liable instead of the principal. These are the settlement and election concepts previously noted in sections 9 and 10.

With respect to contractual matters in general, an agent may become bound to the third party by the way the agent signs the agreement or due to the language of the actual contract; that is, the agent may be liable because of the contractual document. An agent can become liable to a third party if the agent exceeds actual and apparent authority and no ratification by the principal occurs. In other words, based on a breach of an implied promise that the agent is representing a principal, the agent and third party legally are bound to one another. Further details of these two methods of binding the agent to the third party follow.

Based on the contract. Three situations may arise that make the agent liable to the third party due to the contract itself. First, if the agent carelessly executes a written agreement, he may fail to bind his principal and may incur personal liability. For example, when an agent signs a simple contract or commercial paper, he should execute it in a way that clearly indicates his representative capacity. If the signature fails to indicate the actual relationship of the parties and fails to identify the party intended to be bound, the agent may be personally liable on the instrument. Many states permit the use of oral evidence to show the intention of the agent and the third party when the signature is ambiguous—the agent is allowed to offer proof that it was not intended that he assume personal responsibility. The Code contains express provisions on the liability of an agent who signs a commercial paper. These are discussed in Chapter 39. The following case is an example of an agent failing to sign in a representative capacity.

CASE

Plaintiff Moore entered into a contract to market apples grown by Pioneer Orchards Company. The defendants Seabaugh and Weiss had entered into a financial management contract with Pioneer Orchards that required their approval of all Pioneer contracts. In order to indicate their approval of the Moore contract, Seabaugh and Weiss signed without stating their capacity or reasons for signing. Later, when a dispute arose, Moore sued Pioneer, Seabaugh, and Weiss for breach of contract. Seabaugh and Weiss argued that, as agents, they could not be held personally liable.

ISSUE: Are these agents personally liable on the Moore contract?

DECISION: Yes.

REASONS:
1. Generally, where a third party and an agent for a disclosed principal make a contract, the agent is not personally liable to the third party for a breach of the contract.
2. An agent of a disclosed principal may be held personally liable to a third party for a breach of the contract if the parties to the contract agree upon personal liability of the agent.
3. An agent incurs personal liability, regardless of disclosure of the principal, where the agent contracts in his own name rather than on behalf of his principal.
4. Where an individual signs an agreement without indicating that the signature is only given as an agent, personal liability can be established.

Moore v. Seabaugh, 684 S.W.2d 492 (Mo. App. 1984).

Second, if the agent does not disclose his agency or name his principal, he binds himself and becomes subject to all liabilities, express and implied, created by the contract and transaction, in the same manner as if he were the principal. If an agent wishes to avoid personal liability, the duty is upon the agent to disclose the agency. There is no duty on the third party to discover the agency.

An agent who purports to be a principal is liable as a principal. The fact that the agent is known to be a commission merchant, auctioneer, or other professional agent is immaterial. He must disclose not only that he is an agent but the identity of his principal if the agent is not to have personal liability. Any agent for an undisclosed or partially disclosed principal assumes personal liability on the contract into which he enters, as occurred in the following case.

CASE

This case arises out of the breach of an employment contract. Sound West, Inc., is a Montana corporation that owns a chain of stores. Jim Rhines is the president and a shareholder of Sound West. Gary Como, who has worked as an accountant and with computers, sought employment in Montana. Through an employment agency's reference, Como met with Rhines about possible employment. After a series of interviews in April 1978, Rhines agreed to hire Como and to pay his moving expenses. They agreed Como would begin working for Sound West in June. After Como moved and settled his family, he contacted Rhines about beginning his employment. Rhines was noncommittal. Following several more requests by Como for a starting date, Rhines told Como there was no job for him at Sound West. Como secured employment elsewhere and sued Rhines for lost wages and moving expenses. Rhines argued he was acting as an agent for Sound West, Inc.; therefore he was not personally liable to Como.

ISSUE: Was Rhines liable to Como for damages resulting from the breach of the employment contract?

DECISION: Yes.

REASONS:
1. The managing officer of a corporation, even though acting for the company, becomes liable as a principal where he deals

with a third party who is ignorant of the company's existence or the manager's relationship to that company.

2. Rhines was not able to refute Como's proof that Como believed Rhines was an individual doing business as Sound West. Apparently, Rhines never disclosed to Como that Rhines simply was an agent for a corporation called Sound West, Inc.

Como v. Rhines, 645 P.2d 948 (Mont. 1982).

Third, the third party may request the agent to be bound personally on the contract. This request may be due to lack of confidence in the financial ability of the principal because the agent's credit rating is superior to that of the principal, or some personal reason. When the agent voluntarily assumes the burden of performance in his personal capacity, he is liable in the event of nonperformance by his principal.

Based on breach of warranty. An agent's liability may be implied from the circumstances as well as being the direct result of the contract. Liability in such situations is usually said to be implied and to arise from the breach of an implied warranty. Two basic warranties are used to imply liability: the warranty of authority and the warranty that the principal is competent.

As a general rule, an agent implicitly warrants to third parties that he possesses power to effect the contractual relations of his principal. If in any particular transaction the agent fails to possess this power, the agent violates this implied warranty, and he is liable to third parties for the damages resulting from his failure to bind the principal. The agent may or may not be aware of this lack of authority, and he may honestly believe that he possesses the requisite authority. Awareness of lack of authority and honesty is immaterial. If an agent exceeds his authority, he is liable to the third parties for the breach of the warranty of authority.

The agent may escape liability for damages arising from lack of authority by a full disclosure to a third party of all facts relating to the source of the agent's authority. Where all the facts are available, the third party is as capable of judging the limits of the agent's powers as is the agent.

Every agent who deals with third parties warrants that his principal is capable of being bound. Consequently, an agent who acts for a minor or a corporation not yet formed may find himself liable for the nonperformance of his principal. The same rule enables the third party to recover from the agent when his principal is an unincorporated association, such as a club, lodge, or other informal group. An unincorporated association is not a legal entity separate and apart from its members. In most states it cannot sue or be sued in the name it uses, but all members must be joined in a suit involving the unincorporated group. When an agent purports to bind such an organization, a breach of the warranty results because there is no entity capable of being bound. If the third party is fully informed that the principal is an unincorporated organization and he agrees to look entirely to it for performance, the agent is not liable.

The warranty that an agent has a competent principal must be qualified in one respect. An agent is not liable when, unknown to him, his agency has been cut short by the death of the principal. Death of the principal terminates an agency.

Because death is usually accompanied by sufficient publicity to reach third parties, the facts are equally available to both parties, and no breach of warranty arises.

18. Third Party's Liability to Principals

A disclosed principal may enforce any contract made by an authorized agent for the former's benefit. This right applies to all contracts in which the principal is the real party in interest, including contracts made in the agent's name. Furthermore, if a contract is made for the benefit of a disclosed principal by an agent acting outside the scope of his authority, the principal is still entitled to performance, provided the contract is properly ratified before withdrawal by the third party.

An undisclosed principal is entitled to performance by third parties of all assignable contracts made for his benefit by an authorized agent. It is no defense for the third party to say that he had not entered into a contract with the principal.

If a contract is one that involves the skill or confidence of the agent and is one that would not have been entered into without this skill or confidence, its performance may not be demanded by the undisclosed principal. This rule applies because the contract would not be assignable, since personal rights and duties are not transferable without consent of the other party.

In cases other than those involving commercial paper, the undisclosed principal takes over the contract subject to all defenses that the third party could have established against the agent. If the third party contracts to buy from such an agent and has a right of setoff against the agent, he has this same right to set off against the undisclosed principal. The third party may also pay the agent prior to discovery of the principal and thus discharge his liability.

19. Third Party's Liability to Agents

Normally, the agent possesses no right to bring suit on contracts made by him for the benefit of his principal, because he has no interest in the cause of action. The agent who binds himself to the third party, either intentionally or ineptly by a failure to express himself properly, may, however, maintain an action. An agent of an undisclosed principal is liable on the contract and may sue in his own name in the event of nonperformance by the third party. Thus either the agent or the undisclosed principal may bring suit, but in case of a dispute, the right of the previously undisclosed principal is superior.

Custom has long sanctioned an action by the agent based on a contract in which he is interested because of anticipated commissions. As a result, a factor may institute an action in his own name to recover for goods sold. He may also recover against a carrier for delay in the shipment of goods sold or to be sold.

Similarly, an agent who has been vested with title to commercial paper may sue the maker of the paper. The same is true of any claim held by the principal that he definitely places with the agent for collection and suit, where necessary. In all cases of this character, the agent retains the proceeds as a trust fund for his principal.

CHAPTER SUMMARY

Basic Principles

Actual Authority	1. Actual authority is transmitted directly by the principal to the agent. 2. Such authority may be expressed by the principal in either written or spoken form. 3. In the alternative, actual authority may be implied from the actions of the principal and agent or from the nature of either party's position (such as a corporate officer).
Apparent or Ostensible Authority	1. When actual authority is missing, the doctrine of estoppel may create apparent authority. 2. The basis of apparent authority is the indication of an agency relationship by the principal to third parties. This authority is possible only with fully disclosed principals. 3. Apparent authority is most likely to exist when an agent is terminated and the principal fails to give notice to third parties of termination.
Ratification	1. If neither actual nor apparent authority can be found, ratification by the principal may still bind the principal and third party contractually. 2. Ratification of an unauthorized agent's acts can occur only when the principal is fully disclosed. 3. Furthermore, principal must have full knowledge of all material facts and give a clear indication (expressed or implied) of ratification.

Liability of Principals

Disclosed Principal's Liability to Agents	1. As long as agents act in an authorized manner, principals must indemnify agents. 2. When an agent exceeds the actual authority, the principal is not liable to the agent unless the unauthorized acts were ratified.
Disclosed Principal's Liability to Third Parties	1. If an agent negotiates a contract within either actual or apparent authority, the principal is legally bound to the third party. 2. If an agent exceeds authority, the principal is bound to the third party only if ratification occurs before the third party withdraws.
Undisclosed Principal's Liability to Agents	1. These rules apply to partially disclosed and undisclosed principals alike. 2. A principal is liable to hold an agent harmless if the agent acted within actual authority granted. (There is no apparent authority in these situations.) 3. A principal has no liability to an agent who exceeds actual authority. (Ratification is not possible.)
Undisclosed Principal's Liability to Third Parties	1. These rules apply to partially disclosed and undisclosed principals alike. 2. A principal is contractually bound to third parties if the agent acted within actual authority, and the contract can be assigned to the principal without the third parties' consent.
Election	1. These rules apply only to fully undisclosed principals. 2. Third parties must elect to hold either the agent or the previously undisclosed (now revealed) principal liable on the contract.

3. What constitutes an election is not clear. Most states follow the theory that a final judgment is an election.

Settlement

1. This applies only to fully undisclosed principals.
2. A principal is not contractually bound to a third party if that principal settles with the agent after the contract is negotiated but before the principal becomes disclosed.

Special Situations

1. Principals are liable for the knowledge possessed by the agent unless the third party has requested that the agent keep the information confidential.
2. In general, principals are liable only for the agent's actions. Agents must be given clear authority to appoint subagents.
3. Principals generally are not liable for an agent's abuse of financial powers. Such powers are very limited and must be explicitly granted by the principal to the agent.

Liability of Agents and Third Parties

Agent's Liability to Principals

1. In general, an agent is not liable to the principal if that agent followed instructions and did not breach any fiduciary duties.
2. An agent of an undisclosed principal becomes liable to perform the contract if that principal has settled with the agent.
3. An agent is liable to the principal if the agent exceeded the actual authority granted unless the disclosed principal ratified the unauthorized actions.

Agent's Liability to Third Parties

1. Generally, an agent does not become contractually bound to third parties. (Recall, one purpose of the agency relationship is to substitute the principal for the agent as the party contractually liable to the third party.)
2. An agent of an undisclosed principal does become contractually bound to the third party if that principal settles with the agent or if the third party elects to hold the agent liable.
3. An agent becomes bound to the third party if that agent fails to indicate his representative capacity.
4. An agent becomes bound to the third party when that agent breaches the implied warranty that the agent is acting within the authority granted or the warranty that there is a competent principal.

Third Party's Liability to Principals

1. A third party is contractually liable to a disclosed principal when the agent acts within the authority granted or when the principal ratifies the unauthorized acts prior to the third party's withdrawing from the contract.
2. A third party is bound to a partially disclosed or undisclosed principal if the contract is assignable by the agent without the third party's consent.

Third Party's Liability to Agents

1. A third party is contractually liable to an agent when that agent is liable to third party.
2. Examples of these situations might include the application of the concepts of settlement or election when an undisclosed principal is involved, the agent failing to sign in a representative capacity, and the agent breaching the warranty of authority.

REVIEW QUESTIONS AND PROBLEMS

1. Match each term in column A with the appropriate statement in column B.

A	B
(1) Actual authority	(a) The required step to bind a disclosed principal and third party to a contract if the agent's actions are unauthorized.
(2) Apparent authority	(b) An event that constitutes an election.
(3) Ratification	(c) Because of the personal nature of the principal-agent relationship, an agent must be given clear authority to do this.
(4) Election	(d) Breach of this is one example of how an agent becomes contractually liable to a third party.
(5) Judgment theory	(e) Its existence is possible only when the principal is fully disclosed.
(6) Settlement	(f) The process whereby a third party chooses to hold the agent or a previously undisclosed principal liable on a contract.
(7) Appointment of subagents	(g) This type of authority may be conveyed by a principal to an agent by written or spoken words or by the parties' conduct.
(8) Warranty of authority	(h) Method whereby an undisclosed principal is relieved of liability to a third party prior to the principal becoming disclosed.

2. Pat, the owner of a grocery store chain, hires Amy to manage one store. Pat tells Amy to stock the store. Pat also tells Amy: (a) "Be sure to buy soup"; (b) "Don't buy soup"; (c) nothing about soup. Amy then proceeds to buy 40 cases of soup from Tom. In which situations, if any, is Pat liable to Tom? Explain.

3. A real estate broker prepared an earnest money agreement, which included terms different from those actually agreed to by the selling owner. The owner signed the agreement, and upon discovery of the mistake, he sued the real estate dealer for causing the error. Is the agent liable to his principal? Why or why not? No, cause owner ratified by signing the contract

4. Jim applied for health insurance coverage with Great American. The application was taken by an independent insurance agent who was not an agent of Great American. The brochure stated that a policy would be issued after investigation. At the time, Jim was told that the insurance would be effective immediately upon payment of the premium. Later Great American denied coverage and returned his check. Is it liable on the contract? Why or why not?

5. Kapp authorized Schlad to have an engine repaired. Kapp specified that he would not pay more than $3,000 in repair costs. Schlad spent $6,500 on the repairs. Is Kapp or Schlad liable for the additional $3,500? Explain. Schlad, he exceeded his authority

6. A buyer sued the Farm Corporation for specific performance of a contract for the sale of farmland. The contract had been signed by the president of the corporation. The board of directors had authorized the president to discuss the sale of land but had not authorized the sale. The land described in the contract was 35 percent of the corporation's assets. Is the Farm Corporation bound to perform the contract signed by its president? Explain.

7. Jerry, the managing agent of Pet Shop, Inc., borrowed $3,500 from Turner on the shop's behalf for use in the business. The company had not authorized Jerry to borrow the money, but it did repay $500 of the amount to Turner. Is Turner entitled to collect the balance due from the shop? Why or why not? Yes, Shop ratified by paying the $500

8. Oxford operates a janitorial service and cleans commercial buildings. Oxford contracted with Gresham to clean several buildings on a regular basis, not knowing that Gresham

was only an agent hired to manage these buildings. Gresham failed to make several payments owed to Oxford. When Oxford sued Gresham for the money owed, Gresham argued he was not liable, since he was merely an agent. Is Gresham correct? Why or why not?

9. Ann worked for Perry's Grocery as purchasing agent for poultry and farm produce. In all transactions with farmers, Ann acted as the principal and purchased on the strength of her own credit. Ann failed to pay for some of the produce purchased. The farmers, having ascertained that Perry's Grocery was the true principal, seek to hold it responsible. May they do so? Suppose that Perry's had previously settled with Ann? Explain.

10. Alice was hired by Petro Chemical to be a member of the land acquisitions department. While investigating the possible purchase of a large tract of land, Alice learned that there was neither oil nor gas under the land. Trion, the owner of this land, was dismayed by Alice's findings. Trion persuaded Alice not to tell her employer of her knowledge. Indeed, if Petro Chemical purchased his land, Trion agreed to pay Alice \$25,000. Trion was able to convince Petro Chemical to buy his land since it had the possibility of containing oil and gas. After this purchase, Petro Chemical discovered it had been defrauded. It sued Trion, but he claimed he could not be liable since Alice's knowledge of the barren land was imputed to Petro Chemical. Was this agent's knowledge notice to her principal? Explain.

11. Patricia owned a retail clothing store. As her agent, Patricia's father did business in the store's name. Indeed, a power of attorney signed by Patricia gave her father the authority "to sign and indorse all checks and drafts and to transact all business." Patricia's father borrowed money from a bank for the store's benefit. Did the power of attorney give her father the authority to approve this loan? Explain.

12. Alex, thinking he had authority to do so, signed a promissory note as an agent of Patterson's Paint Corporation. Later Alex and the payee learned Patterson's was not bound, owing to Alex's lack of authority to borrow money. Is Alex liable if the note was signed "Patterson's Paint Corporation, by Alex Ander, as agent"? Why?

Agency and the Law of Torts

23

CHAPTER PREVIEW

BUSINESS MANAGEMENT DECISION

You are the president of a soft-drink bottling company. Your products are delivered by drivers who own their trucks and who are paid on a commission basis. These drivers work their own hours, and they pay their assistants. You consider these drivers to be independent contractors.

What risks are present and what should you do to minimize them?

FUNDAMENTAL PRINCIPLES

1. Introduction

The fundamental principles of tort liability in the law of agency, which are discussed in this chapter, can be summarized as follows:

1. Agents, servants, and independent contractors are personally liable for their own torts.
2. Agents, servants, and independent contractors are not liable for the torts of their employers.
3. A master is liable under a doctrine known as *respondeat superior* for the torts of his servant if the servant is acting within the scope of his employment.
4. A principal, proprietor, employer, or contractee (each of these terms is sometimes used) is not, as a general rule, liable for the torts of an independent contractor.
5. Injured employees may have rights against their employers as well as against third parties who cause their injuries.

Master *In agency relationships involving torts, this party is in a position similar to that of a principal.*

Servant *A person employed by another and subject to the direction and control of the employer in performance of his duties.*

The terms **master** and **servant** are technically more accurate than the terms *principal* and *agent* in describing the parties when tort liability is discussed. Courts, nevertheless, frequently describe the parties as *principal* and *agent*. A principal, however, is liable for torts of only those agents who are subject to the kind of control that establishes the master-servant relationship. For the purpose of tort liability, a *servant* is a person who is employed with or without pay to perform personal services for another in his affairs, and who, in respect to the physical movements in the performance of such service, is subject to the master's right of power of control. A person who renders services for another but retains control over the manner of rendering such services is not a servant, but an independent contractor.

2. Tort Liability of Agents, Servants, and Independent Contractors

Every person who commits a tort is personally liable to the individual whose body or property is injured or damaged by the wrongful act. An agent or officer of a corporation who commits or participates in the commission of a tort, whether or not he acts on behalf of his corporation, is liable to third persons injured. One is not relieved of tort liability by establishing that the tortious act was committed under the direction of someone else or in the course of employment of another.

The following case is typical of those holding corporate officers personally liable for torts committed in their official capacity.

CASE

The Mississippi Printing Company, Inc., filed suit against Maris, West & Baker, Inc., and its president, executive vice president, and production manager. The plantiff alleged that these three individuals wrote a letter to the Better Business Bureau in Jackson, Mississippi. This letter supposedly contained libelous statements about the "very unbusiness-like conduct" of the plaintiff. The three individual defendants sought a directed verdict in their favor since they signed the letter in their representative capacities.

ISSUE: Is a directed verdict appropriate?

DECISION: No.

REASONS:

1. The potentially libelous letter was signed by the corporation's president, the executive vice president, and the production manager. Each signed in his official capacity on Maris, West & Baker stationery. It is clear that the individuals named participated directly in the publication of the letter.
2. The general rule is well established that when a corporate officer directly participates in or authorizes the commission of a tort, even on behalf of the corporation, he may be held personally liable.
3. Therefore it is appropriate to allow the jury to determine the individual defendants' personal liablity, if any.

Mississippi Printing v. Maris, West & Baker, Inc., 492 So.2d 977 (Miss. 1986).

The fact that the employer or principal may be held liable does not in any way relieve the servant or agent from liability. The agent's or servant's liability is joint and several with the liability of the principal. Of course, the converse is not true. An agent, servant, or independent contractor is not liable for the torts of the principal, master, or employer.

Assume that an employer is liable as the result of a tort committed by an agent or servant. Is the employer upon paying the judgment entitled to recover from the agent or servant? The answer is technically "yes" because a servant is liable for this own misconduct either to others or to his employer.

Suits by masters against servants for indemnity are not common, for several reasons. First, the servant's financial condition frequently does not warrant suit. Second, the employer knows of the risk of negligence by his employees and covers this risk with insurance. If indemnity were a common occurrence, the ultimate loss would almost always fall on employees or workers. If this situation developed, it would have an adverse effect on employee morale and would make labor-management relations much more difficult. Therefore few employers seek to enforce the right to collect losses from employees.

Just as a master may have a right to collect from the servant, under certain situations the servant may maintain a successful action for reimbursement and indemnity against the master. Such a case would occur when the servant commits a tort by following the master's instructions if that servant did not know his conduct was tortious. This was discussed in Chapter 21.

Example: Matthews, a retail appliance dealer, instructs Stewart to repossess a TV set from Trevor, who had purchased it on an installment contract. Matthews informs Stewart that Trevor is in arrears in his payments. Actually, Trevor is current in his payments. A bookkeeping error had been made by Matthews. Despite Trevor's protests, Stewart repossesses the TV set pursuant to Matthew's instructions. Stewart has committed the torts of trespass and wrongful conversion. Matthews must indemnify Stewart and satisfy Trevor's claim if Trevor elects to collect tort damages from Stewart.

TORT LIABILITY OF MASTERS

3. Respondeat Superior

A master is liable to third persons for the torts committed by his servants *within the scope of their employment* and in prosecution of the master's business. This concept, frequently known as *respondeat superior* (let the master respond), imposes vicarious liability on employers as a matter of public policy. Athough negligence of the servant is the usual basis of liability, the doctrine of *respondeat superior* is also applicable to intentional torts, such as trespass, assault, libel, and fraud, which are committed by a servant acting within the scope of his employment. It is applicable even though the master did not direct the willful act or assent to it.

This vicarious liability imposed on masters, which makes them pay for wrongs they have not actually committed, is not based on logic and reason but on business and social policy. The theory is that the master is in a better position to pay for the wrong than is the servant. This concept is sometimes referred to as the "deep pocket" theory. The business policy theory is that injuries to persons and property are hazards of doing business, the cost of which the business should bear rather than have the loss borne by the innocent victim of the tort of society as a whole.

There is universal agreement that a master is vicariously liable for the actual damages caused by a servant acting within the scope of employment. However, there is disagreement about when the master is liable for punitive damages that may be awarded to punish the servant's wrong. One theory that has been widely adopted by courts in some states is called the *vicarious liability rule*. This rule states that the master always is liable for punitive damages awarded against the servant if the wrong commited occurred within the scope of the servant's employment. The logic behind this rule involves the belief that making the master liable for punitive damages will help deter reckless or intentional torts.

The more modern view of punitive damages that has been adopted by a growing number of states has been called the *complicity rule*. The advantage of this rule is that it allows for a determination of whether a master actually is blameworthy before making that master liable for punitive damages. In essence, under this second principle, in order to collect punitive damages from the master, an injured third party must be able to prove that either (1) the master had authorized the servant to commit the tort, (2) the master was reckless in employing or retaining the servant, (3) the servant was employed in a managerial position, or (4) the master had ratified the servant's tortious conduct. The following case illustrates the application of the complicity rule.

CASE

Richard Welch was employed as a truck driver by Mercury Motors Express. While driving in an intoxicated condition. Welch drove off the road and hit David Faircloth. As a result of this wreck, Faircloth died. The representative of Faircloth's estate sued Mercury Motors Express under the doctrine of ***respondeat superior.*** The trial jury awarded the plaintiff $400,000 in compensatory damages and $250,000 in punitive damages. Since it did not dispute the fact that its driver was under the influence of alcohol at the time of the wreck, Mercury paid the compensatory damages. However, Mercury appealed and argued it is not responsible to pay the punitive damages awarded.

ISSUE: Is a master liable in punitive damages for the willful and wanton misconduct of its employee acting within the scope of employment?

DECISION: No.

REASONS:

1. Before an employer may be held vicariously liable for punitive damages under the doctrine of *respondeat superior,* there must be some fault on his part.
2. The employer's fault does not have to amount to willful and wanton misconduct independent of the servant's conduct.
3. For example, in this case Mercury Motors would have become liable for punitive damages if it knew its driver was drinking when he reported to work or if it knew this driver had a history of a drinking problem.
4. In this case, the plaintiff proved no separate fault on Mercury Motors' part. Relying solely on the master-servant relationship is insufficient to make the master liable for punitive damages.

Mercury Motors Express v. Smith, 393 So.2d 545 (Fla. 1981).

The application of the doctrine of *respondeat superior* usually involves the issue of whether the servant was *acting within the scope of his employment* at the time of the commission of the tort. The law imposes liability on the master only if the tort occurs while the servant is carrying on the master's business or if the master authorizes or ratifies the servant's actions. The master's liability does not arise when the servant steps aside from his employment to commit the tort or when the servant does a wrongful act to accomplish a personal purpose. This is discussed further in section 5 in this chapter.

It is not possible to state a simple test to determine if the tort is committed within the scope of the employment. Factors to be considered include the nature of the employment, the right of control "not only as to the result to be accomplished but also as to the means to be used," the ownership of the instrumentality such as an automobile, whether the instrumentality was furnished by the employer, whether the use was authorized, and the time of the occurrence. Most courts inquire into the intent of the servant and the extent of deviation from expected conduct involved in the tort.

As a general rule, the master cannot avoid liability by showing that he has instructed the servant not to do the particular act complained of. When a servant disobeys the instructions of his master, the fact of disobedience alone does not insulate the master from liability. In addition, the master is not released by evidence that the servant was not doing the work his master had instructed him to do, when the servant had misunderstood the instruction. As long as the servant is attempting to further his master's business, the master is liable, because the servant is acting within the scope of his employment.

The issue of whether a servant is acting within the scope of employment usually is one of fact. Therefore this issue typically must be resolved by a jury. Seldom will a judge be able to make a ruling involving the doctrine of *respondeat superior* as a matter of law. One of the most difficult situations to resolve is going to or coming from work. Although general statements could be made, the peculiar facts of each case are crucial in determining whether an employer is liable for the employee's acts, as the following case illustrates.

CASE

Anthony Barajas was an employee of the Trojan Fireworks Company. On December 21, 1979, Trojan held a Christmas party at its factory from noon until 4:00 P.M. The employees were not required to perform their regular duties that afternoon. Instead, they were encouraged to attend the party and to enjoy the alcoholic beverages provided. Barajas attended the party and drank heavily. He then attempted to drive home. Barajas was involved in a wreck that killed James Harris and injured two others. Suits were filed against Trojan asserting that the company was liable for Barajas's actions since he was within the scope of employment. On Trojan's motion, the trial court dismissed the complaints since it concluded, as a matter of law, that Barajas was not within the scope of employment at the time of the accident. The plaintiffs appealed.

ISSUE: Did the trial court err in dismissing the complaint?

DECISION: Yes.

REASONS:
1. As a general rule, employers are exempt from liability for injury caused to or by employees while the employees are traveling to and from work. This rule often is referred to as the "going and coming" rule.
2. However, there are exceptions to the going and coming rule. It is socially desirable that an employer compensate an innocent third party injured by a negligent employee where the risk is inherent in or created by the employment.
3. The employer's liability attaches where a nexus exists between the employment and the activity that results in a foreseeable injury.
4. Trojan should not be excused from liability, as a matter of law, when the company created and perhaps encouraged a situation that permitted an intoxicated employee to drive home.
5. Plaintiffs' complaints contain sufficient alleged facts, which, if proved, would support a jury's finding that Barajas was within the scope of employment at the time the accident occurred.

Harris v. Trojan Fireworks Company, 174 Cal. Rptr. 452 (App., 4th Dist. 1981).

4. Expanding Vicarious Liability

In recent years, the law has been expanding the concept of vicarious liability, even to acts of persons who are not employees. A person engaged in some endeavor gratuitously may still be a ''servant'' within the scope of the master-servant doctrine. The two key elements for determination of whether a gratuitous undertaking is a part of the master-servant relationship are (1) whether the actor has submitted himself to the directions and to the control of the one for whom the service is done, and (2) whether the primary purpose of the underlying act was to serve another. If so, the "master" is liable for the torts of the unpaid "servant."

Most of the expansion of the application of *respondeat superior* and vicarious liability has been by statute. Liability for automobile accidents has been a major area of expansion. Some states have adopted what is known as the "family car doctrine." Under it, if the car is generally made available for family use, any member of the family is presumed to be an agent of the parent-owner when using the family car for his or her convenience or pleasure. The presumption may be rebutted, however. Other states have gone further and provided that anyone driving a car with the permission of the owner is the owner's agent, and the owner has vicarious liability to persons injured by the driver.

5. Exceptions—Frolics and Detours

Although it often is difficult to know with certainty whether a servant is or is not within the scope of employment, the law has recognized that the master is *not* liable when the servant is on a frolic or when the servant has detoured in a substantial manner from the master's instructions. A *frolic* exists whenever a servant pursues his personal interests while neglecting the master's business. For example, a route salesman who leaves his route to accomplish a personal errand is on a frolic. If an accident occurs while this salesman is on the frolic, his master would not be liable for the third party's injuries. A very hard question to answer is this: When does a frolic or detour end so that the servant is again within the scope of employment?

Not every deviation from the strict course of duty is a departure that will relieve a master of liability for the acts of the servant. The fact that a servant, while performing his duty to his master, incidentally does something for himself or a third person does not automatically relieve the master from liability for negligence that causes injury to another. To sever the servant from the scope of his employment, the act complained of must be such a divergence from his regular duties that its very character severs the relationship of master and servant.

Another difficult situation is presented when the servant combines his own business with that of his master. As a general rule, this fact does not relieve the master of liability. Furthermore, the doctrine of *respondeat superior* has been extended to create the master's liability for the negligence of strangers while assisting a servant in carrying out the master's business if the authority to obtain assistance is given or required, as in an emergency.

6. Intentional Torts

Intentional or willful torts are not as likely to occur within the scope of the servant's employment as are those predicated upon a negligence theory. If the willful misconduct of the servant has nothing to do with his master's business and is animated entirely by hatred or a feeling of ill will toward the third party, the master is not liable. Nor is the master liable if the employee's act has no reasonable connection with his employment. However, the injured third party generally does not have to prove that the master actually instructed the servant to commit the intentional tort. Once again, the key issue for determining the master's liability is whether the servant was within the scope of employment, as is illustrated in the following case.

CASE

Alden and Winthrop Condict, who are brothers, operate a ranch. Wynn Condict, the son of Winthrop (and nephew of Alden), works on this ranch. There is an area on the Condict ranch where gas pumps are located close to a bridge, and, because of its weakened condition, the bridge had been designated for use by lightweight vehicles only. One morning Wynn Condict was at the gas pumps assigning his father's employees their various tasks for the day. At the same time, Ted Jenkins and another employee of Alden Condict were gassing two vehicles, one of which was a heavy army surplus six-by-six truck utilized in haying operations. An altercation occurred between Jenkins and Wynn Condict when Jenkins made known his intent to drive the large truck over the bridge, it being Wynn Condict's position that this was one of the heavy vehicles for which the bridge was not to be used. Wynn Condict became alarmed because his new pickup truck was blocking the bridge and he proceeded to back his pickup across the bridge. In the meantime, Jenkins had commandeered the army surplus vehicle, crashed it through a gate, and headed toward Wynn's vehicle. Somewhere near the end of the bridge or just off the other side, Jenkins rammed the pickup with the truck. As a result of this impact, Wynn Condict claims that he suffered severe injury to his back, which resulted in his bringing a personal injury action against Alden Condict, as Jenkins's employer, in which he sought both compensatory and punitive damages. The trial judge directed a verdict in favor of Alden Condict, finding that Wynn Condict had failed to prove that Jenkins was acting in the scope of employment at the time of this incident. Wynn Condict appealed.

ISSUE: Must the plaintiff prove that the defendant authorized his employee to commit this intentional tort in order to find the act within the scope of employment?

DECISION: No.

REASONS:

1. The correct burden of proof to be placed on the plaintiff with regard to the scope of employment issue is to demonstrate that the employee was at least in part seeking to further the interest of the employer.
2. An important factor in determining whether the master is liable for the intentional tort of the employee is whether the "use of force is not unexpectable by the master."
3. The judge erred in finding plaintiff did not discharge his burden of proof. Plaintiff was required to show that, at least in part, the defendant was seeking to further the master's business and that the acts were foreseeable. The case should have been submitted to the jury.

Condict v. Condict, 664 P.2d 131 (Wyo. 1983).

7. Tort Suits—Procedures

As previously noted, the law of torts in most states, unlike the law of contracts, allows joinder of the master and servant as defendants in one cause of action or permits them to be sued separately. Although the plantiff is limited to one recovery, the master and servant are jointly and severally liable. The party may collect from either or both in any proportion until the judgment is paid in full. If the servant is sued first and a judgment is obtained that is not satisfied, the suit is not a bar to a subsequent suit against the master, but the amount of the judgment against the servant fixes the maximum limit of potential liability against the master.

If the servant is found to be free of liability, either in a separate suit or as a codefendant with the master, then the suit against the master on the basis of *respondeat superior* will fail. The master's liability is predicated upon the fault of the servant; if the servant is found to be free of fault, the master has no liability as a matter of law.

INDEPENDENT CONTRACTORS' TORTS

8. Control over Independent Contractors

An *independent contractor* has power to control the details of the work he performs for his employer. Because the performance is within his control, he is not a servant, and his only responsibility is to accomplish the result contracted for. For example, Rush contracts to build a boat for Ski-King at a cost of $40,000, according to certain specifications. It is clear that Rush is an independent contractor; the completed boat is the result. Had Ski-King engaged Rush by the day to assist in building the boat under Ski-King's supervision and direction, the master-servant relationship would have resulted. Keep in mind that an agent with authority to represent his principal contractually will, at the same time, be either a servant or an independent contractor for the purpose of tort liability.

The hallmark of a master-servant relationship is that the master not only controls the result of the work but also has the right to direct the manner in which the work will be accomplished. The distinguishing feature of a proprietor–independent contractor relationship is that the person engaged to do the work has exclusive control of the manner of performing it, being responsible only to produce the desired result. In ascertaining whether a person is a servant or an independent contractor, the basic inquiry is whether such person is subject to the alleged employer's control or right to control his physical conduct in the performance of services for which he was engaged. Whether the relationship is master-servant or proprietor–independent contractor is usually a question of fact for the jury or for a fact finder if the issue arises in an administrative proceeding, as occurred in the following case.

CASE

Emida Cedar had timber harvesting rights to some land. Cedar and Eugene Sines entered into an agreement wherein he would harvest and transport the timber to various mills for a price of $90.00 per 1,000 board feet. This agreement was entered into as an oral one some time in January or February 1982. On May 20, 1982, while attempting to load logs, Sines caught his hand in the loader's gears. That he has serious permanent injury is not in dispute.

Sines made a claim on Cedar for medical expenses and income benefits. The claim was denied by Cedar's surety, Mission National Insurance Company, on the basis that Sines was not an employee of Cedar. Following a hearing, the Industrial Commission concluded that Sines was an independent contractor at the time of his accident, and denied benefits. Sines has appealed that determination.

ISSUE: Was the commission's conclusion supported by the evidence?

DECISION: Yes.

REASONS: 1. The current test in Idaho for determining whether an individual is an employee or an independent contractor is the "right to control test." The test generally focuses upon consideration of four factors: (a) direct evidence of the right, (b) the method of payments, (c) furnishing major items of equipment, and (d) the right to terminate the employment relationship at will and without liability.

2. Whether an individual is an employee or an independent contractor is an issue that must be decided on a case-by-case approach, with the decision to be reached based upon all the facts and circumstances established by the evidence.
3. The commission found that Sines hired, controlled, and paid his own assistants; furnished his own equipment and tools; paid his own expenses; and decided when his crew was to begin work, end work, and take breaks. He even hired his replacement after he was injured.
4. Substantial and competent evidence supports the facts found by the commission, and it properly applied the law based upon those facts.

Sines v. Sines, 718 P.2d 1214 (Idaho 1986).

Without changing the relationship from that of proprietor and independent contractor or the duties arising from that relationship, an employer of an independent contractor may retain a broad general power of supervision of the work to ensure satisfactory performance of the contract. He may inspect, stop the work, make suggestions or recommendations about details of the work, or prescribe alterations or deviations.

9. General Rule—No Liability

The destinction between servants and independent contractors is important because, as a general rule, the doctrine of *respondeat superior* and the concept of vicarious liability in tort are not applicable to independent contractors. There is no tort liability, as a general rule, because the theories that justify liability of the master for the servant's tort are not present when the person engaged to do the work is not a servant. Nor is any liability imputed to one who controls certain activities of persons not employed by him.

The application of the doctrine of *respondeat superior* and the tests for determining if the wrongdoer is an independent contractor are quite difficult to apply to professional and technically skilled personnel. It can be argued that a physician's profession requires such high skill and learning that others, especially laymen, cannot as a matter of law be in control of the physician's activities. That argument, if accepted, would eliminate the liability of hospitals for acts of medical doctors.

Notwithstanding the logic of this argument, courts usually hold that *respondeat superior* may be applied to professional persons and that such persons may be servants. Of course, some professional and technical persons are independent contractors. Hospitals and others who render professional service through skilled employees have the same legal responsibilities as everyone else. If the person who commits a tort is an employee acting on the employer's behalf, the employer is liable, even though no one actually "controls" the employee in the performance of his art or skill. These concepts are appplicable to doctors, chemists, airline pilots, lawyers, and other highly trained specialists.

Since it is generally understood that one is not liable for the torts of an independent contractor, contracts frequently provide that the relationship is that of proprietor–independent contractor, not master-servant. Such a provision is not binding on third parties, and the contract cannot be used to protect the contracting parties from the actual relationship as shown by the facts.

10. Exceptions—Liability Created

The rule of insulation from liability in the independent contractor situation is subject to several well-recognized exceptions. The most common of these is related to work inherently dangerous to the public, such as blasting with dynamite. The basis of this exception is that it would be contrary to public policy to allow one engaged in such an activity to avoid his liability by selecting an independent contractor rather than a servant to do the work.

Another exception to insulation from vicarious liability applies to illegal work. An employer cannot insulate himself from liability by hiring an independent contractor to perform a task that is illegal. Still another common exception involves employees' duties considered to be duties that cannot be delegated. In discussing the law of contracts, we noted that personal rights and personal duties could not be transferred without consent of the other party. Many statutes impose strict duties on parties such as common carriers and innkeepers. If an attempt is made to delegate these duties to an independent contractor, it is clear that the employer upon whom the duty is imposed has liability for the torts of the independent contractor. In a contract to perform a service or supply a product, liability for negligence cannot be avoided by engaging an independent contractor to perform the duty. Finally, an employer is liable for the torts of an independent contractor if the tort is ratified. If an independent contractor wrongfully repossesses an automobile, and the one hiring him refuses to return it on demand, the tort has been ratified, and both parties have liability.

Tort liability is also imposed on the employer who is himself at fault, as he is when he negligently selects the employee. This is true whether the party performing the work is a servant or an independent contractor, as is illustrated in the following case.

CASE

K.M.S. Investments, owners of a large apartment complex, rented an apartment to Jorge and Stephanie Pontiac in May 1978. In August, K.M.S. hired Dennis Graffice as the complex's resident manager. Graffice was hired despite his criminal record indicating he had been convicted of four felonies in two different states. K.M.S. made no attempt to conduct a firsthand investigation of Graffice's background. It relied solely on the completed application and personal interview. In September 1978, while Jorge was out of town, Stephanie Pontiac was raped at knife point by a person she recognized as Dennis Graffice. He had entered the Pontiac apartment with his passkey. After Graffice was convicted of this sexual assault, the Pontiacs sued K.M.S. for damages.

ISSUE: Is K.M.S. liable to the Pontiacs?

DECISION: Yes, K.M.S. is liable for being negligent in hiring Dennis Graffice as a resident manager.

REASONS: 1. An employer is not criminally liable for the crimes of employees whether they are agents or independent contractors.

2. An employer has a duty to exercise reasonable care in hiring individuals who may pose a threat of injury to members of the public.
3. K.M.S. breached this duty of care by failing to conduct a reasonable investigation of a prospective employee who would be given a passkey to all the tenants' apartments.
4. The negligence in hiring Graffice was the only reason he was on the premises, had contact with Mrs. Pontiac, and was provided with a passkey facilitating his entry to her apartment.

Pontiacs v. K.M.S. Investments, 331 N.W.2d 907 (Minn. 1983).

TORT LIABILITY TO EMPLOYEES

11. Common Law Principles

An employer owes certain nondelegable duties to his employees. These include the duties to warn employees of the hazards of their employment, supervise their activities, furnish a reasonably safe place to work, and furnish reasonably safe instrumentalities with which to work. As part of the obligation to provide a safe place to work, the employer must instruct his employees in the safe use and handling of the products and equipment used in and around the employer's plant or facilities. What is reasonable for the purposes of these rules depends on all the facts and circumstances of each case, including the age and ability of the worker as well as the condition of the premises. It might be negligent to put a minor in charge of a particular instrument without supervision, although it would not be negligent to assign an adult or experienced employee to the same equipment.

Fellow-servant doctrine *Precludes an injured employee from recovering damages from his employer when the injury resulted from the negligent act of another employee.*

Assumption of the risk *Negligence doctrine that bars the recovery of damages by an injured party on the ground that such party acted with actual or constructive knowledge of the hazard causing the injury.*

At common law, the employer who breached these duties to his employees was liable in tort for injuries received by the employees. The employer was not an insurer of his employee's safety, but liability was based on negligence. In turn, the employee in his tort action was confronted with overcoming three defenses available to the employer, one or more of which frequently barred recovery. The first of these defenses was that the employee was *contributorily negligent*. If the employee was even partially at fault, this defense was successful, even though the majority of the fault was the employer's. Second, if the injury was caused by some other employee, the **fellow-servant doctrine** excused the employer and limited recovery to a suit against the other employee who was at fault. Finally, in many jobs that by their very nature involved some risk of injury, the doctrine of **assumption of the risk** would allow the employer to avoid liability.

The common law rules resulted for the most part in imposing on employees the burdens that resulted from accidental injuries, occupational diseases, and even death. Through the legislative process, society has rather uniformly determined that this result is undesirable as a matter of public policy. Statutes known as *workers' compensation* have been enacted in all the states. These laws impose liability without fault (eliminate the common law defenses) on most employers for injuries, occupational diseases, and death of their employees.

12. Workers' Compensation

In general. Workers' compensation laws vary a great deal from state to state in their coverage of industries and employees, the nature of the injuries or diseases that are compensable, and the rates and source of compensation. In spite of these wide variances, certain general observations can be made.

State workers' compensation statutes provide a system of paying for death, illness, or injury that arises out of and in the course of the employment. The three defenses the employer had at common law are eliminated. The employers are strictly liable without fault. Furthermore, states have begun to hold employers liable even though an employee cannot prove the employer solely responsible for the damages done. This legal principle is applied especially when occupational diseases, as opposed to accidental injuries, are involved, as occurred in the following case.

CASE

Frank Tavares began his employment career as an insulation worker in 1953. During his career, he worked for many different companies, always as an insulation worker. During 1977, Tavares worked for A.C.&S., Inc. In January 1978, Tavares became ill. After consulting several doctors, it was determined that Tavares suffered from pulmonary asbestosis, which was caused by his exposure to asbestos dust found in insulation materials. Tavares sued A.C.&S., Inc., for workers' compensation benefits. The company argued it was not liable since Tavares could not prove that his disease was caused during his employment with the company during 1977.

ISSUE: Should Tavares be able to collect workers' compensation benefits from his last employer?

DECISION: Yes.

REASONS:
1. An occupational disease, unlike an accidental injury, commonly is characterized by a long history of injurious exposure without actual disability.
2. Due to the difficulty of determining the actual date a disease occurs, the date of disability controls the rights and liabilities of the employer and employee.
3. The last employer is liable under workers' compensation laws if either (a) the employee's work with the last employer aggravated a preexisting disease, or (b) the last employment was of the same nature and type that caused the disease, even though the employee's condition was not aggravated.

Tavares v. A.C.&S., Inc., 462 A.2d 977 (R.I. 1983).

Most state statutes exclude certain types of employment from their coverage. Generally, domestic and agricultural employees are not covered. In the majority of states, the statutes are compulsory. In some states, employers may elect to be subject to lawsuits by their employees or their survivors. In such cases, the plaintiff must prove that the death or injury resulted proximately from the negligence of the employer. But the plaintiff is not subject to common law defenses. In addition, there is no statutory limit to the amount of the damages recoverable. Thus few employers elect to avoid coverage.

Benefits. The workers' compensation acts give covered employees the right to certain cash payments for their loss of income. A weekly benefit is payable during periods of disability. In the event of an employee's death, benefits are provided for the spouse and minor children. The amount of such awards is usually subject to a stated maximum and is calculated by using a percentage of the wages of the employee. If the employee suffers permanent partial disability, most states provide compensation for injuries that are scheduled in the statute and those that are non-scheduled. As an example of the former, a worker who loses a hand might be awarded 100 weeks of compensation at $90 per week. Besides scheduling specific compensation for certain specific injuries, most acts also provide compensation for nonscheduled ones, such as back injuries, based on the earning power the employee lost owing to his injury. In addition to the payments above, all statutes provide for medical benefits and funeral expenses.

In some states, employers have a choice of covering their workers' compensation risk with insurance or being self-insured (i.e., paying all claims directly) if they can demonstrate their capability to do so. In other states, employers pay into a state fund used to compensate workers entitled to benefits. In these states, the amounts of the payments are based on the size of the payroll and the experience of the employer in having claims filed.

Burden of proof. Although the right to workers' compensation benefits is given without regard to fault of either the employer or the employee, employers are not always liable. The tests for determining whether an employee is entitled to workers' compensation are simply: (1) Was the injury accidental? and (2) Did the injury arise out of and in the course of the employment? Since workers' compensation laws are remedial in nature, they have been very liberally construed. In recent years, the courts have tended to expand coverage and scope of the employer's liability. It has been held that heart attacks and other common ailments are compensable as "accidental injuries," even though the employee had either a preexisting disease or a physical condition likely to lead to the disease. Likewise, the courts have been more and more liberal in upholding awards that have been challenged on the ground that the injury did not arise out of and in the course of the employment.

Federal statutes. Several federal statutes pertain to the liability of certain kinds of employers for injuries, diseases, and deaths arising out of the course of employment. Railroad workers are covered by the Federal Employers' Liability Act (FELA). This statute does not provide for liability without fault, as in the case of workers' compensation, but it greatly increases the chances of a worker's winning a lawsuit against his employer by eliminating or reducing the defenses the latter would have had at common law. While fault of the carrier must be proved for an employee to recover for injuries under the FELA, and a regular lawsuit must be filed in court, the act provides the worker with a distinct advantage over many workers' compensation systems. There is no limit or ceiling to the amount an employee can recover for injuries. The Jones Act gives maritime employees the same rights against their employers as railway workers have against theirs under the FELA.

13. Liability of Third Parties

Irrespective of other legal relationships, any person injured by the commission of a tort has a cause of action against the wrongdoer. An employee who is injured by the wrongful conduct of the third person may recover from the third person. If the employee has been compensated for his injuries by his employer under the applicable workers' compensation law, the employer is entitled to recover any worker's compensation payments from the sum that the employee recovers from the wrongful third party.

Three rather unusual tort situations have a direct relation to the employment contract. First, any third party who maliciously or wrongfully influences a principal to terminate an agent's employment thereby commits a tort. The wrongful third party must compensate the agent for any damages that result from such conduct. Second, any third person who wrongfully interferes with the prospective economic advantage of an agent has liability to the agent for the loss sustained. Third, any person who influences another to breach a contract in which the agent is interested renders himself liable to that agent as well as to the principal. These three torts by third parties were discussed in further detail in Chapter 6.

CHAPTER SUMMARY

Fundamental Principles

1. Agents, servants, and independent contractors are personally liable for their own torts.
2. Agents, servants, and independent contractors are not liable for the torts of their employers.
3. A master is liable under the *respondeat superior* doctrine for the torts of his servant if the servant is acting within the scope of employment.
4. A principal, proprietor, employer, or contractee (each of these terms is sometimes used) is not, as a general rule, liable for the torts of an independent contractor.
5. Injured employees may have rights against their employer as well as against third parties who cause their injuries.

Tort Liability of Masters

Respondeat Superior

1. Literally means "let the master respond."
2. Legal doctrine that places liability as a matter of public policy on employers for the torts of their employees.
3. This doctrine allows injured persons to recover from the party with the "deeper pocket."
4. The basic issue is whether the servant was acting within the scope of employment at the time the tort occurred.
5. This issue is a factual one which usually must be decided by a jury.

Expanding Vicarious Liability

1. A person who is not paid may be a gratuitous "servant" and may make the "master" liable.

2. The family car doctrine is an expansion of vicarious liability beyond the traditional master-servant relationship.

Exceptions—Frolics and Detours

1. Typically, a servant is outside the scope of employment if the servant is on a frolic of his own or detours from his assigned tasks.
2. A *frolic* exists when a servant pursues his personal interests instead of the master's business.
3. A *detour* may occur when a servant fails to follow the master's instructions.

Intentional Torts

1. Intentional or willful torts are less likely to occur within the servant's scope of employment than are torts caused by negligence. Thus masters generally are not liable for harm intentionally caused by servants.

Tort Suits—Procedures

1. Masters and servants generally are jointly and severally liable for the servants' torts. If the servant is not liable, neither is the master.
2. Although legal actions may be filed against both a master and a servant, the third party is limited to only one recovery.

Independent Contractors' Torts

Control over Independent Contractors

1. If one has the power to control the details of the work, he is an independent contractor.
2. In the master-servant relationship, the master has the right to direct the manner of performing the work.

General Rule—No Liability

1. The doctrine of *respondeat superior* and the concept of vicarious liability are not applicable to torts caused by independent contractors.
2. Therefore proprietors generally are not personally liable to third parties who are injured by independent contractors.

Exceptions—Liability Created

Proprietors are liable if:

1. the work of the independent contractor is inherently dangerous.
2. the independent contractor's work is illegal.
3. the work to be done by the independent contractor is nondelegable.
4. the proprietor ratifies the independent contractor's tort.
5. the independent contractor is negligently selected by the proprietor.

Liability to Employees

Common Law Principles

1. Employers owe duties to their employees to furnish a safe place to work, and they may be liable for breach of these duties.
2. An employer was only liable for negligence, and the three common-law defenses were available.

Worker's Compensation

1. State statutes passed to ensure that injured employees do not bear the loss caused by the injury.
2. Because employees no longer have to sue, employers are no longer protected by common law defenses of contributory negligence, assumption of risk, and fellow-servant rule.
3. Employees' benefits include payment of medical bills, loss of income, and rehabilitation income for disabilities suffered.
4. Employees must prove that their injuries, illnesses, or deaths arose out of and in the course of employment.
5. The Federal Employers' Liability Act and the Jones Act protect injured railroad and maritime employees, respectively.

Liability of Third Parties

1. Third parties who interfere with the employer-employee relationship may become liable for damages to either the employer or the employee or both.

REVIEW QUESTIONS AND PROBLEMS

1. Match the terms in column A with the appropriate statement in column B.

A	B
(1) *Respondeat superior*	(a) Example of when a proprietor becomes liable for torts of an independent contractor.
(2) Family car doctrine	(b) Proof that an employee must make in order to recover under workers' compensation laws.
(3) Frolic	(c) Type of tort for which a third party is liable for money damages.
(4) Inherently dangerous work	(d) An expansion of vicarious liability that makes the owner of a vehicle liable for the torts of a family member.
(5) Workers' compensation	(e) Exists when a servant pursues his personal interests instead of the master's business.
(6) Arising out of and in the course of employment	(f) State statutes passed to ensure that injured employees receive benefits from employers.
(7) Interference with economic relationships	(g) Doctrine that allows injured persons to recover from the party with the ''deeper pocket.''

2. Which party, the master or the servant, has the ultimate liability for torts that are the servant's rather than the master's fault? How would your answer change if the tort by a servant was caused by the master's improper instructions?

3. While a guest at the Marshview Inn, Tom was severely beaten by Seth, a night watchman for the Inn. Tom sued the Inn and Seth, as an agent for the Inn. Because Marshview Inn was not the proper company name, Tom's suit against the Inn was dismissed. Tom's suit against Seth was dismissed since Seth was not technically an agent for the Inn. (He was an agent for the Inn's corporate owner.) Tom appealed the dismissal of his claim against Seth. What is the basis for this appeal? Should Tom be allowed to continue his claim against Seth? Why or why not?

4. Employees of Multi-Media Cablevision were working on the campus of Central College. In the course of their employment, they removed a manhole cover. While the cover was displaced, Kline, president of the college, rode by the work site on his bicycle. His bicycle hit the open manhole, throwing him violently forward over the handlebars. He suffered injuries, including a broken shoulder. Is Kline entitled to collect punitive damages? Why or why not?

5. Steve was employed by Greta as a trainee photographer. Late one night after photographing a wedding, Steve was returning the camera equipment to the studio (he was not required to return the equipment that night) when his auto collided with Tim's auto, and Tim was killed. Tim's estate sues Greta and Steve. What should be the result? Why?

6. Yancey, an offshore oil rigger, was employed by Texaco. Yancey had a schedule of seven days on and seven days off. On the seventh day of work, Yancey traveled 30 miles by boat and then drove 150 miles in his car to his home. Yancey was paid for oil-field work and for boat travel time, but his pay stopped when he disembarked. While traveling to his home, Yancey struck a car and killed Theresa. Her estate sued Texaco for her wrongful death. Is an employer liable for the torts of its employees while the employees are on their way to or from work? Why or why not?

7. Stanfield brought this action for damages arising out of an accident in which Roy's truck collided with an automobile in which Stanfield was a passenger. Roy was returning

from a trip where he had performed several errands for his parents, who owned and operated several businesses. Did the accident occur while Roy was within the scope of employment, so as to place liability on Roy's parents under the doctrine of *respondeat superior?* Why or why not?

8. A father allowed his son, a minor, to drive the family car. Contrary to his father's instructions, the son permitted a friend to drive the car while he (the son) rode in the front seat. The friend was negligent and collided with a car driven by Tracy. Tracy sued the father to recover for her damages. Was the fatheı liable? Why or why not?

9. Sam was an employee of the Munchie Company. Sam's job was to drive an ice-cream truck and sell ice cream from the truck. One day the truck stalled, and Sam ask Ted and his friends to push the truck. They agreed, and Sam gave each of them a can of whipped cream as compensation for their help. Ted's can exploded and injured his eye. When sued by Ted, Munchie Company argued that Sam was acting outside his scope of employment at the time he gave Ted the can of whipped cream. Is this a valid argument? Explain.

10. White, an employee of Inter-City Auto Freight, Inc., was driving a large tractor-trailer truck. In attempting to pass Mr. Kuehn, a motorist, White swerved his truck toward Kuehn. After Kuehn had moved to the next lane, he stepped on the gas, caught up with the truck, and motioned with his fist for White to pull over. White again forced Kuehn into another lane. After Kuehn regained control of his car, both parties stopped on the highway's shoulder. White got out of his cab carrying a 2-foot-long metal pipe. As he approached Kuehn, White swung the pipe. It grazed the side of Kuehn's face and knocked Kuehn's glasses to the ground. As Kuehn bent over to pick up his glasses, White hit him two more times. Prior to this incident, White's record as a driver had been very good. Kuehn sued both White and his employer, Inter-City. Should Inter-City be liable for White's assault on Kuehn? Explain.

11. Joiner employed an independent contractor to spray pesticide on his crops. During the application process, the spray damaged a nearby fishing lake owned by Boroughs. When Boroughs sued, the trial court held that Joiner was not liable as a matter of law since the injury was inflicted by an independent contractor. Boroughs contends that Joiner is liable because the work done was inherently or intrinsically dangerous. On appeal, does Borough's argument have merit? Why or why not?

12. Dr. Keldene was employed at a regular salary by the QRS shipping lines to serve aboard ship and treat passengers. Keldene treated Barry, a passenger, who died as a result of Keldene's negligence. May Barry's heirs recover from QRS? Explain.

13. Everson, a Lockheed employee, was assigned to work out of town for one week. After dinner following the third day of this job, Everson and three friends decided to "go out on the town." They drove to a bar and dance hall where they had some drinks, listened to the music, and talked about the work to be done. About 12:30 A.M., Everson left to drive back to the motel. On the way, he failed to round a curve and died as a result of the accident. Can Everson's spouse collect workers' compensation benefits? Explain.

14. Dr. Chung suffered a heart attack after office hours while jogging around the Kalani High School track. At the time of his heart attack, Chung was employed as the president of Animal Clinic. He was also the sole director and sole stockholder of the corporation. A physician testified that the heart attack was work connected. Is Chung entitled to workers' compensation? Why or why not?

15. Roberts, an engineer for Southern Railway Company, was injured when the train he was operating derailed. The track slopes downhill at that point and curves sharply. A 7-foot section of broken rail was found at the site of the accident. Whether the rail was cause or effect of the accident was an issue at trial. Southern Railway was found to be negligent by the jury, and Roberts was awarded $100,000. Will a jury's verdict in a FELA case be overturned on appeal where there is some evidence to support it? Why or why not?

Termination of the Agency Relationship

24

CHAPTER PREVIEW

- TERMINATION BY OPERATION OF LAW

  Death
  Insanity
  Bankruptcy
  Destruction or Illegality of Subject Matter

- TERMINATION BY PARTIES' ACTIONS

  Mutual Agreement
  Unilateral Action
  Traditional Notions of Terminations at Will
  Exceptions to Termination at Will
  Good-faith termination • Public policy exception
  Rights of Wronged Employees

- GENERAL EXCEPTIONS TO TERMINATION

  Agency Coupled with an Interest
  Agency Coupled with an Obligation

- ISSUES INVOLVING THIRD PARTIES

  Problems with Apparent Authority
  Notice Required

BUSINESS MANAGEMENT DECISION

You are the personnel manager for a manufacturing firm. You developed a handbook for employees that states "no employee will be discharged without good cause." One of the plant workers has a reputation for being late to work, slow in his performance, and a general troublemaker. However, this employee's supervisor has no documentation to support this reputation. This supervisor asks you whether he can discharge this employee.

What would you advise?

Two issues are basic to termination of an agency relationship. First, what acts or facts are sufficient to terminate the authority of the agent insofar as the immediate parties are concerned? Second, what is required to terminate the agent's authority insofar as third parties are concerned? The latter question recognizes that an agent may continue to have the *power* to bind the principal, but not the *right* to do so. The first part of this chapter is concerned with how an agency relationship is terminated. Sections 8 through 12 examine exceptions to the general rules on termination. The last part of this chapter answers how termination may affect the third parties who have dealt with an agent. In other words, the answer to the first question asked above is the subject matter of the bulk of this chapter. The second question is answered in sections 13 and 14.

With respect to the actual termination of the relationship between a principal and an agent, two methods are crucial. The next section contains information on how an agency can be terminated by operation of law. The other method—termination by the acts of the principal or agent—follows.

TERMINATION BY OPERATION OF LAW

The occurrence of certain events is viewed as automatically terminating the agency. As a legal principle, any one of four happenings may end the principal-agent relationship: the death of either party, the insanity of either party, the bankruptcy of either party under specific conditions, and the destruction or illegality of the agency's subject matter.

1. Death

The death of an individual acting as a principal or agent immediately terminates the agency even if the other party is unaware of the death. Once the time of death is established, there should not be any controversy about an agency ceasing to exist. Such an event is often quite significant, as the following case illustrates.

CASE

On March 28, 1975, R.V. McCoy opened a checking account in his name at the Virginia Citizens Bank. In October 1976, McCoy telephoned the bank's president and inquired about adding another person to his checking account. McCoy had the bank add Kaye Stanley as an authorized party to sign checks. In essence, Kaye Stanley became an agent of McCoy as opposed to a co-owner of the account. On December 4, 1976, McCoy died, and the bank's president learned of this event that day. On December 6, Kaye Stanley wrote a check for $13,748.58 on McCoy's account and received that amount in cash from the bank. McCoy's executor now is attempting to collect this $13,748.58 from the bank for the benefit of McCoy's estate.

ISSUE: Is the bank liable to the McCoy estate?

DECISION: Yes.

REASONS:
1. Kaye Stanley was an agent of McCoy with authority to make deposits and withdrawals and sign checks to be paid from his account.
2. Death of a principal automatically terminates an agent's authority; therefore, Kaye Stanley had no authority to sign a check on December 6, two days after McCoy's death.
3. The bank knew about McCoy's death (through its president's knowledge) within a reasonable time to deny Kaye Stanley's request for a withdrawal.
4. Since the bank has dealt with an unauthorized agent, it must pay the money to the McCoy estate and attempt to recover from Kaye Stanley.

Sturgill v. Virginia Citizens Bank, 291 S.E. 2d 207 (Va. 1982).

2. Insanity

Insanity of a party does not always provide a distinctive time of termination. For example, if the principal has not been adjudged insane publicly, courts have held that an agent's contracts are binding on the principal unless the third party was aware of the principal's mental illness. This ruling has occurred especially when the contract has been beneficial to the insane principal's estate.

3. Bankrupty

The timing of the termination of an agency due to bankruptcy also is not always clear. Bankruptcy has the effect of termination only when it affects the subject matter of the agency. Assume that a business organization files for reorganization under the bankruptcy laws. Since the court's order of relief will allow this organization to continue its business activity, its agency relationships will not be terminated. However, if the debtor's petition sought Chapter 7 liquidation, the organization's bankruptcy would terminate all its agencies. This result occurs because the organization will cease to exist as a viable principal. When a bankruptcy case will act to terminate an agency, its impact happens at the time the court grants an order of relief. At that time, a trustee typically is appointed to hold the debtor's assets. (See Chapter 45, on bankruptcy.)

4. Destruction or Illegality of Subject Matter

Events that destroy the agency's subject matter may be things other than bankruptcy. For example, if the purpose of the agency relationship becomes illegal or impossible to perform, termination occurs automatically. Whereas it may be unlikely for the purpose of most business relationships to become illegal, the purpose may become impossible to perform whenever the agency's subject matter is destroyed. Suppose that an owner of real estate hires a real estate agent to find a ready, willing, and able buyer for his four-bedroom, two-bathroom house. If that house is destroyed by fire or wind or other causes, the agent's appointment would be terminated, since the house could not now be sold in its former condition.

TERMINATION BY PARTIES' ACTIONS

5. Mutual Agreement

Termination of an agency may occur due to the terms of the principal-agent agreement. For example, an agency may be created to continue for a definite period of time. If so, it ceases, by virtue of the terms of the agreement, at the expiration of the stipulated period. If the parties consent to the continuation of the relationship beyond the period, the courts imply the formation of a new contract of employment. The new agreement contains the same terms as the old one and continues for a like period of time, except that no implied contract can run longer that one year because of the statute of frauds.

Another example is an agency created to accomplish a certain purpose, which ends automatically with the accomplishment of the purpose. Furthermore, when it is possible for one of several agents to perform the task, such as selling certain real estate, it is held that performance by the first party terminates the authority of the other agents without notice of termination being required.

An agency may always be terminated by the mutual agreement of the principal and agent. Even if their original agreement does not provide for a time period of duration, the parties may agree to cancel their relationship. Since the agency is, in essence, based on a consensual agreement, the principal and agent can agree to end their association.

6. Unilateral Action

In addition to the principal and agent's mutually agreeing to end their relationship, the law generally allows either one of these parties to act independently in terminating an agency unilaterally. As a general rule, either party to an agency agreement has full *power* to terminate the agreement whenever he desires, even though he possesses no *right* to do so. For example, if the Paulson Company agreed to employ Alicia for one year, an agency for a definite stated period has been created. That is, these parties have agreed to be principal and agent, respectively, for a one-year period. Despite this agreement, the courts are hesitant to force either an employer or employee to remain in an unhappy situation. Therefore these parties generally do have the power to terminate this employment contract. A premature breach of the agreement is considered to be a wrongful termination, and the breaching party becomes liable for damages suffered by the other party. Of course, if an agent is discharged for cause, such as for failing to follow instructions, he may not recover damages from the employer.

7. Traditional Notions of Termination at Will

Many, and perhaps most, agency contracts do not provide for the duration of the agreement. When an agency is to last for an unspecified or indefinite time period, the relationship may be terminated at the will of either the princpial or the agent. There is some controversy about whether a contract for permanent employment is terminable at the employer's will. Many courts have followed the traditional view that a promise for permanent employment, not supported by any consideration other than the performance of duties and payment of wages, is a contract for an indefinite period and terminable at the will of either party at any time. However, there is an opposing view that requires the employer to prove good cause or reason to dismiss an employee who has been promised permanent employment. The following case is one example of this latter view.

CASE

James Eales was hired in 1974 to be a physician's assistant at the Tanana Medical Clinic. Eales was told when he was hired that he could work for the clinic until he retired. However, on April 2, 1980, Eales was fired. He sued the clinic for damages on the basis that he was wrongfully discharged. The trial court held for the clinic, and Eales appealed.

ISSUE: Did the clinic's promise to employ Eales until he retired create an employment contract for a definite or indefinite period?

DECISION: Eales's contract was for a definite period.

REASONS:
1. Eales's normal retirement age can be easily determined. Thus the contract for employment until retirement can be considered to be one for a definite period.
2. Implicit in the foregoing conclusion is a rejection of those authorities that hold contracts for permanent employment are terminable at the employer's will. These authorities are based on the lack of mutuality of obligation that exists since an employee cannot be bound to work permanently for a particular employer. Therefore they hold that the employer is not bound to pay the employee indefinitely.
3. This logic is rejected. There is no requirement of mutuality of obligation with respect to contracts formed with a bargained-for exchange of consideration.
4. Since Eales's contract was to run for a definite period of time, he could be discharged only for good cause. There having been no showing of such justification, the clinic's discharge of Eales was wrongful.

Eales v. Tanana Valley Medical-Surgical Group, Inc., 663 P.2d 958 (Alaska 1983).

As a general rule, when an agency agreement is terminable at the will of either party, both the principal and agent have the legal *right* as well as the power to terminate their relationship. When a party has the right to do so, a termination is not a breach of contract and no liability is incurred. In other words, both the principal and agent have had the ability to end an agency at any time for any reason as long as the relationship was not to last for a definite time. For a number of reasons, in recent years courts have established many exceptions to this "terminable at will" notion. The next section examines these exceptions.

8. Exceptions to Termination at Will

In England at common law, an employment contract for an indefinite period was presumed to extend for one year unless there were reasonable grounds for discharge. Early American courts followed this approach, but late in the nineteenth century, apparently influenced by the laissez-faire climate of the Industrial Revolution, the American courts rejected the English rule and developed the employment-at-will doctrine, discussed in section 7. The doctrine recognized that where an employment was for an indefinite term, an employer could discharge an employee "for good cause, for no cause, or even for cause morally wrong, without being thereby guilty of legal wrong."

By the turn of the twentieth century, the at-will doctrine was absolute. Since the 1930s, however, government regulation in the workplace has increased dramatically as legislative bodies recognize the need to curb harsh applications and abuse of the rule, especially in labor relations.

Statutory modifications of the at-will doctrine are numerous. Laws prohibiting discrimination make it unlawful for an employer to discharge an employee because of race, color, religion, sex, age, or national origin. Labor laws prevent discharges for union activities. Other forms of discriminatory discharges have also been prohibited by various state legislatures. See Table 24–1, which lists typical statutory protections against the discharge-at-will rule.

Consistent with the philosophy of the statutory modifications, many state courts have recognized the need to protect workers who are wrongfully discharged under circumstances not covered by any legislation or whose job security is not safeguarded by a collective bargaining agreement or civil service regulations. The courts have

TABLE 24–1 EXAMPLES OF EXCEPTIONS TO DISCHARGE AT WILL

Often Based on Statutes	Usually Based on Case Law
Alleged Improper Ground for Discharge	
1. Jury service	1. Refusing to commit perjury
2. Military service	2. Refusing to lobby
3. Union activity	3. Refusing to perform an illegal act or to violate a statute
4. Discrimination	4. Complaining of sexual harrassment
5. Wages garnished	5. Voting against management as an employee-shareholder
6. Refusing lie-detector test	6. Supplying information to the police
7. Responding to subpoena to testify in legal proceedings	7. Refusing to handle radioactive materials in violation of federal guidelines
8. Testifying in wage law violation cases, OSHA violation cases	8. Whistle blowing
9. Filing workers' compensation claim	9. Suing employer for unpaid commissions

Note: Not every state or every court would find liability on each of these grounds.

accomplished this objective by requiring employers to act in good faith and by finding liability if a discharge is contrary to public policy.

Good-faith termination. The first, and the more expansive of the two theories, is imposing upon an employer an implied duty to terminate an employee only in good faith. This contract theory often uses personnel handbooks and work rules to find that a unilateral contract exists and thus requires good faith in performing it. Many of these handbooks contain a statement that the employee will be terminated only if good cause is proved. The handbook's language reinforces the court's inclination to find that the employer is bound to an implied promise that makes the concept of termination at-will inapplicable. In one case, a female employee was terminated because she refused to date her foreman. The court held that the employment contract contained an implied covenant of good faith and fair dealing and that a discharge made in bad faith constituted a breach.

Public policy exception. The second, and more popular of the two theories, is widely known as the *public policy exception.* This theory allows the discharged employee to recover if the termination violates a well-established and important public policy. Some of the examples of protected public policy preventing discharge without liability are set forth in Table 24–1. Many are based on statutes prohibiting discharge for specific reasons, and others are based on the court's view of public policy as it is needed to protect employees.

The courts of various states have different attitudes about the public policy exceptions to the at-will rule. Most states will take a strict view of what public policies support an action for wrongful discharge. Employees have a cause of action for wrongful discharge when the discharge is contrary to a fundamental and well-defined public policy as evidenced by existing law. That is, a wrongful discharge is actionable when the termination clearly contravenes the public welfare and gravely violates paramount requirements of public interest. The public possibly must be evidenced by constitutional or statutory provisions. An employee cannot be fired for refusing to violate the Constitution or a statute. Employers will be held liable for those terminations that effectuate an unlawful end. However, they will not be liable for discharge that may still have a "bad motive" in the eyes of the employee. Table 24–2 list examples of discharges that courts have held not to be actionable. The following case is typical of those in which the grounds for discharge were questionable but there was no liability.

TABLE 24–2 EXAMPLES OF REASONS FOR DISCHARGE HELD NOT TO BE ACTIONABLE AS AGAINST PUBLIC POLICY

1. Objecting to the marketing of a potentially dangerous product
2. Refusing to work on drug research that employee believed was medically unethical
3. Being insubordinate and uncooperative
4. Planning to go into competition with employer
5. Accepting rebates
6. Filing health insurance claim
7. Reporting to employer that company was violating various statutes and its societal obligations
8. Making complaints about company honesty

CASE

Defendant J. C. Penney Company hired David Patton (plaintiff) in 1969. Plaintiff worked in Eugene until 1980, when he was tranferred to Portland where he worked as a merchandising manager. In 1981, the store manager, defendant McKay, told plaintiff to break off a social relationship with a female co-employee. Plaintiff responded by telling McKay that he did not socialize with the co-employee at work and that he intended to continue seeing her on his own time. Apparently, the social relationship did not interfere with plaintiff's performance at work, for during this time he earned several awards for "Merchant of the Month" and one for "Merchant of the Year."

McKay later made statements to the effect that if plaintiff wanted to keep working he had to discontinue the relationship. Although no written or unwritten policy, rule or regulation proscribed socializing between employees, other employees told plaintiff that McKay disfavored plaintiff's fraternization with the female co-employee. Nevertheless, plaintiff continued seeing the co-employee. In February 1982, McKay terminated plaintiff's employment for unsatisfactory job performance. The district manager, defendant Chapin, approved the termination. Plaintiff filed suit against J. C. Penney Company and McKay for wrongful discharge.

ISSUE: Was the discharge of plaintiff wrongful so as to justify damages or reinstatement?

DECISION: No.

REASONS:

1. Generally, an employer may discharge an employee at any time for any reason, absent a contractual, statutory, or constitutional requirement. Termination of employment ordinarily does not create a tortious cause of action. However, there are exceptions to this general rule.
2. Plaintiff does not allege that his discharge was for pursuing statutory rights related to his status as an employee. Nor does plaintiff allege interference with an interest of public importance.
3. Plaintiff claims that the employer invaded his personal right of privacy and that the employer could not fire him for pursuing a private right. But these claims blur "rights" against governmental infringement with "rights" against a private employer.
4. Plaintiff's acts were voluntary, and no state or federal law mandates or prohibits discrimination on that account. It may seem harsh that an employer can fire an employee because of dislike of the employee's personal lifestyle, but because the plaintiff cannot show that the actions fit under an exception to the general rule, plaintiff is subject to the traditional doctrine of "fire at will."

Patton v. J. C. Penney, Co., 719 P.2d 854 (Oreg. 1986).

9. Rights of Wronged Employees

The employee whose employment has been wrongfully cut short is entitled to recover compensation for work done before his dismissal and an additional sum for damages. Most states permit him to bring an action either immediately following the breach, in which event he recovers prospective damages, or after the period has expired, in which event he recovers the damages actually sustained. In the latter case, as a general rule, he is compelled to deduct from the compensation called for in the agreement the amount that he has been able to earn during the interim.

Under such circumstances, a wrongfully discharged employee is under a duty to exercise reasonable diligence in finding other work of like character. Idleness is not encouraged by the law. Apparently, this rule does not require him to seek employment in a new locality or to accept work of a different kind or more menial character. The duty is to find work of like kind, provided it is available in the particular locality. One way that damages for wrongful discharges may be mitigated is for the employer to rehire the employee. A discharged employee often seeks this remedy in addition to accrued back pay.

In some cases, an employer wrongfully discharges an employee but has no liability because the employee either fails to prove damage or fails to mitigate damages. The following case reached just such a result.

CASE

Patrick Dawson filed suit against the *Billings Gazette* on September 23, 1982, alleging that he had been wrongfully terminated from his employment as a reporter with the newspaper on June 21, 1982, and that the *Gazette* had violated its duty of good faith and fair dealing. At the trial, a jury found that the *Gazette* had breached its duties of good faith and fair dealing, that Dawson was not entitled to any compensatory damages, and that the *Gazette* was not liable for punitive damages. Dawson appealed these findings.

ISSUE: Is it permissible to award zero damages to an employee who was wrongfully discharged?

DECISION: Yes.

REASONS:

1. Dawson had three sources of income from the time he was fired until the time of trial. He received four and one-half weeks' pay for unused vacation and holiday time and two weeks' severance pay from the *Gazette*. He received unemployment compensation, and he performed free-lance work for several publications.
2. Dawson failed to mitigate his damages. An injured party is not required to seek employment in another line of work or to move to a different locality. However, he or she must exercise ordinary diligence to procure other employment. After he was fired, Dawson applied to just four newspapers, restricted his job search to papers of equal or greater circulation than that of the *Gazette*, and only those located in the western United States. He totally rejected the idea of working for a smaller newspaper in fear of the resulting harm to his career. The *Sacramento Bee* indicated that a position might be available; but Dawson rejected the inquiry because of the salary cut he would be taking.
3. Dawson could have obtained full-time employment with a reputable newspaper soon after his firing if he had vigorously sought to do so. By failing to pursue comparable full-time work in the journalism field, Dawson failed to mitigate his damages.

Dawson v. Billings Gazette, 726 P.2d 826 (Mont. 1986).

GENERAL EXCEPTIONS TO TERMINATION

10. Introduction

In addition to the public policy reasons for not making employment relationships terminable at will, there are two other exceptions to the general rules on when and how agency relationships may be terminated. The exceptions to termination at will are usually related to employment situations and do not stop termination. They simply create liability for wrongful termination. There are also general exceptions applicable to any principal-agent relationship that actually prevent termination of the relationship. These two general exceptions are known as an agency coupled with either an interest or an obligation.

While reading the next two sections, keep in mind that agencies generally may be terminated by operation of law or by the parties' actions. Also keep asking why these general exceptions are necessary. That is, look for the answers to the following questions: What is so important about the agency discussed to justify making it not subject to termination? Why is imposing liability for wrongful termination an inadequate remedy?

11. Agency Coupled with an Interest

Agency coupled with an interest *When an agent has an actual interest in the property of his principal and has a right of action against interference by third parties with that property.*

The first general exception to how and when an agency is terminated is the factual situation described as an **agency coupled with an interest.** This term describes the relationship that exists when the agent has an actual beneficial interest in the property that is the subject matter of the agency. A mortgage or a security agreement usually contains a provision naming the lender as the agent to sell the described property in the event of a default. Thus this lender becomes an agent with a security interest in the subject matter of the principal-agent relationship. In other words, these documents do create an agency coupled with an interest. A more modern phrase used to describe this situation is a *power given as security*. Mortgages and security agreements that give the lender the power to sell the collateral as security for repayment cannot be cancelled unilaterally by the principal.

An agency coupled with an interest in property cannot be terminated unilaterally by the principal and is not terminated by events (such as death or bankruptcy of the principal) that otherwise terminate agencies by operation of law. The net effect is that an agency coupled with an interest in property cannot be terminated without the consent of the agent, as illustrated by the following case.

CASE

While of sound mind, William Grady Head signed a general power of attorney in March 1976. This document appointed his wife, Emma, to act on his behalf in all matters. Also while he was mentally competent, Mr. Head along with Mrs. Head created a revocable trust for the benefit of their two natural daughters and a third woman (Esther Taute) they had raised. Each daughter's interest in the trust assets was 40 percent, and Esther Taute's interest was 20 percent. Six days after the trust agreement was signed, Mr. Head signed a document called a First Amendment, which removed Taute's 20 percent interest. It was established that Mr. Head was not mentally competent when this amendment was signed. Three weeks later, Mrs. Head acting for herself and as Mr. Head's attorney in fact, ratified the amended trust document. After both Mr. and Mrs. Head had died, the beneficiaries of this trust sought a declaration of their respective interests. The trial court ruled that the trust was valid as originally written. The natural daughters appealed, arguing that their mother's ratification of the amendment removed Esther Taute's interest.

ISSUE: Could Mrs. Head continue to act as Mr. Head's agent even after he became mentally incompetent?

DECISION: Yes.

REASONS: 1. In general, a power of attorney is revoked by operation of law upon an adjudication of insanity.

2. However, if the agent's authority is "coupled with an interest," the principal's insanity does not terminate the agency.

3. "Coupled with an interest" means that the agent must have a present interest in the property upon which the power is to operate. There must be a beneficial interest in the thing itself that is the subject of the power.

4. As a co-creator of the trust, Mrs. Head had a present existing interest in the trust property and in its distribution. She could designate the beneficiaries or even revoke the trust agreement. This power was independent of her authority as Mr. Head's agent.

5. Since Mrs. Head's status as an agent was coupled with her independent interest in the trust, her authority to act on Mr. Head's behalf was not terminated by his insanity.

6. Therefore her ratification of the trust agreement as amended was effective to destroy Esther Taute's 20 percent interest.

Matter of Estate of Head, 615 P.2d 271 (N.M. App. 1980).

12. Agency Coupled with an Obligation

An agency coupled with an interest in property must be distinguished from an **agency coupled with an obligation.** This agency is created as a source of reimbursement to the agent. For example, an agent who is given the right to sell a certain automobile and to apply the proceeds on a claim against the principal is an agency coupled with an obligation. Such an agency is a hybrid between the usual agency and the agency coupled with an interest in property. The agency coupled with an obligation cannot unilaterally be terminated by the principal, but death or bankruptcy of the principal will terminate the agency by operation of law.

Agency coupled with an obligation *When an agent is owed money by his principal and the agency relationship is created to facilitate the agent collecting this money from a third party, an agency coupled with an obligation is created.*

Under either type of agency, it should be clear that the interest in the subject matter must be greater than the mere expectation of profits to be realized or in the proceeds to be derived from the sale of the property. The interest must be in the property itself. A real estate broker is not an agent coupled with an interest, even though he expects a commission from the proceeds of the sale. Likewise, a principal who has appointed an agent to sell certain goods on commission has the power to terminate the agency at any time, although such conduct might constitute a breach of the agreement.

ISSUES INVOLVING THIRD PARTIES

13. Problems with Apparent Authority

As this chapter has explained to this point, issues involving the termination of agencies concern both the principal and agent. Indeed, subject to some exceptions, termination of an agency occurs by operation of law or by the actions of the principal or agent. Whereas these parties, by the nature of the relationship, will learn of the termination, the third parties who know of the agency may not be aware that a particular relationship is terminated. Whenever a third party has been induced by the principal to believe an agency exists, there is an opportunity for the principal to become bound to the third party due to apparent authority. The existence of apparent or ostensible authority is discussed in Chapter 22.

In order to prevent the existence of apparent authority, the law requires the principal to give notice of termination to all third parties who have learned of the agency. How and when this required notice is to be given to third parties involve whether these parties had dealt personally with the agent or had just known of the agency's existence. Also of importance is whether the notice required be personally delivered or constructively given.

14. Notice Required

Notice of an agency's termination may be delivered in one of two ways. First, the notice may be personally or privately given. Examples of this type of notice include oral communication, face to face, or over the phone. Sending notice through the mail also is considered to be personally delivered when properly addressed and stamped. Second, the alternative type of notice is public or constructive notice. Such notices include an announcement in a newspaper or other periodical. Furthermore, notice can be constructively given over radio, television, or other media of communication.

The type of notice of termination required to cut off an agent's apparent authority depends on the third party's relationship to the agent. When the agency is terminated by the acts of the principal or agent, the principal has the duty to give personal notice of the termination to those third parties who have dealt with the agent. When a third party has not previously dealt with the agent, the principal satisfies his duty to give notice by providing for public notice. If the principal fails to give the type of notice required, that principal is allowing the agent's apparent authority to exist, as happened in the following case.

CASE

In the early 1970s, the Moores purchased siding during the construction of their home. This siding, which was manufactured by Puget Sound Plywood, Inc., began to come apart during 1977. The problem became so severe in 1979 that the Moores attempted to contact their source of the siding. They discovered that the company no longer existed. However, they learned that Rehcon, Inc., represented Puget Sound concerning the defective siding. Thereafter, in March 1980, Rehcon quit in its representative capacity of Puget Sound because of a lack of cooperation. No efforts were made by Puget Sound to notify the public that Rehcon was no longer its agent. On June 24, 1980, Mr. Moore notified Rehcon of his defective siding. Subsequently, the Moores sued Puget Sound for $4,550, which was the cost of replacing the siding. The basis of this suit was a breach of warranty concerning the siding. Puget Sound defended by asserting that it had not been notified, as required, of the Moores' problem with the siding. The trial court dismissed the Moores' complaint, and they appealed.

ISSUE: Was the notice given to Rehcon, a former agent, sufficient to satisfy the notice required to be given to Puget Sound?

DECISION: Yes.

REASONS:
1. Rehcon, in fact, had been Puget Sound's agent hired to handle complaints about the siding.
2. When Rehcon ceased to be Puget Sound's agent, the principal failed to give any notice, personal or public, to third parties who knew Rehcon was an agent.

3. An agent's apparent authority may exist beyond termination of the principal-agent relationship when notice of the termination has not been given.
4. Therefore Mr. Moore's notice of the breach of warranty to Rehcon was sufficient notice to Puget Sound.

Moore v. Puget Sound Plywood, Inc., 332 N.W.2d 212 (Neb. 1983).

By fulfilling the duty to give notice of termination to third parties according to the factual situation and the local requirements, the principal prevents apparent authority from existing. A third party who has not dealt with the agent may not learn of the notice given publicly. If that third party relies on the continuation of the agency, he does so to his own detriment. In other words, the principal does not become liable to the third party in such a situation. If a third party who did deal with the agent has not received direct personal notice from the principal but has learned indirectly of the agency's termination or of facts sufficient to place him on inquiry, he is no longer justified in dealing as if the agent represents the principal. In other words, a third party who has dealt with the agent cannot rely on apparent authority to bind the principal when that third party learns of the agency's termination via public, rather than personal, notice.

When the agency is terminated by action of law, such as death, insanity, or bankruptcy, no duty to notify third parties is placed on the principal. Such matters receive publicity through newspapers, official records, and otherwise, and third parties normally become aware of the termination without the necessity for additional notification. If the death of the principal occurs before an agent contracts with a third party, the third party has no cause of action against either the agent or the estate of the principal unless the agent is acting for an undisclosed principal. In the latter case, since the agent makes the contract in his own name, he is liable to the third party. Otherwise, the third party is in as good a position to know of the death of the principal as is the agent.

A special problem exists in regard to notice in cases of special agents as distinguished from general agents. Ordinarily, notice is not required to revoke the authority of a special agent, since the agent possesses no continuing authority, and no one will be in the habit of dealing with him. Only if the principal has directly indicated that the agent has authority in a certain matter or at a certain time will notice be required, to prevent reliance on the principal's conduct by a party dealing with the agent. This is especially true if the agent is acting under a special power of attorney. Actual notice of termination is required in these cases.

CHAPTER SUMMARY

Termination by Operation of Law

1. Death of either principal or agent ends the relationship.
2. Insanity of either principal or agent ends the relationship.
3. Bankruptcy of principal or agent may end the relationship if subject matter of relationship is affected.
4. Destruction or illegality of the agency's subject matter ends the relationship.

Termination by Parties' Actions

Mutual Agreement

1. Due to its contractual nature, agency relationships can be terminated by the principal's and agent's consent at any time.
2. Such consent may be reflected in an original agreement that is to last for a stated time period.
3. Consent to terminate also occurs if the purpose of the relationship is accomplished or if the parties agree to end the relationship prior to the stated date of termination.

Unilateral Action

1. In general, even if the agency is to last for a stated time, either the principal or agent can end the relationship at any time.
2. The parties have the power of termination even if they lack the legal right.
3. If a party exercises the power of termination while lacking the right, that party is liable for money damages that the premature termination causes.

Termination at Will

1. Traditionally, if there was no stated period of duration, both the principal and agent had the right and power to terminate the relationship at their desire or will.
2. If the agency is terminable at will, the party terminating the relationship has no liability for damages.

Exception to Termination at Will

1. There is a growing trend to require that employers support their decisions to fire employees on a reasonable basis.
2. Many statutes prohibit discharge for stated reasons. Case law also imposes liability contract that must be performed in good faith.
3. Language taken from employees' handbooks has been used to create a unilateral contract which must be performed in good faith.
4. Protected rights include those listed in Table 24–1.

Rights of Wronged Employees

1. An employee is entitled to recover actual damages sustained.
2. Actual earnings are deducted from what would have been earned.
3. There is a duty to mitigate damages by seeking similar work in the same community.

General Exceptions to Termination

Agency Coupled with an Interest

1. This relationship occurs when an agent has an actual beneficial interest in the property that is the subject matter of the agency.
2. This also is described as a power given as security.
3. This type of agency cannot be terminated by operation of law or by the unilateral acts of the principal.

Agency Coupled with an Obligation

1. A relationship created as a source of reimbursement to the agent.
2. This relationship cannot be terminated by the unilateral acts of the principal. However, it can be terminated by operation of law.

Issues Involving Third Parties

Problems with Apparent Authority

1. Although an agent's actual authority is removed when the agency is terminated, apparent authority may still exist from the third parties' perspective.
2. The principal is required to give notice of termination to third parties in order to cut off the agent's apparent authority.

Notice Required	1. Notice of termination may be given personally or publicly. 2. Personal notice include that given face to face, over the phone, or by mail. 3. Public notice is that given constructively through newspaper, radio, television, or other means of public communication. 4. When termination occurs by the acts of the parties, personal notice must be given to the third parties who have dealt with the agent. Public notice is sufficient to cut off an agent's apparent authority when a prospective third party has not previously dealt with the agent. 5. When termination occurs by operation of law, generally no notice needs to be given by the principal to third parties.

REVIEW QUESTIONS AND PROBLEMS

1. Match each term in column A with the appropriate statement in column B.

A	B
(1) Operation of law	(a) Generally present even though the legal right of termination is lacking.
(2) Power of termination	(b) One example of an employee's protected right.
(3) Termination at will	(c) Often used as a basis for proving that an employer breached an implied duty or agreement.
(4) Employees' handbook	(d) A relationship created as a source of reimbursement to the agent.
(5) Jury service	(e) Termination by death, insanity, bankruptcy, destruction, or illegality.
(6) Agency coupled with an interest	(f) Given constructively through the newspaper, radio, or television.
(7) Agency coupled with an obligation	(g) Also known as a power given as security.
(8) Public notice	(h) A traditional legal concept whereby the terminating party has the right and power to end a relationship.

2. As a matter of law, the occurrence of any one of four events operates to terminate a principal-agent relationship. List these four events.

3. In addition to termination by operation of law, an agency may be terminated by the mutual agreement of the principal and agent. Describe three factual situations wherein the parties' agreement ends their relationship.

4. When agency relationships are terminated by the actions of the parties involved, the concepts of the *power* to terminate and *right* to terminate become important. Explain the distinction between the legal significance of these terms.

5. The Dixie Company offered Papageorge a contract of employment as a regional manager. Dixie's offer contained a proposed annual salary of $35,000. Papageorge accepted this offer, but he was not allowed to begin work. Dixie canceled the contract. When Papageorge sued, Dixie denied liability and contended that without an agreed-upon duration, this employment was terminable at will. Papageorge argued that the stated annual salary implied a contract to last at least a year. Which party is correct? Why?

6. Weiner was informed that his employer's policy was not to terminate employees without just cause. His employment application stated that his employment would be subject to the provisions of the employer's "Handbook on Personnel Policies and Procedures." The handbook represented that "[t]he company will resort to dismissal for just and sufficient cause only, and only after all practical steps toward rehabilitation or salvage of the employee have been taken and failed. However, if the welfare of the company indicates that dismissal is necessary, then that decision is arrived at and is carried out forthrightly." Is this employment relationship terminable at will? Explain.

7. Palmateer was fired both for supplying information to local law enforcement authorities that an IH employee might be involved in a violation of the Criminal Code and for agreeing to assist in the investigation and the employee's trial if requested. He filed suit against IH alleging retaliatory discharge. What result? Why?

8. Andy was hired as a computer salesman on commission. A dispute arose over the commission, and Andy filed suit against his employer and asked the court to resolve the dispute. The employer admitted to error on the commission but discharged Andy anyway for disloyalty. The employment contract was for a definite period, which had not expired. Is Andy entitled to damages for retaliatory discharge? Why or why not?

9. Ludwick, a seamstress, worked as an at-will employee in Carolina's sewing plant. Ludwick was served with a subpoena to appear before the South Carolina Employment Security Commission. Shortly thereafter she was advised by her boss that if she obeyed the subpoena, she would be fired. Ludwick honored the subpoena and testified at the hearing. Upon returning to her job at Carolina on the following day, she was fired. Is she entitled to damages for retaliatory discharge? Explain.

10. A police officer still on probationary status with a small-town police force helped gain the release of a man who had been arrested for vagrancy under an obsolete statute. The prisoner had been jailed for twenty-one days without arraignment. The police chief, not inclined to let "big-city cops" tell him how to run his department, fired the probationary officer, who then responded with an action for wrongful discharge. What result? Why?

11. Vincent was hired as vice-president for sales by Robert's Hawaii Tours. This employment agreement was dated July 3, 1988, and it was to last for five years. Vincent was to be paid between $1,500 to $2,200 a month by Robert's. Despite this five-year agreement and for no apparent reason, Vincent was fired on February 21, 1989. Vincent sued for the salary provided by the employment contract. Robert's argued that Vincent refused to mitigate the damages since he refused possible employment opportunities. The best offer Vincent had, to mitigate damages, was $400 per month plus a commission. He refused to accept this offer of employment. Is Vincent entitled to money damages despite his unwillingness to mitigate the damages as shown by his refusal to take the lower-paying sales job? Explain.

12. Ann, a real estate agent, was authorized by Peter to sell several lots at specified prices. Ann was to receive an 8 percent commission on each lot sold. Before any lots were sold, Peter revoked the authorization granted. Since Ann had spent her own money advertising these lots, she claimed that her authority was irrevocable as an agency coupled with either an interest or obligation. Is Ann correct? Why?

13. Dr. Thompson's malpractice insurance was obtained through the Duncan Insurance Agency. During 1979 and 1980, Thompson's insurance was with Aetna Casualty & Surety Company. In 1981, the Duncan Agency ceased being an agent for Aetna, and it became an agent for St. Paul Insurance Company. Duncan changed Thompson's coverage to St. Paul without explaining why the change occurred. In 1981, Thompson was sued for an alleged act of malpractice that occurred in July 1979. Thomspon immediately notified the Duncan Agency, which mistakenly notified St. Paul. St. Paul began defending Thompson, but it then discovered it was not the doctor's insurer in 1979. Aetna was notified, but it refused to defend the malpractice since it was not promptly and timely notified of the filed suit as the insurance policy required. Thompson sued Aetna, relying on the immediate notice given to Duncan Agency. Is Aetna liable for not defending the malpractice case against Thompson? Why?

14. Alicia, a buyer for Patterson's Department Store, was discharged. Although Turner Manufacturers knew of Alicia's position with Patterson's, it had never sold merchandise to Alicia. After Alicia was discharged, an article about her changing jobs appeared in the local newspapers, but Turner did not read it. If Alicia now purchases goods on credit from Turner and charges them to Patterson's, is Patterson's liable to Turner? Explain.

Choosing the Form of Business Organization

25

CHAPTER PREVIEW

BUSINESS MANAGEMENT DECISION

You and a business associate decide to make a movie concerning the 1988 presidential campaign. This project will require $1,500,000 in capital, an amount that must be raised. You and your associate desire to maintain editorial and production control over this project.

What type of business organization should be created to achieve your objectives?

INTRODUCTION

Business organizations may operate under a variety of legal forms. The common ones are sole proprietorships, partnerships, limited partnerships, and corporations. There are also some specialized organizations, such as professional service corporations that are authorized by statute. These allow doctors, lawyers, dentists, and other professional persons to have many of the advantages of incorporation.

This chapter examines the various forms of organization and the factors that influence the actual selection of a particular form. The factors involved in this selection are applicable to all businesses, from the smallest to the largest, but the relative influence of the various factors varies greatly, depending on the size of the business. As a practical matter the very large business usually is incorporated, because that usually is the method that can bring a large number of owners and investors together for an extended period of time.

The difficulty of deciding which is the best form of organization to select is most often encountered in the closely held business. Taxation is usually the most significant factor. Although a detailed discussion of the tax laws is beyond the scope of this text, some of the general principles of taxation will be presented in order to illustrate the influence of taxation in choosing among organizational forms.

1. General Partnerships

Partnership *A business organization consisting of two or more owners who agree to carry on a business and to share profits and losses.*

Partnerships developed logically in the law, and the common law of partnerships has been codified in the Uniform Partnership Act. A **partnership** is an association of two or more persons to carry on, as co-owners, a business for profit. It is the result of an agreement.

Advantages. A partnership form of organization has many advantages:

1. Since it is a matter of contract between individuals, to which the state is not a party, it is easily formed.
2. Costs of formation are minimal.
3. It is not a taxable entity.
4. Each owner, as a general rule, has an equal voice in management.
5. It may operate in more than one state without being required to comply with many legal formalities.
6. Partnerships are generally subject to less regulations and less governmental supervision than corporations.

The fact that a partnership is not a taxable entity does not mean that partnership income is tax-free. A partnership files an information return allocating its income among the partners, and each partner pays income tax on the portion allocated to him.

Disadvantages. Several aspects of partnerships may be considered disadvantageous. First, as a practical matter, only a limited number of people may own such a business. Second, a partnership is dissolved every time a new member is added as a new partner or an old member ceases to be a partner either by withdrawal or by death. Although dissolution is the subject matter of Chapter 28, it should be observed here that the perpetual existence of a corporation is often a distinct advantage, compared with easily dissolved partnerships.

Third, the liability of a partner is unlimited, contrasted with the limited liability of a shareholder. The unlimited liability of a partner is applicable both to contract and tort claims. Fourth, since a partner is taxed on his share of the profits of a partnership, whether distributed to him or not, a partner may be required to pay income tax on money that is not received. This burden is an important consideration in a new business that is reinvesting its profits for expansion. A partner in such a business would have to have an independent means of paying the taxes on such income.

2. Joint Venture

A *joint venture,* or *joint adventure,* occurs when two or more persons combine their efforts in a particular business enterprise and agree to share the profits or losses jointly or in proportion to their contributions. It is distinguished from a partnership in that the joint venture is a less formal association and contemplates a single transaction or a limited activity, whereas a partnership contemplates the operation of a general business. A joint venture is a specific venture without the formation of a partnership or corporation.

A partnership in most states is a legal entity, apart from the partners; a joint venture is not. A joint venture cannot sue or be sued. A suit must be by, on behalf of, or against the joint venturers individually.

Joint ventures file a partnership tax return and have many of the other legal aspects of partnerships. The parties stand in a fiduciary relationship with each other and are agents for purposes of tort liability.

LIMITED PARTNERSHIPS

3. Characteristics

A **limited partnership,** like other partnerships, comes into existence by virtue of an agreement. Like a corporation, it is authorized by statute, and the liability of one or more, but not all, of the partners is limited to the amount of capital contributed at the time of the creation of the partnership. For liability purposes, a limited partnership is, in effect, a hybrid between the partnership and the corporation.

One or more *general partners* manage the business and are personally liable for its debts. One or more *limited partners* also contribute capital and share in

Limited partnership *A partnership in which one or more individuals are general partners and one or more individuals are limited partners. The limited partners contribute assets to the partnership without taking part in the conduct of the business. They are liable for the debts of the partnership only to the extent of their contributions.*

profits and losses, but they take no part in running the business and incur no liability with respect to partnership obligations beyond their contribution to capital. A limited partner's position is analogous to that of a corporate shareholder whose role is that of an investor with limited liability. Note that in the following case, the general partners act like the board of directors of a corporation and make decisions on such matters as paying out profits to the limited partners. It is from the limited liability of the limited partners that the organization gets its name.

CASE

Plaintiffs are three of eighteen limited partners in Mt. Hood Meadows, Oregon, Ltd., a limited partnership established to carry on the business of constructing and operating a winter sports development in the Hood River Meadows area of the Mt. Hood National Forest. They brought this action against the general partner to compel the distribution of all retained profits.

ISSUE: Do limited partners have a right to compel the general partner to distribute to them all of the profits allocated under the provisions of the partnership agreement?

DECISION: No.

REASONS:

1. A limited partner's position is analogous to that of a corporate shareholder, whose role is that of an investor with limited liability, and with no voice in the operation of the enterprise.
2. A general partner's relationship to the limited partners is analogous to the relationship of a corporate board of directors to the corporate shareholders; the general partner functions as a fiduciary with a duty of good faith and fair dealing. Like the corporate director's fiduciary responsibility to the shareholders for the declaration of dividends, the general partner's duty to the limited partners in the distribution of profit is discharged by decisions made in good faith that reflect legitimate business concerns.
3. The only section of the agreement that addresses the partners' right to profits describes the percentage of profits to which each partner is "entitled." It does not address the distribution of profits; it merely provides the method of calculating and allocating profits. The agreement contains no provision expressly directing the general partner to distribute profits to the limited partners.
4. A broad grant of authority to manage a business, such as that applicable here, includes the authority to conduct all affairs reasonably necessary or incidental to the expressly authorized business. Decisions regarding the management, including the distribution of profits, fall within that broad authority.
5. Profit is an accounting concept; its allocation takes place in the partnership books, and it may bear little or no relationship to cash on hand. Each partner is taxed on his distributable share of the profits, regardless of whether cash is actually distributed or whether it is available for distribution. For that reason, the partnership agreement must specify how the profits are to be allocated. The availability of cash for distribution, however, depends strictly on management's operation of the business. The business's

future cash needs are also determined by management. That is why the decision as to how much, if any, of a limited partner's share of the profits is to be distributed is a management decision. If a limited partner were to take part in that aspect of the control of the business, the partner would risk the loss of his limited liability.

Brooks v. Mt. Hood Meadows, Oregon, Ltd., 725 P.2d 925 (Oreg. App. 1986).

Limited partnerships are governed in most states by the Uniform Limited Partnership Act provisions. The purpose of this statute is to encourage trade by permitting persons to invest in a business and reap their share of the profits without becoming liable for debts or risking more than the capital contributed. This reduced risk is based on the investor's not being a general partner or participating actively in the conduct of the business. The risk cannot be further reduced by taking a security interest in the property of the limited partnership.

4. Creation

To create a limited partnership under the Uniform Limited Partnership Act, the parties must sign and swear to a certificate containing, among other matters, the following information about the limited partnership agreement: the name of the partnership, the character of the business, its location, the name and place of residence of each member, those who are to be the general and those who are to be the limited partners, the term for which the partnership is to exist, the amount of cash or the agreed value of property to be contributed by each partner, and the share of profit or compensation each limited partner shall receive. Strict compliance with the statutory requirement is necessary if the limited partners are to achieve the goal of limited liability. Some states by statute require only substantial compliance, however, especially between the partners.

The certificate must be recorded in the county where the partnership has its principal place of business, and a copy must be filed in every community where it conducts business or has a representative office. Most states require notice by newspaper publication. In the event of any change in the facts relative to the partnership agreement contained in the certificate as filed—such as a change in the name of the partnership, the capital, or other matters—a new certificate must be filed. If such a certificate is not filed and the partnership continued, the limited partners immediately become liable as general partners. The terms of the agreement are often quite important, and they should be carefully reviewed and fully understood by all partners, including the limited partners. The following case demonstrates the type of conflict that may arise over the meaning of language in limited partnership agreements and its importance to investing limited partners.

CASE

TRL is a limited partnership consisting of seventeen limited partners and CCK and RMI, both as general partners. The limited partnership agreement contained the following language:

> . . . any amendment to this Agreement which would adversely affect the general liabilities of the Limited Partners, or change the

> method of allocation of the profits or losses or the distribution of the Partnership funds or assets shall require the consent in writing of all Limited Partners . . . any other amendment to this Agreement shall require the approval in writing of Partnership Percentages aggregating sixty-six and two-thirds percent (66 ⅔).

On March 13, 1984, RMI and CCK proposed to amend the limited partnership agreement in the following two ways:

1. To change the value for which newly issued units of TRL could be issued from at least $50,000 to at least their fair market value determined by the managing general partner of TRL on an annual basis; [and]
2. To change the number of authorized units of TRL from 300 to an unlimited number.

These amendments were approved by the general partners and five limited partners, who together represented more than 66 ⅔ percent of the organization's ownership. Eleven limited partners did not vote, and one limited partner voted against the amendments.

A limited partner (plaintiff) sued to enjoin the enforcement of these amendments since they were not adopted with unanimous consent.

ISSUE: Does the language of the limited partnership agreement require a unanimous vote to approve these amendments?

DECISION: No.

REASONS:

1. An amendment that would adversely affect the general liability of the limited partners is one that would make a limited partner liable beyond the amount of his contribution to the partnership. It is not, as plaintiff suggests, one that would create an unlimited right of forced capital contribution, or create a "liability" to a partnership. If the drafters had meant the term *general liability* to include capital contributions, the term *capital contributions* would have been used. The amendments do not adversely affect the general liabilities of the limited partners.
2. Plaintiff is correct in recognizing that a certain number of dollars in profits distributed by the method indicated in the amendment to, for instance, 1,000 partners, is going to result in each of the partners getting a lesser amount than, for instance, if these profits were distributed to only ten partners. In other words, the more partners there are, the lesser amount each is going to get of the profits. However, when the number of partners is increased, this is not a change in the method of allocation of the profits and losses. Instead, this is simply a change in the number of people to whom the profits and losses will be allocated.
3. A change in the method of the allocation of profits and losses would be if the amendment was changed so that the managing general partner received as his share of profits and losses a different percentage. Another example would be an amendment that gave the general partners a set amount rather than allocating to them their share in proportion to the total of units owned by them to the total units owned by all the partners.

4. Since neither the *general liability* nor the method of allocation of the profits or losses has been changed by these amendments, they were properly approved by those owners representing at 66 ⅔ percent of the organization.

Reilly v. Rangers Management, Inc., 717 S.W.2d 442 (Tex. App. 1986).

The statutes of most states require the partnership to conduct its business in a firm name that does not include the name of any of the limited partners or the word *company*. Some states specify that the word *limited* shall be added.

The 1980s saw the development of limited partnerships with characteristics of publicly traded corporations. These limited partnerships with thousands of limited partners are usually referred to as *master limited partnerships*. The units of the limited partners are traded like stocks and are traded on stock exchanges. They first developed in the petroleum industry as a means of passing cash flow to investors without corporate taxation. Today they are used in financing theatrical productions, health care organizations, TV stations, and professional sports teams.

Master limited partnerships distribute cash flow to partners. The distributions are a tax-free return of capital until they exceed the original investment. Losses, however, are not deductible under the 1986 tax law revision. Many master limited partnerships have been outstanding investments, but many have failed and the market has tended to be very volatile. Cash payouts are often less than the projection, and most are thinly traded. These organizations are taxed as corporations if they are publicly traded (more than 5% of their interests change hands during a taxable year).

5. Operation and Dissolution

Unless a limited partner participates in management and control of the business, his liabililty to creditors does not extend beyond his contribution to the business. Participation in management makes the limited partner a general partner with unlimited liability.

In many states, but not all, this unlimited liability cannot be avoided by making the general partner a corporation if the limited partners would be in control of the corporate general partner. Thus, in some states, the officers and directors of a corporate general partner who are also individually limited partners have liability as general partners, and in other states they do not. The following case adopts the former view.

CASE

A limited partnership was formed with a corporation as the general partner. The limited partners were officers and directors of the corporation. Delaney, a creditor of the limited partnership, sought to collect a partnership debt individually from the limited partners. The law provides that a limited partner who takes part in the control of a business is liable as a general partner.

ISSUE: Can the personal liability that attaches to a limited partner when he takes part in control of the business be evaded by acting through a corporation?

DECISION: No.

REASONS:
1. Strict compliance with the limited partnership statute is required if limited partners are to avoid liability as general partners.
2. An exception to the rule that corporate officers are insulated from personal liability arising from their activities or those of a corporation exists where the corporate fiction is used to circumvent a statute.
3. The limited partners effectively controlled the business in their individual capacities. Their personal liability cannot be avoided by the corporate fiction.
4. A limited partner need not hold himself out as a general partner for liability to attach. The liability is statutory, not based on any theory of estoppel.

Delaney v. Fidelity Lease Limited, 526 S.W.2d 543 (Tex. 1975).

While a limited partner has no right to participate in management, a limited partner does have the right (1) to have the partnership books kept at the principal place of business of the partnership, and at all times to inspect and copy any of them, (2) to have on demand true and full information of all things affecting the partnership and a formal account of partnership affairs whenever circumstances render it just and reasonable, (3) to have the right to receive a share of the profits or other compensation by way of income, (4) to have dissolution and winding up by decree of court, and (5) to have his contribution returned upon dissolution. He is a quasi-shareholder. In addition, in most states the limited partner does not become a general partner by engaging in activities that are of an advisory nature and do not amount to control of the business.

To dissolve a limited partnership voluntarily before the time for termination stated in the certificate, notice of the dissolution must be filed and published. Upon dissolution, the distribution of the assets of the firm is prescribed by statute. As a general rule, the law gives priority to limited partners over general partners after all creditors are paid.

A limited partnership is dissolved only when there is a change in the general partners. Because limited partners have no active voice in the daily management of the organization, the limited partners' interests are treated like corporate shareholders' stock. Therefore, unless there is an agreement to the contrary, limited partners are free to transfer their interests without causing a dissolution of the limited partnership.

The limited partnership as a tax shelter is of special value in many new businesses, especially real estate ventures such as shopping centers and apartment complexes. It gives the investor limited liability and the operators control of the venture. It allows the use of depreciation to provide a tax loss that can be deducted by the limited partner to the extent of risk in the investment. Offsetting this tax loss, usually, is a positive cash flow that gives a limited partner an income at the same time that he has a loss for tax purposes.

6. Revised Uniform Limited Partnership Act

In 1976, the Commissioners on Uniform State Laws issued a revised Uniform Limited Partnership Act. This act has been adopted by most states, and in all probability it will become the law in the other states in the future. The revised act tends to make a limited partnership even more like a corporation than does the original act.

Under the revised act, the name of the limited partnership must contain the words *limited partnership*. The name may not contain the name of a limited partner unless his name is also the name of a general partner or one that had been used prior to the admission of that limited partner.

A limited partnership under the revised act is required to maintain a registered office within the state and an agent to receive notices for it. The law requires that certain records, such as a list of all partners and a copy of the certificate of the limited partnership, be maintained at this office. Copies of the partnership tax returns and copies of all financial statements must be kept for three years.

Under the revised act, the certificate creating the partnership is filed with the state's secretary of state. If it is later amended or canceled, the certificates of amendment and cancellation are also filed in that office.

The revised act makes a substantial change in the liability of a limited partner who participates in control of the business. The liability of a general partner is imposed on a limited partner who participates in the control of the business only if the third party had knowledge of the participation. In addition, the act provides that a limited partner does not participate in the control of the business by (1) being an agent or employee of the business, (2) consulting with or advising a partner with respect to the partnership, (3) acting as surety for the limited partnership, (4) approving or disapproving of an amendment to the certificate, and (5) voting on matters such as dissolution, sale of assets, or a change of name.

THE BUSINESS CORPORATION

7. Advantages and Disadvantages

The corporation comes into existence when the state issues the corporate charter. A **corporation** is a legal entity that usually has perpetual existence. The liability of the owners is limited to their investment, unless there is a successful "piercing of the corporate veil." (See Chapter 29 for a further discussion of "piercing the corporate veil.")

Corporation *A collection of individuals created by statute as a legal person, vested with powers and capacity to contract, own, control, convey property, and transact business within the limits of the powers granted.*

A corporation, as a general rule, is a taxable entity paying a tax on its net profits. Dividends paid to stockholders are also taxable, giving rise to the frequently made observation that corporate income is subject to double taxation. The accuracy of this observation will be discussed later.

The advantages of the corporate form of organization may be briefly summarized as follows:

1. It is the easiest method that will raise substantial capital from a large number of investors.
2. Tax laws have several provisions that are favorable to corporations.
3. Control can be vested in those with a minority of the investment by using techniques such as nonvoting or preferred stock.
4. Ownership may be divided into many separate and unequal shares.
5. Investors have limited liability.
6. The organization can have perpetual existence.

7. Certain laws, such as those relating to usury, are not applicable to corporations.
8. Investors, notwithstanding their status as owners, may also be employees entitled to benefits such as workers' compensation.

Among the frequently cited disadvantages of the corporate form of organization are these:

1. Cost of forming and maintaining the corporate form with its rather formal procedures.
2. Expenditures such as license fees and franchise taxes that are assessed against corporations but not against partnerships.
3. Double taxation of corporate income and the frequently higher rates.
4. The requirement that it must be qualified to do business in all states where it is conducting intrastate business.
5. Subject to more regulations by government at all levels than are other forms.
6. Being required to use an attorney in litigation, whereas an ordinary citizen can proceed on his or her own behalf.

The fact that corporations are required to use an attorney in litigation is listed as a disadvantage of the corporate form of organization. As a practical matter, all forms of organization must use an attorney in any litigation of much significance, so to that extent the requirement is not a significant disadvantage. It does emphasize, however, the fact that corporations do require the services of lawyers on an ongoing basis. The role of the lawyer and his relationship to a business corporation is colorfully stated by Roy A. Redfield in *Factors of Growth in a Law Practice:*

> When the business corporation is born, the lawyer is the midwife who brings it into existence; while it functions he is its philosopher, guide and friend; in trouble he is its champion, and when the end comes and the last sad rites must be performed, the lawyer becomes the undertaker who disincorporates it and makes final report to the Director of Internal Revenue.

The following case explains the rationale behind the rule of law that requires corporations to be represented by a licensed attorney in all litigation.

CASE

Plaintiff is incorporated to do business in the state of Maine, where the parties to any legal proceeding must be represented by an attorney authorized to practice law in the state. An exception exists for a person pleading or managing his own cause of action. The plaintiff corporation filed a lawsuit and was represented in court by its president, who concededly was not authorized to practice law in the state. The defendant moved for dismissal on the ground that the plaintiff was not properly represented. The corporation contended that it could appear on its own behalf by an agent such as its president.

ISSUE: May a corporation designate a nonattorney agent to represent it in a legal proceeding?

DECISION: No.

REASONS: 1. Although an individual may represent himself in court, state law prohibits a corporation from being represented by a nonattorney.

2. A corporation is an artificial entity created by law, and as such it can neither practice law nor appear or act in person. To allow a corporation to be represented by its officer would allow persons not qualified to practice law and unamendable to the general discipline of the court to maintain litigation.

Land Management v. Department of Environmental Protection, 368 A.2d 602 (Me. 1977).

8. Taxation of Corporate Income

The fact that taxation is listed as both an advantage and a disadvantage of the corporate form illustrates the importance of the tax factor in choosing this particular form of organization. Corporate tax law provisions change from time to time, depending on the economy and the effect of tax policy on employment, economic growth, and so on. The current rates are as follows:

Income ($)	Tax Rate
0–50,000	15 percent
50–75,000	25 percent
Over 75,000	34 percent

Among the tax laws that favor corporations over partnerships are the following:

1. Health insurance premiums are fully deductible and are not subject to the limitations applicable to individuals.
2. Deferred compensation plans may be adopted.
3. Retained earnings are taxed at graduated rates that may be lower than the individual tax rates of the shareholders.
4. Income that is needed to be retained in the business is not taxed to persons who do not receive it, as occurs in a partnership.
5. The corporation may provide some life insurance for its employees as a deductible expense.
6. Medical expenses in excess of health insurance coverage may be paid on behalf of employees as a deductible expense.

The corporate form of organization also has some major tax disadvantages. First of all, corporate losses are not available as a deduction to shareholders, whereas partnership losses are immediately deductible on the individual returns of partners. Corporate losses can only be used to offset corporate profits during different taxable years.

Second, a major disadvantage to corporations occurs when a profit is made and the corporation pays a dividend to its shareholders. The dividend will have been taxed at the corporate level and then taxed again to the shareholder. The rate of the second tax depends on the personal tax rate of each shareholder receiving the dividend. This is known as the "double tax" on corporate income. (The next section explains why the "double tax" may not be as big a disadvantage as it first seems.)

Third, the corporate form is frequently at a disadvantage from a tax standpoint because the 34 percent rate over $75,000 exceeds the individual rate of the owners of the business. Finally, some states impose a higher income tax on corporate income than on individual income. In addition, many other forms of taxes are imposed on corporations that are not imposed on individuals or partnerships.

9. Avoidance of Double Taxation

Certain techniques may be used to avoid, in part, the double taxation of corporate income. First of all, reasonable salaries paid to corporate employees may be deducted in computing the taxable income of the business. Thus, in a closely held corporation in which all or most shareholders are officers or employees, this technique can be used to avoid double taxation of much of the corporate income. The Internal Revenue Code disallows a deduction for excessive or unreasonable compensation, and unreasonable payments to shareholder employees are taxable as dividends. Therefore the determination of the reasonableness of corporate salaries is an ever-present tax problem in the closely held corporation that employs shareholders.

Second, the capital structure of a corporation may include both common stock and interest-bearing loans from shareholders. Envision a company that needs $200,000 to begin business. If $200,000 of stock is purchased, there will be no expense to be deducted. But suppose that $100,000 is loaned to the company at 10 percent interest. In this case, $10,000 of interest each year is deductible as an expense of the company, and thus subject to only one tax as interest income to the owners. Just as in the case of salaries, the Internal Revenue Code contains a counteracting rule relating to corporations that are undercapitalized. If the corporation is undercapitalized, interest payments will be treated as dividends and disallowed as deductible expenses.

The third technique for avoiding double taxation—or to at least delay it—is simply not to pay dividends and to accumulate the earnings. Here again we have tax provisions designed to counteract the technique. There is a special income tax imposed on "excessive accumulated earnings" in addition to the normal tax rate.

Finally, a special provision in the Internal Revenue Code treats small, closely held business corporations and partnerships similarly for income tax purposes. These corporations are known as Sub-Chapter S corporations.

10. Sub-Chapter S Corporations

The limited partnership is a hybrid between a corporation and a partnership in the area of liability. A similar hybrid known as a *tax-option* or *Sub-Chapter S corporation* exists in the tax area of the law. Such corporations have the advantages of the corporate form without the double taxation of income.

The tax-option corporation is one that elects to be taxed in a manner similar to that of partnerships—that is, to file an information return allocating income and losses among the shareholders for immediate reporting, regardless of dividend distributions, thus avoiding any tax on the corporation.

Sub-Chapter S corporations cannot have more than thirty-five shareholders, each of whom must sign the election to be taxed in the manner similar to a partnership. There are many technical rules of tax law involved in Sub-Chapter S corporations. But as a rule of thumb, this method of taxation has distinct advantages for a business operating at a loss, because the loss is shared and immediately deductible on the returns of shareholders active in the business. It is also advantageous for a business capable of paying out net profits as earned, thereby avoiding the corporate tax. If net profits must be retained in the business, Sub-Chapter S tax treatment is somewhat disadvantageous because income tax is paid by the shareholders on earnings not received.

11. The Professional Service Associations

Traditionally, professional services, such as those of a doctor, lawyer, or dentist, could be performed only by an individual and could not be performed by a corporation, because the relationship of doctor and patient or attorney and client was considered a highly personal one. The impersonal corporate entity could not render the personal services involved.

For many years there were significant tax advantages in corporate profit-sharing and pension plans that were not available to private persons and to partnerships to the same extent. An individual proprietor or partner was limited to a deduction of 15 percent of income or $15,000 under a *Keogh* pension plan provision. Professional persons therefore often incorporated or created professional associations in order to obtain the greater tax advantages of corporate pension and profit-sharing plans. To make this possible, every state enacted statutes authorizing *professional associations*. As legal entities similar to corporations, their payments to qualified pension and profit-sharing plans qualify for deductions equal to those of business corporations.

The tax laws were changed in 1984 in an attempt to equalize the tax treatment of Keogh plans and corporate pension and profit-sharing plans. While this has generally been achieved, there remain a few advantages to corporate plans. Most professional corporations that were created earlier remain in existence, and new ones are still being formed.

The law authorizing professional corporations does not authorize business corporations to practice a profession such as law or medicine. Professional corporations are special forms of business organizations that must meet strict statutory requirements. In addition, professional persons practicing a profession as a professional corporation do not obtain any limitation on their professional liability to third persons. However, as the following case illustrates, the shareholders of a professional corporation do have limited liability for corporate debts that do not directly involve the practice of the profession.

CASE

We're Associates leased office space to Cohen, Stracher & Bloom, a professional service corporation, engaged in the practice of law. The lease was in the name of the corporation. However, when the rent was not paid, We're Associates filed suit and attempted to hold the individual shareholders liable. The trial court reviewed the following statutory language:

> Each shareholder, employee or agent of a professional service corporation shall be personally and fully liable and accountable for any negligent or wrongful act or misconduct committed by him or by any person under his direct supervision and control while rendering professional services on behalf of such corporation.

The trial judge dismissed the plaintiff's suit against the individual defendants, and the plaintiff appealed.

ISSUE: May shareholders of a professional service corporation be held liable in their individual capacities for rents due under a lease naming only the professional service corporation as tenant?

DECISION: No.

REASONS:

1. The general rule is that shareholders of a corporation are not personally liable for corporate debts.
2. The plain words of the statute, imposing personal liability only in connection with the rendition of professional services on behalf of the professional service corporation, cannot be defeated by a liberal construction that would include ordinary business debts within the definition of professional services.
3. The rationale that shareholders of a professional service corporation should be held personally liable for ordinary business debts of the corporation because they are "closer" to the management of such corporation than are shareholders of an ordinary business corporation has not prevailed in our state over the general policy of allowing corporations to be formed for the express purpose of limited liability.
4. This decision should work no injustice on those who enter into leases or any other contracts with professional service corporations, who are free to seek the personal assurances of the shareholders that the commitments of the professional service corporation will be honored.

We're Associates v. Cohen, Stracher & Bloom, 480 N.E.2d 357 (N.Y. 1985).

In some ways, the total liability of a professional association may be greater than if the profession were practiced as a partnership. For example, a professional association may have liability for discriminating against owner-employees because of age, whereas a partnership would not have liability to a partner because of age discrimination. Several laws that protect shareholder employees do not protect partners.

Today, there are thousands of professional corporations in all states. They can be identified by the letters *S.C.* (Service Corporation), *P.C.* (Professional Corporation), or *Inc.* (Incorporated), or by the word *company* in the name of the professional firm.

MAKING THE DECISION

A few pages back, we listed advantages of incorporating a business with substantial capital. If the business is to be owned and operated by relatively few people, their choice of form of organization will be made with those factors in mind—expecially taxation, control, liability, perpetual existence, and legal capacity. *Legal capacity* is the power of the business, in its own name, to sue or be sued, own and dispose of property, and enter into contracts.

In evaluating the impact of taxation, an accountant or attorney will look at the projected profits or losses of the business, the ability to distribute earnings, and the tax brackets of the owners. An estimate of the tax burden under the various forms of organization will be made. The results will be considered along with other factors in making the decision on the form of business organization.

The generalization that partners have unlimited liability and shareholders limited liability must be qualified in the case of a closely held business. A small, closely held corporation with limited assets and capital will find it difficult to obtain credit on the strength of its own credit standing alone; and as a practical matter, the shareholders will usually be required to add their individual liability as security for the debts. If Tom, Dick, and Jane seek a loan for their corporation, they usually will be required to guarantee repayment of the loan. This is not to say that closely held corporations do not have some degree of limited liability. The investors in those types of businesses are protected with limited liability for contractlike obligations imposed as a matter of law (such as taxes) and for debts resulting from torts committed by company employees while engaged in company business. If the tax aspects dictate that a partnership and limited liability are desired by some investors, the limited partnership will be considered.

Issues of liability are not restricted to the investors in the business or to financial liability. Corporation law has developed several instances in which the directors and officers of the corporation will have liability to shareholders or the corporation for acts or omissions by those directors or officers in their official capacity. These matters are discussed more fully in Chapter 30.

The significance of the law relating to control will be apparent in the discussions on formation and operation of partnerships and corporations in the chapters that follow. The desire of one or more individuals to control the business is a major factor in selecting the form, and the control issues are second only to taxation in importance.

CHAPTER SUMMARY

Introduction

General Partnerships

1. The partnership is easily formed, and the costs of formation are minimal.
2. The partnership is not a taxable entity, and losses are immediately deductible.
3. Each partner as a general rule has an equal voice in management.
4. It can operate in any state and is subject to less government regulation.
5. A partnership may involve only a limited number of people and is easily dissolved.
6. Partners have unlimited liability.
7. Income is taxed to a partner whether received or not.

Joint Ventures

1. It is like a partnership but for a single transaction.
2. A joint venture is not a legal entity but is treated as a partnership for tax purposes.

Limited Partnerships

Characteristics

1. A limited partnership has at least one general partner with unlimited liability.

2. It is not a taxable entity, and any losses are immediately deductible.
3. The general partners manage the business.

Creation

1. A certificate containing vital information is filed in a public office.
2. Limited partners do not participate in management and are thus similar to shareholders.
3. The name used gives notice of the limited liability of some owners.
4. The steps necessary to establish a limited partnership are governed by a statute and must be followed closely.

Operation and Dissolution

1. Usually, the limited partners forgo their right to participate in management in exchange for having their liability limited to their investment.
2. Limited partners do have the right to inspect the books, to have an accounting, to dissolve the organization by court decree, and to share in the distribution of profits.
3. In general, the transfer of a limited partner's interest does not dissolve the limited partnership.

Revised Uniform Limited Partnership Act

1. Limited partnerships have additional requirements concerning their offices and records.
2. Limited partners who participate in management assume unlimited liability only to persons who know of the participation.

The Business Corporation

Advantages

1. Investors have limited liability, and the business may have perpetual existence.
2. It is a method by which even hundreds of thousands of persons can own a business together and in varying percentages of ownership.
3. Several provisions in the tax law favor corporations.
4. As a separate entity, there are many laws covering only corporations.

Disadvantages

1. There are significant costs in forming and maintaining a corporation.
2. Corporate income is taxed to the corporation, and dividends are taxed to the shareholders.
3. It must qualify in every state where it conducts intrastate business and is subject to greater government regulation.
4. It must have an attorney represent it in litigation.

Taxation of Corporate Income

1. Several provisions of the Internal Revenue Code, such as those relating to health insurance, have special advantages for corporations.

Avoidance of Double Taxation

1. There are several techniques for avoiding double taxation of corporate income, such as the payment of salaries and expenses on behalf of the owners of the corporation.

Sub-Chapter S Corporations

1. The Sub-Chapter S corporation, which is a corporation taxed in the same manner as a partnership, is of special importance in avoiding the double taxation of corporate income.

Professional Services Associations

1. Such associations were created to give professional persons some of the tax advantages of corporations.
2. A business corporation cannot practice these professions.
3. Shareholders of professional associations do not have limited malpractice liability but do have limited liability for other debts of the associations.

Making the Decision

1. Those responsible for deciding the form of organization must weigh all of the factors with special emphasis on taxation.

REVIEW QUESTIONS AND PROBLEMS

1. Match each term in column A with the appropriate statement in column B.

A	B
(1) Partnership	(a) A business owned by one person who is personally liable for all losses.
(2) Proprietorship	(b) An artificial being created by a state.
(3) Limited partnership	(c) Two or more persons combine their efforts for a single transaction.
(4) Corporation	(d) Created when shareholders elect to be treated as partners for tax purposes.
(5) Legal capacity	(e) Created by an agreement between two or more persons who agree to share profits and losses.
(6) Buy and sell agreement	(f) Provides for compensation to a deceased or withdrawing owner of a business in return for that owner's interest.
(7) Sub-Chapter S corporation	(g) The ability of an organization to sue or to own property.
(8) Joint venture	(h) Exists when some partners are treated like shareholders for liability purposes.

2. Garrett and Lewis signed an agreement creating a limited partnership. Garrett was the general partner and Lewis was a limited partner. Neither the agreement nor the certificate required by statute were filed with the secretary of state. This limited partnership purchased merchandise on credit from Products, Ltd., which assumed that the business was a general partnership. Should the failure to file pertinent documents related to the limited partnership make Lewis liable to Products, Ltd., as if he were a general partner? Explain.

3. The partners of a limited partnership had their signatures acknowledged by a notary, but they did not swear to the truth of the document. Is the certificate valid to the extent that the limited partners have limited liability? Explain.

4. A general partner agreed to provide a limited partner with a unilateral refund of his partnership contribution if the limited partner became dissatisfied with the conduct of the business. The other parties did not consent to the modification of the partnership agreement. Is the agreement enforceable? Why or why not?

5. Oklahoma prohibits the sale of alcoholic beverages in an "open saloon." Roby, in an attempt to circumvent this prohibition, formed a limited partnership whose capital would be used to purchase liquor. The limited partners would be individual consumers of alcoholic beverages. The partnership would enter into storage and service agreements with various private clubs to store the liquor and serve it to the partners upon proof of identification. Is the activity a legal limited partnership? Why or why not?

6. Kramer, a limited partner in a McDonald's franchise, invested $90,000 in the limited partnership. To secure his investment, he took a security agreement from the franchise covering all equipment, inventory, and receivables. Is he entitled to do so? Why or why not?

7. Lane and Louis were limited partners in a real estate venture. After the business was in financial difficulty, these limited partners had two meetings with the general partners to discuss the problems of the venture. In addition, Lane visited the construction site and "obnoxiously" complained about the work that was being conducted. Do these actions constitute taking part in the control of the business enough to make the limited partners liable as general partners? Explain.

8. Gerald and Lionel purchased a tavern. They orally agreed that Lionel would manage the business at a stated salary and receive 50 percent of all profits for his interest as a *limited* partner. Subsequently, the Internal Revenue Service assessed a deficiency in cabaret taxes in the amount of $46,000. Lionel contended that since he was a limited partner, he was not personally liable for the taxes. Is Lionel correct? Explain.

9. Vaughan is a limited partner in the Grand Limited Partnership, a real estate syndication. He purchased his interest for $5,000 when the partnership was created. The partnership has prospered, and Vogel has offered to buy Vaughan's limited partnership interest for $6,500. The general partners are opposed to the sale because they dislike Vogel. Is Vaughan entitled to sell the interest without the consent of the general partners? Why or why not?

10. John Thompson and Richard Allenby wish to enter the camping equipment manufacturing business. If the following facts exist, which type of business organization would be most advantageous?
    a. Thompson is an expert in the field of camping gear production and sale but has no funds. Allenby knows nothing about such production but is willing to contribute all necessary capital.
    b. Camping gear production requires large amounts of capital, much more than Thompson and Allenby can raise personally or together, yet they wish to control the business.
    c. Some phases of production and sale are rather dangerous, and a relatively large number of tort judgments may be anticipated.
    d. Sales will be nationwide.
    e. Thompson and Allenby are both sixty-five years old. No profits are expected for at least five years, and interruption of the business before that time would make it a total loss.
    f. Several other persons wish to put funds into the business but are unwilling to assume personal liability.
    g. The anticipated earnings over cost, at least for the first few years, will be approximately $70,000. Thompson and Allenby wish to draw salaries of $25,000 each; they also want a hospitalization and retirement plan, all to be paid from these earnings.
    h. A loss is expected for the first three years, owing to the initial capital outlay and the difficulty in entering the market.

26 Formation of Partnerships

CHAPTER PREVIEW

- WHEN DOES A PARTNERSHIP EXIST?

    Express Partnerships
    Implied Partnerships
    Partnership by Estoppel

- THE PARTNERSHIP AGREEMENT

    Profit-and-Loss Provision
    Partnership Capital Provision
    Partnership Property
    Firm Name
    Goodwill
    Buy and Sell Provisions

BUSINESS MANAGEMENT DECISION

You and two friends agree to practice public accounting together as partners. Each of you agrees to pay $50,000 in capital to begin the practice.

What concerns do you have at the outset of this relationship?

WHEN DOES A PARTNERSHIP EXIST?

1. Introduction

A *partnership* is defined as an association of two or more persons to carry on as co-owners of a business for profit. It is the result of an agreement between competent parties to place their money, property, or labor in a business and to divide the profits and losses. Each partner is personally liable for the debts of the partnership, since the partnership is in effect a mutual agency relationship. The following case illustrates the impact of sharing profits.

CASE

Beck and Kirk entered into a "land development agreement" that provided that Beck would contribute land and Kirk would furnish her expertise to create a residential housing development to be called Beckhaven Estates. Beck and Kirk agreed to divide any profits. Kirk employed the plaintiff, Indiana Surveying, to plot the development. When Kirk failed to pay for the survey, suit was instituted against Beck and Kirk as partners.

ISSUE: Did Beck and Kirk's business venture constitute a partnership?

DECISION: Yes.

REASONS:

1. A partnership is an association of two or more persons to carry on as co-owners of a business for a profit.
2. The receipt by a person of a share of the profits of a business is prima facie evidence that he is a partner in the business. The "land development agreement" between Beck and Kirk provided that the two parties would split any profit. This sharing of profits is evidence that a partnership existed.
3. The agreement signed by the parties clearly intended the creation of a housing development, which is a business enterprise for profit. Moreover, the development was to be called Beckhaven Estates, after Beck. The use of a firm name is additional evidence of the existence of a partnership.

Beck v. Indiana Surveying Co., 429 N.E.2d 264 (Ind. 1981).

2. Express Partnerships

Express partnership agreements may be either oral or written, but a carefully prepared written agreement is highly preferable to an oral one. The provisions usually contained in articles of partnership are discussed in section 5 of this chapter.

Issues concerning the existence of a partnership may arise between the parties or between the alleged partnership and third parties. The legal issues in these two situations are substantially different. When the issue is between the alleged partners, it is essentially a question of intention. Between the alleged partners, a partnership arises only from an express or implied agreement between them. It is never established by operation of law. When the issue concerns liability to a third person, the question involves not only intention to create the partnership but issues of estoppel as well. Insofar as third persons are concerned, conduct of an alleged partner is often more important than intent.

3. Implied Partnerships

Between the parties, the intention to create a partnership may be expressed or implied from their conduct. The basic question is whether the parties intend a relationship that includes the essential elements of a partnership, not whether they intend to be partners. In fact, under certain circumstances, a corporation may be held to be a partnership at least between the owners of the business.

If the essential elements of a partnership are present, the mere fact that the parties do not think they are becoming partners is immaterial. If the parties agree upon an arrangement that is a partnership in fact, it is immaterial whether they call it something else or declare that they are not partners. On the other hand, the mere fact that the parties themselves call the relation a partnership will not make it so if they have not, by their conduct, agreed upon an agreement that by the law is a partnership in fact.

The essential attributes of a partnership are a common interest in the business and management and a share in the profits and losses. This common interest may be established by a holding of property and a sharing of the profits and losses related to the property. If there is a sharing of profits, a partnership may be found to exist even though there is no sharing of losses.

The presence of a common interest in property and management is not enough to establish a partnership by implication. Nor, of itself, does an agreement to share the gross returns of a business, sometimes called gross profits, prove an intention to form a partnership. If a person receives a share of real or net profits in a business, that is prima facie but not conclusive evidence of partnership. It may be overcome by evidence that the share in the profits is received for some other purpose, such as payment of a debt by installments, wages, rent, annuity to a widow of a deceased partner, interest on a loan, or payment of goodwill by installments. Bonuses are frequently paid as a percent of profit, but they do not make the employee a partner. Likewise, many leases provide for rent based on profits. Such provisions do not create a partnership as the following case illustrates.

CASE

Defendant Holler owned grazing land and was looking for someone to pasture cattle on his land. P&M Cattle Company, a cattle rancher, entered into a grazing contract with Holler, which provided in part that "net money" from the sale of cattle was to be split evenly between the parties. For many years the operation was a success. However, in 1974 P&M suffered an $89,000 loss. P&M sued, contending that the agreement made the parties "partners" and that Holler was liable for one-half of the loss. Holler contended that he was not a partner but only a landlord receiving profits as rent.

ISSUE: Were the parties partners?

DECISION: No.

REASONS:
1. As with any contractual relationship, the intent of the parties is controlling. Here, there was no evidence of intent to form a partnership.
2. The agreement was not labeled a partnership contract, nor was a partnership federal income tax return ever filed. Plaintiff described his payments to defendant on his tax return as "contract feeding."
3. The agreement was a mere contract for grazing cattle.

P&M Cattle Co. v. Holler, 559 P.2d 1019 (Wyo. 1977).

4. Partnership by Estoppel

Insofar as third pesons are concerned, partnership liability, like the apparent authority of an agent, may be predicated upon the legal theory of estoppel. If a person by words spoken or written or by conduct represents himself, or consents to another's representing him, as a partner in an existing partnership, that person is not a partner but is liable to any party to whom such representation has been made. If the representation is made in a public manner either personally or with consent of the apparent partner, the apparent partner is liable if credit is extended to the partnership, even if the creditor did not actually know of the representation. This is an exception to the usual estoppel requirement of actual reliance.

The courts are not in accord as to whether a person must affirmatively disclaim a reputed partnership that he did not consent to or claim. Some court cases hold that if a person is held out as a partner and he knows it, he should be chargeable as a partner unless he takes reasonable steps to give notice that he is not, in fact, a partner. These courts impose a duty on a person to deny that he is a partner, once he knows that third persons are relying on representations that he is a partner. Other cases indicate that there is no duty to deny false representations of partnership if the ostensible partner did not participate in making the misrepresentation. Also there is no duty to seek out all those who may represent that he is a partner, so that he may deny it.

In most states, the statutory law of partnerships recognizes partnerships by estoppel. These statutes usually incorporate the common law elements of estoppel, as the following case illustrates.

CASE

Glenn Smith and David Wright contracted with Mike Norman, doing business as Norman Construction Company, to build two houses. During the early stages of construction, Mike's father, Max Norman, lead Smith and Wright to believe that Max was in partnership with his son, Mike. In fact, no such partnership existed. The construction projects were not completed. Smith and Wright filed a suit against Mike and Max Norman. The plaintiffs argued that Max Norman, although he was in actuality not a partner of his son, should be estopped from denying liability for the losses sustained by the plaintiffs from the alleged poor workmanship and failure to complete their homes. (The plaintiffs' claim against Mike Norman was stayed when Mike filed for bankruptcy.)

ISSUE: Did Max Norman, based on his representations, become a partner by estoppel?

DECISION: No.

REASONS:

1. An estoppel has three important elements. The actor, who usually must have knowledge of the true facts, communicates something in a misleading way, either by words, conduct, or silence. The other relies upon that communication. And the other would be harmed materially if the actor is later permitted to assert any claim inconsistent with his earlier conduct.
2. In this case, there is not a scintilla of evidence that the plaintiffs entered into their contracts with Mike Norman based upon any conduct or declaration by his father. Plaintiff Glenn Smith testified that when he entered into the contract with Mike Norman, he did not think Max Norman was a partner in Mike Norman's business. Plaintiff David Wright testified that he likewise dealt only with Mike Norman and knew of no involvement by Max Norman in the business.
3. Had the alleged representations by Max Norman been made prior to or at the time the plaintiffs entered into their contracts with Mike Norman, the decision in this case might have been different. Because the alleged representations came after the plaintiffs had obligated themselves to make the payments, however, it cannot be said that they relied upon those alleged representations to their detriment.

Smith v. Norman, 495 S. 2d 536 (Ala. 1986).

THE PARTNERSHIP AGREEMENT

5. Introduction

The partnership agreement, usually called the *articles of partnership,* vary from business to business. Among the subjects usually contained in such agreements are the following: the names of the partners and of the partnership, its purpose and duration, the capital contributions of each partner, the method of sharing profits and losses, the effect of advances, the salaries (if any) to be paid the partners, the method of accounting and the fiscal year, the rights and liabilities of the parties upon the death or withdrawal of a partner, and the procedures to be followed upon dissolution.

The Uniform Partnership Act or other partnership statute is a part of the agreement as if it had actually been written into the contract or had been made part of its stipulations. The following sections discuss some or the more important provisions of the partnership agreement and indicate the effect of the Uniform Partnership Act on the agreement.

6. Profit-and-Loss Provision

Unless the agreement is to the contrary, each partner has a right to share equally in the profits of the enterprise, and each partner is under a duty to contribute equally to the losses. Capital contributed to the firm is a liability owing by the firm to the contributing partners. If, on dissolution, there are not sufficient assets to repay each partner his capital, the amount is considered as a loss; and like any other loss of the partnership, it must be met.

Example: A partnership is composed of A, B, and C. A contributed $20,000, B contributed $10,000, and C contributed $4,000. The firm is dissolved, and upon the payment of debts only $10,000 of firm assets remain. Because the total contribution to capital was $34,000, the operating loss is $24,000. If these partners have not agreed otherwise, this loss must be borne equally by A, B, and C, so that the loss for each is $8,000. This means that A is entitled to be reimbursed to the extent of her $20,000 contribution less $8,000, her share of the loss, or net of $12,000. B is entitled to $10,000, less $8,000, or $2,000. Because C has contributed only $4,000 he must now contribute to the firm an additional $4,000, in order that his loss will equal $8,000. The additional $4,000 contributed by C, plus the $10,000 remaining, will now be distributed so that A will receive $12,000 and B $2,000.

Occasionally, articles of copartnership specify the manner in which profits are to be divided, but they neglect to mention possible losses. In such cases the losses are borne in the same proportion that profits are to be shared. In the event that losses occur when one of the partners is insolvent and his share of the loss exceeds the amount owed him for advances and capital, the excess must be shared by the other partners. They share this unusual loss in the same ratio that they share profits. Thus, in the above example, if C were insolvent, A and B would each bear an additional $2,000 loss.

In addition to the right to be repaid his contributions, whether by way of capital or advances to the partnership property, the partnership must indemnify every partner for payments made and personal liabilities reasonably incurred by him in the ordinary and proper conduct of its business or for the preservation of its business or property.

7. Partnership Capital Provision

Partnership *capital* consists of the total credits to the capital accounts of the various partners, provided the credits are for permanent investments in the business. Such capital represents the amount that the partnership is obligated to return to the partners at the time of dissolution, and it can be varied only with the consent of all the partners. Undivided profits that are permitted by some of the partners to accumulate in the business do not become part of the capital. They, like temporary advances by firm members, are subject to withdrawal at any time unless the agreement provides to the contrary.

The amount that each partner is to contribute to the firm, as well as the credit he is to receive for assets contributed, is entirely dependent upon the partnership agreement. A person may become a partner without a capital contribution. For example, he may contribute services to balance the capital investment of the other partners. Such a partner, however, has no capital to be returned at the time of liquidation. Only those who receive credit for capital investments—which may include goodwill, patent rights, and so forth, if agreed upon—are entitled to the return of capital when dissolution occurs. As the following case holds, business experience is not a contribution to capital.

CASE

Plaintiff Badran and defendant Bertrand executed a partnership agreement on June 23, 1976, to sell Indian jewelry. The agreement provided that each partner should contribute $50,000 to the capital of the partnership. Bertrand contributed her share. Badran, however, did not do so. He chose instead to contribute personal business expertise. When the business failed, Bertrand took possession of the unsold merchandise as a return of capital. Badran brought the suit for an accounting and distribution of the remaining partnership assets held by Bertrand.

ISSUE: Does a partner's contribution of services constitute a capital contribution?

DECISION: No.

REASONS:
1. Capital furnished by any partner is a debt owing by the partnership to the contributing partner and should be repaid to him if the firm's assets are sufficient after paying the firm's liabilities to outsiders.
2. Upon dissolution, where one has contributed capital and another services, the one contributing the capital is entitled to withdraw its value and the other has contributed nothing which is to be returned.

Badran v. Bertrand, 334 N.W.2d 184 (Neb. 1983).

If the investment is in a form other than money, the property no longer belongs to the contributing partner. He has vested the firm with title, and he has no greater equity in the property than has any other party. At dissolution, he recovers only the amount allowed to him for the property invested.

8. Partnership Property

In conducting its business, a partnership may use its own property, the property of the individual partners, or the property of some third person. It frequently becomes important, especially on dissolution and where claims of firm creditors are involved, to ascertain exactly what property constitutes partnership property, in order to ascertain the rights of partners and firm creditors in specific property.

As a general rule, the agreement of the parties will determine what property is properly classified as partnership property. In the absence of an express agreement, what constitutes partnership property is ascertained from the conduct of the parties and from the purpose for, and the way in which, property is used in the pursuit of the business.

The Uniform Partnership Act provides that all property specifically brought into partnership or acquired by it is partnership property. Therefore, unless a contrary intention appears, property acquired with partnership funds is partnership property. In other words, there is a presumption that property acquired with partnership funds is partnership property, but this presumption is rebuttable.

Property acquired by a partner individually is often transferred to the partnership as a part of a partner's contribution to capital. If this property is purchased on credit, the creditor has no claim against the partnership, even though the property can be traced to it. A personal loan made to a partner does not become a partnership debt unless it is expressly assumed by the partnership. The following case used this basic rule to deny partnership liability.

CASE

The defendants loaned money to Dalton Waldrop in 1974. In mid-1975, Dalton Waldrop and Thomas Waldrop, his brother, formed a partnership for the drilling of wells. In January 1976, this partnership was incorporated as Waldrop Drilling & Pipe Company, Inc. In May 1976, Dalton Waldrop left the corporation and his interest was taken over by Thomas Waldrop. Neither the partnership nor the corporation assumed the obligation of Dalton Waldrop to the defendants for the loan to Dalton Waldrop by the defendants in 1974. In August 1976, defendants employed Waldrop Drilling & Pipe to repair one of their pumps. This repair work was completed on August 24, 1976, at a reasonable cost of $2,873.75. On November 4, 1976, at the request of the defendants, the corporation performed additional repair services in the reasonable amount of $710.54. Neither of these bills was paid. The corporation brought this action to collect the amount due. Defendants sought to offset these amounts against the balance owed to them by Dalton Waldrop. The trial court rejected the offset and entered judgment in favor of the corporation for these amounts plus interest and costs. The defendants appealed.

ISSUE: Does a partnership become liable for a loan previously made to an individual who becomes a partner simply because the loan proceeds were used to purchase equipment that became partnership property?

DECISION: No.

REASONS:

1. A loan made to a partner in his individual capacity before formation of the partnership is not a partnership debt unless it is expressly assumed by the partnership.
2. Thomas Waldrop testified he was unaware of this obligation until the business entity performed some work for defendants, and the defendants thereafter sought to offset the cost of the work against the amount of their loan to Dalton Waldrop.
3. Neither the partnership nor the corporation in fact assumed Dalton Waldrop's personal obligation to the defendants. In these circumstances, the trial court was correct in concluding that neither entity became obligated for Dalton Waldrop's personal obligation to the defendants.
4. Therefore the defendants may not offset the amount Dalton Waldrop owes them against the amount they owe the successor corporation.

Waldrop v. Holland, 588 P.2d 1237 (Wash. App. 1979).

Because a partnership has the right to acquire, own, and dispose of personal property in the firm name, legal documents affecting the title to partnership personal property may be executed in the firm name by any partner. The Uniform Partnership Act also treats a partnership as a legal entity for the purposes of title to real estate that may be held in the firm name. Title so acquired can be conveyed in the partnership name. Many of the legal principles relating to partnership property are discussed in the next chapter.

9. Firm Name

Because a partnership is created by the agreement of the parties, they select the name to be used. This right of selection is subject to two limitations by statute in many states. First, a partnership may not use the word *company* or other language that would imply the existence of a corporation. Second, if the name is other than that of the partners, they must comply with assumed name statutes that require the giving of public notice as to the actual identity of the partners. Failure to comply with this assumed name statute may result in the partnership's being denied access to the courts to sue its debtors, or it may result in criminal actions being brought against those operating under the assumed name.

The firm name is an asset of the firm, and as such it may also be sold, assigned, or disposed of in any manner upon which the parties agree. At common law, a partnership was not a legal entity that could sue and be sued in the firm name. All actions had to be brought in behalf of, or against, all the partners as individuals. Today, statutes in most states have changed the common law and allow partnerships to sue or be sued in the firm name. Most states also consider the partnership a legal entity for purposes of litigation even in the absence of a statute. The following case, involving a joint venture of corporate partners, reached this result.

CASE

Decker Coal Company is a joint venture between Wytana, Inc., a Delaware corporation, and Western Minerals, Inc., an Oregon corporation. It is engaged in the surface mining of low-sulfur coal and operates its plant in Decker, Montana. Decker brought suit against Commonwealth Edison Company. Edison moved to dismiss the complaint, asserting, among other things, that Decker lacked the capacity to sue in its own name. The trial court held that Decker did have the capacity to sue in its own name, and Edison appealed.

ISSUE: Does Decker Coal Company, as a joint venture between two out-of-state corporations, have capacity to bring suit as a plaintiff against a corporation under Montana law?

DECISION: Yes.

REASONS:
1. Under Montana law, a joint venture (such as Decker) is treated like a partnership.
2. While a partnership at common law was not considered a distinct entity from the partners composing it, the modern tendency is the other way, that is, to treat a partnership as an entity distinct from and independent of the individuals composing it.
3. There is a tendency to treat a partnership as an entity in the business world, and no good reason is apparent why the law should not conform to business custom and usage.
4. It is undoubtedly true, as Edison suggests, that the Montana legislature could have enacted a statute permitting partnerships to sue in their own names. Conversely, it could have enacted a statute prohibiting a partnership from suing in its own name. The fact is that it did neither. In the absence of express guidance from the legislature, this court must follow what we submit is the

clear intent of the legislature to treat partnerships as distinct entities with power to sue.

Decker Coal Co. v. Commonwealth Edison Co., 714 P.2d 155 (Mont. 1986).

Partnerships may also declare bankruptcy as a firm. To this extent, and to the extent that it can own and dispose of property in the firm name, a partnership is a legal entity. It is not a legal entity to the extent that a corporation is, however.

10. Goodwill

Goodwill, which is usually transferred with the name, is based upon the justifiable expectation that a firm's good reputation, satisfied customers, established location, and past advertising will result in continued patronage of old customers and the probable patronage of new customers. Goodwill is usually considered in an evaluation of the assets of the business, and it is capable of being sold and transferred. Upon dissolution caused by the death of one of the partners, the surviving partner must account for it to the legal representative of the deceased partner, unless otherwise agreed upon in the *buy and sell agreement.*

When goodwill and the firm name are sold, an agreement not to compete is usually part of the sales agreement. Such an agreement may be implied but should be a part of the buy and sell provisions.

11. Buy and Sell Provisions

Either as part of the partnership agreement or by separate contract, the partners should provide for the contingency of death or withdrawal of a partner. This contingency is covered by a *buy and sell agreement,* and it is imperative that the terms of the buy and sell provisions be agreed upon before either party knows whether he is a buyer or a seller. After the status of the parties becomes known, agreement is extremely difficult, if not impossible. If such agreement is lacking, many additional problems will arise upon the death or withdrawal of a partner, and there are many possibilities of litigation and economic loss to all concerned.

A buy and sell agreement avoids these types of problems by providing a method whereby the surviving partner or partners can purchase the interest of the deceased partner, or the remaining partner or partners can purchase the interest of the withdrawing partner. A method of determining the price to be paid for such interest is provided. The time and method of payment are usually stipulated. The buy and sell agreement should specify whether a partner has an option to purchase the interest of a dying or withdrawing partner or whether he has a duty to do so.

It is common for partners to provide for life insurance on each other's lives as a means of funding the buy and sell provisions. In the event of a partner's death, proceeds of the insurance are used to purchase the deceased partner's interest. Premiums on such life insurance are not deductible for tax purposes but are usually treated as an expense for accounting purposes. There are a variety of methods for holding title to the insurance. It may be individually owned or business owned. The provisions of the policy should be carefully integrated into the partnership agreement; each partner's estate plan should also properly consider the ramifications of this insurance and of the buy and sell agreement.

CHAPTER SUMMARY

When Does a Partnership Exist?

Express Partnerships

1. A partnership may be created by express agreement or may be implied from conduct. In either case it is a question of the intent of the parties.

Implied Partnerships

1. The essential elements of a partnership are a common interest in the business and a share in the profits and losses.
2. The receipt of a share of the profits is prima facie evidence of a partnership, but this presumption may be overcome by evidence that the share of profits is for some other purpose.

Partnership by Estoppel

1. While parties may not be partners as between themselves, a partnership may exist insofar as third parties are concerned.
2. A partnership by estoppel is created if a person by words or conduct represents himself or consents to another's representing him as a partner.

The Partnership Agreement

Profit-and-Loss Provision

1. Unless there is an agreement to the contrary, profits and losses are shared equally.
2. If the agreement does not cover losses, they are shared in the same manner as profits.

Partnership Capital Provision

1. Partnership capital is the amount contributed by a partner and the amount that is to be returned on dissolution.
2. Undivided profits are not a part of capital.
3. A party may become a partner without a capital contribution.

Partnership Property

1. All property brought into the partnership or acquired by it is partnership property.
2. Property contributed as part of a capital contribution is partnership property.
3. Partnership property may be acquired and disposed of in the partnership name.

Firm Name

1. The partnership may not use words indicating that it is a corporation.
2. The partnership is other than the names of the partners and must comply with the assumed name statute.
3. The firm name is an asset and may be treated as such.
4. Partnerships can sue and be sued in their firm name.

Goodwill

1. Goodwill is an asset that may be transferred to others and that must be accounted for upon the death of a partner.

Buy and Sell Provisions

1. The partnership agreement must provide for the contingency of the death, withdrawal, or expulsion of a partner.
2. Such agreements are usually funded with life insurance as an expense of the partnership.

REVIEW QUESTIONS AND PROBLEMS

1. Match each term in column A with the appropriate statement in column B.

A	B
(1) Partnership by estoppel	(a) An agreement that covers the rights of parties on dissolution.

(2) Implied partnership
(3) Ostensible partner
(4) Articles of partnership
(5) Partnership capital
(6) Advance
(7) Assumed name statute
(8) Buy and sell agreement

(b) The contribution of partners to the partnership.
(c) A partnership created by conduct.
(d) Failure to comply may be a crime.
(e) Partnership liability that is imposed on one who has held himself out to be a partner when in fact he is not a partner.
(f) Synonymous with a partner by estoppel.
(g) The agreement creating a partnership
(h) A loan to the partnership by a partner.

2. Les and Turner entered into a written agreement whereby Turner was to farm Les's land in exchange for one-third of the crop as rental. The contract also provided that Les was to advance financing and Turner was to furnish the equipment. It was also agreed that after delivery of the one-third of the crops, all net proceeds and losses were to be shared equally. The contract specifically stated that Les and Turner were not partners, but landlord and tenant. Are Les and Turner partners? Why or why not?

3. A son sued his father, claiming a partnership interest in a business. The father had purchased all the assets of the business in his own name and was solely liable on all business debts. All the taxes were paid by the father, and no partnership tax return had been filed. The parties had equal access to the proceeds of the business. Was the son a partner? Explain.

4. David was employed by Walter to sell and service boilers. He was paid 50 percent of the net profit of each sale. Are David and Walter partners? Why or why not.

5. Charlotte and Gia, both attorneys, agreed to share office space and other overhead expense, but they did not agree to form a partnership. The sign outside their offices and their common letterhead read "Charlotte Gifford and Gia Hammond, Attorneys at Law." Using this stationery, Charlotte purchased some office equipment from Descor. Gia did not join in the contract in any way. Charlotte did not pay for the equipment. Is Gia liable to Descor? Discuss.

6. Defendants Marquart and Roth entered into a written agreement with plaintiff, whereby defendants were designated as the service agent for plaintiff in Missoula, Montana. Under the agreement, defendants were authorized to merchandise tires, batteries, and accessories delivered to them by plaintiff. According to the plaintiff, Marquart informed him that he and defendant Roth were going into a joint venture together to merchandise plaintiff's goods. Roth testified that the agreement was blank when Roth signed it and that Marquart was the actual operator of the business. When the goods were not paid for, plaintiff sued both parties. Did a partnership exist between Marquart and Roth, making Roth liable for the merchandise delivered? Explain.

7. Pursuant to an oral agreement, Andy and Jeff formed a partnership to do kitchen remodeling. It was agreed that Andy was to invest $10,000 and manage the business affairs. Jeff, who would invest $1,000, was to work as job superintendent and manage the work. Profits were to be split fifty-fifty, but possible losses were not discussed. The business proved unprofitable, and Andy brought action against Jeff for one-half of the losses. To what extent is Jeff liable? Explain.

8. A partnership is to be liquidated. Smith has contributed $6,000 to capital; Charles $3,000 to capital; and Black has made no contribution to capital but has merely contributed his services. Liabilities of the partnership exceed assets by $9,000. How much must each partner contribute to pay off the liabilities? Explain.

9. Alex, Ben, and Carl formed the ABC Company, a partnership, with Alex contributing $12,000 of capital, Ben contributing $8,000, and Carl contributing $6,000. The partnership agreement provided that the partnership was to exist for twenty years, but the partners made no provision as to the proportions in which profits and losses were to be shared. During the course of operating the partnership, A made a loan of $1,000 to the partnership that has not been repaid, and the partnership also owes outside creditors additional amounts that exceed the value of partnership assets by $3,000. How much will each be required to pay, and how much will each receive upon dissolution? Explain.

10. Pat and Doris were equal partners in a real estate business. Doris purchased a piece of real estate in her own name; however, she reimbursed herself for the down payment from the partnership's checking account. This property was shown on the partnership's books, and all expenses connected with it were paid by the partnership. Is this real estate partnership property, each partner being entitled to one-half of the profits from its sale? Why or why not?

11. A partnership known as Stein Properties brought suit in its firm name against a trustee on a deposit receipt contract. The partnership had not complied with the state's fictitious name statute. The defendant moved to dismiss the suit, contending that the partnership could not sue because of its failure to comply with the state statute. Will the suit be dismissed? Why or why not?

12. Why should a buy and sell provision be included in a partnership agreement? How can the partnership be sure of having sufficient funds to comply with a buy and sell provision?

27 Operation of Partnerships

CHAPTER PREVIEW

BUSINESS MANAGEMENT DECISION

The partners in an existing partnership decide to make you a partner. You are not required to make any contribution to the firm's capital, but you are expected to work full time.

To what must you get the existing partners to agree?

The operation of a partnership is governed by the provisions of the partnership agreement and the applicable statutory law, which in most states is the Uniform Partnership Act. Thus the rights, duties, and powers of partners are both expressed (those in the agreement) and implied (those created by law). Many of the expressed rights, duties, and powers are discussed in Chapter 26, on typical provisions of the partnership agreement. Those that are implied are discussed in this chapter, along with additional observations about the partnership agreement as it affects operations. Throughout this discussion remember that a partner is essentially an agent for the other partners and that the general principles of the law of agency are applicable.

Before examining the rights, duties, and powers of partners, certain terminology must be understood. A **silent partner** in a general partnership is one who does not participate in management. If the silent partner is to have limited liability, the provisions of the Uniform Limited Partnership Act must be followed. A **secret partner** is unknown to third parties. He may advise management and participate in decisions, but his interest is not known to third parties. A **dormant partner** is both secret and silent.

Silent partner *A partner who has no voice in the management of the partnership.*

Secret partner *A partner whose existence is not known to the public.*

Dormant partner *A partner who is both secret and silent.*

THE RIGHTS OF PARTNERS

1. To Participate in Management

All partners have equal rights in the management and conduct of the firm's business. These rights are not determined by the share that each partner has invested in the business. The partners may, however, agree to place the management within the control of one or more partners.

The majority of the partners decide ordinary matters arising in the conduct of the partnership business. If the firm consists of only two persons who are unable to agree, and the articles of partnership make no provision for the settlement of disputes, dissolution is the only remedy. If a partner refuses to agree to a demand by another, it is usually not a breach of the fiduciary duties owed by one partner to another. In the following case, notice the failure to anticipate the disagreement and the deadlock.

CASE

Covalt and High formed a partnership to own real estate containing an office building and warehouse. The property was leased to CSI Corporation of which Covalt owned 25 percent and High 75 percent of the stock. After the original lease expired, Covalt resigned his corporate position and went to work for a competitor of CSI. He continued in the partnership and demanded that the rent be increased. When CSI did not agree, Covalt sued High for breach of his fiduciary duties as a partner.

ISSUE: Can a partner recover damages against his copartner for the copartner's failure or refusal to negotiate and obtain an increase in the amount of rental of partnership property?

DECISION: No.

REASONS:
1. At the time of the formation of the partnership, both Covalt and High were officers and shareholders of CSI. Each was aware of the potential for conflict between their duties as corporate officers to further the business of the corporation and that of their role as partners in leasing realty to the corporation for the benefit of the partnership business. In the posture of being both landlord and representatives of the tenant, they had conflicting loyalties and fiduciary duties. Each party's conflict of interest was known to the other and was acquiesced in when the partnership was formed.
2. Covalt and High were legally invested with equal voices in the management of their partnership's affairs.
3. As between the partners themselves, in the absence of an agreement of a majority of the partners, an act involving the partnership business may not be compelled by one partner upon the other.
4. Under the facts herein, in the absence of a mutual agreement between the partners to increase the rent of the partnership realty, we hold that one partner may not recover damages for the failure of the copartner to acquiesce in a demand by the plaintiff that High negotiate and execute an increase in the monthly rentals of partnership property with CSI. Thus there was no breach of fiduciary duty.

Covalt v. High, 675 P.2d 999 (N.M. App. 1983).

As the result of the type of disagreement that occurred in the foregoing case, partnership agreements usually provide for some form of arbitration of deadlocks between partners. Such provisions avoid dissolution and should always be used when there are an even number of partners.

The majority cannot, however, without the consent of the minority, change the essential nature of the business by altering the partnership agreement or by reducing or increasing the capital of the partners. It cannot embark upon a new business or admit new members to the firm. In a limited partnership, the agreement cannot be modified without the unanimous consent of all partners.

Certain acts other than those enumerated previously require the unanimous consent of the partners in order to bind the firm, namely: (1) assigning the firm property to a trustee for the benefit of creditors; (2) confessing a judgment; (3) disposing of the goodwill of the business; (4) submitting a partnershp agreement to arbitration; and (5) doing any act that would make impossible the conduct of the partnership business.

2. To Be Conpensated for Services

It is the duty of each partner, in the absence of an agreement to the contrary, to give his entire time, skill, and energy to the pursuit of the partnership affairs. No partner is entitled to payment for services rendered in the conduct of the partnership business unless an agreement to that effect has been expressed or may be implied from the conduct of the partners. Note that in the following case the unsuccessful partner-plaintiff probably expected to be compensated.

CASE

In July 1976, Sharp, Zelinsky, and Laubersheimer entered into a written agreement to form a general partnership doing business as Maple Investments. Shortly thereafter, Salo joined as a fourth partner. Sharp contributed land valued at $50,000 to the partnership; Zelinsky, Salo, and Laubersheimer made cash contributions of $10,000, $10,000 and $5,000, respectively. The partnership agreement did not provide for compensation to the partners for services rendered.

Maple Investments began construction of commercial warehouses on the partnership property. These warehouses were sold. Laubersheimer handled the closing for the partnership. Instead of depositing the proceeds of the sale ($104,000) into the partnership's account, he placed the money in a new account that only Laubersheimer and Salo had access to. When these partners refused to release the $104,000 of partnership assets, Sharp and Zelinsky sued to recover the assets, to dissolve the partnership, and to recover compensation owed Sharp for services rendered. The trial court ruled for the plaintiffs, including the payment of $60,000 as compensation to Sharp.

ISSUE: Is a partner entitled to compensation for services rendered to the partnership when the partnership agreement does not expressly provide for such compensation?

DECISION: No.

REASONS:

1. According to the partnership agreement, each partner was required to contribute reasonable time and attention to the business and affairs of the partnership. Apart from the partners' sharing of profits, no other form of remuneration is provided for.
2. Since the partnership agreement is silent regarding compensation, the law will not allow plaintiffs to be reimbursed for services rendered on behalf of the partnership. The partnership agreement governs the rights and duties of the partners in relation to the partnership.
3. The trial court's award to Sharp of $60,000 for services rendered must be reversed.

Sharp v. Laubersheimer, 347 N.W.2d 268 (Minn. 1984).

An agreement to compensate may be implied from the practice of actually paying a salary. If an agreement or practice contemplates a salary to one or more partners but no amount is specified, it may be presumed that the payment of reasonable compensation is intended. This often occurs when one partner is actually engaged in the business and others are not. Often, one of the partners does not desire to participate in the management of the business. The partnership agreement in such case usually provides that the active partners receive a salary for their services in addition to their share in the profits. A surviving partner is entitled to reasonable compensation for his services in winding up the partnership affairs unless he is guilty of misconduct in winding up the affairs.

3. To Interest

Contributions to capital are not entitled to draw interest unless they are not repaid when the repayment should be made. The partner's share in the profits constitutes the earnings on his capital investment. In the absence of an expressed provision for the payment of interest, it is presumed that interest will be paid only on advances above the amount originally contributed as capital. Advances in excess of the prescribed capital, even though credited to the capital account of the contributing partners, are entitled to draw interest from the date of the advance.

Unwithdrawn profits remaining in the firm are not entitled to draw interest. They are not considered advances or loans merely because they are left with the firm, although custom, usage, and circumstances may show an intention to treat them as loans.

4. To Information and to Inspection of Books

Every partner is entitled to full and complete information concerning the conduct of the business and to inspect the books to secure that information. The partnership agreement usually contains provisions relative to the records that the business will maintain. Each partner is under a duty to give the person responsible for keeping the records whatever information is necessary to carry on the business efficiently and effectively. It is the duty of the person keeping the records to allow each partner access to them, but no partner has a right to remove the records from the agreed-upon location without the consent of the other partners. Each partner is entitled to make copies of the records, provided he does not make his inspection for fraudulent purposes.

Each partner has implied authority to receive notices and information for all other partners concerning matters within the pursuit of the partnership business. Knowledge held by any partner in his mind but not revealed to the other partners is nevertheless notice to the partnership. Knowledge of one partner is legally knowledge of all partners, provided that the facts became known or were knowledge obtained within the scope of the partnership business. A partner has a duty to communicate known facts to the other partners and to add them to the records of the partnership. Failure to do so is fraud on the partnership by the partner possessing the knowledge. This failure to inform is also a breach of the duty to assist in the maintenance of accurate records.

5. To an Accounting

The partners' proportionate share of the partnership assets or profits, when not determined by a voluntary settlement of the parties, may be ascertained in a suit for an accounting. Such suits are equitable in nature; and in states that still distinguish between suits at law and suits in equity, these actions must be filed in the court of equity.

As a general rule, a partner cannot maintain an *action at law* against other members of the firm on the partnership agreement because until there is an accounting and all partnership affairs are settled, the indebtedness among the firm members is undetermined. This general rule is subject to a few commonsense exceptions. For example, if the partnership is formed for the carrying out of a single venture or transaction, or the action involves a segregated or single unadjusted item of account, or a personal covenant or transaction entirely independent of the partnership affairs, a suit at law may be filed. Since the affairs of a partnership usually involve multiple and complicated transactions, the requirement of an accounting before a suit for damages is usually applied, as it was in the following case.

CASE

C&S Builders, Inc., sued Mitchell Resort Enterprises, Inc., for the reasonable profit of joint ventures between them. The joint ventures involved the construction and sale of townhouses. The lower court awarded the plaintiff $75,000 for undivided profits, and the defendant appealed.

ISSUE: Can C&S Builders sue Mitchell Resort Enterprises before an accounting and settlement of partnership affairs has been made?

DECISION: No.

REASONS:
1. The law is well settled that one partner may not sue another partner on a claim arising out of partnership business until an accounting and settlement of partnership affairs is made.
2. There are several exceptions to this rule, as where the partnership was formed for the carrying out of a single venture or transaction, or the action involves a segregated or single unadjusted item of account, or a personal covenant or transaction entirely independent of the partnership affairs.
3. The exceptions not being applicable, C&S Builders' claim is precluded until an accounting and settlement of partnership affairs has been made.

Mitchell Resort Enterprises, Inc. v. C&S Builders, Inc., 570 S.W.2d 465 (Tex. 1978).

Because partners ordinarily have equal access to the partnership records, there is usually no need for formal accountings to determine partnership interests. A suit for an accounting is not permitted for settling incidental matters or disputes between the partners. If a dispute is of such grievous nature that the continued existence of the partnership is impossible, a suit for an accounting in equity is allowed.

In all cases, a partner is entitled to an accounting upon the dissolution of the firm. Without a dissolution of the firm, he has a right to a formal accounting in the following situations.

1. There is an agreement for an accounting at a definite date.
2. One partner has withheld profits arising from secret transactions.
3. There has been an execution levied against the interest of one of the partners.

4. One partner does not have access to the books.
5. The partnership is approaching insolvency, and all parties are not available.

Upon an agreement between themselves, the partners may make a complete accounting and settle their claims without resort to a court of equity.

6. Partnership Property Rights

A partner is a co-owner with his partners of partnership property. Subject to any agreement among partners, a partner has an equal right among his partners to possess partnership property for partnership purposes. He has no right to possess partnership property for other purposes without the consent of the partners.

A partner has a right that the property will be used in the pursuit of the partnership business and to pay firm creditors. Since a partner does not own any specific item of the partnership property, he has no right in specific partnership property that is transferable by him. A partner has no right to use the firm property in satisfaction of his personal debts; conversely, his personal creditors cannot make a levy upon specific partnership property.

When a partner dies, his interest in specific partnership property passes to the surviving partner or partners, who have the duty of winding up the affairs of the partnership in accordance with the partnership agreement and the applicable laws. When the winding-up process is complete, the estate of the deceased partner will be paid whatever sum the estate is entitled to, according to law and the partnership agreement. The surviving partner may sell the property, real and personal, of the partnership in connection with winding up the business, in order to obtain the cash to pay the estate of the deceased partner.

A partner's interest *in the firm* consists of his rights to share in the profits that are earned and, after dissolution and liquidation, to the return of his capital and undistributed profits. This assumes, of course, that his capital has not been absorbed or impaired by losses.

A partner may assign his interest, or his right to share, in the profits of the partnership. Such an assignment will not of itself work a dissolution of the firm. The assignee is not entitled to participate in the management of the business. The only right of the assignee is to receive the profits to which the assignor would otherwise have been entitled and, in the event of dissolution, to receive his assignor's interest.

A partner's interest in the partnership cannot be levied upon by his separate creditors and sold at public sale. A judgment creditor of a partner must proceed by obtaining a "charging order" from the court. This order charges the interest of the debtor partner with the unsatisfied amount of the judgment debt. The court will ordinarily appoint a receiver, who will recieve the partner's share of the profits and any other money due or to fall due to him in respect of the partnership and apply that money upon the judgment. Likewise, the court may order that the interest charged be sold. Such a sale is not a sale of the partnership assets or property. Neither the charging order nor the sale of the interest will cause a dissolution of the firm unless the partnership is one that is terminable at will. The following case illustrates these principles.

CASE

Amerco obtained a judgment against Bohonus, a partner in an operating partnership. Amerco sought a charging order against Bohonus's interest in the partnership from the court pursuant to the Uniform Partnership Act. The court granted the request for a charging order. As a part of that order, the court ordered the sale of property of the partnership business.

ISSUE: May the trial court order the sale of partnership property to satisfy the individual debt of a partner?

DECISION: No.

REASONS:
1. A partner's right in specific partnership property is not subject to attachment or execution, except on a claim against the partnership.
2. By statute, only the "interest in the partnership" may be charged and there is no provision for the sale of assets or property of the partnership.
3. The Uniform Partnership Act prohibits the sale of partnership property in order to satisfy the nonpartnership debts of individual partners.

Bohonus v. Amerco, 602 P.2d 469 (Ariz. 1979).

If there is more than one judgment creditor seeking a charging order, the first one to seek it is usually paid in full before others are paid anything. There is no pro rata distribution unless the partnership is dissolved.

DUTIES AND POWERS OF PARTNERS

7. Duties

A partnership is a fiduciary relationship. Each partner owes the duty of undivided loyalty to the other. Therefore every partner must account to the partnership for any benefit and hold as a trustee for it any profits gained by him without consent of the other partners. This duty also rests upon representatives of deceased partners engaged in the liquidation of the affairs of the partnership.

The partnership relation is a personal one, obligating each partner to exercise good faith and to consider the mutual welfare of all the partners in his conduct of the business. If one partner attempts to secure an advantage over the others, he thereby breaches the partnership relation, and he must account for all benefits that he obtains. This includes transactions with partners and with others. It also includes transactions connected with winding up the business. The duty continues, even though the partnership is dissolved, if the partnership opportunity arose prior to dissolution.

8. Power to Contract

A partner is an agent of the partnership for the purpose of its business, and the general rules of agency are applicable to all partnerships. Each partner has authority to bind the partnership with contractual liability whenever he is apparently carrying on the business of the partnership in the usual way. If it is apparent that he is not carrying on business of the partnership in the usual way, his act does not bind the partnership unless it is authorized by the other partners, as in the following case.

CASE

Plaintiff Hodge sued for specific performance of a contract for the sale of a small parcel of land belonging to a partnership. The contract was signed by Rex E. Voeller, the managing partner of the partnership, which operated a drive-in theater. The parcel, adjacent to the theater, was part of the theater's driveway. The other partners contended that Voeller did not have authority to sell the parcel of land.

ISSUE: Did Voeller have authority to sell the partnership property?

DECISION: No.

REASONS:
1. This contract is enforceable if Voeller had the actual authority to sell the property. Even if Voeller did not have such actual authority, the contract is still enforceable if the sale is the usual way of carrying on the business and Hodge did not know that Voeller did not have this authority.
2. The authority of one partner to make and acknowledge a deed for the firm will not be presumed.
3. Selling real estate is not the usual or customary business of a partnership that operates a movie theater. Thus, even if Hodge believed that Voeller as exclusive manager had authority to transact all business of the firm, Voeller still could not bind the partnership through a unilateral act that was not in the usual business of the partnership.

Hodge v. Garrett, 614 P.2d 420 (Idaho 1980).

The rules of agency relating to authority, ratification, and secret limitations on the authority of a partner are applicable to partnerships, but the extent of implied authority is generally greater for partners than for ordinary agents. Each partner has implied power to do all acts necessary for carrying on the business of the partnership. Admissions or representations pertaining to the conduct of the partnership business and made by a partner may be used as evidence against the partnership.

The nature and scope of the business and what is usual in the particular business determine the extent of the implied powers. Among the common implied powers are the following: to compromise, adjust, and settle claims or debts owed by or to the partnership; to sell goods in the regular course of business and to make warranties; to buy property within the scope of the business for cash or upon credit; to buy insurance; to hire employees; to make admissions against interest; to enter into contracts within the scope of the firm; and to receive notices. In a trading partnership, a partner has the implied authority to borrow funds and to pledge the assets of the firm. Some of these implied duties are discussed more fully in the sections that follow.

9. Power to Impose Tort Liability

A partner has the power to impose tort liability through the doctrine of *respondeat superior*. The law imposes tort liability upon a partnership for all wrongful acts or omissions of any partner acting in the ordinary course of the partnership and for its benefit.

CASE

A jury returned a verdict for the plaintiff Martin in the amount of $125,000 against Drs. Barbour and Egle. The case was based on allegations of negligence by Barbour in performing an operation for a rectal condition that resulted in permanent incontinence. The defendant Egle did not assist or participate in the surgery and did not treat the plaintiff. However, Egle was a partner in the practice of medicine with Barbour at the time of the surgery.

ISSUE: Is Egle liable for the negligence of Barbour in performing the operation?

DECISION: Yes.

REASONS:
1. Pursuant to general rules, partners in the practice of medicine are all liable for an injury to a patient resulting from the lack of skill or the negligence, either in omission or commission, of any one of the partners within the scope of their partnership business.
2. Since Egle was a partner of the medical partnership, he is liable for the negligence of Barbour.

Martin v. Barbour, 558 S.W.2d 200 (Mo. 1977).

If a partnership has liability because of a tort of a partner, the firm has the right to collect its losses from the partner at fault. In effect, a partnership that is liable in tort to a third person has a right of indemnity against the partner at fault. Likewise, if the injured third party collects directly from the partner at fault, the partner cannot seek contribution from his copartners.

10. Powers over Property

Each partner has implied authority to sell to good-faith purchasers personal property that is held for the purpose of resale and to execute any documents necessary to effect a transfer of title. Of course, if his authority in this connection has been limited, and that is known to the purchaser, the transfer of title will be ineffective or voidable. A partner has no power to sell the fixtures and equipment used in the business unless he has been duly authorized. His acts are not a regular feature of the business, and a prospective purchaser should make certain that the particular partner has been given authority to sell. The power to sell, where it is present, also gives the power to make warranties that normally accompany similar sales.

The right to sell a firm's real property is to be inferred only if the firm is engaged in the real estate business. In other cases there is no right to sell and convey realty unless it has been authorized by a partnership agreement. In most states, a deed by one partner without authority is not binding on the firm, but it does convey the individual interest of the parties executing and delivering the deed. This conveyance, however, is subject to the rights of creditors of the partnership.

Under the Uniform Partnership Act, title to real property may be taken in the firm name as a "tenancy in partnership," and any member of the firm has power to execute a deed thereto by signing the firm name. If that happens, what is the effect of a wrongful transfer of real estate that has been acquired for use in the business and not for resale? The conveyance may be set aside by the other partners, because the purchaser should have known that one partner has no power to sell real estate without the approval of the others. However, if the first purchaser has resold and conveyed the property to an innocent third party, the latter takes good title.

If the title to real estate is held in the firm name, a conveyance by the partners as individuals is not effective to convey title to the real estate. The conveyance must be in the firm name. This is true even if the conveyance is to a partner as part of a settlement agreement between the partners.

If the title to firm property is not held in the firm name but is held in the names of one or more of the partners, a conveyance by those in whose names the title is held passes good title, unless the purchaser knows or should know that title was held for the firm. There is nothing in the record title in such a situation to call the buyer's attention to the fact that the firm has an interest in the property.

The power to mortgage or pledge a firm's property is primarily dependent upon the power to borrow money and bind the firm. A partner with authority to borrow may, as an incident to that power, give the security normally demanded for similar loans. Because no one partner without the consent of the others has the power to commit an act that will destroy or terminate the business, the power to give a mortgage on the entire stock of merchandise and fixtures of a business is usually denied. Such a mortgage would make it possible, upon default, to liquidate the firm's assets and thus destroy its business. Subject to this limitation, the power to borrow carries the power to pledge or mortgage.

11. Financial Powers

To determine the limit of a partner's financial powers, partnerships are divided into two general classes—trading and nontrading partnerships. A *trading partnership* is one that has for its primary purpose the buying and selling of merchandise. In such a trading firm, each partner has an implied power to borrow money and to extend the credit of the firm, in the usual course of business, by signing negotiable paper.

A *nontrading partnership* is one that does not buy and sell commodities but has for its primary purpose the production of commodities or is organized for the purpose of selling services: for example, professional partnerships in law, medicine, or accounting. In such partnerships, a partner's powers are more limited, and a partner does not have implied power to borrow money. However, if the partner's act is within the scope of partnership business, a member of a nontrading partnership may bind the firm by the exercise of implied authority, just as a partner in a trading partnership may.

CHAPTER SUMMARY

Rights of Partners

Management	1. Unless the agreement provides to the contrary, each partner has an equal right to manage and to conduct the firm's business.

2. The majority of partners can make final decisions concerning normal operations.
3. Certain actions require unanimous consent to bind the firm.

Compensation

1. Partners are not generally compensated other than with a share of the profits, unless the agreement provides otherwise.
2. A partner engaged in winding up the partnership is entitled to compensation for doing so.
3. Unless the agreement is to the contrary, partners have a duty to devote all of their time, skill, and energy to partnership affairs.

Interest

1. Capital contributions do not earn interest.
2. Interest is paid on advances above capital contributions.
3. Interest is not paid on unwithdrawn profits.

Information and Inspection of Books

1. Each partner is entitled to all information concerning the business and to inspect the books and records of the partnership.
2. Partners have a duty to furnish information necessary to operate the business.
3. Partners have a right to make copies of partnership records.

Accounting

1. In the event of a dispute as to the rights of the parties to assets or income, the equity action of an accounting is available to determine the rights of the partners.
2. As a general rule, partners are not allowed to sue each other in courts of law for dollar damages.
3. The suit for an accounting cannot be brought for minor disputes.
4. The suit for an accounting is usually a part of the dissolution process.

Property

1. Each partner has an equal right to possess partnership property for partnership purposes.
2. A partner has no right in specific partnership property and no right to use partnership property for personal purposes.
3. Upon the death of a partner, the property belongs to the surviving partners, who have a duty to wind up the affairs. These surviving partners must pay the deceased partner's estate the sum to which the deceased partner was entitled.
4. A partner's interest cannot be levied upon by his separate creditors. Creditors are entitled to obtain a charging order and to collect the partner's share of profits to satisfy the judgment.

Duties and Powers of Partners

Duties

1. A partnership is a fiduciary relationship, and each partner must act only on behalf of the partnership.
2. A partner cannot take for himself an opportunity of the partnership, and any gains that should have belonged to the partnership must be paid to it.
3. All acts of partners are subject to the good-faith standard.
4. Since knowledge of any partner is charged to all partners, there is a duty on one partner to inform all other partners of all facts affecting the partnership business.

Power to Contract

1. A partner is an agent of the partnership business, and the general rules of agency are applicable.
2. The implied authority of a partnership is greater than that of an ordinary

agent. A partner has the implied power to do all acts necessary to carry on the business.

Power to Impose Tort Liability

1. The doctrine of *respondeat superior* is applicable to the partnership relationship.
2. If the partnership incurs liability because of the tort of a partner, it has the right to collect the loss from the partner.

Powers over Property

1. Partners have authority to sell personal property held by the partnership for resale in the ordinary course of business.
2. A partner has no right to sell firm real estate unless it is engaged in the business of selling real estate.
3. Real property held in the partnership name can be conveyed only with the agreement of all partners.

Financial Powers

1. In a trading partnership, each partner has the implied power to borrow money to extend the credit of the firm in the usual course of business.
2. In a nontrading partnership, a partner does not have the implied power to borrow money.

REVIEW QUESTIONS AND PROBLEMS

1. Match each term in column A with the appropriate statement in column B.

A	B
(1) Silent partner	(a) A partnership that is engaged in the buying and selling of goods.
(2) Secret partner	(b) Describes the title to property held in the partnership name.
(3) Dormant partner	(c) A partner that does not participate in management.
(4) Tenancy in partnership	(d) A partnership engaged in providing services.
(5) Changing orders	(e) A loan to a partnership by a partner.
(6) Trading partnership	(f) A partner that is unkown to third parties.
(7) Nontrading partnership	(g) A court procedure for collecting an undivided debt of a partner from the partnership.
(8) Advance	(h) A partner that is both secret and silent.

2. The partners in a partnership composed of seven members have differing views on several partnership issues. If the partnership agreement makes no provision for the number of partners required to decide particular issues, how many votes does it take:

   a. To discharge a clerk accused of stealing?
   b. To cause the dissolution of the partnership?
   c. To require the change of the partnership business from a wholesale to a retail operation?
   d. To require the submission of a partnership claim for arbitration?
   e. To submit to a confession of judgment on behalf of the partnership?

3. Peter, John, and James were partners in the ownership and operation of a fishing vessel. Peter had perfected a new type of net for catching sharks. Getting the nets ready for use took a lot of time, but their use saved the partnership time and money. Is Peter entitled to extra compensation for this contribution? Explain.

4. Two people have been partners for a number of years. Upon the death of one, the other spent considerable time in winding up the partnership affairs. Is the surviving partner legally entitled to compensation for services? Why or why not?

5. Albert and Maria were partners in a grocery business. The firm was in need of additional working capital, and Albert advanced $20,000. Is Albert entitled to interest on the advance? Why or why not?

6. Huffington was the managing partner of an oil and gas investment firm. He learned of an Indonesian oil deal and acquired 10 percent of it for himself. Is the partnership entitled to the investment? Explain.

7. Preston obtained a judgment against Daniel. He sought a charging order against Daniel's interest in a general partnership in order to collect the judgment. Jeff also obtained a judgment against Daniel. Jeff seeks to intervene in Preston's suit for a charging order, so that he (Jeff) may share in it. Preston claims that he has a right to full payment before Jeff is entitled to anything. Should the charging order against Daniel's partnership interest pro rate the payment between Preston and Jeff? Explain.

8. Bedford and Eckhart formed a partnership and built a shopping center. Three years later, Bedford, the managing partner, informed Eckhart that the business was in deep financial trouble and that he had tried to sell the complex but had failed. Bedford said that the best thing to do would be for one to buy the other out, and that their equity in the business was not worth more than $3 million. Eckhart sold his half interest in the partnership to Bedford for $1.5 million. Later he discovered that their equity in the business amounted to over $10 million and that Bedford had received several offers to purchase the business. Eckhart brought suit to rescind the sale, to have the partnership dissolved, and for accounting. Should Eckhart succeed? Why or why not?

9. A partnership was in the real estate business. It was formed to buy and sell apartment buildings. Two of the three partners signed a contract to sell one of the partnership's buildings. Is the third partner bound by the contract? Why or why not?

10. Martin, Lewis and Davis are partners in a CPA firm. Martin negligently causes an automobile accident while on his way to perform an audit. Are the firm and the other partners liable? Explain.

11. A patient sued Dr. Flynn for medical malpractice. Flynn, who is a partner in a medical partnership, sought contributions from his partners. He contended that his negligence, if any, occurred in the course of the partnership's business. Is Flynn entitled to contributions from his partners? Why or why not?

12. Wood and Simmons took title to certain land as partners and leased it to the defendant. Later, when they dissolved the partnership, Wood and his wife conveyed all their interest in the property to Simmons and his wife. Simmons and his wife then separated, and he conveyed the property to her as part of their settlement. When Mrs. Simmons filed suit for possession of the property, the defendant contended that the title to the land remained with the partnership. Was the defendant correct? Why or why not?

13. Defendants Smith and Brook were partners in the automobile business under the name of Greenwood Sales and Service. Defendant Brook borrowed $6,000 from plaintiff and gave a partnership note in return. Is Smith liable on the note? Why or why not?

14. A partner in an accounting firm borrowed $10,000 in the firm name and used the proceeds to pay an individual debt. Is the firm liable for this debt? Explain.

28 Dissolution of Partnerships

C H A P T E R   P R E V I E W

BUSINESS MANAGEMENT DECISION

You are a partner in a twenty-member law firm. One of your partners, Anderson, retires from the practice of law and leaves the partnership. Anderson's duties included purchasing equipment and library materials for the firm. You assume these duties upon Anderson's retirement.

What is the first action you need to take?

TERMINOLOGY

Three steps are necessary to end a partnership: dissolution, winding up, and termination. **Dissolution,** the legal destruction of the partnership relation, occurs whenever any partner ceases to be a member of the firm or whenever a new partner is admitted. It is the change in the relation of the partners caused by any partner's ceasing to be associated in carrying on—as distinguished from winding up—the business. Dissolution alone does not terminate the partnership but, rather, designates the time when partners cease to carry on business together. **Winding up** involves the process of reducing the assets to cash, paying off the creditors, and distributing the balance to the partners. **Termination** occurs only when the winding-up process is completed. Prior to termination, a partnership even though dissolved, still has the right to collect its debts, as the following case illustrates:

Dissolution *Occurs any time there is a change in the partners, either by adding a new partner or by having a preexisting partner die, retire, or otherwise leave.*

Winding up *The process of liquidating a business organization.*

Termination *Occurs when the winding up or liquidation is completed. This is the end of the organization and its business.*

CASE

A claim was brought against the estate of Earl E. Howe, deceased. The claim was filed on behalf of and in the name of a law partnership, Horton, Davis & McCaleb. The claim was for the balance due on an outstanding bill for legal services rendered to decedent by the claimant law firm. During a hearing on the claim, the trial court learned that claimant law firm had dissolved. The court dismissed the claim.

ISSUE: Does a dissolved partnership have the right to collect outstanding accounts when it is winding up its business?

DECISION: Yes.

REASONS:

1. Dissolution does not terminate the partnership and does not end completely the authority of the partners. The order of events is (a) dissolution, (b) winding up, and (c) termination. Termination extinguishes their authority. It is the ultimate result of the winding up and occurs at the conclusion of the windup.
2. Part of the winding up includes collections of debts owed the partnership. The filing of this claim and the remarks of claimant's counsel to the trial court indicate that the claimant was in the process of winding up its affairs by attempting to collect an amount due for legal services rendered to decedent.

Howe v. Horton, Davis & McCaleb, 407 N.E.2d 766 (Ill. App. 1980).

Dissolutions will occur without violation of the partnership agreement (1) at the end of the stipulated term or particular undertaking specified in the agreement, (2) by the express will of any partner when no definite term or particular undertaking is specified, (3) by the agreement of all the partners, or (4) by the expulsion, in good faith, of any partner from the business, in accordance with power conferred by the partnership agreement. Dissolutions also may occur by operation of law or by an order of a court of equity.

METHODS OF DISSOLUTION

1. Act of Partners

When a definite term of a particular undertaking is not specified, it is a *partnership at will*. In such a partnership, any partner may, without liability, legally dissolve it at any time. Dissolution may be accomplished by giving notice to the other parties.

No particular form of notice is required; it will be implied from circumstances inconsistent with the continuation of the partnership. When a partner whose services are essential leaves the community, his departure is an act and notice of dissolution.

Expulsion of a partner is a breach of the partnership agreement unless the agreement confers the power of expulsion upon a majority of the partners. Assume that A, B, and C are partners. A and B cannot expel C unless that power is specifically granted in the agreement. Without power to expel, partners may seek judicial dissolution if one partner is guilty of violating the partnership agreement (see section 3). If C in the above case was not devoting his time to the business, as he was required to do in the partnership agreement, A and B could seek a dissolution on these grounds, although they could not expel C.

It should be noted that subject to a few exceptions, breach of a partnership agreement does not mean that the breaching partner loses his interest in the partnership. The law does not favor forfeitures; therefore, such breaches as the failure of a partner to devote all his time to the firm business do not cause him to lose his interest in the firm property. However, where the partnership agreement provides for the forfeiture of his interest in the firm property by a partner who withdraws within a stated period, such a provision will be enforced.

Breaches of the partnership articles, whether or not committed in bad faith, also do not cause a partner to lose his rights to share in the profits. But a partner who refuses to contribute funds essential to the operation of a partnership business may be excluded from participation in any profit. And if one of the partners abandons the business, he may forfeit some or all of his share of the profits.

Dissolution may also occur in violation of the partnership agreement. Although the agreement stipulates the length of time the partnership is to last, dissolution is always possible because the relationship is essentially a mutual agency not capable of specific performance. Each partner therefore has the *power*, but not the *right*, to revoke the relationship. In the event of wrongful dissolution, the wrongdoer is liable for damages.

2. Operation of Law

If during the period of the partnership, events make it impossible or illegal for the partnership to continue, it will be dissolved by operation of law. Such events or conditions are the death or bankruptcy of one of the partners or a change in the law that makes the continuance of the business illegal. Of course, a partnership may also be illegal at its inception. In such a case, the courts will leave the partners where it finds them and will not grant relief to a partner in a suit against the other partner or partners.

Since a partnership is a personal relationship existing by reason of contract, when one of the partners dies, the partnership is dissolved. It is not terminated on dissolution, but it continues for the purpose of winding up the partnership's affairs. The process of winding up is, in most states, the exclusive obligation and right of the surviving partner or partners. The executor or administrator of the deceased partner has no right to participate in, or interfere with, the winding-up processes, unless, of course, the deceased was the last surviving partner. The only right of the personal representative of a deceased partner is to demand an accounting upon completion of the winding up of the partnership's affairs. As a general rule, the estate of the deceased partner is not bound on contracts entered into by the surviving partners if the contracts are unconnected with the winding up of the affairs of the partnership. This is discussed more fully later in the chapter.

The bankruptcy of a partner will dissolve the partnership because the control of his property passes to the trustee in bankruptcy for the benefit of the creditors. The mere insolvency of a partner will not be sufficient to justify a dissolution. The bankruptcy of the firm itself is a cause for dissolution, as is a valid assignment of all the firm's assets for the benefit of creditors.

3. Court Decree

When a partnership by its agreement is to be continued for a term of years, circumstances sometimes make continued existence of the firm impossible and unprofitable. Upon application of one of the partners to a court of equity, the partnership may be dissolved. Under the following circumstances and situations, a court of equity may order dissolution:

1. Total incapacity of a partner to conduct business and to perform the duties required under the contract of partnership
2. A declaration by judicial process that a partner is insane
3. Willful and persistent commitment of a breach of the partnership agreement, misappropriation of funds, or commitment of fraudulent acts
4. An innocent party's application for dissolution because the partnership was entered into as a result of fraud
5. Gross misconduct and neglect or breach of duty by a partner to such an extent that it is impossible to carry out the purposes of the partnership agreement
6. In some states, any grounds that make dissolution equitable or in the best interests of the partners

Courts will not interfere and grant a decree of dissolution for mere discourtesy, temporary inconvenience, minor differences of opinion, or errors in judgment. The misconduct must be of such gross nature that the continued operation of the business would be unprofitable. In those states that have incorporated item 6 into their law, courts of equity will order dissolution if there is serious disharmony among the partners.

In cases arising out of the dissolution of a partnership, a court of equity may appoint a receiver to liquidate the partnership, obtain an accounting of the proceeds, and distribute the assets. A receiver may be appointed when the evidence indicates that it is necessary to preserve the property and to protect the rights of the parties. For example, a receiver may be appointed where the remaining parties are delaying the winding-up process or are breaching any of the fiduciary duties of partners.

THE EFFECT OF DISSOLUTION

4. Powers of Partners

The process of winding up, except when the agreement provides for continuation by purchase of former partners' shares, involves liquidation of the partnership assets so that cash may be available to pay creditors and to make a distribution to the partners. When the agreement provides for continuation and purchase of a deceased partner's interest, the technical dissolution is followed by valuation and payment, and the new firm immediately commences business.

As a general rule, dissolution terminates the actual authority of any partner to act for the partnership except as far as necessary to wind up partnership affairs, to liquidate the assets of the firm in an orderly manner, or to complete transactions begun but not finished. Insofar as third persons who had dealings with the firm are concerned, apparent authority still exists until notice of termination is given.

This apparent authority means that one partner of a dissolved partnership binds the firm on contracts unconnected with winding up the firm's affairs. When he does so, issues arise as to whether or not the new obligations may be met with partnership funds or whether the contracting partner is entitled to contribution toward payment of the debt or obligation from the other partners.

The resolution of these issues depends on the cause of the dissolution. If the dissolution is caused by (1) the act of a partner, (2) bankruptcy of the partnership, or (3) the death of a partner, each partner is liable for his share of any liability incurred on behalf of the firm after dissolution, just if there had been no dissolution, unless the partner incurring the liability had knowledge of the dissolution. Of course, such knowledge is usually present. In these situations, if knowledge of the dissolution is present, the partner incurring the liability is solely responsible and cannot require the other partners to share the burden of an unauthorized act. If the dissolution is not caused by the act, bankruptcy, or death of a partner but by some event such as a court decree, no partner has authority to act and therefore has no right to contribution from other partners for liabilities incurred after dissolution.

When dissolution results from the death of a partner, title to partnership property remains in the surviving partner or partners for purposes of winding up and liquidation. Thus, both real and personal property are, through the survivors, made available to a firm's creditors. All realty is treated as though it were personal property. It is sold, and the surviving partners finally account, usually in cash, to the personal representative of the deceased partner for the latter's share in the proceeds of liquidation.

5. Rights of Partners

Upon dissolution, a withdrawing partner who has not breached the partnership agreement has certain options with regard to his interest in the dissolved partnership.

He may require the partnership to be wound up and terminated. The partnership will be liquidated and the assets distributed among the partners. The alternative is to allow the business to continue, or accept the fact that it has continued.

If the withdrawing partner allows the business to continue, the value of his interest in the partnership as of the date of dissolution is ascertained. He then has the right to receive, at his option after an accounting, either the value of this interest in the partnership with interest or, in lieu of interest, the profits attributable to the use of his rights in the property of the dissolved partnership. The portion of profits to which a withdrawing partner is entitled because of the use of property will usually be less than his portion prior to dissolution. This is true because a portion of the profit is usually attributable to services of the continuing partners, and most courts allow for compensation to be paid to the continuing partners. The following case discusses the elections available to former partners upon the dissolution of a partnership.

CASE

Art Lange and Bert Bartlett worked together for several years on a part-time basis installing swimming pools. In 1972, they verbally agreed to form the partnership "Pool Boys" and began operating the business full time. This arrangement continued until April 1975, when Lange told Bartlett that he no longer wanted to participate in the partnership. It is clear that Lange was not expelled as a partner; rather, he retired from the partnership. Bartlett eventually offered Lange $3,000 in payment for Lange's share of the partnership; Lange refused this offer. In 1978, Lange sued to recover his share of the partnership.

ISSUE: Upon dissolution, what rights does the former partner have?

DECISION: The former partner can either force the business to wind up and take his part of the proceeds, sharing in profits and losses after dissolution, or he can permit the business to continue and claim as a creditor the value of his interest at dissolution.

REASONS:

1. When a partner dies or retires, the partnership is dissolved. However, the partnership is not terminated upon dissolution; it continues until the windup of the partnership affairs is completed.
2. The first task for a trial court faced with making a settlement of a former partner's account after dissolution is to determine what election the retiring partner made at the point of dissolution. Every partnership dissolution causes a windup rather than a continuation unless the outgoing partner "consents" to a continuation.
3. If a trial court determines that a business was engaged in a windup, the former partner receives the value of his or her interest at the date of liquidation or final settlement. In other words, the outgoing partner shares in both profits and losses until termination.
4. If the former partner elects to allow the business to continue, this partner is not responsible for the debts of the continuing partnership. The former partner becomes a creditor of the firm to the extent of his interest in the firm at dissolution.
5. The former partner's election does not have to be made until the final accounting, so that the former partner is able to make an informed choice.

Lange v. Bartlett, 360 N.W.2d 702 (Wis. App. 1984).

When dissolution is caused in any way other than breach of the partnership agreement, each partner has a right to insist that all the partnership assets be used first to pay firm debts. After firm obligations are paid, remaining assets are used to return capital contributions and then to provide for a distribution of profits. All the partners except those who have caused a wrongful dissolution of the firm have the right to participate in the winding up of the business. The majority selects the method and procedures to be followed in the liquidation. The assets are turned into cash unless all agree to distribute them in kind.

If a partnership that is to continue for a fixed period is dissolved by the wrongful withdrawal of one partner, the remaining members may continue as partners under the same firm name for the balance of the agreed term of the partnership. They are required to settle with the withdrawing partner for his interest in the partnership and to compensate him, but they are allowed to subtract from the amount due in cash the damages caused by his wrongful withdrawal. In the calculation of his share, the goodwill of the business is not taken into consideration. The fact that a partner breached the agreement does not take away the right to an accounting and to receive his share of the partnership after deducting any damages caused by the breach of the agreement.

Upon dissolution, it is the duty of the remaining partner or partners to wind up the affairs. If they fail to do so and instead continue the business, they have liability to the withdrawing partner, his assignee, or personal representative for use of partnership assets. The liability may include interest if the value of the former partner's portion of the partnership can be ascertained, or it may include liability for a share of post-dissolution profits. This liability arises because the business is continuing to use the assets of all the former partners and the continuing partners have failed to wind up the business and terminate it.

Is a partner entitled to be paid for services rendered during the winding-up process? If the dissolution is caused by the death of a partner, the answer is "yes." If the dissolution is caused by some other act or occurrence, most courts hold that a partner is not entitled to extra compensation for services rendered in completing unfinished business unless the partnership agreement authorizes it. Income during the winding-up process is allocated to former partners according to their respective shares.

It is often difficult to value accurately the interest of a withdrawing or deceased partner when the business continues. The buy and sell provisions will control the method for establishing the value of the interest as of the date of dissolution. If there are no buy and sell provisions and the parties cannot agree, a judicial decision on the value may be required. This decision may sometimes involve which of the parties is to continue the business, as well as the amount to be paid the withdrawing partner, but it cannot be made with mathematical certainty.

6. Third Parties

Dissolution of a partnership terminates the authority of the partners to create liability, but it does not discharge any existing liability of any partner. An agreement between the partners themselves that one or more of the partners will assume the partnership liabilities and that a withdrawing partner will not have any liability does not bind the firm's creditors. However, a partner may be discharged from any existing liability by an agreement to that effect with the creditors. Such an agreement may be express or even implied from the conduct of the parties.

When a firm's assets are insufficient to pay its debts, the individual property of partners, including the estate of a deceased partner, is subject to claims of third parties for all debts created while the partnership existed. This liability is subject to the payment of individual debts, however.

After dissolution, two categories of parties are entitled to notice of the dissolution. First of all, the firm's creditors, including all former creditors, are entitled to actual notice of the dissolution. Transactions entered into after dissolution without such notice continue to bind withdrawing partners and the estate of deceased partners. If proper notice is given, former partners are not liable for contracts unconnected with winding up the partnership's affairs. Notice eliminates the apparent authority to bind the former firm and its partners. Failure to give notice and the continuation of apparent authority in effect creates a partnership estoppel. As between the parties, the original partnership is dissolved, but as to third parties, a partner carrying on the business of the former partnership binds the partners. The following case illustrates the dangers of failing to give notice of dissolution.

CASE

On September 27, 1977, Roger Allen sought a short-term loan of $60,000 from plaintiff, the Royal Bank and Trust Company, to enable him to obtain a larger loan from another source. Allen advised plaintiff that the $60,000 would be kept in an escrow account belonging to his attorneys, the firm of Weintraub, Gold & Alper. Allen gave Royal Bank a letter dated September 27, 1977, on the law firm's stationery, addressed to him and signed by Alfred Weintraub (one of the three named partners), acknowledging that the check would be received by the firm as escrow agent, that it would be placed in the firm's trust account (identified by number) at the Madison Avenue branch of Marine Midland Bank, and that the money would be returned to plaintiff by October 5, 1977. Plaintiff called its New York attorneys, who advised that they had not heard of the firm Weintraub, Gold & Alper, and that the three named individuals were listed separately in an attorney directory as practicing law at the address given on the firm stationery. Plaintiff's credit officer found the firm listed in the current Manhattan telephone directory, at the address and number corresponding to the letterhead. When he dialed the number a receptionist answered "Weintraub, Gold and Alper." He then spoke to Weintraub and confirmed the escrow arrangement set forth in the September 27 letter. Plaintiff that day made the loan, giving Allen a $60,000 check payable to the law firm, which was acknowledged in writing by Weintraub. Despite demand, the check has never been returned. Plaintiff sued Allen and the firm as well as Weintraub, Gold and Alper individually, to recover the funds.

In support of its motion for summary judgment against the firm, and the lawyers individually, plaintiff produced the following additional uncontroverted evidence to establish the continued existence of the law firm in the year 1977. The three individuals continued to share what had been the partnership offices until at least November 1977. The receptionist answered the telephone in the firm name to give the appearance to firm clients that the firm still existed. The $60,000 check received September 27, 1977, was deposited in a special account maintained in the firm name. In July 1977, the three partners signed bank documents certifying that the partnership existed, received a loan, and opened new accounts. Liability insurance was obtained for the firm from January 9, 1977 through January 9, 1978. Firm letterhead was used for court correspondence in October 1977. The partnership filed no certificate of dissolution and made no public announcement of dissolution until the withdrawal of Alper in November 1977 when formal notices were sent out and use of the firm name ceased.

The crux of defendants' opposition to plaintiff's summary judgment motion is that as of January 1, 1976 the firm, which had existed since 1972 or 1973, dissolved by oral agreement between Messrs. Weintraub and Gold, that it took no new clients thereafter, that its conduct in 1977 was fully consistent with winding up, and that Weintraub therefore had no authority to bind the partnership in September 1977. Continued use of the firm name and letterhead, defendants insist, was to be only for limited duration, as an aid in the transition to individual practices.

ISSUE: Did the lawyers' failure to give notice of dissolution to the Royal Bank justify the court holding these lawyers liable for not returning the check?

DECISION: Yes.

REASONS:

1. Acts of a partner in apparently carrying on the partnership business in the usual way are binding on the partnership unless the partner has no authority to act, and the person dealing with that partner knows that fact.
2. Weintraub's acts with respect to the escrow deposit were apparently for the benefit of a client and in furtherance of the partnership business. If indeed Weintraub lacked authority to act for the partnership in the particular matter, there is no evidence that plaintiff knew of this.
3. Whether or not the plaintiff knew that Weintraub, Gold & Alper continued in 1977 despite the intent of its members is an issue we need not resolve. A partner who makes, and consents to, continued representation that a partnership in fact exists is estopped to deny that a partnership exists to defeat the claim of a creditor. Here, defendants are estopped to deny their relationship as against plaintiff.
4. Nearly two years after alleged dissolution, the public indicia of the partnership remained undisturbed. Where the firm space, telephone number, telephone book listing, and stationery continued in use by the individuals, with no discernible sign of dissolution, we conclude that the partnership continued to be liable as such to a party reasonably relying to its detriment on the impression of an ongoing entity.

Royal Bank v. Weintraub, Gold & Alper, 497 N.E.2d 289 (N.Y. 1986).

Notice of dissolution is required, whether the dissolution is caused by an act of the parties or by operation of law, unless a partner becomes bankrupt or the continuation of the business becomes illegal. Therefore, upon death of a partner, the personal representative should give immediate notice of the death and dissolution in order to avoid further liability.

The second category of parties entitled to notice of dissolution consists of persons who knew about the partnership but who were not creditors. When the dissolution is caused by an act of the parties, the partners will continue to be liable to all such parties unless public notice of dissolution is given. Notice by publication in a newspaper in the community where the business has been transacted is sufficient public notice.

If a partner has not actively engaged in the conduct of the partnership business, if creditors have not learned that he was a partner and have not extended credit to the firm because of their faith in him, there is no duty to give notice to either of the groups mentioned above on his withdrawal.

7. New Partners and New Firms

A person admitted as a partner into an existing partnership is liable to the extent of his capital contribution for all obligations incurred before his admission, as though he had previously been a partner. The new partner is not personally liable for such obligations, and the creditors of the old firm can look only to the firm's assets and to members of the old firm. However, prior debts sometimes become new debts, as for example, upon the renewal of a note. In the following case, if the note had not been renewed, the liability of the new partner would have been limited to $100,000—his capital contribution. As a result of the renewal, the liability was over $300,000 and the partner was not involved in the renewal of the note. This case demonstrates the risk of unlimited liability in a partnership.

CASE

On September 17, 1980, five individuals formed a partnership named Southern Distilleries in order to engage in the business of producing fuel grade alcohol (gasahol). The partners signed an agreement providing that any three partners having an aggregate interest in the partnership of at least 60 percent were authorized to borrow money and execute promissory notes on behalf of the partnership. On December 19, 1980, three partners, Adams, Fitch, and Moulthrop, executed two promissory notes on behalf of Southern Distilleries to Commercial State Bank. Both notes came due on March 19, 1981, but Southern Distilleries failed to pay. On April 2, 1981, an amended partnership agreement was executed by the five original partners and by three other individuals, including Julius Moseley. The purpose of the amendment was to "change the percentage interests of the partners and to admit new partners." The document indicates that Moseley contributed $100,000 to the capital account of the partnership and acquired a "profit and loss interest in the partnership" slightly in excess of 6 percent.

On July 21, 1981, Southern Distilleries paid the interest due on the December 19 notes, and Adams, Fitch, and Moulthrop executed a new note. The bank marked the notes dated December 19 "paid" and returned them to Southern Distilleries. Southern Distilleries failed to satisfy the July 21 note when it matured and the bank brought this action to enforce payment. Upon its findings, the trial court found that Moseley was liable for $303,241.52. Moseley appealed.

ISSUE: Does Moseley, a new partner as of April 2, 1981, have unlimited liability for a debt that preexisted his becoming a partner if this debt was renegotiated on July 21, 1981?

DECISION: Yes.

REASONS:

1. A person admitted as a partner into an existing partnership is liable for partnership obligations arising before his admission into the partnership. His liability for preexisting obligations can be satisfied only out of partnership property, however.
2. Although Moseley categorizes the debt created by the note sued on as the renewal of a preexisting debt, it is clear that the obliga-

tion created by the old note terminated when the bank accepted the new note. Prior to the execution of the new note, the bank could have brought an action to collect the debt. After it accepted the new note and satisfied the old one, there was no obligation that was due and payable to the bank until the new note matured.

3. In agreeing to the forebearance of its rights to collect the money owed it by Southern Distilleries, the bank relied on the representations of the partnership agreement that the partners, including Moseley, would be bound by the new note. Since the contract sued on was entered into by a partnership that included Moseley, the bank is entitled to enforce the contract against Moseley.

Moseley v. Commercial State Bank, 457 So.2d 967 (Ala. 1984).

If a business is continued without liquidation of the partnership affairs, creditors of the first, or dissolved, partnership are also creditors of the partnership continuing the business. Likewise, if the partners assign all their interest to a former partner or a third person who continues the business without liquidation of the partnership affairs, creditors of the dissolved partnership are also creditors of the person continuing the business.

DISTRIBUTION ON DISSOLUTION

8. Solvent Partnerships

Upon the dissolution of a solvent partnership and winding up of its business, an accounting is made to determine its assets and liabilities. Before the partners are entitled to participate in any of the assets, whether or not the firm owes them money, all firm creditors other than partners are entitled to be paid. After firm creditors are paid, the assets of the partnership are distributed among the partners as follows:

1. Each partner who has made advances to the firm or has incurred liability for, or on behalf of, the firm is entitled to be reimbursed.
2. Each partner is then entitled to the return of the capital that he has contributed to the firm.
3. Any balance is distributed as profits in accordance with the partnership agreement.

In many partnerships, one partner contributes capital, the other contributes labor, so the partner contributing labor has nothing to be returned in step 2. Of course, the original agreement could place a value on such labor; but unless it does, only the partner who contributes cash or other property will be repaid in step 2.

In the absence of agreement to the contrary, goodwill is a partnership asset that should be accounted for on termination of a partnership. If the dissolution is caused by the wrongful act of one seeking an accounting, most courts hold that the dissolution will not have goodwill considered in the determination of the value of the partnership interest.

Goodwill is usually defined as "the advantage or benefit, which is acquired by an establishment, beyond the mere value of the capital, stock, funds, or property employed therein, in consequence of the general public patronage and encouragement, which it receives from constant or habitual customers, on account of its local position, or common celebrity, or reputation for skill or affluence, or punctuality, or from other accidental circumstances or necessities, or even from ancient partialities or prejudices." A much narrower definition has been stated as the probability that the old customers will resort to the old place.

Most partnerships build goodwill as an asset. Difficult ethical questions arise, however, in professional partnerships. Traditionally, the prevailing rule relative to professional partnerships was that goodwill did not exist at dissolution, as the reputation of the business entity was dependent on the individual skills of each member.

There appears, however, to be a growing trend throughout the country which recognizes that a professional service partnership possesses goodwill. An ever-increasing number of jurisdictions have held that goodwill may lawfully exist in a professional partnership, and the actual existence of this asset in a particular partnership is a question of fact. The rationale for many of these cases is that the reputation for skill and learning in a particular profession often creates an intangible but valuable asset by gaining the confidence of clients who will speak well of the practice.

If one partner appropriates the goodwill or retains it for his own use, he must account for it to the other partner unless the other partner is in breach of the agreement. The following case discusses goodwill and the various methods that may be used to determine its value.

CASE

The defendants, the Mitchells, own and operate an automobile dealership called Mitchell Motors. The dealership operated as a corporation from 1940 until 1954, and as a partnership thereafter. Swann served as business manager of Mitchell Motors from 1940 until 1967. In 1966 Swann entered into the partnership with an agreement that provided he would receive 5 percent of the profits and losses of the partnership. The agreement also provided that upon Swann's death, the partnership would pay his estate any undistributed profits of the partnership. In 1967, Swann retired. On June 30, 1979, the Mitchells dissolved the partnership without notifying Swann. They transferred all the partnership's assets to a corporation and issued stock to themselves. Swann discovered the conversion to corporate form in 1980 when he received a final payment from the Mitchells intended to represent his percentage of the profits of the business to the date of dissolution. Swann sues for wrongful dissolution of the partnership and to recover a portion of the capital surplus, including the value of the goodwill of the business.

ISSUE: Should the goodwill of the business be considered in determining the value of the partnership and the plaintiff's damages?

DECISION: Yes.

REASONS: 1. The goodwill of a business may be defined as the advantage or benefit the business has beyond the mere value of its property and capital. Goodwill is usually evidenced by general public patronage and is reflected in the increase in profits beyond those that may be expected from the mere use of capital.

2. Goodwill is an asset of a business, and it must be taken into account in any sale or valuation of assets of a business.
3. Goodwill is an asset subject to consideration or an accounting between partners on dissolution of a partnership.
4. Where some or all the partners retain possession of any of the partnership's assets after dissolution for use in another business venture, they must account to the partnership for the value of those assets at the time of dissolution.

Swann v. Mitchell, 435 So.2d 797 (Fla. 1983).

9. Insolvent Partnerships

Marshaling of assets *A principle in equity for a fair distribution of a debtor's assets among his creditors.*

When the firm is insolvent and a court of equity is responsible for making the distribution of the assets of the partnership, the assets are distributed in accordance with a rule known as **marshaling of assets.** Persons entering into a partnership agreement implicitly agree that the partnership assets will be used for the payment of the firm debts before the payment of any individual debts of the partners. Consequently, a court of equity, in distributing the assets, will give them to the firm's creditors before awarding them to separate creditors or individual partners. The court will give separate assets of the partners to their private creditors before awarding these assets to the firm's creditors. Neither class of creditors is permitted to use the funds belonging to the other until the claims of the other have been satisfied. The firm's creditors have available two funds out of which to seek payment: assets of the firm and the individual assets of the partners. Individual creditors of the partners have only one fund: the personal assets of the partners. Because of this difference, equity compels the firm's creditors to exhaust the firm's assets before having recourse to the partners' individual assets.

The doctrine of marshaling of assets does not apply if a partner conceals his existence and permits the other member of the firm to deal with the public as the sole owner of the business. Under these circumstances, the secret partner's conduct has led the creditors of the active partner to rely on the firm's assets as the separate property of the active partner; and by reason of his conduct, the secret partner is estopped from demanding an application of the equity rule that the firm's assets shall be used to pay the firm's creditors first and individual assets used to pay individual creditors. Thus the firm's assets must be shared equally with its creditors and the individual creditors of the active partner. In such a case, because the firm's assets may not be sufficient to pay all its debts when depleted by payments to individual creditors, there may be unpaid firm creditors, and secret partners will be personally liable.

Just as the individual creditors are limited to individual assets, firm creditors are limited to firm assets. Therefore firm creditors are not entitled to payment out of the individual assets of the partners until the individual creditors have been paid. This rule applies even though the firm creditors may at the same time be individual creditors of a member of the firm. There are two main exceptions to this general rule: (1) The rule for the limit of firm creditors to firm assets applies only where there are firm assets. If no firm assets or no living solvent partner exists, the firm creditors may share equally with the individual creditors in the distribution of the individual estates of the partners. (2) If a partner has fraudulently converted the firm assets to his own use, the firm's creditors will be entitled to share equally with individual creditors in the guilty partner's individual assets.

The doctrine of marshaling of assets is not applicable to tort claims under the Uniform Partnership Act. Partners are individually liable in tort for the acts of the firm, its agent, and servants. The liability is joint and several. Thus the injured party may sue the partners individually or as a partnership. The firm assets need not be first used to collect a judgment, and direct action may be taken against individual assets.

CHAPTER SUMMARY

Terminology

1. Dissolution occurs whenever there is a change (deletion or addition) in the partners as members of a partnership.
2. Winding up involves the process of reducing the assets to cash paying creditors, and distributing the balance to the partners.
3. Termination of a partnership occurs when the winding-up process is completed.

Methods of Dissolution

Act of Partners

1. In a partnership at will, any partner may dissolve the partnership at any time without liability.
2. Expulsion of a partner is a breach of the partnership agreement unless it provides for such expulsion.
3. Dissolution may occur in violation of the partnership agreement, in which case there is liability for wrongful dissolution.

Operation of Law

1. Any event that makes it impossible or illegal to continue the partnership operates as a dissolution.
2. Death or bankruptcy of a partner or the partnership operates as a dissolution.
3. Insolvency of a partner is not a basis for dissolution.

Court Decree

1. A court of equity may order dissolution if a partner is incapacitated or is in willful and persistent breach of the partnership agreement.
2. Other grounds such as gross misconduct also may justify a court in ordering dissolution.

The Effect of Dissolution

Powers of Partners

1. Dissolution terminates the authority of a partner to act except to wind up partnership affairs.
2. The winding-up process includes liquidating the assets, completing transactions, paying debts, and distributing the balance.
3. Partners possess apparent authority to bind the dissolved partnership unless persons dealing with the partners have actual or constructive notice of the dissolution.
4. On the death of a partner, title to partnership property remains with the surviving partners for the purpose of winding up the partnership.

Rights of Partners

1. A withdrawing partner has the right to be paid the value of his interest in the partnership as of the date of dissolution.
2. A partner has the right to have partnership property used to pay firm debts.
3. If a partnership is wrongfully dissolved, the remaining partners may continue for the agreed term of the partnership. They must settle with the withdrawing partner but may deduct damages caused by the wrongful dissolution.
4. If the partnership is terminated, the former partner is entitled to a share of the net profits earned during the winding-up process.
5. If the partnership is continued, the former partner is entitled to either interest on the value of his share of the partnership or a share of the profits until he is paid off in the final accounting.
6. The winding-up parties are not entitled to be paid for services in completing unfinished business except in the case of dissolution caused by the death of a partner.

Third Parties

1. An agreement between partners that a withdrawing partner will have no liability is not binding on firm creditors.
2. A withdrawing partner or the estate of a deceased partner has liability for firm debts in the event firm assets are insufficient to discharge them.
3. Notice of dissolution must be given to third parties in order to abolish the partners' apparent authority to act on behalf of the firm.
4. This notice may be actual (personal) or constructive (public).
5. All creditors (past and present) must receive actual notice of dissolution if the dissolution is caused by the acts of partners or by a partner's death or incompetency.
6. All other third parties can be informed by constructive notice.
7. No notice needs to be given any third party if the dissolution was caused by bankruptcy or illegality.

New Partners and New Firms

1. A new partner in an existing partnership is liable for firm debts incurred prior to admission only to the extent of his capital contribution.
2. If the partnership is continued without liquidation, creditors of the dissolved partnership are creditors of the new partnership.

Distributions on Dissolution

Solvent Partnerships

1. After firm creditors are paid, the assets are distributed in the following order: (1) partnership advances, (2) partnership capital, and (3) undistributed profits.
2. Goodwill is a partnership asset that must be accounted for if either partner retains it.

Insolvent Partnerships

1. If the partnership is unable to pay all of its debts, the doctrine of marshaling of assets will be followed.
2. Firm assets are paid to firm creditors. Individual assets are used to pay individual creditors. Each class must be paid in full before assets can be used to pay the other class.
3. If a firm has no assets, the firm creditors may share in the individual assets. The same is true if a partner has fraudulently converted firm assets to his own use.
4. The doctrine of marshalling of asets is not applicable to tort claims.

REVIEW QUESTIONS AND PROBLEMS

1. Match each term in column A with the appropriate statement in column B.

A	B
(1) Dissolution	(a) Notice in a newspaper of general circulation.
(2) Winding up	(b) This partnership may be dissolved at any time for any reason.
(3) Termination	(c) The process of reducing assets to cash, paying creditors, returning capital contributions, and distributing the balance to the partners.
(4) Partnership at will	(d) The advantage or benefit a business has beyond its tangible assets.
(5) Marshaling of assets	(e) The legal destruction of the partnership relationship that occurs whenever any partner ceases to be a member of the firm or whenever a new partner joins the firm.
(6) Accounting	(f) A method for allocating property among the firm creditors and the individual creditors of the partner.
(7) Notice by publication	(g) A formal determination of the partnership's financial condition.
(8) Goodwill	(h) The completion of the winding-up process.

2. Plaintiff and defendant were partners in a motel, restaurant, and condominium development. Plaintiff was responsible for building and selling the condominiums; defendant ran the motel and restaurant. After the condominiums were sold, plaintiff charged defendant with failure to pay taxes and with commingling partnership funds with his own money. Defendant accused plaintiff of improper accounting methods on the condominiums. Will a court order a dissolution? Why or why not?

3. A partnership that operated an apartment building had a negative cash flow during fifteen of seventeen months prior to filing a dissolution suit. The lease continued after the court ordered dissolution. There was evidence that appreciation of the value of the building offset the operating losses. Was the court correct in ordering dissolution? Explain.

4. Mark and Stacy, brother and sister, were partners who had irreconcilable differences. In a suit to dissolve the partnership, a referee was appointed. The referee, in order to dispose of the assets, asked each partner to submit a bid. The brother submitted a bid for $65,000, but the sister did not bid. She now objects to the sale to her brother. The parties had stipulated that one of them could continue the business. On dissolution, is it permissible for the court to order a sale of partnership property to one of the partners for the purpose of continuing the business? Explain.

5. Hoppen and Powell were partners. Powell breached his fiduciary duties by engaging in a similar business in competition with the partnership. Hoppen filed suit for dissolution, and the court awarded all partnership property to Hoppen because of Powell's conduct. Was the court correct? Explain.

6. Anderson, Ernst, and Sells were partners in an accounting firm. Their partnership agreement did not expressly grant the power to expel any partner. Anderson and Ernst decided that they should carry on the business without Sells, who proved to be lazy and inefficient in producing revenue. How should Anderson and Ernst proceed in removing Sells? Explain.

7. Ashley, Butler, and O'Hara operated a large canning company as a partnership. O'Hara died suddenly and unexpectedly. Scarlett, an attorney, has been appointed as executor of O'Hara's estate. Does Scarlett have a right to participate in the winding up of this partnership? Why or why not?

8. Metals Suppliers was a partnership that bought and sold precious gems and metals. Cooper, one of the partners, flew to New York City to negotiate a major contract.

While Cooper was away, Golden died in an automobile accident. Before he received the news of Golden's death, Cooper signed a contract committing the partnership to buy $500,000 worth of diamonds. Is the partnership bound to this contract? Why or why not?

9. Peter and Robert Scalera operated a partnership known as Constructors I. They agreed to build a house for the Munns. The project fell into default almost immediately. The partnership ran into severe financial difficulties and the brothers dissolved their business. Peter and Robert individually met with the Munns to inform them that the brothers were no longer doing business as partners. Each of them offered to complete the construction contract individually, and the Munns elected to have Robert do so. Robert Scalera resumed construction on plaintiff's house but was unable to finish it. The Munns had to pay another contractor to finish the job and were forced to pay for materials that Robert Scalera had charged at a supply company. The plaintiffs sued both brothers to recover damages for breach of contract. Peter Scalera defended by stating that he was discharged from his obligations under the contract because the Munns, after having been notified of the dissolution of the partnership, agreed that Robert alone would complete performance. When a partnership is dissolved, and one partner assumes the partnership's obligations with the consent of the creditors, does this free the discharged partner from liability? Explain.

10. Bush and Baker formed a partnership, but one year later mutually agreed to dissolution. The only notice of dissolution was by publication in a newspaper in the community where their business had been transacted. By agreement, Bush continued to operate the business. O'Neill Company, a previous creditor of the partnership, continued to extend credit to the business. When O'Neill Company was not paid, it brought suit against both Baker and Bush. Should Baker be held liable for the credit extended after dissolution? Why or why not?

11. I.B.M. sold machinery to a limited partnership on credit. Before this debt was paid in full, the partnership was dissolved, and the capital contributions were returned to the limited partners. Thereafter, the partnership could not pay its debts. Can I.B.M. collect from the limited partners? To what extent? Explain.

12. Patrick and Douglas operated a sawmill business as partners. The First Bank made a loan to the partnership, which was secured by a deed of trust on Patrick's home. When the partnership defaulted on this loan, the bank commenced foreclosure proceedings on the house. Patrick seeks to enjoin this foreclosure until a partnership accounting is completed. He contends that partnership assets will discharge this and all other debts. Should an injunction be issued? Why or why not?

13. A partnership consists of three partners, Monroe, Adams, and Madison, who share profits equally. The partnership agreement is silent on the sharing of losses. Monroe loaned the partnership $10,000 and made a capital contribution of $20,000; Adams made a $10,000 capital contribution; Madison made no capital contribution. The partnership now has assets of $80,000 and owes outside creditors $55,000. The partners have decided to dissolve the firm. How much is each partner entitled to receive on dissolution? Explain.

14. Bradley and Smith are the only partners in an insolvent partnership. The firm has assets of $10,000 and liabilities of $100,000. The creditors are Donaldson ($50,000), Charles ($40,000), and Williams ($10,000). The three creditors rank equally in order of priority. Bradley does not have any personal assets or liabilities. Smith has personal assets of $80,000 but he owes the Security Bank $50,000. Smith has no other personal debts. How much are Donaldson, Charles, Williams, and Security Bank each entitled to receive? Explain.

Formation of Corporations

29

CHAPTER PREVIEW

- PROCEDURE FOR INCORPORATION

  The Charter
  Corporate Name
  Powers of Corporations
  Bylaws
  Domestic and Foreign Corporations
  Promoters
  Liability • No liability • Theories of corporate liability. • Avoidance of liability

- DISREGARDING THE CORPORATE ENTITY

  To "Pierce the Corporate Veil"
  Alter Ego Theory
  Promotion of Justice Theory

- CORPORATE STOCK

  Kinds of Stock
  Stocks vs. bonds • Common and preferred stock • No-par stock • Stock warrant • Watered stock • Treasury stock
  Stock Subscriptions
  Right to Transfer Stock
  Mechanics of Transfer

BUSINESS MANAGEMENT DECISION

You are a promoter for a corporation to be formed. Among other activities, you hire an attorney to draft the incorporation papers, you rent office space, and you contract for printing services.

What should you do to avoid becoming personally liable on these transactions?

Corporations may be classified in a variety of ways: public or private, for profit (business corporations) or not-for-profit. Each state classifies corporations doing business within the state as foreign or domestic, to denote the state where incorporation took place. Moreover, each state has a variety of statutes relating to specialized corporations such as cooperatives, church and religious corporations, and fraternal organizations. In this chapter and those that follow, we are primarily concerned with the private business corporations.

Statutes relating to business corporations vary from state to state, yet they are quite similar. For our discussion, the basic principles of the Model Business Corporation Act will be used as the basic statute. This model act, prepared by the Commission on Uniform State Laws, has been wholly adopted by a few states, largely adopted by others. A major influence on the law of corporations throughout the country, its application to any particular issue must nevertheless be checked in each state.

A *corporation* is an artificial, intangible person or being, created by the law. Incorporating is a method by which individual persons are united into a new legal entity. For this new legal entity, they select a common name and the purposes that it is to accomplish. As a legal entity separate and apart from the persons who had it created, the corporate existence is not affected by the death, incapacity, or bankruptcy of any of the persons involved in its creation or in its operation. Its owners do not have personal liability on its contracts, and it has no liability for the obligations of its shareholders. As a legal entity, a corporation is able to own property and to sue or be sued in its own name in the same manner as a natural person. It has rights and duties separate and apart from its shareholders and the law recognizes this separation in a variety of situations.

A corporation is also a person for purposes of both tort and criminal law. As an impersonal entity, it can act only through agents and servants, but the corporation is subject to the doctrine of *respondeat superior* and may be punished for certain criminal acts of its agents or servants.

Although a corporation is considered a person under most statutes, there are a few, such as those allowing the appointment of "suitable persons" as parole officers, in which it is not a "person." A corporation is a person for purpose of the due process clause of the Fifth and Fourteenth Amendments to the United States Constitution. For purposes of the privilege against compulsory self-incrimination, it is not a person.

PROCEDURE FOR INCORPORATION

1. The Charter

The law prescribes the steps to be taken for the creation of the corporation. Most corporate laws provide that a specified number of adult persons, usually not less than three, may file an application for a **charter.** The application contains the names and addresses of the incorporators, the name of the proposed corporation, the object for which it is to be formed, its proposed duration, the location of its registered office, the name of its registered agent, and information about the stock of the corporation.

Charter *The document issued by a state that creates the corporation.*

The *registered agent* is the person designated to receive notices for the corporation. The *registered office* is the location where notices may be delivered. A registered agent of a corporation need not simultaneously serve as an officer or director of such corporation, but an officer usually serves as registered agent. If a corporation fails to maintain a registered agent at its registered office, then the secretary of state becomes the agent of the corporation to receive service of process. Such an event usually means loss of any lawsuit because of lack of actual knowledge of it, as happened in the following case.

CASE

In 1982, a dispute arose between S. Donald Norton Properties, Inc. (Norton), and Triangle Pacific, Inc. (Triangle). Triangle claimed Norton owed it $8,120 under a sales contract. Counsel for both parties tried to reach an agreement, but negotiations broke down and Triangle filed suit seeking the disputed amount. Triangle attempted service of process upon the registered agent of Norton at the registered address. When the marshal was unable to locate the agent at the address, service was perfected upon the secretary of state. Norton failed to answer or appear within forty-five days after service was perfected and a default judgment was entered against it. Norton filed a petition in equity to have the default judgment set aside. Triangle filed a motion for judgment on the pleadings, which was granted, and Norton appeals.

ISSUE: Did the court's award in favor of Triangle of a judgment on the pleadings, which thereby supported the default judgment against Norton, deprive Norton of its right to due process?

DECISION: No.

REASONS:
1. A corporation is a creature of statute, and it has no rights or existence but what the statutes give it. If the corporation complies with statutory requirements for doing business in this state, it will not be deprived of service or notice.
2. A corporation is required to have and continuously maintain a registered office and agent.
3. Whenever a corporation fails to appoint or maintain a registered agent in this state, or whenever its registered agent cannot with reasonable diligence be found at the registered office, then the secretary of state shall be an agent of such corporation.

S. Donald Norton Properties v. Triangle Pacific, 325 S.E.2d 160 (Ga. 1985).

The information supplied about the corporate stock usually includes (1) whether there will be preferred stock or only common stock, (2) the stated or par value of the stock (if the stock has no stated value, then it is called no-par stock), (3) the number of shares of stock that will be authorized, and (4) the number of shares of stock that will actually be issued.

Some states also require the names and addresses of the subscribers to the stock and the amount subscribed and paid in by each. Most applications usually indicate whether the stock is to be paid for in cash or in property.

The application, signed by all the incorporators, is forwarded to a state official, usually the secretary of state. If the application is in order, the official then issues a charter. If the application is not in proper form or if the corporation is being formed for an illegal purpose, the secretary of state will refuse to create the corporation and deny it a charter.

Upon return of the charter properly signed by the secretary of state, it is filed by the incorporators in the proper recording office. The receipt of the charter and its filing are the operative facts that bring the corporation into existence and give it authority and power to do business. It is not necessary that stock be issued or bylaws be adopted for the corporation to exist as a legal entity.

After the charter has been received and filed, the incorporators and all others who have agreed to purchase stock meet and elect a board of directors. They may also approve the bylaws of the corporation if the applicable law so provides. In most instances, the bylaws are approved by the board, not by the shareholders. The board of directors that has been elected then meets, approves the bylaws, elects the officers, calls for the payment of the subscription price for the stock, and makes whatever decisions are necessary to commence business.

2. Corporate Name

One of the provisions in the application for a corporate charter is the proposed name of the corporation. In order that persons dealing with a business will know that it is a corporation and that the investors therefore have limited liability, the law requires that the corporate name include one of the following words or end with an abbreviation of them: *corporation*, *company*, *incorporated*, or *limited*. A corporate name must not be the same as, or deceptively similar to, the name of any domestic corporation or a foreign corporation authorized to do business in the state in which the application is made.

Most states have procedures for reserving a corporate name for a limited period. Inquiry is usually made concerning the availability of a name; if it is available, it is reserved while the articles are being prepared. The name may be changed by charter amendment at any time without affecting corporate contracts or title to corporate property in any way.

3. Powers of Corporation

The application for a charter includes a statement of the powers desired by the corporation. These are usually stated in quite broad language. A corporation has only such powers as are conferred upon it by the state that creates it. The charter, together with the statute under which it is issued, sets forth the express powers of the corporation. All powers reasonably necessary to carry out the expressed powers are implied.

The following general powers are ordinarily granted to the corporation by statute: (1) to have perpetual existence; (2) to sue and be sued; (3) to have a corporate name and corporate seal; (4) to own, use, convey, and deal in both real and personal property; (5) to borrow and lend money other than to officers and directors; (6) to purchase, own, and dispose of securities; (7) to enter into contracts of every kind; (8) to make charitable contributions; (9) to pay pensions and establish pension plans; and (10) all powers necessary or convenient to effect any of the other purposes.

Any acts of a corporation that are beyond the authority, express or implied, given to it by the state in the charter are said to be ***ultra vires*** acts—''beyond the authority.'' If a corporation performs acts or enters into contracts to perform acts that are *ultra vires*, the state creating such a corporation may forfeit its charter for misuse of its corporate authority. The extent of the misuse is controlling in determining whether the state will take away its franchise or merely enjoin the corporation from further *ultra vires* conduct.

Ultra vires *''Beyond power.'' The acts of a corporation are ultra vires when they are beyond the power or authority of the corporation as granted by the state in its charter.*

Although third parties have no right to object to the *ultra vires* acts of a corporation, a stockholder may bring court action to enjoin a corporation from performing an *ultra vires* contract. If the corporation sustains losses or damages because of the *ultra vires* venture, the corporation may recover from the directors who approved the contracts. When the directors exceed corporate powers, they may become personally liable for resulting losses.

At common law, a corporation had no liability on contracts beyond its corporate powers because the corporation had capacity to do only those things expressly authorized within its charter or incidental thereto. Most modern statutes, including the Model Business Corporation Act, provide that all *ultra vires* contracts are enforceable. Neither party to such a contract may use *ultra vires* as a defense. *Ultra vires* conduct on the part of the corporation may be enjoined by the state or any shareholder; but otherwise, contracts previously made are binding, whether they be wholly executory, partially executed, or fully performed.

4. Bylaws

A **bylaw** is a rule governing and managing the affairs of the corporation. It is binding upon all shareholders but not third parties, unless the third parties have knowledge of it. The bylaws contain provisions establishing the corporate seal and the form of the stock certificate, the number of officers and directors, the method of electing them and removing them from office, as well as the enumeration of their duties. Bylaws specify the time and place of the meetings of the directors and the shareholders. Together with the articles of incorporation and the applicable statute, the bylaws provide rules for operating the corporation. The bylaws are subservient to the articles of incorporation and the statute but are of greater authority than, for instance, a single resolution of the board. Failure to follow the bylaws constitutes a breach of the fiduciary duties of a director or officer.

Bylaws *Rules for government of a corporation or other organization.*

Bylaws are valid if they are reasonable and are consistent with the corporate charter and the applicable statutes. Bylaws may be illegal and void. For example, a bylaw of a corporation gave the president the power to manage the corporation's affairs. Such a bylaw is void because the law provides that the affairs of corporations shall be managed by a board of directors.

The power to alter, amend, or revoke the bylaws is vested in the board of directors unless reserved to the shareholders by statute or by the articles of incorporation. The board cannot, however, repeal, amend, or add to the bylaws if the change will affect the vested rights of a shareholder.

5. Domestic and Foreign Corporations

To a state or country, corporations organized under its laws are *domestic* corporations; those organized under the laws of another state or country are *foreign* corporations.

Domestic corporations become qualified to do business upon receipt and recording of their charter. Foreign corporations with significant intrastate activities must also "qualify" to do business by obtaining a certificate of authority and by paying the license fees and taxes levied on local businesses. A foreign corporation engaged wholly in *interstate* commerce through a state need not qualify in that state.

Most state statutes require foreign corporations to qualify to do business by filing a copy of their articles of incorporation with the secretary of state. They are also required to appoint an agent upon whom service of process may be served and to maintain an office in the state. Failure to comply results in a denial of the right of access to the courts as a plaintiff. Some states allow a plaintiff that has failed to obtain a certificate of authority a continuance in the case for a short time in order to obtain the certificate. In the following case, this liberal view was not enough to save the plaintiff, which only challenged the constitutionality of the requirement and lost.

CASE

Christian Services, a Missouri corporation, filed a lawsuit against Northfield Villa, Inc., seeking damages for breach of contract. The complaint did not contain an allegation that Christian Services possessed a certificate of authority to conduct business in Nebraska. On October 18, 1984, Northfield Villa filed a motion for summary judgment. On November 13, Christian Services asked for and was granted a continuance of the hearing on the summary judgment motion. The court granted Christian Services until December 31 to comply with the Nebraska law regarding a certificate of authority. During a hearing on January 21, 1985, the court concluded that Christian Services still lacked authority to do business in Nebraska. The court granted Northfield Villa's motion for summary judgment.

ISSUE: Was this motion properly granted?

DECISION: Yes.

REASONS:

1. Nebraska statutes provide as follows: "No foreign corporation transacting business in this state without a certificate of authority . . . shall be permitted to maintain any action . . . in any court of this state, until such corporation shall have obtained a certificate of authority."
2. Objection to a nonauthorized corporation's maintaining a lawsuit may be raised at any time during the pendency of such litigation, and the court may, in its discretion, limit the time that the plaintiff can have for procuring the necessary certificate of authority.

3. Christian Services was allowed in excess of sixty days to obtain the necessary proof, and when time ran out, it did not request any extension. There was no abuse of discretion on the part of the trial court.

Christian Services v. Northfield Villa, Inc., 385 N.W.2d 904 (Neb. 1986).

Of course, a corporation that cannot be a plaintiff because of lack of a certificate could be sued in a state if it had sufficient minimum contacts to satisfy due process. Generally, subjecting a foreign corporation to a state's qualification statutes requires more activity within a state than for service of process or for taxation of its income and property. Qualification is essential if there are local activities that constitute transacting business.

In a real sense, this denial of access to the courts as a plaintiff prevents a corporation from conducting business, because its contracts are not enforceable by suit, and debtors would thus be able to avoid payment to the corporation. Transacting business within the state without complying with the statute also subjects the corporation and its officers to statutory penalties, such as fines.

The term *doing business* is not reducible to an exact and certain definition. The Model Business Corporation Act defines the term by saying that a foreign corporation is *doing business* when "some part of its business substantial and continuous in character and not merely casual or occasional" is transacted within a state. A corporation is not *doing business* in a state merely because it is involved in litigation or maintains a bank account or an office within a state for the transfer of its stock. It also states that a foreign corporation is not required to obtain a license to do business by reason of the fact that (1) it is in the mail-order business and receives orders from a state that are accepted and filled by shipment from without the state, and (2) it uses salespeople within a state to obtain orders that are accepted outside the state. If the orders are accepted or filled within the state, or if any sale, repair, or replacement is made from stock physically present within the state in which the order is obtained, a foreign corporation is required to obtain a license.

6. Promoters

A *promoter*, as the name implies, promotes the corporation and assists in bringing it into existence. One or more promoters will be involved in making application for the charter, holding the first meeting of shareholders, entering into preincorporation subscription agreements, and engaging in other activities necessary to bring the corporation into existence. Promoters are responsible for compliance with the applicable **blue-sky laws** (statutes relating to the sale of securities), including the preparation of a prospectus if required.

Blue-sky laws *Popular name for state acts providing for the regulation and supervision of investment securities.*

Liability. Many of these activities involve the incurring of contractual obligations or debts. Preparation of the application for a charter usually requires the assistance of a lawyer, and it must be accompanied by the required filing fee. Legal questions about who has liability for these obligations and debts frequently arise. Is the promoter liable? Is the corporation after formation liable? Are both liable?

Certain general principles of contract and agency law prevent simple answers to these questions. First of all, a promoter is not an agent prior to incorporation, because there is no principal. A party who purports to act as an agent for a nonexistent principal is generally liable as a principal. Thus a promoter is liable on preincorporation contracts unless the other party is aware that the corporation has not been formed and agrees that the promoter is not to be bound by the contract personally. Second, the corporation technically cannot ratify the contracts of promoters because ratification requires capacity to contract both at the time of the contract and at the time of the ratification.

No liability. To avoid the difficulties caused by these legal theories, the law has used certain fictions to create an obligation on the part of the corporation and to provide a means to eliminate liability on the part of the promoters. One fiction is that a novation occurs. This theory proceeds on the premise that when the corporation assents to the contract, the third party agrees to discharge the promoter and to look only to the corporation. Establishing a novation often fails because of a lack of proof of any agreement to release the promoter, as occurred in the following case, even though the original contract required that the promoter incorporate and transfer the contract to the new corporation.

CASE

Plaintiff, an underwear manufacturer, contracted to sell its business to the defendant Cormier. Plaintiff was to receive commissions on subsequent sales of underwear and other products. The agreement provided that Cormier "shall have a new corporation, 'Polypro, Inc.' formed and shall assign all of its right and obligation" under the agreement to the corporation. Pursuant to the agreement, inventory was transferred to Cormier in late June 1981. On July 22, 1981, Polypro, Inc., was formed and capitalized in the amount of $2,500. Correspondence between the parties indicates that thereafter the plaintiff conducted business with both Cormier and Polypro, Inc. When it did not receive its commissions, plaintiff sued Cormier personally. Cormier argues that Polypro, Inc., is liable since he acted only as a promoter, or, in the alternative, he is relieved of liability since a novation occurred.

ISSUE: Is Cormier relieved of personal liability for the nonpayment of commissions to plaintiff?

DECISION: No.

REASONS:

1. As a general rule, promoters are personally liable on contracts that they have entered into personally, even though they have contracted for the benefit of a projected corporation; the promoter is not discharged from liability by the subsequent adoption of the contract by the corporation when formed, unless there is a novation.
2. A promoter may be discharged from liability on a preincorporation contract by a novation if the corporation assumes the contract and the other contracting party assents to the substitution of the corporation for the promoter.
3. Cormier could not unilaterally discharge himself from the contract he signed with the plaintiff; some affirmative action by the plaintiff was needed to release Cormier individually. The evidence indi-

cates that the plaintiff relied on Cormier's personal wealth in entering into this unsecured agreement. We find no express or implied intent on the plaintiff's part to release Cormier from liability. Furthermore, Polypro, Inc., took no action to accept the assignment of rights from Cormier.

4. Accordingly, no express or implied novation occurred.

Skandinavia, Inc. v. Cormier, 514 A.2d 1250 (N.H. 1986).

Theories of corporate liability. Another theory that is used to determine liability on preincorporation obligations may be described as the *offer and acceptance theory*. Under this theory, a contract made by a promoter for the benefit of the corporation is an offer that may be accepted by the corporation after it comes into existence. Acceptance of the benefits of the contract constitutes a formal ratification of it. If the corporation does not accept the offer, it is not liable. The promoter may or may not be liable, depending on the degree of disclosure. Corporations have also been held liable on promoters' contracts on theories that may be called the *consideration theory* and the *quasi-contract theory*. After incorporation, directors may promise to pay for expenses and services of promoters. Under the consideration theory, their promise will be binding and supported by sufficient consideration, on the theory of services previously rendered.

The quasi-contract theory holds that corporations are liable by implication for the necessary expenses and services incurred by the promoters in bringing them into existence, because such expenses and services accrue or inure to the benefit of the corporation. The corporation would be unjustly enriched if liability did not exist.

Finally, it should be noted that some states have abandoned trying to justify corporate liability with a legal theory and have simply provided by statute that corporations are liable for the reasonable expenses incurred by promoters.

Avoidance of liability. The parties frequently do not intend the promoter to be liable on a preincorporation contract. A promoter may avoid personal liability by informing the other party that he does not intend to be liable and that he is acting in the name of, and solely on, the credit of a corporation to be formed. But if the promoter represents that there is an existing corporation when there is none, the promoter is liable. A promoter should make sure that contracts entered into on behalf of the proposed corporation are worded to relieve him of personal liability if that is the intent.

Promoters occupy a fiduciary relationship toward the prospective corporation. Their position does not give them the right to secure any benefit or advantage over the corporation itself or over other shareholders. A promoter cannot purchase property and then sell it to the corporation at a profit, nor has he a right to receive a commission from a third party for the sale of property to the corporation. In general, however, he may sell property acquired by him prior to the time he started promoting the corporation, provided he sells it to an unbiased board of directors after full disclosure of all pertinent facts.

DISREGARDING THE CORPORATE ENTITY

7. To "Pierce the Corporate Veil"

One of the basic advantages of the corporate form of business organization is the limitation of shareholder liability. Corporations are formed for the express purpose of limiting one's risk to the amount of his investment in the stock. Sometimes suits are brought to hold the shareholders personally liable for an obligation of a corporation or to hold a parent corporation liable for debts of a subsidiary.

Such suits attempt to "pierce the corporate veil." They ask the court to look behind the corporate entity and take action as though no entity separate from the members existed. They may not ask that the corporate entity be disregarded simply because all the stock is owned by the members of a family or by one person or by another corporation.

The lending of money to a corporation one controls or guaranteeing its debts is not enough to justify piercing the corporate veil. It would frustrate the purposes of corporate law to expose directors, officers, and shareholders to personal liability for the debts of the corporation when they contribute funds to, or on behalf of, a corporation for the purpose of assisting the corporation to meet its financial obligations. The loan or guarantee may assist the corporate efforts to survive, thus benefiting the creditors. If such acts were grounds to eliminate the separate corporate entity, such loans and guarantees usually would not be forthcoming.

8. Alter Ego Theory

Notwithstanding the foregoing general principles, courts today frequently disregard the separate corporate entity and "pierce the corporate veil." They do so to hold parent corporations liable for the debts of a subsidiary and to hold individual shareholders liable for corporate obligations. Many cases use a theory known as the "alter ego theory," while others pierce the corporate veil in order to prevent fraud or injustice or to prevent violation for a statute.

The alter ego theory disregards the separate corporate existence when one corporation is organized, controlled, and conducted to make it a mere instrumentality of another corporation or when individual shareholders conduct themselves in disregard of the separate entity. If the corporate entity is disregarded by the shareholders themselves, so that there is such a unity of ownership and interest that separateness of the corporation has ceased to exist, the alter ego doctrine will be followed.

Some of the factors considered significant in justifying a disregard of the corporate entity using the alter ego theory are (1) undercapitalization of a corporation, (2) failure to observe corporate formalities such as annual meetings, (3) nonpayment of dividends, (4) siphoning of corporate funds by the dominant stockholders, (5) nonfunctioning of other officers or directors, (6) absence of corporate records, and (7) use of the corporation as a facade for operations of the dominant stockholders.

9. Promotion of Justice Theory

In addition to the alter ego theory, courts will pierce the corporate veil if the ends of justice require it. Justice will require the disregarding of the corporate entity if the liability-causing activity did not occur only for the benefit of the corporation, if the liable corporation has been gutted and left without funds by those controlling it in order to avoid actual or potential liability, or if the corporation has been used to defraud or otherwise promote injustice.

For example, assume that A and B sold a business and agreed not to compete with the buyer for a given number of years. In violation of the contract, A and B organized a corporation in which they became the principal stockholders and managers; the buyer may enjoin the corporation from competing with him, and he may do so effectively, as he could have enjoined A and B from establishing a competing business. Similarly, assume that a state law provides that a person may not hold more than one liquor license at a time. This law cannot be circumvented by forming multiple corporations. The attempt to evade the statute would justify piercing the corporate veil. The following case distinguishes between these two theories and adopts the modern trend of liberally piercing the corporate veil.

CASE

Joe Castleberry owned shares in Texan Transfer, Inc., a closely held organization. Due to severe competition, Texan Transfer was not as successful as projected. Castleberry agreed to sell his shares back to the corporation, but he was not paid. Thereafter, Castleberry discovered that his fellow shareholders in Texan Transfer, Inc., had formed other corporations to compete with Texan Transfer. Castleberry sued the corporation and its shareholders, Byron Branscum and Michael Byboth, individually. The jury found that Branscum and Byboth defrauded Castleberry by manipulating Texan Transfer, Inc., and by forming competing businesses to ensure that Castleberry did not get paid. The court pierced the corporate veil of Texan Transfer, Inc., and held Branscum and Byboth personally liable. They appealed and argued that the corporate entity of Texan Transfer could not be disregarded.

ISSUE: Was it proper for the court to pierce the corporate veil and hold these shareholders personally liable?

DECISION: Yes.

REASONS:

1. Many cases have blurred the distinction between alter ego and other bases for disregarding the corporate fiction and treated alter ego as a synonym for the entire doctrine of disregarding the corporate fiction. However, alter ego is only one of the bases for disregarding the corporate entity.
2. Alter ego applies when there is such unity between corporation and individual that the separateness of the corporation has ceased and holding only the corporation liable would result in injustice. It is shown from the total dealings of the corporation and the individual, including the degree to which corporate formalities have been followed and corporate and individual property have been kept separately, the amount of financial interest, ownership, and control the individual maintains over the corporation, and whether the corporation has been used for personal purposes. Alter ego's rationale is: "If the shareholders themselves disregard the separation of the corporate enterprise, the law will also disregard it so far as necessary to protect individual and corporate creditors."
3. We disregard the corporate fiction, even though corporate formalities have been observed and corporate and individual prop-

erty have been kept separately, when the corporate form has been used as part of a basically unfair device to achieve an inequitable result.

4. Specifically, we disregard the corporation fiction:
   (a) When the fiction is used as a means of perpetrating fraud;
   (b) Where a corporation is organized and operated as a mere tool or business conduit of another corporation;
   (c) Where the corporate fiction is resorted to as a means of evading an existing legal obligation;
   (d) Where the corporate fiction is employed to achieve or perpetrate monopoly;
   (e) Where the corporate fiction is used to circumvent a statute; and
   (f) Where the corporate fiction is relied upon as a protection of crime or to justify wrong.
5. Because disregarding the corporate fiction is an equitable doctrine, Texas takes a flexible fact-specific approach focusing on equity, and the jury's findings in this case support piercing the corporate veil and holding the wrongful shareholders personally liable.

Castleberry v. Branscum, 721 S.W.2d 270 (Tex. 1986).

CORPORATE STOCK

10. Kinds of Stock

A *stock certificate* is written evidence of the ownership of a certain number of *shares of stock* of a corporation. The certificate recognizes a certain person as being a *shareholder* with rights in the corporation—primarily, the right to share in profits, to participate indirectly in the control of the corporation, and to receive a portion of the assets at time of dissolution. A share of stock gives the holder no right to share in the active management of the business.

Stocks vs. bonds. Stock must be distinguished from a bond. A *bond* is an obligation of the corporation to pay a certain sum of money in the future at a specified rate of interest. It is comparable to a corporation's promissory note. A bondholder is a creditor of the corporation, whereas a shareholder is an owner of the corporation. A shareholder has a right to receive dividends if they are declared by the board of directors and to participate in the assets of the corporation after all creditors have been paid. A bondholder has no right to vote or to participate in the management and control of a corporation. A shareholder has a right to participate in management to the extent of electing the directors and voting on matters such as dissolution.

Common and preferred stock. *Common stock* is the simplest type of corporate stock. It entitles the owner to share in the control, profits, and assets of the corporation in proportion to the amount of common stock held. Such a shareholder has no advantage, priority, or preference over any other class of shareholders unless otherwise specified.

Preferred stock has priority over other classes of stock in claiming dividends or assets on dissolution. The most important right given to a preferred shareholder is the right to receive a certain specified dividend, even though the earnings are not sufficient to pay like dividends to common shareholders.

Preferred stock may be cumulative or noncumulative. If *cumulative*, any dividends that are not paid because of lack of earnings accrue and are paid when earnings are available. If *noncumulative*, only the current year's preferred dividend is paid out of current earnings. If nothing is stated about the payment of the dividends, the preferred stock is cumulative, and preferred dividends and all arrears thereon must be paid before a dividend is declared on common stock.

No-par stock. The statutes of most states provide that a corporation may issue stock with *no par value*. The value of no-par stock is determined by its sale price in the open market or by the price set by the directors as a "stated value." Shareholders, creditors of the corporation, and the public are not misled or prejudiced by this type of stock, because there is no holding out that the stock has any particular face value. All persons dealing in no-par stock are put on notice that they should investigate the corporation's assets and its financial condition. Stock with no par value represents its proportionate part of the total assets of the corporation.

Stock warrant. A **stock warrant** is a certificate that gives its holder the right to subscribe for and purchase a given number of shares of stock in a corporation at a stated price. It is usually issued in connection with the sale of other shares of stock or of bonds, although the law of some states permits the issuance of stock warrants entirely separate and apart from the sale of other securities. Warrants are transferable. The option to purchase contained in the warrant may or may not be limited as to time or otherwise conditioned. Warrants have value and can readily be sold on the market in the same fashion as other securities.

Stock warrant *A certificate that gives the holder the right to subscribe for and purchase, at a stated price, a given number of shares of stock in a corporation.*

Watered stock. **Watered stock** is stock that has been issued as fully paid, when in fact its full *par value* has not been paid in money, property, or services. The original owner of watered stock has liability for the unpaid portion of its stated value. If Catherine exchanges property worth $200 for 1,000 shares of $1 par value stock, she owes the corporation $800. If the corporation becomes insolvent, a creditor may require that the balance due be paid.

The liability for watered stock arises because the capital stock of a corporation represents the total par value of all the shares of the corporation (plus the stated value of no-par stock). The public, including corporate creditors, has a right to assume that the capital stock issued has been paid for in full. The corporation in effect represents that assets have been received in payment equal in amount to its issued capital stock. If stock is issued in excess of the actual assets in money value received for it by the corporation, there is watered stock.

Watered stock *Corporate stock issued by a corporation for property at an overvaluation, or stock issued for which the corporation receives nothing in payment.*

Treasury stock. **Treasury stock** is that which has been issued by the corporation for value and returned to the corporation by gift or purchase. It may be sold at any price, including below par, and the proceeds returned to the treasury of the corporation for working capital. It differs from stock originally issued below par in that the purchaser is not liable for the difference between par and the sale price. It may be sold at any price the company sees fit to charge.

Treasury stock *Stock of a corporation that has been issued by the corporation for value but is later returned to the corporation by way of gift or purchase.*

A corporation is restricted in its power to purchase treasury stock because the purchase might effect a reduction of its capital, to the detriment of creditors. In most states a corporation is permitted to purchase treasury stock only out of accumulated profits or surplus. This restriction retains stockholders' investment, equivalent to the original capital, as a protective cushion for creditors in case subsequent losses develop.

A corporation may redeem its preferred stock if there is no injury to, or objection by, creditors. Here, again, many of the states require the preferred stock to be redeemed out of surplus, or they demand that authority to reduce the capital stock be obtained from the state.

11. Stock Subscriptions

A *preincorporation stock subscription* is an agreement to purchase stock in a corporation. It is a binding agreement (a subscriber cannot revoke his subscription) created among the subscribers for stock in a corporation to be formed. The subscription is usually drafted in a manner that creates a contract. Some states by statute have provided that a preincorporation subscription constitutes a binding, irrevocable offer to the corporation, by reason of the mutual promises of the parties. The offer is usually limited to a specified period of time, such as six months.

Certain conditions are inherent in the preincorporation subscription contract. The subscriber will not be liable unless the corporation is completely organized; the full amount of the capital stock is subscribed; and the purpose, articles, and bylaws of the corporation are as originally stated and relied upon by the subscriber. Conditions, expressed or implied, are often waived by the subscriber if, with knowledge of the nonperformance, he participates in stockholders' meetings, pays part or all of his subscription, or acts as an officer or director of the corporation.

A subscription to stock of a corporation already in existence is a contract between the subscriber and the corporation. Such a contract may come into existence by reason of an offer either made by the corporation and accepted by the subscriber or made by the subscriber and accepted by the corporation. If the corporation opens subscription books and advertises its stock, it is seeking for an offer to be made by the subscriber. The corporation may, however, make a general offer to the public, which may be accepted by the subscriber in accordance with the terms of the general offer.

12. Right to Transfer Stock

A share of stock is personal property, and the owner has the right to transfer it just as he may transfer any other personal property. The right to transfer freely one's share in the corporation is one of the features of corporate life that distinguishes it from a partnership. A share of stock is generally transferred by an indorsement and the delivery of the certificate of stock and by surrender of the certificate to the stock transfer agent for reissue.

Shareholders of close corporations usually attempt to restrict the transfer of stock. Such attempts may be part of a contract or they may be included in the bylaws. These restrictions may be a simple right of first refusal to either the corporation, the other shareholder, or both, or there may be a binding buy and sell agreement among the shareholders. In the latter case, there is a sale of the stock upon the happening of a specified event even if the owner or the estate of the owner does not desire to sell, as illustrated in the following case.

CASE

In 1963, the shareholders of a closely held corporation executed an agreement that provided that upon the death of any shareholder, the survivors had an option for one year from the date of death to buy a deceased shareholder's shares at a price set by the majority shareholders each year. If no price was established for a given year, the most recently set price prevailed.

Dorothy Renberg died April 22, 1978. During April 1979, the surviving shareholders notified Dorothy's husband that they wished to purchase her shares pursuant to the buy-sell agreement. The husband refused to sell and initiated this suit to prevent the transfer of stock.

ISSUE: Is a buy-sell agreement that grants the surviving shareholders an option to purchase deceased party's shares valid?

DECISION: Yes.

REASONS:
1. The purpose of such buy-sell agreements is to prevent transfers of stock to outsiders without first providing an opportunity for the existing shareholders to acquire the stock. These agreements assure the purchase by persons most likely to act in harmony with other stockholders.
2. A basic reason for buy-sell agreements is to provide a way to determine the value of stock. This is important because stock in a closely held corporation is not publicly traded, and therefore the value cannot be readily ascertained.
3. Courts give great deference to a buy-sell agreement. Mere disparity between the price specified and the actual value of the stock is not enough to invalidate the agreement.
4. Dorothy throughout her life stood to benefit the most from the buy-sell agreement because she was the youngest shareholder. Further, she was consistently advised as to the value of the stock and she had access to the corporation's records and could have called a meeting of the shareholders to reassess the value of the stock had she so desired.

Renberg v. Zarrow, 667 P.2d 465 (Okla. 1983).

A corporate bylaw that makes shares of stock transferable only to the corporation or to those approved by the board of directors is unenforceable. It places too severe a restraint upon the alienation of property. Society is best protected when property may be transferred freely, but an agreement or bylaw approved by all shareholders to the effect that no transfer of stock shall be made until it has first been offered to the other shareholders or to the corporation is generally enforced. Notice of the bylaw or agreement should be set forth in the stock certificate because an innocent purchaser without notice of the restriction on alienation receives ownership free from the restriction.

In a close corporation, sometimes the buy and sell agreements between shareholders provide for matters such as salary continuation in the event of death or disability and the amount of dividends to be paid in the future. Some agreements even commit the shareholders to vote for certain persons in the election of directors. Such agreements are valid in closely held corporations, providing the duration of the agreement is not so long that it becomes contrary to public policy and providing the agreement does not adversely affect minority interests in the corporation. These agreements are used by the majority owners to ensure the election of the desired board of directors. Corporations are governed by the republican principle that the whole are bound by lawful acts of the majority. It is not against public policy nor is it dishonest for shareholders to contract for the purpose of control.

The importance of shareholder buy and sell provisions must not be overlooked. It is just as important to have a means of getting a shareholder out of a closely held corporation as it is to have a means of getting a partner out of a partnership.

Shareholder buy and sell provisions should be worked out before any shareholder knows whether he is a buyer or a seller. Although withdrawal from active participation will not effect a dissolution, it can have the serious effect of precipitating a lawsuit, or a shareholder may continue to participate in management when he does not desire to do so. Frequently, a withdrawing shareholder will be forced to sell his stock for less than it is worth because a buy and sell agreement was not worked out in advance.

13. Mechanics of Transfer

A share may be transferred or assigned by a bill of sale or by any other method that will pass title to a chose in action (a right to recover money or property from another through judicial procedure) or other intangible property. Whenever a share of stock is sold and a new stock certificate issued, the name of the new owner is entered on the stock records of the corporation. In a small corporation, the secretary of the corporation usually handles all transfers of stock and also the canceling of old certificates and issuing of new. Large corporations, in which there are hundreds and even thousands of transactions, employ transfer agents. The transfer agents transfer stock, cancel old certificates, issue new ones, keep an up-to-date list of the names of shareholders of the corporation, distribute dividends, mail out shareholders' notices, and perform many functions to assist the corporation secretary. Stock exchange rules provide that corporations listing stock for sale must maintain a transfer agency and registry, operated and maintained under exchange regulations. The registrar of stock is an agent of the corporation whose duty is to see that no stock certificates are issued in excess of the authorized capitalization of the corporation.

Article 8 of the Uniform Commercial Code deals with investment securities. The general approach of Article 8 is that securities are negotiable instruments and that bona fide purchasers have greater rights than they would have "if the things bought were chattels or simple contracts." The particular rules of Article 3 that relate to the establishment of preferred status for commercial paper are applied to securities. Defenses of the issuer are generally not effective against a purchaser for value who has received the securities without being given notice of the particular defense raised.

A bona fide purchaser is one who purchases in good faith and without notice of any adverse claim. He is the equivalent of a holder in due course of a negotiable instrument, which is discussed in Chapter 38. A bona fide purchaser takes free of "adverse claims," which include a claim that a transfer was wrongful or that some other person is the owner of, or has an interest in, the security.

CASE

On June 18, 1973, Tom executed an assignment of a stock certificate of defendant corporation representing sixty shares of 4½ percent preferred stock, and he gave the certificate to plaintiff. On February 21, 1976, Tom told plaintiff that the stock certificate had to be exchanged for other stock (6½ percent preferred) paying a higher dividend. Plaintiff gave Tom the stock certificate, but the sixty shares of 6½ percent preferred stock were never delivered to plaintiff, and Tom refused to return the 4½ percent stock certificate.

Plaintiff sued the corporation, contending that he is entitled to dividends as of June 18, 1973. It contended that plaintiff's complaint does not state a cause of action, because there was no allegation that the certificate was ever presented for registration.

ISSUE: Is a party entitled to a transfer of shares of stock in the absence of a showing that the certificate was presented to the transfer agent?

DECISION: No.

REASONS:
1. Article 8 of the Uniform Commercial Code governs transactions in securities that are in registered form.
2. A registrar has a duty to register a transfer of ownership of a security in registered form only upon satisfaction of several conditions, including presentation of the security with a request to register transfer.
3. Plaintiff did not present the certificate; therefore this condition was not satisfied.

Wanland v. C. E. Thompson Co., 338 N.E.2d 1012 (Ill. App. 1978).

CHAPTER SUMMARY

Procedure for Incorporation

The Charter	1. The incorporators prepare an application for a charter that includes basic information such as the purpose of the corporation, the location of its office and registered agent, and information about its stock. 2. The application will indicate the amount of authorized stock and the amount to be issued. 3. When the application is approved, it is returned as a charter, which is filed in the proper recording office.
Corporate Name	1. The name of a corporation must include words such as *corporation*, *company*, *incorporated*, or *limited*, which provides notice of the limited liability of the shareholders. 2. A corporate name must not be deceptively similar to names of other corporations.
Powers of Corporations	1. A corporation has all the powers granted in its charter and those set forth in the statutes of the state of incorporation. 2. The usual powers include the power to sue and be sued, to own, convey, and deal in property, to enter into contracts, and to purchase and dispose of securities. 3. The *ultra vires* act is one beyond the authority of the corporation. 4. Neither the corporation nor parties dealing with it may avoid liability on the ground of *ultra vires*.

5. *Ultra vires* conduct on the part of the corporation may be enjoined at the request of the shareholders or may be the basis of a revocation of the charter by the state.

Bylaws

1. After filing the charter, the incorporators meet with all stock subscribers and elect a board of directors. The board in turn meets and adopts bylaws.
2. The bylaws provide the rules for managing the corporation. They cover such activities as the corporate seal, stock certificates, the number and manner of election of officers, and the time and place of meetings of shareholders as well as the board of directors.

Domestic and Foreign Corporations

1. A corporation organized under a state's laws is a *domestic* corporation in that state; a corporation incorporated in one state is a *foreign* corporation in all other states.
2. Foreign corporations transacting local business in a state must qualify to do business in that state. If they fail to do so, they are denied access to the courts as well as being subject to other sanctions.
3. If a business is only engaged in interstate commerce and is not conducting intrastate activities, it is not required to obtain a license to do business.

Promoters

1. A promoter is usually an incorporator and is active in obtaining preincorporation agreements. Promoters are responsible for compliance with all applicable laws.
2. A promoter may be personally liable to contracts prior to incorporation, but this liability may be avoided.
3. A corporation after it is formed may have liabliity on preincorporation agreements under a variety of theories.
4. Promoters stand in a fiduciary relationship to the corporation and cannot secure benefits at the expense of other shareholders or the corporation.

Disregarding the Corporate Entity

To "Pierce the Corporate Veil"

1. Creditors may seek to look through the corporation to the shareholders and seek to impose liability as if the corporate entity did not exist.
2. The corporate entity is not disregarded simply because all of the stock is owned by one person.

Alter Ego Theory

1. The alter ego theory is used to pierce the corporate veil where a corporation is actually nothing more than the alter ego of another corporation or of an individual.
2. This theory is used where the business is actually operated as if the separate corporate entity did not exist.

Promotion of Justice Theory

1. Courts will pierce the corporate veil to avoid fraud and to promote the ends of justice.

Corporate Stock

Kinds of Stock

1. Some stock is preferred over others in either dividends, distributions on dissolution, or both.
2. Stock may be issued without par value in which case the directors provide a stated value for balance sheet purposes.
3. A stock warrant gives a person a right to subscribe and to purchase corporate stock at a stated price. Such warrants are transferable.

4. Watered stock is stock that is issued as fully paid when in fact an equivalent value has not been paid to the corporation.
5. Treasury stock is stock of the corporation that has been purchased by or returned to the corporation.
6. Treasury stock may only be purchased out of accumulated earnings. Otherwise, the purchase could constitute a reduction of capital.

Stock Subscriptions

1. A preincorporation stock subscription is binding and irrevocable for a stated period of time after its execution.
2. Preincorporation subscriptions are usually conditioned on such things as final organization of the corporation and subscription to all the stock.
3. Stock may also be subscribed after incorporation, and such contracts are subject to the same rules as other contracts.

Right to Transfer Stock

1. In a close corporation, the bylaws may grant a right of first refusal to the corporation or to other shareholders.
2. A buy and sell agreement may require the purchase of stock on death or withdrawal of a shareholder.

Mechanics of Transfer

1. Stock is transferred on the records of the corporation by surrender of the stock certificate and issuing a new one. Large corporations retain stock transfer agents to perform this task.
2. Article 8 of the Uniform Commercial Code deals with investment securities. If its provisions are complied with, a party purchasing stock has greater rights than the seller.

REVIEW QUESTIONS AND PROBLEMS

1. Match each term in column A with the appropriate statement in column B.

A	B
(1) Incorporator	(a) A theory used to pierce the corporate veil.
(2) Bylaw	(b) Stock repurchased by the issuing corporation.
(3) Foreign corporation	(c) Right to subscribe for stock.
(4) Promoter	(d) One who signs an application for a corporate charter.
(5) *Ultra vires*	(e) One who assists in organizing a corporation.
(6) Alter ego	(f) A corporation operating in a state other than the state that issues its charter.
(7) Treasury stock	(g) Stock not fully paid for.
(8) Stock warrant	(h) A rule for governing a corporation.
(9) Watered stock	(i) A contract defense that is unavailable to the parties to a contract today.
(10) Stock dividend	(j) A transfer of earned surplus to capital stock and the issue of stock to current shareholders in the proportion of their current holdings.

2. LST Company was the parent company and BAG Company was a subsidiary. LST Company extended credit to BAG Company. The latter became insolvent, and the other creditors objected to LST's sharing equally in the assets. Is LST entitled to its pro rata share of BAG's assets? Why or why not?

3. The plaintiffs entered into a series of contracts involving coal excavations with Doral Coal Company and Dean Coal Company. Robert W. William, defendant, was president of both coal companies. When royalty payments owed were not made by the corporations as agreed, plaintiffs canceled the agreements and filed suit against the defendant individually. They contended that the defendant was personally liable because he was the sole shareholder of each corporation. Is the defendant liable? Why or why not?

4. Smith attempted to file articles of incorporation on behalf of a mortgage company. The articles expressed the rates of interest the mortgage company would charge its borrowers. These rates of interest were usurious under state law. May the secretary of state lawfully reject the articles of incorporation? Why or why not?

5. The First National Bank of Lander, which was the Wyoming Bancorporation's subsidiary in Lander, Wyoming, planned to change its name to First Wyoming Bank, N.A.—Lander. First Wyoming Savings and Loan Association filed a complaint seeking permanently to enjoin the defendant from making the name change. First Wyoming Savings alleged that it had established a trade name in the words "First Wyoming" and that the use of the name "First Wyoming Bank—Lander" would result in confusion and deception to the general public. What result? Why?

6. Through its president, a religious corporation leased liquor-dispensing equipment from the Drink-n-Drown Beverage Company. When the lessee defaulted, Drink-n-Drown filed suit for the unpaid rent. The religious corporation's board of directors asserted *ultra vires* as a defense. Is the defense justified? Explain.

7. Plaintiff, MPL Leasing, a California corporation, sold equipment to Johnson and shipped it to Alabama. When Johnson failed to pay, MPL sued Johnson in Alabama. Johnson moved to dismiss on the ground that MPL was a foreign corporation not qualified to do business in Alabama and that the state's constitution prevented unqualified corporations from enforcing their contracts in Alabama's courts. What result? Why?

8. Plaintiff does virtually all its business in Mississippi and less than 1 percent of its business in Arkansas. It is not registered to do business in the state of Arkansas as required by law. Its agents went to Arkansas and entered into a contract in Arkansas to do some work on a residence near Lake Village. It was not paid for its work and filed an action to impose a lien against the Arkansas residence. May the lien be judicially enforced? Why or why not?

9. The XYZ Corporation was to be formed by Peter, a promoter. In order to operate the corporation after incorporation, it was necessary for Peter to lease certain facilities. Peter executed a lease in the corporate name for office space without revealing to the lessor that the corporation had not yet been organized. The corporation subsequently came into existence, and the board declined to accept the lease of office space that Peter had executed in the corporate name.
   a. Can the corporation validly decline the lease of office space? Explain.
   b. Does Peter have any liability on any of the leases he made? Explain.

10. Plaintiff corporation, engaged in the sale of plastics, entered into a preincorporation contract which was initiated and concluded by two persons who later became officers of the corporation. It formed the basis for the subsequent sale to defendant of over $1 million in goods. Suit was brought to recover balance due on goods sold. The defendant denied liability because the plaintiff was not incorporated at the time of the contract. What result? Why?

11. Dearmin was president and the sole shareholder of Dearmin Brothers Excavating, Inc. The corporation experienced severe cash flow problems in 1975. To help alleviate this problem, Dearmin loaned $30,000 to the corporation and personally guaranteed several loans that were made to the corporation. Hill sold oil products to the corporation. When his bill for $6,268.46 was not paid, he instituted this suit against Dearman personally using the alter ego doctrine. What result? Explain?

12. David formed a corporation for tax purposes. No directors' meetings were held. David retained total control of the corporation's operations, and he took money from the corporate account for personal purchases. Creditors sought to pierce the corporate veil. Should they proceed? Explain.

13. Define the following terms:
    a. Preferred stock
    b. Cumulative preferred stock
    c. Noncumulative preferred stock
    d. Watered stock
    e. Treasury stock

14. A corporation decided to repurchase stock of a shareholder who recently died. The corporation was in existence for three years and had lost $50,000 during this period. The original shareholders had invested $25,000 in the business of which the deceased had invested $5,000. How much may the corporation pay for the stock of the deceased? Explain.

15. Albert sold Betty some stock representing ownership of the Cobra Corporation. Albert delivered the stock certificate to Betty, but he failed to indorse it. Albert died, and the executor of his estate claims that the stock certificate should be returned, since it was not indorsed. Betty contends she is entitled to have the certificate indorsed by Albert's representative. Who is correct? Explain.

30 Operating Corporations

C H A P T E R   P R E V I E W

BUSINESS MANAGEMENT DECISION

You serve as an outside director on the board of the All-at-Once Corporation. During a board meeting, the president of All-at-Once makes a fifteen-minute presentation on the benefits and detriments of merging All-at-Once with Take-Your-Time, Inc. After this presentation, the president asks for a vote of the directors approving the merger.

Do you have any concerns about casting your vote?

The preceding chapter is concerned with the legal aspects of forming a corporation. Many of the legal principles discussed there are also applicable to the operation of a corporate entity. Many bylaw provisions, for example, are directly concerned with operations. Because some of the subjects dealt with in this chapter, such as the rights of shareholders, have a bearing on formation problems, the preceding chapter and this one should be considered complementary.

Three distinct groups participate in the management of a corporation. *Shareholders* or *stockholders* (the words are synonymous) comprise the basic governing body. Shareholders exercise their control by electing the *board of directors*, sometimes by approving the bylaws, and by voting on matters such as merger, consolidation, or dissolution. The board of directors is the policy-making group, with responsibility for electing *officers*, who carry out the policies. The duties and powers of the shareholders, the board of directors, and the various officers are regulated by statute, by the bylaws of the corporation, and by corporate resolutions passed by the board of directors.

SHAREHOLDERS

1. Rights in General

A shareholder has the following rights, usually created by statute and reiterated in the bylaws: (1) the right to inspect the books and papers of the corporation, (2) the right to attend shareholders' meetings and to vote for directors and on certain other matters such as dissolution or merger, (3) the right to share in the profits when a dividend is declared, (4) the preemptive right, and (5) the right to bring a shareholder's derivative suit. In some states a shareholder has the additional right to cumulative voting.

The right to inspect the books and papers is limited to good-faith inspections for proper and honest purposes at the proper time and the proper place. The general rule applied by the courts reviewing inspection statutes has been that the primary purpose of the inspection must not be one that is adverse to the best interests of the corporation. A *proper purpose* is one that seeks to protect the interests of the corporation as well as the interests of the shareholder seeking the information. A shareholder is legitimately entitled to know anything and everything that the records, books, and papers of the company would show to protect his interests. A shareholder must have an honest motive and not proceed for vexatious or speculative reasons. He must seek something more than satisfaction of his curiosity and must not be conducting a general fishing expedition. A shareholder's desire to learn the reasons for lack of dividends or low dividends, and suspicion of mismanagement arising from such dividend policy, will constitute a proper purpose. Most courts, as in the following case, consider an attempt to oust present management to be a proper purpose.

CASE

Delmarmo Associates owned 13 percent of the stock issued by New Jersey Engineering & Supply Company. Delmarmo sought a list of stockholders and the bylaws of this corporation. When Delmarmo was denied the information requested, this lawsuit was filed seeking the court's assistance. According to affidavits on behalf of the corporation, Delmarmo's purpose was to solicit purchase of stock from other stockholders in order to gain control and assume management himself, to accomplish his employment by the corporation as a consultant, to merge or sell the corporation, or to initiate a public offering of its stock.

ISSUE: Does Delmarmo have a right to the information sought?

DECISION: Yes.

REASONS:

1. The purpose of gaining voting control of a corporation through purchase of stock or solicitation of proxies is not improper. An intent antagonistic towards present management is not evidence of bad faith or ulterior motive detrimental to the corporation itself.
2. Any person who shall have been a shareholder of record of a corporation for at least six months immediately preceding his demand, or any person holding, or so authorized in writing by the holders of, at least 5 percent of the outstanding shares of any class or series, upon at least five days' written demand shall have the right for any proper purpose to examine in person or by agent or attorney, during usual business hours, the minutes of the proceedings of its shareholders and record of shareholders and to make extracts therefrom.
3. As a 13 percent stockholder, plaintiff enjoys the right to purchase stock and solicit proxies from other stockholders for the ultimate purpose of ousting present management and assuming management under Delmarmo.

Delmarmo Associates v. New Jersey Engineering & Supply Co., 424 A.2d 847 (N.J. 1980).

The court in the preceding case held that the burden of proof rests on the corporation to prove the shareholder's purpose is improper. Courts in other states have held that the burden of proving good faith and proper purpose for a shareholder's examination of corporate records rests on him, but proof of actual mismanagement or wrongdoing is not necessary, and good-faith fears of mismanagement are sufficient.

The business hours of the corporation are the reasonable and proper hours in which stockholders are entitled to inspect the books. They also have the right to the assistance of accountants and attorneys in that inspection. The assistance of qualified professionals is often required to understand the books and records and to know what to ask for.

In some states, a shareholder who is refused access to the books and records is entitled to damages as provided by statute. A typical statute provides that a shareholder who is denied the right to inspect books and records is entitled to damages equal to 10 percent of the value of the stock owned. This right to inspect includes contracts and correspondence as well as books and records. The right extends even to confidential records.

2. Meetings

Action by the shareholders normally binds the corporation only when taken in a regular or properly called special meeting after notice required by the bylaws or statute has been given. It is generally conceded, however—and most states so provide by statute—that action approved informally by *all* shareholders will bind the corporation. If there is less than unanimous approval, informal action is not possible.

Notice. Notice of a special meeting must include a statement concerning matters to be acted upon at the meeting; any action taken on other matters will be ineffective. If unusual action, such as a sale of corporate assets, is to be taken at the regular annual meeting, notice of the meeting must call specific attention to that fact; but otherwise, any business may be transacted at the annual meeting.

Failure to give proper notice of a meeting generally invalidates the action taken at the meeting. A stockholder who has not received notice but attends and participates in a meeting waives the lack of notice by his presence.

Quorum. A quorum of shareholders must be present in person or by proxy (a **proxy** is the authority to vote another's stock) in order to transact business. If shareholders leave the meeting, they can no longer be counted as present. A *quorum* is usually a majority of the voting shares outstanding, unless some statute or the bylaws provide for a larger or smaller percentage. Affirmative action is approved by majority vote of the shares represented at a meeting, provided a quorum exists. Under common law, certain unusual matters such as a merger or sale of all corporate assets require a unanimous vote. Today, statutes usually provide that such actions can be taken by vote of two-thirds or three-fourths of the shareholders. Many of these statutes also provide that the dissenting shareholders have the right to surrender their shares and receive their fair value if they disapprove of the action taken.

Proxy *Authority to act for another, used by absent stockholders to have their votes cast by others.*

Purposes. In large, publicly held corporations, the annual meeting of shareholders serves a variety of purposes. Management has usually solicited enough proxies in advance to control any vote that is taken, so the outcome is usually a certainty. Nevertheless, many shareholders attend meetings in order to question management on a variety of issues and to lobby for certain policies. Management uses the annual meeting of shareholders of large corporations as a public relations opportunity, to educate the shareholders on company accomplishments as well as its problems.

3. Voting

Statutes of the states and the charters issued under their authority prescribe the matters on which shareholders are entitled to vote. Usually, they vote on the election of directors; on major policy issues such as mergers, consolidations, and dissolution; and, in some instances, on a change in the bylaws.

Some state laws allow a corporation to deny some shareholders the vote on certain issues, such as the election of directors. This denial allows a minority of shareholders to obtain control. But since public policy supports the right of an investor to vote, the status of stock as nonvoting must be communicated to the investor, or the stock purchase may be rescinded.

As a general rule, every shareholder is entitled to as many votes as he owns shares of stock. The shareholder whose name appears in the corporate records is usually designated by the bylaws as the person entitled to vote. Owners of preferred stock, depending on their contract with the corporation, may or may not be entitled to vote.

Cumulative voting *In voting for directors, a stockholder may cast as many votes as he has shares of stock multiplied by the number to be elected. His votes may be all for one candidate or distributed among as many candidates as there are offices to be filled.*

The statutes of some states provide for **cumulative voting** in the election of directors. In cumulative voting, a shareholder may cast as many votes for one board candidate as there are board members to be filled, multiplied by the number of his shares of stock, or he may distribute this same number of votes among the candidates as he sees fit. A shareholder owning 100 shares of stock has 300 votes if three directors are to be elected. He may cast all 300 for one candidate, or they may be spread among the candidates.

A shareholder is entitled to vote only by virtue of his ownership of the stock, but he may specifically authorize another to vote his stock. Authorization is made by power of attorney and must specifically state that the agent of the shareholder has power to vote his principal's stock. This *voting by proxy* is a personal relationship that the shareholder may revoke before the authority is exercised. Laws pertaining to principal and agent control this relationship.

A shareholder, unlike a director, is permitted to vote on a matter in which he has a personal interest. Although in certain respects he represents the corporate welfare in his voting, in most respects he votes to serve his interest. But a majority of shareholders is not permitted to take action that is clearly detrimental to the corporate and minority interest.

4. Preemptive Right

The original application for a charter specifies the amount of stock the corporation will be authorized to issue and the amount that will be issued without further notice to the state. The amount of authorized stock and the amount of issued stock are used to compute the license fees and franchise taxes due to the state of incorporation. These limitations on stocks cannot be increased or exceeded without the authority of the state.

Shareholders may authorize an increase in the authorized capital stock, but such action may not be taken by the directors. An increase in the authorized capital stock is an amendment to the corporate charter, which requires state approval.

The board of directors may sell unissued capital stock when the amount previously issued is less than that authorized. This sale does not require an amendment to the charter. All that is required is that the state be informed of the additional issue of the stock so that the correct taxes may be collected.

When an increase in the capital stock has been properly authorized, the existing shareholders have a prior right over third parties to subscribe to the increased capital stock. This right is called the shareholder's *preemptive right*. It is based on the shareholder's right to protect and maintain his proportionate control and interest in the corporation. The preemptive right may be limited or waived by contract and by provisions in the charter or bylaws of the corporation in most states. In many states it is not applicable to treasury stock. Many publicly held corporations, such as IBM, have eliminated it.

The preemptive right is applicable to new authorizations of stock. It is generally not applicable to new issues of stock previously authorized. If the new issue of an original authorization takes place a long time after the original issue, many states provide that the preemptive right exists. Most states approve the issuance of stock to employees under stock option plans without regard to the preemptive right.

5. Derivative Suits

A shareholder cannot maintain an *action at law* for injuries to the corporation, because the corporation is a legal entity and by law has a right to bring a suit in its own name. Any cause of action based on conduct injurious to the corporation accrues in the first instance to the corporation. Nor can a shareholder bring a suit against the directors or other officers of the corporation for negligence, waste, and mismanagement in the conduct of the corporate business. The right to sue for injuries to the corporation rests strictly with the corporation itself, unless modified by statute.

A shareholder may, however, bring a *suit in equity* known as a shareholder's *derivative suit* to enjoin the officers of a corporation from entering into *ultra vires* contracts or from doing anything that would impair the corporate assets. Likewise, the shareholder has a right to bring suit for dollar damages on behalf of the corporation if the officers are acting outside the scope of their authority, are guilty of negligent conduct, or are engaging in fraudulent transactions that are injurious to the corporation itself. Thus, the purposes of a derivative action are twofold: first, it is the equivalent of a suit by the shareholders to compel the corporation to sue; and second, it is a suit by the corporation, asserted by the shareholders on its behalf, against those liable to it. As a general rule, the shareholder bringing the derivative suit must have been a shareholder at the time of the action complained of and at the time the suit was filed. Individuals are not allowed to acquire stock for the purpose of filing a derivative action or to reacquire it, as occurred in the following case.

CASE

Plaintiff (Vista) brought a stockholders' derivative action against a corporation, its officers, and its directors alleging fraud, negligence, and breach of fiduciary duties. Plaintiff was a stockholder at the time of the transactions complained of, but later sold its stock. Just prior to filing the suit, plaintiff repurchased 100 shares of stock in the defendant corporation. Plaintiff had made a proper demand on the corporation to take action itself.

ISSUE: Must a plaintiff in a shareholder's derivative suit have owned stock at the time the claim arose and continuously from that time until the suit is filed?

DECISION: Yes.

REASONS:

1. A derivative action is one brought by one or more shareholders. The use of the term "shareholders" requires that the plaintiff own stock in the corporation at the time he brings suit.
2. The policy of the law requires continuous stock ownership. The share ownership requirement is intended to prevent the litigating of purchased grievances or speculating in wrongs done to corporations. Once a shareholder has sold his stock he is in the same position as any other nonshareholder.

Vista Fund v. Garis, 227 N.W.2d 19 (Minn. 1979).

Before a shareholder may bring a derivative suit, he must show that he has done everything possible to secure action by the managing officers and directors and that they have refused to act. He must first seek to persuade the officers and directors to take action. Shareholders upset at a corporate failure to bring a lawsuit may not initiate a derivative suit without first demanding it of the directors. If the directors refuse and the derivative action challenges that refusal, courts normally accept the business judgment of the directors. The directors' decision will hold unless bad faith is proved. The corporate decision not to file a lawsuit against directors or others will rarely be set aside by a court if it is made on the basis of a recommendation by outside directors or disinterested investigators. This deference to objective board decisions is based on the *business judgment rule*, which is discussed in section 12 of this chapter.

However, the futility of a stockholder's demand upon a board of directors will excuse the demand. Futility of a stockholder's demand upon a board of directors to redress an alleged wrong to the corporation is gauged by circumstances existing at the commencement of the derivative suit. For example, if the officers and directors are under an influence that sterilizes their discretion, they cannot be considered proper persons to conduct litigation on behalf of the corporation; thus, if there is a conflict of interests in the directors' decision not to sue because the directors themselves have profited from the transaction underlying the litigation, no demand need be made and the shareholders can proceed directly with the derivative suit. In such cases, the business judgment rule does not come into play.

Any judgment received in such an action is paid to the corporation. The shareholder who initiates the action is permitted to recover the expenses involved in the suit.

Mere dissatisfaction with the management of the corporation will not justify a derivative suit. In the law of corporations, it is fundamental that the majority shareholders control the policies and decisions of the corporation. Every shareholder implicitly agrees that he will be bound by the acts and decisions of a majority of the shareholders or by the agents of the corporation they choose. Courts will not undertake to control the business of a corporation, although it may be seen that better decisions might be made and the business might be more successful if other methods were pursued.

The majority of shares of stock are permitted to control the business of a corporation. They may not act in violation of its charter or some public law or corruptly, oppressively, and fraudulently subversive of the rights and interests of the corporation or of a shareholder. If a majority of disinterested directors acting in good faith and with reasonable business judgment adopt a course of action, it will not be overturned by a derivative suit.

6. Dividends

Dividend *A stockholder's pro rata share in the distributed profits of a corporation.*

Although a shareholder has a right to share in **dividends** when declared, whether or not a dividend is declared is within the discretion of the board of directors. Shareholders are not entitled to the payment of a dividend simply because earned surplus exists. The board of directors may see fit to continue the profits in the business for the purpose of expansion, but it must act reasonably and in good faith. Where fraud or a gross abuse of discretion is shown, and there are profits out of which dividends may be declared, the shareholders may compel the board of directors to declare dividends. Before there is a right to interfere by asking a court to order the payment of dividends, however, it must be clear that the board of directors has illegally, wantonly, and without justification refused to declare a dividend.

When a cash dividend is declared, it becomes a debt of the corporation. It will be paid to the person whose name appears on the corporate stock records as the owner of the share on the record date the dividend is payable. This is known as the *ex-dividend date*. The fact that it is paid to this person does not necessarily mean that the payee is entitled to keep it. If the stock has been sold prior to the dividend date but not transferred on the books of the corporation, the buyer is entitled to the dividend. On the other hand, if there is only a contract to sell the stock, the seller is entitled to any dividend paid prior to the delivery of the stock as held in the following case.

CASE

Milliken contracted to purchase the stock of Albany Felt owned by Clark Estates. Under each contract, delivery of the stock certificates was to take place when the total purchase price was paid. Absent from both contracts was any provision as to which party would be entitled to dividends declared by Albany Felt between the dates of the agreements and the dates of transfer of the shares. A dividend distribution was made during this period and Milliken claimed that it was entitled to these dividends.

ISSUE: Absent agreement, does a seller retain the right to receive dividends until the stock is paid for and delivered?

DECISION: Yes.

REASONS:
1. Critical to the determination whether buyer or seller were entitled to the dividend is the question whether present sales—current transfers of substantial beneficial interest—or only agreements to make future sales were manifested by the execution of the contracts.
2. In the absence of an agreement to the contrary, the buyer under an executory contract to sell stock is not entitled to dividends until the legal title to the stock has passed to him, which is not until delivery is made to him or is due to him and is offered to be made.
3. All terminology in the contract looked to future occurrences and is inconsistent with a present transfer of beneficial ownership of the stock. Therefore the sellers retained the right to receive the dividends.

Deering Milliken v. Clark Estates, Inc., 373 N.E.2d 1212 (N.Y. 1979).

A *cash dividend*, once its declaration has been made public, may not be rescinded. A declaration of dividends is proper so long as it does not impair the capital stock. Any declaration that reduces the net assets of the corporation below the outstanding capital stock is illegal.

Dividends are permissible only after provision has been made for all expenses, including depreciation. In industries with wasting or depleting assets, such as mines and oil wells, it is not necessary to allow for depletion before declaring dividends.

Directors are personally liable to creditors for dividends improperly declared.

In most states, shareholders who receive such dividends may be compelled to return them.

Stock dividend New shares of its own stock issued as a dividend by a corporation to its shareholders, in order to transfer retained earnings to capital stock.

Stock split A readjustment of the financial plan of a corporation, whereby each existing share of stock is split into new shares, usually with a lowering of par value.

A **stock dividend** is a transfer of retained earnings to capital and is used when the earnings are required for growth of the business. Stock dividends of the issuing company are not taxable income to shareholders. A **stock split** differs from a stock dividend in that in the former there is no transfer of surplus to capital but only a reduction in par value and an increase in the number of shares.

7. Fiduciary Aspects

The law as it relates to shareholders' relationships in close corporations is somewhat different from the law as it relates to them in publicly held corporations. Publicly held corporations have many shareholders, none of whom owns a majority of the stock. As a general rule, there is no fiduciary relationship between shareholders in publicly held corporations. One owner of stock listed on the New York Stock Exchange owes no duty to other owners of the same stock unless, of course, the shareholder is also an insider subject to regulation by the Securities and Exchange Commission.

A *close corporation* is one in which management and ownership are substantially identical, to the extent that it is unrealistic to believe that the judgment of the directors will be independent of that of the shareholders. The shareholders in a close corporation owe one another substantially the same fiduciary duty that partners owe one another. They must discharge their management and shareholder responsibilities in conformity with the strict good-faith standard, and they may not act out of avarice, expediency, or self-interest in derogation of their loyalty to other shareholders and to the corporation. A shareholder in a close corporation may not permit his private interests to clash with those of the corporation and other shareholders.

Some courts have called close corporations "incorporated partnerships." They are corporations for liability, perpetual existence, and taxation, but the shareholders expect to act and to be treated as partners in their dealings among themselves. The practical realities dictate that the relationship be considered a fiduciary one, demanding fairness, honesty, and full disclosure of all functions. Close corporations are held to a higher moral standard than that of the marketplace. However, there are limits to the duties owed even in a close corporation. As the following case illustrates, in the absence of a buy and sell agreement, the fiduciary aspects do not require redemption of stock on the death of a shareholder.

CASE

Alice M. Marr owned 800 shares of the 11,340 shares outstanding of common stock of Gloucester Ice & Cold Storage Company, a close corporation. No provisions restricting the transfer of stock or requiring the corporation or remaining shareholders to redeem its stock on the death of a shareholder appear in the corporation's articles of organization or bylaws or in any agreement among the shareholders.

After Marr's death in 1977, the administrator of her estate (Mr. Goode) informed the management of Gloucester of his desire to sell, or to have redeemed, the 800 shares of Gloucester stock owned by the Marr estate. By a letter dated April 4, 1978, North Shore offered to purchase the 800 shares from the Marr estate at $12.50 a share. The unaudited financial statement of Gloucester for the year ending December 31, 1977, indicated that the book value of the stock was $38.87 a share. The plaintiff did not accept the North Shore offer and, after a short time, the offer was withdrawn.

At an annual meeting of stockholders in 1982, the administrator again requested redemption but the corporation denied any obligation to do so. He then brought this action seeking a declaration that the fiduciary obligation shareholders of a close corporation owe one another requires that majority shareholders purchase, or cause the corporation to purchase, the shares of a minority shareholder on the death of the minority shareholder. The trial court entered summary judgment for the defendant. Goode appealed.

ISSUE: Absent any agreement to do so, are the majority shareholders of a close corporation bound to buy a deceased minority shareholder's stock?

DECISION: No.

REASONS:

1. One of the identifying characteristics of a close corporation is the absence of a ready market for corporate stock. A shareholder wishing to convert an investment in a close corporation to cash for personal financial reasons or because of unhappiness with the management of the enterprise will have only a limited number of opportunities for disposing of the asset.
2. However, in the absence of an agreement among shareholders or between the corporation and the shareholder, or a provision in the corporation's articles of organization or bylaws, neither the corporation nor a majority of shareholders is under any obligation to purchase the shares of minority shareholders when minority shareholders wish to dispose of their interest in the corporation.
3. While the plaintiff's predicament in not being able to dispose of the Gloucester stock to facilitate prompt settlement of the Marr estate is unfortunate, the situation was not caused by the defendants but is merely one of the risks of ownership of stock in a close corporation. It is not the proper function of this court to reallocate the risks inherent in the ownership of corporate stock in the absence of corporate or majority shareholder misconduct.
4. The majority shareholders made no effort to curtail, or interfere with, any benefits to which Marr or her estate was entitled as a minority stockholder in Gloucester. The majority shareholders simply refused to purchase the Marr estate stock. This refusal violated no agreement or corporate governance provision and did not violate any fiduciary obligation they owed to the plaintiff.

Goode v. Ryan, 489 N.E.2d 1001 (Mass. 1986).

Suits alleging a breach of fiduciary duty often involve the purchase of stock by a majority shareholder or director from a minority shareholder. Such purchases usually involve the use of inside information. A seller under these circumstances should be aware that the buyer has superior knowledge. In deciding such cases, there are three different views among the various states. The majority view is that a director does not stand in a fiduciary relationship to a shareholder in the acquisition of stock and therefore has no duty to disclose inside information. The minority view is that a director is under a duty to disclose all material information. The third view is that although a director ordinarily owes no fiduciary duty to shareholders when acquiring stock, under special circumstances a fiduciary relationship arises.

The special facts creating the fiduciary relationship may include the familial relationship of the parties, the forthcoming sale of corporate assets, the director's initiation of the sale, and the relative ages and experience in financial affairs of the directors and the selling shareholder.

DIRECTORS

8. Powers

Directors of a corporation are elected by the shareholders. They ordinarily attend meetings, exercise judgment on propositions brought before the board, vote, and direct management, although they need not be involved actively in the day-to-day operation of the business. A director has no power to issue orders to any officer or employee, nor can he institute policies by himself or command or veto any other action by the board.

It is not essential that directors hold stock in the corporation. Because they are to supervise the business activities, select key employees, and plan for the future development of the enterprise, they are presumably selected for their business ability.

At one time, most directors of major publicly held corporations were insiders—officials of the corporation. Today, insider-dominated corporate boards seem to be on the way out. Outside directors now constitute the majority on almost nine out of ten boards of directors. These outside directors provide greater independence, more minority representation, and greater diversification in the backgrounds of the directors. Moreover, many people feel that such boards accept more corporate social responsibility and greater accountability for their actions. They also demand higher standards of performance by corporate officers.

Directors have power to take action necessary or proper to conduct the ordinary business activities of the company. They may not amend the charter, approve a merger, or bring about a consolidation with another corporation without the approval of the shareholders.

9. Meetings

The bylaws usually provide for the number of directors. Historically, at least three directors were required; but in recent years, many corporate statutes have authorized two directors—and in some cases, one director. This development is especially prevalent in professional associations or corporations, which frequently have only one shareholder and thus only one director.

Since the board of directors must act as a unit, it is traditional that it assemble at board meetings. The bylaws provide for the method of calling directors' meetings and for the time and the place of the meetings. A record is usually kept of the activities of the board of directors, and the evidence of the exercise of its powers is stated in resolutions kept in the corporate minute book. A majority of the members of the board of directors is necessary to constitute a quorum unless a bylaw provides to the contrary. Special meetings are proper only when all directors are notified or are present at the meetings. Directors may not vote by proxy, having been selected as agents because of their personal qualifications.

Modern statutes make it possible for a board to take informal action (usually by telephone), provided the action is subsequently reduced to writing and signed by all of the directors. This gives a board the flexibility and capability to make decisions without delay. Failure to have unanimous approval of such informal action or to give proper notice is fatal to actions attempted by the board of directors.

Traditionally, a director was forbidden to vote on any matter in which he had a personal interest. Even though his vote was not necessary to carry the proposition considered, many courts would regard any action voidable if it was taken as a result of that vote. Some courts went so far as to hold that if he was present at the meeting, favorable action was not binding. Most courts held that if his presence was required to make a quorum, no transaction in which he was interested could be acted upon. These rather severe rules were developed so that directors would not be tempted to use their position to profit at the expense of the corporation.

Today, many states have somewhat relaxed traditional rules on directors' voting and participation. The trend of the law is to allow interested directors to be present and to be counted as a part of the quorum. Actions taken with interested directors are valid if the participating director's interest is fully and completely disclosed, provided the action is approved by a majority of disinterested directors. Even in states that have changed the earlier common law view, a director with a personal interest in a subject is not allowed to vote on the matter. The problem of acting in good faith is discussed later in this chapter.

10. Compensation

The charter, bylaws, or a resolution by the shareholders usually stipulates payment of directors' fees. If not, service as a director is uncompensated. Directors who are appointed as officers of the corporation should have their salaries fixed at a meeting of the shareholders or in the bylaws. Because directors are not supposed to vote on any matter in which they have a personal interest, director officers of small corporations usually vote on salaries for each other but not their own, and the action to determine salaries should be ratified by the shareholders in order to ensure the validity of the employment contracts.

Some states by statute allow a majority of directors to fix all salaries irrespective of financial interest. In these states, courts are often called upon to review the reasonableness of approved salaries. The following is typical of such cases.

CASE

Nick Soulas, plaintiff-appellant, one-third owner of Troy Donut University, Inc. ("Troy"), an Ohio corporation, filed a complaint against George L. Sauter and James Barouxis, each of whom also owned one-third of the stock in the corporation. He alleged that in June 1980, they had engaged in a course of conduct designed to minimize the profits available to the corporate shareholders and to eliminate Soulas from participation in the benefits of the corporation by causing their salaries to be increased to unreasonably high levels. Soulas also alleged that Sauter and Barouxis had breached the fiduciary duty owed by them as majority directors and officers to Soulas, a minority shareholder, to act in good faith in relation to the corporation's affairs.

Soulas had been engaged in the donut business since 1954 and started a Jolly Roger Donut Shop in 1961. Thereafter, he brought Sauter and Barouxis into the donut business as employees and trained them to be bakers. In 1970, Soulas, Sauter, and Barouxis formed a Sub-Chapter S corporation for ownership of a Jolly Roger Donut Shop in the university area. The three persons each owned one-third of the corporation and were to split profits on a one-third basis.

In July 1980, Sauter and Barouxis called a meeting of the corporation directors, without notifying Soulas, and greatly increased each of their salaries. Sauter's salary was increased from $380 a week to $700 a week, and Barouxis' salary was increased from $340 a week to $660 a week. The result of those increases in salary was that the labor cost of their donut shop far exceeded the labor costs of any other donut shop analyzed. In 1981, their labor charge amounted to 52.68 percent of the gross income compared to an average in the industry of 32.41 percent. A further result of the salary increases was that the profits generated by the corporation became almost nonexistent. Hence, Soulas, a one-third owner of the corporation, was effectively eliminated from receiving any profits from the corporation.

ISSUE: Were the increases in salary reasonable and justified?

DECISION: No.

REASONS:

1. The burden is upon the director employees to justify their salaries and to show the reasonableness thereof. This rule applies with particular force in this case since their salaries were increased at a meeting to which Soulas, the minority director, was not invited.
2. The compensation paid to corporate officers and directors must bear a reasonable relationship to the value of services rendered. In determining the reasonableness of the compensation, all relevant factors should be considered, which would primarily include (1) whether there has been an increase in the business of the corporation, (2) the amount of compensation paid to employees for comparable work by similar corporations in the same industries, and (3) whether there has been a proportionate increase in the duties and responsibilities of the officer employees in connection with the substantial increase in their compensation.
3. Looking at the pertinent factors, the evidence shows that there has not been a significant increase in the business of the corporation since 1979. The donut shop has proceeded at about the same level of gross income. All of the evidence shows that the compensation paid to managers and assistant managers of donut shops with a similar gross income was far less than that voted by Sauter and Barouxis to themselves. Actually, the wages paid them prior to the increase voted in 1980 were at the top of the industry pay scale.
4. Based on this evidence, the reasonable conclusion is that Sauter and Barouxis failed to meet the burden of justifying their salary increases.

Soulas v. Troy Donut University, Inc., 460 N.E.2d 310 (Ohio App. 1983).

LIABILITY OF OFFICERS AND DIRECTORS

11. In General

The officers and directors of a corporation may have personal liability both in tort and in contract. The principles of the law of agency are applicable; liability is usually to the corporation, although it may extend to shareholders and third parties as well.

The liability of corporate officers and directors for tortious conduct is predicated on basic common law principles. Those who personally participate in a tort have personal liability to the third party on the usual common law tort theories, as does any other agent or servant. This liability is based on the participation theory.

Several statutes impose liability on directors and officers. Officers and directors who have responsibility for federal withholding and social security taxes may be liable to the federal government for failure to collect and transfer these taxes for their employees. In the following case, notice the lengths the state government and the court went to in order to impose liability for sales taxes on an employee who had no financial interest in the corporation other than a job.

CASE

The state of Maryland levied an assessment of $4,865.80 in retail sales tax against Margo Cardellino, because of her status as secretary-treasurer of Prince Frederick Auto Parts, Inc. This corporation's articles of incorporation stated that one of its purposes was to retail auto parts. Michael Finkle was the only director named, and Finkle testified that he owned, operated, and appointed himself president of the corporation. After the filing of the articles of incorporation, none of the routine corporate formalities were undertaken: no bylaws were adopted, no shares of stock were issued, and no organizational or annual meetings were held.

Cardellino was hired as a secretary and bookkeeper for the business, with duties that included sending out bills, keeping a record of inventory, answering the telephone, and writing checks. She was an authorized signature on the Prince Frederick Auto Parts, Inc., checking account and had the responsibility of filing monthly sales tax returns. Finkle testified that although the accountant had recommended that appellant be made secretary and treasurer, this was never actually done.

When Cardellino filed the sales tax returns, she added "Secy-Treas." in the blank below her signature. She was listed as a corporate officer on personal property tax returns also. Cardellino appealed the levy of the assessment, arguing that the corporation was not properly formed and that, even if the corporation was properly formed, she was not an officer liable for the assessed taxes.

ISSUE: Is Cardellino, as an officer, liable for the taxes owed by the corporation?

DECISION: Yes.

REASONS:

1. The filing of the articles was conclusive proof of the existence of the corporation. By filing documents as a corporate officer, appellant implicitly represented to the state that the corporation was validly organized, and cannot now seek to avoid the liabilities that flow from being a corporate officer by asserting the lack of the formal steps of organization.
2. Though ordinarily a vote of shareholders or directors is necessary to elect or appoint officers, it has been held that the appointment of an officer may be "inferred." Persons acting as officers are presumed to be such and rightfully in office in the absence of proof to the contrary.
3. Finkle, the sole director of the corporation, appointed appellant to undertake tasks utilizing the title of secretary-treasurer. Appel-

lant prepared and signed the retail sales tax returns as secretary-treasurer, was specified as secretary-treasurer on personal property tax returns, and signed the personal property tax returns as an officer of the corporation.

4. Even if the formal requirements of installing appellant as a corporate officer were not met, there was sufficient evidence to sustain a conclusion that appellant was the de facto secretary-treasurer of the corporation. As such, appellant became personally liable for the unpaid retail sales tax.

Cardellino v. Comptroller, 511 A.2d 573 (Md. App. 1986).

There are numerous other statutes that impose liability on officers and directors of corporations. For example, they are subject to third-party liability for aiding a corporation in such acts as patent, copyright, or trademark infringements, unfair competition, antitrust violations, violation of the laws relating to discrimination, or violations of the securities laws. They are also personally liable when they issue stock as fully paid when it is not paid in full, or when dividends are declared or treasury stock is purchased without the requisite retained earnings.

The relationship between the officers and directors and a corporation is a fiduciary one. The existence and exercise of the statutory power of directors, rather than shareholders, to manage the business and the affairs of a corporation carries with it certain fundamental fiduciary obligations to the corporation and its shareholders. These fiduciary duties of corporate directors require that they act in the best interests of the corporation's shareholders, and this duty extends to protecting the corporation and its owners from perceived harm whether a threat originates from third parties or other shareholders. Liability is often imposed for violation of these fiduciary duties owed to the corporation. When liability is sought, the usual defense is the business judgment rule discussed in the next section. The fiduciary relationship requires that directors act in good faith and with due care. It prohibits conflicts of interest and imposes a duty of undivided loyalty on officers and directors. This rule is discussed further in the sections that follow.

12. The Business Judgment Rule

The *business judgment rule* means that courts honoring principles of corporate self-government will not inquire into the good-faith decisions involving business judgment. Directors are not liable for breach of fiduciary duties because of mere mistakes of judgment. The rule protects directors from personal liability in damages. It applies to cases of transactional justification where an injunction is sought against board action or against its decision. It puts the focus on the decision of the board as contrasted with any possible liability of the board of directors. The rule arises from the fiduciary duties of directors. It creates a presumption that places the burden of demonstrating bad faith on the party attacking an action of a board of directors. The presumption is that the directors of corporations act on an informed basis in good faith and in the honest belief that the action taken was in the best interests of the company. Thus they are presumed not to be personally liable.

The presumption is also based on the belief that directors are better equipped than courts to make business judgments and that directors act independently, without self-dealing or personal interest, and exercise reasonable diligence. There are exceptions to the business judgment rule. The business judgment rule can only sustain corporate decision making or transactions that are within the power or authority of the board of directors. If the directors are guilty of fraud, bad faith, gross overreaching, an abuse of discretion, or gross negligence, then the business judgment rule does not prevent a court from imposing personal liability on directors or from changing a board decision. If corporate directors are not entitled to protection of the business judgment rule, the courts scrutinize directors' decisions as to their intrinsic fairness to the corporation and to its minority shareholders.

The business judgment rule is asserted in a variety of cases. As was previously indicated, many cases involve derivative suits and a board decision to sue on behalf of the corporation. In recent years corporate takeover issues have frequently been litigated. For example, boards of directors have amended corporate bylaws to change the rights of shareholders and have restructured corporations in order to avoid takeovers. Boards have granted officers of corporations "golden parachutes" in order to protect them should a takeover occur. Preferred stock has been issued to avoid proxy fights. In cases such as these, the corporation usually defends its action by using the business judgment rule. In doing so, the directors must show that they had reasonable grounds for believing that a danger to corporate policy and effectiveness existed which required the action taken. The proof in takeover cases that a defense is reasonable in relation to the defenses posed is materially enhanced where a majority of the board favoring the proposal consisted of outside independent directors who have acted on an informed basis, in good faith, and in the honest belief that the action taken was in the best interests of the company. This also applies to a decision of disinterested directors, made in good faith and in the exercise of honest judgment, not to litigate a claim of the corporation.

13. Loyalty and Good Faith

A director occupies a position of trust and confidence with respect to the corporation and cannot, by reason of his position, directly or indirectly derive any personal benefits that are not enjoyed by the corporation or the shareholders. This duty of loyalty or the duty to act in good faith prohibits directors from acting with a conflict of interest. The most common violation of this duty occurs when a director enters into a contract with, or personally deals with, the corporation. A conflict of interest also arises in transactions between the director's corporation and another entity in which he may be a director, employee, investor, or one who is otherwise interested. In all circumstances, the director or officer must fully disclose his conflict of interest to the corporation. If he fails to do so, the contract may be rescinded.

Under common law, a contract between a corporation and one of its directors was voidable unless it was shown to be approved by a disinterested board *and* "fair" to the corporation, in that its terms were as favorable as those available from any other person. Under some modern statutes, the transaction is valid if it is approved, with knowledge of the material facts, by a vote of disinterested directors or shareholders *or* if the director can show it to be "fair."

Issues of good faith frequently arise when a corporation is in financial difficulty. For example, the good faith of a director or officer is an issue when such a person is attempting to collect a personal loan to the corporation. Directors and officers may make loans to their corporations, and they may use the same methods as other creditors to collect bona fide corporation debts owed to them, but only as long as the corporation is solvent. When a corporation is insolvent or on the verge of insolvency, its directors and officers become fiduciaries of corporate assets for the benefit of creditors. As fiduciaries, directors and officers cannot by reason of their special position give themselves preference over the other creditors in collecting bona fide business debts.

Many cases involve the *corporate opportunity doctrine*. This doctrine precludes corporate fiduciaries from diverting to themselves business opportunities in which the corporation has an expectancy, property interest, or right, or which in fairness should otherwise belong to the corporation. The doctrine follows from a corporate fiduciary's duty of undivided loyalty to the corporation. The good-faith requirement is lacking when a director or officer takes for himself an opportunity that the corporation should have had.

A director must present all possible corporate opportunities to the corporation first. Only after disinterested, informed directors have determined that the corporation should not pursue such opportunities can a director pursue them for his own benefits. If a corporate director acquires property for himself, knowing the corporation desires it, he breaches his fiduciary relation to the corporation, and it may obtain the property.

Persons charged with violating the corporate opportunity doctrine sometimes seek to avoid liability by claiming that the corporation was not in a financial position to take advantage of the opportunity. In most states, if the corporation is solvent, financial inability to undertake an opportunity does not absolve a corporate fiduciary from liability for diverting what is otherwise a corporate opportunity. Financial insolvency will, however, excuse corporate fiduciaries from liability in most states. The fiduciary has the burden of proving insolvency; mere financial difficulty is not enough.

To allow a corporate fiduciary to take advantage of a business opportunity when the fiduciary determines the corporation to be unable to avail itself of it would create the worst sort of temptation for the fiduciary. He could rationalize an inaccurate and self-serving assessment of the corporation's financial ability and thereby compromise the duty of loyalty to the corporation. If a corporate fiduciary's duty of loyalty conflicts with his personal interest, the latter must give way.

The appropriate method to determine whether or not a corporate opportunity exists is to let the corporation decide at the time the opportunity is presented. If a fiduciary is uncertain whether a given opportunity is corporate or not, or whether the corporation has the financial ability to pursue it, he needs merely to disclose the existence of the opportunity to the directors and let them decide. Disclosure is a fundamental fiduciary duty. It cannot be burdensome, and it resolves the issue for all parties concerned and eliminates the necessity for a judicial determination after the fact.

A corporate officer or director does not become free to appropriate a business opportunity of the corporation by resigning his office. The duty continues after the resignation.

14. Due Care

In addition to good faith, directors must exercise due care. In its simplest terms, the duty to exercise *due care* is synonymous with a duty not to be negligent. As a general rule, directors owe that degree of care that a businessman of ordinary prudence would exercise in the management of his own affairs. The nature and extent of reasonable care depend on the type of corporation, its size, and its financial resources. A bank director is held to stricter accountability than the director of an ordinary business. In large corporations many duties must be delegated, so intimate knowledge of details by the directors is not possible. In corporations invested with a public interest—such as insurance companies, banks, building and loan associations, and public utilities—rigid supervision and specific obligations are imposed upon directors. If a director fails to exercise the requisite degree of care and skill, the corporation will have a right of action against him for any resulting losses.

As a general rule, a director should acquire at least a rudimentary understanding of the business of the corporation and should be familiar with the fundamentals of that business. Since directors are bound to exercise ordinary care, they cannot set up as a defense to a suit against them lack of knowledge needed to exercise the requisite degree of care. If one has not had sufficient business experience to perform the duties of a director, he should either acquire the knowledge by inquiry or refuse to serve.

Directors must keep informed about the activities of the corporation. Otherwise, they may not be able to participate in the overall management of corporate affairs. Directors may not shut their eyes to corporate misconduct and then claim that because they did not see the misconduct, they did not have a duty to look. They have a duty to protect the corporation. This does not require a detailed inspection of day-to-day activities but a general monitoring of corporate affairs and policies. Accordingly, a director should attend board meetings regularly. Indeed, a director who is absent from a board meeting is presumed to concur in action taken on a corporate matter, unless a dissent is filed with the secretary of the corporation within a reasonable time after learning of such action.

Although directors are not required to audit corporate books, they should be familiar with the financial affairs of the corporation through a regular review of its financial statements. In some circumstances, directors may be charged with ensuring that bookkeeping methods conform to industry custom and usage. The extent of review, as well as the nature and frequency of financial statements, depends not only on the customs of the industry but also on the nature of the corporation and the business in which it is engaged. Financial statements of some small corporations may be prepared internally and only on an annual basis; in a large, publicly held corporation, the statements may be produced monthly or at some other regular interval. Adequate financial review normally would be more informal in a private corporation than in a publicly held corporation.

Generally directors are immune from liability if, in good faith, they rely on the opinion of counsel for the corporation or on written reports prepared by a certified public accountant or on financial statements, books of account, or reports of the corporation represented to them to be correct by the president, the officer of the corporation having charge of its books of account, or the person presiding at a meeting of the board. The review of financial statements, however, may give rise to a duty to inquire further into matters revealed by those statements. Upon discovery of an illegal course of action, a director has a duty to object, and if the corporation does not correct the conduct, to resign.

In certain circumstances, the fulfillment of the duty of a director may call for more than mere objection and resignation; sometimes a director may be required to seek the advice of legal counsel. A director may require legal advice concerning the propriety of his own conduct, the conduct of other officers and directors, or the conduct of the corporation. A director should consult with corporate counsel or his own legal adviser whenever there is doubt regarding a proposed action. Sometimes the duty of a director may require more than consulting with outside counsel. A director may have a duty to take reasonable means to prevent illegal conduct by co-directors, including the threat of suit.

A director is not an ornament, but an essential component of corporate governance. Consequently, a director cannot protect himself behind a paper shield bearing the motto "dummy director." A director may incur liability by failing to do more than passively rubber-stamp the decisions of the active managers. Directors must use their best business judgment. As previously discussed, they have no liability for honest mistakes. Directors are liable to the corporation for negligence in management. As a general rule, since no duty extends to third-party creditors, there is no liability to them or to the shareholders individually, as the following case illustrates.

CASE

Plaintiff held a corporate note secured by a chattel mortgage and by a mortgage on real property. The note was not paid, so a foreclosure suit was instituted. The foreclosure sale did not bring enough to satisfy the obligation. Plaintiff brought action against the officers and directors of the corporation, alleging that they had mismanaged the corporate business. The lower court ruled that a creditor had no standing to sue.

ISSUE: Do creditors of a corporation have a claim against officers and directors for *negligent* mismanagement of its affairs?

DECISION: No.

REASONS:

1. Directors or officers may be liable to the corporation or shareholders for mismanagement of the business of the corporation or waste of its assets, but they are not liable to its creditors for mere mismanagement or waste of assets constituting a wrong or breach of duty to the corporation.
2. A creditor of a corporation may not maintain a personal action at law against the officers or directors of a corporation who have, by their mismanagement or negligence, committed a wrong against the corporation to the consequent damage of the creditor. The reason given for the rule is the entire lack of privity between the parties.
3. The duty to exercise diligence and care is one owed to the corporation, and it is elementary law that one person cannot maintain an action against another for a wrong to a third person who is injured only incidentally.

Equitable Life & Casualty Co. v. Inland Printing Co., 454 P.2d 162 (Utah 1971).

15. Indemnification and Insurance

In recent years, dissenting shareholders, public interest groups, and government regulators have caused a dramatic increase in the number of lawsuits filed against directors and officers of publicly held corporations. Many of the lawsuits result from the failure of directors to prevent activities such as bribery of foreign officials and illegal political contributions. Most large corporations carry liability insurance for directors, and costs for this insurance are soaring because of the increased number of suits.

In order to reimburse directors and officers for the expenses of defending lawsuits if the insurance is nonexistent or inadequate, most states provide by statute for indemnification by the corporation. The Model Business Corporation Act provides that the standard for indemnification is that the director must have "acted in good faith and in a manner he reasonably believed to be in or not opposed to the best interests of the corporation" and if a criminal action, "had no reasonable cause to believe his conduct was unlawful." The indemnification is automatic if the director has been successful in the defense of any action.

CHAPTER SUMMARY

Shareholders

Rights in General	1. Shareholders have rights created by statute. These usually include the right to inspect the books and papers of the corporation, the right to attend meetings and to vote, and the right to dividends. 2. The right to inspect the books and papers is limited to good-faith inspections for proper and honest purposes at the proper time and the proper place. 3. An attempt to oust present management is a proper purpose for inspection. 4. Shareholders have the right to the assistance of accountants and attorneys in that inspection.
Meetings	1. Shareholders are entitled to notice of the annual meeting and of special meetings as well. The notice must include the matters to be acted upon at special meetings and all unusual matters that are on the agenda of the annual meeting. 2. Informal action by all shareholders may be taken without an actual meeting. 3. A quorum is usually a majority of the voting stock.
Voting	1. Shareholders usually vote to elect directors and on issues such as dissolution. 2. Election of directors by cumulative voting is possible in some states. 3. Shareholders may vote by proxy. 4. Shareholders may vote on matters in which they have a personal interest.
Preemptive Right	1. A shareholder also may have a preemptive right, which is the right to buy a proportionate share of new stock issues.
Derivative Suits	1. A shareholder has the right to bring a suit on behalf of the corporation when the directors fail to do so. Shareholders usually must demand that the directors take action before filing such a suit. 2. The minority shareholders of a corporation agree tacitly to be bound by the acts of the majority. The majority controls the business unless acting illegally, oppressively, or fraudulently.
Dividends	1. A shareholder has a right to dividends declared but has no right to have dividends declared. 2. It is generally up to the board of directors to declare a dividend.

3. A stock dividend is a transfer of retained earnings to capital and in effect gives the shareholder nothing of additional value.

Fiduciary Aspects

1. In a publicly held corporation, the shareholders do not stand in a fiduciary relationship with each other.
2. In a closely held corporation, the shareholders do stand in a fiduciary relationship to the enterprise and to each other.
3. Shareholders in a close corporation must act in good faith. In many states, this includes the duty to disclose relevant information.

Directors

Powers

1. The directors determine policy in the ordinary course of business and elect the officers.
2. Directors need not be shareholders.

Meetings

1. The bylaws provide the procedures for calling and conducting directors' meetings, and minutes of them are maintained.
2. The majority of the directors constitute a quorum, and action is usually by a majority.
3. Directors may not vote by proxy, but informal action that is unanimous is allowed in most states.
4. Directors may not vote on matters in which they have a personal interest, although their presence may be used to constitute a quorum.

Compensation

1. Directors are compensated as provided in the bylaws.
2. Directors fix the salary of officers, but generally they cannot vote on their own salary.

Liability of Officers and Directors

In General

1. Directors and officers may have personal liability both in tort and in contract. This liability may be to the corporation or to third parties.
2. Directors are liable to the corporation for breach of their fiduciary duties or of duties imposed by statute.

The Business Judgment Rule

1. Directors are not liable for breach of fiduciary duties because of mere mistakes of judgment.
2. The presumption is that the directors of corporations act on an informed basis in good faith and in the honest belief that the action taken was in the best interests of the company.
3. The presumption is based on the belief that directors are better equipped than courts to make business judgments.
4. If the directors are guilty of fraud, bad faith, gross overreaching, an abuse of discretion, or gross negligence, then the business judgment rule does not prevent a court from imposing personal liability on directors or from changing a board decision.

Loyalty and Good Faith

1. Directors must act in good faith. The duty of good faith creates liabliity if there is a conflict of interest.
2. The *corporate opportunity doctrine* precludes corporate fiduciaries from diverting to themselves business opportunities in which the corporation has an expectancy, property interest, or right, or which in fairness should otherwise belong to the corporation.

Due Care

1. As a general rule, directors owe that degree of care that a businessman of ordinary prudence would exercise in the management of his own affairs.

	2. Directors may rely on experts such as accountants or attorneys in exercising their responsibilities.
	3. Directors are not liable to third parties for negligence in management.
Indemnification and Insurance	1. Corporations usually carry liability insurance to protect directors.

REVIEW QUESTIONS AND PROBLEMS

1. Match each term in column A with the appropriate statement in column B.

A	B
(1) Cumulative voting	(a) A lawsuit filed on behalf of a corporation by a shareholder as a result of the failure of the officers and directors to file the suit.
(2) Preemptive right	(b) A majority of the shares of a coroporation.
(3) Derivative suit	(c) The record date on which a dividend is payable.
(4) Quorum	(d) A reduction in par value and an increase in the number of shares outstanding.
(5) Proxy	(e) Prevents some derivative suits.
(6) Ex-dividend date	(f) A shareholder is entitled to the number of votes in electing directors that is the product of number of shares times number of directors to be elected. All the shareholder's votes may be cast for one director.
(7) Stock split	(g) The right to vote someone else's stock.
(8) Business judgment rule	(h) The right of a shareholder to purchase additional stock of subsequent stock issues so that he may maintain his overall percentage of total stock outstanding.

2. Miles a bank shareholder, requested an unlimited inspection of the bank's books and records. He said that he wanted to ascertain whether any action had been taken contrary to the best interests of the stockholders, such as misuses of corporate funds; abuse of corporate office; diversion of corporate assets to the personal benefit of any officer, director, employee, or stockholder; misapplication of corporate assets; or favoring of certain customers of the bank because of personal connections with officers or directors of the bank. He also wanted to determine whether the directors had lived up to their fiduciary obligation to the stockholders. Must the bank honor his request? Explain.

3. All stockholders were present at the annual stockholders' meeting of a corporation whose bylaws required only a majority of shareholders to constitute a quorum. During the meeting, two stockholders who owned a majority of the stock withdrew from the meeting while it was in progress. Following their withdrawal, the remaining stockholders elected five members to the board of directors. Should the election of the directors be invalidated? Why or why not?

4. A corporation board authorized a director, Wilson, to negotiate the purchase of some land. Instead, Wilson secretly bought the land himself and sold it to the corporation at a profit. After learning of the deceit, the corporation failed to act. Do the minority shareholders have any remedy? Explain.

5. Able, Baker, and Charlie were directors of the ABC Corporation. During the early years the corporation met with moderate success and showed a small annual profit each year. There was nothing in the corporate charter or bylaws in respect to compensation for directors, and during this initial period the directors did not seek or receive any compensation. In 1980, the corporation had a banner year, several new contracts were obtained, and a new product line that the directors decided the corporation should make and sell proved highly profitable. The directors performed the usual and customary services and duties of their office in a highly competent and skillful manner and their efforts were to a large extent responsible for the large profit obtained in 1980. After the 1980 income statement was received and examined by the directors, they met on March 15, 1981, and voted themselves retroactive bonus of $10,000 each as the reasonable

value of services for the past years. Sherman, a stockholder of record, objected to this action and now brings a derivative stockholder's action against the directors and seeks to obtain a judgment against each of the directors to the extent of the bonus he received. What result? Why?

6. On March 1, a company declared a cash dividend of $1 per share, payable on June 1 to all stockholders of record on May 1. On April 10, Ann sold ten shares of her stock to Bob, but the transfer was not recorded on the corporation's books until May 15. To whom will the company pay the dividend? Who is entitled to the dividend? Explain.

7. There were two equal shareholders of Bonanza, Inc., a shopping center operation. Hunt, as president, managed the business. Sampson was secretary but inactive. Hunt purchased Sampson's stock for $75,000. At the time of the sale, Hunt did not inform Sampson of (1) additional leases that had been obtained, (2) a commitment for the financing of a third phase of the development, and (3) sale of part of the stock to three doctors. Is Sampson entitled to recover the difference between the selling price and the fair market value of the stock at the time of the sale? Why or why not?

8. Abner owned a majority of the stock of Lum Company, and he ran the corporation by himself. The balance of the stock was owned by Abner's brother and sister, who agreed to sell all their stock to him. At the time of the purchase, Abner was negotiating a sale of the company, but he did not reveal this fact to his brother and sister. The sale of the company resulted in a great profit to Abner. The brother and sister brought suit to recover the difference. Should the brother and sister succeed? Why?

9. Wilkes and three other individuals formed a corporation to operate a nursing home many years ago. The four corporate shareholders were also elected directors, and they served as employees of the close corporation. Plaintiff had a quarrel with one of the other directors after years of successful operation. As a result, the other board members canceled plaintiff's salary, refused to reelect him as director, and stopped paying dividends in an attempt to freeze him out. He sued for damages on the ground that the majority had breached the fiduciary duty owed to him. With what result? Why?

10. Alan is chairman of the board of directors of Shipping Corporation. The bylaws of the corporation provide for a seven-person board of directors, one of whom has just died. The bylaws have no provision for filling a vacancy and Alan would like to appoint his brother. Alan attempted to telephone the other directors and inform them of what he would like to do. He contacted two directors, who agreed by telephone. A third director could not be reached. The fourth director agreed to Alan's plan on behalf of himself and the fifth director, who had given his proxy to the fourth director. The substance of the telephone calls was not reduced to writing. Can Alan legally appoint his brother as a director? Explain.

11. A Michigan statute requires all corporations to provide funds to meet any workers' compensation claim presented by an employee. Failure to so provide, by insurance or otherwise, renders the officers and directors jointly and severally liable. Plaintiff was injured during the course of his employment with the corporate defendant and was awarded 215 weeks of compensation. Shortly thereafter, the corporation went bankrupt without paying the claim. Plaintiff seeks to hold the directors and officers personally liable. With what result? Why?

12. A company was in arrears on five of its preferred dividends but paid the sixth dividend anyway because the stock subscription agreement provided that if six dividends were omitted, the preferred stockholders were entitled to assume control of the company. The dividends were paid while the capital was impaired. Are the directors personally liable for the dividends paid? Why or why not?

13. Plaintiffs sued the president, vice president, and secretary of the corporation that built them new houses. They alleged that due to faulty planning, their homes were built in an area that was often flooded by the drainage of the other areas of the development. Do the officers have personal liability? Why or why not?

Corporate Dissolutions, Mergers, and Consolidations

31

CHAPTER PREVIEW

- VOLUNTARY DISSOLUTION

  Procedures
  Notice to Creditors
  Distributions

- INVOLUNTARY DISSOLUTIONS

  Commenced by the State
  Commenced by Shareholders
  Deadlocks • Best interest • Illegal, fraudulent, or oppressive conduct
  Commenced by Creditors
  Procedures
  Liability of Shareholders

- CONSOLIDATIONS, MERGERS, AND ACQUISITIONS

  Definitions
  Procedures
  Rights of Dissenting Shareholders
  Liability of Successors
  Antitrust Considerations
  Statutes • Clayton act—section 7

BUSINESS MANAGEMENT DECISION

You are major shareholder, director, and officer of a corporation that is interested in acquiring the capability to manufacture explosives. Your corporation has the opportunity to buy the Powder Keg Company. This company has a history of manufacturing dynamite and fireworks.

If your company acquires Powder Keg, what steps should be taken to reduce your company's liability for any defective products previously manufactured by Powder Keg?

Corporate existence terminates upon the expiration of the period set forth in the charter or upon the voluntary or involuntary dissolution of the corporation. This chapter discusses the various methods of terminating the corporate existence. It also discusses the impact of the antitrust laws on mergers and acquisitions. Since a corporation is a creation of a statute, it can be dissolved only according to statute. Thus the statute of the state of incorporation is very important.

Most corporate charters provide for perpetual existence. If the charter stipulates that the corporation shall exist for a definite period, it automatically terminates at the expiration of the period, unless application to continue the corporation is made and approved by the authority granting the charter. Since almost every corporation has perpetual existence, formal action is almost always required to end the life of a corporation.

VOLUNTARY DISSOLUTION

1. Procedures

A corporation that has obtained its charter but has not commenced business may be dissolved by its incorporators. The incorporators file articles of dissolution with the state, and a certificate of dissolution is issued if all fees are paid and the articles are in order.

A corporation that has commenced business may be voluntarily dissolved either by the written consent of *all* its shareholders or by corporate action instituted by its board of directors and approved by the requisite percentage (usually two-thirds) of the shareholders. The board action, usually in the form of a recommendation, directs that the issue be submitted to the shareholders. A meeting of shareholders is called to consider the dissolution issue, and if the vote is in favor of it to the degree required by statute, the officers follow the statutory procedures for dissolution.

These procedures require the corporate officers to file a statement of intent to dissolve. The statement is filed with the state of incorporation, and it includes either the consent of all shareholders or the resolutions instituted by the board of directors. Upon filing the statement of intent to dissolve, the corporation must cease to carry on its business, except for winding up its affairs, even though corporate existence continues until a certificate of dissolution is issued by the state.

The filing of a statement of intent to dissolve is revocable. If the shareholders change their minds before the articles of dissolution are issued, the decision may be revoked by filing a statement of revocation of voluntary dissolution proceedings. When such a statement is filed, the corporation may resume its business.

2. Notice to Creditors

In winding up its affairs, the corporation must give notice to all known creditors of the corporation. If notice is not given, the corporation remains liable on the debts, and statutes of limitation, which eventually wipe out claims against corporations and its shareholders, do not start to run. In addition, directors become personally liable for any debt of which notice is not given. These debts include tort claims as well as contract claims, as the following case illustrates.

CASE

Bonsall was injured in a "slip and fall" accident while shopping at the defendant's grocery store. She telephoned the store and notified it of her injury. Defendant notified its insurance company and an adjuster contacted the plaintiff and her attorney.

Later, the defendant corporation was dissolved. It failed to give actual notice of intent to dissolve to the plaintiff, although it published notice of dissolution in the newspaper. The South Carolina law on corporate dissolution provides:

> After the filing by the Secretary of State of a statement of intent to dissolve, . . . (b) The corporation shall immediately cause notice of the filing of the statement of intent to dissolve to be mailed to each known creditor of the corporation. . . .

ISSUE: Was the plaintiff a "known creditor" entitled to notice?

DECISION: Yes.

REASONS:
1. The plaintiff was clearly known to the defendant.
2. A tort claim makes a person a creditor.
3. Since notice was not given to plaintiff, who was a known creditor, the corporation was not dissolved insofar as her rights are concerned and it remains liable.

Bonsall v. Piggly Wiggly Helms, Inc., 274 S.E.2d 298 (S.C. 1981).

3. Distributions

In dissolution proceedings, corporate assets are first used to pay debts. After all debts are paid, the remainder is distributed proportionately among the shareholders. If there are insufficient assets to pay all debts, a receiver will be appointed by a court, and the proceedings will be similar to those of involuntary dissolutions, discussed later.

When all funds are distributed, the corporation will prepare duplicate "articles of dissolution" and forward them to the state for approval. When signed by the appropriate state official, usually the secretary of state, one copy is filed with state records and one copy is returned to the corporation to be kept with the corporate records.

INVOLUNTARY DISSOLUTIONS

4. Commenced by the State

Quo warranto *A proceeding in court by which a governmental body tests or inquires into the authority or legality of a corporation's existence.*

The state, having created the corporation, has the right to institute proceedings to cancel the charter. Suits by a state to cancel or forfeit a charter are known as **quo warranto** proceedings. They are filed by the attorney general, usually at the request of the secretary of state. Statutes often allow charters to be canceled by executive action also.

Charters may be canceled by suit or executive action if a corporation (1) did not file its annual report, (2) neglected to pay its franchise tax and license fees, (3) procured its charter by fraud, (4) abused and misused its authority, (5) failed to appoint and maintain a registered agent for the service of notices and process or had not informed the state of the name and address of its registered agent, or (6) ceased to perform its corporate functions for a long period of time. By proper proceedings and without charter forfeiture, the attorney general may also enjoin a corporation from engaging in a business not authorized by its charter. If a corporation is dissolved for any of the foregoing reasons, it may not continue its business. Its officers and directors may wind up the business, but any other contract is null and void.

By statute in most states, the officers and directors do not have personal liability for debts incurred on behalf of the corporation when its charter is suspended for failure to comply with state laws. Such statutes only suspend the right of a corporation to transact business while the corporation is delinquent for failure to file its annual report or pay its annual fees to the state. They do not expose the corporation's officers of directors to personal liability for debts incurred during the period of delinquency.

5. Commenced by Shareholders

Deadlocks. Involuntary dissolution may be ordered by a court of equity at the request of a shareholder when the directors are deadlocked in the management of corporate affairs or the shareholders are deadlocked and unable to elect a board of directors. Deadlocks require proof that irreparable injury is likely and that the deadlock cannot be broken. A mere deadlock in voting to elect directors is not sufficient in itself in most states to cause a court to order dissolution.

CASE

Shareholders of Cooper-George, Inc., failed to elect new directors at two successive annual meetings due to a deadlock in voting power. The corporation has continued, however, to transact business. In April 1979, a shareholder initiated this suit, seeking dissolution under a Washington statute granting courts jurisdiction to liquidate the assets and business of a corporation when it is established that the shareholders are deadlocked in voting power and have failed for a period of at least two years to elect successor directors. The trial court interpreted the code section to be mandatory and the grounds sufficient for dissolution of a corporation.

ISSUE: Is the failure of shareholders at two consecutive annual meetings to elect new directors, by itself, sufficient grounds for dissolution of a corporation?

DECISION: No.

REASONS:
1. The provision is not mandatory but gives the court jurisdiction to exercise its discretion in the best interest of all the shareholders.
2. In determining whether to grant dissolution, the principal inquiry is whether dissolution would be beneficial to all the shareholders.
3. Determining the shareholders' best interest involves use of a balancing test. The courts must consider the seriousness of the deadlock and whether the corporation is able to conduct business profitably despite the deadlock.
4. Because the trial court dissolved the corporation simply because it met the jurisdictional requirements of the statute, the case is reversed and remanded to allow the court to consider the facts of the case and determine if dissolution would be in the best interests of the shareholders.

Henry George & Sons, Inc. v. Cooper-George, Inc., 632 P.2d 512 (Wash. 1981).

Since the proceedings are in a court of equity, the issue is whether dissolution will be beneficial to the shareholders and not injurious to the public. The power to order dissolution is discretionary. In exercising its discretion, the court considers the seriousness of the deadlock and whether the corporation is able to conduct business profitably despite the deadlock. It also considers whether such a dissolution will be beneficial or detrimental to all shareholders, or injurious to the public. For example, the court may consider such factors as the length of time the company has been in business, the stated purpose of the business, the original incorporators, whether one shareholder has shown a clear design to take over the business and is in a financial posture to do so to the detriment of other shareholders who may be injured financially by tax consequences, what the market for sale and purchase is at the instant time, whether the shareholders are in a relatively equal bargaining position, and whether it is in the best interests of all the shareholders to leave them to find their own solutions by one party buying out the others in a fair market value situation rather than by a forced sale.

Illegal, fraudulent, or oppressive conduct. The general rule throughout the United States is that a minority shareholder or group of shareholders of a going and solvent corporation cannot, without statutory authority, maintain a suit to have it dissolved. Most states have statutes that authorize courts of equity to liquidate a corporation at the request of a shareholder when it is proved that those in control of the corporation are acting illegally, fraudulently, or oppressively. It is so difficult to define oppressive conduct that each case must be decided on its own facts.

Actions intended to squeeze out or freeze out minority shareholders may provide grounds for dissolution or other equitable relief. Minority shareholders have been granted relief when the majority have refused to declare dividends but have paid out all profits to themselves in the form of salaries and bonuses. Relief was also granted in a recent case where the majority shareholders of a corporation that was *not* in need of funds sold additional stock in order to dilute the percentage of control of the minority, who the majority knew were unable financially to exercise their preemptive right. Such conduct is a breach of the fiduciary relationship.

Today, conduct that is not illegal or fraudulent may be held to be oppressive. Although controlling shareholders in a closely held corporation are not fiduciaries in the strict sense of the word, the general concepts of fiduciary duties are useful in deciding if conduct is oppressive. The law imposes equitable limitations on dominant shareholders. They are under a duty to refrain from using their control to profit for themselves at the expense of the minority. Repeated violations of these duties will serve as a ground for dissolution. Even though it takes a substantially less evidence to to justify dissolution of a partnership than of a close corporation, the trend is to treat the issues as similar. *Oppressive conduct* may be summarized as conduct that is burdensome, harsh, and wrongful. It is a substantial deviation from fair dealing and a violation of fair play. It is a violation of the fiduciary duty of good faith in those states that recognize such a duty.

All states allow minority shareholders to obtain dissolution when it is established that corporate assets are being wasted or looted or the corporation is unable to carry out its purposes. Some states have by statute broadened the grounds for court-ordered dissolution. These states allow courts to order dissolution when it is reasonably necessary for the protection of the rights or interests of minority shareholders. Even in these states a corporation will not be dissolved by a court for errors of judgment or because the court confronted with a question of policy would decide it differently than would the directors. Dissolutions by decree at the request of a shareholder are rare; but as previously noted, the trend is to give greater protection to the minority shareholders.

6. Commenced by Creditors

A corporation is in the same position as a natural person insofar as its creditors are concerned. A suit may be brought against it; and when a judgment is obtained, an execution may be levied against its property, which may then be sold. Corporate assets may be attached; and if the corporation has no property subject to execution, its assets may be traced by a bill in a court of equity.

The creditors have no right, because they are creditors, to interfere with the management of the business. A creditor who has an unsatisfied judgment against a corporation may bring a bill in equity to set aside conveyances and transfers of corporate property that have been fraudulently transferred for the purpose of delaying and hindering creditors. Creditors may also, under the above circumstances, ask for a receiver to take over the assets of the corporation and to apply them to the payment of debts.

When there is an unsatisfied execution and it is established that the corporation is insolvent, a court may order a dissolution. The same is true if the corporation admits its insolvency. Dissolution in such cases proceeds in the same manner as if instituted by the state or by voluntary proceedings when insolvent. These procedures are discussed in the next section.

Receiver *An officer of the court appointed on behalf of all parties to the litigation to take possession of, hold, and control the property involved in the suit, for the benefit of the party who will be determined to be entitled thereto.*

7. Procedures

In liquidating a corporation, courts have the full range of judicial powers at their disposal. They may issue injunctions, appoint **receivers,** and take whatever steps are necessary to preserve the corporate assets for the protection of creditors and shareholders. The receiver will usually collect the assets, including any amount owed to the corporation for shares. The receiver will then sell the assets, pay the debts and expenses of liquidation, and if any funds are left, divide them proportionately among the shareholders. Courts usually require creditors to prove their claims in court in a manner similar to that in bankruptcy proceedings. When all funds in the hands of a receiver are paid out, the court issues a decree of dissolution that is filed with the secretary of state. Funds due persons who cannot be located are deposited with the state treasurer and held for a specified number of years. If not claimed by the creditor or shareholder within the declared period, the funds belong to the state.

8. Liability of Shareholders

As a general rule, shareholders are not personally liable for the debts of the firm, but a shareholder who has not paid the corporation for his original issue of stock in full is liable to the receiver or to a creditor for the unpaid balance. In addition, statutes in most states allow creditors to reach assets of the former corporation that are in the hands of shareholders. The assets of a corporation are a trust fund for the payment of creditors, and the directors must manage this fund for their benefit. The liability of shareholders to creditors of the corporation is predicated on the theory that the transfer of corporate assets on dissolution is in fraud of creditors, and a shareholder knowingly receiving such assets ought to have liability.

Claims that existed before dissolution may be enforced afterward by statute in most states. For a specified period after dissolution, remedies survive against a corporation, its directors, officers, and shareholders. Suits against the corporation may be prosecuted or defended in the corporate name even though the corporate existence has technically ended. A judgment on such a claim may be collected from the corporation if it has property or from any former insurance carrier of the corporation. A claim may also be collected from property distributed to shareholders on dissolution, or the creditor may proceed directly against the shareholder receiving property. As previously noted, failure to give notice to creditors of intent to dissolve stops the time period from running.

The time period to sue after dissolution was created to protect creditors from losses that could easily result from the ''death'' of the corporate debtor. However, this protection is limited to whatever period is specified by the law of the state of incorporation; liability does not continue indefinitely. In addition, there is no liability for postdissolution causes of action unless a statute imposes it. The following case discusses the common law trust fund theory and a statutory replacement on the issue of survival of claims against a dissolved corporation.

CASE

Theodore Moeller was injured in 1975 by an elevator installed by the Hunter-Hayes Elevator Company in 1960. The injured worker brought an action against former shareholders of the company because the business had been dissolved in 1964. The shareholders moved for summary judgment on the grounds that a state statute required actions against dissolved corporations and their shareholders be brought within three years after the company is dissolved. The trial court granted the motion.

ISSUE: May the plaintiff sue the former shareholders of a dissolved corporation for injuries occurring eleven years after dissolution?

DECISION: No.

REASONS:
1. The statute clearly sets up a three-year statute of limitations for suits against shareholders of dissolved corporations. As harsh as it may seem, the statute is a great deal better than the common law rule, which held that a plaintiff's cause of action terminated when a corporation was dissolved with no recourse against the shareholders.
2. Although equitable doctrines, such as the "trust fund" theory, arose to alleviate the harshness of the common law rule, this statute sets a maximum three-year time limit that cannot be abridged by the courts.

Hunter v. Fort Worth Capital Corporation, 620 S.W.2d 547 (Tex. 1981).

CONSOLIDATIONS, MERGERS, AND ACQUISITIONS

9. Definitions

A business may acquire other businesses in a variety of ways. It may singly purchase the assets of the other firm. Such purchases include the plant, equipment, and even the goodwill of the other business. In such cases, the selling business retains its liabilities and its corporate structure.

Businesses may also consolidate or merge. Consolidation is the uniting of two or more corporations. A new corporation is created and the old entities are dissolved. The new corporation takes title to all the property, rights, powers, and privileges of the old corporations, subject to the liabilities and obligations of the old corporations. In a *merger,* one of the corporations continues its existence but absorbs the other corporation, which ceases to have an independent existence. The continuing corporation may expressly or impliedly assume and agree to pay the debts and liabilities of the absorbed corporation, whose creditors become third-party creditor beneficiaries. By statute in most states, the surviving corporation is deemed to have assumed all the liabilities and obligations of the absorbed corporation.

10. Procedures

The procedures for consolidations and mergers are statutory. Usually, the board of directors gives its approval by resolution that sets forth in detail all facts of the planned merger or consolidation. The plan is submitted to the shareholders for approval. Notice of the meeting typically includes the resolution passed by the directors. If proxies are submitted for the vote, proxy material must disclose all material facts required for an intelligent decision by the shareholders. In most states, the shareholders must approve the plan by a two-thirds vote of all shares and two-thirds of each class if more than one class of stock is voting. If the consolidation or merger is approved by the shareholders of both corporations, articles of consolidation or articles of merger will be prepared and filed with the state. If the papers are in order and all fees are paid, a certificate of consolidation or a certificate of merger will be issued.

11. Rights of Dissenting Shareholders

Statutes of the appropriate state may be strictly complied with, yet the courts may block a merger or acquisition. A merger may not be effected for the purpose of freezing out or squeezing out minority shareholders. If a merger has no valid business purpose other than the elimination of minority shareholders, courts will enjoin the merger or consolidation. Even if the minority shareholders receive the investment value of their interest in the merged corporation, the policy favoring corporate flexibility is not furthered by permitting the elimination of minority interests for the benefit of the majority, when no benefit thereby accrues to the corporation. Moreover, the majority shareholders owe the minority shareholders a fiduciary obligation in dealing with corporate assets. This duty includes the protection of corporate interests and restraint from doing anything that would injure the corporation or deprive it of profits or the ability to exercise its powers. Since dissolution may cause these effects, the majority may not dissolve when the only purpose is to get rid of the minority.

A shareholder who dissents from a consolidation or merger, and who makes his dissent a matter of record prior to the decision by serving a written demand that the corporation purchase his stock, is entitled to be paid the fair value of his stock on the day preceding the vote on the corporate action. Procedures are established for ascertaining the fair value and for a judicial decision of that issue if necessary. Once committed to the procedure, a shareholder cannot change his mind and keep his stock. This stops a party from finding out the price and then accepting or rejecting it. Among the relevant factors to be considered in evaluating a dissenting shareholder's stock are the nature of the corporation, the market demand for the stock, the business of the corporation, its earnings, dividends, net assets, general economic conditions, the market prices of comparable companies, the market price and earnings ratio, management and policies, revenues for various contingencies, tax liabilities, future earnings, and the permanency of the business.

The law requires procedures to determine a fair price for the stock of the dissenting shareholders. One method for determining this fair price is known as the *weighted average method*. This method assigns a particular weight to the elements of value: assets, market price, and earnings. The results are added to determine the value per share, as illustrated by the following case.

CASE

Hedahl's-QB&R, Inc., was a closely held corporation. The owners of a majority of the stock voted to merge the corporation with another corporation. Brown, a minority stockholder, dissented. The statute provides that a dissenting shareholder who objects to a merger is entitled to be paid the "fair value" of his shares on the date preceding the vote. Brown contended that the stock was worth $322 per share, but the corporation took the position that it was worth only $100 per share. The lower court found that the fair value was $230 per share.

ISSUE: Was the lower court's determination of the fair value of the stock correct?

DECISION: No. (The fair value of the stock was $138.65 per share.)

REASONS:
1. There are three methods used by the court in determining the fair value of shares of dissenting shareholders: (a) the market value method, (b) the asset value method, and (c) the investment or earnings value method.
2. Although there was no established market for the stock, the average sale price over four years was $69 per share.
3. The fair market value of all assets minus all liabilities gave an asset value of $242.81 per share.
4. The earnings value or investment value method produced a value of zero, because the corporation had lost money for several years.
5. The court assigned weights to each system and computed the value.

Brown v. Hedahl's-QB&R, Inc., 185 N.W.2d 249 (N.D. 1971).

There is no rule of thumb for the weight to be given any factor. Moreover, the weighted average method is not exclusive, and many courts today believe it is outmoded. Other techniques that are acceptable in the financial community, such as discounted cash flow analysis and comparisons with other tender offers, may be used. All relevant factors are considered in determining a fair price; fair value cannot be computed according to any precise mathematical formula. If the stock is regularly traded in an exchange, market value may be the dominant factor.

The laws relating to dissenting shareholders petitioning for appraisal and the right to be paid the fair values of their stock apply to a cash-for-stock merger as well as a stock-for-stock merger. Also, a shareholder who dissents from a sale or exchange of all or substantially all the assets or property of the corporation, other than in the usual course of business, has the same right to be paid for his stock. When the statutory procedures are followed, the dissenting shareholder ceases to be a shareholder when notice is given; he then becomes a creditor.

Tender offers create problems in valuing the stock of dissenting shareholders. Such offers usually include a premium, in order to overcome objections of many shareholders; but dissenting shareholders who refuse a tender offer and insist on a judicial determination of the fair value of shares are not entitled to receive the tender offer premium. A premerger tender offer price does not establish a floor on the amount that the court may fix as the value of shares in an appraisal proceeding, but it does have some evidentiary significance.

12. Liability of Successors

In the case of a merger or a consolidation of corporations, the changed entity ordinarily remains liable for prior debts; a business cannot shrug off personal liability to its creditors simply by merging, consolidating, switching from the partnership to the corporate form or vice versa, or changing its name. By statute in most states, the surviving corporation is deemed to have assumed all the liabilities and obligations of the absorbed corporation or of the former corporations, as the following case held. These liabilities may even include punitive damages.

CASE

Pickett was employed in a Jacksonville shipyard from 1965 through June 1968, where, as part of his employment as an insulator of ships, he extensively used Philip Carey asbestos cement. Pickett developed severe lung problems, due to the devastating effects on the human body that result from exposure to asbestos. The Picketts sued, on the grounds of negligence and strict liability, several defendants, including the petitioner (Celotex) in its capacity as the corporate successor to Philip Carey. Finding that Philip Carey was negligent in placing "defective" asbestos-containing insulating products on the market that caused Pickett's injuries, the jury awarded compensatory damages of $500,000 to Pickett and $15,000 to his wife. The jury also determined that Philip Carey had acted so as to warrant punitive damages in the amount of $100,000 against Celotex. Celotex appealed the imposition of punitive damages.

ISSUE: May punitive damages be properly assessed against a successor corporation when such damages arise from the actions of an acquired corporation?

DECISION: Yes.

REASONS:

1. Celotex's claim that the imposition of punitive damages here contravenes the purpose of such damages is unpersuasive. Punitive damages are imposed as a punishment of the defendant and as a deterrent to others.
2. Were we to hold that the potential for punitive damages disappears at merger, this may well encourage reckless conduct. Our holding here recognizes that since reckless wrongdoing by the predecessor can result in liability for punitive damages against the successor, acquisition candidates are deterred from such actions. Realization that their companies will sell for less, or not at all, if they engage in reckless behavior provides an incentive for acquisition candidates to conform their behavior to socially acceptable norms.
3. Liability for the reckless misconduct of Philip Carey legally continues to exist within, and under the name of, Celotex.

Celotex Corp. v. Pickett, 490 So.2d 35 (Fla. 1986).

In order to avoid assuming the debts and liabilities of corporations that are being acquired, the acquiring businesses often purchase the assets of a corporation without assuming the liabilities and without any change of organization. The buyer does not become involved with the seller, and there is no merger or consolidation. As a general rule, if one corporation acquires only the assets of another corporation, the acquiring corporation is not liabile for the debts and liabilities of the transferor. An exception exists if the transfer is an attempt to defraud creditors.

This general rule is subject to attack today. Under what circumstances should an acquiring corporation have liability for the debts and the obligations of the business whose assets it acquired? This becomes a difficult question when the assets acquired include the firm name and its product line. The contract of acquisition usually provides for no assumption of liabilities, but should such a provision bind third parties when the selling corporation dissolves as soon as the sale is complete? This issue arises quite frequently in product liability cases. It is not surprising that the courts of different states have answered the liability issue differently in product liability cases. The majority view is to find no liability, but many states take the opposite view. The following case notes the various theories used to impose product liability upon a successor corporation, especially the ''product line'' theory.

CASE

On March 6, 1981, Carolyn Hamaker severed the second, third, fourth, and fifth fingers of her left hand when it became caught in a notcher machine (model 3072) manufactured by Kenwel Machine Company, Inc. (Kenwel).

On December 31, 1975, Kenwel sold its assets to John S. and Rosemary H. Jackson, husband and wife, for the cash sum of $140,000.00. Thereafter, Kenwel ceased business operations, and its corporate existence was terminated eighteen months later in August 1977.

Pursuant to the purchase agreement executed between Kenwel and the Jacksons on January 30, 1976, the Jacksons bought the following assets: machinery, equipment, hand tools, furniture, fixtures, leasehold improvements, patent rights, accounts receivable, inventory, and goodwill. They did not purchase the patent for notcher model 3072. Nor did the Jacksons purchase any corporate stock from Kenwel.

Following the sale, the Jacksons formed Kenwel-Jackson Machine, Inc., which began its corporate existence on February 2, 1976. No officer or director of Kenwel was ever an officer, director, stockholder, or employee of Kenwel-Jackson. Nor was there any transfer of top management personnel from the old to the new corporation.

After her accident, Carolyn Hamaker sued Kenwel-Jackson, seeking damages based on various theories of products liability. The trial court found that Kenwel-Jackson was not liable, and Carolyn Hamaker appealed.

ISSUE: Is Kenwel-Jackson, as the successor corporation, liable for Hamaker's injuries under "continuity of enterprise," "merger," or "product line" theories of strict tort liability?

DECISION: No.

REASONS:

1. The general rule is that a corporation that purchases the assets of another corporation does not succeed to the liabilities of the selling corporation. There are, however, four exceptions to the general rule under which liability may be imposed on a purchasing corporation:
   a. When the purchasing corporation expressly or implicitly agrees to assume the selling corporation's liability;
   b. When the transaction amounts to a consolidation or merger of the purchaser and seller corporations;
   c. When the purchaser corporation is merely a continuation of the seller corporation; or
   d. When the transaction is entered into fraudulently to escape liaiblity for such obligations.
2. There is no language in the contract between these parties to suggest that Kenwel-Jackson impliedly assumed responsibility for future products liability actions against Kenwel. In fact, the purchase agreement expressly conditioned the sale of assets upon Kenwel's promise to discharge or to provide for all of its current or long-term liabilities incurred or unsatisfied as of the date of closing.
3. Kenwel-Jackson's cash purchase of Kenwel's assets does not fall within the "merger" or "continuation" exceptions to the general rule.

4. The fact that Hamaker's accident occurred some six years after the sale disposes of any suggestion that Kenwel-Jackson and its predecessor entered into the transaction fraudulently to escape liability. Accordingly, we hold that Kenwel-Jackson is not liable for Hamaker's injuries under any of the exceptions to the general rule in relation to successor corporate purchasers.
5. Hamaker argues that Kenwel-Jackson is liable for her injuries under the "product line" theory, which was created to ensure that the costs of injuries are borne by the manufacturers that put such products on the market rather than the injured persons, who are powerless to protect themselves.
6. Kenwel-Jackson did not acquire the patent for the model 3072 notcher when it purchased the assets of Kenwel. Kenwel-Jackson never participated in the design, manufacture, distribution, or chain of sale of the model 3072 notcher. Kenwel-Jackson neither invited use of its predecessor's model 3072 notcher, nor represented to the public at large, and Hamaker in particular, that the notcher was safe and suitable for use.

Hamaker v. Kenwel-Jackson Machine, Inc., 387 N.W.2d 515 (S.D. 1986).

13. Antitrust Considerations

Mergers and acquisitions are usually classified as horizontal, market extension, vertical, or conglomerate. A **horizontal merger** combines two businesses in the same field or industry, reducing the number of competitors. A *market extension merger* is an acquisition in which the acquiring company extends its markets. This market extension may be either in new products (product extension) or in new areas (geographical extension). A **vertical merger** brings together two companies, one being the customer of the other. Such a combination usually removes the customer from the market as far as other suppliers are concerned. It may remove a source of supply also if the acquiring company is a customer of the acquired one. A **conglomerate merger** is one in which the businesses involved are neither competitors nor related as customer and supplier in any given line of commerce.

Horizontal merger *Merger of corporations that were competitors prior to the merger.*

Vertical merger *A merger of corporations, one corporation being the supplier of the other.*

Conglomerate merger *Merging of companies that have neither the relationship of competitors nor that of supplier and customer.*

Statutes. The law of mergers is based primarily on three statutes—the Sherman Act, the Bank Merger Act, and the Clayton Act. A horizontal merger violates the Sherman Act if it is a combination in unreasonable restraint of trade or if it results in monopolization of a line of commerce or if it is an attempt to monopolize.

A great deal of merger litigation involves banks. Their mergers are subject to the provisions of the Bank Merger Acts of 1960 and 1966, as well as the usual antitrust laws. Bank mergers are illegal unless approved by one of the agencies that regulate banks. If the merger involves a national bank, the approval of the Comptroller of the Currency is required. If the banks are state banks that are members of the Federal Reserve System, the approval of the Federal Reserve Board is necessary. Other mergers of banks insured by the Federal Deposit Insurance Corporation require approval of that agency.

Clayton act—section 7. Section 7 of the Clayton Act is the major statute in the merger and acquisition area. It was originally adopted in 1914 and later amended by the Celler-Kefauver amendment in 1950. Section 7 of the Clayton Act as amended provides essentially that no business engaged in commerce shall acquire any of the stock or assets of another such business if the effect may be substantially to lessen competition or to tend to create a monopoly in any line of commerce in any section of the country. The phrase "engaged in commerce" as used in Section 7 means engaged in the flow of interstate commerce. It was not intended to reach all businesses engaged in activities that affect commerce. Hence, the phrase does not encompass businesses engaged in intrastate activities substantially affecting interstate commerce, only those that are engaged in interstate commerce. Violations require only a finding and conclusion that a given acquisition has a reasonable probability of lessening competition or tendency toward monopoly. Section 7 does not deal with certainties, only with probabilities. The goal of the law is to arrest incipient anticompetitive effects and trends toward undue concentration of economic power. In determining whether or not a merger or acquisition is illegal, courts examine both the product market and the geographic market affected.

The law has neither adopted nor rejected any particular tests for measuring relevant markets. Both the product market and geographic market of the companies involved are factual issues. The more narrowly the product line or geographic area is defined, the greater the impact of a merger or acquisition on competition. Thus the relevant market frequently determines the probable anti-competitive effects of the merger. A decision that enlarges the line of commerce may be important in establishing that a merger is not anticompetitive.

For a violation of Section 7, courts must also find that within the market the effect of the merger "may be substantially to lessen competition or to tend to create a monopoly." The degree of market concentration prior to the merger and the relative position of the merged parties are important factors to be considered. If there has been a history of tendency toward concentration in an industry, increases in further concentration may be prohibited because of the policy of the law to curb such tendencies before they become harmful. A significant concept in the merger field is the *potential entrant doctrine*. This doctrine finds that the prohibited effect may exist where an acquisition or a merger involves a potential entrant into a market. An acquisition of a competitor by a potential competitor is thus illegal where the effect may be substantially to lessen competition. The potential entrant doctrine has been used to prevent a soap company from acquiring a major bleach company. Since the soap company was a potential entrant into the bleach business, the acquisition was reviewed as anticompetitive. The same doctrine may be used also to stop geographic expansion by mergers and acquisitions. The potential entrant doctrine is applied not only because entry would bring in an additional competitor but also because the mere presence of a potential competitor at the edge of the market has positive effects on those companies actually competing.

Today those responsible for enforcing this law are primarily concerned with horizontal acquisitions. Vertical acquisitions and conglomerate mergers are likely to be challenged only if they involve a highly concentrated industry or monopoly is likely. Many large mergers and acquisitions have been consummated without legal challenge. It seems that every day there are more large mergers proposed and consummated. Although many of these involve billions of dollars, there is very little enforcement of the Clayton Act.

CHAPTER SUMMARY

Voluntary Dissolution

Procedures

1. A corporation with a charter that has not commenced business may be dissolved by its incorporators filing articles of dissolution.
2. A corporation that has commenced business may be dissolved by all of its shareholders.
3. A corporation that has commenced business may be dissolved by its board of directors with the approval of two-thirds of the shareholders.

Notice to Creditors

1. A corporation must give notice to all creditors of its intent to dissolve. The directors are personally liable to creditors to whom notice is not given.

Distributions

1. Corporate assets are first used to pay debts. Any remaining assets are distributed proportionately among the shareholders.
2. If there are insufficient assets to pay debts, a receiver will be appointed, and the dissolution will proceed as if it were involuntary.

Involuntary Dissolutions

Commenced by the State

1. The state may file a ''quo warranto'' proceeding to cancel a corporate charter.
2. Such proceedings are brought to failure of the corporation to comply with the law in such areas as annual reports, franchise taxes, and registered agents.

Commenced by Shareholders

1. Shareholders may petition a court of equity to dissolve a corporation if there is a deadlock in management and irreparable injury is likely.
2. Shareholders may obtain dissolution if the directors are acting illegally, fraudulently, or oppressively.
3. Modern statutes do not allow the majority to freeze out minority shareholders, and dissolution is an appropriate remedy in such cases.
4. Shareholders in closely held corporations have duties similar to partners in a partnership.

Commenced by Creditors

1. Creditors have no right to interfere with the management of a corporation.
2. Creditors may ask for a receiver to be appointed when they have an unsatisfied judgment. If insolvency is established, dissolution is possible.

Procedures

1. Courts of equity have the full range of procedures to protect corporate assets, the creditors, and shareholders.
2. Creditors are required to prove their claims before they share in assets.

Liability of Shareholders

1. Shareholders have no personal liability to creditors unless the stock is not paid for in full or assets have been transferred to them in default of creditors.
2. Claims against the corporation exist for a specified time after dissolution and may be enforced against shareholders receiving corporate assets.

Consolidations, Mergers and Acquisitions

Definitions

1. A consolidation is the uniting of two or more corporations into a newly created one.

2. A merger occurs when one corporation absorbs another, with the latter one being dissolved.

Procedures

1. There are statutory procedures that must be followed. These usually require submission to the shareholders for approval.
2. Each class of shareholders must approve the plan and usually by a two-thirds vote.

Rights of Dissenting Shareholders

1. Minority shareholders who dissent to a merger or consolidation are entitled to be paid the fair value of their stock immediately prior to the change in the corporation. Various methods are in use for determining fair market value.
2. A tender offer does not establish fair market value, but it is evidence of the value.

Liability of Successors

1. In a merger or consolidation, the new corporation is liable for the debts of the old corporation.
2. When one corporation acquires the assets of another, there may be liability in some states, if the facts warrant it.

Antitrust Considerations

1. The Clayton Act provides that a merger or acquisition is illegal if the effect may be to substantially lessen competition or tend to create a monopoly.
2. The law covers mergers between competitors that are known as horizontal mergers, mergers between buyer and seller that are vertical mergers, and mergers where there is no connection between the parties, which are called conglomerate mergers.
3. In judging the legality of a merger, the court examines the product market, the geographic market, and the impact on competiton.

REVIEW QUESTIONS AND PROBLEMS

1. Match each term in column A with the appropriate statement in column B.

A	B
(1) Consolidation	(a) A merger in which the acquired corporation previously competed with its acquirer.
(2) Merger	(b) By what authority.
(3) Horizontal merger	(c) A merger between two firms that have nothing in common.
(4) Vertical merger	(d) One corporation absorbs another.
(5) Conglomerate merger	(e) A technique for valuing the stock of a dissenting shareholder.
(6) Quo warranto	(f) Uniting two corporations into a new third one.
(7) Weighted average method	(g) A merger between a supplier and one of its customers.
(8) Product line	(h) A theory used to extend liability for personal injuries to a successor corporation.

2. What persons must approve a voluntary dissolution of a corporation if business has not been commenced? What persons must approve a voluntary dissolution if the corporation has commenced business activities?

3. Adams, the owner of all capital stock of the Gazette Corporation, a newspaper business, sold all his shares to Burr and promised to serve as adviser to the newspaper for a period of five years in return for an annual salary of $20,000. After three years, Burr petitioned for dissolution, which was obtained. Does Adams have a right to collect the balance of the salary from the corporation? Explain.

4. Pauline, the past president of a dissolved corporation, brought suit against two shareholders of the corporation to recover the amount of her unpaid salary. The state statute provided that the shareholders are personally liable for unpaid salaries and wages of employees and laborers in an amount equal to the value of the stock owned by them. The stockholders contend that the statute is not applicable to the chief executive officer, who had complete control of the corporation. Should Pauline succeed? Why or why not?

5. Bob and David, father and son, entered into an agreement whereby each was 50 percent stockholder of a close corporation operating a luncheonette. The agreement provided that the death of either party would constitute an automatic option to the survivor to purchase, at book value, the shares of stock of the deceased. Upon Bob's death, his daughter Ann (David's sister and administrator of Bob's estate) refused to sell for the value shown on the books. Having created a deadlock in management, Ann then petitioned for dissolution. Should it be granted? Explain.

6. Plaintiff was injured in a laundromat. The laundromat was incorporated and the defendant was its sole shareholder. The corporation was insured under a $100,000 liability policy. Plaintiff obtained a $150,000 judgment against the corporation, on which the insuror paid $100,000. Defendant liquidated the assets of the corporation and as sole shareholder retained the proceeds of the liquidation. This suit is against the defendant individually for the $50,000 of the judgment not covered by the insurance. May a judgment creditor of a dissolved corporation proceed against the sole shareholder for the value of the liquidated assets of the corporation necessary to satisfy the judgment? Why or why not?

7. A father and his two sons formed a corporation to conduct a general contracting business with each owning one-third of the stock. Three years later, one of the sons ceased to be employed by the corporation. There had been a dispute, and the plaintiff had been removed as an officer and director of the corporation. The corporation pays no dividends but invests its profits in real estate. Is the plaintiff entitled to have the corporation dissolved? Why or why not?

8. Majority shareholders of a close corporation award de facto dividends to all shareholders except for two former employees who were also minority shareholders. Is this grounds for a court to order dissolution? Explain.

9. David was president of Music, Inc. He owned 53 percent of the common stock. David received a salary of $10,000 per year and bonuses of $7,000 per year. The corporation had a net worth of $100,000 and sales of $245,000. The net profit of the company had been under $2,000 each year, and dividends were either small or nonexistent. Minority shareholders brought suit to compel dissolution of the corporation on the ground of waste, alleging that the waste occurred in the payment of bonuses to David. Should the company be dissolved? Why or why not?

10. A corporation filed its notice of intent to dissolve with the secretary of state of the state of incorporation. It failed to give notice of dissolution to the local tax collector. Suit was filed six years later against the directors to collect the unpaid corporate property taxes. The law provided that suits against corporations survive for two years after dissolution. With what result? Why?

11. Dissenting shareholders to a merger filed a suit for damages against the merging corporations and their directors. They alleged breach of fiduciary duties, fraud, and conspiracy to violate the securities laws. The defendants moved to dismiss, contending that the only remedy available to the plaintiffs was to be paid the fair value of their shares. What result? Why?

12. The shareholders of a corporation met to vote on a proposed merger. After the vote was taken and the meeting adjourned, a minority shareholder gave written notice of objection to the proposed merger. Are the majority shareholders entitled to obtain the fair cash value for their shares? Why or why not?

13. Von's Grocery, a retail grocery chain doing business in the Los Angeles area, acquired a direct competitor, Shopping Bag Food Store. As a result, Von's became the second largest grocery chain in Los Angeles, with sales of which amounted to 7.5 percent of the market. Before the merger, both companies were rapidly growing, aggressive competitors. The Los Angeles market was characterized by an increasing trend toward concentration through acquisitions and a marked decline in the number of single-store owners. Is the merger illegal under Section 7 of the Clayton Act? Explain.

Introduction to the Law of Property 32

CHAPTER PREVIEW

BUSINESS MANAGEMENT DECISION

You are a commercial loan officer at a local financial institution. You commit to loan $1,000,000 to an investor who plans to buy an apartment complex. In addition to having an interest in the land and the buildings, you want the heating and air-conditioning units, the carpeting, and the appliances to be part of your security.

What should you do to make certain you have the interests as security you desire?

INTRODUCTION

Property *All rights, powers, privileges, and immunities that one has concerning tangibles and intangibles. The term includes everything of value subject to ownership.*

While most people tend to think of **property** as a thing owned or possessed by someone, this is not the way the law thinks of and analyzes property. In the law, property is thought of as "a bundle of rights" that one or more persons may have with respect to a thing. These rights may include the right to physically control the thing (possession); the right to transfer the thing to another by sale, gift, or will; or even the right to destroy it. The *bundle of rights* concept means that property is a series of legal relationships in which some people have rights and all others have duties that are negative in character. For example, each of us has a duty not to interfere with another's use and enjoyment of his property. As you study Part VI of this text, you should always keep the bundle of rights concept in mind.

The concept of property as a bundle of rights is meaningless unless it is associated with people or with legal entities that qualify as persons. Some of the terms frequently used in expressing this association are *ownership*, *title*, and *possession*. The word *owner* usually describes someone who possesses all the rights or interest associated with the thing involved. The word *title* is often used synonymous with *ownership*. *Title* is also used to signify the method by which ownership is acquired, as by a transfer of title. It may also be used to indicate the evidence by which ownership is established—a written instrument called a title, as a car title. Thus the word *title* has a variety of meanings, depending on the context.

The word *possession* is equally difficult to define accurately. Its meaning is also dependent somewhat on the context in which it is used. Possession implies the concept of physical control by a person over property and the personal and mental relationship to it. While it is physically possible to possess a watch or a ring, it is obviously physically impossible to possess 1,000 acres of land in the same manner. Yet the word *possession* as a legal term is used in both instances. Possession describes not only physical control but the power to obtain physical control by legal sanctions, if necessary. In general, the concepts of possession and title should be kept separate and distinct. In other words, having possession of property does not mean the possessor also has title. The reverse is also true—a person who has title to property does not always have possession of that property. For example, a landlord of an apartment building owns (has title to) each unit; the tenants have physical control (possession) of the premises.

Part VI includes materials on a variety of topics related to property. The subsequent chapters concentrate on various transactions involving property; this chapter is concerned with some introductory principles of property. In particular, this chapter discusses the distinction among categories of property, the property status of personal property added to land called fixtures, and the variety of ownership interests that may be held in land.

CLASSIFICATIONS OF PROPERTY

1. Real versus Personal Property

From the standpoint of its physical characteristics, property is classified as either **real property** or **personal property**. When describing property, the adjective *real* refers to land and things attached to the land. Therefore land as part of the earth's surface, buildings, fences, and trees are examples of things classified as *real property*. *Personal property* consists of all other things that are not real property. By definition, all items of property are classified as either real or personal property, although lawyers sometimes refer to *mixed property* to describe such things as real estate leases.

Real property *The legal interests in land and things attached to or growing on land.*

Personal property *The rights, powers, and privileges a person has in things that are not real property.*

2. Real Property

The legal terms *real property* and *real estate* are very similar and frequently confused. In fact, these terms are often used interchangeably. However, there is a technical distinction between real property and real estate. The term *real estate* refers to the physical aspects of land and its attachments. For example, the dirt on the land is real estate, as are any actual improvements, such as buildings, roads, fences, and landscaping. Also included in the definition of real estate are the spaces above and below the land's surface. Included in these spaces are mineral, water, and air rights. Historically, real estate included unlimited subsurface (mineral rights) and air rights. Today, these rights are limited to a reasonable distance. Despite this limitation, these rights still have great value to the landowner. Indeed, interference with mineral and air rights is treated similarly to trespass on the land's surface.

The term *real property* is used to describe the legal rights that a person can have in real estate. For instance, the ownership interest a person may have in land and its improvements is classified as a real property interest. Because the distinction between real property and real estate is a subtle one, the text and cases included in this book use the terms as synonyms.

The three most important areas of the law of real property concern (1) ownership interests, (2) methods of acquiring title, and (3) transactions. The various ownership interests that can be created in land are discussed in this chapter. The next chapter includes a discussion of the methods used to acquire real property. Also important to this discussion is Chapter 35, wills, trusts, and estate planning. Transactions involving leases and bailments are reviewed in Chapter 34.

Tangible *Describes property that is physical in character and capable of being moved.*

3. Personal Property

Personal property may be classified as **tangible** or **intangible.** The term *tangible personal property* includes objects such as goods. The term *intangible personal property* refers to things such as accounts receivable, goodwill, patents, and trade-

Intangible *Something which represents value but has no physical nature.*

marks. Intangible personal property has value, as tangible property has, and each can be transferred.

The term *chattel* is used to describe personal property generally, but chattels may also be classified as chattels real and chattels personal. *Chattels real* describes an interest in land, such as a leasehold; *chattels personal* is applied to movable personal property. When the term *chattel* is used in connection with intangible personal property, the property is referred to as chattels personal in action. A *chattel personal in action*—or *chose in action,* as it is frequently called—is something to which one has a right to possession, but concerning which he may be required to bring some legal action in order ultimately to enjoy possession. A contract right may be said to be a chose in action because a lawsuit may be necessary to obtain the rights under the contract. A negotiable instrument such as a note or check is a common form of chose in action. Although the instrument itself may be said to be property, in reality it is simply evidence of a right to money, and it may be necessary to maintain an action to reduce the money to possession.

In this text, three aspects of personal property are considered most important. First, what happens if an item of personal property becomes permanently attached to real estate? This question is answered in sections 6 through 10 of this chapter dealing with fixtures. Second, how does a person acquire or transfer ownership of personal property? This issue is discussed in Chapter 33. Third, what transactions involving personal property are most important? Chapter 34 concentrates on personal property transactions, especially the legal aspects of bailments.

4. Reasons for Distinguishing between Real and Personal Property

The distinction between real and personal property, significant in a variety of situations, is important in determining the law applicable to a transaction that has contact with more than one state. Such issues are known as *conflict of laws* problems. Chapter 1 may be reviewed for an overview of conflict of laws problems.

Situs *"Place, situation." The place where a thing is located. The situs of land is the state or county where it is located.*

Conflict of laws principles. As a general rule, conflict of laws principles provide that the law of the **situs**—the law of the state where real property is located—determines all legal questions concerning real property. Legal issues concerning conflict of laws relating to personal property are not so easily resolved. Conflict of laws rules may refer to the law of the owner's domicile to resolve some questions and to the law of the state with the most significant contacts with the property to resolve others. The law of the situs of the property is also used to resolve some legal issues. Therefore the description of property as real or personal has a significant impact on the determination of the body of substantive law used to decide legal issues concerning the property.

Inheritance and transfer of property. In most states, real and personal property are handled under different rules of law and procedures when their owner dies. Insofar as inheritance is concerned, however, many modern statutes abolish any distinction between the two. The law as it relates to the passing of property on the death of the owner is discussed in Chapter 35.

During the lifetime of the owner, the distinction between real and personal property is significant, since the methods of transferring them are substantially different. Formal instruments such as deeds are required to transfer an interest in land, whereas few formalities are required in the case of personal property. A bill of sale may be used in selling personal property; but it is not generally required, and it does not, in any event, involve the technicalities of a deed. The transfer of personal property is, as as rule, quite simply accomplished (a motor vehicle transfer may require the delivery of a certificate of title), whereas formality is required to transfer real property.

Taxes. Systems for taxing real estate are different from those for taxing personal property in many states. Property taxes on real estate are significant in every state, while personal property taxes often are less significant. Typical of the issues that may arise are those relating to mobile homes. Is a mobile home that is placed on a foundation real estate and thus subject to real estate taxation, or is it personal property? Similar questions make it apparent that parties to various transactions and courts are frequently called upon to label property as real or personal. If the issue is likely to arise, it should always be covered in agreements.

5. The Doctrine of Equitable Conversion

In contracts for the sale of real estate, there is frequently a substantial time lag between the execution of the contract and its performance. During this period, one or more of the parties may die, the property may be destroyed, or the original parties may enter into other transactions, such as an assignment of the contract. The legal effect of these events and transactions is frequently affected by whether or not the interest of a party is real estate or personal property. In community property states, for example, one spouse may transfer personal property without the other joining in the transfer, whereas if the interest is real estate, the other spouse must join in conveyance.

The interest of a party to a contract involving real estate is not determined by legal title to the property involved. Rather, the interest is determined by equitable principles and a doctrine known as the doctrine of **equitable conversion.** The doctrine of equitable conversion operates on the execution of a contract involving real estate and converts the interest of the seller who has legal title to real property to an interest in personal property, and it converts the interest of the buyer who owes money to an interest in real estate. In other words, after the execution of a contract, the law considers that the seller's interest in the transaction is personal property and that the buyer's interest is real property. This result comes from the concept that equity regards the transaction as being completed.

Equitable conversion *An equitable principle that, for certain purposes, permits real property to be converted into personalty, and vice versa.*

To illustrate the foregoing, assume that your Aunt Agatha, in her will, leaves all her real estate to you and all her personal property to me. Aunt Agatha then enters into a contract to sell her house for $50,000 but dies before receiving the money. Although Aunt Agatha has legal title to the real estate at the time of her death, the doctrine of equitable conversion converts that to personal property, and the $50,000 would be paid to me, not you, under Agatha's will.

FIXTURES

6. What is a Fixture?

The classification of property as real or personal may be very difficult at times, and it may change from time to time. For example, when a dishwasher is purchased at an appliance store, it is clearly personal property. However, what is its status if it is built into your kitchen cabinets? Does this dishwasher remain an item of personal property, or has it become a part of the real estate? The answers to these questions are determined by the *law of fixtures*. A **fixture** is personal property that has become a part of real estate.

Fixture *An item of personal property that has become attached or annexed to real estate. Fixtures generally are treated as part of the real estate.*

To understand better what a fixture is, it is helpful to review the reasons for distinguishing between personal and real property. Also important is being able to know when personal property is likely to have become a fixture. There are three tests, discussed below, that courts have used to determine fixture status. These are often called the intention, annexation, and adaptation tests. As you read the following sections, keep in mind that once personal property becomes a fixture, it is treated as a part of the real estate. The tests are not cumulative and their use depends on the factual situation.

7. Reasons for Determining Fixture Status

The question of whether or not an item is a fixture and thus part of the real estate arises in determining (1) the value of real estate for tax purposes; (2) whether or not a sale of the real estate includes the item of property in question; (3) whether or not the item of property is a part of the security given by a mortgagor of the real estate to a mortgagee; and (4) whether the item belongs to the owner of the building or to the tenant on termination of a lease. Fixture issues also arise under Article 9 of the Uniform Commercial Code in disputes between secured creditors and persons with an interest in the land. The UCC provides that no security interest exists in "goods incorporated into a structure in the manner of lumber, bricks, tile, cement, glass, metal work and the like." A party with a security interest in such goods loses it when the goods are incorporated into the real estate.

If property is a fixture, (1) it is included in the value of real estate for tax purposes; (2) it is sold, and title passes with the real estate; (3) it is a part of the security covered by a mortgage; and (4) it belongs to the landlord owner, not to the tenant on termination of a lease.

8. Annexation Test

The degree of attachment of personal property to the real estate is the essence of the annexation test. Furthermore, whether the article can be removed without material injury to the article, building, and land are important considerations in determining whether the article is a fixture.

The common law required the chattel to be "let into" or "united" to the land. The test of annexation alone is inadequate, for many things attached to the soil or buildings are not fixtures, and many things not physically attached to the soil or buildings are considered fixtures. Articles of furniture substantially fastened but easily removed are not necessarily fixtures. Physical annexation may be only for the purpose of more convenient use. On the other hand, machinery that has been annexed but detached for repairs or other temporary reasons may still be considered a fixture, although severed.

Doors, windows, screens, storm windows, and the like, although readily detachable, are generally considered fixtures because they are an integral part of the building and pertain to its function. Electric ranges connected to a building by a plug or vent pipe generally are not fixtures, but the removal of wainscoting, wood siding, fireplace mantels, and water systems would cause a material injury to the building and land; therefore these items usually are fixtures.

9. Adaptation Test

Because the annexation test alone is inadequate to determine what is a fixture, the adaptation test has been developed. Adaptation means that the article is used in promoting the purpose for which the land is used. Thus, if an article is placed upon, or annexed to, land to improve it, make it more valuable, and extend its use, it is a fixture. Pipes, pumps, and electric motors for an irrigation system are chattels that may be adapted to become fixtures. This test alone is not adequate, because rarely is an article attached or placed upon land except to advance the purpose for which the land is to be used.

10. Intention Test

Because of the inherent weaknesses with the annexation and adaptation tests, it is always best for parties to specify their intentions concerning the issue of fixtures. However, when the parties' intent is not clear, in addition to annexation and adaptation, the following situations and circumstances may be useful in determining the parties' intent: (1) the kind and character of the article affixed; (2) the purpose and use for which the annexation has been made; and (3) the relation and situation of the parties making the annexation. The relation of landlord and tenant suggests that items such as showcases, acquired and used by the tenant, are not intended to become permanently part of the real property. Such property, called **trade fixtures,** is an exception to the general rule of fixtures because they are generally intended to be removed by the tenant at the end of the lease. Trade fixtures continue to be classified as personal property.

Trade fixtures *Personal property placed upon or annexed to real estate leased by a tenant for the purpose of carrying on a trade or business. The tenant generally is allowed to remove this property at the end of the lease.*

The most important factor to consider in determining whether personal property has become a fixture is the intent of the parties. In other words, as between a buyer and seller of real estate, those parties may clearly state in their contract that an attached ceiling fan will be removed by the seller. Likewise, mortgage documents, security agreements, and leases should all be written in a way to indicate whether the parties intend the property to be treated as personal property or as a fixture. If the parties neglect to state their intentions, courts have turned to the annexation and adaptation tests as a way to predict what the parties' intent really was. However, when the parties' intent is clear, courts have used this factor as the controlling one in determining fixture status, as occurred in the following case.

CASE

Lawrence and Donna Reeves borrowed money from the Metropolitan Life Insurance Company. To secure this loan, the Reeves signed a mortgage describing their real estate. This mortgage was properly recorded by Metropolitan. The Reeves then contracted with Production Sales to have a grain storage facility constructed on their land. This facility consists of a number of steel structures bolted onto concrete slabs that are partially embedded into the ground, and includes 50 to 60 feet of underground tubing through which air is electronically pumped in order to move grain from the dryer to either of two storage bins. Most of the structures were transported to the site in a disassembled state, assembled with numerous bolts (over 1,000 of them in each of the two storage bins), lifted into the air, and then placed and bolted onto the slabs. Disassembly and removal of the steel structures would require a period of over two weeks. This facility cost $171,185.30. Production Sales financed this facility and filed an Article 9—secured transactions—financing statement.

The contract of sale between Production Sales and the Reeves stated that the facility would not become part of the Reeves' real estate until full payment had been made. After paying only $16,137.77, the Reeves defaulted. When Production Sales began to remove the facility, Metropolitan, as the real estate mortgagee, filed suit to have the parties' rights determined.

ISSUE: Did the grain storage facility become a part of the real estate so that Metropolitan's mortgage has priority over Production Sales' security interest?

DECISION: No.

REASONS:

1. If the facility is a fixture, the interest of Production Sales is subordinate to the liens of the mortgagee; if it is not a fixture, the interest of Production Sales never becomes subject to the mortgage and thus is free of the lien created by the mortgage.
2. Three factors determine whether an article, or combination of articles, is a fixture: (1) whether the article or articles are actually annexed to the reality, or something appurtenant thereto; (2) whether the article or articles have been appropriated to the use or purpose of that part of the realty with which it is or they are connected; and (3) whether the party making the annexation intended to make the article or articles a permanent accession to the freehold.
3. The third factor, the intention of the annexing party to make the article or articles a permanent accession to the realty, is the factor that is typically given the most weight. Courts generally will uphold the characterization put on the property by the parties to a purchase contract.
4. Therefore the provision of the purchase agreement, that the facility not become a part of the realty until after full payment, is to be enforced. Since full payment had not been made, the facility did not become a fixture, and Production Sales has priority to remove the facility.

Metropolitan Life Insurance Co. v. Reeves, 389 N.W.2d 295 (Neb. 1986).

REAL PROPERTY OWNERSHIP INTERESTS

11. Bundle of Rights

We have emphasized that property interests are best defined as the bundle of rights a person has in a thing. Property is an object or a thing over which someone exercises legal rights.

Defining property interests as a bundle of rights enables courts and the law to develop a variety of such interests in property. A person may possess all of the bundle of rights in relation to a thing, in which case he is the only owner. On the other hand, the bundle of rights may be divided among several people, in which case there is multiple ownership of the rights. For example, the owner of a tract of land may authorize the local public utility companies to install power and telephone lines through his land. The utility companies are granted what is called an *easement*, which is a property right. As a result, the owner has less than the full bundle of rights, and the rights of others result in what is known as an **encumbrance.**

Encumbrance *A burden on the title to land. A mortgage or other lien is an encumbrance upon the title.*

Furthermore, this bundle of rights concept allows owners of real property to create a variety of ownership interests. In essence, the type of real property ownership interest is determined by the rights of an owner to possess, use, and transfer the land. In order to understand the possible variations of ownership interests, keep in mind that the complete bundle of rights must be accounted for at all times. In the case of multiple ownership, the rights of each will vary depending on the type of multiple ownership. Multiple ownership is discussed in detail in Chapter 35.

12. Fee Simple Estates

When used in connection with land, the legal term *estate* is synonymous with ownership interests. *Fee simple estates* are those interests classified as either absolute or qualified present interests. *Present interests* are those that allow the owner to possess the land now. In the alternative, the owner of a present interest may transfer the right of possession to another party. A **fee simple absolute** is the most complete ownership interest possible. It contains the largest bundle of rights of any estate in land. The fee simple absolute is the interest usually received by the grantee in a real estate sales transaction. The language used to create this unlimited interest does not contain words of limitation. A fee simple interest that may be defeated in the future by the occurrence or nonoccurrence of a stated event or condition is called a *qualified* or *conditional fee simple*.

Fee simple absolute *The most complete interest a person may have in land. Such an estate is not qualified by any other interest, and it passes upon the death of the owners to the heirs, free from any conditions. It includes the entire bundle of rights.*

The possible variations of these fee simple estates are complex and beyond the scope of this text. It is sufficient for you to keep two points in mind about qualified fee simple estates. First, these interests do not contain the complete bundle of rights that exists with every piece of land. Therefore there is a future ownership interest that may become possessory, causing the holder of this future interest to gain superior title relative to the owner of the qualified fee simple interest. Second, these qualified interests usually are less valuable when compared with a fee simple absolute interest. Thus you should always be aware of the ownership interest involved in a real estate transaction. Generally you would not be willing to pay as much for a qualified fee simple as you would for a fee simple absolute interest. A gift of land "to my grandson as long as he remains married" is an example of a qualified or conditional fee simple interest.

13. Life Estates

One of the most widely used ownership interests in estate planning is the **life estate.** When properly used, the life estate enables landowners to provide for those they desire while reducing both income and estate taxes. The life estate interest may be

Life estate *An interest in real property that lasts only as long as a designated person lives.*

created either by will or by deed. A life estate may be for the life of the grantee, or it may be created for the duration of the life of some other designated person. It may be conditional upon the happening of an event, such as the marriage of the life tenant. A husband may convey property to his wife for life or until she remarries. Unless the instrument that creates the life estate places limitations upon it, the interest can be sold or mortgaged like any other interest in real estate. The buyer or mortgagee must, of course, take into consideration the fact that the life estate may be terminated at any time by the death of the person for whose life it was created.

The life tenant is obligated to use reasonable care to maintain the property in the condition in which it was received, ordinary wear and tear excepted. There is a duty to repair, to pay taxes, and, out of the income received, to pay interest on any mortgage that may have been outstanding at the time the life estate was created. The life tenant has no right to **waste** the property or to do anything that tends to deplete the value of the property. A life tenant would have no right to drill for oil, mine coal, or cut timber from the land, unless those operations were being conducted at the time the life estate was created. If the extraction of minerals is begun by a life tenant, the proceeds are put into a trust. The income of the trust is paid to the life tenant, and upon the death of the life tenant, the principal of the trust estate is paid to the person who has the future interest that follows the life estate. Likewise, a life tenant has no duty to make lasting improvements to the property. If such improvements are made, the holder of the future interest cannot be required to contribute to their cost.

Waste *Damage to the real property, so that its value as security is impaired.*

14. Remainders and Reversions

Because a life estate represents less than the complete bundle of rights, there must be a future interest accompanying every life estate. After the termination of a life estate, the remaining estate may be given to someone else, or it may go back to the original owner or to his heirs. If the estate is to be given to someone else upon the termination of a life estate, it is called an *estate in remainder*. If it is to go back to the original owner, it is called a *reversion*. When a reversion exists and the original owner of that interest is dead, the property reverts to the heirs of that original owner. Regardless of whether a remainder or a reversion follows a life estate, these future interests may be sold, mortgaged, or otherwise transferred as if they were any other real property interest. This right to transfer these interests exists even before the life estate ends and the remainder or reversion becomes present possessory interests. Upon the death of the life tenant, the remainder or reversion generally converts into a fee simple absolute interest once again.

Since the owners of remainders and reversions have a valuable real property interest, they have the right to enforce the life tenant's duty not to waste the land's value. The timing for filing a suit to recover damages for or to enjoin waste depends on the type of waste occurring. For example, the holder of a life estate may actively destroy an improvement on the real estate or it may only be passive—the neglect of an improvement, allowing it to deteriorate. In general, the statute of limitations for filing an action against waste begins to run when active waste occurs and when the life tenant dies if the passive type of waste has occurred. The following case makes this distinction and discusses the relationship between a life tenant and the remainderman.

CASE

At her husband's death in 1962, Ada Brannan was given a life estate in some farmland that contained a house. The remainder interests were left to Dorothy Moore and Kent Reinhardt. Ada lived in or rented the farmhouse until 1965. From then until her death in 1976, the house was unoccupied, and as a result, it slowly deteriorated. Due to poor family relationships, the remaindermen were estranged from Ada. Although they checked on the house from time to time, the remaindermen took no official action to stop the ongoing waste. However, Dorothy (Ada's daughter) did mention to her mother many times the need to fix up the farmhouse. At Ada's death, Dorothy and Kent filed a claim against Ada's estate for $16,159, the amount of damage done to the house during the life estate. The representative of Ada's estate did not deny that waste had occurred. Instead, she asserted the defense that the remaindermen were barred from filing a claim since they unreasonably delayed taking action to prevent Ada's waste.

ISSUE: Under these circumstances, was the remaindermen's suit for damages timely filed?

DECISION: Yes. An award of $10,433 was affirmed.

REASONS:

1. It is the duty of a life tenant to keep property subject to the life estate in repair so as to preserve the property and to prevent decay or waste.
2. Waste may be either voluntary or permissive. Voluntary waste consists of the commission of some deliberate destructive act. Permissive waste is the failure of the life tenant to exercise the ordinary care of a prudent person for the preservation and protection of the estate.
3. Although remaindermen do not have to wait until a life tenant dies to sue for waste, the statute of limitations does not commence to run in favor of the tenant until the life estate ends when the remainderman's action is based on permissive waste and the injury is continuing in its nature.

Moore v. Phillips, 627 P.2d 831 (Kan. App. 1981).

15. Easements and Licenses

An **easement** is a right granted for the use of real property. The grantor may convey to the grantee a right of way over his land, the right to erect a building that may shut off light or air, the right to lay drain tile under the land, or the right to extend utilities over the land. If these rights of easement are reserved in the deed conveying the property or granted by a separate deed, they pass along with the property to the next grantee and are burdens upon the land. An easement made by special contract is binding only on the immediate parties to the agreement. If a right to use another's land is given orally, it is not an easement but a **license.** The owner of the land may revoke a license at any time unless it has become irrevocable by conduct constituting estoppel. An easement given by grant cannot be revoked except by deed, since such a right of way is considered a right in real property; nor can it be modified without the consent of the owner of the easement.

Easement *An easement is an interest in land—a right that one person has to some profit, benefit, or use in or over the land of another. Such right is created by a deed, or it may be acquired by prescription (the continued use of another's land for a statutory period).*

License (privilege) *A mere personal privilege given by the owner to another to do designated acts upon the land of the owner.*

An owner of land may create an easement for the benefit of another by deed. Usually, a party desiring an easement purchases it from the owner of the *servient land* (the land on which the easement exists). Or a seller of real estate may reserve an easement in his favor when deeding the property to someone else. This situation will occur when a party sells only part of his land and the portion retained requires the easement. Assume that Farmer Brown sells half of his farm to a neighbor. Since the half sold borders on the only road touching the farm, Farmer Brown will need to reserve an easement for ingress and egress. The land retained is often called the *dominant land*, and the land transferred subject to an easement is called the *servient estate*.

Easements may be obtained through adverse use. Such easements are known as *easements by prescription*. These concepts of adverse use or possession are developed more fully in the next chapter. For now, suffice it to say that if a party uses an easement for a long period of time, the owner of the land may not deny the existence of the easement. Easements may also be obtained through judicial proceedings in certain cases. Since the law takes the position that an owner of land should be entitled to access to that land, owners of land that would otherwise be landlocked may be entitled to an *easement by necessity*. Such an easement is, in effect, granted by the owner of the servient land to the owner of the other land by implication. Government bodies and public utilities may obtain easements by condemnation proceedings without the consent of the owner. Of course, the owner of the land is entitled to just compensation in such cases.

Tenancy in common *The most usual method of two or more persons owning property at the same time. None of the formalities or unities required for other specialized forms of co-ownership are essential for this method.*

Joint tenancy *Two or more persons to whom land is deeded in such manner that they have "one and the same interest, accruing by one and the same conveyance, commencing at one and the same time, and held by one and the same undivided possession." Upon the death of one joint tenant, his property passes to the survivor or survivors.*

16. Multiple Ownership

There are three distinct methods by which two or more people may own property at the same time: tenancy in common, joint tenancy, and tenancy by the entirety. The first two types of co-ownership are applicable to every kind of property, real or personal. However, *tenancy by the entirety* is a type of joint tenancy held by spouses in real estate only. Several states have modified the common law characteristics of these forms of ownership, so it is essential that each state's law be consulted for the technicalities of these tenancies.

A basic distinction between a **tenancy in common** and a **joint tenancy** is the effect of death on the tenancy. In the event of the death of a tenant in common, his or her share in the property passes to the executor named in the will or to the administrator of the deceased's estate. If property is held in joint tenancy, the interest of a deceased owner automatically passes to the surviving joint owner. Such property is not subject to probate or to the debts of the deceased joint tenant. Thus joint tenancy with the right of survivorship passes the title of the deceased by operation of law to the survivor or survivors, free of the claims of anyone else except for taxes that may be due. The case following demonstrates the impact of the death of a joint tenant on his creditors.

CASE

On February 1, 1980, the plaintiff, Irvin L. Young Foundation, Inc., obtained a default judgment against the original defendant, Frank K. Damrell, in a Massachusetts state court in the amount of $148,511.19. On November 12, 1982, the plaintiff filed a diversity action in the federal court against Frank Damrell to enforce the Massachusetts judgment. At that time, the court granted an *ex parte* attachment in the amount of $150,000 on a parcel of property situated in the town of Southport. Frank Damrell and his wife, Evelyn Damrell, held title to the property as joint tenants, having acquired it on

August 1, 1953. On August 30, 1983, Frank Damrell died. He was survived by his wife. On January 7, 1985, Evelyn Damrell moved to intervene as a defendant, seeking a discharge of the attachment on the ground that as a result of her husband's death, she held exclusive title to the property. Before her motion was granted, the district court, on May 7, 1985, entered judgment for the plaintiff and against the defendant, Estate of Frank K. Damrell, in the amount of $148,533.49, with interest. Execution of the attachment was stayed on August 9, 1985, when Evelyn Damrell was allowed to join this litigation to assert her claim to the property.

ISSUE: Does an attachment on property survive the death of debtor who owned the property as a joint tenant?

DECISION: No.

REASONS:
1. The general rule is that the lien created by an attachment, like a lien created by a judgment, attaches only to the interest of the debtor joint tenant. When that tenant dies, the lien terminates; it does not continue to encumber the real estate the whole of which becomes vested in the surviving joint tenant. Thus the surviving tenant becomes the sole owner of the property free of any liens that may have existed on the extinguished interest of the deceased.
2. This rule derives from the theory that the "right of survivorship" interest of a joint tenant is an estate in land that vests on creation of the joint tenancy, making a joint tenancy interest with right of survivorship analogous to a life estate. Thus the surviving joint tenant of real property does not take any new or additional interest by virtue of the death of his joint tenant under the laws of descent and distribution, but rather under the original conveyance by which the joint tenancy was created, his interest in the property is merely freed from the participation of the other.
3. It therefore follows that because the death of a joint tenant does not result in a transfer of that tenant's interest to the survivor, but merely terminates any interest the decedent may have had, any liens existing against the deceased joint tenant's interest are likewise extinguished, and the survivor becomes the sole owner of the entire property free from any liens which may have previously existed on the now extinguished interest of the joint tenant debtor.

Irvin L. Young Foundation, Inc. v. Damrell, 511 A.2d 1069 (Me. 1986).

Both joint tenancy and tenancy in common ownership may include two or more persons who may or may not be related. In tenancy in common, the share of the tenants may differ. One may own an undivided two-thirds; the other an undivided one-third. In joint tenancy, the interests must not only be equal, they must be created at the same time. These requirements and other aspects of joint tenancy are discussed in Chapter 35.

Community property *All property acquired after marriage by husband and wife, other than separate property acquired by devise, bequest, or from the proceeds of noncommunity property.*

Eight states—Arizona, California, Idaho, Louisiana, Nevada, New Mexico, Texas, and Washington—have what is known as **community property,** having inherited it in part from their French and Spanish ancestors. In these states, most property acquired after marriage other than by devise, bequest, or from the proceeds of noncommunity property becomes the joint property of husband and wife. Upon the death of one of the parties, title to at least half the community property passes to the survivor. In most of the states, the disposition of the remainder may be by will or under the rules of descent.

17. Condominiums and Cooperatives

A *condominium* is an individually owned apartment, town house, or office in a multiunit structure such as an apartment building or in a complex. As a method of owning and transferring property, it possesses some of the characteristics of individual ownership and some of multiple ownership. In addition to the individual apartment, town house, or office, the owner has an undivided interest in the common areas of the building and land, such as hallways, entrances, yard, recreation, and other public areas. Thus the deed to a condominium covers the housing unit involved and undivided fractional interest in the common areas. Taxes, expenses, and liabilities arising from these common areas usually are divided on a proportional basis, using each owner's fractional interests in the undivided common areas. The following case illustrates the logic of the pro rata allocation.

CASE

J. A. Dutcher owned a condominium apartment in the Eastridge Terrace Condominium complex. This unit was leased to Ted and Christine Owens. Due to a faulty lighting fixture in a common area, a fire occurred, and the Owens lost property valued at $69,150. The Owenses filed suit against Dutcher, the other owners of units within the complex, and the Eastridge Terrace Condominium Association. For procedural reasons only Dutcher was found liable for the Owens' losses. The trial court ruled that Dutcher was liable for only $1,087.04. This figure is based on the total damages proven ($69,150) times the proportional interest Dutcher owned in the common areas (1.572 percent). The appellate court reversed this ruling and held that Dutcher was jointly and severally liable for the Owens's total damages. The Supreme Court granted this review.

ISSUE: Is a condominium owner jointly and severally liable or liable only for a proportional share of the damages created by the complex's common areas?

DECISION: This liability must be calculated on a pro rata basis.

REASONS:

1. In essence, condominium ownership is the merger of two estates in land into one: the fee simple ownership of an apartment or unit in a condominium project and a tenancy in common with other owners in the common elements.
2. The Texas Condominium Act proportionately allocates various financial responsibilities. For example, the act provides for pro rata contributions by owners toward expenses of administration and maintenance, insurance, taxes, and assessments. Pro rata provisions also exist for the application of insurance proceeds.
3. Because of the limited control afforded a unit owner, the liability of a condominium owner is limited to his pro rata interest in the whole, where such liability arises from those areas held in tenancy in common.

Dutcher v. Owens, 647 S.W.2d 948 (Tex. 1983).

Condominiums are of growing importance in commercial offices as well as residential uses. Due to its structural nature, a determination of an owner's full rights and duties requires an understanding of not only the law of property but also the law of business organizations. In a condominium complex there is an organization created to operate the common areas, to make repairs, and to make improvements. This organization usually is a corporation. Each owner of a unit has one vote in an election of a board of directors or governors. This board of the owners' association operates the development subject to the owners' approval.

There is a distinction between a *condominium* and a *cooperative* insofar as the ownership of real estate is concerned. A *cooperative* venture may involve an activity such as a retail store, or it may involve the ownership and operation of a residential development. If a person buys an interest in a cooperative, he is purchasing a share of a not-for-profit corporation. Strictly speaking, the owner of an interest in a cooperative does not own real estate. He owns personal property—his share of the cooperative. The cooperative would pay taxes and upkeep out of the assessments to its members. A condominium contains multiple units for taxing purposes; the cooperative is a single unit. The same may be said for financing. Each owner of a condominium may mortgage his or her own portion. In a cooperative, if there is financing, there will be only one mortgage. In both the condominium and the cooperative there is a special form of business organization to coordinate the operation of the property.

RESTRICTIONS ON OWNERSHIP INTERESTS

18. Introduction

There can be no property rights without a government and a legal system to create and enforce them. Private property rights cannot exist without some method of keeping the bundle of rights for the true owner and for restoring these rights to him if he is deprived of them. It should also be recognized that no one person has a totally unrestricted bundle of rights. To some extent, the law always limits private property rights and the use of private property in order to protect the public's interest.

There are two basic methods of restricting ownership interests in land. First, governing bodies at the federal, state, and local levels may require an owner to sell his land so that it may be utilized for a public purpose. These governing bodies may also regulate the use of land through statutes and ordinances. For example, there are many environmental protection laws designed to control the use of land. Furthermore, zoning regulations are typical of the ordinances intended as land-use controls. Collectively, governmental regulations of an ownership interest are called *public restrictions*.

The second method of restricting ownership interests is that referred to as *private restrictions*. By *private*, we mean that nongovernmental parties limit an owner's use and enjoyment of the land. Examples of private restrictions, discussed in section 21, include easements, licenses, conditions, and covenants. Although these items may be considered to be interests in the hands of those that can enforce them, they are restrictions on the ownership interests on which they exist. They restrict the bundle of rights and create rights in others.

19. Public Restrictions—Eminent Domain

Eminent domain *The right that resides in the United States, state, county, city, or other public body to take private property for public use upon payment of just compensation.*

One of the inherent rights our forefathers recognized was the right of individuals to own property. Indeed, the United States Constitution, in the Fifth Amendment, states that property shall not be taken from any person for a public use without just compensation. This language has been interpreted to be applicable to all levels of government. In essence, the Constitution not only protects the property owner, it also gives the governing body the power to buy private property when two conditions are satisfied. First, the property being acquired must be needed for the public's use and benefit. Second, the property owner must be justly compensated. This constitutional power is known as the power of **eminent domain.** In other words, the government may terminate an owner's interest by acquiring it for a public purpose upon payment of the fair market value.

Without question, the public use requirement is satisfied when land is needed for the construction of a public highway, park, hospital, school, or airport. Indeed, in similar cases, the issue of public use for the condemned land is seldom litigated. However, more recently there has been an expansion of the public use doctrine. For example, the exercise of the eminent domain power has been justified even when the property taken was not actually to be used by the public, as occurred in the following case.

CASE

The Detroit Economic Development Corporation (DEDC) was created with the state's authority by the city of Detroit to provide for the public's general health, safety, and welfare through alleviating unemployment, providing economic assistance to industry, assisting the rehabilitation of blighted areas, and fostering urban redevelopment. DEDC, through its eminent domain powers, planned to purchase a large tract of land. This land was then to be conveyed to General Motors Corporation for a site for construction of an assembly plant. A neighborhood association and individuals filed suit to prevent this taking of private land. They argued that DEDC's action was for the ultimate benefit of private corporation. Therefore, they claimed that the power of eminent domain was not available since the land being acquired was not for a public use.

ISSUE: Can a municipality use the power of eminent domain to condemn property for transfer to a private corporation to build a plant to promote industry and commerce, thereby adding jobs and tax receipts to the economic base of the municipality and state?

DECISION: Yes.

REASONS:

1. The term *public use* has not received a narrow or inelastic definition. Indeed, the meaning of "public use" changes with changing conditions of society. The right of the public to receive and enjoy the benefit of the use determines whether the use is public or private.
2. The city presented substantial evidence of the severe economic conditions facing the residents of Detroit and Michigan, the need for new industrial development to revitalize local industries, the economic boost the proposed project would provide, and the lack of other adequate available sites for this GM plant.

3. The power of eminent domain is to be used in this instance primarily to accomplish the essential public purposes of alleviating unemployment and revitalizing the city's economic base. The benefit to a private corporation is merely incidental.

Poletown Neighborhood Council v. City of Detroit, 304 N.W.2d 455 (Mich. 1981).

Today, the more difficult issue to resolve when property is being condemned is how much is just compensation. Indeed, the question of property's fair market value usually is the basic factual issue to be answered by the court in eminent domain cases. Expert appraisers are called to testify, and the final determination of what is just compensation frequently is left to a jury. With respect to the concept of just compensation, you should realize it is not equal to full compensation. Although some statutes have been adopted by legislatures defining the items a property owner must be paid for, the Constitution does not require that the owner be reimbursed for attorneys' fees, expert witnesses' fees, costs of relocating, or loss of business goodwill.

The Supreme Court has given new vigor to the Fifth Amendment rights of property owners. Previously, the Supreme Court had refused to decide whether a demand for just compensation could be a remedy sought by a landowner claiming to have had his land taken by the application of an excessive land-use regulation. In a 1987 decision, the Supreme Court held that any temporary taking of property requires just compensation. If the state occupies your property for even a short period, it must pay rental. The case involved a church summer camp whose buildings were destroyed by a flood. The state restricted all use of the land because it was in a flood plain. A state court lifted the restriction but denied compensation to the owners for the loss of use prior to the decision. The Supreme Court said the state had to pay for the time the restriction was in effect. Any governmental action that even temporarily denies a landowner use of land is a taking requiring just compensation within the Fifth Amendment.

A second case involved a landowner seeking a building permit. The state conditioned granting the permit on the owner's creating an easement on his land for the public to pass across his property to reach the beach. This condition was held by the Supreme Court to be a taking and unconstitutional without just compensation. If state and local governments attach conditions to building permits that are unrelated to the purpose of the development, the result is a taking for which the government must compensate the landowners. The issuance of building permits cannot be used to achieve unrelated goals. The law recognizes that the government's power to forbid particular land uses under the police power includes the power to condition such uses on some concession by the owner so long as the concession furthers the same governmental purpose advanced to justify prohibiting the use.

20. Public Restrictions—Zoning Regulations

The primary method local governments use to restrict a landowner's interest is the adoption of a *zoning ordinance*. These ordinances typically divide a community into zones and regulate the use of land within each zone. The type and intensity of the land's use in these zones can be classified as open space, residential, commercial, or industrial. Within each classification there can be several categories that further regulate the owner's use of his land. For example, property zoned R-1 might be reserved for single-family residences with lot sizes of not under one-half acre. R-5 could represent that zone wherein multiple-family residences (apartments or condominiums) are permitted.

A community's comprehensive zoning plan also restricts the use of land regarding the density of development allowed. Restrictions on buildings' height and bulk are not uncommon. Height limitations usually restrict the maximum height of buildings in feet or stories. Bulk regulations control the percentage of the lot the building may occupy. Setback and lot size requirements are examples of typical bulk restrictions.

The overall purpose of zoning ordinances is to provide a more aesthetically pleasing environment for all citizens of the community. Few people want their residence located in or near the site of a major industrial facility. Although it is a restriction on ownership interests, properly designed and implemented zoning regulations can enhance property values. Despite these benefits, you should know that there are methods for changing zoning classifications when they become unreasonable. In other words, in most communities the local zoning ordinances are subject to a continuous review process.

21. Private Restrictions—Conditions and Covenants

An ownership interest in land may be restricted by *conditions* or *covenants*. In section 12, qualified fee simple estates are discussed. In essence, these interests are conditioned on the occurrence of a stated event. For example, land may be conveyed by a grantee, Albert, on the condition that he marry before his twenty-fifth birthday. If Albert does not satisfy the condition of marriage, he loses all ownership interest in the property conveyed. In other words, a breach of a stated condition may result in termination of all interests previously held.

Quite often a grantor of land may wish to restrict the use of the land conveyed, but not wish to use the harshness of stated conditions. Restrictive covenants give such a grantor an alternative. These restrictions may be contained in the deed, or they may be made applicable to several tracts of land by attaching them to a plat of a subdivision. A *plat* is a diagram of the lot lines contained in a subdivision. This plat often is recorded in the public records so that reference can be made to it. Where such restrictions are contained in a plat, they are binding on all subsequent purchasers, and they supplement the applicable zoning laws.

The typical restrictions contained in a plat or a deed may provide that the land shall be used exclusively for residential purposes, that the style and cost of the residence must meet certain specifications, and that certain restrictions inserted in the deed are covenants or promises on the part of the grantee to observe them and are said to run with the land. Even though the grantee fails to include them in a subsequent deed made by him, any new owner is nevertheless subject to them. They remain indefinitely as restrictions against the use of the land, although they may not be enforced if conditions change substantially after the inception of the covenants.

Most of these covenants are inserted for the benefit of surrounding property. They may be enforced by surrounding owners, particularly when the owner of a subdivision inserts similar restrictions in each deed or in the plat. The owner of any lot subject to the restrictions is permitted to enforce the restrictions against other lot owners in the same subdivision. Note that in the following case, the court traced the chain of title of both parties to a common land developer. This is sometimes referred to as *vertical privity* in the law of real property.

CASE

Hanna owned four lots in the Browncroft Extension residential neighborhood. He planned to construct duplexes on these lots. Malley, the owner of one lot in this neighborhood, filed suit to enjoin Hanna's construction plans. Malley argued that Hanna's plans, if allowed, would violate a restrictive covenant found in both Hanna's and Malley's chain of title. This restrictive covenant, originally placed in the deeds from the developer to the parties' predecessors in title, stated the following:

> Each lot in the Browncroft tract shall be used for residence purposes only and no double house, Boston flat, or apartment house, shall ever be built upon any lot in said tract.

Hanna asserted that Malley lacked the privity to enforce the restrictive covenant.

ISSUE: Does Malley have the privity required to enforce the restrictive covenant?

DECISION: Yes.

REASONS:

1. In order to establish the privity requisite to enforce a restrictive covenant, a party need only show that his property derives from the original grantor who imposed the covenant and whose property was benefited thereby and that the party to be burdened derives his property from the original grantee who took the property subject to the restrictive covenant. This "vertical privity" arises wherever the party seeking to enforce the covenant has derived his title through a continuous lawful succession from the original grantor.
2. Here, the undisputed facts establish the requisite vertical privity. Plaintiff Malley derives title to his property from Brown Brothers. The latter burdened the property conveyed to defendant's predecessor by subjecting the conveyance to the restrictive covenant in question, and this covenant, in turn, accrued to the benefit of the property retained by Brown Brothers, including that lot ultimately obtained by Malley.
3. The succession of conveyances from Brown Brothers to Malley was continuous and lawful. Nothing in the record indicates otherwise. Likewise, the succession of conveyances to defendant was continuous and lawful, and each transfer was subject to the covenant in question originally imposed by Brown Brothers upon defendant's predecessor in title. Vertical privity requires nothing more.

Malley v. Hanna, 480 N.E.2d 1068 (N.Y. 1985).

Restrictions in a deed, however, are strictly construed against the party seeking to enforce them. Doubts about restrictions are resolved in favor of freedom of the land from servitude, as a matter of public policy.

Occasionally, a covenant is inserted for the personal benefit of the grantor and will not run with the land. If a grantee, as part of the consideration, covenants to repair a dam on land owned by the grantor, the covenant will not run with the land and will not place a duty upon a subsequent grantee. The promise neither touches nor concerns the land; it is only a personal covenant for the benefit of the grantor.

It should be emphasized that covenants and conditions that discriminate on the grounds of race, creed, color, or national origin are unconstitutional as a denial of equal protection of the laws. Such covenants were common at one time, and many are still incorporated in restrictions that accompany plats. When challenged, they have been held to be unconstitutional. They should be considered void.

CHAPTER SUMMARY

Introduction

1. *Ownership* is synonymous with *title*.
2. *Title* means the right or legal interest in a property item.
3. *Possession* represents the physical control a person may exert over property.

Classifications of Property

Real Property

1. The legal interests a person may have in land and things attached to or growing on the land.
2. These interests may include the right to the use and benefit of the land's surface, air space, subsurface area, or any combination of these.

Personal Property

1. The legal interest in all property other than real property.
2. Personal property may be tangible, such as a car or book.
3. Personal property also includes intangible items, such as accounts receivables, goodwill, and rights to enforce contracts.
4. A name for personal property in general is *chattel*.

Reasons for Distinguishing between Real and Personal Property

1. Conflict of laws principles apply differently, depending on the type of property.
2. Real and personal property may be treated differently when the owner dies.
3. Transactions involving real property generally are more formal than personal property transactions.
4. These types of property are treated differently from the standpoint of taxation.

The Doctrine of Equitable Conversion

1. Courts of equity often treat an interest in real estate as personal property, and vice versa.
2. This doctrine is important when there is a lag between making a contract and performing it.

Fixtures

What Is a Fixture?

1. A fixture is an item of personal property that has become part of the land.

Reasons for Determining Fixture Status

1. Fixtures increase the value of real estate.
2. Fixtures generally are included in the sale of real property—personal property can be retained by the seller.
3. Fixtures generally are part of the security given to the creditor taking real property as security. Personal property items are excluded from this security.
4. Fixtures usually remains as the landlord's property at the end of a lease, whereas personal property can often be taken by the tenant.

Tests

1. The annexation test states that the more firmly personal property is attached to real estate, the more likely it is to be a fixture.
2. The adaptation test states that the more the personal property item is used to promote the use and enjoyment of the land, the more likely it is to be a fixture.
3. The intention test, which is the most important, relies on the parties involved to agree whether an item is a fixture or whether it remains as personal property.

Real Property Ownership Interests

Bundle of Rights

1. The rights described by the bundle of rights theory may be held by one person, or they may be divided among two or more people.
2. How these rights are divided determines the ownership interests that may be created. Regardless of how many interests are created, the entire bundle of rights must be accountable with respect to each piece of land.

Fee Simple Estates

1. The basic types of interests presently held by the owner.
2. A fee simple absolute represents the most complete bundle of rights possible.
3. Qualified or conditional fee simple ownership interests may be defeated by the future occurrence of a stated event.

Life Estates

1. The life estate is an important tool in estate planning.
2. This type of ownership interest will terminate upon the death of a designated person.
3. The life tentant has a duty to preserve the value of the real property and not to waste the land's resources or improvements.
4. A life estate must be followed by a future interest known as a remainder or reversion.

Remainders and Reversions

1. A remainder is held by a third party, and a reversion is held by the grantor of the life estate.

Easements and Licenses

1. An easement is the right of one person to use the land owned by another person. Usually an easement is thought of as a permanent restriction that passes from one owner to the next.
2. A license is a less permanent grant of use of land as compared with an easement.

Multiple Ownership

1. Property may be owned by two or more persons as tenants in common, in joint tenancy, or as tenants by the entireties.
2. Tenancy is common in the type of multiple ownership generally most favored by courts. There is no right of survivorship, and the deceased co-owner's interest passes by will or by interstate succession.
3. Since a joint tenant's interest ceases on death, the property is not subject to the debts of a deceased joint tenant.

Condominiums and Cooperatives

1. A condominium is an individually owned apartment or town house in a multiunit complex.
2. In addition to the individual unit, a condominium owner has an undivided interest in the common areas.
3. A person with an interest in a cooperative owns at least one share in a corporation that owns the real property. This personal property interest allows the owner to lease a portion of the real estate.

Restrictions on Ownership Interests

Public Restrictions

1. The power of eminent domain allows a government body to take private property for the public use upon the payment of just compensation.
2. Through its zoning regulations, a local community can restrict the use of land. Typically the zones include open space, residential, commercial, and industrial uses.

Private Restrictions

1. Restrictive covenants are commonly seen in subdivisions. Their purpose is to enhance the value of neighboring property by having all owners agree not to use their land in destructive or unpleasing ways.
2. These covenants must be distinguished from conditions. A breach of a covenant may make the owner liable for damages. However, a breach of a condition usually causes the loss of the ownership interest.

REVIEW QUESTIONS AND PROBLEMS

1. Match each term in column A with the appropriate statement in column B.

A	B
(1) Title	(a) The legal interests a person may have in land and things attached to or growing on the land.
(2) Possession	(b) This power allows the government to take private property for public use upon the payment of just compensation.
(3) Real property	(c) An item of personal property that has become attached to land and is treated as real property.
(4) Chattel	(d) The legal interest in property; synonymous with ownership.
(5) Fixture	(e) The most important method for determining fixture status.
(6) Intention test	(f) Another name for personal property.
(7) Fee simple absolute	(g) The most complete ownership interest in real property.
(8) Remainder	(h) A permanent right of one person to use the land of another person.
(9) Eminent domain	(i) The right to physical control of the use and enjoyment of property.
(10) Easement	(j) The future interest that follows a life estate and is held by a third party.

2. The state of New Jersey sought to tax as real property cranes used in the loading and unloading of ships designed to carry freight in containers. These large cranes were mounted and movable on tracks at the pier. Each crane weighed 1,000,000 pounds and required special concrete piles for the base of the piers. Each crane was 50 feet wide and stood 170 feet above the rail. The boom could be raised to 245 feet. Complex electrical systems were required for operation of the cranes. The cranes were movable by barge. Were the cranes fixtures and thus taxable as part of the real estate? Explain.

3. Turner owned and operated a comprehensive cable TV system that contained about 630 miles of feeder cable. The cable was annexed to telephone poles owned by the telephone company, under a lease that required removal if the telephone company should need the space for its own service needs. The county assessed the TV cable system as real property, contending that the cable is a fixture under common law principles. Should the TV cable be classified as as fixture? Why or why not?

4. Following an oral agreement with Marley, the owner and operator of Marley's Store, The Oil Company installed gasoline pumps and storage tanks. The agreement included a clause that the equipment would remain on the property as long as Marley purchased gasoline solely from The Oil Company. Marley sold the property to Clarence, who decided to purchase gasoline from another source. The Oil Company offered to sell the equipment to Clarence or remove it. Clarence claimed that the equipment was firmly annexed to the property and was a part of the real estate he purchased. Was Clarence correct? Explain.

5. In his will, C. W. Chandler left his entire estate to his wife, Mazelle. His will also stated the following: "I further desire that at her death, my estate go to our son, Mose G. Chandler." The issue arose asking what interest this will actually gave to Mazelle Chandler. A lawsuit to have the will interpreted was filed. What interest is conveyed to Mazelle by the language in C. W. Chandler's will? Explain.

6. A husband willed certain land to his wife for life, with the remainder to their children. After the husband's death, his wife leased the property to a coal company, which strip-mined the land. Is it legal for a holder of a life estate to transfer her interest? Do the children have a good cause of action against the coal company? Why or why not?

7. Harris, by will, devised land to his wife for the duration of her life with the remainder to pass to the Audubon Society to be used as a "wildlife refuge" on her death. On the property there is a commercially operated kennel for cats and dogs that is leased to a third party. This lease produces about \$3,600 a year in rental income for the life tenant. The Department of Health inspected the kennel and ordered improvements to the kennel facility as a condition of license renewal. The cost of these improvements is estimated at \$28,570. Is the remainder interest responsible for paying any of the cost of the improvements? Why or why not?

8. Marguerite sold land to Joe reserving her right of free egress and ingress over the private road. Joe sold the land to Kim, but the deed did not mention that Kim was taking the land subject to the easement contained in the conveyance by Marguerite to Joe. Is the easement effective against Kim? Why or why not?

9. James and Bessie Egan had a life estate in a tract of land, and Melford Egan owned the remainder. An agreement between these parties provided for a fifty-fifty division of the proceeds of any sale of the property. Under a threat of condemnation, these parties signed a contract and a deed to the state of Missouri. On October 5, this contract and deed were placed in escrow to be held until a check for the purchase price was received. On October 25, James and Bessie were killed in an accident. On November 9, the state delivered its check to the escrow agent. A dispute arose concerning who was entitled to the sales proceeds. Was the delivery of the signed deed to an escrow agent on October 5 effective to pass title to the state, so that James and Bessie were entitled to half the proceeds? Why?

10. A school district condemned a parcel of land. On the land there was a propane storage tank that was cradled on concrete piers. The piers were four feet high and were buried approximately six feet beneath the surface of the ground. They were constructed of steel and concrete. Related equipment consisting of an electric motor, pump, and various valves to load and unload propane was welded in place and attached to a concrete foundation and to an electric conduit on the site. The tank and related equipment weigh approximately twelve to fourteen tons. Must the school district pay for the propane tank and its related equipment and foundation? Why or why not?

11. Alan owned land in a subdivision and planned to construct two apartment buildings on the land. Some residents of the subdivision brought suit for an injunction, contending that the construction would violate the covenants contained in the subdivision plat, which restrict buildings to single-family residences. Alan claimed that the covenant was no longer effective because the land had been rezoned for multifamily buildings. Should the restrictive covenant remain enforceable? Why or why not?

12. Terry planned to construct an apartment building on land he owned in a subdivision. The plat of the subdivision contained a restrictive covenant prohibiting use of its land for business purposes. Some residents of the subdivision contended this covenent prohibited Terry's plans. Terry sought a court decision determining the impact of the covenant on his proposal. Should the covenant be interpreted to prevent the construction of an apartment building? Explain.

13. The Hubers purchased two adjoining lots. On one of the lots they started construction of a storage building to store their boats, car, tractor, camper, 32-foot travel-trailer, washer and dryer, rock-cutting equipment, and canned goods. The Declaration of Restrictions stated: ''No lot shall be used for any purpose other than for residential purposes.'' Is the construction of the storage building a violation of the restrictions? Why or why not?

Acquiring Title to Property

33

C H A P T E R   P R E V I E W

BUSINESS MANAGEMENT DECISION

As the property manager employed by a large wood products company, you learn that a business located adjacent to a piece of your company's timberland is using a portion of this land to park vehicles.

Should you be concerned? If so, why? What should you do?

In addition to the general legal principles of property, discussed in Chapter 32, it is important to understand how title to both personal and real property is acquired. The legal requirements for obtaining an ownership interest differ greatly, depending on whether the property involved is personal or real. Therefore this chapter examines the methods of acquiring title to personal property. It then concentrates on both voluntary and involuntary transfers of real property. An understanding of acquiring title to property will allow us to understand transactions involving property.

ACQUIRING TITLE TO PERSONAL PROPERTY

1. Methods

Title to personal property may be acquired through any of the following methods: *original possession*, *transfer*, *accession*, or *confusion*. Original possession is a method of extremely limited applicability. It may be used to obtain title over wild animals and fish or things that are available for appropriation by individuals. Property that is in its native state and over which no one as yet has taken full and complete control belongs to the first person who reduces such property to his exclusive possession. Property once reduced to ownership, but later abandoned, belongs to the first party next taking possession.

In addition to the above, it might be said that property created through mental or physical labor belongs to the creator unless he has agreed to create it for someone else for compensation. Books, inventions, and trademarks would be included under this heading. This kind of property is usually protected by the government through means of copyrights, patents, and trademarks.

2. Title by Transfer—In General

As a general rule, a transferee receives the rights of the transferor, and a transferee takes no better title than the transferor had. If the transferor of the personal property did not have title to the property, the transferee would not have title either, even though the transferee believes that his transferor had a good title. Suppose Pastor Jones purchases a new stereo set for a church from parishioner Tithe. Unknown to Pastor Jones, Tithe had stolen the stereo from the Bulldog Music Store. The stereo set still belongs to Bulldog Music, and the church has no title to it. An innocent purchaser from a thief obtains no title to the property purchased, and no subsequent purchaser stands in any better position. Because the thief had no title or ownership, persons who acquired the property from or through the thief have no title or ownership.

In Chapter 17, section 11, we discuss the concept of a good-faith purchaser of personal property. We emphasize that if the transferor of the property has a voidable title, and he sells property to an innocent purchaser, the transferee may obtain good title to the property. Assume that through fraudulent representations, Fred acquires title to Sam's property. Sam could avoid the transaction with Fred and obtain a return of his property. If Fred sells the property to Ann, and she does not know about his fraudulent representations, Sam cannot disaffirm against Ann. Ann has good title to the property, since she is a good-faith purchaser for value.

Title to personal property may be transferred by sale, gift, will, or operation of law. Since it is probably most relevant in business transactions, the law relating to transfer by sale is discussed in the chapters on Article 2 of the Uniform Commercial Code. Transfers of title by gift is taken up in section 3 of this chapter. Wills and intestate succession are discussed in Chapter 35. Finally, transfer of title to personal property may occur at a judicial sale or lien foreclosures. Chapter 41, on the Article 9 secured party's rights under a security agreement upon default by the debtor, illustrates how the law operates to transfer title to personal property.

3. Transfer by *Inter Vivos* Gift

The phrase ***inter vivos*** refers to gifts made voluntarily during the life of the party transferring title. A testamentary gift is one that is effective only at the owner's death.

Requirements. Generally there are just two people required to accomplish an *inter vivos* gift. The *donor* is the party making the gift. The *donee* is the one receiving or acquiring title to the property. The law requires that three elements be satisfied in order to have a valid *inter vivos* gift. These elements are (1) the donor's intent to make a gift, (2) delivery of possession by the donor, and (3) acceptance of the gift by the donee. From a legal standpoint, the element of *delivery* usually is most important. Unless a contrary intent is clear and obvious, the physical change of possession of personal property creates a presumption that both the donor and donee consent to a gift. However, in the event there is a dispute over the true ownership of personal property, all three elements must be established in order to have a valid gift. Many times disputes concerning gifts arise after the donor dies, as is illustrated by the following case.

CASE

Rayford A. Barham, special administrator (Administrator) of the estate of his mother, Leona C. Barham (Decedent), brought an action to recover certain personal property from Rhena Jones (Jones), the sister of the Decedent, which the Administrator claims belongs to the estate of the Decedent. The Administrator specifically alleged that after his making proper demand, Jones wrongfully retained possession of a set of diamond rings, a house trailer and its contents, $328.98 from the Decedent's bank accounts, and a grandfather clock. The Administrator denies Jones's claim that she owns the property as a result of valid and completed gifts by the Decedent. The trial court found in favor of Jones, and the Administrator appealed.

ISSUE: Did the trial court correctly rule that the disputed items were the property of Jones?

DECISION: Yes, except for the clock.

REASONS:
1. The Decedent, in an emotionally upset state, gave the rings to Jones. Jones returned the rings the next day, telling the Decedent to wear them. The return did not nullify an otherwise valid acceptance of the gift.
2. The Decedent made an *inter vivos* gift of the trailer and contents. She changed title to the name of Jones and her husband. The trailer was registered thereafter in the Jones's name and they obtained the title. Jones had access and use of the trailer before the Decedent's death. The elements of a completed gift are present.
3. Jones was a joint party on bank accounts with the Decedent. She had limited authority to write checks for the Decedent and pay bills after the death. The accounts were joint accounts that were "payable on request to one or more of the two or more parties whether or not mention is made of any right of survivorship." A right of survivorship is presumed on a joint account. Jones qualifies as the surviving party and the legal presumption is controlling.
4. The Decedent intended to give the clock in the future—it was on layaway at the time of death and transfer was not completed. Thus the requirement of delivery for a gift was not fulfilled.

Barham v. Jones, 647 P.2d 397 (N.M. 1982).

The delivery can be actual or constructive or symbolic, if the situation demands. Thus, if the property is in storage, the donor could make a delivery by giving the donee the warehouse receipt. A donor may also accomplish delivery by giving the donee something that is a token representing the donee's dominion and control. A delivery of the keys to an automobile may be a valid symbolic delivery, although a symbolic or constructive delivery will not suffice if actual delivery is reasonably possible.

***Gift* causa mortis** *A gift made in anticipation of death. If the donor survives, the gift is revocable.*

Gift *causa mortis.* In general, an executory promise to make a gift is not enforceable, since the donee typically has not given consideration to support the donor's promise. However, subject to one exception, an executed or completed gift cannot be rescinded by the donor. **Gifts *causa mortis*** constitute this exception to the general rule on the finality of completed gifts. A gift *causa mortis* is in contemplation of death and refers to the situation in which a person who is, or who believes he is, facing death makes a gift on the assumption that death is imminent. A person about to embark on a perilous trip or to undergo a serious operation or one who has an apparently incurable and fatal illness might make a gift and deliver the item to the donee on the assumption that he may soon die. If he returns safely or does not die, the donor is allowed to revoke the gift and recover the property from the donee.

4. Title by Accession

Accession literally means "adding to." In the law of personal property, accession has two basic meanings. First of all, it refers to an owner's right to all that his property produces. The owner of a cow is also the owner of each calf born, and the owner of lumber is the owner of a table made from the lumber by another. *Accession* is also the legal term used to signify the acquisition of title to personal property when it is incorporated into other property or joined with other property.

When accession occurs, who has title is frequently in issue. The general rule is that when the goods of two different owners are united without the willful misconduct of either party, the title to the resulting product goes to the owner of the major portion of the goods. This rule is based on the principle that personal property permanently added to other property and forming a minor portion of the finished product becomes part of the larger unit. Since title can be in only one party, it is in the owner of the major portion. The owner of the minor portion might recover damages if his portion were wrongfully taken from him. The law of accession simply prevents the owner of the minor portion from recovering the property itself.

The law of accession distinguishes between the rights of innocent and willful trespassers, although both are wrongful. An *innocent* trespasser to personal property is one who acts through mistake or conduct that is not intentionally wrongful. A *willful* trespasser cannot obtain title against the original owner under any circumstances because of the wrongful intent.

Suppose that Garrod owns some raw materials, and that Durham inadvertently uses these materials to manufacture a product. The product belongs to Garrod. If Durham also adds some raw materials of his own, the manufactured product belongs to the party who contributed the major portion of the materials. If Durham becomes the owner, Garrod is entitled to recover her damages. If Garrod is the owner, Durham is not entitled to anything, since he used Garrod's materials without authority to do so. If Durham had knowingly used Garrod's raw materials, Durham could not recover the completed product under any circumstances due to his willful misconduct.

In order to make this example an even clearer illustration of the law of accession, suppose that each of the labels on the chart in Figure 33–1 describes actions by Durham. The owner of the finished product is indicated in each box. As you can see, the real distinction occurs when Durham makes a major addition to Garrod's raw materials. It is under these circumstances that the innocent or intentional nature of Durham's trespass becomes most important.

Similar issues arise when unauthorized repairs are made to an owner's personal property and when property subject to an accession is sold. In general, the owner is entitled to goods as repaired, irrespective of the repair's value, unless the parts

	NO ADDITION	MINOR ADDITION	MAJOR ADDITION
INNOCENT WRONGDOER	Garrod	Garrod	Durham
INTENTIONAL WRONGDOER	Garrod	Garrod	Garrod

FIGURE 33–1

added during the repair can be severed without damaging the original goods. If the property that is the subject of accession is sold to a good-faith purchaser, the rights and liabilities of this third party are the same as those of the seller. If the seller is a willful trespasser, he has no title and can convey none. The true owner can recover the property without any liability to the third party. If the innocent third party made improvements or repairs, he has the right to remove his additions if they can be removed without damaging the original goods.

5. Title by Confusion

Property of such a character that one unit may not be distinguished from another unit and that is usually sold by weight or measure is known as *fungible property*. Grain, hay, logs, wine, oil, and similar property are of this nature. When personal property belongs to various parties, it may be mixed by intention, accident, mistake, or wrongful misconduct of an owner of some of the goods. Confusion of fungible property belonging to various owners, assuming that no misconduct (confusion by consent, accident, or mistake) is involved, results in an undivided ownership of the total mass. To illustrate: Grain is stored in a public warehouse by many parties. Each owner holds an undivided interest in the total mass, his particular interest being dependent on the amount stored by him. Should there be a partial destruction of the total mass, the loss would be divided proportionately.

Confusion of goods that results from the wrongful conduct of one of the parties causes the title to the total mass to pass to the innocent party. If the mixture is divisible, an exception exists. The wrongdoer, if he is able to show that the resultant mass is equal in value per unit to that of the innocent party, is able to recover his share. If the new mixture is worth no less per unit than that formerly belonging to the innocent party, the wrongdoer may claim his portion of the new mass by presenting convincing evidence of the amount added by him. If two masses are added together and the wrongdoer can only establish his proportion of one mass, he is only entitled to that proportion of the combined mass.

For example, Farmers Smith and Jones grow corn on adjoining property. Farmer Smith agrees to store Jones's corn in return for 25 percent of the corn stored. Without measuring the amount of corn stored for Jones, Smith adds this corn to a silo containing corn grown by Smith. Since there is no certainty as to how much corn belongs to Jones, a court would probably award him 75 percent of all the corn stored. Smith is limited to a one-fourth interest of even his corn, since he wrongfully commingled a fungible product. This result is necessary in order to ensure that Jones recovers at least his share of the corn.

6. Abandoned, Lost, and Mislaid Property

Abandonment *The giving up dominion and control over property, with the intention to relinquish all claims to it. Losing property is an involuntary act; abandonment is voluntary.*

Property is said to be **abandoned** whenever it is discarded by the true owner who, at that time, has no intention of reclaiming it. The property belongs to the first individual again reducing it to possession.

Property is *lost* whenever, as a result of negligence, accident, or some other cause, it is found at some place other than that chosen by the owner. Title to lost property continues to rest with the true owner. However, until this owner has been ascertained, the finder may keep the property found. The finder's title is good against everyone except the true owner. The rights of the finder are superior to those of the person in charge of the property upon which the lost article is found unless the finder is a trespasser. Occasionally, state statutes provide for newspaper publicity concerning articles that have been found. If the owner cannot be located, the found property or a portion of it reverts to the state or county if the property's value exceeds an established minimum. Otherwise, it goes to the finder.

Property is *mislaid* or *misplaced* if its owner has intentionally placed it at a certain spot, but the manner of placement indicates that he has forgotten to pick it up. The presumption is that he will eventually remember where he left it and return for it. The finder must turn it over to the owner of the premises, who may hold it until the owner is located. The distinctions between abandoned, lost, and mislaid property are subtle and frequently litigated. As the following case illustrates, the factual situations in such cases are amazing and seem more fictional than real.

CASE

Zibton purchased numerous file cabinets from First National Bank of Chicago. Some of the cabinets were locked and some had miscellaneous papers in them. Zibton sold four cabinets to Strayve, who gave one to Michael. Six weeks later, while Michael was moving the cabinet, it fell over, and several of the locked drawers opened, revealing stacks of certificates of deposit, seven of which were unpaid and valid and totaled over $6 million. Six of the CDs were payable to bearer. Michael called the FBI, which took possession of the CDs. Michael sued for a declaratory judgment to determine ownership of the CDs. Michael argued that First National Bank had abandoned any ownership interest in these CDs.

ISSUE: Were the CDs abandoned by the bank?

DECISION: No, they were mislaid.

REASONS:

1. Mislaid property is that which is intentionally put in a certain place and later forgotten; property is lost when it is unintentionally separated from the dominion of its owner; and property is abandoned when the owner, intending to relinquish all rights to the property, leaves it free to be appropriated by any other person.
2. A finder of property acquires no rights in mislaid property, is entitled to possession of lost property against everyone except the true owner, and is entitled to keep abandoned property.
3. Abandonment is generally defined as an intentional relinquishment of a known right. As a general rule, abandonment is not presumed and the party seeking to declare an abandonment must prove the abandoning party intended to do so.
4. The CDs were originally stored in the cabinet marked "Paid Negotiable CDs." When custody of paid CDs was transferred to another bank division, the CDs were to be moved and placed in storage. The CDs were removed and the cabinets randomly checked. Ultimately, the cabinets were sold.
5. It is readily apparent from the evidence that the certificates of deposit were to be transferred to other storage and some simply were overlooked and left in the file cabinets. The relinquishment of possession, under the circumstances here, without a showing of an intention to permanently give up all right to the certificates of deposit is not enough to show an abandonment.

Michael v. First Chicago Corp., 487 N.E.2d 403 (Ill. App. 1985).

ACQUIRING TITLE TO REAL PROPERTY—VOLUNTARY TRANSFERS

7. Introduction

Title to real property may be acquired (1) by original entry, called title by occupancy; (2) by a deed from the owner; (3) by judicial sale; (4) by benefit of the period of the statue of limitations, called adverse possession; (5) by accretion, which may happen when a river, lake, or other body of water creates new land by depositing soil; and (6) by will or descent under intestacy statues (discussed in Chapter 35).

8. Original Entry

Original entry refers to a title obtained from the sovereign. Except in those portions of the United States where the original title to the land was derived from grants that were issued by the king of England and other sovereigns who took possession of the land by conquest, title to all the land in the United States was derived from the United States government. Private individuals who occupied land for the period of time prescribed by federal statue and met other conditions established by law acquired title by patent from the federal government.

Delivery of a valid deed is the most common method of voluntarily transferring real property ownership interests. Sections 9 through 15 examine the essential requirements and types of deeds frequently used. The next part of this chapter discusses some of the ways in which title to land may be lost by the owner involuntarily. These topics include transfers by judicial sales, adverse possession, and accretion.

9. Transfer by Deed—Legal Descriptions

Deed *A written instrument in a special form, signed, sealed, delivered, and used to pass the legal title of real property from one person to another.* (See *Conveyance.*) *In order that the public may know about the title to real property, deeds are recorded in the Deed Record office of the county where the land is situated.*

A **deed** is the legal document that represents the ownership interest in or title to land. Although there are other essential elements of deeds, one of the most important parts of any deed is the legal description of the land involved. By reference to the deed, people must be able to get the information that allows them to determine the exact location of the land described. This description is based on one of the following acceptable systems: (1) the metes and bounds system, (2) the rectangular survey system, or (3) the plat system.

Metes and bounds. The *metes and bounds* system establishes boundary lines by reference to natural or artificial monuments, that is, to fixed points, such as roads, streams, fences, trees. A metes and bonds description starts with a monument, determines the angle of the line and the distance to the next monument, and so forth, until the tract is fully enclosed and described. Because surveyors may not always agree, the law of metes and bounds creates an order of precedence. Reference to monuments controls over courses (angles), and courses control over distances. In general, the least important factor to consider is the amount of acres or area contained in a description.

Rectangular survey. The term *rectangular survey* refers to a system of describing land by using a known baseline and principal meridians. The baseline runs from east to west, and principal meridians run from north to south. Townships are thus

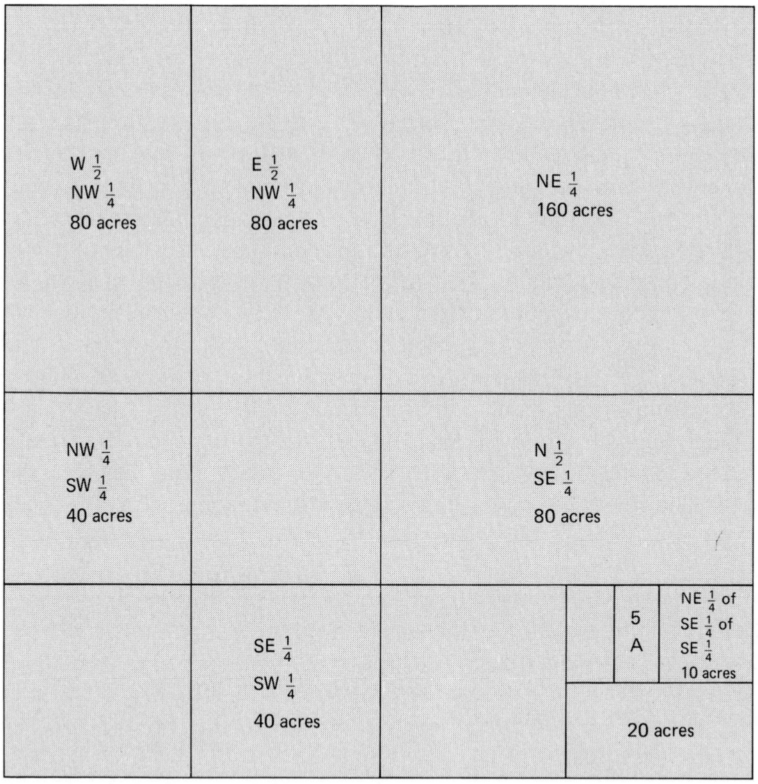

W $\frac{1}{2}$ NW $\frac{1}{4}$ 80 acres
E $\frac{1}{2}$ NW $\frac{1}{4}$ 80 acres
NE $\frac{1}{4}$ 160 acres
NW $\frac{1}{4}$ SW $\frac{1}{4}$ 40 acres
N $\frac{1}{2}$ SE $\frac{1}{4}$ 80 acres
SE $\frac{1}{4}$ SW $\frac{1}{4}$ 40 acres
5 A
NE $\frac{1}{4}$ of SE $\frac{1}{4}$ of SE $\frac{1}{4}$ 10 acres
20 acres

FIGURE 33–2

located in relation to these lines. For example, a township may be described as 7 North, Range 3 East of the third Principal Meridian. This township is seven townships north of the baseline and three east of the third principal meridian. The townships, then, would be divided into 36 sections, each section being one square mile, which consists of 640 acres. Parts of the section are described by their locations within it, as Figure 33–2 illustrates.

Plat. A *plat* is a recorded document dividing a tract described by metes and bounds or rectangular survey into streets, blocks, and lots. The land may thereafter be described in relation to the recorded plat simply by giving the lot number, block, and subdivision name. Lot 8 in Block 7 of Ben Johnson's Subdivision in the City of Emporia, Kansas, might describe real property located in that municipality.

10. Other Essential Requirements of All Deeds

The statutes of the various states provide the necessary form, language, and execution requirements of deeds. For example, these statutes usually require that the parties involved be identified at the beginning of the deed. Often these parties are referred to as the **grantor** and **grantee.** All deeds must contain language that indicates the type of ownership interest being conveyed. Also the deed must state clearly that this interest is being transferred to the grantee. A properly drafted deed needs to

Grantor *A person who executes the deed by which he divests himself of title.*

Grantee *A person to whom a grant is made; one named in a deed to receive title.*

Notary public *A public officer authorized to administer oaths.*

be signed by the grantor and, in some states, sealed, witnessed, or acknowledged in the presence of a **notary public.** Finally, the deed must be delivered.

A deed is not effective until it is delivered—that is, placed entirely out of the control of the grantor. This delivery usually occurs by the handing of the instrument to the grantee or to some third party known as an *escrow agent*. The delivery by the grantor must occur during the lifetime of the grantor. It cannot be delivered by someone else after the grantor's death, even if the grantor has ordered the delivery.

In order that the owner of real estate may notify all persons of the change in title to the property, the statutes of the various states provide that deeds shall be recorded in the recording office of the county in which the land is located. Failure to record a deed by a new owner makes it possible for the former owner to convey and pass good title to the property to an innocent third party, although the former owner has no right to do so and would be liable to his first grantee in such a case.

Although the recording of a deed is necessary to give public notice of a change of ownership, the recording is not necessary to pass title as between the grantor and grantee. The following case illustrates this distinction concerning recording.

CASE

Plaintiff, Yolanda Blakely, bought, developed, improved, and then attempted to sell land. The land in question was leased to defendants, Reider and Delores Kelstrup, rent-free for five years. During the lease period, Blakely assigned her interest in the leased property to the Triple B Trust. The assignment was recorded. Triple B later reassigned the interest to her through a deed, which was not recorded. At the end of the lease period the Kelstrups refused to vacate the premises and Blakely filed a complaint against them under Montana's forceable entry and detainer statutes. The Kelstrups defended, alleging Blakely was not the proper party to bring the action because she was not the real party in interest, due to a lack of record title.

ISSUE: Is Blakely, as owner of the land, the real party in interest despite her failure to record the deed?

DECISION: Yes.

REASONS:

1. The Kelstrups mistake record title with legal title. The two are not synonymous. A property owner can have valid legal title to property without recordation. The rule is an unrecorded deed affecting title to land is valid between the parties.
2. Documents are recorded to alert those persons who might change their position in reliance on the condition of title, specifically subsequent purchasers and mortgages. The Kelstrups are holdover tenants. Their only interest in the property was a rent-free five-year lease. They do not fall within the scope and protection afforded by the recording statutes. Their legal position is not affected whether Blakely or the Triple B holds title to the property. In any event, Blakely holds title because, though unrecorded, she holds a valid deed from Triple B Trust.
3. The Kelstrups' argument that Blakely is not the proper party to bring the action due to the earlier assignment is without merit. The law in Montana for over eighty years has been a plaintiff vested with legal title is the real party in interest.

Blakely v. Kelstrup, 708 P.2d 253 (Mont. 1985).

11. Optional Elements of Deeds

In addition to the essential requirements of all deeds, a deed may contain all, some, or none of the optional elements referred to as *covenants* or *warranties*. These covenants or warranties are promises or guarantees made by the grantor pertaining to the land and the grantor's bundle of rights with respect to it. These covenants may include a promise that (1) at the time of making the deed, the grantor has fee simple title and the right and power to convey it (*covenant of seizin*); (2) the property is free from all encumbrances except those noted in the deed (*covenant against encumbrances*); (3) the grantee and his successors will have the quiet and peaceful enjoyment of the property (*covenant of quiet enjoyment*); and (4) the grantor will defend the title of the grantee if anyone else should claim the property (*covenant of further assurances*).

Many different kinds of deeds are used throughout the United States, the statutes of each state providing for the various types. The common types are the *warranty deed*, the *grant deed*, the *bargain and sale deed*, and the *quitclaim deed*. There are also special types of deeds used when the grantor holds a special legal position at the time of conveyance. Special deeds are used by the executors and administrators of estates, by guardians, and by sheriffs or other court officials executing deeds in their official capacity. The major distinction among types of deeds relates to the covenants or warranties the grantor of the deed makes to the grantee. A deed may contain several warranties or none at all, depending on the type of deed and the language used.

12. Warranty Deed

From the grantee's perspective, the *warranty deed* provides the broadest protection that the grantor is conveying clear title to the land described in the deed. This protection is provided because the warranty deed contains all four of the covenants mentioned above. Therefore the warranty deed is the type of deed grantees usually insist upon in traditional real estate sales transactions.

The covenant of seizin is breached when the grantor's title is inferior to another person's ownership interest. The warranty against encumbrances is the one that is most likely to be breached. All real estate is encumbered at least to the extent of taxes that are a lien. Moreover, unsatisfied judgments against the owners constitute an encumbrance in most states, as do both visible and recorded easements. In fact, there is a breach of warranty even if the grantee has knowledge of the encumbrance and it is not an exception in the deed. As the following case demonstrates, the deed must be carefully prepared and must except all encumbrances or there will be liability for breach of warranty.

CASE

Lockhart agreed to purchase a parcel of real property located in Phenix City from Phenix City Investment Company. On February 2, 1981, a warranty deed conveying title to the property was executed by Phenix City Investment Company to Lockhart. This deed contained the following covenants of warranty:

> And, we do for ourselves and for our heirs, executors, administrators and assigns, covenant with the said Grantee, his heirs and assigns, that we are lawfully seized

in fee simple of said premises; that they are free from all encumbrances, unless otherwise noted above; that we have a good right to sell and convey the same as aforesaid; that we will and our heirs, executors, administrators, and assigns, shall warrant and defend the same to the said Grantee, his heirs and assigns, forever, against the lawful claims of all persons.

At the same time, Lockhart signed a note payable to Phenix City Investment Company in the principal amount of $18,000, payable in monthly installments. As security for this note, he executed a purchase money mortgage on the real property. This statement appeared on the mortgage: "This is a second mortgage subject to the first mortgage executed to the American Federal Savings and Loan Association of Columbus, Georgia."

Later, Lockhart learned that he would have to pay $16,000 to satisfy the first mortgage held by American Federal Savings and Loan. Lockhart sued Phenix City Investment Company for breach of its covenant against encumbrances. Phenix City argued that since Lockhart had knowledge of the first mortgage, no express exception of this encumbrance had to be noted in the warranty deed.

ISSUE: Does a covenant against encumbrance protect the grantee against an encumbrance the grantee knew or should have known about?

DECISION: Yes.

REASONS:
1. Although Lockhart was given notice of the prior encumbrance when he signed his mortgage, such notice is not sufficient to overcome the covenant in the deed which warranted that there were no encumbrances on the property.
2. A covenant of freedom from encumbrances, like a covenant of seizin and good right to convey, is broken as soon as made if there is an outstanding prior encumbrance diminishing the value of the property conveyed; and knowledge of the encumbrance at the time of the covenant does not bar the right of the covenantee, because such covenants are taken as indemnity against known, as well as unknown, encumbrances.

Lockhart v. Phenix City Investment Co., 488 So.2d 1353 (Ala. 1986).

Whether public restrictions on ownership interests, such as zoning ordinances, constitute an encumbrance has created some controversy. In general, the mere existence of a public restriction on the use of real estate does not constitute an encumbrance. However, an existing violation of a public restriction is an encumbrance within the meaning of the covenant against encumbrances.

The lawyer drafting a deed must ascertain which encumbrances actually exist and except them in the deed. A typical deed might provide that the conveyance is "subject to accrued general taxes, visible easements, and easements and restrictions of record." If there is an outstanding mortgage, it would also be included as an exception to the warranty against encumbrances. The warranty of quiet enjoyment and the covenant of further assurances are promises by the grantor to defend the title in legal proceedings if someone else claims it. Such defense includes paying court costs and attorneys' fees.

13. Grant Deed

In some states (California being one) a deed known as a grant deed is in more common use than is the warranty deed. In a *grant deed,* the grantor covenants that no interest in the property has been conveyed to another party, that the property has not been encumbered except as noted, and that any title to the property the grantor might receive in the future will be transferred to the grantee. A grantor under a grant deed has liability only as a result of encumbrances or claims that arose while the property was owned by the grantor. A grant deed does not protect the grantee against encumbrances that existed prior to the grantor taking title. As a result, the grant deed is much narrower than the warranty deed in the promises made to the grantee.

14. Bargain and Sale Deed

A *bargain and sale deed* warrants that the grantor has title to the property and the right to convey, but it does not contain any express covenants as to the title's validity. This deed also is sometimes called a *warranty deed without covenants.* The bargain and sale deed simply states that the grantor "does hereby grant, bargain, sell, and convey" his interest in the real property to the grantee. In states that authorize a bargain and sale deed, a grantee who desires the covenants and warranties of a warranty deed must require that the sales contract state that a warranty deed will be delivered by the grantor. If the sales contract is silent about the type of deed, the grantor is obligated only to sign and deliver a bargain and sale deed.

15. Quitclaim Deed

A grantor who does not wish to make warranties with respect to the title may execute a **quitclaim** deed, merely transferring all the "right, title, and interest" of the grantor to the grantee. Whatever title the grantor has, the grantee receives, but the grantor makes no warranties. A quitclaim deed is used when the interest of the grantor is not clear; for example, where a deed will clear a defective title. It is also used to eliminate possible conflicting interests or when, in fact, there may be no interest in the grantor.

Quitclaim *A deed that transfers all rights or interests in land but does not include any covenants of warranty. The grantor transfers only that which he has.*

The grantee who takes property under a quitclaim deed must understand that he may be receiving nothing at all. A person could give a quitclaim deed to the Brooklyn Bridge to anyone willing to pay for it. The grantee obviously is not given anything at all by such a deed. The grantor simply conveyed all of his interest in the bridge, without assurances that any rights of ownership did, in fact, exist. To transfer all of a person's rights in someone else's property is to transfer nothing at all.

The amount of protection each deed gives to the grantee is the most important distinction to remember. The order in which these types of deeds is discussed is also the order of the amount of protection provided. The warranty deed contains the greatest protection for the grantee. The grant deed protects the grantee from encumbrances placed on the land's title by the grantor but not by others. The bargain and sale deed simply states that the grantor has the right to convey the title involved, but all other covenants and warranties are missing. Finally, the grantor who gives a quitclaim deed does not even promise that he has any rights in the land at all.

16. Escrow Arrangements

As previously noted, a deed to be effective must be delivered in the lifetime of the grantor. This delivery may be to the grantee or to some third party to hold and later deliver to the grantee. Such a party is known as an escrow agent or escrowee.

Escrow An agreement under which a grantor places the deed with a third person called escrow agent. The performance of a condition or the happening of an event stated in the agreement permits the escrow holder to make delivery to the grantee.

An **escrow** provision is desirable because it is always possible for the grantor to die or otherwise become incapacitated between the time of executing the contract and the date of delivery of possession and final payment. Therefore the deed should be executed concurrently with the contract. The deed is then delivered to a third person known as the *escrowee* or *escrow agent*, to be delivered to the grantee upon final payment. If the seller-grantor dies in the meantime, the transaction can be closed without delay.

The escrow arrangement also prevents a claim of a creditor or the rights of a new spouse from interfering with the rights of the buyers if the creditor's claim arose or the marriage occurred after a contract was signed but before the closing. The escrow in effect removes title from the seller. In essence, the law presumes at the actual closing that the transfer or title relates back to the time the escrow was established. Although an escrow arrangement may be created as a separate contract, it is often included as part of the sales contract, especially when the time period until closing is long.

ACQUIRING TITLE TO REAL PROPERTY—INVOLUNTARY TRANSFERS

17. Transfer by Judicial Sale

Judicial sale A sale authorized by a court that has jurisdiction to grant such authority. Such sales are conducted by an officer of the court.

Title to land may be acquired by a purchaser at a sale conducted by a sheriff or other proper official and made under the jurisdiction or a court having competent authority to order the sale. In order to raise money to pay a judgment obtained against an owner, a **judicial sale** of that owner's property may be necessary. To collect unpaid taxes, land owned by a delinquent taxpayer is sold at a public *tax sale*. The purchaser at a tax sale acquires a tax title. A mortgage foreclosure sale is a proceeding in equity by which a mortgagee obtains, by judicial sale, money to pay the obligation secured by the mortgage. The word *foreclosure* is also applied to the proceedings for enforcing other types of liens, such as mechanic's liens, assessments against realty to pay public improvements, and other statutory liens. The character of title acquired by a purchaser at a judicial sale is determined by state statute.

18. Title by Adverse Possession

Adverse possession Acquisition of legal title to another's land by being in continuous possession during a period prescribed in the statute.

Although the concepts of title and possession usually are treated as separate and distinct, physical control of land may result in the possessor's acquiring title under the principle known as **adverse possession.** A person who enters into actual possession of land and remains thereon openly and notoriously for the period of time prescribed in the statute of limitations, claiming title in denial of, and adversely to, the superior title of another, will at the end of the statutory period acquire legal title.

The owner's knowledge that his land is occupied adversely is not essential to the claim, but possession must be of a nature that would charge a reasonably diligent legal owner with knowledge of the adverse claim. In other words, the possessor must not try to hide his present use of the land. Indeed, any time the legal owner or anyone else asserts his rights to the land, the possessor must deny his claim and be steadfast in his right to the property's use.

Claim of right. The possessor's claim to be the owner of land must be based on some legal right. Obviously, some mistake leads to the application of the principles of adverse possession. The possessor must be more than a squatter. He must believe that he has a *claim of right* as the true owner of the property. *Color of title* is an expression that refers to a title that has a defect but is otherwise good. A mistake in a deed does not convey clear title but does convey color of title. In many states adverse possession by one with color of title who pays real estate taxes will ripen into title in a much shorter period than is required for adverse possession without color of title. For example, a state with a twenty-year requirement may require only ten years if there is color of title and payment of the taxes. This use of adverse possession is very important in clearing defective titles. Errors can be ignored after the statutory period if there is adverse possession, color of title, and payment of taxes.

Adverse possession may still be one method by which a landowner of a large tract involuntarily ''transfers'' an ownership interest in that tract. However, today the bulk of reported adverse-possession cases deal with boundary disputes involving strips of land just a few feet wide. This factual situation frequently arises when neighbors discover that a fence or hedge has been located on their common boundary for a number of years. As the following case illustrates, sometimes a structure is actually on another's property and title may be obtained by adverse possession.

CASE

Joseph and Helen Naab and Roger and Cynthia Nolan are the owners of contiguous tracts of land in a subdivision of Williamstown, West Virginia. Mr. and Mrs. Naab purchased their property in 1973. At the time of purchase there was both a house and a small concrete garage on the property. The garage had been erected some time prior to 1952 by one of the Naabs' predecessors in title. Immediately following the construction of the garage, a gravel driveway was established leading from the garage to an alley located behind the Naab property.

In 1975, Roger and Cynthia Nolan purchased their lot, which, the following year, they had surveyed. The survey indicated that one corner of the Naabs' garage encroached 1.22 feet onto the Nolans' property and the other corner encroached 0.91 feet over their property line.

In 1979, after notifying the Naabs of the survey, the Nolans requested that their neighbors tear down the garage and discontinue using the driveway. When the Naabs refused, the Nolans erected a 4-foot fence to deny access to the garage and use of the driveway. In 1980, the Nolans placed a detached metal outbuilding further to frustrate their neighbors' use of the driveway and access to the garage.

The Naabs sought judicial determination of their rights regarding the garage and driveway. The Circuit Court of Wood County held that the Naabs acquired title by adverse possession to that portion of the Nolans' lot upon which the garage was built. The Nolans appealed.

ISSUE: Have the Naabs gained title to that portion of the Nolans' land occupied by the garage?

DECISION: Yes.

REASONS:

1. An elementary principle of property law states that the owner of a burdened premise is bound by the actions or inactions of his predecessors in title. The record discloses that the predecessors in title of both the Naabs and the Nolans accepted the erection of the concrete garage and accompanying gravel driveway some time before 1952.
2. One who seeks to assert title to a tract of land under the doctrine of adverse possession must prove each of the following elements for the requisite statutory period: (1) that he has held the tract adversely or hostilely; (2) that the possession has been actual; (3) that it has been open and notorious (sometimes stated in the cases as visible and notorious); (4) that possession has been exclusive; (5) that possession has been continuous; (6) that possession has been under claim of title or color of title.
3. Element one, unquestionably, is present. The survey clearly indicated that the garage occupied a portion of the appellants' lot. Such physical dominion is sufficient to satisfy the first adverse or hostile element. This same fact of exercising physical dominion over a portion of the lot satisfies the second requirement, that the possession be "actual."
4. The third requirement, that possession be open and notorious, requires that the acts asserting dominion over the property "must be of such a quality to put a person of ordinary prudence on notice of the fact that the possessor is claiming the land as his own." Proof of actual knowledge on the part of the true owner is not ordinarily required.
5. The fourth element in proving a successful transfer of title to property by adverse possession does not defeat the sporadic use of the property by others; it only need be the type of possession that would characterize an owner's use. The record does not indicate that anybody but the appellees and their predecessors in title ever used the garage.
6. Possession is continuous when the preponderance of the evidence shows continuous possession by one asserting adverse possession for the statutory period of ten years. It is uncontradicted that the Naabs and their predecessors in title have occupied the garage at least since 1952.
7. The sixth and final requirement for successful assertion of title by adverse possession has also been met. A claim of title is generally nothing more than the possessor entering upon the land with the intent to claim it as his own. The appellees fulfilled this requirement when they proceeded as if they had title to that portion of the Nolans' lot upon which the garage was located. No permission was either asserted or proved.
8. The circuit court, therefore, was correct in finding that the Naabs had acquired title to the land on which their garage sits.

Naab v. Noland, 327 S.E.2d 151 (W. Va. 1985).

Tacking. In our mobile society, it is a fact that residential property typically is transferred every few years. Therefore the issue of how the statutory period of adverse possession is satisfied often arises. The answer to this issue is found in the principle of *tacking*. Tacking allows successive owners to add their time periods of ownership together to satisfy the long statutory period required for adverse possession. In order for tacking to occur, successive owners must claim under the same chain of title. In other words, a buyer may be able to tack to the seller's period of ownership. Likewise, an heir may tack to his ancestor's ownership period.

Although adverse possession does occur among private owners of land, it has been held that a municipal corporation or other governmental body cannot lose its interests in land to one claiming to be the owner, regardless of how long that person has possessed the land. In other words, governmental land cannot be adversely possessed.

19. Title by Accretion

Soil added to land by action of water is an **accretion.** If a shore or bank is extended by gradual addition of sand or mud deposited by water, the extension also is called an *alluvion*. If water recedes and exposes more land, the increase in the shore or bank is a *reliction*.

Accretion *Gradual, imperceptible accumulation of land by natural causes, usually next to a stream or river.*

A sudden deposit of land such as that caused by a flood does not make a change in ownership or boundary lines; but if the change is slow and gradual by alluvion or reliction, the newly formed land belongs to the owner of the bed of the stream in which the new land was formed. If opposite banks of a private stream belong to different persons, it is a general rule that each owns the bed to the middle of the stream; however, title to lands created by accretion may be acquired by adverse possession. In public waters, such as navigable streams, lakes, and the sea, the title of the bed of water, in the absence of special circumstances, is in the United States. Accretion to the land belongs to the **riparian** owner; islands created belong to the government.

Riparian *A person is a riparian owner if his land is situated beside a stream or other body of water, either flowing over or along the border of the land.*

EVIDENCE OF TITLE

20. Abstract of Title

Ownership of real estate is a matter of public record. Every deed, mortgage, judgment, lien, or other transaction that affects the title to real estate must be made a matter of public record in the county in which the real estate is located. Deeds and other documents are usually recorded in the county recorder's office. The records of the probate court furnish the public documents necessary to prove title by will or descent. Divorce proceedings and other judicial proceedings that affect the title to real estate are also part of the public record.

In order to establish title to real estate, it is necessary to examine all the public records that may affect the title. In a few states, lawyers actually examine all the public records to establish the title to real estate. Because it is extremely difficult for an individual or his attorney to examine all the records, in most states businesses have been formed for the express purpose of furnishing the appropriate records for any given parcel of real estate. These *abstract companies* are usually well-established firms that have maintained tract indexes for many years and keep them current on a daily basis. Upon request, an abstract company prepares an abstract of the records that sets forth the history of the parcel in question and all matters that may affect the title. The abstract of title is examined by an attorney, who writes his opinion concerning the title, setting forth any defects in the title as well as encumbrances against it. The abstract of title must be brought up to date each time the property is transferred or proof of title is required, in order that the chain of title will be complete. The opinion on title will be useless unless all court proceedings, such as foreclosures, partitions, transfers by deed, and probate proceedings, are shown. It should be noted that an attorney's opinion on title is just that—an opinion. If the attorney makes a mistake—his opinion states that his client has title to Blackacre when in fact he does not have title to Blackacre—the client does not have title. The client's recourse would be a malpractice suit against the attorney.

21. Title Insurance

Because of limited resources, many lawyers are unable to respond in damages to pay losses caused by their mistakes. Therefore the abstract of title and attorney's opinion as a means of protecting owners are often not satisfactory. There may be title defects that do not appear in the record and that the attorney does not cover in his title opinion. An illegitimate child may be an unknown heir with an interest in property, as may a spouse in a secret marriage. To protect owners against such hidden claims and to offset the limited resources of most lawyers, *title insurance* has developed.

Title insurance is, in effect, an opinion of the title company instead of the lawyer. The opinion of the title company is backed up to the extent of the face value of the title insurance policy. If the purported owner loses his property, he collects the insurance just as if it were life insurance and the insured had died. Title insurance can cover matters beyond those in a title opinion. It has the financial backing of the issuing company, which is financially more secure than any law firm. Modern real estate practice uses title policies rather than abstracts and title opinions. Title insurance companies usually maintain their own tract records, thus eliminating the cost of bringing the abstract up to date. Generally, title insurance companies issue a *title commitment letter* at the seller's request. This commitment becomes the basis of the title insurance policy issued to protect the buyer. Title insurance companies that are negligent in searching a title become liable for the damages such negligence causes, as occurred in the following case.

CASE

Paul Malinak owned 640 acres of land in Montana. During his ownership, St. Regis Paper Company acquired rights to timber on this land. Malinak mistakenly believed these rights expired in 1974. During early 1975, Malinak agreed to sell his land, and he requested a title insurance commitment from Safeco Title Insurance Company. This commitment deleted any mention of possible rights of St. Regis. Although that sale of the land fell through, Malinak sold his land to Lowell Novy in late 1975. Relying on the title commitment previously received, Malinak warranted the title to Novy without timber reservations. Safeco issued a title insurance policy to Novy that also made no mention of St. Regis's timber rights. Shortly after the sales transaction was closed, St. Regis notified Novy of its plans to cut timber. Novy sued Safeco under the title policy. Safeco notified Malinak that it would seek to recover from him if the company was liable to Novy. Malinak argued that Safeco was liable to him for his expenses in defending the title transferred to Novy. Malinak asserted that his warranty of clear title was based on Safeco's title commitment.

ISSUE: Is the seller (Malinak) protected by a title insurance company's (Safeco's) commitment?

DECISION: Yes.

REASONS:

1. Title *insurance* is a contract to indemnify the insured against loss through defects in the insured title or against liens or encumbrances that may affect the insured title at the time the policy is issued.
2. A title *commitment* is in a somewhat different category from the title policy that follows it. Ordinarily, a commitment is ordered by the seller for the purpose of exhibiting it to the buyer as a representation of the quality of the title seller expects to sell to the buyer.
3. It is within the expectations of the parties—the seller ordering the title commitment and the title insurer inspecting the public records—that the title commitment will accurately reflect the insurability of the title, or the condition of the public records, as the case may be, with respect to that title.
4. The failure of the title company to base its commitment on a reasonably diligent search of the public records makes it liable to the seller for negligence.

Malinak v. Safeco Title Insurance Company of Idaho, 661 P.2d 12 (Mont. 1983).

22. Torrens System

Another method used to prove ownership in some localities is known as the *Torrens system*, based on a registered title that can be transferred only upon the official registration records. The original registration of any title usually requires a judicial determination as to the current owner, and then all subsequent transfers merely involve the surrender of the registered title, in much the same way that an automobile title is transferred. The Torrens system is a much simpler system to use after a title has once been registered, but the high cost of obtaining the original registration has prevented it from replacing abstracts and title policies as proof of title in most areas.

CHAPTER SUMMARY

Acquiring Title to Personal Property

Title by Transfer—In general	1. The most common way title to personal property is transferred is by an Article 2 sales transaction (see Chapters 17 and 18).

2. Title to personal property also may be transferred by will at the owner's death (see Chapter 35).
3. Title to personal property also can be transferred as a gift or by operation of law.

Transfer by *Inter Vivos* Gift

1. An *inter vivos* gift is one made voluntarily during the life of the giver.
2. The person making a gift is called a *donor*. The *donee* is the person receiving the gift.
3. In order to have a valid *inter vivos* gift, there must be donative intent, delivery, and acceptance.
4. In general, a promise to make a gift is not enforceable. However, once the gift is made, it generally cannot be revoked. A gift *causa mortis* is an exception to the irrevocability of completed gifts.

Title by Accession

1. Literally means "adding to."
2. This concept governs the acquisition of title to personal property when it is incorporated into or joined with other property.
3. The principles of accession depend on whether the wrongdoer was an innocent or willful trespasser.

Title by Confusion

1. *Fungible property* usually is sold by weight or measure. One unit of this type of property cannot be distinguished from another unit.
2. Confusion or commingling of fungible property may cause title to all or some portion of the property to pass from a wrongdoer to an innocent party.

Abandoned, Lost, and Mislaid Property

1. Abandoned property is discarded by the true owner who has no intent to reclaim it. The first person to take possession of abandoned property is considered the new owner.
2. Lost property is that found in some place other than that chosen by the owner. The person who finds lost property has superior rights to everyone except for the true owner.
3. Mislaid property are those items that the owner has forgotten to pick up. The owner of the real estate on which the mislaid property is discovered holds the property subject to the claims of the true owner.

Acquiring Title to Real Property—Voluntary Transfers

Original Entry

1. Title is obtained from the government by a patent. It seldom occurs today.

Transfer by Deed

1. A deed is the legal document that represents title to land.
2. A valid deed must contain an accurate legal description based on the metes and bounds, the rectangular survey, or the reference to the plats system of describing land's boundaries.

Other Essential Requirements of All Deeds

1. A valid deed must also identify the parties involved, contain language transferring an ownership interest, be signed by the grantor, and be delivered to the grantee in the grantor's lifetime.

Optional Elements of Deeds

1. By including or deleting optional covenants or warranties, various types of deeds can be created.
2. Deeds vary in the amount of protection they give to the grantee. From the most to least protection provided, these deeds include the warranty deed, the grant deed, the bargain and sale deed, and the quitclaim deed.

Escrow Arrangements

1. The escrow may be a part of the sales contract or a separate agreement.
2. This arrangement involves the constructive delivery of a deed from the seller to the buyer.
3. The deed is delivered to a disinterested third party who holds it until closing.
4. The delivery to the buyer relates back to the time of delivery to the escrow. This concept avoids many problems that arise with respect to either party's death or the claims of the seller's creditors.

Acquiring Title to Real Property—Involuntary Transfers

Transfer by Judicial Sale

1. A court with proper jurisdiction may order that real property be sold in order to satisfy the owner's creditors.
2. Examples of judicial sales include tax sales and foreclosures of mortgages, mechanic's liens, assessment for public improvements, and other statutory liens.

Title by Adverse Possession

1. An example of when possession may result in legal title.
2. The essential elements of adverse possession are satisfied if a person possesses land openly, notoriously, hostilely, and continuously for the statutory period under a claim of right.
3. In essence, the record owner is prevented from claiming title if possession has adversely continued for the statutory time period.

Title by Accretion

1. Soil added to land by the action of a body of water.
2. The gradual extension of a shoreline by matter being deposited by water is called *alluvion*.
3. If more land is exposed by the water receding, *reliction* occurs.
4. The gradual increase in land belongs to the owner of the streambed in which the new land was formed.

Evidence of Title

1. The seller typically is required to transfer marketable title.
2. In order to establish the marketability of the seller's title, a lawyer's title opinion letter or a title insurance policy should be obtained.
3. A few states allow a title registration, known as the Torrens system, as an alternative method of showing marketable title.

REVIEW QUESTIONS AND PROBLEMS

1. Match each term in column A with the appropriate statement in Column B.

A	B
(1) *Inter vivos* gift	(a) Discarded by the owner with no intent to reclaim it.
(2) Accession	(b) An example of when possession of real property may result in legal title.
(3) Fungible property	(c) Legal documents that represent title to real property.
(4) Abandoned property	(d) Usually sold by weight or measure. Subject to confusion.
(5) Mislaid property	(e) The deed that assures the grantee of the most protection possible.

(6) Deeds	(f) This concept governs the acquisition of title to personal property when it is incorporated into or joined with other property.
(7) Rectangular survey system	(g) Made voluntarily during the life of the donor.
(8) Warranty deed	(h) Occurs when land is exposed by water receding.
(9) Adverse possession	(i) A method used to describe accurately the boundaries of real estate.
(10) Reliction	(j) Held by the owner of the real estate on which it is found, subject to the true owner's claims.

2. Aunt Bee bought ten lottery tickets, each representing a chance to win an automobile. She wrote her minor niece's name on the back of one of these tickets and mailed it to her niece's mother. The niece was never informed that this ticket was received. At the drawing for the car, the niece's ticket was selected. Aunt Bee claimed the car belonged to her since the niece had not accepted the gift. Is Aunt Bee correct? Explain.

3. Vivian lived with and cared for her uncle, Mr. Evans, throughout the last years of his life. One month before he died, Mr. Evans went to his bank and examined the contents of his safe deposit box. He asked for both keys to this box. Upon arriving home, he gave Vivian one of these keys and told her that the contents belonged to her when he died. The safe deposit box contained stocks, bonds, and other items worth approximately $800,000. Although Vivian had a key, she could not have obtained access to its contents, since the box remained registered in Mr. Evans's name alone. When Mr. Evans died, his heirs claimed the contents of his deposit box. Vivian argued that she was the donee of an *inter vivos* gift of the box's contents. Which element of an *inter vivos* gift is an issue? Make the arguments for each side and indicate the likely outcome of the case.

4. An automobile owned by Perkins was stolen. The thief installed a new engine, and sold the car to a used-car dealer. The dealer, in turn, sold the car to Moseley, who added a sun visor, seat covers, and a gasoline tank. May Perkins reclaim the automobile and keep the items added? Explain.

5. Troop, who is in the oil business, is the sole owner of a well named Gusher. Troop also is in partnership with Wright, and together they have equal interests in Spindletop. These parties have agreed that Troop will store the oil produced by Spindletop and will make monthly reports to Wright. After several months passed without a report, Wright discovered that Troop was storing oil produced from Gusher and Spindletop in the same holding tank. If Troop has not kept accurate records of both wells' production, how much of the stored oil is Wright entitled to, if any? Explain.

6. Bernice rented a safe deposit box from the Old Orchard Bank. In May, while examining the contents of her own box, Bernice discovered $6,325 in cash on a chair that was pushed under an examination table. Bernice turned this money over to the bank, which sent a notice to its safe deposit box customers that property had been discovered in the safety vault. No one responded to this ad, and on July 1, Bernice claimed that she was entitled to this lost money. The bank refused to give her the money since it argued that the money had been mislaid. Bernice filed a suit to recover the cash. Who is entitled to the $6,325? Explain.

7. Edward executed a warranty deed to his home to his daughter, Elizabeth. The deed was placed in his safe deposit box. He told Elizabeth that she would get the house on his death. Elizabeth had a key to the safe deposit box. She removed the deed and had it recorded. Edward brought suit to have the deed declared invalid. What result? Why?

8. Campbell entered into a sales contract to buy real estate from Storer. To complete this transaction, a warranty deed was delivered to Campbell in 1985. Although he received it, Campbell failed to record this deed. In 1990, Storer conveyed by deed the same land to a third person. When he discovered he no longer was the record owner, Campbell sued Storer for damages. Storer defended his second conveyance on the grounds that Campbell's failure to record his deed prevented him from acquiring legal title to the real estate. Did Campbell acquire legal title in 1985? Why or why not?

9. Bryan and Linda contracted to have Pioneer Homes build a house. In return for $52,000, Pioneer Homes deeded a house and lot to them. The deed delivered specifically stated the title conveyed was good, marketable, and free of all encumbrances. Later, Bryan and Linda decided to sell this house and lot. It was then that they discovered their house was only 3.5 feet from the side boundary. This location of the house violated the local minimum side-lot requirement of 15 feet. To resolve this violation, Bryan and Linda purchased a strip of land for $1,500. They then sued Pioneer Homes for breach of the covenant against encumbrances. Did Pioneer Homes breach this covenant? Why or why not?

10. In 1947, J. G. Head's Farms, Inc., conveyed Lot 12, Block 8 of Unit A to Lottie Morrison. Lottie failed to record and then lost her deed. In 1960, J. G. Head's Farms, Inc., signed and delivered a quitclaim deed covering all the land it owned in Unit A to the Miami Holding Corporation. In 1963, J. G. Head's Farms, Inc., conveyed Lot 12 of Block 8 to Lottie Morrison by quitclaim deed. This deed, which replaced the 1947 warranty deed that had been lost, was recorded on March 4, 1963. Lottie Morrison conveyed Lot 12 to Matthews in 1970. Thereafter, a dispute arose between Matthews and the Miami Holding Corporation as to who had superior title to Lot 12. Who does have superior title to Lot 12? Explain.

11. Dick and Dan owned adjoining property. By an honest mistake, Dick built a fence that was 5 feet onto Dan's property. Both owners recognized the fence as the boundary. Twenty-five years after the fence was built, Dan had his property surveyed. The survey revealed the fence's improper location. Dan sought to have the fence removed, but Dick sued, claiming that he now owned the disputed 5-foot strip through adverse possession. Should Dick be declared to own this land? Why? (Assume a twenty-year statutory period.)

transfered by adverse possession - 21 yrs

34 Leases and Bailments

CHAPTER PREVIEW

- LEASE TRANSACTIONS

  Classification of Leases
  Stated period • Period to period • At will • At sufferance
  Tenants—Rights and Duties
  Landlords—Rights and Duties
  Warranty of Habitability
  Liability to Third Parties
  Uniform Residential Landlord and Tenant Act

- BAILMENTS

  Required Elements
  Types of Bailments
  Degree of Care Owed by Ballor

- BAILEES: RIGHTS AND DUTIES

  Degree of Care Owed by Bailees
  Disclaimers of Liability by Bailees
  Other Rights and Duties of Bailees
  Common Carriers as Bailees
  Innkeepers as Bailees

BUSINESS MANAGEMENT DECISION

You are president of a company that owns several apartment complexes. Your company rents mainly to college students. Due to a number of news reports, you become concerned about your company's liability for excessive drinking and drug use by your tenants. You desire to have the opportunity to inspect the apartments.

What should you do to accomplish this goal?

There are many ways to classify transactions involving property interests. One way is to look at real property versus personal property transactions. Another way is to examine the interest transferred. It is this latter method we have chosen to utilize in this chapter. In Chapters 17 and 18, we focused on Article 2's coverage of the *sale* of movable personal property. In sales transactions, the seller transfers both ownership and possession of the property to the buyer. In this chapter, we cover those transactions involving real and personal property in which possession but not ownership is transferred. The following sections are concerned with leases of real estate and bailments of personal property.

LEASE TRANSACTIONS

1. In General

A **lease** is a transfer of possession of real estate from a landlord (lessor) to a tenant (lessee) for a consideration called rent. A lease may be oral or written, expressed, or simply implied from the facts and circumstances. A lease differs from a mere *license*, which is a privilege granted by one person to another to use land for some particular purpose. A license is not an interest in the land. A license to the licensee is personal and not assignable.

Lease *A contract by which one person divests himself of possession of land and grants such possession to another for a period of time.*

2. Classification of Leases

A lease may be a tenancy for a stated period, from period to period, at will, or at sufferance.

Stated period. As its name implies, a *tenancy for a stated period* lasts for the specific time stated in the lease. The statute of frauds requires a written lease if the period exceeds one year. The lease for a stated period terminates without notice at the end of the period. It is not affected by the death of either party during the period. A lease of land for a stated period is not terminated by destruction of the improvements during the period unless the lease so provides. If a lease covers *only* the improvements on land, destruction of them creates impossibility of performance.

Period to period. A *tenancy from period to period* may be created by the terms of the lease. A lease may run from January 1, 1989 to December 31, 1989, and from year to year thereafter unless terminated by the parties. Many leases from period to period arise when the tenant, with the consent of the landlord, holds over after the end of a lease for a stated period. When a *holdover* occurs, the landlord may object and evict the former tenant as a trespasser. Or he may continue to treat the tenant as a tenant; in which case the lease continues from period to period, with the period being identical to that of the original lease, not to exceed one year. The one-year limitation results from the language of the statute of frauds. The amount of rent is identical to that of the original lease.

Leases from year to year or from month to month can be terminated only upon giving proper notice. The length of the notice is usually prescribed by state statute—usually thirty days for a month-to-month lease and sixty to ninety days for one that is year to year. Statutes usually provide the time of the notice, such as on the day the rent is due. Farm leases usually have a special notice period so that the tenant will have notice before planting the next year's crops.

At will. A *tenancy at will*, by definition, has no fixed period and can be terminated by either party at any time upon giving the prescribed statutory notice. A few states do not require notice, but if legal action is necessary to obtain possession for the lessor, a time lag will be automatically imposed.

At sufferance. A *tenancy at sufferance* occurs when a tenant holds over without the consent of the landlord. Until the landlord decides to evict him or to allow him to stay, he is a tenant at sufferance.

3. Tenants—Rights and Duties

The rights and duties of the parties to the lease are determined by the lease itself and by the statutes of the state in which the property is located. Several rights of tenants are frequently misunderstood. For example, the tenant is entitled to exclusive possession and control of the premises unless the lease provides to the contrary. The landlord has no right to go upon the premises except to collect rent. This means that the owner of an apartment building cannot go into the leased apartments and inspect them unless the lease specifically reserves the right to do so. At the end of the lease, the landlord may retake possession of the premises and inspect for damage. A landlord may also retake possession for purposes of protecting the property if the tenant abandons the premises.

Unless the lease so provides, a tenant has no duty to make improvements or substantial repairs. A tenant is not obligated to replace a worn-out heating or air-conditioning system, but it is his duty to make minor repairs such as replacing a broken window. Because of the difficulty in classifying repairs, the lease should spell out the exact obligations of both parties. If the lease obligates the tenant to make repairs, the obligation includes significant items such as replacing a rotten floor or a defective furnace. The duty to repair usually does not extend to replacing the whole structure if it is destroyed.

An important right in many leases of commercial property is the tenant's right to remove *trade fixtures* that he has installed during the lease period. Remember the distinction between fixtures and trade fixtures. The former become a part of the real estate and belong to the owner of the land. The latter remain personalty and belong to the tenant. The right of removal terminates with the lease, and unremoved trade fixtures become the property of the lessor.

Another important right of the tenant relates to his corresponding duty to pay rent. The duty to pay rent is subject to setoffs for violations of the provisions of the lease by the landlord. The duty to pay rent is released in the event of an **eviction**, actual or constructive. *Constructive eviction* occurs when the premises become untenantable, not because of any fault of the tenant, or when some act of the landlord deprives the tenant of quiet enjoyment of the premises. (One example of such an act involves the landlord's breach of an implied warranty of habitability, which is discussed in section 5 of this chapter.) Assume that Joe College rents a basement apartment on campus. A spring rain floods the apartment and makes it uninhabitable. Joe has been constructively evicted. He may move out, and his duty to pay rent is released. Failure to vacate the premises is a waiver of constructive eviction grounds, however. A tenant who continues in possession despite grounds for constructive eviction must continue to pay rent unless this duty is relieved by statute.

Eviction *An action by a landlord to expel a tenant.*

Some states and cities in recent years have enacted laws in an attempt to force landlords to maintain their property in a tenantable condition. These laws allow tenants to withhold rent where the premises are in such disrepair that the health and safety of the tenant is jeopardized. Such laws protect low-income tenants from slum landlords.

Unless prohibited by the lease, a tenant may assign the lease or sublet the premises without the consent of the landlord. In an *assignment*, the assignee becomes liable to the landlord for the rent (of course, the assignor remains liable also). In a *sublease*, the sublessee is liable to the tenant, and the tenant is liable to the landlord. An assignment transfers the original leasehold to the assignee. A sublease creates a new leasehold estate. Ordinarily, an assignment is for the balance of the original lease, whereas a sublease is only for part of the term.

If a lease prohibits assignment, it does not necessarily prevent a sublease; if a lease prohibits subleasing, it does not necessarily prevent assignment; if both are to be prohibited, the lease should so provide. Most leases provide that any assignment or sublease must have the approval of the landlord. Whether the landlord can withhold consent arbitrarily is an issue that has frequently arisen. Historically, the landlord's consent to a proposed assignment or sublease could be withheld without any reason. However, the trend now is to require that the landlord's lack of consent be reasonable under the factual circumstances. This is based on the requirement of good faith and commercial reasonableness, as was discussed by the court in the following case.

CASE

Jose Fernandez leased retail office space from Oscar Vazquez. The lease contained a clause that required the tenant to obtain the landlord's written consent to any assignment of the lease. When Fernandez's business failed, he attempted to assign his rights and duties under the lease to a third party. Without providing any reasons, Vazquez refused to agree to the assignment. When Vazquez sued for unpaid rent, Fernandez counterclaimed that Vazquez improperly refused to consent to the assignment.

ISSUE: May a landlord arbitrarily refuse to consent to an assignment?
DECISION: No.

REASONS: 1. The law generally favors free alienation of property, and under common law a tenant has the right to assign his leasehold interest without the consent of the lessor unless the lease provides otherwise.

2. A lease is a contract and, as such, should be governed by the general contract principles of good faith and commercial reasonableness. One established contract principle is that a party's good-faith cooperation is an implied condition precedent to performance of a contract.

3. A landlord may not arbitrarily refuse consent to an assignment of a commercial lease that provides, even without limiting language, that a tenant shall not assign or sublease the premises without the written consent of the landlord.

4. Whether a landlord breached the lease by acting unreasonably in withholding consent of a commercial tenant is to be determined by a jury according to the facts of that case. The following factors are among those that a jury may properly consider in applying the standards of good faith and commercial reasonableness: (a) financial responsibility of the proposed subtenant, (b) the "identity" or "business character" of the subtenant, i.e., suitability for the particular building, (c) the need for alteration of the premises, (d) the legality of the proposed use, and (e) the nature of the occupancy, i.e., office, factory, clinic, etc.

Fernandez v. Vazquez, 397 So.2d 1171 (Fla. 1981).

4. Landlords—Rights and Duties

Lien *The right of one person, usually a creditor, to keep possession, or control, of the property of another for the purpose of satisfying a debt.*

Distress for rent *The taking of personal property of a tenant in payment of rent.*

The landlord's foremost right is to collect payment for rent. In many states and by the express terms of many leases, the landlord has a **lien** for unpaid rent on the personal property of the tenant physically located on the premises. This lien right is exercised in a statutory proceeding known as **distress for rent.** By following the prescribed procedures, the landlord is able to physically hold personalty on the premises until the rent is paid. If not paid, the tenant's personal property may be sold pursuant to court order. The proceeds of the sale, after deducting court costs, are applied to the rent.

A second basic right belonging to the landlord is to have the tenant vacate the premises upon termination of the tenancy. If the tenancy is terminated lawfully, the landlord's right to possession is absolute. The tenant may not deny the landlord's title. Furthermore, tenants have a duty to redeliver physical control of the premises in the same condition as received, ordinary wear and tear excepted. The motive of the landlord in terminating the lease usually is immaterial. However, because of federal statutes, a landlord may not discriminate in leasing or terminating a lease on the basis of race, color, religion, sex, or national origin.

A landlord also is entitled to recover from either the tenant or third parties for injuries to or waste of property. Tenants may not make any material changes to improvements without the landlord's permission. They may not move walls, install new ones, or do anything else that would constitute a material change in the premises without permission.

Tenants sometimes vacate the premises and refuse to pay any further rent prior to the expiration of the lease's full term. This is especially true in long-term commercial leases. What are the rights and duties of the parties when the tenant breaches the lease contract by abandoning the premises? Does the landlord have a duty to seek a new tenant? The answer to these questions depends on state law. In some states a landlord need not seek a new tenant, and the full obligation of the tenant remains. In these states, the tenant can look for someone to take over the lease, but the lessor need not. The modern view is that the landlord has a duty to mitigate the tenant's damages. If the landlord fails to attempt to mitigate the damages, the tenant's liability is eliminated.

It is common practice for a landlord to require that the tenant deposit a stated sum of money, such as one month's rent, as security for the lease. This security deposit covers nonpayment of rent and possible damage to the premises. Many landlords have been reluctant to return these security deposits, contending in most cases that damages were present, requiring repairs. As a result, many tenants have refused to pay the last month's rent, demanding that the security deposit be applied. Such practices by landlords and tenants have created a great deal of animosity and litigation. To alleviate this problem, the legislatures of many states have passed laws governing lease security deposits. Such laws usually require that the landlord pay interest on the deposits and itemize the cost of any repairs that were made from the deposit. They further require the landlord to return the deposit promptly and prohibit the landlord from using it to repair conditions caused by normal wear and tear. In the event a tenant is required to sue the landlord to recover the deposit, the tenant is entitled to collect attorney's fees. Finally, under these statutes, the tenant usually is not allowed to set off the deposit against the last month's rent.

Tort liability is sometimes imposed on landlords for injuries to their tenants. Such liability only exists where there is a duty owed by the landlord to the tenant and the duty is breached. For example, the modern view is that the owner of a residential dwelling unit, who leases it to a tenant for residential purposes, has a duty to reasonably inspect the premises before allowing the tenant to take possession, and to make the repairs necessary to transfer a reasonably safe dwelling unit to the tenant unless defects are waived by the tenant. This duty may be modified by agreement of the parties.

After the tenant takes possession, the landlord has a continuing duty to exercise reasonable care to repair dangerous defective conditions upon notice of their existence by the tenant, unless waived by the tenant. In most states, a landlord has no duty to maintain in a safe condition any part of the premises under the tenant's exclusive control. The landlord does, however, have a duty to use ordinary care to maintain in a reasonably safe condition any part of the leased premises that was reserved for the common use of all tenants. Further, if the landlord, after delivering possession of the premises to a tenant, enters to make repairs or improvements, he must use reasonable care in making them.

This expansion of the liability of landlords is not unlimited. The court in the following case found no duty and thus no liability. Many courts have been faced with similar factual issues.

CASE

In her petition, plaintiff alleged that she was a tenant in residence at an apartment complex owned and operated by the defendant. She stated that on November 27, 1982, at an unspecified time, while at her car, which was parked in the defendant's parking lot provided for tenants, she was sexually assaulted by a male assailant. Plaintiff further alleged that defendant's manager had actual knowledge of an earlier sexual assault occurring in the same area within two months prior to this assault and that the defendant was negligent in failing to warn plaintiff of that assault.

ISSUE: Did the landlord have a duty to warn this and other tenants of possible dangers?

DECISION: No.

REASONS:
1. In order to impose liability on the landlord, a duty must exist. Whether a duty exists is ultimately a question of fairness.
2. Factors to consider in imposing a duty on a landlord include weighing the relationship of the parties against the nature of the risk and the public interest in the proposed solution, as well as the likelihood of injury, the magnitude of the burden of guarding against it, and the consequences of placing that burden on a defendant.
3. No cases were found that impose liability on a landlord based on a *single* prior criminal act perpetrated upon a tenant. A landlord should not be held liable for the failure to warn tenants against events that are unlikely to occur or events about which the tenants are equally aware.

C.S. v. Sophir, 368 N.W.2d 444 (Neb. 1985).

5. Warranty of Habitability

In recent years, courts have been called upon to decide if there is an implied *warranty of habitability* in a lease of residential property. (This is similar to the issue of warranties on the sale of new housing and is part of the broadened protection given the consuming public, which is discussed more fully in Chapter 44.) Some courts have held in all housing leases that there is an implied warranty of habitability. One court held that the fact that a tenant knew of a substantial number of defects when he rented the premises and that rent was accordingly reduced did not remove the tenant from protection of the warranty. The court reasoned that permitting that type of bargaining would be contrary to public policy and the purpose of the doctrine of implied warranty of habitability. In determining the kinds of defects that will be deemed to constitute a breach of warranty of habitability, several factors are considered. Among the common factors are (1) the violation of any applicable housing code or building or sanitary regulations; (2) whether the nature of the deficiency affects a vital facility; (3) the potential or actual effect upon safety and sanitation; and (4) whether the tenant was in any way responsible for the defect. A breach of this warranty may allow a tenant to terminate the lease. It may serve as a defense to a suit for rent and as a means to obtain a rent reduction.

Defects in vital portions of the premises that may affect health are more important than defects in extras such as swimming pools or recreational facilities, which are not likely to render the premises uninhabitable. It should be kept in mind that not all states recognize an implied warranty of habitability in residential leases. Also, most states have not extended implied warranties to commercial leases. In general, implied warranties of habitability are created either by courts on a case-by-case basis or by statutory enactment.

6. Liability to Third Parties

Difficult legal questions arise in cases involving the landlord's and tenant's liability for injuries to persons on the premises. As a general rule, a landlord makes no warranty that the premises are safe or suitable for the intended use by the tenant, and third persons are on the premises at their own peril. A landlord owes no greater duty to a tenant's guests than is owed to the tenant. A landlord does have a duty to give notice of latent defects of which he has knowledge, and some states add unknown defects of which he should have knowledge in the exercise of ordinary care. In recent years, the liability of landlords under this view has expanded, but there still must be a duty that is breached before there is liability.

Knowing that business invitees of the tenant will be constantly entering the premises to transact business, the owner of business property has an increased responsibility known as the *public use* exception to the general rule. The basis of the exception is that the landlord leases premises on which he knows or should know that there are conditions likely to cause injury to persons, that the purpose for which the premises are leased involve the fact that people will be invited upon the premises as patrons of the tenant, and that the landlord knows or should know that the tenant cannot reasonably be expected to remedy or guard against injury from the defect. Thus a landlord of a business owes a higher duty than does the landlord of essentially private premises. Moreover, landlords of business premises often undertake to care for the common areas. In such cases, they have a duty to inspect, repair, and maintain common areas in a reasonably safe condition.

Many suits against lessors by third persons result from falls on the premises, often associated with ice, snow, or waxed floors. Historically, a landlord had no duty to remove ice and snow. In recent years, many courts have changed this rule as it is applied to multiple-family dwellings and businesses. Many tenants are simply unequipped to perform the task of snow and ice removal. They sometimes lack the physical wherewithal, capability, or the equipment (and storage space) necessary to the task.

Even in those states that do not require removal of ice and snow, if the landlord does undertake to remove snow and ice, he must do so with ordinary care, taking into account dangerous conditions caused by subsequent thawing and freezing of snow placed near the walkway.

7. Uniform Residential Landlord and Tenant Act

The National Conference of Commissioners on Uniform State Laws has proposed that state legislatures adopt the Uniform Residential Landlord and Tenant Act (URLTA). To date, at least seventeen states have followed this recommendation. The URLTA or a substantially similar version has been adopted and is law in Alaska, Arizona, Connecticut, Florida, Hawaii, Iowa, Kansas, Kentucky, Michigan, Montana, Nebraska, New Mexico, Oklahoma, Oregon, Tennessee, Virginia, and Washington.

In addition to making the laws governing residential lease transactions simpler, clearer, and more uniform, URLTA attempts to assure equal bargaining power between landlord and tenant. Many of the rights and duties already discussed are part of URLTA. For example, the landlord cannot collect a security deposit that exceeds one month's rent. Failure to return this deposit without justification makes the landlord liable for twice the amount of this deposit, plus the tenant's attorney's fees. The landlord must deliver possession of the premises at the beginning of the lease term, and the landlord must maintain the premises in a habitable condition.

A tenant's basic responsibilities are to pay rent, to keep the dwelling safe and clean, and to allow the landlord to enter the premises under reasonable circumstances. Examples of when the landlord must be allowed to enter would include the making of periodic inspections, repairs, or improvements. The tenant also must cooperate in showing the premises to potential buyers or tenants. URLTA provides the landlord with the right to enter in all emergency situations.

URLTA also contains an article on the remedies available to either tenant or landlord when the other party breaches the lease agreement. For the most part, URLTA adopts the common law remedies and defenses, such as constructive and retaliatory eviction, previously discussed. Furthermore, provisions allow the tenant to make minor repairs and deduct the cost from the rent if the landlord fails to make the repair after being notified of the defect. A minor repair is defined as one costing less than $100 or one-half the periodic rent, whichever amount is greater. The common law remedy available to the landlord known as distress for rent (see section 4) is abolished. However, if the tenant holds over in bad faith after the lease expires, the landlord can sue for possession and three times the actual damages suffered or three months' rent, whichever is greater.

BAILMENTS

8. Required Elements

Possession of personal property is often temporarily surrendered by the owner to another person. The person to whom the goods are delivered may perform some service pertaining to the goods, such as a repair, after which the goods are returned to the owner. Or someone may borrow or lease an article from its owner. Another temporary transfer of possession occurs when the owner causes the goods to be stored in a warehouse. In general, the provisions of the Uniform Commercial Code are applicable to these transactions involving the temporary transfer of possession of personal property.

Bailment *Delivery of personal property to another for a special purpose. Delivery is made under a contract, either expressed or implied, that upon the completion of the special purpose, the property shall be redelivered to the bailor or placed at his disposal.*

An agreement whereby possession of personal property is surrendered by the owner with provision for its return at a later time is known as a **bailment.** The owner of the goods is called the *bailor*. The one receiving possession is called the *bailee*. There are three distinct requirements for a bailment: retention of title by the bailor, possession and temporary control of the property by the bailee, and ultimate possession to revert to the bailor or to someone designated by the bailor.

9. Types of Bailments

Bailments can be categorized naturally into three classes: bailments for the benefit of the bailor, bailments for the benefit of the bailee, and bailments for the mutual benefit of bailor and bailee. Typical of the first group are those cases in which the bailor leaves goods in the safekeeping of the bailee without any provision for paying the bailee for caring for the article. Because the bailee is not to use the goods or to be paid in any manner, the bailment is for the exclusive benefit of the bailor.

A bailment for the benefit of the bailee is best illustrated by a loan of some article by the bailor to the bailee without any compensation to the bailor. Assume a student borrows a professor's automobile for a weekend date. The bailment is one for the sole benefit of the student, the bailee.

The most common type of bailment is the one in which both parties are to benefit. Contracts for repair, carriage, storage, or pledge of property fall within this class. The bailor receives the benefit of some service; the bailee benefits by the receipt of certain agreed compensation. Thus both parties benefit as a result of the bailment.

To constitute a bailment for mutual benefit, it is not essential that the bailee actually receive compensation in money or tangible property. If the bailment is an incident of the business in which the bailee makes a profit, or it was accepted because of benefits expected to accrue, it is a mutual benefit bailment.

10. Degree of Care Owed by Bailor

Property leased by a bailor to a bailee (a mutual benefit bailment) must be reasonably fit for the intended purpose. For this reason, it is the duty of the bailor to notify the bailee of all defects in the property leased of which the bailor might reasonably have been aware. The bailor is responsible for any damage suffered by the bailee as the result of such defects, unless the notice is given. This rule holds even though the bailor is not aware of the defect if, by the exercise of reasonable diligence, the defect could have been discovered.

If, on the other hand, an article is merely loaned to a bailee—a bailment for the benefit of the bailee—the bailor's duty is to notify the bailee only of known defects. A bailor who fails to give the required notice of a known defect is liable to any person who might be expected to use the defective article as a result of the bailment. Employees of the bailee and members of the bailee's family may recover from the bailor for injuries received as a consequence of known defects.

BAILEES: RIGHTS AND DUTIES

11. Degree of Care Owed by Bailees

Provided that proper care has been exercised by the bailee, any loss or damage to the property bailed falls on the bailor. Each type of bailment requires a different degree of care by the bailee. In a bailment for the benefit of the bailor, the bailee is required to exercise only slight care. In a bailment for the benefit of the bailee, extraordinary care is required. A bailment for the mutual benefit of the parties demands ordinary care on the part of the bailee. *Ordinary care* is defined as care that the average individual usually exercises over his own property. The following case is typical of those distinguishing among the three types of bailments and the duties owed by the bailee to the bailor.

CASE

Morris and Hamilton were guests at a dinner party. While working in the kitchen, Hamilton removed her wristwatch and placed it on a counter. Hamilton returned to the party, but she left her watch on the counter since she intended to do further work in the kitchen. Hamilton became ill and left the party without getting her watch from the kitchen. Morris picked up the watch for the purposes of giving it back to Hamilton at the party. She failed to find Hamilton and thereafter lost track of the watch. Hamilton sued, alleging Morris was a bailee of the watch and negligently lost the watch while it was in her possession. Morris conceded there was a bailment but maintained it was gratuitous, thereby requiring a duty of only slight care.

ISSUE: Is Morris a gratuitous bailee of Hamilton? If so, what duty of care is owed?

DECISION: Yes, Morris held the watch for the sole benefit of Hamilton. Only a duty of slight care is owed by a gratuitous bailee.

REASONS:

1. When one person takes possession of and exercises control over another's personal property, a bailment is created by operation of law.
2. The evidence shows that Morris acted solely for the benefit of Hamilton; therefore Morris was a gratuitous bailee.
3. A bailee who acts gratuitously is not held to the same standard of care as one who enters upon the same undertaking for pay. The latter owes a duty of reasonable or ordinary care, while a gratuitous bailee owes only a duty of slight care. Thus, in order for a bailor to recover from a gratuitous bailee, he must prove the bailee was guilty of gross negligence.
4. Gross negligence is that degree of negligence that shows indifference to others as constitutes an utter disregard of prudence. It must be such a degree of negligence as would shock fair-minded people.
5. Hamilton failed to prove that Morris acted in a grossly negligent manner regarding her possession of the watch. Therefore Morris is not liable for losing that watch despite the fact that a bailment was created.

Morris v. Hamilton, 302 S.E.2d 51 (Va. 1983).

The amount of care demanded of a bailee varies with the nature and value of the article bailed. The care found to be sufficient in the case of a carpenter's tool chest would probably not be ample for a diamond ring worth $10,000. A higher standard of protection is required for valuable articles. Moreover, when damages are assessed against a bailee, they are based on retail replacement value, not the wholesale cost to a bailee.

In addition to the duty to exercise due care, the bailee promises to return the property to the bailor undamaged upon termination of the bailment. This promise can be used to create a prima facie case of negligence. A bailor who proves that property delivered in good condition was returned from the bailee in bad condition establishes a presumption of negligence, and that bailor is entitled to recover from the bailee unless the presumption is rebutted. If there is no other evidence, the bailor will win the suit. The bailee may rebut this prima facie case by introducing evidence to establish that there was no negligence on its part, but the bailee has the burden of proving that it has used reasonable care and caution after the prima facie case has been established. This prima facie case of negligence exists only if all elements of a bailment are present. If there is no bailment, there is no prima facie case upon nondelivery or damage to the goods. The following case demonstrates the application of this prima facie case concept.

CASE

Ronald Knight brought his Corvette to H&H for some warranty repair work. H&H's service adviser told Knight the car would be ready within two days. On the second day the service adviser called Knight, explaining it was necessary to order parts, that the car was not repaired, and that Knight could retrieve the car and use it until the parts were obtained. Knight did not pick up his car, and the car was parked in a fenced lot beside H&H's garage. Knight's car was stolen from H&H's lot two days later. After an investigation failed to locate his car, Knight filed suit. He alleged that H&H had breached its contractual duties under a mutually beneficial bailment by failing to redeliver his Corvette. H&H acknowledged the bailment for hire, but argues Knight must prove H&H was negligent and that such negligence was the cause of Knight's car being stolen.

ISSUE: In a bailment for hire, if the bailee fails to return the property to the bailor, is this proof of the bailee's negligence?

DECISION: Yes.

REASONS:
1. The loss or injury of bailed property while in the hands of the bailee ordinarily creates a presumption of negligence.
2. Where the property is in the sole possession of the bailee, that bailee may well be the only party in a position to explain the circumstances under which the property was lost or damaged.
3. Once the bailor proves delivery of property in good condition to the bailee and failure to redeliver upon timely demand, the burden is irrevocably fixed on the bailee to prove by a preponderance of the evidence that he has exercised due care to prevent the loss, damage, or destruction of the property.

Knight v. H&H Chevrolet, 337 N.W.2d 742 (Neb. 1983).

12. Disclaimers of Liability by Bailees

Bailees frequently attempt to disclaim liability for damage to property while it is in their possession. Such a clause in a contract is known as an *exculpatory clause*. Dry cleaners' tickets often bear statements disclaiming liability for damage to property delivered to them for cleaning. An exculpatory clause disclaiming liability for negligence is illegal if the bailee is a quasi-public institution, because such contracts are against public policy. This is discussed in Chapter 12.

More and more bailees are being classified as quasi-public businesses because of the inequality of bargaining power between many bailors and their bailees. Not all exculpatory clauses seek to eliminate liability completely; some seek to limit the amount of damages. Contracts limiting the amount of damages are looked upon more favorably than absolute disclaimers because it is fair for both parties to know the value of the property and the risk present. In accordance with this theory, the Uniform Commercial Code provides that the **warehouse receipt** or storage agreement

Warehouse receipt *An instrument showing that the signer has in his possession certain described goods for storage. It obligates the signer, the warehouseman, to deliver the goods to a specified person or to his order or bearer upon the return of the instrument.*

may limit the amount of liability in case of loss or damage to the covered property, but the agreement cannot disclaim the obligation of reasonable care.

Carrier *A natural person or a corporation who receives goods under a contract to transport for a consideration from one place to another.*

Carriers also attempt to limit their liability. A carrier may not contract away its liability for goods damaged in shipment, but it may limit the liability to a stated amount. A carrier may also, where lower rates are granted, relieve itself from the consequences of causes or conduct over which it has no control.

Because a carrier may limit liability to an agreed valuation, the shipper is limited in recovery to the value asserted in the bill of lading. The rate charged for transportation will vary with the value of the property shipped. For this reason, the agreed valuation is binding.

13. Other Rights and Duties of Bailees

The bailment agreement governs the rights and duties of the bailee. If the bailee treats the property in a different manner or uses it for some purpose other than that contemplated by the bailment contract, the bailee becomes liable for any loss or damage to the property, even though the damage can in no sense be attributed to the conduct of the bailee. Let us assume that Murray stores a car for the winter in Plante's public garage. Because of a crowded condition, Plante has the car temporarily moved to another garage without Murray's consent. As a result of a tornado, the car is destroyed while at the second location. The loss falls upon Plante, who breached the terms of the bailment contract. In a restricted sense, the bailee is guilty of conversion of the bailor's property during the period in which the contract terms are being violated.

The bailee has no right to deny the title of the bailor unless the bailee has yielded possession to one having a better title than the bailor. The bailee has no right to retain possession of the property merely because he is able to prove that the bailor does not have legal title to the goods. In order to defeat the bailor's right to possession, the bailee must show that the property has been turned over to someone having better title or that he is holding the property under an agreement with the true owner.

14. Common Carriers as Bailees

Common carrier *One who is engaged in the business of transporting personal property from one place to another for compensation. Such person is bound to carry for all who tender their goods and the price for transportation. A common carrier operates as a public utility and is subject to state and federal regulations.*

The contract for carriage of goods constitutes a mutual benefit bailment, but the care required of the carrier greatly exceeds that of the ordinary bailee. A **common carrier** is an absolute insurer of the safe delivery of the goods to their destination. Proof of delivery to a carrier of a shipment in good condition and its arrival at the destination in a damaged condition creates a prima facie case against the carrier.

This absolute liability of a common carrier is subject to only five exceptions. Any loss or damage must fall upon the shipper if it results from (1) an act of God, (2) action of an alien enemy, (3) order of public authority, (4) inherent nature of the goods, or (5) misconduct of the shipper. Thus any loss that results from an accident or the willful misconduct of some third party must be borne by the carrier. A person who wanted to injure a certain railway company set fire to several boxcars loaded with freight. Losses due to damage to the goods fell upon the carrier. On the other hand, if lightning, an act of God, had set fire to the cars, the loss would have fallen upon the shipper. However, the defense of an act of God is narrowly construed to include only events that were not foreseeable.

The shipper must suffer any damage to goods in shipment if damage results from the very nature of the goods, improper crating, or failure to protect the property. Thus, if a dog dies because his crate was poorly ventilated, the shipper is unable to recover from the carrier. Remember, though, that the carrier has the burden of proving that it was free from negligence and that the damage falls within one of the exceptions to the rule establishing the carrier's liability as an insurer of the shipment.

The burden is on the shipper to prove that the goods were in good condition at the time and place of shipment. Although proof that the goods were in good condition when delivered to the carrier and that they were damaged when delivered by the carrier creates a prima facie case of liability, there is no presumption that the goods were in good condition when delivered to the carrier. Actual proof is required.

The liability of the carrier attaches as soon as the goods are delivered. The extreme degree of care required of the carrier may be terminated before the goods are actually delivered to the **consignee.** Three views in the United States determine when the relationship of the carrier ceases. Some states hold that the duties of the carrier end, and those of a **warehouseman** begin, as soon as the local shipment is unloaded from the car into the freight house. Others hold the carrier to strict liability until the consignee has had a reasonable time in which to inspect and remove the shipment. Still other states hold that the consignee is entitled to notice—and that he has reasonable time after notice—in which to remove the goods before the liability of the carrier as a carrier is terminated. For example, assume that the goods arrive at their destination and are unloaded and placed in the freight house. Before the consignee has had time to take them away, the goods are destroyed by fire, although the carrier has exercised ordinary care. Under the first of these views, the loss would fall upon the shipper because at the time of the fire, the railway was no longer a carrier but a warehouseman. Under the other two views, the loss would fall on the carrier, whose extreme liability had not yet terminated because no time had been given for delivery.

Consignee *A person to whom a shipper usually directs a carrier to deliver goods.*

Warehouseman *A person engaged in the business of storing goods for hire.*

A common carrier, while not an insurer of its passengers' safety, owes the highest degree of care to them. In other words, a common carrier will be liable to passengers for injuries caused by even the slightest negligence. This high duty is not owed to persons who are on the premises of the carrier but are not on board the carrier. To these people, the carrier owes only ordinary care. Passengers who are in the process of boarding or exiting are considered to be on board and are protected by the carrier's duty to exercise extraordinary care, as is illustrated by the following case.

CASE

Isabel Carey was a passenger on a bus owned and operated by Jack Rabbit Lines, Inc. She was seventy-nine years oid at the time she was a passenger. Upon arrival, the bus was parked twelve to eighteen inches from a crub. The area where the passengers were to unload was dimly lit. As Carey stepped off the bus, she stepped into a gutter instead of on the sidewalk, resulting in a fall. She suffered injuries to her shoulder and wrist, resulting in some permanent physical impairment. The bus driver parked twelve to eighteen inches from the curb for convenience in unloading baggage. He did not warn passengers of the danger in disembarking from the bus.

Carey sued the bus lines and was awarded damages by the trial court. Jack Rabbit Lines appealed.

ISSUE: Did the bus driver provide a reasonably safe place for disembarking passengers?

DECISION: No.

REASONS:
1. A carrier of persons for reward must use the utmost care and diligence and a reasonable degree of skill and provide everything necessary for the passengers' safe carriage. This duty extends to passengers who are in the process of alighting from the bus.
2. The failure of appellant's driver to park the bus close enough to the curb to permit appellee and the other passengers to step safely onto the sidewalk and his failure to warn them of the possible danger or to assist them in alighting constituted negligence that supports the trial court's award of damages.

Carey v. Jack Rabbit Lines, Inc., 309 N.W.2d 824 (S.D. 1981).

15. Innkeepers as Bailees

Issues similar to those involved with common carriers frequently arise in suits against hotel and motel operators. Under common law, an innkeeper was an insurer of the safety of the goods of its guests. The law imposed liability as a matter of public policy because the innkeeper and his employees had easy access to the guests' rooms. Exceptions to this general rule relieved the innkeeper from liability for loss caused by an act of God, a public enemy, an act of public authority, the inherent nature of the property, or the fault of the guest.

Most states have enacted statutes pertaining to hotel or motel operators' liability. These statutes usually provide that if the operator appropriately notifies guests that a safe or lockbox is maintained for their use, there is no liability if guests' property is stolen from their rooms. Such laws usually cover property of "small compass," which includes money, negotiable instruments, jewelry, and precious stones. The requirement that notice of the availability of the safe be given with notice of the liability limitation is usually strictly enforced.

Some states also have laws that limit the maximum liability of hotel and motel operators to a stated amount, such as $500. Others have changed the liability from that of an insurer to that of a bailee of a mutual benefit bailment (ordinary care as the duty). In all states, the liability of the innkeeper is limited to the value of the property. There is no liability for consequential damages that may flow from the loss of the property.

CHAPTER SUMMARY

Lease Transactions

Classification of Leases

1. A tenancy for a stated period lasts for the time specified in the lease.
2. A tenancy from period to period may run from month to month or

year to year. Such a lease often is created when a tenant holds over, with the landlord's consent, after a lease for a stated period.

3. A tenancy at will has no definite duration and can be terminated by either the landlord or tenant after proper notice is given.
4. A tenancy at sufferance occurs when a tenant holds over without the landlord's consent.

Tenants—Rights and Duties

1. In general, the tenant has the right to exclusive possession free from interference.
2. Tenant has the right to have the premises suitable for the intended use.
3. Unless the lease provides otherwise, the tenant is free to assign or sublease his interest to a third party. (Note that leases frequently require the landlord's approval prior to such transfer.)
4. The tenant's basic duty is to pay the rent and to return possession at the end of the lease term.

Landlords—Rights and Duties

1. The landlord has the right to expect the tenants to pay rent.
2. The landlord has legal remedies such as distress for rent and eviction powers to encourage the tenant's performance.
3. The landlord generally has the duty to maintain the premises. Although tenants may be liable for damages caused, the landlord cannot unreasonably retain a security deposit.

Warranty of Habitability

1. Many courts have held that landlords implicitly warrant that residential property is habitable.
2. A breach of this warranty allows the tenant to reduce rental payments or to terminate the lease without further liability.

Liability to Third Parties

1. In general, a landlord has no greater duty to protect third parties from injuries than is owed to the tenants.
2. The "public use" exception means that a landlord of a business owes a higher duty to third parties than does a landlord of private premises.

Uniform Residential Landlord and Tenant Act

1. This act is an attempt to make all state laws uniform in the area of residential leases.
2. At least seventeen states have adopted substantial portions of this act.

Bailments

Required Elements

1. A bailment involves the temporary transfer of possession of personal property with the understanding that possession must be returned. There is no transfer of ownership interests.
2. A *bailor* is the owner who transfers physical possession to another person. A *bailee* is the person receiving possession who understands that the possession will be returned to the bailor or a designated party.

Types of Bailments

1. A bailment for the sole benefit of the bailor usually occurs when a bailee is not compensated.
2. A bailment for the sole benefit of the bailee is illustrated by a bailee borrowing some item of personal property.
3. A bailment for the mutual benefit of the parties is the most common in commercial transactions. Rental agreements, warehouse arrangements, and shipping contracts are examples of this third type of bailment.

Degree of Care Owed by Bailor

1. This duty of care depends on the type of bailment.
2. In bailments for the sole benefit of the bailee, bailor must give notice of any defects of which he is aware.

3. In other types of bailment, the bailor must inspect the personal property and give notice of those defects known or those that should have been discovered.

Bailees: Rights and Duties

Degree of Care Owed by Bailees

1. This degree of care depends on the type of bailment.
2. In bailments for the sole benefit of the bailor, the bailee owes only slight care.
3. In bailments for the sole benefit of the bailee, the bailee owes extraordinary care.
4. In bailments for the mutual benefit of the parties, bailees owe ordinary reasonable care.
5. Regardless of type of bailment, the bailee must return possession to the bailor or there is a presumption of negligence.

Disclaimers of Liability by Bailees

1. Courts tend to declare disclaimers of liability, known as exculpatory clauses, invalid as against public policy.
2. Clauses limiting a bailee's liability are viewed more favorably and often enforced.

Other Rights and Duties of Bailees

1. A bailee is liable if the bailed property is treated in a manner contrary to the bailment agreement.
2. A bailee may deny the bailor the property only if the bailee can prove someone else has better title to the property.

Common Carriers as Bailees

1. As a bailee, a common carrier owes a duty of absolute assurance of the property's safe delivery.
2. A common carrier's liability is limited by five exceptions. These are damage to the property being caused by (a) an act of God, (b) an action of an alien enemy, (c) an order of public authority, (d) the inherent nature of the property, and (c) the misconduct of the shipper.

Innkeepers as Bailees

1. Originally, innkeepers were considered absolute insurers of the safety of guests and the guests' belongings.
2. Today, most states have statutes that limit the innkeeper's liability with respect to guests' personal property.

REVIEW QUESTIONS AND PROBLEMS

1. Match each term in column A with the appropriate statement in column B.

A	B
(1) Tenancy for a stated period	(a) Occurs when a tenant holds over without the landlord's consent.
(2) Tenancy at will	(b) The transfer of possession but not ownership of personal property.
(3) Tenancy at sufferance	(c) An absolute insurer of safe delivery of goods being transported.
(4) Distress for rent	(d) A lease for a specific period of time.
(5) Bailment	(e) One of the landlord's legal remedies when a tenant refuses to pay rent.
(6) Bailor	(f) The owner of personal property who transfers possession to a bailee.
(7) Ordinary care	(g) A lease with no stated duration which can be terminated by either the landlord or the tenant after proper notice is given.

(8) Exculpatory clause	(h) A disclaimer of liability.
(9) Common carrier	(i) The degree of care owed by the bailee in a bailment for the mutual benefit of the parties.

2. Lambert owned an apartment building and leased an apartment to Tammy. While Tammy was out of town, Lambert entered the apartment and found some illegal drugs. When Tammy returned, Lambert asked her to move out or face criminal prosecution. Tammy sued, claiming that Lambert had trespassed. Was Lambert guilty of trespass? Why?

3. The Kroger Company opened a supermarket as one of the original tenants of a shopping center owned by Developer's Unlimited. Kroger signed a ten-year lease. However, due to declining sales, Kroger subleased the store space to Thomas, who operated a discount department store. Thomas agreed to assume all of Kroger's obligations under the original lease. Developer's claims that Kroger's sublease to Thomas is inconsistent with the terms of the original lease. Assuming there is no clause in the lease concerning Kroger's right to assign or sublease, does Developer's have any basis for denying Thomas the right to use the store space? Explain.

4. Grocers, Inc., as a tenant, entered into a five-year lease with Properties, Unltd., as a landlord. The leased property was to be used as a grocery store. Grocers, Inc., had financial difficulties and vacated the premises when it closed the store. The landlord listed the premises with a broker, but it asked for an annual rent of $33,600, which was $12,600 greater than the rent provided in the original lease with Grocers, Inc. When the premises were not relet at the higher rent, Properties, Unltd., sued Grocers, Inc., for accrued rent. Is this landlord entitled to accrued rent? Explain.

5. Jeff and four friends leased a house owned by Amanda Hogg. At the commencement of the lease, each tenant gave Ms. Hogg $100 as a security deposit. When the lease term legally expired, these tenants asked that their deposits be returned to Jeff. Ms. Hogg was given Jeff's forwarding address. Ms. Hogg failed to send a list of damages with itemized repair costs within thirty days after the premises were vacated. Ms. Hogg also refused to refund any of the tenants' security deposits. Are these tenants entitled to receive their deposits plus damages? Why or why not?

6. Stewart, while walking on the sidewalk, tripped and fell. The sidewalk was dilapidated and in a bad state of repair. An antiques store abutted the sidewalk. Stewart sued the owner of the store for his injuries. What result? Explain.

7. Miller's car was parked in a large self-service parking garage owned by the Central Parking System. The parking garage is the type where a machine automatically gives a ticket to a driver before he enters the garage. The driver then parks in a place of his choice, leaves his car, and takes his keys with him. The only employee on duty is the attendant who collects the money from the driver upon exiting. Miller parked his car in the garage following this procedure. The wheels were stolen from his car. Is the garage company liable for the stolen wheels without a showing of negligence? Why?

8. Noble ordered a stereo tuner, which was delivered by United Parcel Service to his apartment building. Paulette, the receptionist/switchboard operator, signed the appropriate receipt for and received the tuner, and she placed it on a shelf in a small room next to her desk where packages for tenants were kept. Later the tuner was stolen. Noble sued the landlord for the value of his property. Has he made a prima facie case? Explain.

9. Patrick left some of his clothes at Douglas Dry Cleaners, Inc. Through no negligence of Douglas, an arsonist started a fire that destroyed the company's building and its contents. Patrick is suing to recover the value of his clothes. Should he recover? Why?

10. Lloyd Groat was licensed as a common carrier. Arnold Albrecht, a logger, hired Groat to transport a 45-ton crawler log loader from one job site to another. Some of Albrecht's employees accompanied Groat during this transfer. While the equipment was being moved, the truck carrying the loader bogged down on a steep, freshly graveled logging road. Groat and Albrecht's employees used a Caterpillar bulldozer to extract the truck from the mire. While the truck was being pulled free, the log loader came loose from the trailer. The loader cascaded down an embankment, where it came to rest in a damaged

condition. Albrecht filed suit, claiming Groat was strictly liable for the damage to the log loader, since he was a common carrier. Groat contended he should be able to reduce his liability due to the negligence of Albrecht's employees, which contributed to the damaging of the loader. Is strict liability the proper standard of liability of a common carrier? Explain.

11. Core Company shipped by railroad four carloads of apples from Seattle, Washington, to Washington, D.C. The apples arrived spoiled, and Core brought suit, alleging that the negligence of the railroad caused the apples to arrive in improper condition. An employee of Core, who was not present when the apples were inspected or shipped, testified that the apples were in good condition when delivered to the carrier. His testimony was based on inspection reports of the Department of Agriculture, which were prepared six weeks prior to shipment. Should the railroad be held liable? Explain.

12. Goncalves was a guest at Regent, a luxury hotel. He traveled with a jewelry collection worth $1 million, and he delivered it to Regent for safekeeping. The room containing the individual safe deposit boxes was a plasterboard room easily accessible to the public. It was broken into, and Goncalves's box was broken into and emptied. He sued Regent to recover the value of his jewelry. A state statute limited hotel liability to $500 for each loss of property regardless of the cause. Goncalves sued for the total value of his property. What result? Why?

Wills, Trusts, and Estate Planning

35

CHAPTER PREVIEW

BUSINESS MANAGEMENT DECISION

You have been appointed the senior trust officer of a financial institution. Your position makes you responsible for the administration, as trustee, of a large number of trusts. You learn that one of your trust officers is buying stocks on margin.

What should you do?

Perhaps no aspect of the ownership of property is of greater significance than the various methods available for disposing of that property upon death. This significance is due in part to transfer taxes imposed by the federal and some state governments. As a result of transfer taxes, income tax problems, and other related concerns, specialists are actively engaged in estate planning.

Estate planning involves much more than the transfer of property at the owner's death. Proper planning includes the creation of an estate, as well as the distribution of estate assets. For example, a young couple with small children may be very concerned about providing for their children's college education. How this goal is achieved is one part of estate planning. Acquisition of a principal residence, a vacation home, or other assets may play a major part in planning an estate. How one provides for loved ones in the event of death or disability should be considered. Retirement plans also are an important part in estate planning.

Estate planning is a lifelong, ever-changing process; it is not a one-time transaction. This chapter presents material on some of the legal principles involved in the estate planning process. For instance, a valid will often is considered the cornerstone or foundation of a well-planned estate. However, substitutes for wills may be useful in particular circumstances. Furthermore, trusts can be utilized separate from or in conjunction with a will. Wills, substitutes for wills, and trusts are discussed in the following sections.

WILLS

1. Terminology

Will *The formal instrument by which a person makes disposition of his property, to take effect upon his death.*

Guardian *A person appointed by the court to look after the property rights and person of minors.*

Testator *A person who has died leaving a will.*

Executor (of an estate) *The person whom the testator names or appoints to administer his estate upon his death and to dispose of it according to his intention.*

A **will** is a document that expresses a person's intention as to the disposition of his property on death. It also serves several additional functions. It designates the personal representative who is to be responsible for settling the affairs of the deceased. A will may make provision for the appointment of **guardians** of the person and the estate of a minor child. Indeed, for young parents who have not yet amassed much financial wealth, the appointment of a guardian for their minor children usually is the most important reason to have a will. Many wills also provide for payment of taxes that may be due on the death of the deceased and for matters such as whether or not the personal representative should be required to have sureties on the official bond.

A person who dies leaving a valid will is said to die *testate*. This person, upon signing a will, generally is referred to as the **testator**. The personal representative of a testator is an **executor**. A person who dies without leaving a valid will dies *intestate*. The personal representative of a person who dies intestate is called an **administrator.** This personal representative (whether an executor or an administrator) is in charge of gathering the deceased's assets, paying the lawful debts, and distributing the assets to the appropriate persons. A *guardian* is the personal representative in charge of the well-being of a minor's person or property or both. A *conservator* may be appointed when the care of a mentally incompetent adult is involved. Some states use the term *guardian* as well.

Administrator *A person to whom letters of administration have been issued by a probate court, giving such person authority to administer, manage, and close the estate of a person who died intestate.*

A gift by will of real estate usually is called a *devise;* a gift of personal property other than money is called a *bequest;* and a gift of money is referred to as a *legacy*. Devises, bequests, and legacies are further classified as specific, general, or residuary. A *specific gift* (devise, bequest, or legacy) is a gift of particular property described to identify and distinguish it from all other parts of the deceased's property. If property described in a specific gift is not owned by the testator at death, the gift fails or is said to be *adeemed*. A *general gift* is one that does not describe any particular property, and it may be satisfied by delivery of any property of the general kind described. A gift of a specified sum of money is a general legacy. A *residuary gift* is one that includes all the property not included in the specific or general devises, bequests, or legacies. All of these terms are important in the payment and distribution of the shares of an estate and in determining which party actually receives a specific item of property.

2. Testamentary Capacity

Testamentary capacity does not require a perfect mind or average intelligence. Testamentary capacity, first of all, requires a minimum age, such as eighteen years. The person executing the will must have sufficient mental capacity to comprehend and remember who are the natural objects of his affection, to comprehend the kind and character of his property, and to understand that he is engaged in making a will. Less mental capacity is required to execute a will than is required to execute ordinary business transactions and contracts. Since many people at the time of making a will are in poor health, the law recognizes that many testators will not be of perfect mind, and all that is required is a minimum capacity to understand the nature and extent of one's property and to formulate the plan involved in making the will. While the widow in the following case failed to have the will set aside, she would have been entitled in most states to a portion of the estate by renouncing the will. Had she been successful in the suit, she would have received all of the estate instead of a portion that would be half in many states.

Testamentary capacity *A person is said to have testamentary capacity when he understands the nature of his business and the value of his property, knows those persons who are natural objects of his bounty, and comprehends the manner in which he has provided for the distribution of his property.*

CASE

Robert Bass, a habitual drunkard, executed a will in 1974, devising his entire estate to a church to the exclusion of his widow. When he died, his widow contested the validity of the will on the ground that he lacked the capacity to make a will. However, the witnesses testified that Mr. Bass was not drunk or mentally unstable when the will was executed.

ISSUE: Does a habitual drunkard, in a lucid moment, have the mental capacity to make a valid will?

DECISION: Yes.

REASONS:

1. In order to have testamentary capacity, an individual does not have to be absolutely of sound mind and memory in every respect. All that is required is that he have sufficent mental capacity to comprehend and remember who are the natural objects of his bounty and to comprehend the kind and character of his property according to some plan formed in his mind.
2. Alcoholism, illness, eccentricity, and offensive or disgusting personal habits do not constitute unsoundness of mind.
3. Since the evidence did not show that alcoholism, illness, or insane delusions in any way affected or entered into the execution of the will, Robert Bass's will was valid.

Hellams v. Ross, 233 S.E.2d 98 (S.C. 1977).

3. Formalities of Execution

In general, the testator must sign the will. In the alternative, since many people who are physically incapacitated may not be able to sign the will, it may be signed by someone else in the testator's presence and at his direction. It will not be set aside simply by proving that the signature on it is not that of the deceased.

In most states, the testator need not sign in the presence of witnesses if he acknowledges to them that the instrument is his own and that it bears his signature. The witnesses need not be informed that the document is a will, but only that it is the testator's instrument. The signature aspect of attestation is that the testator watch the witnesses sign, and in most states it is essential that the witnesses testify that the testator watched them sign as attesting witnesses.

A credible witness is one who is competent to testify in support of the will. If the witness is an interested party because he takes something under the will, that the witness generally will not be allowed to receive any more property as a result of the will than he would have received had there been no will. In other words, a witness to the will cannot profit or gain any property as a result of the will. He will be required to testify and will lose whatever the will gives him in excess of his intestate share of the deceased's estate.

The most important thing to remember about executing a will is that the number of credible witnesses and the formalities required vary from state to state. Consultation with a lawyer licensed in the state involved is always recommended.

4. Grounds for Challenging a Will's Validity

Very often a disinherited or disappointed party will challenge the validity of a will by proving that a testator lacked the mental capacity to make that will. Another challenge might be that the formal requirements of signing and witnessing the will were not met. In addition, the validity of a testator's will may be challenged on the grounds that the testator was unduly influenced to make a will that provides for a distribution scheme contrary to that testator's expected wishes and desires. This ground for challenging a will is defined as influence that overpowers the mind of the testator and deprives him of his free agency in the execution of the will. It is the equivalent of saying, "This is not my wish, but I must do it." It is more than mere persuasion, for here there is an exercise of independent judgment and deliberation. A presumption of undue influence is often found to exist where there is a fiduciary relationship between a testator and a beneficiary who takes substantial benefits from the will. This is especially true if the beneficiary is a nonrelated dominant party and the testator a dependent party and the will is written, or its preparation procured, by the beneficiary, as occurred in the following case.

CASE

An undertaker had served as confidential adviser to a now deceased woman eighty years of age. He managed all of her affairs. At a time when her mind was deteriorating, the undertaker called in his attorney to draw a will for her. The will left virtually all of the estate to the undertaker. The will was contested, and the probate court disallowed it on the ground of undue influence.

ISSUE: Did the conduct of the undertaker constitute undue influence?

DECISION: Yes.

REASONS:

1. When a confidential or trust relationship exists between a testator and a beneficiary under a will, the law requires the closest scrutiny and most careful examination of all the circumstances. Here, the facts clearly establish a relationship of trust and confidence and an elderly spinster with a weakened mind.
2. In connection with the execution of the will and operating at the time the will is made, undue influence means influence that amounts to moral coercion or that destroys free agency, so that the testator—unable to withstand the influence or too weak to resist it—was constrained to do that which was not her actual will.

Barton v. Beck Estate, 195 A.2d 63 (Me. 1963).

5. Revocation, Republication, Revival, and Renunciation

A will is said to be *ambulatory*, or not effective, until the death of the testator. It may be revoked at any time. Among the common methods of revoking a will are physical destruction, making a will declaring the revocation, a later will that is inconsistent with the prior will, marriage, and divorce. In many states, divorce revokes the will only to the extent of bequests or devises to the former spouse. Marriage revokes a will because it is presumed that the testator would want a different plan of distribution as the result of the marriage. It is therefore important that whenever there is a marriage or a divorce, the law of the state of the domicile be consulted to determine its effect on a prior will.

State laws usually prohibit partial revocation of a will except by a duly signed and attested instrument. Additions, alterations, substitutions, interlineations, and deletions on the face of a will are therefore ineffective, and the will stands as originally executed. The law prohibits partial revocation because of the ease with which such minor changes could be made by third parties even after the death of the person whose will is involved.

Unless a provision is made for a child born after the execution of the will, or unless the will by clear and convincing language indicates that after-born children are to be disinherited, the after-born child in most states takes from the estate whatever he or she would have received had there been no will. A legal adoption has the same effect. This stipulation is based on the assumption that the testator at the time of the execution of the original will would not have considered the after-born child and that a provision would have been intended had the child been considered. The following case illustrates the courts' desire to benefit after-born children, whether they are natural-born or adopted children.

CASE

David H. Darling's mother, Frances Roberts Darling, died testate in 1967. Her will, in pertinent part, established a trust that required the trustees

> (1) To pay whatever costs of the funeral and burial of my son David are proper in the judgment of the Trustees and promptly upon his death to divide, distribute and transfer the remaining property of the trust fund equally to the children of the said David H. Darling who survive him. In the event that any of my said grandchildren entitled to share in my estate under the terms of this, my last will and testament, shall not be of the age of 25 years at the time of the death of my said son, David H. Darling, then and in that event, the share of my estate to which they are entitled shall be held by my trustees, under the provisions of said trust, and paid by said trustees to said grandchildren upon their attaining the age of twenty-five years.

Darling, the son referred to in the foregoing passage, was married four times. His first marriage produced a son, Stephen, in 1949. Bruce and Mark, born in 1958 and 1960, respectively, were products of Darling's second marriage. The third marriage produced another son, John, in 1966. David married a fourth time, after his mother's death, in 1972. In 1977, he adopted his last wife's children, namely, Kimberly Sue, David, and Jayne. Darling then died in December 1982.

The natural children of David Darling filed suit and asked the court to declare that the adopted children should not share in this trust.

ISSUE: Are the adopted children of David Darling entitled to share in the benefits of the trust established prior to the adoption?

DECISION: Yes.

REASONS:

1. After a decree of adoption is entered, the usual relation of parent and child and all the rights, duties, and other legal consequences of the natural relation of child and parent shall thereafter exist between such adopted child and the person or persons adopting such child and his, her, or their kindred.
2. An adopted child, in the absence of specific testamentary directions to the contrary, inherits from the antecedents of an adoptive parent to the same extent as do the adoptive parent's natural children.
3. It is true, as certain of the natural children argue, that their grandmother could not have known of the adoptions, for she had both executed her will and died before they took place. Her

lack of knowledge, however, is not significant. She would have been equally ignorant of any natural children sired by Darling after her death. The important point is that she had no control over who became Darling's children or by what means. She chose to benefit Darling's children.

4. Darling elected to make the children produced by his fourth wife his own by adopting them. Having become his, those children qualify as beneficiaries of the testamentary trust.

In Re Estate of Darling, 365 N.W.2d 821 (Neb. 1985).

In most states, a will that is in any manner totally revoked can be revived only by the republication or reexecution of the will or by an instrument in writing declaring the revival and executed in the same manner as a new will. To illustrate, assume that a person during her lifetime has executed four wills, each specifically revoking the former. None of these wills had been destroyed until the testator, shortly before her death, physically destroyed will number four. Is number three then valid? In most states, the answer is no. Wills are not stacked one on the other so that the revocation of the latest will revives the earlier will. In the situation described, the person would die without a will.

Some states have recognized an exception to the general rule that a revoked will is ineffective unless the testator's intent indicates otherwise. This exception is known as the *doctrine of dependent relative revocation*. In essence, this doctrine applies when the testator intends to revoke one will and substitute a new will in its place. If the new will is not made or is not valid for some reason, this doctrine allows the previously revoked will to remain valid. In order for the doctrine to apply, it must be proved that the testator intended the revocation of an old will to be conditioned on the validity of a new will. Usually the nature of a deceased person's intent is very difficult to prove. Therefore the doctrine of dependent relative revocation will be applied to a very narrow factual situation. As a practical matter, an old will should not be destroyed prior to the execution of a new one.

A similar issue as to a will's validity arises when a person executes a **codicil** or a minor change to a will. When a codicil is executed and it specifically refers to a former will, it has the effect of bringing the former will down to the date of the codicil, and the will is then construed as of the date of the codicil. A codicil can validate a previously invalid will. It can also validate a will that has been revoked by marriage or divorce.

Codicil *An addition to, or a change in, an executed last will and testament. It is a part of the original will and must be executed with the same formality as the original will.*

The law in most states gives a spouse certain rights that cannot be denied by will. These rights include support during the period of administration, with a statutory minimum usually provided. The court will determine the exact amount, based on the size of the estate and the standard of living of the surviving spouse. A spouse may also *renounce* a will and take a statutory share in lieu of provisions made by the will. In other words, one spouse cannot completely prevent his or her property from passing to a surviving spouse by making different provisions in the will. In many states, a spouse receives one-half the estate upon renunciation, irrespective of the provisions of the will. It should be recognized that the right to renounce usually exits for spouses only—children can be completely disinherited.

ALTERNATIVES TO WILLS

6. Introduction

Numerous methods, legal devices, and techniques can serve as a valid substitute for a will. The law of intestacy may be viewed as a substitute for a will because it is, in effect, a state-made will for people who have not taken the trouble to execute one for themselves. Among the most common substitutes for wills are contracts, including life insurance contracts, trusts, and joint tenancy property.

Life insurance policies name a beneficiary to receive the proceeds on the death of the insured. This beneficiary may be the estate of the insured, in which case the proceeds will pass under the will of the deceased; or if the insured dies without a will, the proceeds will be distributed according to the laws of intestacy. The usual arrangement is to name an individual beneficiary and successive beneficiaries in the event the primary beneficiary predeceases the insured. In that case, the provisions of the will are immaterial, and the life insurance will be paid in accordance with the terms of the policy, even if the will purports to cover life insurance.

Individuals enter into numerous contracts that have the effect of disposing of property on death. Some contracts stipulate the terms of a will or surrender rights to renounce a will or take an intestate share. For example, contracts known as *antenuptial agreements* are often entered into by parties contemplating marriage, especially when one or both have children by a prior marriage.

In Part V, "Business Organizations," reference is made to *buy* and *sell* agreements between partners and between the shareholders of closely held corporations. These contracts, in effect, dispose of the interests of partners and shareholders on death. The contractual agreement will dispose of the property, irrespective of any provision in a will, in much the same manner as does life insurance. Other contracts, including employment contracts and leases, may have a similar effect.

A *living trust* is another substitute for a will when it contains provisions as to the disposition of property on the death of a life tenant. Since this device is so important and so commonly used, it is discussed more fully in sections 10 through 14.

Finally, the use of some methods of *joint ownership* are used as substitutes for wills because ownership automatically passes to the surviving owner on the death of the other. In particular, joint tenancies and tenancies by the entirety are used to accomplish this purpose.

Prior to examining the various forms of multiple ownership, the next section discusses what happens when a person dies without leaving a valid will.

7. Intestate Succession

Succession *The transfer by operation of law of all rights and obligations of a deceased person to those who are entitled to them.*

As stated previously, a person who dies without leaving a valid will is said to die *intestate*. When a person dies intestate, the state law provides how the deceased's property will be distributed. In this sense, a state's **intestate succession law** acts as an alternative to a will. Although all of the states attempt to provide a scheme of distribution that a reasonable person likely would have intended, the statutes of intestacy do vary from state to state. To complicate matters, the intestate laws of two or more states may have to be used in settling the estate of a person who dies without a will. For example, when real estate is a part of the deceased's estate, the appropriate intestate statute is that one of the state in which the land is located.

When personal property is to be distributed, the law of the deceased's domicile generally controls.

The typical intestate succession statute provides that the deceased's assets are to be inherited by that deceased's closest living relatives. However, the intestate succession statute in one state may provide that a spouse of the deceased receives the entire estate if there are no surviving children. In another state, under similar circumstances the intestate statute may require that the property be divided between the deceased's spouse and parents. If a person is survived by a spouse and children, most states provide that the estate is divided among the spouse and children. Often this is an undesirable result, because of the unmarketability of property owned by minors. This problem arises due to the fact that minors generally can void contractual transactions prior to reaching the age of majority.

Everyone over the legal age of testamentary capacity should be aware of his state's scheme of intestate succession. If that scheme contradicts a person's desires for distributing assets, that person should have a valid will prepared and executed. Indeed, as an alternative to a valid will that can be personalized to the testator's specific needs, the intestate succession scheme is considered inferior as an estate planning tool.

8. Joint Tenancy

Joint tenancy as one form of multiple ownership is discussed in Chapter 32. Remember that because joint tenants own property subject to a right of survivorship, the law favors tenancy in common, and joint tenancy property is not subject to the debts of a deceased joint tenant.

Joint tenancy *Two or more persons to whom land is deeded in such manner that they have "one and the same interest, accruing by one and the same conveyance, commencing at one and the same time, and held by the same undivided possession." Upon the death of one joint tenant, his property passes to the survivor or survivors.*

In order to establish a valid joint tenancy, certain requirements must be satisfied. These requirements are known as the four unities of time, title, interest, and possession. The *unity of time* requires that the joint tenants' ownership be created in the same conveyance. To have the *unity of title*, each owner must have the same estate, such as a fee simple absolute, a remainder, or any other estate, which is created by the same conveyance. The *unity of interest* exists when each owner has the same percentage interest subject to the other owners' interest. For example, two joint tenants must each own 50 percent of the undivided property, three own 33 percent each, four own 25 percent each, and so forth. Finally, the *unity of possession* is present when each joint tenant has the right to possess all the property subject to the other owners' rights of possession.

When there is a question about which form of ownership exists in any specific case, the law usually favors tenancy in common and property passing by will or intestacy, rather than its passing by right of survivorship. Courts do not find that property is held in joint tenancy with the right of survivorship unless there is a contract between the two co-owners clearly stating that such is the case and that the right of survivorship is to apply. Bank signature cards and stock certificates that use the term *joint tenancy* or "with the right of survivorship" create such a contract, as does the language "as joint tenants and not as tenants in common." In most states, the contract must be signed by both parties to be effective. Failure to use the proper language or have a properly executed contract results in a tenancy in common.

Several additional aspects of holding property in joint tenancy frequently result in litigation. First of all, joint tenancy is often used as a substitute for a will. A party wishing to leave property to another on death sometimes puts the property in joint tenancy. Is a present gift intended? Does the new joint tenant have the right to share in the income of the property prior to the death of the original owner? Such issues are frequently litigated, and the answers depend on the intent of the parties.

A similar issue arises when one person in ill health or incapacitated adds another person's name to a savings or a checking account in order to allow the latter to pay bills and handle the former's business transactions. The signature card often provides for a joint tenancy. Was a joint tenancy or mere agency intended? Joint tenancy arrangements are frequently challenged successfully on the ground that the right of survivorship was not intended.

Another difficulty involves describing the property held in joint tenancy. Frequently, a contract covering a safe deposit box will provide that it be held in joint tenancy. Does such a contract cover the contents of the box as well? The following case is typical of those involving this issue.

CASE

Mrs. Morak, an elderly woman, and Dwight and Kathleen Davison were close friends. Indeed, the Davisons took care of Mrs. Morak because she had no close relatives. On June 11, 1981, the Davisons and Mrs. Morak rented a safe deposit box as joint tenants with right of survivorship. Mrs. Morak used this box exclusively during her life. Mrs. Morak died on July 8, 1984 intestate and with no known heirs. On January 4, 1985, Dwight and Kathleen Davison filed a petition alleging they were joint tenants with a right of survivorship in the contents of the safe deposit box worth $324,987.35 and $4,020 in currency. The bonds show Mrs. Morak and various members of her family, all of whom are apparently deceased, as the owners. The administrator of the estate filed an answer alleging that the agreement of joint tenancy with right of survivorship between the Davisons and the decedent was merely for the use of the box and not for the disposition of the contents.

ISSUE: Were the Davisons entitled to the contents of the safe deposit box they rented with Mrs. Morak as joint tenants?

DECISION: No.

REASONS:
1. The only evidence offered indicating that the Davisons had a right to the contents of the lock box was provided by the Davisons. Mr. Davison testified that Mrs. Morak told him he and his wife were to become joint owners of what was in the box. He also stated, however, that he did not know what the box contained and that he never entered the box during Mrs. Morak's lifetime.
2. A joint lease of a safe deposit box in and of itself is insufficient to support the contention that a gift has been made of the contents.
3. The deposit of articles in a jointly leased safe deposit box of itself works no change in title, absent an express agreement that the contents of the box shall be joint property. This is so even if the language in the lease describes a joint tenancy with the right of survivorship, unless it specifically refers to the contents.
4. In conclusion, the agreement between these parties was only for the rental of the safe deposit box and not for the disposition of its contents.

Newton County v. Davison, 790 S.W.2d 810 (Ark. 1986).

What is the effect of a mortgage by one joint tenant that purports to cover all the property held in joint tenancy? In some states, the mortgage operates to sever the joint tenancy, and the mortgage is valid against the undivided interest of the mortgagor. This result is not reached in states that treat a mortgage as merely a lien. In these states, there is no severance, and upon the death of the mortgagor, the property is free of the mortgage. In almost every state, the courts have held that one joint tenant cannot encumber the interest of the other co-tenant without consent. A grantor can only give what he owns, and a grantee can only receive what the grantor is entitled to convey. A mortgagee's claim is thus limited to the interest of the mortgagor.

Another disadvantage of the joint tenancy arrangement is the ease with which it may be severed or terminated. Each joint tenant has the power to terminate the right of survivorship by a simple transfer or conveyance of his interest to a third party. The severance of the unities of time, title, interest, or possession converts the joint tenancy to a tenancy in common. This severance may occur either by one of the co-owner's actions or by order of a court in a suit for partition of the owners' interests, as occurred in the following case.

CASE

Robert Hall, James Hall, and Beverly Hamilton are brothers and sister. Their parents deeded the family home to these three as "joint tenants with right of survivorship and not as tenants in common." After their father died, Beverly moved into this house to live with their mother. When their mother died in 1980, Beverly continued to live in the house. Because she refused to agree to sell this property, Robert and James filed this suit for partition of three owners' interests. Beverly objected and argued that a joint tenancy cannot be ended by court order.

ISSUE: Is property held in joint tenancy subject to partition?

DECISION: Yes.

REASONS:

1. Partition provides a method whereby two or more persons who own property together may put an end to the multiple ownership, so that each may own a separate portion of the property or, if a division in kind is not feasible, the property may be sold and each owner given an appropriate share of the proceeds.
2. The right of partition is considered an incident of common ownership. The general rule, therefore, is that all property capable of being held in co-tenancy is subject to partition by judicial proceedings.
3. A joint tenant is a co-tenant owning an undivided interest in property, and partition may be had as between joint tenants to the same extent as between tenants in common.
4. A joint tenancy may be so created that partition of it cannot be had; but in the absence of such a provision, a joint tenancy may be divided by the courts at the request of one owner without the consent of the other owners.

Hall v. Hamilton, 667 P.2d 350 (Kan. 1983).

9. Tenancy by the Entirety

If the owners are related by marriage and the state law so provides, a conveyance to a husband and wife creates a specialized joint tenancy, which is called tenancy by the entireties. A tenancy by the entirety in states that authorize such common ownership of real estate can exist only between husband and wife. A conveyance of real estate to a husband and wife in these states is automatically a tenancy by the entirety if all four unities, discussed above, are present. Neither tenant can unilaterally sever or end the tenancy. It may be terminated only by divorce, a joint transfer to a third party, or a conveyance by one spouse to the other. The inability of either spouse to terminate the tenancy unilaterally is the primary difference between a joint tenancy and a tenancy by the entireties, as the basic characteristic of each is the right of survivorship.

In most states that authorize tenancy by the entireties, not only is there a prohibition on one tenant making a voluntary transfer of his share, but there are also severe restrictions on the rights of creditors to collect an individual debt from one tenant of the property. Suppose a husband and wife own their home as tenants by the entireties. A creditor has a judgment for $10,000 against the husband alone. In most states, the creditor could not cause a sale of the house to collect the debt. Of course, if the creditor had a judgment against both husband and wife, he could collect from a judicial sale of the property.

TRUSTS

10. Introduction

Trust *A relationship between persons by which one holds property for the use and benefit of another. The relationship is called fiduciary in nature. The person entrusted with the property is called a trustee. The person for whose benefit the property is held is called a beneficiary.*

The word **trust** is generally used to describe an *express* private trust. An *express private trust* is a fiduciary relationship with respect to property, which subjects the person with legal title to property (the *trustee)* to equitable duties to deal with the property for the benefit of another (the *beneficiary*). In other words, a *trust* is a fiduciary relationship under which one person, the trustee, holds title to property and deals with it for the benefit of another person, the beneficiary. The most important single aspect of the relationship is its fiduciary character. The trustee is under an absolute obligation to act solely for the benefit of the beneficiary in every aspect of the relationship. Both real and personal property may be held in trust.

11. Creation of Trusts

A trust may be created by a transfer of property during one's lifetime (a *living*, or *inter vivos*, *trust*), or it may be created by a transfer on death (a *testamentary trust*). The person creating the trust is usually called the *settlor*, although he is sometimes referred to as the *creator* or the *trustor* in estate planning literature. The settlor may create the trust by a transfer of property to the trustee, or the settlor may declare himself to be trustee of described property for the benefit of designated beneficiaries.

Consideration is not required to create a trust. Although consideration may support the creation of an *inter vivos* trust, it is rarely present in a testamentary trust. A trust involving real estate requires written evidence of the intention to create the trust and an exact description of the property held in trust. This writing requirement must be satisfied since the statute of frauds is applicable to trusts containing real estate. In general, personal property may be held in a trust that is created orally. Although it is preferable to state clearly that a trust is being created, not all trusts are created by a formally drafted trust agreement.

A trust may have several beneficiaries, and their rights may be dependent on several variable factors. The trustee may be authorized to determine which beneficiaries shall receive the income of the trust and how much each shall receive. The right of a trustee to allocate the income of the trust among the beneficiaries is sometimes referred to as a *sprinkling trust* provision. It has the advantage of allowing the trustee with actual knowledge of the needs of the beneficiaries to take those needs into account in the distribution of income. A trust may also have successive beneficiaries. A trust could provide that the income would go to the deceased's spouse for life; and on the death of the spouse, to their children for life; on the children's death, to grandchildren.

A settlor may be a trustee as well as one of the beneficiaries of a trust. A trustee may be one of the beneficiaries of a trust, but the sole trustee cannot be the sole beneficiary. If the sole trustee is the sole beneficiary of a trust, there is a merger of the legal and equitable interests, causing a termination of the trust by operation of law.

When the settlor is also the trustee and life beneficiary, the trust operates in effect as a will. It is nevertheless valid in most states, even though it is not executed with the formality required of a will. In such case, it is used to avoid probate proceedings and to save the costs involved in such proceedings.

12. Types of Trusts

In addition to the express private trust, the law recognizes trusts created by operation of law: constructive trusts, resulting trusts, and charitable trusts. A court of equity may create a *constructive trust* in order to prevent unjust enrichment, as in a transfer of property procured by fraud or violation or some fiduciary duty. Courts of equity also create *resulting trusts*, which result when the person with legal title is not intended to have it. For example, if a child purchases property in the name of a parent, there is no presumption of a gift, and the child may establish that the parent holds title in trust for the child.

The *charitable trust* is a valuable estate planning tool. It differs from a private trust in that it can benefit an indefinite group and can have perpetual existence. Among typical charitable purposes for which a trust can be created are the promotion of religion, education, health, public comfort, and the relief of poverty.

Perhaps the single most important principle in the law of charitable trusts is the doctrine of *cy pres*, which provides that if a particular charitable purpose cannot be carried out in the manner directed by the settlor, the court can direct the application of the trust property to another charitable purpose consistent with the general charitable intention. The words *cy pres* mean ''as nearly as,'' and the courts simply choose another charitable purpose that is as nearly as possible like the one designated by the settlor. The following case is typical of those applying this very important doctrine.

CASE

Leta Puckett's will established a trust to be funded by the residue of her estate after specific bequests were completed. The trust was established in order to provide two annual one-year scholarships for students going to college. One scholarship was to benefit a student studying science, chemistry, or premedicine. The other scholarship was to benefit a student studying religion. The trust provided that after expenses were paid for the trust's administration, all the net income was to be divided equally between these two scholarships. Lena Lee Myers, a first cousin of Leta Puckett, challenged this testamentary trust on the grounds that the trust property would produce net income far in excess of that needed to establish the two scholarships. Ms. Myers argues that she is entitled to this excess property as the deceased's closest intestate heir.

ISSUE: If the property included in a charitable trust exceeds that needed to accomplish the charitable purpose, what should be done with the excessive property?

DECISION: It should be used for charitable purposes.

REASONS:

1. *Cy pres* is an equitable power that makes it possible for a court to carry out a testamentary trust established for a particular charitable purpose if the testator has expressed a general charitable intent, and for some reason his purpose cannot be accomplished in the manner specified in the will. The court is empowered to direct the disposition of the property to some related charitable purpose in order to carry out the testator's purpose as nearly as possible.
2. A testator is said to have had a "general charitable purpose" when the particular gift is of a generally charitable nature rather than to benefit a specific charitable entity.
3. Where the income of a trust fund is directed by a will to be used for certain charitable purposes, but at the time of the testator's death it is greater than appears reasonably required for such purposes, *cy pres* can be used to apply the surplus to similar charitable purposes.
4. Therefore, if in the present case the trust's net income is more than is needed to furnish two scholarships, scholarships may be provided for additional students.

Estate of Puckett, 168 Cal. Rptr. 311 (Cal. App. 1980).

13. Administration of Trusts

Since a trust is fiduciary relationship, the trustee owes a high duty of loyalty to the beneficiary. The trustee is not allowed to enter individually into transactions with the trust. Such contracts or transactions are voidable without regard to fairness, and good faith is no defense. A trustee also has a duty not to delegate his responsibility to another.

Perhaps the most important duty of the trustee is in regard to investments. The trustee has a duty not to commingle trust funds with his individual funds and a duty to earmark and segregate trust property. The trustee has a duty to diversify investments. This diversity is sometimes horizontal, sometimes vertical. *Horizontal diversity* means that the trustee should diversify his investments geographically and in various industries throughout the country. *Vertical diversity* means that he should diversify by investing in different companies within the same industry.

It is frequently stated that a trustee, in the selection of trust investments, must exercise a degree of care that men of prudence and intelligence exercise in the management of their own affairs, not in regard to speculation, but in regard to the permanent disposition of their funds, considering probable income as well as the probable safety of the investment. This is generally known as the *prudent man rule*.

To obtain the requisite diversification, especially in trusts with relatively small amounts of assets, *common trust funds* have developed. They allow a trustee, such as a bank or a trust company that holds several trusts, to invest the trust funds together. The duty not to commingle is not violated, because each trust fund has its stated proportion of the total investment.

The trustee has all necessary powers to carry out the appropriate duties. These generally include the power to sell if necessary, to lease, to incur necessary expenses, to settle claims, and to retain investments. A trustee generally has no power to borrow money or to mortgage the trust assets. A trustee is liable to the beneficiary for any loss caused by a breach of trust and for any personal profit made in breach of his duty of loyalty. A trustee who makes improper investments cannot set off the gains on one against the losses on the other. Any gain in an improper investment remains in the trust, and the trustee is required to make up the losses on improper investments.

14. Termination of Trusts

In the absence of fraud or mistake, a settlor cannot revoke a trust unless he has specifically reserved the power to do so. The same principle applies to modifications of the trust. A trust may be terminated when its purposes have been accomplished or if the trust purpose becomes illegal. A trust may be terminated by the consent of all beneficiaries, provided that are all of legal age and all consent, and provided also that termination will not defeat the purpose for which the trust was created. This last-mentioned provision is especially important in the so-called *spendthrift* trust, which is to protect one or more beneficiaries who are unable to manage financial matters. Such trusts cannot be terminated even with the beneficiaries' consent.

In regard to spendthrift trusts, it should be noted that all trusts are spendthrift trusts to a certain extent. That is, as a general rule, a creditor cannot collect a debt of the beneficiary directly from the trust estate if the trust was created by someone other than the beneficiary. One of the purposes of a trust is to protect the beneficiary from the claims of his creditors, and allowing a creditor to collect directly from the trust estate would defeat this purpose. Therefore, with the exception of a few claims, such as alimony, child support, and taxes, the trustee is not obligated to pay over the income or principal of the trust estate to anyone other than the beneficiary. Of course, after the beneficiary has received the income, a creditor may use legal process to collect a claim. The fact that all trusts are spendthrift regarding involuntary transfers is a major reason for use of the trust device.

CHAPTER SUMMARY

Wills

Terminology	1. A person who leaves a valid will dies *testate*. This person is known as a *testator*.

2. An *executor* settles the estate of a person dying testate. An *administrator* is appointed by a court to settle the estate of a person dying intestate. A *guardian* is the personal representative of the person of a minor and his estate. A *conservator* is the personal representative of a person who is not competent to handle his own affairs.
3. A gift of real property as a term of the will is a *devise*. A *bequest* is a gift of personal property in general under a will. A *legacy* is a gift of a specific amount of money.

Testamentary Capacity

1. A testator must be the minimum statutory age, such as 18.
2. A testator must have the capacity to know the kind and character of his property, to know and remember the natural objects of his affection, and to make a scheme of distribution.

Formalities of Execution

1. A will must be signed by the testator or by someone else in his presence and at his direction.
2. A will must be attested in the presence of the testator by two or three (depending on the state) disinterested and competent witnesses.

Grounds for Challenging a Will's Validity

1. The lack of the testator's capacity to make a will and the lack of proper execution are two grounds for having a will declared void.
2. Proof that the testator was unduly influenced, which means his true desires were not folllowed, is another important method for challenging a will.

Revocation, Republication, Revival, and Renunciation

1. A will is ambulatory and can be changed at any time during the testator's life.
2. A will may be revoked by destruction, a later will, marriage, or divorce.
3. Once a will is revoked, it cannot be revived automatically. In order to be valid, a revoked will must be republished.
4. A spouse may renounce a will and claim a statutory interest against the estate.

Alternatives to Wills

Intestate Succession

1. A person who dies without leaving a valid will is said to die *intestate*.
2. In such a case, the deceased person's property is distributed according to the scheme of distribution provided by state statute.

Joint Tenancy

1. A joint tenancy is characterized by the right of survivorship. However, the right may be severed by one of the co-owners conveying his interest to a third party.

Tenancy by the Entirety

1. A tenancy by the entirety is a special type of joint tenancy. This method of co-ownership is limited to real property interests jointly held by a husband and wife. Generally, this right of survivorship cannot be severed without the consent of both spouses.

Trusts

Creation of Trusts

1. A trust is used by one person to transfer legal title to real or personal property to another person for the benefit of a third person.
2. These parties are known as the settlor, trustee, and beneficiary, respectively.
3. An *inter vivos* trust is created during the lifetime of the settlor. A *testamentary* trust is created in a settlor's will.

Types of Trusts	1. An express private trust is created by a settlor for the benefit of an individual or a non-charitable organization. 2. A constructive trust can be created by a court of equity in order to prevent unjust enrichment. 3. A resulting trust also can be created by a court of equity when a person who actually has legal title to property is supposed to hold that property for the benefit of another party. 4. A charitable trust occurs when the beneficiary is a charitable organization. This trust is an important estate planning tool since it can be used to reduce estate taxes. The doctrine of *cy pres* often is applied to accomplish the settlor's charitable intent.
Administration of Trusts	1. All trustees are in the fiduciary position of trust and confidence. 2. Trustees must use the trust property only for the beneficiary. 3. Trustees must handle and invest the trust property as a reasonably prudent person would.
Termination of Trusts	1. Generally, a settlor cannot revoke an established trust unless the right of revocation is reserved. 2. Trusts usually are terminated when their purpose has been accomplished or when all the beneficiaries (assuming that they are competent) agree to the termination.

REVIEW QUESTIONS AND PROBLEMS

1. Match each term in column A with the appropriate statement in Column B.

A	B
(1) Testator	(a) Created during the lifetime of the settlor.
(2) Executor	(b) Dying without leaving a valid will.
(3) Bequest	(c) A person who dies and leaves a valid will.
(4) Undue influence	(d) A special method whereby spouses can own real property with a right of survivorship.
(5) Intestate	(e) A gift of personal property under the terms of a will.
(6) Joint tenancy	(f) A method whereby two or more people may own either real or personal property.
(7) Tenancy by the entirety	(g) The personal representative who manages the estate of a testator.
(8) Settlor	(h) An equitable principle used to accomplish a settlor's charitable intent.
(9) *Inter vivos* trust	(i) A ground for challenging a will's validity requiring proof that the testator lacked freedom of choice.
(10) *Cy pres*	(j) The creator of a trust.

2. Jud executed a will in his hospital room, where he was dying from acute alcoholism and cancer. He was under sedation and had been given two ounces of whisky. The will provided that Jud's property was to be divided between his wife and daughter. When the will was challenged, witnesses testified that the will had been read to Jud and that he appeared to understand it. Did Jud have sufficient testamentary capacity to make the will valid? Explain.

3. Ted died January 12, 1990. His widow presented for probate a will dated October 18, 1989. Betsy, one of the witnesses on the will, testified that she did not see Ted sign this will and that Ted was not present when she signed as a witness. Was this will properly executed? Why or why not?

4. A testator was hospitalized with terminal cancer. When he executed his will, it was read to him by the attorney who prepared it. Being quite feeble, the testator signed it with an *X* and it was attested to by the lawyer and a nurse. Is the will validly executed? Explain.

5. Woodrow Larrick died on June 27, 1979. A few days before he died, Woodrow tore up his will and burned it. This will provided that $30,000 be given to his brother, Arthur, and that the rest of his estate go to his wife, Verna, to whom he had been married since 1974. As the surviving wife, Verna was appointed administratrix on July 23, 1979. Under the Arkansas intestate succession statute, she was to receive Woodrow's entire estate. Arthur, the brother, sought to have a copy of Woodrow's will probated. He contended that Woodrow revoked his old will only on the condition that a new will was made as a substitute. Since Woodrow's sudden death prevented the will from being signed, the old will should not be considered revoked. Does the doctrine of dependent relative revocation operate to save Woodrow's will and the gift to Arthur? Explain.

6. Lloyd, a car dealer, individually owned a house and his business building in joint tenancy with his wife. Lloyd died suddenly, leaving a million-dollar insurance policy payable to his wife and the aforesaid real estate. His corporate business was insolvent by $250,000. Is the wife obligated to pay off the business debt? Is the real property or insurance encumbered by it? Explain.

7. A mother deposited $10,000 of her money in a joint account with her son in a savings and loan association. Both signatures were required for withdrawal, and the signature card contained the following: "Any funds placed in, or added to, the account by any one of the parties is and shall be conclusively intended to be a gift to the other party to the extent of his pro rata share." The mother retained possession of the passbook and subsequently brought suit, claiming that she is the sole owner of the funds. Is the mother correct? Why?

8. Halliburton executed a warranty deed to himself and Morgan, as joint tenants. Later a bank loaned Halliburton $100,000, which was secured by a note and mortgage covering the real property jointly owned by Halliburton and Morgan. Morgan was not a party to the loan or the mortgage. Halliburton dies. Does the bank have a valid claim against the property? Why or why not?

9. After Henry married Wilma, he transferred a house he owned to himself and Wilma, as joint tenants. Later, Henry filed a declaration to sever the survivorship right of the joint tenancy. He then executed a will devising his interest in the house to his daughter by a previous marriage. Upon Henry's death, Wilma claimed ownership of the property. Should Wilma receive the property as the surviving joint tenant? Why?

10. Would you answer to problem 9 change if a tenancy by the entirety had been created instead of a joint tenancy? Explain.

11. Donald and Mary Alice were husband and wife. As a result of their divorce and property settlement, the parties agreed as follows:

    That income derived from the interest held by the parties in the real estate syndicate known as the Big Bear Property in San Bernardino County, California, should be established as a family trust . . . with the Plaintiff and Defendant as Trustees with the restriction and requirement that said funds be accumulated for the education of the minor children of the parties. . . .

    Throughout the next several years, these parties had the income from their Big Bear Property deposited into an account at a local bank. Mary Alice sought to have this account closed and one-half of the $5,914.28 on deposit given to her. After her former husband objected, Mary Alice filed suit and argued that a formal trust was never created. Was this money deposited in a local bank pursuant to a divorce decree and property settlement agreement held in trust? Why or why not?

12. Theresa established a trust of certain farmland in which she was both trustee and income beneficiary during her lifetime. The trust agreement provided that upon Theresa's death the earnings were to go to her brother for his life. Theresa died intestate. Her nieces claimed that the trust arrangement, though an attempted substitution for a will, was void, since it was not executed formally as a will must be. Is the trust valid? Explain.

13. Marcia, a trustee, was given broad authority by the trust instrument in the administration of the trust. Using trust funds, she made a personal profit from a real estate investment. Valerie, a beneficiary to the trust, sued to recover the profits for the estate. Has Marcia breached her fiduciary duty? Explain.

36 Introduction to Commercial Paper

C H A P T E R   P R E V I E W

BUSINESS MANAGEMENT DECISION

As treasurer of a large company, you are charged with overseeing all your company's relationships with financial institutions.

What procedures should you and your staff follow with respect to the company checking account and bank statements?

This part of the text covers the law as it relates to contract obligations that are in the form of **commercial paper.** These principles are primarily found in Article 3 of the Uniform Commercial Code. Such contracts are often referred to as negotiable instruments. The word *negotiable* means that such instruments can move freely in financial transactions as a substitute for money. For example, checks are negotiable instruments used to pay for goods and services. Negotiable instruments are also credit devices. When one borrows money or purchases goods on credit, the usual practice is for the debtor to execute a promissory note payable to the creditor.

Commercial paper *Negotiable instruments that serve as a substitute for money or as a credit transaction.*

There are two basic types of negotiable instruments. The *note* is a promise to pay and the *draft* is an order to someone else to pay. The *check* is a typical draft, an order from the drawer, directing the drawee (bank) to pay money to the payee of the check.

This chapter discusses the basic concepts of negotiable instruments with a major emphasis on checks. The following chapters cover the law as it relates to negotiable instruments and the rights and liabilities of the various parties.

CONCEPT OF NEGOTIABILITY

Negotiable instruments developed because of the commercial need for something that would be readily acceptable in lieu of money and would accordingly be readily transferable in trade or commerce. Substantial protection and assurance of payment must be given to any person to whom the paper might be transferred. To accomplish this protection, it is necessary to insulate the transferee from most of the defenses that a primary party, such as the maker of a note, might have against the payee. The purpose of the negotiability trait is to prevent the primary party from asserting defenses to the instrument against the person to whom the paper was transferred.

To accomplish the foregoing, Article 3 of the Code provides that a person to whom negotiable paper is negotiated takes it free of personal defenses arising out of the agreement from which the negotiable paper was created.

This basic theory of negotiability can be further explained by noting the difference between the *assignment* of a contract and the *negotiation* of a negotiable instrument. Assume that the dealer owes the manufacturer $1,000 but has a counterclaim because the product was defective. If a third party such as a bank purchased the contract right to collect the $1,000 from the manufacturer, it would be subject to the dealer's defense of failure of consideration. The bank, as assignee, would secure no better right against the dealer than the original right held by the manufacturer, the assignor. The bank therefore could not collect the full $1,000 from the dealer.

In this example, if the evidence of the debt is not a simple contract for money but a negotiable promissory note given by the dealer to the manufacturer, and if it is properly negotiated, the bank is in a position superior to that which it occupied when it was an assignee. Assuming that it is a "holder in due course," the bank has a better title because it is free of the personal defenses that are available against the manufacturer, the original party to the paper. The dealer, therefore, cannot use the defense of failure of consideration, and the bank can collect the $1,000.

Transfer of the instrument free of personal defenses is the very essence of negotiability. Three requirements must be met before a transferee is free from personal defenses. First, the instrument must be negotiable; that is, it must comply with the statutory formalities and language requirements. An instrument that does not qualify is nonnegotiable, and any transfer is an assignment subject to all defenses. Second, the instrument must be properly *negotiated* to the transferee. If the instrument is not properly negotiated, the transfer is an assignment subject to all defenses. Third, the party to whom negotiable commercial paper is negotiated must be a *holder in due course* or have the rights of a holder in due course. Each of these concepts is discussed in detail in the next chapters.

The defenses that cannot be asserted against a holder in due course are called *personal defenses*. *Real defenses*, on the other hand, may be asserted against anyone, including a holder in due course. Real defenses are matters that go to the very existence of the instruments. Personal defenses such as failure of consideration involve less serious matters and usually relate to the transaction out of which they arose, or events such as payment of the note. The following case illustrates the importance of obtaining the return of a negotiable instrument when payment is made.

CASE

Florida City Express, Inc., in return for merchandise, executed promissory notes payable to Latin American Tire Company. The payee indorsed and discounted the notes with the Bank of Miami. The bank took the notes before maturity for value, and without notice of the existence of any defenses to them; hence, it was a holder in due course.

When the notes matured, the Bank of Miami sought to collect them. In the meantime, the maker of the notes had paid the payee the principal due on the notes. These payments were not recorded on the notes.

ISSUE: Must the maker pay the notes again?

DECISION: Yes.

REASONS:

1. A holder in due course takes and holds a negotiable instrument free of all defenses of which he is not on notice. It is very clear that this rule includes the defense of discharge or payment.
2. When an instrument is paid in whole or in part before maturity, it is the duty of the party making payment to have the payment noted on or to require surrender of the instrument. If he omits these precautions and the instrument is transferred before maturity to a holder in due course without notice of the payments, he may not avail himself of the personal defense of prior payment against such a holder in due course.

Bank of Miami v. Florida City Express, Inc., 367 So.2d 683 (Fla. App. 1979).

KINDS OF COMMERCIAL PAPER

1. Terminology

Article 3 of the Code, Commercial Paper, is restricted in its coverage to the negotiable note, certificate of deposit, draft, and check. A note is two-party paper, as is a certificate of deposit. The parties to a note are the *maker*, who promises to pay, and the *payee*, to whom the promise is made. The draft and the check are three-party instruments. A draft presupposes a debtor-creditor relationship between the *drawer* and the *drawee* or some other obligation on the part of the drawee in favor of the drawer. The drawee is the debtor; the drawer is the creditor. The drawer-creditor orders the drawee-debtor to pay money to a third party, who is the *payee*. The mere execution of the draft does not obligate the drawee on the paper. The drawee's liability on the paper arises when it formally *accepts* the obligation to pay in writing upon the draft itself. By accepting, the drawee becomes primarily liable on the paper [3–410(1)]. Thereafter, the drawee is called an *acceptor*, and its liability is similar to the liability of the maker of a promissory note.

2. Notes

A *note* initially is a two-party instrument in which the issuer (the *maker*) promises to pay to the order of a *payee* or to **bearer** (see Figure 36–1). A note is used to evidence an obligation to pay in the future and is typically employed in loan and secured sales transactions.

Bearer *The person in possession of an instrument.*

3. Certificates of Deposit

A *certificate of deposit* (commonly called a CD) is a two-party, usually short-term, instrument in which a bank is the maker [3–104(2)(c)]. A CD is a bank's written acknowledgment of money on deposit that the bank promises to pay to the depositor or to his order or to some third person. The promise to repay distinguishes the CD from a deposit slip. A CD basically is a promissory note issued by a bank as a means of investment. People buy CDs to earn the interest they bear. The bank may pay higher rates of interest than on a savings account, since a CD may not be redeemed until the date specified without significant penalties. Figure 36–2 is an example of a negotiable CD.

$5,000 July 1, 19XX

For value received, I, the undersigned, promise
to pay to the order of Paul Payee on demand
the principal sum of $5,000 (five thousand dollars).

/s/ ______________________ (seal)

FIGURE 36–1

CERTIFICATE OF DEPOSIT
First Athens Bank
Athens, GA

Has received on deposit and on May 1, 1996 will pay to the order of Darlene Depositor $20,000.00 (twenty thousand dollars) with interest at a rate of ten percent (10%) payable upon return of this certificate properly indorsed. No payment before maturity. No interest after maturity.

First Athens Bank

May 1, 1990 /s/
(date of issue) (authorized signature)

FIGURE 36–2

4. Drafts

A *draft* (sometimes called a bill of exchange) is a simple order to pay money [3–104(2)(a)]. It is addressed by one person (the *drawer*) to another person (the *payor* or *drawee*), requiring that person to pay on demand or at a fixed future time a definite amount to the order of a named person (the *payee* or *holder*) or to bearer. A seller of goods or services may draw a draft on the buyer for purchase price of the goods, making the instrument payable to himself. In this case, the seller is both the drawer and the payee, while the buyer is the drawee of the draft. In drawing this draft, the seller implicitly promises to pay its amount to any holder if it is not paid by the drawee [3–413(2)]. By putting his demand for payment in the stylized form of a draft, the seller thereby facilitates the transfer of his right to receive payment from the buyer.

Drafts may be payable on demand or at a fixed or determinable time. Usually demand drafts are presented to the drawee for payment and are said to be payable *on sight*. Time drafts may be presented to the drawee for payment or *acceptance*. They are said to be payable at a fixed time after sight.

5. Checks

A *check* is a demand draft drawn on a bank. A check drawn by a bank upon itself is a *cashier's check*. *Travelers' checks* are like cashier's checks in that the financial institution issuing them is both the drawer and the drawee. Travelers' checks are negotiable when they have been completed by the identifying signature. A *bank draft* is a banker's check; that is, it is a check drawn by one bank on another bank, payable on demand.

A *certified check* is one that has been accepted by the drawee bank. Either the drawer or the holder of a check may present it to the drawee bank for certification. The bank will stamp "certified" on the check, and an official of the bank will sign it and date it. By certifying, the bank assumes responsibility for payment and sets aside funds from its customer's account to cover the check.

Certification may or may not change the legal liability of the parties upon the instrument. When the *drawer* has a check certified, such a certification merely acts as additional security and does not relieve the drawer of any liability. On the other hand, when the *holder* of a check secures certification by the drawee bank, he thereby accepts the bank as the only party liable thereon. Such an act discharges the drawer and all prior indorsers from any liability [3–411(1)]. The effect of such certification is similar to a payment by the bank and redeposit by the holder.

The refusal of a bank to certify a check at the request of a holder is not a dishonor of the instrument. The bank owes the depositor a duty to pay but not necessarily the duty to certify checks that are drawn on it, unless there is a previous agreement to certify [3–411(2)]. A drawer cannot stop payment on a check after the bank has certified it.

Checks are sometimes postdated. A *postdated check* creates different legal relationships than does a "regular" check. It does not represent that funds are currently available to cover the check. A postdated check is, in effect, a credit transaction.

BANK DEPOSITS AND COLLECTIONS

6. Terminology

Article 4 of the Code, Bank Deposits and Collections, provides uniform rules to govern the collection of checks and other instruments for the payment of money. These rules govern the relationship of banks with one another and with depositors in the collection and payment of items.

The following terminology of Section 4–105 of the Code is significant with regard to the designation of the various banks in the collection process for checks:

1. "**Depositary bank**" means the first bank to which an item is transferred for collection even though it is also the payor bank.
2. "**Payor bank**" means a bank by which an item is payable as drawn or accepted.
3. "**Intermediary bank**" means any bank to which an item is transferred in course of collection except the depositary or payor bank.
4. "**Collecting bank**" means any bank handling the item for collection except the payor bank.
5. "**Presenting bank**" means any bank presenting an item to a payor bank.
6. "**Remitting bank**" means any payor or intermediary bank remitting for an item.

It should be kept in mind that a bank may occupy more than one status in the collection process. For example, a bank that receives a customer's deposit drawn on another bank is both a depositary and a collecting bank. A bank accepting a deposit of a check drawn by another customer is both a depositary and a payor bank.

Timing is important in the check collection process. Many of the technical rules of law refer to a *banking day,* which is defined as "that part of any day on which a bank is open to the public for carrying on substantially all of its banking functions" [4–104(1)(c)]. A bank is permitted to establish a cutoff hour of 2 P.M. or later, so that the bank may have an opportunity to process items, prove balances, and make the necessary entries to determine its position for the day. If an item is received after the cutoff hour or after the close of the banking day, it may be treated as having been received at the opening of the next banking day [4–107]. The term *midnight deadline* with respect to a bank means midnight on its banking day following the banking day on which it receives a check or a notice regarding the check [4–104(1)(h)].

7. The Bank Collection Process

If a check is deposited in a bank other than the bank on which it is drawn, it must be sent to the payor bank for payment. This collection process may involve routing the item through a number of banks that typically credit or debit accounts they maintain with one another. In particular, the regional Federal Reserve Banks, with which most banks have accounts, play a major role in this process. An example may help you understand the collection process.

Suppose that Carson in Athens, Georgia, mails his check drawn on the First Athens Bank to Exxon in Houston, Texas, in payment of an obligation. Exxon deposits the check in the First National Bank of Houston, which forwards it to the Federal Reserve Bank of Houston, which sends it to the Federal Reserve Bank of Atlanta, which presents it to the First Athens Bank for payment. The relationship of these parties is depicted in Figure 36–3.

As Figure 36–3 indicates, the collection process begins when the customer (Exxon) deposits a check to its account. The account is provisionally credited by the bank. The check then passes through the collecting banks, each of which provisionally credits the account of the prior bank. When the check finally reaches the payor-drawee bank (First Athens Bank), that bank debits the drawer's (Carson's) account.

Clearinghouse *An association of banks or other payors regularly clearing items.*

Honor *To pay or to accept the instrument.*

The payor bank then credits the account of the presenting bank, remits to it or, if both belong to the same **clearinghouse,** includes the check in its balance there. If the payor bank **honors** the check, the settlement is final. Transactions

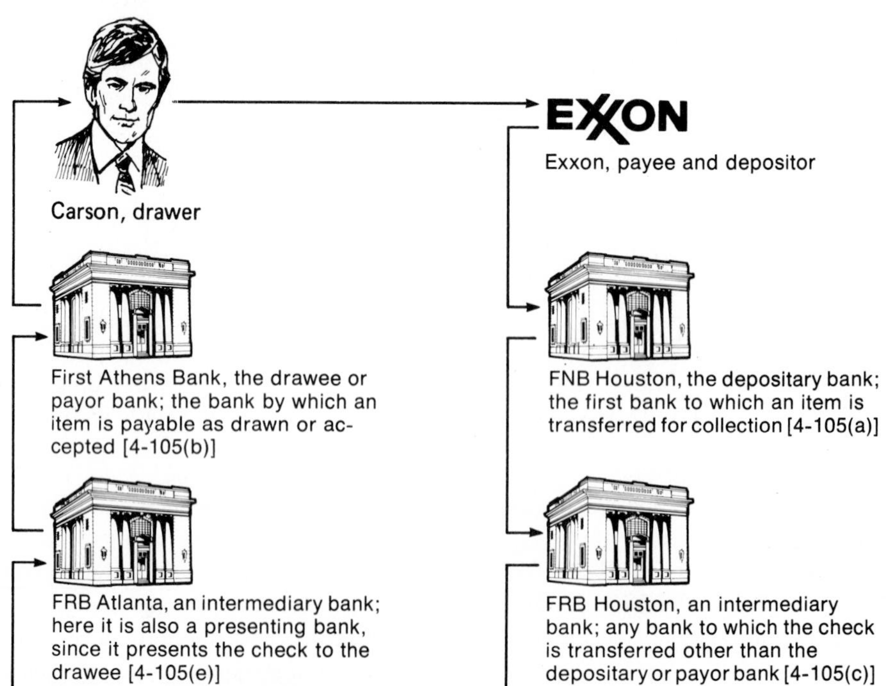

FIGURE 36–3 Process of Collecting Transit Item

prior to this final settlement by the payor bank are called "provisional settlements," because it is not known until final settlement whether the check is "good." If the payor bank **dishonors** the check, as in the case of an "N.S.F." (not sufficient funds) check, the presenting bank will revoke its provisional settlement and charge the item back to the account of the prior collecting bank. Likewise, other banks in the chain of collection will charge back. The final step is a chargeback to the **customer's** account by the depositary bank and the return of the check to the customer. Each of the collecting banks must return the item or send notification of the facts by its midnight deadline. The right to charge back by the depositary bank is not affected by the fact that the depositor may have drawn against the provisional credit.

Dishonor *Acceptance or payment is refused or cannot be obtained.*

Customer *A person having an account with a bank or for whom a bank has agreed to collect items.*

A depositor does not have the right to draw against uncollected funds. Accordingly, he is not entitled to draw against an item payable by another bank until the provisional settlement his depositary bank has received becomes final [4–213(4)(a)].

Availability of funds. Because of complaints by customers that the check collection process allowed financial institutions to "hold" the availability of funds for excessive periods, Congress passed and President Ronald Reagan signed the Expedited Funds Availability Act. The regulations issued by the Federal Reserve Board have established when funds from deposited checks must be available to customers.

Beginning September 1, 1990, funds from cashier's checks, certified checks, government checks, and electronic deposits must be available to the customer on the next business day after deposit. Funds from local checks (those written on financial institutions within the same Federal Reserve check-processing region as the depositary bank) must be made available within two business days after deposit. Finally, funds represented by out-of-town checks must be made available within five business days after deposit.

These time periods on making funds available do not apply to new accounts (those less than thirty days old) or to checks written for more than $5,000. Customers under these circumstances must inquire of their banks how long the check collection process will likely take. Of course, banks may allow their customers to draw against uncollected funds during a time period shorter than that just discussed.

Indorsements. A customer who deposits an item for collection should indorse it, but quite frequently a customer forgets that signature. The depositary bank may supply the missing **indorsement.** If the bank states on the item that it was deposited by a customer or credited to his account, such a statement is as effective as the customer's indorsement. This is a practical rule intended to speed up the collection process by making it unnecessary to return to the depositor any items he may have failed to indorse [4–205]. The term *customer* is broadly construed and may include parties other than depositors.

Indorsement *Writing one's name upon paper for the purpose of transferring the title. When a payee of a negotiable instrument writes his name on the back of the instrument, his writing is an indorsement.*

Presentment *A demand for acceptance or payment made upon the maker, acceptor, drawee, or other payor by, or on behalf of, the holder.*

8. Collecting Banks

When a bank has received a check for collection, it has the duty to use ordinary care in performing its collection operations. These operations include presenting the check to the drawee or forwarding it for **presentment,** sending notice of nonpayment if it occurs and returning the check after learning that it has not been paid, and **settling** for the check when it receives final payment. Failure of the collecting

Settle *To pay in cash, by clearinghouse settlement, or by remittance or otherwise as instructed. A settlement may be either provisional or final.*

bank to use ordinary care in handling a check subjects the bank to liability to the depositor for any loss or damage sustained.

To act seasonably, a bank is generally required to take proper action before the midnight deadline following the receipt of a check, a notice, or a payment. Thus, if a collecting bank receives a check on Monday and presents it or forwards it to the next collecting bank any time prior to midnight Tuesday, it has acted seasonably. If it fails to do so, it has liability unless it is excused by matters beyond its control. In this case the bank must use due diligence, and excuses are difficult to establish, as the following case illustrates.

CASE

A bank's normal operating procedure was as follows: (1) collect the day's checks and send them for processing to the computer center in a nearby town; (2) return any dishonored checks to the bank in order that notice of dishonor may be sent before the midnight deadline. One of the bank's customers, as payee, deposited a check in its own account at the payor bank. As usual the check was sent to the computer center for processing. There, the drawer's account was found to have insufficient funds to cover the check. However, before the check was returned to the bank, the main road between the computer center and the bank was blocked by a flood. Rather than send the check by an alternate mountain road route, the computer center gave the check to an air freight service. The air service did not deliver on time, and notice of dishonor was sent to the customer past the midnight deadline. The funds were withdrawn from the customer's account who sued for wrongful dishonor of the check.

ISSUE: Does the flood excuse the bank's post–midnight deadline dishonor?

DECISION: No.

REASONS:
1. Although the disruption of a normal procedure was caused by factors beyond the control of the bank, the situation could have been prevented by due diligence.
2. The somewhat slower but more trustworthy mountain road route provided a safer alternative than the unproven air freight service.
3. Thus, because notice of dishonor was not sent before the midnight deadline, the item was then settled.

First Wyoming Bank v. Cabinet Craft Distrib., 624 P.2d 227 (Wyo. 1981).

9. Payor Banks

An item is finally paid by a payor bank when the bank (1) pays the item in cash, (2) settles for the item without reserving the right to revoke the settlement, (3) completes the process of posting the item, or (4) makes a provisional settlement and fails to revoke it within the time prescribed [4–213(1)]. Upon final payment, the payor bank is accountable for the item, and it has substituted its own obligation for that of the drawer. Final payment usually occurs whenever the payor bank makes a provisional settlement for the item (a credit) and then fails to revoke its credit within its midnight deadline after receipt of the item.

A payor bank that is not also the depositary bank must make a provisional settlement for an item on the banking day it is received. However, that bank has until final payment of the check—but not later than its midnight deadline—to decide whether or not the item is good [4–302(a)]. Within this time, the bank may revoke the settlement and return the item or, if this is not possible, send written notice of nonpayment. This enables the bank to defer posting until the next day.

When a check drawn by one customer of a bank is deposited by another customer of the same bank for credit on its books, the bank may return the item and revoke any credit given at any time prior to its midnight deadline [4–302(b)]. The deposit of an item on which the depositary bank is itself the payor bank becomes available for withdrawal on the opening of the second banking day following receipt of the item [4–213(4)(b)].

Failure of the payor-drawee bank to take action within the prescribed time limits may make it accountable to the person who deposited the check if the check is not paid. This liability is imposed if the bank (1) retains a check presented to it by another bank without settling for it by midnight of the banking day of receipt or (2) does not pay or return the check or send notice of dishonor within the period of its midnight deadline [4–302(a)].

Another problem relates to the *order of payment of checks*. There is no priority among checks drawn on a particular account and presented to a bank on any particular day. The checks and other items may be accepted, paid, certified, or charged to the indicated account of its customer in any order convenient to the bank [4–303(2)].

An item does not always proceed through the clearinghouse. It may be presented directly to the payor bank by a customer of that bank for payment over the counter. If the payor bank pays the item in cash, it may not later collect back the payments if its customer had insufficient funds on deposit [4–213(1)(a)].

BANKS AND THEIR CUSTOMERS

10. The Debtor-Creditor Relationship

The legal relationship between a bank and its depositors is that of debtor and creditor. If the depositor is a borrower of the bank, the reverse relationship (creditor-debtor) also exists between the bank and its customers. The dual relationship provides the bank with a prompt and easy method of protecting itself in the event of a depositor's default or pending insolvency. A bank can ''seize'' bank deposits under its right of *setoff* (an independent right to deduct debts from customers' accounts) if such action becomes necessary to protect its account receivable.

A bank is under a duty to honor properly payable checks drawn by its customer when there are sufficient funds in his account to cover the checks. A check is not properly payable if it has been altered or if it contains a forgery. If a bank pays a check that is not properly payable, the customer may insist on the account being recredited.

If there are insufficient funds, the bank may honor the properly payable checks, even though this action creates an overdraft. The customer is indebted to the bank for the overdraft and implicitly promises to reimburse the bank [4–401(1)]. While most overdrafts are dishonored, they are sometimes paid and the customer owes the bank for the check, as occurred in the following case.

CASE

Louise Kalbe signed a check that was later lost or stolen. The check was drafted for $7,260 payable to cash and cashed at a Florida bank. Kalbe's bank, the Pulaski State Bank, received the check on Thursday, January 8, 1982, and paid it the following Monday. The check created an overdraft of $6,542.12. The bank then commenced this action to recover $7,260 from Kalbe. The trial court awarded the bank the amount of the check plus costs.

ISSUE: Although the honoring of this check created a large overdraft, could the bank properly pay the check and retain its right to recover the amount of the check from Kalbe?

DECISION: Yes.

REASONS:

1. Section 4–401(1) of the Uniform Commercial Code unambiguously states that a bank may charge a customer's account for an item otherwise properly payable even though the charge creates an overdraft. A bank's payment of an overdraft check is treated as a loan to the depositor, because a check signed by a depositor on his or her account carries an implied promise to reimburse the bank.
2. Kalbe does not claim that the bank honored an altered check or a check bearing a forged or unauthorized drawer's signature. The check was therefore otherwise properly payable, and under UCC Section 4–401(1) the bank could charge Kalbe's account for the check.
3. Under UCC Section 4–302, the bank, as a payor bank, was required to pay, return, or otherwise dishonor the check by midnight on the next banking day following the banking day on which it received the check. Under this section, by failing to act on the check by midnight on Friday, January 9, the bank became accountable for the item to the Florida bank presenting the check.
4. However, Section 4–302 did not change the bank's relation with Kalbe. This section establishes payor bank collection practices. By delaying action past the deadline, the bank in effect paid the check. It could then charge Kalbe's account.
5. The alleged negligence of the bank in missing the midnight deadline is irrelevant. Section 4–401 places no duty of ordinary care on a bank in creating overdrafts.
6. Therefore the bank's actions were proper, and Kalbe must reimburse the bank for the check.

Pulaski State Bank v. Kalbe, 364 N.W.2d 162 (Wis. App. 1985).

If a bank in good faith pays an altered check, it can charge the account of its customer only according to the original tenor of the check. Thus, if a check is raised, the bank can charge its customer's account only with the original amount of the check [4–401(2)(a)]. If a person signs his name to an incomplete check and it is thereafter completed and presented to the drawee bank that pays it, the bank can charge the customer's account for the full amount if it pays in good faith and does not know that the completion was improper [4–401(2)(b)]. The improperly completed check is not an altered check.

11. Wrongful Dishonor

If a bank wrongfully dishonors a check, it is liable to its customer for damages proximately caused by the wrongful dishonor. When the dishonor occurs by mistake, as distinguished from a malicious or willful dishonor, liability is limited to the *actual damages proved* [4–402]. These damages may include *consequential damages* proximately caused by the wrongful dishonor, damages such as for arrest or prosecution of the customer. If the wrongful dishonor is willful, punitive damages in addition to actual damages may be awarded. The Code rejects early common law decisions holding that, if the dishonored item were drawn by a merchant, he was defamed in his business because of the reflection on his credit. Consequently, a merchant cannot recover damages on the basis of defamation because of wrongful dishonor of a check.

Some recent cases have allowed customers to collect for mental suffering as a part of consequential damages. The following case is an example of this trend. Notice that the bank's customer also collected punitive damages.

CASE

On Sunday, May 13, 1979, Kenneth and Vicki Issacs discovered that their checkbook was missing. They reported the loss promptly to Twin City Bank on Monday, and later learned that two forged checks totaling $2,050 had been written on the account and honored on May 11 and May 12. Their account had contained approximately $2,500 before the forgeries occurred. A few checks cleared Monday morning before the bank decided to issue a hold order to freeze the Isaacs' account. Mr. Isaacs had been convicted of burglary and the bank put the initial hold on the account out of some concern that the Isaacs' were somehow involved with the forged checks. The individual responsible for the forgeries was later charged and convicted. The police told the bank on May 30 there was no evidence to connect the Isaacs with the person arrested. Nevertheless, the bank dishonored checks written on the Isaacs' account and further denied the Isaacs their funds for some four years. The Isaacs filed suit in mid-June 1979 for wrongful dishonor and wrongful withholding of their funds. The jury awarded the Isaacs $18,500 in compensatory damage and $45,000 in punitive damages. The compensatory award included damages for mental anguish, loss of credit, and loss of the bargain on a house.

ISSUE: Was there sufficient evidence to support the award of compensatory and punitive damages?

DECISION: Yes.

REASONS:

1. Section 4–402 of the Uniform Commercial Code provides that "[a] payor bank is liable to its customer for damages proximately caused by the wrongful dishonor of an item," such as a check. This section also allows recovery for any consequential damages that are proven and proximately caused by the wrongful dishonor. Whether the consequential damages were proximately caused by the wrongful dishonor is a question of fact to be determined in each case.
2. Although few courts have considered recovery for mental suffering under UCC Section 4–402, a majority of those addressing the issue have allowed recovery.

3. There was sufficient evidence to support an award of damages for the loss of credit. Prior to the forgery incident, the Isaacs' credit reputation with the bank was described by the bank as "impeccable." The freezing of funds had a traumatic effect on their lives. They lost their credit standing with the bank and were unable to secure credit commercially at other institutions because of their status at the bank. This denial of credit contributed to some money loss in addition to its being a reasonable element of mental suffering.
4. The bank dishonored an earnest money check for a home the Isaacs were planning to buy, ending prospects for the purchase at that time. Additionally, this evidence was admissible as an element of mental suffering.
5. There was sufficient evidence to sustain damages for mental suffering. In addition to the anguish caused by the loss of credit and inability to pursue the purchase of the house, the Isaacs had to borrow from friends and family because of the wrongful withholding. They were left in a precarious position financially. There was testimony that the financial strain contributed to marital difficulties, leading at one point to the filing of a divorce suit, which was later dropped.
6. The punitive damage award for intentional wrongful dishonor was not excessive. The deterrent effect of punitive damages has some correlation to the financial condition of the party against whom punitive damages are allowed. Viewing the circumstances of this case in their entirety, the amount awarded was not grossly excessive or prompted by passion or prejudice.
7. In summary, there was substantial evidence to support the amount of the award for compensatory damages, and the punitive damage award was proper. Therefore the trial court's decision is affirmed.

Twin City Bank v. Isaacs, 672 S.W.2d 651 (Ark. 1984).

12. Stop Payment Orders

A customer has the right to stop payment on checks drawn on his account. Only the drawer has this right; it does not extend to holders—payees or indorsers. To be effective, a stop payment order must be received at a time and in a manner that will afford the bank a reasonable opportunity to stop payment before it has taken other action on the item [4–403]. For example, if a check has been certified, the depositor cannot stop payment, whether he or the payee procured the certification.

A bank must act reasonably in complying with a valid stop payment order. It cannot avoid liability by asserting immaterial differences between the check and the stop payment order. An oral stop order is binding on the bank for only fourteen days unless confirmed in writing within that period. Unless renewed in writing, a written stop order is effective for only six months [4–404].

A bank that honors a check upon which payment has been stopped is liable to the drawer of the check for any loss he has suffered because of the failure to obey the stop order. The burden is on the customer to establish the amount of his loss. Thus, if the drawer did not have a valid reason to stop payment, he cannot collect from a bank that fails to obey the stop payment order [4–403(3)]. Because of the concept of negotiability previously noted, a stop order on a check gives the drawer only limited protection. If the check is negotiated by the payee to a holder in due course, that holder can require payment of the amount by the drawer of the check, notwithstanding the stop order.

The bank cannot by agreement disclaim its responsibility for its failure to obey stop payment orders [4–103(1)]. Thus a form signed by a customer agreeing not to hold the bank responsible for failure to stop payment could not be enforced.

13. Banks' Rights and Duties

A bank is entitled, but not *obligated*, to pay a check that is over six months old, and it may charge the check to the customer's account [4–404]. Certified checks do not fall within the six-month rule; they are the primary obligation of the certifying bank, and the obligation runs directly to the holder of the check.

In paying *stale checks*, the bank must act in good faith and exercise ordinary care. It must ask questions, and if a reasonable person would be put on notice that something is wrong, it should contact the drawer for authority to pay the stale item.

As a general proposition, the death or incompetence of a person terminates the authority of others to act on his behalf. If this principle were applied to banks, a tremendous burden would be imposed upon them to verify the continued life and competence of drawers. A bank's authority to pay checks therefore continues until it knows that a customer has died or has been judged incompetent and the bank has had a reasonable opportunity to act [4–405].

14. Depositors' Rights and Duties

Banks make available to their customers a statement of account and canceled checks. Within a reasonable time after they are received, the customer must examine them for forgeries and for alterations. The bank does not have the right to charge an account with forged checks, but the customer's failure to examine and to notify will prevent him from asserting the forgery (or alteration) against the bank if the bank can establish that it suffered a loss because of this failure. The bank may be able to prove that prompt notification would have enabled it to recover from the forger [4–406(2)].

The Code does not specify the period of time within which the customer must report forgeries or alterations. It does specify that if the same wrongdoer commits successive forgeries or alterations, the customer must examine and notify the bank within fourteen days after the first item and statement were available to him. Otherwise, he cannot assert the same person's forgeries or alterations paid in good faith by the bank [4–406(2)(b)]. This rule is intended to prevent the wrongdoer from having the opportunity to repeat his misdeeds. If the customer can establish that the bank itself was negligent in paying a forged or altered item, the bank cannot avail itself of a defense based on the customer's tardiness in examining and reporting [4–406(3)]. The customer must prove that the bank did not use ordinary care in processing the checks. As the following case illustrates, this is often difficult.

CASE

Bill J. Knight is the president and majority stockholder of K&K Manufacturing, Inc. K&K Manufacturing employed only Knight and a bookkeeper, Eleanor Garza. The bookkeeper's duties at K&K were very broad, including picking up the company mail and Knight's personal mail from a common post office box, preparing checks for Knight's signature to pay both company and personal bills, and making entries in a cash disbursement journal reflecting the expenses for which the checks were written. Most importantly, it was her responsibility to reconcile the monthly statements prepared and sent by appellee Union Bank, where Knight kept both his business and personal checking and savings accounts.

Between March 1977 and January 1978, Miss Garza forged Knight's signature on some sixty-six separate checks drawn on his personal or business accounts at Union Bank. The majority of these checks were made payable to her. The total amount of the forgeries on the K&K account was $49,859.31. The total on Knight's personal account was $11,350. The bank paid each such check and Miss Garza received or was credited with the proceeds.

Knight sued the Union Bank for breach of contract, seeking repayment of the funds the bank paid out on checks with unauthorized signatures. After a court trial, judgment was entered in favor of appellant Knight for $5,500, representing the amount paid out of his personal account on forged checks from March 28 to May 20, 1977. This figure included eight forged checks paid by the bank prior to the mailing of its monthly statement containing a record of the payments and the checks themselves to Knight on May 6, plus a fourteen-day period. Since no forged checks on the K&K account were paid prior to May 20, judgment was entered for the bank against it. Both Knight and K&K have appealed.

ISSUE: Did Union Bank exercise reasonable care in paying the checks forged by Miss Garza?

DECISION: Yes.

REASONS:

1. Section 4–406(1) requires a customer to examine with care and promptness the checking statement sent by the bank in order to discover unauthorized signatures or alterations.
2. Section 4–406(2) precludes the customer who fails to comply with subsection (1) from recovering against the bank unless the customer establishes the bank also was negligent.
3. The mere fact that the bank has paid a forged check does not mean the bank has breached its duty of ordinary care.
4. At trial, an operations officer for Union Bank testified as to the methods employed during the period the forgeries occurred to discover unauthorized signatures on depositors' checks. She testified that checks were organized so that a bundle from the same account could be compared with the authorized signature on the bank's signature card. A staff of five filing clerks handled an average of approximately 1,000 checks each per hour in this manner. She testified it was common for a file clerk to become familiar with the drawer's signature in large accounts such as Knight's and K&K's.
5. An official of a large Arizona bank testified that tellers and file clerks are not trained to be handwriting experts. He testified that, in his opinion, because most large banks have completely abandoned physical comparison of checks with the signature card, the system employed by appellee was better than the norm of

the banking community in southern Arizona. Similar methods of comparing drawers' signatures have been upheld as constituting ordinary care and being within reasonable commercial standards across the country.

6. Because Union Bank exercised reasonable care and because Knight failed to examine promptly his personal and business checking statements, the loss due to the forgeries properly was placed on Knight and K&K.

K&K Manufacturing, Inc. v. Union Bank, 628 P.2d 44 (Ariz. 1981).

The same principles and rules apply when a bank processes an item that has been materially altered or contains an unauthorized indorsement. If a person's negligence contributes to the alteration or unauthorized signature, the bank is not liable for the item paid unless the bank failed to observe reasonable commercial standards. Thus, if both parties are "at fault," the bank is liable, because its fault prevents it from asserting the fault of the other party.

A customer is precluded from asserting a forgery of the drawer's signature or alteration on a check after one year from the time the check and statement were made available even though the bank was negligent. Forged indorsements must be reported within three years [4–406(4)]. If a payor bank, as a matter of policy or public relations, waives its defense of tardy notification by its customer, it cannot thereafter hold the collecting bank or any prior party for the forgery [4–406(5)].

CHAPTER SUMMARY

Concept of Negotiability

1. An assignee of a contract takes it subject to any defense the obligor may have against the assignor.
2. The goal of negotiability is to insulate a transferee from personal defenses that a primary party, such as a maker of a note, might have against the transferor.
3. For a holder to take an instrument free of personal defenses, the instrument must be negotiable, must be properly negotiated, and the holder must be a holder in due course.

Kinds of Commercial paper

Notes

1. A promissory note is a two-party instrument in which the maker promises to pay a stated amount to the payee.

Certificates of Deposit

1. A certificate of deposit is a two-party instrument in which a financial institution such as a bank promises to repay a stated sum with interest on a certain date.

Drafts

1. A draft is a bill of exchange in which a drawer orders a drawee to pay a stated amount to a payee.

Checks

1. A check is a demand draft drawn on a bank.
2. A check drawn by a bank on itself is a cashier's check. Travelers' checks are cashier's checks in which the financial institution is both the drawer and the drawee.
3. A certified check is one that has been accepted by the drawee bank, and by the acceptance it assumes the obligation of the drawer. Certification at the request of a holder releases the drawer from any further liability. A bank has no duty to certify a check.

Bank Deposits and Collections

Terminology

1. Depositary bank—the first bank to which an item is transferred for collection.
2. Payor bank—the bank by which an item is payable as drawn or accepted.
3. Intermediary bank—any bank to which an item is transferred in the course of collection except the depositary or payor bank.
4. Collecting bank—any bank handling the item for collection except the payor bank.
5. Presenting bank—any bank presenting an item to a payor bank.
6. Remitting bank—any payor or intermediary bank remitting an item.
7. A banking day is that part of the day in which a bank is open, and which usually ends at 2:00 P.M. so that the bank may process items before it closes. Items received after 2:00 P.M. are generally posted the following day.
8. A midnight deadline is midnight on the banking day following the banking day the item or notice is received by the bank.

The Bank Collection Process

1. A check deposited in the account is a provisional settlement until the check is honored by the payor bank.
2. If the payor bank dishonors a check, provisional settlements are revoked. This must occur for each bank by its midnight deadline.
3. Depositors do not have the right to draw against provisional settlements, although many banks allow them to do so.
4. Items deposited for collection without indorsement may be indorsed by the depositary bank on behalf of its customer. The indorsement indicates that it was deposited to the account of the customer.
5. Depositary banks may not supply indorsements of persons who are not customers.

Collecting Banks

1. Banks have a duty to use ordinary care in the collection process. Failure to do so creates liability for losses sustained.
2. Banks must take action before the midnight deadline on checks, notices from other banks, and making payments.

Payor Banks

1. An item is paid by a payor bank when it actually pays the item, settles for it without reserving the right to revoke the settlement, completes the posting of the item, or makes a provisional settlement and does not revoke it within the time allowed.
2. A provisional settlement may be revoked until the midnight deadline.
3. If a check is drawn on the payor bank by a customer of the same bank, the bank may revoke the credit any time until the close of business the next day.
4. There is no priority in the order of paying checks presented on the same day.

Banks and Their Customers

The Debtor-Creditor Relationship

1. The relationship between a bank and its depositors is that of debtor and creditor. If the depositor borrows money from the bank, the opposite relationship also exists.
2. A bank can seize deposits and set them off against debts to the bank.
3. A bank has a duty to honor checks when there are sufficient funds on deposit. It may also pay other checks and collect the amounts from its depositors.
4. A bank can charge a customer's account for an altered check only to the extent of the original amount of the check.
5. If an incomplete check is signed by a depositor and it is completed improperly, a bank can, in good faith, charge the account with the completed amount.

Wrongful Dishonor

1. A bank is liable for all damages caused by wrongful dishonor.
2. If the dishonor is willfully wrong, punitive damages may be collected.
3. Wrongful dishonor is not defamation of a merchant.

Stop Payment Orders

1. A customer has the right to stop payment on checks drawn on his account.
2. The stop order must be received in a time and manner that will allow the bank a reasonable opportunity to stop payment.
3. Oral stop orders expire in fourteen days unless confirmed in writing.
4. Written stop orders are effective for only six months but may be renewed in writing.
5. A bank that fails to stop payment upon proper notice is liable to the drawer of the check for any proven losses.
6. A bank may not contractually disclaim liability for failure to obey a stop order.

Banks' Rights and Duties

1. A bank may pay a check more than six months old but need not do so.
2. The death or incompetence of a customer terminates the bank's authority to honor checks written on the customer's account.
3. Notice of these events must be given to the bank.

Depositors' Rights and Duties

1. Upon receipt of the statement of account and canceled checks, the depositor has a duty to examine them within a reasonable time for forged, unauthorized, or altered checks.
2. Although the bank does not initially have the right to charge the customer's account for forged, unauthorized, or altered checks, the customer's failure to examine and notify may prevent him from asserting the improper charge to his account.
3. If both the customer and the bank are at fault in allowing the forged, altered, or unauthorized check to be paid, the bank is liable.
4. The customer cannot assert a forged, altered, or unauthorized check after one year from the time the canceled check or the statement of account was available for examination.
5. Forged indorsements must be reported within three years.

REVIEW QUESTIONS AND PROBLEMS

1. Match each term in column A with the appropriate statement in Column B.

A	B
(1) Depositary bank	(a) Period after which a forged indorsement may no longer be asserted.
(2) Personal defense	(b) Period after which written stop payment order expires.
(3) Midnight deadline	(c) Period after which a forged check may no longer be asserted by depositor.
(4) Six months	(d) The first bank to which an item is transferred for collection.
(5) Fourteen days	(e) Part of next banking day.
(6) Certification	(f) Period after which an oral stop payment order expires.
(7) Real defense	(g) Precludes a bank from honoring a stop order.
(8) One year	(h) May not be asserted against a holder in due course.
(9) Three years	(i) May be asserted against a holder in due course.
(10) Presenting bank	(j) Any bank presenting an item except a payor bank.

2. Give the *name* of each of the following three *forms* and parties to the form.

John E. Murray, Jr.
School of Law
Pittsburgh, PA

NO. 157

8-26
430

January 4, 19XX

PAY TO THE ORDER OF George Harlin $ 70.00

Seventy and no/100 DOLLARS

Pleasant Hills Office
MELLON BANK

John E. Murray Jr.

:0430--0026: 243--7716: 0157 :0000000007000:

(a)

FIRST CITY BANK OF NEW YORK
New York, New York

No. 4762 May 1, 19XX

THIS CERTIFIES THAT THERE HAS BEEN DEPOSITED with the undersigned the sum of $400,000.00

four hundred thousand DOLLARS

Payable to the order of Dana Oil Company on July 27, 1989, with interest only to maturity at the rate of TWELVE per cent (12%) per annum upon surrender of this certificate properly indorsed.

FIRST CITY BANK OF NEW YORK BY:
M. Hopkins, Vice President
Authorized Signature

(b)

Moscow, Idaho June 7, 19XX

One year from date pay to the order of Betty Stein

Four thousand Dollars

Andre Pellier

To: Robert Shaw
47 Peachtree Street
Atlanta, Georgia 30303

(c)

3. A check was issued payable jointly to Sam and Chuck. Sam indorsed the check and deposited it in his account with National Bank. Chuck did not indorse the check, nor has Chuck ever been a customer of National Bank. National Bank supplied Chuck's missing indorsement and forwarded the check to the drawee bank. Chuck sued National Bank for cashing the check without his indorsement. May the bank supply the missing indorsement of a joint payee who is not a customer-depositor with the bank? Explain.

4. Pearl is the holder of a check drawn by Sharpe on Washington State Bank. Pearl also maintains an account at Washington State Bank. The check is deposited at the bank on Monday. On that same day, Sharpe's account is overdrawn, but she promises to make a substantial deposit, so the bank holds the check until Thursday. Sharpe does not make the deposit, and the bank, on Friday, returns the check to Pearl marked "Insufficient Funds." Can Pearl require the bank to make good on the check? Why or why not?

5. Equipment Company bought equipment from Wells and paid him with a check drawn upon Citizens Bank. When the equipment was not delivered the next day, Equipment Company stopped payment on the check. Wells cashed the check at his own bank, Fargo Bank. When the check was presented to Citizens Bank, it refused to honor the check because of the stop order. Can Fargo Bank successfully collect from Wells? Why or why not?

6. Grain Elevator Company owed State Bank $272,000 on certain promissory notes. Grain, in negotiating a new loan, told State Bank's officers that it lost $22,000 during the last year and that its checking account has been overdrawn by $35,000. The bank turned down the new loan request. It set off Grain's $71,000 checking account balance against the old loans and returned all of Grain's checks when presented for payment. Is State Bank liable for refusing to cash the checks? Why?

7. On January 29, Edwards, a wholesale grocer, made a large deposit in cash to his account at Cattlemen's Bank. In error, Edwards's deposit was posted to the account of Edmunds, another depositor. On the following day, Nevins, a local producer jobber, deposited a check to his account at Watermill bank drawn on Cattlemen's Bank to Nevins's order by Edwards. When the check was presented for payment, Cattlemen's Bank refused to honor it and stamped it "Insufficient Funds." The check was promptly returned to Nevins by Watermill Bank. If Edwards's deposit on January 29 had been properly posted, his bank account balance would have been substantially greater than the amount of his check to Nevins. Edwards sues the Cattlemen's Bank for damages. What result? Why?

8. The facts are as in problem 7. Assume that Edwards's check had been given to Nevins in payment for a carload of produce which Edwards had arranged to resell at a large profit, that the bank was aware of this, that on dishonor of the check Nevins stopped the goods in transit, and that Edwards as a result lost his profit on the resale of the goods. May Edwards recover such lost profits from the bank? Explain.

9. Franklin, a depositor of the Milltown Bank, orally ordered the cashier of the bank to stop payment on a check he had issued. The check was issued in payment for goods that were not received. Franklin learned that the seller was a notorious confidence man. The cashier in turn notified the tellers that an oral stop order had been given. Ten days later one of the tellers, who was not paying much attention to his business, paid the seller's wife, who had been sent to the bank to cash the check for the seller. Franklin, while examining his canceled checks at the end of the month, discovered the error and promptly demanded that his account be credited for the amount of the check. Is he entitled to the credit? Why?

10. Alex drew check #896 in the amount of $1,844.98 on the Fidelity Bank. When he telephoned Fidelity Bank and ordered a stop payment on the check, he incorrectly stated the amount as $1,844.48. Fidelity Bank's computer is programmed to stop payment only if the amount of the check is correct. Upon presentation, the computer overlooked the check and the check was paid. Is the bank liable for failure to comply with the stop payment order? Why or why not?

11. On June 30, 1985, Charles issued check #2668 drawn on Community State Bank in the amount of $5,000 to Southern Masonry. Subsequently, Charles was advised by the payee that the check had been lost, and a replacement check was issued and cashed. In July 1988, check #2668 was deposited by the payee in its account at Community State Bank. Is the bank entitled to charge Charles's account? Why or why not?

12. Newton, a holder in due course, presented a check to the Marshall Bank, the drawee bank named on the face of the instrument. The bank examined the signature of the drawer very carefully, but the signature was such an exact forgery of the drawer's signature that only a handwriting expert could have detected a difference. The bank therefore paid the check. Assume that the check was promptly returned to the drawer-depositor but that he did not discover the forgery until thirteen months after the check was returned to him. Can he compel the bank to credit his account for the loss? Why?

13. Jensen opened a checking account and directed that the bank statements be mailed to his attorney. The attorney forged Jensen's signature on a check in April 1985. The attorney's theft was discovered in 1986 and Jensen notified the bank of the forging in July 1987. Is Jensen entitled to collect the amount of the forged check from the bank? Why or why not?

Negotiable Instruments 37

CHAPTER PREVIEW

- GENERAL REQUIREMENTS

  Writing Signed by a Maker or Drawer
  Necessity of a Promise or Order
  Unconditional Promise or Order
  The Particular Fund Concept
  Sum Certain in Money
  Certain Time of Payment
  Acceleration and Extension Clauses

- THE MAGIC WORDS OF NEGOTIABILITY

  Order Paper
  Bearer Paper

- OTHER FACTORS AFFECTING NEGOTIABILITY

  Terms and Omissions Not Affecting Negotiability
  Incomplete Instruments
  Ambiguous Terms and Rules of Construction

- TRANSFER OF COMMERCIAL PAPER

  Transfer by Negotiation
  Types of Indorsements
  Blank Indorsements
  Special Indorsements
  Restrictive Indorsements

BUSINESS MANAGEMENT DECISION

One of your responsibilities as an officer of a financial institution is to decide whether or not to purchase (at a discount) the promissory notes that are payable to your customers.

What criteria should you use in making your decision to purchase these notes?

Chapter 36 introduced the concept of negotiability. We learned that a holder in due course of a negotiable instrument is not subject to personal defenses asserted by prior parties to the instrument. The negotiability principle is our first concern in this chapter. We will examine the legal requirements that must be met if an instrument is to qualify for the special treatment afforded negotiable instruments. We will then discuss the second requirement for a party to be free of personal defenses—proper negotiation.

GENERAL REQUIREMENTS

The negotiability of an instrument is determined by the terms written on the face of the instrument. In order to be negotiable, an instrument must satisfy four basic requirements: It must (1) be signed by the maker or drawer, (2) contain an unconditional promise or order to pay a sum certain in money, (3) be payable on demand or at a definite time, and (4) be payable to order or to bearer [3–104(1)].

1. Writing Signed by a Maker or Drawer

The first requirement is simply that there be a writing signed by the maker or drawer [3–104(1)(a)]. It is not required that any particular type or kind of writing be used, nor is it necessary that the signature be at any particular place upon the instrument. The instrument may be in any form that includes "printing, typewriting, or any other intentional reduction to tangible form" [1–201(46)]. A symbol is a sufficient signature if "executed or adopted by a party with present intention to authenticate a writing" [1–201(39)]. The use of the word *authenticate* in the definition of *signed* makes it clear that a complete signature is not required. The authentication may be printed or written and may be placed on the instrument by stamp.

For purposes of internal control, many businesses and other organizations require that instruments be signed by at least two persons or that they be countersigned. When the agreement requires two signatures, the drawee may not pay on only one signature, even if the one signing is authorized. The authority is limited or divided; both must sign.

2. The Necessity of a Promise or Order

A negotiable note must contain a *promise* to pay. Although the word *promise* is used in almost all notes, a word or words expressing an undertaking to pay may be substituted. The promise must be derived from the language of the instrument, not from the fact that a debt exists. A mere acknowledgment of a debt in writing (an IOU) does not contain a promise. Even though an IOU is a valid enforceable instrument upon which recovery may be had, it is not negotiable.

A draft must contain an **order** to pay. The purpose of the instrument is to order the drawee to pay money to the payee or his order. The drawer must use plain language to show an intention to make an order and to signify more than an authorization or request. It must be a direction to pay. Thus an instrument in the following form would not be negotiable: "To John Doe. I wish you would pay $1,000 to the order of Richard Roe. [Signed] Robert Lee." This would nevertheless be a valid authorization for John Doe to make payment to Richard Roe. The correct method to create an order to pay would be: "To John Doe. Pay $1,000 to the order of Richard Roe. [Signed] Robert Lee."

Order *A direction to pay that must be more than an authorization or request. It must, with reasonable certainty, identify the person to pay.*

3. Unconditional Promise or Order

Negotiable instruments serve as a substitute for money and as a basis for short-term credit. If these purposes are to be served, it is essential that the instruments be readily received in lieu of money and freely transferable. Conditional promises or orders would defeat these purposes, for it would be necessary that every person determine whether or not the condition had been performed prior to his taking the instrument. The instruments would not freely circulate. In recognition of these facts, the law requires that the promise or order be unconditional.

The question of whether or not the promise or order is conditional arises when the instrument contains language in addition to the promise or order to pay money. The promise or order is conditional if the language of the instrument provides that payment is controlled by, or is subject to, the terms of some other agreement [3–105(2)(a)]. Clearly, a promise or order is conditional if reference to some other agreement is *required* and if payment is *subject* to the terms of another contract. Such a reference imposes the terms of the other writing.

However, a mere reference to some other contract or document does not condition the promise or order and does not impair negotiability. Such reference simply gives information about the transaction that gave rise to the instrument. Thus the words "subject to contract" condition the promise or order, but the words "as per contract" do not render the promise or order conditional. The latter is informative rather than restrictive.

Statements of the consideration for which the instrument was given and statements of the transaction out of which the instrument arose are simply informative [3–105(1)(b)]. A draft may have been drawn under a letter of credit, and a reference to this fact does not impose a condition [3–105(1)(d)]. Notes frequently contain a statement that some sort of security has been given, such as a mortgage on property, or that title to goods has been retained as security for the payment of the note. In either case, the purpose is to make clear to the holder that the promise to pay is secured by something in addition to the general credit of the maker; and as a consequence, a mere reference to the security does not destroy negotiability [3–105(1)(e)].

Normally implied or constructive conditions in an agreement that underlies the instrument do not make the instrument conditional. For example, a promise that payment will be made when the contract is performed does not make the promise to pay conditional [3–105(1)(a)]. However, express conditions stated in the instrument itself can make the promise to pay conditional. The following case illustrates this rule and also discusses the close relationship between an unconditional promise and the requirement that the time of payment be fixed.

CASE

D. C. Stewart Company owned the Astro Motel in Cedar City, Utah. Roland Vance, a real estate agent for C. J. Realty, approached Stewart about listing the motel for sale with C. J. Realty. The listing agreement was entered into, and Vance subsequently obtained a potential buyer. On September 24, 1979, Stewart and Wendell and Connie Downward entered into a lease agreement and option to purchase. This agreement provided that the Downwards, as lessees, could exercise an option to purchase the motel on or before May 1, 1980. The same day this agreement was entered into, Stewart executed a promissory note for $15,900, payable to C. J. Realty to secure the real estate commission to which C. J. Realty would be entitled if the Downards exercised their option to purchase. The promissory note provided that it would be payable "in full upon the final closing between D. C. Stewart Co. and . . . [the Downwards] . . . which shall be on or before May 1, 1980, when . . . [the Downwards] . . . exercise their option to purchase the Astro Motel. . . ." On September 27, 1979, the promissory note was sold by Vance, acting on behalf of C. J. Realty, to Angelo Calfo for $12,720. The Downwards never exercised their option to purchase the motel. After May 1, 1980, Calfo made demand for payments upon Stewart. Stewart refused to pay since the note's validity was conditioned on an event that had not occurred. Calfo brought suit on the note, and the trial court held for Calfo without allowing Stewart to assert his defense.

ISSUE: Was the promissory note enforceable despite Stewart's defense?

DECISION: No.

REASONS:

1. Under Section 3–104(1) of the Uniform Commercial Code, a note must meet four criteria to be negotiable. First, the instrument must evidence a signature by the maker; second, it must contain an unconditional promise or order to pay a certain sum in money; third, it must be payable on demand or at a definite time; and fourth, it must be payable to order or to bearer. Stewart and Calfo agree the promissory note satisfies the first and fourth requirements, but disagree as to whether the second and third are met.
2. Negotiable notes must contain unconditional promises to serve the purposes for which they were created. Conditional promises do not perform the currency and credit functions of negotiable instruments.
3. The idea of the facilitation of easy transfer of notes requires that a transferee be able to trust what the instrument says and be able to determine the validity of the note and its negotiability from the language in the note itself. Therefore, in addition to having the qualities of negotiability, an instrument must display those qualities on its face, without reference to extrinsic facts. This requirement protects transferees from defenses to payment that are not readily apparent from the document.
4. The promissory note involved in this case is conditional and indefinite on its face. It specifically states that it is due only upon a final closing "when buyers [the Downwards] exercise their option to purchase." The language clearly places the holder on notice that the note will become due only upon a contingency that the holder cannot control. As for definiteness, the date merely defines when the option to purchase expires, and does not establish a time when the note will certainly become due.

5. Therefore the promissory note sued upon is not a negotiable instrument. Thus Stewart should be allowed to assert his defenses to Calfo's claim for payment.

Calfo v. D. C. Stewart Co., 717 P.2d 697 (Utah 1986).

4. The Particular Fund Concept

A maker or drawer must engage or pledge his general credit, or his promise or order is conditional. A statement that an instrument is to be paid only out of a particular fund imposes a condition [3–105(2)(b)]. Such an instrument does not carry the general personal credit of the maker or drawer. It is contingent on the sufficiency of the fund on which it is drawn. For example, if a note states: "I promise to pay to the order of John only out of my corn profits," the note is conditioned on having corn profits. The promise is conditional, and the instrument is nonnegotiable. This result is due to the *particular fund doctrine*.

There are three exceptions to this doctrine. First, an instrument is not considered conditional merely because it makes reference to a particular source or fund from which payment is expected but not required. For example, although a check indicates it will be paid out of a particular account, it still may be negotiable.

The second exception involves an instrument that is issued by a government or governmental unit and is limited to payment out of a particular fund [3–105(1)(g)]. The following case illustrates this exception to the particular fund concept.

CASE

To finance construction of a public golf course, Sarpy County sold short-term, interest-bearing notes. The notes stated that they were "to be paid from funds gathered by property tax collections." When the company hired to build the golf course went out of business, the golf course project was abandoned. Holders of the notes sued the county. The county defended, claiming that the notes were nonnegotiable because they were payable out of a particular fund. The county further contended that since the notes were nonnegotiable, the holders took the notes subject to the defense of failure of consideration since the golf course was not completed. Plaintiffs contend that the notes were negotiable and that they took the notes free of the defense of failure of consideration.

ISSUE: Are notes issued by a governmental unit payable only out of a particular fund negotiable?

DECISION: Yes.

REASONS:

1. In general, if an instrument states that it is payable out of a particular fund, the instrument makes payment conditional, which destroys negotiability.
2. However, Code Section 3–105(1)(g) provides that the promise to pay from a particular fund is not a conditional promise if the instrument is issued by a government or governmental unit. Sarpy County is such a governmental unit.

Sanitary and Imp. Dist. v. Continental Western, 343 N.W.2d 314 (Neb. 1983).

Third is when an unincorporated association, such as a partnership, trust, or an estate, limits its obligation to pay the instrument only from the assets of the organization and eliminates liability of the individual members, such as partners. The instrument may still be negotiable. For purposes of negotiability, the Code recognizes partnerships and other unincorporated associations as ''commercial entities'' that may execute negotiable instruments as an entity [3–105(1)(h)].

5. Sum Certain in Money

To be negotiable, an instrument must be payable in money. Instruments payable in chattels such as wheat or platinum are not payable in money. *Money* means a medium of exchange that is authorized or adopted by a domestic or foreign government as a part of its currency [1–201(24)]. The amount payable may be stated in foreign as well as domestic money [3–107(2)]. If the sum payable is stated in foreign currency, payment may be made in the dollar equivalent unless it is specified in the instrument that the foreign currency is the only medium of payment.

The language used in creating commercial paper must be certain with respect to the amount of money promised or ordered to be paid. Otherwise, its value at any period could not be definitely determined. If the principal sum to be paid is definite, negotiability is not affected by the fact that it is to be paid with interest, in installments, with exchange at a fixed or current rate, or with cost of collection and attorney's fees in case payment is not made at maturity [3–106].

If at any time during the term of the paper its full value can be ascertained, the requirement that the sum must be certain is satisfied. The obligation to pay costs and attorney's fees is part of the security contract, separate and distinct from the primary promise to pay money; therefore, it does not affect the required sum certain. The certainty of amount is not affected if the instrument specifies different rates of interest before and after default; nor is the certainty affected by a provision for a stated discount for early payment or an additional charge if payment is made after the date fixed [3–106(1)(c)]. The principal amount to be paid, however, must be certain in order for the note to be negotiable.

The issue of whether an instrument specifies a sum certain often arises with guaranty agreements, as illustrated in the following case.

CASE

DeWitt, an officer of K&G Corporation, signed a guaranty agreement with Peoples National Bank that guaranteed a bank loan to K&G "to the extent of $30,000." The guaranty agreement did not state the amount loaned to K&G. The holder of the note sued DeWitt for $30,000. DeWitt sought to assert the defense of embezzlement by the company president. (He could assert the defense only if the instrument were not negotiable.)

ISSUE: Is a guaranty instrument that guarantees payment "to the extent of $30,000" a negotiable instrument?

DECISION: No.

REASONS: 1. The guaranty did not within itself indicate the amount of the loan guaranteed. For an instrument to be negotiable, it must contain a sum certain in money. That sum must be stated in the instrument itself.

2. Here, DeWitt's liability could have been $10,000 or $20,000 or $30,000, depending on the amount loaned to K&G. "To the extent of $30,000" only establishes a ceiling on the amount to be paid; it does not state a sum certain to be paid.

Gillespie v. DeWitt, 280 S.E.2d 736 (N.C. 1981).

6. Certain Time of Payment

As a substitute for money, negotiable instruments would be of little value if the holder were unable to determine when he could demand payment. A negotiable instrument, therefore, must be payable on demand or at a "definite time" [3–104(1)(c)].

An instrument is payable on *demand* when it so states, when payable at sight or on presentation, or when no time of payment is stated [3–108]. In general, the words *payable on demand* are used in notes, and the words *at sight* in drafts. If nothing is said about the due date, the instrument is demand paper. A check is a good illustration of such an instrument. The characteristic of demand paper is that its holder can require payment at any time by making a demand upon the person who is obligated on the paper.

Not every instrument that indicates no time of payment is a demand instrument. If the instrument provides for periodic payment of interest or contains an acceleration clause without specifying the actual due date, such instruments are nonnegotiable. The interest clauses and acceleration clauses clearly indicate an intent that it not be payable on demand. As the following case illustrates, such clauses must be carefully worded if negotiability is to be retained.

CASE

McGuire bought Tursi's clothes boutique, paying $10,000 in cash and executing a promissory note for $65,000. The note had an acceleration clause and stated that "interest payments of $541.66 shall be due and payable on the fifth day of October, November and December, 1979." Tursi refused to close the sale to McGuire and sold the note to Parker in another deal. When Parker sued McGuire on the $65,000 note, McGuire defended on the basis of failure of consideration since Tursi refused to close the sale of her boutique. Parker contended that failure of consideration on a negotiable instrument is not a defense against a holder in due course. McGuire responded that the note was nonnegotiable because the note was not payable on demand or at a definite time.

ISSUE: Is the $65,000 note negotiable?

DECISION: No.

REASONS:

1. The note was not payable at a definite time because no specific time for repayment of the principal amount of $65,000 was stated therein.
2. The note was not payable on demand since it specified a fixed amount of interest to be paid over three months. A demand note also has no need for an acceleration clause.
3. Since the note was not payable on demand or at a definite time, it was nonnegotiable.

PP, Inc. v. McGuire, 509 F. Supp. 1079 (1981) (applying N.J. law).

The requirement of a definite time is in keeping with the necessity for certainty in instruments. It is important that the value of an instrument can always be determined. This value will be dependent on the ultimate maturity date of the instrument. If an instrument is payable only upon an act or event, the time of its occurrence being uncertain, the instrument is not payable at a definite time even though the act or event has occurred [3–109(2)]. Thus an instrument payable "thirty days after my father's death" would not be negotiable.

The requirement of certainty as to the time of payment is satisfied if it is payable on or before a specified date [3–109(1)(a)]. Thus an instrument payable "on or before" June 1, 1990, is negotiable. The obligor on the instrument has the privilege of making payment prior to June 1, 1990, but is not required to pay until the specified date. An instrument payable at a fixed period after a stated date, or at a fixed period after sight, is payable at a definite time [3–109(1)(b)]. The expressions "one year after date" or "sixty days after sight" are definite as to time.

7. Acceleration and Extension Clauses

Two types of provisions appearing on the face of instruments may affect the definite time requirement. One, an *acceleration clause*, hastens or accelerates the maturity date of an instrument. Accelerating provisions may be of many different kinds. A typical one provides that in case of default in payment, the entire note shall become due and payable. Another kind gives the holder an option to declare the instrument due and payable when he feels insecure about ultimate payment. An instrument payable at a definite time subject to any acceleration is negotiable [3–109(1)(c)]. If, however, the acceleration provision permits the holder to declare the instrument due when he feels insecure, the holder must act in good faith in the honest belief that the likelihood of payment is impaired. The presumption is that the holder has acted in good faith, placing the burden on the obligor-payor to show that such act was not in good faith [1–208].

The second type of provision affecting time is an *extension clause*, the converse of the acceleration provision. It lengthens the time for payment beyond that specified in the instrument. A note payable in two years might provide that the maker has the right to extend the time of payment six months. An instrument is payable "at a definite time subject to extension at the option of the holder, or to extension to a further definite time at the option of the maker or acceptor or automatically upon or after a specified act or event" [3–109(1)(d)]. If an extension is at the option of the holder, no time limit is required. The holder always has a right to refrain from undertaking collection. An extension at the option of the maker or acceptor, however, or an automatic extension must specify a definite time for ultimate payment or negotiability is destroyed.

THE MAGIC WORDS OF NEGOTIABILITY

8. Introduction

The *words of negotiability* express the intention to create negotiable paper. The usual words of negotiability are *order* and *bearer* [3–110, 3–111]. When these words are used, the maker or drawer has in effect stated that the instrument may be negotiated to another party. When the word *bearer* is used, it means that payment will be made to anyone who *bears* or possesses it. When the word *order* is used, it means that it will be paid to the designated payee or anyone to whom the payee orders it to be paid.

Other words of equivalent meaning may be used, but to ensure negotiability it is preferable to use the conventional words. If the instrument is not payable to "order" or to "bearer," it is not negotiable, and all defenses are available in suits on the instrument. The following case illustrates how easy it is to overlook the magic words.

CASE

Andersen gave a promissory note to Great Lakes in return for Great Lakes's promise to deliver 65,000 trees for Andersen's nursery business. The note recited: "For value received, Andersen promises to pay to Great Lakes $9,000 to be paid $100 per month beginning October 1 for ninety months." In return for a loan, Great Lakes transferred the note to First Investment. When Great Lakes failed to deliver the trees, Andersen refused to pay First Investment. First Investment sued Andersen, claiming that the note was negotiable, so it took free of Andersen's defense of failure of consideration.

ISSUE: Is Andersen's note negotiable?

DECISION: No.

REASONS: 1. To be negotiable, the note would have to be payable to Great Lakes or its order. It could also state "payable to the order of Great Lakes." It did neither but was only payable to Great Lakes.

2. Since the note was nonnegotiable, First Investment was not a holder in due course but was an assignee taking subject to the defense of failure of consideration.

First Investment Company v. Andersen, 621 P.2d 683 (Utah 1980).

9. Order Paper

If the terms of an instrument provide that it is payable to the order or assigns of a person who is specified with reasonable certainty, the instrument is payable to order [3–110(1)]. The expressions "Pay to the order of John Doe" or "Pay to John Doe or order" or "Pay to John Doe or assigns" create order paper (see Figure 37–1).

An instrument may be payable to the order of two or more payees together, such as A and B, or in the alternative, A or B. An instrument payable to A and B must be indorsed by both. One payable to the order of A or B may be indorsed and negotiated by either [3–116].

An instrument may be payable to the order of an estate, a trust, or a fund. Such instruments are payable to the order of the representative of the estate, trust, or fund [3–110(1)(e)]. An instrument payable to the order of a partnership or an unincorporated association such as a labor union is payable to such partnership or association. It may be indorsed by any person authorized by the partnership or association [3–110(1)(g)].

10. Bearer Paper

The basic characteristic of bearer paper (see Figure 37–2) as distinguished from order paper is that it can be negotiated by delivery without indorsement. An instrument

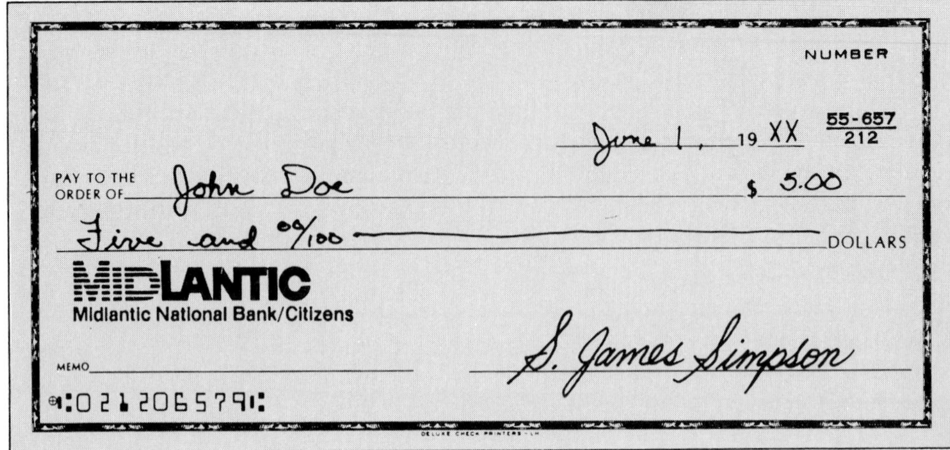

FIGURE 37–1 Order paper payable to the order of John Doe [3–110(1)]. It requires John Doe's indorsement if it is to be negotiated.

is payable to bearer when created if it is payable (1) to bearer, (2) to the order of bearer (as distinguished from the order of a specified person or bearer), (3) to a specified person or bearer (notice that it is not to *the order of* a specified person or bearer), or (4) to "cash" or "the order of cash," or any other indication that does not purport to designate any specific payee [3–111]. An instrument will be considered bearer paper only after it is determined that it cannot be order paper.

Although bearer paper can be negotiated without indorsement, the person to whom it is transferred will often require an indorsement. The reason for this is that an indorser has a greater liability than one who negotiates without indorsement. Also, if the instrument is dishonored, identification of the person who negotiated the paper becomes easier with an indorsement.

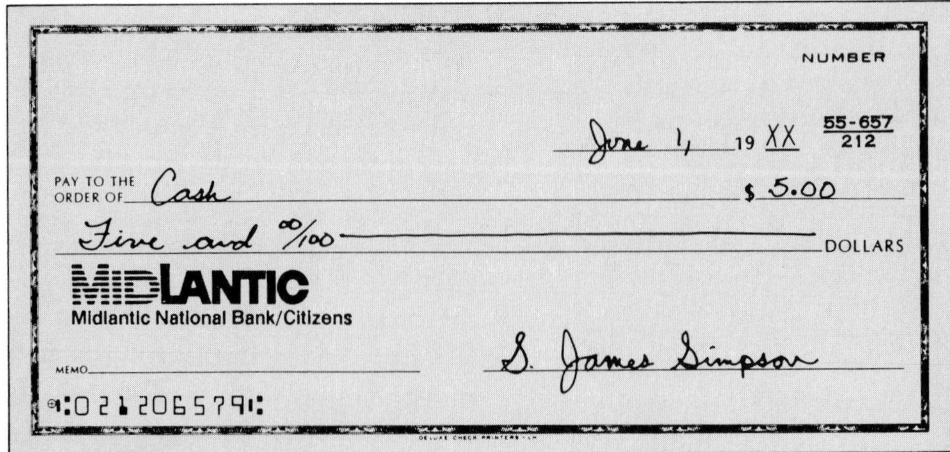

FIGURE 37–2 Bearer paper. Its negotiation is effective without an indorsement [3–111].

OTHER FACTORS AFFECTING NEGOTIABILITY

11. Terms and Omissions Not Affecting Negotiability

Some additional terms, usually for the benefit of the payee or other holder, may be included in commercial paper without impairing negotiability. Many instruments contain statements indicating that collateral has been given. These statements, including provisions relating to the rights of the payee or holder in the collateral, do not affect negotiability [3–112(1)(b)(c)].

The drawer of a check or draft may include a provision that the payee, by indorsing or cashing it, acknowledges full satisfaction of an obligation of the drawer. The provision will not affect negotiability [3–112(1)(f)]. Checks or drafts drawn by insurance companies in settlement of claims usually contain such a provision.

Often, the consideration for which an instrument was given is set forth in the instrument, and it is common to include words such as "for value received" or "in payment for services rendered." The omission of words stating the consideration for which an instrument was given will not affect its negotiability. Nor is the negotiable character of an instrument otherwise negotiable impaired by omission of a statement of the place where the instrument is drawn or payable [3–112(1)(a)].

Whether there is no date, a wrong date, an antedate, or a postdate is not important from the standpoint of negotiability [3–114(1)]. Any date that does appear on the instrument is presumed correct until evidence is introduced to establish a contrary date [3–114(3)]. Any fraud or illegality connected with the date of the instrument does not affect its negotiability but merely gives a defense.

12. Incomplete Instruments

A person may sign an instrument that is incomplete in that it lacks one or more of the necessary elements of a complete instrument. Thus a paper signed by the maker or drawer, in which the payee's name or the amount is omitted, is incomplete.

An incomplete instrument cannot be enforced until it is completed [3–115(1)]. If the blanks are subsequently filled in by any person in accordance with the authority or instructions given by the party who signed the incomplete instrument, it is then effective as completed. A person might leave blank, signed checks with an employee who must pay for goods to be delivered. When the employee fills in the amounts and names of the payees, the checks are perfectly valid.

A date is not required for an instrument to be negotiable; however, if a date is necessary to ascertain maturity ("payable sixty days from date"), an undated instrument is an incomplete instrument. The date may be inserted by the holder. If an instrument is payable on demand or at a fixed period after date, the date that is put on the instrument controls, even though it is antedated or postdated [3–114(2)].

13. Ambiguous Terms and Rules of Construction

In view of the millions of negotiable instruments that are made and drawn daily, it is to be expected that a certain number of them will be ambiguously worded. Accordingly, the Code provides a number of rules to be applied in interpreting negotiable instruments.

Some instruments are drawn in such a manner that it is doubtful whether the instrument is a draft or a note. It may be directed to a third person but contain a promise to pay, rather than an order to pay. The holder may treat it as either a draft or a note and present it for payment to either the person who signed it or the apparent drawee. Where a draft is drawn on the drawer, it is treated as a note [3–118(a)].

An instrument may contain handwritten terms, typewritten terms, or printed terms. Where there are discrepancies in the instrument, handwritten terms control typewritten and printed terms, and typewritten terms control printed terms [3–118(b)]. Thus a printed note form may state that it is payable on demand, but there may be typed or written on the note "payable thirty days from date." Such an instrument would be payable in thirty days.

There may also be a conflict between the words and the figures on an instrument. Thus a check may have the words "fifty dollars" and the figures "$500." The words control, and the check would be for $50. If the words are ambiguous, the figures will control [3–118(c)]. In a check with the words "Five seventy-five dollars" and figures "$5.75," the figures will control. In some cases, the ambiguity may arise from the context of the words.

If an instrument provides for the payment of interest but does not state the rate, the rate will be at the judgment rate at the place of payment. An unsatisfied money judgment bears interest at a rate specified by statute, and whatever this judgment rate is in a particular state will thus be applicable in this situation. Interest will run from the date of the instrument or, if it is undated, from the date of issue [3–118(d)].

If two or more persons sign an instrument as maker, acceptor, drawer, or indorser as part of the same transaction, they are jointly and severally liable unless the instrument otherwise specifies. This means that the full amount of the obligation could be collected from any one of them or that all of them might be joined in a single action. Joint and several liability is imposed even though the instrument contains such words as "I promise to pay" [3–118(e)].

TRANSFER OF COMMERCIAL PAPER

14. Introduction

The general rule governing the transfer of almost all types of property is that a person can transfer no greater interest than he owns. *Assignments* follow that general rule. The general law of assignments is discussed in Chapter 16. When one attempts to transfer rights by assignment, it is generally stated that the assignee steps into the shoes of the assignor. Thus the transfer of an instrument by assignment, whether negotiable or nonnegotiable, vests in the assignee only those rights the assignor had.

By contrast, the key feature of negotiability is that a *negotiation* might confer on a transferee greater rights than were held by the transferor. If the transfer is by negotiation, the transferee becomes a *holder* [3–202(1)]. A holder has, for example, the legal power to transfer the instrument by assignment or negotiation; he can usually enforce it in his own name [3–301]; he can discharge the liability of any party in several ways (as we shall later explain); and he enjoys several procedural advantages. Moreover, the holder has the opportunity to become a *holder in due course* with rights not granted by the instrument.

Thus, in an *assignment*, only the rights of the transferor are passed to the transferee, but in a *negotiation*, there is the possibility of granting greater rights. Any contract can be assigned; only a negotiable instrument can be negotiated.

15. Transfer by Negotiation

Two methods of negotiating an instrument make the transferee a holder. If the instrument is payable to bearer, it may be negotiated by delivery alone; if it is order paper, indorsement and delivery are required [3–202(1)]. The indorsement must be placed on the instrument itself or on a paper so firmly affixed to it that it becomes a part thereof. The indorsement paper that is annexed is called an *allonge*. The indorsement must be made by the holder or by someone who has the authority to do so on behalf of the holder [3–202(2)]. If the payee is a corporation, an officer will indorse on its behalf. The indorsement should include the corporate name, but this is not actually required.

The indorsement, to be effective as a negotiation, must convey the entire instrument or any unpaid balance due on the instrument. If it purports to indorse less than the entire instrument, it will be effective only as a partial assignment [3–202(3)]. An indorsement reading "Pay to A one-half of this instrument" would not be a negotiation, and A's position would be that of an assignee.

The indorser may add to his indorsement words of assignment, condition, waiver, guarantee, or limitation or disclaimer of liability, and the like. The indorsement is nevertheless effective to negotiate the instrument [3–202(4)]. Thus if A, the payee of a negotiable instrument, signs his name on the reverse side with the words "I hereby assign this instrument to B," he has effectively indorsed the instrument, and upon delivery to B, B is a holder.

If the name of the payee is misspelled, the payee may negotiate by indorsing either the name appearing on the instrument or in his true name, or both. A person who pays the instrument or gives value for it may require that both names be indorsed [3–203]. The desirable practice is to indorse in both names when the name of the payee is misspelled.

Instruments payable to multiple parties must be indorsed by all parties in order to negotiate the instrument. If authorized, one party may sign for the other. A bank may supply missing indorsements for its depositors. If there is a joint account, it may add the indorsement of either party or both in the event an item is payable to both. Note the significance of this right for banks in the following case.

CASE

Fred Beyer and his wife Peggy Beyer opened a joint account at the defendant bank. Both deposited checks to the account and wrote checks on it. As a part of a settlement with an insurance company, they received a check payable to both of them. It was deposited to the joint account without indorsement. The bank negotiated the check after a bank employee stamped the check with the following indorsement:

> Deposited to the account of the within named payee in accordance with payee's instruction. Absence of the indorsement guaranteed by the First National Bank of Dillon, Montana.

The Beyers had marital difficulties and Peggy took all of the money out of the account. Fred sued the bank for the funds, alleging that it was liable to him for the check because he had not indorsed it.

ISSUE: Is the bank liable?

DECISION: No.

REASONS:
1. A check made payable to a husband and wife together must be indorsed by both in order to negotiate the instrument. Although one may be authorized to sign for the other, the mere fact that copayees are husband and wife does not authorize one to sign for the other.
2. A depositary or collecting bank may add the indorsement of a depositor if it does so in good faith and in accordance with reasonable commercial standards.
3. Both parties used the account and the bank acted properly.

Beyer v. First National Bank of Dillon, 612 P.2d 1285 (Mont. 1980).

16. Types of Indorsements

The ordinary indorsements used in negotiating paper are either special or blank. If added terms condition the indorsement, it is also a restrictive indorsement, which limits the indorsee's use of the paper. Also, the indorser may *limit* or *qualify* his liability as an indorser by adding words such as "without recourse." This qualified indorsement has the effect of relieving the indorser of his contractual liability as an indorser—that he will pay if the primary obligor refuses to do so. A qualified indorsement will also be a blank or a special indorsement. These indorsements are discussed in the following sections.

17. Blank Indorsements

A blank indorsement consists of the indorser's name written on the instrument. If an instrument drawn payable to order is indorsed in blank (see Figure 37–3), it becomes payable to bearer [3–204(2)]. After the blank indorsement, if it is indorsed

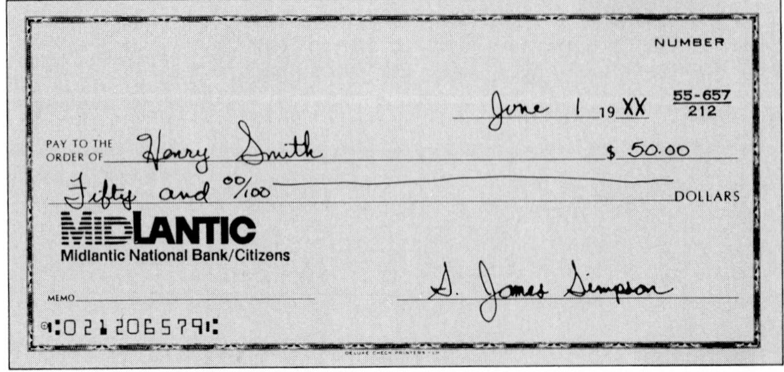

FIGURE 37–3 Order paper, payable to the order of Henry Smith. With his blank indorsement, shown at right, the order paper becomes bearer paper, negotiable by mere delivery.

specially, it reverts to its status as order paper, and an indorsement is required for further negotiation [3–204(1)]. If a check, on its face payable to the order of Henry Smith, is indorsed "Henry Smith," it becomes bearer payable and can be negotiated by mere delivery. A thief or finder could pass title to the instrument.

18. Special Indorsements

A special indorsement specifies the person to whom or to whose order it makes the instrument payable (see Figure 37–4). When an instrument is specially indorsed, it becomes payable to the *order of* the special indorsee and requires his indorsement for further negotiation. Thus an indorsement "Pay to John Jones" or "Pay to the order of John Jones" is a special indorsement and requires the further indorsement by John Jones for negotiation. If a bearer instrument is indorsed specially, it requires further indorsement by the indorsee. This is true if the instrument was originally bearer paper or if it became bearer paper as the result of a blank indorsement. In other words, the last indorsement determines whether the instrument is order paper or bearer paper [3–204].

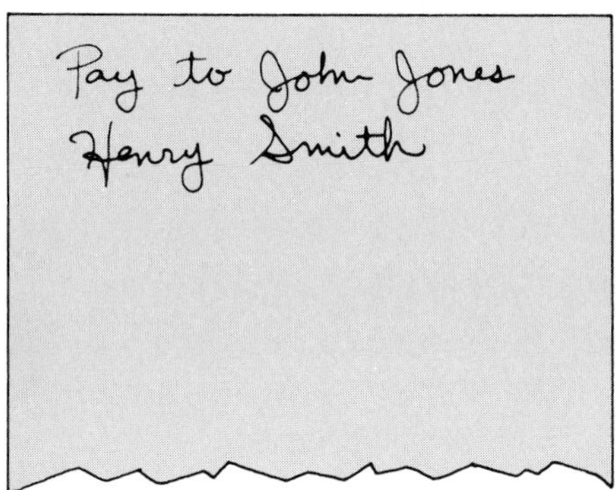

FIGURE 37–4 A special indorsement by Henry Smith. For negotiation, it requires further indorsement by John Jones.

The holder of an instrument may convert a blank indorsement into a special indorsement by writing above the blank indorser's signature any contract consistent with the character of the indorsement [3–204(3)]. Thus Richard Roe, to whom an instrument has been indorsed in blank by John Doe, could write above Doe's signature, "Pay to Richard Roe." The paper would require Roe's indorsement for further negotiation.

19. Restrictive Indorsements

A person who indorses an instrument may impose certain restrictions upon his indorsement; that is, the indorser may protect or preserve certain rights in the paper and limit the rights of the indorsee. Of the four types of restrictive indorsement, one is conditional (for example, "Pay John Doe if Generator XK-711 arrives by June 1, 1989"). Or the indorsement may purport to prohibit further transfer of the instrument, such as "Pay to John Doe only" [3–205(a)(b)]. When a check is deposited in a bank and will be processed through bank collection, the indorsements "For collection," "For deposit only," and "Pay any bank" are restrictive [3–205(c)]. In the fourth type, the indorser stipulates that it is for the benefit or use of the indorser or some other person, such as "Pay John Doe in trust for Richard Roe" [3–205(d)].

A restrictive indorsement does not prevent further transfer or negotiation of the instrument [3–206(1)]. Thus an instrument indorsed "Pay to John Doe only" could be negotiated by John Doe in the same manner as if it had been indorsed "Pay to John Doe."

The most common restrictive indorsement is "For deposit only" (see Figure 37–5). It is a common practice for payees of checks to use such an indorsement in order to safeguard checks. Once a check is stamped "For deposit only," a thief or finder of the check cannot cash it. The only action the bank can take is to deposit it into the indorser's account. If it fails to do so, it has liability to the indorser, as occurred in the following case.

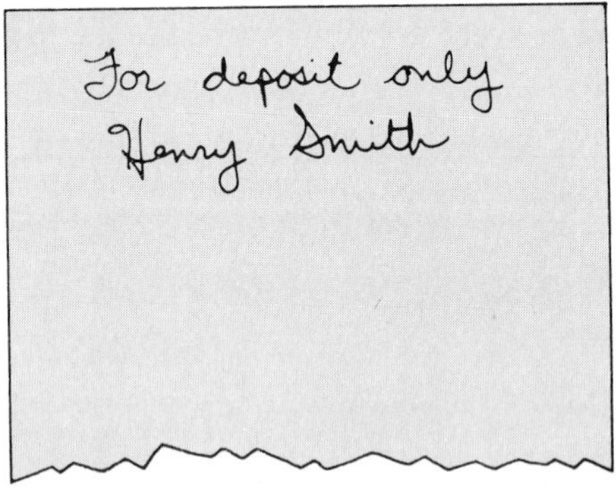

FIGURE 37–5 A restrictive indorsement by Henry Smith. Subsequent holders should be only the banks in the collection process.

CASE

Darwin, a general partner of two different partnerships, drew funds against a construction loan made to one of the partnerships. He received a money order payable to that partnership and he indorsed it "Deposit to the account of Rancho Village Partners, Ltd." However, he deposited the money order in the defendant bank with a deposit slip for the other partnership's (Settlement Ltd.) account. The bank accepted the deposit in spite of the restrictive indorsement. Darwin then embezzled the money from the Settlement Ltd. account. The first partnership sued both Darwin and the bank.

ISSUE: Was the bank liable for its payment because of the restrictive indorsement?

DECISION: Yes.

REASONS:
1. UCC Section 3–206 imposes a duty on the bank to pay consistent with the restrictive indorsement, and this duty gives rise to liability if it fails to do so.
2. There can be no waiver of the restrictive indorsement.

Rutherford v. Darwin, 622 P.2d 245 (N.M. 1980).

The effect of restrictive indorsements is substantially limited when applied to banks. An intermediary bank or a payor bank that is not a depositary bank can disregard any restrictive indorsement except that of the bank's immediate transferor. This limitation does not affect whatever rights the restrictive indorser may have against the bank of deposit or his right against parties outside the bank's collection process [3–206(2)]. Under a conditional indorsement or an indorsement for collection or deposit, a transferee (other than an intermediary bank) becomes a holder for value if it pays consistent with the indorsement [3–206(3)].

When the indorsement is for the benefit of the indorser or another person, such as "Pay to John Doe in trust for Richard Roe," only the first taker is required to act consistently with the restrictive indorsement [3–206(4)]. John Doe has the obligation to use the instrument or the proceeds from it for the benefit of Richard Roe. John Doe could negotiate the instrument to John Smith, who could qualify as a holder and ignore the restriction.

CHAPTER SUMMARY

General Requirements

Signed Writing	1. The negotiable instrument must be signed by the maker or drawer. 2. The signature can be anything intended to authenticate the instrument and it can be applied by mechanical means.
Promise or Order	1. A note must contain a promise, and a draft must contain an order.
Unconditional Promise or Order	1. The promise or order must be unconditional. A promise is conditional if reference to some other document is required or the instrument is subject to the terms of another document. 2. A recital of consideration does not destroy negotiability.
Particular Fund Concept	1. A promise that is limited to a particular fund is conditional and the instrument is not negotiable. 2. Exceptions to the particular fund concept involve instruments specifying an account to be debited and instruments issued by governmental units, partnerships, or unincorporated associations.
Sum Certain in Money	1. The unconditional promise or order must involve a sum certain in money. 2. Money is any currency adopted by a government. 3. A sum certain is present if the amount of money involved can be calculated from the information contained on the face of the instrument.
Certain Time of Payment	1. An instrument to be negotiable must be payable on demand or at a definite time. 2. An instrument is payable on demand when no time of payment is stated.
Acceleration and Extension Clauses	1. An acceleration clause that changes the maturity date does not destroy negotiability. 2. An extension clause that extends the time of payment at the option of the maker or acceptor without specifying the time of ultimate payment destroys negotiability. 3. An extension clause exercised by the holder does not destroy negotiability.

The Magic Words of Negotiability

Order Paper

1. To be negotiable, a note must be payable to the order of some person or to bearer. A note or check that is simply payable to a specified person is nonnegotiable.
2. An instrument payable to the order of two people must be indorsed by both.
3. An instrument payable to an estate, trust, or fund may be indorsed by the appropriate representative.

Bearer Paper

1. Bearer paper may be negotiated without indorsement by delivery.
2. An instrument is bearer paper if it specifies that it is payable to bearer or to cash.
3. Bearer paper may be negotiated by a finder or thief, and anyone in possession of it is entitled to collect.

Other Factors Affecting Negotiability

Terms and Omissions

1. Many terms do not affect negotiation. For example, a statement acknowledging satisfaction of an obligation on a check does not destroy negotiability.
2. An undated instrument is nevertheless negotiable as is a postdated instrument.

Incomplete Instruments

1. An incomplete instrument cannot be enforced until it is completed.
2. Instruments may be completed as authorized or unauthorized. Unauthorized completion is a personal defense that cannot be asserted against a holder in due course.

Ambiguous Terms and Rules of Construction

1. Handwritten terms prevail over typewritten terms or printed terms, and typewritten terms control printed terms.
2. If there is a conflict between words and figures, the words control.
3. If an instrument provides for interest without stating the rate, the rate on judgments will be followed.

Transfer of Commercial Paper

Negotiation

1. The term *negotiation* is used to describe the method of transferring a negotiable instrument in a manner that makes the transferee a holder.
2. A transfer that is not a proper negotiation is an assignment, and the assignee has the same rights as the assignor.
3. For proper negotiation, the whole instrument must be negotiated.
4. Bearer paper is negotiated by delivery. Order paper requires indorsement and delivery.

Blank Indorsement

1. A blank indorsement consists of the indorser's name, usually written on the back of the instrument.
2. A blank indorsement converts order paper to bearer paper.

Special Indorsements

1. Special indorsements indicate the person to whom the instrument is payable. Special indorsements require the indorsement of such person for further negotiation.

Restrictive Indorsements

1. Restrictive indorsements allow the indorser to preserve rights and limit the options of the indorsee.
2. The most common restrictive indorsement is "For deposit only." This means that the bank may not cash the check but must deposit the proceeds into the account of the indorser.
3. A restrictive indorsement when applied to banks does not prevent further negotiation and is applicable only to the immediate indorsee.

REVIEW QUESTIONS AND PROBLEMS

1. Match each term in column A with the appropriate statement in column B.

A	B
(1) IOU	(a) Varying exchange rates have no impact.
(2) Particular fund concept	(b) A statement of the transaction out of which the instrument arose.
(3) Sum certain in money	(c) Requires good faith in its execution.
(4) Restrictive indorsement	(d) Without recourse.
(5) Negotiability unaffected	(e) Not a promise.
(6) Acceleration clause	(f) Does not destroy negotiability if a governmental unit is the maker or drawer.
(7) Extension clause	(g) May or may not destroy negotiability.
(8) Blank indorsement	(h) For deposit only.
(9) Qualified indorsement	(i) Pay to John Jones./s/Paul Pringle.
(10) Special indorsement	(j) A signature

2. Comment briefly on the provisions described in these instruments as to their bearing on negotiability; in each instance the other portions of the instrument are in proper form.
   a. A bill of exchange drawn by Y on Z directs Z to pay $1,000 to the order of A and charge this amount to Y's "Book Fund."
   b. The XYZ Company (a partnership) signed a note promising to pay $1,000 and bearing the notation "limited to payment out of the entire assets of the maker."
   c. X signed a note promising to pay $5,000 or deliver 100 barrels of oil at the option of the holder.
   d. One of the notes is payable "five days after the death of the maker."
   e. A note containing the following notation: "with interest at bank rates."
3. Mitchell executed a construction contract and note payable to a contractor. The note was payable ninety days from its date or upon completion of the improvements provided for in the lien contract, whichever occurred first. Payment of the note was secured by the lien created in the lien contract and was subject to and governed by said contract. Was the note negotiable? Why or why not?
4. Skyblast Freight executed a note that contained the following provisions: "This note is payable only from the proceeds of the sale of the Skyblast Freight Building." Is the note negotiable? Why or why not?
5. Nestrick executed a note with the Bank of Viola to secure an uninterrupted line of credit. The note, in pertinent part, recited that it was "payable in installments of $80.00 per week from the *Jack and Jill* contract." Is this note negotiable? Explain.
6. Employer gave Pension Fund and Company a note stating that Employer promises to pay Pension Fund Company "all current contributions as they become due under the collective bargaining agreement in addition to the sum of $15,606.44 with interest." Is this note negotiable? Why or why not?
7. A draft stated on its face that it was payble "upon acceptance." Is the draft conditional and thus nonnegotiable? Why or why not?
8. Horace Brace has in his possession the following instrument:

November 1, 1985

I, Walter Forgel, hereby promise to pay Charles Smidlap ONE THOUSAND DOLLARS ($1,000.00) one year after date. This instrument was given for the purchase of FIVE HUNDRED (500) shares of Beefstake Mining Corporation. Interest at 10 percent.

Walter Forgel (Signature)

Horace Brace purchased the instrument from Charles Smidlap at a substantial discount. Smidlap specializes in the sale of counterfeit mining stock. Walter Forgel is one of his innocent victims. What are the rights of Brace against Forgel on the instrument? Explain.

9. Roberts was a holder in due course of a properly drawn check payable to "Bearer." He indorsed the check as follows:

   Pay to the order of Wilson Hall without recourse.
   /s/Peter Roberts

   What type of indorsement did Roberts make? If Hall wishes to negotiate the instrument, what is required? Explain.

10. Casey held a negotiable instrument payable to his order. He transferred the instrument to Dale for value. At the time of transfer Casey failed to indorse his name on the back of the instrument and Dale accepted the instrument as given to him. What rights does Dale have on the instrument? Explain.

11. A caterer, holder of a check, wishes to protect herself against its loss or theft. It has been indorsed to her in blank. Describe two methods by which she may gain this protection. Explain.

12. Quincy signed a promissory note payable to the order of Unger, who indorsed the note in blank over to Pritchard. Pritchard then transferred the note to Truax by delivery. Is Truax a holder of the instrument? Why or why not?

13. Bob issued a check payable to the order of Gary, who lost it without indorsing it. Can a finder of the check negotiate it? Why or why not?

Holders in Due Course and Defenses

38

CHAPTER PREVIEW

- STATUS OF THIRD PARTIES
  Assignee • Holder • Holder in due course • Contract provisions

- HOLDER IN DUE COURSE
  Requirements
  Value
  Good Faith
  Without Notice
  Before Overdue
  Holder from a Holder in Due Course

- DEFENSES
  Classifications
  Personal Defenses
  Real Defenses

- FTC RULE FOR CONSUMERS
  Introduction
  FTC Rule

BUSINESS MANAGEMENT DECISION

You are the senior loan officer of your bank. Among your many customers is a mobile home dealer, whose inventory your bank finances. This dealer typically takes promissory notes from its customers. The dealer then indorses these notes to your bank as partial payment for its debt. A dissatisfied customer of the dealer refuses to pay your bank until the defects with the mobile home are corrected.

Should you sue this dissatisfied customer of the mobile home dealer to collect on the note?

STATUS OF THIRD PARTIES

The original party to whom an instrument is issued or drawn has the right to transfer the instrument to someone else. The party to whom it is transferred may be an *assignee*, a *holder*, or a *holder in due course*.

Assignee. The party is an *assignee* if the instrument is not negotiable, and he has the status of an assignee if it has not been properly negotiated. (Remember that a thief or finder may negotiate bearer, but not order, paper.) If a negotiable instrument is properly negotiated, the party receiving it is a *holder*. If certain requirements are met, the holder may qualify as a *holder in due course* and have a special status [3–302]. If a holder does not qualify as a holder in due course, his position is equivalent to that of an assignee, and any defense available to the original parties may be asserted against the instrument.

Holder. Either the original payee or a third party may qualify as a holder of an instrument and may transfer or negotiate it. A holder may legally discharge it or enforce payment in his own name [3–301]. A thief or finder may qualify as a holder of a bearer instrument. As we will see later, a thief or finder cannot qualify as a holder in due course because he gave no value for the instrument.

Holder in due course. If there is no claim or defense to the instrument, it is immaterial whether the party seeking to enforce it is a holder or a holder in due course. The Code makes all holders the functional equivalent of holders in due course until a defense is claimed. The burden of proving a defense is on the party asserting it. When the defense is proved, the holder has the burden of proving that he is a holder in due course [3–307(3)]. If he can prove that, he can enforce payment, notwithstanding the presence of a personal defense to the instrument. (Later in the chapter we discuss both types of defenses: personal and real.) A holder in due course will not be able to enforce the instrument in the event that a real defense is proven. The preferred status of a holder in due course exists only where the defense to the instrument is a personal defense.

Issues as to whether or not a party is a holder in due course usually arise when the party seeks to collect on the instrument. But occasionally a party is sued on a negligence theory for losses incurred in transactions involving an instrument.

To avoid liability, the defendant must establish that he is or was a holder in due course. Thus a holder in due course is free of claims and is not subject to personal defenses.

Contract provisions. Contract provisions frequently attempt to give a status equivalent to a holder in due course to an assignee of contract. These provisions purport to waive defenses if the contract is assigned. Some states have declared such provisions to be illegal as against public policy if the drawer or maker is a consumer. Other states have enforced waiver of defense clauses provided the assignee meets the requirements to qualify as a holder in due course and the defense waived is a personal defense. Thus the material in this chapter is significant for many nonnegotiable contracts as well as negotiable instruments.

HOLDER IN DUE COURSE

1. Requirements

In order to qualify as a holder in due course, a holder must meet three basic requirements. He must take the instrument (1) for value, (2) in good faith, and (3) without notice that it is overdue, that it has been dishonored, or that any other person has a claim to it or defense against it [3–302(1)].

A payee may be a holder in due course if all the requirements are met. Most payees deal with the maker or drawer. However, a payee may be a holder in due course when the instrument is not delivered to the payee by the maker but is delivered by an intermediary or agent of the maker. A payee that participates in the transaction out of which the instrument arises cannot be a holder in due course.

When an instrument is acquired in a manner other than through the usual channels of negotiation or transfer, the holder will not be a holder in due course. Thus, if an instrument is obtained by an executor in taking over an estate, is purchased at a judicial sale, is obtained through legal process by an attaching creditor, or is acquired as a transaction not in the regular course of business, the party acquiring it is not a holder in due course [3–302(3)].

2. Value

A holder must have given *value* for an instrument in order to qualify as a holder in due course. A person to whom an instrument was transferred as a gift would not qualify as a holder in due course. *Value* does not have the same meaning as *consideration* in the law of contracts. A mere promise is consideration, but it is not value. As long as a promise is executory, the value requirement to be a holder in due course has not been met [3–303].

While a mere promise is not value, if the promise to pay is negotiable in form, it does constitute value [3–303(c)]. A drawer who issues his check in payment for a negotiable note that he is purchasing from the holder becomes a holder for value even before his check is cashed. A bank that cashes a check has given value.

A holder who takes an instrument in payment of an existing debt is a holder for value [3–303(b)]. Thus, if Ada owed Brenda $500 on a past-due account and transferred a negotiable instrument to Brenda in payment of such account, Brenda would qualify as a holder for value. The same holds true if the instrument is received as collateral for an existing debt, whether the debt is due or not.

A purchaser of a limited interest in paper can be a holder in due course only to the extent of the interest purchased [3–302(4)]. If a negotiable instrument is transferred as collateral for a loan, the transferee may be a holder in due course, but only to the extent of the debt that is secured by the pledge of the instrument. For example, George loans Gerry $2,500. To secure the loan, Gerry negotiates Ron's note in the amount of $4,000 to George. George is a holder in due course only to the extent of $2,500.

A person who purchases an instrument for less than its *face value* can be a holder in due course to the full amount of the instrument. Cora is the payee of a note for $1,000. She may discount the note and indorse it to Wick for $800. Wick has nevertheless paid value and is entitled to collect the full $1,000.

3. Good Faith

A holder must take the instrument in good faith in order to qualify as a holder in due course [3–304]. *Good faith* is defined as ''honesty in fact in the conduct or transaction concerned'' [1–201(19)]. If a person takes an instrument under circumstances that clearly establish the fact that there is a defense to the instrument, he does not take it in good faith. Failure to follow accepted business practices or to act reasonably by commercial standards, however, does not establish lack of good faith. Good faith is a subjective rather than an objective determination. Honesty rather than diligence or negligence is the issue, as the following case illustrates.

CASE

John Ryan owed David Taves approximately $18,500. In partial payment of the debt, Ryan delivered to Taves three checks, two for $1,500 each in October 1982 and the third for $10,000 in November 1982. The checks were drawn by Gene Griebel on two business accounts. Griebel was another individual involved in financing Ryan's business projects. Griebel had authority to sign these checks. He delivered them to Ryan without having filled in the payee or amount, but with instructions to pay the salary of an employee of one of the businesses and to pay rent on some farmland. Ryan's delivery to Taves was contrary to these instructions. Griebel stopped payment on each of these checks. After the third check did not clear, Taves telephoned Griebel to ask why payment had been stopped. It was only then that Taves learned of Ryan's dishonest completion of Griebel's checks. Nevertheless, Taves sued Griebel, claiming he was entitled to payment on the three checks because he was a holder in due course. The trial court granted Taves's motion for summary judgment, and Griebel appealed.

ISSUE: Was Taves a holder in due course of the checks signed by Griebel?

DECISION: Yes.

REASONS: 1. In order to acquire the status of a holder in due course, an individual must take an instrument for value, in good faith, without notice that it is overdue or has been dishonored, and without notice of any defense against or claim to it on the part of any person.

While it is conceded that Taves took the checks for value, the existence of Taves's good faith is disputed.

2. Good faith in a subjective determination, rather than an objective one. An individual need not satisfy some standard of reasonable conduct that would require him to act on circumstances that would have caused a careful purchaser to investigate further. Even if such circumstances existed, the individual will not fail to meet the good-faith requirement if he honestly believed his conduct was proper.
3. Taves acted in good faith. Taves does not fail to meet the good-faith requirement even though he accepted checks drawn on corporate accounts in payment of his loan. Accepting the second of two checks after a stop payment order had been made by the same drawer also does not impugn Taves's good faith. Taves never learned of Ryan's dishonesty until he contacted Griebel. Taves believed that he acted properly, and there are no facts to suggest he lacked good faith.
4. As the drawer of the check, Griebel created the opportunity for misuse of funds. Therefore, although both he and Taves are relatively innocent victims of Ryan's misconduct, Griebel should bear the loss. He entrusted the check to Ryan without imposing any limitations whatsoever on the check faces, and continued to do so after he became aware that Ryan was misusing them.
5. Therefore Taves is a holder in due course because he took the checks for value in good faith and had no notice that they were misused. The trial court's decision is affirmed.

Taves v. Griebel, 363 N.W.2d 73 (Minn. App. 1985).

Taking a note on large discount does not in and of itself establish lack of good faith. A large discount may result from factors other than the existence of a defense to the instrument. The burden is on the party seeking to deny the holder in due course status to prove lack of good faith. Good faith is presumed in the absence of facts to show bad faith.

Under a doctrine known as *close connectedness*, a transferee does not take an instrument in good faith when the transferee is so closely connected with the transferor that the transferee may be charged with knowledge of an infirmity in the underlying transaction. The rationale for the close connectedness doctrine is the basic philosophy of the holder in due course concept: to encourage free negotiability of commercial paper by removing certain anxieties from one who takes the paper as an innocent purchaser, knowing no reason why the paper is not sound as its face would indicate. Therefore the more the holder knows about the underlying transaction, and particularly the more he controls or participates or becomes involved in it, the less he fits the role of a good-faith purchaser for value. The closer his relationship to the underlying agreement that is the source of the note, the less need there is for giving him the tension-free rights.

Among the factors that tend to establish the close connection are (1) drafting by the transferee of forms for the transferor; (2) approval of the transferor's procedures by the transferee (e.g., setting the interest rate); (3) an independent check by the transferee on the credit of the debtor; (4) heavy reliance by the transferor on the transferee (e.g., transfer by the transferor of all or substantial part of his paper to the transferee); and (5) common or connected ownership or management of the transferor and transferee. Close connectedness exists also (1) when the transferee or assignee has substantial voice in, or control of, a vested interest in the underlying transaction, or (2) if the transferee has knowledge of the particular transaction or of the way the seller does business, so that he knows of claims the buyer has against the seller. The basic question is whether the holder of the instrument is actually a party to the transaction. As the following case illustrates, the issue is one of fact.

CASE

Denise and Timothy St. James operated the Las Vegas Chiropractic Center. They purchased a debt collection service from National Revenue Corporation (NRC). John Walker, an NRC employee, sold them the debt collection service and had them sign two promissory notes payable to Diversified Commercial Finance Corporation. Diversified provided financing for NRC by lending the money to individuals to pay for NRC's services and providing NRC with preprinted promissory notes for NRC's customers to sign. The St. Jameses stopped making payments on the notes after several months because NRC was allegedly not providing the services promised. Diversified sued the St. Jameses, seeking the balance due on the note. The St. Jameses responded with the defense of failure of consideration. They claimed NRC's failure to provide the services promised in the service agreement excused their payment. The trial court granted Diversified's motion for summary judgment, concluding that Diversified was a holder in due course and therefore immune from the defenses to payment that were available against the seller, NRC.

ISSUE: Was Diversified immune, as a holder in due course, from all the defenses that the St. Jameses could invoke against NRC to avoid payment on the notes?

DECISION: No.

REASONS:

1. Although Diversified is a party with whom the St. Jameses have dealt, under traditional analysis they cannot assert the defense of failure of consideration against Diversified. Diversified has fulfilled the requirements to be a holder in due course free from the personal defenses of the maker.
2. However, many jurisdictions have broken with the traditional analysis of the holder in due course rule and have limited its application either by statutory enactment or judicial adoption of the close connectedness doctrine. This doctrine holds a lender subject to the defenses that a buyer has against his seller where the lender and seller are closely connected.
3. Although the Uniform Consumer Credit Code and the Federal Trade Commission rules apply the close connectedness doctrine only to consumer transactions, we adopt the doctrine with respect to all transactions where the buyer can demonstrate a close connection between the seller and a lender. The reasons for the doctrine are equally applicable in nonconsumer transactions.
4. The record discloses that a genuine issue of fact, whether NRC and Diversified are closely connected, remains to be tried. The

promissory notes on their face were sufficient to demonstrate that a material fact remains to be tried. They indicate that Diversified may have been in reality a party to the service agreement.

5. Therefore, because a genuine issue of material fact remained to be tried, Diversified was not entitled to summary judgment. The case is reversed and remanded to the trial court.

St. James v. Diversified Commercial Financial Corp., 714 P.2d 179 (Nev. 1986).

As a result of the close connectedness doctrine, many courts have held that a transferee of a negotiable note does not take in ''good faith'' and is not a holder in due course of a note given in the sale of consumer goods where the transferee is a finance company involved with the seller of the goods, and which has a pervasive knowledge of factors relating to the terms of the sale. As the foregoing case illustrates, the concept of close connection may also be used to protect a business as well as a consumer in many states.

The good-faith requirement has often been challenged by consumers using the close connectedness doctrine when a consumer note was immediately transferred by a seller to a bank. If the bank qualified as a holder in due course, the consumer would have to pay, even though the goods were defective. This issue has been significantly eliminated today by a 1976 Federal Trade Commission (FTC) ruling allowing consumers to use all defenses when sued on a negotiable note. This FTC rule is discussed in detail later in this chapter.

4. Without Notice

Closely related to good faith is the requirement that the transferee must not have **notice** of any claim or defense to the instrument, that it is overdue, or that it has been dishonored [3–304]. A person has notice of a fact if he has actual knowledge of it, has received notification of it, or (from the facts and circumstances known to him) has ''reason to know'' that it exists [1–201(25)]. The law generally provides that a person has reason to know a fact if his information would indicate its existence to a person of ordinary intelligence (or of the intelligence of the person involved, if that is above the ordinary). He also has reason to know the facts if they are so highly probable that a person exercising reasonable care will assume their existence.

__Notice__ A person has ''notice'' of a fact when (a) he has actual knowledge of it; or (b) he has received a notice or notification of it; or (c) from all the facts and circumstances known to him at the time in question, he has reason to know that it exists.

If there is visible evidence of forgery or alteration, a purchaser is put on notice of a claim or defense [3–304(1)(a)]. Certain irregularities on the face of an instrument also put a purchaser on notice that there may be a claim or defense to the instrument. Many are obvious, such as a signature that is obviously affixed by someone else, as happened in the following case.

CASE

Ken Hessler was in the business of raising hogs for J and J Farms, Inc. JJ Farms would deliver the hogs to Hessler and require him to sign a promissory note payable to JJ Farms to cover the cost of the hogs and feed. After the hogs were raised, JJ Farms would take them to be sold at auction. The proceeds were applied to satisfy Hessler's notes and his fees for raising the hogs. Business went well until January 4, 1977, when

JJ Farms' representative asked Hessler to sign his wife's name to the promissory note for the hogs delivered that week. Hessler signed his wife's name, then placed his initials "K.H." after the signature. JJ Farms then immediately sold the note to Arcanum National Bank. Unfortunately for Hessler, the hogs delivered to him on January 4 had previously been sold by JJ Farms to another buyer, who repossessed the hogs from Hessler. The note became due and Arcanum demanded payment from Hessler. Arcanum claimed to be a holder in due course. Hessler contended that Arcanum was subject to the defense of lack of consideration since the note on its face gave notice of a defense.

ISSUE: Does a promissory note in which the wife's name is signed by the husband followed by his initials constitute "notice" so as to preclude a buyer of the note from being a holder in due course?

DECISION: Yes.

REASONS:

1. The defect on the face of the note calls into question the validity of the note, the terms of the note, and created an ambiguity as to the party who is to pay the note. The bank should have realized that the defect on the note signaled the possibility of defenses on the underlying obligation.
2. The bank handled Hessler's finances and had a signature card on Mr. and Mrs. Hessler. Therefore the bank had constructive notice that Mrs. Hessler's signature was not valid.

Arcanum National Bank v. Hessler, 433 N.E.2d 204 (Ohio 1982).

If an instrument is incomplete in some important respect at the time it is purchased, notice is imparted [3–304(1)(a)]. Blanks in an instrument that do not relate to material terms do not give notice of a claim or defense; but if the purchaser has notice that the completion was improper, he is not a holder in due course [3–304(4)(d)].

Knowledge that a defense exists or that the instrument has been dishonored prohibits the status of a holder in due course. In some situations, knowledge of certain facts does *not*, of itself, give the purchaser notice of a defense or claim. Awareness that an instrument is antedated or postdated does not prevent a holder from taking in due course [3–304(4)(a)]. Knowledge of a separate contract is not notice. Although a defense will arise if the contract is not performed, such knowledge does not prevent one from becoming a holder in due course. Of course, if the purchaser is aware that the contract has been breached or repudiated, he will not qualify as a holder in due course.

Actual notice to prevent a party from being holder in due course must be received at a time and in a way that will give a reasonable opportunity to act on it [3–304(6)]. A notice received by the president of a bank one minute before the bank's teller cashes a check is not effective in preventing the bank from becoming a holder in due course.

5. Before Overdue

To be a holder in due course, a purchaser of an instrument must take it without notice that it is overdue [3–304(1)(c)]. A purchaser of overdue paper is charged with knowledge that some defense may exist. A purchaser has notice that an instrument is overdue if he has reason to know that any part of the principal amount is overdue [3–304(3)(a)]. Past-due interest does not impart notice to the holder [3–304(4)(f)]. The instrument itself will usually indicate if it is past due, as in the following case.

CASE

Girner executed a $5,000 promissory note to First Realty Corporation on September 25, 1980. Monthly payments on the note were to commence on January 15, 1981. A schedule was printed on the back of the note. The note was assigned by First Realty to Imran Bohra in exchange for property. On July 27, 1981, Bohra transferred the note to his attorney, F. Eugene Richardson, in payment for legal services rendered by Richardson. At that time there was no entry of any payment on the back of the note. Richardson sued Girner for the amount of the note. Girner argued no payments were due since Bohra owed Girner more than the $5,000 represented in this note. Richardson asserted that he was a holder in due course of the note and thus free from Girner's claim of a setoff. The trial court held Richardson was not a holder in due course and was subject to Girner's setoff against Bohra. Richardson appealed.

ISSUE: Did Richardson take the note with notice that it was overdue, thereby making him subject to Girner's setoff against Bohra?

DECISION: Yes.

REASONS:
1. Unless a person is a holder in due course, the note is subject to all valid claims to it on the part of any person and to all defenses, counterclaims, and setoffs.
2. The facts in this case clearly reveal that at the time Richardson acquired the note no payments had been entered in the schedule on the back of the note. Six payments should have been made at the time of the transfer to Richardson.
3. In the present case, Bohra knew that Girner had claims against him far in excess of the amount of the note here in question. From the record there is an indication that Bohra had been told by Girner, prior to assignment of the note to Richardson, that he should consider the note paid.
4. In view of the fact that Richardson had notice that payments on the note were overdue at the time he took the note, he was not a holder in due course. Therefore the note was subject to the defense by Girner against Bohra.

Richardson v. Girner, 668 S.W.2d 523 (Ark. 1984).

Demand paper poses a special problem, since it does not have a fixed date of maturity. A purchaser of demand paper cannot be a holder in due course if he has reason to know that he is taking it after a demand has been made, or if he takes it more than a reasonable length of time after its issue [3–304(3)(c)]. What is a reasonable or an unreasonable time is determined on the basis of a number of factors—the kind of instrument, the customs and usages of the trade or business, and the particular facts and circumstances involved. In the case of a check, a reasonable time is presumed to be thirty days [3–304(3)(c)]. The thirty-day period is a presumption rather than an absolute rule.

6. Holder from a Holder in Due Course

A transferee may have the rights of a holder in due course, even though he personally does not meet all the requirements. Because a transferee obtains all the rights that the transferor had, a person who derives title through a holder in due course also has those rights. Code Section 3–201(1) states this principle, the *shelter provision*, which advances the marketability of commercial paper.

The main significance of the shelter provision is that it permits one who is not a holder in due course to share the shelter from claims and defenses enjoyed by the holder in due course from whom he got the instrument.

EXAMPLE: Paul fraudulently induces Mary to execute and deliver a note to him. Paul then negotiates the note to Tom, who qualifies as a holder in due course. Tom makes a gift of the note to Al, who sells it to Bob, a friend of Paul's, who knew of Paul's fraud. Bob sells it to Carl after maturity. Is Carl a holder in due course? No. Were Bob and Al holders in due course when they owned the instrument? No. Is Carl subject to Mary's defense? No. While Al, Bob, and Carl are not and were not holders in due course, they have the rights of a holder in due course. They have Tom's rights and are free of the personal defense. Mary's defense was cut off by Tom's status as a holder in due course. (See Figure 38–1.)

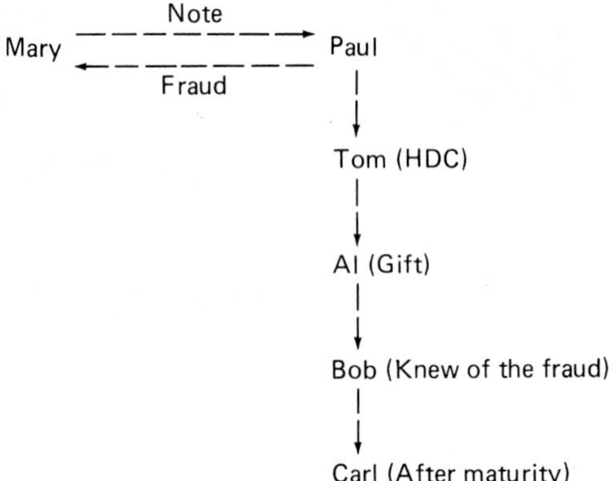

FIGURE 38–1

The shelter provision is subject to a limitation. A person who formerly held the paper cannot improve his position by later reacquiring it from a holder in due course. If a former holder was himself a party to any fraud or illegality affecting the instrument, or if he had notice of a defense or claim against it as a prior holder, he cannot claim the rights of a holder in due course by taking from a later holder in due course.

DEFENSES

7. Classifications

A holder in due course takes commercial paper free from the *personal defenses* of the parties to the paper [3–305]. One who is not a holder in due course or who does not have the rights of one under the shelter provision is subject to such defenses.

All transferees, including holders in due course, are subject to what are referred to as *real defenses*.

In general, real defenses relate to the existence of any obligation on the part of the person who asserts them. The most obvious real defense is forgery of the signature of the maker of a note or the drawer of a check. The person whose signature was forged has not entered into any contract, and he has an absolute defense even against a holder in due course.

The Code generally specifies which defenses are real and which are personal. A few defenses—infancy being one—are real in some states and personal in others. Table 38–1 groups them according to their usual status. The basic aspects of most personal defenses are discussed in the materials on contracts.

TABLE 38–1 COMMERCIAL PAPER: TYPICAL DEFENSES

Personal Defenses	Real Defenses
Lack or failure of consideration	Unauthorized signature
Nonperformance of a condition precedent	Material alteration
Nondelivery, conditional delivery, or delivery for a special purpose	Infancy, if it is a defense to a simple contract
Payment	Lack of capacity
Slight duress	Extreme duress
Fraud in the inducement	Fraud in the execution
Theft by the holder or one through whom he holds	Illegality
Violation of a restrictive indorsement	Discharge in bankruptcy
Unauthorized completion	Discharge of which the holder has notice
Other defenses to a simple contract	
Any real defense where the party was negligent	

8. Personal Defenses

A distinction exists between *fraud in the inducement* and *fraud in the execution*. Inducement pertains to the consideration for which an instrument is given. The primary party intended to create an instrument but was fraudulently induced to do so. Such a defense is personal and is not available against a holder in due course. Fraud in the execution exists where a negotiable instrument is procured from a party when circumstances are such that the party does not know that he is giving a negotiable instrument. Fraud in the execution is a real defense [3–305(2)(c)]. The theory is that since the party primarily to be bound has no intention of creating an instrument, none is created. Such fraud is rare because persons are usually charged with knowledge of what they sign, as occurred in the following case.

CASE

W. G. and Betty Ellis executed a promissory note for $25,000 in favor of Standard Finance Company for the purpose of getting a loan. Mr. Ellis took the money and left the vicinity. When the note was due, Mrs. Ellis refused payment. She contended that Mr. Ellis had tricked her into signing the note. She claimed that Mr. Ellis assured her that her signature was a mere "formality," that he alone was liable, and that the debt would be repaid without any participation by her. Standard Finance contended that Mrs. Ellis's defense was fraud in the inducement, a personal defense, which is ineffective to defeat the rights of a holder in due course.

ISSUE: Is the fraud in this case a real or a personal defense?

DECISION: Personal defense.

REASONS:

1. Fraud in the execution, which is a real defense and effective against a holder in due course, requires the signer to sign an instrument on a false representation without knowing the character or essential terms of the instrument. An example is an illiterate person signing a note on the false representation that the instrument is a receipt.
2. The case here is one of fraud in the inducement. No representation was made to Mrs. Ellis that the note was anything but a note and Mr. Ellis explained to her the essential terms of the instrument prior to execution. Her error was relying on Mr. Ellis's statement. The paper on its face was valid.
3. The signer must exercise caution of a reasonably prudent man when he signs commercial paper. Here, reliance on Mr. Ellis's statements that she would not be liable constituted negligence on her part.

Standard Finance Company Limited v. Ellis, 657 P.2d 1056 (Hawaii 1983).

Another personal defense, acquisition of title by or through a thief, is easily preventable. Conversion of bearer paper to order paper precludes its negotiation by a thief or finder.

A holder in due course is not subject to the defense of unauthorized completion of an instrument [3–407(3)]. The defense is personal. The person who left the blank space must bear the risk of wrongful completion.

Negligence of a party, frequently present in situations of fraud and material alteration, will reduce a real defense to a personal defense [3–406]. A check written with a wide, blank space preceding the amount offers a wrongdoer an easy place to raise that amount. The negligent check writer has reduced the defense to a personal one. The defense may be asserted, however, if the bank fails to follow reasonable commercial standards. The issue is a question of fact for the jury, which often finds for the customer, as it did in the following case.

CASE

Sam Crisp was approached by Bill Carter to do some repair work on Crisp's lightning rod. Carter said he would do the work for $12.50. Crisp made out the check for $12.50 but left the name of payee blank and an open space preceding the amount for which the check was issued. Carter took the check and altered the amount to where it read $6,212.50. Owensboro National Bank paid the check and Crisp sued the bank to recover his losses. The bank claimed Crisp's negligence precluded him from asserting the alteration and that it paid the check in good faith. At the trial the judge submitted the issues to the jury in an interrogatory that required the jury to decide whether the employees of the bank failed to follow reasonable commercial standards in paying the check. Ten of the twelve jurors found in the affirmative. Accordingly, a judgment was entered in Crisp's favor in the sum of $6,200. The bank appealed.

ISSUE: Despite Crisp's negligence in leaving an open space on his check, must the bank exercise commercially reasonable care before honoring the raised check?

DECISION: Yes.

REASONS:

1. Crisp was negligent as that term is used in UCC Section 3–406. His negligence substantially contributed to the alteration. However, this section also requires that the check be paid in "good faith and in accordance with the reasonable commercial standards of the drawee's or payor's business."
2. Although Crisp was negligent, his negligence may be overcome by the negligence of the bank in cashing the check. This was a question of fact, which properly was submitted to the jury. The jury found that the cashier of the bank failed to follow reasonable commercial standards in paying Crisp's check and that such failure was a substantial factor in causing Crisp's loss.
3. Not only does it appear to be clearly reasonable from the evidence for the jury to find in favor of Crisp, but, as a matter of fact, the jury did find in his favor. The trial court did not err in refusing to direct a verdict for the bank.

Owensboro National Bank v. Crisp, 608 S.W.2d 51 (Ky. 1980).

9. Real Defenses

The real defense of unauthorized signature includes signatures by agents without authority and forgeries [3–404(1)]. It applies to indorsements as well as to the signature creating the instrument.

The most common example of a material alteration is the "raising" of a check [3–407]. A check drawn in the amount of $50 might be raised by alteration to $500. This creates a real defense to the extent of the alteration. A subsequent holder in due course could enforce the check only in the amount of its original $50.

The defense of lack of capacity is a real defense if the state law so provides. If it is a defense to a simple contract, it is a real defense [3–305(2)(a)]. The same is true for all forms of illegality. If a contract is merely voidable, the defense is personal; if the contract is void or unenforceable, the defense is a real one. If state law provides that usurious contracts are null and void, usury is a real defense.

FTC RULE FOR CONSUMERS

10. Introduction

The holder in due course concept was predicated on the need for commercial paper to move quickly, freely, and as "a courier without luggage" in the financial community. Negotiable instruments were intended to be the equivalent of money. Use of commercial paper was encouraged by freeing it of personal defenses if its holder is a holder in due course. Today, consumer advocates argue that protection of the consumer is more important than the reasons for the holder in due course concept, and that all defenses should always be available to the consumer-debtor. They feel that the best protection for a consumer is the right to withhold payment if goods are defective or not delivered.

A number of states have enacted statutes prohibiting the use or enforcement of clauses that cut off defenses in contracts such as leases. Courts in many states have held that a holder was not a holder in due course when the finance company was closely connected with the seller (the close connectedness doctrine previously discussed). Courts have also strictly construed the application of the holder in due course rule. Doubts about the negotiability of instruments have been resolved against negotiability. Several states have achieved this result by the enactment of the Uniform Consumer Credit Code, whose provisions are applicable to instruments other than checks. This code offers two alternative approaches to the problem. A state legislature can select the one it considers best suited to the needs of the state.

One alternative simply gives maximum protection to the consumer by allowing him to assert all claims and defenses against the assignee of any paper that he signed. The other alternative provides that the assignee can give written notice of the assignment to the debtor. The consumer is then given the right to assert defenses for three months. After the three-month period, the assignee is free of any defense, and the debtor's only remedy is against the seller.

11. FTC Rule

Since these state efforts were not universal, in 1976 the Federal Trade Commission, acting under its authority to prohibit unfair or deceptive methods of competition, adopted a rule that prohibits the use of the holder in due course concept against consumers. It also provides that a contract clause purporting to cut off defenses is an unfair method of competition and illegal.

The FTC rule is designed to eliminate substantial abuses often inflicted upon the purchaser of consumer goods. Under the holder in due course concept, consumers were often required to pay for defective merchandise and even for merchandise not received. Since consumer paper was usually sold to a bank or other financial institution, the purchaser of the paper would qualify as a holder in due course. As such, it would be able to collect, and the consumer was left to fight it out with the seller when a problem arose.

The FTC rule is applicable to any sale or lease of goods or services to consumers in commerce. In such a transaction, it is an unfair or deceptive act or practice for a seller to receive a credit contract that does not contain the following provision in at least 10-point bold type:

NOTICE

**ANY HOLDER OF THIS CONSUMER CREDIT CONTRACT
IS SUBJECT TO ALL CLAIMS AND DEFENSES
WHICH THE DEBTOR COULD ASSERT AGAINST THE SELLER
OF GOODS OR SERVICES OBTAINED PURSUANT HERETO
OR WITH THE PROCEEDS HEREOF.**

Thus the holder could not be a holder in due course, because the holder agrees to be subject to all defenses.

To prevent sellers from sending buyers directly to the lender and thus circumventing the law, the rule has a special provision relating to lending institutions. It declares that it is an unfair or deceptive practice for a seller to accept in payment the proceeds of a purchase-money loan unless a similar notice is included in the loan agreement in 10-point bold type.

For the purpose of the foregoing rule, a purchase-money loan exists if the seller refers the consumer to the creditor or is affiliated with the creditor by common control, contract, or business arrangement. This means that if the lending institution regularly does business with the seller or has an understanding that its customers may obtain financing, the provision must be included in the loan contract. Again, it provides that all defenses are available to the consumer.

As a result of the FTC rule, if a consumer-purchaser or buyer has any defense against the seller, it may assert that defense against the bank or other financial institution that seeks to collect the debt. Thus banks and other financial institutions must make sure that the seller stands behind the products sold. In addition, they must deal only with responsible parties on a recourse basis if losses are to be avoided.

CHAPTER SUMMARY

Status of Third Parties

Status Possibilities	1. A transferee of commercial paper may be an assignee, a holder, or a holder in due course. 2. An assignee is a transferee of a simple contract, or one to whom a negotiable instrument has not been properly negotiated. 3. A holder has a negotiable instrument that has been properly negotiated. 4. A holder that meets certain requirements is a holder in due course and takes instruments free of personal defenses.
Contract Provisions	1. Contracts often contain clauses that waive defenses in the event the contract is assigned. 2. Such clauses are illegal in some states and legal in others. 3. If legal, most states require that the assignee meet the same requirements as a holder in due course, and these states waive only personal defenses.

Holder in Due Course

Value	1. A holder in due course must take the instrument for value and not as a gift. A mere promise is not value, but a preexisting debt is value.
Good Faith	1. A holder in due course must take in good faith. Good faith is honesty in fact. If the holder knows that there is a defense, he is not a good-faith taker.
Without Notice	1. A holder in due course must take without notice that it is overdue, has been dishonored, or that there is a claim or defense to the instrument. A person has notice if he has actual knowledge or reason to know the fact.

Before Overdue

1. An instrument is overdue if it is demand paper and more than a reasonable length of time has passed. In the case of a check this time period is thirty days.

Holder from a Holder in Due Course

1. A transferee from a holder in due course has the rights of a holder in due course and thus is free of personal defenses. A person may take by gift, with knowledge of a defense, or after maturity and still be able to collect on an instrument if it has passed through the hands of a holder in due course.
2. The shelter provision is not applicable to a reacquirer.

Defenses

Personal Defenses

1. A personal defense is one that arises out of the transaction that created the instrument. They are generally based on the law of contracts.
2. Payment is a very important personal defense.
3. Negligence reduces a real defense to a personal defense.

Real Defenses

1. A real defense may be asserted against any party, including a holder in due course.
2. Real defenses go to the essence of the instrument. The most important real defense is forgery.

FTC Rule for Consumers

1. The FTC rule prevents the use of the holder in due course concept in a consumer credit transaction.
2. In such transactions involving consumers, the contract must contain a notice in 10-point bold type informing all holders that any defense available against the seller of goods can be asserted against the holder.
3. The same notice must be contained in purchase-money loan documents.

REVIEW QUESTIONS AND PROBLEMS

1. Match each term in column A with the appropriate statement in column B.

A	B
(1) Shelter provision	(a) May be a real defense or a personal one depending on state law.
(2) Value	(b) Prohibits consumers from holder in due course status.
(3) Good faith	(c) Always a real defense.
(4) Holder	(d) Eliminates real defenses.
(5) FTC rule	(e) Allows a transferee to have the rights of a holder in due course.
(6) Fraud in the execution	(f) A mere promise does not qualify as this.
(7) Infancy	(g) Has possession of a negotiable instrument that has been properly negotiated.
(8) Negligence	(h) Honesty in fact.

2. Siegman, a diamond merchant, issued a note for diamonds purchased. The seller indorsed the note to a bank "as collateral for his preexisting obligations to the banks and as collateral for the diamonds shipped to defendants." Did the bank give value so as to qualify as a holder in due course? Explain.

3. A bank received a check to deposit in Seve's account. Seve subsequently wrote checks withdrawing most of the proceeds of the deposited check. The bank paid these checks before receiving notice that the deposited check was dishonored. Does the bank qualify as a holder in due course? Explain.

4. Evans wrote and delivered a promissory note to Cey Cheese, Inc. Cey Cheese indorsed the note to a law firm for legal services to be performed. Cey Cheese had obtained the notes from Evans by fraudulent representations but the law firm was unaware of this. When the firm tried to collect on the note, Evans asserted the defense of fraud in the inducement. Is this defense effective against the law firm? Why?

5. Andrews owed Martin, his accountant, a fee for services rendered. Andrews drew a check on his bank payable to "Cash" and signed it. He left the amount blank because he was not sure of the exact amount owed. On his way to Martin's office Andrews lost the check. Oliver found the check, filled it in for $500, and handed it to Ernest to satisfy a $500 debt that Oliver owed to Ernest. Ernest accepted the check in good faith as payment for the debt and immediately presented it to the drawee bank. The drawee bank refused to cash it because of a stop payment order. Is Andrews liable to Ernest for the $500? Why?

6. C&S Bank sued Johnson to collect a $50,000 note. Johnson had signed the note payable to Peek. Peek had transferred the note to the bank as security for a $20,000 loan. Johnson seeks to assert a defense of fraud and lack of consideration. Is the bank a holder in due course? Why or why not?

7. Pat fraudulently misrepresented certain goods he was attempting to sell Mike. Mike relied on these misstatements and purchased the goods, giving Pat in exchange a negotiable promissory note for $100, made by Mike, payable to Pat's order, and maturing on November 14, 1989. Pat indorsed and delivered the note to Art, a holder in due course. On November 15, 1989, Art indorsed and delivered the note to Harry, in exchange for Harry's promise to pay Art $95. Harry did not know of Pat's fraud until he attempted to collect from Mike and Mike refused payment. Is Harry a holder in due course? Why? Is Harry free of the defense? Why?

8. Charles was appointed guardian for his seven-year-old son, Chad, who was the beneficiary of his grandfather's life insurance policy. The insurance company issued a check for $30,588.39 made payable to "Charles, Guardian of the Estate of Chad a Minor." Charles opened a personal account with the check and absconded with the proceeds. When the bank was sued by Chad, it claimed to be a holder in due course. Was it? Explain.

9. Nevers executed a note payable to the order of Young due on January 1, 1990. On March 1, 1990, Young negotiated the note to Glassen. Will Glassen be subject to the personal defenses of Nevers? Why?

10. Wells issued a check on its account at First National Bank payable to the order of Tayman in the amount of $4,200. Wells stopped payment on the check early the next banking day. Later that day Tayman attempted to cash the check at First National, and when payment was refused, he took the check to his own bank, Second National, which cashed it. Is Second National a holder in due course? Why or why not?

11. Arthur purchased securities from William, giving William his check payable to William's order and drawn on Produce Bank in payment. William immediately indorsed the check to the order of Robert, and it was accepted by Robert in payment of a debt owed him by William. Robert indorsed the check in blank and delivered it to his son, Charles, as a birthday gift. Arthur has discovered that the securities sold him by William are worthless and has directed Produce Bank to stop payment. When Produce Bank refuses to pay Charles on the check and Charles sues Arthur, may Arthur assert the defense of failure of consideration against Charles? Explain.

12. Pam bought equipment from a dealer who was to supply additional equipment weekly. These additional items would permit Pam to make tapes that the dealer was to purchase. Pam gave the dealer a note for the equipment; but the additional equipment was never delivered and the dealer went out of business. Before closing, the dealer discounted the note at a bank that had purchased other notes from the dealer. The bank had a very close relationship with the dealer and apparently knew of the dealer's shady business practices. The bank now sues Pam to collect the proceeds of the note. Is it a holder in due course? Why?

13. Hilda executed a note payable to Home Improvements, Inc., for various improvements to her house. The company negotiated the note to a bank, which sued Hilda. If the bank is a holder in due course, can Hilda raise the defense that Home Improvements made several material misrepresentations in inducing her to sign the note? Explain.

14. Smith delivered to Janett his check drawn on National Bank payable to Janett. Janett had the check certified and delivered it to Cook as payment on account. The certification was stamped on the face of the check. It said ''Certified payable as originally drawn.'' The original check was for $1,000. Janett had raised the amount to $4,000 prior to the certification. No one but an expert would have realized that the check had been raised. How much can Cook collect on the check? How much can the bank charge to Smith's account? Explain.

Liability of Parties to Commercial Paper

39

CHAPTER PREVIEW

- **LIABILITY BASED ON SIGNATURES**

  In General
  Capacity of the Signature
  Agency Principles
  Exceptions: Impostors and Fictitious Payees

- **LIABILITY BASED ON STATUS**

  Classification of Parties
  Liability of Primary Parties

- **LIABILITY OF SECONDARY PARTIES**

  Accommodation Parties and Guarantors
  Drawers
  Indorsers
  Transferors without Indorsement
  Forgeries
  Double Forgeries

- **CONDITIONAL LIABILITY**

  Presentment— In General
  Presentment—How and Where
  Presentment—When
  Dishonor
  Notice of Dishonor
  Protest
  Excuses for Failure to Perform Conditions Precedent

- **DISCHARGE OF LIABILITY**

BUSINESS MANAGEMENT DECISION

You are the president of a closely held corporation that runs a retail clothing store. Your business has grown to the point where your store needs expanding and remodeling. These needs will cost $150,000, an amount you wish to borrow on behalf of the corporation.

How should you sign a promissory note on behalf of the corporation to avoid becoming personally liable?

In our discussions of the rights of holders and holders in due course, we usually assumed that the party being sued had liability unless a valid defense could be asserted against the plaintiff. In this chapter, we go to the basic issue of the liability of a defendant in the absence of a defense.

In a transaction involving commercial paper, liability may be predicated on either the instrument itself or on the underlying contract. No person is liable on the instrument itself unless his signature appears thereon, but the signature may be affixed by a duly authorized agent [3–401(1)]. Persons whose signatures appear on instruments may have different types of liability, depending on their status. This chapter discusses the liability of various parties to commercial paper transactions. Unless indicated otherwise, liability is predicated on the instrument itself and on the rules of the Code relating to commercial paper.

LIABILITY BASED ON SIGNATURES

1. In General

A person's liability on commercial paper results from his signature on the instrument. The signature may be affixed as a maker, drawer, or acceptor on the face of the instrument, or it may be an indorsement on the back. Liability varies, based on the capacity of the signer. However, the signature generally must be genuine or signed by an authorized agent to impose liability on the signer. As with almost every general rule, this one is subject to exceptions, which are discussed in section 4.

2. Capacity of the Signature

The liability of makers of notes is different from the liability of drawers of drafts and checks, which is different from that of indorsers of commercial paper. The liability of these parties varies because of the different capacities in which they sign commercial paper. A person signing commercial paper may do so to assist or accommodate someone else. This signer may enjoy a special status insofar as liability is concerned. These various liabilities are described throughout this chapter.

The capacity in which a person signs is usually obvious because of the location of the signature. Makers and drawers usually sign in the lower right-hand corner of an instrument, and indorsers sign on the back of an instrument. A drawee normally places his signature of acceptance on the face of the instrument, but his signature on the back would clearly indicate that he was signing as an acceptor unless he could establish otherwise. When the signature does not reveal the obligation of the party who signs, the signature is an indorsement [3–402].

3. Agency Principles

The general principles of the law of agency are applicable to commercial paper. A principal is bound when a duly authorized agent signs the principal's name on commercial paper. If the agent is not authorized to sign, the principal is not bound unless the principal (1) ratifies the signature or (2) is estopped from asserting lack of authority. An agent who fails to bind his principal because of lack of authority will usually be personally liable to third parties.

An agent is also personally liable if he fails to show his representative capacity [3–403(2)(a)]. This may occur when the principal is not named on the instrument. Even if the principal's name appears on the instrument, the agent may fail to indicate that he is signing in a representative capacity. In such cases, the agent is also personally liable [3–403(2)(a)].

An agent can relieve himself of liability to the person to whom he issued the paper by proving that such party knew he was acting only as an agent for his principal [3–403(2)(b)]. Between the parties, parol evidence is admissible to show the intent of the parties where the principal's name appears on the instrument and the status of the agent's signature is ambiguous. In the case of checks, the imprinting of the corporate name constitutes substantial evidence that the drawer signed in a representative capacity on behalf of the corporation. The payee of a corporate check expects less from the drawer than does the payee of a corporate note. It is common for creditors to demand the individual promise of corporate officers on notes, especially in the case of small corporations.

To avoid personal liability, the signer has the burden of establishing representative capacity. The proof may be an agreement, understanding, or course of dealing that shows an intent between the parties for the signer to act in a representative capacity. Failure to meet the burden of proof results in personal liability, as the following case demonstrates.

CASE

John Madera signed a promissory note payable to A. Duda & Sons, Inc., in the amount of $47,872. The note began "for value received, we promise to pay A. Duda & Sons, Inc. . . ." Madera signed the note beneath the name and address of Tomatoes, Inc., as follows:

TOMATOES, INC.
3118 Produce Row
Houston, Texas 77023

/s/ John Madera

When the note was not paid, Duda & Sons filed suit against Tomatoes and against Madera individually, alleging that the two defendants were jointly and severally liable for the balance due on the note. The trial court entered final judgment in favor of Duda against Tomatoes, but the court found Madera not liable on the note.

ISSUE: Was Madera liable on the note in an individual capacity?

DECISION: Yes.

REASONS:

1. Under Section 3–403(2)(a) of the Uniform Commercial Code, an authorized representative who signs his own name to an instrument is personally obligated if the instrument neither names the party represented nor shows that the person signed in a representative capacity. Under Section 3–403(2)(b), unless the parties agree otherwise, if just one of these requirements—either the party represented or the representative capacity of the signer—does not appear on the instrument, the signer is also personally liable.
2. According to Code Section 3–403(3), the name of an organization preceded or followed by the name and office of the authorized signer is a signature made in a representative capacity. However, even though the particular office or position of the signer is not indicated on the instrument, the instrument may disclose on its face that a signature was executed only in a representative capacity.
3. Nothing on the face of the note or in testimony to the court reflects that Madera signed the note only in a representative capacity, with no intention of incurring personal liability. Madera signed the promissory note below the name of the company, but Madera's office does not appear on the note. Therefore Madera's representative capacity is not indicated as mandated by Section 3–403(3). Additionally, the instrument does not indicate on its face that Madera signed in a representative capacity. The language "we promise to pay" shows that payment was promised from more than one source.
4. Madera provided no evidence at trial to rebut the presumption of personal liability. Duda presented evidence that Madera made representations that he would stand by the note. Madera offered no evidence to rebut his status of individual signer as shown by the face of the note and the testimony of Duda's witness.
5. Therefore, as a matter of law, Madera is liable in an individual capacity. The trial court's decision is reversed, and the case is remanded.

Duda & Sons, Inc. v. Madera, 687 S.W.2d 83 (Tex. App. 1985).

4. Exceptions: Impostors and Fictitious Payees

An exception to the requirement that signatures be genuine arises when an instrument is made payable to an impostor or to a fictitious person. The drawer's signature is genuine, but the instrument is indorsed in the name of the person who is being impersonated or in the fictitious name.

In the impostor situation, one person poses as someone else and induces the drawer to issue a check payable to the order of the person being impersonated. In the fictitious payee case, the person who induces the issuance of the instrument simply makes up the name of the payee. In both cases the instrument is then indorsed in the name of the person being impersonated or the name made up. The indorsement in the name of the payee is effective because it was made by the person that the drawer intended to indorse, and the named payee was not intended to have an interest in the check. The loss falls on the drawer rather than on the person who took the check or the bank that honored it [3–405(1)(a)]. *Note:* If the check is intended for the party named but is diverted and forged by an employee, the indorsement is not effective because the instrument is not indorsed by the party intended by the drawer.

A typical fictitious payee case involves a dishonest employee authorized to sign his employer's name to checks, or one who draws checks that he presents to his employer for the latter's signature. Thus the employee may draw payroll checks or checks payable to persons with whom the employer would be expected to do business. He either signs the checks or obtains his employer's signature and then cashes the checks, indorsing the name of the payee. If he is in charge of the company's books, he is able to manipulate the books when the canceled checks are returned and may thus avoid detection. The Code imposes this loss on the employer; the dishonest employee can effectively indorse in the payee's name [3–405(1)(c)]. The following case is typical of those illustrating this very important principle.

CASE

One of plaintiff's employees, who was authorized to draw checks on plaintiff's account, drew several checks to firm creditors. He indorsed the checks in the name of the payees and cashed them. The depositary bank presented the checks to the payor bank, which paid them and debited plaintiff's accounts. When the embezzlement was discovered, plaintiff sued its bank.

ISSUE: Is the bank liable for the amount of the forged checks?

DECISION: No.

REASONS:
1. Under the "fictitious payee" rule of UCC Section 3–405, if the person signing on behalf of the maker or drawer intends the payee to have no interest in the instrument, the indorsement by the wrongdoer is effective.
2. Plaintiff's employee never intended the payees to have any interest in the checks; his indorsement is effective.
3. The loss is shifted from the bank to the employer, who is in a better position to prevent such forgeries by exercising reasonable care in the selection and supervision of its employees.

Brighton, Inc. v. Colonial First National Bank, 422 A.2d 433 (N.J. 1980).

LIABILITY BASED ON STATUS

5. Classification of Parties

Primary party *The one all other parties expect to pay. The maker of a note and the acceptor of a draft are the primary party to those instruments.*

For the purposes of liability, the Code divides the parties to commercial paper into two groups—primary parties and secondary parties. The **primary parties** are the makers of notes and acceptors of drafts. These parties have incurred a definite obligation to pay and are the parties who, in the normal course of events, will *actually* pay the instrument.

The *secondary parties* are drawers of drafts, drawers of checks, and indorsers of any instrument. These parties do not expect to pay the instrument but assume, rather, that the primary parties will fulfill their obligations. The drawer and indorsers expect that the acceptor will pay the draft. The indorsers of a note expect that the maker will pay when the note matures. Drawers and indorsers have a responsibility to pay if the primary parties do not, *provided* that certain conditions precedent are satisfied. The drawer and the indorser are, in effect, saying that they will pay if the primary party (acceptor or maker) does not, but only if the party entitled to payment has made proper demand upon the primary party and due notice of the primary party's dishonor of the instrument has then been given to the secondary parties [3–413(2), 3–414(1)].

6. Liability of Primary Parties

A primary party engages that he will pay the instrument according to its terms. The maker thus assumes an obligation to pay the note as it was worded at the time he executed it. The acceptor assumes responsibility for the draft as it was worded when he gave his acceptance [3–413(1)].

If a maker signs an incomplete note, when the note is completed—even though the completion is unauthorized—it can be enforced against him by a holder in due course. On the other hand, if an instrument is materially altered after it is made, the maker has a real defense in the absence of negligence. The maker confirms to all subsequent parties the existence of the payee and his capacity to indorse [3–413(3)].

The drawee of a check or draft is not liable on the instrument until acceptance. Upon acceptance, the acceptor is primarily liable. An acceptance must be in writing on the draft and signed by the drawee-acceptor [3–410(1)]. Acceptance is usually made by the drawee's writing or stamping the word *Accepted,* with the name and the date, across the face of the instrument. The usual means for accepting a check is to have it certified.

A party presenting a draft for acceptance is entitled to an *unqualified acceptance* by the drawee. Thus, when the drawee offers an acceptance that in any manner varies or changes the direct order to pay or accept, the holder may refuse the acceptance [3–412(1)]. The paper is dishonored; and upon notice of dishonor or protest, the holder may hold responsible all prior parties on the paper—back to, and including, the drawer.

LIABILITY OF SECONDARY PARTIES

7. Accommodation Parties and Guarantors

One who signs an instrument for the purpose of lending his name and credit to another party to an instrument is an *accommodation party* [3–415(1)]. He may sign as an indorsor, maker, or acceptor or as a co-maker or co-acceptor. The accommodation party is liable in the capacity in which he signed [3–415(2)]. As an indorser, he does not indorse for the purpose of transferring the paper, but rather to lend security to it.

Since any party, including a co-maker, may be an accommodation party, and accommodation parties are treated somewhat differently from other parties, issues as to the status of a party frequently arise. The intention of parties is the significant element in determining whether one who signs a note is an accommodation party or a principal maker. The primary factors to be considered in determining the intent of the parties are (1) whether or not the proceeds of the instrument are received by the party, and (2) whether the signature was required as a condition of the loan. If the party did not receive the proceeds but the creditor demanded the signature as a condition for the loan, the party signing is an accommodation party. Whether the signature is as a co-maker or indorser, it should be recognized that the liability of an accommodation party is supported by the consideration that flows from the creditor to the principal debtor, and the fact that no consideration flowed directly to the accommodation party is no defense. Lack of benefit to a party does tend to show the status of the party, however.

The significance of being an accommodation party is found in the law of **suretyship.** An accommodation party is a **surety.** In some situations a surety is entitled to a discharge from liability where other parties are not. The right to discharge may be asserted against one who is not a holder in due course [3–415(3)]. Sureties have a right of contribution from co-sureties. Sureties are not liable to the party accommodated. If a surety is required to pay, he can obtain reimbursement from the accommodated party [3–415(5)]. The following case demonstrates the importance of clearly indicating the status of an accommodation party on the instrument itself.

Suretyship *The legal relationship whereby one person becomes a surety for the benefit of the creditor and debtor.*

Surety *A person who agrees to become liable to the creditor for the debtor's obligation in the event the debtor fails to perform as promised.*

CASE

Dixie Neeley executed a note to the City Bank and Trust Company. King executed a separate guaranty agreement for the debt. Ms. Neeley had financial difficulty and was not making payments on the note. She arranged for her former husband, Finnell, to lend his name to the note by adding his signature to the back of the note. After Finnel signed, King paid off the note and it was assigned to him. King then sued Finnell to collect the note.

ISSUE: To what extent is Finnell liable on the note?

DECISION: One-half of the amount due.

REASONS:
1. Since the signature on the back of the instrument does not contain any indication of the capacity in which it was signed, it is an indorsement.
2. An indorsement not in the chain of title is an accommodation indorsement, and Finnell is therefore an accommodation indorser.
3. An accommodation indorser is liable only after presentment, dishonor, and notice of dishonor.
4. The plaintiff and the defendant are bound for the same debt. They are co-sureties. As co-sureties, the right of contribution exists for only a pro rata share and not the total debt.

King v. Finnell, 603 P.2d 754 (Okla. 1979).

The liability of an accommodation party arises without express words. A guarantor's liability is based on words of guaranty. If the words "Payment guaranteed" or their equivalent are added to a signature, the signer engages that if the instrument is not paid when due, he will pay it without previous resort by the holder to other parties on the paper [3–416(1)]. If the words "Collection guaranteed" are added to a signature, the signer becomes liable only after the holder has reduced his claim against the maker or acceptor to judgment, and execution has been returned unsatisfied, or after the maker or acceptor has become insolvent or it is otherwise apparent that it is useless to proceed against him [3–416(2)].

A guarantor waives the conditions precedent of presentment, dishonor, notice of dishonor, and protest. The words of guarantee do not affect the indorsement as a means of transferring the instrument but impose on such indorser the liability of a co-maker [3–416(5)]. Such a person in effect becomes a primary party.

8. Drawers

The drawer engages that upon *dishonor* of the draft and any necessary notice of dishonor or protest, he will pay the amount of the draft to the holder or to any indorser who has paid it [3–413(2)]. In effect, the drawer assumes a conditional liability on the instrument. The party who draws a draft or check, like one who makes a note or accepts a draft, affirms to all subsequent parties the existence of the payee and the payee's capacity to indorse [3–413(3)]. In addition, most drawers have liability on the underlying contract or transaction in which they deliver the instrument as drawer. In other words, if the drawer delivered a check for goods and the check is dishonored, the drawer has liability for the goods that were not paid for, in addition to any liability on the check itself.

9. Indorsers

Indorsers of checks, drafts, or notes have two kinds of liability. First, they are liable on their *contract of indorsement* [3–414(1)]. The indorsement contract can be either unqualified or qualified. The majority of transferors indorse without qualification. The unqualified indorser has what is known as conditional liability. There are conditions precedent to liability. The indorser does not say "I will pay," but rather says "I will pay if the instrument is properly presented, dishonored, and notice of dishonor is given or any necessary protest is made." The unqualified indorser's conditional liability, which runs to subsequent parties [3–414(1)], is discussed later in this chapter. A *qualified* indorser indorses with the words "without recourse." By indorsing "without recourse," the qualified indorser disclaims conditional liability.

Second, an indorser has *unconditional* liability. This unconditional liability is based on breach of warranty. An indorser makes warranties with reference to the instrument that is transferred [3–417(2)]. He warrants that he has good title to the instrument, that all signatures are genuine or authorized, that the instrument has not been materially altered, and that no defense of any party is good against him. He also warrants that he does not know of any insolvency proceedings with respect to any of the parties involved [3–417(2)(e)]. If any of these warranties are breached, there is liability.

Chapter 36 includes discussion of the bank collection process. As checks move through this process, they are usually negotiated by indorsement and delivery. Depositary banks are authorized to add missing indorsements of customers by certifying that the check is forwarded for collection, without the need to obtain an actual signature. Banks that forward checks for collection make warranties the same as other parties. They are liable for breach of any of the warranties, as occurred in the following case.

CASE

On June 2, 1977, Elmer Chilson wrote a check for $4,550 on his account with Merchants National Bank of Topeka, Kansas. The check was made payable to Murlas Brothers Commodities, Inc., and it was in payment for the purchase of gold futures. Later, Caribbean Bronze, Inc., presented the check, without indorsement by Murlas Brothers or any other party, to Capital Bank of Miami, Florida, for deposit. Capital credited Caribbean Bronze's account, stamped the back of the check with "P.E.G. [prior endorsements guaranteed] Capital Bank of Miami, N.A.," and sent the check through the banking channels for payment by Merchants. On June 13, Merchants paid the check and charged Chilson's account. On September 1, Chilson brought the absence of an indorsement to Merchants' attention and demanded that his account be credited. Merchants asked Capital to provide the missing indorsement, but none was provided. On May 20, 1982, Merchants paid Chilson $4,550. Merchants then filed an action charging Capital with breach of the implied warranties of title and presentment. The trial court granted summary judgment to Merchants, and Capital appealed.

ISSUE: Is Capital liable to Merchants for payment of this check that had no indorsement?

DECISION: Yes.

REASONS:

1. According to Section 4–401 of the Uniform Commercial Code, if a bank pays on a check that has been drawn on a customer's account, but which has a forged indorsement, the bank must recredit its customer's account or be liable to the indebted payee in conversion.
2. However, under UCC Section 4–207, every collecting bank warrants that it has good title to the check. Therefore, under a theory of breach of this warranty, a bank may be able to transfer liability for payment of an item to a bank from which the check was received.
3. Forged indorsements breach the warranty of good title under Section 4–207(1)(a). Therefore Section 4–207 allows the drawee bank, the bank that receives a depositor's check for payment, to shift liability for forged indorsements and material alterations to prior collecting banks. This rule of liability directly places the burden of making sure that the indorsement is valid on the first bank in the collection chain, because it has the best opportunity to verify the indorsement.
4. This reason for imposing liability on the first bank in situations involving forged indorsements also applies when an indorsement is missing. Therefore payment on a check without any indorsement also breaches the warranty of good title, and a drawee bank may shift liability in these situations to prior collecting banks.
5. Therefore Capital is liable to Merchants under the Code for the amount of the check.

Chilson v. Capital Bank of Miami, Fla., 701 P.2d 903 (Kan. 1985).

The warranties are made whether the transfer is by delivery only, by qualified indorsement (without recourse), or by unqualified indorsement. A qualified indorsement eliminates only conditional liability; it does not eliminate unconditional liability or prevent a breach of warranty. The qualified indorser's warranty about defenses is simply that he has no *knowledge* of any defense [3–417(3)]. It is also important to note that liability is automatic if any of the warranties are breached. The indorser and transferor by delivery must make good without regard to the performance or notice of dishonor.

10. Transferors without Indorsement

A transferor without an indorsement (bearer paper) also makes warranties to the transferee. They are the same warranties an unqualified indorser makes, except the warranties run only to the immediate transferee, whereas the indorser's warranties extend to all subsequent holders [3–417(2)].

As noted in the preceding section, all secondary parties have unconditional liability because this liability is based on a theory of breach of warranty. Technically speaking, the party who presents an instrument for payment and signs it is not an indorser. The signature is a receipt for the payment; but in presenting the instrument, the person warrants that no indorsements are forged, that so far as he knows the signature of the maker or drawer is genuine, and that it has not been materially altered [3–417(1)]. The person who pays or accepts will thus have recourse against the presenting party if these warranties are breached.

11. Forgeries

Forgery *False writing or alteration of an instrument with the fraudulent intent of deceiving and injuring another. Writing another's name upon a check without consent.*

Banks have a special problem in connection with **forgeries.** Checks presented to payor banks for payment may bear forged signatures of drawers or forged indorsements. If the drawer's signature was forged, the bank that honors the check has not followed the order of the drawer and cannot charge the account [3–418]. If charged, it must be recredited. Likewise, the bank will have to make restitution to the party whose name was forged on the check as an indorsement [3–419(1)(c)]. In either case, the loss initially is that of the bank that pays the instrument bearing the forgery.

In the case of a forged drawer's signature, the payor bank as a general rule cannot collect payment from the party who received it. The bank has the signature of the drawer on file and is charged with knowledge of the forgery. This general rule is subject to the exception that if the party receiving payment is the forger or dealt with the forger and was negligent in doing so, the payor may recover the payment. Thus, if a collecting bank was negligent, the payor bank that paid on a forged drawer's signature could recover from the collecting bank.

A payor bank who pays on a forged indorsement has greater rights in seeking to recover the payment than does the payor who pays on a forged drawer's signature. In the case of a forged indorsement, the payor has no way of knowing about the forgery, and thus it can collect from the person to whom payment was made, who in turn can collect from all prior parties back to the forger.

A bank sometimes cashes a check indorsed by an agent who lacks authority. When it does, the bank is held liable to the payee if the bank is charged with knowledge of the lack of authority. Just as in the case of forgery by a stranger, the drawer can insist that the drawee recredit his account with the amount of any unauthorized payment. An unauthorized signature is a forgery and a real defense.

12. Double Forgeries

Assume that a drawer's signature is forged and that there is no indorsement by the payee or that the payee's indorsement is also forged. Which party bears the loss if the check is paid by the drawee bank? If the rule applicable to forged drawer's signature is followed, the drawee bears the loss because of the prescription that it is familiar with the drawer's signature. If the loss allocation scheme for a check with a forged indorsement is followed, the loss would be on the party who dealt with the forger because that party was in the best position to notice the flaw in the indorsement and to verify the identity of the person forging the indorsement.

The courts that have faced this conflict have resolved it in favor of placing the loss on the drawee bank. A check bearing a double forgery is treated like a check bearing only a forged drawer's signature. This rationale is that in a double forgery situation, no true payee can make a legitimate claim to the check, so any loss suffered by the drawer is attributable to the forged drawer's signature rather than the forged indorsement. The fictitious payee rule is not applicable to cases of double forgeries because the forged indorsement does not cause the drawer's loss. The drawer did not intend payment to any payee, so no payee can appear and demand payment. It is irrelevant whether the payee is real or fictitious and whether the indorsement is forged, missing, or otherwise defective.

CONDITIONAL LIABILITY

13. Introduction

We previously noted that the term *conditional liability* is used to describe the secondary liability that results from the status of parties as drawers or unqualified indorsers. The adjective *conditional* refers to the fact that certain conditions precedent must be fulfilled to establish liability [3–501]. The conditions precedent are *presentment, dishonor, notice of dishonor,* and in some instances *protest.* The importance of exact compliance with the conditions precedent cannot be overemphasized. Failure to comply may result in the discharge of the secondary parties. It should also be kept in mind that defenses may be asserted by an indorser against an immediate transferee to avoid conditional liability.

14. Presentment—In General

Presentment is a demand made upon a maker or drawee [3–504(1)]. In relation to a note, it is a demand for payment made by the holder on the maker. In the case of a draft, it may be either a demand for acceptance or a demand for payment.

The drawee of a draft is not bound on the instrument as a primary party until acceptance. The holder will usually wait until maturity and present his draft to the drawee for payment, but he may present it to the drawee for acceptance before maturity in order to give credit to the instrument during the period of its term. The drawee is under no legal duty to the holder to accept. If the acceptance is refused, the draft must be presented for payment. If dishonor occurs, liability may be passed to the indorsers and the drawer upon proper notice of dishonor.

In most instances, it is not necessary to present an instrument for acceptance. Presentment for payment alone is usually sufficient, but presentment for acceptance must be made in order to charge the drawer and indorsers of some drafts. For example, if the date of payment depends on presentment, as in the case of a draft payable after sight, presentment for acceptance is required in order to fix the maturity date of the instrument [3–501(1)(a)]. Failure to make a proper presentment for payment results in the complete discharge of an indorser [3–501(1)(b)].

15. Presentment—How and Where

Presentment may be made by personally contacting the primary party and making a demand for acceptance or payment. Presentment may be made by mail or through a clearinghouse [3–504(2)(a)(b)]. Presentment by mail is effective when received. If the instrument specifies the place of acceptance or payment, presentment is made there. If no place is specified, presentment may be made at the place of business of the party to accept or to pay. Presentment is excused if neither the party to accept or pay nor anyone authorized to act for him is present or accessible at such place [3–504(2)(c)]. A draft accepted or a note made payable at a bank in the United States must be presented at that bank [3–504(4)]. Presentment of a check to the data processing center of the payor bank is effective if the records are maintained at the center. This is important when a bank has several branches, as occurred in the following case.

CASE

Chrysler Credit Corporation and Al Barry, Inc., signed certain financing agreements. Chrysler Credit thereby agreed to finance the purchase of new and used vehicles for sale by the dealer. Barry drew ten checks on January 18 and 19 payable to Chrysler Credit Corporation in the total amount of $53,337.75. The checks were drawn on Barry's account at Charleroi branch office of First National Bank & Trust. Chrysler deposited the checks in its account at the Monroeville branch of Mellon Bank on January 19, 1979. The checks were routed through the Federal Reserve and received at the main branch and data processing center at First National in Washington, Pennsylvania, on January 22, 1979. The checks were processed and posted in a reject journal because they were drawn on uncollected funds. The Charleroi branch received a copy of the posting reject journal at approximately 10:30 A.M. on January 23, 1979. The manager decided to pay the checks that day, but reversed the decision on January 24 and notified the center.

Chrysler Credit sues for the amount of the checks. Chrysler Credit argues that the checks were "presented on and received by" the Charleroi branch within the meaning of the Uniform Commercial Code on January 22, 1979. Thus Chrysler Credit contends the bank is liable for the amount of each check because it failed to dishonor within its midnight deadline.

ISSUE: Does presentment of a check at the data processing center of a payor bank require the bank to give notice of dishonor or return the check prior to midnight of the next banking day?

DECISION: Yes.

REASONS:

1. The Uniform Commercial Code provides that a payor bank must pay, return, or dishonor a check within the midnight deadline following presentment to or receipt by the bank. The Code defines midnight deadline as "midnight on its next banking day following the banking day on which it receives the relevant item."
2. The policy underlying a midnight deadline that must be met by the payor bank is to protect against the rights of others being compromised. Also, in such a setting, a number of banks are extending credit to each other. The considerations of this policy dictate that First National was required to pay, return, or dishonor the ten checks before midnight on the day following presentment.
3. First National is incorrect in asserting that the instrument was "presented on and received by" the payor bank when the Charleroi branch received the posting reject journal of January 23. Consideration of the official comments UCC Section 4–106 supports the conclusion that presentment at the processing center triggered the midnight deadline. The center was a designated place of presentment and performed an integral and necessary check processing function. First National is accountable for the face value of the ten checks plus interest because of its failure to meet the midnight deadline.

Chrysler Credit Corp. v. First National Bank & Trust, 582 F. Supp. 1436 (W.D. Pa. 1984).

To balance the liberal attitude regarding what will suffice as a presentment, Section 3–505(1) empowers the party on whom presentment is made to require

1. Exhibition of the instrument
2. Reasonable identification of the person making presentment
3. Evidence of authority if presentment is made for another
4. Production of the instrument at a place specified in it or (if none is specified) at any reasonable place
5. A signed receipt on the instrument for any partial or full payment and its surrender upon full payment

If the primary party does not avail himself of these rights, the presentment is perfectly valid, no matter how or where the presentment is made. If he does require proper presentment, a failure to comply invalidates the presentment, but the instrument is not dishonored. The requirement of identification of the presenting party applies to bearer paper as well as order paper [3–505].

16. Presentment—When

In general, an instrument must be presented for payment on the day of maturity. The presentment must be made at a reasonable hour and, if at a bank, during banking hours.

When an instrument is payable on demand, it must be presented or negotiated within a reasonable time after such secondary party became liable, for example, after his indorsement [3–503(1)(e)]. Thus, in the case of a demand note, an indorser would be discharged if presentment were not made within a reasonable time after he indorsed the note.

Note that presentment within a ''reasonable time'' is required when a definite maturity date is not included in the instrument, that is, sight and demand instruments. A reasonable time for presentment is determined by the nature of the instrument, any usage of banking or trade, and the facts of the particular case [3–503(2)].

The drawer of a check is liable for it for a reasonable time, presumed to be thirty days after date or issue, whichever is later. In that time, a check should be presented for payment or to initiate bank collection [3–504(2)(a)]. The presumed reasonable time for presentment in order to hold the indorser liable is seven days after the indorsement [3–503(2)(b)].

17. Dishonor

The party who presents an instrument is entitled to have the instrument paid or accepted. If the party to whom the instrument is presented refuses to pay or accept, the instrument is *dishonored* [3–507(1)]. The presenting party then has recourse against indorsers or other secondary parties, provided he gives proper notice of such dishonor.

When a draft is presented to the drawee for *acceptance,* the drawee may wish to ascertain some facts from the drawer before he assumes the obligation of an acceptor. As a result, the law allows the drawee to defer acceptance until the close of the next business day following presentment [3–506(1)]. If the drawee needs more time within which to obtain information, the holder can give him one additional business day within which to accept. The secondary parties are not discharged by the one-day postponement. The holder who presents the draft for *acceptance* is seeking the drawee's obligation on the paper and will not receive payment until a later date. For this reason, the Code permits a longer period of time within which to accept a draft than is allowed when the draft is presented for payment. When an instrument is presented for *payment,* the party to whom presentment is made is allowed a reasonable time to examine the instrument, to determine whether the instrument is properly payable, but payment must be made in any event on the same day that it is presented and before the close of business on that day [3–506(2)].

18. Notice of Dishonor

When an instrument has been dishonored on proper presentment, the holder must give prompt *notice of the dishonor* in order to have a right of recourse against unqualified indorsers [3–507(2)]. Failure to give prompt and proper notice of dishonor results in the discharge of indorsers.

Notice of dishonor should also be given to the drawer, even though failure to do so discharges the drawer only to the extent of a loss caused by the improper notice. Such a loss could arise if the bank failed after dishonor and before notice to the drawer [3–502(1)]. Although this is a rare occurrence, the notice will expedite settlement for the item.

Generally, notice is given to secondary parties by the holder or by an indorser who has received notice. Any party who may be compelled to pay the instrument may notify any party who may be liable on it [3–508(1)].

Except for banks, notice must be given before midnight of the third business day after dishonor [3–508(2)]. A person who has received notice of dishonor and wishes to notify other parties must do so before midnight of the third business day after receipt of the notice.

Banks must give any necessary notice before the bank's "midnight deadline"—before midnight of the next banking day following the day on which a bank receives the item or notice of dishonor [3–508(2)].

Notice may be given in any reasonable manner, including oral notice, notice by telephone, and notice by mail. The notice must identify the dishonored instrument and state that it has been dishonored. Written notice is effective when sent, even though it is not received, if it bears proper address and postage [3–508(4)].

Proper notice preceded by any necessary presentment and dishonor imposes liability upon secondary parties to whom such notice of dishonor is given. Proper notice operates for the benefit of all parties who have rights on the instrument against the party notified [3–508(8)]. Thus it is necessary to notify a party only once for his liability to be fixed. Assume that A, B, C, and D are indorsers in that order.

- Holder gives notice to A and C only.
- C will not be required to give additional notice to A.
- If C is compelled to pay, he would have recourse against A.
- B and D are discharged if they are not notified by the holder or one of the indorsers.

This occurs because indorsers are, in general, liable in the order of their indorsement. An indorser who is required to pay can recover from an indorser prior to him. But each indorser is entitled to notice of dishonor, so that he can take appropriate steps to pass the responsibility on to those prior to him on the paper.

19. Protest

Protest is a certificate stating the following: an instrument was presented for payment or acceptance, it was dishonored, and the reasons, if any, given for refusal to accept or pay [3–509]. It is a formal method for satisfying the conditions precedent and is required only for drafts that are drawn or payable outside the United States. The protest requirement is in conformity with foreign law in this respect. In other cases, protest is optional with the holder. Protest serves as evidence both that presentment was made and that notice of dishonor was given. It creates a presumption that the conditons precedent were satisfied.

20. Excuses for Failure to Perform Conditions Precedent

An unexcused delay in making any *necessary* presentment or in giving notice of dishonor discharges parties who are entitled to performance of the conditions precedent. Indorsers are completely discharged by such delay; and drawers, makers of notes payable at a bank, and acceptors of drafts payable at a bank are discharged to the extent of any loss caused by the delay [3–502]. Delay in making presentment, in giving notice of dishonor, or in making protest is excused when the holder has acted with reasonable diligence and the delay is not due to any fault of the holder. He must, however, comply with these conditions or attempt to do so as soon as the cause of the delay ceases to exist [3–511(1)].

The performance of the conditions precedent is entirely excused if the party to be charged has *waived* the condition. When such waiver is stated on the face of the instrument, it is binding on all parties; when it is written above the signature of the indorser, it binds him only [3–511(6)]. Most promissory notes contain such a waiver.

The performance of the conditions precedent is also excused if the party to be charged has himself dishonored the instrument or has countermanded payment or otherwise has no reason to expect or right to require that the instrument be accepted or paid [3–511(2)(b)]. If a drawer of a check has stopped payment on the check, the drawer is not in a position to complain about slow presentment or any lack of notice of dishonor.

DISCHARGE OF LIABILITY

The liability of various parties may be discharged in a variety of ways, many of them previously noted [3–601]. Certification of a check at the request of a holder discharges all prior parties [3–411]. Any ground for discharging a simple contract also discharges commercial paper [3–601(2)].

Payment usually discharges a party's liability. This is true even if the payor has knowledge of the claim of another person. Payment does not operate to discharge liability if the payor acts in bad faith and pays one who acquired the instrument by theft. Payment is also no defense if paid in violation of a restrictive indorsement [3–603].

A holder may discharge any party by intentionally canceling the instrument or by striking out or otherwise eliminating a party's signature. The surrender of the instrument to a party will also discharge that party [3–605].

If a holder agrees not to sue one party or agrees to release *collateral,* then all parties with rights against such party or against the collateral are discharged from liability. This assumes that there is no express reservation of rights by the holder and that the party claiming discharge did not consent to the holder's actions [3–606].

When an instrument is reacquired by a prior party, he may cancel all intervening indorsements. In this event, all parties whose indorsements are canceled are discharged [3–208].

Fraudulent and material alteration of an instrument discharges any party whose liability is affected by the alteration. Of course, this is not true if the alteration is agreed to or if the party seeking to impose liability is a holder in due course [3–407]. In fact, no discharge is effective against a holder in due course unless he has notice of the discharge when he takes the instrument [3–602].

CHAPTER SUMMARY

Liability Based on Signatures

In General	1. Signatures of makers, drawers, and acceptors are affixed to the front of an instrument. Indorsements generally are on the back of the paper. 2. All signatures generally must be genuine to hold the signer liable.

Capacity of the Signature

1. Liability of the signer varies, depending on whether the signature is that of a maker, acceptor, drawer, or indorser.
2. The signature also may indicate the accommodation nature of the signer.
3. The capacity of the signature usually is reflected by its location.
4. When the signature is not clear as to the capacity, the signature is an indorsement.

Agency Principles

1. No person is liable on an instrument unless his signature is on the instrument, but it may be affixed by an agent.
2. A principal is bound by acts of his agent. If the agent is not authorized to sign, the principal is not bound unless he ratifies it or is estopped from asserting lack of authority.
3. An agent is personally liable if he fails to show his representative capacity or fails to bind the principal.

Exceptions: Impostors and Fictitious Payees

1. If a check is payable to an impostor or fictitious payee and indorsed by the impostor or by the person supplying the name of the fictitious person, the indorsement is effective as a negotiation. In such a case the loss falls on the drawer and not the bank.
2. These situations usually are a part of an embezzlement scheme, and the loss is placed on the employer who was in a position to prevent it from occurring.

Liability Based on Status

Liability of Primary Parties

1. Makers of notes and acceptors of drafts agree they will pay the instrument according to its terms.
2. The usual means for acceptance of a check is to certify it.

Liability of Secondary Parties

Accommodation Parties and Guarantors

1. An accommodation party is a surety. Such a party may sign as a maker, acceptor, or indorser.
2. Such an indorser does not indorse to negotiate but to lend credit to the instrument.
3. These parties are in the same position as other parties insofar as the conditions precedent to conditional liability are concerned.
4. An accommodation party may collect from co-makers and is not liable to the party accommodated.

Drawers

1. Drawers of drafts and checks and unqualified indorsers agree to pay if the primary party does not.
2. A drawer admits the existence of the payee and its capacity to indorse.

Indorsers

1. Indorsers are liable on their contract of indorsement. If an unqualified indorsement, there is both conditional and unconditional liability.
2. A qualified indorser has only unconditional liability.

Transferors without Indorsement

1. Transferors who do not indorse have unconditional liability to their immediate transferee.
2. Unconditional liability is based on breach of warranty. Secondary parties warrant that they have good title to the instrument, no defense of any party is good against them, all signatures are genuine, and the instrument has not been materially altered.

Forgeries

1. A bank that pays on a forged signature of the drawer cannot charge the drawer's account.
2. A bank paying on the forged signature of an indorser must return the instrument to the party whose name was forged.
3. In the event of the forged signature of a drawer, the bank cannot collect from the party receiving payment unless that party is the forger or the party dealt with the forger negligently.
4. A payor bank that pays on a forged indorsement can collect from the person to whom payment was made.

Double Forgeries

1. If both the drawer's signature and an indorsement are forged, the loss falls on the drawee.
2. If the drawer's signature is forged, it is irrelevant whether the payee is real or fictitious and whether the indorsement is forged, missing, or otherwise defective.

Conditional Liability

Presentment

1. Presentment is a demand on a maker or drawee for payment or acceptance. Failure to make a proper presentment results in complete discharge of indorsers.
2. Presentment by mail or through a clearinghouse is effective. It may also be made at the place of business of the party to accept or pay. The party on whom presentment is made has the power to require exhibition of the instrument.
3. Presentment must be made on the day of maturity, or if payable on demand, it must be presented or negotiated within a reasonable time after such secondary party became liable.
4. Drawer of a check is liable for thirty days after date or issue, whichever is later. An indorser is liable for seven days after his indorsement. Presentment beyond these time periods releases indorsers but the drawer may remain liable.

Dishonor

1. If an instrument is presented and not paid or accepted, it is dishonored.
2. If presentment is for acceptance, the drawee has one additional day to act.
3. If presentment is for payment, the drawee must act on the presentment that day.

Notice of Dishonor

1. When an instrument is dishonored, the presenting party has recourse against indorsers or other secondary parties, provided that he gives notice of dishonor.
2. Notice of dishonor requires the holder to be prompt in order to have a right of recourse against unqualified indorsers. Except for a bank, the notice must be given before midnight of the third business day.
3. Banks must give notice of dishonor before the bank's midnight deadline.
4. Notice may be by any reasonable manner. It may be written, oral, or by phone.

Other Aspects

1. Protest is a certificate stating the instrument was presented for payment, it was dishonored, and the reasons for refusal to accept or pay. It is used in foreign transactions primarily.
2. Conditions precedent of notice of dishonor, presentment, or protest may be waived by the party to be charged. Such waivers are contained in most notes.

Discharge of Liability

1. Discharge of a party's liability may be accomplished by payment, cancellation of the instrument, surrender of the instrument, or fraudulent and material alteration of an instrument.

REVIEW QUESTIONS AND PROBLEMS

1. Match each term in column A with the appropriate statement in column B.

A	B
(1) Presentment	(a) One who signs an instrument for the prupose of lending his name and credit to another party.
(2) Dishonor	(b) The secondary liability that results from the status of parties as drawers or unqualified indorsers.
(3) Notice of dishonor	(c) A person who agrees to pay an instrument according to its terms.
(4) Accommodation party	(d) A person who is primarily liable on a draft.
(5) Protest	(e) The liability of one who negotiates by use of a qualified indorsement.
(6) Primary party	(f) A refusal to pay or to accept.
(7) Acceptor	(g) A requirement for conditional liability
(8) Unconditional liability	(h) A formal method of satisfying conditions precedent.
(9) Conditional liability	(i) A demand made upon a maker or drawee.

2. Bank sues M. O. Cannon personally to collect a promissory note for $60,000. Mr. Cannon was an officer of Slocumb & Cannon, a corporation in serious financial difficulty. The note was signed as follows:

   Slocumb & Cannon
   By: M. O. Cannon
   (Debtor)
   M. O. Cannon
   (Debtor)

   What result? Why?

3. Lee executed and delivered a promissory note due November 1, 1987, to the plaintiff bank. The note was a consolidation of previous loans made to Village Homes, Inc., which were in default. The note was signed by Lee personally. "Village Homes, Inc." does not appear anywhere on the note. Is Lee personally liable on the note? Why or why not?

4. Security Bank sued a corporate borrower, Fastwich, Inc., and certain guarantors of the note. The note was signed as follows:

   [typed] FASTWICH, INC.
   [/s/] John J. Smith II [/s/] Carolyn Smith
   [/s/] Gary D. Smith [/s/] Cheryl J. Smith

   Is the corporation bound on the note? Why or why not?

5. Alex was employed by a brokerage company. He devised a scheme to defraud his employer by issuing fraudulent orders to sell customers' securities. When the brokerage firm issued a check to the customer whose stock had been sold, Alex would obtain the check, forge the customer's indorsement, and pocket the money. When the fraud was discovered, the brokerage company sought to recover its losses from the bank on whom the checks were drawn. Is the bank liable for honoring the checks on a forged indorsement? Explain.

6. Anne loaned Donna's son David money to start a business, which later failed. David offered to sign a promissory note for the debt to prevent Anne from instituting legal proceedings against the remaining assets of the failed business. Anne agreed, but would only accept a note cosigned or indorsed by Donna. Donna signed the back of her son's note. Anne sued Donna to collect the note when David could not be located. What result? Why?

7. A check in settlement of a lawsuit was made payable jointly to the client and to the attorney. The attorney indorsed it in blank and delivered it to the client. When the check was dishonored, the client sued the attorney to collect the face of the check. Is the attorney liable as an indorser? Why or why not?

8. Mark delivers a negotiable promissory note to Peter. Peter specially indorses it and delivers it to Art. Art adds his signature and delivers it to Bill. Bill, without signing it, delivers it to Carl. Carl indorses without recourse and delivers it to Dick. Dick presents the instrument to Mark, who replies, "I'm sorry, but I have no money." From whom can Dick collect the note? What must he do to collect? Explain.

9. The facts are as in problem 8, except Mark informs Dick that the signature on the note is a forgery. From whom can Dick collect the note? Explain.

10. Drawer issues a check "to the order of Payee" for $5,000. Forger steals the check from payee, forges payee's name on the check and sells the check to Jane, who deposits it in her account with Depositary Bank. The check proceeds through the bank collection process, where it is ultimately paid by drawee. Because the check was stolen, payee was not paid.
    a. May payee require drawer to issue another check? Why?
    b. Can drawer now require drawee to recredit his account for the first check that was stolen and forged? Why?
    c. Assume that payee seeks recovery from drawee, rather than requiring drawer to issue a new check. Will payee win? Why?
    d. If drawee has either recredited drawer's account or paid payee for conversion of the check, may drawee now recover from Depositary Bank? Why?
    e. Will Depositary Bank now be able to recover from Jane? Why?
    f. Can Jane now recover from forger? Why?

11. A check was indorsed on the back by three persons, Johns, Baker, and Charles. When Johns was sued, he sought to prove that he signed after Baker and Charles. Is he entitled to offer such proof? Explain the significance of the evidence.

12. Plaintiff forwarded two checks to defendant bank for collection. The checks were not honored because of insufficient funds. The drawee bank failed to give notice of dishonor by its midnight deadline. It claims to be excused because of a computer breakdown. The Code excuses delays by banks if caused by "emergency conditions or other circumstances beyond the control of the bank provided it exercises such diligence as the circumstances require." Is the payor bank excused from giving proper notice of dishonor? Explain.

13. On Thursday, May 15, Fox, the payee on a check drawn by Owens of Riverside Bank, indorsed the check to the order of Granger, who, on the same date, indorsed the check to the order of Hines, a mutual friend of Granger and Owens. On Friday, May 16, Hines presented the check for payment at the bank and payment was refused because of insufficient funds in Owens's account. Not wishing to embarrass Owens, Hines telephoned and advised Owens of the bank's refusal to pay and the reason therefor. Owens promised to make a deposit to his bank account on the following Monday and told Hines to again present the check at the bank on that day and it would be paid. Hines agreed but unexpectedly had to go out of town on business and could not again present the check for payment until the following Thursday, May 22. When Hines again presented the check at the bank, payment was again refused for the same reason. Hines thereupon promptly and properly notified Granger, Fox, and Owens of the dishonor of the check. It was later determined that Owens was insolvent. Does Hines have a cause of action

against Granger and Fox? Explain. Assuming that Hines may recover from Granger and Fox and recovers from Fox only, may Fox recover from Granger? Explain.

14. Winston Corporation purchased five $1,000 thirty-day notes of the Fubor Corporation. The notes were clever forgeries. The forger, William Claude, drew the notes to his own order and signed the name of Oscar Fubor to the notes as the maker. He then indorsed them to Bernard Oldfield, signing his own name in blank. Oldfield negotiated them to Winston Corporation using a ''without recourse'' indorsement. What are the rights, if any, of Winston against Fubor, Claude, and Oldfield? Explain.

15. Sue indorsed a note. Above all indorsements was printed, ''Notice of protest waived.'' The note was not paid when it became due. The holder sent notice to Sue's former address, and she did not receive it. Was she properly notified? Why or why not?

40 Introduction to the Secured Transaction

C H A P T E R   P R E V I E W

- INTRODUCTION

  Unsecured Creditors
  Secured Creditors

- SCOPE OF ARTICLE 9

  In General
  Classifications of Collateral
  Tangible Goods
  Consumer goods • Equipment • Farm products • Inventory
  Documentary Collateral
  Chattel paper • Documents of title • Instruments
  Intangible Collateral
  Accounts • Contract rights • General intangibles

- CREATION OF A SECURITY INTEREST

  Introduction
  The Security Agreement
  Debtor's Rights in Collateral and Creditor's Value

- PERFECTION OF A SECURITY INTEREST

  Introduction
  Perfection by Filing
  Perfection by Possession
  Perfection by Attachment

- FLOATING LIENS

  In General
  After-Acquired Property
  Future Advances
  Proceeds

BUSINESS MANAGEMENT DECISION

As president of a large bank, you are contacted by the president of your community's largest department store. This store seeks an open line of credit of $10 million to finance its inventory worth an estimated $15 million.

Should you grant the line of credit? If so, what should you require of the store?

INTRODUCTION

With this chapter we begin an in-depth examination of the *creditor-debtor* relationship. The creation of this relationship is one of the most common examples of contracts in our society today. The extension of credit occurs at every level of business as well as in our personal lives. For example, manufacturers finance raw materials and equipment; wholesalers and retailers finance inventory; and consumers finance their purchases. The common denominator of all these financial transactions is that the creditor wants to be paid.

1. Unsecured Creditors

Most debtors voluntarily repay their obligations, and most creditors depend only on the debtor's personal promise to pay. Such creditors are said to be *unsecured*. An unsecured creditor does not have any source other than the debtor from which to collect the debt. A credit sales transaction wherein the seller is unsecured is often called a sale on *open account* or *open credit*.

The danger facing unsecured creditors is illustrated by the steps an unsecured creditor must take if the debtor fails to repay voluntarily. The unsecured creditor must first sue the debtor and obtain a judgment. Then, as a *judgment creditor*, it may pursue the enforcement procedures available to a judgment creditor. These postjudgment procedures include obtaining a writ of execution—having a law enforcement official levy on the debtor's property and having the property sold at a public auction. The process of litigation and enforcement of the judgment are costly in terms of both time and money. More importantly, the debtor may not have any property that can be sold to pay the judgment, in which case the creditor will be unable to collect the debt. Many unsecured debts are simply uncollectible.

2. Secured Creditors

In order to avoid the difficulty of collecting unpaid debts, many creditors insist on a second source of repayment in addition to the debtor's personal promise to repay. This second source may take several forms. Very often, if the debtor owns any real estate, it is mortgaged to secure a debt. The use of real estate as security is discussed in Chapter 42. Another source of repayment is a second person's commitment to pay the debt. This source creates a *suretyship*, which is discussed in Chapter 43. A third source is the use of the debtor's personal property as collateral. It is this use of personal property that this chapter and the next one consider.

Article 9 of the Uniform Commercial Code provides for a *secured transaction*. This transaction involves a *security interest* in personal property or fixtures granted by a debtor to a creditor, which the creditor can use to obtain satisfaction of the debt in the event of nonpayment [9–102 (1)(a)]. A *fixture* is an item of personal property that has become attached to real estate. Items of personal property and fixtures used as security are called *collateral* [9–105 (1)(c)]. A creditor who is protected by a valid Article 9 security interest is known as a *secured creditor*. A creditor obtains a security interest by entering into a *security agreement* with the debtor. In order to be secured as to third parties, the creditor must *perfect* the security interest [9–301].

In general, perfected secured creditors are in a much more favorable position than unsecured creditors. For example, the secured creditor, upon the debtor's default, can seize the collateral and have the collateral applied to the payment of the debt. These rights of a secured creditor upon the debtor's default are explained further in Chapter 41.

Secured creditors enjoy an advantage when a debtor becomes insolvent or files for bankruptcy. The secured creditor has personal property from which repayment may be obtained. By having a security interest in the debtor's personal property, a secured creditor, in effect, is given priority over unsecured creditors.

It should be recognized that even secured creditors face the risk that a debt will not be repaid. The value of the collateral may be less than the debt, and under certain circumstances, the collateral may not be sold. As the following case illustrates, creditors must be fully informed about the business conduct of their debtors. If not, they may find that being a secured creditor will not protect them.

CASE

Ely Group borrowed money from Brock and granted Brock a security interest in its inventory. During a period of financial difficulty, Ely Group failed to pay employees in violation of the Fair Labor Standards Act's (FLSA) minimum wage provision. When Ely Group defaulted on the loan owed to Brock, Brock took possession of the inventory made by the uncompensated employees of Ely Group. Such goods are known as "hot goods" under the terms of the FLSA. The Department of Labor filed suit to prohibit Brock from transporting or selling the "hot" inventory made in violation of the FLSA. Brock argued that the FLSA should not apply to holders of collateral who obtain possession in good faith pursuant to a valid security agreement.

ISSUE: Is Brock subject to the FLSA despite a showing of good faith?

DECISION: Yes.

REASONS:

1. The FLSA defines "person" as "an individual, partnership, association, corporation, business trust, legal representative, or any organized group of persons."
2. Section 15(a)(1) contains two exemptions to the general prohibition of interstate shipment of "hot goods." The first, enacted as part of the original FLSA, exempts common carriers from the prohibition on transportation of such goods. The second, added in 1949, exempts a purchaser who acquired the goods for value, without notice of any violation, and "in good faith in reliance

on written assurance from the producer that the goods were produced in compliance with the requirements" of the act.

3. We find no indication that Congress actually considered application of the "hot goods" provision to secured creditors when it enacted the FLSA. By claiming a general exemption for creditors, without any duty to ascertain compliance with the FLSA, petitioner is asking us to put creditors in a better position than good-faith purchasers, for whom Congress specifically added an exemption.
4. While improving working conditions was undoubtedly *one* of Congress's concerns, it was certainly not the *only* aim of the FLSA. In addition to the goal identified by petitioner, the act's declaration of policy reflects Congress's desire to eliminate the competitive advantage enjoyed by goods produced under substandard conditions. This court has consistently recognized this broad regulatory purpose.
5. We hold that Section 15(a)(1)'s broad prohibition on interstate shipment of "hot goods" applies to secured creditors who acquire the goods pursuant to a security agreement. This result is mandated by the plain language of the statute, and it furthers the goal of eliminating the competitive advantage enjoyed by goods produced under substandard labor conditions.

Citicorp Indus. Credit Inc. v. Brock, 107 S.Ct. 2694 (1987).

SCOPE OF ARTICLE 9

3. In General

In general, there have been two versions of Article 9 of the Code. The first was adopted in the early 1960s. By the 1970s there was obvious flaws in the provisions, which prompted the drafting of a revised version. To date, almost every state has adopted the revised version, and it is included in the appendix to this text. Except where noted, all text references are to the 1972 version of Article 9.

In order to gain an appreciation for how an Article 9 secured transaction protects creditors, our study is divided into five parts:

1. The scope of Article 9
2. The creation of a security interest
3. The perfection of a security interest
4. The priorities to the collateral
5. The creditor's rights and duties when a debtor defaults

The first three objectives are discussed in this chapter. Priority issues and the creditors' rights and duties on the debtor's default are discussed in Chapter 41.

Although Article 9 deals primarily with secured transactions, it also covers outright sales of certain types of property, such as accounts receivable [9–102(1)(b)]. Thus a sale of the accounts receivable of a business must comply with the Code requirements as if the accounts were security for a loan.

Except for sales such as those of accounts receivable, the main test to be applied in determining whether a given transaction falls within the purview of Article 9 is whether it was intended to have effect as security. Every transaction with such intent is covered [9–102(1)(a)]. A lease with option to buy may be considered a security transaction rather than a lease if the necessary intent is present.

Certain credit transactions are expressly excluded from Article 9 coverage [9–104]. In general, these exclusions involve transactions that are not of a commercial nature. Examples of common exclusions include a landlord's lien, an assignment of wages, and a transfer of an insurance policy. Another important exclusion is the lien created by state law in favor of those who service or repair personal property, such as automobiles. This lien, known as an *artisan's lien*, is discussed in more detail in Chapter 43.

4. Classifications of Collateral

Collateral *An item of value placed with a creditor to assure the performance of the debtor.*

The broad application of Article 9 can best be seen by examining the various types of **collateral** covered by it. There is not an item of personal property that cannot be used as collateral in a secured transaction. The only limitation to what is acceptable as collateral is the creditor's willingness to accept an interest in a particular item of personal property.

Collateral may be classified according to its physical makeup into (1) tangible, physical property or goods; (2) documentary property that has physical existence, such as a negotiable instrument, but is simply representative of a contractual obligation; and (3) purely intangible property, such as an account receivable. Each type of collateral presents its own peculiar problems, and the framework of Article 9 is structured on the peculiarities of each type. Table 40–1 summarizes the various classifications of personal property that may be the collateral that is the subject of

TABLE 40–1 COLLATERAL SUBJECT TO A SECURITY INTEREST

Tangible Property ("Goods")	Documentary Collateral	Intangible Property
Any personal property that is movable at the time the security interest attaches or that is a fixture [9-105 (1)(h)]. A fixture is a special type of article 9 collateral [9-313]. Goods are classified as one of the following: • Consumer goods [9-109 (1)] • Equipment [9-109 (2)] • Farm products [9-109 (3)] • Inventory [9-109 (4)]	Involves some indispensable piece of paper and has both tangible and intangible aspects. Documentary collateral is classified into one of the following: • Chattel paper [9-105 (1) (b)] • Documents of title [9-105 (1) (f)] • Instruments [9-105 (1) (i)]	Not evidenced by an indispensable writing, which distinguishes it from documentary collateral. Intangible property consists of one of the following: • Account [9-106] • Contract right [9-106 62 Code]; deleted by 72 Code and definition of account, above, reworded to cover it • General intangibles [9-106]

a security interest. The following three sections also discuss each of these three classifications.

5. Tangible Goods

In secured transactions under either version of Article 9, four categories of **tangible** goods are established. These categories include the following:

Tangible Describes property that is physical in character and capable of being moved. A debt is intangible, but a promissory note evidencing such debt is tangible.

1. Consumer goods
2. Equipment
3. Farm products
4. Inventory

In determining the classification of any particular item of goods, it is necessary to take into account not only the physical attributes of the collateral but also the status of the debtor who is buying the property or using it as security for a loan and the use the debtor will make of the goods. Keep in mind that the classification will determine the place of filing to perfect the security interest against third parties. It may also affect the rights of the debtor on default.

Consumer goods. Goods fall into the **consumer goods** classification if they are used or bought primarily for personal, family, or household purposes [9–109(1)].

Consumer goods Goods that are used or bought for use primarily for personal, family, or household purposes.

Equipment. Goods that are used or bought for use primarily in a business, in farming, in a profession, or by a nonprofit organization or governmental agency fall within the **equipment** category [9–109(2)]. The category is something of a catchall, embracing goods that otherwise defy classification. Since equipment often is attached to realty and becomes a fixture, the discussion of fixtures later is especially significant for the equipment classification.

Equipment Goods that are used or bought for use primarily in business or by a debtor which is a nonprofit organization or a governmental subdivision or agency.

Farm products. The **farm products** category includes crops and livestock, supplies used or produced in farming operations, and the products of crops or livestock in their unmanufactured state (ginned cotton, wool, milk, and eggs), provided that the items are in the possession of a debtor who is engaged in farming operations [9–109(3)]. Farm products are *not* equipment or inventory. Note that goods cease to be farm products and must therefore be reclassified when (1) they are no longer in the farmer's possession or (2) they have been subjected to a manufacturing process. Thus, when the farmer delivers his farm products to a marketing agency for sale or to a frozen-food processor as raw materials, the products in the hands of the other party are inventory. Likewise, if the farmer maintained a canning operation, the canned product would be inventory, even though it remained in his possession.

Farm products Crops or livestock used or produced in farming operations.

Inventory. **Inventory** consists of goods that are held by a person for sale or lease or are to be furnished under a contract of service. They may be raw materials, work in process, completed goods, or material used or consumed in a business [9–109(4)]. The basic test to be applied in determining whether goods are inventory is whether they are held for immediate or ultimate sale or lease. The reason for the inclusion of materials used or consumed in a business (e.g., supplies of fuel, boxes,

Inventory Goods that a person holds for sale or lease or goods that are raw materials, work in process, or materials used or consumed in a business.

and other containers for packaging the goods) is that they will soon be used in making an end product for sale.

The proper classification of goods is determined on the basis of its nature and intended use by the debtor. For example, a television set in a dealer's warehouse is inventory to the dealer. When the set is sold and delivered to a consumer customer, it becomes a consumer good. If an identical set were sold on the same terms to the owner of a tavern, to be used for entertaining customers, the set would be equipment in the hands of the tavern owner. The secured party generally cannot rely on the classification furnished by the debtor. The secured party must analyze all facts to ensure proper classification of the collateral and proper perfection of the security interest. The following case illustrates that collateral may fall into a different classification than might be apparent at first glance.

CASE

James Faden, a farmer and rancher, borrowed money from the First State Bank. To secure the bank, Faden granted to it a security interest in all his current and future acquired livestock held as part of his farming operations. A controversy arose when some of Faden's cattle were sold by the Producers Livestock Marketing Association. This association retained the proceeds from the sale of the cattle. The bank sued, claiming that it was entitled to the proceeds since it had been secured by the cattle. The association argued that Faden had purchased the cattle to resell them one or two days later; therefore these cattle were inventory and not farm products subject to the bank's security interest.

ISSUE: Can cattle be classified as inventory rather than as farm products?

DECISION: Yes.

REASONS:

1. Livestock used or produced in farming operations are farm products. If goods are farm products, they are neither equipment nor inventory.
2. Goods held for sale or lease are classified as inventory.
3. The classifications of goods are mutually exclusive. In borderline cases the principal use to which the property is put should be considered determinative.
4. The cattle purchased and resold one or two days later were goods held for immediate sale. There is nothing to indicate that they had any connection with Faden's farming and ranching operation. Under these facts, these cattle were inventory as a matter of law.

First State Bank v. Producers Livestock Marketing Association Non-Stock Cooperative, 261 N.W.2d 854 (Neb. 1979).

6. Documentary Collateral

In secured transactions, three types of paper are considered to represent such valuable property interests that they are included as potential collateral. These items of paper property include chattel paper, documents of title, and instruments. These items comprise various categories of paper frequently used in commerce. These papers may be negotiable or nonnegotiable. Each of these items of potential collateral is evidenced by a writing, and each represents rights and duties of the parties who signed the writing.

Chattel paper. **Chattel paper** refers to a writing or writings that evidence both (1) an obligation to pay money and (2) a security interest in, or a lease of, specific goods [9–105(1)(b)]. The chattel paper is *itself* a security agreement. A security agreement in the form of a conditional sales contract, for example, is often executed in connection with a negotiable note or a series of notes. The group of writings (the contract plus the note) taken together as a composite constitutes *chattel paper*.

Chattel paper A writing that evidences both a monetary obligation and a security interest in, or a lease of, specific goods.

A typical situation involving chattel paper as collateral is one in which a secured party who has obtained it in a transaction with his customer may wish to borrow against it in his own financing. To illustrate: A dealer sells an electric generator to a customer in a conditional sales contract, and the customer signs a negotiable installment note. At this point, the contract is the security agreement; the dealer is the secured party; the customer is the debtor; and the generator is the collateral (equipment). The dealer, needing funds for working capital, transfers the contract and the note to a financing agency as security for a loan. In the transaction between dealer and finance company, the contract and note are the collateral (chattel paper), the finance company is the secured party, the dealer is the debtor, and the customer is now designated as the **account debtor.**

Account debtor The person who is obligated on an account, chattel paper, contract right, or general intangible.

Documents of title. Included under the heading of **documents of title** are **bills of lading, warehouse receipts,** and any other document that in the regular course of business or financing is treated as sufficient evidence that the person in possession of it is entitled to receive, hold, and dispose of the document and the goods it covers [1–201(15)].

Document of title Includes bill of lading, dock warrant, dock receipt, warehouse receipt, or order for the delivery of goods.

Bill of lading A document evidencing the receipt of goods for shipment, issued by a person engaged in the business of transporting or forwarding goods.

Warehouse receipt Issued by a person engaged in the business of storing goods for hire.

Instruments. As distinguished from chattel paper, an *instrument* means (1) negotiable instrument, (2) an investment security such as stocks and bonds, or (3) any other writing that evidences a right to the payment of money and is not itself a security agreement or lease [9–105(1)(i)]. To qualify as an instrument, the other writing must also be one that is in the ordinary course of business transferred by indorsement or assignment. Thus the classification includes, in addition to negotiable instruments, those that are recognized as having some negotiable attributes. Instruments are frequently used as collateral, and they present certain problems in this connection because of their negotiable character. These problems are discussed further in the part of this chapter concerning perfection. Due to the readily transferable nature of negotiable instruments, priority issues also are complicated when this type of collateral is used in a secured transaction. These complications are explained in the next chapter.

7. Intangible Collateral

In the law of secured transactions, there is a third basic classification of collateral called *intangibles*. This classification includes the following three categories: (1) accounts, (2) contract rights, and (3) general intangibles. These categories are distinguished from documentary collateral by virtue of the fact that they are not represented by a writing. In other words, these three categories of potential collateral are truly lacking any physical characteristics.

Accounts. An **account** is any right to payment arising out of a sale of goods or services if that right is not evidenced by a writing, such as with an instrument or chattel paper [9–106]. An account receivable, which arose from a sale on open credit, is a typical example of an account.

Account A right to payment that is not evidenced by a writing.

Contract right *Under a contract, any right to payment not yet earned by performance and not evidenced by an instrument or chattel paper.*

Contract rights. A **contract right** is the right to payment under a contract that has not yet been performed [9–106]. In other words, a contract right exists only until the party performs his obligations under the contract. After contractual performance occurs, the contract right becomes an account receivable. Due to the slight distinction between this and the previous category of collateral, the concept of contract rights was deleted in the 1972 revision of Article 9. In that revision, the word ''account'' is redefined to include contract rights.

General intangibles *Any personal property (including things in action) other than goods, accounts, contract rights, chattel paper, documents, and instruments.*

General intangibles. The **general intangibles** category includes miscellaneous intangible personal property that may be used as commercial security but does not fall within any of the preceding classifications of collateral. Examples of general intangibles include goodwill, literary rights, patents, and copyrights [9–106].

CREATION OF A SECURITY INTEREST

8. Introduction

Attachment *A four-step process of creating an enforceable security interest.*

The ultimate goal of the secured party is to have an enforceable, attached, and perfected security interest. The remainder of this chapter is devoted to these three concepts: *enforceability*, *attachment*, and *perfection*. Completing the steps as outlined in Section 9–203 causes a security interest to spring into existence. This moment of creation is called **attachment.** At the time of attachment, the security interest is also enforceable against the debtor and third parties [9–203(1), 9–201]. However, third parties may defeat the security interest if it is not perfected. Perfection is discussed later in this chapter.

The following steps are required of creditors to create a security interest:

1. Make a security agreement with the debtor.
2. Make sure the debtor has ''rights in the collateral.''
3. Give value.
4. Make the security interest enforceable either by putting the security agreement in writing, which the debtor signs, or by taking possession of the collateral pursuant to the agreement.

The four steps can occur in any order. A security agreement may be executed and the secured party may give value (such as a loan) before the debtor acquires rights in the collateral. Assume that Sewall, a small manufacturing company, is seeking a loan of $5,000 from a bank. Sewall intends to buy a Model 711 Reaper sewing machine, which will be the collateral. Assume that the following progressive steps occur:

1. *A security agreement is signed by Sewall, but not by the bank. Sewall has yet to deal with Reaper.* Only the debtor is required to sign this document.
2. *Now Sewall contracts with Reaper to buy the Model 711 machine.* According to Article 2, a buyer does not have any rights in the goods until the goods are identified to the contract [2–501(1)(b)].
3. *Reaper removes a Model 711 machine from its inventory and marks it for delivery to Sewall.* Now the goods are identified to the contract. Therefore the debtor, Sewall, has rights in the collateral [2–501].

4. *The bank, for the first time, makes a binding commitment to lend Sewall the $5,000.* The requirement that the secured party give value is met. Agreeing to lend money, as well as actually making a loan, is the giving of value [1–201(44)].

Not until step 4 is completed does an Article 9 security interest exist. Only after these four steps are completed has a security interest attached to the collateral (sewing machine). After step 4, we find a written security agreement signed by the debtor; the debtor has rights in the collateral; and the secured party has given value. Thus an attached and enforceable security interest comes into existence. The following three sections describe a few more rules about the elements of creating a valid security interest.

9. The Security Agreement

The basic instrument in a secured transaction is the *security agreement* [9–105(1)(1)]. It must be in writing unless the security arrangement is a possessory one and the secured party is in possession of the collateral [9–203(1)]. Allowing the creditor to possess the collateral is not always feasible. Indeed, most circumstances require that the debtor have possession of the collateral. In these situations, the security agreement must be in writing, and it must be signed by the debtor. Regardless of whether the security agreement is in oral or written form, this agreement must describe the collateral in a manner sufficient so that it can be reasonably identified [9–110].

When it is in a written form, the security agreement usually will contain many other provisions. The forms in general use include a statement of the amount of the obligation and the terms of repayment; the debtor's duties in respect to the collateral, such as insuring it; and the rights of the secured party on default. In general, the parties can include such terms and provisions as they may deem appropriate to their particular transactions.

10. Debtor's Rights in Collateral and Creditor's Value

Another requirement for attachment (or creation of a valid security interest) is that the debtor must have rights in the collateral. It is clear that the debtor-buyer gets rights in the collateral against his seller upon delivery of the goods. A number of recent cases have held that the buyer can acquire rights prior to shipment, the earliest time being when the seller identifies the goods to the contract. The rights acquired by the buyer are subject to the seller's right of reclamation if the buyer fails to pay or if the buyer's check bounces. If a security interest created by the buyer attaches to the goods prior to the seller exercising a right to reclaim, the secured party generally prevails over the unpaid seller holding the bounced check.

A debtor's rights in the collateral must be more than a mere right to possession. Possession alone is not enough to create a security interest, as the court held in the following case.

CASE

Charles and Desideria Manesa entered into an agreement with Vigil whereby the Manesas were to purchase a restaurant and equipment from Vigil. At the time of the agreement, Vigil was leasing the restaurant premises to Dan Quintana. The Manesas and Ernest and Rosina Archuleta obtained a $59,000 loan from the First National

Bank of Santa Fe. The loan was secured by a mortgage on real estate and by a security agreement and financing statement on the restaurant equipment that the Manesas were intending to purchase from Vigil. The bank disbursed the loan on June 16, 1982, but did not file the financing statement on the equipment until October 29, 1982. The Manesas never purchased the equipment from Vigil.

On June 22, 1982, subsequent to the failure of the Manesa-Vigil purchase agreement, Quintana agreed to buy the restaurant and equipment from Vigil. Quintana, in turn, then agreed to sell the restaurant and equipment to the Manesas and Archuletas, and on the same day Quintana entered into a purchase agreement with them to that effect. The purchase price was to be $63,500, and required the Manesas and Archuletas to pay $29,000 upon execution of the purchase agreement. The Manesas paid Quintana $16,000; however, Quintana never received any of the remaining money that was due to him by the Manesas and Archuletas.

The Archuletas and Manesas failed to make first payments either to the bank on the note or to Quintana in the amounts required by the lease and by the purchase agreement. Quintana immediately gave notice to the Archuletas and the Manesas to vacate the premises, but they failed or refused to do so. Quintana then asserted his landlord's lien against the collateral. The bank filed suit, arguing that its security interest in the restaurant equipment had priority over Quintana's landlord's lien.

ISSUE: Did the bank have a valid security interest that gave it priority to the collateral described?

DECISION: No.

REASONS:

1. In order for a security interest to attach, there must be an agreement that it attach, value must be given, and the debtor must have rights in the collateral.
2. The purchase agreement between Quintana and the Manesas and the Archuletas contained a condition precedent that was never performed; therefore, as a matter of law, the contract was never consummated.
3. The Manesas and the Archuletas failed to comply with the initial requirements of the contract, that is, payment of the full $29,000 required under the purchase agreement, which would have given them more than mere possession of the equipment. Naked possession of collateral by the debtor provides an insufficient acquisition of rights in the collateral. Thus, the bank's security interest has not attached. As a matter of law, the bank had neither a valid security interest in the collateral nor a claim against the property of Quintana, much less a perfected security interest superior to Quintana's claimed landlord's lien.

First National Bank of Santa Fe v. Quintana, 733 P.2d 858 (N.M. 1987).

For purposes of attachment, value is defined somewhat differently than it is in commercial paper (Article 3). Basically, *value* means that a secured party has furnished to the debtor any consideration sufficient to support a simple contract [1–201(44)]. When a bank loans money or makes a binding executory promise to extend credit to a merchant and takes a security interest in the merchant's inventory, value is given. Value is also given when the secured party takes his security interest to secure a preexisting claim against the debtor.

PERFECTION OF A SECURITY INTEREST

11. Introduction

Between the debtor and secured party, the security agreement protects the secured party's security interest. But the secured party also wants protection against third parties, who may later make claims against the secured collateral. **Perfection** of the security interest will give this desired protection to the secured party. Perfection is designed to give notice to third parties that financing is occurring on the basis of collateral described. In general, an unperfected secured party's claim is subordinate to the claims of others who acquire an interest in the collateral without knowledge of the unperfected security interest.

Perfection *This process is essential to inform the public that a creditor has an interest in the debtor's personal property. Perfection may occur by attachment, by filing a financing statement, by possession, and by noting the security interest on a certificate of title.*

Article 9 provides numerous ways in which a security interest can be perfected. The methods of perfection include (1) filing a financing statement, (2) taking possession of the collateral, or (3) simply creating a security interest (automatic perfection). Several factors must be taken into account in determining which of the three methods is appropriate in any given transaction: (1) the kind of collateral in which security interest was created, (2) the use the debtor intends to make of the collateral, and (3) the status of the debtor in relation to the secured party.

12. Perfection by Filing

The most common method of perfecting a security interest occurs when the creditor files a *financing statement* in the appropriate public office. This financing statement, which is to be distinguished from the security agreement, is signed by the debtor only but includes the addresses of both parties. This statement must contain a description of the collateral. It also must indicate that the debtor and secured party have entered into a security agreement. Simple forms are available with spaces for additional provisions as agreed upon by the parties, but this basic information is all that is required. If crops or fixtures constitute the collateral, then the financing statement must include a description of the real estate concerned [9–402].

Often there are errors made in completing financing statements. A financing statement is effective even though it contains minor errors that are not seriously misleading. A mistake in a legal description of land would be misleading. The following case illustrates minor errors that did not prevent perfection.

CASE

The Post, Inc., borrowed money from the Citizens National Bank of Evansville. This bank created a security interest in Post's inventory. The bank properly filed a financing statement with the Secretary of State. Subsequent to these events, Raymond Wedel purchased a used boat from Post. Because of Post's default, the bank sought to repossess the boat Wedel claims to have purchased.

Wedel challenges the validity of the perfected security interest on two grounds. He first asserts the financing statement is ineffective because the debtor's name was erroneously listed on the financing statement as "Post, Inc. d/b/a Osborn Boats & Motors" instead of "The Post, Inc." He argues the missing "The" invalidates the statement because the statute requires the correct name of the debtor to appear on the financing statement.

Wedel's second challenge to the validity of the bank's perfected security interest concerns the description of the collateral in the financing statement. The statement describes the collateral as "new boats—all types of trailers, new jet boats." Wedel argues the financing statement would not alert a creditor of any security interest in the 1979 Ambassador boat because it was used and not new. Thus he reasons the financing statement is ineffective to perfect the bank's security interest in the 1979 Ambassador boat.

ISSUE: Did the bank perfect its interest in Post's inventory by filing a sufficient fianancing statement?

DECISION: Yes.

REASONS:

1. The test of the sufficiency of financing statement is whether, under all the facts, the filing would have given a file searcher notice to justify placing a duty upon him to make further inquiry concerning the possible security interest. Essentially, all that is required of the creditor is to file something publicly that will alert credit searchers to the existence of a security agreement.
2. We hold the omission of an article such as "The" from the beginning of the debtor's name as a minor error that is not seriously misleading. We judicially note that initial articles—"A," "An," and "The"—are commonly omitted when titles are organized alphabetically. Thus a filing that omits the initial article of a corporation name fulfills the test of a minor error that is not seriously misleading because such a filing should alert searches to the existence of a security agreement.
3. The collateral description requirement for financing statements is somewhat less demanding than the requirement for security agreements. The financing statement statute requires only a description "indicating the types" of collateral, while the security interest statute states the security agreement must contain "a description of the collateral," a more demanding test.
4. The financing statement covering new boats was sufficient, as a matter of law, to direct further inquiry by Wedel to determine whether the 1979 Ambassador boat was included as collateral, especially because the financing statement was filed in 1979, the same year as the model of the boat in question. An opposite result would require a secured party to have to update the status of the collateral after every new model is introduced, and this would contravene the inquiry notice which is the purpose of the collateral description in the financing statement.

Citizens National Bank of Evansville v. Wedel, 489 N.E.2d 1203 (Ind. App. 1986).

A financing statement is not a substitute for a security agreement. A security agreement may be filed as a financing statement if it contains the required information and is signed by the debtor. However, a financing statement usually will not qualify as a security agreement. Most businesspeople use a separate financing statement, because filing a security agreement would make public some information the parties might prefer to keep confidential.

The purpose of filing is to give notice that the secured party has a security interest in the described collateral. Potential creditors are charged with the task of going to a public office to check to see if the proposed collateral is already encumbered. A person searching the records finds only minimal information and may obtain more from the parties listed in the financing statement.

A secured party can file a financing statement before the security interest attaches to the collateral. In fact, since the filing serves as notice to third parties, it is wise for the secured party to file at the earliest possible moment. Nevertheless, the filing of a financing statement does not perfect a security interest until it is in existence by attachment [9–303(1)].

The financing statement may provide a maturity or expiration date, but more often it is silent on this point. In the absence of such data, the filing is effective for a period of five years, subject to being renewed by the filing of a continuation statement signed by the secured party [9–403(2)]. In order to be effective, a continuation statement must be filed within six months of the financing statement's termination. If it is properly renewed, the original financing statement continues to be valid for another five years [9–403(3)].

The presence in the records of a financing statement constitutes a burden upon the debtor, since it reveals to all persons with whom he may be dealing that his property is or may be subject to the claims of others. The Code therefore provides for the filing of a *termination statement* to clear the record when the secured party is no longer entitled to a security interest. Failure of the secured party to send a termination statement within ten days after written demand by the debtor subjects the secured party to a $100 penalty and makes him liable for any loss suffered by the debtor [9–404(1)].

Filing a financing statement is *required* in order to perfect a nonpossessory security interest in most secured transactions. As a general rule, filing is required in the case of an assignment of accounts receivable or contract rights. An exception exists for certain isolated transactions. If the assignment does not encompass a significant portion of the outstanding accounts or contract rights of the assignor, filing is not required [9–302(1)(e)].

The Code allows the states to require that the financing statement be filed in a central filing system, a local filing system, or a combination [9–401]. A central filing system means that all filing is in the state capital except for fixtures, which are filed locally. Local filing means that filing is at the county level. Most states have enacted dual filing systems. The usual system requires local filing for fixtures, local filing for farm-related collateral and consumer goods, and central filing for other business-related collateral, such as inventory and equipment. If the appropriate office for filing is unclear, the secured party should file the financing statement in every office that might be considered proper.

The Code makes special provisions for goods such as motor vehicles that have a certificate of title. The filing requirements of the Code do not apply, and the usual method of indicating a security interest is to have it noted on the certificate of title [9–302(3)]. If the security interest is properly perfected on the certificate of title, the security interest is valid even though a substitute certificate of title fails to disclose the interest of the secured party. In most states, taking title in the name of the secured party is not a valid means of perfection. The following case explains the reason behind this rule of law.

CASE

Louis Bonnett borrowed money from his mother, Lila. In order to give her security in case he could not repay the loan, Louis transferred the title to his 1971 Dodge to his mother. Louis and Lila agreed that Louis would remain the owner of this car, but that Lila would hold the title in her possession as a security device. Shortly, thereafter, the Nobles levied a judgment they had against Louis on the Dodge which Louis was still driving. Lila objected to this levy on the grounds her security interest in the Dodge had priority over the Nobles' claim.

ISSUE: Did Lila have a properly perfected security interest in the Dodge?

DECISION: No.

REASONS:

1. In order to perfect an interest in an automobile, the secured party must deposit a copy of the instrument creating the security interest with the motor vehicle division along with the certificate of title last issued for the vehicle. If the vehicle has not yet been registered, the copy of the instrument creating the lien must be accompanied by the owner's application for an original registration and certificate of title.
2. Once the motor vehicle division is satisfied as to the genuineness of the title application, it issues a new certificate of title. This certificate lists the name of the owner and contains a statement of all encumbrances or liens existing against the vehicle.
3. This new certificate of title constitutes constructive notice to creditors or purchasers of all liens against the vehicle.
4. Since Lila failed to follow these steps for perfecting a security interest in an automobile, her interest is not perfected and is subject to the judgment creditors' claim.

Noble v. Bonnett, 577 P.2d 248 (Ariz. 1978).

13. Perfection by Possession

Pledge ***Pledge*** *Personal property, as security for a debt or other obligation, deposited or placed with a person called a pledgee.*

The simplest way to give notice of a security interest is for the secured party to take possession of the collateral [9–305]. This transfer of the collateral's possession from the debtor to the secured party is called a **pledge.** Since a secured party's possession of the collateral gives notice of his security interest, no public filing is required. As noted previously, the possessory security interest is very easy to accomplish because a written security agreement is not required. However, the use of possession as perfection is quite limited because most debtors either need or want possession of the collateral.

Possession is the required method of perfection of a security interest in instruments. Filing a financing statement is deemed inappropriate, since instruments are created to be freely transferable in commercial transactions. Because a third party accepting an instrument as security or as payment would not think to check for the existence of a financing statement, the Code limits the method of perfection in instruments to possession.

Possession is an optional method of perfection if the collateral consists of goods, negotiable documents of title, and chattel paper [9–305]. Since intangible collateral lacks a physical existence, it cannot be possessed. Therefore the filing of a financing statement is essential for perfection if the collateral is an account, a contract right, or a general intangible.

Although it usually is considered an alternative to filing, possession of the collateral is the only method whereby complete protection in documents and chattel paper can be obtained. The reason possession of documents is necessary for absolute perfection is that the rights of good-faith holders to whom a document has been negotiated by the debtor will prevail over the secured party, even though there has been a filing. Possession of chattel paper is necessary in order to prevent buyers who purchase chattel paper in the ordinary course of their business from obtaining a superior claim in the paper [9–308]. These situations involving issues of priority to the collateral are discussed in more detail in the next chapter.

For a variety of commercial reasons, it may be necessary or desirable that the secured party with a possessory security interest temporarily release possession of the collateral to the debtor. Since the release is of short duration, it would be cumbersome to require a filing. The Code therefore provides that a security interest *remains perfected* for a period of twenty-one days without filing when a secured party having a perfected security interest releases the collateral to the debtor. This grace period applies only to (1) instruments, (2) negotiable documents, and (3) goods in the hands of a bailee not covered by a negotiable document of title.

If an *instrument* is temporarily released to the debtor, the purpose must be to enable the debtor to make a presentation of it, collect it, renew it, obtain registration of a transfer, or make an ultimate sale or exchange. The risks associated with such a release involve the debtor's improper or unauthorized negotiation of the instrument, or the debtor's sale of the instrument to a bona fide purchaser. If the debtor has possession of the instruments, these risks always are present.

The purposes for which *goods* or *documents* may be released to the debtor are limited. The release to the debtor of these items of collateral must be for the purpose of (1) ultimate sale or exchange or (2) loading, unloading, storing, shipping, transshipping, manufacturing, processing, or otherwise dealing with them in a manner preliminary to their sale or exchange [9–302(5)].

14. Perfection by Attachment

Another method of perfection simply involves the attachment of the security interest to the collateral. In other words, in some situations, the creation of the security interest, which is attachment, is also perfection. In these situations, the secured party is automatically perfected by attachment. One example of this type of perfection is the twenty-one-day time period mentioned in the preceding section. A much more common application of perfection by attachment occurs in transactions involving a **purchase-money security interest.**

Purchase-money security interest *A security interest that is taken or retained by the seller of the collateral to secure all or part of its price; or taken by a person who, by making a loan, gives value to enable the debtor to acquire rights in, or the use of, collateral.*

There are two types of *purchase-money security interests* (often referred to as PMSI). The first one is called the seller's PMSI. This occurs when a seller of goods finances the purchase price and retains a security interest in the goods sold as collateral [9–107(1)(a)]. The second example of a PMSI involves the lender's PMSI. This situation arises when a lender advances money to enable a debtor to acquire the collateral, and the money is, in fact, used to buy the collateral [9–107(1)(b)].

Perfection by attachment is possible when a PMSI is created in any item of consumer goods [9–302]. Creditors are allowed to be automatically perfected when they have taken a PMSI in consumer goods because it would be very burdensome to have to file a financing statement after every consumer credit sales transaction. Furthermore, this perfection by attachment prevents the official record keepers from being overworked with a multitude of filings.

A secured party perfected by attachment enjoys only limited protection from third-party claims. In Chapter 41 we examine some situations in which the secured party who relies on perfection by attachment loses rights in the collateral to good-faith buyers.

FLOATING LIENS

15. In General

Often a creditor may create a security interest in collateral that is likely to be sold by the debtor. This event is very common when the collateral is inventory. In order to remain secured, the creditor will want to create a *floating lien.* A floating lien is created when the security agreement describes the collateral as including property acquired in the future by the debtor [9–204(1)]. The security agreement may also provide that future advances made to the debtor will be covered [9–204(3)]. The secured party can also have a security interest in the proceeds of the sale of collateral in the debtor's ordinary course of business.

The secured party's floating lien is protected against the claims of third parties by virtue of the public notice that such a financing arrangement has been made. The amount of the debt and the actual collateral can be constantly changing if the security agreement is worded to include after-acquired property, future advances of money, and the proceeds of any sale. This sort of arrangement allows the secured party to tie up most of the assets of a debtor, a possibility considered acceptable in business financing but restricted toward consumers, as the next section indicates.

16. After-Acquired Property

The security agreement may provide that property acquired by the debtor at any later time shall also secure some or all of the debtor's obligation under the security agreement. Many security agreements contain an *after-acquired property clause* such as the following:

> The security interest of the secured party under this security agreement extends to all collateral of the type that is the subject of this agreement and is acquired by the debtor at any time during the continuation of this agreement.

Under this clause, as soon as the debtor acquires rights in new property, a security interest in the new property vests in favor of the secured party [9–204(1)].

This clause obviously binds a debtor severely. The Code limits the effect of after-acquired property clauses in relation to consumer goods, since the clauses seem best suited to commercial transactions and might work undue hardship on a consumer. Unless a consumer obtains goods within ten days after the secured party gives value, a security interest usually cannot attach under an after-acquired property clause in consumer goods contracts [9–204(2)].

17. Future Advances

A creditor may include in a security agreement that the collateral protects him with respect to future advances in addition to the original loan. Such a provision is usually referred to as a *dragnet clause*. Dragnet clauses are also used to pick up existing debts. A *future advance* occurs when the secured party makes another loan to the debtor. This additional loan is a future advance covered by a properly worded security agreement even if the secured party was not obligated to make the second loan. A problem that arises with future advances occurs in this context: SP-1 lends money, files a financing statement, and has perfected his security interest. SP-2 later lends money, files, and perfects his interest in the same collateral. SP-1 generally would have priority, since he was the first to file. But what happens when SP-1 lends additional money after SP-2 has filed and perfected? SP-1 still has priority.

If the future advance is made while a security interest is perfected, the secured party with priority to the original collateral has the same priority with respect to the future advance. Likewise, if a perfected secured party makes a commitment to lend money later, that party has the same priority regarding the future advance as he has with respect to the original collateral. These rules are justified by the necessity of protecting the filing system. In other words, a secured party that is perfected by filing remains perfected when future advances are made without having to check for filings made later than his financing statement.

18. Proceeds

Proceeds Whatever is received when collateral is sold, exchanged, collected, or otherwise disposed of.

The passing of the security interest from goods to the **proceeds** of the sale is an important part of the floating lien concept. A debtor may sell or otherwise dispose of the collateral, but the secured party may have an interest in the identifiable proceeds. These proceeds may take the form of cash or noncash proceeds. Examples of noncash proceeds include accounts receivable, instruments, chattel paper, documents of title, or any form of goods [9–306(1)]. In those states that have adopted the 1972 revision, insurance payments also clearly are proceeds.

Two different factual situations concerning proceeds may arise. A debtor may have the authority to dispose of the collateral, as in a sale of inventory. Or he may dispose of the collateral without authority to do so. In either situation, the secured party has an interest in the proceeds. In the former, he loses his security interest in the collateral that is sold in the ordinary course of business, but he retains an interest in the proceeds. If the debtor sells the collateral without authority, the secured party retains a security interest in the original collateral, and he gains an interest in the proceeds [9–306(2)].

An interest in the proceeds from the sale of collateral may remain perfected even if the original financing statement does not specifically mention proceeds. This continuous perfection occurs if the original financing statement's description of collateral includes the type of collateral that covers the proceeds. For example, suppose that the original financing statement describes the collateral as inventory and accounts. If an item of inventory is sold on account, the proceed is an account receivable. The secured party is perfected with respect to this account by the original financing statement. However, suppose that the item of inventory is sold and the buyer signs a promissory note. This note, as an instrument, is not covered by the original financing statement. Indeed, in order to be perfected the secured party must take possession of this note. In this situation, the 1972 revision provides that the secured party is automatically perfected for ten days with regard to the proceeds not covered by the original financing statement. In order to remain perfected, the secured party must perfect the interest in these proceeds by some acceptable method during this ten-day period [9–306(3)].

Special provisions relate to the secured party's interest in proceeds if the debtor becomes involved in bankruptcy or other insolvency proceedings [9–306(4)]. In general, the secured party is entitled to reclaim from the trustee in bankruptcy proceeds that can be identified as relating to the original collateral. If the proceeds are no longer identifiable because they have been commingled or deposited in an account, the secured party nonetheless has a perfected security interest in an amount up to the proceeds received by the debtor within ten days prior to the commencement of the bankruptcy proceedings. Other priority issues are discussed in the next chapter.

CHAPTER SUMMARY

Introduction

Unsecured Creditors

1. An unsecured creditor has only the debtor to look to for payment of a debt or performance of a contractual promise.
2. If the debtor fails to perform, the unsecured creditor must file suit and try to collect.
3. An unsecured creditor who has obtained a judgment is a judgment creditor. This creditor must obtain a writ of execution, have the writ levied on the debtor's property, and have the property, if any, sold at public auction.

Secured Creditors

1. In order to avoid the time and expenses of seeking a judgment and having the debtor's property sold, creditors often seek an interest in collateral.
2. Collateral may take many forms. However, Article 9 is limited to the debtor's personal property and fixtures.
3. Secured creditors have many advantages in collecting unpaid debts over unsecured creditors.

Scope of Article 9

In General

1. Article 9 includes any commercial transaction wherein the purpose is to use the debtor's personal property or fixtures as collateral.
2. Article 9 also covers transactions involving the outright sale of accounts receivable.
3. Article 9 does not govern transactions involving security interests that are not commercial in nature.
4. Such excluded transactions are the creation of a landlord's lien, an assignment of wages, and a transfer of an insurance policy.

Classifications of Collateral

1. Collateral is classified on the basis of its physical characteristics and on the basis of the debtor's use of the collateral.
2. Article 9 collateral can be classified as tangible goods, documentary collateral, or intangible collateral.
3. Tangible goods can be categorized as consumer goods, equipment, farm products, and inventory.
4. Documentary collateral can be subdivided into documents of title, chattel paper, and instruments.
5. Intangible collateral consists of accounts, contract rights, and general intangibles. Contract rights, as a category of collateral, were eliminated by the 1972 revision of Article 9.

Creation of a Security Interest

Introduction

1. To create a valid Article 9 security interest, the interest must attach to the collateral and become enforceable.
2. This process is achieved by (a) the existence of a security agreement, (b) the debtor having rights in the collateral, (c) the creditor granting value, and (d) the debtor signing the agreement or the creditor taking possession of the collateral.
3. These steps of attachment may occur in any order as long as all have occurred.

The Security Agreement

1. The agreement is the grant of a security interest by the debtor to the creditor.
2. The agreement must name the parties and describe the collateral involved.
3. The agreement may be oral if the creditor takes possession of the collateral. If possession remains with the debtor, this agreement must be in writing and signed by the debtor.

Debtor's Rights in Collateral and Creditor's Value

1. In general, a debtor has rights in the collateral when it is identified to a sales contract.
2. Normally, the debtor has rights in the collateral when the debtor has possession. However, a debtor-lessee may not have sufficient rights in items possessed to create a security interest in these items.
3. Value is defined as consideration sufficient to support a contract.
4. A creditor's executory promise to lend money is value.

Perfection of a Security Interest

Introduction

1. Perfection is that step which notifies the public that a creditor has an interest in the described collateral.
2. Perfection generally gives a secured creditor priority to collateral over the claims of third parties.

Perfection by Filing

1. The most common method of perfection is filing a financing statement.
2. The financing statement is a separate document from a security agreement. The debtor must sign a written financing statement.
3. A financing statement is effective for five years unless a shorter time period is clearly stated or unless a continuation statement is filed to extend the statement's duration.
4. To be valid, a financing statement must be filed in the appropriate office, as required by state law.

Perfection by Possession

1. Notice of the creditor's interest in collateral clearly is given if the creditor has possession of the collateral.
2. Possession is an optional method of perfection if the collateral is tangible goods, negotiable documents, or chattel paper.
3. Possession is mandatory if the collateral is instruments.
4. An interest in intangible collateral cannot be perfected by possession. A financing statement must be filed when the collateral is intangible in form.

Perfection by Attachment

1. In some situations, the creation (or attachment) of a security interest automatically perfects the secured creditor.
2. The twenty-one-day exceptions to the creditor's having possession of instruments is one example of perfection by attachment.
3. The more common example of perfection by attachment involves the secured party's PMSI in consumer goods.

Floating Liens

In General

1. A floating lien is created when a creditor's security interest covers after-acquired collateral, future advances, and proceeds.
2. This concept avoids the necessity of the secured party having to create a new security interest and file a new financing statement every time the debtor acquires additional property or borrows additional money.

After-Acquired Property

1. A clause granting the creditor an interest in new property acquired by the debtor may be included in the security agreement.
2. This clause's application is limited to a ten-day period if the property is consumer goods.

Future Advances

1. A security agreement may state that the security interest covers future loans made by the creditor.
2. In general, priority with respect to future advances made is determined by the date of original perfection.

Proceeds

1. A secured party's floating lien also gives that party's interest in the proceeds of a sale of collateral.
2. These proceeds may be in the form of cash or noncash collateral.
3. Under the 1972 Code, an interest in proceeds continues as perfected if the original financing statement included a description of the type of collateral that covers the proceeds. Otherwise, the secured party is perfected by attachment for a ten-day period.

REVIEW QUESTIONS AND PROBLEMS

1. Match each term in column A with the appropriate statement in column B.

A	B
(1) Unsecured creditor	(a) The essential element in the creation and enforceability of a security agreement.
(2) Tangible goods	(b) Exists when either a seller or lender, as a secured party, lends the money that enables the debtor to buy the collateral.
(3) Inventory	(c) A general classification of collateral that has a physical nature.
(4) Chattel paper	(d) The document that must be filed to perfect a security interest.
(5) General intangible	(e) A category of collateral held by a business debtor for resale.
(6) Attachment	(f) A party whose only collateral is the debtor's promise to repay.
(7) Security agreement	(g) A catchall category for collateral.
(8) Financing statement	(h) Another name for perfection by attachment.
(9) Automatic perfection	(i) A writing that evidences both an obligation to pay money and a security interest or lease.
(10) Purchase money security interest	(j) An essential document which must be signed by the debtor if he retains possession of the collateral if a security interest is to be created.
(11) Floating lien	(k) Arises from the sale of collateral.
(12) Proceeds	(l) Created when a creditor's security interest covers after-acquired collateral or future advances or both.

2. Clark rented a TV from Rental Service. The rental agreement provided that Clark would lease the set for at least one week. Title would remain with Rental Service unless Clark rented the TV set for seventy-eight consecutive weeks and fulfilled all the terms of the agreement. After a few months, Rental Service repossessed the TV set. Clark contended the agreement was really an installment sales agreement disguised as a lease. Is this transaction a secured sale or a lease? Explain.

3. Classification of collateral is not always easy. Classify the following collateral:
   a. Burns Rentals leases and sells TV sets and cars. Burns obtains financing from City Bank, enabling him to buy twenty-five cars and 100 new TV sets.
   b. Burns has fifty cars on his lot for lease.
   c. Burns sells a truck to Boyce and retains a security interest in the truck. Boyce uses the truck exclusively for weekend camping and fishing trips.
   d. Burns assigns Boyce's promissory note and security agreement to City Bank as collateral for a loan.
   e. Burns Rentals buys 300 new Philco TV sets for his annual summer sale. Classify the TV sets in the hands of Philco; in Burns's possession. Virgil, owner of Virgil's Truck City and Bar, buys a TV set during the sale. The set is delivered to Virgil in its original carton and put in the back of his 16 wheeler. What type of goods did Virgil buy?
   f. When Philco sells TV sets to Burns, it packages them in special shipping cartons, using packaging materials such as Styrofoam and excelsior. Philco maintains a large supply of these materials
   g. Burns has a large supply of diesel fuel and oil for his fleet of trucks.

4. Jim Gibbs purchased a used truck and delivered it to Vernie King for needed repairs. After one month, Gibbs was notified that the truck was repaired. The total cost of the repairs was more than Gibbs could afford. King agreed to lend Gibbs $1,250 as a partial payment for the repairs. Gibbs orally agreed to give King a security interest in the truck in return for the loan. However, no written security agreement was prepared or signed. Gibbs took possession of the truck and later defaulted on his repayment of the $1,250. King sought to repossess the truck as a secured creditor. Gibbs argued King did not have a security interest in this truck. Can a creditor be secured on the basis of an oral security agreement if the debtor has possession of the collateral? Explain.

5. A bank entered into a security agreement with a farmer. It covered "all crops in bin or stored in commercial elevator" and "all crops growing or to be grown." The agreement did not include any description of the land concerned. The farmer harvested the grain and took it immediately to the grain company for sale, without prior storage. Is the grain subject to the bank's security interest? Why or why not?

6. Gil sold office furniture to Fireside Realty Company. To secure the sale, the parties executed a security agreement that described the collateral as "furniture as per the attached listing." No listing was attached, nor was any listing included in the financing statement. Does Gill have a security interest in the furniture? Explain.

7. Chapman entered into a franchise agreement with Senter, which provided for an initial inventory and assistance in opening an auto parts store. When Senter's check in payment of the inventory was dishonored, Chapman notified Senter that the franchise agreement was revoked and that Chapman was repossessing the inventory. Chapman had the locks changed on the store to effect its repossession. Senter then borrowed $4,500 from a bank using the inventory of the store as collateral. Chapman claims that this security interest never was perfected because it had never "attached" to the collateral. Is he correct? Why or why not?

8. Walker purchased Terminal Moving & Storage Company by making a small down payment and signing a promissory note for the remainder of the purchase price. On the same day, Walker, as sole owner, executed a security interest in all of the corporation's assets in favor of the seller. The seller later assigned the security interest and the note to a third party, who assigned them to Putnam. When the corporation filed for bankruptcy a few years later, the bankruptcy trustee contended that Putnam did not have a valid

security interest. The trustee argued that the security interest was given without any consideration being given to the corporation itself. Therefore the security interest did not attach because no value had been given. Did Putnam have a valid security interest? Explain.

9. A financing statement listed the debtor as ''Elite Boats, Division of Glasco, Inc.'' rather than as ''Glasco, Inc.,'' the correct name of the company. Is the financing statement adequate to perfect a security interest? Why or why not?

10. Francis executed a security agreement and a financing statement securing a debt with his growing crops. Both documents described the farmland as ''the southeast one-quarter of section 24, township 71 north, range 32 in Grant Township, Adams County, Iowa.'' That description was in error; the secured party had intended to refer not to section 24 but to section 25 (where Francis lived on a farm his father owned). Is the security interest in the crops perfected? Why or why not?

11. Paula, an accountant, lent money to a company that was already indebted to her for services rendered. As security for the loan and to secure payment for the services, the company assigned to Paula a portion of its expected recovery of a pending lawsuit. Paula did not file a financing statement with regard to the assignment. Subsequently, Debra was awarded a judgment against the company in another lawsuit. Debra, without knowledge of the assignment to Paula, had the sheriff levy against the company's property. At the sheriff's execution sale, all of the company's rights in the pending lawsuit were sold to Debra. When the lawsuit was settled, Paula claimed rights to the proceeds. Is Paula entitled to the proceeds of the lawsuit pursuant to her security interest? Explain.

12. Tom and Marie Shafer purchased a household washing machine and dishwasher on credit from the Georgia Power Company (GPC). GPC took purchase money security interests in each of these appliances that were perfected by attachment. Later, the Shafers granted security interests in these same appliances to Personal Thrift as collateral for a loan. Personal Thrift perfected its interests by filing a proper financing statement. The Shafers defaulted on all these loans, and Personal Thrift took possession of the appliances. GPC sued Personal Thrift, seeking to recover the two appliances. Personal Thrift argued that GPC's automatic perfection was unconstitutional as a violation of equal protection and due process. Is perfection by attachment constitutional? Explain.

13. Nelson, a farmer, signed a security agreement to Farmer's Bank covering his crops. The agreement contained a dragnet clause. Nelson had debts from a former crop year and later borrowed to plant his current crops. When he sold the crops to a grain elevator, the elevator used the proceeds to satisfy debts due it rather than pay the proceeds to Farmer's Bank as it had demanded. Farmer's Bank sues the elevator for the value of the crops. What resulted? Why?

14. Cable Services of Florida, Inc., purchased a backhoe and financed the purchase with ITT Industrial Credit Company. ITT prepared a security agreement that required Cable to insure the backhoe. Cable did acquire insurance through the Insurance Management Corporation (IMC), which agreed to lend Cable the money for the insurance premium. This insurance actually was issued by U.S.F.&G. Company. The backhoe was stolen, and the parties claimed the benefits under this insurance policy. IMC received a check from U.S.F.&G. as payment under the policy. ITT, as a secured party, claimed this insurance money as a proceed from the backhoe. IMC claimed a portion of these insurance benefits as payment of its loan to Cable for the insurance premiums. Is money paid under an insurance policy a proceed to which the secured party is entitled? Why or why not?

15. By answering the following, check your knowledge of the business decisions involved in secured transactions:
    a. Assume that you are a retailer with a large amount of outstanding accounts receivable and you are in need of cash to pay expenses. How might you raise the necessary cash? Explain.

b. Assume that you are considering lending to Fred Tauber of Tauber & Sons and taking a security interest in certain property of Tauber & Sons. What should you do prior to lending the money? Explain.
c. Assume that you are arranging to finance another's business. It will be a secured financing plan that works on a continuing basis. What provisions should you require for inclusion in the security agreement and in the financing statement? Explain.
d. Assume that you are a secured party and are in doubt about whether you have to file and, if so, where to file. What do you do? Explain.

41 Issues in Article 9 Transactions

CHAPTER PREVIEW

- **PRIORITY ISSUES IN GENERAL**
- **SECURED PARTY VERSUS BUYERS OF COLLATERAL**

  General Rule
  Buyers in the Ordinary Course of Business
  Buyers of Consumer Goods
  Buyers of Chattel Paper and Instruments
    Proceeds from sale of inventory collateral • Proceeds from sale of noninventory collateral or as original collateral

- **SECURED PARTY VERSUS SECURED PARTY**

  General Rule
  PMSI in Inventory Collateral
  PMSI in Noninventory Collateral
  Fixtures
  Accessions
  Commingled and Processed Goods

- **SECURED PARTY VERSUS LIEN CREDITORS**

  General Rule
  Laborer's, Artisan's, and Materialman's Liens
  Judgment Creditor's Lien
  Bankruptcy Trustee's Lien

- **RIGHTS AND DUTIES ON DEBTOR'S DEFAULT**

  Repossession of Collateral
    Self-Help • Judicial action • Alternatives to repossession
  Rights and Duties of Secured Party in Possession
  Foreclosure Sale
    Notice required • Time of sale • Commercial reasonableness
  Rights of Parties after Foreclosure
  Strict Foreclosure
    Notice required • Prevention of strict foreclosure
  Debtor's General Remedies

BUSINESS MANAGEMENT DECISION

A customer of your bank operates an appliance store. This customer wants to borrow $500,000 to finance a new line of VCRs. As the chief commercial loan officer, you have the Article 9 records examined, and you learn that this customer has granted a security interest in the store's inventory to a competing financial institution. You believe that the new line of VCRs will be profitable to your customer.

Should you make the loan? If so, what can you do to obtain a priority claim to the VCRs over that of the competing financial institution?

The preceding chapter describes how a security interest is created and how it is perfected. For the most part, in this chapter we assume that these essential steps have been accomplished. The dominant theme of this chapter is whether a perfected secured party has priority over others claiming an interest in the personal property being used as collateral. By "priority," we mean the party first in line to have its claim paid from the proceeds made from the sale of the collateral.

This chapter examines two questions: First, when does a perfected secured party not have priority to the collateral? Second, what are the secured parties' rights and duties when the debtor defaults?

PRIORITY ISSUES IN GENERAL

Collateral is frequently the subject of conflicting claims. Two or more persons may claim a security interest in the same collateral, or a person may claim that he has a better right to the collateral than does the secured party. Interests that may compete with the secured party's claim of priority fall into the following two basic categories: (1) those who purchase the collateral from the debtor and (2) those who are creditors of the debtor. These creditors may be further subdivided into those who have a conflicting security interest in the same collateral and those who have some other lien on the collateral. Among the many ways in which conflicting claims to collateral may arise, the following are some of the more important situations:

1. A debtor sells the collateral to a good-faith purchaser who may or may not know of the security interest.
2. A debtor gives more than one security interest in the same collateral.
3. Collateral becomes attached to real property, so that it is a fixture.
4. Collateral becomes attached to personal property that belongs to another or in which another has security interest.
5. Collateral has been processed (such as raw material, in which there is a security interest, being converted into a finished product).
6. The government or some other creditor claims a lien on the property.
7. Collateral has been repaired or improved by the services or materials of another.
8. A trustee in bankruptcy claims the collateral in connection with a bankruptcy case involving the debtor.

In all these situations, as well as in many others, it is necessary to sort out the conflicting interests and determine the priority among them. Keep in mind that the priority of a secured party's claim often is determined by whether or not the secured party has perfected his security interest. If it is not properly perfected, there is no priority. The general rule of Article 9 of the Uniform Commercial Code regarding priority is that after proper perfection, the secured party has priority over (1) those who purchase the collateral from the debtor, (2) those who are also creditors of the debtor, and (3) those who represent creditors in insolvency proceedings instituted by, or against, the debtor.

The bulk of the following material involves exceptions to this general rule. In addition to these exceptions, a secured party that has priority to collateral may agree, explicitly or implicitly, to subordinate its claim in preference to the rights of a third party. We assume in these discussions that this has not occurred.

SECURED PARTY VERSUS BUYERS OF COLLATERAL

1. General Rule

We now turn our attention to the secured party's priority when the collateral is sold or transferred to a third party. In general, the secured party's security interest continues in any collateral sold or transferred unless the security agreement authorizes such a sale or transfer free of the security interest. This general rule makes sense, since the secured party and the debtor are free to make any legal agreement they wish and a secured party may voluntarily give up the security interest. A more likely issue arises when the debtor sells the collateral without the secured party's approval. Under Section 9-306(2), if the debtor makes an unauthorized sale or transfer, the security interest usually continues in the collateral in the hands of the buyer, as was held in the following case.

CASE

Matteson sold a bulldozer to the Thorson Group and retained a security interest in the bulldozer. A financing statement was filed on October 6, 1980. The Thorson Group defaulted on payments and delivered the bulldozer to Walker, an auctioneer. When Matteson learned of the transfer, he wrote Walker a letter specifying that the minimum sale price for the bulldozer would have to be $22,400 plus other fees and costs. Matteson specified that only under these conditions would he consent to the sale. The auctioneer never responded to the letter. The bulldozer was sold to Harper for $20,500. The auctioneer kept the proceeds and filed for bankruptcy. Matteson demanded that Harper return the bulldozer. Harper contended that Matteson's letter discontinued Matteson's security interest by authorizing the sale. Also, Harper maintained that Matteson had a duty to post a notice of his security interest on the bulldozer to warn potential buyers. The trial court granted summary judgment for Matteson, and Harper appealed.

ISSUES: Did Matteson's letter to the auctionner discontinue the security interest in the bulldozer? Did Matteson have a duty to affix a notice on the bulldozer at the place of sale informing potential buyers of his security interest?

DECISIONS: No. No.

REASONS:
1. Matteson expressly conditioned the sale of the bulldozer requiring a sales price of at least $22,400 plus fees and costs. The sale of the bulldozer to Harper for $20,500 violated the condition imposed by Matteson and does not constitute an authorized sale.
2. The Uniform Commercial Code's purpose of providing a simple and unified structure for secured financing transactions is furthered by a comprehensive system in which parties can perfect by filing and rely on that perfection.
3. Requiring the secured party to follow the collateral to every sale and post a notice to unwary buyers would undermine the simplicity, uniformity, and reliability of the filing system.

Matteson v. Harper, 682 P.2d 766 (Oreg. 1984).

There are three situations in which the buyers take priority over the secured party, even though the sale was unauthorized. These situations are considered in the next three sections.

2. Buyers in the Ordinary Course of Business

A **buyer in the ordinary course of business** "takes free of a security interest created by his seller even though the security interest is perfected and even though the buyer knows of its existence" [9-307(1)]. A buyer in the ordinary course of business is a buyer who buys goods from a seller who is in the business of selling goods of that kind [1-201(9)]. When you buy goods at the grocery store, department store, and gas station, you are a buyer in the ordinary course of business. In general, a transaction in the ordinary course of business involves the sale of a seller's inventory. The following case illustrates a buyer in the ordinary course of business and indicates why it is important that the secured party have accurate information about the debtor's business.

Buyer in ordinary course of business *A person who, in good faith and without knowledge that the sale to him is in violation of the ownership rights or security interest of a third party in the goods, buys in ordinary course from a person in the business of selling goods of that kind.*

CASE

Peggy Sparks purchased a horse trailer from Walter Hoffmeister. Her purchase from Hoffmeister was financed by the Antigo Co-op Credit Union. She picked up the trailer from Hoffmeister on May 7, 1974. On May 18, 1974, Sparks displayed the trailer at a horse show. James L. Miller saw the "for sale" sign on the trailer, looked it over, and eventually bought the trailer from Sparks on July 2, 1974. The sum of $2,700 was paid by Miller to Sparks for the trailer. Miller believed that Sparks was in the business of selling horse trailers.

Sparks failed to pay Antigo Co-op Credit Union. Because of Sparks's default, Antigo brought an action against Miller, claiming that the trailer was subject to Antigo's perfected security interest. Miller answered, denying any knowledge of the prior security interest and asked for the dismissal of the plaintiff's complaint. Miller argued that, as a buyer in the ordinary course of business, he took the trailer free of Antigo's security interest. The trial court agreed with Miller.

ISSUE: Does a buyer in the ordinary course of business take free of a security interest when the secured party did not know that the seller was in the business of selling goods of the kind that constituted the collateral?

DECISION: Yes.

REASONS:

1. The only contested factual issue was whether Peggy Sparks, at the time Miller bought the horse trailer, was "in the business of selling goods of that kind." Sparks showed the trailer at a horse show and advertised it for sale. There was another new trailer on Sparks's farm on the date of the sale. Sparks bought trailers from Hoffmeister with the intent of reselling them. She carried trailer parts for resale and color charts, which were provided by Hoffmeister. When she conveyed the trailer to Miller, she did so by the means of a "Sales and Production Order," which had been furnished her by Hoffmeister. She signed the sales instrument on the line provided for the dealer's signature. In addition to having a new trailer on the premises on the date she sold the trailer to Miller, she had sold another trailer immediately before she purchased the trailer eventually sold to Miller. Whether she was a "dealer" in the sense that she had a manufacturer's franchise to sell is irrelevant. She was in the business of selling trailers.
2. The knowledge or lack of knowledge, whether actual or constructive, of a security holder is immaterial to the rights of a buyer in the ordinary course of business. The status of a buyer in the ordinary course of business does not depend on what the secured party knew.
3. Article 9 of the Uniform Commercial Code is not designed to reward a secured party for its ignorance of the business of its debtor. The philosophy of the Uniform Commercial Code is that it is more reasonable to expect a secured party to investigate its debtor's business than to impose such a duty on a good-faith consumer.
4. The fact that in this case Antigo Co-op Credit Union financed Peggy Sparks without knowing her ordinary course of business was selling horse trailers does not change the law's basic policy to protect the consumer. Antigo properly must bear the burden of failing to investigate its debtor.

Antigo Co-op Credit Union v. Miller, 271 N.W.2d 642 (Wis. 1978).

The reason for giving priority to a buyer in the ordinary course of business is obvious. When you buy goods from a professional seller, you expect to get clear title to the goods and would never think that they might be subject to a security interest. This rule, then, simply codifies the customary expectations of buyers in our society. It has been applied to buyers of new cars from a dealership and to a dealer buyer who buys from another dealer. Generally, this rule would not apply if you bought a used car from a car repair garage, since the garage is not in the business of selling cars on a daily basis. In other words, the garage does not sell cars in the ordinary course of its business.

The buyer-in-ordinary-course-of-business rule does not apply to a person buying farm products from a person engaged in farming operations [9-307(1)]. Typically, farmers or ranchers get loans and grant security interest in their crops or cattle. This rule allows the secured party to follow its security interest into the hands of a cattle buyer or a grain elevator or food processor. To understand the reason for this exception, you should recognize that most farmers borrow money to plant and raise their crops. These loans are repaid when the crops are sold. If the law did not grant priority to creditors of farmers, these farmers would not be able to function. Creditors of farmers and those who do business with farmers must keep this exception to the buyer-in-ordinary-course-of-business rule clearly in mind.

3. Buyers of Consumer Goods

The rule of continuing priority for the secured party does not apply when a consumer-buyer purchases consumer goods from a consumer-debtor. The consumer-debtor, by definition, cannot sell his property in the ordinary course of business. This is because, as a consumer, the seller is not engaged in a business activity. In Chapter 40, we discuss that a secured party with a purchase-money security interest (PMSI) in consumer goods is automatically perfected when the security interest is created. In other words, a PMSI in consumer goods is perfected by attachment. Nevertheless, a secured party who relies on this automatic perfection may lose his priority. As the next paragraph explains, a secured party with a PMSI in consumer goods has to file a financing statement to be assured of priority over a consumer-buyer of the collateral.

Section 9-307(2) allows a consumer-buyer of consumer goods from a consumer-debtor to take free of the PMSI ''unless prior to the purchase the secured party has filed a financing statement covering such goods.'' Suppose that Smith buys a sofa from Furniture Company and gives it a PMSI in the sofa for the unpaid purchase price. Furniture Company does not file a financing statement. A few months later, Smith sells the sofa to her next-door neighbor, Jones, who uses the sofa in his home. Although Furniture Company has an automatically perfected security interest in the sofa, the sale is free of that PMSI if Jones paid value, did not know of the PMSI, and uses the sofa for consumer purposes [9-307(2)]. If Furniture Company had filed a financing statement, Jones's purchase would be subject to the PMSI. In the alternative, if Jones had purchased this sofa from Smith for a resale in his used-furniture store, Jones's purchase would be subject to the Furniture Company's security interest even if the Furniture Company had not filed a financing statement. This result is because Jones would not be a consumer-buyer in this latter example.

4. Buyers of Chattel Paper and Instruments

In the preceding chapter, we note that perfection by attachment is possible with respect to an interest in instruments for twenty-one days and with respect to proceeds for ten days. Since security interests in chattel paper or instruments perfected by attachment may be in conflict with security interests in those items perfected by filing, Article 9 has priority rules to cover such conflicts. Perfection by attachment when the collateral is chattel paper or instruments is used in three situations:

1. The chattel paper or instruments or both are *proceeds* from the sale of *inventory* collateral.

2. The chattel paper or instruments or both are *proceeds* from the sale of *noninventory* collateral.
3. The instruments are the original collateral. (If chattel paper is the original collateral, the secured party must file a financing statement or take possession in order to perfect the interest in chattel paper. Perfection by attachment is not possible if the original collateral is chattel paper.)

Proceeds from sale of inventory collateral. To illustrate the first situation, assume that a retail merchant has financed its inventory with the First State Bank. This bank has a security interest in the merchant's inventory, and it has perfected this interest by filing a financing statement describing the inventory. As a part of its daily business, the merchant sells some of its inventory to a buyer who signs an installment sales contract, which grants the merchant a security interest in the items sold. This installment sales contract, as a proceed from the sale of inventory, is chattel paper. Further assume that another buyer simply signs a promissory note when buying some of the merchant's inventory. This transaction creates an instrument as a proceed. To replenish the inventory, the merchant sells within five days the chattel paper and instrument proceeds to the Second State Bank. Which bank has priority proceeds?

The First State Bank would claim to have priority with respect to these proceeds as a secured party perfected under the ten-day rule of automatic perfection. The Second State Bank would claim priority as a buyer who has possession of and who has paid value for these proceeds. *Answer:* A purchaser of chattel paper or an instrument who pays value and who takes possession of it in the ordinary course of business takes priority over a security interest in the chattel paper or instrument that is claimed merely as proceeds from the sale of inventory [9-308(b)]. This rule applies even if the purchaser had knowledge of the secured party's security interest in these proceeds. Thus, the Second State Bank has priority.

Proceeds from sale of noninventory collateral or as original collateral. The rule that governs the other two situations, is a little different. If the chattel paper or instruments were proceeds from the sale of noninventory collateral or if the instruments were the original collateral, a buyer of these items in the ordinary course of business has priority only if he does not have any knowledge of the secured party's security interest in the chattel paper or instruments [9-308(a)]. For example, suppose that the merchant granted to the First State Bank a security interest in equipment as well as inventory. Assume that this bank files a financing statement describing the collateral as inventory, equipment, and chattel paper. Now suppose that the merchant sells a piece of equipment in return for chattel paper and then sells the chattel paper to the Second State Bank. That bank is subject to the First State Bank's interest in the chattel paper, since Second State Bank had constructive knowledge of First State Bank's interest in chattel paper via the financing statement's being properly filed.

Of course, a financing statement describing the collateral as instruments does not protect a secured party. Remember, perfection in instruments can be achieved only through possession. Indeed, the real lesson of Section 9-308 and of this discussion is that a secured party has not *absolutely* perfected its interest in chattel paper as proceeds or in instruments as proceeds or original collateral until it has taken possession of these items of collateral.

SECURED PARTY VERSUS SECURED PARTY

5. General Rule

Two or more creditors may obtain security interests covering the same collateral. If the value of the collateral is less than the total of the claims it secures, upon the debtor's default it will be necessary to determine the priority of competing security interests.

Section 9-312 governs most secured party versus secured party priority contests. It contains special rules to be applied when the conflicting security interests are regular or when at least one of the interests is a purchase-money security interest. The general rule governing priority between regular perfected security interests in the same collateral is found in Section 9-312(5)(a) of the Code.

This section basically provides a *first-in-time-rule*. In other words, the first creditor to file or to perfect, if filing is not required, will have priority. This rule emphasizes the special status of filing a financing statement. Remember, filing can occur at any time, even prior to attachment. The Code adopts a pure "race type" statute: The first to file or perfect wins. Knowledge is unimportant. The benefit of a race statute is that it provides for certainty and predictability. Whichever party wins the race has priority.

This first-in-time rule also makes it advantageous to be perfected by attachment. Suppose a retail merchant sold a refrigerator to Smith to be used in Smith's home. Assume the merchant sold this refrigerator to Smith on credit, and the merchant had Smith sign a security agreement. This merchant is automatically perfected by attachment, sinc he has a PMSI in consumer goods. If Smith then granted a security interest in this refrigerator to a bank in return for a loan, the bank must file a financing statement to be perfected. If Smith defaults on his payments to both the merchant and the bank, which party has priority to the refrigerator? The merchant has priority, since he was perfected before the bank filed. Section 9-312(5)(a) states that the creditor who files *or* perfects first has priority.

There are a number of exceptions to this general rule, and each is designed to meet the needs of a specific commercial situation. The next five sections examine some of these exceptions. For example, a secured party with a PMSI enjoys a preferred status in some situations.

6. PMSI in Inventory Collateral

In order to be really protected, a secured party with a security interest in inventory usually will insist upon having the security agreement contain an after-acquired inventory clause. If that security interest is perfected by filing, the general rule is that this secured party will have priority over a later secured party, since he was first in time. However, what happens if the debtor wants to finance a new line of inventory? This general rule effectively stops the debtor unless the secured party is willing to make a future advance. For the purpose of allowing the debtor more control over his inventory, Section 9-312(3) creates an exception to this general rule.

For example, a bank lends a store money secured by all the store's inventory now owned or hereafter acquired. The bank properly files a financing statement. A year later, a loan company advances money to allow the store to acquire a new line of appliances. Before the new appliances arrive, the loan company properly files a financing statement covering the appliances. The loan company then notifies the bank that the loan company intends to finance the new appliances for the store on a PMSI. The loan company now has priority over the bank, but only in relation to the new appliances.

The requirements of Section 9-312(3) are rather simple. First, the PMSI secured party must perfect its PMSI and give the other secured party *written* notice that it has (or expects to have) a PMSI in certain described inventory. Perfection and notice must occur prior to the debtor's receiving the inventory. The purpose of the notice is to protect the first secured party so that he will not make new loans based on the after-acquired inventory or otherwise rely on the new inventory as his collateral.

It is not important whether the perfection of the PMSI or the notification to the preexisting secured party occurs first. What is important is that these steps must occur before the debtor takes possession of the new inventory. Proof of the time that each of the steps was accomplished is essential if the PMSI creditor is to have priority. In the following case, the matter was returned for a trial on the time issues. A paper trail showing compliance is essential for a lender financing inventory.

CASE

C&S Bank had a perfected security interest in the debtor TV store's inventory. In order to expand its store and to begin selling household appliances, the debtor entered into an "Inventory Financing Agreement" with the Appliance Buyers Credit Corporation (ABCC). On November 29, 1978, ABCC filed a financing statement covering the inventory it financed. On December 1, 1978, ABCC sent to C&S Bank notice that it had acquired a purchase-money security interest in the debtor's inventory of appliances. The debtor then took possession of the household appliances. When the debtor defaulted, C&S Bank took possession of all the inventory and announced its intention to sell it to satisfy the amount owed it by the debtor. ABCC claimed that it had a superior security interest in the debtor's appliance inventory. C&S Bank argued that its security interest had priority since ABCC had filed a financing statement before giving C&S written notice of the PMSI in inventory.

ISSUE: Does ABCC's purchase money security interest have priority over C&S Bank's interest?

DECISION: Yes.

REASONS:
1. Section 9-312(3) provides that a perfected purchase-money security interest in inventory has priority over a preexisting security interest in the same property if the purchase-money security interest was perfected and written notice was given to the holders of the prior conflicting security interests before the debtor receives possession of the newly financed inventory.
2. The order of when a PMSI in inventory is perfected and when the written notice is given are irrelevant so long as they both occur prior to the debtor's possession of the inventory.

King's Appliance v. Citizens and Southern Bank, 278 S.E.2d 733 (Ga. 1981).

7. PMSI in Noninventory Collateral

For collateral other than inventory, a purchase-money security interest is superior to conflicting security interests in the same collateral, provided the purchase-money security interest is perfected at the time the debtor receives the collateral or within ten days thereafter [9-312(4)]. Thus prior notice to other secured parties is not required in cases of equipment if the security interest is perfected within ten days after the debtor receives the equipment. The prior notice requirement is limited to a PMSI in new inventory under Section 9-312(3).

Why is prior notice required for inventory but not other classifications of collateral? The answer is that secured parties are likely to rely on the debtor's inventory more than on other types of collateral as a primary source of repayment. In other words, the sale of inventory is much more likely to produce regular income from which debts can be paid. Therefore the secured parties need to be informed more readily about the fact that they cannot rely on new inventory. The lack of prior notice about new equipment being purchased on credit, for example, does not create a problem for the preexisting secured parties, since their reliance on that equipment should be minimal.

A secured party with a purchase-money security interest in noninventory collateral is given a special status for ten days after the debtor receives the property. The protection during this period is limited. It gives priority over the rights of only (1) transferees in bulk (buyers of all or a substantial portion of a business) from the debtor and (2) lien creditors to the extent that such rights arise between the time the purchase-money security interest attaches and the time of filing [9-301(2)]. The purchase-money secured party is not protected against (1) a sale by the debtor to another party or (2) a secured transaction in which the collateral is given as security for a loan during the period prior to filing. Of course, to remain continuously perfected, the secured party must file a financing statement or otherwise perfect during this ten-day period.

8. Fixtures

Personal property that is collateral for a secured party may be annexed to real estate. This annexation transforms the personal property into a *fixture*. Examples of fixtures would include an installed heating/air-conditioning unit, a built-in kitchen appliance, and lighting and plumbing fixtures. The use of fixtures or potential fixtures as collateral raises a question of priority between the Article 9 secured party and one who has an interest in the real estate. These third parties with possible conflicting interests could include the owner of the real estate or a party who has a security interest in that real estate. (Chapter 42 discusses in detail the use of real property as security.)

The party that has priority is entitled, upon default, to remove the fixtures. This party is required to reimburse an encumbrancer or owner other than the debtor for the cost of repair of any physical damages caused by the removal [9-313(5)].

Building materials are clearly not classified as fixtures [9-313(2)]. The revised Code recognizes three categories of goods: (1) those that retain their chattel character and are not part of the real estate, (2) building materials that lose their chattel character entirely and are a part of the real estate, and (3) an intermediate class that becomes a part of the real estate for some purposes but may be a part of a secured transaction. The third category is *fixtures*.

The term *fixture filing* is used to require filing where a mortgage on real estate would be filed. The financing statement for fixture filing must (1) show that it covers fixtures, (2) recite that it is to be filed in the real estate records, (3) describe the real estate, and (4) show the name of the record owner if the debtor does not own the real estate. A creditor's failure to meet these requirements of a fixture filing destroys that creditor's claim of priority, as illustrated by the following case.

CASE

A dispute arose between two banks as to which one had ihe better rights to grain bins located on the debtor's real estate. The Bank of Rector had financed the debtor's purchase of the real estate involved and had recorded its mortgage on May 17, 1976. The Corning Bank had previously financed the grain bins and had filed a financing statement on March 19, 1976. This financing statement did not describe the real estate where the bins were located, nor was it referenced into the real estate records. When the debtor became insolvent, these banks sought a judicial determination establishing which one had priority to the grain bins.

ISSUE: Does the filing of a financing statement prior to the recording of a mortgage give the Corning Bank priority to the grain bins?

DECISION: No.

REASONS:
1. The court held that these grain bins were firmly attached to the real estate and thus were fixtures.
2. Under the applicable 1972 revision of Section 9-313, a financing statement filed as a fixture filing must contain a sufficient description of the real estate involved so that constructive notice of the financier's interest will be given to anyone searching the applicable real estate records. Furthermore, the Corning Bank failed to have its financing statement cross-referenced in the real estate records.
3. Failure to abide by these essential requirements results in a subsequent mortgagee having priority to the grain bins located on the secured real estate.

Corning Bank v. Bank of Rector, 576 S.W.2d 949 (Ark. 1979).

A mortgage may describe fixtures and thus be used as a financing statement. In such cases, the mortgage is exempt from the five-year limitation on financing statements.

Two basic priority rules are based on fixture filing. First, there is the general rule that governs the potential conflict between a nonpurchase-money security interest in fixtures and a real estate interest. This rule is another one based on the first-in-time principle. For example, if the Article 9 security interest is fixture-filed before a mortgage is recorded, the fixture filer has priority. Of course, if the mortgage is recorded first, it has priority [9-313(4)(b)]. The second rule concerns purchase-money security interest in fixtures. If the fixture filing for a PMSI occurs before the goods become fixtures or within ten days thereafter, the security interest is superior to any *earlier* realty interest, such as a prior recorded mortgage [9-313(4)(a)].

A special filing rule applies to *soft fixtures* (readily removable factory or office machines or readily removable replacements of domestic appliances). These fixtures can be perfected by any method allowed under Article 9, such as filing, taking possession, fixture filing, or automatic perfection. If you replace a stove (a fixture) in your house and give a PMSI to the seller, the PMSI in consumer goods (stove) would thus automatically be perfected [9-313(4)(c)].

A special priority provision for a construction loan gives it total priority [9-313(6)]. Thus a security interest in fixtures added as part of new construction is always subordinate to the construction mortgage on file or to a mortgage given to refinance a construction mortgage.

9. Accessions

In addition to being affixed to real estate, goods may be installed in or affixed to other goods. In general, this occurs when parts are added to personal property in order to repair that object. These parts are called **accessions.** When accessions are present, there is a possibility for conflict between a party with an interest in the repaired object and a party with an interest in the accessions. The confusing thing in determining which of these parties has priority is that the attachment (creation) of a security interest is as important as the perfection of that interest.

Accessions *Items of personal property that become incorporated into other items of personal property.*

Two basic rules govern priority to accessions. First, a security interest that attaches to goods *before* they become accessions generally has priority over all persons' claims to the whole object. This rule applies regardless of whether the claims to the whole object arose before or after the accessions were installed [9-314(1)]. The second rule is applied when a security interest in goods attaches *after* they become accessions. In general, this security interest is superior to all subsequent claims to the whole object. However, preexisting claims to the whole object have priority over the security interest in the accessions [9-314(2)].

To help in your understanding of Section 9-314, consider the following:

EXAMPLE: The Houston Oil Company owns a large air compressor which it uses in its oil and gas drilling operations. This compressor is part of the equipment in which the Bank of the Southwest has perfected a security interest. The basis of the bank's perfection is a financing statement. Last month, the oil company had the compressor repaired by the Hughes Tool Company. These repairs cost $30,000, and the oil company signed a security agreement granting to Hughes an interest in the parts installed in the compressor. If the oil company defaults on its payments to both the bank and Hughes, the rules stated above determine which party has priority to the accessions. If the Hughes Tool Company created its security interest before the repairs were made, it has priority. If the repairs were made and then the security interest was created (attached), the bank has priority. Upon the debtor's default, the secured party with priority can remove its collateral from the whole. However, this party must make payment for the cost of repair of any physical damage caused by removal [9-314(4)].

These general rules on priority to accessions are subject to two exceptions. First, any party with an interest in the whole object who has priority can consent to subordinate his interest in favor of the party with an interest in the accessions. To be binding, this consent must be in writing. The second exception is a bit more confusing, since it reintroduces the concept of perfection as the basis for priority. Notice that in the example above we never mentioned that Hughes had to perfect its interest in the parts in order to have priority over the bank. If Hughes does not perfect its interest by filing a financing statement, it can lose whatever priority it has to (1) a subsequent purchaser of the whole object, (2) a subsequent judgment creditor who levies on the whole object, and (3) a creditor with a prior perfected security interest to the extent that this creditor makes subsequent advances [9-314(3)]. Therefore, to be assured of priority to the parts installed, the repairer who extends credit must create and perfect its security interest in the parts (accessions) prior to installing them.

10. Commingled and Processed Goods

In a manufacturing process, several items—including raw materials and components, each of which may be subject to different security interests—may combine to make a finished product. The collateral to which the financing party is entitled will ultimately be the product that results from the combination of the materials in which he has a security interest. If a security interest in the raw materials was perfected, the security interest continues in the product if the identity of the goods is lost *or* the original financing statement provided for a security interest that covered the ''product'' [9-315(1)]. In a situation in which component parts are assembled into a machine, the secured party would generally have a choice of claiming either (1) a security interest in the machine or (2) an interest in a component part as provided for security interests in accessions [9-314(1)]. If he stipulates ''product,'' he cannot claim an accession. When more than one security interest exists in the product, the secured parties share in the product in proportion to the costs of their materials used [9-315(2)].

SECURED PARTY VERSUS LIEN CREDITORS

11. General Rule

In addition to other secured parties and buyers of the collateral, a secured party's security interest can conflict with parties holding *liens* arising from operation of law. Four types of liens created by law may come into conflict with an Article 9 security interest: (1) federal tax lien; (2) laborer's, artisan's, or materialman's lien; (3) judgment creditor's lien; and (4) the bankruptcy trustee's lien. In general, the rule determining priority between a secured party and a lienholder is the first-in-time rule. In other words, the party that is first to indicate its interest on the public record has priority.

For example, failure to pay federal taxes allows the Internal Revenue Service to file a notice of a tax lien on any property of the delinquent taxpayer. The property described in a federal tax lien may also be subject to an Article 9 security interest. The secured party has a priority claim to this property if the notice of the tax lien is filed *after* the security interest is perfected. If the notice of the tax lien is filed *before* the security interest is perfected, the Internal Revenue Service has priority.

Although the federal tax lien follows the first-in-time rule, other liens do create some exceptions to this general rule as discussed in the following sections.

12. Laborer's, Artisan's, and Materialman's Lien

Laborer's, *artisan's*, and *materialman's liens* are discussed in detail in Chapter 43. For now, it is sufficient to know that these liens may be created under common law or by statute. The *common law lien* on goods—allowed for repair, improvement, storage, or transportation—is superior to a perfected security interest as long as the lien claimant retains possession of the property. *Statutory liens* also may have such priority. Even though a lien is second in point of time, it will be granted priority over a perfected security interest in the goods unless the statute creating the lien provides that it is subordinate [9-310]. The reason for giving superiority to a second-in-time lien is the presumption that the service rendered by the lienholder has added to or protected the value of the collateral.

13. Judgment Creditor's Lien

Article 9 defines a **lien creditor** as a creditor who acquired a lien on the debtor's property by a sheriff's levy based on the creditor's judgment, or a trustee in bankruptcy [9-301(3)]. The lien creditor is more generally called a judgment creditor as discussed in the introduction to Chapter 40. This creditor, having obtained a judgment in a lawsuit, seeks to collect that judgment by levy, attachment, execution, or the like on the debtor's property. The Code provides a first-in-time rule. A secured party who perfects before the judicial lien creditor levies will prevail. Assume that a levy is made on October 3. If the secured party has perfected at any time prior to October 3, the secured party's security interest has priority over the judicial lien creditor. Priority goes to the lien creditor if the security interest is perfected after October 3.

Lien creditor *A creditor who has acquired a lien on property involved by attachment, levy, or the like.*

There is one important exception to this general first-in-time rule. Under Section 9-301(2), the Code provides a ten-day grace period for filing a PMSI, regardless of the type of collateral. Assume that a secured party makes a PMSI loan to a debtor on May 1 and that the secured party files to perfect on May 8. Since filing was within the ten-day period, the security interest relates back to May 1 under Section 9-301(2). Therefore, if a lien is levied on May 3, the security interest is perfected and is superior to a lien creditor under Section 9-301(a)(b).

14. Bankruptcy Trustee's Lien

The subject of bankruptcy is covered in Chapter 45. Bankruptcy is a remedy for financial difficulties granted by the federal Bankruptcy Reform Act of 1978. When a debtor (voluntarily or involuntarily) is put into bankruptcy, his nonexempt assets are required to be turned over to a trustee to be sold to satisfy the claims of unsecured creditors. If a secured party has a security interest in some of those assets, then the security interest is threatened. The bankruptcy trustee is another third party who may attempt to defeat certain Article 9 secured parties. It is the trustee's job to gather and liquidate the debtor's estate, reduce it to cash, and make a pro rata payment to the bankrupt-debtor's *unsecured* creditors.

The trustee will attempt to show that the Article 9 security interest is ineffective. If the attempt is successful, it will increase the available assets and, in turn, increase the pro rata distribution to the unsecured creditors. The acid test for an Article 9 security interest is said to be its ability to survive the trustee's attack. Several sections of the 1978 Bankruptcy Act give the trustee powers to avoid an Article 9 security interest; many of them—such as the power to avoid the security interest as a *preference* under Section 547—are considered in Chapter 45. For now, we analyze one important right of the bankruptcy trustee in his quest to set aside a security interest.

The most frequent clash between the secured party and the trustee occurs when the security interest is not perfected. The trustee will prevail over an unperfected security interest by using the bankruptcy law and the Code. The trustee generally has the rights of a hypothetical lien creditor. This allows the trustee to pretend to be a lien creditor on the date the bankruptcy petition is filed. In essence, on this date, the trustee can assert the same rights that a lien creditor would have on that same date under Article 9. (See the preceding section for the rights of a lien creditor.) The following example illustrates that this rule is easy to apply.

Assume that the bankruptcy petition was filed on October 10, and the secured party filed a financing statement on October 11. As we already know, the lien creditor's levy has priority over an unperfected security interest but is inferior to a previously perfected security interest. Now apply that reasoning to the time the bankruptcy petition is filed. If before that date (October 10 in our example) the security interest is perfected, the trustee loses. But in our example, perfection occurred on October 11. Since the security interest was unperfected on October 10, the trustee will have priority.

The following case gives another example of this first-in-time rule. It also emphasizes the importance of being a *perfected* secured party.

CASE

On May 20, 1974, Verlan J. Rumbaugh and his wife, Gladys, borrowed $30,000 from the Southwest Bank of Omaha. A security agreement and financing statement were prepared by the bank. The collateral described in these documents was inventory, fixtures, and accounts receivable in Rumbaugh's hardware business. The financing statement was not signed by Verlan J. Rumbaugh, who was the sole owner of the business. However, in the place for the debtor's signature appeared "By Gladys H. Rumbaugh." This financing statement was filed in the appropriate office on May 21, 1974. On Jaunary 31, 1977, Rumbaugh's hardware store voluntarily filed a petition in bankruptcy. The bank's claim of priority to Rumbaugh's inventory and fixtures was objected to by the trustee in bankruptcy.

ISSUE: Does the bank have priority to the collateral when compared to the bankruptcy trustee?

DECISION: No.

REASONS:
1. An unperfected security interest is inferior to, among others, a lien creditor's claim. A trustee in bankruptcy has the rights of a lien creditor from the date the bankruptcy petition is filed.
2. To be effective, a financing statement must be signed by the debtor. The term "debtor" means the owner of the collateral.
3. The financing statement in this case, which was not signed by the debtor, is insufficient to perfect a security interest. Therefore the bankruptcy trustee has priority, and the bank is treated as being an unsecured general creditor.

Southwest Bank of Omaha v. Moritz, 227 N.W.2d 430 (Neb. 1979).

RIGHTS AND DUTIES ON DEBTOR'S DEFAULT

15. Introduction

A debtor's default is the event that illustrates the real benefits of being an Article 9 secured party. Article 9 defines the rights and duties of both secured parties and debtors in default situations. The provisions of Part 5 of Article 9 permit the secured party to take possession of the collateral and dispose of it to satisfy his claim. He may obtain the collateral by self-help (if this procedure does not breach the peace) or by court action [9-503]. Once the collateral is in hand, the secured party has two alternatives. The first one is to conduct a *foreclosure sale* with the proceeds to be applied to the unpaid debt. The second option is *strict foreclosure*, which occurs when the secured creditor retains the collateral in satisfaction of the debt. At any time before either alternative regarding disposition of the collateral becomes final, the debtor has the right to *redeem* his interest in the collateral by paying off the debt.

The first event that a secured party must establish is a *default* by the debtor. The security agreement will set forth the debtor's obligations, which, if breached, will constitute a default. A default may occur even though payments on the debt are current. For example, a note may require that the debtor insure the collateral. Failure to maintain proper insurance coverage may justify the creditor's repossessing the collateral and selling it according to the procedures described in the sections that follow.

These following sections discuss the parties' rights and duties on the debtor's default from a chronological perspective. First, the secured party must take possession of the collateral. This act often is called *repossession*, since the secured party may have sold the collateral to the debtor. Next, the secured party must decide whether to sell the collateral or to to keep it. Finally, the secured party must give the debtor the opportunity to exercise his rights to redeem.

Prior to discussing the secured party's ability to repossess the collateral, a special rule concerning some types of collateral should be noted. If the collateral is accounts, chattel paper, instruments, or general intangibles, repossession is not necessary because the secured party is already in possession of the collateral. The secured party can simply proceed to collect whatever may become due on the collateral. He may give reasonable notice to the person who owes the account receivable or instrument to make payment directly to the secured party [9-502(1)]. A failure to give reasonable notice prevents the secured party from collecting these debts from any party other than the original debtor.

16. Repossession of Collateral

Self-help. Generally, a secured party will attempt "peaceable," **self-help** repossession, since it is swift and inexpensive. The main drawback is that self-help techniques must not result in a breach of the peace. Countless judicial options have considered whether self-help repossession is peaceable or not under particular situations.

Self-help *A creditor's attempt to take possession of collateral without the court's assistance.*

The following three sets of circumstances usually are deemed peaceable in connection with a repossesion. First, the secured party removes the collateral (a car) from the street or parking lot without the knowledge or objection of the debtor. More than likely, starting the car without the use of the ignition key will be considered peaceful. If the removal is from the debtor's open premises such as a driveway, it is not objectionable. Second, removal without the debtor's consent (or even if debtor knows but does not make an express objection) is not a breach of the peace. Finally, removal of the collateral from the premises of a third party (such as a garage, parking lot, neighbor's yard) is lawful so long as neither the debtor nor third person expressly objects.

Breach of the peace *This occurrence invalidates the creditor's legal right to take possession of the collateral without the assistance of a court. This event occurs whenever the possession by the creditor is accompanied by violence, deception, or an objection by the debtor.*

In four situations, repossession will usually involve a **breach of the peace.** First, it is a breach to threaten or to appear to threaten violence to the debtor or other person who is present, whether or not any violence occurs. Second, removal of the collateral over the express objection of the debtor (even if there is no violence) is a breach of the peace. Most courts also find a breach of the peace when the removal is over the express objection of a third party in possession of the collateral. Third, the use of trickery is a breach of the peace. For example, posing as a police officer would be considered an illegal repossession. Fourth, unauthorized entry into the debtor's home, garage, or other building for the purpose of repossession is unlawful. The following case is an example that illustrates this situation.

CASE

The Barnette Bank had a perfected security interest in the assets of Quest and Sea-Sky Travel Agency. Due to the debtor's deliquency in repaying a loan, the bank decided to take possession of the agency's assets. A bank official called the owner, Quest, who was at home sick. Nevertheless, this official asked Quest to come to her place of business so that the bank could close it down. Quest asked for some time to retrieve some valuable papers in her office. The bank official agreed to her request. Despite this agreement, when Quest arrived at her office, bank employees already had removed most of the contents of her office. Indeed, Quest's records were scattered on the floor. Quest brought an action contending that the bank's self-help measures were a breach of the peace.

ISSUE: Is the bank liable to Quest for its actions in taking possession of her travel agency's assets?

DECISION: Yes.

REASONS:

1. The bank's self-help measures constituted a breach of the peace and were therefore unlawful.
2. There is a two-pronged test to determine if a breach of the peace occurred: (a) whether the creditor entered the debtor's premises and (b) whether the debtor or someone acting in his behalf consented to the entry and repossession.
3. The debtor's consent must be freely and voluntarily given before a creditor can enter an enclosed space.
4. A breach of peace also can occur if the creditor damages property of the debtor while taking possession of the collateral.
5. A creditor is liable for any negligence resulting in damage to the debtor's collateral.

Quest v. Barnette Bank of Pensacola, 397 So.2d 1020 (Fla. 1981).

Judicial action. If a secured party cannot obtain possession of the collateral by the peaceful self-help method, a judicial action becomes necessary. Repossession by judicial action may be accomplished by several means. The secured party may bring a *replevin* action, which is a judicial action for the actual recovery of the possession of an item of personal property. Or the action may be for a personal judgment against the debtor, with that judgment being levied on the collateral. In some states, the judicial action may be brought to obtain a foreclosure sale of specific personal property.

Obviously, repossession by judicial action is more expensive than self-help; however, the Code does make the debtor liable for most court costs, including attorney's fees. The secured party is well advised to use the courts when the debtor will not part with the goods without a fight. Under the typical judicial action, the plaintiff files a complaint, makes an affidavit, and posts a required bond. Then the sheriff seizes the property. Unless the debtor objects within a specified time, the property is delivered to the secured party.

Alternatives to repossession. By including specific provisions in the security agreement, a secured party can tailor his rights on the debtor's default to suit his particular needs. In other words, secured parties may provide for alternative remedies to the self-help repossession or the judicial action allowed by Article 9. The security agreement can, for instance, put the debtor to work. It can provide that the debtor assemble the collateral and make it available to the secured party at a place reasonably convenient to both parties [9-503]. If the debtor refuses, the secured party may use judicial help in requiring a debtor in possession of collateral that is spread out over a number of places to gather the collateral at one place.

In the case of collateral such as heavy equipment, the physical removal from the debtor's plant and storage elsewhere pending resale may be excessively expensive and, in some cases, impractical. Thus the Code allows the secured party, without removal, to render equipment unusable and to dispose of the collateral on the debtor's premises [9-503]. Any such action must, of course, be "commercially reasonable."

17. Rights and Duties of Secured Party in Possession

The secured party has certain rights against the debtor who has defaulted. First, any reasonable expenses incurred in connection with the collateral are chargeable to the debtor and are secured by the collateral [9-207(2)(a)]. Second, the risk of accidental loss or damage to the collateral is on the debtor to the extent that the loss is not covered by insurance [9-207(2)(b)]. Finally, the secured party is entitled to hold as additional security any increase in or profits received from the collateral, unless the increase or profit is money [9-207(2)(c)].

Once the secured party has obtained possession of the collateral, that party must decide what to do with the collateral. The secured party may sell the collateral and apply the sale proceeds to satisfy the debt. Or the secured party may decide to keep the collateral in satisfaction of the debt. Because of the potential harshness of strict foreclosure, there are situations when a debtor or other interested party can force the secured party to sell the collateral.

The Code imposes certain duties on a secured party in possession of the collateral [9-207]. The most important is to exercise reasonable care in the custody and preservation of the collateral. If the collateral is chattel paper or instruments, reasonable care includes taking steps to preserve rights against prior parties unless otherwise agreed.

EXAMPLE: Debtor pledged its stock in ABC Corporation to creditor to secure a loan. While creditor was in possession, ABC issued rights to current stockholders to buy additional shares, which rights would expire if not exercised by a stated date. Knowing of this right, creditor failed to notify debtor about it before the expiration date. Creditor thus failed to exercise due care and would be liable to debtor for any loss caused by the failure to notify.

18. Foreclosure Sale

Foreclosure *The forced sale of a defaulting debtor's property at the insistence of the creditor.*

After default, a secured party may sell, lease, or otherwise dispose of the collateral [9-504]. The usual disposition is by public or private **foreclosure** sale. The primary goal is to get the best possible price on the resale, since that benefits both the debtor and the secured party. For example, the higher the foreclosure sale price, the greater the likelihood of a surplus for the debtor. Also, the likelihood of a deficiency is diminished.

The foreclosure sale can be public or private, and it can be by one or more contracts [9-504(3)]. A *public sale* is a sale by auction open to the general public. A public sale often occurs on the courthouse steps. A *private sale* is a sale through commercial channels to a buyer arranged by the secured party. Such a buyer could be a dealer who regularly buys and sells goods like the collateral.

Although the Code provides flexible rules for the foreclosure sale, it does not leave the debtor unprotected and at the secured party's mercy. Indeed, the Code imposes definite restrictions on the secured party, who must adhere to these restrictions or risk losing the remedies provided by the Code. Of these restrictions, three are the most important: (1) *reasonable notification* of the foreclosure sale given to the debtor by the secured party, (2) *reasonable timing* of the foreclosure sale, and (3) *commercial reasonableness* of every aspect of the foreclosure sale.

However, nowhere does the Code specify the consequences of a creditor's failure to meet the requirements of proper notice and commercially reasonable disposition. Courts have reached varying results in cases where a creditor has failed to comply with the Code's provisions governing disposition of the collateral.

One line of authority holds that the creditor's failure to comply with the requirements governing disposition of repossessed collateral serves as an absolute bar to the creditor's right to a *deficiency judgment*. These courts view the Code's requirements as conditions precedent to the creditor's right to recover a deficiency judgment.

A second line of authority, adopted by only a few courts, permits the secured party to recover a deficiency judgment despite his noncompliance with the requirements subject to the debtor's rights to recover from the secured party any loss occasioned by the creditor's failure to comply with the Code. Under this approach, the debtor's claim for damages is generally asserted as a counterclaim in the creditor's action for a deficiency judgment.

The third approach on failure to follow the statute is that the failure is not an absolute bar to the recovery of a deficiency, but there is a presumption that the fair market value of collateral at the time of repossession was equal to the amount of the total debt that it secured. The presumption arises when it has been determined that the secured party has disposed of the collateral in a commercially unreasonable manner. The burden to prove that the fair market value of the collateral was less than the debt at that time is then on the secured party.

Notice required. A secured party is not free to assume that repossession of the collateral serves as *notice* of a possible public or private foreclosure sale. The Code requires the secured party to give reasonable notice of either the time and place of any public sale or of the time after which a private sale may occur [9-504(3)]. This notice gives the debtor a deadline within which to protect himself in whatever manner he sees fit.

When notification is required by the Code, it must be reasonable in all situations. Upon the failure to give reasonable notice of a foreclosure sale, the secured party usually is denied the right to sue the debtor for a deficiency judgment, although the other approaches noted above may be followed. It should be emphasized that this notice must be given, not necessarily received.

The notice must be sent to the debtor and (to be reasonable) must be sent in time for the debtor to take appropriate steps to protect his interests if he so desires. The notice of resale need not be given if the debtor has signed *after default* a statement renouncing or modifying his right to notification of sale.

In the case of consumer goods, notice must be given only to the debtor. With the exception of consumer goods, the Code requires that notice be sent to any other secured party from whom the secured party has received written notice of an interest.

Notification of an impending disposition is not required if the collateral is (1) perishable or (2) threatens to decline speedily in value or (3) is of a type customarily sold on a recognized market [9-504(3)]. Examples of goods sold on a recognized market include commodities or corporate stock sold on a public exchange. Used cars and similar items are not considered customarily sold in a recognized market, since there is no established price for these items.

Time of sale. In general, the Code does not establish any stated *time* limitation within which the foreclosure sale or disposition of collateral must occur. This absence of a stated time period for resale conforms to the Code philosophy of encouraging disposition by private sale through regular commercial channels. For example, it may not be wise to dispose of goods if the market collapses. Likewise, the sale of large amounts of inventory in parcels over time may be more reasonable than a forced sale of the entire amount in bulk. The foreclosure sale must be commercially reasonable. The secured party is not allowed to delay when no reason exists for not making a prompt sale.

An exception to this general rule of no time restriction does apply if the collateral is consumer goods and if the debtor has paid over 60 percent of the purchase price or loan amount. Under these circumstances, the consumer goods must be sold within ninety days after the secured party has taken possession of the collateral. This exception is necessary to protect the debtor, since, in most cases, a sale of the consumer goods will produce proceeds in excess of the debt.

Commercial reasonableness. Every aspect of the resale, including the *method*, *manner*, *time*, *place*, and *terms* must be commercially reasonable. The term *commercially reasonable* is not defined in the Code, but case law has developed some rules to assist in making the determination in future cases. First, the fact that a better price could have been obtained at another time or by another method is not of itself sufficient to establish that the resale was unreasonable. However, recent case law indicates that a resale at a price substantially under what might well have been received is not commercially reasonable. In particular, if the sale is followed by a second sale at a substantially greater price, it is not reasonable. If the secured party has not exerted much effort (as in failing to contact a number of prospective buyers), the sale may be held not commercially reasonable. The following case is typical of those involving the issue of commercial reasonableness.

CASE

In April of 1982 Fraker and Deere entered into a five-year leasing agreement that obligated Fraker to make ten semiannual $12,219.73 payments to Deere in exchange for the use of a combine and attachments. The lease also gave Fraker the option to purchase the equipment at the expiration of the lease for an additional $26,242.75. The lease provided that upon default Deere had the right to take possession of the leased equipment and sell it. After Fraker had used the combine for one year he was unable to make further payments. In May 1983, he returned the combine to Deere. The following December, Deere sent notice of private sale to Fraker and over 300 John Deere dealers in Iowa and Illinois. The combine was sold on January 20, 1984, for $63,227, and Fraker was notified of a $25,045.21 deficiency. When Deere sued for this deficiency, Fraker argued that Deere did not give adequate notice of the private sale and that Deere's sale did not meet reasonable commercial standards. The trial court granted Deere's motion for summary judgment. Fraker appealed.

ISSUE: Was the grant of summary judgment proper in light of the factual issues raised by Fraker?

DECISION: No.

REASONS:

1. Deere's written letter to Fraker, entitled "Notice of Private Sale," gave him sufficient opportunity to purchase the harvester, advised him a private sale was contemplated, and plainly satisfied the statutory notice requirement.
2. However, the burden of proving commercial reasonableness was on Deere, the secured party. Deere also had the burden to show the absence of a genuine fact issue, with the record viewed in the light most favorable to Fraker.
3. The commercial reasonableness of a sale of collateral is ordinarily a question of fact. At the outset, the secured party must choose between a private and a public sale, and that choice itself may present a question of fact on commercial reasonableness of the sale of collateral. In choosing between a public and a private sale in the context of resale of goods after contract breach, the character of the goods must be considered and relevant trade practices and usages must be observed.
4. One of the specific "terms" of sale that is relevant to the issue of commercial reasonableness is the adequacy or insufficiency of the price itself. However, the price is only one aggregate of circumstances that should be emphasized in determining whether a sale was commercially reasonable. A second circumstance of this private sale was that Deere held the combine from May until the end of the fall harvest season without renting or attempting to sell it, then gave notice in December and sold it in January. Deere conceded the obvious: It is more difficult to sell a harvester in January than in the fall.
5. On this summary judgment record, considering all the elements of this private sale as an aggregate, a finder of fact could reasonably conclude that the price Deere received for the combine was grossly inadequate, the timing of the sale inappropriate, and consequently that Deere had not satisfied those burdens on the question of commercial reasonableness.

John Deere Leasing Co. v. Fraker, 395 N.W.2d 885 (Iowa 1986).

The Code allows the secured party to buy the collateral at any public sale, but the right to buy at a private sale is restricted. Only if the collateral is of a type normally sold in a recognized market or is subject to universal price quotations can the secured party buy at a private sale [9-504(3)]. This prohibition against the creditor's buying at a private sale acknowledges that creditors can overreach the debtor's rights by conducting a sham sale. A *sham sale* occurs if the collateral is purchased by the creditor at an unreasonably low price that allows the creditor to make the debtor liable for a substantial deficiency. Obviously, this type of resale is commercially unreasonable.

A resale is recognized as commercially reasonable if the secured party either (1) sells the collateral in the customary manner in a recognized market or (2) sells at a price current in such market at the time of resale or (3) sells in conformity with reasonable commercial practices among dealers in the type of property sold.

19. Rights of Parties after Foreclosure

The buyer of the collateral at a foreclosure sale receives it free of the security interest under which the sale was held. This buyer also is free of any inferior security interest [9-504(4)]. Thus the good-faith purchaser at a disposition sale receives substantial assurance that he will be protected in his purchase.

After the sale has been made, the proceeds of the sale will be distributed and applied as follows. First, the expenses the secured party incurred in taking repossession and conducting the foreclosure sale will be paid. After these expenses are paid, the sale's proceeds are used to satisfy the debt owed to the secured party. Third, any indebtedness owed to persons who have inferior security interest in the collateral will be paid. Fourth and finally, any surplus remaining after all these debts are satisfied will be returned to the debtor [9-504(1)]. If the foreclosure sale is commercially reasonable in all respects but does not produce enough to satisfy all these charges, the debtor is liable for any deficiency [9-504(2)].

20. Strict Foreclosure

Notice required. The secured party who intends to keep the collateral in satisfaction of the debt rather than conduct a foreclosure sale must send written notice to the debtor indicating this intent [9-505(2)]. This notice is not required if the debtor has signed, after default, a statement modifying or renouncing his right to this notice. If the collateral is consumer goods, only the debtor needs to be given notice of the proposed **strict foreclosure.** Notice to other interested parties is not necessary when consumer goods are involved, since most of the secured parties claiming a conflicting interest will have PMSI and will be relying on perfection by attachment. Thus the secured party proposing a strict foreclosure will not even know of conflicting interests.

Strict foreclosure *The agreement by the creditor and debtor to allow the creditor to retain possession of the debtor's property in satisfaction of the creditor's claim.*

When collateral other than consumer goods is involved, written notice proposing strict foreclosure must be sent to all persons who have filed a financing statement covering the collateral or who are known to have a security interest in it. Within the time period (discussed in the next subsection), the debtor or any interested party may object in writing to the proposed strict foreclosure. If no objections are received, the secured party can retain the collateral in satisfaction of the debt [9-505(2)].

Prevention of strict foreclosure. Strict foreclosure is disallowed in two situations. First, special provisions relate to consumer transactions. Disposition of consumer goods may be *compulsory*, and, if so, a sale must be made within ninety days after possession is taken by the secured party. This resale of the collateral is mandatory when there exists either (1) a purchase-money security interest in consumer goods and 60 percent of the purchase price has been paid or (2) an interest in consumer goods to secure a nonpurchase-money loan and 60 percent of the loan has been repaid [9–505(1)]. As stated previously, these rules exist because there is a presumption that the resale will result in surplus proceeds. The resale within ninety days ensures that the consumer debtor will not be deprived of this surplus. Of course, it is possible that even though a large percentage of the purchase price or loan amount has been paid, the resale of the collateral clearly will not produce a surplus. Thus the consumer debtor is allowed to waive the right of mandatory resale. This waiver must be in writing and must be signed by the debtor after default [9-505(1)].

The second situation when strict foreclosure may be prevented involves an objection to the secured party keeping the collateral. As noted in the preceding section, the debtor and all other interested parties must be sent written notice that a strict foreclosure is proposed. Any of these parties may object to this proposal. This objection must be made in writing, and it must be received by the secured party's proposing the strict foreclosure within twenty-one days of the original notice's being sent. If these requirements for objecting to a strict foreclosure are met, the collateral must be sold [9-505(2)].

21. Debtor's General Remedies

Except for the ninety-day period for consumer goods, the secured party is not required to make disposition of the repossessed goods within any time limit. The debtor has the right to *redeem* or reinstate his interest in the collateral until (1) that property has been sold or contracted to be sold, or (2) the obligation has been satisfied by the retention of the property. The debtor must, as a condition of **redemption,** tender the full amount of the obligation secured by the collateral plus expenses incurred by the secured party in connection with the collateral and (if so provided in the security agreement) attorneys' fees and legal expenses [9-506].

Redemption *To buy back. A debtor buys back or redeems his mortgaged property when he pays the debt.*

If the secured party fails to comply with the provisions of the Code relating to default, a court may order disposition or restrain disposition, as the situation requires. If the sale has already taken place, the secured party is liable for any loss resulting from his noncompliance, and he may lose his right to recover any deficiency. If the collateral is consumer goods, the consumer debtor is entitled to recover from the secured party (1) the credit service charge plus 10 percent of the principal amount of the debt or (2) the time-price differential plus 10 percent of the cash price, whichever is greater [9-507(1)]. The secured party who forecloses a security interest in consumer goods must be very careful to comply with the law as it relates to their sale.

Note that if the creditor fails to follow the compulsory sale of consumer goods under the 60 percent–ninety-day rule of Section 9-505(1), the debtor may recover in conversion or under the liability provisions of Section 9-507(1). Under the latter provision, the debtor may recover any loss caused by the secured party's failure to comply with Code provisions. In addition to recovering damages caused by the secured party, if consumer goods are involved the debtor also can recover the Code penalty discussed in the preceding paragraph.

CHAPTER SUMMARY

Secured party versus Buyers of Collateral

General Rule

1. Secured parties who are perfected generally have priority over buyers of collateral. However, there are at least three exceptions.

Buyers in the Ordinary Course of Business

1. Such a buyer takes free from a perfected secured party's interest.
2. A buyer in the ordinary course of business is a buyer who buys goods from a seller who is in the business of selling goods of that kind from inventory.
3. This rule of priority does not apply when the collateral is farm products.

Buyers of Consumer Goods

1. A buyer of consumer goods from a consumer cannot make this purchase in the ordinary course of business, since the consumer is not in business.
2. A buyer of consumer goods from a consumer has priority over a secured party who has relied on perfection by attachment of a purchase-money security interest if the buyer has no knowledge of the security interest and if the buyer uses the goods as consumer goods.
3. A secured party can be assured of priority with respect to consumer goods if a financing statement is properly filed.

Buyers of Chattel Paper and Instruments.

1. A buyer of chattel paper or instruments that are proceeds from the sale of inventory collateral has priority over a secured party even if that buyer has knowledge of the security interest. This buyer must make the purchase in the ordinary course of business for value and must take possession of the chattel paper or instruments.
2. A buyer of chattel paper or instruments that are proceeds from the sale of noninventory collateral takes priority over a secured party only if that secured party relies on the ten-day automatic perfection rule and if the buyer lacks knowledge of the security interest.
3. A buyer of instruments that were original collateral takes priority over a secured party only if that secured party relies on the twenty-one-day automatic perfection rules and if the buyer lacks knowledge of the security interest.

Secured Party versus Secured Party

General Rule

1. The secured party who is first to file or perfect has priority to the described collateral. When PMSIs are involved, exceptions do exist.

PMSI in Inventory Collateral

1. A second-in-time secured party who has a PMSI in inventory may have priority over a preexisting secured party.
2. This purchase-money secured party must notify the preexisting secured party in writing and must file a financing statement before the debtor gets possession of the collateral.

PMSI in Noninventory Collateral

1. A second-in-time secured party who has a PMSI in noninventory collateral may have priority over a preexisting secured party.
2. This purchase-money secured party does not have to give notice of its PMSI. However, this party must file a financing statement before or within ten days after the debtor takes possession of the collateral.

Fixtures

1. The financing of fixtures or potential fixtures creates the possible conflict between an Article 9 secured party and a party with an interest in the real estate.

2. The Code requires a fixture filing. It specifically provides rules concerning priority in certain situations when a fixture-secured party and a real estate secured party have conflicting interests.
3. These situations include the financing of building materials, the financing of soft fixtures, the creation of PMSI and non-PMSI in fixtures, and the rights of construction mortgages.

Accessions

1. An *accession* is a good or part that is added to or installed in a larger good. Accessions typically arise in repairs of personal property.
2. A secured party who creates a security interest in accessions before they are affixed to the whole object has priority to the accessions.
3. If the security interest in accessions is created after the parts are added to the whole object, the party secured by the accessions has priority over anyone who subsequently takes an interest in the whole. However, this secured party's interest is inferior to parties who have a preexisting interest in the whole object.
4. To be assured of priority, the party who is secured by accessions should perfect as well as create the security interest *prior* to the parts being added to the wole object.

Commingled and Processed Goods

1. A creditor with a perfected security interest in raw materials or component parts generally has a security interest in the finished product as well.
2. Secured parties with conflicting interests in the finished products must share in proportion to the costs of the materials used in manufacturing the finished products.

Secured Party versus Lien Creditors

General Rule

1. Whichever party, the secured party or the lien creditor, who is on record first in time has priority.
2. Federal tax liens follow this general rule. A tax lien is considered to be on record when the notice of the lien is filed.

Laborer's, Artisan's, and Materialman's Liens

1. These liens may be of common law or statutory origin.
2. Article 9 provides an exception to the general priority rule because it is presumed that the repairs increase the value of the collateral.

Judgment Creditor's Lien

1. These lienholders usually are subject to the general rule stated above. A judicial lien is on record when it is levied on the debtor's property.
2. A PMSI-secured party may defeat a preexisting judgment creditor's lien if the secured party perfects within ten days after debtor receives possession of collateral and if the judicial lien is levied between the time the security interest attaches and the time it is perfected.

Bankruptcy Trustee's Lien

1. The bankruptcy trustee is considered a hypothetical lien creditor. Therefore the trustee is in the same priority position as the judgment creditor.
2. The bankruptcy trustee's lien arises on the date the bankruptcy petition is filed.

Rights and Duties on Debtor's Default

Repossession of Collateral

1. The secured party's basic right on the debtor's default is to obtain possession of the collateral.
2. The collateral may be possessed through peaceful self-help or through judicial action.

3. This judicial action may take the form of a replevin action, a suit for judgment and levy, or a suit for an order of foreclosure.
4. The secured party can include any legal provision in the security agreement providing an alternative remedy to repossession.
5. These provisions can require the debtor to assemble all collateral in one location, or the secured party may be allowed to make heavy equipment unusable and sell it from the debtor's place of business.

Rights and Duties of Secured Party in Possession

1. The secured party can recover the cost of repossession from the debtor.
2. Any increase in the collateral is additional security protecting the secured party.
3. Once the secured party has possession of the collateral, that party must decide to conduct a foreclosure sale or to keep the collateral in satisfaction of the debt, which is called strict foreclosure.
4. In general, the secured party must handle the collateral with reasonable care.

Foreclosure Sale

1. A foreclosure sale may be public or private. A public sale is open to the general public and usually is an auction.
2. A private sale is arranged by the secured party who locates one or more buyers of the collateral.
3. The secured party always must give the debtor notice of the foreclosure sale. This notice must include the time and place of a public sale. The notice need only inform the debtor of the time after which a private sale may occur.
4. If the collateral is consumer goods, notice of resale needs to be given only to the debtor. If other types of collateral are involved, notice also must be given to the other secured parties who have notified the secured party arranging the sale of their interest.
5. This type of notice is not required if the collateral is perishable, threatens to decline in value rapidly, or is sold on a recognized market.
6. In general, there is no time limit within which a foreclosure sale must occur.
7. The applicable standard is that the sale must occur within a reasonable time.
8. All aspects of a foreclosure sale must be handled in a commercially reasonable manner.
9. This standard has been and continues to be developed by case law, since the Code does not provide a definition.

Rights of Parties after Foreclosure

1. A buyer at a commercially reasonable foreclosure sale takes the property free from the security interest of the seller and all inferior security interests.
2. The proceeds of a resale of collateral will be distributed to the secured party to pay for the expenses of repossession and resale and for the debt. Any remaining proceeds will be paid to other parties secured by the same collateral. Any surplus is paid to the debtor. Any deficiency is owed by the debtor.

Strict Foreclosure

1. A secured party who proposes to keep the collateral in satisfaction of the debt must send the debtor written notice of this proposal unless the debtor has waived after default the right to such notice.
2. If the collateral is not consumer goods, written notice of strict foreclosure also must be sent to all other known interested parties.
3. If the collateral is consumer goods and 60 percent of the purchase price or loan amount has been paid, the consumer goods must be sold within ninety days of the secured party's possession of them.

4. Any debtor or interested party may object to the strict foreclosure and force a foreclosure sale. This objection must be given in writing within twenty-one days of the secured party's notice of strict foreclosure being sent.

Debtor's General Remedies

1. The debtor has a right to redeem his interest in the collateral any time prior to final action being taken by the secured party.
2. To redeem interests in default, the debtor must pay all amounts owed to the secured party.
3. If the secured party fails to comply with any Code provision, the debtor can sue for actual damages plus any applicable Code remedy.

REVIEW QUESTIONS AND PROBLEMS

1. Match each term in column A with the appropriate statement in column B.

A	B
(1) Buyer in the ordinary course of business	(a) May be of common law or statutory origin.
(2) Accession	(b) A judicial action seeking possession of personal property.
(3) Laborer's lien	(c) The reinstatement of a defaulting debtor's interest in collateral.
(4) Judicial lien	(d) A foreclosure sale involving an unreasonably low price.
(5) Self-help	(e) A party who purchases an item from a seller in the business of selling such items.
(6) Replevin	(f) A foreclosure when anyone may be the buyer.
(7) Public sale	(g) The rights of a judgment creditor who levies on the debtor's property.
(8) Sham sale	(h) A secured party's retention of collateral in satisfaction of the debt.
(9) Strict foreclosure	(i) Personal property affixed to personal property.
(10) Redemption	(j) A method of repossession that is available as long as it is peaceful.

2. Assume that the following events occur. Answer each part based on these and any additional facts given.

   The First National Bank agrees to lend $500,000 to Custom Sound Stereo and Television Company. To secure its position, the bank takes a security interest in Custom Sound's inventory, equipment, accounts, and chattel paper and in its after-acquired inventory, equipment, accounts, and chattel paper. A security agreement and financing statement is filed in the proper location to give the bank a perfected security interest.

   a. Corliss purchases a TV set for her personal use. If Custom Sound defaults on its loan payments, who has priority between the bank and Corliss? Explain.
   b. Deborah, a doctor, purchases a stereo for her office waiting room. If Custom Sound defaults on its loan payments, who has priority to the stereo between the bank and Deborah? Explain.
   c. Suppose Deborah purchased her stereo on credit. She signed a promissory note, but not a security agreement. Does the bank have any interest in this note? If so, how is this interest perfected? Explain.
   d. If Custom Sound sells Deborah's note to the Second Financial Institution three days after she signed it, who has priority to the note between the bank and the Institution? Explain.

e. Suppose Corliss purchased her TV set on credit. She signed a promissory note and a security agreement. What are all the ways that Custom Sound can perfect its interest in Corliss's TV set?
f. Assume Corliss, while still owing Custom Sound, sells the TV set to Freddie, a neighbor. Who has priority to the TV set between Custom Sound and Freddie if Corliss defaults on her payments to Custom Sound?
g. Suppose Custom Sound is in need of new computerized stereo testing equipment. It agrees to buy on credit new equipment worth $50,000 from Hi-Fi Diagnostic Corporation. This corporation wants to keep a security interest in the equipment sold to Custom Sound. What must Hi-Fi Diagnostic Corporation do to be sure of having priority to the equipment in case Custom Sound defaults?

3. Acme Glass Company sells Welch four mirrors on credit and installs the mirrors in Welch's house. The glass company retains a security interest in the mirrors and immediately fixture-files. Will the company's security interest be superior under the Code to that of (a) First Bank, which has a mortgage on the house? (b)A new owner who buys the house from Welch? Explain both answers.

4. Krueger left his car with Gomer for extensive repairs. State Bank has a perfected security interest in the car. Gomer's bill is $1,152, which Krueger cannot pay. Can Gomer sell the car to get his bill paid? Why or why not?

5. SP-1 takes a security interest in Don's inventory on February 1. Don files a bankruptcy petition on February 5. SP-1 files a financing statement on February 9 to perfect its security interest in Don's inventory. May the trustee prevail over SP-1's security interest? Would your answer change if SP-1's security interest were a PMSI? Explain.

6. To answer parts a through g of this problem, rely on the following situation: A debtor was in arrears in his auto payments. When he failed to respond to requests for payment from the secured party, the secured party sent an agent to repossess the car. Is the agent's repossession of the car peaceful in the following instances?
   a. When the agent repossesses, the car is parked in front of the debtor's house.
   b. The agent at 11:00 P.M. tows away the car from the parking lot at the apartment house complex where the debtor had an assigned space.
   c. The car is parked in the debtor's unlocked garage.
   d. The car is parked in the debtor's locked garage. The agent unlocks the garage door, removes the car, and locks the garage.
   e. The car is parked at a service station after a tuneup. The station owner permits the agent to remove the car.
   f. The car is parked on the road in front of the debtor's house. As the agent starts to enter the car, the debtor bursts from the door of his house, shouting epithets and demanding that his car not be moved. But the agent is able to start the car and drive away before the debtor can get to the car.
   g. The agent comes to the debtor's house and states that he is from the city water department and needs to check the debtor's pipe system. The agent then sneaks into the garage and drives the car away.

7. Clark Equipment lent Armstrong Equipment Company $1,800,000. This loan was secured by heavy road-building equipment used by Armstrong in a five-state area. The security agreement signed by Armstrong contained a clause that allowed Clark to "require borrower to assemble the collateral and make it available at a place to be designated which is reasonably convenient to all parties." When Armstrong defaulted, Clark asked Armstrong to assemble the equipment. This request was ignored, and Armstrong continued to conduct work through all five states. Clark sued to enjoin Armstrong's operation and to force the assembling of the collateral. Armstrong argued that the injunction remedy is not provided for by the Code. Is Clark entitled to an injunction compelling Armstrong to assemble all the collateral in one location? Explain.

8. Scott Trucking purchased several trucks and financed the transaction through Mack Financial Corporation. Scott became delinquent and returned the trucks to Mack in February 1985. These trucks remained in Mack's possession until they were sold at a public

auction on January 25, 1988. In February 1985, Scott owed Mack $127,600. In January 1988, the trucks were sold for $44,700. Is Scott Trucking liable for the deficiency? Why or why not?

9. Hansen borrowed $258,218 from the State Bank of Towner. As security for this loan, Hansen granted to State Bank interests in his cattle and farm machinery. When Hansen defaulted, the State Bank took possession of the cattle and machinery. Without ever providing any notice of sale to Hansen, the bank sold these items at an auction. The bank then sued Hansen for the deficiency between the debt and the sale's proceeds. Hansen argued that the bank's failure to give prior notice of a foreclosure sale prevents it from obtaining a deficiency judgment. Was the bank entitled to a deficiency judgment? Why or why not?

10. Carol granted a security interest in her mobile home to the bank. When Carol defaulted on her payments, the bank sent a certified letter to her at her last known address. This letter contained notice of the time when and the place where the bank would be selling Carol's mobile home. Since Carol had moved, the letter was forwarded to her new address. Twice the post office attempted to deliver this certified letter, but no one would come to the door. Notices that a certified letter was at the post office were left in Carol's mailbox. Ultimately, the letter was returned to the bank. The mobile home was sold, and a deficiency balance remains. Is the bank entitled to collect it from Carol? Why or why not?

11. A furniture manufacturer, secured by a security agreement, sold furniture to Daniel on credit. When Daniel did not pay as agreed, the creditor repossessed the furniture. This creditor approached one possible buyer for the items but failed to sell them. The creditor then bought the collateral at a private sale and sued Daniel for a deficiency of $7,000. Daniel contends that he is entitled to credit for the full value of the repossessed goods because the private sale was improper. Is Daniel correct? Why or why not?

12. McIlroy Bank lent money to Seven Day Builders (SDB) to enable SDB to lease some equipment. This equipment was used as collateral to secure the bank that repayment would be made. When SDB defaulted, the bank took possession of the equipment. Although it never notified SDB of its intentions, the bank planned to retain possession of this equipment in satisfaction of the debt. SDB argued that the bank could not keep the collateral and that the bank was liable for damages caused to SDB. Did the bank fail to follow proper procedures such that it is liable to the debtor? Explain.

13. The secured party repossessed Crosby's personal pickup truck after Crosby had paid over 60 percent of the cash price. The secured party failed to sell the truck within the ninety days required by the Code. Crosby sued for the statutory penalty under Section 9-507(1). Is Crosby entitled to collect this penalty? How is this penalty calculated?

Real Property as Security

42

CHAPTER PREVIEW

BUSINESS MANAGEMENT DECISION

You operate a building supply business, and you have supplied on credit lumber and other materials for the construction of a large apartment complex. The general contractor of this project has been one of your best customers. However, sixty days have passed since the apartment complex was completed, and you have not received a payment for the materials furnished.

What should you do to protect your chances of being paid?

The chapters on contracts and the Uniform Commercial Code deal with many aspects of the law that are of substantial consequence to creditors. We saw basic legal procedures available to creditors—their right to sue for breach of contract and to use certain collection methods to enforce judgments obtained in such suits. The secured transaction, discussed in the previous chapters, involves the use of personal property as a significant method used by creditors to ensure the collection of debts.

In this chapter and the next one, we are concerned with additional aspects of the law that protect creditors. The use of real estate as security is the topic of this chapter; we discuss real estate mortgages and mechanic's liens. The next chapter includes material on other laws assisting creditors, especially the use of a third party's commitment as assurance to the creditor that a debt will be repaid.

MORTGAGE TRANSACTIONS

1. Terminology

Mortgage *A conveyance of an interest in real property for the purpose of creating a security for a debt.*

A real estate **mortgage** is an interest in real property, an interest created for the purpose of securing the performance of an obligation, usually the payment of a debt. A mortgage is not a debt—only security for a debt. The owner of the estate in land that is being used as security for the debt is called the *mortgagor*, since that owner is granting a mortgage interest to the creditor. This party to whom the security interest in the real estate is conveyed is called the *mortgagee*.

2. Theories of Mortgages

Title theory. Three distinct legal theories relate to mortgages. The first of these, the *title theory*, was developed under common law. Originally, a mortgage on land was an absolute conveyance of the title to the land by the owner to the mortgagee. However, title reverted to the mortgagor when the obligation was performed or the money was repaid. If the mortgagor failed to repay the debt, the property remained the property of the mortgagee. Under the title theory, the mortgagee could not be forced to sell the land to satisfy the debt. The process of not having a forced sale is known as *strict foreclosure*. Furthermore, any time after default, the mortgagor lost all rights to redeem the interest in the real property. Due to the harshness of its application, the title theory has very little support today.

Lien (or equitable) theory. The second theory of mortgages is usually known as the *lien theory*, although it is sometimes called the *equitable theory*. Under this theory, a mortgage is not a conveyance of title, but only a method of creating a *lien* on the real estate. The lien or equitable theory avoids the harshness that results under the title theory. Under the lien theory, a mortgagee does not have title when the mortgagor defaults; he simply has a lien that can be foreclosed. Upon foreclosure of the lien, any proceeds of the sale are used to pay the debt and the costs of the sale. Any excess from the proceeds remains the property of the mortgagor. In addition, the lien theory grants to the mortgagor a right to redeem his property after the default and foreclosure. These rights to redeem are discussed in section 12 of this chapter.

Intermediate theory. Many states do not follow the title or the lien theory; they have reached a compromise between the two, an *intermediate theory*. Under it, a mortgage is a conveyance of title, but the equitable theories are applied to it. Mortgages must be foreclosed; and the mortgagor has the right to redeem the interest prior to the foreclosed sale. This right of redemption exists even though the mortgagee has "title."

3. Documents Involved

Remember that a mortgage is evidence of the security interest a lender is receiving; it is not evidence of the loan being made. Therefore typically there are two documents involved in the mortgage financing transaction.

The promissory note is the piece of paper that evidences the borrower's agreement to repay the amount of the loan. This note should include the principal borrowed, the interest rate charged, the term or the life of the loan, and the amount of the periodic payments.

In addition to the note, the *mortgage document* must be prepared. Since a mortgage is a contract, it must meet all the requirements of an enforceable agreement. A mortgage must be in writing and contain (1) the names of the mortgagor and mortgagee, (2) an accurate description of the mortgaged property, (3) the terms of the debt (incorporated from the note), and (4) the mortgagor's signature. This document must be executed with all the formalities of a deed.

In order that the mortgagee may give notice to third parties that he has an interest in the real estate, it is necessary that the mortgage be recorded in the recording office of the county where the real estate is situated. Recording serves to notify subsequent parties of the lien or encumbrance of the mortgage.

4. Mortgage Clauses

In addition to the essential requirements just mentioned, mortgage documents are often several pages long because they contain many optional clauses. Some of the more typical mortgage provisions include an acceleration clause, a prepayment penalty clause, and a dragnet clause. These clauses are discussed below. A mortgage also usually contains provisions on the rights and duties of the mortgagor and mortgagee. These rights and duties are discussed in the next section.

Acceleration clauses. An acceleration clause enables the mortgagee to declare the entire outstanding balance of the loan immediately due and payable if stated conditions occur. For example, a *due-on-default clause* allows the mortgagee at his option to demand full payment if the mortgagor has failed to make a payment or a series of payments within a stated time period. A default may also occur whenever the mortgagor fails to comply with any other provision of the mortgage.

A *due-on-encumbrance clause* allows the mortgagee to accelerate the debt owed any time the mortgagor encumbers the real property without the mortgagee's consent. Examples of encumbering the property might include creating an easement in favor of a third party, agreeing to the application of restrictive covenants on the use of the land, failing to pay for work done to improve the property, or failing to pay taxes as they become due. The occurrence of any of these events entitles the mortgagee to demand full payment in order to protect the security interest the mortgagee already has.

The most controversial acceleration clause has been the *due-on-sale clause*. This type of clause permits the mortgagee to call the loan due whenever the mortgagor sells the collateral. The purpose of this clause originally was to protect the mortgage from purchasers with a questionable ability to repay the loan. In other words, with the due-on-sale acceleration clause, the mortgagee could prevent the assumption of the mortgage-secured loan by a buyer who was not creditworthy. Many states required proof of **impairment of the security** as a condition to enforcement of the clause.

Impairment of security *A decrease in the value of the collateral from which the debt may be collected.*

During periods of rapidly increasing interest rates, the due-on-sale clause has been utilized by mortgagees to adjust their below-market interest rates to a higher level without proof of impairment of the security. This clause has been used to prevent assumptions without an upward adjustment of the interest rate being charged. During the late 1970s and early 1980s, many states passed laws limiting the use of due-on-sale clauses as a means of adjusting the mortgagee's portfolio regarding interest rates. In addition, the courts in several states held due-on-sale clauses to be illegal as against public policy because they prevented the easy transfer of property.

In 1982, the United States Supreme Court upheld an administrative rule that federally chartered institutions are exempt from state laws and regulations limiting the enforceability of due-on-sale clauses, regardless of the mortgagee's purpose. The Court held that the federal rule preempted state laws. Congress subsequently by statute allowed states meeting certain requirements to postpone federal preemption until October 15, 1985. Since this decision, some states have decided that state-chartered financial institutions should be allowed to enforce due-on-sale clauses regardless of the circumstances. This trend has been necessary to keep state and federally created institutions on an equal competitive level. Other states have held such clauses valid in commercial loans but invalid when applied to homeowners. Thus the legality of these clauses depends on the lender and its location.

The right of acceleration may be waived if it is not exercised within a reasonable time. In the following case, note that the decision is made in a court of equity and, as a result, prompt action to accelerate is essential.

CASE

In September 1980, the Rakestraws sold property to Dozier Associates, Inc., and financed the purchase by accepting a mortgage containing a standard due-on-sale clause. By deed recorded in January 1981, Dozier Associates transferred the property without the mortgagee's prior written consent to respondents William and Nancy Dozier, the owners of the Dozier Corporation. The mortgagee admitted receiving an insurance endorsement reflecting the change of ownership and accepting timely mortgage payments from the Doziers individually for seventeen months before calling in the loan in the spring of 1982 for violation of the due-on-sale clause. The Doziers objected to the loan amount being accelerated since their payments had been accepted for seventeen months.

ISSUE: Must a due-on-sale acceleration clause be exercised, if at all, within a reasonable time after the unauthorized sale occurs?

DECISION: Yes.

REASONS:

1. Since an action to foreclose a mortgage is in equity, the election to accelerate must be made within a reasonable time or the equitable defenses of laches, waiver, and estoppel may be raised against the mortgagee.
2. We hold the election of the holder to declare the acceleration of the due date of the entire debt represented by a mortgage note containing a due-on-sale clause must be exercised within a reasonable time after notice of default.
3. The Rakestraws waived the right to accelerate by accepting payments for seventeen months and are now estopped from asserting it.

Rakestraw v. Dozier Associates, Inc., 329 S.E.2d 437 (S.C. 1985).

Prepayment penalty clause. A mortgagor has the right without penalty to pay the loan off earlier than the agreed time unless the mortgage or note includes a prepayment penalty clause. This clause is used to protect the mortgagee when interest rates are falling. The prepayment penalty clause usually is limited to the situation where the mortgagor borrows funds at a lower rate in order to pay off the original loan. This clause is not applicable when the mortgagor prepays the loan due to the sale of the mortgaged property. This use would likely be prohibited as a restraint on the transferability of property.

If a mortgage contains both a due-on-sale and a prepayment penalty clause, the mortgagee probably is taking unfair advantage of the mortgagor—especially if the mortgagor is a consumer borrower. Most courts probably would refuse to allow the combined effect of these clauses. These clauses could be declared unenforceable as being unconscionable or contrary to public policy.

Dragnet clause. A mortgage may be created prior to the time when money is advanced to the mortgagor. Such a mortgage is called a *mortgage to secure future advances*. The clause in a mortgage that makes the security interest cover future advances is referred to as a *dragnet clause*. This clause gives the mortgagee a valid interest in the real property described in the mortgage as of the date the mortgage is recorded to the extent of the amount stated in the mortgage.

For example, assume Rick E. Olsen, an owner of real estate, signs a mortgage containing a dragnet clause naming First Federal Savings and Loan as the mortgagee. This mortgage secures a loan First Federal makes to Rick in the amount of $50,000 and is recorded on September 2, 1987. Suppose Second National Bank then lends Rick $20,000 and receives a mortgage describing the same land as that described in the mortgage protecting First Federal. Second National's mortgage is recorded on April 10, 1988. Further assume that as of today's date, Rick has paid off half of the loan he owes First Federal ($25,000 of the $50,000), and it lends him another $15,000 without taking any new security. If Rick defaults the next day and if his land is sold for $45,000, who gets what of the proceeds? *Answer*: First Federal would get the full $40,000 Rick owes it, and Second National would get the remaining $5,000 of the proceeds. Second National would then be unsecured with respect to the remainder of what Rick owed it. The lesson of this example is to beware of dragnet clauses unless they are protecting you.

5. Rights and Duties of the Parties

Payment of the mortgage debt terminates the mortgage. Upon payment, the mortgagor is entitled to a release or satisfaction of the mortgage. This release should be recorded in order to clear the title to the land; otherwise, the unreleased mortgage will remain a **cloud on the title.** If the mortgagee refuses to give a release, he can be compelled to do so in a court of equity.

Cloud the title *A defect, encumbrance, or other interest that exists in the record title to land.*

The mortgagor is entitled to retain possession of the real estate during the period of the mortgage unless a different arrangement is provided for in the mortgage. The mortgagor may not use the property in a manner that will materially reduce its value. Mining ore, pumping oil, or cutting timber are operations that cannot be conducted by the mortgagor during the period of the mortgage unless the right to do so is reserved in the mortgage agreement. The rights will be implied when they are being conducted at the time the mortgage is created.

Any parcel of real estate may be subject to more than one mortgage. In addition, mortgaged land may be subject to a lien for property taxes. A mortgagee has a right to pay off any superior mortgage in order to protect his security, and he can charge the amount so paid to the mortgagor. Likewise, he may pay taxes or special assessments that are a lien on the land and recover the sum expended. The mortgagor is under a duty to protect the security; but should he fail to do so, the mortgagee has the right to make any reasonable expenditures necessary to protect the security for a debt.

The rights and duties of the parties may change when the mortgaged property is transferred. This situation, involving the transfer of the mortgage itself, is discussed in the next section.

6. Transfer of Mortgaged Property

The mortgagor may sell, will, or give away the mortgaged property, subject, however, to the rights of the mortgagee. A transferee from a mortgagor has no greater rights than the mortgagor. For example, a grantee of the mortgagor's interest may redeem the land by paying off the debt. A grantee of mortgaged property is not personally liable for the mortgage debt unless he impliedly or expressly assumes and agrees to pay the mortgage. An assumption of a debt secured by a mortgage must be established by clear and convincing evidence. A purchase "subject to" a mortgage is usually considered not to be a legally enforceable assumption. If the grantee assumes the mortgage, he becomes personally liable for the debt, even when the land is worth less than the mortgage.

To illustrate, assume that Berg purchases real estate worth $88,000, which is subject to a mortgage of $60,000. Berg pays the former owner $28,000 cash. If she assumes and agrees to pay the mortgage, she is personally liable for the $60,000 debt. If the property is sold at a foreclosure sale, Berg is liable for any deficiency. However, if she merely purchased the property "subject to" the mortgage when she paid the $28,000, Berg would have no liability for any deficiency on foreclosure.

If the grantee of the mortgaged property assumes and agrees to pay the indebtedness, he thereby becomes the person primarily liable for the debt. Between the grantee and the mortgagor, by virtue of his promise to the mortgagor to pay the debt, he is the principal debtor, and the mortgagor is a surety. This assumption by the grantee does not relieve the mortgagor of his obligation to the mortgagee, and the mortgagor continues to be liable unless he is released from his indebtedness by the mortgagee. Such a release must comply with all the requirements for a novation.

7. Alternatives to the Mortgage

Now that some of the basic principles of a mortgage have been discussed, at least three alternatives to the mortgage should be considered.

Deed of trust *An instrument by which title to real property is conveyed to a trustee to hold as security for the holder of notes.*

Deed of trust. A document known as a **deed of trust** or *trust deed* may be used as a substitute for a mortgage for the purpose of securing debts. Through this document, title to the real property is conveyed to a third party, who is the trustee, to be held for the benefit of the creditor. Whereas a mortgage involves two parties—the mortgagor (debtor) and the mortgagee (creditor)—the deed of trust involves three parties—the trustor (debtor), the trustee, and the beneficiary (creditor).

The trustee's title does not affect the debtor's use of the land as long as the loan is being repaid. If the debt is fully paid at the time required by the contract, the trustee reconveys the title to the debtor and releases the lien thereon. If there is a default, the trustee sells the property and applies the proceeds to the payment of the secured loan. Under this power of sale, the trustee transfers to the new purchaser all right, title, and interest that the debtor had at the time the deed trust was executed.

Deeds of trust are used instead of mortgages when the note is likely to be negotiated and when numerous notes are secured by the same property. The nature of the deed of trust is that the note secured by it can be freely transferred, separate and apart from the deed of trust. When the debtor pays the note, he surrenders it to the trustee under the trust deed, and the latter makes it a matter of record that the obligation has been satisfied.

Deed absolute on its face. A second alternative concerns a deed absolute on its face (one that purports to be only a deed with no qualifications) that may be shown by parol evidence to be a mortgage. If such evidence indicates that the intention of the parties was to make the transfer as security for a loan, the deed will be construed as a mortgage. The grantor of the deed must prove by clear, precise, and positive evidence that it was the intention of the parties to use the deed for the purpose of securing a loan. The burden is often difficult to sustain, as the plaintiff learned in the following case.

CASE

Frank, Louis, and Robert Stava were brothers and beneficiaries of the estate of Cecilia Stava. In an attempt to settle their respective claims, the brothers agreed that Frank receive the trailer court property. To gain full use of this land, Frank granted a mortgage describing this land to Louis and Robert. This transaction was necessary to protect the interests of Louis and Robert pending the final distribution of the estate. When Frank failed to pay his brothers, they sought to foreclose their mortgage. Prior to the foreclosure sale occurring, Frank deeded the trailer court property to his brothers. When they attempted to remove Frank from the property, Frank filed this suit, arguing that the deed should be interpreted as an equitable mortgage.

ISSUE: Was the warranty deed transferred from Frank to Louis and Robert an absolute conveyance or an equitable mortgage?

DECISION: An absolute conveyance.

REASONS:
1. It is clear that in order to prove an agreement to treat a deed as a mortgage, it must be shown that such was the intention of all parties to the deed.
2. Plaintiff, having alleged the deed is such a mortgage, has the burden of proving the same, and must do so by clear and convincing evidence. One of the principal tests is whether the relation of the parties to each other as debtor and creditor continues after the conveyance is made. If it does, then the transaction will be considered a mortgage, otherwise, not. The intention of the parties may be evidenced not only by the documents in question but by the declarations and conduct of the parties.
3. It is clear the delivery of the deed by plaintiff to defendants was considered by the latter to pay the debt and satisfy the foreclosure action they brought.
4. All of defendants' actions are consistent with the deed's being given to satisfy the debt and their conduct in asserting their rights as the owners of the property. We find nothing in the record to show that defendants ever regarded plaintiff as their debtor after the deed was delivered.

Stava v. Stava, 383 N.W.2d 765 (Neb. 1986).

8. A Third Alternative: Contract for a Deed

The third alternative to a mortgage occurs when the seller of real estate finances the transaction through a *contract for a deed* rather than with the use of a formal mortgage. It is actually a conditional sale of real estate in which the seller retains title to the land and the buyer makes payments for an extended period of time. In essence, the seller finances the sales transaction. A contract for a deed providing for payments over five, ten, or twenty years is not unusual. The buyer's right to a deed to the property is conditioned on all payments being made. The seller is protected against nonpayment, since he retains legal ownership of the property until all payments are made.

Sometimes this type of sales agreement is known as an *installment land contract*. Regardless of its name, this contract contains many of the usual provisions found in the traditional sales contract. In addition, the purchaser has the risk of loss if improvements are destroyed during the period of the contract, unless there is an agreement or state statute to the contrary. The escrow provision is essential in contracts for a deed because several years usually intervene between execution of the contract and delivery of the deed. The buyer usually makes payments to the escrow agent, who must at all times be aware of the status of the contract.

Two additional clauses in most installment land contracts are of particular significance. One of them is known as the acceleration clause; the other is known as the forfeiture clause. The *acceleration clause* allows the seller to declare the full amount of the contract due and payable in the event the buyer fails to make any of the payments or fails to perform any other of the contract's provisions as agreed. The *default* or *forfeiture clause* allows the seller, when the buyer is in default, to terminate the contract and to get the deed back from the escrow agent. The net effect of this clause is to allow the seller to keep all payments and improvements made as liquidated damages for breach of contract and to regain possession of the premises even if leased to a third party.

After a buyer has made substantial payments or has a substantial equity in the land, forfeiture of a contract for a deed might be inequitable. The principles discussed in Chapter 8 that apply to liquidated damages and forfeitures are also applicable to these contracts because courts of equity abhor forfeitures. When the buyer's equity is substantial and forfeiture would be inequitable, a court, upon proper application, may prohibit the forfeiture. The court orders the property to be sold and the proceeds distributed to the seller, to the extent necessary to pay off the contract. The balance is paid to the buyer. No general rule can be stated to describe cases in which a forfeiture will be allowed or not. As a part of its equitable jurisdiction, the court will examine all the facts. If the buyer has paid only a small amount, forfeiture usually will be permitted. If the buyer has made only a slight default with regard to the amount and time of payment, or the amount of the unpaid purchase price is much less than the value of the property involved, forfeiture will be denied. Forfeiture clauses are easily waived, but usually a buyer must be notified if the clause is to be reinstated after he has defaulted without having been required to forfeit.

MORTGAGE FORECLOSURE

9. Introduction

The issue of how the mortgage really protects the mortgagee is based on the assumption that the mortgagor has defaulted or will default prior to the loan being paid fully. If no default occurs, the mortgagee will recover that which it wants—repayment of the loan. However, upon a default, the real property described in the mortgage can be used as leverage to encourage the mortgagor to pay what is owed. If payment still is not forthcoming, **foreclosure** becomes the valuable, albeit last, means of collection. In the following sections, you will read about the methods of foreclosure, the priority of claims to the proceeds, the mortgagor's rights to redeem his interest in the real property, and the mortgagee's rights to seek a deficiency.

Foreclosure *The forced sale of property, which is used as security, to satisfy the obligation of a defaulting debtor.*

10. Types of Foreclosures

The statutes of the various states specify the procedure by which mortgages are foreclosed. The common types of foreclosure proceedings are strict foreclosure, foreclosure by judicial action, and foreclosure by exercise of the power of sale.

Strict foreclosure. Strict foreclosure gives the mortgagee clear title to the land. A decree of strict foreclosure provides that if the debt is not paid by a certain date, the mortgagor loses the described real estate and the mortgagee takes it free from the rights of junior mortgagees and lienholders. It is used only where it is clear that the mortgaged property is not worth the mortgage indebtedness, the mortgagor is insolvent, and the mortgagee accepts the property in full satisfaction of the indebtedness. The substitution of the property for the debt has a historical basis in the United States in those states that followed the absolute title theory. Since the title theory has very little impact today, strict foreclosure seldom arises by operation of law.

Today the mortgagor may agree to transfer title to the mortgagee in satisfaction of a debt by use of a *deed in lieu of foreclosure*. Obtaining title by this deed is not synonymous with the strict foreclosure process. Unlike foreclosure, a deed in lieu of foreclosure does not extinguish all the junior liens that may be on the property. Therefore the mortgagee who accepts a deed in lieu of foreclosure may become involved in legal disputes with other creditors. These disputes usually involve the issue of whether the mortgagee took advantage of a defaulting mortgagor and thereby received property of more value than the debt satisfied.

Foreclosure by judicial action. The usual method of foreclosing a mortgage is a proceeding in a court of equity. If the mortgagor is in default, the court will authorize the sale of all the land at public auction. Following the sale, the purchaser receives a deed to the land. The funds received from the sale are used to pay court costs, the mortgage indebtedness, and inferior liens in the order of their priority. If any surplus remains, it is paid to the former owner of the property.

Statutes in many states provide a period of time after the sale within which the mortgagor or other persons having an interest are entitled to redeem the property. Where such statutes are in force, the purchaser is not entitled to a deed until after the expiration of the period within which redemption may be made. If the mortgagor remains in possession of the property sold, the purchaser may request that the court appoint a receiver and order the mortgagor to pay rent during the redemption period. The purchaser is entitled to the net rent during this period.

Foreclosure by power of sale. Particularly in states following the intermediate theory of mortgages, the mortgage often provides that, upon default by the mortgagor, the mortgagee may sell the real property without resorting to judicial action. This method of foreclosure can be made only in strict conformity with the mortgage's provisions. Such provisions usually require the mortgagee to advertise several times in the local newspaper the time and location of the public auction.

This type of power of sale makes the mortgagee the agent of the mortgagor for the purpose of selling the property. The power of sale creates in the mortgagee's favor an agency coupled with an interest, which means that the mortgagee's appointment as the mortgagor's agent is irrevocable. Therefore the mortgagor's death, insanity, bankruptcy, or withdrawal of consent does not destroy the validity of the power of sale. This type of agency and its termination are discussed in more detail in Chapter 24.

As the mortgagor's agent, the mortgagee cannot purchase the property at the sale unless there is an explicit grant of such authority. Whoever the purchaser is at a foreclosure pursuant to a power of sale receives only the title the mortgagor had when he made the mortgage. In some states, a power of sale is expressly forbidden from appearing in a mortgage. In these jurisdictions, foreclosures can occur only after a judicial hearing.

11. Priority to Proceeds

A mortgage that holds senior priority on a property and that will be paid first in the event of default and foreclosure is known as a *first mortgage*. The amount of money that can be raised through a first mortgage is often less than the borrower needs to complete a purchase. In such cases *junior mortgages*—that is, second, third, and fourth mortgages, which are subordinate to the first mortgage—are sometimes used. Such mortgages carry more risk than first mortgages and usually are issued for shorter periods of time and at higher interest rates.

The priority given to various mortgages on the same real estate normally is determined by which mortgagee is the first to record the mortgage document with the public records. However, order of recording does not always determine priority. One mortgagee whose mortgage is already on record may agree to subordinate its priority to another mortgagee. For example, a mortgagee that holds a security interest on a vacant land probably would agree to let a second mortgagee who has lent funds for a construction project have priority if the construction of an improvement will increase the land's value by more than the amount of the additional mortgage.

Junior mortgages also are commonly used to help in the financing of the sale of an existing home or income properties. For example, a homeowner may be able to get a higher price for his house if the purchaser can assume an existing mortgage at an interest rate lower than those currently charged by banks. The required down payment may be larger than the buyer can pay, however, and the seller may be willing to take a second mortgage for part of the purchase price. Furthermore, second mortgages commonly are used for home-improvement loans. A family that wants to add a room or make extensive repairs to its home can usually get the money to do so at a lower rate through a junior mortgage than by taking out a personal installment loan.

Foreclosure of an inferior mortgage is made subject to all superior liens. In other words, the foreclosure of a second mortgage does not affect a first mortgage. The buyer at the foreclosure sale takes title, and the first mortgage remains a lien on the property. A foreclosure does cut off the enforceability of all inferior liens. For instance, the foreclosure of a first mortgage eliminates the rights of the second and subsequent mortgages.

12. Mortgagor's Rights of Redemption

Equitable. A mortgagor who is in default on a note secured by a mortgage can terminate the foreclosure process prior to its completion by exercising a right called the **equity of redemption.** Upon the mortgagor's payment of an amount equal to the debt then owing plus interest and any expenses incurred by the mortgagee, the mortgagor's interest in the property is restored. In other words, the debt and the mortgage will be reinstated if the mortgagor redeems his interest by making payment prior to the foreclosure sale.

Equity of redemption *The right a mortgagor has before final foreclosure to redeem or get back his property after it has been forfeited for nonpayment of the debt it secured.*

Any person who acquires the mortgagor's interest while a default situation exists also acquires the right to redeem the property interest equitably prior to foreclosure. Because the mortgagee may have the right to accelerate the amount owed upon default, the entire debt may have to be paid in order to redeem the interest. Normally the mere payment of the amount in the default is not sufficient if the debt has been accelerated properly, as was the situation in the following case.

CASE

Bay Side, Inc., borrowed money from the MFS Service Corporation and secured the loan by signing a mortgage that contained a due-on-default acceleration clause. When Bay Side failed to make a loan payment, MFS declared the entire amount due and payable. MFS also began foreclosure proceedings to sell the real estate described in the mortgage. Bay Side sought to terminate the foreclosure proceedings by paying MFS the amount of the original default plus expenses. When MFS refused to withdraw the foreclosure action, Bay Side appealed.

ISSUE: After a mortgage-secured debt has been accelerated due to the debtor's default, can the equity of redemption be exercised by a partial payment?

DECISION: No.

REASONS: 1. The parties are governed by any legal agreement into which they enter. The right to accelerate a debt in default is lawful.

2. Partial payment made after acceleration of the entire debt is not sufficient to cure the default and thus redeem interest and terminate the foreclosure process.

Bay Side, Inc. v. MFS Service Corp., 407A.2d 206 (Del. 1979).

Statutory. In many states (including Alabama, Arizona, California, Colorado, Connecticut, Hawaii, Idaho, Illinois, Indiana, Iowa, Kansas, Kentucky, Maine, Michigan, Minnesota, Missouri, Montana, Nevada, New Jersey, North Dakota, Oregon, South Dakota, Utah, and Washington), the mortgagor is allowed to redeem his property even after foreclosure. This right to redeem property after a foreclosure sale is called the *statutory right of redemption*. The statutory redemption period varies from state to state, being as short as six months and as long as two years. In some states, the period is shortened if the mortgagee waives any right to a deficiency. The most common statutory period is one year. In states that have this statutory right of redemption, the purchaser at a foreclosure sale does not obtain full and clear title until the statutory period of redemption has passed.

13. Mortgagee's Rights to Deficiency Judgments

A person who executes the note or bond secured by the mortgage is personally liable for the debt. If the property that is the security for the debt does not sell for a sum sufficient to pay the indebtedness, the mortgagor remains liable for the deficiency, and a *deficiency judgment* may be entered for this unpaid balance. This judgment may be collected from the mortgagor's other property or income. In other words, additional assets of the mortgagor may be seized and sold by an officer of the court to satisfy the mortgagee's claim of deficiency.

Property that is sold at a foreclosure sale seldom brings a price that reflects the market value of the property under normal circumstances. During the Great Depression of the 1930s, prices at foreclosure sales fell to extremely low levels, often leaving debtors with large deficiency judgments against them even after they had lost their mortgaged property. As might be expected, a great deal of antideficiency legislation was passed during that period. To recover the full amount of a deficiency, the mortgagee must be able to prove the foreclosure sale was conducted according to commercially reasonable standards. Indeed, the mortgagee should have the foreclosure price approved by the appropriate court prior to or concurrent with the filing of a motion for a deficiency judgment. In the alternative, the mortgagee may waive the right to collect the amount of a deficiency. The following case discusses the extent to which a mortgagee is entitled to collect a deficiency on foreclosure.

CASE

On February 9, 1970, Richard Hammer borrowed $7,000 from the Danvers Savings Bank and executed a promissory note in favor of the bank. The note was secured by land in Boxford, Massachusetts. After the defendant defaulted, the bank foreclosed on his property. No potential buyers attended the foreclosure sale except bank representatives. They purchased the defendant's real estate for $100, and later resold it for $2,025. The bank sought a $10,040.02 deficiency judgment against Hammer, consisting of the sum of the $7,000 principal due under the note, $1,523.55 in accrued interest, $1,237.88 in taxes, $709.50 for legal notices of the foreclosure sale, $150 for an auctioneer, and $1,444.09 for legal fees and expenses, less a credit of $2,025, the resale price. Hammer argued that the price paid for his land was so inadequate that the sale should be invalidated. The trial court granted the bank's motion for summary judgment in the amount of $10,040.02. Hammer appealed.

ISSUE: Was the grant of summary judgment proper in light of the price paid at foreclosure?

DECISION: No.

REASONS:

1. When a mortgagee seeks to uphold a foreclosure sale in order to bring a deficiency action against the mortgagor, courts scrutinize the sale price very closely to ensure that the mortgagee acted with strict impartiality. We will review this sale with particular caution because the bank purchased the mortgaged property at its own foreclosure sale.
2. Generally, an inadequate price will not invalidate a sale or entitle the debtor to damages. A grossly disproportionate price, however, indicates that the sale was improperly conducted, entitling the debtor to relief.
3. The price paid by the bank was so grossly disproportionate to Hammer's debt and the value of the property as to indicate bad faith or lack of reasonable diligence.
4. Because title to the property has passed to bona fide purchasers, we will not set aside the foreclosure sale. We therefore remand for a reassessment of damages. The trial court must first determine the fair market of the real estate at the time of foreclosure. The damages should consist of the difference between that market value and the defendant's outstanding debt plus costs.

Danvers Savings Bank v. Hammer, 440 A.2d 435 (N.H. 1982).

In order not to impose too great a hardship on mortgagors, different schemes have been devised to limit the amount of these parties' liability for deficiencies. Some states, including Nebraska, New Jersey, and Oregon, have simply outlawed all deficiency judgments. Many other states have antideficiency statutes that are applicable only to purchase-money mortgages. When a mortgage is given to secure payment of the balance of the purchase price of real property, the mortgagee is not entitled to a deficiency judgment. In these states, if the mortgage proceeds are not used to finance the purchase of the real property, deficiency judgments are allowed. The elimination of liability for deficiencies rests on several theories: that the mortgagee lent his money on the security of the real estate and not the personal credit of the purchaser; that a mortgagee should share with the mortgagor the risk of declining real estate values; and that if the real estate is the limit of the security, sounder loans and fewer inflationary ones will be made.

MECHANIC'S LIENS

14. Introduction

Mechanic's lien *A lien for the value of material and labor expended in the construction of buildings and other improvements.*

Mechanic's lien laws provide for the filing of liens upon real estate that has been improved. An improvement is any addition to the land. While the term *improvement* does not always mean that the land's value has been increased, most improvements usually do increase the real estate's value. The purpose of a mechanic's lien is to protect contractors, laborers, and materialmen in the event of nonpayment of their accounts. Because state laws vary slightly in the protection accorded and the procedure required to obtain these liens, the laws of the state in which the property is located should be consulted.

To gain an understanding of how mechanic's liens generally are used to secure payment for one who contributed to an improvement, the following sections discuss potential lienholders, the perfection and enforcement of liens, priority issues, and protection against liens.

15. Potential Lienholders

The persons usually entitled to a lien include those who (1) deliver material, fixtures, apparatus, machinery, or forms to be used in repairing, altering, or constructing a building upon the premises; (2) fill, sod, or do landscape work in connection with the premises; (3) act as architect, engineer, or superintendent during the construction of a building; or (4) furnish labor for repairing, altering, or constructing a building.

Persons who contract with the owner, whether they furnish labor or material or agree to construct the building, are known as *contractors*. Thus virtually any contract between the owner and another that has for its purpose the improvement of real estate gives rise to a lien on the premises in favor of those responsible for the improvement. Improvements include fixtures.

In addition to contractors, anyone who furnishes labor, materials, or apparatus to contractors or anyone to whom a distinct part of the contract has been sublet, has a right to a lien. These latter parties are customarily referred to as *subcontractors*. Their rights differ slightly from those of contractors, and some of these differences are considered in later sections.

Prior to studying the nature of a mechanic's lien, you must understand that not every act related to real estate is an improvement and leads to a lien. The statutes creating mechanic's liens are crucial in determining who is protected by these liens.

16. Perfection and Enforcement

In some states, a contractor has a lien as soon as the contract to repair or to improve the real estate is entered into. In others, the lien attaches as soon as the work is commenced. A supplier of materials usually has a lien as soon as the materials are furnished. A laborer has a lien when the work is performed. The statutes relating to mechanic's liens provide for the method of perfecting these mechanic's liens and for the time period during which they may be perfected. The time period begins when the work is substantially completed. Minor corrections to the work or trivial work done after substantial completion does not extend the period.

The usual procedure is that the party seeking to perfect a mechanic's lien files or records a notice of lien in the office of the county in which deeds to real estate are recorded. Some statutes provide for filing in the county of residence of the owner. A copy of the notice is sent to the owner of record and to the party contracting for the repair or improvement. This notice must be filed within the prescribed statutory period. The law then requires a suit to foreclose the lien and specifies that it be commenced within an additionally prescribed period such as one year. Anything less than strict observance of the filing requirements eliminates the mechanic's lien, but not the debt. The following case illustrates the importance of an accurate legal description in the notice.

CASE

William A. Mead was a trustee for a trust that owned adjacent parcels of real property in Maricopa County. Smith Pipe & Steel Company sold and furnished construction materials to Flood Plumbing Company, a licensed plumbing subcontractor, for use in the construction of structures and improvements on the *south* parcel of the adjacent lots. Flood completed the work but subsequently went bankrupt and failed to pay Smith for the materials. Smith then recorded a Notice and Claim of Lien. The Notice and Claim of Lien, however, gave the legal description of the *north* parcel instead of the south parcel upon which the improvements were made. After Smith filed a complaint to foreclose the lien, Mead moved for summary judgment, arguing that the erroneous description rendered the lien invalid. The trial court agreed and granted Mead's motion. Smith appealed.

ISSUE: May a lien claimant perfect its lien when the Notice and Claim of Lien contain erroneous legal descriptions of the land involved?

DECISION: No.

REASONS:
1. With regard to the content of the lien, in 1973, the legislature amended Section 33-993 to provide that the notice and claim of lien contain "[t]he *legal description* of the lands and improvements to be charged with a lien."
2. The inexact provision under former Section 33-993(1), "[a] description . . . sufficient for identification" did not give any indication

whether a legal description, street address, or physical description of the land or improvements would suffice.

3. The amended version, however, removed this obvious ambiguity by requiring a legal description to be used when describing the property to be charged with the lien. Significantly, the legislature not only added the legal description requirement, but at the same time omitted the "sufficient for identification" language from the old statute.
4. We believe this reflects a legislative intent that substantial compliance with the legal description requirement is necessary in order to perfect a lien.

Smith Pipe & Steel Company v. Mead, 634 P.2d 962 (Ariz. 1981).

Most mechanic's lien laws provide a relatively long period, such as one year, during which a contractor may file a mechanic's lien and proceed to enforce it against the property interest of the party with whom he contracted. This time period is relatively long because the obligation is known to the owner, and he is in no way prejudiced if the lien is not promptly filed.

A much shorter time period is set for subcontractors, laborers, and materialmen to file a mechanic's lien. The owner of the premises may not know the source of materials and may not know the names of all persons performing services on the premises. To this extent, the liens of subcontractors, materialmen, and workers may be secret, and the owner may pay the wrong person. Therefore the time period in which the statutory procedures must be followed is relatively short, such as sixty to ninety days.

If the property is sold or mortgaged, the existence of any mechanic's lien often would be unknown to the purchaser or mortgagee. For this reason the statutes on mechanic's liens usually specify the same short period of time for the perfection of the mechanic's lien—whether by a contractor, subcontractor, materialmen, or laborer—if it is to be effective against good-faith purchasers of the property or subsequent mortgagees. Under these statutory provisions, a mechanic's lien that could be enforced against the property interest of the original contracting owner cannot be enforced against the property interest of the new owner or mortgagee after the expiration of the prescribed statutory period. Thus, during the relatively short statutory period, a mechanic's lien is good against innocent third parties even though it has not been properly perfected. Consequently, a purchaser of real estate should always ascertain if any repairs or improvements have been made to the premises within the time period for filing mechanic's liens. If it is determined that repairs or improvements have been made, the procedures outlined in the next section should be followed.

If a contractor, subcontractor, supplier of material, or laborer fails to file his notice of lien within the appropriate prescribed time period or fails to commence suit within the additional period, the lien is lost.

Since a person entitled to a mechanic's lien has a prescribed period within which to file his lien, the date on which this time period starts to run is frequently quite important. Most statutes provide that in the case of a supplier, the time period starts to run from the date the materials are delivered; and in the case of a contractor or subcontractor performing services, the time for filing starts to run from the completion of the work. This latter concept requires further clarification, however.

Should a contractor or subcontractor be able to postpone the time for filing by performing additional services at a later date? Assume that a contractor has allowed the time for filing his lien to elapse. Should the time period start all over if he makes a minor repair, such as adjusting a doorknob or touching up a paint job? Common sense would say no, and most statutes provide that a contractor or subcontractor cannot extend the statutory period of time by performing minor, trifling repairs after the work has been substantially completed. In other words, trivial work done or materials furnished after the contract has been substantially completed will not extend the time in which a lien claim can be filed.

17. Priorities

Two basic situations create issues of priorities concerning mechanic's liens. The first concerns priority among similar mechanic's liens. The second situation involves the priority of a mechanic's lienholder compared with the rights of a mortgagee to the proceeds from the forced sale of the real estate.

Among mechanic's lienholders. If there are several mechanic's liens filed as the result of the same improvement project, the liens are entitled to priority on the basis of when the lienholder began work on the project. If several liens are considered equal in priority and there are insufficient funds to satisfy all these claims, the lienholders must share the proceeds on a pro-rata basis. Each lienholder is entitled to that portion of the proceeds which his work represented of the entire improvement.

Between mechanic's lienholder and mortgagee. When determining the priority of a mechanic's lien and a mortgage on the same property, the date of attachment is crucial. Nearly all states provide that a mortgage attaches when it is properly recorded. If the state where the land is located is one of the few providing that a mechanic's lien attaches when a notice of lien is filed, then priority is given to the creditor who is first to file.

The majority of states' laws on mechanic's liens say that these liens attach when work first begins or when supplies are first delivered. In these states a mortgage may be filed before a notice of lien is filed, and yet the lien has priority. A mortgagee must therefore make sure there are no potential mechanic's liens or obtain an agreement from contractors, laborers, and suppliers that their liens are subordinated to the mortgage. Without these actions, a mortgagee may lose all or at least part of the foreclosure proceeds to a mechanic's lienholder.

Still other states give priority to mechanic's liens over a previously recorded mortgage because the lienholder has increased the value of the real property. This added value should be evident in the greater proceeds obtained at the foreclosure sale. After the lienholder is paid, the mortgagee still has the remaining proceeds, which should be the same as if no improvement had been made. This priority given to the mechanic's lien may not apply if the items added to the real estate become inseparable from the entire improvement.

Some states by statute give priority to a construction mortgage over mechanic's liens. This preference is given because all the parties intend that the contractors and suppliers will be paid out of the proceeds of the construction loan. As the following case illustrates, this priority is usually limited to the amounts that the construction mortgagee is obligated to advance. If the funds do not have to be advanced by the mortgagee, an unpaid perfected mechanic's lien will have priority over the prior mortgage.

CASE

On April 27, 1984, the First American Federal Savings Bank loaned Pat H. McGowan and his wife, Charlotte C. McGowan, the sum of $105,200 for the purchase of a lot and the construction of a house. A mortgage and promissory note were executed in conjunction with the loan. On the same date, $30,150 of the loan proceeds was applied as payment for the lot. The balance of the loan proceeds was placed in a trust fund that was to be used for the purpose of the construction. The mortgage contained a typed-in provision which stated:

> That the purpose of this loan is to pay $30,150 on the purchase price of said property and the lender is unequivocally obligated and committed to advance the balance to the borrower for the purpose of erecting improvements on the mortgaged property, and lender's lien shall extend to, and include, all improvements erected upon said property and be prior to any lien for labor or material furnished to such improvements. . . .

The mortgage was recorded on April 27, 1984, and construction commenced on May 2, 1984. During the construction, Dempsey provided material. When he was not paid, Dempsey filed a mechanic's lien and sued to enforce his valid lien.

ISSUE: Does the construction mortgagee have priority over the mechanic's lienholder?

DECISION: Yes, under these circumstances.

REASONS:

1. In order to establish a construction money mortgagee's priority over materialmen's liens, the following conditions must be satisfied: (1) the mortgage must be executed and recorded before commencement of the building; (2) the mortgagee must be unequivocally bound to advance money for construction; and (3) the recorded mortgage must show the mortgagee is unequivocally bound.
2. The requirement that a lender be unequivocally bound to advance the construction money in order to have priority over other lienholders means that the construction money lender must have no discretion in advancing construction funds if the borrower satisfies the standard requirements included in their contract. A literal requirement that a lender can have absolutely no discretion or any conditions relating to future advances in a mortgage would defeat the purpose of the loan and probably bring an end to construction money loans.
3. Under the circumstances of this case we hold that the mortgagee was unequivocally obligated and committed to advance the balance of the trust fund to the borrower for the purpose of erecting improvements on the mortgaged property.

Dempsey v. McGowan, 722 S.W.2d 848 (Ark. 1987).

18. Protection against Liens

Mechanic's lien statutes usually provide that an owner is not liable for more than the contract price if he follows the procedures outlined in the law. These usually require that the owner, prior to payment, obtain from the contractor a sworn statement setting forth all the creditors and the amounts due, or to become due, to each of them. It is then the duty of the owner to retain sufficient funds at all times to pay the amounts indicated by the sworn statements. In addition, if any liens have been filed by the subcontractors, it is the owner's duty to retain sufficient money to pay them. He is at liberty to pay any balance to the contractor.

An owner has a right to rely on the truthfulness of the sworn statement of the contractor. If the contractor misstates the facts and obtains a sum greater than that to which he is entitled, the loss falls upon the subcontractors who dealt with him, rather than upon the owner. Under such circumstances, the subcontractors may look only to the contractor for payment. Payments made by the owner, without his first obtaining a sworn statement, may not be used to defeat the claims of subcontractors, materialmen, and laborers. Before making any payment, the owner has the duty to require the sworn statement and to withhold the amount necessary to pay the claims indicated.

The owner may also protect himself by obtaining waivers of the contractor's lien and of the liens of subcontractors, suppliers, and laborers. A *waiver* is the voluntary relinquishment of the right to a lien before a notice of lien is filed. In a few states, a waiver of the lien by the contractor is also a waiver of the lien of the subcontractors, as they derive their rights through those of the contractor. However, in most states, lien waivers are effective only against those who agree not to claim a mechanic's lien and who executes a waiver.

Even after a notice of lien is filed, lienholders may extinguish their right to enforce the lien. This postfiling process is known as a *release* of the lien. Very often, the concept of waivers and that of releases is confused. A waiver occurs before a notice of lien is filed, whereas a release is used after there is a public filing. A mechanic's lien commonly is released when the landowner pays the lienholder after a notice of lien has been filed.

CHAPTER SUMMARY

Mortgage Transactions

Terminology	1. A *mortgage* is the document wherein a borrower grants to a lender a security interest in the borrower's real estate. 2. A *mortgagor* is the borrower who grants the security interest in real estate to the lender. 3. A *mortgagee* is the lender who receives a security interest in real estate.
Theories of Mortgages	1. Originally, a mortgage conveyed legal title or ownership to the mortgagee. 2. Today, the law of a state usually views a mortgage as creating only a lien on the real estate or, in the alternative, a mortgagee has title that is created as a lien for security purposes.

3. These modern theories are known as the lien (or equity) theory and the intermediate theory, respectively.

Documents Involved

1. The borrower in a mortgage transaction usually signs a promissory note, which is evidence of the borrower's personal obligation to repay.
2. The borrower also signs a mortgage, which is the document that grants the lender a security interest in described real estate.

Mortgage Clauses

1. Mortgages often include acceleration clauses that allow the mortgagee to make the entire debt due and payable upon the occurrence of certain events. These clauses may be classified as due on default, due on encumbrance, and due on sale.
2. A prepayment penalty clause is often included in a mortgage. It allows the mortgagee to collect a penalty if the debt is paid off early without permission.
3. A dragnet clause allows one mortgage to serve as security for any future loan the mortgagee grants to the mortgagor.

Transfer of Mortgaged Property

1. When real estate and the mortgage describing such real estate are transferred, the question arises about whether the original mortgagor or the transferee or both are liable.
2. The transferee who takes the property "subject to" the mortgage does not become personally liable for any deficiency should there be a foreclosure sale.
3. The transferee who takes the property and who "assumes" the mortgage does become personally liable for any deficiency.
4. In either of the two situations above, the original mortgagor remains personally liable for the debt unless there has been a novation.

Alternatives to the Mortgage

1. In many states, a three-party document, known as a deed of trust, is often used instead of a mortgage.
2. A deed, which is absolute on its face, may be treated as a mortgage if the parties' intent was for the deed to serve as security and not as an outright conveyance.

Contract for a Deed

1. A conditional sales contract of real estate.
2. The seller finances the transaction and retains title as security.
3. Payments are made over a substantial time period.
4. An escrow arrangement is essential in such contracts.
5. During the extended time of performance, the doctrine of equitable conversion shifts the seller's and buyer's legal interests.

Mortgage Foreclosure

Types of Foreclosures

1. Strict foreclosure occurs when a mortgagee simply keeps title to the real estate rather than conducting a foreclosure sale. This process was most closely associated with the title theory. Due to the rejection of the title theory, strict foreclosure seldom is allowed today.
2. Foreclosure by judicial action requires court approval to conduct a sale of the mortgaged real estate. In states that follow a lien theory of mortgages, this type of foreclosure is most common.
3. Foreclosure by the power of sale usually is allowed in states that have adopted an intermediate theory of mortgages if the mortgage contains a power-of-sale clause.

Priority to Proceeds

1. Mortgagees have priority to the proceeds of a sale in the same order in which their mortgages were recorded.

2. An exception to this order occurs if a mortgagee with a superior priority subordinates its claim to an inferior mortgagee.
3. Upon the foreclosure of a superior mortgage, all inferior mortgages are extinguished. However, the buyer at a foreclosure sale of an inferior mortgage takes subject to all superior mortgages.

Mortgagor's Rights of Redemption

1. A mortgagor in default has the right to redeem or reinstate his interest in the real estate by paying the debt plus necessary expenses.
2. All mortgagors may exercise the equitable right of redemption prior to the foreclosure sale.
3. Even after the foreclosure sale, some states allow the mortgagor to exercise a statutory right of redemption. This statutory right is more likely to exist in states recognizing the lien theory of mortgages.

Mortgagee's Rights to Deficiency Judgment

1. After a foreclosure sale that has not produced proceeds equal to the debt, the mortgagee may sue the mortgagor for the deficiency.
2. In order to recover a deficiency judgment, the mortgagee must prove that the foreclosure sale was commercially reasonable.
3. A few states have abolished this right to collect a deficiency judgment, particularly when a purchase-money mortgage is involved.

Mechanic's Liens

Introduction

1. A mechanic's lien gives security to any party who has contributed to an improvement of real estate.
2. An improvement does not necessarily increase the value of real estate.

Potential Lienholders

1. Those parties who contract directly or indirectly with an owner for an improvement are potential lienholders. Typically, these parties include general contractors and subcontractors.
2. Suppliers of materials and laborers who provide work also are potential lienholders.

Perfection and Enforcement

1. Since mechanic's liens are created by state law, each state's requirements for a valid lien vary to some degree.
2. In general, a lienholder must file a notice of a lien within a statutory time period after work is completed.
3. In addition to the notice of lien, a lawsuit must be filed within the time provided.
4. As a result of the lawsuit, a court may order that the improved real estate be sold in order to satisfy the lienholder's claim for payment.

Priorities

1. Among mechanic's lienholders, priority usually is determined by the beginning of that lienholder's work or delivery of materials.
2. If lienholders are equal in priority, they share the proceeds on a pro rata basis. Each should receive the same percentage of the proceeds that his work contributed to the whole improvement.
3. The priority between mechanic's liens and mortgages depends on the state's law and the time each claim attached to the real estate.

Protection against Liens

1. A real estate owner who is improving his land should obtain a sworn statement from the contractor prior to making any payment. This statement should explain who are potential lienholders. The owner can then take steps to satisfy these parties' claims.
2. An owner generally can prevent claims by making payment to the lienholders or by having these lienholders waive or release their rights to a mechanic's lien.

REVIEW QUESTIONS AND PROBLEMS

1. Match each term in column A with the appropriate statement in column B.

A	B
(1) Mortgagee	(a) A clause that allows one mortgage to secure future advances.
(2) Mortgagor	(b) Allows the mortgagor to reinstate his interest after a foreclosure sale has occurred.
(3) Lien theory	(c) A clause found in a mortgage that permits the mortgagee to conduct a foreclosure sale without court approval.
(4) Due on default	(d) The party who lends money and is secured by an interest in real estate.
(5) Dragnet	(e) The voluntary relinquishment of the right to a mechanic's lien prior to a notice of lien being filed.
(6) Strict foreclosure	(f) A view of mortgages that does not involve the conveyance of title.
(7) Power of sale	(g) A seldom-used process whereby the mortgagee gets to keep mortgaged property regardless of the property's value and the amount of the debt.
(8) Equitable right of redemption	(h) The voluntary relinquishment of a mechanic's lien after the notice of lien has been filed.
(9) Statutory right of redemption	(i) The filing of this is a required step in the perfection and enforcement of a mechanic's lien.
(10) Notice of a lien	(j) A type of acceleration clause often included in a mortgage.
(11) Waiver	(k) A borrower of money who grants the creditors a security interest in real estate.
(12) Release	(l) Allows the mortgagor to reinstate his interest after default but before a foreclosure sale occurs.

2. New Mexico Bank & Trust sued Lucas Bros. and Liberty National Bank to foreclose on a mortgage. Liberty National Bank held a mortgage on Lucas Bros. property recorded subsequent to a New Mexico Bank & Trust mortgage in the amount of $20,000. The New Mexico Bank & Trust mortgage contained a dragnet clause which provided that the mortgaged real estate would secure all future loans made to Lucas Bros. Does the dragnet clause in the mortgage allow all subsequent loans made by New Mexico Bank & Trust to enjoy the same priority as the original mortgage? Why or why not?

3. Mort owned real estate that he had mortgaged. Mort sold this property to Pat, who agreed to take it "subject to" the mortgage. Pat ascertained the balance of the debt Mort owed at the date of purchase of the land. When Pat failed to make payments, the mortgage was foreclosed. What does the term "taking subject to a mortgage" mean? Explain. Is Mort liable for the balance due? Why or why not?

4. Johnson was heavily in debt. He deeded his land to a state bank and leased it back for one year with an option to repurchase it. For the deed he received cash to apply to his debts in an amount equal to approximately one-half the value of the land. Johnson sued the state bank to have the deed declared to be a mortgage. Is he likely to succeed? Why or why not?

5. Garland paid $72,000 down and signed a purchase-money mortgage note for the $287,000 balance due on realty. When Garland defaulted, over $300,000 in principal and interest was still owing. At a public auction, Hill, the mortgagee, bid $25,000 for the property

and agreed to forgive the balance of principal and interest due. Garland filed suit to enjoin the sale on the equitable ground that the price was "shockingly inadequate." May an inadequate purchase price be made adequate by the mortgagee's waiver of his right to claim a deficiency against the mortgagor? Explain.

6. A merchant sold materials to Vendor, who in turn sold them to a subcontractor who incorporated them into a structure at the request of the contractor. Which of the parties are entitled to a mechanic's lien? Explain.

7. Johnson, a surveyor, was employed by Barnhill to survey, plat, and lay out 194 acres of land. A dispute arose as to payment, and Johnson filed a mechanic's lien and instituted this action to foreclose it. Barnhill moved to dismiss the action on the ground that the work done by Johnson did not entitle him to a mechanic's lien since the real estate had not been improved. Is the surveyor entitled to a mechanic's lien? Why or why not?

8. At the time Bill bought a new home, his attorney examined the recorded documents affecting interests in the property. No mechanic's liens were revealed. A short time after Bill had bought this home, Ralph, a roofer, demanded payment for a roof installed prior to Bill's purchase. Is it possible that Ralph has any rights against Bill's property? Why?

9. On November 10, 1987, an architect signed a certificate acknowledging the substantial completion of the construction of a building. Thereafter, the contractor continued to do finishing work until January 2, 1988. A mechanic's lien was filed March 11, 1988. The state law required that mechanic's liens be filed within ninety days after the completion of any building. Does the contractor have a valid lien? Why or why not?

10. The Graffs, plaintiffs, brought this action to invalidate a mechanic's lien claimed against their property by Boise Cascade on the grounds that the notice of lien was invalid because it did not set forth the name of the person who requested the materials and because it was not properly verified. The defendant, Boise Cascade Corporation, argued that the omissions were inconsequential and that the notice of the lien complied with the statutory requirements. Are the statutory requirements that the notice of lien contain the name of the person to whom the material was furnished and a proper verification of the claim mandatory conditions precedent to the creation and existence of a lien?

11. Carver Lumber filed a suit to foreclose a mechanic's lien. Commercial Bank, which held a purchase-money mortgage on the same property, claimed priority over Carver Lumber's lien. Commercial Bank's mortgage was recorded after Carver Lumber began work on the property. Is the bank correct? What assumptions have you made in reaching your answer? Explain.

12. Swann contracted with Diver Company for the construction of a house on his property. Upon completion, Swann made a substantial payment to Diver and instructed him to pay Materials, Inc., for building material supplied for the house. Diver delivered a $3,400 check and a $3,400 promissory note to Materials in exchange for its waiver of lien. But the check and the note proved to be worthless, and Materials informed Swann that the waiver was rescinded. Is Materials entitled to a mechanic's lien? Why or why not?

43 Additional Laws Assisting Creditors

C H A P T E R   P R E V I E W

- ARTISAN'S LIENS
- BULK TRANSFERS

  Terminology
  Duties of the Transferee
  Rights of the Creditors

- SURETYSHIP IN GENERAL

  Terminology
  Surety • Guarantor • Guaranty agreements
  Suretyship versus Indemnity
  Creation of Suretyship Contracts
  Liability of the Parties in General

- CREDITOR-SURETY RELATIONSHIP

  Fiduciary Aspects
  Principal's Default—Notice
  Surety-creditor agreement • Surety as drawer or indorser of commercial paper • Surety as collection guarantor
  Surety's Performance and Subrogation Rights

- CREDITOR-PRINCIPAL RELATIONSHIP

  Principal's Defenses
  Lack of capacity and discharge in bankruptcy • Statute of limitations
  Releases
  The surety's consent • Reservation of rights • Principal's fraud
  Extensions of Time for Payment
  Other Modifications
  Surety's consent • Uncompensated sureties • Compensated sureties

- PRINCIPAL-SURETY RELATIONSHIP

  Surety's Duty to Account
  Surety's Right to Reimbursement
  Liability of Co-Sureties

BUSINESS MANAGEMENT DECISION

You operate an electronics repair business. A customer's television has cost $200 for repairs. When the customer comes to pick up the television, he can pay only $50. He promises to pay the remaining $150 when he gets paid next Friday.

Should you let this customer have the television?

Chapter 42 deals with the use of mortgages or similar documents as one way a creditor has security. Chapters 40 and 41 discuss the taking of a security interest in personal property as another way a creditor can be secured when extending credit. These discussions on the methods of how creditors become secured are incomplete. In this chapter we examine three more legal areas designed to assist creditors in the collection of debts: artisan's liens, Article 6 on bulk transfers, and suretyship. In essence, this chapter discusses additional laws designed to give creditors security, or a source in addition to the debtor, from which the debt can be collected.

ARTISAN'S LIENS

An **artisan's lien** is a security interest in personal property in favor of one who has performed services on the personal property. Such services often take the form of a repair. From a very early date, the common law permitted one who expended labor or materials on the personal property of another to retain possession of the property as security for his compensation. This right to possession creates a lien against the owner's personal property when the task is completed. By court decisions, such a lien typically has been interpreted to exist in favor of public warehousemen and common carriers of goods entrusted to their care. Today, in almost every state, the artisan's lien has been extended by statute to cover all cases of storage or repair.

Artisan's lien *The claim against an item of personal property that arises when one has expended labor upon, or added to, the property. This person is entitled to possession of the property as security until paid for the value of labor or material.*

Because the artisan's lien is perfected by possession, voluntary surrender of the property generally terminates the lien. If the artisan parts with possession, reacquisition of the goods involved will not re-create the lien, as was attempted in the following case.

CASE

Plaintiff, known as 660 Syndicate, owned an airplane which had been leased to Wyoming Airlines. The Wyoming Airlines had Rocky Mountain Turbines (R.M.T.) service and repair the airplane. Although it had not been paid, R.M.T. returned the airplane to Wyoming Airlines. After it could not collect the money it was owed, R.M.T. reacquired possession of the repaired airplane. R.M.T. planned to enforce its lien by selling the airplane. Plaintiff filed suit claiming that it was entitled to possession of the airplane. Plaintiff argued that R.M.T.'s lien was unenforceable.

Issue: Was R.M.T.'s lien on the plane made valid by the subsequent acquisition of the plane?

Decision: No.

Reasons: 1. Statutory language clearly states that the lien established by R.M.T. is a possessory lien which terminates upon the "voluntary surrender of possession" unless "a lien statement has previously been filed."
2. Common law liens also last only as long as possession of the property is retained.
3. Reacquistiion of the property after the lien is terminated does not act to restore the prior lien.

Rocky Mountain Turbines v. 660 Syndicate, 623 P.2d 758 (Wyo. 1981).

The artisan's lien is personal to the party who performs the services and is not assignable. A lienholder may temporarily surrender possession, with an agreement that the lien will continue. However, if rights of a third party arise while the lienholder is not in possession of the property, the lien is lost. Surrender of part of the goods will not affect the lien on the remaining goods. However, the release of possession will not terminate the lien if a notice of lien is recorded in accordance with state lien and recording statutes prior to surrender of possession of the goods. Notice of an artisan's lien in the public records serves as an adequate substitute for possession.

Under common law, the lienholder had to retain the property until a judgment was obtained; then he levied execution on the property. Modern statutes permit the lienholder to have the property sold to satisfy the claim. These statutes usually require notice to the owner prior to the sale. With respect to the proceeds of a forced sale, the artisan generally has a superior claim when compared with a preexisting Article 9 secured party. The lienholder has priority because the law presumes that the work of improvement done on the personal property has increased that property's value at least in an amount equal to the lienholder's claim. Therefore the secured creditor has not been damaged by having inferior status. Any surplus proceeds left after all claims against the property are satisfied are paid to the owner of the property.

BULK TRANSFERS

1. Terminology

Chapter 41 explains that a buyer in the ordinary course of business takes free of a security interest previously created in the personal property purchased. Purchases in the ordinary course of business are often items to be used as inventory. However, Article 9 does not address the purchase of inventory that is not in the ordinary course of business. For example, what happens when all the inventory is purchased? What are the rights of the creditors of the seller? What are the rights of the purchaser to whom the inventory has been transferred? Is the purchaser liable for the debts of the seller, or is the purchaser free of them?

Article 6 of the Uniform Commercial Code is concerned with these bulk transfer situations, and it provides answers to the questions just asked. Prior to reading the following material, an understanding of the terminology used in Article 6 is essential. A *bulk transfer* covers sales of inventory if (1) the sale is in bulk and not in the ordinary course of business; (2) it is of the major part of the materials, supplies, merchandise, or other inventory; and (3) the seller's principal business is the sale of merchandise from stock. Ordinarily, a sale of a manufacturing concern is not subject to the law; however, this sale would be subject to Article 6 if the firm included a retail outlet that also was being sold. Enterprises that manufacture what they sell—certain bakeries, for example—would be subject to the law. Enterprises whose principal business is the sale of services rather than merchandise are not covered. Article 6 is applicable to transfers of a substantial part of the equipment of an enterprise only if the equipment is sold in connection with the bulk transfers of inventory. A sale of just the equipment of a business is not subject to the law.

The parties involved in a bulk transfer are usually referred to as the transferor, the transferee, and the creditors of the transferor. The *transferor* is the business selling the bulk of its inventory. The *transferee* is the party who is the buyer in the bulk transfer.

In a bulk transfer, the transferor's creditors have presumably extended credit on the strength of the assets transferred. The sale of these assets could jeopardize the ability of the creditor to collect the debt, since the transferor might fail to pay the debt after receiving the proceeds of the sale. Article 6 has attempted to remedy this situation by imposing certain requirements on the transferee who purchases inventory in bulk, if the sale is to pass title to the property free of the claims of creditors.

Article 6 does not change the relationship between a transferor and transferee. A contract of sale is valid without compliance. However, if the statutory requirements are not met, the property in the hands of the transferee is subject to the claim of the transferor's creditors. The following sections describe the duties of the transferee and the rights of the transferor's creditors under Article 6.

2. Duties of the Transferee

Article 6, as adopted in most states, does not require transferees to protect the interests of the transferor's creditors. They are not required to withhold or to pay the purchase price even to known creditors of the transferor. An optional provision of Article 6 requires the transferee to make mandatory payment to the transferor's creditors to satisfy their claims. The states are free to adopt or not adopt this provision, and some states have adopted it. You must check the applicable state law to see if this provision has been adopted.

Regardless of whether this optional provision has been enacted. Article 6 imposes two other requirements on the transferee. This party must first obtain from the transferor a schedule of the property tranferred and a sworn list of the transferor's creditors. This list must include the creditors' addresses and the amount owed to each. The transferee can rely on the accuracy of this list. This schedule of property and list of creditors must be kept for at least six months and be always available to creditors. Or the transferee can file these documents in the designated public office.

The second requirement concerns the notification process. The transferee must give notice personally or by registered mail to all persons on the list of creditors and to all other persons who are known to the transferee to have claims against the transferor. Notice must be given at least ten days before the transferee takes possession of the goods or pays for them (whichever happens first). This notice must contain the following information: (1) that a bulk transfer is about to be made; (2) names and business addresses of both the transferor and transferee; and (3) whether the debts of the creditors are to be paid in full as a result of the transaction. If the debts are to be paid, the address to which the creditors should send their bills must be included. If no provision is made for payment in full of the creditors, the notice must contain the following additional information: (1) estimated total of transferor's debts; (2) location and description of property to be tranferred; (3) the address where the creditor list and property schedule may be inspected; (4) whether the transfer is in payment of, or security for, a debt owing to transferee and, if so, the amount of the debt; and (5) whether the transfer is a sale for a new consideration and, if so, the amount of the consideration and the time and place of payment.

In states that have adopted the optional provision of Article 6, the transferee is obligated, in effect, to see that creditors are paid in full or pro rata from the "new consideration" paid by the transferee. Failure to do so creates personal liability up to the value of the property. In all other states, the notice tells the creditors to take action if they want to be paid out of the inventory or the proceeds of the sale. The purchaser is not under a duty to see that they are paid, and the purchaser-transferee of the inventory has no personal liability if the two steps are taken. Notwithstanding the notice, most creditors fail to take action—apparently because they do not understand the foregoing.

Article 6 is applicable to bulk sales by auction. The auctioneer is required to obtain a list of creditors and of the property to be sold. All persons who direct, control, or are responsible for the auction are collectively called the *auctioneer*. The auctioneer is also required to give ten days' notice of sale to all persons on the list of creditors.

3. Rights of the Creditors

If the required procedures have been followed, the transferor's creditors will have had ample opportunity to take any necessary steps to protect their interests. Their action might include the levying of execution against the property or obtaining a writ of attachment or a temporary injunction to stop the sale. If Code procedures have not been followed, the transfer is ineffective as to the creditors, and they may collect the debt from the transferee to the extent of the value of the transferred property.

In order to collect from the transferee, the creditors must take action within six months after the transferee takes possession if the Article 6 provisions have not been followed. If the transferee and the bulk transfer are concealed, the creditors must act within six months after they learn of the transfer. A purchaser who buys for value and in good faith from the transferee obtains the property free of any objection based on noncompliance with the Code. However, the transferee who sells the property becomes personally liable to the transferor's creditors to the extent of the value received.

The failure to comply with Article 6 by those in charge of an auction sale of the bulk of a business's inventory creates personal liability to the extent of the auction's proceeds.

SURETYSHIP IN GENERAL

4. Introduction

Suretyship provides security for a creditor without involving an interest in property. In suretyship, the security for the creditor is provided by a third person's promise to be responsible for the debtor's obligation.

Suretyship may have commenced with the beginning of civilization. Although there is evidence of surety contracts as far back as 2750 B.C., and in the Code of Hammurabi, about 2250 B.C., the earliest written contract of suretyship that has been found dates to 670 B.C. By A.D. 150, the Romans had developed a highly technical law of suretyship. The concept of a corporate surety did not evolve until the Industrial Revolution. Today, suretyship plays a major role in many business transactions, especially construction contracts. Suretyship also is involved in a substantial percentage of loan transactions.

5. Terminology

A *principal,* or *principal debtor*, or *obligor* is the party who borrows money or assumes direct responsibility to perform a contractual obligation. The party entitled to receive payment or performance is called the *creditor* or *obligee*. Any party who promises the creditor to be liable for a principal's payment of performance is either a *surety* or *guarantor*. The word *party* includes individuals as well as all types of business organizations.

What is the difference between a surety and a guarantor? Historically, the distinction has involved the difference between a third party being primarily and secondarily liable. Also involved is the distinction between assuring a creditor that the principal will perform a noncredit contractual promise and that the principal will repay money borrowed.

Surety. A surety's promise to be liable for a principal's obligation is created as a part of and dependent on the principal's agreement to perform. In a narrow sense, a surety is considered primarily liable for the principal's performance. In other words, a creditor could demand performance from the surety rather than the principal. From this concept came the general rule that no notice of the principal's default had to be given in order for the creditor to hold the surety liable. This notice requirement and its ramifications are discussed in section 10.

Since a surety's promise is part of the creditor-debtor relationship, a creditor may sue the surety simultaneously when action is taken against the principal. Finally, a surety's obligation can be summarized as being a promise to do what the principal agreed to do.

Guarantor. On the other hand, a guarantor's promise to be liable for a principal's obligation is created separate from and independent of the principal's agreement to perform. In other words, a guarantor's promise is only related to, but not an essential part of, the principal's obligation. A guarantor will become liable to the creditor only when the principal has defaulted. Therefore the principal is primarily liable and the guarantor is secondarily liable. Historically, this concept has required the creditor to give the guarantor notice of the debtor's default before action could be commenced against the guarantor. Furthermore, a creditor, if necessary, must bring two legal actions—first against the principal and, second and separately, against the guarantor. To summarize—a guarantor promises that the principal will do what the principal promised to do.

Guaranty agreements. There are two types of guaranty agreements: general and special. A *general guarantor* is a party whose promise is not limited to a single transaction or to a single creditor. For example, a principal may have an open line of credit and may borrow from the creditor many times within the overall credit limitation. A guarantor who promises to be liable upon the principal's default regardless of the number of transactions within the credit line is called a general guarantor. The general guarantor has significant potential liability, as the following case illustrates.

CASE

In 1972, the Damsel Corporation sought financing from Chemical Bank. In order to receive the financing, the officers of the corporation were required to execute personal guaranty contracts with the bank. The identical instruments provided that they were continuing guaranties and that they were to remain in effect irrespective of any interruptions in the business relations of Damsel with the bank. The officers had the right to terminate the guaranties by giving written notice at any time.

By 1975, Damsel had paid off its debt to Chemical Bank. However, the bank continued to factor accounts receivable for several of Damsel's suppliers. As a result of this arrangement, Damsel wrote hundreds of checks to the bank. Some of the checks were dishonored. In 1980, Damsel filed for bankruptcy protection under a Chapter 11 reorganization proceeding. In an attempt to collect the dishonored checks, the bank sued the Damsel officers on their personal guaranties. These officers argued that Damsel's repayment in 1975 had terminated their guaranty agreements.

ISSUE: Did the personal guaranties of the Damsel Officers survive the corporation's payment of the 1972 debt?

DECISION: Yes.

REASONS:

1. Where a guaranty is continuing, applicable to after-acquired obligations, and terminable only by writing, it does not end upon the repayment of the loan that created the necessity for the guaranty contracts.
2. Here the parties expressly provided that the guaranty would be continuing irrespective of any interruptions in the business relations of the debtor and the bank. No clearer showing of intent to keep a guaranty alive is needed.
3. If the guarantors had wanted out of their agreement, all they had to do was give the bank written notice. They did not do that, so they are bound by their continuing guaranties.

Chemical Bank v. Sepler, 457 N.E.2d 714 (N.Y. 1983).

A *special guarantor* is a party who limits the promise made to a single transaction or to a single creditor or both. A special guarantor's obligation would not protect a creditor to the full extent of an open line of credit if the initial loan transaction was for a lesser amount. In addition, a creditor cannot assign the special guarantor's promise to a new creditor.

Guaranty agreements also are classified as absolute or conditional. Under an *absolute guaranty*, a creditor can go directly to the guarantor to collect. In a *conditional guaranty*, the creditor must have made reasonable but unsuccessful attempts to collect from the principal before the guarantor can be held liable.

Fortunately, today the distinction between a surety and a guaranty has very little significance. This result is due in large part to the *Restatement of Security*, a legal treatise on the subject of suretyship. Although the *Restatement* is not the law, its influence on the law is quite substantial. Those scholars who prepared the *Restatement of Security* considered *surety* to be interchangeable with *guarantor*. Therefore, unless stated otherwise, the general principles presented below are applicable to sureties as well as guarantors. Keep in mind that the statute of frauds applies only to guaranty contracts involving secondary promises and not to contracts involving a primary promise.

6. Suretyship versus Indemnity

A contract of suretyship should be distinguished from a contract of *indemnity*. Both contracts ultimately provide protection that what has been promised will be performed. However, the approach to accomplishing this purpose is vitally different. A surety makes a promise to a person (creditor) who is *to receive* the performance of an act or payment of a debt by another (principal). In a contract of indemnity, the assurance of performance is made to the party (principal) who is promising *to do* an act or *to pay* a debt. Whereas suretyship provides security to creditors, indemnity provides security to principal debtors. In other words, indemnity is a promise to the debtor, or obligor, to hold him harmless from any loss he may incur as a result of nonpayment of a debt or nonperformance of a promise. Most insurance contracts are examples of indemnification agreements between the insurer and the insured.

7. Creation of Suretyship Contracts

Two basic situations exist when a surety's promise would benefit the creditor: (1) when the creditor is concerned about the principal's ability to repay a loan and (2) when the creditor is concerned about the principal's completion of a contractual promise other than repayment.

Typically, a surety's promise to the creditor to pay the principal's loan is made gratuitously. The consideration (or money) given to the principal is sufficient consideration to make the surety's promise enforceable. Such sureties are generally known as *uncompensated sureties*, and their liabilities may be limited by law.

Performance bonds and fidelity bonds are also examples of suretyship. A *performance bond* provides protection against losses that may result from the failure of a contracting party to perform the contract as agreed. The surety (bonding company) promises the party entitled to performance to pay losses caused by nonperformance by the principal in an amount not to exceed the face of the bond. *Fidelity bonds* give protection against the dishonest acts of a person. In other words, such a bonding company promises to repay the employer any loss, not to exceed a stated amount, caused by the covered employees' embezzlement. Bonding companies are sureties in the sense that the term *surety* includes security either for the payment of money or for the faithful performance of some other duty. Bonding companies usually are compensated sureties.

Whereas uncompensated sureties are given special protection as favorites of the law, *compensated sureties* are perceived as being able to take care of themselves. This difference is illustrated in the interpretation of the contract. Ambiguous provisions of surety agreements are construed in favor of the unpaid surety and against the creditor. Ambiguous provisions of surety agreements involving compensated sureties are resolved against the surety. This distinction results from the fact that ambiguous language is generally construed against the party writing it. In the case of unpaid sureties, the language is usually framed by the creditor and signed by the surety. In the case of compensated sureties, the contract is usually prepared by the surety.

Suretyship agreements are usually express written contracts, whereby the surety assumes responsibility for the principal's performance for the creditor. The surety agrees that he may be called upon to pay or to perform in case the principal defaults.

Contracts of suretyship also may result by operation of law. Assume that Jones sells his retail lumber business to Smith, who assumes and agrees to pay, as part of the purchase price, all of Jones's outstanding liabilities. Between Smith and Jones, Smith has now become the primary debtor. Jones is a surety and secondarily liable. As soon as the creditors are notified of the sale, they are obligated to respect the new relationship by attempting to recover from Smith before looking to Jones for payment.

8. Liablity of the Parties in General

The surety's liability is dependent on the many factors that exist in a three-party relationship. Therefore the following discussion is divided into three parts, each based on the following relationships:

1. Creditor-surety (sections 9 through 11)
2. Creditor-principal (sections 12 through 16)
3. Principal-surety (sections 17 through 19)

CREDITOR-SURETY RELATIONSHIP

9. Fiduciary Aspects

The suretyship relationship has some fiduciary aspects. It requires good faith and fair dealing. For this reason, a creditor possessing information affecting the risk must communicate such information to the surety before the contract is made. This duty applies only to information that is *significant* to the risk. It does not cover *all* matters that might affect the risk. If some facts make the risk a materially greater one than the surety intends to assume, and if the creditor knows this, he has a duty to disclose those facts. The duty to disclose exists only if the creditor has reason to believe that the surety does not know the facts and the creditor has a reasonable opportunity to communicate them to the surety. The following case held that a failure to communicate facts to the surety creates a defense for the surety.

CASE

Gary Levitz was, in 1977, the chief executive officer and a substantial owner of M. D. Pruitt Furniture Company. In order to obtain credit for Pruitt with Williams Furniture, a division of Georgia Pacific Corporation, Levitz executed a personal guaranty of Pruitt's debts to Williams. That guaranty was revocable only by written notice. In January 1981, at a time when no money was owing from Pruitt to Williams, Levitz severed his relationship with Pruitt and sold his interest to another. Levitz never revoked his guaranty although Williams was aware that he no longer was involved with Pruitt. Williams also knew that Levitz had revoked similar guaranties with other furniture manufacturers. Its credit manager assumed that Levtiz had simply overlooked notifying Williams. Despite substantial concerns about the financial stability of Pruitt, Williams shipped furniture to it in the summer of 1981. Shortly thereafter, Pruitt went bankrupt. Suit was brought on the Levitz guaranty; and Levitz appeals from the summary judgment granted against him.

ISSUE: May a creditor financially bind a surety when the creditor suspects the surety has no intention to act as a surety and when the debtor's financially weak condition is unknown to the surety?

DECISION: No.

REASONS:

1. Where before the surety has undertaken his obligation, the creditor knows facts unknown to the surety that materially increase the risk beyond that which the creditor has reason to believe the surety intends to assume, and the creditor also has reason to believe that these facts are unknown to the surety and the creditor has a reasonable opportunity to communicate them to the surety, failure of the creditor to notify the surety of such facts is a defense to the surety.
2. Williams' credit manager advised his superiors not to extend credit to Pruitt in the summer of 1981 because he feared Pruitt to be on the edge of insolvency. Because Williams knew that Levitz had not been involved in Pruitt's operations for six months, it also had reason to know that Levitz would not know of Pruitt's declining fortunes.
3. A continuing guaranty of debts is, in effect, an offer accepted serially by each extension of credit. Each extension of credit creates a new suretyship contract because a revocable continuing guarantee is merely a continuing offer which the creditor accepts each time he extends credit to the principal.
4. This being so, we believe the principle applicable that an offer, known by the offeree to have been extended under a unilateral mistake of fact, cannot be accepted so as to bind the offeror.

Georgia Pacific Corp. v. Levitz, 716 P.2d 1057 (Ariz. App. 1986).

When we concentrate on a typical loan transaction, the surety generally will have as much, if not more, knowledge about the principal than will the creditor. Therefore the fiduciary duty of disclosure will seldom arise if the surety is a relative of or otherwise related in a business sense to the principal. However, in keeping with conservative lending practices—when in doubt about its appropriateness—the creditor should disclose what it knows about the principal when the surety inquires.

Since the contract is between the surety and the creditor, any misconduct of the principal that induces a party to become a surety does not allow that surety to avoid the contract. At the time of the contract, however, a creditor who is aware of the principal's misrepresentation is obligated to inform the surety of the misrepresentation. This duty to inform probably occurs most frequently when a creditor learns that a principal has misrepresented its financial condition to a prospective surety. Particularly when the surety does not have access to the principal's records and books, the creditor is obligated to warn the surety of the increased risk. In this situation, a creditor's failure to warn the surety will release that surety from liability.

Perhaps the most common application of these fiduciary duties occurs when a financial institution is bonding its employees. An employer who knows of an employee's past financial transgressions (such as embezzlement) must inform the bonding company of this fact at the time a bond is sought. Furthermore, an employer who discovers that a bonded employee has been guilty of misappropriation of funds should immediately discharge the employee unless the surety assents to his continued employment. To allow the employee to continue subjects the surety to a risk not contemplated. Rehabilitation of the employee by giving him a second chance can be undertaken only with the consent of the surety. If the surety does not consent, and if the employee is guilty of misappropriation a second time, the surety is not liable on the surety bond.

10. Principal's Default—Notice

By the nature of the agreement, a surety has no obligation to the creditor unless the principal fails to perform. Although no performance is owed prior to that time, a surety is liable to the creditor *as soon as* the principal defaults. This simple-sounding rule means that the creditor usually does not have to exhaust his remedies against the principal before seeking to recover from the surety. Additionally, a creditor may take action against the surety without having to give notice to the surety that the principal has defaulted. The action will provide the notice. The rule that notice need not be given the surety is subject to the following three exceptions:

1. The contract may require notice to the surety.
2. A surety who is a drawer or indorser of commercial paper is entitled to notice unless waived in the paper.
3. A surety who only guarantees collection is entitled to notice.

Surety-creditor agreement. A surety may insist on including a clause in the contract with the creditor requiring the notice of the principal's default be given within a specified time. Whenever such a clause is included, courts will enforce it. If such a clause is binding on the parties, the creditor's failure to notify the surety of the principal's default discharges the surety from liability. However, the notice requirement must be reasonably, and not strictly, interpreted, as occurred in the following case.

CASE

The Floor Covering Association agreed with Local Union No. 1179 to fund certain health, welfare, pension, and other fringe benefits payments. As a part of its collective bargaining agreement, the association was required to furnish a surety bond covering the agreed-upon payments. Merchants Mutual Bonding Company signed a bond covering up to $10,000 of the association's fringe benefits payment. This bond contained a requirement that Merchants Mutual be notified within thirty days of the association's failure to perform. In March 1975, the association defaulted on making its fringe benefits payment. In March or April, an agent of the union orally told Merchants Mutual that there may be a claim filed on the bond. Formal written notice of a claim was not sent until September 1975. The union, as a creditor, filed suit against Merchants Mutual. This defendant argued it was not liable since the bond's notice requirement had not been satisfied. Furthermore, there had been no action taken against the defaulting association.

ISSUE: Is the surety liable on the bond despite the delay in receiving formal written notice of the principal's default and despite no action having been filed against the principal?

DECISION: Yes.

REASONS:

1. The notice given was adequate. The bond required notice of default within thirty days after the union (creditor) gained knowledge of the default.
2. Here, the union found out that the association was in arrears on its payments in March 1975. In either March or April, a union official, by telephone, notified the surety of the default. Such notice was sufficient, especially when there has been no evidence that the surety was disadvantaged by any delay. There was substantial compliance with the notice requirement.
3. A judgment against the association was not a prerequisite to a suit against the surety by the union. It would be of no use since no one would benefit. Because the law does not require one to do useless things, a judgment against the association is not a requirement to justify a suit against the surety.

Local No. 1179 v. Merchants Mutual Bonding Co., 613 P.2d 944 (Kan. 1980).

Surety as drawer or indorser of commercial paper. Any drawer of a draft (check) and any indorser of a note, draft, or certificate of deposit becomes liable on the instrument signed if (1) presentment for payment or acceptance was made within a reasonable time, (2) dishonor occurred, and (3) notice of dishonor was given within the time allowed. Since this notice of dishonor must be given, parties who become a surety through their status as an accommodating drawer or indorser or both are entitled to be notified of the principal's (primary party's) default (dishonor). Chapter 39 on the liability of parties to commercial paper gives further details of the notice requirement in this exception.

Surety as collection guarantor. Chapter 39 also explains that a collection guarantor under the terms of the Uniform Commercial Code assures the creditor that collection can be obtained from the guarantor if all efforts to collect from the principal prove unsuccessful. Due to the nature of this assurance, equity requires that the guarantor's potential liability not be unresolved indefinitely while the creditor pursues its claim against the principal.

To the extent a collection guarantor suffers from a lack of notice, that guarantor is discharged. For example, assume that a creditor attempts to collect a debt owed by the principal for two years without notifying that collection guarantor of any such actions. Then the creditor seeks to collect from the guarantor. Also assume that the guarantor can prove that two years before, the guarantor could have recovered 75 percent of the obligation owed from the principal, but now the guarantor can recover nothing. The creditor's lack of notice relieves the guarantor of 75 percent of the original obligation.

The collection guarantor is not damaged by a lack of notice if that guarantor is aware of what actions the creditor is taking to collect from the principal. In the example above, if the guarantor knew of the creditor's efforts despite no notice being received, that guarantor has not been prejudiced in any way. In other words, the guarantor could have satisfied its potential obligation at any time and pursued its rights against the principal. Therefore, in this situation, the collection guarantor remains liable for 100 percent of the obligation.

11. Surety's Performance and Subrogation Rights

In general, when a principal defaults, the surety immediately becomes liable to the creditor. The surety can satisfy its obligation to the creditor by performing as promised or by showing that it has a valid excuse for not performing. The following sections present several situations in which the surety is relieved of liability. However, for the time being, assume that upon the principal's default, the surety does perform as promised. When performance has been completed, the surety's most important right involves the concept of **subrogation.**

Subrogation *The substitution of one person in another's place, whether as a creditor or as the possessor of any lawful right, so that the substituted person may succeed to the rights, remedies, or proceeds of the claim.*

The term *subrogation* literally means the substitution of one person in the place of another. The surety who fully performs the obligation of the principal is subrogated to the creditor's rights against the principal. The surety who pays the principal's debt becomes entitled to any security interest the principal has granted to the creditor regarding the debt paid. Furthermore, whenever the creditor obtains a judgment against the principal, the surety receives the benefit of this judgment when the surety satisfies the principal's debts.

Because of the right of subrogation, a creditor in possession of collateral given to him by the principal is not at liberty to return it without the consent of the surety. Any surrender of security releases the surety to the extent of its value, his loss of subrogation damaging him to that extent. Failure of the creditor to make use of the security, however, does not release the surety, since the latter is free to pay the indebtedness and to obtain the security for his own protection. If the creditor loses the benefit of collateral by inactivity—failure to record a mortgage or notify an indorser—the surety is released to the extent that he is injured. In general, if the person who is entitled to protection under the contract of suretyship does anything that will materially prejudice the rights of the surety, the surety will, to that extent at least, be discharged.

The right of subrogation protects the creditor as well as the surety. In other words, a creditor has the right to step into the shoes of the surety and to enforce the surety's rights against the principal. Assume that the principal delivered corporate stock to the surety in order to protect the surety in the event of the principal's default. The creditor, to the extent of his claim, may substitute his position for that of the surety with reference to the stock. In the event of the return of the stock by the surety to the principal, the creditor is entitled to follow the stock into the hands of the debtor and subject it to a lien. The creditor may also secure an injunction against return of the stock to the principal, thus having it impounded by the court until the principal debt falls due, at which time the stock may be sold for the benefit of the creditor.

CREDITOR-PRINCIPAL RELATIONSHIP

12. Introduction

As has been stated previously, a surety generally becomes liable only when the principal defaults. Therefore, if the principal does not default, the surety never becomes liable to the creditor; no default occurs if the principal performs as promised. However, there may be other situations in which the principal has not defaulted because he has a valid excuse for nonperformance. These situations may involve a defense the principal can assert against the creditor, a release of the principal by the creditor, or a modification of the creditor-principal relationship. Any of these possible situations may have an impact on the surety's liability.

13. Principal's Defenses

In general, any defense the principal can use to reduce liability to the creditor may also be used by a surety to reduce his liability. This idea of making the principal's defenses available to the surety is not conditioned on the principal's utilizing the defense first. The surety is protected by the defense regardless of whether or not the principal is relieved of liability.

One important defense is that of lack of a primary obligation. In other words, the surety is not bound if the principal is not bound. This may occur when the principal fails to sign a contract, although expected to do so. Other common examples of defenses that may be available to the principal and surety include mutual mistake, fraud, duress, undue influence, illegality, impossibility, and lack or failure of consideration.

Setoffs and counterclaims of both the principal and the surety may be used as a defense by the surety under certain circumstances. The surety can set off any claim it has against the creditor and use the setoff to reduce or eliminate the liability. If the debtor is insolvent, if the principal and surety are used jointly, or if the surety has taken an assignment of the claim of the debtor, the surety is entitled to use as a defense any setoff that could be used by the principal debtor in a suit by the creditor.

There are three important exceptions to the general rule that defenses available to the principal may be used by the surety to avoid liability to the surety; (1) the principal's lack of capacity, (2) the principal's discharge in bankruptcy, and (3) the principal's performance excused due to the statute of limitations having run.

Lack of capacity and discharge in bankruptcy. Lack of capacity and discharge in bankruptcy are not available to the surety as defenses because the surety promised in the first instance to protect the creditor against the principal's inability to perform. Most creditors, particularly those in loan transactions, anticipate the principal's lack of capacity or discharge in bankruptcy. A creditor is likely to protect against the consequences of these possible events by insisting that a surety becomes involved.

When a principal who lacks capacity avoids a contract and fails to return the consideration that was received from the creditor, the surety is required to make up any deficiency between the value of whatever the principal has performed and the complete performance. If, on the other hand, the principal returns all or some of the consideration received from the creditor, the surety's liability is reduced by the value of the consideration returned.

Statute of limitations. The principal's defense that the statute of limitations prevents collection by the creditor may not be used by the surety. The principal and the surety have separate time periods for which they remain liable to the creditor, and that period may be longer for the surety. For example, the principal may be liable only on the basis of an oral promise (two-year statute of limitations, for instance). The surety's obligation may be based on a written agreement subject to a six-year statute of limitations. Obviously, the creditor who waits for three years after the principal's default cannot recover from the principal. Nevertheless, in this situation, the surety remains liable.

14. Releases

In general, a creditor who voluntarily releases the principal from liability also releases the surety. The logic of this general rule is based on the fact that the surety becomes liable only upon the principal's default. If the principal never defaults since the creditor relinquishes its claim against the principal, the surety never becomes liable either. Any conclusion to the contrary would mean the creditor could indirectly require the principal's performance even after a release. If a creditor could hold the surety liable, the surety could seek reimbursement from the principal. Therefore the creditor would indirectly be requiring the principal's performance.

As always, we must consider some exceptions to this general rule. The following three are discussed here: (1) A surety that consents to a principal's release is not released; (2) a creditor that reserves rights against a surety does not release that surety; and (3) a release obtained by that principal's fraud does not release the surety if the creditor rescinds the release prior to the surety's performance.

The surety's consent. It is hard to imagine why any commercial surety would voluntarily consent to remain liable when a principal is released from liability. Indeed, most situations involving a surety's consent to remain personally liable probably will involve a friendship or kinship between the surety and the principal. For example, a surety may wish to help a friend or relative by improving that principal's financial record. In order to achieve this result, the surety may actually seek the principal's release by consenting to remain liable.

Furthermore, a surety may be secured by the principal in return for acting as a surety. We could assume that a business, as principal, granted its president, as surety, a security interest in all its accounts and general intangibles. A creditor may be willing to take the surety's security interest in full satisfaction of the performance owed. The creditor might agree to release the principal from further personal liability if the surety consents to the creditor's having the right to pursue its claim against the accounts and general intangibles. The basis for this conclusion is the creditor's right of subrogation, discussed in section 11.

Reservation of rights. Even a nonconsenting surety is not released when a principal is released if the creditor reserves rights against the surety. In essence, the creditor's reservation of rights is interpreted to be a promise by the creditor that the principal will not be sued. The creditor can still hold the surety liable, and the surety can seek reimbursement from the principal upon the surety's performance. Therefore, in essence, the principal ultimately remains liable despite the prior release. The creditor really has promised only that the creditor will not sue the principal. In order to protect the surety's potential claim against the principal, the surety may perform for the creditor any time after that creditor has released the principal and has reserved rights against the surety. Due to its vital importance and its impact on the surety's liability, notice of the reservation of rights against a surety should be given in writing to both the surety and the principal.

Principal's fraud. With the use of false financial statements, the principal may induce a creditor to accept less than full performance from the principal or no performance at all in return for the creditor's release. Once that creditor learns of this fraudulent scheme by the principal, the creditor may rescind its release agreement. What impact these events have on a surety's liability depends on the factual situation. Normally a surety (that has not consented and has not had rights reserved against it) is released when the principal is released. However, if the release is obtained by fraud by the principal, the creditor would be greatly disadvantaged if the surety is released altogether. Therefore, if the surety had no knowledge of the fraud, that surety is released only to the extent it has relied on the release and the changed legal position as a result of the release. If the surety had knowledge of the principal's wrongful acts, the surety is not justified in relying on the release. In this latter situation, the creditor still may hold the surety liable for the principal's uncompleted performance.

15. Extension of Time for Payment

Before discussing the rules regarding the surety's liability, we need to have a clear understanding of what is meant by an extension of time for performance. To affect the surety's liability, the extension agreement must be a binding, enforceable contract. As such, it must be for a definite time and supported by consideration. In other words, the principal must induce the creditor to extend the time originally involved by promising something in addition to what the principal is already obligated to do. A principal's consideration for an extension may take the form of a refinancing agreement or an advance payment of interest. Merely promising to pay the original debt at a future date will not supply the consideration, because performance of a preexisting obligation is not consideration.

The creditor's gratuitous indulgence or passive permission to the principal to take more time than the contract provides has no impact on the surety's liability. Such conduct by the creditor does not injure the surety in any way. Upon the principal's default, the surety is free to perform at any time and pursue all available remedies.

If there is a formalized agreement between creditor and principal whereby the time for performance is extended to a definite time, a nonconsenting, uncompensated surety is discharged from liability. This rule is necessary, since the extension of time delays any potential default by the principal. Such a delay could adversely affect the surety's ability to recover from the principal if the surety has to perform. During the extension, the principal's financial condition could worsen, which could increase the surety's ultimate risk of loss.

As with releases, this general rule does not apply if the surety consents to the extension. Furthermore, a surety is not discharged by a formal extension of time if the creditor expressly reserves rights against the surety. This reservation of rights must be a part of the extension agreement. The creditor's stipulation that rights are reserved against the surety does not bind the surety to the extension agreement. Thus the surety may proceed to satisfy the creditor's claim and sue the principal for reimbursement at any time. The principal, therefore, is not really protected by an extension agreement that includes the creditor's reservation of rights against the surety. This type of extension agreement simply is a limited promise by the creditor not to sue the principal during the extension period.

Finally, a formalized extension of the time for performance discharges a compensated surety only to the extent that surety is injured by the extension. Of course, this rule assumes that the surety does not consent to the extension agreement. A compensated surety is perceived as being capable of protecting itself by anticipating possible extension agreements and charging a premium in accordance with expectations.

16. Other Modifications

In addition to an extension of the time for payment, any other modification of the creditor-principal agreement generally discharges the surety. The logic behind this general rule is that a surety should not be liable for the performance of some agreement made after the surety's commitment to the creditor. A modification agreed to by creditor and principal is a novation that relieves the surety from its obligation. In general, evidence of a renewed obligation is not considered to be a modification that relieves the surety of liability. However, if the renewal note increases the principal's obligation, the surety is relieved of further liability unless the surety consents to the renewal agreement.

An examination of the exceptions or qualifications to this general rule may make the philosophy behind it clearer. These exceptions include the following: (1) A surety that consents to the modification is not discharged. (2) An uncompensated but nonconsenting surety is not discharged to the extent the modification benefits the surety. (3) A compensated surety is not discharged if the modification does not materially increase the surety's risk.

Surety's consent. As in other areas of suretyship, the parties can override the application of the general rule on modification by this agreement. A surety who consents to remain liable is not discharged by a modification to the creditor-principal agreement. This exception is applicable regardless of when the surety consents. Whether consent to modifications occurs before, at the time of, or after the modification, the consenting surety remains liable to the creditor.

If the surety's consent is not a part of the original agreement signed by the surety, the creditor has the responsibility to notify the surety of the modification and to obtain the surety's consent. Failure to obtain this consent upon full notice of the modification automatically discharges the surety.

Uncompensated sureties. The surety who is not paid is a favorite of the law. In fact, the uncompensated surety is so protected in some states that any modification to the principal's obligation results in an absolute discharge of this surety, assuming no consent, as occurred in the following case.

CASE

On June 18, 1976, 3-W Enterprises, Inc. (3-W), entered into a franchise agreement with Inter-Sport, Inc. As a part of the franchise agreement, Steve and Vicki Wilson executed a guaranty agreement covering the payment of royalties arising from the agreement. The Wilsons were not compensated for their guaranty. On May 10, 1981, 3-W and Inter-Sport entered into a compromise agreement, evidenced by a promissory note. This note reduced the amount due under the franchise agreement to a sum certain. The compromise also varied some of the terms of the original 1976 agreement. When 3-W failed to perform as promised in the note, Inter-Sport sued the Wilsons to collect under their guaranty agreement. The Wilsons argued that they were no longer liable due to the modifications without their consent.

ISSUE: Are the Wilsons personally liable for 3-W's debts under the guaranty contract after a promissory note has been executed by the corporation to pay the debt?

DECISION: No.

REASONS:

1. A material alteration in the obligation assumed under a guaranty contract, made without the assent of the uncompensated sureties, discharges them from further liability.
2. Uncompensated sureties are entitled to have their promises narrowly interpreted. They cannot be held liable beyond the strict terms of their commitment.
3. Here the underlying agreement between the parties was a guaranty of the franchise agreement. The subsequent execution of the promissory note from 3-W to Inter-Sport, Inc., in satisfaction of sums owed on the franchise agreement constituted a material change in both the form and substance of the original undertaking. Therefore any liability the Wilsons may have had as sureties of the franchise agreement has been extinguished.

Inter-Sport, Inc. v. Wilson, 661 S.W.2d 367 (Ark. 1983).

Courts in some states have disliked the harshness of the rule that discharges an uncompensated surety whenever any modification is made without that surety's consent. Therefore there are decisions that hold that an uncompensated (and nonconsenting) surety should not be discharged if the creditor-principal modification benefits the surety. This benefit must be so obvious that there is no way to doubt its beneficial nature. Typically, such a modification occurs only when the creditor agrees to reduce the amount due or the rate of interest. In some states, a change in interest rates (up or down) does not discharge a continuing surety. Since interest rates are expected to change in today's economy, that change should not discharge the continuing surety.

Compensated sureties. Sureties that receive consideration (separate from that received by the principal) in return for their promises are *not* protected by the law to the same extent as uncompensated sureties. Thus, with respect to the impact of creditor-principal modifications, a compensated surety is discharged altogether only if that surety's risk has materially increased. If the increased risk to the surety cannot be readily determined, it is immaterial. To the extent that a compensated surety's risk is increased only slightly by the modification, that surety is discharged only to the extent of the increased risk. And if the compensated surety's risk is not affected by the modification, the surety remains liable as promised.

Why is an extension of time for payment treated differently from other modifications? This distinction in treatment basically is due to the creditor's ability to reserve rights against the surety upon an extension of the time of performance. In this section on modification, there has been no mention of reservation of rights. A creditor cannot reserve rights against a surety when a general modification of the principal's agreement is made.

PRINCIPAL-SURETY RELATIONSHIP

17. Surety's Duty to Account

Not only does the principal owe a duty to perform to the creditor, but the principal also owes that same duty to the surety. This duty arises by express agreement or by implication. Whenever a surety is present, the principal owes the duty to protect that surety from liability regardless of whether the surety has a contract with that principal or with the creditor. The only exception to this general rule is when the principal is relieved of liability due to a defense assertable against the creditor's claim. It is this general duty the principal owes the surety that justifies the surety's right to be reimbursed by the principal after the surety has satisfied the creditor's claim.

The surety owes a duty to account to the principal for any profits obtained after the surety performs. For example, suppose a principal gave a creditor a security interest in some equipment. And assume that a surety personally paid $100,000 in order to satisfy the principal's delinquent obligation. As noted previously, the surety has the right to the security interest via subrogation. If the surety sold the equipment for $175,000, that surety would have to return $75,000 to the principal. This surety's duty to account emphasizes the fact that the surety is liable for the principal's performance of an obligation. In essence, the surety should be liable for no more than, and should not benefit from, the commitment made.

18. Surety's Right to Reimbursement

Generally, after the surety has performed, the surety is entitled to be reimbursed by the principal. As you have come to expect, this general rule on the surety's right to be reimbursed is subject to at least two exceptions. First, a principal may inform a surety of a valid defense that a principal can assert to deny the creditor's claim. If the surety fails to use this defense as a means of reducing liability, the surety is not entitled to be reimbursed by the principal. Basically, the law requires the principal to bear the burden of informing the surety of available defenses. However, this requirement to inform does not apply when the principal's defense cannot be asserted by the surety. For example, the principal's defenses of (1) lack of capacity, (2) discharge in bankruptcy, and (3) expiration of the statute of limitations cannot be asserted by the surety. Regardless of whether a surety knows of these defenses, that surety cannot force the principal to reimburse expenses after the surety has satisfied the creditor's claim. In other words, these defenses extinguish the principal's liability altogether.

A second exception to the principal's duty to reimburse occurs when a surety has performed for a creditor after a principal has been released. A surety that performs is not entitled to be reimbursed by the principal if the principal has been released by the creditor's agreement. This rule makes logical sense, since it would be fraudulent for a creditor of a discharged or released principal to seek performance from a surety. If a surety does perform under the circumstances, the surety has a right to have the value of performance returned from the creditor.

This rule relieving the principal of the duty to reimburse the surety is not applicable when the creditor releasing the principal reserves rights against the surety. As discussed in sections 14 and 15, a surety remains liable to perform the principal's obligations if the creditor reserves rights against the surety. If the surety must perform for the creditor, it is only fair that the surety be reimbursed by the principal. The use of the concept of reservation of rights is allowed when a principal is released by a creditor or when time for payment is extended formally. In both cases, the principal debtor remains liable to the surety.

19. Liability of Co-Sureties

Throughout this chapter, there has been an implicit assumption that only one surety was involved in protecting the creditor. This assumption is too simplistic to reflect the actual situation in the marketplace. In any contract, a creditor may insist upon or otherwise be benefited by the existence of two or more sureties. Generally, these sureties may exist as co-sureties or as sub-sureties. *Co-sureties* are jointly and severally liable to the creditor. The term *joint and several* means the creditor may sue the co-sureties jointly for the performance promised or may sue each surety separately for the entire performance due. A *sub-surety* promises to be liable only in the event that the surety refuses to perform and thereby defaults. A sub-surety is a surety's surety. Unless the sureties involved in a transaction agree otherwise, they are considered co-sureties. A sub-suretyship normally must be created by the agreement of the parties, whereas a co-suretyship may be created by implication.

Numerous legal principles govern the rights of all the parties involved in a transaction with two or more sureties. In general, all the basic rules and exceptions discussed in this chapter remain applicable. For example, a release of the principal is a release of the surety if the surety does not consent to the release and if the creditor does not reserve rights against the surety. When a creditor releases one surety but not the other sureties, the general rule is that the remaining sureties are released to the extent that they cannot seek contribution against the released surety. Once again, this rule is not applicable if the remaining sureties consent or if the creditor reserves rights against the remaining sureties.

In addition to the applicability of the legal principles discussed above, there are rules that govern the liability of co-sureties one to another. Similar to the surety's right to be reimbursed by the principal, the fundamental rule among co-sureties is their right of contribution. This right is how co-sureties work out among themselves their fair share of the performance completed for the creditor. Whereas a creditor can hold one surety liable for all of the principal's obligation, that surety is liable for only a pro-rata share (among the co-sureties) of the performance rendered. The right of contribution works to allocate the liability 50–50 among two co-sureties, 33⅓–33⅓–33⅓ among three co-sureties, and so forth. Before one co-surety can collect from another, proof of payment of the obligation is required. In general, any recovery does not include attorneys' fees, although interest calculated at the statutory rate may be recovered, as held in the following case.

CASE

Plaintiff Throckmorton and defendant Collins were the officers, directors, and sole shareholders of Central Ceilings, Inc. (Central). A bank loan to Central was guaranteed by the plaintiff, his wife, the defendant, and his wife. After plaintiff left Central, the company folded and the note was left unpaid. Subsequently, Throckmorton and his wife took out a loan and repaid the outstanding note, with the bank assigning the note to Throckmorton. Throckmorton sued for contribution from defendants.

ISSUE: Are co-sureties liable for the stated interest on the note and for attorney's fees?

DECISION: No.

REASONS:
1. The plaintiff's rights to recover from the defendants are based on the equitable principles governing contribution between co-sureties, not the terms of the instrument on which the co-sureties have become liable. Based on these principles, a co-surety is liable for his proportionate share of the principal.
2. The judgment against defendant sureties should carry interest at the statutory rate and should not impose an attorney's fee in the absence of any express contract between co-sureties or statute providing for such fee. Therefore, the award of attorney's fees is reversed, and the award of interest is reduced from 8¾ percent to 6 percent, the statutory rate.

Collins v. Throckmorton, 425 A.2d 146 (Del. 1980).

CHAPTER SUMMARY

Artisan's Liens

1. The right to possess, for leverage in the collection process, personal property that one has serviced or repaired.
2. The "improved" personal property must be possessed at all times.
3. If possession is surrendered voluntarily, the lien is lost unless a claim of lien is filed in the public records.
4. Artisan's liens are personal and cannot generally be assigned.

5. The property is sold and the proceeds are used to satisfy the lienholder's claim.
6. In general, artisan's lienholders have priority to the sale proceeds.

Bulk Transfers

Terminology

1. A bulk transfer is the sale of such a large amount of inventory that the sale is not in the ordinary course of business.
2. The parties involved in a bulk transfer are called the transferor, the transferee, and the transferor's creditor.

Duties of the Transferee

1. The transferee must obtain and then maintain for six months a schedule of property being transferred and a list of the transferor's creditors.
2. The transferee also must give notice to all the transferor's creditors that a bulk transfer is occurring.

Rights of the Creditors

1. The creditors' action upon receiving notice of a bulk transfer is to levy against the property transferred or enjoin that transfer.
2. This action must be taken within six months of the transfer if Article 6 is not followed.

Suretyship in General

Terminology

1. A principal is a debtor or one who is obligated to perform a contractual promise.
2. A creditor is the party to whom money is owed or who is entitled to some other contractual performance.
3. A surety is a party who assures the creditor that the principal will perform as promised.
4. The term *surety* should be compared and contrasted with *guarantor* and *indemnitor*.

Creation of Suretyship Contracts

1. These contracts usually arise in relationship to the principal's obligation to repay a debt or to complete some other promised performance.
2. These contracts may be created as expressed written agreements or by operation of law.

Creditor-Surety Relationship

Fiduciary Aspects

1. A suretyship is based on trust and confidence.
2. Both creditor and surety must share any information that may adversely affect that party's potential liability.

Principal's Default—Notice

1. A surety becomes liable to the creditor when the principal defaults.
2. In general, the creditor does not have to give notice of default in order to hold the surety liable.
3. However, notice of default is required if the creditor-surety agreement requires it, if the surety is a drawer or indorser of commercial paper, of if the surety is a collection guarantor.

Surety's Performance and Subrogation Rights

1. A surety satisfies its obligation upon performance.
2. Having performed, the surety is entitled to any rights of the creditor.
3. Likewise, the creditor is entitled to be protected by any rights held by the surety.

Creditor-Principal Relationship

Principal's Defenses

1. Sureties generally can utilize any defense a principal has against the creditor to reduce liability.
2. The principal's defenses of lack of capacity, discharge in bankruptcy, and expiration of the statute of limitations cannot be asserted by the surety.

Releases

1. In general, a creditor who releases a principal from liability also releases any surety.
2. The principal's release does not relieve the surety of liability if the surety consents to the release, if the creditor reserves rights against the surety, or if the release is obtained by the principal's fraud.

Extensions of Time for Payment

1. An extension must be a valid agreement supported by consideration if it is to have an impact on the surety's liability.
2. A formal extension does discharge the surety's liability unless the surety consents, unless the creditor reserves rights against the surety, or unless the surety is compensated and not injured by the extension.

Other Modifications

1. In general, any modification of the creditor-principal relationship discharges the surety.
2. Exceptions to this general rule include the surety's consent to the modification, the uncompensated surety to the extent of any benefit, and the compensated surety as long as the modification does not materially increase that surety's risk.

Principal-Surety Relationship

Surety's Duty to Account

1. The surety must account to the principal for any benefits the surety receives from performance.

Surety's Right to Reimbursement

1. In general, after performance a surety is entitled to be reimbursed by the principal. This right of the surety is based on the principal's obligation not to default.
2. The surety's right to reimbursement does not apply if the principal has informed the surety of a valid defense that would defeat the creditor's claim of performance.
3. The right to reimbursement is also lacking if the surety performs after the principal has been discharged or released by the creditor, unless the creditor reserves rights against the surety.

Liability of Co-Sureties

1. In general, the liability of co-sureties is based on the same principles as the liability of one surety.
2. Co-sureties are jointly and severally liable. Generally, the right of contribution assures that co-sureties share liability on a pro rata basis.

REVIEW QUESTIONS AND PROBLEMS

1. Match each term in column A with the appropriate statement in column B.

A	B
(1) Artisan's lien	(a) In modern law, another term for a guarantor.
(2) Bulk transfer	(b) The right that exists between co-sureties.
(3) Schedule of property	(c) Literally means to stand in the place of another.
(4) Surety	(d) A sale of a large quantity of inventory outside the ordinary course of business.
(5) Indemnity	(e) Usually associated along with a list of creditors.
(6) Subrogation	(f) Not created when a repairman agrees to do work on credit.
(7) Reimbursement	(g) A promise to hold someone harmless.
(8) Contribution	(h) A surety's right against a principal.

2. Al's garage repaired William's automobile by installing a rebuilt engine. Al wished to retain a lien on the car to cover his costs for the parts and labor. How can he accomplish this? Explain.

3. Mary took her car to the local Chevrolet dealer for service and necessary repairs. After the dealer performed the desired work, Mary paid the bill in full. However, the dealer refused to relinquish possession of her car, since Mary had not paid for repairs previously made on the same car. Does the dealer have a lien on her car so that Mary cannot regain possession of it? Why or why not?

4. National Bank failed to file the financing statement necessary to perfect its security interest in Frye's inventory. Therefore the bank was a general, unsecured creditor. Before Frye filed a petition in bankruptcy, he sold all his inventory in bulk to Unclaimed Freight. Frye and Unclaimed Freight did not comply with Article 6 of the UCC. Specifically, Unclaimed Freight did not demand that Frye provide it with a list of all existing creditors and the amounts owed to each. The bank filed suit to recover Frye's inventory from Unclaimed Freight. Does a general, unsecured creditor have priority over a transferee in bulk who failed to comply with Article 6 requirements? Why or why not?

5. Ernest purchased an operating livestock feed and supply store. However, Ernest did not satisfy the requirements of the Bulk Transfers Act. ACCO was a creditor of Ernest's transferor. ACCO filed a lawsuit seeking to hold Ernest personally liable for the debts owed to ACCO. What result? Why?

6. Sam wrote a letter of guaranty to Carl on behalf of Rex, a retailer. The letter stated that Sam "does guarantee payment of any credit granted by you not to exceed ten thousand dollars ($10,000)." Rex was involved in a series of individual transactions with Carl, of which none exceeded $10,000. Rex failed to pay, but Sam contends that his total liability is limited to one transaction. Is Sam correct? Why or why not?

7. Lee signed as guarantor of a promissory note signed by Akins and payable to Vaughn. Lee expressly inserted a provision into the note that if the principal debtor defaulted, Lee must be notified promptly if he was to be liable. After the maker defaulted, no notice was given of that fact by Vaughn to Lee. When Vaughn sued Lee for payment, Lee contended that the lack of notice discharged this liability. When a surety contract expressly requires notice of the default, is the surety liable on the note if the payee does not promptly notify the surety? Why or why not?

8. Owens hired Terry, a general contractor, to build a house. Terry, in turn, hired Paint-It-All, a subcontractor, to paint the house. Being concerned about Paint-It-All's reputation, Terry required that a performance bond be obtained. Paint-It-All paid the Aetna Insurance Company to assure its performance. Paint-It-All failed to do the job, and Terry brought an action against Aetna alone. May he do so? Explain.

9. Donald Dunwoody borrowed money from the First National Bank and in return granted a security interest in his office equipment. In addition to this security, the bank required that Donald's sister, Sarah, sign as surety of her brother's performance. Donald did default on his payment. Sarah paid the loan in full and now claims to have rights in her brother's office equipment. Is she correct? Explain.

10. Lamar and Carolyn Upshaw guaranteed payment up to $4,000 on a loan from First State Bank to James Chaney. The Upshaws gave the bank a mortgage to a parcel of property they owned as security for payment. Subsequently, Chaney signed a new note with the bank renewing his obligations and canceling all prior notes. Chaney defaulted, and the bank seeks to foreclose on the Upshaw realty. Could the bank foreclose on the Upshaw property based on their surety agreement in the original note? Explain.

11. A newspaper entered into a contract with Alan by the terms of which Alan was to purchase newspapers at wholesale and deliver them to residential buyers. Alan's father agreed to serve as accommodation surety. Although the contract called for weekly payments by Alan, the newspaper allowed him to pay monthly. Did this allowance relieve Alan's father from any liability as surety? Why or why not?

12. Panworld purchased bicycles on credit from Heide. AMR corporation guaranteed Panworld's debt as a compensated surety. Later Panworld and Heide modified the original contract without the consent of the surety. No injury to AMR resulted from the modifications. Is AMR still liable? Explain.

13. A corporate note was guaranteed by four persons. When the corporation failed, two of the guarantors paid off the note and sued the other two for half the amount paid including accrued interest at the rate specified in the original note and for attorney's fees. What result? Explain.

Laws Assisting Debtors and Consumers

44

CHAPTER PREVIEW

BUSINESS MANAGEMENT DECISION

As the general manager of a collection agency, you are told by one of your collectors that a debtor does not want to be contacted again. This debtor informed your collector that the debtor has retained a lawyer.

What guidance should you give your collector?

The four preceding chapters discuss laws designed to assist creditors in the collection of debts. Numerous laws also attempt to protect consumers from financial and physical harm. These laws seek to protect consumers in their contracts, especially those that involve credit, and from injury caused by products.

Debtor and consumer protection involves all branches of government. There are protection statutes enacted by federal and state governments. Courts have also extended protection to consumers. The demise of privity of contract in breach of warranty cases is an example of judicial consumer protection. Finally, administrative agencies such as the Federal Trade Commission and Federal Reserve Board have responsibilities to assist in the protection of consumer-debtors.

The law has been aiding debtors and consumers for several reasons. Debtors and consumers frequently have less bargaining power than creditors and sellers. Many are financially unsophisticated, easily deceived, and lack information needed to make intelligent decisions. Therefore much of the consumer movement has been directed at providing all the relevant information so that borrowers and purchasers will be able to make reasonably intelligent decisions in the marketplace. Other laws are aimed at equalizing the bargaining power between buyer and seller. This equalization is often accomplished by declaring contract provisions illegal if they would not be agreed to by a party with equal bargaining power.

This chapter covers the laws regulating both debtor and consumer protection. The concerns for debtors and consumers are so interrelated that many laws were enacted specifically to protect consumer debtors. Sections 1 through 14 concentrate on the laws that assist such debtors. The last portion of this chapter deals with laws that protect consumers who are not necessarily debtors.

DEBTOR PROTECTION IN GENERAL

As of June 1987, consumer debt in the United States reached a record $586.7 billion. More and more of it is becoming delinquent. It is estimated that approximately 3.5 percent of all bank card accounts are delinquent. It is not surprising, therefore, that the law is constantly concerned with the debtor-creditor relationship and with balancing their competing interests.

This chapter is basically concerned with the laws and regulations affecting consumer credit transactions. The laws discussed are applicable to all consumer credit transactions regardless of whether the lender is a secured or unsecured creditor or whether the loan is secured by personal property, by an individual's promise, or by real property.

The term *consumer* means those individuals involved in transactions concerning personal, family, or household needs as opposed to commercial or business purposes. The term *credit* involves any situation in which money is lent with repayment to be made in the future.

The following materials discuss the lender's requirements (1) to refrain from discriminatory lending practices, (2) to use and report the consumer's credit history accurately, (3) to disclose pertinent information about the loan, and (4) to collect the debt properly.

CREDIT APPLICATIONS

1. Equal Credit Opportunity Act

The Equal Credit Opportunity Act (ECOA) originally prohibited discrimination in credit transactions on the basis of sex or marital status. The ECOA was enacted in response to findings of studies that indicated that women had a much more difficult time borrowing money than did their male counterparts. Later the ECOA was amended to add age, race, color, religion, national origin, receipt of public assistance benefits, and the good-faith exercise of any right under the Consumer Credit Protection Act as categories of prohibited discrimination in credit transactions.

A *creditor* subject to the ECOA is an individual or a business organization, in the ordinary course of business, participating in a decision whether or not to extend credit. Creditors include financial institutions, retail stores, and credit card issuers. *Discrimination* occurs when an applicant is treated less favorably than other applicants. An *applicant* is any individual or business organization requesting or receiving an extension of credit from a creditor. An *application* is defined as an oral or written request for an extension of credit made in accordance with procedures established by a creditor for the type of credit requested. The terms and the provisions of the ECOA are applicable to lease transactions as well as sales transactions if credit decisions are involved, as was held in the following case.

CASE

Patricia Ann Brothers attempted to lease an automobile from First Leasing. As a part of the lease transaction, Mrs. Brothers was required to submit an application for credit. She informed the company that she intended to lease the automobile in her own name rather than jointly with her husband. Nevertheless, she was required to include information concerning her husband's financial history, and he was required to sign the application. Her application for credit was denied because her husband had applied for bankruptcy.

ISSUE: Is there a violation of the Equal Credit Opportunity Act?

DECISION: Yes.

REASONS:
1. The ECOA, a comprehensive statute designed to protect debtors, prohibits discrimination by any creditor "against any applicants, with respect to any aspect of a credit transaction . . . on the basis of . . . sex or marital status."
2. A consumer lease is a *credit transaction* under ECOA.

3. There is nothing in the literal language or the legislative history that suggests that the ECOA does not apply to consumer leases. Interpreting "credit transactions" so that the ECOA applies to consumer lease transactions as well as credit sales is essential to the accomplishment of its antidiscriminatory goal.

Brothers v. First Leasing, 724 F.2d 789 (9th Cir. 1984).

The ECOA allows suits for dollar damages by victims of credit discrimination. Individual victims are entitled to recover actual damages, which can include a recovery for embarrassment and mental distress. In addition to actual damages, victims can sue for attorney's fees, other legal costs, and punitive damages up to $10,000. Punitive damages may be awarded even in the absence of actual damages being proved. In addition to these private remedies, governmental entities may bring suit to enjoin violations of the ECOA and to assess civil penalties. Punitive damages may not be recovered by the government.

Generally any action to enforce the ECOA must be begun within two years from the date the violation occurred. An exception to this statute of limitations arises if an administrative agency or the attorney general begins enforcement action within two years of the violation's occurrence. Any applicant who has been a victim of wrongful discrimination then has one year after the governmental enforcement action is commenced to bring a civil action to enforce the ECOA.

2. Discrimination Prohibited

A creditor must not advertise the availability of credit in any way that implicitly discriminates. For example, a picture of potential applicants must not include only males or females, whites or blacks, young or old, and so on. Such a picture must be representative of all potential applicants. Furthermore, an ad campaign must not be directed to a target audience that could result in possible discrimination due to the makeup of the target audience. Advertising must be directed to the entire community in a nondiscriminatory manner. A creditor found guilty of discriminatory advertising may be ordered to conduct an affirmative advertising campaign specifically aimed at the group suffering from past discrimination.

In addition to concerns about advertising, creditors must be aware of what information can be properly requested on an application. Recall that the purpose of the ECOA is to prohibit discrimination when extending credit on the basis of the applicant's race, color, religion, national origin, sex, marital status, age, receipt of income from a public assistance program, or exercise of a right under the law. The best way to avoid discrimination is not to request any information on which a discrimination charge can be based. With respect to the application form, the following are six general rules regarding information that should *not* be requested from the applicant:

1. A creditor should not inquire about an applicant's spouse or former spouse.
2. A creditor should not inquire about the applicant's marital status when the applicant will be individually liable.

3. A creditor should not inquire whether an applicant's income is derived from alimony, child support, or separate maintenance payments.
4. A creditor should not inquire about the sex of an applicant.
5. A creditor should not inquire about the applicant's birth control practices, capacity to bear children, or intention to have children.
6. A creditor should not inquire about an applicant's race, color, religion, or national origin.

3. Fair Credit Reporting Act

Shortly after an applicant has applied for a loan, the creditor normally will check on the applicant's credit history. This check may be conducted simply by examining the applicant's past record with this creditor. Or the creditor may contact a third party for a credit report. When this latter step occurs, the Fair Credit Reporting Act (FCRA) must be followed. The basic reason for the FCRA's enactment was to prevent abuses in credit-reporting systems. Furthermore, with this law, Congress provided a means to protect all individuals' privacy and to ensure accuracy with respect to the information in the reports covered.

The FCRA covers the compilation, distribution, and utilization of credit reports on consumers. Reports on businesses are not within the scope of this law. The FCRA governs the activities of both the consumer reporting agencies and the users of information provided by such agencies. The term *consumer reporting agency* includes any person who or entity that regularly collects information on consumers and furnishes it to third parties. In essence, these agencies are in the business of selling consumer reports for a fee. A *consumer report* is a written or oral communication relating to a consumer's creditworthiness, credit standing, credit capacity, character, general reputation, personal characteristics, or mode of living.

From these definitions, it is clear that a report containing information solely about transactions or experiences between the consumer and the party making the report is not covered by the FCRA. For example, a financial institution may be asked about its credit experience with one of its customers. If that institution reports only its experience with the customer, a consumer report, as defined in the FCRA, is not involved. The FCRA covers only consumer reporting agencies.

4. Consumer Reporting Agencies

To be covered, a consumer report must be for use in connection with at least one of the following:

1. Extending credit
2. Hiring, transferring, promoting, or firing an employee
3. Selling insurance
4. Issuing a license, particularly one of a professional nature
5. Determining eligibility for governmental financial assistance

A reporting agency must take steps not to include obsolete information. In general, adverse information over seven years old is obsolete and should not be included in a consumer report. Information on bankruptcy cases over ten years old also is considered obsolete. Furthermore, all consumer reporting agencies must establish procedures that, when implemented, will prevent improper or inaccurate information from being included in a consumer report. In the following case the attorney's fee award exceeded the verdict.

CASE

An application for a federally insured home loan was initially denied on the basis of the mortgage reports supplied by a credit-reporting agency to the mortgage company. Although the reporting agency accurately reported the information supplied to it by the applicant's creditors, certain information supplied by the creditors was inaccurate. The applicant sued the reporting agency for negligence.

ISSUE: May credit-reporting agencies that accurately report inaccurate information furnished by creditors be liable for damages under the Fair Credit Reporting Act?

DECISION: Yes.

REASONS:

1. The FCRA requires credit-reporting agencies to "follow reasonable procedures to assure maximum possible accuracy" of credit information. With this requirement, Congress demonstrated its desire that agencies that assemble credit reports be more than a conduit of information.
2. Liability is not automatically imposed when an agency reports inaccurate information. The adequacy of an agency's procedures is governed by what a reasonably prudent person would do under similar circumstances.

Bryant v. TRW, Inc. 689 F.2d 72 (6th Cir 1982).

5. Users of Information

Those parties that decide whether a consumer will be extended credit, sold insurance, employed, or licensed may use information from two sources other than themselves. These two outside sources of information are consumer reporting agencies or someone else. Users of this information have an obligation to disclose the source of such information to the consumer. However, the duty to disclose and the extent of such disclosure depend on the source of information.

First, assume that adverse action was taken regarding a consumer's credit, insurance, or employment application because of some information contained in a consumer report. When the user of this information notifies the consumer of the adverse action, the user automatically must disclose the name and address of the consumer reporting agency that furnished the report. Without this requirement, the consumer would find it difficult to determine whether the information in the report was accurate.

Second, again assume that adverse action was because of some information furnished to the user by a party other than a consumer reporting agency. Before the FCRA requires the user to disclose the information relied on, that user and the consumer must follow several steps: (1) At the time notice of adverse action is given to the consumer, the user also must notify the consumer that he has the right to request in writing the reasons for the adverse action being taken. (2) Within sixty days after receiving the user's notice, the consumer must make a written request for an explanation of why this adverse action was taken. (3) After receiving the consumer's request for an explanation, the user must disclose the information on which the adverse decision was based.

6. Rights of Consumer Debtors

Any consumer debtor has the right to and the consumer reporting agency has the duty to disclose the following items contained in that consumer's file:

1. The nature and substance of all information except medical records
2. The sources of that information
3. The parties receiving a consumer report for employment purposes within the prior two years and the parties receiving a consumer report for any other purposes within the prior six months

Before disclosing the information contained in the consumer's file, the consumer reporting agency must ask the consumer to provide proper identification. When information from the consumer's file is made available to the consumer, he has the right to have the information explained by a competently trained employee of the consumer reporting agency.

The consumer has a right to the information in his file without any charge if the request is made within thirty days after the consumer receives either (1) notice of adverse action on an application for credit, insurance, or employment or (2) notice from a debt collection agency that his credit rating may be adversely affected. In other situations, consumers may be charged a reasonable fee when examining the contents of their files. This fee is collected by the consumer reporting agency.

Another important protection of consumers is their right to challenge the accuracy of information contained in the file. For instance, suppose that a consumer examines his file and has a justifiable reason to dispute the correctness or relevance of some information. The consumer must communicate this dispute's existence to the consumer reporting agency. Upon receiving this notice of dispute, the agency must reinvestigate the appropriateness of this information being in the consumer's file. As a result of such a reinvestigation, one of two steps must be followed.

First, if the consumer reporting agency determines that the information is inaccurate or cannot be verified, such information must be deleted from the file. Second, the reinvestigation may result in a finding that the disputed information is accurate and relevant. This second finding by the consumer reporting agency means that the dispute is not resolved. In this event, the consumer must be allowed to write a brief statement describing his position, to be included in that consumer's file. This statement may be limited to 100 words if the consumer reporting agency provides assistance to the consumer regarding the writing of the statement.

The consumer has the right to insist that this or some similar statement be included in any future consumer report furnished by the agency. Furthermore, upon the consumer's request, the agency must give notice that information has been deleted or give notice of a statement of the consumer's position to any user of a consumer report if that user received (1) a report related to an employment purpose within a two-year period or (2) a report related to any other purpose within a six-month period prior to the consumer's request.

To encourage enforcement of its provisions, the FCRA provides for both civil and criminal sanctions. Regarding civil liability, any consumer reporting agency or user of credit reports that *negligently* fails to comply with FCRA is liable to the consumer for that person's actual damages plus costs of the action and reasonable attorney's fees. Additionally, if the consumer reporting agency or user is shown to have *willfully* violated the FCRA's provisions, that party is liable for any punitive damages the court might award. Civil actions must be filed within two years of the date the violation occurred. If the violation involves misrepresentation of information, the statute of limitations begins running when the misrepresentation is discovered.

In the cases in which someone obtains information about a consumer from a consumer reporting agency under false pretenses, criminal sanctions may be imposed. When false pretenses are knowingly and willfully utilized, the perpetrator may be fined up to $5,000 or confined for up to one year or both.

The decision to extend the applicant credit also creates a number of legal requirements that must be satisfied. These requirements are found in the federal Truth-in-Lending Act and in the Uniform Consumer Credit Code if your state has adopted this code.

CREDIT TRANSACTIONS

7. Truth-in-Lending Act—General Approach

The Truth-in-Lending Act (TILA) and Regulation Z issued by the Federal Reserve Board to implement the statute apply to any individual or business organization offering or extending credit. They apply whenever the following four conditions are met:

1. The applicant for credit is an individual consumer as contrasted with a corporation or other business organization.
2. Credit is offered or extended on a regular basis, which means the creditor extended consumer credit more than twenty-five times during the previous calendar year. If the creditor extended consumer credit secured by a dwelling at least five times, the regularity requirement is met.
3. The repayment of the credit extended is subject to a finance charge or is evidenced by a written agreement that allows for more than four installments.
4. Finally, the credit is for family, household, or personal uses. This fourth element of TILA's coverage once again emphasizes the consumer versus business nature of the loan covered by the act.

The following case discusses the philosophy of TILA and illustrates some typical violations.

CASE

Marjorie Dehning purchased consumer goods from Wise Furniture on four separate occasions between February 9, 1979, and October 22, 1979. Each sales contract refinanced the previous contract and retained a security interest in all the goods purchased. On March 4, 1981, Dehning defaulted on the last contract with an outstanding balance of $811.23 due. Dehning had made payments of $947.55 prior to default.

Dehning then brought this action alleging that Wise had violated the Truth-in-Lending Act and Regulation Z by failing to disclose adequately its finance charge and retained security interests.

ISSUE: Did Wise's failure to disclose its finance charge and failure to unequivocally describe its retained security interests violate the Truth-in-Lending Act?

DECISION: Yes.

REASONS:

1. The purpose of the Truth-in-Lending Act is to assure meaningful disclosure of credit terms so that the consumer will be able to avoid the uninformed use of credit. Its goal is the protection of unsophisticated consumers.
2. The Truth-in-Lending Act requires that the finance charge be accurately and fairly disclosed. When there is a refinancing transaction, Regulation Z requires that new disclosures be made to the consumer. In this case, each contract financed the previous one. However, the contracts do not clearly disclose whether the unpaid finance charges were added to the amount owed in the new refinancing agreements. If these additions were made, a new finance charge could be computed on the new larger amount. It is clear that the credit terms were unclear and in violation of the Truth-in-Lending Act.
3. Wise also violated the Truth-in-Lending Act by its failure to describe clearly and unequivocally its retained security interest.
4. Damages under the Truth-in-Lending Act are twice the amount of any finance charge in connection with the transaction. The plaintiff may subtract from her damages what she owes Wise to pay off the furniture and have Wise pay her the remainder. This is called *recoupment* and is allowed under the Truth-in-Lending Act.

Wise Furniture v. Dehning, 343 N.W.2d 26 (Minn. 1984).

Consumer credit transactions are exempt from the act if the amount of credit extended exceeds $25,000. The reason for this exemption seems to be that consumer debtors who borrow over $25,000 have the sophistication to protect themselves. However, even untrained and inexperienced consumers borrow substantially more than $25,000 when they purchase a personal residence and use that residence as security. Therefore mortgage transactions involving personal residences are not exempted from the act's requirements regardless of the dollar amount involved.

8. Disclosures Required

The basic purpose ot TILA has been, and continues to be, to encourage potential consumer debtors to shop for credit. In order to facilitate this comparison shopping, the Act requires the creditor to disclose certain items of information. Although there are numerous and technical disclosure requirements, the most important items to be revealed include the following:

1. The identity of the creditor
2. The amount financed
3. An itemization of the amount financed
4. The finance charge
5. The annual percentage rate
6. The payment schedule
7. The total amount of all payments

Of these, items 2, 4, 5 and 7 frequently are the most important.

Amount financed. The amount financed by the creditor is calculated by taking the amount of the loan's principal, adding other amounts financed by the creditor that are not a part of the finance charge, and then subtracting the amount of any prepaid finance charge. This amount must be stated as a dollar figure and must be clearly marked as the "Amount Financed."

Finance charge. This item is considered one of the most important, and it is one of the most complex to calculate. Once again, this disclosure is in the form of a dollar figure. This finance charge figure quickly shows the consumer applicant what this credit transaction is costing over its term. In essence, this figure includes all charges paid by the consumer applicant when securing the extension of credit. This dollar figure is more than the total amount of all interest payments. The finance charge also includes all fees charged by the creditor as a cost of extending credit. Especially in long-term mortgage-secured loans, it is not unusual for the finance charge to be greater than the amount financed.

Annual percentage rate. Along with the finance charge, the annual percentage rate (APR) is the second part of the all-important disclosure requirement of TILA. The APR can be used by consumer applicants to compare the cost of obtaining credit. This cost is expressed in terms of a percentage rate rather than in dollars, as with the finance charge. The APR is the cost of the credit expressed as a yearly rate. This rate is a measure that relates the amount and timing of the credit received by the consumer applicant to the amount and timing of the payments to be made by the applicant. The complex method of calculating the APR is beyond our purpose in this chapter. However, since the finance charge includes items in addition to interest payments, the APR is almost always higher than the quoted interest rate.

Total amount of all payments. Under the heading "Total Amount of All Payments," the creditor must disclose in a dollar figure the total amount the consumer debtor will have paid after all the payments have been made. A simple way to check the accuracy of this figure is to add the amount financed and the finance charge. This addition should equal the total amount of all payments. If the consumer applicant desires to do so, this figure can be a helpful source in comparing credit opportunities.

TILA also protects borrowers by prohibiting misleading advertising, such as representing lower down payments and lower installment payments than are actually available. If an advertisement contains any details of a credit plan, it must also include as disclosures substantial information on finance charges, rates, cash price, down payment, and other information included in the specific regulations used to enforce the law.

9. Sanctions for Truth-in-Lending Violations

TILA provides for both civil and criminal sanctions against creditors that fail to comply with the applicable provisions. For example, in a civil suit based on the creditor's failure to make all necessary disclosures, an individual plaintiff may recover two times the finance charge subject to a minimum of $100 and a maximum of $1,000. In a class action for improper disclosures, there is no limit on an individual's claim, but the class can recover only the lesser of $500,000 or 1 percent of the creditor's net worth.

Not all improper disclosures result in civil liability. Creditors that make bona fide errors in their disclosures are not necessarily liable. A bona fide error may include an inaccurate disclosure due to clerical, printing, or computer malfunctions. Technical but immaterial violations do not create a ground to hold creditors liable for dollar damages.

Although it is rare, the Justice Department can bring criminal charges against a creditor for violating TILA. To be a crime, failure to make adequate and accurate disclosures must be done knowingly and willfully. The criminal violation is punishable by up to a $5,000 fine or up to one year in confinement or some combination of the two.

10. Uniform Consumer Credit Code

All the federal laws discussed in this chapter do not preempt state consumer credit protection laws so long as these state laws do not narrow the protection provided by Congress. Because of the diversity among the states concerning protection of consumers in credit transactions, the Commissioners on Uniform State Laws have prepared a proposed uniform law similar to many of the federal laws. The Uniform Consumer Credit Code (UCCC) attempts to protect consumers by utilizing the technique of full disclosure of all pertinent facts about the credit transaction to buyers. The UCCC is applicable to virtually every transaction involving credit: retail installment sales, consumer credit, small loans, and usury.

The UCCC does not fix rates of interest but rather sets maximums that may be charged. When the amount financed is $300 or less, the maximum is 36 percent per year; and when the amount is more than $300 but less than $1,000, it is 21 percent per year. The credit code has detailed provisions covering matters such as delinquency charges, deferral charges, service charges on refinancing or loan consolidation, and revolving charge accounts. It also prohibits most deficiency judgments when goods sold as a part of a consumer credit sale are repossessed.

The UCCC requires a written disclosure that *conspicuously* sets forth the required facts prior to a sale or loan. Just as in the Truth-in-Lending Act, the annual percentage rate is the key fact that must be disclosed. The difference between the cash price and the credit price is also essential as a part of the disclosure. The provisions on advertising generally require that the ad include the rate of the credit service charge as well as the amount of the charge.

In addition to regulating the cost of credit, the UCCC prohibits certain types of agreements. It prohibits the use of the holder-in-due course concept and outlaws agreements cutting off defenses. It prohibits the use of multiple agreements to obtain higher interest. It also prohibits *balloon payments*. If any scheduled payment is more than twice as large as the average payment, the buyer has the right to refinance the balloon payment, without penalty, on terms no less favorable than the original terms. The balloon-payment provision is not applicable to a sale for agricultural purposes or one pursuant to a revolving charge account.

The UCCC prohibits debtors from assigning their earnings as part of a credit sale. In addition, lenders are not allowed to take an assignment of earnings for payment of a debt arising out of a consumer loan. The UCCC also prohibits referral sales schemes in which the buyer is given credit on a purchase for furnishing the names of other possible purchasers.

Violations of the UCCC may be punished criminally. In addition, debtors are relieved of their obligation to pay the finance charge, and they are entitled to recover, from creditors who violate the law, up to three times the finance charge actually paid. Of course, debtors are not obligated to pay charges in excess of those allowable by the act. If a debtor entitled to a refund is refused a refund, the debtor is entitled to recover the total amount of the credit service charge or ten times the excess charge, whichever is greater. If the excess charge was in deliberate violation of the act, the penalty may be recovered even if the excess has been repaid.

This UCCC proposal has received modest approval, being adopted by only nine states: Colorado, Idaho, Indiana, Iowa, Kansas, Maine, Oklahoma, Utah, and Wyoming. South Carolina and Wisconsin have legislation substantially similar to the UCCC.

DEBT COLLECTION

11. Fair Credit Billing Act

From the creditor's perspective, after credit has been extended the next stage of the transaction is collection from the debtor. Prior to being able to collect an amount owed, the creditor must inform the consumer debtor what is owed. This information is conveyed through a *billing*. Due to the problem a mistake in a billing could cause, the Fair Credit Billing Act (FCBA) was enacted. The FCBA is applicable only to open-ended consumer credit transactions. A billing error associated with any business loan or with a consumer closed-end transaction is *not* covered by the FCBA.

Definitions. The term *billing error*, as used in the FCBA, can consist of a periodic statement containing any of the following: (1) a reflection of credit not actually extended, (2) a reflection of credit extended of which the debtor seeks clarification, (3) a reflection of the cost of goods and services not received by the debtor or by an authorized agent, (4) a reflection of a computational error made by the creditor, (5) a failure to reflect a payment made by the debtor, and (6) a failure to reflect the type of transaction involved. A billing error also occurs when the creditor fails to send the periodic statement to the borrower's last known address if that address has been given to the creditor at least twenty days before the end of a billing cycle.

A *billing error notice* is a written notice received by a creditor from a consumer debtor. This notice must contain the consumer debtor's statement that a billing error exists, and there must be a statement as to why the consumer believes such error exists. Furthermore, this notice must enable the creditor to identify the following items: (1) the consumer debtor's name, (2) his account number, and (3) the type, date, and amount of the billing error. Finally, this notice must be received by the creditor within sixty days after the first periodic statement containing the error was sent by the creditor for the provisions of the act to apply.

Creditor's general duties. If a creditor receives a billing error notice, that creditor must, first of all, acknowledge in writing to the consumer debtor the receipt of the notice within thirty days of its actual receipt. Second, the creditor, within two billing cycles but not more than ninety days after the notice is received, must either (1) correct the error, credit the account for the correct amount, and send a notice of the correction made; or (2) send a written statement of clarification to the consumer debtor as to why the creditor believes no error has been made.

Until a billing error has been corrected or until an explanation of the billing's accuracy has been sent and received, the creditor cannot (1) restrict the credit available to the consumer debtor, (2) close that account, and (3) report or even threaten to report the consumer debtor's nonpayment to a credit rating organization. A report to a credit-reporting agency may be made after the creditor has sent an explanation of why there is no billing error and after the time for payment has passed if the consumer debtor has not reasserted the billing error's existence. If a dispute continues to exist, the creditor may make a credit report if the following steps are satisfied: (1) The report must indicate that the amount or account is in dispute, (2) the creditor must mail or otherwise deliver to the consumer debtor a written notice of the name and address of all persons receiving the credit report, and (3) the creditor promptly must make a report of any subsequent resolution of the dispute to all those who received the original report.

The FCBA also regulates some of the accounting practices of creditors. For example, prompt posting of all payments is required in order to prevent additional finance charges being billed to the consumer debtor's account. Furthermore, creditors of revolving charge accounts cannot impose finance charges on a new purchase made by the consumer debtor unless a statement including the amount upon which the finance charge for that period is based is mailed at least fourteen days before the date the finance charge will be imposed if full payment is not made.

12. Credit Card Protection

Lost or stolen credit cards are often used for unauthorized purchases, resulting in a loss to (1) the business that dealt with the wrong person, (2) the credit card company, which may be the same as (1), as in the case of an oil company's gasoline credit card, or (3) the actual cardholder. TILA seeks to limit the cardholder's loss and to impose most of the losses on the issuer of the card. For example, the law prohibits the issuance of credit cards except upon application or upon the renewal of an existing card. Thus the person to whom a card is issued has no liability for unauthorized purchases if that card was issued without being requested.

TILA further provides that a cardholder is liable only up to the lesser of the amount charged or $50 for the unauthorized use of a credit card, and then only if all the following conditions are met:

1. The credit card is an accepted card, one that the cardholder had requested.
2. The charge is made prior to the cardholder's giving notice to the issuer that the card was lost or stolen.
3. Within two years before the unauthorized use, the issuer warned the cardholder of his potential liability for unauthorized use.
4. The issuer had provided the cardholder with a preaddressed notice form that may be mailed to the issuer in the event the card is lost or stolen.

The warning to the cardholder mentioned in condition 3 may be given by printing it on the card. This notice must state that the liability in the case of loss or theft shall not exceed $50. The cardholder also must be informed in a clear manner that the notice of loss or theft may be given orally as well as in writing.

Finally, no cardholder is liable unless the issuer has provided a method whereby the user of the card can be identified as the person authorized to use it. This identification traditionally has been by the cardholder's signature, photograph, or fingerprint on the card. In order to reduce the problem of counterfeiting credit cards, the means of identifying the cardholder has shifted to mechanical and electronic devices.

13. Fair Debt Collection Practices Act

The Fair Debt Collection Practices Act (FDCPA) was adopted to prevent the use of abusive, deceptive, and unfair debt collection practices by debt collectors. This law is also intended to ensure the competitiveness of those debt collectors that are not utilizing abusive tactics.

The FDCPA is directed toward those that are in the business of collecting debts owed to someone else. For example, creditors are not subject to the FDCPA's provisions unless they attempt to collect a debt by using a name that does not reveal that creditor's identity. Creditors are exempt from this law because it is believed that creditors will not engage in unfair debt collection practices with their customers. This belief is based on the fact that creditors will not jeopardize their goodwill with their debtors by using questionable practices.

The FDCPA is applicable only to the collection of consumers' debts. The law presumes that business debtors are able to protect themselves from unfair debt collection practices.

The law permits a bill collector to communicate with third parties, such as neighbors or employers of the debtor, but it limits the contact. Third parties may not be informed that the consumer owes a debt. When an attorney represents the debtor and the bill collector knows it, the collector may not get in touch with anyone else except the attorney, unless the attorney fails to respond to the collector's communication.

The act also restricts the methods that may be used in the collection process. The collector may not (1) physically threaten the debtor, (2) use obscene language, (3) pretend to be an attorney, (4) threaten the debtor with arrest or garnishment unless the collector or creditor is legally entitled to such action and intends to take it, or (5) telephone the debtor repeatedly with intent to annoy. In telephoning the debtor, the collector must make a meaningful disclosure of his identity and may not telephone collect or call before 8:00 A.M. or after 9:00 P.M. In addition to these specific prohibitions, the Act forbids the collector from using any "unfair or unconscionable" means to collect the debt.

If a debtor desires to stop repeated contacts, he need only notify the collector in writing of this wish. Any further contact by the collector following such notification violates the Act. The collector's sole remedy in such cases is to sue the debtor. Violations of the law entitle the debtor to sue the collector for actual damages, including damages for invasion of privacy and infliction of mental distress, court costs, and attorney's fees. In the absence of actual damages, the court may still order the collector to pay the debtor up to $1,000 for violations.

Many states have enacted laws similar to the FDCPA. In general, these laws are interpreted very liberally in order to provide the greatest protection reasonably possible. Note the danger for creditors and bill collectors in the following decision in Texas.

CASE

Clara Campbell brought suit against Beneficial Finance Company and its employee, Raymond Johnson, alleging a cause of action for harassment and abusive debt collection practices in violation of the Texas Debt Collection Act. Campbell's daughter and son-in-law, Sue and Bobby Rice, were indebted to Beneficial and were delinquent in their payments. Campbell alleged that Mr. Johnson threatened and harassed her because she would not disclose the whereabouts of the Rices. The trial court granted Beneficial a summary judgment on the basis that Mrs. Campbell had no standing to sue for injuries under provisions of the Debt Collection Act because she was not a debtor. Mrs.Campbell appealed.

ISSUE: May a third party who suffers harm when credit company abuses her in an attempt to locate a debtor sue for violation of the Debt Collection Act?

DECISION: Yes.

REASONS:
1. The statute clearly allows *anyone* who is harmed by a debt collector a cause of action for damages, regardless of whether that person is a debtor. To hold otherwise would protect the debtor, but leave his family and friends subject to abuse by the collector.
2. It is clear that while the threat, coercion, harassment, or abuse must occur in connection with the collection or attempted collection of a debt alledgedly owed by a consumer, persons other than the debtor may maintain an action for violation of the Act.

Campbell v. Beneficial Finance Company of Dallas, 616 S.W.2d 375 (Tex. 1981).

14. Limitations on Garnishment

A logical source from which a debt can be collected from a consumer borrower is that person's earnings. Legal action may be taken to use the debtor's earnings to pay a debt. This legal process is known as *garnishment*. Because garnishment may adversely affect the consumer's employment and his family's welfare, Congress has statutorily limited the amount of earnings that can be subject to garnishment.

Disposable earnings are that part of a consumer's earnings left after all withholdings required by law are deducted from the earnings. In general, the federal maximum amount of the total disposable earnings subject to garnishment in any week may not exceed the *lesser* of the following: (1) 25 percent of the disposable earnings for the week or (2) the amount by which the disposable earnings for that week exceed thirty times the federal minimum hourly wage prescribed by the Fair Labor Standards Act. For example, suppose that a consumer debtor has disposable earnings of $200 per week and these earnings are subject to garnishment. What is the federal limit on the amount garnished? The answer is $50. The calculation of 25 percent of disposable earnings is $50, whereas this amount of disposable earnings exceeding thirty times the minimum wage ($3.35 per hour) is $99.50. Since $50 is the lesser of the amounts calculated, it is the garnishment limit.

In the past some employers have discharged employees when their earnings were garnished. The federal law now prohibits this discharge on the basis that the employee's earnings have been subject to garnishment for only one indebtedness. (By implication, the law seems to permit the dismissal of an employee from employment if there are garnishments involving two or more indebtednesses owed by that employee.) If an employer violates this provision limiting the discharge of employees, the employer may be fined up to $1,000 or imprisoned up to one year, or any combination of these two sentences.

The federal law does not preempt the field of garnishment or affect any state law. Many state laws exempt larger amounts than does the federal law, and the net effect of the federal law is to exempt the larger amount that either provides. Both the state and the federal laws illustrate a public policy against using a wage earner's income to pay judgment debts. In some states, the amount exempt is left to the courts, in order to avoid undue hardship on the debtor.

OTHER CONSUMER PROTECTION LAWS

15. Magnuson-Moss Warranty Act

In the past, warranties have been written in language so technical and misleading that many so-called warranties on products were actually disclaimers of warranties. Prior to the adoption of the federal law on warranties and the Federal Trade Commission (FTC) rules designed to accomplish its goals, a wide gap separated what the consumer was led to believe and what the manufacturer and seller would do under a warranty. To alleviate this problem, to provide consumers with adequate information about express warranties, and to prevent deceptive warranties, Congress enacted the Magnuson-Moss Warranty Act. This law and the FTC rules adopted under it are applicable to the sale of all consumer products costing over $5. The law is not applicable to service contracts or to leases. The following case illustrates the limited applicability of this law.

CASE

James A. Corral sued the Rollins Protective Services Company for damages. Rollins had installed and agreed to service a fire and burglary alarm system in the Corral home. A fire occurred, the alarm system failed to function, and Corral sustained substantial damage. Among other theories the plaintiff alleged a violation of the federal Magnuson-Moss Warranty Act. The lower court granted Rollins's motion for a summary judgment on the basis that in the absence of a sale there were no warranties that were protected by the Act. Corral appealed.

ISSUE: Does the Magnuson-Moss Warranty Act apply to this Corral-Rollins transaction?

DECISION: No.

REASON:

1. The Magnuson-Moss Warranty Act was passed by Congress in 1975 and applies to the *sale* of consumer products manufactured after July 4, 1975.
2. Rollins maintains that the Act is inapplicable, and relies upon language found in the definitional section of the law that refers only to sales transactions. A "consumer" is described as a *buyer* of any consumer product, that is, personal property used for personal, family, or household purposes.
3. Warranties on services are not covered under the Act. Also, the Act does not apply to leases of consumer products since a "written warranty" under the Act only arises in connection with the "sale" of a consumer product. Thus the Act literally covers only warranties on a consumer product "sold" to a consumer.
4. The agreement here, whether it be a lease, service agreement, or a lease/service agreement, has none of the characteristics of a sale and is clearly not subject to the terms of the Act.

Corral v. Rollins Protective Services, 732 P.2d 1260 (Kan. 1987).

This law does not require that a warranty be given. However, if a warranty is made by the seller, that warranty must satisfy the requirements stated in the following paragraphs. Specifically, the Magnuson-Moss Act provides guidance concerning express warranties, implied warranties, and mechanisms for resolving disputes.

Express warranties. The first requirement of the law is that a warrantor of a consumer product must, by means of a written warranty, fully and conspicuously disclose in simple and readily understood language the terms and conditions of the warranty. The law and the rules then specify what must be included in the written warranty. Such a warranty must include, among other things, a statement of what the warrantor will do in the event of a defect or breach of warranty, at whose expense, and for what period of time. Furthermore, the warranty must set forth the step-by-step procedure the consumer is to follow in order to obtain performance of the warranty.

Any exceptions or limitations of the warranty must be indicated. A warrantor may not exclude or limit consequential damages for breach of any warranty unless the exclusion or limitation appears conspicuously on the face of the warranty.

The law also requires that each warranty be labeled ''full'' or ''limited'' if the product sells for over $15. A *full warranty* must indicate its duration. Products covered by a full warranty must be repaired or replaced by the seller without charge and within a reasonable time in the event there is a defect, malfunction, or failure to conform to the written warranty. A purchaser of a *limited warranty* is put on notice to find out its limits.

To assist the consumer in making an intelligent purchase decision, sellers are required to make available all information about the warranties. Prior to the sale, this information must be clearly and conspicuously displayed in close connection with the warranted product. If the contract involves a used car, the FTC has issued specific rules that must be complied with in order to provide consumers with accurate warranty information.

Implied warranties. Under the federal law, a warrantor may not impose any limitation on the duration of any implied warranty. No supplier may disclaim or modify any implied warranty if there is a written warranty or if, at the time of sale or within ninety days, the supplier enters into a service contract with the buyer. The latter restriction does not prevent a seller from limiting the time period of a written warranty. The time period of the warranty must also be set forth in clear and unmistakable language on the face of the warranty.

Mechanisms to resolve disputes. A significant aspect of the federal law deals with informal mechanisms for the resolution of consumer disputes. The law does not require such mechanisms, but it strongly encourages sellers to use them. If a seller establishes a procedure for an independent or government entity to resolve disputes with its buyers, the consumer must resort to the procedure before filing suit against the seller. Consumers are given access to these informal dispute procedures free of charge.

Violations of the warranty law subject the business to a suit for damages. This cause of action is in addition to a suit under the Uniform Commercial Code. The law also authorizes class action suits for damages for breach of warranty if at least 100 persons are affected. The law also allows consumers to collect attorney's fees if legal counsel is required to enforce a warranty. This makes litigation a reasonable alternative even though the cost of the product is not substantial. Without the provision authorizing attorney's fees, consumer suits in breach of warranty cases would rarely be the subject of litigation.

16. Housing Warranties

Due to the nature of the transaction, the buyer of real estate normally will have had very little opportunity to inspect the real estate and its improvements prior to the signing of a contract. Therefore, during the time prior to the closing, the buyer should make an effort to inspect the property thoroughly. A smart buyer would seek the assistance of experts to inspect, when applicable, the roof, the air-conditioning and heating unit, the plumbing, the electrical wiring, and other major appliances and utilities. Even after such inspections, the buyer may not discover some substantial defect that adversely affects the property's value.

Buyers have been allowed to rescind purchases on the ground of fraud or misrepresentation, but historically warranties were found to exist only when specifically included in the contract. In other words, the seller of housing was not held responsible for the habitability of the structure or the quality of workmanship and materials. In recent years, most states have changed the law as it relates to the sale of housing but have retained the doctrine of *caveat emptor* for vacant real estate. The courts in these states have imposed liability on sellers and builders of housing by use of a variety of theories. Some courts have held that there is an implied warranty against structural defects, similar to the implied warranty of fitness in the sale of personal property, and that there is no rational basis for differentiating between the sale of a newly constructed house by the builder-vendor and the sale of any other manufactured product. These courts usually have not extended the warranty against structural defects to the individual who builds a house himself and later decides to sell it. Casual sales and resales are not included because the warranty arises when the seller is in the business of selling housing. Furthermore, warranties of habitability usually are not implied in the sale of vacant land.

Other courts have created an implied warranty that a home is built and constructed in a reasonably workmanlike manner and that it is fit for its intended purpose—habitation. In one case, there was no water supply, and the subdivider-seller was held liable for breach of this warranty. In another case, the air-conditioning system did not work properly, and the seller was held to have breached an implied warranty. In some cases, the buyer is entitled to damages. If the breach is so great that the home is unfit for habitation, rescission is an available remedy. However, the theory of implied warranty does not impose on the builder an obligation to build a perfect house.

The issue of whether the builder's liability is limited to the first purchaser or extends to subsequent purchasers has caused courts a great deal of difficulty. Some courts have held that subsequent purchasers are protected by the builder's implied warranty. Other courts have ruled that the subsequent purchaser can recover when it is proved the builder was negligent. The distinctions between implied warranty and negligence theories are subtle and at times confusing, as is illustrated in the following case.

CASE

Shirley Mae Weller and William S. Weller are the fourth owners of a house designed, built, and sold in 1973 by the defendants, Cosmopolitan Homes, Inc., Hutchinson Construction Company, and Builders' Research Engineering Company (the builders). Although the Wellers seek to recover for deficiencies in workmanship, design, and materials in the house attributable to negligent design and construction by the defendants, the facts alleged in the complaint relate to cracking in the foundation from movement or settling of the house that had not occurred at the time the Wellers made their purchase on January 4, 1977.

The district court dismissed the Wellers' complaint on the ground that there was no privity of contract between the defendants and the Wellers because the Wellers were not the first purchasers or users of the house, and therefore the defendants did not owe the Wellers a duty of reasonable care. The court of appeals reversed the district court ruling, holding that regardless of lack of privity of contract, the purchaser of a used home may recover for property damage caused by the negligence of the builder. The builder then sought further review.

ISSUE: May a subsequent owner of improved real estate hold the original builder liable for negligence even though such owner cannot recover under a breach of contractual warranty theory?

DECISION: Yes, to the extent of damages caused by latent defects.

REASONS:
1. An obligation to act without negligence in the construction of a home is independent of contractual obligations such as implied warranty of habitability.
2. Given the mobility of most potential homeowners, it is foreseeable that a house will be sold to subsequent purchasers, and any structural defects are as certain to harm the subsequent purchaser

as the first. We see no reason for disallowing a subsequent purchaser to state a claim in negligence.

3. Negligence requires that a builder or contractor be held to a standard of reasonable care in the conduct of its duties to the foreseeable users of the property. Negligence in tort must establish defects in workmanship, supervision, or design as a responsibility of the individual defendant.
4. In the context of the purchase of a used home, the owner must demonstrate that the defect is latent or hidden, and must show that the defect was caused by the builder.

Cosmopolitan Homes, Inc. v. Weller, 663 P.2d 1041 (Colo. 1983).

This issue of how to protect subsequent purchasers may be of less importance today because of the variety of builder-supported programs that give the buyers of new homes an express warranty for a stated period. These warranties require the builder or an insurance company to repair major defects discovered within the period of coverage. Actually these warranties can be positive selling points for the property, since they can be transferred during the time provided. Express warranty programs as well as court-adopted remedies involving implied warranties and negligence make it clear that consumer protection has been extended to housing.

17. Consumer Product Safety Act

In 1972, Congress enacted the Consumer Product Safety Act, creating the Consumer Product Safety Commission and a Product Safety Advisory Council. This law imposes safety standards on manufacturing and commercial operations relating to consumer products and, with a few exceptions, identifies and regulates almost all aspects of safety in products sold to the public. Since there is no requirement that the goods be sold, the law covers free samples and products sold to others but used by consumers. The breadth of the law is apparent from its definition of *consumer product*. The term includes any article produced or distributed for sale to, or use by, a consumer in or around a permanent or temporary household or residence, a school, in recreation, or otherwise.

Manufacturers of consumer products are required to furnish information about their products to the commission. This information may include technical data; it must include all information on new products. The law also requires manufacturers to notify the commission whenever they learn that a product is defective or fails to meet applicable standards. Notice also must be given to the general public and to known purchasers whenever it is found that a product is defective or in violation of a safety rule.

Once a product safety rule has been adopted, a variety of private and public enforcement procedures are available. Courts are authorized to issue injunctions, which may result in the removal of a product from the market. The law provides a penalty of $2,000 for each violation, up to a maximum of $500,000 for each product involved in a violation. A consumer is authorized to sue in federal courts for injuries caused by a product if the manufacturer is knowingly in violation of a product safety rule, provided the claim meets the jurisdictional amount ($50,000) of the federal courts.

18. Unfair Business Practices

By federal statute, the Federal Trade Commission is responsible for preventing unfair or deceptive acts or practices in commerce. As a result of this law, the FTC has a Bureau of Consumer Protection actively engaged in regulating advertising and the sale of goods. Advertising is unfair or deceptive if it has a tendency or capacity to mislead consumers.

The FTC has found numerous unfair and deceptive promotional devices and advertisements. One ad violated the law by comparing the seller's price with a higher "regular" price or a manufacturer's list price. It is deceptive to refer to a "regular price" unless the seller usually and recently sold the items at that price in the regular course of business. Also it has been held deceptive to refer to the "manufacturer's list price" when that list price is not the ordinary and customary retail sales price of the item in the locality. Bait and switch promotions are another violation of the FTC Act. In a *bait and switch* sales technique, a product is advertised at a low price that will bring in customers whom the advertiser then tries to switch to other products he prefers to sell.

Ads that are false or misleading about the quality of a product or its source are also unfair and deceptive. Disparaging the product of a competitor may be stopped by the FTC on the ground that such ads are unfair. Words that are technically not false may be held to be deceptive if they give the wrong impression to consumers. The words "guaranteed for life" were held to be deceptive when the seller intended the life to be the life of the product, and consumers thought that the guarantee was for the life of the purchaser of the product.

Many states have laws designed to aid and protect consumers in a multitude of transactions. These laws, which are enacted pursuant to the police power, are usually enforced by the state attorney general, but they may be enforced by consumers and class action suits.

19. Home Solicitation

Under its authority to prevent unfair deceptive business practices, the Federal Trade Commission has regulated door-to-door selling. The FTC rule covers any sale, lease, or rental of consumer goods with a purchase price of $25 or more at places of business other than the normal place of business of the seller. It does not cover mail-order or telephone sales or sales in which the buyer has requested the seller to visit his home.

The law requires the seller to furnish the buyer with a copy of the contract in the same language—for example, Spanish—used in the oral presentation. The contract must, in 10-point type, notify the buyer that the transaction may be canceled at any time prior to midnight of the third business day after the date of the transaction. The seller is required to furnish the buyer with a form to be used to cancel, so that all the buyer is required to do is to sign the form and send it to the seller. The seller also must orally inform the buyer of the right to cancel.

The law requires the seller to honor the notice of cancellation within ten days, refund all payments made and all property traded in, and return any instruments assigned by the buyer. If the purchase is canceled, all security arrangements are null and void. If the goods have been delivered to the buyer prior to cancellation, the seller must, within ten days, notify the buyer whether the seller intends to repossess or to abandon the goods.

20. Real Estate Settlement Procedures Act

Since the purchase of a home is the most significant transaction ever entered into by most people, the law contains provisions aimed at assisting buyers with this transaction. At one time, the amount of settlement costs or closing costs in real estate transactions often came as a surprise, if not a shock, to many purchasers. To aid home buyers and borrowers, Congress, in 1974, enacted a law requiring the disclosure of all costs to buyers and borrowers prior to the consummation of a real estate transaction. The law assumes that the disclosure of the total cost will allow buyers and borrowers to shop for credit and thus reduce the settlement costs in many cases. The disclosure statement also gives advance notice of the cash required at settlement.

The law requires the use of a standard form for advance disclosure of closing costs and for recording the actual charges incurred at settlement in all covered transactions. Some settlement costs are typically paid by sellers; others are the obligation of buyers. The form covers both categories of expenses. Among the common items disclosed are loan origination fees, loan discount points, appraisal fees, attorney's fees, inspection fees, title charges, and the cost of surveys.

The law also outlaws certain practices that are contrary to the interest of the home-buying public. Among these are giving kickbacks for referring a borrower to a lender, charging or accepting a fee for something other than services actually performed, and requiring that a home seller purchase title insurance from any particular title company. For the title insurance violation, there is a liability equal to three times the cost of the title insurance.

In addition to the foregoing, this law prevents a lender from requiring that an unreasonable amount be paid in advance for the purposes of paying real property taxes and insurance when they are due. These payments generally are known as *escrow* payments. A lender can require the borrower to pay at closing, as escrow, the amount equal to the number of months between the closing date and the last time the bill was paid. In addition, the lender can collect at closing a cushion of two months of the total estimated bill for taxes and insurance.

CHAPTER SUMMARY

Debtor Protection in General

1. The federal government has enacted into law numerous statutes designed to protect the consumer debtor in credit transactions.
2. A consumer debtor is an individual involved in a credit transaction for the purpose of satisfying personal, family, or household needs.
3. Credit is applicable to any transaction in which money is lent with repayment to be made in the future.

Credit Applications

Equal Credit Opportunity Act

1. This law prevents discrimination in granting credit on the basis of sex, race, color, age, religion, national origin, the receipt of welfare, or the exercise of any right under the law.
2. Victims of illegal discrimination may collect actual damages, attorney's fees, other legal expenses, and punitive damages.
3. The ECOA prohibits discriminatory advertising concerning the availability of credit.
4. The creditor must take care not to request on a credit application any information that may lead to discrimination in the extension of credit.

Fair Credit Reporting Act

1. This law was designed to prevent abuses in the credit reporting industry and to ensure a person's right to privacy.
2. The FCRA's protection is limited to reports on consumers. Businesses are presumed to be able to protect themselves.
3. The FCRA regulates those who distribute reports on consumers and the users of such reports.

Consumer Reporting Agencies

1. Such an agency exists when it regularly collects information on consumers and furnishes it to third parties.
2. These agencies must make certain that consumer reports are used for a justifiable purpose.
3. These agencies also must take precautions to ensure the accuracy of the information distributed. Such information must not be obsolete.

Users of Information

1. Whenever a user of a consumer report takes adverse action on a consumer's credit, insurance, employment, or license application, that user must disclose from which reporting agency the information was obtained.

Rights of Consumer Debtors

1. A consumer debtor has the right to inspect the report an agency has compiled on him.
2. This debtor may challenge the accuracy of any information.
3. If the information is retained by the consumer reporting agency, the consumer debtor may prepare and require the agency to include in any report a written statement about the dispute.

Credit Transactions

Truth-in-Lending Act

1. TILA is applicable only if the credit transaction involves a consumer debtor who will repay a debt that is payable in more than four installments or is subject to a finance charge.
2. TILA attempts to encourage consumer debtors to shop for the best credit opportunities. This purpose is accomplished through disclosure requirements that provide the information to make comparison possible.

Disclosures Required

1. TILA's most important required disclosures are the amount financed, the finance charge, the annual percentage rate, and the total amount of all payments.

Sanctions for Violations

1. Failure to make these disclosures accurately exposes the creditor to liability for twice the finance charge within the range of $100 to $1,000.

Uniform Consumer Credit Code

1. This law has been adopted by a few states.
2. It does not fix interest rates but does set maximum rates of interest.
3. This law prohibits certain types of transactions such as those requiring balloon payments after the end of a relatively short period of time.

4. The law prohibits a seller from taking a wage assignment from a consumer.

Debt Collection

Fair Credit Billing Act

1. This law specifies the rights of consumer debtors and the duties of creditors if there is a billing error in an open-ended credit transaction.
2. After a consumer debtor has submitted a billing error notice, the creditor must respond by correcting the error or explaining why the bill is accurate.
3. The FCBA establishes criteria for how the creditor is to treat the consumer debtor during the resolution of a dispute.
4. This law also provides creditors with accounting principles that must be followed when a payment is credited to the consumer debtor's bill.

Credit Card Protection

1. A cardholder is liable only up to $50 for the unauthorized use of a credit card.
2. There is no liability for unauthorized purchases by credit card that were not requested by the cardholder.
3. There is no liability unless the card has a method for identification of the user.

Fair Debt Collection Practices Act

1. The FDCPA was passed to prevent the abuses that may occur in the debt collection process.
2. This law regulates only third parties who act as debt collectors. Creditors who collect from their own debtors are exempt.
3. The FDCPA covers only the collection of consumer debts. Again, businesses are presumed to be able to protect themselves.
4. A number of collection practices are allowed and a number are considered illegal under the FDCPA.
5. Any person abused during a third party's efforts to collect a consumer debt may recover actual damages, attorney's fees, and other legal expenses.

Limitations on Garnishments

1. Both federal and state governments limit the amount of wages that can be used to pay debts.
2. The federal law limits garnishment to 25 percent of take-home pay or the amount that disposable earnings exceed thirty times the federal minimum wage, whichever is less.
3. Employers may not discharge an employee because one garnishment proceeding has been instituted against that employee.

Other Consumer Protection

Magnuson-Moss Warranty Act

1. Warranties of consumer products must be in writing and must fully and conspicuously disclose in simple, readily understood language the terms of the warranty.
2. The warranty must include a statement of what the warrantor will do in the event of a breach of warranty, at whose expense, and for what time period.
3. The warranty must inform the consumer of the steps to be followed to obtain performance.
4. Warranties must be labeled full or limited, and information about warranties must be readily available.

5. A warrantor may exclude or limit consequential damages only in conspicuous writing on the face of the warranty.
6. Informal procedures established by the warrantor in order to resolve disputes concerning warranties must be followed by the customers.

Housing Warranties	1. Prior to closing, the buyer should inspect the real property thoroughly for possible problems. 2. To protect buyers from the hard-to-discover defects, courts have held that builders implicitly warrant that a residence is habitable. 3. Many builders have begun to give express warranties that houses are free from structural defects.
Consumer Product Safety Act	1. The Consumer Product Safety Commission imposes safety standards on manufacturers of consumer products. Manufacturers are required to furnish information to the commission. 2. There are sanctions in addition to common law liability, and the statute allows suits in the federal courts in the event that product safety rules are violated.
Unfair Business Practices	1. The Federal Trade Commission may prohibit deceptive business practices by issuing cease and desist orders. 2. State statutes also attempt to prohibit deception of consumers. They generally create liability not only to consumers but also to competitors for false and deceptive advertising.
Home Solicitation	1. The Federal Trade Commission has rules regulating door-to-door selling. These cover goods costing $25 or more. 2. The rules require written contracts in at least 10-point type, and the contract must allow cancellation any time prior to midnight of the third business day after the transaction. 3. The buyer must be orally informed of the right to cancel and obtain a refund.
Real Estate Settlement Procedures Act	1. This law applies to the purchase of homes. It requires the disclosure of all costs to buyers and borrowers in advance of the closing of the transaction. 2. The buyer is furnished a completed standard form informing him as to the amount of such costs and which party is expected to pay them.

REVIEW QUESTIONS AND PROBLEMS

1. Match each term in column A with the appropriate statement in column B.

A	B
(1) Consumer debtor	(a) A third party who collects information on consumers and furnishes it to creditors, insurers, employers, and similar parties.
(2) Equal Credit Opportunity Act	(b) Designed to inform buyers of closing costs.
(3) Fair Credit Reporting Act	(c) Enacted to encourage consumer applicants to shop for the best credit opportunity.
(4) Consumer reporting agency	(d) Exists to ensure that buyers of housing are protected against defects.
(5) Truth-in-Lending Act	(e) An individual involved in a credit transaction for the purposes of satisfying personal, family, or household needs.

(6) Billing error	(f) Passed to prevent abuses that may occur in the debt collection process.
(7) Fair Debt Collection Practices Act	(g) Law that regulates those parties that either distribute or use information on consumers.
(8) Housing Warranties	(h) Regulated by the Federal Trade Commission and state laws.
(9) Magnuson-Moss Warranty Act	(i) Law enacted to prevent discrimination based on several factors in the granting of credit.
(10) Consumer Product Safety Act	(j) The federal law that establishes requirements concerning manufacturers' warranties.
(11) Unfair business practices	(k) A mistake in an open-ended credit statement.
(12) Real Estate Settlement Procedures Act	(l) Enacted to impose safety standards on manufacturers of consumer products.

2. The Equal Credit Opportunity Act was passed to prevent discrimination in the credit extension transaction. What are the criteria on which the credit decision cannot be legally based?

3. An insurance company requested a credit investigating company to investigate a person who had filed a suit against the insurance company. Is the report prepared subject to the provisions of the Fair Credit Reporting Act? Why or why not?

4. Lamb's automobile insurance policy was canceled due to information in a report furnished by Equifax Services, Inc. (Equifax), to the insurance company. Lamb contacted Equifax to discover the contents of the report. He was verbally told the contents but was not given a copy. Lamb disputed the following two items contained in the report: (1) the reason for his first divorce and (2) information concerning an arrest. Because of the dispute, Equifax reinvestigated Lamb's background and issued a new report. It deleted the first disputed item but retained the second based on a verification by police records. Lamb was given a copy of this second report, and he took no exception to it. The second report was furnished to another source, but Lamb was not told this fact. When he learned that Equifax had reported the information about his arrest, Lamb instituted this suit alleging defamation and violation of the FCRA. Did Equifax violate the disclosure requirements of the FCRA? Explain.

5. Friendly Finance held a mortgage on Dandy's six-unit apartment building. Dandy fell behind on his payments and, to avoid foreclosure, agreed to execute a mortgage on his home in favor of Friendly. This second mortgage secured a note for the amount that Dandy was in arrears on his payments. When the second mortgage was entered, Friendly did not comply with the Truth-in-Lending law. Dandy now sues Friendly for his actual damages plus twice the amount of the finance charge. Should Dandy suceed? Why?

6. The purchaser of an automobile entered into an installment sales transaction with an automobile dealer. Prior to completion of the transaction, the dealer submitted the buyer's credit application to a credit company. Once the dealer had been notified that the buyer met that company's credit standards, the buyer and the dealer executed a retail installment contract. It stated: "The foregoing contract hereby is accepted by the Seller and assigned to the credit company in accordance with terms of the Assignment set forth on the reverse side hereof." The credit company purchased the contract without recourse against the dealer. Is the credit company subject to TILA? Explain.

7. A salesman for Plumbing Company sold a water-softening unit to Baker. The sales agreement included a "referral sale" credit. For every sale to a buyer Baker had referred to Plumbing, Baker would get a $40 credit toward payment for Baker's unit. Is this a valid sales agreement? Explain.

8. Plaintiff, a former credit card holder, alleged a violation of the Fair Credit Billing Act. The credit card was issued to a corporation for a company account with the plaintiff, as president, authorized to use it and he agreed to be jointly liable. Later a dispute arose over the account and the card was canceled. Is this dispute subject to the Fair Credit Billing Act? Why or why not?

9. The Charge-It Company issued a credit card to Albert at his request. Albert's card was stolen, and he immediately notified Charge-It. The thief used Albert's card for motel and gasoline purchases. Who bears the loss in this situation? Why?

10. Mr. Boudreaux owed the Allstate Company $185, payable in twenty-four monthly installments. When Boudreaux became unemployed, he fell behind in his payments. Allstate hired the Debtor's Collection Agency to collect the amount owed by Boudreaux. This agency began calling his neighbors repeatedly, since the Boudreaux phone was disconnected. It used insulting language in speaking to these neighbors about Boudreaux. Mrs. Boudreaux also was insulted when an agent attempted to collect the amount owed. Does Boudreaux have any recourse against the agency for these debt collection actions? Explain.

11. Harry, a wage earner, earns $200 per week. His employer witholds 20 percent for income and FICA taxes. A garnishment proceeding is commenced against Harry and his employer to collect a judgment owed by Harry. Under the applicable federal law, how much of Harry's wages may be garnished each week? Explain your calculations.

12. Tom purchased a BMW that was warranted for 36,000 miles or three years. Within the warranty period, the engine failed. The seller contended that the failure was caused by buyer abuse. Tom sued under the Magnuson-Moss Warranty Act and the Uniform Commercial Code. Are both remedies available? Explain. Why would a plaintiff want to use both?

45 Bankruptcy

CHAPTER PREVIEW

- **TYPES OF PROCEEDINGS**

  In General
  Liquidation Proceedings
  Reorganization Proceedings
  Adjustment of Individuals' Debts
  Adjustment of Family Farmer's Debts

- **GENERAL PRINCIPLES**

  Property of the Estate
  Exemptions
  Debts That Are Not Discharged
  Grounds for Denying Discharge

- **PROCEDURAL STEPS**

  Voluntary Commencement
  Involuntary Commencement
  Conversion of Cases
  Automatic Stay
  Meeting of Creditors

- **TRUSTEE AND CASE ADMINISTRATION**

  Trustee and the Estate
  General Duties and Powers
  Executory Contracts and Unexpired Leases
  Voidable Preferences
  Fraudulent Transfers

- **CREDITORS**

  Creditors and Claims
  Right of Setoff
  Priorities

BUSINESS MANAGEMENT DECISION

Your company, which is self-insured, faces thousands of products liability suits. The potential liability could reach hundreds of millions of dollars. Other than these suits, your company is financially sound and profitable.

Should your company consider filing for bankruptcy protection?

The law of bankruptcy provides possible solutions to problems that arise when a person, partnership, corporation, farmer, or municipality is unable, or finds it difficult to satisfy obligations to creditors. Bankruptcy has its roots in the law of the Roman Empire and has been a part of English jurisprudence since 1542. The bankruptcy laws in the United States have been amended periodically. The last major revision is known as the Bankruptcy Reform Act of 1978. This law became effective on October 1, 1979. Additional amendments to it occurred in 1984 and in 1986.

The basic concept underlying bankruptcy is to allow a debtor who is in a difficult financial situation a fresh financial start. In other words, the bankruptcy laws permit a deserving debtor the opportunity to come out from under overwhelming financial burdens and to begin life anew. However, this "fresh start" is not granted without the debtor's paying something for the opportunity. In essence, the bankruptcy laws have always attempted to balance the rights of the debtor with the rights of the creditors. In order to protect the creditors, the debtor must turn over his assets to court supervision. Loss of every asset would deprive the debtor of the opportunity for a fresh financial start. Therefore the debtor may exempt certain items from the bankruptcy estate and retain them as the basis for a new beginning.

As you study this chapter, keep in mind that the bankruptcy laws provide an acceptable alternative for debtors in financial difficulty. Filing for bankruptcy is no longer socially unacceptable or an admission of failure. More than ever before, bankruptcy has become an acceptable solution to the financial distress individuals or businesses could not otherwise overcome.

The 1984 amendment was necessitated by a Supreme Court decision relative to the status of bankruptcy judges. It also responded to criticisms that the law was too pro-debtor in its exemptions. The 1986 amendments created a new chapter to assist farmers in their attempts to survive a difficult period in agriculture.

The following materials describe the types of bankruptcy proceedings, some procedural aspects of a bankruptcy case, and rights and duties of the parties involved in a bankruptcy case.

Prior to studying these materials, you should be aware of some terminology used in the bankruptcy law. For example, the debtor is an individual, a business organization, or a municipality that the bankruptcy case concerns. A **claim** is a right to payment from the debtor. Claims are held and asserted by creditors. An **order of relief** is entered by the bankruptcy judge when he finds that the debtor is entitled to the protection of the bankruptcy law. A trustee is the person responsible for managing the debtor's assets.

Claim *A creditor's right to payment in a bankruptcy case.*

Order of relief *The ruling by a bankruptcy judge that a particular case is properly before the bankruptcy court.*

TYPES OF PROCEEDINGS

1. In General

The federal bankruptcy laws have two distinct approaches to the problems of debtors. One approach is to liquidate debts. The liquidation approach recognizes that misfortune and poor judgment often create a situation in which a debtor will never be able to pay his debts by his own efforts, or at least it will be very difficult to do so.

The second approach is to postpone the time of payment of debts or to reduce some of them to levels that make repayment possible. This approach is found in the reorganization sections for businesses and in the adjustment of debts provisions for municipalities, farmers, and individuals with regular incomes. The reorganization and adjustment provisions are aimed at rehabilitation of debtors. These procedures, if utilized, prevent harassment of debtors and spare them undue hardship while enabling most creditors eventually to obtain some repayment.

There are five types of bankruptcy proceedings, each identified by a chapter of the statute. Chapter 7, Liquidation; Chapter 9, Adjustment of Debts of a Municipality; Chapter 11, Reorganization; Chapter 12, Adjustment of Debts of a Family Farmer; Chapter 13, Adjustment of Debts of an Individual with Regular Income. Chapter 9 adjustment proceedings recognize the financial plight of many governmental units such as New York City and Cleveland, Ohio. A municipal governmental entity may be a debtor under Chapter 9 if state law or a public official authorized by state law permits it. The municipality must be unable to meet its debts as they mature, and it must desire to effect a plan to adjust its debts. Because of the special and limited use of this proceeding, it will not be discussed further in this text.

2. Liquidation Proceedings

Liquidation *The process of winding up the affairs of a corporation or firm for the purpose of paying its debts and disposing of its assets.*

Discharge *An order by a bankruptcy court that a debt is no longer valid; in essence, the debtor's obligation is forgiven.*

Liquidation proceedings are used to eliminate most of the debts of a debtor. In exchange for having the debts declared uncollectible, the debtor must allow many, if not most, of his assets to be used to satisfy creditors' claims. Cases under Chapter 7 of the statute may involve individuals, partnerships, or corporations, but only individuals may receive a **discharge** from the court. A discharge voids any judgment against the debtor to the extent that it creates a personal liability. A discharge covers all scheduled debts that arose before the date of the order for relief. It is irrelevant whether or not a claim was filed or allowed. A discharge also operates as an injunction against all attempts to collect the debt—by judicial proceedings, telephone calls, letters, personal contacts, or other efforts. Under all types of proceedings, once they are commenced, creditors are prohibited from attempting to collect their debts.

The debts of partnerships and corporations that go through liquidation proceedings are not discharged. These businesses are still technically liable for their debts; however, the lack of discharge is immaterial unless the partnership or corporation acquires assets later. This lack of discharge stops people from using "shell" businesses after bankruptcy for other purposes.

Certain businesses are denied the right to liquidation proceedings. Railroads, insurance companies, banks, savings and loan associations, homestead associations, and credit unions may not be debtors under Chapter 7 of the Bankruptcy Act. These organizations are subject to the jurisdiction of administrative agencies that handle all aspects of such organizations, including problems related to insolvency.

Under this arrangement, there are alternative legal provisions for their liquidation.

Chapter 7 has special provisions relating to liquidation proceedings involving stockbrokers and commodity brokers. These special provisions are necessary to protect their customers, because bankruptcies of this kind usually involve large indebtedness and substantial assets. Stockbrokers and commodity brokers are subject only to Chapter 7. Chapter 11 and Chapter 13 proceedings are not available to them.

3. Reorganization Proceedings

Reorganization proceedings are utilized when debtors wish to restructure their finances and attempt to pay creditors over an extended period, as required by a court-approved plan. Such cases almost always involve a business, and approximately 20,000 such petitions are filed annually. Chapter 11 of the 1978 Bankruptcy Act contains detailed provisions on all aspects of the plan of reorganization and its execution.

As soon as practicable after the order for relief, the court appoints a committee of creditors holding unsecured claims. The committee ordinarily consists of persons with the seven largest claims, and it may employ attorneys, accountants, or other agents to assist it. Working with the trustee and the debtor concerning the administration of the case, it represents the interests of the creditors. It may investigate the financial condition of the debtor and will assist in the formulation of the reorganization plan.

The court in reorganization cases will usually appoint a trustee before approval of the plan of reorganization. If the court does not appoint a trustee, it will appoint an examiner who conducts an investigation into the affairs of the debtor, including any mismanagement or irregularities.

After the trustee or the examiner conducts the investigation of the acts, conduct, assets, liabilities, financial conditions, and other relevant aspects of the debtor, a written report of this investigation is filed with the court. The trustee may file a plan of reorganization if the debtor does not, or it may recommend conversion of the case to liquidation proceedings. The trustee will also file tax returns for the debtor, file reports with the court, and may even operate the debtor's business unless the court orders otherwise. The debtor may file a plan of reorganization with the voluntary petition or later, in an attempt to extricate the business from its financial difficulties and help it to survive. The plan will classify claims, and all claims within a class will be treated the same. All unsecured claims for less than a specified amount may be classified together. The plan will designate those classes of claims that are unimpaired under the plan and will specify the treatment to be given claims that are impaired.

The plan must provide a means for its execution. It may provide that the debtor will retain all or part of the property of the estate. It may also propose that property be sold or transferred to creditors or other entities. Mergers and consolidations may be proposed. In short, the plan will deal with all aspects of the organization of the debtor, its property, and its debts. Some debts will be paid in full, some will be partially paid over an extended period of time, and others may not be paid at all. The only limitation is that all claimants must receive as much as they would receive in liquidation proceedings.

Holders of claims or interests in the debtor's property are allowed to vote and to accept or reject the proposed plan of reorganization. A class of claims has accepted a plan if at least two-thirds in amount and more than half in number of claims vote yes. Acceptance by a class of interests such as equity holders requires a two-thirds yes vote.

A hearing is held on the confirmation of a plan, to determine if it is fair and equitable. The statute specifies several conditions, such as good faith, which must be met before the plan is approved. Also before approval, it must be established that each holder of a claim or interest has either accepted the plan or will receive as much under the reorganization plan as would be received in liquidation proceedings. For secured creditors, this means that they will receive the value of their security either by payment or by delivery of the property. Confirmation of the plan makes it binding on the debtor, equity security holders, and creditors. Confirmation vests the property of the estate in the debtor and releases the debtor from any payment not specified in the reorganization plan.

As a general rule, any debtor subject to liquidation under the statute (Chapter 7) is also subject to reorganization (Chapter 11). An exception exists for railroads. The public interest in railroads prevents their liquidation, but the law recognizes that financial reorganization of railroads is not only possible but often desirable.

4. Adjustment of Individuals' Debts

Chapter 13 proceedings are used to adjust the debts of individuals with regular income whose debts are small enough and whose income is significant enough that substantial repayment is feasible. Such persons often seek to avoid the stigma of bankruptcy. Unsecured debts of individuals utilizing Chapter 13 proceedings cannot exceed \$100,000, and the secured debts cannot exceed \$350,000. Persons utilizing Chapter 13 are usually employees earning a salary, but persons engaged in business also qualify. Self-employed persons who incur trade debts are considered to be engaged in business.

The debtor files a plan that provides for the use of all or a portion of his future earnings or income for the payment of debts. The income is under the supervision and control of the trustee. Except as provided in the plan, the debtor keeps possession of his property. If the debtor is engaged in business, the debtor continues to operate his business. The plan must provide for the full payment of all claims entitled to priority unless the creditors with priority agree to a different treatment. If a plan divides unsecured claims into classes, all claims within a class must be given the same treatment.

Unsecured claims not entitled to priority may be repaid in full or reduced to a level not lower than the amount that would be paid upon liquidation. Since this amount is usually zero, any payment to unsecured creditors will satisfy the law. The secured creditors may be protected by allowing them to retain their lien, by payment of the secured claim in full, or by the surrender of the property to the secured claimant. The usual plan will provide for payments over three years, but the court may extend the payment period up to a total of five years. A typical plan allocates one-fourth of a person's take-home pay to repay debts.

The plan may modify the rights of holders of secured and unsecured claims, except that the rights of holders or real estate mortgages may not be modified. Claims arising after the filing of the petition may be included in the plan. This is a realistic approach, because all the debts of the debtor must be taken into account if the plan is to accomplish its objectives.

When the court conducts a hearing on the confirmation of the plan, if it is satisfied that the debtor will be able to make all payments to comply with it, the plan will be approved. Of course, the plan must be proposed in good faith, be in compliance with the law, and be in the best interest of the creditors.

As soon as the debtor completes all payments under the plan, the court grants the debtor a discharge of all debts, unless the debtor waives the discharge or the debts are not legally dischargeable (see sections 8 and 9).

Courts, after a hearing, may also grant a discharge, even though all payments have not been made, if the debtor's failure to complete the payments is due to circumstances for which the debtor should not justly be held accountable. In such cases, the payments under the plan must be not less than those that would have been paid on liquidation, and modification must not be practicable.

5. Adjustment of Family Farmer's Debts

In 1986, the dire economic plight of the nation's farmers prompted Congress to enact Chapter 12 of the bankruptcy law. Chapter 12 is a reorganization and adjustment law designed to help family farmers stay in business. Without it Congress feared that tens of thousands of farmers would be forced off their farms notwithstanding the fact that farmers may not be put into Chapter 7 involuntarily. This exemption from involuntary bankruptcy is discussed further in section 12.

Chapter 12 of the bankruptcy law is directed at both the short-term and long-term debt of farmers. Under this new law, farmers with as much as $1.5 million in debt are allowed to write down the debt to the current value of their collateral—forcing lenders to write off the difference between a loan's face value and the depressed value of most farm assets. This became necessary because land values had declined sharply, and thus the value of collateral was often less than the debt. If a farmer obtained a discharge in bankruptcy, the creditor would only receive the value of the collateral anyway, so Congress decided to keep the farmers on the farm and to limit the secured creditors to what they would receive in liquidation proceedings.

Under the provisions of Chapter 12, a farmer must file a reorganization plan within ninety days after filing a bankruptcy petition. The plan includes a statement of the farmer's opinion of the current market value of his land and other collateral. Secured creditors have an opportunity to challenge the farmer's estimate of collateral value. Once the plan is approved by the court, creditors cannot veto it.

The farmer must use all of his income that is not needed to support the farm family and current operating expenses for the next three to five years to pay off unsecured creditors such as feed and fuel dealers. If these debts are not paid after five years, they are forgiven. The farmer must pay secured creditors the current market value of the collateral in installments. This will usually be over the life of the original loan.

The net effect of the law is to reduce the amount of the yearly payments from that originally agreed upon to whatever it takes to amortize the new value of the collateral. In a sense, the farmer is repurchasing his farm at its new and lower value.

The new law may make it more difficult for farmers to get new loans or to renew them. It may make cash flow more important than collateral in many loan decisions. It may also give a farmer seeking to renew a loan a negotiating tool. If the loan is not renewed, the farmer threatens to file under Chapter 12 and this would force some write-off of his loan. A few years' experience is needed before the impact of this new chapter of the bankruptcy law is known.

GENERAL PRINCIPLES

6. Property of the Estate

The *bankruptcy estate* consists of all legal or equitable interests of the debtor in property, wherever located. The property may be tangible or intangible and includes causes of action. All property is included in the estate to begin with, but the debtor may exempt portions entitled to exemption, as discussed in the next section.

The estate includes property that the trustee recovers by using his power to avoid prior transactions. It also includes property inherited by the debtor or received as a beneficiary of life insurance within 180 days of the petition. Proceeds, products, offspring, rents, and profits generated by or coming from property in the estate are also part of the estate.

In general, property acquired by the debtor after commencement of the case—including earnings from employment—belongs to the debtors. Property held in trust for the benefit of the debtor under a *spendthrift trust* does not become a part of the estate. In essence, the trustee in bankruptcy acquires the same interest with the same restrictions as the debtor had at the time the bankruptcy petition was filed. However, the trustee can require creditors to turn over possession of assets that were held by the creditors at the time the petition was filed. In return, the trustee must provide adequate protection for these creditors' claims. These concepts apply to the IRS and other government agencies, as the following case illustrates.

CASE

Whiting Pools, Inc., sold, installed, and serviced swimming pools. When the corporation became obligated for $92,000 in taxes, the Internal Revenue Service (IRS) seized all of the corporation's tangible personal property. The estimated liquidation value of this property was $35,000, at most. However, its estimated going-concern value in Whiting's hands was $162,876. One day after the seizure, Whiting filed a petition for Chapter 11 reorganization protection. The trustee in bankruptcy sought to require the IRS to turn over the property seized.

ISSUE: When the IRS has seized property of a debtor before that debtor files a petition in bankruptcy, is the trustee entitled to recover the property after the petition has been filed?

DECISION: Yes.

REASONS:

1. By authorizing reorganization, Congress recognized the fact that the assets of a debtor are more valuable if used in a reorganized business rather than if they are sold for scrap.
2. The reorganization effort would have little chance of success if property essential to running the business was not allowed to remain in the hands of the debtor.
3. Under the Bankruptcy Reform Act, secured parties must turn over property seized to the trustee. The IRS is bound to the same extent as any secured creditor.
4. Therefore the IRS must turn over to the trustee Whiting's tangible personal property.

United States v. Whiting Pools, Inc., 103 S.Ct. 2309 (1983).

7. Exemptions

Technically, all property of the debtor becomes property of the bankruptcy estate, but an individual debtor is then permitted to claim some of it as exempt from the proceedings. That property is then returned to the debtor. Exemptions are granted by federal, state, and local laws. The 1978 Bankruptcy Act, as it has been amended, allows the following exemptions in the debtor's property:

1. Real property used as a residence, up to $7,500
2. The debtor's interest, not to exceed $1,200, in one motor vehicle
3. The debtor's interest, not to exceed $200 in any particular item or $4,000 in aggregate value, in household furnishings, wearing apparel, appliances, books, animals, crops, or musical instruments that are held primarily for the personal family or household use of the debtor and his dependents
4. The debtor's interest in jewelry, not to exceed $500
5. The debtor's interest in other property, not to exceed $400, plus up to $3,750 of any unused real property exemption
6. The debtor's interest, not to exceed $750, in any implements, professional books, or tools of the trade of the debtor, or the trade of his dependents
7. Unmatured life insurance contracts
8. The cash value of life insurance, not to exceed $4,000
9. Professionally prescribed health aids
10. The debtor's right to receive benefits such as social security, unemployment compensation, public assistance, disability benefits, alimony, child support and separate maintenance reasonably necessary, and current payments of pension, profit-sharing, annuity, or similar plans
11. The debtor's right to receive payment traceable to the wrongful death of an individual on whom the debtor was dependent or to life insurance on the life of such a person or to payments for personal injury not to exceed $7,500

The 1984 amendments placed a cap of $4,000 on the total amount of household items that can be exempt. These amendments also restrict tenants to an additional amount of $3,750 when exempting personal property under exemption 5 above. Prior to this change, debtors who did not own a residence could use the entire real estate exemption of $7,500 (see exemption 1) to exempt additional personal property not exempted by another provision of the federal exemptions. Creditors have praised these amendments as a more equitable balance of debtors' and creditors' rights.

Every state has enacted statutes granting exemptions to debtors domiciled there, but these exemptions vary greatly from state to state. For example, some state exemptions exceed those provided by the federal bankruptcy laws. Other state exemptions are too small to give a debtor a real chance at a fresh financial start. Debtors may claim the larger exemptions offered by their state if it is to their advantage to do so. In order to encourage some states to raise their exemptions, the 1978 Act provides that the federal exemptions will be available to debtors unless the state specifically passes a law denying its residents the federal exemptions. Over half the states have adopted laws denying debtors the use of the federal exemptions; however, these states have substantially increased their own exemptions. The following case demonstrates the broad protection that is given by some state exemption statutes.

CASE

A West Virginia statute limits a creditor who seeks a debtor's wages to 20 percent of the wages or the excess over thirty times the minimum wage, whichever is less. The West Virginia constitution also authorizes a $1,000 personal exemption from debts. A debtor's employer was served with successive executions against that employee's wages. The employee debtor claimed the $1,000 personal exemption with respect to each successive execution. The lower court held that when the accumulated amount of wages the debtor exempted in each successive pay period totaled $1,000, the personal exemption would be exhausted with regard to his wages. Thereafter, the debtor's wages would be subject to the executions without any personal exemption available to the debtor. The debtor appealed this ruling.

ISSUE: Does the full personal exemption apply to each successive execution filed against the employer for the debtor's wages?

DECISION: Yes.

REASONS:

1. From the statutory provisions, we reach the following conclusions. First, the $1,000 personal exemption is based upon the fair market value of the personal property claimed exempt on the date the exemption is asserted. Second, wage payments can be exempted under the personal exemption. Third, where wages are claimed to be exempt, a successive exemption affidavit must be filed for each pay period. Finally, the personal exemption covers the property claimed or selected by the debtor as contained in his exemption affidavit.
2. An exemption statute must be liberally construed to accomplish its object, which is for the protection and benefit of a poor debtor and his helpless family, to give them the bread of life, and a pillow whereon to lay the head, to save them from destitution and absolute want.
3. The personal exemption may be asserted as often as a creditor seeks to attach the debtor's personal property, but it can only shield $1,000 of personal property each time it is filed.
4. The personal exemption applies as to the value of the property owned at the time the exemption affidavit is filed without regard to any exemptions claimed on prior occasions.
5. A judgment debtor who successively claims his accrued wages as part of his $1,000 personal exemption is not subject to having his personal exemption reduced by the prior amounts of accrued wages so exempted.

Miller v. Barron, 352 S.E.2d 41 (W. Va. 1986).

As a general rule, exempt property is not subject to any debts that arise before the commencement of the case. Exceptions to the general rule apply to tax claims, alimony, child support, and separate maintenance. Exempt property can be used to collect such debts after the proceeding. The discharge in bankruptcy does not prevent enforcement of valid liens against exempt property; however, judicial liens and nonpossessory, nonpurchase money security interests in household goods, wearing apparel, professional books, tools, and professionally prescribed health aids may be avoided. A debtor may redeem such tangible personal property from a lien securing a dischargeable consumer debt by paying the lien holder the amount of the secured claim. Exempt property is free of such liens after the proceedings. Waivers of exemptions are unenforceable, to prevent creditors from attempting to deny debtors the necessary property to gain a fresh start.

8. Debts That Are Not Discharged

A debt is a liability on a claim. A claim may be based on the right to payment that could be enforced in a proceeding at law, or it may be based on the right to an equitable remedy for breach of performance if the breach gives a right to payment. Claims based on equitable remedies may be dischargeable the same as those based on legal remedies, as the following case indicates. Note what the court did not hold as well as what it held.

CASE

Kovacs operated a hazardous waste disposal business in Ohio. The state filed suit against Kovacs for polluting public waters in violation of environmental laws. Kovacs settled the suit by agreeing to stop the pollution, to clean up the waste site, and to pay the state $75,000. The agreement was made part of an injunction. When Kovacs did not clean up the waste site or pay the $75,000, the state had a receiver appointed who took possession of the property. Kovacs then filed a petition in bankruptcy. The state argued that Kovacs's obligation to clean up the waste site was not a debt within the meaning of the bankruptcy law. The state then contended that since this obligation was not a debt, the obligation could not be discharged. The lower courts held the obligation was dischargeable, and the state's petition for a writ of certiorari was granted.

ISSUE: Is Kovacs's obligation to clean up a waste site a "debt" subject to discharge under the bankruptcy law?

DECISION: Yes.

REASONS:

1. For bankruptcy purposes, a debt is a liability on a claim. A claim is defined by section 101(4) of the UCC as follows:

   (A) right to payment, whether or not such right is reduced to judgment, liquidated, unliquidated, fixed, contingent, matured, unmatured, disputed, undisputed, legal, equitable, secured, or unsecured; or

   (B) right to an equitable remedy for breach of performance if such breach gives rise to a right to payment, whether or not such right to an equitable remedy is reduced to judgment, fixed, contingent, matured, unmatured, disputed, undisputed, secured, or unsecured.

2. The state resorted to the courts to enforce its environmental laws against Kovacs and secured a negative order to cease polluting, an affirmative order to clean up the site, and an order to pay a sum of money to recompense the state for damage done to the fish population. Each order was one to remedy an alleged breach of Ohio law; and if Kovacs' obligation to pay $75,000 to the state is a debt dischargeable in bankruptcy, which the state freely concedes, it makes little sense to assert that because the cleanup order was entered to remedy a statutory violation, it cannot likewise constitute a claim for bankruptcy purposes.

3. At oral argument in this court, the state's counsel conceded that after the receiver was appointed, the only performance sought from Kovacs was the payment of money. Had Kovacs furnished the necessary funds, either before or after bankruptcy, there seems little doubt that the receiver and the state would have been satisfied. On the facts before it, and with the receiver in control of the site, we cannot fault the court of appeals for concluding that the cleanup order had been converted into an obligation to pay money, an obligation that was dischargeable in bankruptcy.

Ohio v. Kovacs, 105 S.Ct. 705 (1985).

As the court noted in the preceding case, not all debts are discharged in Chapter 7 cases. A discharge in bankruptcy does not discharge an individual debtor from the following debts:

1. Certain taxes and customs duties
2. Debts for obtaining money, property, services, or credit by false pretenses, false representations, or actual fraud
3. Consumer debts over $500 for luxury goods and services incurred within forty days of the order of relief
4. Cash advances over $1,000 that are extensions of consumer credit under an open end credit plan within twenty days of the order of relief
5. Unscheduled debts
6. Debts for fraud or defalcation while acting in a fiduciary capacity and debts created by embezzlement or larceny
7. Alimony, child support, and separate maintenance
8. Liability for willful and malicious torts
9. Tax penalties if the tax is not dischargeable
10. Student loans less than five years old
11. Debts incurred as a result of an accident caused by driving while intoxicated
12. Debts owed before a previous bankruptcy to which discharge was denied for grounds other than the 6-year rule
13. Fines and penalties payable to and for the benefit of governmental units that are not compensation for actual pecuniary losses

The taxes that are not discharged are the same ones that receive priority under the second, third, and seventh categories discussed in section 23 on priorities. If debtors fail to file a return, file it beyond its last due date, or file a fraudulent return, those taxes are not discharged. One of the most common tax liabilities that is not discharged in bankruptcy is the one for unpaid withholding and social security taxes.

Items 3 and 4, which were added by the 1984 amendments, now prevent the debtor from going on a spending spree or "loading up" at creditors' expense just before filing a bankruptcy petition. The phrase "luxury goods and services" is defined as not including goods or services acquired for the support or maintenance of the debtor or his dependents.

For a debt to be denied discharge because of fraud, the creditor must have placed reasonable reliance on a false statement in writing. The denial of unscheduled debts means that the claim of any creditor who is not listed or who does not learn of the proceedings in time to file a claim is not discharged. The debtor, under such circumstances, remains liable for it unless he can prove that the creditor did have knowledge of the proceeding in time to file a claim. Proof of actual knowledge is required, and although such knowledge often exists, care should be taken to list all creditors so that all claims will unquestionably be discharged.

Tort liability claims based on negligence are discharged. Tort liability claims arising from willful and malicious acts are not discharged. A judgment arising out of an assault and battery is not discharged. Item 11 was added by the 1984 amendments. The logic behind making this tort liability nondischargeable indicates support in the battle to discourage drunk driving.

The provision generally denying discharge to student loans was added in the 1978 revision. It seeks to give creditors and the government five years to collect student loans. There is an exception if the debtor is able to convince the court that undue hardship on him and his dependents will result if the student loan debt is not discharged. If the debtor fails to prove the undue hardship caused by the student loan, a general discharge will not relieve the debtor of the obligation to pay that student loan. Student loans are not discharged automatically. A person seeking a discharge of them must prove undue hardship in the bankruptcy court.

As a result of item 13, criminals will not be able to use the bankruptcy laws to avoid fines that have been levied. The Supreme Court has extended this nondischargeable debt to include restitution obligations imposed on debtors in state criminal proceedings. Great deference is given to state criminal proceedings, and amounts owed to accomplish the penal goals of a state such as the deterrence of crime are not dischargeable, as the court held in the following case.

CASE

In 1980, Carolyn Robinson pleaded guilty to larceny in the second degree. The charge was based on her wrongful receipt of $9,932.95 in welfare benefits from the state of Connecticut. As a part of her sentence, Robinson was required to make restitution at the rate of $100 per month during her probationary period. On February 5, 1981, Robinson filed a Chapter 7 bankruptcy petition. She sought to have her obligation to make restitution discharged. Although they received notice of the Chapter 7 petition, the staff members of the Connecticut Department of Income Maintenance and of the Probation Office did not respond. Robinson's obligation to make restitution was discharged. Later the Probation Office objected when the restitution payments ceased. Robinson filed this action to have the discharge affirmed.

ISSUE: Were the restitution payments, as required as a condition of Robinson's probation, dischargeable in a Chapter 7 bankruptcy proceeding?

DECISION: No.

REASONS: 1. Federal bankruptcy courts should not invalidate the results of state criminal proceedings. The right to formulate and enforce penal sanctions is an important aspect of the sovereignty retained by the states.

2. The relevant portion of Section 523(a)(7) protects from discharge any debt "to the extent such debt is for a fine, penalty, or forfeiture payable to and for the benefit of a governmental unit, and is not compensation for actual pecuniary loss."
3. Section 523(a)(7) creates a broad exception for all penal sanctions, whether they be called fines, penalties, or forfeitures. Congress included two qualifying phrases; the fines must be both "to and for the benefit of a government unit," and "not compensation for actual pecuniary loss."
4. Neither of the qualifying clauses of Section 523(a)(7) allows the discharge of a criminal judgment that takes the form of restitution. The criminal justice system is not operated primarily for the benefit of victims, but for the benefit of society as a whole. Thus it is concerned not only with punishing the offender, but also with rehabilitating him.
5. Because criminal proceedings focus on the state's interests in rehabilitation and punishment, rather than the victim's desire for compensation, we conclude that restitution orders imposed in such proceedings operate "for the benefit of" the state. Similarly, restitution payments are not assessed "for compensation" of the victim.
6. These interests are sufficient to place restitution orders within the meaning of Section 523(a)(7).

Kelly v. Robinson, 107 S.Ct. 353 (1986).

9. Grounds for Denying Discharge

A discharge in bankruptcy is a privilege, not a right. Therefore, in addition to providing that certain debts are not discharged, the 1978 Bankruptcy Act specifies the following grounds for denying an individual debtor a discharge:

1. Fraudulent transfers
2. Inadequate records
3. Commission of a bankruptcy crime
4. Failure to explain a loss of assets or deficiency of assets
5. Refusing to testify in the proceedings or to obey a court order
6. Any of the above within one year in connection with another bankruptcy case of an insider
7. Another discharge within six years
8. Approval by the court of a waiver of discharge

The first three grounds for denying discharge are predicated on wrongful conduct by the debtor in connection with the case. Fraudulent transfers involve such acts as removing, destroying, or concealing property with the intent to hinder, delay, or defraud creditors or the trustee. The conduct must occur within one year preceding the case, or it may occur after the case is commenced.

A debtor is also denied a discharge if he has concealed, destroyed, mutilated, falsified, or failed to keep or preserve any books and records relating to his financial condition. A debtor is required to keep records from which his financial condition may be ascertained, unless the failure is justified.

Bankruptcy crimes are generally related to the proceedings. They include a false oath, the use or presentation of a false claim, or bribery in connection with the proceedings and with the withholding of records.

The six-year rule, which allows a discharge only if another discharge has not been ordered within six years, extends to Chapter 11 and Chapter 13 proceedings, as well as to those under Chapter 7. Confirmation of a plan under Chapter 11 or 13 does not have the effect of denying a discharge within six years if all the unsecured claims were paid in full, or if 70 percent of them were paid and the debtor has used his best efforts to pay the debts.

Either a creditor or the trustee may object to the discharge. The court may order the trustee to examine the facts to see if grounds for the denial of the discharge exist. Courts are also granted the authority to revoke a discharge within one year if it was obtained by fraud on the court.

PROCEDURAL STEPS

10. Introduction

Chapter 3 of the 1978 Bankruptcy Reform Act is concerned with procedural aspects and administration of all types of bankruptcy cases, regardless of the chapter under which the case is filed. The provisions of Chapter 3 give guidance in how to and who can file a case, in how the automatic stay prohibits any action against the debtor, and in how creditors are informed of the debtor's status. These provisions are discussed in the next five sections. The most technical portion of Chapter 3 is entitled "administrative powers." These provisions grant the bankruptcy court and the trustee a wide range of powers to accomplish the purposes of the bankruptcy law. Sections 16 through 20 present a more detailed examination of these powers and duties.

11. Voluntary Commencement

A debtor may voluntarily instigate a bankruptcy case under any appropriate chapter by filing a petition with the bankruptcy court. In recognition of the fact that husbands and wives often owe the same debts, a joint case may be filed. A *joint case* is a voluntary one concerning a husband and wife, and it requires only one petition. The petition must be signed by both spouses, since one spouse cannot take the other into bankruptcy without the other's consent. Insolvency is not a condition precedent to any form of voluntary bankruptcy action.

All petitioners must pay a filing fee of $60, in installments if they prefer. Only one filing fee is required in a joint case. A petition filed by a partnership as a firm is not a petition on behalf of the partners as individuals. If they intend to obtain individual discharges, separate petitions are required.

The petition contains lists of secured and unsecured creditors, all property owned by the debtor, property claimed by the debtor to be exempt, and a statement of affairs of the debtor. This statement includes current income and expenses so that the judge can dismiss a case if he believes that a substantial abuse of the bankruptcy code has occurred. This is an important consideration when a debtor's liabilities do not exceed assets and the filing is based on some fact other than that the debtor cannot pay his debts as they come due. The statement of affairs of a debtor engaged in business is much more detailed than the one filed by a debtor not in business.

In general, the filing of a voluntary petition constitutes an order of relief indicating that the debtor is entitled to the bankruptcy court's protection. This concept of an automatic order of relief upon the debtor's filing caused creditors to argue that some debtors were filing voluntary petitions when the debtor did not need the court's protection. In 1984, Congress amended Chapter 7 to allow the bankruptcy judge, on his own initiative, to dismiss a case filed voluntarily if the debtor's obligations are primarily consumer debts and if the order of relief would be an abuse of the bankruptcy law. However, there is a presumption in favor of granting the relief requested by the debtor.

If the bankruptcy judge decides the petition was properly filed and an order of relief is effective, an interim trustee will be appointed. The roles of this trustee and the permanent one are discussed in sections 16 through 20.

12. Involuntary Commencement

Involuntary cases are commenced by one or more creditors filing a petition. If there are twelve or more creditors, the petition must be signed by at least three creditors whose unsecured claims are not contingent and aggregate at least $5,000. If there are fewer than twelve creditors, only one need sign the petition, but the $5,000 amount must still be met. Employees, insiders, and transferees of voidable transfers are not counted in determining the number of creditors. ''Insiders'' are persons such as relatives, partners of the debtor, and directors and officers of the corporation involved. The subject of voidable transfers is discussed later in this chapter.

Creditors may commence involuntary proceedings in order to harass the debtor. To protect the debtor, the court may require the petitioning creditors to file a bond to indemnify the debtor. This bond will cover the amounts for which the petitioning creditors may have liability to the debtor. The liability may include court costs, attorney's fees, and damages caused by taking the debtor's property.

Until the court enters an order for relief in an involuntary case, the debtor may continue to operate his business and to use, acquire, and dispose of his property. However, the court may order an interim trustee appointed to take possession of the property and to operate the business. If the case is a liquidation proceeding, the appointment of the interim trustee is mandatory unless the debtor posts a bond guaranteeing the value of the property in his estate.

Since some debtors against whom involuntary proceedings are commenced are, in fact, not bankrupt, the debtor has a right to file an answer to the petition of the creditors and to deny the allegations of the petition. If the debtor does not file an answer, the court orders relief against the debtor. If an answer is filed, the court conducts a trial on the issues raised by the petition and the answer. A court will order relief in an involuntary proceeding against the debtor only if it finds that the debtor is generally not paying his debts as they become due. Insolvency in the balance sheet sense (liabilities exceeding assets) is not required. Relief may also be ordered if, within 120 days before the filing of the petition, a custodian, receiver, or agent has taken possession of property of the debtor for the purpose of enforcing a lien against the debtor.

The statute specifies which debtors under each chapter are subject to involuntary proceedings. Farmers and not-for-profit corporations are not subject to involuntary proceedings, under either Chapter 7 or Chapter 11. A *farmer* is defined as a person who receives more than 80 percent of gross income for the taxable year preceding the bankruptcy case from a farming operation he owns and operates. The term *farming operation* includes tillage of the soil; dairy farming; ranching; production or raising of crops, poultry, or livestock; and production of poultry or livestock products in an unmanufactured state.

Creditors also are prohibited from forcing any debtor into a Chapter 13 proceeding. The reason for this rule is that a Chapter 13 debtor is required to pay off his debts pursuant to an approved plan. To force an individual debtor to work to pay his debts is equivalent to involuntary servitude, which violates the Thirteenth Amendment of the Constitution.

13. Conversion of Cases

Because a case may be filed voluntarily or involuntarily under the various chapters, the issue arises as to whether the debtor or the creditors can convert a filing to another type of proceeding. If the original filing is under Chapter 7, the debtor can request a conversion to a Chapter 11 or 13 proceeding. Creditors can have a Chapter 7 case converted to Chapter 11, but not to Chapter 13. If the case was filed voluntarily as a Chapter 11 reorganization proceeding, the debtor may request that the case be converted to a Chapter 7 or 13 proceeding. However, if the Chapter 11 proceeding was begun involuntarily, the creditors must consent to a conversion to Chapter 7. Creditors may seek to convert a Chapter 11 proceeding to Chapter 7 as long as the debtor is neither a farmer nor a nonprofit corporation. Creditors cannot convert a case from Chapter 11 to Chapter 13 without the debtor's consent.

In general, a debtor may convert a Chapter 13 proceeding to Chapter 7 or 11, whichever is more appropriate. Creditors also may ask the court to convert a case filed under Chapter 13 to Chapter 7 or 11 unless the debtor is a farmer. If the debtor is a farmer, any conversion must be agreed to by that farmer before that conversion will occur.

14. Automatic Stay

Bankruptcy cases operate to **stay** other judicial or administrative proceedings against the debtor. These stays of proceedings may operate to the detriment of a creditor or third party. For example, a stay would prevent a utility company from shutting off service. Despite this potential harm to creditors, the stay automatically becomes applicable immediately upon the bankruptcy petition being filed, as occurred in the following case.

Stay *The order of relief. This order prevents all creditors from taking any action to collect debts owed by the protected debtor.*

CASE

On September 8, 1980, William and Katherine Arens filed a voluntary petition in bankruptcy. The notice of bankruptcy was not issued until September 10, 1980. On September 9, 1980, United Northwest Federal Credit Union sued the Arenses to recover money and foreclose its security interest on their mobile home. The Arenses were notified of this suit when they received a summons from the sheriff on September 16, 1980. No further action was taken on the credit union's lawsuit in state court until after the bankruptcy court dismissed the debtors' petition on May 4, 1981, for their failure to appear in court. On May 11, 1981, the state trial court entered a default judgment against the couple in the credit union's lawsuit. Mr. and Mrs. Arens now challenge the entry of a default judgment against them as contrary to the bankruptcy law's automatic stay provision.

ISSUE: May a creditor begin a lawsuit against a debtor when a bankruptcy petition has been filed?

DECISION: No.

REASONS:
1. The bankruptcy law provides for an automatic stay of all proceedings against the debtor once the petition in bankruptcy is filed. That means no lawsuit can be filed once the debtor institutes a bankruptcy case. It does not matter that the creditor had no notice of the filing by the debtor. The stay is automatic.
2. The purpose of the stay is to protect the debtor. It gives him a breathing spell from his creditors, and allows him to be free of creditor harassment, a foreclosure, or collection actions. It gives him time to attempt repayment or time to develop a reorganization or liquidation plan.
3. The stay also protects the creditors. Without it, certain creditors would be able to pursue their own remedies against the debtors' property. Those who acted first would obtain payment in preference to and to the detriment of other creditors.

United Northwest Federal Credit Union v. Arens, 664 P.2d 881 (Kan. 1983).

The stay provision often works to the disadvantage of secured creditors; especially in reorganization cases under Chapter 11. If the value of the property securing the debt does not cover the full debt, the creditor will lose because he cannot sell the property during the period of the stay. Creditors whose collateral is worth less than the loan amount are not entitled to compensation for the period of the stay in the bankruptcy court.

When the trustee continues to operate the debtor's business, it is frequently necessary to use, sell, or lease property of the debtor. In order to prevent irreparable harm to creditors and other third parties as a result of stays, a trustee may be required to provide "adequate protection" to third parties. In some cases, adequate protection requires that the trustee make periodic cash payments to creditors. In others, the trustee may be required to provide a lien to the creditor. When the sale, lease, or rental of the debtor's property may decrease the value of an entity's interest in property held by the trustee, a creditor may be entitled to a lien on the proceeds of any sale, lease, or rental. The court is empowered to determine if the trustee has furnished adequate protection; and when the issue is raised, the burden of proof is on the trustee.

The automatic stay is designed to protect both debtor and creditor. The stay provides the debtor time and freedom from financial pressures to attempt repayment or to develop a plan of reorganization. Creditors are protected by the stay, since it forces them to comply with the orderly administration of the debtor's estate. In other words, the stay prevents some creditors from grabbing all the debtor's assets while other creditors receive nothing. It also allows for orderly trials of claims such as those for personal injury or wrongful death. Such claims are tried in the federal district courts and not in the bankruptcy courts.

Despite these advantages of staying all proceedings against the debtor who files a bankruptcy petition, there are exceptions to the application of the automatic stay. These exceptions apply to proceedings that are not directly related to the debtor's financial situation. Proceedings that are not automatically stayed when a bankruptcy petition is filed include (1) criminal actions against the debtor; (2) the collection of alimony, maintenance, or support from property that is not part of the estate; and (3) the commencement or continuation of an action by a governmental unit to enforce that governmental unit's police power. Although these actions are not stayed automatically by the filing of a bankruptcy petition, the trustee may seek to enjoin these actions if they harm the debtor's estate.

15. Meeting of Creditors

In a voluntary case, the debtor has filed the required schedules with the petition. In an involuntary case, if the court orders relief, the debtor will be required to complete the same schedules as the debtor in a voluntary proceeding. From this point, the proceedings are identical. All parties are given notice of the order for relief. If the debtor owns real property, notice is usually filed in the public records of the county where the land is situated. The notice to creditors will include the date by which all claims are to be filed and the date of a meeting of the creditors with the debtor. This meeting of creditors must be within a reasonable time after the order for relief. The debtor appears at the meeting with the creditors, and the creditors are allowed to question the debtor under oath. The court may also order a meeting of any equity security holders of the debtor.

At the meeting of creditors, the debtor may be examined by the creditors to ascertain if property has been omitted from the list of assets, if property has been conveyed in defraud of creditors, and other matters that may affect the right of the debtor to have his obligations discharged.

In liquidation cases, the first meeting of creditors includes the important step of electing a *permanent trustee*. This trustee will replace the interim trustee appointed by the court at the time the order for relief was entered. The unsecured creditors who are not insiders elect this permanent trustee. To have a valid election, creditors representing at least 20 percent of the amount of unsecured claims held against the debtor must vote. The election is then determined by a majority of the unsecured creditors voting.

TRUSTEE AND CASE ADMINISTRATION

16. Trustee and the Estate

The trustee may be an individual or a corporation that has the capacity to perform the duties of a trustee. In a case under Chapter 7 or 13 of the act, an individual trustee must reside or have an office and the corporate trustee must have an office in the judicial district in which the case is pending or in an adjacent district. Prior to becoming a trustee in a particular case, the trustee must file with the court a bond in favor of the United States. This bond may be used as a source of collection if the trustee should fail to faithfully perform his duties.

The trustee is the representative of the estate and has the capacity to sue and to be sued. Trustees are authorized to employ professional persons such as attorneys, accountants, appraisers, and auctioneers and to deposit or invest the money of the estate during the proceedings. In making deposits or investments, the trustee must seek the maximum reasonable net return, taking into account the safety of the deposit or investment.

The statute has detailed provisions on the responsibilities of the trustee under the tax laws. As a general rule, the trustee has responsibility for filing tax returns for the estate. After the order for relief, income received by the estate is taxable to it and not to an individual debtor. The estate of a partnership or a corporation debtor is not a separate entity for tax purposes. While the technical requirements of the tax laws are beyond the scope of this text, it should be remembered that the bankruptcy laws contain detailed rules complementary to the Internal Revenue Code in bankruptcy cases, and both must be followed by the trustee.

17. General Duties and Powers

The statutory duties of the trustees in liquidation proceedings are to (1) collect and reduce to money the property of the estate; (2) account for all property received; (3) investigate the financial affairs of the debtor, (4) examine proofs of claims and object to the allowance of any claim that is improper; (5) oppose the discharge of the debtor if advisable; (6) furnish information required by a party in interest; (7) file appropriate reports with the court and the taxing authorities, if a business is operated; and (8) make a final report and account and file it with the court.

A trustee that is authorized to operate the business of the debtor is authorized to obtain unsecured credit and to incur debts in the ordinary course of business. These debts are paid as administrative expenses.

A trustee in bankruptcy has several rights and powers with respect to the property of the debtor. First of all, the trustee has a judicial lien on the property, just as if the trustee were a creditor. Second, the trustee has the rights and powers of a judgment creditor who obtained a judgment against the debtor on the date of the adjudication of bankruptcy and who had an execution issued that was returned unsatisfied.

Third, the trustee has the rights of a bona fide purchaser of the real property of the debtor as of the date of the petition. Finally, the trustee has the rights of an actual unsecured creditor to avoid any transfer of the debtor's property and to avoid any obligation incurred by the debtor that is voidable under any federal or state law. As a result of these rights, the trustee is able to set aside transfers of property and to eliminate the interests of other parties where creditors or the debtor could do so.

The trustee also has the power to avoid certain liens of others on the property of the debtor. Liens that first become effective on the bankruptcy or insolvency of the debtor are voidable. As a general rule, liens that are not perfected or enforceable against a bona fide purchaser of the property are also voidable. Assume that a seller or creditor has an unperfected lien on goods in the hands of the debtor on the date the petition is filed. The lien is perfected later. That lien is voidable if it could not be asserted against a good-faith purchaser of the goods. Liens for rent and for distress for rent are also voidable.

The law imposes certain limitations on all these rights and powers of the trustee. A purchase-money security interest under Article 9 of the Code may be perfected after the petition is filed if it is perfected within ten days of delivery of the property. Such a security interest cannot be avoided by the trustee if properly perfected.

The rights and powers of the trustee are subject to those of a seller of goods in the ordinary course of business who has the right to reclaim goods if the debtor was insolvent when the debtor received them. The seller must demand the goods back within ten days, and the right to reclaim is subject to any superior rights of secured creditors. Courts may deny reclamation and protect the seller by giving his claim priority as an administrative expense.

18. Executory Contracts and Unexpired Leases

Debtors are frequently parties to contracts that have not been performed. Also, there are often lessees of real property, and the leases usually cover long periods of time. As a general rule, the trustee is authorized, subject to court approval, to assume or to reject an executory contract or unexpired lease. If the contract or lease is rejected, the other party has a claim subject to some statutory limitations. A rejection by the trustee creates a prepetition claim for the rejected contract or lease debt subject to these limitations.

If the contract or lease is assumed, the trustee will perform the contract or assign it to someone else, and the estate will presumably receive the benefits. If the trustee assumes a contract or lease, he must cure any default by the debtor and provide adequate assurance of future performance. In shopping-center leases, adequate assurance includes protection against declines in percentage rents and preservation of the tenant mix, among other things.

A trustee may not assume an executory contract that requires the other party to make a loan, deliver equipment, or issue a security to the debtor. A party to a contract based on the financial strength of the debtor is not required to extend new credit to a debtor in bankruptcy.

Contracts and leases often have clauses prohibiting assignment. The law also prohibits the assignment of certain contract rights, such as those that are personal in nature. The trustee in bankruptcy is allowed to assume contracts, notwithstanding a clause prohibiting the assumption or assignment of the contract or lease. The trustee is not allowed to assume a contract if applicable nonbankruptcy law excuses the other party from performance to someone other than the debtor, unless the other party consents to the assumption.

The statute invalidates contract clauses that automatically terminate contracts or leases upon filing of a petition in bankruptcy or upon the assignment of the lease or contract. The law also invalidates contract clauses that give a party other than the debtor the right to terminate the contract upon assumption by the trustee or assignment by the debtor. Such clauses hamper rehabilitation efforts and are against public policy. They are not needed, because the court can require the trustee to provide adequate protection and can ensure that the other party receives the benefit of its bargain.

Debtors are sometimes lessors instead of lessees. If the trustee rejects an unexpired lease of a debtor lessor, the tenant may treat the lease as terminated or may remain in possession for the balance of the lease. There is a similar provision for contract purchasers of real estate. They may treat the rejection as a termination, or they may remain in possession and make the payments due under the contract. A purchaser that treats a contract as terminated has a lien on the property to the extent of the purchase price paid.

If the trustee assigns a contract to a third party and the third party later breaches the contract, the trustee has no liability. This is a change of the common law in which an assignor is not relieved of his liability by an assignment. An assignment by a trustee in bankruptcy is, in effect, a novation if the assignment is valid.

In 1984, the United States Supreme Court held that the trustee's power gave the trustee the right to terminate employees who were working under a collective bargaining contract. Unions were so upset by this ruling that they convinced Congress that the court's decision had to be changed by legislation. Indeed, the union's efforts were a major reason that the 1984 amendments were passed by Congress and signed by President Ronald Reagan. When an employer files a petition under Chapter 11, the amended law requires the trustee to apply to the court to reject the collective bargaining contract. After the application is filed, the trustee and the employees' representative must negotiate about how the collective bargaining contract can be changed to allow the debtor-employer to reorganize successfully. If these negotiations are unsuccessful in reaching a mutual agreement, the trustee may seek the bankruptcy court's approval to reject the collective bargaining contract. The court must conduct a hearing within fourteen days after the trustee filed an application to reject the contract. The court's ruling on this application must be announced within thirty days of the hearing.

19. Voidable Preferences

Preference *If an insolvent debtor pays some creditors a greater percentage of the debts than he pays other creditors in the same class, and if the payments are made within ninety days prior to his filing a bankruptcy petition, those payments constitute illegal and voidable preference. An intention to prefer such creditors must be shown.*

One of the goals of bankruptcy proceedings is to provide an equitable distribution of a debtor's property among his creditors. To achieve this goal, the trustee in bankruptcy is allowed to recover transfers that constitute a **preference** of one creditor over another. As one judge said, "A creditor who dips his hand in a pot which he knows will not go round must return what he receives, so that all may share." To constitute a recoverable preference the transfer must (1) have been made by an insolvent debtor; (2) have been made to a creditor for, or on account of, an antecedent debt owed by the debtor before the transfer; (3) have been made within ninety days of the filing of the bankruptcy petition; and (4) enable the creditor to receive a greater percentage of his claim than he would receive under a distribution from the bankruptcy estate in a liquidation proceeding.

Insofar as the time period is concerned, there is an exception when the transfer is to an insider. Then, the trustee may avoid the transfer if it occurred within one year of the date of filing the petition, provided the insider had reasonable cause to believe the debtor was insolvent at the time of the transfer.

A debtor is presumed to be insolvent during the ninety-day period prior to the filing of the petition. Any person contending that the debtor was solvent has the burden of coming forward with evidence to prove solvency. Once credible evidence is introduced, the party with the benefit of the presumption of insolvency has the burden of persuasion on the issue.

Recoverable preferences include not only payments of money but also the transfer of property as payment of, or as security for, a prior indebtedness. Since the law is limited to debts, payments by the debtor of tax liabilities are exempt from the preference provision and are not recoverable. A mortgage or pledge may be set aside as readily as direct payments. A pledge or mortgage can be avoided if received within the immediate ninety-day period prior to the filing of the peition in bankruptcy,. provided it was obtained as security for a previous debt. The effective date of a transfer or a mortgage of real property may be questioned if the date the legal documents are signed is different from the date these documents are recorded. A logical solution to this potential problem seems to be to rely on the date the document is recorded in the public records. This was the court's approach in the following case.

CASE

The trustee in bankruptcy seeks to avoid a transfer of real property by the debtor to the Jerrolds on the basis that the transfer was a preference. A warranty deed was signed by the debtor and delivered to the Jerrolds on May 25, 1982. For some unexplained reason, the deed was not recorded until August 17, 1982. A Chapter 7 voluntary petition was filed on September 10, 1982. Therefore the deed involved in the disputed transfer was delivered more than ninety days before the date of the filing of the debtor's petition in bankruptcy. However, the deed was filed for registration within the ninety-day period.

ISSUE: For the purposes of determining whether a transfer of real property is voidable as preferential, is a deed effective on the date of delivery or on the date of recording?

DECISION: The date of recording.

REASONS:
1. A bona fide purchaser without notice from the debtor could have acquired an interest in the real property involved which is superior to any interest of Jerrolds prior to the deed's being recorded.
2. Therefore the transfer in question was not "made" until the deed was recorded on August 17, 1982, which is within ninety days of the bankruptcy petition's being filed.
3. Since the other essential elements of a voidable preference (debtor was insolvent, transfer was in satisfaction of an antecedent debt, and creditor was preferred over other creditors), the trustee is empowered to void this transfer of real property.

In re Brown Iron & Metal, Inc., 28 B.R. 426 (E.D. Tenn. 1983).

Payment of a fully secured claim does not constitute a preference and therefore may not be recovered. Transfers of property for a contemporaneous consideration may not be set aside, because there is a corresponding asset for the new liability. A mortgage given to secure a contemporaneous loan is valid even when the mortgagee took the security with knowledge of the debtor's insolvency. An insolvent debtor has a right to attempt to extricate himself, as far as possible, from his financial difficulty. If the new security is personal property, it must be perfected within ten days after the security interest attaches. The trustee's power to avoid a preference does not apply in a case filed by an individual debtor whose debts are primarily consumer debts if the aggregate value of the property subject to the preferential transfer is less than $600.

The law also creates an exception for transfers in the ordinary course of business or in the ordinary financial affairs of persons not in business. The payment of such debts within forty-five days after they are incurred is not recoverable if the payment is made in the ordinary course of business. This exception covers ordinary debt payments such as utility bills. The law on preferences is directed at unusual transfers and payments, not those occurring promptly in the ordinary course of the debtor's affairs.

20. Fraudulent Transfers

Fraudulent conveyance A *conveyance of property by a debtor for the intent and purpose of defrauding his creditors.*

A transfer of property by a debtor may be fraudulent under federal or state law. The trustee may proceed under either to set aside a fraudulent conveyance. Under federal law, a **fraudulent conveyance** is a transfer within one year of the filing of the petition, with the intent to hinder, delay, or defraud creditors. Under state law, the period may be longer and is usually within the range of two to five years.

Fraudulent intent may be inferred from the fact that the consideration is unfair, inadequate, or nonexistent. Solvency or insolvency at the time of the transfer is significant, but it is not controlling. Fraudulent intent exists when the transfer makes it impossible for the creditors to be paid in full or for the creditors to use legal remedies that would otherwise be available.

The intent to hinder, delay, or defraud creditors may also be implied. Such is the case when the debtor is insolvent and makes a transfer for less than a full and adequate value. Fraudulent intent is present if the debtor was insolvent on the date of the transfer or if the debtor becomes insolvent as a result of the transfer.

If the debtor is engaged in business or is about to become so, the fraudulent intent will be implied when the transfer leaves the businessperson with an unreasonably small amount of capital. The businessperson may be solvent; nevertheless, he has made a fraudulent transfer if the net result of the transfer leaves him with an unreasonably small amount of capital, provided the transfer was without fair consideration. Whether or not the remaining capital is unreasonably small is a question of fact.

The trustee may also avoid a transfer made in contemplation of incurring obligations beyond the debtor's ability to repay as they mature. Assume that a woman is about to enter business and that she plans to incur debts in the business. Because of her concern that she may be unable to meet these potential obligations, she transfers all her property to her husband, without consideration. Such a transfer may be set aside as fraudulent. The requisite intent is supplied by the factual situation at the time of the transfer and the state of mind of the transferor. The actual financial condition of the debtor in such a case is not controlling but does shed some light on the intent factor and state of mind of the debtor.

The trustee of a partnership debtor may avoid transfers of partnership property to partners if the debtor was or thereby became insolvent. This rule was made to prevent a partnership's preferring partners who are also creditors over other partners. Such transfers may be avoided if they occurred within one year of the date of filing the petition.

If a transferee is liable to the trustee only because the transfer was to defraud creditors, the law limits the transferee's liability. To the extent that the transferee does give value in good faith, the transferee has a lien on the property. For the purpose of defining value in the fraudulent transfer situation, the term includes property or the satisfaction or securing of a present or existing debt. It does not include an unperformed promise to support the debtor or a relative of a debtor.

CREDITORS

21. Creditors and Claims

Creditors are required to file proof of their claims if they are to share in the debtor's estate. Filed claims are allowed unless a party in interest objects. If an objection is filed, the court conducts a hearing to determine the validity of the claim. A claim may be disallowed if it is (1) unenforceable because of usury, unconscionability, or failure of consideration, (2) for unmatured interest, (3) an insider's or attorney's claim and exceeds the reasonable value of the services rendered, (4) for unmatured alimony or child support, (5) for rent, and (6) for breach of an employment contract. These latter two claims may be disallowed to the extent that they exceed the statutory limitations for such claims.

Illegality can be raised, because any defense available to the debtor is available to the trustee. Postpetition interest is not collectible, because interest stops accruing at the date of filing the petition. Bankruptcy operates as an acceleration of the principal due. From the date of filing, the amount of the claim is the total principal plus interest to that date.

Unreasonable attorney's fees and claims of insiders are disallowed because they encourage concealing assets or returning them to the debtor. Since alimony claims are not dischargeable in bankruptcy, there is no reason to allow a claim for postpetition alimony and child support.

The amount of rent that may be included in a claim is limited. The law is designed to compensate the landlord for his loss, but not to allow the claim to be so large that other creditors will not share in the estate. A landlord's damages are limited to the rent for the greater of one year or 15 percent of the remaining lease term, not to exceed three years. In liquidation cases, the time is measured from the earlier of the date of filing the petition and the date of surrender of possession. In cases filed under Chapters 9, 11, and 13 of the Act, the claim is limited to three years' rent. Of course, these limitations are not applicable to rent owed by the trustee, an administrative expense for which the estate is liable.

Landlords often have a security deposit for rent. To the extent that the security deposit exceeds the rent allowed as a claim, it must be paid over to the trustee to be a part of the bankruptcy estate. If the security deposit is less than the claim, the landlord keeps the security deposit, and it will be applied in satisfaction of the claim. The limitations on claims for rent are applicable to bona fide leases, not to leases of real property that are financing or security leases.

The limitation for damages resulting from termination of employment contracts is similar to the one for rent. Damages are limited to compensation for the year following the earlier of the date of the petition and that of the termination of employment.

Claims are sometimes contingent or otherwise unliquidated and uncertain. Personal injury and wrongful death claims against a debtor that cannot be settled are tried in federal district courts and not in bankruptcy courts. The law authorizes the bankruptcy court to estimate and to fix the amount of such claims, if necessary, to avoid undue delay in closing the estate or approving of a plan of reorganization. The same is true of equitable remedies such as specific performance. Courts will convert such remedies to dollar amounts and proceed to close the estate or approve the plan.

If a secured claim is undersecured—that is, if the debt exceeds the value of the collateral—the claim is divided into two parts. The claim is secured to the extent of the value of the collateral. It is an unsecured claim for the balance.

22. Right of Setoff

Any person owing money to the debtor may set off against the amount owed any sum that the debtor owes him, provided such amount would be allowable as a claim. To the extent of this *setoff,* he becomes a preferred creditor, but he is legally entitled to this preference. This, however, does not apply when the claim against the debtor has been purchased or created for the purpose of preferring the creditor. Assume that a bank has lent a debtor $2,000 and that the debtor has $1,500 on deposit at the time of bankruptcy. The bank is a preferred creditor to the extent of the deposit. This setoff will be allowed unless the evidence discloses that the deposit was made for the purpose of preferring the bank. In that case, the deposit becomes a part of the debtor's estate because of the collusion.

Since the filing of the petition in bankruptcy operates as a stay of all proceedings, the right of setoff operates at the time of final distribution of the estate. Since the law allows the trustee to use the funds of the debtor with court approval, parties who wish to exercise the right of setoff should seek "adequate protection."

The right to setoff will usually be exercised by a creditor against a deposit that has been made within ninety days of the filing of a petition in bankruptcy. Quite frequently, there are several such deposits, and there may also have been several payments on the debt during the ninety-day period. As a result of these variables, the application of setoff principles is sometimes difficult.

The law seeks to prohibit a creditor from improving his position during the ninety-day period. It does so by allowing the trustee to recover that portion of the setoff which would be considered a preference. This amount recoverable by the trustee is the insufficiency between the amount owed and the amount on deposit on the first day of the ninety-day period preceding the filing of a bankruptcy petition that a deficiency occurred to the extent that this insufficiency is greater than the insufficiency existing on the day the petition is filed. If the deposit on the first day of the preceding ninety-day period exceeds the creditor's claim, look for the first insufficiency during the ninety-day period and calculate the setoff based on the first insufficiency.

Assume that a bankruptcy petition was filed on September 2. Throughout the ninety days prior to this filing, the debtor owes $2,000 to the creditor. On June 4, the debtor has on deposit with the creditor $1,500. On July 15, the amount on deposit is reduced to $700. On September 1, the debtor's balance is increased to $1,800. At the time of the filing, the creditor seeks to use the entire $1,800 on deposit to set off its claim against the debtor. The trustee would be able to recover $300 of this attempted setoff, since there was a greater insufficiency of that amount on the first day of the ninety-day period prior to the petition's being filed. In other words, the creditor's setoff would be limited to $1,500.

23. Priorities

The bankruptcy law establishes certain priorities in the payment of claims. After secured creditors have had the opportunity to benefit from a security interest in collateral, the general order of priority is as follows:

1. Administrative expenses
2. Involuntary GAP creditors
3. Wages, salaries, and commissions
4. Contributions to employee benefit plans
5. Suppliers of grain to a grain storage facility or of fish to a fish produce storage or processing facility
6. Consumer deposits
7. Governmental units for certain taxes

Administrative expenses include all costs of administering the debtor's estate, including taxes incurred by the estate. Typical costs include attorney's fees, appraiser's fees, and wages paid to persons employed to help preserve the estate.

The term *involuntary GAP creditor* describes a person who extends credit to the estate after the filing of an involuntary petition under Chapter 11 and before a trustee is appointed or before the order for relief is entered. Such claims include taxes incurred as the result of the conduct of business in this period.

The third class of priority is limited to amounts earned by an individual within ninety days of the filing of the petition or the cessation of the debtor's business, whichever occurred first. The priority is limited to $2,000 for each individual, but it includes vacation, severance, and sick leave pay as well as regular earnings. The employee's share of employment taxes is included in the third priority category, provided the wages and the employee's share of taxes have been paid in full. The category does not include fees paid to independent contractors.

The fourth priority recognizes that fringe benefits are an important part of many labor-management contracts. The priority is limited to claims for contributions to employee benefit plans, arising from services rendered within 120 days before commencement of the case or cessation of the debtor's business, whichever occurs first. The priority is limited to $2,000 multiplied by the number of employees less the amount paid under priority 3. The net effect is to limit the total priority for wages and employee benefits to $2,000 per employee.

The fifth priority was included in the 1984 amendments. It is designed to protect the farmer who raises grain and the fisherman if their grain or fish are held by the owner of a production or storage facility. If the farmers or fishermen have not been paid for the grain or fish transferred, they have a priority claim to the extent of $2,000 per creditor.

The sixth priority was added in 1978 as an additional method of consumer protection. It protects consumers who have deposited money in connection with the purchase, lease, or rental of property or the purchase of services for personal, family, or household use that were not delivered or provided. The priority is limited to $900 per consumer.

The seventh priority is for certain taxes. Priority is given to income taxes for a taxable year that ended on or before the date of filing the petition. The last due date of the return must have occurred not more than three years before the filing.

Employment taxes and transfer taxes such as gift, estate, sale, and excise taxes are also given sixth-class priority. Again the transaction or event that gave rise to the tax must precede the petition date, and the return must have been due within three years. The bankruptcy laws have several very technical aspects relating to taxation, and they must be reviewed carefully for tax returns filed by the trustee and claims for taxes.

In liquidation cases, the property available is first distributed among the priority claimants in the order just discussed. Then the property is distributed to general unsecured creditors who file their claims on time. Next, payment is made to unsecured creditors who tardily file their claims. Thereafter distribution is made to holders of penalty, forfeiture, or punitive damage claims. Punitive penalties, including tax penalties are subordinated to the first three classes of claims, as a matter of policy. Regular creditors should be paid before windfalls to persons and entities collecting penalties. Finally, postpetition interest on prepetition claims is paid if any property is available to do so. After the interest is paid, any surplus goes to the debtor. Claims within a particular class are paid pro rata if the trustee is unable to pay them in full.

CHAPTER SUMMARY

1. Of major importance today is the Bankruptcy Reform Act of 1978 as it has been amended in 1984 and in 1986.
2. The basic purpose of the bankruptcy law is to give a debtor in financial difficulty an opportunity to overcome this problem.
3. Terms to remember include *debtor*, *claim*, *order of relief*, and *trustee*.

Types of Proceedings

In General

1. The bankruptcy law has two basic approaches to resolving a debtor's financial problems—one is liquidation and the other is reorganization.

Liquidation Proceedings

1. This proceeding is governed by Chapter 7 of the statute.
2. In general, a debtor surrenders all assets from which creditors are paid as much as possible.
3. Individual debtors generally have all unpaid debts discharged or forgiven. Technically, a business organization's debts are not discharged.

Reorganization Proceedings

1. This proceeding is governed by Chapter 11 of the statute.
2. In essence, the debtor attempts to restructure the financial situation so that creditors can be substantially paid over time.
3. The key to a successful reorganization is the court's approval of a reasonable confirmation plan.

Adjustment of Individuals' Debts

1. This proceeding is governed by Chapter 13 of the statute.
2. The debtor must be an individual who has regular income and who has unsecured debts not exceeding $100,000 and secured debts not exceeding $350,000.
3. Again, a plan of repayment must be approved. The unsecured creditors must receive at least as much as they would under a Chapter 7 liquidation proceeding.

Adjustment of Family Farmer's Debts	1. A farmer may have his debts reduced to the value of his collateral. 2. Farmers must use all income that is not required for support to pay off unsecured debts. Any debts not paid within five years are discharged. 3. Periodic payments are paid on secured debts to pay off the value of the collateral.

General Principles

Property of the Estate	1. All the property interests of a debtor are used to create an estate. 2. The trustee, in essence, has whatever interests a debtor had at the time a bankruptcy petition was filed.
Exemptions	1. To enhance the debtor's fresh start, the debtor may exempt certain property from the estate. 2. These exemptions are governed by either federal or state law, whichever the state law provides.
Debts That Are Not Discharged	1. Certain debts are not discharged; therefore they survive the bankruptcy case and remain payable to the creditor.
Grounds for Denying Discharge	1. There also are grounds for denying a discharge. 2. Basically, in its balancing process, the drafters of the law decided that debts created in certain situations should not be forgiven.

Procedural Steps

Voluntary Commencement	1. Any proceeding may be started by a debtor filing a petition in bankruptcy. 2. The voluntary filing acts as an order of relief unless the bankruptcy judge decides that a consumer debtor is not entitled to Chapter 7 protection.
Involuntary Commencement	1. In general, cases may also be started by creditors with at least $5,000 in claims filing a petition. This creditor-commenced action is known as an involuntary case. 2. In an involuntary case, the bankruptcy judge must decide whether an order of relief is appropriate. 3. An involuntary case cannot be filed under Chapter 13 of the statute regardless of who the debtor is. And an involuntary case under Chapters 7 and 11 cannot be filed when the debtor is a farmer or a nonprofit corporation.
Automatic Stay	1. The filing of a bankruptcy petition protects the debtor against any action taken by creditors. 2. This stay is automatic even before the creditors learn of the petition's being filed. 3. The stay remains in effect until the bankruptcy judge permits actions by creditors.
Meeting of Creditors	1. After the order of relief is entered, a meeting of the creditors will be scheduled. At this meeting, creditors can question the debtor and examine documents. 2. Also at this meeting, unsecured creditors will elect a permanent trustee.

Trustee and Case Administration

Trustee and the Estate

1. The trustee must satisfy statutory prerequisites before he, she, or it is qualified.
2. The trustee has the responsibility for preserving the estate for the benefit of all creditors.
3. The trustee must fulfill the administrative duties with regard to taxes and similar matters.
4. In general, the trustee is a fiduciary of the estate.

General Duties and Powers

1. The trustee may employ professionals in representing the estate. The trustee also may sue and be sued in a representative capacity.
2. The trustee has several statutory duties designed to ensure the proper workings of the bankruptcy law.
3. The trustee may operate the business of the debtor and may incur expenses associated with such an operation.
4. The trustee may assume the position of a lienholder or a good-faith purchaser if such positions enhance the estate.
5. The trustee also may avoid certain liens on the debtor's property.

Executory Contracts and Unexpired Leases

1. The trustee has the general power to perform or avoid executory contracts and unexpired leases, regardless of what the agreement may state about the debtor's right to assign.
2. The trustee's power to avoid or modify a collective bargaining contract has been limited, but not removed, by the 1984 amendments.

Voidable Preferences

1. In order to keep all creditors on an equal basis, the trustee can avoid any transfer or payment to a creditor if such was made within ninety days of the petition being filed, if such was made to satisfy all or part of antecedent debts, if such was made while the debtor was insolvent, and if such was indeed a preference.
2. The debtor is presumed to be insolvent during the ninety days prior to the petition's being filed.
3. If the preferred creditor is an insider, the time period of concern is one year, not ninety days, before the petition was filed.

Fraudulent Transfers

1. A transfer of property may be fraudulent under either federal or state law.
2. In general, any transfer within a statutory time period prior to the filing of a bankruptcy petition is fraudulent if the debtor intended to hinder, delay, or defraud creditors.
3. The trustee has the power to declare these transfers invalid in order to protect the estate for the creditors' benefit.

Creditors

Creditors and Claims

1. Creditors must be able to prove their claims in order to be paid from the debtor's estate.
2. There are numerous reasons why a claim may be disallowed altogether or otherwise limited.

Right of Setoff

1. Because the debtor may have a claim against the creditor, that creditor can set off the amount owed to the debtor against the claims the creditor makes on the debtor's estate.

2. This setoff must not give an unreasonable preference to the creditor. The trustee will examine all events during the ninety days prior to the filing of the bankruptcy in order to determine the proper amount of the setoff.

Priorities

1. The creditors' claims are subject to payment according to the priority established by the bankruptcy law.
2. Seven categories of priority claims must be paid before the first general unsecured creditor's claim is paid.

REVIEW QUESTIONS AND PROBLEMS

1. Match each term in column A with the appropriate statement in column B.

A	B
(1) Liquidation	(a) A creditor's right to payment.
(2) Reorganization	(b) Entered by bankruptcy judge whenever debtor is entitled to the court's protection.
(3) Claim	(c) The creditor's right to reduce the amount of its claim by the amount it owes the debtor.
(4) Discharge	(d) The type of proceeding pursued under Chapter 7.
(5) Order of relief	(e) A transfer that gives a creditor an unfair advantage over other creditors.
(6) Meeting of creditors	(f) The legal forgiveness of a debt.
(7) Voidable preference	(g) The type of proceeding pursued under Chapter 11.
(8) Right of setoff	(h) The event when, among other things, a permanent trustee is elected.

2. The bankruptcy court approved a repayment plan proposed by debtors, Eddie and Angela Freeman, pursuant to Chapter 13. Under the plan, the Freemans agreed to pay their secured creditors in full, but their unsecured creditors were to receive nothing. Public Finance is an unsecured creditor and appeals the affirmation of the plan, arguing that a plan which proposes no payment to unsecured creditors fails to meet the good-faith requirement of the bankruptcy law. Does "good faith" exist only when the debtor proposes payment to unsecured creditors? Explain.

3. Pauline lives in a state that exempts $800 for an automobile owned by a debtor in a bankruptcy proceeding. Pauline's car was worth more than $800, so she sought to recover $800 of the sales price when the court sold the car to satisfy her debts. Her creditors contend that she is not entitled to any exemption for a car worth more than $800. Who is correct? Explain.

4. Clark, a 43-year-old licensed family therapist, filed a Chapter 7 petition in bankruptcy and claimed an exemption for his Keogh retirement plan. Contributions to such a plan are tax-deductible, and income tax on the fund and its earnings is deferred until withdrawn. Funds may be withdrawn when a participant becomes 59½, dies, or is disabled. If funds are withdrawn before these events, the participant must pay a penalty tax of 10 percent in addition to regular income taxes and is barred from making contributions to the plan for five years. Is the Keogh plan asset exempt? Explain.

5. A state court awarded a wife $100,000 in alimony. The husband did not pay it and later filed a petition under Chapter 7 of the bankruptcy law. He proved that his ex-wife did not need the money, as she was now gainfully employed and was in fact quite wealthy. Is this debt dischargeable? Explain.

6. Taylor borrowed money pursuant to the Guaranteed Student Loan Program. Three years later he filed a petition in voluntary bankruptcy and included his student loans on his list of debts. Taylor was given a general discharge in bankruptcy. Is he still liable for his student loans? Why or why not?

7. Fred Murray owns 350 acres of farmland on which he raises cattle, pigs, and other livestock. He also grows hay and has a large garden. In addition to these responsibilities related to his farming operations, Fred works for the state labor department. In fact, 50 percent of his income comes from his salary paid by the state. Through mismanagement, Fred became involved in financial difficulties and was not paying his debts as they became due. His creditors commenced an involuntary bankruptcy proceeding against him. Is the creditors' action proper? Explain.

8. A husband and wife filed a joint voluntary petition under Chapter 13 of the bankruptcy law. The husband, an attorney specializing in bankruptcy law, admitted that he "filed this Chapter 13 for the sole purpose of rejecting an option agreement" that granted a company the option to purchase a particular parcel of land owned by the petitioners. Should the court approve the plan and allow the rejection of the option? Why or why not?

9. The Chocolate Cookie Company entered into a twenty-year lease at an annual rental of $4,000 a year. This lease contained a clause that the lease was not assignable without the lessor's consent. Eighteen months after the lease was signed, the Chocolate Cookie Company commenced voluntary liquidation proceedings. The trustee sought to enforce the lease, despite the nonassignability clause. May the trustee enforce the lease as written? Why?

10. With the facts as in problem 9, how much could the lessor claim in the bankruptcy proceeding if the trustee terminated the lease six months after the petition was filed (after two years of the lease term had passed)? Explain.

11. Despite financial difficulties, Barney bought two suits for $500. When he received a bill for the suits, two weeks later, he was insolvent, but he fully paid this bill in cash. One month later he filed a petition in bankruptcy. The appointed trustee sued to recover the $500 paid, contending that the payment was a preferential transfer. Was the trustee correct? Why?

12. Tracy filed a bankruptcy petition on November 2. The State Bank seeks to establish its right to setoff, based upon the following facts. For the six months prior to the petition's being filed, Tracy owed the bank $2,000 at all times. Tracy had a savings account that had the balances:

July 1–August 30	$3,000.00
August 31–September 15	1,000.00
September 16–October 2	500.00
October 3–November 2	2,000.00

What is the maximum amount of setoff to which the bank is entitled? Why? Would your answer change if the balance on November 2 were only $500.00? Explain.

13. Afer filing for Chapter 11 reorganization, an employer continued to pay wages to its employees and to withhold the required amounts of FICA and income taxes from their paychecks. However, it did not pay the withheld amount to the IRS. Subsequently, the bankruptcy court appointed a trustee to supervise the liquidation of the estate. The government filed a claim for the taxes due from the reorganization period. Which priority claim does the government have? Explain.

14. White is an attorney who performed professional services for Smith & Smyth Insurance Company. This company did not pay White before it filed a voluntary liquidation proceeding. White seeks to have his claim given priority in the distribution of the debtor's estate, since his fees should qualify as a wage claim. Is White's contention correct? Why or why not?

UNIFORM COMMERICAL CODE

UNIFORM COMMERCIAL CODE

AN ACT

To be known as the Uniform Commercial Code, Relating to Certain Commercial Transactions in or regarding Personal Property and Contracts and other Documents concerning them, including Sales, Commercial Paper, Bank Deposits and Collections, Letters of Credit, Bulk Transfers, Warehouse Receipts, Bills of Lading, other Documents of Title, Investment Securities, and Secured Transactions, including certain Sales of Accounts, Chattel Paper, and Contract Rights, Providing for Public Notice to Third Parties in Certain Circumstances; Regulating Procedure, Evidence and Damages in Certain Court Actions Involving such Transactions, Contracts or Documents; to Make Uniform the Law with Respect Thereto; and Repealing Inconsistent Legislation.

ARTICLE 1

GENERAL PROVISIONS

PART 1

SHORT TITLE, CONSTRUCTION, APPLICATION AND SUBJECT MATTER OF THE ACT

Section 1-101. Short Title. This act shall be known and may be cited as Uniform Commercial Code.

Section 1-102. Purposes; Rules of Construction; Variation by Agreement.

(1) This Act shall be liberally construed and applied to promote its underlying purposes and policies.

(2) Underlying purposes and policies of this Act are

(a) to simplify,clarify and modernize the law governing commercial transactions;

(b) to permit the continued expansion

of commercial practices through custom, usage and agreement of the parties;

(c) To make uniform the law among the various jurisdictions.

(3) The effect of provisions of this Act may be varied by agreement, except as otherwise provided in this Act and except that the obligations of good faith, diligence, reasonableness and care prescribed by this Act may not be disclaimed by agreement but the parties may by agreement determine the standards by which the performance of such obligations is to be measured if such standards are not manifestly unreasonable.

(4) The presence in certain provisions of this Act of the words "unless otherwise agreed" or words of similar import does not imply that the effect of other provisions may not be varied by agreement under subsection (3).

(5) In this Act unless the context otherwise requires

(a) words in the singular number include the plural, and in the plural include the singular;

(b) words of the masculine gender include the feminine and the neuter, and when the sense so indicates the words of the neuter gender may refer to any gender.

Section 1-103. Supplementary General Principles of Law Applicable. Unless displaced by the particular provisions of this Act, the principles of law and equity, including the law merchant and the law relative to capacity to contract, principal and agent, estoppel, fraud, misrepresentation, duress, coercion, mistake, bankruptcy, or other validating or invalidating cause shall supplement its provisions.

Section 1-104. Construction Against Implicit Repeal. This Act being a general act intended as a unified coverage of its subject matter, no part of it shall be deemed to be impliedly repealed by subsequent legislation if such construction can reasonable be avoided.

Section 1-105. Territorial Application of the Act; Parties' Power to Choose Applicable Law.

(1) Except as provided hereafter in this section, when a transaction bears a reasonable relation to this state and also to another state or nation the parties may agree that the law either of this state or of such other state or nation shall govern their rights and duties. Failing such agreement this Act applies to transactions bearing an appropriate relation to this state.

(2) Where one of the following provisions of this Act specifies the applicable law, that provision governs and a contrary agreement is effective only to the extent permitted by the law (including the conflict of laws rules) so specified:

Rights of creditors against sold goods. Section 2-402.

Applicability of the Article on Bank Deposits and Collections. Section 4-102.

Bulk transfers subject to the Article on Bulk Transers. Section 6-102.

Applicability of the Article on Investment Securities. Section 8-106.

Policy and scope of the Article on Secured Transactions. Sections 9-102 and 9-103.

Section 1-106. Remedies to be Liberally Administered.

(1) The remedies provided by this Act shall be liberally administered to the end that the aggrieved party may be put in as good a position as if the other party had fully performed but neither consequential or special nor penal damages may be had except as specifically provided in this Act or by other rule of law.

(2) Any right or obligation declared by this Act is enforceable by action unless the provision declaring it specifies a different and limited effect.

Section 1-107. Waiver or Renunciation of Claim or Right After Breach. Any claim or right arising out of an alleged breach can be discharged in whole or in part without consideration by a written waiver or renunciation signed and delivered by the aggrieved party.

Section 1-108. Severability. If any provision or clause of this Act or application thereof to any person or circumstances is held invalid, such invalidity shall not affect other provisions or applications of the Act which can be given effect without the invalid provisions or application, and to this end the provisions of this Act are declared to be severable.

GENERAL DEFINITIONS AND PRINCIPLES OF INTERPRETATION

Section 1-201. General Definition. Subject to additional definitions contained in the subsequent Articles of this Act which are applicable to specific Articles or Parts thereof, and unless the context otherwise requires, in this Act:

(1) "Action" in the sense of a judicial proceeding includes recoupment, counterclaim, set-off, suit in equity and any other proceedings in which rights are determined.

(2) "Aggrieved party" means a party entitled to resort to a remedy.

(3) "Agreement" means the bargain of the parties in fact as found in their language or by implication from other circumstances including course of dealing or usage of trade or course of performance as provided in this Act (Sections 1-205 and 2-208). Whether an agreement has legal consequences is determined by the provisions of this Act, if applicable; otherwise by the law of contracts (Section 1-103). (Compare "Contract.")

(4) "Bank" means any person engaged in the business of banking.

(5) "Bearer" means the person in possession of an instrument, document of title, or security payable to bearer or indorsed in blank.

(6) "Bill of lading" means a document evidencing the receipt of goods for shipment issued by a person engaged in the business of transporting or forwarding goods, and includes an airbill. "Airbill" means a document serving for air transportation as a bill of lading does for marine or rail transportation, and includes an air consignment note or air waybill.

(7) "Branch" includes a separately incorporated foreign branch of a bank.

(8) "Burden of establishing" a fact means the burden of persuading the triers of fact that the existence of the fact is more probable than its non-existence.

(9) "Buyer in ordinary course of business" means a person who in good faith and without knowledge that the sale to him is in violation of the ownership rights or security interest of a third party in the goods buys in ordinary course from a person in the business of selling goods of that kind but does not include a pawnbroker. "Buying" may be for cash or by exchange of other property or on secured or unsecured credit and includes receiving goods or documents of title under a pre-existing contract for sale but does not include a transfer in bulk or as security for or in total or partial satisfaction of a money debt.

(10) "Conspicuous": a term or clause is conspicuous when it is so written that a reasonable person against whom it is to operate ought to have noticed it. A printed heading in capitals (as: NON-NEGOTIABLE BILL OF LADING) is conspicuous. Language in the body of a form is "conspicuous" if it is in larger or other contrasting type or color. But in a telegram any stated term is "conspicuous." Whether a term or clause is "conspicuous" or not is for decision by the court.

(11) "Contract" means the total legal obligation which results from the parties' agreement as affected by this Act and any other applicable rules of law. (Compare "Agreement.")

(12) "Creditor" includes a general creditor, a secured creditor, a lien creditor and any representative of creditors, including an assignee for the benefit of creditors, a trustee in bankruptcy, a receiver in equity and an executor or administrator of an insolvent debtor's or assignor's estate.

(13) "Defendant" includes a person in the position of defendant in a cross-action or counterclaim.

(14) "Delivery" with respect to instruments, documents of title, chattel paper or securities means voluntary transfer of possession.

(15) "Document of title" includes bill of lading, dock warrant, dock receipt, warehouse receipt or order for the delivery of goods, and also any other document which

in the regular course of business or financing is treated as adequately evidencing that the person in possession of it is entitled to receive, hold and dispose of the document and the goods it covers. To be a document of title a document must purport to be issued by or addressed to a bailee and purport to cover goods in the bailee's possession which are either identified or are fungible portions of an identified mass.

(16) "Fault" means wrongful act, omission or breach.

(17) "Fungible" with respect to goods or securities means goods or securities of which any unit is, by nature or usage of trade, the equivalent of any other like unit. Goods which are not fungible shall be deemed fungible for the purposes of this Act to the extent that under a particular agreement or document unlike units are treated as equivalents.

(18) "Genuine" means free of forgery or counterfeiting.

(19) "Good faith" means honesty in fact in the conduct or transaction concerned.

(20) "Holder" means a person who is in possession of a document of title or an instrument or an investment security drawn, issued or indorsed to him or to his order or to bearer or in blank.

(21) To "honor" is to pay or to accept and pay, or where a credit so engages to purchase or discount a draft complying with the terms of the credit.

(22) "Insolvency proceedings" includes any assignment for the benefit of creditors or other proceedings intended to liquidate or rehabilitate the estate of the person involved.

(23) A person is "insolvent" who either has ceased to pay his debts in the ordinary course of business or cannot pay his debts as they become due or is insolvent within the meaning of the federal bankruptcy law.

(24) "Money" means a medium of exchange authorized or adopted by a domestic or foreign government as a part of its currency.

(25) A person has "notice" of a fact when

(a) he has actual knowledge of it; or

(b) he has received a notice or notification of it; or

(c) from all the facts and circumstances known to him at the time in question he has reason to know that it exists.

A person "knows" or had "knowledge" of a fact when he has actual knowledge of it. "Discover" or "learn" or a word or phrase of similar import refers to knowledge rather than to reason to know. The time and circumstances under which a notice or notification may cease to be effective are not determined by this Act.

(26) A person "notifies" or "gives" a notice or notification to another by taking such steps as may be reasonably required to inform the other person in ordinary course whether or not such other actually comes to know of it. A person "receives" a notice or notification when

(a) it comes to his attention; or

(b) it is duly delivered at the place of business through which the contract was made or at any other place held out by him as the place for receipt of such communications.

(27) Notice, knowledge or a notice or notification received by an organization is effective for a particular transaction from the time when it is brought to the attention of the individual conducting that transaction, and in any event from the time when it would have been brought to his attention if the organization had exercised due diligence. An organization exercises due diligence if it maintains reasonable routines for communicating significant information to the person conducting the transaction and there is reasonable compliance with the routines. Due diligence does not require an individual acting for the organization to communicate information unless such communication is part of his regular duties or unless he has reason to know of the transaction and that the transaction would be materially affected by the information.

(28) "Organization" includes a corporation, government or governmental subdivision or agency, business trust, estate, trust, partnership or association, two or more persons having a joint or common interest, or any other legal or commercial entity.

(29) "Party," as distinct from "third party," means a person who has engaged in a transaction or made an agreement within this Act.

(30) "Person" includes an individual or an organization (See Section 1-102).

(31) "Presumption" or "presumed" means that the trier of fact must find the existence of the fact presumed unless and until evi-

dence is introduced which would support a finding of its non-existence.

(32) "Purchase" includes taking by sale, discount, negotiation, mortgage, pledge, lien, issue or re-issue, gift or any other voluntary transaction creating an interest in property.

(33) "Purchaser" means a person who takes by purchase.

(34) "Remedy" means any remedial right to which an aggrieved party is entitled with or without resort to a tribunal.

(35) "Representative" includes an agent, an officer of a corporation or association, and a trustee, executor or administrator of an estate, or any other person empowered to act for another.

(36) "Rights" includes remedies.

(37) "Security interest" means an interest in personal property or fixtures which secures payment or performance of an obligation. The retention or reservation of title by a seller or goods notwithstanding shipment or delivery to the buyer (Section 2-401) is limited in effect to a reservation of a "security interest." The term also includes any interest of a buyer of accounts, chattel paper, or contract rights which is subject to Article 9. The special property interest of a buyer of goods on identification or such goods to a contract for sale under Section 2-401 is not a "security interest," but a buyer may also acquire a "security interest" by complying with Article 9. Unless a lease or consignment is intended as security, reservation of title thereunder is not a "security interest" but a consignment is in any event subject to the provisions on consignment sales (Section 2-326). Whether a lease is intended as security is to be determined by the facts of each case; however (a) the inclusion of an option to purchase does not of itself make the lease one intended for security, and (b) an agreement that upon compliance with the terms of the lease the lessee shall become or has the option to become the owner of the property for no additional consideration or for a nominal consideration does make the lease one intended for security.

(38) "Send" in connection with any writing or notice means to deposit in the mail or deliver for transmission by any other usual means of communication with postage or cost of transmission provided for and properly addressed and in the case of an instrument to an address specified thereon or otherwise agreed, or if there be none to any address reasonable under the circumstances. The receipt of any writing or notice within the time at which it would have arrived if properly sent has the effect of a proper sending.

(39) "Signed" includes any symbol executed or adopted by a party with present intention to authenticate a writing.

(40) "Surety" includes guarantor.

(41) "Telegram" includes a message transmitted by radio, teletype, cable, any mechanical method of transmission, or the like.

(42) "Term" means that portion of an agreement which relates to a particular matter.

(43) "Unauthorized" signature or indorsement means one made without actual, implied or apparent authority and includes a forgery.

(44) "Value." Except as otherwise provided with respect to negotiable instruments and bank collections (Sections 3-303, 4-208 and 4-209) a person gives "value" for rights if he acquires them

(a) in return for a binding commitment to extend credit or for the extension of immediately available credit whether or not drawn upon and whether or not a charge-back is provided for in the event of difficulties in collection; or

(b) as security for or in total or partial satisfaction of a pre-existing claim; or

(c) by accepting delivery pursuant to a pre-existing contract for purchase; or

(d) generally, in return for any consideration sufficient to support a simple contract.

(45) "Warehouse receipt" means a receipt issued by a person engaged in the business of storing goods for hire.

(46) "Written" or "writing" includes printing, typewriting or any other intentional reduction to tangible form.

Section 1-202. Prima Facie Evidence by Third Party Documents. A document in due form purporting to be a bill of lading, policy or certificate of insurance, official weigher's or inspector's certificate, consular invoice, or any other document authorized or required by the contract to be issued by a third party shall be prima facie evidence of its own authenticity and genuineness and of the facts stated in the document by the third party.

Section 1-203. Obligation of Good Faith. Every contract or duty within this Act imposes an obligation of good faith in its performance or enforcement.

Section 1-204. Time; Reasonable Time; "Seasonably."

(1) Whenever this Act requires any action to be taken within a reasonable time, any time which is not manifestly unreasonable may be fixed by agreement.

(2) What is a reasonable time for taking any action depends on the nature, purpose and circumstances of such action.

(3) An action is taken "seasonably" when it is taken at or within the time agreed or if no time is agreed at or within a reasonable time.

Section 1-205. Course of Dealing and Usage of Trade.

(1) A course of dealing in a sequence of previous conduct between the parties to a particular transaction which is fairly to be regarded as establishing a common basis of understanding for interpreting their expressions and other conduct.

(2) A usage of trade is any practice or method of dealing having such regularity of observance in a place, vocation or trade as to justify an expectation that it will be observed with respect to the transaction in question. The existence and scope of such a usage are to be proved as facts. If it is established that such a usage is embodied in a written trade code or similar writing the interpretation of the writing is for the court.

(3) A course of dealing between parties and any usage of trade in the vocation or trade in which they are engaged or of which they are or should be aware give particular meaning to and supplement or qualify terms of an agreement.

(4) The express terms of an agreement and an applicable course of dealing or usage of trade shall be construed wherever reasonable as consistent with each other; but wher such construction is unreasonable express terms control both course of dealirg and usage of trade and course of dealing controls usage of trade.

(5) An applicable usage of trade in the place where any part of performance is to occur shall be used in interpreting the agreement as to that part of the performance.

(6) Evidence of a relevant usage of trade offered by one party is not admissible unless and until he has given the other party such notice as the court finds sufficient to prevent unfair surprise to the latter.

Section 1-206. Statute of Frauds for Kinds of Personal Property Not Otherwise Covered.

(1) Except in the cases described in subsection (2) of this section a contract for the sale of personal property is not enforceable by way of action or defense beyond five thousand dollars in amount or value of remedy unless there is some writing which indicates that a contract for sale has been made between the parties at a defined or stated price, reasonably identifies the subject matter, and is signed by the party against whom enforcement is sought or by his authorized agent.

(2) Subsection (1) of this section does not apply to contracts for the sale of goods (Section 2-201) nor of securities (Section 8-319) nor to security agreements (Section 9-203).

Section 1-207. Performance or Acceptance under Reservation of Rights. A party who with explicit reservation of rights performs or promises performance or assents to performance in a manner demanded or offered by the other party does not thereby prejudice the rights reserved. Such words as "without prejudice," "under protect" or the like are sufficient.

Section 1-208. Option to Accelerate at Will. A term providing that one party or his successor in interest may accelerate payment of performance or require collateral or additional collateral "at will" or "when he deems himself insecure" or in words of similar import shall be construed to mean that he shall have power to do so only if he in good faith believes that the prospect of payment or performance is impaired. The burden of establishing lack of good faith is on the party against whom the power has been exercised.

SALES

PART 1

SHORT TITLE, GENERAL CONSTRUCTION AND SUBJECT MATTER

Section 2-101. Short Title. This Article shall be known and may be cited as Uniform Commercial Code–Sales.

Section 2-102. Scope; Certain Security and Other Transactions Excluded from this Article. Unless the context otherwise requires, this Article applies to transactions in goods; it does not apply to any transaction which although in the form of an unconditional contract to sell or present sale is intended to operate only as a security transaction nor does this Article impair or repeal any statute regulating sales to consumers, farmers or other specified classes of buyers.

Section 2-103. Definitions and Index of Definitions.

(1) In this Article unless the context otherwise requires

(a) "Buyer" means a person who buys or contracts to buy goods.

(b) "Good faith" in the case of a merchant means honesty in fact and the observance of reasonable commercial standards of fair dealing in the trade.

(c) "Receipt" of goods means taking physical possession of them.

(d) "Seller" means a person who sells or contracts to sell goods.

(2) Other definitions applying to this Article or to specified parts thereof, and the sections in which they appear are:

"Acceptance." Section 2-606.
"Banker's credit." Section 2-325.
"Between merchants." Section 2-104.
"Cancellation." Section 2-106(4)
"Commercial unit." Section 2-105.
"Confirmed credit." Section 2-325.
"Conforming to contract." Section 2-106.
"Contract for sale." Section 2-106.
"Cover." Section 2-712.
"Entrusting." Section 2-403.
"Financing agency." Section 2-104.
"Future goods." Section 2-105.
"Goods." Section 2-105.
"Identification." Section 2-501.
"Installment contract." Section 2-612.
"Letter of Credit." Section 2-325.
"Lot." Section 2-105.
"Merchant." Section 2-104.
"Overseas." Section 2-323.
"Person on position of seller." Section 2-707.
"Present sale." Section 2-106.
"Sale." Section 2-106.
"Sale on approval." Section 2-326.
"Sale or return." Section 2-326.
"Termination." Section 2-106.

(3) The following definitions in other Articles apply to this Article:

"Check." Section 3-204.
"Consignee." Section 7-102.
"Consignor." Section 7-102.
"Consumer goods." Section 9-109.
"Dishonor." Section 3-507.
"Draft." Section 3-104.

(4) In addition Article 1 contains general definitions and principles of construction and interpretation applicable throughout this Article.

Section 2-104. Definitions: "Merchant"; "Between Merchants"; Financing Agency."

(1) "Merchant" means a person who deals in goods of the kind or otherwise by his occupation holds himself out as having knowledge or skill peculiar to the practices or goods involved in the transaction or to whom such knowledge or skill may be attributed by his employment of an agent or broker or other intermediary who by his occupation holds himself out as having such knowledge or skill.

(2) "Financing agency" means a bank, finance company or other person who in the ordinary course of business makes advances against goods or documents of title or who by arrangement with either the seller or the buyer intervenes in ordinary course to make or collect payment due or claimed under the contract for sale, as by purchasing or paying the seller's draft or making advances against it or by merely taking it for collection whether or not documents of title accompany the draft. "Financing agency" includes also a bank or other person who similarly intervenes between persons who are in the position of seller and buyer in respect to the goods (Section 2-707).

(3) "Between merchants" means in any transaction with respect to which both parties are chargeable with the knowledge or skill of merchants.

Section 2-105. Definitions: Transferability; "Goods"; "Future" Goods; "Lot"; "Commercial Unit."

(1) "Goods" means all things (including specially manufactured goods) which are movable at the time of identification to the contract for sale other than the money in which the price is to be paid, investment securities (Article 8) and things in action. "Goods" also includes the unborn young of animals and growing crops and other identified things attached to realty as described in the section on goods to be severed from realty (Section 2-107).

(2) Goods must be both existing and identified before any interest in them can pass. Goods which are not both existing and identified are "future" goods. A purported present sale of future goods or of any interest therein operates as a contract to sell.

(3) There may be a sale or a part interest in existing identified goods.

(4) An undivided share in an identified bulk of fungible goods is sufficiently identified to be sold although the quantity of the bulk is not determined. Any agreed proportion of such a bulk or any quantity thereof agreed upon by number, weight or other measure may to the extent of the seller's interest in the bulk be sold to the buyer who then becomes an owner in common.

(5) "Lot" means a parcel or a single article which is the subject matter of a separate sale or delivery, whether or not it is usfficient to perform the contract.

(6) "Commercial unit" means such a unit of goods as by commercial usage is a single whole for purposes of sale and division of which materially impairs its character or value on the market or in use. A commercial unit may be a single article (as a machine) or a set of articles (as a suite of furniture or an assortment of sizes) or a quantity (as a bale, gross, or carload) or any other unit treated in use or in the relevant market as a single whole.

Section 2-106. Definitions: "Contract"; "Agreement"; "Contract for Sale"; "Sale"; "Present Sale"; "Conforming" to Contract; "Termination"; "Cancellation."

(1) In this Article unless the context otherwise requires "contract" and "agreement" are limited to those relating to the present or future sale of goods. "Contract for sale" includes both a present sale of goods and a contract to sell goods at a future time. A "sale" consists in the passing of title from the seller to the buyer for a price (Section 2–401). A "present sale" means a sale which is accomplished by the making of the contract.

(2) Goods or conduct including any part of a performance are "conforming" or conform to the contract when they are in accordance with the obligations under the contract.

(3) "Termination" occurs when either party pursuant to a power created by agreement or law puts an end to the contract otherwise than for its breach. On "termination" all obligations which are still executory on both sides are discharged but any right based on prior breach or performance survives.

(4) "Cancellation" occurs when either party puts an end to the contract for breach by the other and its effect is the same as that of "termination" except that the cancelling party also retains any remedy for breach of the whole contract or any unperformed balance.

Section 2-107. Goods to Be Severed From Realty: Recording

(1) A contract for the sale of minerals or the like (including oil and gas) or a structure or its materials to be removed from realty is a contract for the sale of goods within this Article if they are to be severed by the seller but until severance a purported present sale thereof which is not effective as a transfer of

an interest in land is effective only as a contract to sell.
(2) A contract for the sale apart from the land of growing crops or other things attached to realty and capable of severance without material harm thereto but not described in subsection (1) or of timber to be cut is a contract for the sale of goods within this Article whether the subject matter is to be severed by the buyer or by the seller even though it forms part of the realty at the time of contracting, and the parties can by identification effect a present sale before severance.
(3) The provisions of this section are subject to any third party rights provided by the law relating to realty records, and the contract for sale may be executed and recorded as a document transferring an interest in land and shall then constitute notice to third parties of the buyer's rights under the contract for sale.

PART 2

FORM, FORMATION AND READJUSTMENT OF CONTRACT

Section 2-201. Formal Requirements; Statute of Frauds.

(1) Except as otherwise provided in this section a contract for the sale of goods for the price of $500 or more is not enforceable by way of action or defense unless there is some writing sufficient to indicate that a contract for sale has been made between the parties and signed by the party against whom enforcement is sought or by his authorized agent or broker. A writing is not insufficient because it omits or incorrectly states a term agreed upon but the contract is not enforceable under this paragraph beyond the quantity of goods shown in such writing.

(2) Between merchants if within a reasonable time a written confirmation of the contract and sufficient against the sender is received and the party receiving it has reason to know its contents, it satisfies the requirements of subsection (1) against such party unless written notice of objection to its contents is given within ten days after it is received.

(3) A contract which does not satisfy the requirements of subsection (1) but which is valid in other respects is enforceable

(a) if the goods are to be specially manufactured for the buyer and are not suitable for sale to others in the ordinary course of the seller's business and the seller, before notice of repudiation is received and under circumstances which reasonably indicate that the goods are for the buyer, has made either a substantial beginning of their manufacture or commitments for their procurement; or

(b) if the party against whom enforcement is sought admits in his pleading, testimony or otherwise in court that a contract for sale was made, but the contract is not enforceable under this provision beyond the quantity of goods admitted; or

(c) with respect to goods for which payment has been made and accepted or which have been received and accepted (Sec. 2-606).

Section 2-202. Final Written Expression: Parol or Extrinsic Evidence. Terms with respect to which the confirmatory memoranda of the parties agree or which are otherwise set forth in a writing intended by the parties as a final expression of their agreement with respect to such terms as are included therein may not be contradicted by evidence of any prior agreement or of a contemporaneous oral agreement but may be explained or supplemented.

(a) by course of dealing or usage of trade (Section 1-205) or by course of performance (Section 2-208); and

(b) by evidence of consistent additional terms unless the court finds the writing to have been intended also as a complete and exclusive statement of the terms of the agreement.

Section 2-203. Seals Inoperative. The affixing of a seal to a writing evidencing a contract for sale or an offer to buy or sell goods does not constitute the writing a sealed instrument and the law with respect to sealed instruments does not apply to such a contract or offer.

Section 2-204. Formation in General.

(1) A contract for sale of goods may be made in any manner sufficient to show agreement, including conduct by both

parties which recognizes the existence of such a contract.

(2) An agreement sufficient to constitute a contract for sale may be found even though the moment of its making is undetermined.

(3) Even though one or more terms are left open a contract for sale does not fail for indefiniteness if the parties have intended to make a contract and there is a reasonably certain basis for giving an appropriate remedy.

Section 2-205. Firm Offers. An offer by a merchant to buy or sell goods in a signed writing which by its terms gives assurance that it will be held open is not revocable, for lack of consideration, during the time stated or if no time is stated for a reasonable time, but in no event may such period of irrevocability exceed three months; but any such term of assurance on a form supplied by the offeree must be separately signed by the offeror.

Section 2-206. Offer and Acceptance in Formation of Contract.

(1) Unless otherwise unambiguously indicated by the language or circumstances

(a) an offer to make a contract shall be construed as inviting acceptance in any manner and by any medium reasonable in the circumstances;

(b) an order or other offer to buy goods for prompt or current shipment shall be construed as inviting acceptance either by a prompt promise to ship or by the prompt or current shipment of conforming or non-conforming goods, but such a shipment of non-conforming goods does not constitute an acceptance if the seller reasonably notifies the buyer that the shipment is offered only as an accommodation to the buyer.

(2) Where the beginning of a requested performance is a reasonable mode of acceptance an offeror who is not notified of acceptance within a reasonable time may treat the offer as having lapsed before acceptance.

Section 2-207. Additional Terms in Acceptance or Confirmation.

(1) A definite and seasonable expression of acceptance or a written confirmation which is sent within a reasonable time operates as an acceptance even though it states terms additional to or different from those offered or agreed upon, unless acceptance is expressly made conditional on assent to the additional or different terms.

(2) The additional terms are to be construed as proposals for addition to the contract. Between merchants such terms become part of the contract unless:

(a) the offer expressly limits acceptance to the terms of the offer;

(b) they materially alter it; or

(c) notification of objection to them has already been given or is given within a reasonable time after notice of them is received.

(3) Conduct by both parties which recognizes the existence of a contract is sufficient to establish a contract for sale although the writings of the parties do not otherwise establish a contract. In such case the terms of the particular contract consist of those terms on which the writings of the parties agree, together with any supplementary terms incorporated under any other provisions of this Act.

Section 2-208. Course of Performance or Practical Construction.

(1) Where the contract for sale involves repeated occasions for performance by either party with knowledge of the nature of the performance and opportunity for objection to it by the other, any course of performance accepted or acquiesced in without objection shall be relevant to determine the meaning of the agreement.

(2) The express terms of the agreement and any such course of performance, as well as any course of dealing and usage of trade, shall be construed whenever reasonable as consistent with each other; but when such construction is unreasonable, express terms shall control course of performance and course of performance shall control both course of dealing and usage of trade (Section 1-205).

(3) Subject to the provisions of the next section on modification and waiver, such course of performance shall be relevant to show a waiver or modification of any term inconsistent with such course of performance.

Section 2-209. Modification, Rescission and Waiver.

(1) An agreement modifying a contract within this Article needs no consideration to be binding.

(2) A signed agreement which excludes modification or rescission except by a signed writing cannot be otherwise modified or rescinded, but except as between merchants such a requirement on a form supplied by the merchant must be separately signed by the other party.

(3) The requirements of the statute of frauds section of this Article (Section 2-201) must be satisfied if the contract as modified is within its provisions.

(4) Although an attempt at modification or rescission does not satisfy the requirements of subsection (2) or (3) it can operate as a waiver.

(5) A party who has made a waiver affecting an executory portion of the contract may retract the waiver by reasonable notification received by the other party that strict performance will be required of any term waived, unless the retraction would be unjust in view of a material change of position in reliance on the waiver.

Section 2-210. Delegation of Performance; Assignment of Rights.

(1) A party may perform his duty through a delegate unless otherwise agreed or unless the other party has a substantial interest in having his original promisor perform or control the acts required by the contract. No delegation of performance relieves the party delegating of any duty to perform or any liability for breach.

(2) Unless otherwise agreed all rights of either seller or buyer can be assigned except where the assignment would materially change the duty of the other party, or increase materially the burden or risk imposed on him by his contract, or impair materially his chance of obtaining return performance. A right to damages for breach of the whole contract or a right arising out of the assignor's due performance of his entire obligation can be assigned despite agreement otherwise.

(3) Unless the circumstances indicate the contrary a prohibition of assignment of "the contract" is to be construed as barring only the delegation to the assignee of the assignor's performance.

(4) An assignment of "the contract" or of "all my rights under the contract" or an assignment in similar general terms is an assignment of rights and unless the language or the circumstances (as in an assignment for security) indicate the contrary, it is a delegation of performance of the duties of the assignor and its acceptance by the assignee constitutes a promise by him to perform those duties. This promise is enforceable by either the assignor or the other party to the original contract.

(5) The other party may treat any assignment which delegates performance as creating reasonable grounds for insecurity and may without prejudice to his rights against the assignor demand assurances from the assignee (Section 2-609).

PART 3

GENERAL OBLIGATION AND CONSTRUCTION OF CONTRACT

Section 2-301. General Obligations of Parties. The obligation of the seller is to transfer and deliver and that of the buyer is to accept and pay in accordance with the contract.

Section 2-302. Unconscionable Contract or Clause.

(1) If the court as a matter of law finds the contract or any clause of the contract to have been unconscionable at the time it was made the court may refuse to enforce the contract, or it may enforce the remainder of the contract without the unconscionable clause, or it may so limit the application of any unconscionable clause as to avoid any unconscionable result.

(2) When it is claimed or appears to the court that the contract or any clause thereof may be unconscionable the parties shall be afforded a reasonable opportunity to present evidence as to its commercial setting, purpose and effect to aid the court in making the determination.

Section 2-303. Allocation or Division of Risks. Where this Article allocates a risk or a burden as between the parties "unless otherwise agreed," the agreement may not only shift the allocation but may also divide the risk or burden.

Section 2-304. Price Payable in Money, Goods, Realty, or Otherwise.

(1) The price can be made payable in

money or otherwise. If it is payable in whole or in part in goods each party is a seller of the goods which he is to transfer.

(2) Even though all or part of the price is payable in an interest in realty the transfer of the goods and the seller's obligations with reference to them are subject to this Article, but not the transfer of the interest in realty or the transferor's obligations in connection therewith.

Section 2-305. Open Price Term.

(1) The parties if they so intend can conclude a contract for sale even though the price is not settled. In such a case the price is a reasonable price at the time for delivery if

(a) nothing is said as to price; or

(b) the price is left to be agreed by the parties and they fail to agree; or

(c) the price is to be fixed in terms of some agreed market or other standard as set or recorded by a third person or agency and it is not so set or recorded.

(2) A price to be fixed by the seller or by the buyer means a price for him to fix in good faith.

(3) When a price left to be fixed otherwise than by agreement of the parties fails to be fixed through fault of one party the other may at his option treat the contract as cancelled or himself fix a reasonable price.

(4) Where, however, the parties intend not to be bound unless the price be fixed or agreed and it is not fixed or agreed there is no contract. In such a case the buyer must return any goods already received or if unable to do so must pay their reasonable value at the time of delivery and the seller must return any portion of the price paid on account.

Section 2-306. Output, Requirements and Exclusive Dealings.

(1) A term which measures the quantity by the output of the seller or the requirements of the buyer means such actual output or requirements as may occur in good faith, except that no quantity unreasonably disproportionate to any stated estimate or in the absence of a stated estimate to any normal or otherwise comparable prior output or requirements may be tendered or demanded.

(2) A lawful agreement by either the seller or the buyer for exclusive dealing in the kind of goods concerned imposes unless otherwise agreed an obligation by the seller to use best efforts to supply the goods and by the buyer to use best efforts to promote their sale.

Section 2-307. Delivery in Single Lot or Several Lots. Unless otherwise agreed all goods called for by a contract for sale must be tendered in a single delivery and payment is due only on such tender but where the circumstances give either party the right to make or demand delivery in lots the price if it can be apportioned may be demanded for each lot.

Section 2-308. Absence of Specified Place for Delivery. Unless otherwise agreed.

(a) the place for delivery of goods is the seller's place of business or if he has none his residence; but

(b) in a contract for sale of identified goods which to the knowledge of the parties at the time of contracting are in some other place, that place is the place for their delivery; and

(c) documents of title may be delivered through customary banking channels.

Section 2-309. Absence of Specific Time Provisions; Notice of Termination.

(1) The time for shipment or delivery or any other action under a contract if not provided in this Article or agreed upon shall be a reasonable time.

(2) Where the contract provides for successive performances but is indefinite in duration it is valid for a reasonable time but unless otherwise agreed may be terminated at any time by either party.

(3) Termination of a contract by one party except on the happening of an agreed event requires that reasonable notification is invalid if its operation would be unconscionable.

Section 2-310. Open Time for Payment or Running of Credit; Authority to Ship under Reservation. Unless otherwise agreed

(a) payment is due at the time and place at which the buyer is to receive the goods even though the place of shipment is the place of delivery; and

(b) if the seller is authorized to send the goods he may ship them under reservation, and may tender the documents of title, but the buyer may inspect the goods after their arrival before payment is due unless such inspection is inconsistent with the terms of the contract (Section 2-513); and

(c) if delivery is authorized and made by way of documents of title otherwise than by subsection (b) then payment is due at the time and place at which the buyer is to receive the documents regardless of where the goods are to be received; and

(d) where the seller is required or authorized to ship the goods on credit the credit period runs from the time of shipment but post-dating the invoice or delaying its dispatch will correspondingly delay the starting of the credit period.

Section 2-311. Options and Cooperation Respecting Performance.

(1) An agreement for sale which is otherwise sufficiently definite (subsection (3) of Section 2-204) to be a contract is not made invalid by the fact that it leaves particulars of performance to be specified by one of the parties. Any such specification must be made in good faith and within limits set by commercial reasonableness.

(2) Unless otherwise agreed specifications relating to assortment of the goods are at the buyer's option and except as otherwise provided in subsections (1) (c) and (3) of Section 2-319 specifications or arrangements relating to shipment are at the seller's option.

(3) Where such specification would materially affect the other party's performance but is not seasonably made or where one party's cooperation is necessary to the agreed performance of the other but is not seasonably forthcoming, the other party in addition to all other remedies

(a) is excused for any resulting delay in his own performance; and

(b) may also either proceed to perform in any reasonable manner or after the time for a material part of his own performance treat the failure to specify or to cooperate as a breach by failure to deliver or accept the goods.

Section 2-312. Warranty of Title and Against Infringement; Buyer's Obligation Against Infringement.

(1) Subject to subsection (2) there is in a contract for a sale a warranty by the seller that

(a) the title conveyed shall be good, and its transfer rightful; and

(b) the goods shall be delivered free from any security interest or other lien or encumbrance of which the buyer at the time of contracting has no knowledge.

(2) A warranty under subsection (1) will be excluded or modified only by specific language or by circumstances which give the buyer reason to know that the person selling does not claim title in himself or that he is purporting to sell only such right or title as he or a third person may have.

(3) Unless otherwise agreed a seller who is a merchant regularly dealing in goods of the kind warrants that the goods shall be delivered free of the rightful claim of any third person by way of infringement or the like but a buyer who furnishes specifications to the seller must hold the seller harmless against any such claim which arises out of compliance with the specifications.

Section 2-313. Express Warranties by Affirmation, Promise, Description, Sample.

(1) Express warranties by the seller are created as follows:

(a) Any affirmation of fact or promise made by the seller to the buyer which relates to the goods and becomes part of the basis of the bargain creates an express warranty that the goods shall conform to the affirmation or promise.

(b) Any description of the goods which is made part of the basis of the bargain creates an express warranty that the goods shall conform to the description.

(c) Any sample or model which is made part of the basis of the bargain creates an express warranty that the whole of the goods shall conform to the sample or model.

(2) It is not necessary to the creation of an express warranty that the seller use formal words such as "warrant" or "guarantee" or that he have a specific intention to make a warranty, but an affirmation merely of the value of the goods or a statement purporting to be merely the seller's opinion or commendation of the goods does not create a warranty.

Section 2-314. Implied Warranty: Merchantability; Usage of Trade.

(1) Unless excluded or modified (Section

2-316) a warranty that the goods shall be merchantable is implied in a contract for their sale if the seller is a merchant with respect to goods of that kind. Under this section the serving for value of food or drink to be consumed either on the premises or elsewhere is a sale.

(2) Goods to be merchantable must be at least such as

(a) pass without objection in the trade under the contract description; and

(b) in the case of fungible goods, are of fair average quality within the description; and

(c) are fit for the ordinary purposes for which such goods are used; and

(d) run, within the variations permitted by the agreement, of even kind, quality and quantity within each unit and among all units involved; and

(e) are adequately contained, packaged, and labeled as the agreement may require; and

(f) conform to the promises or affirmations of fact made on the container or label if any.

(3) Unless excluded or modified (Section 2-316) other implied warranties may arise from course of dealing or usage of trade.

Section 2-315. Implied Warranty: Fitness for Particular Purpose. Where the seller at the time of contracting has reason to know any particular purpose for which the goods are required and that the buyer is relying on the seller's skill or judgment to select or furnish suitable goods, there is unless excluded or modified under the next section an implied warranty that the goods shall be fit for such purpose.

Section 2-316. Exclusion or Modification of Warranties.

(1) Words or conduct relevant to the creation of an express warranty and words or conduct tending to negate or limit warranty shall be construed wherever reasonable as consistent with each other; but subject to the provisions of this Article on parol or extrinsic evidence (Section 2-202) negation or limitation is inoperative to the extent that such construction is unreasonable.

(2) Subject to subsection (3), to exclude or modify the implied warranty of merchantability or any part of it the language must mention merchantability and in case of a writing must be conspicuous, and to exclude or modify any implied warranty of fitness the exclusion must be by a writing and conspicuous. Language to exclude all implied warranties of fitness is sufficient if it states, for example, that "There are no warranties which extend beyond the description on the face hereof."

(3) Notwithstanding subsection (2)

(a) unless the circumstances indicate otherwise, all implied warranties are excluded by expressions like "as is," "with all faults" or other language which in common understanding calls the buyer's attention to the exclusion of warranties and makes plain that there is no implied warranty; and

(b) when the buyer before entering into the contract has examined the goods or the sample or model as fully as he desired or has refused to examine the goods there is no implied warranty with regard to defects which an examination ought in the circumstances to have revealed to him; and

(c) an implied warranty can also be excluded or modified by course of dealing or course of performance or usage of trade.

(4) Remedies for breach of warranty can be limited in accordance with the provisions of this Article on liquidation or limitation of damages and on contractual modification of remedy (Sections 2-718 and 2-719).

Section 2-317. Cumulation and Conflict of Warranties Express or Implied. Warranties whether express or implied shall be construed as consistent with each other and as cumulative, but if such construction is unreasonable the intention of the parties shall determine which warranty is dominant. In ascertaining that intention the following rules apply:

(a) Exact or technical specifications displace an inconsistent sample or model or general language of description.

(b) A sample from an existing bulk displaces inconsistent general language of description.

(c) Express warranties displace inconsistent implied warranties other than an implied warranty of fitness for a particular purpose.

Section 2-318. Third Party Beneficiaries of Warranties Express or Implied. Note: *If this Act is introduced in the Congress of the United States this section should be omitted. (States to select one alternative.)*

Alternative A

A seller's warranty whether express or

implied extends to any natural person who is in the family or household of his buyer or who is a guest in his home if it is reasonable to expect that such person may use, consume or be affected by the goods and who is injured in person by breach of the warranty. A seller may not exclude or limit the operation of this section.

Alternative B

A seller's warranty whether express or implied extends to any natural person who may reasonably be expected to use, consume or be affected by the goods and who is injured in person by breach of the warranty. A seller may not exclude or limit the operation of this section.

Alternative C

A seller's warranty whether express or implied extends to any person who many reasonably be expected to use, consume or be affected by the goods and who is injured by breach of the warranty. A seller may not exclude or limit the operation of this section with respect to injury to the person of an individual to whom the warranty extends.

Section 2-319. F.O.B. and F.A.S. Terms.

(1) Unless otherwise agreed the term F.O.B. (which means "free on board") at a named place, even though used only in connection with the stated price, is a delivery term under which

(a) when the term is F.O.B. the place of shipment, the seller must at that place ship the goods in the manner provided in this article (Section 2-504) and bear the expense and risk of putting them into the possession of the carrier; or

(b) when the term is F.O.B. the place of destination, the seller must at his own expense and risk transport the goods to that place and there tender delivery of them in the manner provided in this Article (Section 2-503);

(c) when under either (a) or (b) the term is also F.O.B. vessel, car or other vehicle, the seller must in addition at his own expense and risk load the goods on board. If the term is F.O.B. vessel the buyer must name the vessel and in an appropriate case the seller must comply with the provisions of this Article on the form of bill of lading (Section 2-323).

(2) Unless otherwise agreed the term F.A.S. vessel (which means "free alongside") at a named port, even though used only in connection with the stated price, is a delivery term under which the seller must

(a) at his own expense and risk deliver the goods alongside the vessel in the manner usual in that port or on a dock designated and provided by the buyer; and

(b) obtain and tender a receipt for the goods in exchange for which the carrier is under a duty to issue a bill of lading.

(3) Unless otherwise agreed in any case falling within subsection (1)(a) or (c) or subsection (2) the buyer must seasonably give any needed instructions for making delivery, including when the term is F.A.S. or F.O.B. the loading berth of the vessel and in an appropriate case its name and sailing date. The seller may treat the failure of needed instructions as a failure of cooperation under this Article (Section 2-311). He may also at his option move the goods in any reasonable manner preparatory to delivery or shipment.

(4) Under the term F.O.B. vessel or F.A.S. unless otherwise agreed the buyer must make payment against tender of the required documents and the seller may not tender nor the buyer demand delivery of the goods in substitution for the documents.

Section 2-320. C.I.F. and C. & F. Terms.

(1) The term C.I.F. means that the price includes in a lump sum the cost of the goods and the insurance and freight to the named destination. The term C. & F. or C.F. means that the price so includes cost and freight to the named destination.

(2) Unless otherwise agreed and even though used only in connection with the stated price and destination, the term C.I.F. destination or its equivalent requires the seller at his own expense and risk to

(a) put the goods into the possession of a carrier at the port for shipment and obtain a negotiable bill or bills of lading covering the entire transportation to the named destination; and

(b) load the goods and obtain a receipt from the carrier (which may be contained in the bill of lading) showing that the freight has been paid or provided for; and

(c) obtain a policy or certificate of insurance, including any war risk insurance, of a kind and on terms then current at the port of shipment in the usual amount, in the currency of the contract, shown to cover the same goods covered by the bill of lading and providing for payment of loss to the order of the buyer or for the account of whom it may concern; but the seller may add to the price the amount of the premium for any such war risk insurance; and

(d) prepare an invoice of the goods and procure any other documents required to effect shipment or to comply with the contract; and

(e) forward and tender with commercial promptness all the documents in due form and with any indorsement necessary to perfect the buyer's rights.

(3) Unless otherwise agreed the term C. & F. or its equivalent has the same effect and imposes upon the seller the same obligations and risks as a C.I.F. term except the obligation as to insurance.

(4) Under the term C.I.F. or C. & F. unless otherwise agreed the buyer must make payment against tender of the required documents and the seller may not tender nor the buyer demand delivery of the goods in substitution for the documents.

Section 2-321. C.I.F. or C. & F.: "Net Landed Weights"; "Payment on Arrival"; Warranty of Condition on Arrival. Under a contract containing a term C.I.F. or C. & F.

(1) Where the price is based on or is to be adjusted according to "net landed weights," "delivered weights," "out turn" quantity or quality or the like, unless otherwise agreed the seller must reasonably estimate the price. The payment due on tender of the documents called for by the contract is the amount so estimated, but after final adjustment of the price a settlement must be made with commercial promptness.

(2) An agreement described in subsection (1) or any warranty of quality or condition of the goods on arrival places upon the seller the risk of ordinary deterioration, shrinkage and the like in transportation but has no effect on the place or time of identification to the contract for sale or delivery or on the passing of the risk of loss.

(3) Unless otherwise agreed where the contract provides for payment on or after arrival of the goods the seller must before payment allow such preliminary inspection as is feasible; but if the goods are lost delivery of the documents and payment are due when the goods should have arrived.

Section 2-322. Delivery "Ex-Ship."

(1) Unless otherwise agreed a term for delivery of goods "ex-ship" (which means from the carrying vessel) or in equivalent language is not restricted to a particular ship and requires delivery from a ship which has reached a place at the named port of destination where goods of the kind are usually discharged.

(2) Under such a term unless otherwise agreed

(a) the seller must discharge all liens arising out of the carriage and furnish the buyer with a direction which puts the carrier under a duty to deliver the goods; and

(b) the risk of loss does not pass to the buyer until the goods leave the ship's tackle or are otherwise properly unloaded.

Section 2-323. Form of Bill of Lading Required in Overseas Shipment; "Overseas."

(1) Where the contract contemplates overseas shipment and contains a term C.I.F. or C. & F. or F. O. B. vessel, the seller unless otherwise agreed must obtain a negotiable bill of lading stating that the goods have been loaded on board or, in the case of a term C.I.F. or C. & F., received for shipment.

(2) Where in a case within subsection (1) a bill of lading has been issued in a set of parts, unless otherwise agreed if the documents are not to be sent from abroad the buyer may demand tender of the full set; otherwise only one part of the bill of lading need be tendered. Even if the agreement expressly requires a full set

(a) due tender of a single part is acceptable within the provisions of this Article on cure of improper delivery (subsection (1) of Section 2-508); and

(b) even though the full set is demanded, if the documents are sent from abroad the person tendering an incomplete set may nevertheless require payment upon furnishing an indemnity which the buyer in good faith deems adequate.

(3) A shipment by water or by air or a contract contemplating such shipment is "overseas" insofar as by usage of trade or agreement it is subject to the commercial, financing or shipping practices characteristic of international deep water commerce.

Section 2-324. "No Arrival, No Sale" Term. Under a term "no arrival, no sale" or terms of like meaning, unless otherwise agreed.

(a) the seller must properly ship conforming goods and if they arrive by any means he must tender them on arrival but he assumes no obligation that the goods will arrive unless he has caused the non-arrival; and

(b) where without fault of the seller the goods are in part lost or have so deteriorated as no longer to conform to the contract or arrive after the contract time, the buyer may proceed as if there had been casualty to identified goods (Section 2-613).

Section 2-325. "Letter of Credit" Term; "Confirmed Credit."

(1) Failure of the buyer seasonably to furnish an agreed letter of credit is a breach of the contract for sale.

(2) The delivery to seller of a proper letter of credit suspends the buyer's obligation to pay. If the letter of credit is dishonored, the seller may on seasonable notification to the buyer require payment directly from him.

(3) Unless otherwise agreed the term "letter of credit" or "banker's credit" in a contract for sale means an irrevocable credit issued by a financing agency of good repute and, where the shipment is overseas, of good international repute. The term "confirmed credit" means that the credit must also carry the direct obligation of such an agency which does business in the seller's financial market.

Section 2-326. Sale on Approval and Sale or Return; Consignment Sales and Rights of Creditors.

(1) Unless otherwise agreed, if delivered goods may be returned to the buyer even though they conform to the contract, the transaction is.

(a) a "sale on approval" if the goods are delivered primarily for use; and

(b) a "sale or return" if the goods are delivered primarily for resale.

(2) Except as provided in subsection (3), goods held on approval are not subject to the claims of the buyer's creditors until acceptance; goods held on sale or return are subject to such claims while in the buyer's possession.

(3) Where goods are delivered to a person for sale and such person maintains a place of business at which he deals in goods of the kind involved, under a name other than the name of the person making delivery, then with respect to claims of creditors of the person conducting the business the goods are deemed to be on sale or return. The provisions of this subsection are applicable even though an agreement purports to reserve title to the person making delivery until payment or resale or uses such words as "on consignment" or "on memorandum." However, this subsection is not applicable if the person making delivery

(a) complies with an applicable law providing for a consignor's interest or the like to be evidenced by a sign, or

(b) establishes that the person conducting the business is generally known by his creditors to be substantially engaged in selling the goods of others, or

(c) complies with the filing provisions of the Article on Secured Transactions (Article 9).

(4) Any "or return" term of a contract for sale is to be treated as a separate contract for sale within the statute of frauds section of this Article (Section 2-201) and as contradicting the sale aspect of the contract within the provisions of this Article on parol or extrinsic evidence (Section 2-202).

Section 2-327. Special Incidents of Sale on Approval and Sale or Return.

(1) Under a sale on approval unless otherwise agreed

(a) although the goods are identified to the contract the risk of loss and the title do not pass to the buyer until acceptance; and

(b) use of the goods consistent with the purpose of trial is not acceptance but failure seasonably to notify the seller of election to return the goods is acceptance, and if the goods conform to the contract acceptance of any part is acceptance of the whole; and

(c) after due notification of election to return, the return is at the seller's risk and expense but a merchant buyer must follow any reasonable instructions.

(2) Under a sale or return unless otherwise agreed

(a) the option to return extends to the whole or any commercial unit of the goods while in substantially their original condition, but must be exercised seasonably; and

(b) the return is at the buyer's risk and expense.

Section 2-328. Sale by Auction.

(1) In a sale by auction if goods are put up in lots each lot is the subject of a separate sale.

(2) A sale by auction is complete when the auctioneer so announces by the fall of the hammer or in other customary manner.

Where a bid is made while the hammer is falling in acceptance of a prior bid the auctioneer may in his discretion reopen the bidding or declare the goods sold under the bid on which the hammer was falling.

(3) Such a sale is with reserve unless the goods are in explicit terms put up without reserve. In an auction with reserve the auctioneer may withdraw the goods at any time until he announces completion of the sale. In an auction without reserve, after the auctioneer calls for bids on an article or lot, that article or lot cannot be withdrawn unless no bid is made within a reasonable time. In either case a bidder may retract his bid until the auctioneer's announcement of completion of the sale, but a bidder's retraction does not revive any previous bid.

(4) If the auctioneer knowingly receives a bid on the seller's behalf or the seller makes or procures such a bid, and notice has not been given that liberty for such bidding is reserved, the buyer may at his option avoid the sale or take the goods at the price of the last good faith bid prior to the completion of the sale. This subsection shall not apply to any bid at a forced sale.

PART 4

TITLE, CREDITORS AND GOOD FAITH PURCHASERS

Section 2-401. Passing of Title; Reservation for Security; Limited Application of this Section. Each provision of this Article with regard to the rights, obligations and remedies of the seller, the buyer, purchasers or other third parties applies irrespective of title to the goods except where the provision refers to such title. Insofar as situations are not covered by the other provisions of this Article and matters concerning title become material the following rules apply:

(1) Title to goods cannot pass under a contract for sale prior to their identification to the contract (Section 2-501), and unless otherwise explicitly agreed the buyer acquires by their identification a special property as limited by this Act. Any retention or reservation by the seller of the title (property) in goods shipped or delivered to the buyer is limited in effect to a reservation of a security interest. Subject to these provisions and to the provisions of the Article on Secured Transactions (Article 9), title to goods passes from the seller to the buyer in any manner and on any conditions explicitly agreed on by the parties.

(2) Unless otherwise explicitly agreed title passes to the buyer at the time and place at which the seller completes his performance with reference to the physical delivery of the goods, despite any reservation of a security interest and even though a document of title is to be delivered at a different time or place; and in particular and despite any reservation of a security interest by the bill of lading

(a) if the contract requires or authorizes the seller to send the goods to the buyer but does not require him to deliver them at destination, title passes to the buyer at the time and place of shipment; but

(b) if the contract requires delivery at destination, title passes on tender there.

(3) Unless otherwise explicitly agreed where delivery is to be made without moving the goods,

(a) if the seller is to deliver a document of title, title passes at the time when and the place where he delivers such documents; or

(b) if the goods are at the time of contracting already identified and no documents are to be delivered, title passes at the time and place of contracting.

(4) A rejection or other refusal by the buyer to receive or retain the goods, whether or not justified, or a justified revocation of acceptance revests title to the goods in the seller. Such revesting occurs by operation of law and is not a "sale."

Section 2-402. Rights of Seller's Creditors Against Sold Goods.

(1) Except as provided in subsections (2) and (3), rights of unsecured creditors of the seller with respect to goods which have been identified to a contract for sale are subject to the buyer's rights to recover the goods under this Article (Sections 2-502 and 2-716).

(2) A creditor of the seller may treat a sale or an identification of goods to a contract

for sale as void if as against him a retention of possession by the seller is fraudulent under any rule of law of the state where the goods are situated, except that retention of possession in good faith and current course of trade by a merchant-seller for a commercially reasonable time after a sale or identification is not fraudulent.

(3) Nothing in this Article shall be deemed to impair the rights of creditors of the seller

(a) under the provisions of the Article on Secured Transactions (Article 9); or

(b) where identification to the contract or delivery is made not in current course of trade but in satisfaction of or as security for a pre-existing claim for money, security or the like and is made under circumstances which under any rule of law of the state where the goods are situated would apart from this Article constitute the transaction a fraudulent transfer or voidable preference.

Section 2-403. Power to Transfer; Good Faith Purchase of Goods; "Entrusting."

(1) A purchaser of goods acquires all title which his transferor had or had power to transfer except that a purchaser of a limited interest acquires rights only to the extent of the interest purchased. A person with voidable title had power to transfer a good title to a good faith purchaser for value. When goods have been delivered under a transaction of purchase the purchaser has such power even though

(a) the transferor was deceived as to the identity of the purchaser, or

(b) the delivery was in exchange for a check which is later dishonored, or

(c) it was agreed that the transaction was to be a "cash sale," or

(d) the delivery was procured through fraud punishable as larcenous under the criminal law.

(2) Any entrusting of possession of goods to a merchant who deals in goods of that kind gives him power to transfer all rights of the entruster to a buyer in ordinary course of business.

(3) "Entrusting" includes any delivery and any acquiescence in retention of possession regardless of any condition expressed between the parties to the delivery or acquiescence and regardless of whether the procurement of the entrusting or the possessor's disposition of the goods have been such as to be larcenous under the criminal law.

(4) The rights of other purchasers of goods and of lien creditors are governed by the Articles on Secured Transactions (Article 9), Bulk Transfers (Article 6) and Documents of Title (Article 7).

PART 5

PERFORMANCE

Section 2-501. Insurable Interest in Goods; Manner of Identification of Goods.

(1) The buyer obtains a special property and an insurable interest in goods by identification of existing goods as goods to which the contract refers even though the goods so identified are non-conforming and he has an opinion to return or reject them. Such identification can be made at any time and in any manner explicitly agreed to by the parties. In the absence of explicit agreement identification occurs

(a) when the contract is made if it is for the sale of goods already existing and identified;

(b) if the contract is for the sale of future goods other than those described in paragraph (c), when goods are shipped, marked or otherwise designated by the seller as goods to which the contract refers;

(c) when the crops are planted or otherwise become growing crops or the young are conceived if the contract is for the sale of unborn young to be born within twelve months after contracting or for the sale of crops to be harvested within twelve months or the next normal harvest season after contracting whichever is longer.

(2) The seller retains an insurable interest in goods so long as title to or any security interest in the goods remains in him and where the identification is by the seller alone he may until default or insolvency or notification to the buyer that the identifica-

tion is final substitute other goods for those identified.

(3) Nothing in this section impairs any insurable interest recognized under any other statute or rule of law.

Section 2-502. Buyer's Right to Goods on Seller's Insolvency.

(1) Subject to subsection (2) and even though the goods have not been shipped a buyer who has paid a part or all of the price of the goods in which he has a special property under the provisions of the immediately preceding section may on making and keeping good a tender of any unpaid portion of their price recover them from the seller if the seller becomes insolvent within ten days after receipt of the first installment on their price.

(2) If the identification creating his special property has been made by the buyer he acquires the right to recover the goods only if they conform to the contract for sale.

Section 2-503. Manner of Seller's Tender of Delivery.

(1) Tender of delivery requires that the seller put and hold conforming goods at the buyer's disposition and give the buyer any notification reasonably necessary to enable him to take delivery. The manner, time and place for tender are determined by the agreement and this Article, and in particular

(a) tender must be at a reasonable hour, and if it is of goods they must be kept available for the period reasonably necessary to enable the buyer to take possession; but

(b) unless otherwise agreed the buyer must furnish facilities reasonably suited to the receipt of the goods.

(2) Where the case is within the next section respecting shipment tender requires that the seller comply with its provisions.

(3) Where the seller is required to deliver at a particular destination tender requires that he comply with subsection (1) and also in any appropriate case tender documents as described in subsections (4) and (5) of this section.

(4) Where goods are in the possession of a bailee and are to be delivered without being moved

(a) tender requires that the seller either tender a negotiable document of title covering such goods or procure acknowledgment by the bailee of the buyer's right to possession of the goods; but

(b) tender to the buyer of a non-negotiable document of title or of a written direction to the bailee to deliver is sufficient tender unless the buyer seasonably objects, and receipt by the bailee of notification of the buyer's rights fixes those rights as against the bailee and all third persons; but risk of loss of the goods and of any failure by the bailee to honor the non-negotiable document of title or to obey the direction remains on the seller until the buyer has had a reasonable time to present the document or direction, and a refusal by the bailee to honor the document or to obey the direction defeats the tender.

(5) Where the contract requires the seller to deliver documents

(a) he must tender all such documents in correct form, except as provided in this Article with respect to bills of lading in a set (subsection (2) of Section 2-323); and

(b) tender through customary banking channels is sufficient and dishonor of a draft accompanying the documents constitutes non-acceptance or rejection.

Section 2-504. Shipment by Seller. Where the seller is required or authorized to send the goods to the buyer and the contract does not require him to deliver them at a particular destination, then unless otherwise agreed he must

(a) put the goods in the possession of such a carrier and make such a contract for their transportation as may be reasonable having regard to the nature of the goods and other circumstances of the case; and

(b) obtain and promptly deliver or tender in due form any document necessary to enable the buyer to obtain possession of the goods or otherwise required by the agreement or by usage of trade; and

(c) promptly notify the buyer of the shipment.

Failure to notify the buyer under paragraph (c)

or to make a proper contract under paragraph (a) is a ground for rejection only if material delay or loss ensues.

Section 2-505. Seller's Shipment Under Reservation.

(1) Where the seller has identified goods to the contract by or before shipment:

(a) his procurement of a negotiable bill of lading to his own order or otherwise reserves in him a security interest in the goods. His procurement of the bill to the order of a financing agency or of the buyer indicates in addition only the seller's expectation of transferring that interest to the person named.

(b) a non-negotiable bill of lading to himself or his nominee reserves possession of the goods as security but except in a case of conditional delivery (subsection (2) of Section 2-507) a non-negotiable bill of lading naming the buyer as consignee reserves no security interest even though the seller retains possession of the bill of lading.

(2) When shipment by the seller with reservation of a security interest is in violation of the contract for sale it constitutes an improper contract for transportation within the preceding section but impairs neither the rights given to the buyer by shipment and identification of the goods to the contract nor the seller's powers as a holder of a negotiable document.

Section 2-506. Rights of Financing Agency.

(1) A financing agency by paying or purchasing for value a draft which relates to a shipment of goods acquires to the extent of the payment or purchase and in addition to its own rights under the draft and any document of title securing it any rights of the shipper in the goods including the right to stop delivery and the shipper's right to have the draft honored by the buyer.

(2) The right to reimbursement of a financing agency which has in good faith honored or purchased the draft under commitment to or authority from the buyer is not impaired by subsequent discovery of defects with reference to any relevant document which was apparently regular on its face.

Section 2-507. Effect of Seller's Tender; Delivery on Condition.

(1) Tender of delivery is a condition to the buyer's duty to accept the goods and, unless otherwise agreed, to his duty to pay for them. Tender entitles the seller to acceptance of the goods and to payment according to the contract.

(2) Where payment is due and demanded on the delivery to the buyer of goods or documents of title, his right as against the seller to retain or dispose of them is conditional upon his making the payment due.

Section 2-508. Cure by Seller of Improper Tender or Delivery; Replacement.

(1) Where any tender or delivery by the seller is rejected because non-conforming and the time for performance has not yet expired, the seller may seasonably notify the buyer of his intention to cure and may then within the contract time make a conforming delivery.

(2) Where the buyer rejects a non-conforming tender which the seller had reasonable grounds to believe would be acceptable with or without money allowance the seller may if he seasonably notifies the buyer have a further reasonable time to substitute a conforming tender.

Section 2-509. Risk of Loss in the Absence of Breach.

(1) Where the contract requires or authorizes the seller to ship the goods by carrier

(a) if it does not require him to deliver them at a particular destination, the risk of loss passes to the buyer when the goods are duly delivered to the carrier even though the shipment is under reservation (Section 2-505); but

(b) if it does require him to deliver them at a particular destination and the goods are there duly tendered while in the possession of the carrier, the risk of loss passes to the buyer when the goods are there duly so tendered as to enable the buyer to take delivery.

(2) Where the goods are held by a bailee to be delivered without being moved, the risk of loss passes to the buyer

(a) on his receipt of a negotiable document of title covering the goods; or

(b) on acknowledgement by the bailee of the buyer's right to possession of the goods; or

(c) after his receipt of a non-negotiable document of title or other written direction to deliver, as provided in subsection (4) (b) of Section 2-503.

(3) In any case not within subsection (1) or (2), the risk of loss passes to the buyer on his receipt of the goods if the seller is a merchant; otherwise the risk passes to the buyer on tender of delivery.

(4) The provisions of this section are subject to contrary agreement of the parties and to the provisions of this Article on sale on approval (Section 2-327) and on effect of breach on risk of loss (Section 2-510).

Section 2-510. Effect of Breach on Risk of Loss.

(1) Where a tender or delivery of goods so fails to conform to the contract as to give a right of rejection the risk of their loss remains on the seller until cure or acceptance.

(2) Where the buyer rightfully revokes acceptance he may to the extent of any deficiency in his effective insurance coverage treat the risk of loss as having rested on the seller from the beginning.

(3) Where the buyer as to conforming goods already identified to the contract for sale repudiates or is otherwise in breach before risk of their loss has passed to him the seller may to the extent of any deficiency in his effective insurance coverage treat the risk of loss as resting on the buyer for a commercially reasonable time.

Section 2-511. Tender of Payment by Buyer; Payment by Check.

(1) Unless otherwise agreed tender of payment is a condition to the seller's duty to tender and complete any delivery.

(2) Tender of payment is sufficient when made by any means or in any manner current in the ordinary course of business unless the seller demands payment in legal tender and gives any extension of time reasonably necessary to procure it.

(3) Subject to the provisions of this Act on the effect of an instrument on an obligation (Section 3-802), payment by check is conditional and is defeated as between the parties by dishonor of the check on due presentment.

Section 2-512. Payment by Buyer Before Inspection.

(1) Where the contract requires payment before inspection non-conformity of the goods does not excuse the buyer from so making payment unless

(a) the non-conformity appears without inspection; or

(b) despite tender of the required documents the circumstances would justify injunction against honor under the provisions of this Act (Section 5-114).

(2) Payment pursuant to subsection (1) does not constitute an acceptance of goods or impair the buyer's right to inspect or any of his remedies.

Section 2-513. Buyer's Right to Inspection of Goods.

(1) Unless otherwise agreed and subject to subsection (3), where goods are tendered or delivered or identified to the contract for sale, the buyer has a right before payment or acceptance to inspect them at any reasonable place and time and in any reasonable manner. When the seller is required or authorized to send the goods to the buyer, the inspection may be after their arrival.

(2) Expenses of inspection must be borne by the buyer but may be recovered from the seller if the goods do not conform and are rejected.

(3) Unless otherwise agreed and subject to the provisions of this Article on C.I.F. contracts (subsection (3) of Section 2-321), the buyer is not entitled to inspect the goods before payment of the price when the contract provides

(a) for delivery "C.O.D." or on other like terms; or

(b) for payment against documents of title, except where such payment is due only after the goods are to become available for inspection.

(4) A place or method of inspection fixed by the parties is presumed to be exclusive but unless otherwise expressly agreed it does not postpone identification or shift the place for delivery or for passing the risk of loss. If compliance becomes impossible, inspection shall be as provided in this section unless the place or method fixed was clearly intended as an indispensable condition failure of which avoids the contract.

Section 3-514. When Documents Deliverable on Acceptance; When on Payment. Unless otherwise agreed documents against which a draft is drawn are to be delivered to the drawee on acceptance of the draft if it is payable more than three days after presentment; otherwise, only on payment.

Section 2-515. Preserving Evidence of Goods in Dispute. In furtherance of the adjustment of any claim or dispute

(a) either party on reasonable notification to the other and for the purpose of ascertaining the facts and preserving evidence has the right to inspect, test and sample the goods including such of them as may be in the possession or control of the other; and

(b) the parties may agree to a third party inspection or survey to determine the conformity or condition of the goods and may agree that the findings shall be binding upon them in any subsequent litigation or adjustment.

PART 6

BREACH, REPUDIATION AND EXCUSE

Section 2-601. Buyer's Rights on Improper Delivery. Subject to the provisions of this Article on breach in installment contracts (Section 2-612) and unless otherwise agreed under the sections on contractual limitations of remedy (Sections 2-718 and 2-719), if the goods or the tender of delivery fail in any respect to conform to the contract, the buyer may
may

(a) reject the whole; or

(b) accept the whole; or

(c) accept any commercial unit or units and reject the rest.

Section 2-602. Manner and Effect of Rightful Rejection.

(1) Rejection of goods must be within a reasonable time after their delivery or tender. It is ineffective unless the buyer seasonably notifies the seller.

(2) Subject to the provisions of the two following sections on rejected goods (Sections 2-603 and 2-604),

(a) after rejection any exercise of ownership by the buyer with respect to any commercial unit is wrongful as against the seller; and

(b) if the buyer has before rejection taken physical possession of goods in which he does not have a security interest under the provisions of this Article (subsection (3) of Section 2-711), he is under a duty after rejection to hold them with reasonable care at the seller's disposition for a time sufficient to permit the seller to remove them; but

(c) the buyer has no further obligations with regard to goods rightfully rejected.

(3) The seller's rights with respect to goods wrongfully rejected are governed by the provisions of this Article on Seller's remedies in general (Section 2-703).

Section 2-603. Merchant Buyer's Duties as to Rightfully Rejected Goods.

(1) Subject to any security interest in the buyer (subsection (3) of Section 2-711), when the seller has no agent or place of business at the market of rejection a merchant buyer is under a duty after rejection of goods in his possession or control to follow any reasonable instructions received from the seller with respect to the goods and in the absence of such instructions to make reasonable efforts to sell them for the seller's account if they are perishable or threaten to decline in value speedily. Instructions are not reasonable if on demand indemnity for expenses is not forthcoming.

(2) When the buyer sells goods under subsection (1), he is entitled to reimbursement from the seller or out of the proceeds for reasonable expenses of caring for and selling them, and if the expenses include no selling commission then to such commission as is usual in the trade or if there is none to a reasonable sum not exceeding ten per cent on the gross proceeds.

(3) In complying with this section the buyer is held only to good faith and good faith conduct hereunder is neither acceptance nor conversion nor the basis of an action for damages.

Section 2-604. Buyer's Options as to Salvage of Rightfully Rejected Goods. Subject to the provisions of the immediately preceding section on perishables if the seller gives no instructions within a reasonable time after notifcation of rejection the buyer may store the rejected goods for the seller's account or reship them to him or resell them for the seller's account with reimbursement as provided in the preceding section. Such action is not acceptance or conversion.

Section 2-605. Waiver of Buyer's Objections by Failure to Particularize.

(1) The buyer's failure to state in connection with rejection a particular defect which is ascertainable by reasonable inspection precludes him from relying on the unstated defect to justify rejection or to establish breach

(a) where the seller could have cured it if stated seasonably; or

(b) between merchants when the seller has after rejection made a request in writing for a full and final written statement of all defects on which the buyer proposes to rely.

(2) Payment against documents made without reservation of rights precludes recovery of the payment for defects apparent on the fact of the documents.

Section 2-606. What Constitutes Acceptance of Goods.

(1) Acceptance of goods occurs when the buyer

(a) after a reasonable opportunity to inspect the goods signifies to the seller that the goods are conforming or that he will take or retain them in spite of their non-conformity; or

(b) fails to make an effective rejection (subsection (1) of Section 2-602), but such acceptance does not occur until the buyer has had a reasonable opportunity to inspect them; or

(c) does any act inconsistent with the seller's ownership but if such act is wrongful as against the seller it is an acceptance only if ratified by him.

(2) Acceptance of a part of any commercial unit is acceptance of that entire unit.

Section 2-607. Effect of Acceptance; Notice of Breach; Burden of Establishing Breach After Acceptance; Notice of Claim or Litigation to Person Answerable Over.

(1) The buyer must pay at the contract rate for any goods accepted.

(2) Acceptance of goods by the buyer precludes rejection of the goods accepted and if made with knowledge of a non-conformity cannot be revoked because of it unless the acceptance was on the reasonable assumption that the non-conformity would be seasonably cured but acceptance does not of itself impair any other remedy provided by this Article for non-conformity.

(3) Where a tender has been accepted

(a) the buyer must within a reasonable time after he discovers or should have discovered any breach notify the seller of breach or be barred from any remedy; and

(b) if the claim is one for infringement or the like (subsection (3) of Section 2-312) and the buyer is sued as a result of such a breach he must so notify the seller within a reasonable time after he receives notice of the litigation or be barred from any remedy over for liability established by the litigation.

(4) The burden is on the buyer to establish any breach with respect to the goods accepted.

(5) Where the buyer is used for breach of a warranty or other obligation for which his seller is answerable over

(a) he may give his seller written notice of the litigation. If the notice states that the seller may come in and defend and that if the seller does not do so he will be bound in any action against him by his buyer by any determination of fact common to the two litigations, then unless the seller after seasonable receipt of the notice does come in and defend he is so bound.

(b) if the claim is one for infringement or the like (subsection (3) of Section 2-312) the original seller may demand in writing that his buyer turn over to him control of the litigation including settlement or else be barred from any remedy over and if he also agrees to bear all expense and to satisfy any adverse judgment, then unless the buyer after seasonable receipt of the demand does turn over control the buyer is so barred.

(6) The provisions of subsections (3), (4) and (5) apply to any obligation of a buyer to hold the seller harmless against infringement or the like (subsection (3) of Section 2-312).

Section 2-608. Revocation of Acceptance in Whole or in Part.

(1) The buyer may revoke his acceptance of a lot or commercial unit whose non-conformity substantially impairs its value to him if he has accepted it

(a) on the reasonable assumption that

its non-conformity would be cured and it has not been seasonably cured; or

(b) without discovery of such non-conformity if his acceptance was reasonably induced either by the difficulty of discovery before acceptance or by the seller's assurances.

(2) Revocation of acceptance must occur within a reasonable time after the buyer discovers or should have discovered the ground for it and before any substantial change in condition of the goods which is not caused by their own defects. It is not effective until the buyer notifies the seller of it.

(3) A buyer who so revokes has the same rights and duties with regard to the goods involved as if he had rejected them.

Section 2-609. Right to Adequate Assurance of Performance.

(1) A contract for sale imposes an obligation on each party that the other's expectation of receiving due performance will not be impaired. When reasonable grounds for insecurity arise with respect to the performance of either party the other may in writing demand adequate assurance of due performance and until he receives such assurance may if commercially reasonable suspend any performance for which he has not already received the agreed return.

(2) Between merchants the reasonableness of grounds for insecurity and the adequacy of any assurance offered shall be determined according to commercial standards.

(3) Acceptance of any improper delivery or payment does not prejudice the aggrieved party's right to demand adequate assurance of future performance.

(4) After receipt of a justified demand failure to provide within a reasonable time not exceeding thirty days such assurance of due performance as is adequate under the circumstances of the particular case is a repudiation of the contract.

Section 2-610. Anticipatory Repudiation. When either party repudiates the contract with respect to a performance not yet due the loss of which will substantially impair the value of the contract to the other, the aggrieved party may

(a) for a commercially reasonable time await performance by the repudiating party; or

(b) resort to any remedy for breach (Section 2-703 or Section 2-711), even though he has notified the repudiating party that he would await the latter's performance and has urged retraction; and

(c) in either case suspend his own performance or proceed in accordance with the provisions of this Article on the seller's right to identify goods to the contract notwithstanding breach or to salvage unfinished goods (Section 2-704).

Section 2-611. Retraction of Anticipatory Repudiation.

(1) Until the repudiating party's next performance is due he can retract his repudiation unless the aggrieved party has since the repudiation cancelled or materially changed his position or otherwise indicated that he considers the repudiation final.

(2) Retraction may be by any method which clearly indicates to the aggrieved party that the repudiating party intends to perform, but must include any assurance justifiably demanded under the provisions of this Article (Section 2-609).

(3) Retraction reinstates the repudiating party's rights under the contract with due excuse and allowance to the aggrieved party for any delay occasioned by the repudiation.

Section 2-612. "Installment Contract"; Breach.

(1) An "installment contract" is one which requires or authorizes the delivery of goods in separate lots to be separately accepted, even though the contract contains a clause "each delivery is a separate contract" or its equivalent.

(2) The buyer may reject any installment which is non-conforming if the non-conformity substantially impairs the value of that installment and cannot be cured or if the non-conformity is a defect in the required documents; but if the non-conformity does not fall within subsection (3) and the seller gives adequate assurance of its cure the buyer must accept that installment.

(3) Whenever non-conformity or default with respect to one or more installments substantially impairs the value of the whole contract there is a breach of the whole. But

the aggrieved party reinstates the contract if he accepts a non-conforming installment without seasonably notifying of cancellation or if he brings an action with respect only to past installments or demands performance as to future installments.

Section 2-613. Casualty to Identified Goods. Where the contract requires for its performance goods identified when the contract is made, and the goods suffer casualty without fault of either party before the risk of loss passes to the buyer, or in a proper case under a "no arrival, no sale" term (Section 2-324) then

(a) if the loss is total the contract is avoided; and

(b) if the loss is partial or the goods have so deteriorated as no longer to conform to the contract the buyer may nevertheless demand inspection and at his option either treat the contract as avoided or accept the goods with allowance from the contract price for the deterioration or the deficiency in quantity but without further right against the seller.

Section 2-614. Substituted Performance.

(1) Where without fault of either party the agreed berthing, loading, or unloading facilities fail or an agreed type of carrier becomes unavailable or the agreed manner of delivery otherwise becomes commercially impracticable but a commercially reasonable substitute is available, such substitute performance must be tendered and accepted.

(2) If the agreed means or manner of payment fails because of domestic or foreign governmental regulation, the seller may withhold or stop delivery unless the buyer provides a means or manner of payment which is commercially a substantial equivalent. If delivery has already been taken, payment by the means or in the manner provided by the regulation discharges the buyer's obligation unless the regulation is discriminatory, oppressive or predatory.

Section 2-615. Excuse by Failure of Presupposed Conditions. Except so far as a seller may have assumed a greater obligation and subject to the preceding section on substituted performance:

(a) Delay in delivery or non-delivery in whole or in part by a seller who complies with paragraphs (b) and (c) is not a breach of his duty under a contract for sale if performance as agreed has been made impracticable by the occurrence of a contingency and the non-occurrence of which was a basic assumption on which the contract was made or by compliance in good faith with any applicable foreign or domestic governmental regulation or order whether or not it later proves to be invalid.

(b) Where the causes mentioned in paragraph (a) affect only a part of the seller's capacity to perform, he must allocate production and deliveries among his customers but may at his option include regular customers not then under contract as well as his own requirements for further manufacture. He may so allocate in any manner which is fair and reasonable.

(c) The seller must notify the buyer seasonably that there will be delay or non-delivery and, when allocation is required under paragraph (b), of the estimated quota thus made available for the buyer.

Section 2-616. Procedure on Notice Claiming Excuse.

(1) Where the buyer receives notification of a material or indefinite delay or an allocation justified under the preceding section he may by written notification to the seller as to any delivery concerned, and where the prospective deficiency substantially impairs the value of the whole contract under the provisions of this Article relating to breach of installment contracts (Sections 2-612), then also as to the whole,

(a) terminate and thereby discharge any unexecuted portion of the contract; or

(b) modify the contract by agreeing to take his available quota in substitution.

(2) If after receipt of such notification from the seller the buyer fails so to modify the contract within a reasonable time not exceeding thirty days the contract lapses with respect to any deliveries affected.

(3) The provisions of this section may not be negated by agreement except in so far as the seller has assumed a greater obligation under the preceding section.

REMEDIES

Section 2-701. Remedies for Breach of Collateral Contracts Not Impaired. Remedies for breach of any obligation or promise collateral or ancillary to a contract for sale are not impaired by the provisions of this Article.

Section 2-702. Seller's Remedies on Discovery of Buyer's Insolvency.

(1) Where the seller discovers the buyer to be insolvent he may refuse delivery except for cash including payment for all goods theretofore delivered under the contract, and stop delivery under this Article (Section 2-705).

(2) Where the seller discovers that the buyer has received goods on credit while insolvent he may reclaim the goods upon demand made within ten days after receipt, but if misrepresentation of solvency has been made to the particular seller in writing within three months before delivery the ten day limitation does not apply. Except as provided in this subsection the seller may not base a right to reclaim goods on the buyer's fraudulent or innocent misrepresentation of solvency or of intent to pay.

(3) The seller's right to reclaim under subsection (2) is subject to the rights of a buyer in ordinary course or other good faith purchaser or lien creditor under this Article (Section 2-403). Successful reclamation of goods excludes all other remedies with respect to them.

Section 2-703. Seller's Remedies in General. Where the buyer wrongfully rejects or revokes acceptance of goods or fails to make a payment due on or before delivery or repudiates with respect to a part or the whole, then with respect to any goods directly affected and, if the breach is of the whole contract (Section 2-612), then also with respect to the whole undelivered balance, the aggrieved seller may

(a) withhold delivery of such goods;

(b) stop delivery by any bailee as hereafter provided (Section 2-705);

(c) proceed under the next section respecting goods still unidentified to the contract;

(d) resell and recover damages as hereafter provided (Section 2-706);

(e) recover damages for non-acceptance (Section 2-708) or in a proper case the price (Section 2-709);

(f) cancel.

Section 2-704. Seller's Right to Identify Goods to the Contract Notwithstanding Breach or to Salvage Unfinished Goods.

(1) An aggrieved seller under the preceding section may

(a) identify to the contract conforming goods not already identified if at the time he learned of the breach they are in his possession or control;

(b) treat as the subject of resale goods which have demonstrably been intended for the particular contract even though those goods are unfinished.

(2) Where the goods are unfinished an aggrieved seller may in the exercise of reasonable commercial judgment for the purposes of avoiding loss and of effective realization either complete the manufacture and wholly identify the goods to the contract or cease manufacture and resell for scrap or salvage value or proceed in any other reasonable manner.

Section 2-705. Seller's Stoppage of Delivery in Transit or Otherwise.

(1) The seller may stop delivery of goods in the possession of a carrier or other bailee when he discovers the buyer to be insolvent (Section 2-702) and may stop delivery of carload, truckload, planeload or larger shipments of express or freight when the buyer repudiates or fails to make a payment due before delivery or if for any other reason the seller has a right to withhold or reclaim the goods.

(2) As against such buyer the seller may stop delivery until

(a) receipt of the goods by the buyer; or

(b) acknowledgement to the buyer by any bailee of the goods except a carrier that the bailee holds the goods for the buyer; or

(c) such acknowledgement to the buyer by a carrier by reshipment or as warehouseman; or

(d) negotiation to the buyer of any negotiable document of title covering the goods.

(3) (a) To stop delivery the seller must so notify as to enable the bailee by reasonable diligence to prevent delivery of the goods.

(b) After such notification the bailee must hold and deliver the goods according to the directions of the seller but the seller is liable to the bailee for any ensuing charges or damages.

(c) If a negotiable document of title has been issued for goods the bailee is not obliged to obey a notification to stop until surrender of the document.

(d) A carrier who has issued a non-negotiable bill of lading is not obliged to obey a notification to stop received from a person other than the consignor.

Section 2-706. Seller's Resale Including Contract for Resale.

(1) Under the conditions stated in Section 2-703 on seller's remedies, the seller may resell the goods concerned or the undelivered balance thereof. Where the resale is made in good faith and in a commercially reasonable manner the seller may recover the difference between the resale price and the contract price together with any incidental damages allowed under the provisions of this Article (Section 2-710), but less expenses saved in consequence of the buyer's breach.

(2) Except as otherwise provided in subsection (3) or unless otherwise agreed resale may be at public or private sale including sale by way of one or more contracts to sell or of identification to any existing contract of the seller. Sale may be as a unit or in parcels and at any time and place and on any terms but every aspect of the sale including the method, manner, time, place and terms must be commercially reasonable. The resale must be reasonably identified as referring to the broken contract, but it is not necessary that the goods be in existence or that any or all of them have been identified to the contract before the breach.

(3) Where the resale is at private sale the seller must give the buyer reasonable notification of his intention to resell.

(4) Where the resale is at public sale

(a) only identified goods can be sold except where there is a recognized market for a public sale of futures in goods of the kind; and

(b) it must be made at a usual place or market for public sale if one is reasonably available and except in the case of goods which are perishable or threaten to decline in value speedily the seller must give the buyer reasonable notice of the time and place of the resale; and

(c) if the goods are not to be within the view of those attending the sale the notification of sale must state the place where the goods are located and provide for their reasonable inspection by prospective bidders; and

(d) the seller may buy.

(5) A purchaser who buys in good faith at a resale takes the goods free of any rights of the original buyer even though the seller fails to comply with one or more of the requirements of this section.

(6) The seller is not accountable to the buyer for any profit made on any resale. A person in the position of a seller (Section 2-707) or a buyer who has rightfully rejected or justifiably revoked acceptance must account for any excess over the amount of his security interest, as hereinafter defined (subsection (3) of Section 2-711).

Section 2-707. "Person in the Position of a Seller."

(1) A "person in the position of a seller" includes as against a principal an agent who has paid or become responsible for the price of goods on behalf of his principal or anyone who otherwise holds a security interest or other right in goods similar to that of the seller.

(2) A person in the position of a seller may as provided in this Article withhold or stop delivery (Section 2-705) and resell (Section 2-706) and recover incidental damages (Section 2-710).

Section 2-708. Seller's Damages for Non-Acceptance or Repudiation.

(1) Subject to subsection (2) and to the provisions of this Article with respect to

proof of market price (Section 2-723), the measure of damages for non-acceptance or repudiation by the buyer is the difference between the market price at the time and place for tender and the unpaid contract price together with any incidental damages provided in this Article (Section 2-710), but less expenses saved in consequence of the buyer's breach.

(2) If the measure of damages provided in subsection (1) is inadequate to put the seller in as good a position as performance would have done then the measure of damages is the profit (including reasonable overhead) which the seller would have made from full performance by the buyer, together with any incidental damages provided in this Article (Section 2-710), due allowance for costs reasonably incurred and due credit for payments or proceeds of resale.

Section 2-709. Action for the Price.

(1) When the buyer fails to pay the price as it becomes due the seller may recover, together with any incidental damages under the next section, the price

(a) of goods accepted or of conforming goods lost or damaged within a commercially reasonable time after risk of their loss has passed to the buyer; and

(b) of goods identified to the contract if the seller is unable after reasonable effort to resell them at a reasonable price or the circumstances reasonably indicate that such effort will be unavailing.

(2) Where the seller sued for the price he must hold for the buyer any goods which have been identified to the contract and are still in his control except that if resale becomes possible he may resell them at any time prior to the collection of the judgment. The net proceeds of any such resale must be credited to the buyer and payment of the judgment entitles him to any goods not resold.

(3) After the buyer has wrongfully rejected or revoked acceptance of the goods or has failed to make a payment due or has repudiated (Section 2-610), a seller who is held not entitled to the price under this section shall nevertheless be awarded damages for non-acceptance under the preceding section.

Section 2-710. Seller's Incidental Damages. Incidental damages to an aggrieved seller include any commercially reasonable charges, expenses or commissions incurred in stopping delivery, in the transportation, care and custody of goods after the buyer's breach, in connection with return or resale of the goods or otherwise resulting from the breach.

Section 2-711. Buyer's Remedies in General; Buyer's Security Interest in Rejected Goods.

(1) Where the seller fails to make delivery then with respect to any goods involved, and with respect to the whole if the breach goes to the whole contract (Section 2-612), the buyer may cancel and whether or not he has done so may in addition to recovering so much of the price as has been paid

(a) "cover" and have damages under the next section as to all the goods affected whether or not they have been identified to the contract; or

(b) recover damages for non-delivery as provided in this Article (Section 2-713).

(2) Where the seller fails to deliver or repudiates the buyer may also

(a) if the goods have been identified recover them as provided in this Article (Section 2-502); or

(b) in a proper case obtain specific performance or replevy the goods as provided in this Article (Section 2-716).

(3) On rightful rejection or justifiable revocation of acceptance a buyer has a security interest in goods in his possession or control for any payments made on their price and any expenses reasonably incurred in their inspection, receipt, transporation, care and custody and may hold such goods and resell them in like manner as an aggrieved seller (Section 2-706)).

Section 2-712. "Cover"; Buyer's Procurement of Substitute Goods.

(1) After a breach within the preceding section the buyer may "cover" by making in good faith and without unreasonable delay any reasonable purchase of or contract to purchase goods in substitution for those due from the seller.

(2) The buyer may recover from the seller as damages the difference between the cost of cover and the contract price together with any incidental or consequential damages as hereinafter defined (Section 2-715), but less expenses saved in consequence of the seller's breach.

(3) Failure of the buyer to effect cover

within this section does not bar him from any other remedy.

Section 2-713. Buyer's Damages for Non-Delivery or Repudiation.

(1) Subject to the provisions of this Article with respect to proof of market price (Section 2-723), the measure of damages for non-delivery or repudiation by the seller is the difference between the market price at the time when the buyer learned of the breach and the contract price together with any incidental and consequential damages provided in this Article (Section 2-715), but less expenses saved in consequence of the seller's breach.

(2) Market price is to be determined as of the place for tender or, in cases of rejection after arrival or revocation of acceptance, as of the place of arrival.

Section 2-714. Buyer's Damages for Breach in Regard to Accepted Goods.

(1) Where the buyer has accepted goods and given notification (subsection (3) of Section 2-607) he may recover as damages for any non-conformity of tender the loss resulting in the ordinary course of events from the seller's breach as determined in any manner which is reasonable.

(2) The measure of damages for breach of warranty is the difference at the time and place of acceptance between the value of the goods accepted and the value they would have had if they had been as warranted, unless special circumstances show proximate damages of a different amount.

(3) In a proper case any incidental and consequential damages under the next section may also be recovered.

Section 2-715. Buyer's Incidental and Consequential Damages.

(1) Incidental damages resulting from the seller's breach include expenses reasonably incurred in inspection, receipt, transportation and care and custody of goods rightfully rejected, any commercially reasonable charges, expenses or commissions in connection with effecting cover and any other reasonable expense incident to the delay or other breach.

(2) Consequential damages resulting from the seller's breach include

(a) any loss resulting from general or particular requirements and needs of which the seller at the time of contracting had reason to know and which could not reasonably be prevented by cover or otherwise; and

(b) injury to person or property proximately resulting from any breach of warranty.

Section 2-716. Buyer's Right to Specific Performance or Replevin.

(1) Specific performance may be decreed where the goods are unique or in other proper circumstances.

(2) The decree for specific performance may include such terms and conditions as to payment of the price, damages, or other relief as the court may deem just.

(3) The buyer has a right of replevin for goods identified to the contract if after reasonable effort he is unable to effect cover for such goods or the circumstances reasonably indicate that such effort will be unavailing or if the goods have been shipped under reservation and satisfaction of the security interest in them has been made or tendered.

Section 2-717. Deduction of Damages from the Price. The buyer on notifying the seller of his intention to do so may deduct all or any part of the damages resulting from any breach of the contract from any part of the price still due under the same contract.

Section 2-718. Liquidation or Limitation of Damages; Deposits.

(1) Damages for breach by either party may be liquidated in the agreement but only at an amount which is reasonable in the light of the anticipated or actual harm caused by the breach, the difficulties of proof of loss, and the inconvenience or non-feasibility of otherwise obtaining an adequate remedy. A term fixing unreasonably large liquidated damages is void as a penalty.

(2) Where the seller justifiably withholds delivery of goods because of the buyer's breach, the buyer is entitled to restitution of any amount by which the sum of his payments exceeds

(a) the amount to which the seller is entitled by virtue of terms liquidating the seller's damages in accordance with subsection (1), or

(b) in the absence of such terms, twenty per cent of the value of the total performance for which the buyer is obligated under the contract or $500, whichever is smaller.

(3) The buyer's right to restitution under subsection (2) is subject to offset to the extent that the seller establishes

(a) a right to recover damages under the provisions of this Article other than subsection (1), and

(b) the amount or value of any benefits received by the buyer directly or indirectly by reason of the contract.

(4) Where a seller has received payment in goods their reasonable value or the proceeds of their resale shall be treated as payments for the purposes of subsection (2); but if the seller has notice of the buyer's breach before reselling goods received in part performance, his resale is subject to the conditions laid down in this Article on resale by an aggrieved seller (Section 2-706).

Section 2-719. Contractual Modification or Limitation of Remedy.

(1) Subject to the provisions of subsections (2) and (3) of this section and of the preceding section on liquidation and limitation of damages,

(a) the agreement may provide for remedies in addition to or in substitution for those provided in this Article and may limit or alter the measure of damages recoverable under this Article, as by limiting the buyer's remedies to return of the goods and repayment of the price or to repair and replacement of nonconforming goods or parts; and

(b) resort to a remedy as provided is optional unless the remedy is expressly agreed to be exclusive, in which case it is the sole remedy.

(2) Where circumstances cause an exclusive or limited remedy to fail of its essential purpose, remedy may be had as provided in this Act.

(3) Consequential damages may be limited or excluded unless the limitation or exclusion is unconscionable. Limitation of consequential damages for injury to the person in the case of consumer goods is prima facie unconscionable but limitation of damages where the loss is commercial is not.

Section 2-720. Effect of "Cancellation" or "Rescission" on Claims for Antecedent Breach. Unless the contrary intention clearly appears, expressions of "cancellation" or "rescission' of the contract or the like shall not be construed as a renunciation or discharge of any claim in damages for an antecedent breach.

Section 2-712. Remedies for Fraud. Remedies for material misrepresentation or fraud include all remedies available under this Article for non-fraudulent breach. Neither rescission or a claim for rescission of the contract for sale nor rejection or return of the goods shall bar or be deemed inconsistent with a claim for damages or other remedy.

Section 2-722. Who can sue Third Parties for Injury to Goods. Where a third party so deals with goods which have been identified to a contract for sale as to cause actionable injury to a party to that contract

(a) a right of action against the third party is in either party to the contract for sale who has title to or a security interest or a special property or an insurable interest in the goods; and if the goods have been destroyed or converted a right of action is also in the party who either bore the risk of loss under the contract for sale or has since the injury assumed that risk as against the other;

(b) if at the time of the injury the party plaintiff did not bear the risk of loss as against the other party to the contract for sale and there is no arrangement between them for disposition of the recovery, his suit or settlement is, subject to his own interest, as a fiduciary for the other party to the contract;

(c) either party may with the consent of the other sue for the benefit of whom it may concern.

Section 2-723. Proof or Market Price: Time and Place.

(1) If an action based on anticipatory repudiation comes to trial before the time for performance with respect to some or all of the goods, any damages based on market price (Section 2-708 or Section 2-713) shall be determined according to the price of such goods prevailing at the time when the aggrieved party learned of the repudiation.

(2) If evidence of a price prevailing at the times or places described in this Article is not readily available the price prevailing within any reasonable time before or after the time described or at any other place which in commercial judgment or under

usage of trade would serve as a reasonable substitute for the one described may be used, making any proper allowance for the cost of transporting the goods to or from such other place.

(3) Evidence of a relevant price prevailing at a time or place other than the one described in this Article offered by one party is not admissible unless and until he has given the other party such notice as the court finds sufficient to prevent unfair surprise.

Section 2-724. Admissibility of Market Quotations. Whenever the prevailing price or value of any goods regularly bought and sold in any established commodity market is in issue, reports in official publications or trade journals or in newspapers or periodicals of general circulation published as the reports of such market shall be admissible in evidence. The circumstances of the preparation of such a report may be shown to affect its weight but not its admissibility.

Section 2-725. Statute of Limitations in Contracts for Sale.

(1) An action for breach of any contract for sale must be commenced within four years after the cause of action has accrued. By the original agreement the parties may reduce the period of limitation to not less than one year but may not extend it.

(2) A cause of action accrues when the breach occurs, regardless of the aggrieved party's lack of knowledge of the breach. A breach of warranty occurs when tender of delivery is made, except that where a warranty explicitly extends to future performance of the goods and discovery of the breach must await the time of such performance the cause of action accrues when the breach is or should have been discovered.

(3) Where an action commenced within the time limited by subsection (1) is so terminated as to leave available a remedy by another action from the same breach such other action may be commenced after the expiration of the time limited and within six months after the termination of the first action unless the termination resulted from voluntary discontinuance or from dismissal for failure or neglect to prosecute.

(4) This section does not alter the law on tolling of the statute of limitations nor does it apply to causes of action which have accrued before this Act becomes effective.

ARTICLE 3

COMMERCIAL PAPER

PART 1

SHORT TITLE, FORM AND INTERPRETATION

Section 3-101. Short Title. This article shall be known and may be cited as Uniform Commercial Code–Commercial Paper.

Section 3-102. Definitions and Index of Definitions.

(1) In this Article unless the context otherwise requires

(a) "Issue" means the first delivery of an instrument to a holder or a remitter.

(b) An "order" is a direction to pay and must be more than an authorization or request. It must identify the person to pay with reasonable certainty. It may be addressed to one or more such persons jointly or in the alternative but not in succession.

(c) A "promise" is an undertaking to pay and must be more than an acknowledgment of an obligation.

(d) "Secondary party" means a drawer or endorser.

(e) "Instrument" means a negotiable instrument.

(2) Other definitions applying to this Article and the sections in which they appear are:

"Acceptance." Section 3-410.
"Accommodation party." Section 3-415.
"Alteration." Section 3-407.
"Certificate of deposit." Section 3-104.
"Certification." Section 3-411.
"Check." Section 3-104.
"Definite time." Section 3-109.
"Dishonor." Section 3-507.
"Draft." Section 3-104.
"Holder in due course." Section 3-302.
"Negotiation." Section 3-202.
"Note." Section 3-104.

"Notice of dishonor." Section 3-508.
"On demand." Section 3-108.
"Presentment." Section 3-504.
"Protest." Section 3-509.
"Restrictive Indorsement." Section 3-205.
"Signature." Section 3-401.

(3) The following definitions in other Articles apply to this Article:

"Account." Section 4-104.
"Banking Day." Section 4-104.
"Clearing house." Section 4-104.
"Collecting bank." Section 4-105.
"Customer." Section 4-104.
"Depositary Bank." Section 4-105.
"Documentary Draft." Section 4-104.
"Intermediary Bank." Section 4-105.
"Item." Section 4-104.
"Midnight deadline." Section 4-104.
"Payor bank." Section 4-105.

(4) In addition Article 1 contains general definitions and principles of construction and interpretation applicable throughout this Article.

Section 3-103. Limitations on Scope of Article.

(1) This Article does not apply to money, documents of title or investment securities.

(2) The provisions of this Article are subject to the provisions of the Article on Bank Deposits and Collections (Article 4) and Secured Transactions (Article 9).

Section 3-104. Form of Negotiable Instruments: "Draft"; "Check"; "Certificate of Deposit"; "Note."

(1) Any writing to be a negotiable instrument within this Article must

(a) be signed by the maker or drawer; and

(b) contain an unconditional promise or order to pay a sum certain in money and no other promise, order, obligation or power given by the maker or drawer except as authorized by this Article; and

(c) be payable on demand or at a definite time; and

(d) be payable to order or to bearer.

(2) A writing which complies with the requirements of this section is

(a) a "draft" ("bill of exchange") if it is an order;

(b) a "check" if it is a draft drawn on a bank and payable on demand;

(c) a "certificate of deposit" if it is an acknowledgment by a bank of receipt of money with an engagement to repay it;

(d) a "note" if it is a promise other than a certificate of deposit.

(3) As used in other Articles of this Act, and as the context may require, the terms "draft," "check," "certificate of deposit" and "note" may refer to instruments which are not negotiable within this Article as well as to instruments which are so negotiable.

Section 3-105. When Promise or Order Unconditional.

(1) A promise or order otherwise unconditional is not made conditional by the fact that the instrument

(a) is subject to implied or constructive conditions; or

(b) states its consideration, whether performed or promised, or the transaction which gave rise to the instrument, or that the promise or order is made or the instrument matures in accordance with or "as per" such transaction; or

(c) refers to or states that it arises out of a separate agreement or refers to a separate agreement for rights as to prepayment or acceleration; or

(d) states that it is drawn under a letter of credit; or

(e) states that it is secured, whether by mortgage, reservation of title or otherwise; or

(f) indicates a particular account to be debited or any other fund or source from which reimbursement is expected; or

(g) is limited to payment out of a particular fund or the proceeds of a particular source, if the instrument is issued by a government or governmental agency or unit; or

(h) is limited to payment out of the entire assets of a partnership, unincorporated association, trust or estate by or on behalf of which the instrument is issued.

(2) A promise or order is not unconditional if the instrument

(a) states that it is subject to or governed by any other agreement; or

(b) states that it is to be paid only out of a particular fund or source except as provided in this section.

Section 3-106. Sum Certain.

(1) The sum payable is a sum certain even though it is to be paid

(a) with stated interest or by stated installments; or
(b) with stated different rates of interest before and after default or a specified date; or
(c) with a stated discount or addition if paid before or after the date fixed for payment; or
(d) with exchange or less exchange, whether at a fixed rate or at the current rate; or
(e) with costs of collection or an attorney's fee or both upon default.

(2) Nothing in this section shall validate any term which is otherwise illegal.

Section 3-107. Money.

(1) An instrument is payable in money if the medium of exchange in which it is payable is money at the time the instrument is made. An instrument payable in "currency" or "current funds" is payable in money.

(2) A promise or order to pay a sum stated in a foreign currency is for a sum certain in money and, unless a different medium of payment is specified in the instrument, may be satisfied by payment of that number of dollars which the stated foreign currency will purchase at the buying sight rate for that currency on the day on which the instrument is payable or, if payable on demand, on the day of demand. If such an instrument specifies a foreign currency as the medium of payment the instrument is payable in that currency.

Section 3-108. Payable on Demand.
Instruments payable on demand include those payable at sight or on presentation and those in which no time for payment is stated.

Section 3-109. Definite Time.

(1) An instrument is payable at a definite time if by its terms it is payable
(a) on or before a stated date or at a fixed period after a stated date; or
(b) at a fixed period after sight; or
(c) at a definite time subject to any acceleration; or
(d) at a definite time subject to extension at the option of the holder, or to extension to a further definite time at the option of the maker or acceptor or automatically upon or after a specified act or event.

(2) An instrument which by its terms is otherwise payable only upon an act or event uncertain as to time of occurrence is not payable at a definite time even though the act or event has occurred.

Section 3-110. Payable to Order.

(1) An instrument is payable to order when by its terms it is payable to the order or assigns of any person therein specified with reasonable certainty, or to him or his order, or when it is conspicuously designated on its face as "exchange" or the like and names a payee. It may be payable to the order of
(a) the maker or drawer; or
(b) the drawee; or
(c) a payee who is not maker, drawer or drawee; or
(d) two or more payees together or in the alternative; or
(e) an estate, trust or fund, in which case it is payable to the order of the representative of each estate, trust or fund or his successors; or
(f) an office, or an officer by his title as such in which case it is payable to the principal but the incumbent of the office or his successors may act as if he or they were the holder; or
(g) a partnership or unincorporated association, in which case it is payable to the partnership or association and may be indorsed or transferred by any person thereto authorized.

(2) An instrument not payable to order is not made so payable by such words as "payable upon return of this instrument properly indorsed."

(3) an instrument made payable both to order and to bearer is payable to order unless the bearer words are handwritten or typewritten.

Section 3-111. Payable to Bearer. An instrument is payable to bearer when by its terms it is payable to
(a) bearer or the order of bearer; or
(b) a specified person or bearer; or
(c) "cash" or the order of "cash," or any other indication which does not purport to designate a specific payee.

Section 3-112. Terms and Omissions Not Affecting Negotiability.

(1) The negotiability of an instrument is not affected by
(a) the omission of a statement of any

consideration or of the place where the instrument is drawn or payable; or

(b) a statement that collateral has been given to secure obligations either on the instrument or otherwise of an obligor on the instrument or that in case of default on those obligations the holder may realize on or dispose of the collateral; or

(c) a promise or power to maintain or protect collateral or to give additional collateral; or

(d) a term authorizing a confession of judgment on the instrument if it is not paid when due; or

(e) a term purporting to waive the benefit of any law intended for the advantage or protection of any obligor; or

(f) a term in a draft providing that the payee by indorsing or cashing it acknowledges full satisfaction of an obligation of the drawer; or

(g) a statement in a draft drawn in a set of parts (Section 3-801) to the effect that the order is effective only if no other part has been honored.

(2) Nothing in this section shall validate any term which is otherwise illegal.

Section 3-113. Seal. An instrument otherwise negotiable is within this Article even though it is under a seal.

Section 3-114. Date, Antedating, Postdating.

(1) The negotiability of an instrument is not affected by the fact that it is undated, antedated or postdated.

(2) Where an instrument is antedated or postdated the time when it is payable is determined by the stated date if the instrument is payable on demand or at a fixed period after date.

(3) Where the instrument or any signature thereon is dated, the date is presumed to be correct.

Section 3-115. Incomplete Instruments.

(1) When a paper whose contents at the time of signing show that it is intended to become an instrument is signed while still incomplete in any necessary respect it cannot be enforced until completed.

(2) If the completion is unauthorized the rules as to material alteration apply (Section 3-407), even though the paper was not delivered by the maker or drawer; but the burden of establishing that any completion is unauthorized is on the party so asserting.

Section 3-116. Instruments Payable to Two or More Persons. An instrument payable to the order of two or more persons

(a) if in the alternative is payable to any one of them and may be negotiated, discharged or enforced by any of them who has possession of it;

(b) if not in the alternative is payable to all of them and may be negotiated, discharged or enforced only by all of them.

Section 3-117. Instruments Payable with Words of Description. An instrument made payable to a named person with the addition of words describing him

(a) as agent or officer of a specified person is payable to his principal but the agent or officer may act as if he were the holder;

(b) as any other fiduciary for a specified person or purpose is payable to the payee and may be negotiated, discharged or enforced by him;

(c) in any other manner is payable to the payee unconditionally and the additional words are without effect on subsequent parties.

Section 3-118. Ambiguous Terms and Rules of Construction. The following rules apply to every instrument:

(a) Where there is doubt whether the instrument is a draft or a note the holder may treat it as either. A draft drawn on the drawer is effective as a note.

(b) Handwritten terms control typewritten and printed terms, and typewritten control printed.

(c) Words control figures except that if the words are ambiguous figures control.

(d) Unless otherwise specified a provision for interest means interest at the judgment rate at the place of payment from the date of the instrument, or if it is undated from the date of issue.

(e) Unless the instrument otherwise specifies two or more persons who sign as maker, acceptor or drawer or indorser and as a part of the same transaction are jointly and severally liable even though the instrument contains such words as "I promise to pay."

(f) Unless otherwise specified consent to extension authorizes a single extension for not longer than the original period. A consent to extension, expressed in the instrument, is binding on secondary parties and accommodation makers. A holder may not exercise his option to extend an instrument over the objection of a maker or acceptor or other party who in accordance with Section 3-604 tenders full payment when the instrument is due.

Section 3-119. Other Writings Affecting Instrument.

(1) As between the obligor and his immediate obligee or any transferee the terms of an instrument may be modified or affected by any other written agreement executed as a part of the same transaction, except that a holder in due course is not affected by any limitation of his rights arising out of the separate written agreement if he had no notice of the limitation when he took the instrument.

(2) A separate agreement does not affect the negotiability of an instrument.

Section 3-120. Instruments "Payable Through" Bank. An instrument which states that it is "payable through" a bank or the like designates that bank as a collecting bank to make presentment but does not of itself authorize the bank to pay the instrument.

Section 3-121. Instruments Payable at Bank.

NOTE: *If this Act is introduced in the Congress of the United States this section should be omitted.*

(States to select either alternative)

Alternative A—

A note or acceptance which states that it is payable at a bank is the equivalent of a draft drawn on the bank payable when it falls due out of any funds of the maker or acceptor in current account or otherwise available for such payment.

Alternative B—

A note or acceptance which states that it is payable at a bank is not of itself an order or authorization to the bank to pay it.

Section 3-122. Accrual of Cause of Action.

(1) A cause of action against a maker or an acceptor accrues

(a) in the case of a time instrument on the day after maturity;

(b) in the case of a demand instrument upon its date or, if no date is stated, on the date of issue.

(2) A cause of action against the obligor of a demand or time certificate of deposit accrues upon demand, but demand on a time certificate may not be made until on or after the date of maturity.

(3) A cause of action against a drawer of a draft or an indorser of any instrument accrues upon demand following dishonor of the instrument. Notice of dishonor is a demand.

(4) Unless an instrument provides otherwise, interest runs at the rate provided by law for a judgment

(a) in the case of a maker, acceptor or other primary obligor of a demand instrument, from the date of demand;

(b) in all other cases from the date of accrual of the cause of action.

PART 2

TRANSFER AND NEGOTIATION

Section 3-201. Transfer: Right to Indorsement.

(1) Transfer of an instrument vests in the transferee such rights as the transferor has therein, except that a transferee who has himself been a party to any fraud or illegality affecting the instrument or who as a prior holder had notice of a defense or claim against it cannot improve his position by taking from a later holder a due course.

(2) A transfer of a security interest in an instrument vests the foregoing rights in the transferee to the extent of the interest transferred.

(3) Unless otherwise agreed any transfer for value of an instrument not then payable to bearer gives the transferee the specifically enforceable right to have the unqualified indorsement of the transferor. Negotiation takes effect only when the indorsement is made and until that time there is no presumption that the transferee is the owner.

Section 3-202. Negotiation.

(1) Negotiation is the transfer of an instrument in such form that the transferee becomes a holder. If the instrument is payable to order it is negotiated by delivery

with any necessary indorsement; if payable to bearer it is negotiated by delivery.

(2) An indorsement must be writted by or on behalf of the holder and on the instrument or on a paper so firmly affixed thereto as to become a part thereof.

(3) An indorsement is effective for negotiation only when it conveys the entire instrument or any unpaid residue. If it purports to be of less it operates only as a partial assignment.

(4) Words of assignment, condition, waiver, guaranty, limitation or disclaimer of liability and the like accompanying an indorsement do not affect its character as an indorsement.

Section 3-203. Wrong or Misspelled Name. Where an instrument is made payable to a person under a misspelled name or one other than his own he may indorse in that name or his own or both; but signature in both names may be required by a person paying or giving value for the instrument.

Section 3-204. Special Indorsement; Blank Indorsement.

(1) A special indorsement specifies the person to whom or to whose order it makes the instrument payable. Any instrument specially indorsed becomes payable to the order of the special indorsee and may be further negotiated only by his indorsement.

(2) An indorsement in blank specifies no particular indorsee and may consist of a mere signature. An instrument payable to order and indorsed in blank becomes payable to bearer and may be negotiated by delivery alone until specially indorsed.

(3) The holder may convert a blank indorsement into a special indorsement by writing over the signature of the indorser in blank any contract consistent with the character of the indorsement.

Section 3-205. Restrictive Indorsements. An indorsement is restrictive which either

(a) is conditional; or

(b) purports to prohibit further transfer of the instrument; or

(c) includes the words "for collection," "for deposit," "pay any bank" or like terms signifying a purpose of deposit or collection; or

(d) otherwise states that it is for the benefit or use of the indorser or of another person.

Section 3-206. Effect of Restrictive Indorsement.

(1) No restrictive indorsement prevents further transfer or negotiation of the instrument.

(2) An intermediary bank, or a payor bank which is not the depositary bank, is neither given notice nor otherwise affected by a restrictive indorsement of any person except the bank's immediate transferor or the person presenting for payment.

(3) Except for an intermediary bank, any transferee under an indorsement which is conditional or includes the words "for collection," "for deposit," "pay any bank," or like terms (subparagraphs (a) and (c) of Section 3-205) must pay or apply any value given by him for or on the security of the instrument consistently with the indorsement and to the extent that he does so he becomes a holder for value. In addition such transferee is a holder in due course if he otherwise complies with the requirements of Section 3-302 on what constitutes a holder in due course.

(4) The first taker under an indorsement for the benefit of the indorser of another person (subparagraph (d) of Section 3-205) must pay or apply any value given by him for or on the security of the instrument consistently with the indorsement and to the extent that he does so he becomes a holder for value. In addition such taker is a holder in due course if he otherwise complies with the requirements of Section 3-302 on what constitutes a holder in due course. A later holder for value is neither given notice nor otherwise affected by such restrictive indorsement unless he has knowledge that a fiduciary or other person has negotiated the instrument in any transaction for his own benefit or otherwise in breach of duty (subsection (2) of Section 3-304).

Section 3-207. Negotiation Effective Although it may be Rescinded.

(1) Negotiation is effective to transfer the instrument although the negotiation is

(a) made by an infant, a corporation exceeding its power, or any other person without capacity; or

(b) obtained by fraud, duress or mistake of any kind; or

(c) part of an illegal transaction; or

(d) made in breach of duty.

(2) Except as against a subsequent holder

in due course such negotiation is in an appropriate case subject to rescission, the declaration of a constructive trust or any other remedy permitted by law.

Section 3-208. Reacquisition. Where an instrument is returned to or reacquired by a prior party he may cancel any indorsement which is not necessary to his title and reissue or further negotiate the instrument, but any intervening party is discharged as against the reacquiring party and subsequent holders not in due course and if his indorsement has been cancelled is discharged as against subsequent holders in due course as well.

PART 3

RIGHTS OF A HOLDER

Section 3-301. Rights of a Holder.
The holder of an instrument whether or not he is the owner may transfer or negotiate it and, except as otherwise provided in Section 3-603 on payment or satisfaction, discharge it or enforce payment in his own name.

Section 3-302. Holder in Due Course.

(1) A holder in due course is a holder who takes the instrument

(a) for value; and

(b) in good faith; and

(c) without notice that it is overdue or has been dishonored or of any defense against or claim to it on the part of any person.

(2) A payee may be a holder in due course.

(3) A holder does not become a holder in due course of an instrument:

(a) by purchase of it at judicial sale or by taking it under legal process; or

(b) by acquiring it in taking over an estate; or

(c) by purchasing it as part of a bulk transaction not in regular course of business of the transferor.

(4) A purchaser of a limited interest can be a holder in due course only to the extent of the interest purchased.

Section 3-303. Taking for Value. A holder takes the instrument for value

(a) to the extent that the agreed consideration has been performed or that he acquires a security interest in or a lien on the instrument otherwise than by legal process; or

(b) when he takes the instrument in payment of or as security for an antecedent claim against any person whether or not the claim is due; or

(c) when he gives a negotiable instrument for it or makes an irrevocable commitment to a third person.

Section 3-304. Notice to Purchaser.

(1) The purchaser has notice of a claim or defense if

(a) the instrument is so incomplete, bears such visible evidence of forgery or alteration, or is otherwise so irregular as to call into question its validity, terms or ownership or to create an ambiguity as the party to pay; or

(b) the purchaser has notice that the obligation of any party is voidable in whole or in part, or that all parties have been discharged.

(2) The purchaser has notice of a claim against the instrument when he has knowledge that a fiduciary has negotiated the instrument in payment of or as security for his own debt or in any transaction for his own benefit or otherwise in breach of duty.

(3) The purchaser has notice that an instrument is overdue if he has reason to know

(a) that any part of the principal amount is overdue or that there is an uncured default in payment of another instrument of the same series; or

(b) that acceleration of the instrument has been made; or

(c) that he is taking a demand instrument after demand has been made or more than a reasonable length of time after its issue. A reasonable time for a check drawn and payable within the states and territories of the United States and the District of Columbia is presumed to be thirty days.

(4) Knowledge of the following facts does

not of itself give the purchaser notice of a defense of claim

(a) that the instrument is antedated or postdated;

(b) that it was issued or negotiated in return for an executory promise or accompanied by a separate agreement, unless the purchaser has notice that a defense or claim has arisen from the terms thereof;

(c) that any party has signed for accommodation;

(d) that an incomplete instrument has been completed, unless the purchaser has notice of any improper completion;

(e) that any person negotiating the instrument is or was a fiduciary;

(f) that there has been default in payment of interest on the instrument or in payment of any other instrument, except one of the same series.

(5) The filing or recording of a document does not of itself consfitute notice within the provisions of this Article to a person who would otherwise be a holder in due course.

(6) To be effective notice must be received at such time and in such manner as to give a reasonable opportunity to act on it.

Section 3-305. Rights of a Holder in Due Course. To the extent that a holder is a holder in due course he takes the instrument free from

(1) all claims to it on the part of any person; and

(2) all defenses of any party to the instrument with whom the holder has not dealt except

(a) infancy, to the extent that it is a defense to a simple contract; and

(b) such other incapacity, or duress, or illegality of the transaction, as renders the obligation of the party a nullity; and

(c) such misrepresentation as has induced the party to sign the instrument with neither knowledge nor reasonable opportunity to obtain knowledge of its character or its essential terms; and

(d) discharge in insolvency proceedings; and

(e) any other discharge of which the holder has notice when he takes the instrument.

Section 3-306. Rights of One Not Holder in Due Course. Unless he has the rights of a holder in due course any person takes the instrument subject to

(a) all valid claims to it on the part of any person; and

(b) all defenses of any party which would be available in an action on a simple contract; and

(c) the defenses of want or failure of consideration, non-performance of any condition precedent, non-delivery, or delivery for a special purpose (Section 3-408); and

(d) the defense that he or a person through whom he holds the instrument acquired it by theft, or that payment or satisfaction to such holder would be inconsistent with the terms of a restrictive indorsement. The claim of any third person to the instrument is not otherwise available as a defense to any party liable thereon unless the third person himself defends the action for such party.

Section 3-307. Burden of Establishing Signatures, Defenses and Due Course.

(1) Unless specifically denied in the pleadings each signature on an instrument is admitted. When the effectiveness of a signature is put in issue

(a) the burden of establishing it is on the party claiming under the signature; but

(b) the signature is presumed to be genuine or authorized except where the action is to enforce the obligation of a purported signer who has died or become incompetent before proof is required.

(2) When signatures are admitted or established, production of the instrument entitles a holder to recover on it unless the defendant establishes a defense.

(3) After it is shown that a defense exists a person claiming the rights of a holder in due course has the burden of establishing that he or some person under whom he claims is in all respects a holder in due course.

PART 4

LIABILITY OF PARTIES

Section 3-401. Signature.

(1) No person is liable on an instrument unless his signature appears thereon.

(2) A signature is made by use of any name, including any trade or assumed name, upon an instrument, or by any word or mark used in lieu of a written signature.

Section 3-402. Signature in Ambiguous Capacity. Unless the instrument clearly indicates that a signature is made in some other capacity it is an indorsement.

Section 3-403. Signature of Authorized Representative.

(1) A signature may be made by an agent or other representative, and his authority to make it may be established as in other cases of representation. No particular form of appointment is necessary to establish such authority.

(2) An authorized representative who signs his own name to an instrument

(a) is personally obligated if the instrument neither names the person represented nor shows that the representative signed in a representative capacity;

(b) except as otherwise established between the immediate parties, is personally obligated if the instrument names the person represented but does not show that the representative signed in a representative capacity, or if the instrument does not name the person represented but does show that the representative signed in a representative capacity.

(3) Except as otherwise established the name of an organization preceded or followed by the name and office of an authorized individual is a signature made in a representative capacity.

Section 3-404. Unauthorized Signatures.

(1) Any unauthorized signature is wholly inoperative as that of the person whose name is signed unless he ratifies it or is precluded from denying it; but it operates as the signature of the unauthorized signer in favor of any person who in good faith pays the instrument or takes it for value.

(2) Any unauthorized signature may be ratified for all purposes of this Article. Such ratification does not of itself affect any rights of the person ratifying against the actual signer.

Section 3-405. Impostors; Signature in Name of Payee.

(1) An indorsement by any person in the name of a named payee is effective if

(a) an impostor by use of the mails or otherwise has induced the maker or drawer to issue the instrument to him or his confederate in the name of the payee; or

(b) a person signing as or on behalf of a maker or drawer intends the payee to have no interest in the instrument; or

(c) an agent or employee of the maker or drawer has supplied him with the name of the payee intending the latter to have no such interest.

(2) Nothing in this section shall affect the criminal or civil liability of the person so indorsing.

Section 3-406. Negligence Contributing to Alteration or Unauthorized Signature. Any person who by his negligence substantially contributes to a material alteration of the instrument or to the making of an unauthorized signature is precluded from asserting the alteration or lack of authority against a holder in due course or against a drawee or other payor who pays the instrument in good faith and in accordance with the reasonable commercial standards of the drawee's or payor's business.

Section 3-407. Alteration.

(1) Any alteration of an instrument is material which changes the contract of any party thereto in any respect, including any such change in

(a) the number or relations of the parties; or

(b) an incomplete instrument, by completing it otherwise than as authorized; or

(c) the writing as signed, by adding to it or by removing any part of it.

(2) As against any person other than a subsequent holder in due course

(a) alteration by the holder which is both fraudulent and material discharges any party whose contract is thereby changed unless that party assents or is precluded from asserting the defense;

(b) no other alteration discharges any party and the instrument may be enforced according to its original tenor, or as to incomplete instruments according to the authority given.

(3) A subsequent holder in due course may in all cases enforce the instrument according to its original tenor, and when an incomplete instrument has been completed, he may enforce it as completed.

Section 3-408. Consideration. Want or failure of consideration is a defense as against any person not having the rights of a holder in due course (Section 3-305), except that no consideration is necessary for an instrument or obligation thereon given in payment of or as security for an antecedent obligation of any kind. Nothing in this section shall be taken to displace any statute outside this Act under which a promise is enforceable notwithstanding lack or failure of consideration. Partial failure of consideration is a defense pro tanto whether or not the failure is in an ascertained or liquidated amount.

Section 3-409. Draft Not an Assignment.

(1) A check or other draft does not of itself operate as an assignment of any funds in the hands of the drawee available for its payment, and the drawee is not liable on the instrument until he accepts it.

(2) Nothing in this section shall affect any liability in contract, tort or otherwise arising from any letter of credit or other obligation or representation which is not an acceptance.

Section 3-410. Definition and Operation of Acceptance.

(1) Acceptance is the drawee's signed engagement to honor the draft as presented. It must be written on the draft, and may consist of his signature alone. It becomes operative when completed by delivery or notification.

(2) A draft may be accepted although it has not been signed by the drawer or is otherwise incomplete or is overdue or has been dishonored.

(3) Where the draft is payable at a fixed period after sight and the acceptor fails to date his acceptance the holder may complete it by supplying a date in good faith.

Section 3-411. Certificate of a Check.

(1) Certification of a check is acceptance. Where a holder procures certification the drawer and all prior indorsers are discharged.

(2) Unless otherwise agreed a bank has no obligation to certify a check.

(3) A bank may certify a check before returning it for lack of proper indorsement. If it does so the drawer is discharged.

Section 3-412. Acceptance Varying Draft.

(1) Where the drawee's proffered acceptance in any manner varies the draft as presented the holder may refuse the acceptance and treat the draft as dishonored in which case the drawee is entitled to have his acceptance cancelled.

(2) The terms of the draft are not varied by an acceptance to pay at any particular bank or place in the United States, unless the acceptance states that the draft is to be paid only at such bank or place.

(3) Where the holder assents to an acceptance varying the terms of the draft each drawer and indorser who does not affirmatively assent is discharged.

Section 3-413. Contract of Maker, Drawer and Acceptor.

(1) The maker or acceptor engages that he will pay the instrument according to its tenor at the time of his engagement or as completed pursuant to Section 3-115 on incomplete instruments.

(2) The drawer engages that upon dishonor of the draft and any necessary notice of dishonor or protest he will pay the amount of the draft to the holder or to any indorser who takes it up. The drawer may disclaim this liability by drawing without recourse.

(3) By making, drawing or accepting the party admits as against all subsequent parties including the drawee the existence of the payee and his then capacity to indorse.

Section 3-414. Contract of Indorser; Order of Liability.

(1) Unless the indorsement otherwise specifies (as by such words as "without recourse") every indorser engages that upon dishonor and any necessary notice of dishonor and protest he will pay the instrument according to its tenor at the time of his indorsement to the holder or to any subsequent indorser who takes it up, even though the indorser who takes it up was not obligated to do so.

(2) Unless they otherwise agree indorsers

are liable to one another in the order in which they indorse, which is presumed to be the order in which their signatures appear on the instrument.

Section 3-415. Contract of Accommodation Party.

(1) An accommodation party is one who signs the instrument in any capacity for the purpose of lending his name to another party to it.

(2) When the instrument has been taken for value before it is due the accommodation party is liable in the capacity in which he has signed even though the taker knows of the accommodation.

(3) As against a holder in due course and without notice of the accommodation oral proof of the accommodation is not admissible to give the accommodation party the benefit of discharges dependent on his character as such. In other cases the accommodation character may be shown by oral proof.

(4) An indorsement which shows that it is not in the chain of title is notice of its accommodation character.

(5) An accommodation party is not liable to the party accommodated, and if he pays the instrument has a right of recourse on the instrument against such party.

Section 3-416. Contract of Guarantor.

(1) "Payment guaranteed" or equivalent words added to a signature means that the signer engages that if the instrument is not paid when due he will pay it according to its tenor without resort by the holder to any other party.

(2) "Collection guaranteed" or equivalent words added to a signature mean that the signer engages that if the instrument is not paid when due he will pay it according to its tenor, but only after the holder has reduced his claim against the maker or acceptor to judgment and execution has been returned unsatisfied, or after the maker or acceptor has become insolvent or it is otherwise apparent that it is useless to proceed against him.

(3) Words of guaranty which do not otherwise specify guarantee payment.

(4) No words of guaranty added to the signature of a sole maker or acceptor affect his liability on the instrument. Such words added to the signature of one of two or more makers or acceptors create a presumption that the signature is for the accommodation of the others.

(5) When words of guaranty are used presentment, notice of dishonor and protest are not necessary to charge the user.

(6) Any guaranty written on the instrument is enforcible notwithstanding any statute of frauds.

Section 3-417. Warranties on Presentment and Transfer.

(1) Any person who obtains payment or acceptance and any prior transferor warrants to a person who in good faith pays or accepts that

(a) he has a good title to the instrument or is authorized to obtain payment or acceptance on behalf of one who has a good title; and

(b) he has no knowledge that the signature of the maker or drawer is unauthorized, except that this warranty is not given by a holder in due course acting in good faith

(i) to a maker with respect to the maker's own signature; or

(ii) to a drawer with respect to the drawer's own signature, whether or not the drawer is also the drawee; or

(iii) to an acceptor of a draft if the holder in due course took the draft after the acceptance or obtained the acceptance without knowledge that the drawer's signature was unauthorized; and

(c) the instrument has not been materially altered, except that this warranty is not given by a holder in due course acting in good faith

(i) to the maker of a note; or

(ii) to the drawer of a draft whether or not the drawer is also the drawee; or

(iii) to the acceptor of a draft with respect to alteration made prior to the acceptance, even though the acceptance provided "payable as originally drawn" or equivalent terms; or

(iv) to the acceptor of a draft with respect to an alteration made after the acceptance.

(2) Any person who transfers an instrument and receives consideration warrants to

his transferee and if the transfer is by indorsement to any subsequent holder who takes the instrument in good faith that

(a) he has a good title to the instrument or is authorized to obtain payment or acceptance on behalf of one who has a good title and the transfer is otherwise rightful; and

(b) all signatures are genuine or authorized; and

(c) the instrument has not been materially altered; and

(d) no defense of any party is good against him; and

(e) he has no knowledge of any insolvency proceeding instituted with respect to the maker or acceptor or the drawer of an unaccepted instrument.

(3) By transferring "without recourse" the transferor limits the obligation stated in subsection (2) (d) to a warranty that he has no knowledge of such a defense.

(4) A selling agent or broker who does not disclose the fact that he is acting only as such gives the warranties provided in this section, but if he makes such disclosure warrants only his good faith and authority.

Section 3-418. Finality of Payment or Acceptance. Except for recovery of bank payments as provided in the Article on Bank Deposits and Collections (Article 4) and except for liability for breach of warranty on presentment under the preceding section, payment or acceptance of any instrument is final in favor of a holder in due course, or a person who has in good faith changed his position in reliance on the payment.

Section 3-419. Conversion of Instrument; Innocent Representative.

(1) An instrument is converted when

(a) a drawee to whom it is delivered for acceptance refuses to return it on demand; or

(b) any person to whom it is delivered for payment refuses on demand either to pay or to return it; or

(c) it is paid on a forged indorsement.

(2) In an action against a drawee under subsection (1) the measure of the drawee's liability is the face amount of the instrument. In any other action under subsection (1) the measure of liability is presumed to be the face amount of the instrument.

(3) Subject to the provisions of this Act concerning restrictive indorsements a representative, including a depositary or collecting bank, who has in good faith and in accordance with the reasonable commercial standards applicable to the business of such representative dealt with an instrument or its proceeds on behalf of one who was not the true owner is not liable in conversion or otherwise to the true owner beyond the amount of any proceeds remaining in his hands.

(4) An intermediary bank or payor bank which is not a depositary bank is not liable in conversion solely by reason of the fact that proceeds of an item indorsed restrictively (Sections 3-205 and 3-206) are not paid or applied consistently with the restrictive indorsement of an indorser other than its immediate transferor.

PART 5

PRESENTMENT, NOTICE OF DISHONOR AND PROTEST

Section 3-501. When Presentment, Notice of Dishonor, and Protest Necessary or Permissible.

(1) Unless excused (Section 3-511) presentment is necessary to charge secondary parties as follows:

(a) presentment for acceptance is necessary to charge the drawer and indorsers of a draft where the draft so provides, or is payable elsewhere than at the residence or place of business of the drawee, or its date of payment depends upon such presentment. The holder may at his option present for acceptance any other draft payable at a stated date;

(b) presentment for payment is necessary to charge any indorser;

(c) in the case of any drawer, the acceptor of a draft payable at a bank or the maker of a note payable at a bank, presentment for payment is necessary, but failure to make presentment discharges such drawer, acceptor or maker only as stated in Section 3-502(1) (b).

(2) Unless excused (Section 3-511)

(a) notice of any dishonor is necessary to charge any indorser;

(b) in the case of any drawer, the acceptor of a draft payable at a bank or the maker of a note payable at a bank, notice of any dishonor is necessary, but failure to give such notice discharges such drawer, acceptor or maker only as stated in Section 3-502(1) (b).

(3) Unless excused (Section 3-511) protest of any dishonor is necessary to charge the drawer and indorsers of any draft which on its face appears to be drawn or payable outside of the states and territories of the United States and the District of Columbia. The holder may at his option make protest of any dishonor of any other instrument and in the case of a foreign draft may on insolvency of the acceptor before maturity make protest for a better security.

(4) Notwithstanding any provision of this section, neither presentment nor notice of dishonor nor protest is necessary to charge an indorser who has indorsed an instrument after maturity.

Section 3-502. Unexcused Delay; Discharge.

(1) Where without excuse any necessary presentment or notice of dishonor is delayed beyond the time when it is due

(a) any indorser is discharged; and

(b) any drawer or the acceptor of a draft payable at a bank or the maker of a note payable at a bank who because the drawee or payor bank becomes insolvent during the delay is deprived of funds maintained with the drawee or payor bank to cover the instrument may discharge his liability by written assignment to the holder of his rights against the drawee or payor bank in respect of such funds, but such drawer, acceptor or maker is not otherwise discharged.

(2) Where without excuse a necessary protest is delayed beyond the time when it is due any drawer or indorser is discharged.

Section 3-503. Time of Presentment.

(1) Unless a different time is expressed in the instrument the time for any presentment is determined as follows:

(a) where an instrument is payable at or a fixed period after a stated date any presentment for acceptance must be made on or before the date it is payable;

(b) where an instrument is payable after sight it must either be presented for acceptance or negotiated within a reasonable time after date or issue whichever is later;

(c) where an instrument shows the date on which it is payable presentment for payment is due on that date;

(d) where an instrument is accelerated presentment for payment is due within a reasonable time after the acceleration;

(e) with respect to the liability of any secondary party presentment for acceptance or payment of any other instrument is due within a reasonable time after such party becomes liable thereon.

(2) A reasonable time for presentment is determined by the nature of the instrument, any usage of banking or trade and the facts of the particular case. In the case of an uncertified check which is drawn and payable within the United States and which is not a draft drawn by a bank the following are presumed to be reasonable periods within which to present for payment or to initiate bank collection:

(a) with respect to the liability of the drawer, thirty days after date or issue which ever is later and

(b) with respect to the liability of an indorser, seven days after his indorsement.

(3) Where any presentment is due on a day which is not a full business day for either the person making presentment or the party to pay or accept, presentment is due on the next following day which is a full business day for both parties.

(4) Presentment to be sufficient must be made at a reasonable hour, and if at a bank during its banking day.

Section 3-504. How Presentment Made.

(1) Presentment is a demand for acceptance or payment made upon the maker, acceptor, drawee or other payor by or on behalf of the holder.

(2) Presentment may be made

(a) by mail, in which even the time of presentment is determined by the time or receipt of the mail; or

(b) through a clearing house; or

(c) at the place of acceptance or payment specified in the instrument or if there be none at the place of business or residence of the party to accept or pay. If neither the party to accept or pay nor anyone authorized to act for him is present or accessible at such place presentment is excused.

(3) It may be made

(a) to any one of two or more makers, acceptors, drawees or other payors; or

(b) to any person who has authority to make or refuse the acceptance or payment.

(4) A draft accepted or a note made payable at a bank in the United States must be presented at such bank.

(5) In the cases described in Section 4-210 presentment may be made in the manner and with the result stated in that section.

Section 3-505. Rights of Party to Whom Presentment is Made.

(1) The party to whom presentment is made may without dishonor require

(a) exhibition of the instrument; and

(b) reasonable identification of the person making presentment and evidence of his authority to make it if made for another; and

(c) that the instrument be produced for acceptance or payment at a place specified in it, or if there be none at any place reasonable in the circumstances; and

(d) a signed receipt on the instrument for any partial or full payment and its surrender upon full payment.

(2) Failure to comply with any such requirement invalidates the presentment but the person presenting has a reasonable time in which to comply and the time for acceptance or payment runs from the time of compliance.

Section 3-506. Time Allowed for Acceptance or Payment.

(1) Acceptance may be deferred without dishonor until the close of the next business day following presentment. The holder may also in good faith effort to obtain acceptance and without either dishonor of the instrument or discharge of secondary parties allow postponement of acceptance for an additional business day.

(2) Except as a longer time is allowed in the case of documentary drafts drawn under a letter of credit, and unless an earlier time is agreed to by the party to pay, payment of an instrument may be deferred without dishonor pending reasonable examination to determine whether it is properly payable, but payment must be made in any event before the close of business on the day of presentment.

Section 3-507. Dishonor; Holder's Right of Recourse; Term Allowing Representment.

(1) An instrument is dishonored when

(a) a necessary or optional presentment is duly made and due acceptance or payment is refused or cannot be obtained within the prescribed time or in case of bank collections the instrument is seasonably returned by the midnight deadline (Section 4-301); or

(b) presentment is excused and the instrument is not duly accepted or paid.

(2) Subject to any necessary notice of dishonor and protest, the holder has upon dishonor an immediate right of recourse against the drawers and indorsers.

(3) Return of an instrument for lack of proper indorsement is not dishonor.

(4) A term in a draft or an indorsement thereof allowing a stated time for representment in the event of any dishonor of the draft by nonacceptance if a time draft or by nonpayment if a sight draft gives the holder as against any secondary party bound by the term an option to waive the dishonor without affecting the liability of the secondary party and he may present again up to the end of the stated time.

Section 3-508. Notice of Dishonor.

(1) Notice of dishonor may be given to any person who may be liable on the instrument by or on behalf of the holder or any party who has himself received notice, or any other party who can be compelled to pay the instrument. In addition an agent or bank in whose hands the instrument is dishonored may give notice to his principal or customer or to another agent or bank from which the instrument was received.

(2) Any necessary notice must be given by a bank before its midnight deadline and by any other person before midnight of the third business day after dishonor or receipt of notice of dishonor.

(3) Notice may be given in any reasonable manner. It may be oral or written and in

any terms which identify the instrument and state that it has been dishonored. A misdescription which does not mislead the party notified does not vitiate the notice. Sending the instrument bearing a stamp, ticket or writing stating that acceptance or payment has been refused or sending a notice of debit with respect to the instrument is sufficient.

(4) Written notice is given when sent although it is not received.

(5) Notice to one partner is notice to each although the firm has been dissolved.

(6) When any party is in insolvency proceedings instituted after the issue of the instrument notice may be given either to the party or to the representative of his estate.

(7) When any party is dead or incompetent notice may be sent to his last known address or given to his personal representative.

(8) Notice operates for the benefit of all parties who have rights on the instrument against the party notified.

Section 3-509. Protest; Noting for Protest.

(1) A protest is a certificate of dishonor made under the hand and seal of a United States consul or vice consul or a notary public or other person authorized to certify dishonor by the law of the place where dishonor occurs. It may be made upon information satisfactory to such person.

(2) The protest must identify the instrument and certify either that due presentment has been made or the reason why it is excused and that the instrument has been dishonored by a nonacceptance or nonpayment.

(3) The protest may also certify that notice of dishonor has been given to all parties or to specified parties.

(4) Subject to subsection (5) any necessary protest is due by the time that notice of dishonor is due.

(5) If, before protest is due, an instrument has been noted for protest by the officer to make protest, the protest may be made at any time thereafter as of the date of the noting.

Section 3-510. Evidence of Dishonor and Notice of Dishonor. The following are admissible as evidence and create a presumption of dishonor and of any notice or dishonor therein shown:

(a) a document regular in form as provided in the preceding section which purports to be a protest;

(b) the purported stamp or writing of the drawee, payor bank or presenting bank on the instrument or accompanying it stating that acceptance or payment has been refused for reasons consistent with dishonor;

(c) any book or record of the drawee, payor bank, or any collecting bank kept in the usual course of business which shows dishonor, even though there is no evidence of who made the entry.

Section 3-511. Waived or Excused Presentment, Protest or Notice of Dishonor or Delay Therein.

(1) Delay in presentment, protest or notice of dishonor is excused when the party is without notice that it is due or when the delay is caused by circumstances beyond his control and he exercises reasonable diligence after the cause of the delay ceases to operate.

(2) Presentment or notice or protest as the case may be is entirely excused when

(a) the party to be charged has waived it expressly or by implication either before or after it is due; or

(b) such party has himself dishonored the instrument or has countermanded payment or otherwise has no reason to expect or right to require that the instrument be accepted or paid; or

(c) by reasonable diligence the presentment or protest cannot be made or the notice given.

(3) Presentment is also entirely excused when

(a) the maker, acceptor or drawee of any instrument except a documentary draft is dead or in insolvency proceedings instituted after the issue of the instrument; or

(b) acceptance or payment is refused but not for want of proper presentment.

(4) Where a draft has been dishonored by nonacceptance a later presentment for payment and any notice of dishonor and protest for nonpayment are excused unless in the meantime the instrument has been accepted.

(5) A waiver of protest is also a waiver of presentment and of notice of dishonor even though protest is not required.

(6) Where a waiver of presentment or

notice or protest is embodied in the instrument itself it is binding upon all parties; but where it is written above the signature of an indorser it binds him only.

PART 6

DISCHARGE

Section 3-601. Discharge of Parties.

(1) The extent of the discharge of any party from liability on an instrument is governed by the section on

(a) payment or satisfaction (Section 3-603; or

(b) tender of payment (Section 3-604); or

(c) cancellation or renunciation (Section 3-605); or

(d) impairment of right of recourse or of collateral (Section 3-606); or

(e) reacquisition of the instrument by a prior party (Section 3-208); or

(f) fraudulent and material alteration (Section 3-407); or

(g) certification of a check (Section 3-411); or

(h) acceptance varying a draft (Section 3-412); or

(i) unexcused delay in presentment or notice of dishonor or protest (Section 3-502).

(2) Any party is also discharged from his liability on an instrument to another party by any other act or agreement with such party which would discharge his simple contract for the payment of money.

(3) The liability of all parties is discharged when any party who has himself no right of action or recourse on the instrument

(a) reacquires the instrument in his own right; or

(b) is discharged under any provision of this Article, except as otherwise provided with respect to discharge for impairment of recourse or of collateral (Section 3-606).

Section 3-602. Effect of Discharge Against Holder in Due Course. No discharge of any party provided by this Article is effective against a subsequent holder in due course unless he has notice thereof when he takes the instrument.

Section 3-603. Payment or Satisfaction.

(1) The liability of any party is discharged to the extent of his payment or satisfaction to the holder even though it is made with knowledge of a claim of another person to the instrument unless prior to such payment or satisfaction the person making the claim either supplies indemnity deemed adequate by the party seeking the discharge or enjoins payment or satisfaction by order of a court of competent jurisdiction in an action in which the adverse claimant and the holder are parties. This subsection does not, however, result in the discharge of the liability

(a) of a party who in bad faith pays or satisfies a holder who acquired the instrument, by theft or who (unless having the rights of a holder in due course) holds through one who so acquired it; or

(b) of a party (other than an intermediary bank or a payor bank which is not a depositary bank) who pays or satisfies the holder of an instrument which has been restrictively indorsed in a manner not consistent with the terms of such restrictive indorsement.

(2) Payment or satisfaction may be made with the consent of the holder by any person including a stranger to the instrument. Surrender of the instrument to such a person gives him the rights of a transferee (Section 3-201).

Section 3-604. Tender of Payment.

(1) Any party making tender of full payment to a holder when or after it is due is discharged to the extent of all subsequent liability for interest, costs and attorney's fees.

(2) The holder's refusal of such tender wholly discharges any party who has a right or recourse against the party making the tender.

(3) Where the maker or acceptor of an instrument payable otherwise than on demand is able and ready to pay at every place of payment specified in the instrument when it is due, it is equivalent to tender.

Section 3-605. Cancellation and Renunciation.

(1) The holder of an instrument may even without consideration discharge any party

(a) in any manner apparent on the face of the instrument or the indorsement, as by intentionally cancelling the instrument or the party's signature by destruction or mutilation, or by striking out the party's signature; or

(b) by renouncing his rights by a writing signed and delivered or by surrender of the instrument to the party to be discharged.

(2) Neither cancellation nor renunciation without surrender of the instrument affects the title thereto.

Section 3-606. Impairment of Recourse or of Collateral.

(1) The holder discharges any party to the instrument to the extent that without such party's consent the holder

(a) without express reservation of rights releases or agrees not to sue any person against whom the party has to the knowledge of the holder a right of recourse or agrees to suspend the right to enforce against such person the instrument or collateral or otherwise discharges such person, except that failure or delay in effecting any required presentment, protest or notice of dishonor with respect to any such person does not discharge any party as to whom presentment, protest or notice of dishonor is effective or unnecessary; or

(b) unjustifiably impairs any collateral for the instrument given by or on behalf of the party or any person against whom he has a right of recourse.

(2) By express reservation of rights against a party with a right of recourse the holder preserves

(a) all his rights against such party as of the time when the instrument was originally due; and

(b) the right of the party to pay the instrument as of that time; and

(c) all rights of such party to recourse against others.

PART 7

ADVICE OF INTERNATIONAL SIGHT DRAFT

Section 3-701. Letter of Advice of International Sight Draft.

(1) A "letter of advice" is a drawer's communication to the drawee that a described draft has been drawn.

(2) Unless otherwise agreed when a bank receives from another bank a letter of advice of an international sight draft the drawee bank may immediately debit the drawer's account and stop the running of interest pro tanto. Such a debit and any resulting credit to any account covering outstanding drafts leaves in the drawer full power to stop payment or otherwise dispose of the amount and creates no trust or interest in favor of the holder.

(3) Unless otherwise agreed and except where a draft is drawn under a credit issued by the drawee, the drawee of an international sight draft owes the drawer no duty to pay an unadvised draft but if it does so and the draft is genuine, may appropriately debit the drawer's account.

PART 8

MISCELLANEOUS

Section 3-801. Drafts in a Set.

(1) Where a draft is drawn in a set of parts, each of which is numbered and expressed to be an order only if no other part has been honored, the whole of the parts constitutes one draft but a taker of any part may become a holder in due course of the draft.

(2) Any person who negotiates, indorses or accepts a single part of a draft drawn in a set thereby becomes liable to any holder in due course of that part as if it were the whole set, but as between different holders in due course to whom different parts have been negotiated the holder whose title first accrues has all rights to the draft and its proceeds.

(3) As against the drawee the first presented part of a draft drawn in a set is the part entitled to payment, or if a time draft to acceptance and payment. Acceptance of any subsequently presented part renders the drawee liable thereon under subsection (2). With respect both to a holder and to the drawer payment of a subsequently presented part of a draft payable at sight has the same effect as payment of a check notwithstanding an effective stop order (Section 4-407).

(4) Except as otherwise provided in this section, where any part of a draft in a set is discharged by payment or otherwise the whole draft is discharged.

Section 3-802. Effect of Instrument on Obligation for Which it is Given.

(1) Unless otherwise agreed where an instrument is taken for an underlying obligation

(a) the obligation is pro tanto discharged if a bank is drawer, maker or acceptor of the instrument and there is no recourse on the instrument against the underlying obligor; and

(b) in any other case the obligation is suspended pro tanto until the instrument is due or if it is payable on demand until its presentment. If the instrument is dishonored action may be maintained on either the instrument or the obligation; discharge of the underlying obligor on the instrument also discharges him on the obligation.

(2) The taking in good faith of a check which is not postdated does not of itself so extend the time on the original obligation as to discharge a surety.

Section 3-803. Notice to Third Party. Where a defendant is sued for breach of an obligation for which a third person is answerable over under this Article he may give the third person written notice of the litigation, and the person notified may then give similar notice to any other person who is answerable over to him under this Article. If the notice states that the person notified may come in and defend and that if the person notified does not do so he will in any action against him by the person giving the notice be bound by any determination of fact common to the two litigations, then unless after seasonable receipt of the notice the person notified does come in and defend he is so bound.

Section 3-804. Lost, Destroyed or Stolen Instruments. The owner of an instrument which is lost, whether by destruction, theft or otherwise, may maintain an action in his own name and recover from any party liable thereon upon due proof of his ownership, the facts which prevent his production of the instrument and its terms. The court may require security indemnifying the defendant against loss by reason of further claims on the instrument.

Section 3-805. Instruments Not Payable to Order or to Bearer. This Article applies to any instrument whose terms do not preclude transfer and which is otherwise negotiable within this Article but which is not payable to order to bearer, except that there can be no holder in due course of such an instrument.

ARTICLE 4

BANK DEPOSITS AND COLLECTIONS

PART 1

GENERAL PROVISIONS AND DEFINITIONS

Section 4-101. Short Title. This Article shall be known and may be cited as Uniform Commercial Code—Bank Deposits and Collections.

Section 4-102. Applicability.

(1) To the extent that items within this Article are also within the scope of Articles 3 and 8, they are subject to the provisions of those Articles. In the event of conflict the provisions of this Article govern those of Article 3 but the provisions of Article 8 govern those of this Article.

(2) The liability of a bank for action or non-action with respect to any item handled by it for purposes of presentment, payment or collection is governed by the law of the place where the bank is located. In the case of action or non-action by or at a branch or separate office of a bank, its liability is gov-

erned by the law of the place where the branch or separate office is located.

Section 4-103. Variation by Agreement; Measure of Damages; Certain Action Constituting Ordinary Care.

(1) The effect of the provisions of this Article may be varied by agreement except that no agreement can disclaim a bank's responsibility for its own lack of good faith or failure to exercise ordinary care or can limit the measure of damages for such lack or failure; but the parties may by agreement determine the standards by which such responsibility is to be measured if such standards are not manifestly unreasonable.

(2) Federal Reserve regulations and operating letters, clearing house rules, and the like, have the effect of agreements under subsection (1), whether or not specifically assented to by all parties interested in items handled.

(3) Action or non-action approved by this Article or pursuant to Federal Reserve regulations or operating letters constitutes the exercise of ordinary care and, in the absence of special instructions, action or non-action consistent with clearing house rules and the like or with a general banking usage not disapproved by this Article, prima facie constitutes the exercise of ordinary care.

(4) The specification or approval of certain procedures by this Article does not constitute disapproval of other procedures which may be reasonable under the circumstances.

(5) The measure of damages for failure to exercise ordinary care in handling an item is the amount of the item reduced by an amount which could not have been realized by the use of ordinary care, and where there is bad faith it includes other damages, if any, suffered by the party as a proximate consequence.

Section 4-104. Definitions and Index of Definitions.

(1) In this Article unless the context otherwise requires

(a) "Account" means any account with a bank and includes a checking, time, interest or savings account;

(b) "Afternoon" means the period of a day between noon and midnight;

(c) "Banking day" means that part of any day on which a bank is open to the public for carrying on substantially all of its banking functions;

(d) "Clearing house" means any association of banks or other payors regularly clearing items;

(e) "Customer" means any person having an account with a bank or for whom a bank has agreed to collect items and includes a bank carrying an account with another bank;

(f) "Documentary draft" means any negotiable or non-negotiable draft with accompanying documents, securities or other papers to be delivered against honor of the draft;

(g) "Item" means any instrument for the payment of money even though it is not negotiable but does not include money;

(h) "Midnight deadline" with respect to a bank is midnight on its next banking day following the banking day on which it receives the relevant item or notice or from which the time for taking action commences to run, whichever is later;

(i) "Properly payable" includes the availability of funds for payment at the time of decision to pay or dishonor;

(j) "Settle" means to pay in cash, by clearing house settlement, in a charge or credit or by remittance, or otherwise as instructed. A settlement may be either provisional or final;

(k) "Suspends payments" with respect to a bank means that it has been closed by order of the supervisory authorities, that a public officer has been appointed to take it over or that it ceases or refuses to make payments in the ordinary course of business.

(2) Other definitions applying to this Article and the sections in which they appear are:

"Collecting bank." Section 4-105.
"Depositary bank." Section 4-105.
"Intermediary bank." Section 4-105.
"Payor bank." Section 4-105.
"Presenting bank." Section 4-105.
"Remitting bank." Section 4-105.

(3) The following definitions in other Articles apply to this Article:

"Acceptance." Section 3-410.
"Certificate of deposit." Section 3-104.
"Certification." Section 3-411.
"Check." Section 3-104.
"Draft." Section 3-104.
"Holder in due course." Section 3-302.

"Notice of dishonor." Section 3-508.
"Presentment." Section 3-504.
"Protest." Section 3-509.
"Secondary party." Section 3-102.

(4) In addition Article 1 contains general definitions and principles of construction and interpretation applicable throughout this Article.

Section 4-105. "Depositary Bank"; "Intermediary Bank"; "Collecting Bank"; "Payor Bank"; "Presenting Bank"; "Remitting Bank." In this Article unless the context otherwise requires:

(a) "Depositary bank" means the first bank to which an item is transferred for collection even though it is also the payor bank;

(b) "Payor bank" means a bank by which an item is payable as drawn or accepted;

(c) "Intermediary bank" means any bank to which an item is transferred in course of collection except the depositary or payor bank;

(d) "Collecting bank" means any bank handling the item for collection except the payor bank;

(e) "Presenting bank" means any bank presenting an item except a payor bank;

(f) "Remitting bank" means any payor or intermediary bank remitting for an item.

Section 4-106. Separate Office of a Bank. A branch or separate office of a bank [maintaining its own deposit ledgers] is a separate bank for the purpose of computing the time within which and determining the place at or to which action may be taken or notices or orders shall be given under this Article and under Article 3.

NOTE: *The words in Brackets are optional.*

Section 4-107. Time of Receipt of Items.

(1) For the purpose of allowing time to process items, prove balances and make the necessary entries on its books to determine its position for the day, a bank may fix an afternoon hour of two P.M. or later as a cut-off hour for the handling of money and items and the making of entries on its books.

(2) Any item or deposit of money received on any day after a cut-off hour so fixed or after the close of the banking day may be treated as being received at the opening of the next banking day.

Section 4-108. Delays.

(1) Unless otherwise instructed, a collecting bank in a good faith effort to secure payment may, in the case of specific items and with or without the approval of any person involved, waive, modify or extend time limits imposed or permitted by this Act for a period not in excess of an additional banking day without discharge of secondary parties and without liability to its transferor or any prior party.

(2) Delay by a collecting bank or payor bank beyond time limits prescribed or permitted by this Act or by instructions is excused if caused by interruption of communication facilities, suspension of payments by another bank, war, emergency conditions or other circumstances beyond the control of the bank provided it exercises such diligence as the circumstances require.

Section 4-109. Process of Posting. The "process of posting" means the usual procedure followed by a payor bank in determining to pay an item and in recording the payment including one or more of the following or other steps as determined by the bank:

(a) verification of any signature;

(b) ascertaining that sufficient funds are are available;

(c) affixing a "paid" or other stamp;

(d) entering a charge or entry to a customer's account;

(e) correcting or reversing an entry or erroneous action with respect to the item.

PART 2

COLLECTION OF ITEMS: DEPOSITARY AND COLLECTING BANKS

Section 4-201. Presumption and Duration of Agency Status of Collecting Banks and Provisional Status of Credits; Applicability of Article; Item Indorsed "Pay any Bank."

(1) Unless a contrary intent clearly appears and prior to the time that a settlement given by a collecting bank for an item is or becomes final (subsection (3) of Section 4-211 and Sections 4-212 and 4-213) the bank is an agent or sub-agent of the owner of the item and any settlement given for the item is provisional. This provision applies regardless of the form of indorsement or lack of indorsement and even though credit given for the item is subject to immediate withdrawal as of right or is in fact withdrawn; but the continuance of ownership of an item by its owner and any rights of the owner to proceeds of the item are subject to rights of a collecting bank such as those resulting from outstanding advances on the item and valid rights of setoff. When an item is handled by banks for purposes of presentment, payment and collection, the relevant provisions of this Article apply even though action of parties clearly establishes that a particular bank has purchased the item and is the owner of it.

(2) After an item has been indorsed with the words "pay any bank" or the like, only a bank may acquire the rights of a holder

(a) until the item has been returned to the customer initiating collection; or

(b) until the item has been specially indorsed by a bank to a person who is not a bank.

Section 4-202. Responsibility for Collection; when Action Seasonable.

(1) A collecting bank must use ordinary care in

(a) presenting an item or sending it for presentment; and

(b) sending notice of dishonor or nonpayment or returning an item other than a documentary draft to the bank's transferor [or directly to the depositary bank under subsection (2) of Section 4-212] (*see note to Section 4-212*) after learning that the item has not been paid or accepted, as the case may be; and

(c) settling for an item when the bank receives final settlement; and

(d) making or providing for any necessary protest; and

(e) notifying its transferor of any loss or delay in transit within a reasonable time after discovery thereof.

(2) A collecting bank taking proper action before its midnight deadline following receipt of an item, notice or payment acts seasonably; taking proper action within a reasonably longer time may be seasonable but the bank has the burden of so establishing.

(3) Subject to subsection (1) (a), a bank is not liable for the insolvency, neglect, misconduct, mistake or default of another bank or person or for loss or destruction of an item in transit or in the possession of others.

Section 4-203. Effect of Instructions. Subject to the provisions of Article 3 concerning conversion of instruments (Section 3-429) and the provisions of both Article 3 and this Article concerning rectrictive indorsements only a collecting bank's transferor can give instructions which affect the bank or constitute notice to it and a collecting bank is not liable to prior parties for any action taken pursuant to such instructions or in accordance with any agreement with its transferor.

Section 4-204. Methods of Sending and Presenting; Sending Direct to Payor Bank.

(1) A collecting bank must send items by reasonably prompt method taking into consideration any relevant instructions, the nature of the item, the number of such items on hand, and the cost of collection involved and the method generally used by it or others to present such items.

(2) A collecting bank may send

(a) any item direct to the payor bank;

(b) any item to any non-bank payor if authorized by its transferor; and

(c) any item other than documentary drafts to any non-bank payor, if authorized by Federal Reserve regulation or operating letter. clearing house rule or the like.

(3) Presenting may be made by a present-

ing bank at a place where the payor bank has requested that presentment be made.

Section 4-205. Supplying Missing Indorsement; No Notice from Prior Indorsement.

(1) A depositary bank which has taken an item for collection may supply any indorsement of the customer which is necessary to title unless the item contains the words "payee's indorsement required" or the like. In the absence of such a requirement a statement placed on the item by the depositary bank to the effect that the item was deposited by a customer or credited to his account is effective as the customer's indorsement.

(2) An intermediary bank, or payor bank which is not a depositary bank, is neither given notice nor otherwise affected by a restrictive indorsement of any person except the bank's immediate transferor.

Section 4-206. Transfer Between Banks. Any agreed method which identifies the transferor bank is sufficient for the item's further transfer to another bank.

Section 4-207. Warranties of Customer and Collecting Bank on Transfer or Presentment of Items; Time for Claims.

(1) Each customer or collecting bank who obtains payment or acceptance of an item and each prior customer and collecting bank warrants to the payor bank or other payor who in good faith pays or accepts the item that

(a) he has a good title to the item or is authorized to obtain payment or acceptance on behalf of one who has a good title; and

(b) he has no knowledge that the signature of the maker or drawer is unauthorized, except that this warranty is not given by any customer or collecting bank that is a holder in due course and acts in good faith

(i) to a maker with respect to the maker's own signature; or

(ii) to a drawer with respect to the drawer's own signature, whether or not the drawer is also the drawee; or

(iii) to an acceptor of an item if the holder in due course took the item after the acceptance or obtained the acceptance without knowledge that the drawer's signature was unauthorized; and

(c) the item has not been materially altered, except that this warranty is not given by any customer or collecting bank that is a holder in due course and acts in good faith

(i) to the maker of a note; or

(ii) to the drawer of a draft whether or not the drawer is also the drawee; or

(iii) to the acceptor of an item with respect to an alteration made prior to the acceptance if the holder in due course took the item after the acceptance, even though the acceptance provided "payable as originally drawn" or equivalent terms; or

(iv) to the acceptor of an item with respect to an alteration made after the acceptance.

(2) Each customer and collecting bank who transfers an item and receives a settlement or other consideration for it warrants to his transferee and to any subsequent collecting bank who takes the item in good faith that

(a) he has a good title to the item or is authorized to obtain payment or acceptance on behalf of one who has a good title and the transfer is otherwise rightful; and

(b) all signatures are genuine or authorized; and

(c) the item has not been materially altered; and

(d) no defense of any party is good against him; and

(e) he has no knowledge of any insolvency proceeding instituted with respect to the maker or acceptor or the drawer of an unaccepted item.

In addition each customer and collecting bank so transferring an item and receiving a settlement or other consideration engages that upon dishonor and any necessary notice of dishonor and protest he will take up the item.

(3) The warranties and the engagement to honor set forth in the two preceding subsections arise notwithstanding the absence of indorsement or words of guaranty or warranty in the transfer or presentment and a collecting bank remains liable for their breach despite remittance to its transferor. Damages for breach of such warranties or engagement to honor shall not exceed the consideration received by the customer or collecting bank responsible plus finance

charges and expenses related to the item, if any.

(4) Unless a claim for breach of warranty under this section is made within a reasonable time after the person claiming learns of the breach, the person liable is discharged to the extent of any loss caused by the delay in making claim.

Section 4-208. Security Interest of Collecting Bank in Items, Accompanying Documents and Proceeds.

(1) A bank has a security interest in an item and any accompanying documents or the proceeds of either

(a) in case of an item deposited in an account to the extent to which credit given for the item has been withdrawn or applied;

(b) in case of an item for which it has given credit available for withdrawal as of right, to the extent of the credit given whether or not the credit is drawn upon and whether or not there is a right of charge-back; or

(c) if it makes an advance on or against the item.

(2) When credit which has been given for several items received at one time or pursuant to a single agreement is withdrawn or applied in part the security interest remains upon all the items, any accompanying documents or the proceeds of either. For the purpose of this section, credits first given are first withdrawn.

(3) Receipt by a collecting bank of a final settlement for an item is a realization on its security interest in the item, accompanying documents and proceeds. To the extent and so long as the bank does not receive final settlement for the item or give up possession of the item or accompanying documents for purposes other than collection, the security interest continues and is subject to the provisions of Article 9 except that

(a) no security agreement is necessary to make the security interest enforceable (subsection (1) (b) of Section 9-203); and

(b) no filing is required to perfect the security interest; and

(c) the security interest has priority over conflicting perfected security interests in the item, accompanying documents or proceeds.

Section 4-209. When Bank Gives Value for Purposes of Holder in Due Course. For purposes of determining its status as a holder in due course, the bank has given value to the extent that it has a security interest in an item provided that the bank otherwise complies with the requirements of Section 3-302 on what constitutes a holder in due course.

Section 4-210. Presentment by Notice of Item Not Payable by, through or at a Bank; Liability of Secondary Parties.

(1) Unless otherwise instructed, a collecting bank may present an item not payable by, through or at a bank by sending to the party to accept or pay a written notice that the bank holds the item for acceptance or payment. The notice must be sent in time to be received on or before the day when presentment is due and the bank must meet any requirement of the party to accept or pay under Section 3-505 by the close of the bank's next banking day after it knows of the requirement.

(2) Where presentment is made by notice and neither honor nor request for compliance with a requirement under Section 3-505 is received by the close of business on the day after maturity or in the case of demand items by the close of business on the third banking day after notice was sent, the presenting bank may treat the item as dishonored and charge any secondary party by sending him notice of the facts.

Section 4-211. Media or Remittance; Provisional and Final Settlement in Remittance Cases.

(1) A collecting bank may take in settlement of an item

(a) a check of the remitting bank or of another bank on any bank except the remitting bank; or

(b) a cashier's check or similar primary obligation of a remitting bank which is a member of or clears through a member of the same clearing house or group as the collecting bank; or

(c) appropriate authority to charge an account of the remitting bank or of another bank with the collecting bank; or

(d) if the item is drawn upon or payable by a person other than a bank, a cashier's check, certified check or other bank check or obligation.

(2) If before its midnight deadline the collecting bank properly dishonors a remittance check or authorization to charge on itself or presents or forwards for collection a remittance instrument of or on another bank which is of a kind approved by subsection (1) or has not been authorized by it, the collecting bank is not liable to prior parties in the event of the dishonor of such check, instrument or authorization.

(3) A settlement for an item by means of a remittance instrument or authorization to charge is or becomes a final settlement as to both the person making and the person receiving the settlement

(a) if the remittance instrument or authorization to charge is of a kind approved by subsection (1) or has not been authorized by the person receiving the settlement and in either case the person receiving the settlement acts seasonably before its midnight deadline in presenting, forwarding for collection or paying the instrument or authorization is finally paid by the payor by which it is payable;

(b) if the person receiving the settlement has authorized remittance by a non-bank check or obligation or by a cashier's check or similar primary obligation of or a check upon the payor or other remitting bank which is not of a kind approved by subsection (1) (b),—at the time of the receipt of such remittance check or obligation; or

(c) if in case not covered by sub-paragraphs (a) or (b) the person receiving the settlement fails to seasonably present, forward for collection, pay or return a remittance instrument of authorization to it to charge before its midnight deadline,—at such midnight deadline.

Section 4-212. Right of Charge-Back or Refund.

(1) If a collecting bank has made provisional settlement with its customer for an item and itself fails by reason of dishonor, suspension of payments by a bank or otherwise to receive a settlement for the item which is or becomes final, the bank may revoke the settlement given by it, charge back the amount of any credit given for the item to its customer whether or not it is able to return the items if by its midnight deadline or within a longer reasonable time after it learns the facts it returns the item or sends notification of the facts. These rights to revoke, charge-back and obtain refund terminate if and when a settlement for the item received by the bank is or becomes final (subsection (3) of Section 4-211 and subsections (2) and (3) of Section 4-213).

[(2) Within the time and manner prescribed by this section and Section 4-301, an intermediary or payor bank, as the case may be, may return an unpaid item directly to the depositary bank and may send for collection a draft on the depositary bank and obtain reimbursement. In such case, if the depositary bank has received provisional settlement for the item, it must reimburse the bank drawing the draft and any provisional credits for the item between banks shall become and remain final.]

NOTE: *Direct returns is recognized as an innovation that is not yet established bank practice, and therefore, Paragraph 2 has been bracketed. Some lawyers have doubted whether it should be included in legislation or left to development by agreement.*

(3) A depositary bank which is also the payor may charge-back the amount of an item to its customer's account or obtain refund in accordance with the section governing return of an item received by a payor bank for credit on its books (Section 4-301).

(4) The right to charge-back is not affected by

(a) prior use of the credit given for the item; or

(b) failure by any bank to exercise ordinary care with respect to the item but any bank so failing remains liable.

(5) A failure to charge-back or claim refund does not affect other rights of the bank against the customer or any other party.

(6) If credit is given in dollars as the equivalent of the value of an item payable in a foreign currency the dollar amount of any charge-back or refund shall be calculated on the basis of the buying site rate for the foreign currency prevailing on the day when the person entitled to the charge-back or refund learns that it will not receive payment in ordinary course.

Section 4-213. Final Payment of Item by Payor Bank; When Provisional Debits and Credits become Final; When Certain Credits become Available for Withdrawal.

(1) An item is finally paid by a payor bank when the bank has done any of the following whichever happens first:

(a) paid the item in cash; or

(b) settled for the item without reserving a right to revoke the settlement and without having such right under statute, clearing house rule or agreement; or

(c) completed the process of posting the item to the indicated account of the drawer, maker or other person to be charged therewith; or

(d) made a provisional settlement for the item and failed to revoke the settlement in the time and manner permitted by statute, clearing house rule or agreement.

Upon a final payment under subparagraphs (b), (c) or (d) the payor bank shall be accountable for the amount of the item.

(2) If provisional settlement for an item between the presenting and payor banks is made through a clearing house or by debits or credits in an account between them, then to the extent that provisional debits or credits for the item are entered in accounts between the presenting and payor banks or between the presenting and successive prior collecting banks seratim, they become final upon final payment of the item by the payor bank.

(3) If a collecting bank receives a settlement for an item which is or becomes final (subsection (3) of Section 4-211, subsection (2) of Section 4-213) the bank is accountable to its customer for the amount of the item and any provisional credit given for the item in an account with its customer becomes final.

(4) Subject to any right of the bank to apply the credit to an obligation of the customer, credit given by a bank for an item in an account with its customer becomes available for withdrawal as of right

(a) in any case where the bank has received a provisional settlement for the item,—when such settlement becomes final and the bank has had a reasonable time to learn that the settlement is final;

(b) in any case where the bank is both a depositary bank and a payor bank and the item is finally paid,—at the opening of the bank's second banking day following receipt of the item.

(5) A deposit of money in a bank is final when made but, subject to any right of the bank to apply the deposit to an obligation of the customer, the deposit becomes available for withdrawal as of right at the opening of the bank's next banking day following receipt of the deposit.

Section 4-214. Insolvency and Preference.

(1) Any item in or coming into the possession of a payor or collecting bank which suspends payment and which item is not finally paid shall be returned by the receiver, trustee or agent in charge of the closed bank to the presenting bank or the closed bank's customer.

(2) If a payor bank finally pays an item and suspends payments without making a settlement for the item with its customer or the presenting bank which settlement is or becomes final, the owner of the item has a preferred claim against the payor bank.

(3) If a payor bank gives or a collecting bank gives or receives a provisional settlement for an item and thereafter suspends payments, the suspension does not prevent or interfere with the settlement becoming final if such finality occurs automatically upon the lapse of certain time or the happening of certain events (subsection (3) of Section 4-211, subsections (1)(d), (2) and (3) of Section 4-213).

(4) If a collecting bank receives from subsequent parties settlement for an item which settlement is or becomes final and suspends payments without making a settlement for the item with its customer which is or becomes final, the owner of the item has a preferred claim against such collecting bank.

PART 3

COLLECTION OF ITEMS: PAYOR BANKS

Section 4-301. Deferred Posting; Recovery of Payment by Return of Items; Time of Dishonor.

(1) Where an authorized settlement for a demand item (other than a documentary draft) received by a payor bank otherwise than for immediate payment over the counter has been made before midnight of the banking day of receipt the payor bank may revoke the settlement and recover any payment if before it has made final payment (subsection (1) of Section 4-213) and before its midnight deadline it

(a) returns the item; or

(b) sends written notice of dishonor or nonpayment if the item is held for protest or is otherwise unavailable for return.

(2) If a demand item is received by a payor bank for credit on its books it may return such item or send notice of dishonor and may revoke any credit given or recover the amount thereof withdrawn by its customer, if it acts within the time limit and in the manner specified in the preceding subsection.

(3) Unless previous notice of dishonor has been sent an item is dishonored at the time when for purposes of dishonor it is returned or notice sent in accordance with this section.

(4) An item is returned:

(a) as to an item received through a clearing house, when it is delivered to the presenting or last collecting bank or to the clearing house or is sent or delivered in accordance with its rules; or

(b) in all other cases, when it is sent or delivered to the bank's customer or transferor or pursuant to his instructions.

Section 4-302. Payor Bank's Responsibility for Late Return of Item. In the absence of a valid defense such as breach of a presentment warranty (subsection (1) of Section 4-207), settlement effected or the like, if an item is presented on and received by a payor bank the bank is accountable for the amount of

(a) a demand item other than a documentary draft whether properly payable or not if the bank, in any case where it is not also the depositary bank, retains the item beyond midnight of the banking day of receipt without settling for it or, regardless of whether it is also the depositary bank, does not pay or return the item or send notice of dishonor until after its midnight deadline; or

(b) any other properly payable item unless within the time allowed for acceptance or payment of that item the bank either accepts or pays the item or returns it and accompanying documents.

Section 4-303. When Items Subject to Notice, Stop-Order, Legal Process or Setoff; Order in which Items may be Charged or Certified.

(1) Any knowledge, notice or stop-order received by, legal process served upon or setoff exercised by a payor bank, whether or not effective under other rules of law to terminate, suspend or modify the bank's right or duty to pay an item or to charge its customer's account for the item, comes too late to so terminate, suspend or modify such right or duty if the knowledge, notice, stop-order or legal process is received or served and a reasonable time for the bank to act thereon expires or the setoff is exercised after the bank has done any of the following:

(a) accepted or certified the item;

(b) paid the item in cash;

(c) settled for the item without reserving the right to revoke the settlement and without having such right under statute, clearing house rule or agreement;

(d) completed the process of posting the item to the indicated account of the drawer, maker or other person to be charged therewith or otherwise has evidenced by examination of such indicated account and by action its decision to pay the item; or

(e) become accountable for the amount of the item under subsection (1) (d) of Section 4-213 and Section 4-302 dealing with the payor bank's responsibility for late return of items.

(2) Subject to the provisions of subsection (1) items may be accepted, paid, certified or charged to the indicated account of its customer in any order convenient to the bank.

PART 4

RELATIONSHIP BETWEEN PAYOR BANK AND ITS CUSTOMER

Section 4-401. When Bank May Charge Customer's Account.

(1) As against its customer, a bank may charge against his account any item which is otherwise properly payable from that account even though the charge creates an overdraft.

(2) A bank which in good faith makes payment to a holder may charge the indicated account of its customer according to

(a) the original tenor of his altered item; or

(b) the tenor of his completed item, even though the bank knows the item has been completed unless the bank has notice that the completion was improper.

Section 4-402. Bank's Liability to Customer for Wrongful Dishonor. A payor bank is liable to its customer for damages proximately caused by the wrongful dishonor of an item. When the dishonor occurs through mistake liability is limited to actual damages proved. If so proximately caused and proved damages may include damages for an arrest or prosecution of the customer or other consequential damages. Whether any consequential damages are proximately caused by the wrongful dishonor is a question of fact to be determined in each case.

Section 4-403. Customer's Right to Stop Payment; Burden of Proof of Loss.

(1) A customer may by order to his bank stop payment of any item payable for his account but the order must be received at such time and in such manner as to afford the bank a reasonable opportunity to act on it prior to any action by the bank with respect to the item described in Section 4-303.

(2) An oral order is binding upon the bank only for fourteen calendar days unless confirmed in writing within that period. A written order is effective for only six months unless renewed in writing.

(3) The burden of establishing the fact and amount of loss resulting from the payment of an item contrary to a binding stop payment order is on the customer.

Section 4-404. Bank not Obligated to Pay Check more than Six Months old. A bank is under no obligation to a customer having a checking account to pay a check, other than a certified check, which is presented more than six months after its date, but it may charge its customer's account for a payment made thereafter in good faith.

Section 4-405. Death or Incompetence of Customer.

(1) A payor or collecting bank's authority to accept, pay or collect an item or to account for proceeds of its collection if otherwise effective is not rendered ineffective by incompetence of a customer of either bank existing at the time the item is issued or its collection is undertaken if the bank does not know of an adjudication of incompetence. Neither death nor incompetence of a customer revokes such authority to accept, pay, collect or account until the bank knows of the fact of death or of an adjudication of incompetence and has reasonable opportunity to act on it.

(2) Even with knowledge a bank may for ten days after the date of death pay or certify checks drawn on or prior to that date unless ordered to stop payment by a person claiming an interest in the account.

Section 4-406. Customer's Duty to Discover and Report Unauthorized Signature or Alteration.

(1) When a bank sends to its customer a statement of account accompanied by items paid in good faith in support of the debit entries or holds the statement and items

pursuant to a request or instructions of its customer or otherwise in a reasonable manner makes the statement and items available to the customer, the customer must exercise reasonable care and promptness to examine the statement and items to discover his unauthorized signature or any alteration on an item and must notify the bank promptly after discovery thereof.

(2) If the bank establishes that the customer failed with respect to an item to comply with the duties imposed on the customer by subsection (1) the customer is precluded from asserting against the bank

(a) his unauthorized signature or any alteration on the item if the bank also establishes that it suffered a loss by reason of such failure; and

(b) an unauthorized signature or alteration by the same wrongdoer on any other item paid in good faith by the bank after the first item and statement was available to the customer for a reasonable period not exceeding fourteen calendar days and before the bank receives notification from the customer of any such unauthorized signature or alteration.

(3) The preclusion under subsection (2) does not apply if the customer establishes lack of ordinary care on the part of the bank in paying the item(s).

(4) Without regard to care or lack of care of either the customer or the bank a customer who does not within one year from the time the statement and items are made available to the customer (subsection (1)) discover and report his unauthorized signature or any alteration on the face or back of the item or does not within three years from that time discover and report any unauthorized indorsement is precluded from asserting against the bank such unauthorized signature or indorsement or such alteration.

(5) If under this section a payor bank has a valid defense against a claim of a customer upon or resulting from payment of an item and waives or fails upon request to assert the defense the bank may not assert against any collecting bank or other prior party presenting or transferring the item a claim based upon the unauthorized signature or alteration giving rise to the customer's claim.

Section 4-407. Payor Bank's Right to Subrogation on Improper Payment. If a payor bank has paid an item over the stop payment order of the drawer or maker, or otherwise under circumstances giving a basis for objection by the drawer or maker, to present unjust enrichment and only to the extent necessary to prevent loss to the bank by reason of its payment of the item, the payor bank shall be subrogated to the rights

(a) of any holder in due course on the item against the drawer or maker; and

(b) of the payee or any other holder of the item against the drawer or maker either on the item or under the transaction out of which the item arose; and

(c) of the drawer or maker against the payee or any other holder of the item with respect to the transaction out of which the item arose.

PART 5

COLLECTION OF DOCUMENTARY DRAFTS

Section 4-501. Handling of Documentary Drafts; Duty to Send for Presentment and to Notify Customer of Dishonor. A bank which takes a documentary draft for collection must present or send the draft and accompanying documents for presentment and upon learning that the draft has not been paid or accepted in due course must seasonably notify its customer of such fact even though it may have discounted or bought the draft or extended credit available for withdrawal as if right.

Section 4-502. Presentment of "On Arrival" Drafts. When a draft or the relevant instructions require presentment "on arrival," "when goods arrive" or the like, the collecting bank need not present until in its judgment a reasonable time for arrival of the goods has expired. Refusal to pay or accept because the goods have not arrived is not dishonor; the bank must notify its transferor of such refusal but need not present the draft again until it is instructed to do so or learns of the arrival of the goods.

§ 4-503

Section 4-503. Responsibility of Presenting Bank for Documents and Goods; Report or Reasons for Dishonor; Referee in Case of Need. Unless otherwise instructed and except as provided in Article 5 a bank presenting a documentary draft

(a) must deliver the documents to the drawee on acceptance of the draft if it is payable more than three days after presentment; otherwise, only on payment; and

(b) upon dishonor, either in the case of presentment for acceptance or presentment for payment, may seek and follow instructions from any referee in case of need designated in the draft or if the presenting bank does not choose to utilize his services it must use diligence and good faith to ascertain the reason for dishonor, must notify its transferor of the dishonor and of the results of its effort to ascertain the reasons therefor and must request instructions.

But the presenting bank is under no obligation with respect to goods represented by the documents except to follow any reasonable instructions seasonably received; it has a right to reimbursement for any expense incurred in following instructions and to prepayment of or indemnity for such expenses.

Section 4-504. Privilege of Presenting Bank to Deal with Goods, Security Interest for Expenses.

(1) A presenting bank which, following the dishonor of a documentary draft, has seasonably requested instructions but does not receive them within a reasonable time may store, sell, or otherwise deal with the goods in any reasonable manner.

(2) For its reasonable expenses incurred by action under subsection (1) the presenting bank has a lien upon the goods or their proceeds, which may be foreclosed in the same manner as an unpaid seller's lien.

ARTICLE 6

BULK TRANSFERS

Section 6-101. Short Title. This Article shall be known and may be cited as Uniform Commercial Code–Bulk Transfers.

Section 6-102. "Bulk Transfers"; Transfers of Equipment; Enterprises Subject to this Article; Bulk Transfers Subject to this Article.

(1) A "bulk transfer" is any transfer in bulk and not in the ordinary course of the transferor's business of a major part of the materials, supplies, merchandise or other inventory (Section 9-109) of an enterprise subject to this Article.

(2) A transfer of a substantial part of the equipment (Section 9-109) of such an enterprise is a bulk transfer if it is made in connection with a bulk transfer of inventory, but not otherwise.

(3) The enterprises subject to this Article are all those whose principal business is the sale of merchandise from stock, including those who manufacture what they sell.

(4) Except as limited by the following section all bulk transfers of goods located within this state are subject to this Article.

Section 6-103. Transfers Excepted from this Article. The following transfers are not subject to this Article:

(1) Those made to give security for the performance of an obligation;

(2) General assignments for the benefit of all the creditors of the transferor, and subsequent transfers by the assignee thereunder;

(3) Transfers in settlement or realization of a lien or other security interest;

(4) Sales by executors, administrators, receivers, trustees in bankruptcy, or any public officer under judicial process;

(5) Sales made in the course of judicial or administrative proceedings for the dissolution or reorganization of a corporation and of which notice is sent to the creditors of the corporation to order of the court or administrative agency;

(6) Transfers to a person maintaining a known place of business in this State who becomes bound to pay the debts of the transferor in full and gives public notice of

that fact, and who is solvent after becoming so bound;

(7) A transfer to a new business enterprise organized to take over and continue the business, if public notice of the transaction is given and the new enterprise assumes the debts of the transferor and he receives nothing from the transaction except an interest in the new enterprise junior to the claims of creditors;

(8) Transfers of property which is exempt from execution.

Public notice under subsection (6) or subsection (7) may be given by publishing once a week for two consecutive weeks in a newspaper of general circulation where the transferor had its principal place of business in this state an advertisement including the names and addresses of the transferor and transferee and the effective date of the transfer.

Section 6-104. Schedule of Property, List of Creditors.

(1) Except as provided with respect to auction sales (Section 6-108), a bulk transfer subject to this Article is ineffective against any creditor of the transferor unless:

(a) The transferee requires the transferor to furnish a list of his existing creditors prepared as stated in this section; and

(b) The parties prepare a schedule of the property transferred sufficient to identify it; and

(c) The transferee preserves the list and schedule for six months next following the transfer and permits inspection of either or both and copying therefrom at all reasonable hours by any creditor of the transferor, or files the list and schedule in (a public office to be here identified).

(2) The list of creditors must be signed and sworn to or affirmed by the transferor or his agent. It must contain the names and business addresses of all creditors of the transferor, with the amounts when known, and also the names of all persons who are known to the transferor to assert claims against him even though such claims are disputed. If the transferor is the obligor of an outstanding issue of bonds, debentures or the like as to which there is an indenture trustee, the list of creditors need include only the name and address of the indenture trustee and the aggregate outstanding principal amount of the issue.

(3) Responsibility for the completeness and accuracy of the list of creditors rests on the transferor, and the transfer is not rendered ineffective by errors or omissions therein unless the transferee is shown to have had knowledge.

Section 6-105. Notice to Creditors. In addition to the requirements of the preceding section, any bulk transfer subject to this Article except one made by auction sale (Section 6-108) is ineffective against any creditor of the transferor unless at least ten days before he takes possession of the goods or pays for them, whichever happens first, the transferee gives notice of the transfer in the manner and to the persons hereafter provided (Section 6-107).

Section 6-106. Application of the Proceeds. In addition to the requirements of the two preceding sections:

(1) Upon every bulk transfer subject to this Article for which new consideration becomes payable except those made by sale at auction it is the duty of the transferee to assure that such consideration is applied so far as necessary to pay those debts of the transferor which are either shown on the list furnished by the transferor (Section 6-104) or filed in writing in the place stated in the notice (Section 6-107) within thirty days after the mailing of such notice. This duty of the transferee runs to all the holders of such debts, and may be enforced by any of them for the benefit of all.

(2) If any of said debts are in dispute the necessary sum may be withheld from distribution until the dispute is settled or adjudicated.

(3) If the consideration payable is not enough to pay all of the said debts in full distribution shall be made pro rata]

NOTE: *This section is bracketed to indicate division of opinion as to whether or not it is a wise provision, and to suggest that this is a point on which state enactments may differ without serious damage to the principle of uniformity.*

In any State where this section is omitted, the following parts of sections also bracketed in the text, should also be omitted, namely:

Section 6-107(2)(e).
6-108(3)(c).
6-109(2).

In any State where this section is enacted, these other provisions should be also.

Optional Subsection (4) [(4) The transferee may within ten days after he takes possession of the goods pay the consideration into the (specify court) in the county where the transferor had its principal place of business in this state and thereafter may discharge his duty under this section by giving notice by registered or certified mail to all the persons to whom the duty runs that the consideration has been paid into that court and that they should file their claims there. On motion of any interested party, the court may order the distribution of the consideration to the persons entitled to it.]

NOTE: *Optional subsection (4) is recommended for those states which do not have a general statute providing for payment of money into court.*

Section 6-107. The Notice.

(1) The notice to creditors (Section 6-105) shall state:

(a) that a bulk transfer is about to be made; and

(b) the names and business addresses of the transferor and transferee, and all other business names and addresses used by the transferor within three years last past so far as known to the transferee; and

(c) whether or not all the debts of the transferor are to be paid in full as they fall due as a result of the transaction, and if so, the address to which creditors should send their bills.

(2) If the debts of the transferor are not to be paid in full as they fall due or if the transferee is in doubt on that point then the notice shall state further:

(a) the location and general description of the property to be transferred and the estimated total of the transferor's debts;

(b) the address where the schedule of property and list of creditors (Section 6-104) may be inspected;

(c) whether the transfer is to pay existing debts and if so the amount of such debts and to whom owing;

(d) whether the transfer is for new consideration and if so the amount of such consideration and the time and place of payment; [and]

[(e) if for new consideration the time and place where creditors of the transferor are to file their claims.]

(3) The notice in any case shall be delivered personally or sent by registered mail to all the persons shown on the list of creditors furnished by the transferor (Section 6-104) and to all other persons who are known to the transferee to hold or assert claims against the transferor.

NOTE: *The words in brackets are optional.*

Section 6-108. Auction Sales; "Auctioneer."

(1) A bulk transfer is subject to this Article even though it is by sale at auction, but only in the manner and with the results stated in this section.

(2) The transferor shall furnish a list of his creditors and assist in the preparation of a schedule of the property to be sold, both prepared as before stated (Section 6-104).

(3) The person or persons other than the transferor who direct, control or are responsible for the auction are collectively called the "auctioneer." The auctioneer shall:

(a) receive and retain the list of creditors and prepare and retain the schedule of property for the period stated in this Article (Section 6-104);

(b) give notice of the auction personally or by registered or certified mail at least ten days before it occurs to all persons shown on the list of creditors and to all other persons who are known to him to hold or assert claims against the transferor; [and]

[(c) assure that the net proceeds of the auction are applied as provided in this Article (Section 6-106).]

(4) Failure of the auctioneer to perform any of these duties does not affect the validity of the sale or the title of the purchasers, but if the auctioneer knows that the auction constitutes a bulk transfer such failure renders the auctioneer liable to the creditors of the transferor as a class for the sums owing to them from the transferor up to but not exceeding the net proceeds of the auction. If the auctioneer consists of several persons their liability is joint and several.

NOTE: *The words in brackets are optional.*

Section 6-109. What Creditors Protected; Credit for Payment to Particular Creditors.

(1) The creditors of the transferor mentioned in this Article are those holding claims based on transactions or events occurring before the bulk transfer, but creditors

who become such after notice to creditors is given (Sections 6-105 and 6-107) are not entitled to notice.

[(2) Against the aggregate obligation imposed by the provisions of this Article concerning the application of the proceeds (Section 6-106 and subsection (3) (c) of 6-108) the transferee or auctioneer is entitled to credit for sums paid to particular creditors of the transferor, not exceeding the sums believed in good faith at the time of the payment to be properly payable to such creditors.]

Section 6-110. Subsequent Transfers. When the title of a transferee to property is subject to a defect by reason of his noncompliance with the requirements of this Article, then:

(1) a purchaser of any of such property from such transferee who pays no value or who takes with notice of such non-compliance takes subject to such defect, but

(2) a purchaser for value in good faith and without such notice takes free of such defect.

Section 6-111. Limitation of Actions and Levies. No action under this Article shall be brought nor levy made more than six months after the date on which the transferee took possession of the goods unless the transfer has been concealed. If the transfer has been concealed, actions may be brought or levies made within six months after its discovery.

NOTE TO ARTICLE 6: *Section 6-106 is bracketed to indicate division of opinion as to whether or not it is a wise provision, and to suggest that this is a point on which State enactments may differ without serious damage to the principle of uniformity.*

In any State where Section 6-106 is not enacted, the following parts of sections, also bracketed in the text, should also be omitted, namely:

Sec. 6-107(2)(e)
6-109(3)(c)
6-109(2).

In any State where Section 6-106 is enacted, these other provisions should be also.

REVISED ARTICLE 9

SECURED TRANSACTIONS; SALES OF ACCOUNTS AND CHATTEL PAPER

PART 1

SHORT TITLE, APPLICABILITY AND DEFINITIONS

Section 9-101. Short Title. This Article shall be known and may be cited as Uniform Commercial Code—Secured Transactions.

Section 9-102. Policy and Subject Matter of Article.

(1) Except as otherwise provided in Section 9-104 on excluded transactions, this Article applies

(a) to any transaction (regardless of its form) which is intended to create a security interest in personal property or fixtures including goods, documents, instruments, general intangibles, chattel paper or accounts; and also

(b) to any sale of accounts or chattel paper.

(2) This Article applies to security interests created by contract including pledge, assignment, chattel mortgage, chattel trust, trust deed, factor's lien, equipment trust, conditional sale, trust receipt, other lien or title retention contract and lease or consignment intended as security. This Article does not apply to statutory liens except as provided in Section 9-310.

(3) The application of this Article to a security interest in a secured obligation is not affected by the fact that the obligation is itself secured by a transaction or interest to which this Article does not apply.

Section 9-103. Perfection of Security Interests in Multiple State Transactions.

(1) Documents, instruments and ordinary goods.

(a) This subsection applies to documents and instruments and to goods other than those covered by a certificate of title described in subsection (2), mobile goods described in subsection (3), and minerals described in subsection (5).

(b) Except as otherwise provided in this subsection, perfection and the effect of perfection or non-perfection of a security interest in collateral are governed by the law of the jurisdiction where the collateral is when the last event occurs on which is based the assertion that the security interest is perfected or unperfected.

(c) If the parties to a transaction creating a purchase money security interest in goods in one jurisdiction understand at the time that the security interest attaches that the goods will be kept in another jurisdiction, then the law of the other jurisdiction governs the perfection and the effect of perfection or non-perfection of the security interest from the time it attaches until thirty days after the debtor receives possession of the goods and thereafter if the goods are taken to the other jurisdiction before the end of the thirty-day period.

(d) When collateral is brought into and kept in this state while subject to a security interest perfected under the law of the jurisdiction from which the collateral was removed, the security interest remains perfected, but if action is required by Part 3 of this Article to perfect the security interest,

(i) if the action is not taken before the expiration of the period of perfection in the other jurisdiction or the end of four months after the collateral is brought into this state, whichever period first expires, the security interest becomes unperfected at the end of that period and is thereafter deemed to have been unperfected as against a person who became a purchaser after removal;

(ii) if the action is taken before the expiration of the period specified in subparagraph (i), the security interest continues perfected thereafter;

(iii) for the purpose of a priority over a buyer of consumer goods (subsection (2) of Section 9-307), the period of the effectiveness of a filing in the jurisdiction from which the collateral is removed is governed by the rules with respect to perfection in subparagraphs (i) and (ii).

(2) Certificate of title.

(a) This subsection applies to goods covered by a certificate of title issued under a statute of this state or of another jurisdiction under the law of which indication of a security interest on the certificate is required as a condition of perfection.

(b) Except as otherwise provided in this subsection, perfection and the effect of perfection or non-perfection of the security interest are governed by the law (including the conflict of laws rules) of the jurisdiction issuing the certificate until four months after the goods are removed from that jurisdiction and thereafter until the goods are registered in another jurisdiction, but in any event not beyond surrender of the certificate. After the expiration of that period, the goods are not covered by the certificate of title within the meaning of this section.

(c) Except with respect to the rights of a buyer described in the next paragraph, a security interest, perfected in another jurisdiction otherwise than by notation on a certificate of title, in goods brought into this state and thereafter covered by a certificate of title issued by this state is subject to the rules stated in paragraph (d) of subsection (1).

(d) If goods are brought into this state while a security interest therein is perfected in any manner under the law of the jurisdiction from which the goods are removed and a certificate of title is issued by this state and the certificate does not show that the goods are subject to the security interest or that they may be subject to security interests not shown on the certificate, the security interest is subordinate to the rights of a buyer of the goods who is not in the business of selling goods of that kind to the extent that he gives value and receives delivery of the goods after issuance of the certificate and without knowledge of the security interest.

(3) Accounts, general intangibles and mobile goods.

(a) This subsection applies to accounts (other than an account described in subsection (5) on minerals) and general intangibles and to goods which are mobile and which are of a type normally used in more than one jurisdiction, such as motor vehicles, trailers, rolling stock, airplanes, shipping containers, road building and construction machinery and commercial harvesting machinery and the like, if the goods are equipment or are inventory leased or held for lease by the debtor to others, and are not covered by a certificate of title described in subsection (2).

(b) The law (including the conflict of laws rules) of the jurisdiction in which the debtor is located governs the perfection or non-perfection of the security interest.

(c) If, however, the debtor is located in a jurisdiction which is not a part of the United States, and which does not provide for perfection of the security interest by filing or recording in that jurisdiction, the law of the jurisdiction in the United States in which the debtor has its major executive office in the United States governs the perfection and the effect of perfection or non-perfection of the security interest through filing. In the alternative, if the debtor is located in a jurisdiction which is not a part of the United States or Canada and the collateral is accounts or general intangibles for money due or to become due, the security interest may be perfected by notification to the account debtor. As used in this paragraph, "United States" includes its territories and possessions and the Commonwealth of Puerto Rico.

(d) A debtor shall be deemed located at his place of business if he has one, at his chief executive office if he has more than one place of business, otherwise at his residence. If, however, the debtor is a foreign air carrier under the Federal Aviation Act of 1958, as amended, it shall be deemed located at the designated office of the agent upon whom service of process may be made on behalf of the foreign air carrier.

(e) A security interest perfected under the law of the jurisdiction of the location of the debtor is perfected until the expiration of four months after a change of the debtor's location to another jurisdiction, or until perfection would have ceased by the law of the first jurisdiction, whichever period first expires. Unless perfected in the new jurisdiction before the end of that period, it becomes unperfected thereafter and is deemed to have been unperfected as against a person who became a purchaser after the change.

(4) Chattel paper.

The rules stated for goods in subsection (1) apply to a possessory security interest in chattel paper. The rules stated for accounts in subsection (3) apply to a non-possessory security interest in chattel paper, but the security interest may not be perfected by notification to the account debtor.

(5) Minerals.

Perfection and the effect of perfection or non-perfection of a security interest which is created by a debtor who has an interest in minerals or the like (including oil and gas) before extraction and which attaches thereto as extracted, or which attaches to an account resulting from the sale thereof at the wellhead or minehead are governed by the law (including the conflict or laws rules) of the jurisdiction wherein the wellhead or minehead is located.

Section 9-104. Transactions Excluded From Article. This Article does not apply

(a) to a security interest subject to any statute of the United States to the extent that such statute governs the rights of parties to and third parties affected by transactions in particular types of property; or

(b) to a landlord's lien; or

(c) to a lien given by statute or other rule of law for services or materials except as provided in Section 9-310 on priority of such liens; or

(d) to a transfer of a claim for wages, salary or other compensation of an employee; or

(e) to a transfer by a government or governmental subdivision or agency; or

(f) to a sale of accounts or chattel paper as part of a sale of the business out of which they arose, or an assignment of accounts or chattel paper which is for the purpose of collection only, or a transfer of a right to payment under a contract to an assignee who is also to do the performance under the contract or a transfer of a single account to an assignee in whole or partial satisfaction of a preexisting indebtedness; or

(g) to a transfer of an interest in or claim in or under any policy of insurance, except as provided with respect to proceeds (Section 9-306) and priorities in proceeds (Section 9-312); or

(h) to a right represented by a judgment (other than a judgment taken on a right to payment which was collateral); or

(i) to any right of set-off; or

(j) except to the extent that provision is made for fixtures in Section 9-313, to the creation or transfer of an interest in or lien on real estate, including a lease or rents thereunder; or

(k) to a transfer in whole or in part of any claim arising out of tort; or

(l) to a transfer of an interest in any deposit account (subsection (1) or Section 9-105), except as provided with respect to proceeds (Section 9-306) and priorities in proceeds (Section 9-312).

Section 9-105. Definitions and Index of Definitions.

(1) In this Article unless the context otherwise requires:

(a) "Account debtor" means the person who is obligated on an account, chattel paper or general intangible,

(b) "Chattel paper" means a writing or writings which evidence both a monetary obligation and a security interest in or a lease of specific goods, but a charter or other contract involving the use or hire of a vessel is not chattel paper. When a transaction is evidenced both by such a security agreement or a lease and by an instrument or a series of instruments, the group of writings taken together constitutes chattel paper;

(c) "Collateral" means the property subject to a security interest, and includes accounts and chattel paper which have been sold;

(d) "Debtor" means the person who owes payment or other performance of the obligation secured, whether or not he owns or has rights in the collateral, and includes the seller of accounts or chattel paper. Where the debtor and the owner of the collateral are not the same person, the term "debtor" means the owner of the collateral in any provision of the Article dealing with the collateral, the obligor in any provision dealing with the obligation, and may include both where the context so requires;

(e) "Deposit account" means a demand, time, savings, passbook or like account maintained with a bank, savings and loan association, credit union or like organization, other than an account evidenced by a certificate of deposit;

(f) "Document" means the document of title as defined in the general definitions of Article 1 (Section 1-201), and a receipt of the kind described in subsection (2) of Section 7-201;

(g) "Encumbrance" includes real estate mortgages and other liens on real estate and all other rights in real estate that are not ownership interests;

(h) "Goods" includes all things which are movable at the time the security interest attaches or which are fixtures (Section 9-313), but does not include money, documents, instruments, accounts, chattel paper, general intangibles, or minerals or the like (including oil and gas) before extraction. "Goods" also includes standing timber which is to be cut and removed under a conveyance or contract for sale, the unborn young of animals, and growing crops;

(i) "Instrument" means a negotiable instrument (defined in Section 3-104), or a security (defined in Section 8-102) or any other writing which evidences a right to the payment of money and is not itself a security agreement or lease and is of a type which is in ordinary course of business transferred by delivery with any necessary indorsement or assignment;

(j) "Mortgage" means a consensual interest created by a real estate mortgage, a trust deed on real estate, or the like;

(k) An advance is made "pursuant to commitment" if the secured party has bound himself to make it, whether or not a subsequent event of default or other event not within his control has relieved or may relieve him from his obligation;

(l) "Security agreement" means an agreement which creates or provides for a security interest;

(m) "Secured party" means a lender, seller or other person in whose favor there is a security interest, including a person to whom accounts or chattel paper have been sold. When the holders of obligations issued under an indenture of trust, equipment trust agreement or the like are represented by a trustee or other person, the representative is the secured party;

(n) "Transmitting utility" means any person primarily engaged in the railroad, street railway or trolley bus business, the electric or electronics communications transmission business, the transmission of goods by pipeline, or the transmission or the production and transmission of electricity, steam, gas or water, or the provision of sewer service.

(2) Other definitions applying to this Article and the sections in which they appear are:

"Account". Section 9-106.
"Attach". Section 9-203.
"Construction mortgage". Section 9-313(1).
"Consumer goods". Section 9-109(1).
"Equipment". Section 9-109(2).
"Farm products". Section 9-109(3).
"Fixture". Section 9-313(1).
"Fixture filing". Section 9-313(1).
"General intangibles". Section 9-106.
"Inventory". Section 9-109(4).
"Lien creditor". Section 9-301(3).
"Proceeds". Section 9-306(1).
"Purchase money security interest". Section 9-107.
"United States". Section 9-103.

(3) The following definitions in other Articles apply to this Article:

"Check". Section 3-104.
"Contract for sale". Section 2-106.
"Holder in due course". Section 3-302.
"Note". Section 3-104.
"Sale". Section 2-106.

(4) In addition Article 1 contains general definitions and principles of construction and interpretation applicable throughout this Article.

Section 9-106. Definitions: "Account"; "General Intangibles." "Account means any right to payment for goods sold or leased or for services rendered which is not evidenced by an instrument or chattel paper, whether or not it has been earned by performance. "General intangibles" means any personal property (including things in action) other than goods, accounts, chattel paper, documents, instruments, and money. All rights to payment earned or unearned under a charter or other contract involving the use or hire of a vessel and all rights incident to the charter or contract are accounts.

Section 9-107. Definitions: "Purchase Money Security Interest." A security interest is a "purchase money security interest" to the extent that it is

(a) taken or retained by the seller of the collateral to secure all or part of its price; or

(b) taken by a person who by making advances or incurring an obligation gives value to enable the debtor to acquire rights in or the use of collateral if such value is in fact so used.

Section 9-108. When After-Acquired Collateral Not Security for Antecedent Debt. Where a secured party makes an advance, incurs an obligation, releases a perfected security interest, or otherwise gives new value which is to be secured in whole or in part by after-acquired property his security interest in the after-acquired collateral shall be deemed to be taken for new value and not as security for an antecedent debt if the debtor acquired his rights in such collateral either in the ordinary course of his business or under a contract of purchase made pursuant to the security agreement within a reasonable time after new value is given.

Section 9-109. Classification of Goods; "Consumer Goods"; "Equipment"; "Farm Products"; "Inventory." Goods are

(1) "consumer goods" if they are used or bought for use primarily for personal, family or household purposes;

(2) "equipment" if they are used or bought for use primarily in business (including farming or a profession) or by a debtor who is a non-profit organization or a governmental subdivision or agency or if the goods are not included in the definitions of inventory, farm products or consumer goods;

(3) "farm products" if they are crops or livestock or supplies used or produced in farming operations or if they are products or

crops or livestock in their unmanufactured states (such as ginned cotton, wool-clip, maple syrup, milk and eggs), and if they are in the possession of a debtor engaged in raising, fattening, grazing or other farming operations. If goods are farm products they are neither equipment nor inventory;

(4) "inventory" if they are held by a person who holds them for sale or lease or to be furnished under contracts of service or if he has so furnished them, or if they are raw materials, work in process or materials used or consumed in a business. Inventory of a person is not to be classified as his equipment.

Section 9-110. Sufficiency of Description. For the purposes of this Article any description of personal property or real estate is sufficient whether or not it is specific if it reasonably identifies what is described.

Section 9-111. Applicability of Bulk Transfer Laws. The creation of a security interest is not a bulk transfer under Article 6 (see Section 6-103).

Section 9-112. Where Collateral is Not Owned by Debtor. Unless otherwise agreed, when a secured party knows that collateral is owned by a person who is not the debtor, the owner of the collateral is entitled to receive from the secured party any surplus under Section 9-502(2) or under Section 9-504(1), and is not liable for the debt or for any deficiency after resale, and he has the same right as the debtor

(a) to receive statements under Section 9-208;

(b) to receive notice of and to object to a secured party's proposal to retain the collateral in satisfaction of the indebtedness under Section 9-505;

(c) to redeem the collateral under Section 9-506;

(d) to obtain injunctive or other relief under Section 9-507(1); and

(e) to recover losses caused to him under Section 9-208(2).

Section 9-113. Security Interests Arising Under Article on Sales. A security interest arising solely under the Article on Sales (Article 2) is subject to the provisions of this Article except that to the extent that and so long as the debtor does not have or does not lawfully obtain possession of the goods

(a) no security agreement is necessary to make the security interest enforceable; and

(b) no filing is required to perfect the security interest; and

(c) the rights of the secured party on default by the debtor are governed by the Article on Sales (Article 2).

Section 9-114. Consignment.

(1) A person who delivers goods under a consignment which is not a security interest and who would be required to file under this Article by paragraph (3) (c) of Section 2-326 has priority over a secured party who is or becomes a creditor of the consignee and who would have a perfected security interest in the goods if they were the property of the consignee, and also has priority with respect to identifiable cash proceeds received on or before delivery of the goods to a buyer, if

(a) the consignor complies with the filing provision of the Article on Sales with respect to consignments (paragraph (3) (c) of Section 2-326) before the consignee receives possession of the goods; and

(b) the consignor gives notification in writing to the holder of the security interest if the holder has filed a financing statement covering the same types of goods before the date of the filing made by the consignor; and

(c) the holder of the security interest receives the notification within five years before the consignee receives possession of the goods; and

(d) the notification states that the consignor expects to deliver goods on consignment to the consignee, describing the goods by item or type.

(2) In the case of a consignment which is not a security interest and in which the requirements of the preceding subsection have not been met, a person who delivers goods to another is subordinate to a person who would have a perfected security interest in the goods if they were the property of the debtor.

PART 2

VALIDITY OF SECURITY AGREEMENT AND RIGHTS OF PARTIES THERETO

Section 9-201. General Validity of Security Agreement. Except as otherwise provided by this Act a security agreement is effective according to its terms between the parties, against purchasers of the collateral and against creditors. Nothing in this Article validates any charge or practice illegal under any statute or regulation thereunder governing usury, small loans, retail installment sales, or the like, or extends the application of any such statute or regulation to any transaction not otherwise subject thereto.

Section 9-202. Title to Collateral Immaterial. Each provision of this Article with regard to rights, obligations and remedies applies whether title to collateral is in the secured party or in the debtor.

Section 9-203. Attachment and Enforceability of Security Interest; Proceeds; Formal Requisites.

(1) Subject to the provisions of Section 4-208 on the security interest of a collecting bank and Section 9-113 on a security interest arising under the Article on Sales, a security interest is not enforceable against the debtor or third parties with respect to the collateral and does not attach unless

(a) the collateral is in the possession of the secured party pursuant to agreement, or the debtor has signed a security agreement which contains a description of the collateral and in addition, when the security interest covers crops growing or to be grown or timber to be cut, a description of the land concerned; and

(b) value has been given; and

(c) the debtor has rights in the collateral.

(2) A security interest attaches when it becomes enforceable against the debtoı with respect to the collateral. Attachment occurs as soon as all of the events specified in subsection (1) have taken place unless explicit agreement postpones the time of attaching.

(3) Unless otherwise agreed a security agreement gives the secured party the rights to proceeds provided by Section 9-306.

(4) A transaction, although subject to this Article, is also subject to ....*, and in the case of conflict between the provisions of this Article and any such statute, the provisions of such statute control. Failure to comply with any applicable statute has only the effect which is specified therein.

Section 9-204. After-Acquired Property; Future Advances.

(1) Except as provided in subsection (2), a security agreement may provide that any or all obligations covered by the security agreement are to be secured by after-acquired collateral.

(2) No security interest attaches under an after-acquired property clause to consumer goods other than accessions (Section 9-314) when given as additional security unless the debtor acquires rights in them within ten days after the secured party gives value.

(3) Obligations covered by a security agreement may include future advances or other value whether or not the advances or value are given pursuant to commitment (subsection (1) of Section 9-105).

Section 9-205. Use or Disposition of Collateral Without Accounting Permissible. A security interest is not invalid or fraudulent against creditors by reason of liberty in the debtor to use, commingle or dispose of all or part of the collateral (including returned or repossessed goods) or to collect or compromise accounts or chattel paper, or to accept the return of goods or make repossessions, or to use, commingle or dispose of proceeds, or by reason of the failure of the secured party to require the debtor to account for proceeds or replace collateral. This section does not relax the requirements of possession where perfection of a security interest depends upon possession of the collateral by the secured party or by a bailee.

Section 9-206. Agreement Not to Assert Defenses Against Assignee; Modification of Sales Warranties Where Security Agreement Exists.

(1) Subject to any statute or decision which establishes a different rule for buyers or lessees of consumer goods an agreement by a buyer or lessee that he will not assert against an assignee any claim or defense which he may have against the seller or lessor is enforceable by an assignee who takes his assignment for value, in good faith and without notice of a claim or defense, except as to defenses of a type which may be asserted against a holder in due course of a negotiable

instrument under the Article on Commercial Paper (Article 3). A buyer who as part of one transaction signs both a negotiable instrument and a security agreement makes such an agreement.

(2) When a seller retains a purchase money security interest in goods the Article on Sales (Article 2) governs the sale and any disclaimer, limitation or modification of the seller's warranties.

Section 9-207. Rights and Duties When Collateral Is In Secured Party's Possession.

(1) A secured party must use reasonable care in the custody and preservation of collateral in his possession. In the case of an instrument or chattel paper reasonable care includes taking necessary steps to preserve rights against prior parties unless otherwise agreed.

(2) Unless otherwise agreed, when collateral is in the secured party's possession

(a) reasonable expenses (including the cost of any insurance and payment of taxes or other charges) incurred in the custody, preservation, use or operation of the collateral are chargeable to the debtor and are secured by the collateral;

(b) the risk of accidental loss or damage is on the debtor to the extent of any deficiency in any effective insurance coverage;

(c) the secured party may hold as additional security any increase or profits (except money) received from the collateral, but money so received, unless remitted to the debtor, shall be applied in reduction of the secured obligation;

(d) the secured party must keep the collateral identifiable but fungible collateral may be commingled;

(e) the secured party may repledge the collateral upon terms which do not impair the debtor's right to redeem it.

(3) A secured party is liable for any loss caused by his failure to meet any obligation imposed by the preceding subsections but does not lose his security interest.

(4) A secured party may use or operate the collateral for the purpose of preserving the collateral or its value or pursuant to the order of a court of appropriate jurisdiction or, except in the case of consumer goods, in the manner and to the extent provided in the security agreement.

Section 9-208. Request for Statement of Account or List of Collateral.

(1) A debtor may sign a statement indicating what he believes to be the aggregate amount of unpaid indebtedness as of a specified date and may send it to the secured party with a request that the statement be approved or corrected and returned to the debtor. When the security agreement or any other record kept by the secured party identifies the collateral a debtor may similarly request the secured party to approve or correct a list of the collateral.

(2) The secured party must comply with such a request within two weeks after receipt by sending a written correction or approval. If the secured party claims a security interest in all of a particular type of collateral owned by the debtor he may indicate that fact in his reply and need not approve or correct an itemized list of such collateral. If the secured party without reasonable excuse fails to comply he is liable for any loss caused to the debtor thereby; and if the debtor has properly included in his request a good faith statement of the obligation or a list of the collateral or both the secured party may claim a security interest only as shown in the statement against persons misled by his failure to comply. If he no longer has an interest in the obligation or collateral at the time the request is received he must disclose the name and address of any successor in interest known to him and he is liable for any loss caused to the debtor as a result of failure to disclose. A successor in interest is not subject to this section until a request is received by him.

(3) A debtor is entitled to such a statement once every six months without charge. The secured party may require payment of a charge not exceeding $10 for each additional statement furnished.

RIGHTS OF THIRD PARTIES; PERFECTED AND UNPERFECTED SECURITY INTERESTS; RULES OF PRIORITY

Section 9-301. Persons Who Take Priority Over Unperfected Security Interests; Rights of "Lien Creditor."

(1) Except as otherwise provided in subsection (2), an unperfected security interest is subordinate to the rights of

(a) persons entitled to priority under Section 9-312;

(b) a person who becomes a lien creditor before the security interest is perfected;

(c) in the case of goods, instruments, documents, and chattel paper, a person who is not a secured party and who is a transferee in bulk or other buyer not in ordinary course of business or is a buyer of farm products in ordinary course of business, to the extent that he gives value and receives delivery of the collateral without knowledge of the security interest and before it is perfected;

(d) in the case of accounts and general intangibles, a person who is not a secured party and who is a transferee to the extent that he gives value without knowledge of the security interest and before it is perfected.

(2) If the secured party files with respect to a purchase money security interest before or within ten days after the debtor receives possession of the collateral, he takes priority over the rights of a transferee in bulk or of a lien creditor which arise between the time the security interest attaches and the time of filing.

(3) A "lien creditor" means a creditor who has acquired a lien on the property involved by attachment, levy or the like and includes an assignee for benefit of creditors from the time of assignment, and a trustee in bankruptcy from the date of filing of the petition or a receiver in equity from the time of appointment.

(4) A person who becomes a lien creditor while a security interest is perfected takes subject to the security interest only to the extent that it secures advances made before he becomes a lien creditor or within 45 days thereafter or made without knowledge of the lien pursuant to a commitment entered into without knowledge of the lien.

Section 9-302. When Filing is Required to Perfect Security Interest; Security Interests to Which Filing Provisions of This Article Do Not Apply.

(1) A financing statement must be filed to perfect all security interests except the following:

(a) a security interest in collateral in possession of the secured party under Section 9-305;

(b) a security interest temporarily perfected in instruments or documents without delivery under Section 9-304 or in proceeds for a 10 day period under Section 9-306;

(c) a security interest created by an assignment of a beneficial interest in a trust or a decedent's estate;

(d) a purchase money security interest in consumer goods; but filing is required for a motor vehicle required to be registered; and fixture filing is required for priority over conflicting interests in fixtures to the extent provided in Section 9-313;

(e) an assignment of accounts which does not alone or in conjunction with other assignments to the same assignee transfer a significant part of the outstanding accounts of the assignor;

(f) a security interest of a collecting bank (Section 4-208) or arising under the Article on Sales (see Section 9-113) or covered in subsection (3) of this section;

(g) an assignment for the benefit of all the creditors of the transferor, and subsequent transfers by the assignee thereunder.

(2) If a secured party assigns a perfected security interest, no filing under this Article is required in order to continue the perfected status of the security interest against creditors of and transferees from the original debtor.

(3) The filing of a financing statement otherwise required by this Article is not necessary or effective to perfect a security interest in property subject to

(a) a statute or treaty of the United States which provides for a national or international registration or a national or international certificate of title or which specifies a place of filing different from that specified in this Article for filing of the security interest; or

(b) the following statutes of this state; [list any certificate of title statute covering automobiles, trailers, mobile homes, boats, farm tractors, or the like, and any central filing statute*.]; but during any period in which collateral is inventory held for sale by a person who is in the business of selling goods of that kind, the filing provisions of this Article (Part 4) apply to a security interest in that collateral created by him as debtor; or

(c) a certificate of title statute of another jurisdiction under the law of which indication of a security interest on the certificate is required as a condition of perfection (subsection (2) of Section 9-103).

(4) Compliance with a statute or treaty described in subsection (3) is equivalent to the filing of a financing statement under this Article, and a security interest in property subject to the statute or treaty can be perfected only by compliance therewith except as provided in Section 9-103 on multiple state transactions. Duration and renewal of perfection of a security interest perfected by compliance with the statute or treaty are governed by the provisions of the statute or treaty; in other respects the security interest is subject to this Article.

Section 9-303. When Security Interest Is Perfected; Continuity of Perfection.

(1) A security interest is perfected when it has attached and when all of the applicable steps required for perfection have been taken. Such steps are specified in Sections 9-302, 9-304, 9-305 and 9-306. If such steps are taken before the security interest attaches, it is perfected at the time when it attaches.

(2) If a security interest is originally perfected in any way permitted under this Article and is subsequently perfected in some other way under this Article, without an intermediate period when it was unperfected, the security interest shall be deemed to be perfected continuously for the purposes of this Article.

Section 9-304. Perfection of Security Interest in Instruments, Documents, and Goods Covered by Documents; Perfection by Permissive Filing; Temporary Perfection Without Filing or Transfer of Possession.

(1) A security interest in chattel paper or negotiable documents may be perfected by filing. A security interest in money or instruments (other than instruments which constitute part of chattel paper) can be perfected only by the secured party's taking possession, except as provided in subsections (4) and (5) of this section and subsections (2) and (3) of Section 9-306 on proceeds.

(2) During the period that goods are in the possession of the issuer of a negotiable document therefor, a security interest in the goods is perfected by perfecting a security interest in the document, and any security interest in the goods otherwise perfected during such period is subject thereto.

(3) A security interest in goods in the possession of a bailee other than one who has issued a negotiable document therefor is perfected by issuance of a document in the name of the secured party or by the bailee's receipt of notification of the secured party's interest or by filing as to the goods.

(4) A security interest in instruments or negotiable documents is perfected without filing or the taking of possession for a period of 21 days from the time it attaches to the extent that it arises for new value given under a written security agreement.

(5) A security interest remains perfected for a period of 21 days without filing where a secured party having a perfected security interest in an instrument, a negotiable document or goods in possession of a bailee other than one who has issued a negotiable document therefor

(a) makes available to the debtor the goods or documents representing the goods for the purpose of ultimate sale or exchange or for the purpose of loading, unloading, storing, shipping, transshipping, manufacturing, processing or otherwise dealing with them in a manner preliminary to their sale or exchange, but priority between conflicting security interests in the goods is subject to subsection (3) of Section 9-312; or

(b) delivers the instrument to the debtor for the purpose of ultimate sale or exchange or of presentation, collection, renewal or registration of transfer.

(6) After the 21 day period in subsections

(4) and (5) perfection depends upon compliance with applicable provisions of this Article.

Section 9-305. When Possession by Secured Party Perfects Security Interest Without Filing. A security interest in letters of credit and advices of credit (subsection (2) (a) of Section 5-116), goods, instruments, money, negotiable documents or chattel paper may be perfected by the secured party's taking possession of the collateral. If such collateral other than goods covered by a negotiable document is held by a bailee, the secured party is deemed to have possession from the time the bailee receives notification of the secured party's interest. A security interest is perfected by possession from the time possession is taken without relation back and continues only so long as possession is retained, unless otherwise specified in this Article. The security interest may be otherwise perfected as provided in this Article before or after the period of possession by the secured party.

Section 9-306. "Proceeds"; Secured Party's Rights on Disposition of Collateral.

(1) "Proceeds" includes whatever is received upon the sale, exchange, collection or other disposition of collateral or proceeds. Insurance payable by reason of loss or damage to the collateral is proceeds, except to the extent that it is payable to a person other than a party to the security agreement. Money, checks, deposit accounts, and the like are "cash proceeds". All other proceeds are "non-cash proceeds".

(2) Except where this Article otherwise provides, a security interest continues in collateral notwithstanding sale, exchange or other disposition thereof unless the disposition was authorized by the secured party in the security agreement or otherwise, and also continues in any identifiable proceeds including collections received by the debtor.

(3) The security interest in proceeds is a continuously perfected security interest if the interest in the original collateral was perfected but it ceases to be a perfected security interest and becomes unperfected ten days after receipt of the proceeds by the debtor unless

(a) a filed financing statement covers the original collateral and the proceeds are collateral in which a security interest may be perfected by filing in the office or offices where the financing statement has been filed and, if the proceeds are acquired with cash proceeds, the description of collateral in the financing statement indicates the types of property constituting the proceeds; or

(b) a filed financing statement covers the original collateral and the proceeds are identifiable cash proceeds; or

(c) the security interest in the proceeds is perfected before the expiration of the ten day period.

Except as provided in this section, a security interest in proceeds can be perfected only by the methods or under the circumstances permitted in this Article for original collateral of the same type.

(4) In the event of insolvency proceedings instituted by or against a debtor, a secured party with a perfected security interest in proceeds has a perfected security interest only in the following proceeds:

(a) in identifiable non-cash proceeds and in separate deposit accounts containing only proceeds;

(b) in identifiable cash proceeds in the form of money which is neither commingled with other money nor deposited in a deposit account prior to the insolvency proceedings;

(c) in identifiable cash proceeds in the form of checks and the like which are not deposited in a deposit account prior to the insolvency proceedings; and

(d) in all cash and deposit accounts of the debtor in which proceeds have been commingled with other funds, but the perfected security interest under this paragraph (d) is

(i) subject to any right to set-off; and

(ii) limited to an amount not greater than the amount of any cash proceeds received by the debtor within ten days before the institution of the insolvency proceedings less the sum of (I) the payments to the secured party on account of cash proceeds received by the debtor during such period and (II) the cash proceeds received by the debtor during such period to which the secured party is entitled under paragraphs (a) through (c) of this subsection (4).

(5) If a sale of goods results in an account

or chattel paper which is transferred by the seller to a secured party, and if the goods are returned to or are repossessed by the seller or the secured party, the following rules determine priorities:

(a) If the goods were collateral at the time of sale, for an indebtedness of the seller which is still unpaid, the original security interest attaches again to the goods and continues as a perfected security interest if it was perfected at the time when the goods were sold. If the security interest was originally perfected by a filing which is still effective, nothing further is required to continue the perfected status; in any other case, the secured party must take possession of the returned or repossessed goods or must file.

(b) An unpaid transferee of the chattel paper has a security interest in the goods against the transferor. Such security interest is prior to a security interest asserted under paragraph (a) to the extent that the transferee of the chattel paper was entitled to priority under Section 9-308.

(c) An unpaid transferee to the account has a security interest in the goods against the transferor. Such security interest is subordinate to a security interest asserted under paragraph (a).

(d) A security interest of an unpaid transferee asserted under paragraph (b) or (c) must be perfected for protection against creditors of the transferor and purchasers of the returned or repossessed goods.

Section 9-307. Protection of Buyers of Goods.

(1) A buyer in ordinary course of business (subsection (9) of Section 1-201) other than a person buying farm products from a person engaged in farming operations takes free of a security interest created by his seller even though the security interest is perfected and even though the buyer knows of its existence.

(2) In the case of consumer goods, a buyer takes free of a security interest even though perfected if he buys without knowledge of the security interest, for value and for his own personal, family or household purposes unless prior to the purchase the secured party has filed a financing statement covering such goods.

(3) A buyer other than a buyer in ordinary course of business (subsection (1) of this section) takes free of a security interest to the extent that it secures future advances made after the secured party acquires knowledge of the purchase, or more than 45 days after the purchase, whichever first occurs, unless made pursuant to a commitment entered into without knowledge of the purchase and before the expiration of the 45 day period.

Section 9-308. Purchase of Chattel Paper and Instruments. A purchaser of chattel paper or an instrument who gives new value and takes possession of it in the ordinary course of his business has priority over a security interest in the chattel paper or instrument

(a) which is perfected under Section 9-304 (permissive filing and temporary perfection) or under Section 9-306 (perfection as to proceeds) if he acts without knowledge that the specific paper or instrument is subject to a security interest; or

(b) which is claimed merely as proceeds of inventory subject to a security interest (Section 9-306) even though he knows that the specific paper or instrument is subject to the security interest.

Section 9-309. Protection of Purchasers of Instruments and Documents. Nothing in this Article limits the rights of a holder in due course of a negotiable instrument (Section 3-302) or a holder to whom a negotiable document of title has been duly negotiated (Section 7-501) or a bona fide purchaser of a security (Section 8-301) and such holders or purchasers take priority over an earlier security interest even though perfected. Filing under this Article does not constitute notice of the security interest to such holders or purchasers.

Section 9-310. Priority of Certain Liens Arising by Operation of Law. When a person in the ordinary course of his business furnishes services or materials with respect to goods subject to a security interest, a lien upon goods in the possession of such person given by statute or rule of law for such materials or services takes priority over a perfected security interest unless the lien is statutory and the statute expressly provides otherwise.

Section 9-311. Alienability of Debtor's Rights: Judicial Process. The debtor's rights in collateral may be voluntarily or involuntarily transferred (by way of sale, creation of a security interest, attachment, levy, garnishment or other judicial process) notwithstanding a provision in the security agreement prohibiting any transfer or making the transfer constitute a default.

Section 9-312. Priorities Among Conflicting Security Interests in the Same Collateral.

(1) The rules of priority stated in other sections of this Part and in the following sections shall govern when applicable: Section 4-208 with respect to the security interests of collecting banks in items being collected, accompanying documents and proceeds; Section 9-103 on security interests related to other jurisdictions; Section 9-114 on consignments.

(2) A perfected security interest in crops for new value given to enable the debtor to produce the crops during the production season and given not more than three months before the crops become growing crops by planting or otherwise takes priority over an earlier perfected security interest to the extent that such earlier interest secured obligations due more than six months before the crops become growing crops by planting or otherwise, even though the person giving new value has knowledge of the earlier security interest.

(3) A perfected purchase money security interest in inventory has priority over a conflicting security interest in the same inventory and also has priority in identifiable cash proceeds received on or before the delivery of the inventory to a buyer if

(a) the purchase money security interest is perfected at the time the debtor receives possession of the inventory; and

(b) the purchase money secured party gives notification in writing to the holder of the conflicting security interest if the holder had filed a financing statement covering the same types of inventory (i) before the date of the filing made by the purchase money secured party, or (ii) before the beginning of the 21 day period where the purchase money security interest is temporarily perfected without filing or possession (subsection (5) of Section 9-304); and

(c) the holder of the conflicting security interest receives the notification within five years before the debtor receives possession of the inventory; and

(d) the notification states that the person giving the notice has or expects to acquire a purchase money security interest in inventory of the debtor, describing such inventory by item or type.

(4) A purchase money security interest in collateral other than inventory has priority over a conflicting security interest in the same collateral or its proceeds if the purchase money security interest is perfected at the time the debtor receives possession of the collateral or within ten days thereafter.

(5) In all cases not governed by other rules stated in this section (including cases of purchase money security interests which do not qualify for the special priorities set forth in subsections (3) and (4) of this section), priority between conflicting security interests in the same collateral shall be determined according to the following rules:

(a) Conflicting security interests rank according to priority in time of filing or perfection. Priority dates from the time a filing is first made covering the collateral or the time the security interest is first perfected, whichever is earlier, provided that there is no period thereafter when there is neither filing nor perfection.

(b) So long as conflicting security interests are unperfected, the first to attach has priority.

(6) For the purposes of subsection (5) a date of filing or perfection as to collateral is also a date of filing or perfection as to proceeds.

(7) If future advances are made while a security interest is perfected by filing or the taking of possession, the security interest has the same priority for the purposes of subsection (5) with respect to the future advances as it does with respect to the first advance. If a commitment is made before or while the security interest is so perfected, the security interest has the same priority with respect to advances made pursuant thereto. In other cases a perfected security interest has priority from the date the advance is made.

Section 9-313. Priority of Security Interests in Fixtures.

(1) In this section and in the provisions of Part 4 of this Article referring to fixture filing, unless the context otherwise requires

(a) goods are "fixtures" when they become so related to particular real estate that an interest in them arises under real estate law

(b) a "fixture filing" is the filing in the office where a mortgage on the real estate would be filed or recorded of a financing statement covering goods which are or are to become fixtures and conforming to the requirements of subsection (5) of Section 9-402

(c) a mortgage is a "construction mortgage" to the extent that it secures an obligation incurred for the construction of an improvement on land including the acquisition cost of the land, if the recorded writing so indicates.

(2) A security interest under this Article may be created in goods which are fixtures or may continue in goods which become fixtures, but no security interest exists under this Article in ordinary building materials incorporated into an improvement on land.

(3) This Article does not prevent creation of an encumbrance upon fixtures pursuant to real estate law.

(4) A perfected security interest in fixtures has priority over the conflicting interest of an encumbrancer or owner of the real estate where

(a) the security interest is a purchase money security interest, the interest of the encumbrancer or owner arises before the goods become fixtures, the security interest is perfected by a fixture filing before the goods become fixtures or within ten days thereafter, and the debtor has an interest of record in the real estate or is in possession of the real estate; or

(b) the security interest is perfected by a fixture filing before the interest of the encumbrancer or owner is of record, the security interest has priority over any conflicting interest of a predecessor in title of the encumbrancer or owner, and the debtor has an interest of record in the real estate or is in possession of the real estate; or

(c) the fixtures are readily removable factory or office machines or readily removable replacements of domestic appliances which are consumer goods, and before the goods become fixtures the security interest is perfected by any method permitted by this Article; or

(d) the conflicting interest is a lien on the real estate obtained by legal or equitable proceedings after the security interest was perfected by any method permitted by this Article.

(5) A security interest in fixtures, whether or not perfected, has priority over the conflicting interest of an encumbrancer or owner of the real estate where

(a) the encumbrancer or owner has consented in writing to the security interest or has disclaimed an interest in the goods as fixtures; or

(b) the debtor has a right to remove the goods as against the encumbrancer or owner. If the debtor's right terminates, the priority of the security interest continues for a reasonable time.

(6) Notwithstanding paragraph (a) of subsection (4) but otherwise subject to subsections (4) and (5), a security interest in fixtures is subordinate to a construction mortgage recorded before the goods become fixtures if the goods become fixtures before the completion of the construction. To the extent that it is given to refinance a construction mortgage, a mortgage has this priority to the same extent as the construction mortgage.

(7) In cases not within the preceding subsections, a security interest in fixtures is subordinate to the conflicting interest of an encumbrancer or owner of the related real estate who is not the debtor.

(8) When the secured party has priority over all owners and encumbrancers of the real estate, he may, on default, subject to the provisions of Part 5, remove his collateral from the real estate but he must reimburse any encumbrancer or owner of the real estate who is not the debtor and who has not otherwise agreed for the cost of repair of any physical injury, but not for any diminution in value of the real estate caused by the absence of the goods removed or by any necessity of replacing them. A person entitled to reimbursement may refuse permission to remove until the secured party gives adequate security for the performance of this obligation.

Section 9-314. Accessions.

(1) A security interest in goods which attaches before they are installed in or affixed to other goods takes priority as to the goods installed or affixed (called in this section "accessions") over the claims of all persons to the whole except as stated in subsection (3) and subject to Section 9-315(1).

(2) A security interest which attaches to goods after they become part of a whole is valid against all persons subsequently acquiring interests in the whole except as stated in subsection (3) but is invalid against any person with an interest in the whole at the time the security interest attaches to the goods who has not in writing consented to the security interest or disclaimed an interest in the goods as part of the whole.

(3) The security interests described in subsections (1) and (2) do not take priority over

(a) a subsequent purchaser for value of any interest in the whole; or

(b) a creditor with a lien on the whole subsequently obtained by judicial proceedings; or

(c) a creditor with a prior perfected security interest in the whole to the extent that he makes subsequent advances

if the subsequent purchase is made, the lien by judicial proceedings obtained or the subsequent advance under the prior perfected security interest is made or contracted for without knowledge of the security interest and before it is perfected. A purchaser of the whole at a foreclosure sale other than the holder of a perfected security interest purchasing at his own foreclosure sale is a subsequent purchaser within this section.

(4) When under subsections (1) or (2) and (3) a secured party has an interest in accessions which has priority over the claims of all persons who have interests in the whole, he may on default subject to the provisions of Part 5 remove his collateral from the whole but he must reimburse any encumbrancer or owner of the whole who is not the debtor and who has not otherwise agreed for the cost of repair of any physical injury but not for any diminution in value of the whole caused by the absence of the goods removed or by any necessity for replacing them. A person entitled to reimbursement may refuse permission to remove until the secured party gives adequate security for the performance of this obligation.

Section 9-315. Priority When Goods Are Commingled or Processed.

(1) If a security interest in goods was perfected and subsequently the goods or a part thereof have become part of a product or mass, the security interest continues in the product or mass if

(a) the goods are so manufactured, processed, assembled or commingled that their identity is lost in the product or mass; or

(b) a financing statement covering the original goods also covers the product into which the goods have been manufactured, processed or assembled.

In a case to which paragraph (b) applies, no separate security interest in that part of the original goods which has been manufactured, processed or assembled into the product may be claimed under Section 9-314.

(2) When under subsection (1) more than one security interest attaches to the product or mass, they rank equally according to the ratio that the cost of the goods to which each interest originally attached bears to the cost of the total product or mass.

Section 9-316. Priority Subject to Subordination. Nothing in this Article prevents subordination by agreement by any person entitled to priority.

Section 9-317. Secured Party Not Obligated on Contract of Debtor. The mere existence of a security interest or authority given to the debtor to dispose of or use collateral does not impose contract or tort liability upon the secured party for the debtor's acts or omissions.

Section 9-318. Defenses Against Assignee; Modification of Contract After Notification of Assignment; Term Prohibiting Assignment Ineffective; Identification and Proof of Assignment.

(1) Unless an account debtor has made an enforceable agreement not to assert defenses or claims arising out of a sale as provided in Section 9-206 the rights of an assignee are subject to

(a) all the terms of the contract between the account debtor and assignor and any defense or claim arising therefrom; and

(b) any other defense or claim of the account debtor against the assignor which accrues before the account debtor receives notification of the assignment.

(2) So far as the right to payment or a part thereof under an assigned contract has not been fully earned by performance, and notwithstanding notification of the assignment, any modification of or substitution for the contract made in good faith and in accord-

ance with reasonable commercial standards is effective against an assignee unless the account debtor has otherwise agreed but the assignee acquires corresponding rights under the modified or substituted contract. The assignment may provide that such modification or substitution is a breach by the assignor.

(3) The account debtor is authorized to pay the assignor until the account debtor receives notification that the amount due or to become due has been assigned and that payment is to be made to the assignee. A notification which does not reasonably identify the rights assigned is ineffective. If requested by the account debtor, the assignee must seasonably furnish reasonable proof that the assignment has been made and unless he does so the account debtor may pay the assignor.

(4) A term in any contract between an account debtor and an assignor is ineffective if it prohibits assignment of an account or prohibits creation of a security interest in a general intangible for money due or to become due or requires the account debtor's consent to such assignment or security interest.

PART 4

FILING

Section 9-401. Place of Filing; Erroneous Filing; Removal of Collateral.

First Alternative Subsection (1)

(1) The proper place to file in order to perfect a security interest is as follows:

(a) when the collateral is timber to be cut or is minerals or the like (including oil and gas) or accounts subject to subsection (5) of Section 9-103, or when the financing statement is filed as a fixture filing (Section 9-313) and the collateral is goods which are or are to become fixtures, then in the office where a mortgage on the real estate would be filed or recorded;

(b) in all other cases, in the office of the [Secretary of State].

Second Alternative Subsection (1)

(1) The proper place to file in order to perfect a security interest is as follows:

(a) when the collateral is equipment used in farming operations, or farm products, or accounts or general intangibles arising from or relating to the sale of farm products by a farmer, or consumer goods, then in the office of the .... in the county of the debtor's residence or if the debtor is not a resident in this state then in the office of the .... in the county where the goods are kept, and in addition when the collateral is crops growing or to be grown in the office of the .... in the county where the land is located;

(b) when the collateral is timber to be cut or is minerals or the like (including oil and gas) or accounts subject to subsection (5) of Section 9-103, or when the financing statement is filed as a fixture filing (Section 9-313) and the collateral is goods which are or are to become fixtures, then in the office where a mortgage on the real estate would be filed or recorded;

(c) in all other cases, in the office of the [Secretary of State].

Third Alternative Subsection (1)

(1) The proper place to file in order to perfect a security interest is as follows:

(a) when the collateral is equipment used in farming operations, or farm products, or accounts or general intangibles arising from or relating to the sale of farm products by a farmer, or consumer goods, then in the office of the .... in the county of the debtor's residence or if the debtor is not a resident of this state then in the office of the .... in the county where the goods are kept, and in addition when the collateral is crops growing or to be grown in the office of the .... in the county where the land is located;

(b) when the collateral is timber to be cut or is minerals or the like (including oil and gas) or accounts subject to subsection (5) of Section 9-103, or when the financing statement is filed as a fixture filing (Section 9-313) and the collateral is goods which are or are to become fixtures, then in the office where a mortgage on the real estate would be filed or recorded;

(c) in all other cases, in the office of the [Secretary of State] and in addition, if the debtor has a place of business in only one county of this state, also in the office of .... of such county, or, if the debtor has no place of business in this state, but resides in the state, also in the office of .... of the county in which he resides.

NOTE: *One of the three alternatives should be selected as subsection (1).*

(2) A filing which is made in good faith in an improper place or not in all of the places required by this section is nevertheless effective with regard to any collateral as to which the filing complied with the requirements of this Article and is also effective with regard to collateral covered by the financing statement against any person who has knowledge of the contents of such financing statement.

(3) A filing which is made in the proper place in this state continues effective even though the debtor's residence or place of business or the location of the collateral or its use, whichever controlled the original filing, is thereafter changed.

Alternative Subsection (3)

[(3) A filing which is made in the proper county continues effective for four months after a change to another county of the debtor's residence or place of business or the location of the collateral, whichever controlled the original filing. It becomes ineffective thereafter unless a copy of the financing statement signed by the secured party is filed in the new county within said period. The security interest may also be perfected in the new county after the expiration of the four-month period; in such case perfection dates from the time of perfection in the new county. A change in the use of the collateral does not impair the effectiveness of the original filing.]

(4) The rules stated in Section 9-103 determine whether filing is necessary in this state.

(5) Notwithstanding the preceding subsections, and subject to subsection (3) of Section 9-302, the proper place to file in order to perfect a security interest in collateral, including fixtures, of a transmitting utility is the office of the [Secretary of State]. This filing constitutes a fixture filing (Section 9-313) as to the collateral described therein which is or is to become fixtures.

(6) For the purposes of this section, the residence of an organization is its place of business if it has one or its chief executive office if it has more than one place of business.

Section 9-402. Formal Requisites of Financing Statement; Amendments; Mortgage as Financing Statement.

(1) A financing statement is sufficient if it gives the names of the debtor and the secured party, is signed by the debtor, gives an address of the secured party from which information concerning the security interest may be obtained, gives a mailing address of the debtor and contains a statement indicating the types, or describing the items, of collateral. A financing statement may be filed before the security agreement is made or a security interest otherwise attaches. When the financing statement covers crops growing or to be grown, the statement must also contain a description of the real estate concerned. When the financing statement covers timber to be cut or covers minerals, or the like, (including oil and gas) or accounts subject to subsection (5) of Section 9-103, or when the financial statement is filed as a fixture filing (Section 9-313) and the collateral is goods which are or are to become fixtures, the statement must also comply with subsection (5). A copy of the security agreement is sufficient as a financing statement if it contains the above information and is signed by the debtor. A carbon, photographic or other reproduction of a security agreement or a financing statement is sufficient as a financing statement if the security agreement so provides or if the original has been filed in this state.

(2) A financing statement which otherwise complies with subsection (1) is sufficient when it is signed by the secured party instead of the debtor if it is filed to perfect a security interest in

(a) collateral already subject to a security interest in another jurisdiction when it is brought into this state, or when the debtor's location is changed to this state. Such a financing statement must state that the collateral was brought into this state or that the debtor's location was changed to this state under such circumstances; or

(b) proceeds under Section 9-306 if the security interest in the original collateral was perfected. Such a financing statement must describe the original collateral; or

(c) collateral as to which the filing has lapsed; or

(d) collateral acquired after a change of name, identity or corporate structure of the debtor (subsection (7)).

(3) A form substantially as follows is sufficient to comply with subsection (1):

Name of debtor (or assignor) ....
Address ....
Name of secured party (or assignee) ....
Address ....

1. This financing statement covers the following types (or items) of property:
   (Describe) ....
2. (If collateral is crops) The above crops are growing or are to be grown on:
   (Describe Real Estate) ....
3. (If applicable) The above goods are to become fixtures on*
   (Describe Real Estate) ....
   and this financing statement is to be filed [for record] in the real estate records. (If the debtor does not have an interest of record) The name of a record owner is ....
4. (If products of collateral are claimed) Products of the collateral are also covered. Signature of Debtor (or Assignor).........................
   Signature of Secured Party (or Assignee).....................
   (use whichever is applicable)

(4) A financing statement may be amended by filing a writing signed by both the debtor and the secured party. An amendment does not extend the period of effectiveness of a financing statement. If any amendment adds collateral, it is effective as to the added collateral only from the filing date of the amendment. In this Article, unless the context otherwise requires, the term "financial statement" means the original financing statement and any amendments.

(5) A financing statement covering timber to be cut or covering minerals or the like (including oil and gas) or accounts subject to subsection (5) of Section 9-103, or a financing statement filed as a fixture filing (Section 9-313) where the debtor is not a transmitting utility, must show that it covers this type of collateral, must recite that it is to be filed [for record] in the real estate records, and the financing statement must contain a description of the real estate [sufficient if it were contained in a mortgage of the real estate to give constructive notice of the mortgage under the law of this state]. If the debtor does not have an interest of record in the real estate, the financing statement must show the name of a record owner.

(6) A mortgage is effective as a financing statement filed as a fixture filing from the date of its recording if

(a) the goods are described in the mortgage by item or type; and

(b) the goods are or are to become fixtures related to the real estate described in the mortgage; and

(c) the mortgage complies with the requirements for a financing statement in this section other than a recital that it is to be filed in the real estate records; and

(d) the mortgage is duly recorded.

No fee with reference to the financing statement is required other than the regular recording and satisfaction fees with respect to the mortgage.

(7) A financing statement sufficiently shows the name of the debtor if it gives the individual, partnership or corporate name of the debtor, whether or not it adds other trade names or names of partners. Where the debtor so changes his name or in the case of an organization its name, identity or corporate structure that a filed financing statement becomes seriously misleading, the filing is not effective to perfect a security interest in collateral acquired by the debtor more than four months after the change, unless a new appropriate financing statement is filed before the expiration of that time. A filed financing statement remains effective

*Where appropriate substitute either "The above timber is standing on . . . ." or "The above minerals or the like (including oil and gas) or accounts will be financed at the wellhead or minehead of the well or mine located on . . . ."

with respect to collateral transferred by the debtor even though the secured party knows of or consents to the transfer.

(8) A financing statement substantially complying with the requirements of this section is effective even though it contains minor errors which are not seriously misleading.

Section 9-403. What Constitutes Filing; Duration of Filing; Effect of Lapsed Filing; Duties of Filing Officer.

(1) Presentation for filing of a financing statement and tender of the filing fee or acceptance of the statement by the filing officer constitutes filing under this Article.

(2) Except as provided in subsection (6) a filed financing statement is effective for a period of five years from the date of filing. The effectiveness of a filed financing statement lapses on the expiration of the five year period unless a continuation statement is filed prior to the lapse. If a security interest perfected by filing exists at the time insolvency proceedings are commenced by or against the debtor, the security interest remains perfected until termination of the insolvency proceedings and thereafter for a period of sixty days or until the expiration of the five year period, whichever occurs later. Upon lapse the security interest becomes unperfected, unless it is perfected without filing. If the security interest becomes unperfected upon lapse, it is deemed to have been unperfected as against a person who became a purchaser or lien creditor before lapse.

(3) A continuation statement may be filed by the secured party within six months prior to the expiration of the five year period specified in subsection (2). Any such continuation statement must be signed by the secured party, identify the original statement by file number and state that the original statement is still effective. A continuation statement signed by a person other than the secured party of record must be accompanied by a separate written statement of assignment signed by the secured party of record and complying with subsection (2) of Section 9-405, including payment of the required fee. Upon timely filing of the continuation statement, the effectiveness of the original statement is continued for five years after the last date to which the filing was effective whereupon it lapses in the same manner as provided in subsection (2) unless another continuation statement is filed prior to such lapse. Succeeding continuation statements may be filed in the same manner to continue the effectiveness of the original statement. Unless a statute on disposition of public records provides otherwise, the filing officer may remove a lapsed statement from the files and destroy it immediately if he has retained a microfilm or other photographic record, or in other cases after one year after the lapse. The filing officer shall so arrange matters by physical annexation of financing statements to continuation statements or other related filings, or by other means, that if he physically destroys the financing statements of a period more than five years past, those which have been continued by a continuation statement or which are still effective under subsection (6) shall be retained.

(4) Except as provided in subsection (7) a filing officer shall mark each statement with a file number and with the date and hour of filing and shall hold the statement or a microfilm or other photographic copy thereof for public inspection. In addition the filing officer shall index the statement according to the name of the debtor and shall note in the index the file number and the address of the debtor given in the statement.

(5) The uniform fee for filing and indexing and for stamping a copy furnished by the secured party to show the date and place of filing for an original financing statement or for a continuation statement shall be $.... if the statement is in the standard form prescribed by the [Secretary of State] and otherwise shall be $....., plus in each case, if the financing statement is subject to subsection (5) of Section 9-402, $..... The uniform fee for each name more than one required to be indexed shall be $..... The secured party may at his option show a trade name for any person and an extra uniform indexing fee of $..... shall be paid with respect thereto.

(6) If the debtor is a transmitting utility (subsection (5) of Section 9-401) and a filed financing statement so states, it is effective until a termination statement is filed. A real estate mortgage which is effective as a fixture filing under subsection (6) of Section 9-402 remains effective as a fixture filing until the mortgage is released or satisfied of

record or its effectiveness otherwise terminates as to the real estate.

(7) When a financing statement covers timber to be cut or covers minerals or the like (including oil and gas) or accounts subject to subsection (5) of Section 9-103, or is filed as a fixture filing, [it shall be filed for record and] the filing officer shall index it under the names of the debtor and any owner of record shown on the financing statement in the same fashion as if they were the mortgagors in a mortgage of the real estate described, and, to the extent that the law of this state provides for indexing of mortgages under the name of the mortgagee, under the name of the secured party as if he were the mortgagee thereunder, or where indexing is by description in the same fashion as if the financing statement were a mortgage of the real estate described.

Section 9-404. Termination Statement.

(1) If a financing statement covering consumer goods is filed on or after ...., then within one month or within ten days following written demand by the debtor after there is no outstanding secured obligation and no commitment to make advances, incur obligations or otherwise give value, the secured party must file with each filing officer with whom the financing statement was filed, a termination statement to the effect that he no longer claims a security interest under the financing statement, which shall be identified by file number. In other cases whenever there is no outstanding secured obligation and no commitment to make advances, incur obligations or otherwise give value, the secured party must on written demand by the debtor send the debtor, for each filing officer with whom the financing statement was filed, a termination statement to the effect that he no longer claims a security interest under the financing statement, which shall be identified by file number. A termination statement signed by a person other than the secured party of record must be accompanied by a separate written statement of assignment signed by the secured party of record and complying with subsection (2) of Section 9-405, including payment of the required fee. If the affected secured party fails to file such a termination statement within ten days after proper demand therefor, he shall be liable to the debtor for one hundred dollars, and in addition for any loss caused to the debtor by such failure.

(2) On presentation to the filing officer of such a termination statement he must note it in the index. If he has received the termination statement in duplicate, he shall return one copy of the termination statement to the secured party stamped to show the time of receipt thereof. If the filing officer has a microfilm or other photographic record of the financing statement, and of any related continuation statement, statement of assignment and statement of release, he may remove the originals from the files at any time after receipt of the termination statement, or if he has no such record, he may remove them from the files at any time after one year after receipt of the termination statement.

(3) If the termination statement is in the standard form prescribed by the [Secretary of State], the uniform fee for filing and indexing the termination statement shall be \$..... and otherwise shall be \$....., plus in each case an additional fee of \$..... for each name more than one against which the termination statement is required to be indexed.

Section 9-405. Assignment of Security Interest; Duties of Filing Officer; Fees.

(1) A financing statement may disclose an assignment of a security interest in the collateral described in the financing statement by indication in the financing statement of the name and address of the assignee or by an assignment itself or a copy thereof on the face or back of the statement. On presentation to the filing officer of such a financing statement the filing officer shall mark the same as provided in Section 9-403(4). The uniform fee for filing, indexing and furnishing filing data for a financing statement so indicating an assignment shall be \$..... if the statement is in the standard form prescribed by the [Secretary of State] and otherwise shall be \$....., plus in each case an additional fee of \$..... for each name more than one against which the financing statement is required to be indexed.

(2) A secured party may assign of record all or part of his rights under a financing statement by the filing in the place where the original financing statement was filed of a separate written statement of assignment signed by the secured party of record and setting forth the name of the secured party of record and the debtor, the file number and the date of filing of the financing

statement and the name and address of the assignee and containing a description of the collateral assigned. A copy of the assignment is sufficient as a separate statement if it complies with the preceding sentence. On presentation to the filing officer of such a separate statement, the filing officer shall mark such separate statement with the date and hour of the filing. He shall note the assignment on the index of the financing statement, or in the case of a fixture filing, or a filing covering timber to be cut, or covering minerals or the like (including oil and gas) or accounts subject to subsection (5) of Section 9-103, he shall index the assignment under the name of the assignor as grantor and, to the extent that the law of this state provides for indexing the assignment of a mortgage under the name of the assignee, he shall index the assignment of the financing statement under the name of the assignee. The uniform fee for filing, indexing and furnishing filing data about such a separate statement of assignment shall be $. . . . . if the statement is in the standard form prescribed by the [Secretary of State] and otherwise shall be $. . . . . , plus in each case an additional fee of $. . . . . for each name more than one against which the statement of assignment is required to be indexed. Notwithstanding the provisions of this subsection, an assignment of record of a security interest in a fixture contained in a mortgage effective as a fixture filing (subsection (6) of Section 9-402) may be made only by an assignment of the mortgage in the manner provided by the law of the state other than this Act.

(3) After the disclosure of filing of an assignment under this section, the assignee is the secured party of record.

Section 9-406. Release of Collateral; Duties of Filing Officer; Fees. A secured party of record may by his signed statement release all or a part of any collateral described in a filed financing statement. The statement of release is sufficient if it contains a description of the collateral being released, the name and address of the debtor, the name and address of the secured party, and the file number of the financing statement. A statement of release signed by a person other than the secured party of record must be accompanied by a separate written statement of assignment signed by the secured party of record and complying with subsection (2) of Section 9-405, including payment of the required fee. Upon presentation of such a statement of release to the filing officer he shall mark the statement with the hour and date of filing and shall note the same upon the margin of the index of the filing of the financing statement. The uniform fee for filing and noting such a statement of release shall be $. . . . . if the statement is in the standard form prescribed by the [Secretary of State] and otherwise shall be $. . . . . , plus in each case an additional fee of $. . . . . for each name more than one against which the statement of release is required to be indexed.

[Section 9-407. Information From Filing Officer].

[(1) If the person filing any financing statement, termination statement, statement of assignment, or statement of release, furnishes the filing officer a copy thereof, the filing officer shall upon request note upon the copy the file number and date and hour of the filing of the original and deliver or send the copy to such person.]

[(2) Upon request of any person, the filing officer shall issue his certificate showing whether there is on file on the date and hour stated therein, any presently effective financing statement naming a particular debtor and any statement of assignment thereof and if there is, giving the date and hour of filing of each such statement and the names and addresses of each secured party therein. The uniform fee for such a certificate shall be $. . . . . if the request for the certificate is in the standard form prescribed by the [Secretary of State] and otherwise shall be $. . . . . Upon request the filing officer shall furnish a copy of any filed financing statement or statement of assignment for a uniform fee of $. . . . . per page.]

Section 9-408. Financing Statements Covering Consigned or Leased Goods. A consignor or lessor of goods may file a financing statement using the terms "consignor," "consignee," "lessor," "lessee" or the like instead of the terms specified in Section 9-402. The provisions of this Part shall apply as appropriate to such a financing statement but its filing shall not of itself be a factor in determining whether or not the consignment or lease is intended as security (Section 1-201(37)). However, if it is determined for other reasons that the consignment or lease is so intended, a security interest of the consignor or lessor which attaches to the consigned or leased goods is perfected by such filing.

Added in 1972.

PART 5

DEFAULT

Section 9-501. Default; Procedure When Security Agreement Covers Both Real and Personal Property.

(1) When a debtor is in default under a security agreement, a secured party has the rights and remedies provided in this Part and except as limited by subsection (3) those provided in the security agreement. He may reduce his claim to judgment, foreclose or otherwise enforce the security interest by any available judicial procedure. If the collateral is documents the secured party may proceed either as to the documents or as to the goods covered thereby. A secured party in possession has the rights, remedies and duties provided in Section 9-207. The rights and remedies referred to in this subsection are cumulative.

(2) After default, the debtor has the rights and remedies provided in this Part, those provided in the security agreement and those provided in Section 9-207.

(3) To the extent that they give rights to the debtor and impose duties on the secured party, the rules stated in the subsections referred to below may not be waived or varied except as provided with respect to compulsory disposition of collateral (subsection (3) of Section 9-504 and Section 9-505) and with respect to redemption of collateral (Section 9-506) but the parties may by agreement determine the standards by which the fulfillment of these rights and duties is to be measured if such standards are not manifestly unreasonable:

(a) subsection (2) of Section 9-502 and subsection (2) of Section 9-504 insofar as they require accounting for surplus proceeds of collateral;

(b) subsection (3) of Section 9-504 and subsection (1) of Section 9-505 which deal with disposition of collateral;

(c) subsection (2) of Section 9-505 which deals with acceptance of collateral as discharge of obligation;

(d) Section 9-506 which deals with redemption of collateral; and

(e) subsection (1) of Section 9-507 which deals with the secured party's liability for failure to comply with this Part.

(4) If the security agreement covers both real and personal property, the secured party may proceed under this Part as to the personal property or he may proceed as to both the real and the personal property in accordance with his rights and remedies in respect of the real property in which case the provisions of this Part do not apply.

(5) When a secured party has reduced his claim to judgment the lien of any levy which may be made upon his collateral by virtue of any execution based upon the judgment shall relate back to the date of the perfection of the security interest in such collateral. A judicial sale, pursuant to such execution, is a foreclosure of the security interest by judicial procedure within the meaning of this section, and the secured party may purchase at the sale and thereafter hold the collateral free of any other requirements of this Article.

Section 9-502. Collection Rights of Secured Party.

(1) When so agreed and in any event on default the secured party is entitled to notify an account debtor or the obligor on an instrument to make payment to him whether or not the assignor was theretofore making collections on the collateral, and also to take control of any proceeds to which he is entitled under Section 9-306.

(2) A secured party who by agreement is entitled to charge back uncollected collateral or otherwise to full or limited recourse against the debtor and who undertakes to collect from the account debtors or obligors must proceed in a commercially reasonable manner and may deduct his reasonable expenses of realization from the collections. If the security agreement secures an indebtedness, the secured party must account to the debtor for any surplus, and unless otherwise agreed, the debtor is liable for any deficiency. But, if the underlying transaction was a sale of accounts or chattel paper, the debtor is entitled to any surplus or is liable for any deficiency only if the security agreement so provides.

Section 9-503. Secured Party's Right to Take Possession After Default. Unless otherwise agreed a secured party has on default the right to take possession of the collateral. In taking possession a secured party may proceed without judicial process if this can be done without breach of the peace or may proceed by action. If the security agreement so provides the secured party may require the debtor to assemble the collateral and make it available to the secured party at a place to be designated by the secured party which is reasonably convenient to both parties. Without removal a secured party may render equipment unusable, and may dispose of collateral on the debtor's premises under Section 9-504.

Section 9-504. Secured Party's Right to Dispose of Collateral After Default; Effect of Disposition.

(1) A secured party after default may sell, lease or otherwise dispose of any or all of the collateral in its then condition or following any commercially reasonable preparation or processing. Any sale of goods is subject to the Article on Sales (Article 2). The proceeds of disposition shall be applied in the order following to

(a) the reasonable expenses of retaking, holding, preparing for sale or lease, selling, leasing and the like and, to the extent provided for in the agreement and not prohibited by law, the reasonable attorneys' fees and legal expenses incurred by the secured party;

(b) the satisfaction of indebtedness secured by the security interest under which the disposition is made;

(c) the satisfaction of indebtedness secured by any subordinate security interest in the collateral if written notification of demand therefor is received before distribution of the proceeds is completed. If requested by the secured party, the holder of a subordinate security interest must seasonably furnish reasonable proof of his interest, and unless he does so, the secured party need not comply with his demand.

(2) If the security interest secured an indebtedness, the secured party must account to the debtor for any surplus, and, unless otherwise agreed, the debtor is liable for any deficiency. But if the underlying transaction was a sale of accounts or chattel paper, the debtor is entitled to any surplus or is liable for any deficiency only if the security agreement so provides.

(3) Disposition of the collateral may be by public or private proceedings and may be made by way of one or more contracts. Sale or other disposition may be as a unit or in parcels and at any time and place and on any terms but every aspect of the disposition including the method, manner, time, place and terms must be commercially reasonable. Unless collateral is perishable or threatens to decline speedily in value or is of a type customarily sold on a recognized market, reasonable notification of the time and place of any public sale or reasonable notification of the time after which any private sale or other intended disposition is to be made shall be sent by the secured party to the debtor, if he has not signed after default a statement renouncing or modifying his right to notification of sale. In the case of consumer goods no other notification need be sent. In other cases notification shall be sent to any other secured party from whom the secured party has received (before sending his notification to the debtor or before the debtor's renunciation of his rights) written notice of a claim of an interest in the collateral. The secured party may buy at any public sale and if the collateral is of a type customarily sold in a recognized market or is of a type which is the subject of widely distributed standard price quotations he may buy at private sale.

(4) When collateral is disposed of by a secured party after default, the disposition transfers to a purchaser for value all of the debtor's rights therein, discharges the security interest under which it is made and any security interest or lien subordinate or lien subordinate thereto. The purchaser takes free of all such rights and interests even though the secured party fails to comply with the requirements of this Part or of any judicial proceedings.

(a) in the case of a public sale, if the purchaser has no knowledge of any defects in the sale and if he does not buy in collusion with the secured party, other bidders or the person conducting the sale; or

(b) in any other case, if the purchaser acts in good faith.

(5) A person who is liable to a secured party

Section 9-505. Compulsory Disposition of Collateral; Acceptance of the Collateral as Discharge of Obligation.

(1) If the debtor has paid sixty per cent of the cash price in the case of a purchase money security interest in consumer goods, and has not signed after default at statement renouncing or modifying his rights under this Part a secured party who has taken possession of collateral must dispose of it under Section 9-504 and if he fails to do so within ninety days after he takes possession the debtor at his option may recover in conversion or under Section 9-507(1) on secured party's liability.

(2) In any other case involving consumer goods or any other collateral a secured party in possession may, after default, propose to retain the collateral in satisfaction of the obligation. Written notice of such proposal shall be sent to the debtor if he has not signed after default a statement renouncing or modifying his rights under this subsection. In the case of consumer goods no other notice need be given. In other cases notice shall be sent to any other secured party from whom the secured party has received (before sending his notice to the debtor or before the debtor's renunciation of his rights) written notice of a claim of an interest in the collateral. If the secured party receives objection in writing from a person entitled to receive notification within twenty-one days after the notice was sent, the secured party must dispose of the collateral under Section 9-504. In the absence of such written objection the secured party may retain the collateral in satisfaction of the debtor's obligation.

Section 9-506. Debtor's Right to Redeem Collateral. At any time before the secured party has disposed of collateral or entered into a contract for its disposition under Section 9-504 or before the obligation has been discharged under Section 9-505(2) the debtor or any other secured party may unless otherwise agreed in writing after default redeem the collateral by tendering fulfillment of all obligations secured by the collateral as well as the expenses reasonably incurred by the secured party in retaking, holding and preparing the collateral for disposition, in arranging for the sale, and to the extent provided in the agreement and not prohibited by law, his reasonable attorneys' fees and legal expenses.

under a guaranty, indorsement, repurchase agreement or the like and who receives a transfer of collateral from the secured party or is subrogated to his rights has thereafter the rights and duties of the secured party. Such a transfer of collateral is not a sale or disposition of the collateral under this Article.

Section 9-507. Secured Party's Liability for Failure to Comply With This Part.

(1) If it is established that the secured party is not proceeding in accordance with the provisions of this Part disposition may be ordered or restrained on appropriate terms and conditions. If the disposition has occurred the debtor or any person entitled to notification or whose security interest has been made known to the secured party prior to the disposition has a right to recover from the secured party any loss caused by a failure to comply with the provisions of this Part. If the collateral is consumer goods, the debtor has a right to recover in any event an amount not less than the credit service charge plus ten per cent of the principal amount of the debt or the time price differential plus ten per cent of the cash price.

(2) The fact that a better price could have been obtained by a sale at a different time or in a different method from that selected by the secured party is not of itself sufficient to establish that the sale was not made in a commercially reasonable manner. If the secured party either sells the collateral in the usual manner in any recognized market therefor or if he sells at the price current in such market at the time of his sale or if he has otherwise sold in conformity with reasonable commercial practices among dealers in the type of property sold he has sold in a commercially reasonable manner. The principles stated in the two preceding sentences with respect to sales also apply as may be appropriate to other types of disposition. A disposition which has been approved in any judicial proceeding or by any bona fide creditors' committee or representative of creditors shall conclusively be deemed to be

commercially reasonable, but this sentence does not indicate that any such approval must be obtained in any case nor does it indicate that any disposition not so approved is not commercially reasonable.

GLOSSARY

Abandonment Applies to many situations. Abandonment of property is giving up dominion and control over it, with intention to relinquish all claims to it. Losing property is an involuntary act; abandonment is voluntary. When used with duty, the word *abandonment* is synonymous with *repudiation*.

Abatement of a nuisance An action to end any act detrimental to the public; e.g., suit to enjoin a plant from permitting the escape of noxious vapors.

Acceptance A statement by one party (called the offeree) that he is prepared to be bound to the contractual position stated in an offer. The acceptance is a second essential element to the meeting of the minds of the contracting parties. *See* Offer.

Acceptance* Under Article 3—Commercial Paper, this is the drawee's signed engagement to honor a draft as presented. It must be written on the draft and may consist of drawee's signature alone. It becomes operative when completed by delivery or notification.

Accessions Items of personal property that become incorporated into other items of personal property.

Accommodation party* In the law of commercial paper, any person who signs an instrument for the purpose of lending his name and his credit.

Accord and satisfaction An agreement between two persons—one of whom has a right of action against the other—that the latter should do or give, and the former accept, something in satisfaction of the right of action—something different from, and usually less than, what might legally be enforced.

Account* Any right to payment for goods sold or leased or for services rendered but not evidenced by an instrument or chattel paper. Under Article 4—Bank Deposits and Collections, *account* is any account with a bank and includes a checking, time, interest, or savings account.

Account debtor The person who is obligated on an account, chattel paper, contract right, or general intangible.

Accretion Gradual, imperceptible accumulation of land by natural causes, usually next to a stream or river.

Action ex contractu An action at law to recover damages for the breach of a duty arising out of contract. There are two types of causes of action: those arising out of contract, ex contractu, and those arising out of tort, ex delicto.

Action ex delicto An action at law to recover damages for the breach of a duty existing by reason of a general law. An action to recover damages for an injury caused by the negligent use of an automobile is an ex delicto action. Tort or wrong is the basis of the action. *See* Action ex contractu.

Adjudicate The exercise of judicial power by hearing, trying, and determining the claims of litigants before the court.

Administrative law The branch of public law dealing with the operation of the various agency boards and commissions of government.

Administrator A person to whom letters of administration have been issued by a probate court, giving such person authority to administer, manage, and close the estate of a deceased person.

Adverse possession Acquisition of legal title to another's land by being in continuous possession during a period prescribed in the statute. Possession must be actual, visible, known to the world, and with intent to claim title as owner, against the rights of the true owner. Claimant

*Terms followed by an asterisk are defined in the Uniform Commercial Code and have significance in connection with Code materials. They are often given a particular meaning in relation to the Code, and their definitions do not necessarily conform with meanings outside the framework of the Code.

usually must pay taxes and liens lawfully charged against the property. Cutting timber or grass from time to time on the land of another is not the kind of adverse possession that will confer title.

Advising bank* A bank that gives notification of the issuance of a credit by another bank.

Affidavit A voluntary statement of facts formally reduced to writing, sworn to, or affirmed before, some officer authorized to administer oaths. The officer is usually a notary public.

Affirmative action program Active recruitment and advancement of minority workers.

Affirmative defense A matter that constitutes opposition to the allegations of a complaint, which are assumed to be true.

A fortiori Latin words meaning "by a stronger reason." Often used in judicial opinions to say that since specific, proven facts lead to a certain conclusion, there are for this reason other facts that logically follow and strengthen the argument for the conclusion.

Agency coupled with an interest When an agent has possession or control over the property of his principal and has a right of action against interference by third parties, an agency with an interest has been created. An agent who advances freight for goods sent him by his principal has an interest in the goods.

Agency coupled with an obligation When an agent is owed money by his principal and the agency relationship is created to facilitate the agent collecting this money from a third party, an agency coupled with an obligation is created. This type of agency cannot be terminated by the actions of the principal, but it may be terminated by operation of law.

Agent A person authorized to act for another (principal). The term may apply to a person in the service of another; but in the strict sense, an agent is one who stands in place of his principal. A works for B as a gardener and is thus a servant, but he may be an agent. If A sells goods for B, he becomes more than a servant. He acts in the place of B.

Agreement* The bargain of the parties in fact as found in their language or by implication from other circumstances, including course of dealing or usage of trade or course of performance as provided in the Uniform Commerical Code.

Amicus curiae A friend of the court who participates in litigation, usually on appeal, though not a party to the lawsuit.

Annuity A sum of money paid yearly to a person during his lifetime. The sum arises out of a contract by which the recipient or another had previously deposited sums in whole or in part with the grantor—the grantor to return a designated portion of the principal and interest in periodic payments when the beneficiary attains a designated age.

Appellant The party who takes an appeal from one court or jurisdiction to another.

Appellee The party in a cause against whom an appeal is taken.

A priori A generalization resting on presuppositions, not upon proven facts.

Arbitration The submission for determination of disputed matter to private, unofficial persons selected in a manner provided by law or agreement.

Architect's certificate A formal statement signed by an architect that a contractor has performed under his contract and is entitled to be paid. The construction contract provides when and how such certificates shall be issued.

Artisan's lien One who has expended labor upon, or added to, another's property is entitled to possession of the property as security until reinbursed for the value of labor or material. A repairs B's watch. A may keep the watch in his possession until B pays for the repairs.

Assignee An assign or assignee is one to whom an assignment has been made.

Assignment The transfer by one person to another of a right that usually arises out of a contract. Such rights are called *choses in action*. A sells and assigns to C his contract right to purchase B's house. A is an assignor. C is an assignee. The transfer is an assignment.

Assignment* A transfer of the "contract" or of "all my rights under the contract" or an assignment in similar general terms is an assignment of rights. Unless the language or the circumstances (as in an assignment for security) indicate the contrary, it is a delegation of performance by the duties of the assignor, and its acceptance by the assignee constitutes a promise by him to perform those duties. This promise is enforceable by either the assignor or the other party to the original contract.

Assignment for the benefit of creditors A, a debtor, has many creditors. An assignment of his property to X, a third party, with directions to make distribution of his property to his creditors, is called an assignment for the benefit of creditors. *See* Composition of creditors.

Assignor One who makes an assignment.

Assumption of the risk Negligence doctrine that bars the recovery of damages by an injured party on the ground that such party acted with actual or constructive knowledge of the hazard causing the injury.

Attachment A legal proceeding accompanying an action in court by which a plaintiff may acquire a lien on a defendant's property as a security for the payment of any judgment that the plaintiff may recover. It is provisional and independent of the court action and is usually provided for by statute. A sues B. Before judgment, A attaches B's automobile, in order to make sure of the payment of any judgment that A may secure.

Attorney at law A person to whom the state grants a license to practice law.

Attorney in fact A person acting for another under a grant of special power created by an instrument in writing. B, in writing, grants special power A to execute and deliver for B a conveyance of B's land to X.

Bad faith "Actual intent" to mislead or deceive another. It does not mean misleading by an honest, inadvertent, or careless misstatment.

Bail (verb) To set at liberty an arrested or imprisoned person after that person or at least two others have given security to the state that the accused will appear at the proper time and place for trial.

Bailee A person into whose possession personal property is delivered.

Bailee* The person who, by a warehouse receipt, bill of lading, or other document of title, acknowledges possession of goods and contracts to deliver it.

Bailment Delivery of personal property to another for a special purpose. Delivery is made under a contract, either expressed or implied, that upon the completion of the special purpose, the property shall be redelivered to the bailor or placed at his disposal. A loans B his truck. A places his watch with B for repair. A places his furniture in B's warehouse. A places his securities in B Bank's safety deposit vault. In each case, A is a bailor and B is a bailee

Bailor One who delivers personal property into the possession of another.

Banking day* Under Article 4—Bank Deposits and Collections, this is the part of any day on which a bank is open to the public for carrying on substantially all of its banking functions.

Bankruptcy The law which provides a process for protecting creditors and debtors when a debtor is unable to pay his obligations.

Bearer* The person in possession of an instrument, document of title, or security payable to bearer or indorsed in blank.

Bearer form* A security is in bearer form when it runs to bearer according to its terms and not by reason of any indorsement.

Beneficiary A person (not a promisee) for whose benefit a trust, an insurance policy, a will, or a contract promise is made.

Beneficiary* A person who is entitled under a letter of credit to draw or demand payment.

Bequest In a will, a gift of personal property.

Bid An offering of money in exchange for property placed for sale. At an ordinary auction sale, a bid is an offer to purchase. It may be withdrawn before acceptance is indicated by the fall of the hammer.

Bilateral contract One containing mutual promises, with each party being both a promisor and a promisee.

Bilateral mistake A situation in which parties to a contract reach a bargain on the basis of an incorrect assumption common to each party.

Bill of lading* A document evidencing the receipt of goods for shipment, issued by a person engaged in the business of transporting or forwarding goods. Includes an airbill, a document that serves air transportation as a bill of lading serves marine or rail transportation. It includes an air consignment note or air waybill.

Bill of particulars In legal practice, a written statement that one party to a lawsuit gives to another, describing in detail the elements upon which the claim of the first party is based.

Bill of sale Written evidence that the title to personal property has been transferred from one person to another. It must contain words of transfer and be more than a receipt.

Blue-sky laws Popular name for acts providing for the regulation and supervision of investment securities.

Bona fide purchaser* A purchaser of a security for value, in good faith, and without notice of any adverse claim, who takes delivery of a security in bearer form or in registered form issued to him or indorsed to him or in blank.

Bond A promise under seal to pay money. The term generally designates the promise made by a corporation, either public or private, to pay money to bearer; e.g., U.S. government bonds or Illinois Central Railroad bonds. Also, an obligation by which one person promises to answer for the debt or default of another—a surety bond.

Breach of the peace* In the law of secured transactions, this occurrence invalidates the creditor's legal right to take possession of the collateral without the assistance of a court. This event occurs whenever the possession by the creditor is accompanied by violence, deception, or an objection by the debtor.

Broker A person employed to make contracts with third persons on behalf of his principal. The contracts involve trade, commerce, buying and selling for a fee (called brokerage or commission).

Broker* A person engaged full or part time in the business of buying and selling securities, who in the transaction concerned acts for, or buys a security from, or sells a security to, a customer.

Bulk transfer* Transfer made outside the ordinary course of the transferor's business but involving a major part of the materials, supplies, merchandise, or other inventory of an enterprise subject to Article 6.

Burden of proof This term has two distinctive meanings.

One meaning is used to identify the party that has the burden of coming forward with evidence of a particular fact. The second meaning is used to identify the party with the burden of persuasion. This second meaning is used in litigation to determine whether one party or another wins regarding an issue in dispute.

Business judgment rule A legal doctrine requiring the officers and directors of corporations to act in good faith as if they were dealing with their own property interests.

Buyer* A person who buys or contracts to buy goods.

Buyer in ordinary course of business* A person who, in good faith and without knowledge that the sale to him is in violation of the ownership rights or security interest of a third party in the goods, buys in ordinary course from a person in the business of selling goods of that kind. Does not include a pawnbroker. "Buying" may be for cash or by exchange of other property or on secured or unsecured credit. Includes receiving goods or documents of title under a preexisting contract for sale but does not include a transfer in bulk or as security for, or in total or partial satisfaction of, a money debt.

Bylaws Rules for government of a corporation or other organization. Adopted by members or the board of directors, these rules must not be contrary to the law of the land. They affect the rights and duties of the members of the corporation or organization, only, not third persons.

Call An assessment upon a subscriber for partial or full payment on shares of unpaid stock of a corporation. Also, the power of a corporation to make an assessment, notice of an assessment, or the time when the assessment is to be paid.

Cancellation* Either party puts an end to the contract because of breach by the other. Its effect is the same as that of "termination," except that the canceling party also retains any remedy for breach of the whole contract or any unperformed balance.

Capital The net assets of an individual enterprise, partnership, joint stock company, corporation, or business institution, including not only the original investment but also all gains and profits realized from the continued conduct of the business.

Carrier A natural person or a corporation who receives goods under a contract to transport for a consideration from one place to another. A railroad, truckline, busline, airline.

Cashier's check A bill of exchange drawn by the cashier of a bank, for the bank, upon the bank. After the check is delivered or issued to the payee or holder, the drawer bank cannot put a "stop order" against itself. By delivery of the check, the drawer bank has accepted and thus becomes the primary obligor.

Cause of action When one's legal rights have been invaded either by a breach of a contract or by a breach of a legal duty toward one's person or property, a cause of action has been created.

Caveat Literally, "let him beware." It is used generally to mean a warning.

Caveat emptor An old idea at common law—"let the buyer beware." When a vendor sells goods without an express warranty as to their quality and capacity for a particular use and purpose, the buyer must take the risk of loss due to all defects in the goods.

Caveat venditor "Let the seller beware." Unless the seller, by express language, disclaims any responsibility, he shall be liable to the buyer if the goods delivered are different in kind, quality, use, and purpose from those described in the contract of sale.

Cease and desist order An administrative agency order directing a party to refrain from doing a specified act.

Certiorari An order issuing out of an appellate court to a lower court, at the request of an appellant, directing that the record of a case pending in the lower court be transmitted to the upper court for review.

Cestui que trust A person who is the real or beneficial owner of property held in trust. The trustee holds the legal title to the property for the benefit of the cestui que trust.

Chancery Court of equity.

Charter Referring to a private corporation, *charter* includes the contract between the created corporation and the state, the act creating the corporation, and the articles of association granted to the corporation by authority of the legislative act. Referring to municipal corporations, *charter* does not mean a contract between the legislature and the city created. A city charter is a delegation of powers by a state legislature to the governing body of the city. The term includes the creative act, the powers enumerated, and the organization authorized.

Chattel A very broad term derived from the word *cattle*. Includes every kind of property that is not real property. Movable properties, such as horses, automobiles, choses in action, stock certificates, bills of lading, and all "good wares, and merchandise" are chattels personal. Chattels real concern real property such as a lease for years, in which case the lessee owns a chattel real.

Chattel paper* A writing or writings that evidence both a monetary obligation and a security interest in, or a lease of, specific goods. When a transaction is evidenced both by such a security agreement or a lease and by an instrument or a series of instruments, the group of writings taken together constitutes chattel paper.

Chose in action The "right" one person has to recover money or property from another by a judicial proceeding. The right arises out of contract, claims for money, debts, and rights against property. Notes, drafts, stock certificates, bills of lading, warehouse receipts, and insurance policies are illustrations of choses in action. They are called tangible choses. Book accounts, simple debts, and obligations not evidenced by formal writing are called intangible choses. Choses in action are transferred by assignment.

Circumstantial evidence If, from certain facts and circumstances, according to the experience of mankind, an ordinary, intelligent person may infer that other connected facts and circumstances must necessarily exist, the latter facts and circumstances are considered proven by circumstantial evidence. Proof of fact A from which fact B may be inferred is proof of fact B by circumstantial evidence.

Civil action A proceeding in a law court or a suit in equity by one person against another for the enforcement or protection of a private right or the prevention of a wrong. It includes actions on contract, ex delicto, and all suits in equity. Civil action is in contradistinction to criminal action, in which the state prosecutes a person for breach of a duty.

Civil law The area of law dealing with rights and duties of private parties as individual entities. To be distinguished from criminal law. Sometimes the phrase refers to the European system of codified law.

Claim A creditor's right to payment in a bankruptcy case.

Class-action suit A legal proceeding whereby one or more persons represent in litigation a larger group of people who might have a claim similar to the representative(s).

Clearinghouse* Under Article 4—Bank Deposits and Collections, clearinghouse is any association of banks or other payors regularly clearing items.

Cloud on title Some evidence of record that shows a third person has some prima facie interest in another's property.

Code A collection or compilation of the statutes passed by the legislative body of a state. Often annotated with citations of cases decided by the state supreme courts. These decisions construe the statutes. Examples: Oregon Compiled Laws Annotated, United States Code Annotated.

Codicil An addition to, or a change in, an executed last will and testament. It is a part of the original will and must be executed with the same formality as the original will.

Coinsurer A term in a fire insurance policy that requires the insured to bear a certain portion of the loss when he fails to carry complete coverage. For example, unless the insured carries insurance that totals 80 percent of the value of the property, the insurer shall be liable for only that portion of the loss that the total insurance carried bears to 80 percent of the value of the property.

Collateral With reference to debts or other obligations, *collateral* means security placed with a creditor to assure the performance of the obligator. If the obligator performs, the collateral is returend by the creditor. A owes B $1,000. To secure the payment, A places with B a $500 certificate of stock in X company. The $500 certificate is called collateral security.

Collateral* The property subject to a security interest. Includes accounts, contract rights, and chattel paper that have been sold.

Collecting bank* Under Article 4—Bank Deposits and Collections, any bank handling the item for collateral except the payor bank.

Collective bargaining The process of good-faith negotiation between employer's and employees' representatives, concerning issues of mutual interest.

Commerce clause Article I, Section 8, Clause 3 of the Constitution of the United States, granting Congress the authority to regulate commerce with foreign nations and among the states.

Commercial unit* A unit of goods that, by commercial usage, is a single whole for purposes of sale. Its division would materially impair its character or value on the market or in use. A commercial unit may be a single article (as a machine) or a set of articles (as a suite of furniture or an assortment of sizes) or a quantity (as a bale, gross, or carload) or any other unit treated in use or in the relevant market as a single whole.

Commission The sum of money, interest, brokerage, compensation, or allowance given to a factor or broker for carrying on the business of his principal.

Commission merchant An agent or factor employed to sell "goods, wares, and merchandise" consigned or delivered to him by his principal.

Common carrier One who is engaged in the business of transporting personal property from one place to another for compensation. Such person is bound to carry for all who tender their goods and the price for transportation. A common carrier operates as a public utility and is subject to state and federal regulations.

Common law That body of law deriving from judicial decisions, as opposed to legislatively enacted statutes and administrative regulations.

Common stock In the law of corporations, the type of ownership interest that must exist.

Community property All property acquired after marriage by husband and wife, other than separate property acquired by devise, bequest, or from the proceeds of noncommunity property. Community property is a concept of property ownership by husband and wife inherited from the civil law. The husband and wife are somewhat like partners in their ownership of property acquired during marriage.

Comparative negligence A modification to the defense of contributory negligence. Under this doctrine, a plaintiff's negligence is compared to that of a defendant.

The plaintiff's right to recover against the defendant is reduced by the percentage of the plaintiff's negligence. *See* Contributory negligence.

Compensatory damages *See* Damages.

Complaint The first paper a plaintiff files in a court in a lawsuit. It is called a pleading. It is a statement of the facts upon which the plaintiff rests his cause of action.

Composition of creditors An agreement among creditors and their debtors by which the creditors will take a lesser amount in complete satisfaction of the total debt. A owes B and C $500 each. A agrees to pay B and C $250 each in complete satisfaction of the $500 due each. B and C agree to take $250 in satisfaction.

Compromise An agreement between two or more persons, usually opposing parties in a lawsuit, to settle the matters of the controversy without further resort to hostile litigation. An adjustment of issues in dispute by mutual concessions before resorting to a lawsuit.

Condemnation proceedings An action or proceeding in court authorized by legislation (federal or state) for the purpose of taking private property for public use. It is the exercise by the judiciary of the sovereign power of eminent domain.

Condition A clause in a contract, either expressed or implied, that has the effect of investing or divesting the legal rights and duties of the parties to the contract. In a deed, a condition is a qualification or restriction providing for the happening or nonhappening of events that, on occurrence, will destroy, commence, or enlarge an estate. "A grants Blackacre to B, so long as said land shall be used for church purposes." If it ceases to be used for church purposes, the title to Blackacre will revert to the grantor.

Condition precedent A clause in a contract providing that immediate rights and duties shall vest only upon the happening of some event. Securing an architect's certificate by a contractor before the contractor is entitled to payment is a condition precedent. A condition is not a promise; hence, its breach will not give rise to a cause of action for damages. A breach of a condition is the basis for a defense. If the contractor sues the owner without securing the architect's certificate, the owner has a defense.

Conditions concurrent Conditions concurrent are mutually dependent and must be performed at the same time by the parties to the contract. Payment of money and delivery of goods in a cash sale are conditions concurrent. Failure to perform by one party permits a cause of action upon tender by the other party. If S refuses to deliver goods in a cash sale, B, upon tender but not delivery of the money, places S in default and thus may sue S. B does not part with his money without getting the goods. If S sued B, B would have a defense.

Condition subsequent A clause in a contract providing for the happening of an event that divests legal rights and duties. A clause in a fire insurance policy providing that the policy shall be null and void if combustible material is stored within 10 feet of the building is a condition subsequent. If a fire occurs and combustible material was within 10 feet of the building, the insurance company is excused from its duty to pay for the loss.

Confirming bank A bank that engages either that it will itself honor a credit already issued by another bank or that such a credit will be honored by the issuer or a third bank.

Conforming* Goods or conduct, including any part of a performance, are "conforming" or conform to the contract when they are in accordance with the obligations under contract.

Conglomerate merger Merging of companies that have neither the relationship of competitors nor that of supplier and customer.

Consequential damages Those damages, beyond the compensatory damages, which arise from special circumstances causing special damages that are not clearly foreseeable. However, before becoming liable for these damages, the breaching party must be aware of the special circumstances that may cause consequential damages.

Consideration An essential element in the creation of contract obligation. A detriment to the promisee and a benefit to the promisor. One promise is consideration for another promise. They create a bilateral contract. An act is consideration for a promise. This creates a unilateral contract. Performance of the act asked for by the promisee is a legal detriment to the promisee and a benefit to the promisor.

Consignee A person to whom a shipper usually directs a carrier to deliver goods; generally the buyer of goods and called a consignee on a bill of lading.

Consignee* The person named in a bill to whom or to whose order the bill promises delivery.

Consignment The delivery, sending, or transferring of property, "goods, wares, and merchandise" into the possession of another, usually for the purpose of sale. Consignment may be a bailment or an agency for sale.

Consignor The shipper who delivers freight to a carrier for shipment and who directs the bill of lading to be executed by the carrier. May be the consignor-consignee if the bill of lading is made to his own order.

Consignor* The person named in a bill as the person from whom the goods have been received for shipment.

Consolidation Two corporations are consolidated when both corporations are dissolved and a new one created, the new one taking over the assets of the dissolved corporations.

Conspicuous* A term or clause is conspicuous when it is written so that a reasonable person against whom it is to operate ought to have noticed it. A printed heading in capitals (as NONNEGOTIABLE BILL OF LADING) is conspicuous. Language in the body of a form is "conspicuous" if it is in larger or other contrasting type or color. But in a telegram, any stated term is "conspicuous." Whether a term or clause is "conspicuous" or not is for decision by the court.

Conspiracy A combination or agreement between two or more persons for the commission of a criminal act.

Constructive delivery Although physical delivery of personal property has not occurred, the conduct of the parties may imply that possession and title has passed between them. S sells large and bulky goods to B. Title and possession may pass by the act and conduct of the parties.

Consumer A person who does not intend to resell an item of property but rather intends to use it for a personal, noncommercial purpose.

Consumer goods* Goods that are used or bought for use primarily for personal, family, or household purposes.

Contingent fee An arrangement whereby an attorney is compensated for services in a lawsuit according to an agreed percentage of the amount of money recovered.

Contract An agreement involving one or more promises that courts will enforce or for the breach of which courts provide a remedy.

Contract right* Under a contract, any right to payment not yet earned by performance and not evidenced by an instrument or chattel paper.

Contributory negligence In a negligence suit, failure of the plaintiff to use reasonable care.

Conversion A legal theory used to create a "sale" of property to a person who interferes with the owner's use of the property to the extent that damages must be paid to compensate the owner for the loss of property.

Conversion* Under Article 3—Commercial Paper, an instrument is converted when a drawee to whom it is delivered for acceptance refuses to return it on demand; or any person to whom it is delivered for payment refuses on demand either to pay or to return it; or it is paid on a forged indorsement.

Conveyance A formal written instrument, usually called a deed, by which the title or other interests in land (real property) are transferred from one person to another. The word expresses also the fact that the title to real property has been transferred from one person to another.

Corporation A collection of individuals created by statute as a legal person, vested with powers and capacity to contract, own, control, convey property, and transact business within the limits of the powers granted.

Corporation de facto If persons have attempted in good faith to organize a corporation under a valid law (statute) and have failed in some minor particular but have thereafter exercised corporate powers, they are a corporation de facto. Failure to notarize incorporators' signatures on applications for charter is an illustration of non-compliance with statutory requirements.

Corporation de jure A corporation that has been formed by complying with the mandatory requirements of the law authorizing such a corporation.

Corporeal Physical; perceptible by the senses. Automobiles, grain, fruit, and horses are corporeal and tangible and are called chattels. *Corporeal* is used in contradistinction to *incorporeal* or *intangible*. A chose in action (such as a check) is corporeal and tangible, or a chose in action may be a simple debt, incorporeal and intangible.

Costs In litigation, an allowance authorized by statute to a party for expenses incurred in prosecuting or defending a lawsuit. The word *costs*, unless specifically designated by statute or contract, does not include attorney's fees.

Counterclaims By cross-action, the defendant claims that he is entitled to recover from the plaintiff. Claim must arise out of the same transaction set forth in the plaintiff's complaint and be connected with the same subject matter. S sues B for the purchase price. B counterclaims that the goods were defective and that he thereby suffered damages.

Course of dealing A sequence of previous conduct between the parties to a particular transaction. The conduct is fairly to be regarded as establishing a common basis of understanding for interpreting their expressions and other conduct.

Course of performance A term used to give meaning to a contract based on the parties having had a history of dealings or an agreement that requires repeated performances.

Covenant A promise in writing under seal. It is often used as a substitute for the word *contract*. There are covenants (promises) in deeds, leases, mortgages, and other instruments under seal. The word is used sometimes to name promises in unsealed instruments such as insurance policies.

Cover* After a breach by a seller, the buyer may "cover" by making in good faith and without unreasonable delay any reasonable purchase of, or contract to purchase, goods in substitution for those due from the seller.

Credit* ("Letter of credit") An engagement by a bank or other person made at the request of a customer and of a kind within the scope of Article 5—Letters of Credit, that the issuer will honor drafts or other demands for payment upon compliance with the conditions specified in the credit. A credit may be either revocable or irrevocable. The engagement may be either an agreement to honor or a statement that the bank or other person is authorized to honor.

Creditor* Includes a general creditor, a secured creditor, a lien creditor, and any representative of creditors, including an assignee for the benefit of creditors, a trustee in bankruptcy, a receiver in equity, and an executor or administrator of an insolvent debtor's or assignor's estate.

Creditor-beneficiary One who, for a consideration, promises to discharge another's duty to a third party. A owes C $100. B, for a consideration, promises A to pay A's debt to C. B is a creditor beneficiary.

Cumulative voting In voting for directors, a stockholder may cast as many votes as he has shares of stock multiplied by the number to be elected. His votes may be all for one candidate or distributed among as many candidates as there are offices to be filled.

Cure* An opportunity for the seller of defective goods to correct the defect and thereby not be held to have breached the sales contract.

Custodian bank* A bank or trust company that acts as custodian for a clearing corporation. It must be supervised and examined by the appropriate state or federal authority.

Custody (personal property) The words *custody* and *possession* are not synonymous. *Custody* means in charge of, to keep and care for under the direction of the true owner, without any interest therein adverse to the true owner. A servant is in custody of his master's goods. *See* Possession.

Customer* Under Article 4—Bank Deposits and Collections, a customer is any person having an account with a bank or for whom a bank has agreed to collect items. It includes a bank carrying an account with another bank. As used in Letters of Credit, a customer is a buyer or other person who causes an issuer to issue a credit. The term also includes a bank that procures insurance or confirmation on behalf of that bank's customer.

Damages A sum of money the court imposes upon a defendant as compensation for the plaintiff because the defendant has injured the plaintiff by breach of a legal duty.

d.b.a. "Doing business as." A person who conducts his business under an assumed name is designated "John Doe d.b.a. Excelsior Co."

Debenture A corporate obligation sold as an investment. Similar to a corporate bond but not secured by a trust deed. It is not like corporate stock.

Debtor* The person who owes payment or other performance of the obligation secured, whether or not he owns, or has rights in, the collateral. Includes the seller of accounts, contract rights, or chattel paper. When the debtor and the owner of the collateral are not the same person, *debtor* means the owner of the collateral in any provision of the Article dealing with the obligation and may include both if the context so requires.

Deceit Conduct in a business transaction by which one person, through fraudulent representations, misleads another who has a right to rely on such representations as the truth or who, by reason of an unequal station in life, has no means of detecting such fraud.

Declaratory judgment A determination by a court on a question of law, the court simply declaring the rights of the parties but not ordering anything to be done.

Decree The judgment of the chancellor (judge) in a suit in equity. Like a judgment at law, it is the determination of the rights between the parties and is in the form of an order that requires the decree to be carried out. An order that a contract be specifically enforced is an example of a decree.

Deed A written instrument in a special form, signed, sealed, delivered, and used to pass the legal title of real property from one person to another. (*See* Conveyance.) In order that the public may know about the title to real property, deeds are recorded in the Deed Record office of the county where the land is situated.

Deed of trust An instrument by which title to real property is conveyed to a trustee to hold as security for the holder of notes or bonds. It is like a mortgage, except the security title is held by a person other than the mortgagee-creditor. Most corporate bonds are secured by a deed of trust.

De facto Arising out of, or founded upon, fact, although merely apparent or colorable. A de facto officer is one who assumes to be an officer under some color of right, acts as an officer, but in point of law is not a real officer. *See* Corporation de facto.

Defendant A person who has been sued in a court of law; the person who answers the plaintiff's complaint. The word is applied to the defending party in civil actions. In criminal actions, the defending party is referred to as the accused.

Deficiency judgment If, upon the foreclosure of a mortgage, the mortgaged property does not sell for an amount sufficient to pay the mortgage indebtedness, the difference is called a deficiency and is chargeable to the mortgagor or to any person who has purchased the property and assumed and agreed to pay the mortgage. M borrows $10,000 from B and as security gives a mortgage on Blackacre. At maturity, M does not pay the debt. B forecloses, and at public sale Blackacre sells for $8,000. There is a deficiency of $2,000, chargeable against M. If M had sold Blackacre to C and C had assumed and agreed to pay the mortgage, he would also be liable for the deficiency.

Defraud To deprive one of some right by deceitful means. To cheat; to withhold wrongfully that which belongs to another. Conveying one's property for the purpose of avoiding payment of debts is a transfer to "hinder, delay, or defraud creditors."

Del credere agency When an agent, factor, or broker guarantees to his principal the payment of a debt due from a buyer of goods, that agent, factor, or broker is operating under a del credere commission or agency.

Delivery A voluntary transfer of the possession of property, actual or constructive, from one person to another, with the intention that title vests in the transferee. In the law of sales, delivery contemplates the absolute giving up of control and dominion over the property by the vendor, and the assumption of the same by the vendee.

Delivery* With respect to instruments, documents of title, chattel paper, or securities, delivery means voluntary transfer of possession.

Delivery order* A written order to deliver goods directed to a warehouseman, carrier, or other person who, in the ordinary course of business, issues warehouse receipts or bills of lading.

Demand A request by a party entitled, under a claim of right, to the performance of a particular act. In order to bind an indorser on a negotiable instrument, the holder must first make a demand on the primary party, who must dishonor the instrument. Demand notes mean "due when demanded." The word *demand* is also used to mean a claim or legal obligation.

Demurrage Demurrage is a sum provided for in a contract of shipment, to be paid for the delay or detention of vessels or railroad cars beyond the time agreed upon for loading or unloading.

Demurrer A common law procedural method by which the defendant admits all the facts alleged in the plaintiff's complaint but denies that such facts state a cause of action. It raises a question of law on the facts, which must be decided by the court.

Dependent covenants (promises) In contracts, covenants are either concurrent or mutual, dependent or independent. Dependent covenants mean the performance of one promise must occur before the performance of the other promise. In a cash sale, the buyer must pay the money before the seller is under a duty to deliver the goods.

Depositary bank* Under Article 4—Bank Deposits and Collections, this means the first bank to which an item is transferred for collection, even though it is also the payor bank.

Descent The transfer of the title of property to the heirs upon the death of the ancestor; heredity succession. If a person dies without making a will, his property will "descend" according to the Statute of Descent of the state wherein the property is located.

Devise A gift, usually of real property, by a last will and testament.

Devisee The person who receives title to real property by will.

Dictum (dicta—plural) The written opinion of a judge, expressing an idea, argument, or rule that is not essential for the determination of the issues. It lacks the force of a decision in a judgment.

Directed verdict If it is apparent to reasonable men and the court that the plaintiff, by his evidence, has not made out his case, the court may instruct the jury to bring in a verdict for the defendant. If, however, different inferences may be drawn from the evidence by reasonable men, then the court cannot direct a verdict.

Discharge The word has many meanings. An employee, upon being released from employment, is discharged. A guardian or trustee, upon termination of his trust, is discharged by the court. A debtor released from his debts is discharged in bankruptcy. A person who is released from any legal obligation is discharged.

Discovery The disclosure by one party of facts, titles, documents, and other things in his knowledge of possession and necessary to the party seeking the discovery as a part of a cause of action pending.

Dishonor A negotiable instrument is dishonored when it is presented for acceptance or payment but acceptance or payment is refused or cannot be obtained.

Dissolution In the law of partnerships, this event occurs any time there is a change in the partners, either by adding a new partner or by having a preëxisting partner die, retire, or otherwise leave.

Distress for rent The taking of personal property of a tenant in payment of rent on real estate.

Divestiture The antitrust remedy that forces a company to get rid of assets acquired through illegal mergers or monopolistic practices.

Dividend A stockholder's pro rata share in the profits of a corporation. Dividends are declared by the board of directors of a corporation. They are paid in cash, script, property, and stock.

Docket A book containing a brief summary of all acts done in court in the conduct of each case.

Documentary collateral* In the law of secured transactions, this category of collateral consists of documents of title, chattel paper, and instruments.

Documentary draft* Under Article 4—Bank Deposits and Collections, this means any negotiable or nonnegotiable draft with accompanying documents, securities, or other papers to be delivered against honor of the draft. Also called a "documentary demand for payment" (Article 5—Letters of Credit). Honoring is conditioned upon the presentation of a document or documents. "Document" means any paper, including document of title, security, invoice, certificate, notice of default, and the like.

Document of title* Includes bill of lading, dock warrant, dock receipt, warehouse receipt, or order for the delivery of goods, and any other document that in the regular course of business or financing is treated as adequately evidencing that the person in possession of it is entitled to receive, hold, and dispose of the document and the goods it covers. To be a document of title, a document must purport to be issued by, or addressed to, a bailee and purport to cover goods in the bailee's possession that are either identified or are fungible portions of an identified mass.

Domicile The place a person intends as his fixed and permanent home and establishment and to which, if he is absent, he intends to return. A person can have but one domicile. The old one continues until the acquisition of a new one. One can have more than one residence at a time, but only one domicile. The word is not synonymous with *residence*.

Dominion Applied to the delivery of property by one person to another, *dominion* means all control over the possession and ownership of the property being separated from the transferor or donor and endowed upon the transferee or donee. *See* Gift.

Donee Recipient of a gift.

Donee-beneficiary If a promisee is under no duty to a third party, but for a consideration secures a promise from a promisor for the purpose of making a gift to a third party, then the third party is a donee-beneficiary. A, promisee for a premium paid, secures a promise from the insurance company, the promisor, to pay A's wife $10,000 upon A's death. A's wife is a donee-beneficiary.

Donor One that gives, donates, or presents.

Dormant partner A partner who is not known to third persons but is entitled to share in the profits and is subject to the losses. Since credit is not extended upon the strength of the dormant partner's name, he may withdraw without notice and not be subject to debts contracted after his withdrawal.

Double jeopardy A constitutional doctrine that prohibits an individual from being prosecuted twice in the same tribunal for the same criminal offense.

Due process Fundamental fairness. Applied to judicial proceedings, it includes adequate notice of a hearing and an opportunity to appear and defend in an orderly tribunal.

Duress (of person) A threat of bodily injury, criminal prosecution, or imprisonment of a contracting party or his near relative to such extent that the threatened party is unable to exercise free will at the time of entering into or discharging a legal obligation.

Duress (of property) Seizing by force or withholding goods by one not entitled, and such person's demanding something as a condition for the release of the goods.

Duty (in law) A legal obligation imposed by general law or voluntarily imposed by the creation of a binding promise. For every legal duty there is a corresponding legal right. By general law, A is under a legal duty not to injure B's person or property. B has a right that A not injure his person or property. X may voluntarily create a duty in himself to Y by a promise to sell Y a horse for $100. If Y accepts, X is under a legal duty to perform his promise. *See* Right.

Earnest money A term used to describe money that one contracting party gives to another at the time of entering into the contract in order to "bind the bargain" and which will be forfeited by the donor if he fails to carry out the contract. Generally, in real estate contracts such money is used as part payment of the purchase price.

Easement An easement is an interest in land—a right that one person has to some profit, benefit, or use in or over the land of another. Such right is created by a deed, or it may be acquired by prescription (the continued use of another's land for a statutory period).

Ejectment An action to recover the possession of real property. It is now generally defined by statute and is a statutory action. *See* Forcible entry and detainer.

Ejusdem generis "Of the same class." General words taking their meaning from specific words which precede the general words. General words have the same meaning as specific words mentioned.

Election A concept applicable in agency relationships when the principal is undisclosed. The third party may elect to hold either the agent or the previously undisclosed principal liable. By electing to hold one party liable, the third party has chosen not to seek a recovery against the other party.

Embezzlement The fraudulent appropriation by one person, acting in a fiduciary capacity, of the money or property of another. *See* Conversion.

Eminent domain The right that resides in the United States, state, county, city, school, or other public body to take private property for public use upon payment of just compensation.

Employment-at-will A doctrine stating that an employee who has no specific agreement as to the length of his employment may be discharged at any time without any reason being given by the employer. This doctrine has been modified in many states in recent years.

Encumbrance A burden on either the title to land or thing or upon the land or thing itself. A mortgage or other lien is an encumbrance upon the title. A right-of-way over the land is an encumbrance upon the land and affects its physical condition.

Enjoin To require performance or abstention from some act through issuance of an injunction.

Entity "In being" or "existing." The artificial person created when a corporation is organized is "in being" or "existing" for legal purposes, thus an entity. It is separate from the stockholders. The estate of a deceased person while in administration is an entity. A partnership for many legal purposes is an entity.

Equal protection A principle of the Fifth and Fourteenth Amendments to the Constitution, ensuring that individuals under like circumstances shall be accorded the same benefits and burdens under the law of the sovereign.

Equipment* Goods that are used or bought for use primarily in business (including farming or a profession) or by a debtor who is a nonprofit organization or a governmental subdivision or agency; or goods not included in the definitions of inventory, farm products, or consumer goods.

Equitable action In Anglo-American law, there have developed two types of courts and procedures for the administration of justice: law courts and equity courts. Law courts give as a remedy money damages only, whereas equity courts give the plaintiff what he bargains for. A suit for specific performance of a contract is an equitable action. In many states these two courts are now merged.

Equitable conversion An equitable principle that, for certain purposes, permits real property to be converted into personalty. Thus, real property owned by a partnership is, for the purpose of the partnership, personal property because to ascertain a partner's interest, the real property must be reduced to cash. This is an application of the equitable maxim, "Equity considers that done which ought to be done."

Equitable estoppel A legal theory used to prevent a party to an oral contract that has been partially performed from asserting the defense of the statute of frauds. *See* Part performance.

Equitable mortgage A written agreement to make certain property security for a debt, and upon the faith of which the parties have acted in making advances, loans, and thus creating a debt. Example: an improperly executed mortgage, one without seal where a seal is required. An absolute deed made to the mortgagee and intended for security only is an equitable mortgage.

Equity Because the law courts in early English law did not always give an adequate remedy, an aggrieved party sought redress from the king. Since this appeal was to the king's conscience, he referred the case to his spiritual adviser, the chancellor. The chancellor decided the case according to rules of fairness, honesty, right, and natural justice. From this there developed the rules in equity. The laws of trust, divorce, rescission of contracts for fraud, injunction, and specific performance are enforced in courts of equity.

Equity of redemption The right a mortgagor has to redeem or get back his property after it has been forfeited for nonpayment of the debt it secured. By statute, within a certain time before final foreclosure decree, a mortgagor has the privilege of redeeming his property by paying the amount of the debt, interest, and costs.

Escrow An agreement under which a grantor, promisor, or obligor places the instrument upon which he is bound with a third person called escrow holder, until the performance of a condition or the happening of an event stated in the agreement permits the escrow holder to make delivery or performance to the grantee, promisee, or obligee. A (grantor) places a deed to C (grantee) accompanied by the contract of conveyance with B bank, conditioned upon B bank delivering the deed to C (grantee) when C pays all moneys due under contract. The contract and deed have been placed in "escrow."

Estate All the property of a living, deceased, bankrupt, or insane person. Also applied to the property of a ward. In the law of taxation, wills, and inheritance, *estate* has a broad meaning. Historically, the word was limited to an interest in land: i.e., estate in fee simple, estate for years, estate for life, and so forth.

Estoppel When one ought to speak the truth but does not, and by one's acts, representations, or silence intentionally or through negligence induces another to believe certain facts exist, and the other person acts to his detriment on the belief that such facts are true, the first person is estopped to deny the truth of the facts. B, knowingly having kept and used defective goods delivered by S under a contract of sale, is estopped to deny the goods are defective. X holds out Y as his agent. X is estopped to deny that Y is his agent. Persons are estopped to deny the legal effect of written instruments such as deeds, contracts, bills and notes, court records, and judgments. A man's own acts speak louder than his words.

Et al. "And other persons." Used in pleadings and cases to indicate that persons other than those specifically named are parties to a lawsuit.

Ethics Conduct based on a commitment of what is right. This conduct often is at a level above that required by legal standards.

Eviction An action to expel a tenant from the estate of the landlord. Interfering with the tenant's right of possession or enjoyment amounts to an eviction. Eviction may be actual or constructive. Premises made uninhabitable because the landlord maintains a nuisance is constructive eviction.

Evidence In law, *evidence* has two meanings. (1) Testimony of witnesses and facts presented to the court and jury by way of writings and exhibits, which impress the minds of the court and jury, to the extent that an allegation has been proven. *Testimony* and *evidence* are not synonymous. Testimony is a broader word and includes all the witness says. *Proof* is distinguished from *evidence*, in that proof is the legal consequence of evidence. (2) The rules of law, called the law of evidence, that determine what evidence shall be introduced at a trial and what shall not; also, what importance shall be placed upon the evidence.

Exclusive dealing contract A contract under which a buyer agrees to purchase a certain product exclusively from the seller or in which the seller agrees to sell all his product production to the buyer.

Ex contractu *See* Action ex contractu.

Exculpatory clause A provision in a contract whereby one of the parties attempts to relieve itself of liability for breach of a legal duty.

Ex delicto *See* Action ex delicto.

Executed Applied to contracts or other written instruments, *executed* means signed, sealed, and delivered. Effective legal obligations have thus been created. The term is also used to mean that the performances of a contract have been completed. The contract is then at an end. All is done that is to be done.

Execution Execution of a judgment is the process by which the court, through the sheriff, enforces the payment of the judgment received by the successful party. The sheriff, by a "writ," levies upon the unsuccessful party's property and sells it to pay the judgment creditor.

Executor (of an estate) The person whom the testator (the one who makes the will) names or appoints to administer his estate upon his death and to dispose of it according to his intention. The terms *executor* and *administrator* are not synonyms. A person who make a will appoints an executor to administer his estate. A court appoints an administrator to administer the estate of a person who dies without having made a will. *See* Intestate.

Executory contract Until the performance required in a contract is completed, it is said to be executory as to that part not executed. *See* Executed.

Exemplary damages A sum assessed by the jury in a tort action (over and above the compensatory damages) as punishment, in order to make an example of the wrongdoer and to deter like conduct by others. Injuries caused by willful, malicious, wanton, and reckless conduct will subject the wrongdoers to exemplary damages.

Exemption The condition of a person who is free or excused from a duty imposed by some rule of law, statutory or otherwise.

Express contract An agreement which is either spoken or written by the parties. *See* Contract.

Express warranty When a seller makes some positive representation concerning the nature, quality, character, use, and purpose of goods, which induces the buyer to buy, and the seller intends the buyer to rely thereon, the seller has made an express warranty.

Factor An agent for the sale of merchandise. He may hold possession of the goods in his own name or in the name of his principal. He is authorized to sell and to receive payment for the goods. *See* Agent.

Factor's lien A factor's right to keep goods consigned to him if he may reimburse himself for advances previously made to the consignor.

Farm products* Crops or livestock or supplies used or produced in farming operations; products of crops or livestock in their unmanufactured states (such as ginned cotton, wool-clip, maple syrup, milk, and eggs); and goods in the possession of a debtor engaged in raising, fattening, grazing, or other farming operations. If goods are farm products, they are neither equipment nor inventory.

Featherbedding In labor relations, a demand for the payment of wages for a service not actually rendered.

Fee simple absolute The total interest a person may have in land. Such an estate is not qualified by any other interest, and it passes upon the death of the owners to the heirs, free from any conditions.

Fellow-servant doctrine Precludes an injured employee from recovering damages from his employer when the injury resulted from the negligent act of another employee.

Felony All criminal offenses that are punishable by death or imprisonment in a penitentiary.

Fiduciary In general, a person is a fiduciary when he occupies a position of trust or confidence in relation to another person or his property. Trustees, guardians, and executors occupy fiduciary positions.

Final decree *See* Decree.

Financing agency* A bank, finance company, or person who, in the ordinary course of business, makes advances against goods or documents of title; or who, by arrangement with either the seller or the buyer, intervenes in ordinary course to make a collect payment due or claimed under the contract for sale, as by purchasing or paying the seller's draft or making advances against it or by merely taking it for collection, whether or not documents of title accompany the draft. "Financing agency" includes a bank or person who similarly intervenes between persons who are in the position of seller and buyer in respect to the goods.

Fine A sum of money collected by a court from a person guilty of some criminal offense. The amount may be fixed by statute or left to the discretion of the court.

Firm offer* An offer by a merchant to buy or sell goods in a signed writing that, by its terms, gives assurance it will be held open.

Fixture An item of personal property that has become attached or annexed to real estate. Fixtures generally are treated as part of the real estate.

Floating lien* In the law of secured transactions, this

concept allows a creditor to become secured with regards to future advances and to collateral acquired by the debtor after the perfection occurs.

Forbearance Giving up the right to enforce what one honestly believes to be a valid claim, in return for a promise. It is sufficient "consideration" to make a promise binding.

Forcible entry and detainer A remedy given to a land owner to evict persons unlawfully in possession of his land. A landlord may use such remedy to evict a tenant in default.

Foreclosure The forced sale of a defaulting debtor's property at the insistence of the creditor.

Forfeiture Money or property taken as compensation and punishment for injury or damage to the person or property of another or to the state. One may forfeit interest earnings for charging a usurious rate.

Forgery False writing or alteration of an instrument with the fraudulent intent of deceiving and injuring another. Writing another's name upon a check, without his consent, to secure money.

Franchise A right conferred or granted by a legislative body. It is a contract right and cannot be revoked without cause. A franchise is more than a license. A license is only a privilege and may be revoked. A corporation exists by virtue of a "franchise." A corporation secures a franchise from the city council to operate a waterworks within the city. *See* License.

Franchise tax A tax on the right of a corporation to do business under its corporate name.

Fraud An intentional misrepresentation of the truth for the purpose of deceiving another person. The elements of fraud are (1) intentionally false representation of fact, not opinion, (2) intent that the deceived person act thereon, (3) knowledge that such statements would naturally deceive, and (4) that the deceived person acted to his injury.

Fraudulent conveyance A conveyance of property by a debtor for the intent and purpose of defrauding his creditors. It is of no effect, and such property may be reached by the creditors through appropriate legal proceedings.

Freehold An estate in fee or for life. A freeholder is usually a person who has a property right in the title to real estate amounting to an estate of inheritance (in fee), or one who has title for life or an indeterminate period.

Full-line forcing An arrangement in which a manufacturer refuses to supply any portion of the product line unless the retailer agrees to accept the entire line.

Fungible* Goods and securities of which any unit is, by nature or usage of trade, the equivalent of any other like unit.

Fungible goods Fungible goods are those "of which any unit is from its nature of mercantile usage treated as the equivalent of any other unit." Grain, wine, and similar items are examples.

Future goods* Goods that are not both existing and identified.

Futures Contracts for the sale and delivery of commodities in the future, made with the intention that no commodity be delivered or received immediately.

Garnishee A person upon whom a garnishment is served. He is a debtor of a defendant and has money or property that the plaintiff is trying to reach in order to satisfy a debt due from the defendant. Also used as a verb: "to garnishee wages or property."

Garnishment A proceeding by which a plaintiff seeks to reach the credits of the defendant that are in the hands of a third party, the garnishee. A garnishment is distinguished from an attachment in that by an attachment, an officer of the court takes actual possession of property by virtue of his writ. In a garnishment, the property or money is left with the garnishee until final adjudication.

General agent An agent authorized to do all the acts connected with carrying on a particular trade, business, or profession.

General intangibles* Any personal property (including things in action) other than goods, accounts, contract rights, chattel paper, documents, and instruments.

General verdict *See* Verdict *in contrast to* Special verdict.

Gift A gift is made when a donor delivers the subject matter of the gift into the donee's hands or places in the donee the means of obtaining possession of the subject matter, accompanied by such acts that show clearly the donor's intentions to divest himself of all dominion and control over the property.

Gift *causa mortis* A gift made in anticipation of death. The donor must have been in sickness and have died as expected, otherwise no effective gift has been made. If the donor survives, the gift is revocable.

Gift *inter vivos* An effective gift made during the life of the donor. By a gift inter vivos, property vests immediately in the donee at the time of delivery, whereas a gift causa mortis is made in contemplation of death and is effective only upon the donor's death.

Good faith* Honesty in fact is the conduct or transaction concerned. Referring to a merchant, good faith means honesty in fact and the observance of reasonable commercial standards of fair dealing in the trade.

Goods* All things that are movable at the time of identification to the contract for sale, including specially manufactured goods but not money in which the price is to be paid, investment securities, and things in action. Includes unborn young animals, growing crops, and other identified things attached to realty as described in the section on goods to be severed from realty.

Goodwill The value, beyond its assets, of a business organization created by its customers.

Grant A term used in deeds for the transfer of the title to real property. The words *convey*, *transfer*, and *grant*, as operative words in a deed to pass title, are equivalent. The words *grant*, *bargain*, and *sell* in a deed, in absence of statute, mean the grantor promises he has good title to transfer free from incumbrances and warrants it to be such.

Grantee A person to whom a grant is made; one named in a deed to receive title.

Grantor A person who makes a grant. The grantor executes the deed by which he divests himself of title.

Gross negligence The lack of even slight or ordinary care.

Guarantor One who by contract undertakes "to answer for the debt, default, and miscarriage of another." In general, a guarantor undertakes to pay if the principal debtor does not; a surety, on the other hand, joins in the contract of the principal and becomes an original party with the principal.

Guardian A person appointed by the court to look after the property rights and person of minors, the insane, and other incompetents or legally incapacitated persons.

Guardian ad litem A special guardian appointed for the sole purpose of carrying on litigation and preserving the interests of a ward. He exercises no control or power over property.

Habeas corpus A writ issued to a sheriff, warden, or other official having allegedly unlawful custody of a person, directing the official to bring the person before a court, in order to determine the legality of the imprisonment.

Hearsay evidence Evidence that is learned from someone else. It does not derive its value from the credit of the witness testifying but rests upon the veracity of another person. It is not good evidence, because there is no opportunity to cross-examine the person who is the source of the testimony.

Hedging contract A contract of purchase or sale of an equal amount of commodities in the future, by which brokers, dealers, or manufacturers protect themselves against the fluctuations of the market. It is a type of insurance against changing prices. A grain dealer, to protect himself, may contract to sell for future delivery the same amount of grain he has purchased in the present market.

Heirs Persons upon whom the statute of descent casts the title to real property upon the death of the ancestor. Consult Statute of Descent for the appropriate state. *See* Descent.

Holder* A person who is in possession of a document of title or an instrument or an investment security drawn, issued, or indorsed to him or to his order or to bearer or in blank.

Holder in due course One who has acquired possession of a negotiable instrument through proper negotiation for value, in good faith, and without notice of any defenses to it. Such a holder is not subject to personal defenses that would otherwise defeat the obligation embodied in the instrument.

Holding company A corporation organized for the purpose of owning and holding the stock of other corporations. Shareholders of underlying corporations receive in exchange for their stock, upon an agreed value, the shares in the holding corporation.

Homestead A parcel of land upon which a family dwells or resides, and which to them is home. The statute of the state or federal governments should be consulted to determine the meaning of the term as applied to debtor's exemptions, federal land grants, and so forth.

Honor* To pay or to accept and pay or, where a creditor so engages, to purchase or discount a draft complying with the terms of the instrument.

Horizontal merger Merger of corporations that were competitors prior to the merger.

Hot-cargo contract An agreement between employer and union, whereby an employer agrees to refrain from handling, using, selling, transporting, or otherwise dealing in the products of another employer or agrees to cease doing business with some other person.

Illegal Contrary to public policy and the fundamental principles of law. Illegal conduct includes not only violations of criminal statutes but also the creation of agreements that are prohibited by statute and the common law.

Illusory That which has a false appearance. If that which appears to be a promise is not a promise, it is said to be illusory. "I promise to buy your lunch if I decide to." This equivocal statement would not justify reliance, so it is not a promise.

Immunity Freedom from the legal duties and penalties imposed upon others. The "privileges and immunities" clause of the United States Constitution means no state can deny to the citizens of another state the same rights granted to its own citizens. This does not apply to office holding. *See* Exemption.

Implied The finding of a legal right or duty by inference from facts or circumstances. *See* Warranty.

Implied-in-fact contract A legally enforceable agreement inferred from the circumstances and conduct of the parties.

Imputed negligence Negligence that is not directly attributable to the person himself but is the negligence of a person who is in privity with him and with whose fault he is chargeable.

Incidental beneficiary If the performance of a promise

would indirectly benefit a person not a party to a contract, such person is an incidental beneficiary. A promises B, for a consideration, to plant a valuable nut orchard on B's land. Such improvement would increase the value of the adjacent land. C, the owner of the adjacent land, is an incidental beneficiary. He has no remedy if A breaches his promise with B.

Indemnify Literally, "to save harmless." Thus, one person agrees to protect another against loss.

Indenture A deed executed by both parties, as distinguished from a deed poll that is executed only by the grantor.

Independent contractor The following elements are essential to establish the relation of independent contractor, in contradistinction to principal and agent. An independent contractor must (1) exercise his independent judgment on the means used to accomplish the result; (2) be free from control or orders from any other person; (3) be responsible only under his contract for the result obtained.

Indictment A finding by a grand jury that it has reason to believe the accused is guilty as charged. It informs the accused of the offense with which he is charged, so that he may prepare its defense. It is a pleading in a criminal action.

Indorsement Writing one's name upon paper for the purpose of transferring the title. When a payee of a negotiable instrument writes his name on the back of the instrument, his writing is an indorsement.

Infringement Infringement of a patent on a machine is the manufacturing of a machine that produces the same result by the same means and operation as the patented machine. Infringement of a trademark consists in reproduction of a registered trademark and its use upon goods in order to mislead the public to believe that the goods are the genuine, original product.

Inherit The word is used in contradistinction to acquiring property by will. *See* Descent.

Inheritance An estate that descends to heirs. *See* Descent.

Injunction A writ of judicial process issued by a court of equity, by which a party is required to do a particular thing or to refrain from doing a particular thing.

In personam A legal proceeding, the judgment of which binds the defeated party to a personal liability.

In rem A legal proceeding, the judgment of which binds, affects, or determines the status of property.

Insolvent* Refers to a person who either has ceased to pay his debts in the ordinary course of business or cannot pay his debts as they become due or is insolvent within the meaning of the federal bankruptcy law.

Installment contract* One which requires or authorizes the delivery of goods in separate lots to be separately accepted, even though the contract contains a clause "each delivery is a separate contract" or its equivalent.

Instrument* A negotiable instrument or a security or any other writing that evidences a right to the payment of money and is not itself a security agreement or lease and is of a type that is in ordinary course of business transferred by delivery with any necessary indorsement or assignment.

Insurable interest A person has an insurable interest in a person or property if he will be directly and financially affected by the death of the person or the loss of the property.

Insurance By an insurance contract, one party, for an agreed premium, binds himself to another, called the insured, to pay the insured a sum of money conditioned upon the loss of life or property of the insured.

Intangible Something which represents value but has no intrinsic value of its own, such as a note or bond.

Intent A state of mind that exists prior to, or contemporaneous with, an act. A purpose or design to do or forbear to do an act. It cannot be directly proven but is inferred from known facts.

Interlocutory decree A decree of a court of equity that does not settle the complete issue but settles only some intervening part, awaiting a final decree.

Intermediary bank* Under Article 4—Bank Deposits and Collections, it is any bank—except the depositary or payor bank—to which an item is transferred in course of collection.

Interpleader A procedure whereby a person who has an obligation, e.g., to pay money, but does not know which of two or more claimants are entitled to performance, can bring a suit that requires the contesting parties to litigate between themselves.

Interrogatory A written question from one party to another in a lawsuit; a type of discovery procedure.

Intestate The intestate laws are the laws of descent or distribution of the estate of a deceased person. A person who has not made a will dies intestate.

Inventory* Goods that a person holds for sale or lease or to be—or which have been—furnished under contracts of service, or goods that are raw materials, work in process or materials used or consumed in a business. Inventory of a person is not to be classified as his equipment.

Irreparable damage or injury *Irreparable* does not mean injury beyond the possibility of repair, but it does mean that it is so constant and frequent in occurrence that no fair or reasonable redress can be had in a court of law. Thus, the plaintiff must seek a remedy in equity by way of an injunction.

Issue* Under Article 3—Commercial Paper, *issue* means the first delivery of an instrument to a holder or a remitter.

Issuer* A bailee who issues a document; but in relation to an unaccepted delivery order, the issuer is the person who orders the possessor of goods to deliver. Issuer includes any person for whom an agent or employee purports to act in issuing a document if the agent or employee has real or apparent authority to issue documents, notwithstanding that the issuer received no goods or that the goods were misdescribed or that in any other respect the agent or employee violated the issuer's instructions.

Item* Under Article 4—Bank Deposits and Collections, *item* means any instrument for the payment of money, even though it is not negotiable, but does not include money.

Jeopardy A person is in jeopardy when he is regularly charged with a crime before a court properly organized and competent to try him. If acquitted, he cannot be tried again for the same offense.

Joint and several Two or more persons have an obligation that binds them individually as well as jointly. The obligation can be enforced either by joint action against all of them or by separate actions against one or more.

Joint ownership The interest that two or more parties have in property.

Joint tenancy Two or more persons to whom land is deeded in such manner that they have "one and the same interest, accruing by one and the same conveyance, commencing at one and the same time, and held by one and the same undivided possession." Upon the death of one joint tenant, his property passes to the survivor or survivors.

Joint tortfeasors When two persons commit an injury with a common intent, they are joint tortfeasors.

Judgment (in law) The decision, pronouncement, or sentence rendered by a court upon an issue in which it has jurisdiction.

Judgment *in personam* A judgment against a person, directing the defendant to do or not to do something. *See In personam.*

Judgment *in rem* A judgment against a thing, as distinguished from a judgment against a person. *See In rem.*

Judicial restraint A judicial philosophy. Those following it believe that the power of judicial review should be exercised with great restraint.

Judicial review The power of courts to declare laws and executive actions unconstitutional.

Judicial sale A sale authorized by a court that has jurisdiction to grant such authority. Such sales are conducted by an officer of the court.

Jurisdiction The authority to try causes and determine cases. Conferred upon a court by the Constitution.

Jury A group of persons, usually twelve, sworn to declare the facts of a case as they are proved from the evidence presented to them and, upon instructions from the court, to find a verdict in the cause before them.

Juvenile court A court with jurisdiction to hear matters pertaining to those persons under a certain age (usually 16 or 18). This court will hear cases involving delinquent behavior.

Laches A term used in equity to name conduct that neglects to assert one's rights or to do what, by the law, a person should have done. Failure on the part of one to assert a right will give an equitable defense to another party.

Latent defect A defect in materials not discernible by examination. Used in contradistinction to patent defect, which is discernible.

Lease A contract by which one person divests himself of possession of lands or chattels and grants such possession to another for a period of time. The relationship in which land is involved is called landlord and tenant.

Leasehold The land held by a tenant under a lease.

Legacy Personal property disposed of by a will. Sometimes the term is synonymous with *bequest*. The word *devise* is used in connection with real property distributed by will. *See* Bequest; Devise.

Legal benefit An analysis used to determine if contractual consideration exists. As an inducement for a party to make a promise, that party (promisor) must receive a legal benefit, or the other party (promisee) must suffer a legal detriment, or both. *See* Consideration; Legal Detriment.

Legal detriment An analysis used to determine if contractual consideration exists. Parties suffer legal detriment when they promise to perform an act that they have no obligation to perform or promise to refrain from taking action that they have the right to take. *See* Consideration; Legal benefit.

Legatee A person to whom a legacy is given by will.

Liability In its broadest legal sense, *liability* means any obligation one may be under by reason of some rule of law. It includes debt, duty, and responsibility.

Libel Malicious publication of a defamation of a person by printing, writing, signs, or pictures, for the purposes of injuring the reputation and good name of such person. "The exposing of a person to public hatred, contempt, or ridicule."

License (governmental regulation) A license is a privilege granted by a state or city upon the payment of a fee. It confers authority upon the licensee to do some act or series of acts, which otherwise would be illegal. A license is not a contract and may be revoked for cause. It is a method of governmental regulation exercised under the police power.

License (privilege) A mere personal privilege given by the owner to another to do designated acts upon the land of the owner. It is revocable at will and creates no estate in the land. The licensee is not in possession. "It is a mere excuse for what otherwise would be a trespass."

Lien The right of one person, usually a creditor, to keep possession of, or control, the property of another for the purpose of satisfying a debt. There are many kinds of liens: judgment lien, attorney's lien, innkeeper's lien, logger's lien, vendor's lien. Consult statute of state for type of lien. *See* Judgment.

Lien creditor* A creditor who has acquired a lien on property involved by attachment, levy, or the like. Includes an assignee for benefit of creditors from the time of assignment and a trustee in bankruptcy from the date of the filing of the petition or a receiver in equity from the time of appointment. Unless all the creditors represented had knowledge of the security interest, such a representative of creditors is a lien creditor without knowledge even though he personally has knowledge of the security interest.

Life estate An interest in real property that lasts only as long as a designated person lives.

Limited partnership A partnership in which one or more individuals are general partners and one or more individuals are limited partners. The limited partners contribute assets to the partnership without taking part in the conduct of the business. They are liable for the debts of the partnership only to the extent of their contributions.

Liquidated A claim is liquidated when it has been made fixed and certain by the parties concerned.

Liquidated damages A fixed sum agreed upon between the parties to a contract, to be paid as ascertained damages by the party who breaches the contract. If the sum is excessive, the courts will declare it to be a penalty and unenforceable.

Liquidation The process of winding up the affairs of a corporation or firm for the purpose of paying its debts and disposing of its assets. May be done voluntarily or under the orders of a court.

Lis pendens "Pending the suit nothing should be changed." The court, having control of the property involved in the suit, issues notice *lis pendens*, that persons dealing with the defendant regarding the subject matter of the suit do so subject to final determination of the action.

Long-arm statute A law which allows courts in the state court systems to extend their personal jurisdiction beyond the state boundaries to nonresident defendants if such defendants have had sufficient minimal contacts with the state to justify the exercise of personal jurisdiction.

Lot* A parcel or a single article that is the subject matter of a separate sale or delivery, whether or not it is sufficient to perform the contract.

Magistrate A public officer, usually a judge, "who has power to issue a warrant for the arrest of a person charged with a public offense." The word has wide application and includes justices of the peace, notaries public, recorders, and other public officers who have power to issue executive orders.

Malice Describes a wrongful act done intentionally without excuse. It does not necessarily mean ill will, but it indicates a state of mind that is reckless concerning the law and the rights of others. *Malice* is distinguished from *negligence*. With *malice* there is always a purpose to injure, whereas such is not true of the word *negligence*.

Malicious prosecution The prosecution of another at law with malice and without probable cause to believe that such legal action will be successful.

Mandamus A writ issued by a court of law, in the name of the state. Writs of mandamus are directed to inferior courts, officers, corporations, or persons, commanding them to do particular things that appertain to their offices or duties.

Mandatory injunction An injunctive order issued by a court of equity that compels affirmative action by the defendant.

Market extension merger A combination of two business organizations allowing one to extend its business to new products or geographical areas. *See* Product extension merger.

Marketable title A title of such character that no apprehension as to its validity would occur to the mind of a reasonable and intelligent person. The title to goods is not marketable if it is in litigation, subject to incumbrances, in doubt as to a third party's right, or subject to lien.

Marshaling of assets A principle in equity for a fair distribution of a debtor's assets among his creditors. For example, a creditor of A, by reason of prior right, has two funds, X and Y, belonging to A, out of which he may satisfy his debt. But another creditor of A also has a right to X fund. The first creditor will be compelled to exhaust Y fund before he will be permitted to participate in X fund.

Master In agency relationships involving torts, this party is in a position similar to that of a principal.

Master in chancery An officer appointed by the court to assist the court of equity in taking testimony, computing interest, auditing accounts, estimating damages, ascertaining liens, and doing other tasks incidental to a suit, as the court requires. The power of a master is merely advisory, and his tasks are largely fact finding.

Maxim A proposition of law that because of its universal approval needs no proof or argument; the mere statement of which gives it authority. Example: "A principal is bound by the acts of his agent when the agent is acting within the scope of his authority."

Mechanic's lien Created by statute to assist suppliers and laborers in collecting their accounts and wages. Its purpose is to subject the land of an owner to a lien for material and labor expended in the construction of buildings and other improvements.

Mediation The process by which a third party attempts

to help the parties in dispute find a resolution. The mediator has no authority to bind the parties to any particular resolution.

Merchant A person who deals in goods of the kind involved in a transaction; or one who otherwise, by his occupation, holds himself out as having knowledge or skill peculiar to the practices or goods involved; or one to whom such knowledge or skill may be attributed because he employs an agent or broker or other intermediary who, by his occupation, holds himself out as having such knowledge or skill.

Merger Two corporations are merged when one corporation continues in existence and the other loses its identity by its absorption into the first. *Merger* must be distinguished from *consolidation*. In *consolidation*, both corporations are dissolved, and a new one is created, the new one taking over the assets of the dissolved corporations.

Metes and bounds The description of the boundaries of real property.

Midnight deadline* Under Article 4—Bank Deposits and Collections, this is midnight on the next banking day following the banking day on which a bank receives the relevant item or notice, or from which the time for taking action commences to run, whichever is later.

Ministerial duty A prescribed duty that requires little judgment or discretion. A sheriff performs ministerial duties.

Minutes The record of a court or the written transactions of the members or board of directors of a corporation. Under the certificate of the clerk of a court or the secretary of a corporation, the minutes are the official evidence of court or corporate action.

Misdemeanor A criminal offense, less than a felony, that is not punishable by death or imprisonment. Consult the local statute.

Misrepresentation The affirmative statement or affirmation of a fact that is not true; the term does not include concealment of true facts or nondisclosure or the mere expression of opinion.

Mistake (of fact) The unconscious ignorance or forgetfulness of the existence or nonexistence of a fact, past or present, which is material and important to the creation of a legal obligation.

Mistake (of law) An erroneous conclusion of the legal effect of known facts.

Mitigation of damages A plaintiff is entitled to recover damages caused by the defendant's breach, but the plaintiff is also under a duty to avoid increasing or enhancing such damages. This duty is called a duty to *mitigate the damages*. If a seller fails to deliver the proper goods on time, the buyer, where possible, must buy other goods, thus mitigating damages.

Monopoly Exclusive control of the supply and price of a commodity. May be acquired by a franchise or patent from the government; or the ownership of the source of a commodity or the control of its distribution.

Mortgage A conveyance or transfer of an interest in property for the purpose of creating a security for a debt. The mortgage becomes void upon payment of the debt, although the recording of a release is necessary to clear the title of the mortgaged property.

Municipal court Another name for a police court. *See* Police court.

Mutual assent In every contract, each party must agree to the same thing. Each must know what the other intends; they must mutually assent or be in agreement.

Mutual mistake *See* Bilateral mistake.

Mutuality The binding of both parties in every contract. Each party to the contract must be bound to the other party to do something by virtue of the legal duty created.

Negligence Failure to do that which an ordinary, reasonable, prudent man would do, or the doing of some act that an ordinary, prudent man would not do. Reference must always be made to the situation, the circumstances, and the knowledge of the parties.

Negotiation* Under Article 3—Commercial Paper, this is the transfer of an instrument in such form that the transferee becomes a holder. If the instrument is payable to order, it is negotiated by delivery with any necessary indorsement; if payable to bearer, it is negotiated by delivery.

Net assets Property or effects of a firm, corporation, institution, or estate, remaining after all its obligations have been paid.

Nexus Connection, tie, or link used in the law of taxation to establish a connection between a tax and the activity or person being taxed.

NLRB National Labor Relations Board

No-fault laws Laws barring tort actions by injured persons against third-party tortfeasors and requiring injured persons to obtain recovery from their own insurers.

Nolo contendere A plea by an accused in a criminal action. It does not admit guilt of the offense charged but does equal a plea of guilty for purpose of sentencing.

Nominal damages A small sum assessed as sufficient to award the case and cover the costs when no actual damages have been proven.

Nonsuit A judgment given against the plaintiff when he is unable to prove his case or fails to proceed with the trial after the case is at issue.

Noscitur a sociis The meaning of a word is or may be known from the accompanying words.

Notary public A public officer authorized to administer oaths by way of affidavits and depositions. Attests deeds and other formal papers, in order that they may be used as evidence and be qualified for recording.

Notice* A person has "notice" of a fact when (a) he

has actual knowledge of it; or (b) he has received a notice or notification of it; or (c) from all the facts and circumstances known to him at the time in question, he has reason to know that it exists. A person "knows" or has "knowledge" of a fact when he has actual knowledge of it. "Discover" or "learn" or a word or phrase of similar import refers to knowledge rather than to reason to know.

Novation The substitution of one obligation for another. When debtor A is substituted for debtor B, and by agreement with the creditor C, debtor B is discharged, a novation has occurred.

Nudum pactum A naked promise—one for which no consideration has been given.

Nuisance Generally, any continuous or continued conduct that causes annoyance, inconvenience, or damage to person or property. *Nuisance* usually applies to unreasonable, wrongful use of property, causing material discomfort, hurt, and damage to the person or property of another. Example: fumes from a factory.

Obligee A creditor or promisee.

Obligor A debtor or promisor.

Offer A statement by one party (called the offeror) that he is prepared to be bound to a contractual position. The offer is the first essential element to the meeting of the minds of the contracting parties. *See* Acceptance.

Oligopoly Control of a commodity or service in a given market by a small number of companies or suppliers.

Option A right secured by a contract to accept or reject an offer to purchase property at a fixed price within a fixed time. It is an irrevocable offer sometimes called a "paid-for offer."

Order* Under Article 3—Commercial Paper, *order* is a direction to pay and must be more than an authorization or request. It must, with reasonable certainty, identify the person to pay. It may be addressed to one or more such persons jointly or in the alternative but not in succession.

Order of relief The ruling by a bankruptcy judge that a particular case is properly before the bankruptcy court.

Ordinance Generally speaking, the legislative act of a municipality. A city council is a legislative body, and it passes ordinances that are the laws of the city.

Ordinary care Care that a prudent man would take under the circumstances of the particular case.

Par value "Face value." The par value of stocks and bonds on the date of issuance is the principal. At a later date, the par value is the principal plus interest.

Pari delicto The fault or blame is shared equally.

Pari materia "Related to the same matter or subject." Statutes and covenants concerning the same subject matter are in pari materia and as a general rule, for the purpose of ascertaining their meaning, are construed together.

Parol evidence Legal proof based on oral statements; with regard to a document, any evidence extrinsic to the document itself.

Part performance A legal doctrine created as an exception to the requirement that contracts be in written form pursuant to the statute of frauds. If the contracting parties have partially performed an oral contract to the extent that a judge is comfortable in ruling that the contract exists, this doctrine is used to enforce the contract. *See* Equitable estoppel.

Partition Court proceedings brought by an interested party's request that the court divide real property among respective owners as their interests appear. If the property cannot be divided in kind, then it is to be sold and the money divided as each interest appears.

Partnership A business organization consisting of two or more owners who agree to carry on a business and to share profits and losses.

Party* A person who has engaged in a transaction or made an agreement within the Uniform Commercial Code.

Patent ambiguity An obvious uncertainty in a written instrument.

Payor bank* Under Article 4—Bank Deposits and Collections, a bank by which an item is payable as drawn or accepted.

Penal bond A bond given by an accused, or by another person in his behalf, for the payment of money if the accused fails to appear in court on a certain day.

Pendente lite "Pending during the progress of a suit at law."

Per curiam A decision by the full court without indicating the author of the decision.

Peremptory challenge An objection raised by a party to a lawsuit who rejects a person serving as a juror. No reason need be given.

Perfection* In the law of secured transactions, this process is essential to inform the public that a creditor has an interest in the debtor's personal property. Perfection may occur by attachment, by filing a financing statement, by possession, and by noting the security interest on a certificate of title.

Perjury False swearing upon an oath properly administered in some judicial proceedings.

Per se "By itself." Thus, a contract clause may be inherently unconscionable—unconscionable *per se*.

Personal property The rights, powers, and privileges a person has in movable things, such as chattels and choses in actions. Personal property is used in contradistinction to real property.

Personal representative The administrator or executor

of a deceased person or the guardian of a child or the conservator of an incompetent.

Personal service The sheriff personally delivers a service of process to the defendant.

Petitioner The party who files a claim in a court of equity. Also the party who petitions the Supreme Court for a writ of certiorari.

Plaintiff In an action at law, the complaining party or the one who commences the action. The person who seeks a remedy in court.

Pleading Process by which the parties in a lawsuit arrive at an issue.

Pledge Personal property, as security for a debt or other obligation, deposited or placed with a person called a pledgee. The pledgee has the implied power to sell the property if the debt is not paid. If the debt is paid, the right to possession returns to the pledgor.

Police court A court with jurisdiction to hear cases involving violations of local ordinances which are punishable as misdemeanors.

Polling jury Calling the name of each juror to inquire what his verdict is before it is made a matter of record.

Possession The method recognized by law and used by one's self or by another to hold, detain, or control either personal or real property, thereby excluding others from holding, detaining, or controlling such property.

Power of attorney An instrument authorizing another to act as one's agent or attorney in fact.

Precedent A previously decided case that can serve as an authority to help decide a present controversy. Use of such case is called the doctrine of *stare decisis*, which means to adhere to decided cases and settled principles. Literally, "to stand as decided."

Preference The term is used most generally in bankruptcy law. If an insolvent debtor pays some creditors a greater percentage of the debts than he pays other creditors in the same class, and if the payments are made within ninety days prior to his filing a bankruptcy petition, those payments constitute illegal and voidable preference. An intention to prefer such creditors must be shown.

Preferred stock Stock that entitles the holder to dividends from earnings before the owners of common stock can receive a dividend.

Preponderance Preponderance of the evidence means that evidence, in the judgment of the jurors, is entitled to the greatest weight, appears to be more credible, has greater force, and overcomes not only the opposing presumptions but also the opposing evidence.

Presenting bank* Under Article 4—Bank Deposits and Collections, this is any bank presenting an item except a payor bank.

Presentment* Under Article 3—Commercial Paper, presentment is a demand for acceptance or payment made upon the maker, acceptor, drawee, or other payor by, or on behalf of, the holder.

Presumption (presumed)* The trier of fact must find the existence of the fact presumed unless and until evidence is introduced that would support a finding of its nonexistence.

Prima facie Literally, "at first view." Thus, that which first appears seems to be true. A prima facie case is one that stands until contrary evidence is produced.

Primary party* In the law of commercial paper, this person is the one all other parties expect to pay. The maker of a note and the drawee of a draft are the primary party to those instruments.

Principal In agency relationships, this party employs the services of an agent to accomplish those goals that he cannot accomplish on his own.

Privilege A legal idea or concept of lesser significance than a right. An invitee has only a privilege to walk on another's land, because such privilege may be revoked at will; whereas a person who has an easement to go on another's land has a right created by a grant, which is an interest in land and cannot be revoked at will. To be exempt from jury service is a privilege.

Privity Mutual and successive relationship to the same interest. Offeror and offeree, assignor and assignee, grantor and grantee are in privity. Privity of estate means that one takes title from another. In contract law, privity denotes parties in mutual legal relationship to each other by virtue of being promisees and promisors. At early common law, third-party beneficiaries and assignees were said to be not in "privity."

Probate court Handles the settlement of estates.

Procedural law The laws which establish the process by which a lawsuit is filed, a trial is conducted, an appeal is perfected, and a judgment is enforced. In essence, these laws can be called the rules of litigation.

Proceeds* Whatever is received when collateral or proceeds are sold, exchanged, collected, or otherwise disposed of. Includes the account arising when the right to payment is earned under a contract right. Money, checks, and the like are "cash proceeds." All other proceeds are "noncash proceeds."

Process In a court proceeding, before or during the progress of the trial, an instrument issued by the court in the name of the state and under the seal of the court, directing an officer of the court to do, act, or cause some act to be done incidental to the trial.

Product extension merger A merger that extends the products of the acquiring company into a similar or related product but one which is not directly in competition with existing products.

Promise* Under Article 3—Commercial Paper, it is an

undertaking to pay, and it must be more than an acknowledgment of an obligation.

Promissory note The legal writing that evidences a debtor's promise to repay an amount of money borrowed.

Property All rights, powers, privileges, and immunities that one has concerning tangibles and intangibles. The term includes everything of value subject to ownership.

Protest* In the law of commercial paper, this event signifies that a proper presentment has been made, that dishonor has occurred, and that notice of dishonor was given in a timely fashion. Protest is required in international commercial paper transactions, but it is optional in domestic transactions.

Proximate cause The cause that sets other causes in operation. The responsible cause of an injury.

Proxy Authority to act for another, used by absent stockholders or members of legislative bodies to have their votes cast by others.

Punitive damages Damages by way of punishment. Allowed for an injury caused by a wrong that is willful and malicious.

Purchase* Includes taking by sale, discount, negotiation, mortgage, pledge, lien, issue or re-issue, gift, or any other voluntary transaction creating an interest in property.

Purchase-money security interest* A security interest that is taken or retained by the seller of the collateral to secure all or part of its price; or taken by a person who, by making advances or incurring an obligation, gives value to enable the debtor to acquire rights in, or the use of, collateral if such value is in fact so used.

Quantum meruit ''As much as he deserves.'' This remedy is used to avoid the unjust enrichment of one party at the expenses of another. This remedy usually is in association with quasi-contracts.

Quasi-contract A situation in which there arises a legal duty that does not rest upon a promise but does involve the payment of money. In order to do justice by a legal fiction, the court enforces the duty as if a promise in fact exists. Thus, if A gives B money by mistake, A can compel B to return the money by an action in quasi-contract.

Quasi-judicial Administrative actions involving factual determinations and the discretionary application of rules and regulations.

Quasi-legislative The function of administrative agencies whereby rules and regulations are promulgated. This authority permits agencies to make enforceable ''laws.''

Quid pro quo The exchange of one thing of value for another.

Quiet title A suit brought by the owner of real property for the purpose of bringing into court any person who claims an adverse interest in the property, requiring him either to establish his claim or be barred from asserting it thereafter. It may be said that the purpose is to remove ''clouds'' from the title.

Quitclaim A deed that releases a right or interest in land but does not include any covenants of warranty. The grantor transfers only that which he has.

Quo warranto A proceeding in court by which a governmental body tests or inquires into the authority or legality of the claim of any person to a public office, franchise, or privilege.

Ratification The confirmation of one's own previous act or act of another: e.g., a principal may ratify the previous unauthorized act of his agent. B's agent, without authority, buys goods. B, by keeping the goods and receiving the benefits of the agent's act, ratifies the agency.

Ratio decidendi Logical basis of judicial decision.

Real property Land with all its buildings, appurtenances, equitable and legal interests therein. In contradistinction to personal property, which refers to movables or chattels.

Reasonable care The care that prudent persons would exercise under the same circumstances.

Receiver An officer of the court appointed on behalf of all parties to the litigation to take possession of, hold, and control the property involved in the suit, for the benefit of the party who will be determined to be entitled thereto.

Recoupment ''A cutting back.'' A right to deduct from the plaintiff's claim any payment or loss that the defendant has suffered by reason of the plaintiff's wrongful act.

Redemption To buy back. A debtor buys back or redeems his mortgaged property when he pays the debt.

Referee A person to whom a cause pending in a court is referred by the court, to take testimony, hear the parties, and report thereon to the court.

Registered form* A security is in registered form when it specifies a person entitled to the security or to the rights it evidences and when its transfer may be registered upon books maintained for that purpose by, or on behalf of, an issuer, as security states.

Reinsurance In a contract of reinsurance, one insurance company agrees to indemnify another insurance company in whole or in part against risks that the first company has assumed. The original contract of insurance and the reinsurance contract are distinct contracts. There is no privity between the original insured and the reinsurer.

Release The voluntary relinquishing of a right, lien, or any other obligation. A release need not be under seal, nor does it necessarily require consideration. The words *release*, *remise*, and *discharge* are often used together to mean the same thing.

Remand To send back a case from the appellate court to the lower court, in order that the lower court may comply with the instructions of the appellate court. Also to return a prisoner to jail.

Remedy The word is used to signify the judicial means or court procedures by which legal and equitable rights are enforced.

Remitting bank* Under Article 4—Bank Deposits and Collections, any payor or intermediary bank remitting for an item.

Replevin A remedy given by statute for the recovery of the possession of a chattel. Only the right to possession can be tried in such action.

Res "Thing."

Res judicata A controversy once having been decided or adjudged upon its merits is forever settled so far as the particular parties involved are concerned. Such a doctrine avoids vexatious lawsuits.

Rescind To cancel or annul a contract and return the parties to their original positions.

Rescission An apparently valid act may conceal a defect that will make it null and void if any of the parties demand that it be rescinded.

Respondeat superior "The master is liable for the acts of his agent."

Respondent One who answers another's bill or pleading, particularly in an equity case. Quite similar, in many instances, to a defendant in a law case.

Responsible bidder In the phrase "lowest responsible bidder," *responsible*, as used by most statutes concerning public works, means that such bidder has the requisite skill, judgment, and integrity necessary to perform the contract involved and has the financial resources and ability to carry the task to completion.

Restitution When a contract is rescinded, all parties must return that which they have received. This remedy attempts to place the parties in the same positions they were in prior to making the contract.

Restraining order Issued by a court of equity in aid of a suit, to hold matters in abeyance until parties may be heard. A temporary injunction.

Restraint of trade Monopolies, combinations, and contracts that impede free competition.

Right The phrase "legal right" is a correlative of the phrase "legal duty." One has a legal right if, upon the breach of the correlative legal duty, he can secure a remedy in a court of law.

Right of action Synonymous with *cause of action*: a right to enforce a claim in a court.

Right-to-work law A state statute that outlaws a union shop contract; one by which an employer agrees to require membership in the union sometime after an employee has been hired, as a condition of continued employment.

Riparian A person is a riparian owner if his land is situated beside a stream of water, either flowing over or along the border of the land.

Sale* The agreement to exchange title to goods for a price.

Satisfaction In legal phraseology, the release and discharge of a legal obligation. Satisfaction may be partial or full performance of the obligation. The word is used with *accord*, a promise to give a substituted performance for a contract obligation; *satisfaction* means the acceptance by the obligee of such performance.

Scienter Knowledge by a defrauding party of the falsity of a representation. In a tort action of deceit, knowledge that a representation is false must be proved.

Seal A seal shows that an instrument was executed in a formal manner. At early common law, sealing legal documents was of great legal significance. A promise under seal was binding by virtue of the seal. Today under most statutes, any stamp, wafer, mark, scroll, or impression made, adopted and affixed, is adequate. The printed word *seal* or the letters *L.S.* (*locus sigilli*, "the place of the seal") are sufficient.

Seasonably* An action is taken "seasonably" when it is taken at, or within, the time agreed; or if no time is agreed, at or within a reasonable time.

Secondary boycott Conspiracy or combination to cause the customers or suppliers of an employer to cease doing business with that employer.

Secondary party* Under Article 3—Commercial Paper, a drawer or indorser.

Secret partner A partner whose existence is not known to the public.

Secured party* A lender, seller, or other person in whose favor there is a security interest, including a person to whom accounts, contract rights, or chattel paper have been sold. When the holders of obligations issued under an indenture of trust, equipment trust agreement, or the like are represented by a trustee or other person, the representative is the secured party.

Security May be bonds, stocks, and other property that a debtor places with a creditor, who may sell them if the debt is not paid. The plural, *securities*, is used broadly to mean tangible choses in action, such as promissory notes, bonds, stocks, and other vendible obligations.

Security* An instrument issued in bearer form or registered form; commonly dealt in on securities exchanges or markets or commonly recognized in any area in which it is issued or dealt in as a medium for invesment; one of a class or series of instruments; evidences a share, a participation or other interest in property or in an enterprise or evidences an obligation of the issuer.

Security agreement* Creates or provides for a security interest.

Security interest* An interest in personal property or fixtures that secures payment or performance of an obligation.

Self-help* In the law of secured transactions, this term describes the creditor's attempt to take possession of collateral without the court's assistance.

Sell To negotiate or make arrangement for a sale. A sale is an executed contract, a result of the process of selling.

Separation of powers The doctrine that the legislative, executive, and judicial branches of government function independently of one another and that each branch serves as a check on the others.

Servant A person employed by another and subject to the direction and control of the employer in performance of his duties.

Setoff A matter of defense, called a cross-complaint, used by the defendant for the purpose of making a demand on the plaintiff. It arises out of contract but is independent and unconnected with the cause of action set out in the complaint. *See* Counterclaims and Recoupment.

Settle* Under Article 4—Bank Deposits and Collections, *settle* means to pay in cash, by clearinghouse settlement, in a charge or credit or by remittance or otherwise as instructed. A settlement may be either provisional or final.

Settlement A concept applicable in agency relationships when the principal is undisclosed. By paying (or settling with) the agent, the principal is relieved of liability to the third party. This third party will look to the agent for performance of their agreement.

Severable contract A contract in which the performance is divisible. Two or more parts may be set over against each other. Items and prices may be apportioned to each other without relation to the full performance of all of its parts.

Shareholders (stockholders) Persons whose names appear on the books of a corporation as owners of shares of stock and who are entitled to participate in the management and control of the corporation.

Share of stock A proportional part of the rights in the management and assets of a corporation. It is a chose in action. The certificate is the evidence of the share.

Silent partner A partner who has no voice in the management of the partnership.

Situs "Place, situation." The place where a thing is located. The situs of personal property is the domicile of the owner. The situs of land is the state or county where it is located.

Slander An oral utterance that tends to injure the reputation of another. *See* Libel.

Small claims court A court with jurisdiction to hear cases involving a limited amount of money. The jurisdictional amount varies among the states and local communities.

Special agent In agency relationships, an agent with a limited amount of specific authority. This agent usually has instructions to accomplish one specific task.

Special appearance The appearance in court of a person through his attorney for a limited purpose only. A court does not get jurisdiction over a person by special appearance.

Special verdict The jury finds the facts only, leaving it to the court to apply the law and draw the conclusion as to the proper disposition of the case.

Specific performance A remedy in personam in equity that compels performance of a contract to be substantial enough to do justice among the parties. A person who fails to obey a writ for specific performance may be put in jail by the equity judge for contempt of court. The remedy applies to contracts involving real property. In the absence of unique goods or peculiar circumstances, damages generally are an adequate remedy for breach of contracts involving personal property.

Standing to sue The doctrine that requires the plaintiff in a lawsuit to have a sufficient legal interest in the subject matter of the case.

Stare decisis "Stand by the decision." The law should adhere to decided cases. *See* Precedent.

Statute A law passed by the legislative body of a state.

Statutes of limitations Laws that exist for the purpose of bringing to an end old claims. Because witnesses die, memory fails, papers are lost, and the evidence becomes inadequate, stale claims are barred. Such statutes are called statutes of repose. Within a certain period of time, action on claims must be brought; otherwise, they are barred. The period varies from six months to twenty years.

Status quo The conditions or state of affairs at a given time.

Stay In the bankruptcy law, this occurs upon the entry of an order of relief. This order prevents all creditors from taking any action to collect debts owed by the protected debtor.

Stock dividend New shares of its own stock issued as a dividend by a corporation to its shareholders, in order to transfer retained earnings to capital stock.

Stock split A readjustment of the financial plan of a corporation, whereby each existing share of stock is split into new shares, usually with a lowering of par value.

Stock warrant A certificate that gives the holder the right to subscribe for and purchase, at a stated price, a given number of shares of stock in a corporation.

Stoppage in transit Upon learning of the insolvency of a buyer of goods, the seller has the right to stop the goods in transit and hold them as security for the purchase price. The right is an extension of the unpaid seller's lien.

Strict foreclosure The agreement by the creditor and debtor to allow the creditor to retain possession of the debtor's property in sastisfaction of the creditor's claim.

Strict liability The doctrine under which a party may be required to respond in tort damages, without regard to that party's use of due care.

Subordinate In the case of a mortgage or other security interest, the mortgagee may agree to make his mortgage inferior to another mortgage or interest.

Subpoena A process issued out of a court requiring the attendance of a witness at a trial.

Subrogation The substitution of one person in another's place, whether as a creditor or as the possessor of any lawful right, so that the substituted person may succeed to the rights, remedies, or proceeds of the claim. It rests in equity on the theory that a party who is compelled to pay a debt for which another is liable should be vested with all the rights the creditor has against the debtor. For example: an insurance company pays Y for damage to Y's car, caused by Z's negligent act. The insurance company will be subrogated to Y's cause of action against Z.

Subsequent purchaser* A person who takes a security other than by original issue.

Substantial performance The complete performance of all the essential elements of a contract. The only permissible omissions or derivations are those that are trivial, inadvertent, and inconsequential. Such performance will not justify repudiation. Compensation for defects may be substituted for actual performance.

Substantive law Law that regulates and controls the rights and duties of all persons in society. In contradistinction to the term *adjective law*, which means the rules of court procedure or remedial law, which prescribe the methods by which substantive law is enforced.

Succession The transfer by operation of law of all rights and obligations of a deceased person to those who are entitled to them.

Summary judgment A judicial determination that no genuine factual dispute exists and that one party to the lawsuit is entitled to judgment as a matter of law.

Summons A writ issued by a court to the sheriff, directing him to notify the defendant that the plaintiff claims to have a cause of action against the defendant and that he is required to answer. If the defendant docs not answer, judgment will be taken by default.

Supremacy Clause Article VI, U.S. Constitution, which states that the Constitution, laws, and treaties of the United States shall be the ''supreme law of the land'' and shall take precedence over conflicting state laws.

Surety A person who agrees to become liable to the creditor for the debtor's obligation in the event the debtor fails to perform as promised.

Suretyship The legal relationship whereby one person becomes a surety for the benefit of the creditor and debtor.

Suspends payments* Under Article 4—Bank Deposits and Collections, with respect to a bank this means that it has been closed by order of the supervisory authorities, that a public officer has been appointed to take it over, or that it ceases or refuses to make payments in the ordinary course of business.

Tangible Describes property that is physical in character and capable of being moved. A debt is intangible, but a promissory note evidencing such debt is tangible. *See* Chattel; Chose in action.

Tenancy The interest in property that a tenant acquired from a landlord by a lease. It may be at will or for a term. It is an interest in land.

Tenancy by the entireties Property acquired by husband and wife whereby upon the death of one, the survivor takes the whole property. The tenancy exists in only a few states. The husband and wife are both vested with the whole estate, so that the survivor takes no new title upon death of the other but remains in possession of the whole as originally granted. For the legal effect of such estate, the state statute should be consulted. *See* Joint tenants.

Tenancy in common The most usual method of two or more persons owning property at the same time. None of the formalities or unities required for other specialized forms of co-ownership are essential for this method.

Tenant The person to whom a lease is made. A lessee.

Tender To offer and produce money in satisfaction of a debt or obligation and express to the creditor a willingness to pay.

Tender of delivery* The seller must put and hold conforming goods at the buyer's disposition and give the buyer any notification reasonably necessary to enable him to take delivery.

Termination In the law of business organizations, this event occurs when the winding up or liquidation is completed. In essence, this is the end of the organization and its business. This term also applies to the destruction of an agency or employment relationship.

Testamentary capacity A person is said to have testamentary capacity when he understands the nature of his business and the value of his property, knows those persons who are natural objects of his bounty, and comprehends the manner in which he has provided for the distribution of his property.

Testator A male who has died leaving a will. A female is a testatrix.

Testimony Statements made by a witness under oath or affirmation in a legal proceeding.

Title This word has limited or broad meaning. When a person has the exclusive rights, powers, privileges, and immunities to property, real and personal, tangible and intangible, against all other persons, he may be said to have the complete title thereto. The aggregate of legal relations concerning property is the title. The term is used to describe the means by which a person exercises control and dominion over property. A trustee has a limited title. *See* Possession.

Tort "Twisted" or "wrong." A wrongful act committed by one person against another person or his property. It is the breach of a legal duty imposed by law other than by contract. X assaults Y, thus committing a tort. *See* Duty; Right.

Tortfeasor One who commits a tort.

Trade fixtures Personal property placed upon, or annexed to, land leased by a tenant for the purpose of carrying on a trade or business during the term of the lease. Such property is generally to be removed at the end of the term, providing removal will not destroy or injure the premises. Trade fixtures include showcases, shelving, racks, machinery, and the like.

Trademark No complete definition can be given for a trademark. Generally it is any sign, symbol, mark, word, or arrangement of words in the form of a label adopted and used by a manufacturer or distributor to designate his particular goods, and which no other person has the legal right to use. Originally, the design or trademark indicated origin, but today it is used more as an advertising mechanism.

Traffic court A court with jurisdiction to hear cases involving violations of the state and local traffic laws.

Transfer In its broadest sense, the word means the act by which an owner sets over or delivers his right, title, and interest in property to another person. A "bill of sale" to personal property is evidence of a transfer.

Treason The offense of attempting by overt acts to overthrow the government of the state to which the offender owes allegiance; or of betraying the state into the hands of a foreign power.

Treasury stock Stock of a corporation that has been issued by the corporation for value but is later returned to the corporation by way of gift or purchase or otherwise. It may be returned to the trustees of a corporation for the purpose of sale.

Treble damages An award of damages allowable under some statutes equal to three times the amount found by the jury to be a single recovery.

Trespass An injury to the person, property, or rights of another person committed by actual force and violence or under such circumstances that the law will infer that the injury was caused by force or violence.

Trust A relationship between persons by which one holds property for the use and benefit of another. The relationship is called fiduciary. Such rights are enforced in a court of equity. The person trusted is called a trustee. The person for whose benefit the property is held is called a beneficiary or "cestui que trust."

Trustee (generally) A person who is entrusted with the management and control of another's property and estate. A person occupying a fiduciary position. An executor, an administrator, a guardian.

Trustee in bankruptcy An agent of the court authorized to liquidate the assets of the bankrupt, protect them, and bring them to the court for final distribution for the benefit of the bankrupt and all the creditors.

Truth-in-lending A federal law that requires disclosure of total finance charges and the annual percentage rate for credit in order that borrowers may be able to shop for credit.

Tying contract Ties the sales of one piece of property (real or personal) to the sale or lease of another item of property.

Ultra vires "Beyond power." The acts of a corporation are ultra vires when they are beyond the power or capacity of the corporation as granted by the state in its charter.

Unauthorized* Refers to a signature or indorsement made without actual, implied, or apparent authority. Includes a forgery.

Unconscionable In the law of contracts, provisions that are oppressive, overreaching, or shocking to the conscience.

Unfair competition The imitation, by design, of the goods of another, for the purpose of palming them off on the public, misleading it, and inducing it to buy goods made by the imitator. Includes misrepresentation and deceit; thus, such conduct is fraudulent not only to competitors but to the public.

Unilateral contract A promise for an act or an act for a promise , a single enforceable promise. C promises B $10 if B will mow C's lawn. B mows the lawn. C's promise, now binding, is a unilateral contract. *See* Bilateral contract.

Usage of trade* Any practice or method of dealing so regularly observed in a place, vocation, or trade that observance may justly be expected in the transaction in question. The existence and scope of such usage are to be proved as facts. If it is established that such a usage is embodied in a written trade code or similar writing, the interpretation of the writing is for the court.

Usurious A contract is usurious if made for a loan of money at a rate of interest in excess of that permitted by statute.

Utter "Put out" or "pass off." To utter a check is to offer it to another in payment of a debt. To "utter a forged writing" means to put such writing in circulation, knowing of the falsity of the instrument, with the intent to injure another.

Value* Except as otherwise provided with respect to negotiable instruments and bank collections, a person gives "value" for rights if he acquires them (a) in return for a binding commitment to extend credit or for the extension of immediately available credit, whether or not drawn upon and whether or not a chargeback is provided for in the event of difficulties in collection; or (b) as security for, or in, total or partial satisfaction of a preexisting claim; or (c) by accepting delivery pursuant to a preexisting contract for purchase; or (d) generally, in return for any consideration sufficient to support a simple contract.

Vendee A purchaser of property. Generally, the purchaser of real property. A *buyer* is usually a purchaser of chattels.

Vendor The seller of property, usually real property. The word *seller* is used with personal property.

Vendor's lien An unpaid seller's right to hold possession of property until he has recovered the purchase price.

Venire To come into court, a writ used to summon potential jurors.

Venue The geographical area over which a court presides. Venue designates the county in which the action is tried. Change of venue means to move to another county.

Verdict The decision of a jury, reported to the court, on matters properly submitted to the jury for consideration.

Vertical merger A merger of corporations, one corporation being the supplier of the other.

Void Has no legal effect. A contract that is void is a nullity and confers no rights or duties.

Voidable That which is valid until one party, who has the power of avoidance, exercises such power. An infant has the power of avoidance of his contract. A defrauded party has the power to avoid his contract. Such contract is voidable.

Voir dire Preliminary examination of a prospective juror.

Voting trust Two or more persons owning stock with voting powers divorce those voting rights from ownership but retain to all intents and purposes the ownership in themselves and transfer the voting rights to trustees in whom voting rights of all depositors in the trust are pooled.

Wager A relationship between persons by which they agree that a certain sum of money or thing owned by one of them will be paid or delivered to the other upon the happening of an uncertain event, which event is not within the control of the parties and rests upon chance.

Waive (verb) To "waive" at law is to relinquish or give up intentionally a known right or to do an act that is inconsistent with the claiming of a known right.

Waiver (noun) The intentional relinquishment or giving up of a known right. It may be done by express words or conduct that involves any acts inconsistent with an intention to claim the right. Such conduct creates an estoppel on the part of the claimant. *See* Estoppel.

Warehouseman* A person engaged in the business of storing goods for hire.

Warehouse receipt* Issued by a person engaged in the business of storing goods for hire.

Warehouse receipt An instrument showing that the signer has in his possession certain described goods for storage. It obligates the signer, the warehouseman, to deliver the goods to a specified person or to his order or bearer upon the return of the instrument. Consult Uniform Warehouse Receipts Act.

Warrant (noun) An order in writing in the name of the state, signed by a magistrate, directed to an officer, commanding him to arrest a person. (verb) To guarantee, to answer for, to assure that a state of facts exists.

Warranty An undertaking, either expressed or implied, that a certain fact regarding the subject matter of a contract is presently true or will be true. The word has particular application in the law of sales of chattels. It relates to title and quality. *Warranty* should be distinguished from *guaranty*, which means a contract or promise by one person to answer for the performance of another.

Warranty of fitness for a particular purpose* An implied promise by a seller of goods that arises when a buyer explains the special needs and relies on the seller's advice.

Warranty of merchantability A promise implied in a sale of goods by merchants: that the goods are reasonably fit for the general purpose for which they are sold.

Waste Damage to the real property, so that its value as security is impaired.

Watered stock Corporate stock issued by a corporation for property at an overvaluation, or stock issued for which the corporation receives nothing in payment.

Will (testament) The formal instrument by which a person makes disposition of his property, to take effect upon his death.

Winding up The process of liquidating a business organization.

Working capital The amount of cash necessary for the convenient and safe transaction of present business.

Workers' compensation A plan for compensating employees for occupational disease, accidental injury, and death suffered in connection with employment.

Writ An instrument in writing, under seal in the name of the state, issued out of a court of justice at the commencement of, or during, a legal proceeding; directed to an officer of the court, commanding him to do some act or requiring some person to refrain from doing some act pertinent or relative to the cause being tried.

Writ of certiorari A discretionary proceeding by which an appellate court may review the ruling of an inferior tribunal.

Writ of *habeas corpus* A court order to one holding custody of another, to produce that individual before the court for the purpose of determining whether such custody is proper.

Yellow-dog contract A worker agrees not to join a union and to be discharged if he breaches the contract.

Zoning ordinance Passed by a city council by virtue of police power. Regulates and prescribes the kind of buildings, residences, or businesses that shall be built and used in different parts of a city.

Index